S0-AHN-532

SCHUBERT'S COMPLETE SONG TEXTS

Volume II

With

International Phonetic Alphabet Transcriptions
Word for Word Translations
and
Commentary

By

BEAUMONT GLASS

SCHUBERT'S COMPLETE SONG TEXTS

Volume II

By

BEAUMONT GLASS

ISBN 1-878617-20-6

LEYERLE PUBLICATIONS
Executive Offices
28 Stanley Street
Mt. Morris, New York 14510

This book may be ordered directly from

LEYERLE
PUBLICATIONS
Box 384
Geneseo, New York 14454

DEDICATION

***To the lieder singer I most admire,
my wife, EVANGELINE NOËL***

im Dezember I965/

LOTTE LEHMANN
4565 VIA HUERTO
HOPE RANCH PARK
SANTA BARBARA. CALIFORNIA

Beaumont Glass hat durch mehrere Saisons meine Liederklassen in der Musik Aka= demie in Santa Barbara(California)begleitet - und ich habe ihn als einen sehr sensitiven,serioesen und musikalischen Begleiter schaetzen gelernt.Er ist wirk= lich viel mehr als das:er durchdringt die Seele der Lieder nachschoepferisch und ist fuer den Singenden eine wahre Inspiration.

Ich kann ihn nur waermstens und aufrichtigst empfehlen.

Lotte Lehmann

English Translation

From Lotte Lehmann, December 1965:

Beaumont Glass has for several seasons accompanied my lieder classes at the Music Academy in Santa Babara [California] -- and I have learned to esteem him as a very sensitive, serious, and musical accompanist. He is really much more than that: he penetrates into the soul of the songs re-creatively and is for the singer a true inspiration. I can only recommend him most warmly and most sincerely.

Lotte Lehmann

ABOUT THE AUTHOR

Professor Beaumont Glass is at present the Director of Opera Theater at the University of Iowa, Iowa City, where he has coached and staged thirty full-scale productions, including *Boris Godunov*, which was telecast in its entirety by Iowa Public Television, and Handel's *Agrippina*, taken on tour to Europe in 1985. He directed *Lucia di Lammermoor*, with Roberta Peters in the title role, for the Utah Opera Company, and *The Magic Flute*, *Fidelio*, *The Marriage of Figaro*, *The Barber of Seville*, and *The Abduction from the Seraglio* for the Cedar Rapids Symphony. He has translated eighteen complete operas, and his translations have been performed by Boston Lyric Opera, the Opera Theater of Springfield, Illinois, the University of Maryland, the Cedar Rapids Symphony, and Anoka Opera, Minnesota, as well as by the University of Iowa.

Before coming to the University of Iowa in 1980, Glass was "*Studienleiter*" (Director of Musical Studies, head of the coaching staff, in charge of the musical preparation of all the operas) at the Zurich Opera, his home theater for nineteen years. He was coach, harpsichordist, and recital accompanist at the Festival of Aix-en-Provence for four summers. In addition to staging forty-eight different operas in Europe and the United States, he has accompanied lieder recitals in the Salzburg, Aix, and Holland Festivals, as well as on tour with Grace Bumbry, Martina Arroyo, and Simon Estes. Glass speaks German, Italian, and French.

He is the author of a biography of soprano Lotte Lehmann, published by Capra Press, Santa Barbara, in 1988. Glass had been Lehmann's assistant for several years at the Music Academy of the West, Santa Barbara, both in art song and in opera. Earlier, he had assisted Maggie Teyte at her studio in London. Glass has written articles for *The Opera Quarterly* and the San Francisco Opera program book, and he has given lectures on opera and art song in Switzerland and in America, including the "Presidential Lecture" at the University of Iowa for the year 1988. Four times in 1994 he was the guest lecturer on the weekly radio program "*Opera Fanatic*" in New York, station WKCR-FM.

Glass made his professional debut as a stage director for the Northwest Grand Opera in Seattle, where his first production was Verdi's *La traviata*, starring Dorothy Kirsten. He has subsequently worked with many of the best-known singers in the world of opera, either as coach or as stage director, or as both.

He is at present preparing a complete edition of the texts of all of Franz Schubert's songs in two volumes, with word-for-word translations, international phonetic alphabet transcriptions, and notes on interpretation, variants, special words, etc., to be published in 1996 and 1997 by Leyerle Publications. He has also created over 150 singing translations of German, French, Spanish, Russian, Finnish, and Norwegian art songs.

Glass is a graduate of Phillips Exeter Academy and the U.S. Naval Academy, Annapolis.

Franz Schubert

Schubert and his Songs
A Brief View

Franz Schubert was born in the Viennese suburb of Lichtenthal on January 31, 1797, the son of a schoolmaster and a domestic servant. The home of his boyhood was filled with music: He learned how to play the violin from his father, the piano from his brother Ignaz; his choirmaster taught him singing, the organ, and basic principles of harmony. When he was eleven he entered the *Stadtkonvikt*, a sort of conservatory-school where specially selected boys were trained to sing in the choir of the Imperial Chapel. He wrote a Fantasy in G for Piano Duet when he was thirteen, his first string quartet at fifteen, his first symphony at sixteen, and, at seventeen, a miraculous, fully mature masterpiece, "*Gretchen am Spinnrade*" from Goethe's *Faust*. A year later came *Erlkönig*, another of his most famous songs. He had been writing songs, copiously, since the age of fourteen. During his adolescence he studied counterpoint and voice with Antonio Salieri, Mozart's notorious rival. An earlier teacher had said of Schubert: "I have nothing more to teach him; he has been taught by God." Papa Schubert expected his son to keep music as an avocation and to prepare for some more practical profession. There was a serious rift between father and son; then Schubert's mother died. A reconciliation took place, but Schubert left home to take up lodgings with various individual friends. Ever since his time at the "Convict," he had enjoyed the company of a wide circle of devoted and admiring young bohemians, poets, and painters, who were drawn to him through his music, especially through his songs. Several of them provided him with lyrics. He was amazingly prolific: on October 19, 1815, for example, he composed seven songs in one day! He wore glasses even while sleeping, so that he could write down an inspiration the moment he woke up. Music, poetry, nature, and convivial friends were everything to him; he ate too much, smoked too much, drank too much (though no one ever saw him drunk), and cared perhaps too little about personal fastidiousness. He was nicknamed "*Schwammerl*"—"Little Sponge." He had a sweet nature, free of cruelty or cynicism. Schubert lived in the city but sang of the country: he and his friends often arranged excursions to the fields and woods just outside Vienna. And in the evening there would be a "*Schubertiade*" at someone's house and Franz would perform his latest compositions and then play for his friends to dance. A distinguished and famous singer, Michael Vogl, took an interest in Schubert's songs and made it his mission to promote them whenever he could in Viennese musical circles. He recognized Schubert's unique ability to capture the essential mood of a poem in his music and to bring the words to new and vivid life. These songs have a remarkable spontaneity and youthfulness, overflowing with feeling, whether joyful, serene, melancholy, or desperate; no matter how sad the subject, there is pain without bitterness. But such songs were ahead of their time. The Viennese aristocrats liked what they knew; the publishers found Schubert's music too difficult, non-commercial. Out of more than a thousand compositions, only a little over one hundred were published during his lifetime. Schubert lived on the borderline of poverty; fame came only after death, a tragically early death before he had reached the age of thirty-two. Today he is recognized as the most significant creator of an art form we call the German *Lied*. He was not the first; *Das Veilchen* by Mozart, for example, and Beethoven's beautiful song cycle, *An die ferne Geliebte*, are worthy precursors. But *Gretchen am Spinnrade* and *Erlkönig* were truly something new and could not have been written by anyone before him. His response to poetry was enthusiastic and instinctive, and he happened to live in an era of poets whose romantic sensibilities reveled in the celebration of nature and in the unashamed expression of personal feelings. If today some of their poems seem overly sentimental, or perhaps too preoccupied with death, too prone to self-pity, we will nevertheless appreciate their best qualities and enjoy them more sympathetically if we can return in imagination to the time that gave them birth. The "Age of Reason" had ended in the chaos of revolution. Political ideologies were ruthlessly suppressed by the censors. But the individual human heart could be explored in poetry. Schubert's songs—he wrote well over six hundred!— represent the German *Lied* in its purest form. They inspired the other great lieder composers who came after him, Robert Schumann, Johannes Brahms, Hugo Wolf, and Richard Strauss. The greatest of Schubert's songs are immortal treasures.

Thoughts on Interpreting Lieder

The singer is an indispensable partner of the composer and of the poet. The singer gives life and expression to the notes and the words and—above all!—to the feelings behind them, the feelings that *inspired* them. This requires, besides a beautiful voice, a rich imagination and the power to communicate. Every poem was born out of a special experience (the mundane and the ordinary are best left to prose); that *specialness* stirred the composer to set it to music. It is our task to try to find—or to imagine—that original, motivating spark of inspiration, and then to illuminate the song from within.

Study the poem, immerse yourself in it! Be sure that you understand its message exactly (one misunderstood word can sometimes alter everything, can even reverse the meaning). Who is speaking those words? Where should you imagine the speaker to be? To whom is he or she addressing those words, and in what frame of mind? Why *that* word, and not another? Why that phrase? What clue to the poet's meaning, what insight do they give us? Every singer is simultaneously an actor, communicating words with the most effective and appropriate expression, ready to move us, to shatter or to charm. But no matter how expressive, the words must be understood: clarity of diction is essential. Even the most exquisite verbal nuance is wasted if the word is not being received by the listener. But clear diction does not mean "spitting out" the consonants in little explosions that break up the line of the melody. Consonants need to be resonantly projected, but not exaggerated, and those voiced consonants that lend themselves to *legato* (especially l, m, n, ng) should be lovingly cherished, to compensate for the many that do not.

The words came first, of course. But the music lifts the words to another realm of the imagination, adding a new dimension, new colors, an intensified spiritual resonance. the union of words and tones is what makes a song; in a truly great *Lied* the combination of poem and music surpasses what either could accomplish alone. In performance, each element must get its individual due and yet be blended in harmony with its counterpart. The consonants and vowels—their sheer sound, apart from the meaning of the word they form,— become part of the musical fabric, the musical effect. Be sensitive to the musical possibilities of the language itself.

To understand the song the singer must study the accompaniment as well as the vocal line. The piano part is full of clues; look for them! The prelude, the postlude, the interludes—they are your world of the moment, your surrounding atmosphere; often they are *you*, your feelings, the "subtext" behind the words you sing. Your eyes, your bearing, your entire expression must be in harmony with what is coming to you from the piano. Imagine where you are, what you see before you, what you are feeling. And communicate all of that to the audience as eloquently as you can, without overstepping the boundary between stage and concert platform. Be totally expressive—but not "theatrical." A great lieder singer invites the audience into the world of the song, to share in moments of beauty and flights of the spirit that the poet and the composer have created and that the interpreter must always endeavor to re-create anew.

It is not nearly enough simply to sing the indicated pitches and note values and to pronounce the words clearly and correctly, no matter how beautiful the voice. Live with the song. Explore its world. Without a special contribution from the imagination, the personality, and the very *soul* of the singer, the performance would at best offer flowers without any fragrance.

Schubert and his poets were deeply sensitive to nature, in all its moods. The Romantics still had a classical education; living as they did among monuments of history and art, they absorbed a rich cultural awareness, which is reflected in their works. Spend time in nature; visit museums; study paintings and literature of the period; listen to recordings by Dietrich Fischer-Dieskau, Elisabeth Schwarzkopf, Lotte Lehmann, Elly Ameling, and other great interpreters of lieder.

Format and Phonetics

An Explanation and Introduction

Format:

The song texts are in alphabetical order by title.

The German text of each song or aria is printed in **bold type**; *above* each word is a transcription of the pronunciation in the characters of the International Phonetic Alphabet ("IPA"); *beneath* each word of the German text is an English word that is as close as practicable to the literal meaning, chosen from among the possible choices offered in a comprehensive German-English dictionary; beneath *that*, usually, in a *fourth* line, is the meaning of the line as it might be expressed in English, with its very different syntax.

Example (from *Die Forelle*, "The Trout"):

ɪn 'la͜enəm 'bɛçla͜en 'hɛlə, daː ʃos |ɪn 'froːɐ(r) |a͜el di 'la͜onɪʃə fo'rɛlə fo'ryːbɐ
In einem Bächlein helle, da schoss in froher Eil die launische Forelle vorüber
In a brooklet clear, there shot in happy haste the capricious trout past
(In a clear little brook, in happy haste, the capricious trout shot past...)

Often different interpretations may be possible; the translator has made a choice according to his own feeling for the language and his own understanding of the poem. A number of definite errors have been discovered in various otherwise excellent books of translations.

After the title, and a translation of the title, the opus number, if any, the year of composition, and the name of the poet are given. Variants in the text are noted beneath or beside the relevant line, with pronunciation (in IPA) and translation of any words different from those in the line. After the end of each song there is a more or less brief commentary, consisting of observations about the nature of the song, with perhaps a hint about the interpretation, some possibly useful background information, an explanation of discrepancies or unusual references, or similar points.

Phonetics:

The pronunciation suggested is based on a combination of two authoritative sources, *Duden—Das Aussprachewörterbuch*, and *Siebs—Deutsche Hochsprache*.

The **diphthongs**, for example, are taken from Siebs, since that version works better for singers, a͜e, a͜o, ɔ͜ø (Siebs) instead of a͜i, a͜u, ɔ͜y (Duden). The treatment of the unaccented ending "**er**" (as in "*Mutter*" or "*aber*") and words or syllables **ending in r** (such as "*der*," "*nur*," "*mehrfach*," "*verlor*") is as recommended in Duden. When the following word or syllable starts with a vowel, it is often advisable *in singing* to pronounce the r, for the sake of clarity and a smoother *legato*. Where that is the case, this collection offers a choice, e.g.: deːɐ̯/deːr, or 'oːdɐ(r). The more formal the mood of the song, the more rhetorical or archaic the wording, the heavier the accompaniment, the more likely that the r's will be sounded distinctly. Some familiarity with current practice among the best German singers is a desirable guide in such, as in all cases.

In general, the pronunciation given is that which would be used in *speaking* the words (an exception: when the composer has given a note to a vowel that would ordinarily be non-syllabic in speech, e.g: e'lyːziʊm—four syllables—instead of e'lyːzi̯ʊm—three syllables). **Double consonants** within a word are not pronounced in speech, but may be treated differently in singing, depending on the length of the note values and the importance of the word itself. For instance, in singing a word like "*Wonne*" (ecstasy) in a slow tempo, the n will be prolonged, both for expressive purposes and to counteract the abnormal rhythm of the word that is dictated by the music, since in speech it would be pronounced quickly with a very short and open ɔ. This subtle distinction has not been observed in the present compilation, and is left to the singer's discretion. If a short vowel is to be sung on a relatively long note, some compromise must be made between the normal pronunciation in quick speech and the demands of the music: this is usually accomplished by doubling the consonant that follows the vowel, to indicate its shorter value. "*Kann*" (can), for instance, must be distinguished from "*Kahn*" (boat).

To remind singers (and speakers) that **t, k, and p** are more or less strongly **aspirated** in German (indicated by Duden only in the introductory pages, later merely assumed), certain IPA symbols have been added to indicate the degree of aspiration: t^h, k^h, p^h strongly aspirated, t‘, k‘, p‘ lightly aspirated. When a word ends with the t, k, or p sound, and the next begins with the same sound, or its voiced equivalent (d, g, or b) the final t, k, or p is *not* aspirated, unless a pause is made between the words (a musical rest, for example). The directors and coaches of German opera houses are very particular about such matters. German audiences expect to understand the words.

A note on the sources:

The compiler and translator has attempted to include the texts of all the solo vocal pieces found in the leading collections of Schubert's lieder, as well as those more recently discovered. Schubert was astoundingly prolific during his tragically brief life. There are 615 different poems or prose poems in these volumes, and many of them he set to music more than once.

The various currently available editions of Schubert's songs are derived, for the most part, from one or the other of two major publications: (1) the *Gesamtausgabe* ("Complete Edition") as edited by Eusebius Mandyczewski and published in 1894 by Breitkopf & Härtel, Leipzig, under the title *Franz Schubert's Werke*, Series 20, in ten volumes; and (2) the more familiar *Edition Peters*, Frankfurt, New York, London, edited by Max Friedländer, in seven volumes. There are many differences between those two publications, and those differences are dealt with in this collection. In many cases, the *Gesamtausgabe* reflects what Schubert actually wrote in the original manuscripts, whereas the Peters edition is often based on the first *published* version, with variants that may or may not have been authorized by the composer himself. Sometimes, where there are discrepancies between Schubert's wording and that of the original poem, the text has been changed by Friedländer (in the Peters edition) to conform with the latter.

Eighteen of the songs included here do not appear in either of the leading collections mentioned above, either because they were lost, or because they were left incomplete by the composer. Performable versions of those songs were completed by Reinhard van Hoorickx and privately published.

The translations:

The translator has endeavored to make the meaning of the text as clear as possible, without any concern for elegance or poetic beauty in the English wording. Some of the original poems are quite straight-forward; others are subject to various interpretations; still others need to be lived in for a while before they yield up a sense of their message. Some German words are encountered only in poetry today; dictionaries usually label them "poetic." But perfectly ordinary words still in daily use are translated into their English equivalents; "*Mädchen,*" for example, is usually going to be "girl" rather than "maiden," unless a medieval atmosphere is an integral factor in the effectiveness of the poem. "*Du*" will be "you" rather than "thou," unless the poem is a prayer.

German diction:

Vowels:

One striking feature of German is the marked **difference in duration** between **long** and **short** vowels. "*Abend*" (ˈa:bənt' - evening), for example, has a long ah; in "*Nacht*" (naxtʰ - night) the *a* is very short. Yet a singer may find the word *Nacht* on a much longer note than the first syllable of *Abend*. How to be true to the sound of the word? No matter how short the note, the *a:* in *Abend* must give the impression of duration through the quality and intensity of the vowel. The *a* in *Nacht* must be prolonged without weight or stress, and the *ch* should be pronounced slightly earlier than if the word were "*nach*" (na:x - after, toward) for instance, which has a relatively long *a*. Another characteristic of German is the obligatory use of the **glottal stop** [|] to separate the end of one word from a following word that begins with a vowel, or to separate certain word elements within a word. Examples: *sie entehren ihn* (zi: |ɛnt'ˈ|e:rən |i:n - they dishonor him), *du und ich* (du: |ʊnt' |ɪç - you and I), *vereinen* (fɛɐ̯ˈ|a̯enən/fɛrˈ|a̯enən - to unite).

—[a] is the IPA symbol for the usual *a* in German. It is basically a brighter, more forward vowel than our American "ah" (except, perhaps, an "ah" in Boston). The *a* in "*Vater*" (ˈfa:t'ɐ - father) or "*haben*" (ˈha:bən - have) is long; in "*Gevatter*" (gəˈfat'ɐ - godfather) the *a* is short.

—[ɑ] is a darker version of *a*, slightly lower and farther back in the mouth; it occurs in the diphthong represented in normal print as *au* and in the IPA as ɑ͜o. Examples: *Baum* (bɑ͜om - tree), *Haus* (hɑ͜os - house).

Besides the difference in duration between "long" and "short," there is a strong phonetic **difference** between the following **"closed"** and **"open"** vowels:

—[e] is a very **closed** vowel that does not exist in American English, and is usually one of the last to be mastered by singers who are not French or German (it is identical with the French *é*). [e] is closer to the position of [i] in the mouth than its nearest approximation in standard English. Examples: *ewig* (ˈe:vɪç - eternal), *Seele* (ˈze:lə - soul). The difference between "*Leben*" (ˈle:bən - life, to live) and "*lieben*" (ˈli:bən - to love) is slight but crucial.

—[ɛ] is similar to the short open *e* in such English words as "let," "egg." It can be long or short; its long version, [ɛ:], is identical to the vowel in "air" without the *r*, and is written as *ä* in German. It is the same sound as *è* in French. That sound must be **avoided** when the [ɛ] is short, as in *Herz* (hɛrt͜s - heart), *Herr* (hɛr - Sir, Mr.), in both of which the vowel is as in "head" and **not** as in "hair" (an important distinction); *ä* can also be short, pronounced [ɛ].

—[ə] is a slightly darkened version of [ɛ] and **should not sound like the English [ʌ]**, the vowel in "love," which in German is only found in the ending *er*, as in *Mutter* (ˈmʊt'ɐ - mother) or *aber* (ˈa:bɐ - but), and is represented in the IPA as [ɐ].

—[i] is a closed vowel identical to the ee in "see."

—[ɪ] is open and short, as in "it" or "if" in English. Some Americans do not distinguish between [ɪ] and [ɛ] in everyday speech, making "bin," "been," and "Ben" sound the same. They must guard against making the same **error** in German. Examples: *ich* (ɪç - I), *bin* (bɪn - am).

—[o] is a **very closed** vowel that, like [e] does not exist in English, but does in French (spelled *ô, au, or eau*). It is closer to the mouth position of [u] than its nearest approximation in American English, which is usually a diphthong [ʌ͜o]. Examples: *ohne* (ˈo:nə - without), *Tod* (tʰo:t' - death), *Boot* (bo:tʰ - boat).

—[ɔ] is very open, almost as much as in French, and always short (whereas the nearest sound in American speech, the vowel in "awe" is generally long). Examples: *noch* (nɔx - still), *Sonne* (ˈzɔnə - sun). There is a big difference between the sound of *offen* (ˈɔfən - open) and *Ofen* (ˈo:fən - oven).

—[u] is closed and similar to the vowel in "moon." Examples: *du* (du: - you), *Ruhe* (ˈru:ə - rest, peace), *tun* (tʰu:n - to do).

—[ʊ] is open and short, similar to the vowel in "foot" or "look" (if pronounced according to standard English; many Americans have a **problem** with this sound in German as in their own regional vernacular). Examples: *Mutter* (ˈmʊt'ɐ - mother), *und* (ʊnt' - and), *Kuss* (kʰʊs - kiss).

—[ø] is closed and does not exist in English. It is pronounced by forming the lips to make a very closed [o] and at the same time trying to say a closed German (or French) [e]. Examples: *schön* (ʃø:n - beautiful), *hören* ('hø:rən - to hear), *König* ('k^{h}ø:nɪç - king). Most Americans make too open a sound when attempting this vowel. It must be distinguished from its open counterpart:
—[œ], the open version of [ø], made by forming the lips to make an open [ɔ] while trying to say [ɛ]. The sound exists in English in "girl," "world," "bird," etc. (before the *r* is added). Examples: *möchte* ('mœçt'ə - would like), *Götter* ('gœt'ɐ - gods), *Töchter* ('t^{h}œçt'ɐ - daughters).
—[y] is closed and does not exist in English. It is made by rounding the lips as if to say [u] and trying to pronounce [i]. Examples: *grün* (gry:n - green), *früh* (fry: - early), *süss* (zy:s - sweet). It is easier than [ø] for Americans because [u] and [i] exist in English, whereas pure [o] and [e] do not.
—[ʏ] is the open version of [y], made by rounding the lips as if to say [ʊ] and trying to pronounce [ɪ]. Examples: *jünger* ('jʏŋɐ - younger), *Küsse* ('k^{h}ʏsə - kisses), *Glück* (glʏk^h - luck).

Diphthongs are always pronounced short in German speech, but may be notated long in music, in which case the first of the two vowel sounds must take up most of the duration of the note (as when singing English diphthongs) Examples: *Wein* (va͜en - wine), *Haut* (hɑ͜ot^h- skin), *Freude* ('frɔ͜ødə - joy).

Consonants:
When the last letter in a word (or word element) is *b, d, g, v,* or *s* that final consonant is unvoiced in German. That means that [b] becomes [p], [d] becomes [t], [g] becomes [k], [v] becomes [f], [z] becomes [s] (exception: when *ich* follows a verb that has lost its final *e* through contraction, as in "*hab' ich,*" the final consonant of the shortened verb may keep its voiced sound). Americans have a particular problem with a final *s* after a voiced consonant, as in *Herzens* ('hɛrt͜səns - heart's), *Lebens* ('le:bəns - life's), *niemals* ('ni:ma:ls - never), because in English an *s* after a voiced consonant is usually voiced (as in "lens"), unless the sound is spelled with a *c*, as in "fence" or "dance." Watch out for this **common fault**! *P, t,* and *k* are usually aspirated in German (that is, mixed with the sound of *h*); this will be indicated by a following [^{h}] if strongly aspirated, or by ['] if slightly aspirated. When *b, d,* and *g* become *p, t,* and *k* at the end of a phrase, they are not as strongly aspirated as the final consonant would be in words actually spelled with *p, t,* or *k*. Example: the difference between *tot* (t^{h}o:t^h - dead) and *Tod* (t^{h}o:t' - death), if the word happens to end a phrase (otherwise both words sound the same).
—*ch* has two pronunciations: [ç] "front *ch*" follows a "front" vowel (*i, e, ä, ö, ü*) or a consonant. It is a light hissing sound, (the lips are not moved, as they are for *sh*). Examples: *ich* (ɪç - I), *Milch* (mɪlç - milk), *durch* (dʊrç - through), *manch* (manç - many a). "Back *ch*" [x] follows a "back" vowel (*a, o, u*). Examples: *ach* (ax - ah!), *noch* (nɔx - still), *Buch* (bu:x - book). There are two **common errors** in pronouncing [x]: either it sounds too much like [ç] or too much like [k]. Example: *Nacht* (naxt^h - night) must not sound like *nackt* (nak't^h - naked).
—*j* [j] is pronounced like *y* in English; sometimes it is aspirated with an *h* for expressive reasons. Examples: *ja* (ja: or hja: - yes), *jung* (jʊŋ or hjʊŋ - young). The possible aspiration has not been indicated in this collection.
—*l* [l] is articulated with the tongue farther toward the front of the mouth than in American speech (but not past the teeth, as in some Russian words). It is a light, lyrical sound, and one of the **problems** for most American speakers. Examples: *Liebe* ('li:bə - love), *Welt* (vɛlt^h - world).
—*m* [m], *n* [n], and *ng* [ŋ] are hummed very resonantly in German singing. Final *n* in the ending *en*, however, is only lightly touched, since such endings serve a grammatical rather than an expressive function.
—*nk* is pronounced [ŋk], as in *denken* ('dɛŋk'ən - to think), *Dunkel* ('dʊŋk'əl - dark).
—*qu* is pronounced [k^{h}v]; that is why German singers often have trouble in Italian with "*questo*" or "*qui*". Examples: *Quelle* ('k^{h}vɛlə - spring, source), *Qual* (k^{h}va:l - torment).
—*r* is uvular in speech (as in French) but trilled or "flipped" by the tongue in singing. Final *r* is a special case, as discussed above under the heading "Phonetics." After a long vowel, in the

prefixes *er, ver, zer,* and in the endings *er, ern,* etc., it is barely indicated and rarely flipped or rolled in modern German speech. Examples: *nur* (nu:ɐ̯ - only), *er* (e:ɐ̯ - he), *vergessen* (fɛɐ̯'gɛsən - to forget), *Mutter* ('mʊt'ɐ - mother). Final double r, as in *starr* (ʃt'ar - rigid) is rolled.
—*st* and *sp* at the beginning of a word element are usually pronounced as if the *s* were *sh* [ʃ]. Examples: *Strasse* ('ʃt'ra:sə - street), *sprechen* ('ʃp'rɛçən - to speak). If *st* or *sp* follow a vowel, or if the *s* and the *t* or *p* belong to different syllables, then the pronunciation is normal. Examples: *erst* (e:ɐ̯st' - first), *lispeln* ('lɪsp'əln - to whisper, to lisp).
—*v* is usually pronounced like *f*, but there are exceptions, especially in names. Venus ('ve:nʊs) keeps the *v* sound; Eva can be pronounced both ways, with [f] for Eve in paradise or the heroine of Wagner's *Die Meistersinger* (e:fa); with [v] for a modern woman, such as Hitler's mistress (e:va). Note that the final *a* is a pure [a] and never [ə] or [ʌ].
—*w* is pronounced [v]. Examples: *Welle* ('vɛlə - wave), *wenn* (vɛn - when, if).
—*z* is pronounced *ts* [t͡s]. Examples: *zu* (t͡su: - to, too), *zwei* (t͡svae̯ - two).
Because there are so many consonants in German, and because they often need to be articulated very strongly and sharply, the singer who wants to sing a beautiful *legato* line must be alert to every opportunity to take advantage of those consonants that lend themselves to *legato* singing, especially *l, m, n, ng*. Those consonants, especially when double, offer the possibility of making a *portamento* or **slur on the consonant itself**, which can give a much needed curve to the otherwise overly angular effect of short choppy syllables bristling with consonants. Seize every chance to exploit those curves! Examples: *Wonne* ('vɔnnə - rapture), *Kummer* ('kʰʊmmɐ - sadness), *Wange* ('vaŋə - cheek), *helle* ('hɛllə - bright). Note that in these examples the *n, m,* and *l* have been doubled in the suggested pronunciation, to illustrate the point. They are not doubled in speech, and therefore not in the phonetic transcriptions in this collection. Doubling at the discretion of the singer is often done for expressive reasons, to add intensity to key words, such as *Liebe!* ('lli:bə - love!), *Mutter!* ('mmʊt'ɐ - Mother!), *Süsse!* ('zzy:sə - sweet one!), etc. Lotte Lehmann, in her master classes, used to call out to her students: "Ten l's!" when they were to sing the word "*Liebe*" in a particularly rapturous phrase.

Stressed syllables: primary stress is indicated with the IPA symbol ['] in front of the syllable; in cases of possible ambiguity, a secondary stress may be indicated with [ˌ].

Some abbreviations:

Op. ... , No. ... = Opus ... , Number ...
GA = *Gesamtausgabe* (ten volumes of Series XX of Schubert's Collected Works, as first published by Breitkopf & Härtel, Leipzig)
P. = Peters Edition (a six-volume collection)
p. = poem (the poet's words, if different from Schubert's text)
subj. = grammatical subject
obj. = grammatical object
obs. = obsolete
masc. = masculine
fem. = feminine

Note: *Lieder* means "songs," the plural of the German word for song which is *das Lied.* In English we can say "lieder singer" or "he sang several lieder," but not "a lieder": the term would be "a *Lied.*" The plural form has become a part of our language, but not yet the singular.

Additional Notes

Spelling has been modernized throughout wherever the pronunciation is unaffected, e.g.: *Träne* for *Thräne, toten* instead of *todten, Los* instead of *Loos.*

This collection contains the texts of all the pieces published as lieder in the Breitkopf & Härtels *Gesamtausgabe* (including those originally intended for chorus), in the seven-volume Peters edition (including solos from Schubert's stage works), and in Bärenreiter's *Neue Schubert Ausgabe*, as well as the texts of all the known songs by Schubert that are not found in any of the above. Every effort has been made to make this collection comprehensive and complete.

A review of Volume I suggested that the use of the IPA symbols [ɐ] and [ɐ̯] should be further clarified. The former represents the sound written "er," when it is the only vowel in a syllable; the latter is the second vowel in a diphthong. Examples: 'mʊtʻɐ (*Mutter* = mother); nuːɐ̯ (*nur* = only). Examples of the sound in English are "mother" and "poor" as those words are pronounced in England or in parts of the eastern United States, without the so-called "mid-western" r. In singing (but not in speech), a flipped r is sometimes sounded at the end of the syllable for the sake of clarity, especially if the next word (or word element) starts with a vowel. In that case the sound of the vowel [ɐ] is preserved before the r; but the [ɐ̯] is not. Care should be taken to distinguish between the endings "er" and "e" in German (examples: *lieber* and *Liebe*); [ə] is lighter and closer to [ɛ], whereas [ɐ] is the only sound in German that is nearly equivalent to the English [ʌ], the vowel in "love." Further clarifications: [|] represents a glottal stop, separating a vowel from the preceding word or word element; [i̯] is a light, short [i] before another vowel, only slightly different from the sound of [j]; example: fa'miːli̯ə (*Familie* = family).

ˈfry:lɪŋsli:tʻ / gəˈlœfnətʻ zɪnt dɛs ˈvɪntʻɐs ˈri:gəl

Frühlingslied / Geöffnet sind des Winters Riegel

Spring Song / Opened are the Bolts of Winter

Posthumously published [composed 1827?] (poem by Aaron Pollak)

gəˈlœfnətʻ zɪnt dɛs ˈvɪntʻɐs ˈri:gəl, lɛntʻˈʃvʊndən lɪstʻ za͜en ˈzɪlbɐflo:ɐ̯;
Geöffnet sind des Winters Riegel, entschwunden ist sein Silberflor;
Opened are the winter's bolts, vanished is its silver crêpe;
(Winter's bolts are opened, its silver crêpe has vanished;)

hɛl ˈblɪŋkʻən de:ɐ̯ gəˈvɛsɐ ˈʃpʻi:gəl, di ˈlɛrçə ʃvɪŋtʻ zɪç ho:x lɛmˈpʰo:ɐ̯;
hell blinken der Gewässer Spiegel, die Lerche schwingt sich hoch empor;
brightly sparkle the waters' mirrors, the lark swings itself high upwards;
(the mirrors of the waters sparkle brightly, the lark soars aloft;)

vi: dʊrç dɛs ˈgra͜ezən ˈkʰø:nɪçs ˈzi:gəl gəˈvɛkʻtʻ lɛɐ̯ˈtʰø:nt de:ɐ̯ ˈfrɔ͜ødə kʰo:ɐ̯.
wie durch des greisen Königs Siegel geweckt ertönt der Freude Chor.
as if through the old king's seal awakened resounds the joy's chorus.
(as if awakened through the seal of old King Winter, a chorus of joy is resounding.)

de:ɐ̯ ˈfry:lɪŋ ʃve:pʻtʻ la͜of das gəˈfɪldə lʊntʻ ˈli:pʻlɪç ˈve:ət ˈt͜se:fy:ɐ̯ nu:ɐ̯,
Der Frühling schwebt auf das Gefilde und lieblich wehet Zephyr nur,
The spring hovers onto the fields and delightfully blows Zephyrus only,
(Spring hovers over the fields and only the gentle west wind is blowing, delightfully;)

de:ɐ̯ ˈblu:mənfʏlə ˈzy:sə ˈmɪldə lɛɐ̯ˈhe:pʻtʻ zɪç lɪn de:ɐ̯ lʊftʻ laˈt͜su:ɐ̯,
der Blumenfülle süsse Milde erhebt sich in der Luft Azur,
the flower- abundance's sweet mildness raises itself in the air's azure,
(the sweet, mild fragrance of abundant flowers rises into the azure air;)

lɪn de:ɐ̯ fɛɐ̯ˈkʰlɛ:rʊŋ ˈvʊndɐbɪldə lɛmˈp͜fɛŋtʻ lʊns ˈlɛçəlnt di naˈtʰu:ɐ̯.
in der Verklärung Wunderbilde empfängt uns lächelnd die Natur.
in the transfiguration's miracle-picture receives us smiling the nature.
(in this picture of miracles and transfiguration Nature receives us, smiling.)

ʃo:n ˈpʰraŋən ˈgɔltʻgəʃmʏkʻtʻ zʏlˈfi:dən lʊntʻ ˈflo:rəns ra͜eç lɛɐ̯ˈbly:tʻ fɛɐ̯ˈʃø:ntʰ,
Schon prangen goldgeschmückt Sylphiden und Florens Reich erblüht verschönt,
Already are resplendent gold-adorned sylphs and Flora's realm blooms beautified,
(Already gold-adorned sylphs are resplendent, and Flora's realm blooms with new beauty;)

rɪŋs ˈvaltʻətʻ lʊstʻ lʊntʻ ˈʃtʻɪlɐ ˈfri:dən, de:ɐ̯ ha͜en lɪstʻ nu:n mɪtʻ la͜opʻ bəˈkʰrø:ntʰ,
rings waltet Lust und stiller Frieden, der Hain ist nun mit Laub bekrönt,
all around reigns pleasure and quiet peace, the grove is now with foliage crowned,
(all around reign pleasure and quiet peace; the grove is now crowned with foliage;)

ve:ɐ̯ ˈfy:lətʰ, li:m lɪstʻ glʏkʻ bəˈʃi:dən, va͜el ˈle:rɔs ˈzy:sɐ ru:f lɛɐ̯ˈtʰø:ntʰ.
wer fühlet, ihm ist Glück beschieden, weil Eros' süsser Ruf ertönt.
whoever feels, to him is happiness granted, because Eros's sweet call is sounding.
(happiness is granted to whoever has feelings, since the sweet call of Eros is sounding.)

ɛmˈp̱faŋət dɛn mɪt ˈtʰrɑ͜otˈəm ˈgruːsə den ˈhɔldən lɛnt͜s, den ʃmʊkˈ deːɐ̯ vɛltʰ,
Empfanget denn mit trautem Grusse den holden Lenz, den Schmuck der Welt,
Receive therefore with intimate greeting the lovely spring, the jewel of the world,
(Therefore receive lovely Spring, the jewel of the world, with an intimate greeting,)

deːɐ̯ ˈva͜eənt ˈlʊns mɪt ˈla͜ezəm ˈkʰʊsə dɛs ˈdaːza͜ens ˈroːzənbaːn lɛɐ̯ˈhɛltʰ,
der weihend uns mit leisem Kusse des Daseins Rosenbahn erhellt,
who consecrating for us with quiet kiss the existence's rose- path brightens,
(Spring, who consecrates and brightens the rose-bordered path of our existence with a quiet kiss,)

deːɐ̯ hɔltˈ lʊns vɪŋkˈt t͜sʊm ˈhoːxgəˈnʊsə lʊntˈ ˈjeːdəs hɛrt͜s mɪtˈ ˈvɔnə ʃvɛltʰ.
der hold uns winkt zum Hochgenusse und jedes Herz mit Wonne schwellt.
who graciously us beckons to the high-enjoyment and every heart with rapture swells.
(who graciously beckons us to sublime delight and swells every heart with rapture.)

[This song does not appear in the Peters edition or in the main collection of the *Gesamtausgabe*, though it is printed in the latter's supplementary volume. It is a version for solo voice and piano of an earlier male-voice quartet. Eros is the god of sensual love, Flora the goddess of flowers.]

Frühlingssehnsucht see *Schwanengesang*

Frühlingstraum see *Winterreise*

ˈfʏlə deːɐ̯ ˈliːbə
Fülle der Liebe
Love's Fullness

Posthumously published [composed 1825] (poem by Friedrich von Schlegel)

a͜en ˈzeːnəntˈ ˈʃtˈreːbən tʰa͜eltˈ miːɐ̯ das hɛrt͜s, bɪs ˈlaləs ˈleːbən zɪç løːstˈ lɪn ʃmɛrt͜s.
Ein sehnend Streben teilt mir das Herz, bis alles Leben sich löst in Schmerz.
A yearning striving divides for me the heart, until all life itself dissolves in pain.
(A yearning striving cleaves my heart, until all life is dissolved into pain.)

ɪn la͜etˈ lɛɐ̯ˈvaxtˈə deːɐ̯ ˈjʊŋə zɪn, lʊntˈ ˈliːbə ˈbraxtˈə t͜sʊm t͜siːl mɪç hɪn.
In Leid erwachte der junge Sinn, und Liebe brachte zum Ziel mich hin.
In sorrow awoke the young mind, and love brought to the goal me hence.
(My young mind awoke in sorrow, and love brought me to the goal.)

iːɐ̯/iːr, ˈledlə ˈflamən, ˈvɛkˈtˈətˈ mɪç la͜of; lɛs gɪŋ mɪtˈˈzamən t͜suː gɔt deːɐ̯ la͜of.
Ihr, edle Flammen, wecktet mich auf; es ging mitsammen zu Gott der Lauf.
You, noble flames, woke me up; it went together to God the course.
(You, noble flames, woke me up; our course sent us together toward God.)

a͜en ˈfɔ͜øɐ vaːɐ̯/vaːr lɛs, das ˈlaləs tʰra͜epˈtˈ; la͜en ˈʃtarkəs, ˈkʰlaːrəs, das ˈleːvɪç bla͜epˈtʰ.
Ein Feuer war es, das alles treibt; ein starkes, klares, das ewig bleibt.
A fire was it, that all drives; a strong, clear one, that eternally remains.
(It was a fire that drives everything, a strong, clear fire that remains forever.)

vas viːɐ̯/viːr lanˈʃtˈreːpˈtˈən, vaːɐ̯ tʰrɔ͜ø gəˈma͜entˈ;
Was wir anstrebten, war treu gemeint;
What we strived toward was faithfully meant;
[*poem:* **was** (what) **treu gemeint** (what was faithfully meant)]

vas vi:ɐ̯ dʊrçˈle:p'tʻən blaep't tʰi:f fɛɐ̯ˈlaentʰ/fɛrˈlaentʰ.
was wir durchlebten bleibt tief vereint.
what we lived through remains deeply united.
[*Peters:* **was wir durchbebten** (dʊrçˈbe:p'tʻən, trembled through)]

da: tʰra:tʻ laen ˈʃaedən mi:ɐ̯/mi:r ɪn di brʊst, das ˈtʰi:fə ˈlaedən de:ɐ̯ ˈli:bəslʊstʰ.
Da trat ein Scheiden mir in die Brust, das tiefe Leiden der Liebeslust.
Then entered a parting to me into the breast, the deep suffering of the love-pleasure.
(Then a parting entered into my heart, the deep suffering, the shadow of love's pleasure.)

ɪm ˈze:ləngrʊndə vo:ntʻ mi:ɐ̯/mi:r laen bɪltʻ, di ˈtʰo:dəsvʊndə vartʻ ni: gəˈʃtʻɪltʰ.
Im Seelengrunde wohnt mir ein Bild, die Todeswunde ward nie gestillt.
In the soul- depths dwells for me an image, the fatal wound was never staunched.
(In the depths of my soul there dwells an image; the fatal wound has never been staunched.)

fi:l ˈtʰaozənt ˈtʰrɛ:nən ˈflɔsən hɪˈnapʻ, laen ˈle:vɪç ˈze:nən tsu: li:ɐ̯/li:r ɪns gra:pʻ.
Viel tausend Tränen flossen hinab, ein ewig Sehnen zu ihr ins Grab.
Many thousand tears flowed down, an eternal yearning to her into the grave.
(Many thousands of tears have flowed; I feel an eternal yearning to follow her into the grave.)

ɪn ˈli:bəsvo:gən ˈvalət de:ɐ̯ gaestʻ, bɪs ˈfɔrtʻgətso:gən di brʊst tsɛɐ̯ˈraestʰ.
In Liebeswogen wallet der Geist, bis fortgezogen die Brust zerreisst.
In love- waves floats the spirit, until dragged away the breast tears apart.
(The spirit floats in waves of love, until, dragged away, the heart is torn apart.)

aen ʃtʻɛrn lɛɐ̯ˈʃi:n mi:ɐ̯ fɔm pʰaraˈdi:s; lʊnt ˈdahɪn fli:n vi:ɐ̯ fɛɐ̯/fɛrˈlaentʻ gəˈvɪs.
Ein Stern erschien mir vom Paradies; und dahin flieh'n wir vereint gewiss.
A star appeared to me from the paradise; and thither flee we united certainly.
(A star appeared to me from Paradise; and to there we shall certainly flee, united.)

hi:ɐ̯ nɔx bəˈfɔøçtʻət de:ɐ̯ blɪkʻ zɪç lɪntʻ, vɛn mɪç lʊmˈlɔøçtʻət di:s ˈhɪməlskʰɪntʻ.
Hier noch befeuchtet der Blick sich lind, wenn mich umleuchtet dies Himmelskind.
Here still moistens the gaze itself gently, when me bathes in light this heavenly child.
(Here tears still gently moisten my eyes, when that heavenly child bathes me in her light.)

aen ˈtsaobɐ ˈvaltʻətʻ jɛtstʻ ˈly:bɐ mɪç, lʊnt de:ɐ̯ gəˈʃtʻaltʻət di:s lal na:x zɪç.
Ein Zauber waltet jetzt über mich, und der gestaltet dies all' nach sich.
A magic rules now over me, and that shapes this all according to itself.
(A magic spell holds me in thrall, and that spell shapes everything according to its own nature.)

als lɔpʻ lʊns fɛɐ̯ˈmɛ:lə ˈgaestʻəsgəvaltʻ, vo: ze:l lɪn ˈze:lə hɪˈny:bɐ valtʰ.
Als ob uns vermähle Geistesgewalt, wo Seel' in Seele hinüber wallt.
As if us joined in marriage spirit-power, where soul in soul to the other side wanders.
(As if a spiritual power were uniting us in marriage,
where one soul crosses over into the other world to merge with the other.)

ɔpʻ laox tsɛɐ̯ˈʃpʻaltʻən mi:ɐ̯/mi:r lɪst das hɛrts, ˈze:lɪç dɔx ˈhaltʻən vɪl lɪç den ʃmɛrts.
Ob auch zerspalten mir ist das Herz, selig doch halten will ich den Schmerz.
If even split for me is the heart, blessed yet hold will I the pain.
(Even though my heart is split apart, I nevertheless shall consider the pain to be blessed.)

[A persistent rhythmic figure and frequent, sometimes surprising modulations characterize this song of love and loss.]

fʊrçt deːɐ̯ gəˈliːpʻtʻən
Furcht der Geliebten
The Beloved's Fear

Posthumously published [composed 1815] (poem by Friedrich Gottlieb Klopstock)

ˈt͡sɪdli, duː ˈva͜enəstʻ, |ʊntʻ |ɪç ˈʃlʊmrə ˈzɪçɐ,
Cidli, du weinest, und ich schlumm're sicher,
Cidli, you weep, and I slumber safely

voː |ɪm ˈzandə deːɐ̯ veːkʻ fɛɐ̯ˈt͡soːgən ˈfɔrtʻʃla͜eçtʰ;
wo im Sande der Weg verzogen fortschleicht;
where in the sand the path twisted steals away;
(where the winding path steals away in the sand;)

a͜ox vɛn ˈʃtʻɪlə naxtʻ |iːn |ʊmˈʃatʻənt ˈdɛkʻətʻ, ʃlʊm rɪç |iːn ˈzɪçɐ.
auch wenn stille Nacht ihn umschattend decket, schlummr' ich ihn sicher.
even if quiet night it overshadowing covers, slumber I it safely.
(even if the quiet night covers it over with shadows, I shall sleep there safely.)

voː |eːɐ̯ zɪç ˈ|ɛndətʻ, voː |a͜en ʃtʻroːm das meːɐ̯ vɪrtʻ,
Wo er sich endet, wo ein Strom das Meer wird,
Where it itself ends, where a river the sea becomes,
(Where that path ends, where a river becomes the sea,)

gla͜etʻ |ɪç ˈ|yːbɐ den ʃtʻroːm, deːɐ̯ ˈzanftʻɐ ˈ|a͜ofʃvɪltʰ;
gleit' ich über den Strom, der sanfter aufschwillt;
glide I over the stream, which more gently swells up;
(I shall glide over the waters, which surge up more gently;)

dɛn, deːɐ̯ mɪç bəˈgla͜etʻət, deːɐ̯ gɔtʻ gəˈboːt͡s |iːm! ˈva͜enə nɪçt, ˈt͡sɪdli.
denn, der mich begleitet, der Gott gebot's ihm! Weine nicht, Cidli.
for He who me accompanies, the God commanded it to it! Weep not, Cidli.
(for God, who accompanies me, commanded the water to do so! Do not weep, Cidli.)

["Cidli" was Klopstock's nickname for his beloved Meta Moller, who later became his wife. In this poem she is worried about him and the future that faces him; he tries to reassure her that God will be beside him on the winding path of his life, and will smooth the turbulent waters for his sake. The *Gesamtausgabe* prints two versions that differ only slightly, most obviously in the last three notes of the vocal phrase that ends in the sixth bar.]

ganyˈmeːtʻ
Ganymed
Ganymede

Op. 19, No. 3 [1817] (Johann Wolfgang von Goethe)

viː |ɪm ˈmɔrgənglant͡sə duː rɪŋs mɪç ˈ|anglyːstʰ, ˈfryːlɪŋ, gəˈliːpʻtʻɐ!
Wie im Morgenglanze du rings mich anglühst, Frühling, Geliebter!
How in the morning-radiance you all around me at-glow, spring, beloved!
(How you glow at me in the radiance of morning all around, beloved Spring!)
["*anglühen*" also means "heat to a glow"]

mɪt ˈtʰɑ͜ozəntˈfaxɐ ˈliːbəsvɔnə
Mit tausendfacher Liebeswonne
With thousandfold love- rapture
(With the thousandfold raptures of love)

zɪç lan ma͜en ˈhɛrtsə drɛŋt ˈda͜enɐ(r) ˈleːvɪgən ˈvɛrmə ˈha͜elɪç gəˈfyːl,
sich an mein Herze drängt deiner ewigen Wärme heilig Gefühl, [*poem:* **Herz** (hɛrts)]
itself to my heart presses your eternal warmth's holy feeling,
(the holy feeling of your eternal warmth surges into my heart,)

ʊnˈlɛntˈlɪçə ˈʃøːnə! das lɪç dɪç ˈfasən mœçtˈ lɪn ˈdiːzən larm!
unendliche Schöne! Dass ich dich fassen möcht' in diesen Arm!
infinite beautiful! That I you grasp might into this arm!
(infinite Beauty! Oh, that I might clasp you in my arms!)

ax, lan ˈda͜enəm ˈbuːzən liːg ɪç lʊntˈ ˈʃmaxtˈə,
Ach, an deinem Busen lieg' ich und schmachte, [*poem:* **lieg' ich, schmachte**]
Ah, on your bosom lie I and languish,
(Ah, upon your bosom I lie and languish,)

ʊnt ˈda͜enə ˈbluːmən, da͜en graːs ˈdrɛŋən zɪç lan ma͜en hɛrts.
und deine Blumen, dein Gras drängen sich an mein Herz.
and your flowers, your grass press themselves against my heart.

duː kʰyːlst den ˈbrɛnəndən dʊrstˈ ˈma͜enəs ˈbuːzəns, ˈliːpˈlɪçɐ ˈmɔrgənvɪntˈ!
Du kühlst den brennenden Durst meines Busens, lieblicher Morgenwind!
You cool the burning thirst of my bosom, lovely morning breeze!

ruːft dra͜en di ˈnaxtˈɪgal ˈliːbəntˈ naːx miːɐ̯/miːr lɑ͜os dem ˈneːbəltʰaːl.
Ruft drein die Nachtigall liebend nach mir aus dem Nebeltal.
Calls into it (= the breeze) the nightingale lovingly to me from the mist- valley.
(From the misty valley the nightingale calls to me lovingly through the morning breeze!)

ɪç kʰɔm, lɪç ˈkʰɔmə! ax! voˈhɪn, voˈhɪn?
Ich komm', ich komme! ach! wohin, wohin? [*poem:* **Wohin? Ach, wohin?**]
I come, I come! Ah! Whither, whither?

hɪˈnɑ͜of ʃtˈreːpˈts, hɪˈnɑ͜of! lɛs ˈʃveːbən di ˈvɔlkˈən ˈlapˈvɛrts,
Hinauf strebt's, hinauf! Es schweben die Wolken abwärts,
Upwards strives it, upwards! There float the clouds downwards,
(Upwards one strives, upwards! The clouds are floating downwards,)
[*poem:* **Hinauf! Hinauf strebt's.**]

di ˈvɔlkˈən ˈna͜egən zɪç deːɐ̯ ˈzeːnəndən ˈliːbə. miːɐ̯! miːɐ̯!
die Wolken neigen sich der sehnenden Liebe. Mir! Mir!
the clouds bend themselves to the yearning love. To me! To me!
(the clouds bend down to yearning love, to me! To me!)

ɪn ˈlɔ͜ørəm ˈʃoːsə ˈlɑ͜ofvɛrts! lʊmˈfaŋəntˈ lʊmˈfaŋən!
In eurem Schosse aufwärts! umfangend umfangen!
In your lap, upwards! Embracing embraced!
(In your lap, upwards! Embracing and embraced!)

'a͜ofvɛrt͜s |an 'da͜enən 'bu:zən, 'lal,li:bəndɐ 'fa:t'ɐ!
aufwärts an deinen Busen, allliebender Vater!
upwards to your bosom, all-loving Father!

[In Greek mythology Zeus, in the form of an eagle, carried Ganymede, a Phrygian youth, up to heaven to become cupbearer to the gods; here Goethe uses that image to suggest a mystical sensation of union with God through love for God's glorious Creation. Schubert's beautiful song begins as fresh and fragrant as a spring morning, with delightful nature painting, grows gradually more and more excitedly ecstatic, and ends in a transcendent experience of infinite divine love.]

gə'be:t' 'vɛ:rənt de:ɐ̯ ʃlaxtʰ
Gebet während der Schlacht
Prayer during Battle

Posthumously published [composed 1815] (poem by Theodor Körner)

'fa:t'ɐ(r), |ɪç 'ru:fə dɪç! 'brʏlənt' |ʊm'vœlk't' mɪç de:ɐ̯ dampf de:ɐ̯ gə'ʃʏt͜sə,
Vater, ich rufe dich! Brüllend umwölkt mich der Dampf der Geschütze,
Father, I call You! Roaring around-clouds me the smoke of the cannons,
(Father, I call upon You! The dense smoke of roaring cannons forms a cloud all around me,)

'ʃp'ry:ənt' |ʊm't͜sʊk'ən mɪç 'rasəlndə 'blɪt͜sə. 'lɛŋk'ɐ de:ɐ̯ 'ʃlaxt'ən, |ɪç 'ru:fə dɪç!
sprühend umzucken mich rasselnde Blitze. Lenker der Schlachten, ich rufe dich!
sparking around-jerk me rattling lightnings. Ruler of the battles, I call You!
(sparks dart around me like lightning flashes, rattling everything. Lord of battles, I call to You!)

'fa:t'ɐ du:, 'fy:rə mɪç! fy:ɐ̯ mɪç t͜sʊm 'zi:gə, fy:ɐ̯ mɪç t͜sʊm 'tʰo:də:
Vater du, führe mich! Führ' mich zum Siege, führ' mich zum Tode:
Father You, lead me! Lead me to the victory, lead me to the death:
(You, Father,—lead me! Lead me to victory, lead me to death:)

hɛr, |ɪç |ɛɐ̯'kʰɛnə 'da͜enə gə'bo:t'ə; hɛr, vi: du: vɪlst', zo: 'fy:rə mɪç.
Herr, ich erkenne deine Gebote; Herr, wie du willst, so führe mich.
Lord, I recognize Your commandments; Lord, as You want, so lead me.
(Lord, I recognize Your commandments; Lord, lead me according to Your will.)

gɔt', |ɪç |ɛɐ̯'kʰɛnə dɪç! zo: |ɪm 'hɛrpst'lɪçən 'ra͜oʃən de:ɐ̯ 'blɛt'ɐ,
Gott, ich erkenne dich! so im herbstlichen Rauschen der Blätter,
God, I recognize You! So in the autumnal rustling of the leaves,
(God, I recognize you! As in the autumnal rustling of the leaves,)

als |ɪm 'ʃlaxt'ən,dɔnɐvɛt'ɐ(r), '|u:ɐ̯kʰvɛl de:ɐ̯ 'gna:də, |ɛɐ̯kʰɛn |ɪç dɪç!
als im Schlachtendonnerwetter, Urquell der Gnade, erkenn' ich dich!
as in the battle- thunderstorm, Source of the Grace, recognize I You!
(thus also in the thunder of battle do I recognize You, Source of all Grace!)

'fa:t'ɐ du:, 'ze:gnə mɪç! |ɪn 'da͜enə hant' bə'fe:l |ɪç ma͜en 'le:bən,
Vater du, segne mich! In deine Hand befehl' ich mein Leben,
Father You, bless me! Into Your hand commend I my life,
(You, Father,—grant me Your blessing! I commend my life into Your hands,)

duː kʰanstʻ lɛs ˈneːmən, duː hastʻ lɛs gəˈgeːbən; t͡sʊm ˈleːbən, t͡sʊm ˈʃtʻɛrbən ˈzeːgnə mɪç!
du kannst es nehmen, du hast es gegeben; zum Leben, zum Sterben segne mich!
You can it take, You have it given; to the life, to the dying bless me!
(You can take it, for You have given it; whether for life or for death, grant me Your blessing!)

ˈfaːtʻɐ(r), lɪç ˈpʰra͡ezə dɪç! sɪstʻ jaː kʰa͡en kʰamp͡f fyːɐ̯ di ˈgyːtʻɐ deːɐ̯/deːr ˈleːɐ̯də;
Vater, ich preise dich! 'Sist ja kein Kampf für die Güter der Erde;
Father, I praise You! 'Tis after all no battle for the goods of the earth;
(Father, I praise You! This is, after all, not a battle for worldly goods;)

das ˈha͡elɪçstʻə ˈʃyt͡sən viːɐ̯ mɪt dem ˈʃveːɐ̯tʻə: drʊm ˈfaləntʻ,
das Heiligste schützen wir mit dem Schwerte: drum, fallend,
the most holy protect we with the sword: therefore, falling,
(we are protecting what is most holy to us with the sword: therefore, whether falling in battle)

lʊntʻ ˈziːgəntʻ, pʰra͡ez ɪç dɪç, gɔt, diːɐ̯/diːr lɛɐ̯ˈgeːb ɪç mɪç!
und siegend, preis' ich dich. Gott, dir ergeb' ich mich!
and victorious, praise I You. God, to You yield I myself!
(or victorious, I praise You. God, I yield myself to You!)

vɛn mɪç di ˈdɔnɐ dɛs ˈtʰoːdəs bəˈgryːsən, vɛn ˈma͡enə ˈlaːdɐn gəˈlœfnətʻ ˈfliːsən:
Wenn mich die Donner des Todes begrüssen, wenn meine Adern geöffnet fliessen:
If me the thunders of the death greet, if my veins opened flow:
(If the thunders of death will greet me, if my opened veins are flowing:)

diːɐ̯, ma͡en gɔt, diːɐ̯/diːr lɛɐ̯ˈgeːb ɪç mɪç! ˈfaːtʻɐ(r), lɪç ˈruːfə dɪç!
dir, mein Gott, dir ergeb' ich mich! Vater, ich rufe dich!
to You, my God, to You yield I myself! Father, I call You!
(to You, my God, to You I yield myself! Father, I call upon You!)

[The poet died in battle soon after he wrote this touching poem in 1813. Schubert set the first stanza as a recitative with exciting, descriptive accompaniment. The following five stanzas are set strophically, to a hymn-like melody with throbbing chords in the piano part.]

Gefrorne Tränen see *Winterreise*

gəˈha͡eməs
Geheimes
Something Secret

Op. 14, No. 2 [1821] (Johann Wolfgang von Goethe)

ˈyːbɐ ˈma͡enəs ˈliːpʻçəns ˈlɔ͡øgəln ʃtʻeːn fɛɐ̯ˈvʊndɐtʻ ˈlalə ˈlɔ͡øtʻə;
Über meines Liebchens Äugeln stehn verwundert alle Leute;
At my sweetheart's ogling stand wondering all people;
(Everyone wonders about the eyes my sweetheart makes;)

ɪç, deːɐ̯ ˈvɪsəndə, daˈgeːgən, va͡es rɛçtʻ guːtʻ vas das bəˈdɔ͡øtʻə.
ich, der Wissende, dagegen, weiss recht gut was das bedeute.
I, the knowing one, on the contrary, know very well what that means.
(I, who share the secret, on the contrary, know very well what those glances mean.)

dɛn lɛs ha͜est‘: lɪç 'li:bə 'di:zən, lʊnt‘ nɪçt‘ lɛtva de:n lʊnt‘ 'je:nən.
Denn es heisst: ich liebe diesen, und nicht etwa den und jenen.
For it means: I love *this* one, and not perchance that one and that (other) one.
(For they mean: "I love *this* man, and not that one or perhaps that other one.")

'lasət‘ nu:ɐ̯/nu:r, li:ɐ̯ 'gu:t‘ən 'lɔ͜øt‘ə, 'lɔ͜øɐ 'vʊndɐn, 'lɔ͜øɐ 'ze:nən!
Lasset nur, ihr guten Leute, euer Wundern, euer Sehnen!
Leave only, you good people, your wondering, your longing!
(So stop, you good people, your wondering, your longing!)

ja:, mɪt‘ 'lʊngəhɔ͜ørən 'mɛçt‘ən 'blɪk‘ət‘ zi: vo:l lɪn di 'rʊndə;
Ja, mit ungeheuren Mächten blicket sie wohl in die Runde;
Yes, with colossal powers gazes she indeed into the company around her;
(Yes, she may gaze into the circle of people around her with colossal power in her eyes;)

dɔx zi: zu:xt‘ nu:ɐ̯ t͜su: fɛɐ̯'kʰyndən li:m di 'nɛçst‘ə 'zy:sə 'ʃt‘ʊndə.
doch sie sucht nur zu verkünden ihm die nächste süsse Stunde.
but she seeks only to make known to him the next sweet hour.
(but she is only trying to let *him—this* man—know the time of their next sweet hour.)

[The poem comes from Goethe's *West-Östlicher Divan* (Western-Eastern Collection of Poetry), 200 poems in twelve books, inspired by the "Divan" of Hafiz (a fourteenth-century Persian poet) and by Goethe's current lady-love, Marianne von Willemer. Schubert's setting is a perfect gem.]

gə'ha͜emnɪs
Geheimnis
A Secret

Posthumously published [composed 1816] (poem by Johann Mayrhofer)

za:k‘ lan, ve:ɐ̯ le:ɐ̯t dɪç 'li:dɐ, zo: 'ʃma͜eçəlnt‘ lʊnt‘ zo: t͜sa:ɐ̯tʰ?
Sag an, wer lehrt dich Lieder, so schmeichelnd und so zart?
Tell to, who teaches you songs, so flattering and so delicate?
(Tell us, who teaches you those songs, so beguiling and so tender?)

zi: 't͜sa͜obɐn 'la͜enən 'hɪməl la͜os 'tʰry:bɐ 'ge:gənvartʰ. ['ru:fən]
Sie zaubern einen Himmel aus trüber Gegenwart. [*GA:* Sie rufen]
They conjure up a heaven out of dreary present. [call, summon]
(They conjure up a heaven out of this dreary present time.)

e:ɐ̯st‘ la:k‘ das lant‘, fɛɐ̯'ʃla͜eɐt‘, lɪm 'ne:bəl fo:ɐ̯/fo:r lʊns da: —
Erst lag das Land, verschleiert, im Nebel vor uns da —
First lay the land, veiled, in the mist before us there —
(First the land lay veiled in mist before us there —)

du: zɪŋst‘, lʊnt‘ 'zɔnən 'lɔ͜øçt‘ən, lʊnt‘ 'fry:lɪŋ lɪst‘ lʊns na:.
du singst, und Sonnen leuchten, und Frühling ist uns nah.
you sing, and suns shine brightly, and spring is to us near.
(you sing, and the sun shines, and spring is near to us.)

den 'ʃɪlfbəkʰrɛnt͜st‘ən 'lalt‘ən, de:ɐ̯ 'za͜enə 'lʊrnə gi:st‘,
Den schilfbekränzten Alten, der seine Urne giesst, [*poem:* Den Alten, Schilfbekränzten]
The reed- crowned old man, who his urn pours,
(The old man crowned with reeds who is pouring from his urn)

lɛɐ̯ˈblɪkst duː nɪçtʻ, nuːɐ̯ ˈvasɐ, viːs dʊrç di ˈviːzən fliːstʰ.
erblickst du nicht, nur Wasser, wie's durch die Wiesen fliesst.
perceive you not, only water, as it through the meadows flows.
(you do not perceive; you see only the water, as it flows through the meadows.)

zoː geːtʻ lɛs la͜ox dem ˈzɛŋɐ(r), leːɐ̯ zɪŋtʰ, leːɐ̯ ʃtʻa͜ontʻ lɪn zɪç;
So geht es auch dem Sänger, er singt, er staunt in sich;
So goes it also for the singer; he sings, he is amazed in himself;
(So it is for the singer, too; he sings, he is amazed, within himself;)
[*poem:* **er singt und** (lʊntʻ, and) **staunt in sich**]

vas ʃtʻɪl la͜en gɔtʻ bəˈra͜etʻətʻ, bəˈfrɛmdətʻ liːn viː dɪç.
was still ein Gott bereitet, befremdet ihn wie dich.
what quietly a god prepares, astonishes him as (it does) you.
(that which a god has quietly prepared astonishes him—the singer—as much as it does you.)

[The poet, one of the composer's close friends, dedicated this poem "to F. Schubert," who obligingly set the compliment to music. The reed-crowned old man with the urn seems to be a reference to the classical portrayal of a river god, as depicted in ancient sculptures. Mayrhofer is suggesting, perhaps, that Schubert's music flows out of him spontaneously, as if the composer himself were unaware of its divine source.]

ga͜est deːɐ̯ ˈliːbə / deːɐ̯ ˈlaːbəntʻ ˈʃla͜eɐtʻ fluːɐ̯ lʊntʻ ha͜en
Geist der Liebe / Der Abend schleiert Flur und Hain
Spirit of Love / The Evening Veils Field and Grove

Posthumously published [composed 1816] (poem by Friedrich von Matthisson)

deːɐ̯/deːr ˈlaːbəntʻ ˈʃla͜eɐtʻ fluːɐ̯/fluːr lʊntʻ ha͜en lɪn ˈtʰra͜olɪç ˈhɔldə ˈdɛmrʊŋ la͜en;
Der Abend schleiert Flur und Hain in traulich holde Dämmrung ein;
The evening veils field and grove in familiar, friendly twilight in;
(The evening veils field and grove in familiar, friendly twilight;)

hɛl flɪmtʻ, voː ˈgɔldnə ˈvœlkʻçən t͜siːn, deːɐ̯ ʃtʻɛrn deːɐ̯ ˈliːbəskʰøːnɪgɪn.
hell flimmt, wo gold'ne Wölkchen ziehn, der Stern der Liebeskönigin.
brightly sparkles, where gold cloudlets drift, the star of the love- queen (= Venus).
(the star of the queen of love is sparkling brightly, there where little golden clouds are drifting.)

di ˈvoːgənfluːtʻ haltʻ ˈʃlʊmɐkʰlaŋ, di ˈbɔ͜ømə ˈlɪspʻəln ˈlaːbəntʻzaŋ;
Die Wogenflut hallt Schlummerklang, die Bäume lispeln Abendsang;
The wave- water sounds slumber- sound, the trees whisper evening-song;
(The undulating waters hum their slumber sounds, the trees whisper an evening song;)

deːɐ̯ ˈviːzə graːs lʊmˈga͜okʻəltʻ lɪntʻ mɪtʻ ˈzʏlfənkʰʊs deːɐ̯ ˈfryːlɪŋsvɪntʻ.
der Wiese Gras umgaukelt lind mit Sylphenkuss der Frühlingswind.
the meadow's grass [obj.]flits about gently with sylph- kiss the spring breeze [subj.].
(the spring breeze flits gently about the grass of the meadow with sylphlike kisses.)

deːɐ̯ ga͜est deːɐ̯ ˈliːbə vɪrkʻtʻ lʊntʻ ʃtʻreːpʻtʻ, voː nuːɐ̯/nuːr la͜en pʰʊls deːɐ̯ ˈʃœp͜fɐ beːpʻtʰ;
Der Geist der Liebe wirkt und strebt, wo nur ein Puls der Schöpfer bebt;
The spirit of the love works and strives where only one pulse of the Creator throbs;
(The spirit of love works and strives wherever even *one* pulse of the Creator throbs;)

ɪm ʃt‘roːm, voː voːg ɪn 'voːgə fliːst‘. lɪm haen, voː blat‘ lan blat‘ zɪç ʃliːstʰ.
im Strom, wo Wog’ in Woge fliesst, im Hain, wo Blatt an Blatt sich schliesst.
in the torrent, where wave into wave flows, in the grove, where leaf to leaf itself joins.
(in the torrent, where wave flows into wave, in the grove, where leaf nestles close to leaf.)

o gaest deːɐ̯ 'liːbə! 'fyːrə duː dem 'jʏŋlɪŋ di lɛɐ̯'kʰoːɐ̯nə tsuː!
O Geist der Liebe! führe du dem Jüngling die Erkorne zu!
O spirit of the love! lead you to the youth the chosen one to!
(O spirit of love, lead to the young man his chosen one!)

aen 'mɪnəblɪk‘ deːɐ̯ 'tʰraot‘ən hɛlt‘ mɪt‘ 'hɪməlsglants di 'leɐ̯dənvɛltʰ!
Ein Minneblick der Trauten hellt mit Himmelsglanz die Erdenwelt!
One love- glance of the dear one brightens with heaven- radiance the earth- world!
(One loving glance from his dear one brightens the whole world with the radiance of heaven!)

[Schubert’s strophic setting has the simple charm of a folksong.]

gaest deːɐ̯ 'liːbə / veːɐ̯ bɪst duː, gaest deːɐ̯ 'liːbə

Geist der Liebe / Wer bist du, Geist der Liebe

Spirit of Love / Who Are You, Spirit of Love

Op. 118, No. 1 [1815] (Ludwig Kosegarten)

veːɐ̯ bɪst duː, gaest deːɐ̯ 'liːbə, deːɐ̯ dʊrç das 'vɛlt‘lal veːp‘tʰ?
Wer bist du, Geist der Liebe, der durch das Weltall webt?
Who are you, spirit of the love, who through the universe weaves?
(Who are you, Spirit of Love, who is active throughout the universe,)

den ʃoːs deɐ̯/deːr 'leːɐ̯də 'ʃvɛŋɐt‘, lʊnt den la'tʰoːm bə'leːp‘tʰ?
den Schoss der Erde schwängert, und den Atom belebt?
the womb of the earth impregnates, and the atom animates?
(who impregnates the womb of the earth and animates the atom,)

deːɐ̯/deːr lele'mɛnt‘ə 'bɪndət‘, deːɐ̯ 'vɛlt‘ənkʰuːgəln baltʰ?
Der Elemente bindet, der Weltenkugeln ballt,
who elements binds, who celestial globes forms,
(who binds elements, who forms the globes that become stars and planets,)

aos 'lɛŋəlharfən 'juːbəlt‘ lʊnt‘ laos dem 'zɔøk‘lɪŋ laltʰ?
aus Engelharfen jubelt und aus dem Säugling lallt?
out of angel-harps exults and out of the suckling babbles?
(who exults through the sounds of angels’ harps and babbles through the voice of a little baby?)

veːɐ̯ bɪst duː, kʰraft deːɐ̯ 'kʰrɛft‘ə, diː 'graezənlaogən hɛltʰ?
Wer bist du, Kraft der Kräfte, die Greisesaugen hellt?
Who are you, power of the powers, which old men’s eyes brightens?
(Who are you, power of powers, which brightens old men’s eyes,)

di: ˈjʏŋlɪŋsvaŋən ˈrø:tʻətʻ, lʊntʻ ˈmɛ:tʻçənbu:zən ʃvɛltʰ? [de:ɐ̯]
die Jünglingswangen rötet, und Mädchenbusen schwellt? [*GA:* **der Jünglingswangen]**
which youth's cheeks reddens, and girl's bosom swells? [who (refers to "*Geist*")]
(which reddens a young man's cheeks and swells a girl's bosom?) [**die** refers to "Kraft"]
[note: "*die*," as in Peters, is preferable to "*der*" in this context.]
[*poem:* **des** (dɛs, the) **Jünglings Wangen... des Mägdleins** (ˈmɛ:kʻtʻla͡ens, maiden's) **Busen]**

de:ɐ̯ ˈli:bə bɔ͡øtʻ lʊntʻ ˈfɔrdɐtʻ, lʊm ˈli:bə rɪŋtʻ lʊntʻ vɪrpʻtʻ,
Der Liebe beut und fordert, um Liebe ringt und wirbt,
Who love offers and demands, for love struggles and woos,
(You who offer love and ask for love, who struggle for love and who woo for love,)

ʊntʻ mɛsiˈa:dən dɪçtʻətʻ, lʊntʻ ˈbru:tʻʊstʰo:də ʃtʻɪrpʻtʰ? [iˈli̯a:dən]
und Messiaden dichtet, und Brutustode stirbt? [*poem:* **und Iliaden dichtet]**
and "Messiahs" writes, and Brutus-death dies? [*Iliads*]
(and write epic *Messiahs* and die a Brutus death?)*

bɪst du: nɪçtʻ ˈlo:dəm ˈgɔtʻəs, lʊnˈʃtʻrɛ:flɪç, vi: za͡en lɪçtʰ?
Bist du nicht Odem Gottes, unsträflich, wie sein Licht?
Are you not breath of God, irreproachable, as His light?
(Are you not the breath of God, as irreproachable as His light,)

ʊntʻ ʃtʻark, vi: ˈza͡enə rɛçtʻə, di: ˈvɛltʻən ba͡otʻ lʊntʻ brɪçtʰ?
und stark, wie seine Rechte, die Welten baut und bricht?
and strong, as His right hand, which worlds builds and breaks?
(and as strong as His right hand, which builds and breaks entire worlds?)

bɪstʻ ˈlʊnzɐs ˈkʰrɔ͡øtstsu:ks ˈfa:nə, lɛntʻˈflamstʻ mɪtʻ ˈha͡elgɐ ʃa:m
Bist unsers Kreuzzugs Fahne, entflammst mit heil'ger Scham
(You) are our crusade's banner, (you) inflame with holy shame
(You are the banner of our crusade, you inflame with holy shame)

den ˈfa͡egən lʊnt den ˈmatʻən, la͡en ˈve:əntʻ ˈlo:riflam.
den Feigen und den Matten, ein wehend Oriflamm'. [*poem & GA:* **Oriflam]**
the coward and the weakling, a fluttering oriflamme.*
(the coward and the weakling, you are a fluttering oriflamme that guides us into righteous battle.)

nu:ɐ̯ de:ɐ̯/de:r lɪstʻ gu:tʻ lʊntʻ ˈle:dəl, de:m du: den ˈbo:gən ʃpʻanstʰ.
Nur der ist gut und edel, dem du den Bogen spannst.
Only he is good and noble for whom you the bow bend.
(Only he is good and noble for whom you bend the bow.)

nu:ɐ̯ de:ɐ̯/de:r lɪstʻ gro:s lʊntʻ ˈgœtʻlɪç, de:n du: t͡sʊm man lɛɐ̯ˈmanstʰ.
Nur der ist gross und göttlich, den du zum Mann ermannst.
Only he is great and godlike, whom you to the man make manly.
(Only he is great and godlike whom you incite to manliness.)

za͡en vɛrkʻ lɪstʻ pʰyraˈmi:də, za͡en vɔrtʻ lɪstʻ ˈmaxtʻgəbo:tʰ.
Sein Werk ist Pyramide, sein Wort ist Machtgebot.
His work is (a) pyramid, his word is authoritative command.
(His work will last like the pyramids, his word commands respect.)

a͜en ʃp'ɔt' lɪst' li:m di 'hœlə, la͜en ho:n lɪst' li:m de:ɐ̯ tʰo:t'.
Ein Spott ist ihm die Hölle, ein Hohn ist ihm der Tod.
A mockery is to him the hell, a defiance is to him the death.
(To him hell is a mockery, and he offers defiance to death.)

[Schubert set twenty poems by Kosegarten, nineteen of them between June and October 1815. Seven were composed in one day (on October 19th). The poet was a village pastor, later a professor of theology. Schubert marked this rousing strophic song to be sung "with vigor." *Note: Brutus was one of Caesar's assassins whom Caesar had loved and trusted; Klopstock's major work was his long poem titled *Messias* ("Messiah"), a sort of German *Paradise Lost* (Kosegarten had referred to Homer's *Iliad*; Schubert made the change, presumably to honor a distinguished German poet instead). The oriflamme was the ancient red silk banner of St. Denis, proudly carried into battle by kings of France.]

'ga͜est'ɐnɛ:ə
Geisternähe
Nearness in Spirit

Posthumously published [composed 1814] (poem by Friedrich von Matthisson)

de:ɐ̯ 'dɛmrʊŋ ʃa͜en dʊrç'blɪŋk't den ha͜en;
Der Dämmrung Schein durchblinkt den Hain;
The twilight's shine through-gleams the grove;
(The glow of twilight gleams through the grove;)

hi:ɐ̯, ba͜em gə'rɔ͜øʃ dɛs 'vasɐfaləs, dɛŋk' lɪç nu:ɐ̯ dɪç, lo: du: ma͜en 'laləs!
hier, beim Geräusch des Wasserfalles, denk' ich nur dich, o du mein Alles!
here, by the sound of the waterfall, think I only you, O you, my all!
(here, by the sound of the waterfall, I am thinking only of you, O you, my everything!)

da͜en 'ʦa͜obɐbɪlt' lɛɐ̯'ʃa͜ent', zo: mɪlt' vi: 'hɛsperʊs lɪm 'la:bənt'gɔldə,
Dein Zauberbild erscheint, so mild wie Hesperus im Abendgolde,
Your magic- image appears, as gentle as Hesperus in the evening-gold,
(Your magical image appears, as gentle as Hesperus in the gold of evening,)

dem 'fɛrnən frɔ͜ønt', gə'li:p't'ə 'hɔldə! le:ɐ̯ ze:nt' vi: hi:ɐ̯ zɪç ʃt'e:ʦ na:x di:ɐ̯;
dem fernen Freund, geliebte Holde! Er sehnt wie hier sich stets nach dir;
to the distant friend, beloved lovely one! He longs as here himself always for you;
(to your distant friend, lovely beloved! He longs for you always, as he does now and here;)

fɛst', vi: den ʃt'am di 'le:fɔ͜øraŋk'ə, lʊm'ʃlɪŋt dɪç 'li:bənt' za͜en gə'daŋk'ə.
fest, wie den Stamm die Epheuranke, umschlingt dich liebend sein Gedanke.
firmly, as the tree-trunk the ivy tendrils, embraces you lovingly his thought.
(his thoughts embrace you lovingly, as firmly as the tendrils of the ivy embrace the tree.)
[*poem:* **Eppich-** ('lɛp'ɪç, ivy—colloquial word) **ranke**]

dʊrç'be:p't dɪç la͜ox lɪm 'la:bənt'ha͜ox dɛs 'bru:dɐga͜est'əs 'la͜ezəs ve:n,
Durchbebt dich auch im Abendhauch des Brudergeistes leises Weh'n,
Through-trembles you too in the evening breath the brother-spirit's soft blowing,
(Does the soft breathing of a kindred spirit quiver through you too in the evening breeze)
[*poem:* **Wehen** ('ve:ən)]

mɪt‘ 'foːɐ̯gəfyːl fɔm 'viːdɐzeːn? leːɐ̯/leːr lɪsts, deːɐ̯ lɪnt, diːɐ̯, 'zyːsəs kʰɪnt‘,
mit Vorgefühl vom Wiederseh'n? Er ist's, der lind, dir, süsses Kind,
with presentiment of the reunion? He is it, who gently, to you, sweet child,
(with a presentiment of our reunion? It is that spirit, sweet child, who gently)
[*poem:* **Wiedersehen** ('viːdɐzeːən)]

dɛs 'ʃlaeɐs 'zɪlbɐˌneːbəl 'kʰrɔøzəlt‘, lʊnt‘ lɪn deːɐ̯ 'lɔk‘ən 'fʏlə 'zɔøzəltʰ.
des Schleiers Silbernebel kräuselt, und in der Locken Fülle säuselt.
the veil's silver mist ruffles, and in the curls' fullness rustles.
(ruffles the silver mist of your veil and rustles in the abundance of your curls.)

ɔft‘ høːɐ̯st duː liːn, viː meloˈdiːn deːɐ̯ 'veːmuːt‘ laos gəˈdɛmpft‘ən 'zaet‘ən
Oft hörst du ihn, wie Melodien der Wehmut aus gedämpften Saiten
Often hear you him, like melodies of the melancholy from muted strings
(Often you hear it, like melancholy melodies from muted strings)

lɪn 'ʃt‘ɪlɐ naxt‘ foˈryːbɐglaet‘ən. laox 'fɛsəlfrae vɪrt‘ leːɐ̯ gəˈtʰrɔø,
in stiller Nacht vorübergleiten. Auch fesselfrei wird er getreu,
in quiet night past- glide. Even free of fetters will he faithfully,
(drifting past in the quiet of the night. Even when he is free of earthly bonds he will faithfully)

diːɐ̯ gants lʊnt‘ 'laentsɪç 'hɪngəgeːbən, lɪn 'lalən 'vɛlt‘ən dɪç lʊmˈʃveːbən.
dir ganz und einzig hingegeben, in allen Welten dich umschweben.
to you totally and solely devoted, in all worlds you about-hover.
(hover near to you, totally and solely devoted to you, in all the worlds beyond.)

[This beautiful song was composed when Schubert was only seventeen, musically already fully mature. Strangely, it is not mentioned in the well-known books by Dietrich Fischer-Dieskau and Richard Capell, and is missing from the Peters collection. The poem expresses a great and happy love that will last even beyond death. Hesperus is another name for Venus, the evening star.]

'gaest‘əs-gruːs / 'gaest‘ɐgruːs
Geistes-Gruss / Geistergruss (Peters title)
A Ghost's Greeting

Op. 92, No. 3 [1815 (?); revisions: 1816, 1818, 1828] (Johann Wolfgang von Goethe)

hoːx laof dem 'lalt‘ən 'tʰʊrmə ʃt‘eːt dɛs 'hɛldən 'leːdlɐ gaest‘,
Hoch auf dem alten Turme steht des Helden edler Geist,
High upon the old tower stands the hero's noble ghost,

deːɐ̯, viː das ʃif foˈryːbɐ geːt‘, lɛs voːl tsuː 'faːrən haestʰ.
der, wie das Schiff vorüber geht, es wohl zu fahren heisst.
which, as the ship past goes, it well to travel bids.
(which, as the ship cruises by, bids it a good voyage.)

ziː, 'diːzə 'zeːnə vaːɐ̯ zoː ʃt‘ark‘, diːs hɛrts zoː fɛst‘ lʊnt‘ vɪlt‘,
"Sieh, diese Sehne* war so stark, dies Herz so fest und wild,
"See, this sinew was so strong, this heart so firm and wild,
("See, these sinew were once so strong, this heart was once so firm and wild,)
[**GA & poem:* **diese Senne** ('zɛnə, sinew—archaic form)]

di ˈkʰnɔxən fɔl fɔn ˈrɪtʻɐmarkʰ, deːɐ̯ ˈbɛçɐ(r) ˈlangəfʏltʰ;
die Knochen voll von Rittermark, der Becher angefüllt;
the bones full of knight-marrow, the cup filled up;
(the marrow in my bones was that of a valiant knight, my cup of life was filled to the brim;)

ma͜en ˈhalbəs ˈleːbən ʃtʻʏrmtʻ lɪç fɔrtʰ, fɛɐ̯ˈdeːnt di hɛlftʻ lɪn ruː,
mein halbes Leben stürmt' ich fort, verdehnt' die Hälft' in Ruh,
my half life stormed I forth, stretched away the half in rest,
(half my life I fought away, stretched out the other half in peace;)

ʊnt duː, duː ˈmɛnʃən- ˈʃifla͜en dɔrtʰ, faːr ˈɪmɐ(r), ˈlɪmɐ t͜suː!
und du, du Menschen-Schifflein dort, fahr' immer, immer zu!"
and you, you human- little ship there, sail ever, ever onward!"
(sail on, little ship of mankind, sail onward, ever onward!")

[Schubert made four slightly differing versions of this song, all four reproduced in the *Gesamtausgabe* (the Peters edition prints the fourth, with an altered title). Goethe wrote the poem during a Rhein and Lahn journey; he was inspired by the sight of an old castle named Lahneck, on a height above the Lahn, and immediately dictated the poem to a friend on the spot.]

Geistliche Lieder see
Dem Unendlichen, Die Gestirne, Das Marienbild, Vom Mitleiden Mariä, Litanei, Pax vobiscum, Gebet während der Schlacht, Himmelsfunken

gəˈnyːkʻzaːmkʰa͜etʰ
Genügsamkeit
Contentedness

Op. 109, No. 2 [1815] (Franz von Schober)

dɔrtʻ ˈraːgətʻ la͜en bɛrkʻ la͜os den ˈvɔlkʻən heːɐ̯
"Dort raget ein Berg aus den Wolken hehr,
"There towers up a mountain out of the clouds sublimely,
("A mountain peak is soaring up sublimely above the clouds,)
[*variant:* **aus den Wolken her** (heːɐ̯, hither)]

liːn lɛɐ̯ˈra͜eçtʻ voːl ma͜en ˈla͜eləndɐ ʃrɪtʰ. dɔx ˈraːgən ˈnɔ͜ʏə lʊntʻ ˈlɪmɐ meːɐ̯,
ihn erreicht wohl mein eilender Schritt. Doch ragen neue und immer mehr,
it reaches probably my hurrying stride. But tower up new and ever more,
(my stride can probably reach it if I hurry. But more and more new ones are rising too,)

fɔrtʻ, daː mɪç deːɐ̯ draŋ nɔx dʊrçglyːtʰ. lɛs tʰra͜epʻtʻ liːn
fort, da mich der Drang noch durchglüht." Es treibt ihn
onward, for me the urge still through-burns." It drives him
(press on, for the urge is still burning within me." It drives him)

fɔm ˈʃveːbəndən ˈroːzənlɪçtʻ, la͜os dem ˈruːɪgən ˈha͜etʻɐn laˈt͜suːɐ̯.
vom schwebenden Rosenlicht, aus dem ruhigen heitern Azur.
from the hovering rosy light, from the calm clear azure.
(away from this hovering rosy light, from the calm cloudless blue of the sky above this valley.)
[*Peters:* **aus den** (dative plural, misprint?)]

lʊnt' 'lɛnt'lɪç 'vaːrəns di 'bɛrgə nɪçt', lɛs vaːɐ̯ 'zaeno 'zeːnzʊxt' nuːɐ̯.
Und endlich waren's die Berge nicht, es war seine Sehnsucht nur.
And in the end was it the mountains not, it was his longing only.
(And in the end it was not the mountains, after all; it was only his longing that drove him on.)

dɔx nuːn vɪrt' lɛs 'rɪŋs'lʊm løːt' lʊnt' flax, lʊnt dɔx kʰan leːɐ̯ 'nɪmɐ tsu'rʏkʰ.
Doch nun wird es ringsum öd' und flach, und doch kann er nimmer zurück.
But now becomes it all around bare and flat, and yet can he never (turn) back.
(But now everything around him is becoming bare and flat; and yet he can never turn back.)

oː 'gœt'ɐ, geːp't' miːɐ̯/miːr laen 'hʏt'əndax lɪm tʰaːl, lʊnt' laen 'friːt'lɪçəs glʏkʰ!
O Götter, gebt mir ein Hüttendach im Tal, und ein friedliches Glück!
O gods, give me a hut- roof in the valley, and a peaceful happiness!
(O gods, give me a hut in the valley as my shelter, and a peaceful kind of happiness!)

[The poet, a close friend of Schubert's, seems to be saying that it is better to be content with a simple, peaceful life in the valley than to strive toward the mountain peaks, however alluring. Schubert's energetic strophic setting treats both sentiments equally—the urge to struggle toward the heights and the wish for an undemanding, less ambitious existence. The poem does not tell us why the climber is unable to return, or why the landscape beyond the mountains is so bleak.]

gə'zaŋ lan di harmo'niː
Gesang an die Harmonie
Song to Harmony

Posthumously published [composed 1816] (poem by Johann Gaudenz von Salis-Seewis)

'ʃœpfərɪn bə'zeːlt'ɐ 'tʰøːnə! 'naːxkʰlaŋ dem lo'lʏmp' lɛnt'haltʰ!
Schöpferin beseelter Töne! Nachklang dem Olymp enthallt!
Creatress of animate tones! Echo from the Olympus reverberated!
(Creatress of tones that have souls! Sounds that have come from Olympus, home of the gods!)

'hɔldə, 'kʰœrp'ɐloːzə 'ʃøːnə, 'zanft'ə 'gaest'ɪgə gə'valt',
Holde, körperlose Schöne, sanfte geistige Gewalt,
Lovely, incorporeal beauty, gentle spiritual power,

diː das hɛrts deːɐ̯/deːr 'leːɐ̯dənzøːnə kʰyːn lɛɐ̯'heːp't' lʊnt' mɪlt' lʊm'valtʰ!
die das Herz der Erdensöhne kühn erhebt und mild umwallt!
which the heart of the earth- sons boldly lifts and tenderly envelops!
(which boldly lifts and tenderly envelops the hearts of mortals,)

diː lɪn 'lɪnrɐ 'ʃt'ʏrmə 'draŋə laːp't' mɪt' 'ʃt'ɪləndɐ ma'giː,
die in inn'rer Stürme Drange labt mit stillender Magie,
which in inner storms' stress comforts with soothing magic,
(which comforts with soothing magic those who feel the stress of inner storms,)

kʰɔm mɪt 'daenəm 'zyːngəzaŋə, 'hɪməlstʰɔxt'ɐ harmo'niː!
komm mit deinem Sühngesange, Himmelstochter Harmonie!
come with your song of reconciliation, heaven's daughter Harmony!

'zɔøftsɐ, diː das hɛrts lɛɐ̯'ʃt'ɪk't'ə, das, mɪs'kʰant', zɪç 'lɛnt'lɪç ʃlɔs —
Seufzer, die das Herz erstickte, das, misskannt, sich endlich schloss —
Sighs, which the heart stifled, that, misjudged, itself finally closed —
(For sighs, which the heart stifled, the heart that, misjudged, finally closed itself to others —)

ˈtʰrɛːnən, diː das ǀɑ͜ok‘ t͜sɛɐ̯ˈdrʏk‘t‘ə, das ǀa͜enst‘ fiːl ǀʊmˈzɔnst‘ fɛɐ̯ˈgɔs,
Tränen, die das Aug’ zerdrückte, das einst viel’ umsonst vergoss,
tears, which the eye pressed back, that once many in vain shed,
(and for tears, which the eyes suppressed, eyes that once shed many tears in vain, —)

dank‘t diːɐ̯ ˈviːdɐ deːɐ̯/deːr ǀɛntˈt͜sʏk‘t‘ə, deːn da͜en ˈlaːbəkʰvɛl ǀʊmˈflɔs.
dankt dir wieder der Entzückte, den dein Labequell umfloss.
thanks you again the enraptured one, whom your refreshing spring flows about.
(the enraptured one, who is bathed in your refreshing spring, thanks you again.)

deːɐ̯/deːr ǀɛmˈp͜fɪndʊŋ ˈt͜saːɐ̯t‘ə ˈbluːmə, diː manç ˈfrɔst‘gɐ blɪk‘ fɛɐ̯ˈzɛŋt‘,
Der Empfindung zarte Blume, die manch frost’ger Blick versengt,
The feeling’s delicate flower, which many a frosty gaze singes,
(The delicate flower of sentiment, which is easily parched by many a frosty stare,)

blyːt‘ ǀɛɐ̯ˈkʰvɪk‘t‘ ǀɪm ˈha͜elɪçtʰuːmə ˈǀa͜enɐ brʊst, diː duː gəˈtʰrɛŋk‘tʰ.
blüht erquickt im Heiligtume einer Brust, die du getränkt.
blooms revived in the sanctuary of a breast, which you (have) watered.
(blooms, revived, in the sanctuary of a breast that has been watered by you.)

dɛs fɛɐ̯ˈgaŋnən ˈtʰrɑ͜omgəˈbɪldə, ˈǀaːmoːɐ̯s ˈmɔrgənfantʰaˈziːn,
Des Vergangnen Traumgebilde, Amors Morgenphantasien,
The past’s dream-vision, Cupid’s morning-fantasies,
(The dream-vision of the past, the morning-fantasies inspired by the god of amorous love,)

ha͜est da͜en ruːf, zoː ʃt‘ɪl viː ˈmɪldə ˈmoːndəsʃat‘ən, ǀʊns ǀʊmˈt͜siːn,
heisst dein Ruf, so still wie milde Mondesschatten, uns umziehn,
bids your call, as quietly as gentle moon- shadows, us to envelop,
(your call bids them envelop us, as quietly as gentle moon-cast shadows,)

ɑ͜of dɛs ˈleːbəns ˈhɛrpst‘gəˌfɪldə lɛŋst‘ fɛɐ̯ˈvɛlk‘t‘ə ˈfa͜elçən blyːn.
auf des Lebens Herbstgefilde längst verwelkte Veilchen blühn.
on the life’s autumnal fields long since withered violets bloom.
(and, on life’s autumnal fields, violets, long since withered, revive and bloom again.)

ˈzyːsɐ ˈtʰɔ͜øʃʊŋ ˈt͜sɑ͜obɐblyːt‘ə, diː ǀɛɐ̯ˈfaːrʊŋ kʰnɪk‘t‘ ǀʊnt‘ raft‘,
Süsser Täuschung Zauberblühte, die Erfahrung knickt und rafft,
Sweet illusion’s magic blossoms, which experience breaks and snatches away,
(The magic blossoms of sweet illusion, so often broken and snatched away by experience,)

vɛk‘t‘ ǀɪm ˈǀøːdəst‘ən gəˈmyːt‘ə ˈda͜enəs ˈvoːllɑ͜ot͜s ˈʃœp͜fʊŋskʰraftʰ.
weckt im ödesten Gemüte deines Wohllauts Schöpfungskraft.
awakens in the most desolate soul your euphony’s creative power.
(are awakened even in the most desolate soul by the creative power of your euphony.)

ˈhɔldɐ, nuːn ǀa͜en ˈzyːsəs ˈvɛːnən, kʰeːɐ̯t das bɪlt‘ fɛɐ̯ˈflɔsnɐ t͜sa͜etʰ;
Holder, nun ein süsses Wähnen, kehrt das Bild verflossner Zeit;
Lovelier, now a sweet imagination, returns the image of flown-by time;
(The image of a time flown by, now only a sweet memory, returns lovelier than ever;)

ˈt͜saːɐ̯t‘ɐ ʃt‘reːp‘t deːɐ̯ ˈliːbə ˈzeːnən, ˈmɪldɐ glyːt di ˈǀɪnɪçkʰa͜etʰ,
zarter strebt der Liebe Sehnen, milder glüht die Innigkeit,
more tenderly struggles the love’s yearning, more gently glows the fervent feeling,
(bereaved love yearns more tenderly, fervent feeling burns more gently,)

vɛn da͜en kʰoːɐ̯ den ˈtʰra͜oɐˌʦseːnən ˈhøːɐn tʰroːstʻ |ʊntʻ ˈ|anmuːtʻ la͜etʰ;
wenn dein Chor den Trauerszenen höhern Trost und Anmut leiht;
when your choir to the scenes of mourning higher solace and grace lends;
(when your choir lends a higher solace and grace to scenes of mourning and grief)

giːpʻtʻ, voː ˈvɔrtʻə nɪçʦ fɛɐ̯ˈmøːgən, ˈlaːpzaːl dem ʦɛɐ̯ˈʃtʻøːɐ̯tʻən ga͜estʰ;
gibt, wo Worte nichts vermögen, Labsal dem zerstörten Geist;
gives, when words nothing can do, comfort to the devastated spirit;
(and, when words have no power to help, gives comfort to the devastated spirit,)

deːɐ̯/deːr |ɛɐ̯ˈgeːbʊŋ ˈʃtʻɪlən ˈzeːgən, voː di tʰrɛːn |ɛɐ̯ˈʃœp͡fəntʻ flɔ͜østʰ.
der Ergebung stillen Segen, wo die Trän' erschöpfend fleusst.
the resignation's quiet blessing, when the tear exhaustingly flows.
(gives the quiet blessing of resignation, when one's font of tears is nearly exhausted.)
[*fleusst* = *fliesst* (from *fliessen* = to flow)]

ˈhɛftʻə |a͜of di ˈlɪçtʻɐn ˈʃtʻɛlən ˈ|ʊnzrɐ baːn deːɐ̯ ˈʃveːɐ̯muːtʻ blɪkʰ;
Hefte auf die lichtern Stellen unsrer Bahn der Schwermut Blick;
Fix upon the brighter places of our pathway the melancholy's gaze;
(When we are melancholy fix our gaze upon the *brighter* places on our pathway;)

tʰraːkʻ den ga͜estʻ |a͜of ˈvoːlla͜oʦ ˈvɛlən |ɪn |a͜en ˈfriːdənslant ʦuˈrʏkʰ..
trag' den Geist auf Wohllauts Wellen in ein Friedensland zurück.
bear the spirit on euphony's waves into a peace- land back.
(bear the spirit back to a land of peace on the waves of euphony.)

zɔlç |a͜en ˈleːbən ʦuː |ɛɐ̯ˈhɛlən bra͜oxtʻ man ˈtʰɔ͜øʃʊŋ |ʊntʻ muˈziːkʰ!
Solch ein Leben zu erhellen braucht man Täuschung und Musik!
Such a life to brighten needs one illusion and music!
(To brighten such a life as this, one needs illusion and music!)

voː deːɐ̯ ʃtʻʊrm dɛs ˈʦa͜etʻəngaŋəs ma͜est deːɐ̯ ˈbɛsɐn plaːn ʦɛɐ̯ˈra͜estʻ,
Wo der Sturm des Zeitenganges meist der Bessern Plan zerreisst,
When the storm of the passing of time mostly the better ones' plan tears up,
(When the storms of passing time mostly destroy the plans made in better times,)

tʰrɔ͜øf |ɪm ˈbalzaːm dɛs gəˈzaŋəs ˈhɔfnʊŋ |ɪn deːɐ̯/deːr ˈ|eːdlən ga͜estʰ.
träufl' im Balsam des Gesanges Hoffnung in der Edlen Geist.
drip in the balm of the song hope into the noble spirit.
(pour hope into the noble spirit with the balm of song.)

kʰɔm, moˈmɛntʻə ʦuː fɛɐ̯ˈʃøːnən deːm, deːɐ̯ nɪçt deːɐ̯ ˈʦuːkʰʊnft tʰra͜otʰ;
Komm, Momente zu verschönen dem, der nicht der Zukunft traut;
Come, moments to beautify for him, who not in the future has confidence;
(Come and bring beauty to present moments for someone who has no confidence in the future;)

ʃlɔ͜øs den blɪkʻ mɪtʻ ˈʃlʊmɐtʰøːnən, deːɐ̯ ʦuː ʃtar |ɪns ˈdʊŋkʻəl ʃa͜otʰ;
schleuss den Blick mit Schlummertönen, der zu starr ins Dunkel schaut;
close the gaze with slumber- tones, that too fixedly into the dark looks;
(with lulling tones close the gaze that stares too fixedly into the darkness;)
[*schleuss* = *schliess'* (from *schliessen* = to close)]

viː den ˈzɔ͜økˈlɪŋ ba͜em lɛntˈˈvøːnən ˈla͜enəs ˈviːgənliːdəs la͜otʰ,
wie den Säugling beim Entwöhnen eines Wiegenliedes Laut,
as the infant at the weaning a lullaby's sound,
(as the sound of a lullaby does the infant that is being weaned,)

lʊl la͜ox lʊns lɪn ˈgɔldnə ˈtʰrɔ͜ømə ˈla͜enɐ ˈbɛsɐn, ˈlɪnɐn vɛltˈ,
lull' auch uns in goldne Träume einer bessern, innern Welt,
lull also us into golden dreams of a better, inner world,
(lull us too into golden dreams of a better, inner world,)

bɪs la͜en ˈzanftˈrəs lɪçt di ˈrɔ͜ømə ˈlʊnzrəs ˈkʰɛrkˈɐs ʃtˈɪl lɛɐ̯ˈhɛltʰ.
bis ein sanftres Licht die Räume unsres Kerkers still erhellt.
till a gentler light the spaces of our prison quietly brightens.
(until a gentler light has quietly come to brighten our prison cell.)

ˈlɛŋəl! deːn t͜sʊm ˈzeːlənkʰraŋkˈən ˈzanftˈəs ˈmɪtˈla͜etˈ ˈniːdɐtʰrɛːkˈtˈ
Engel! den zum Seelenkranken sanftes Mitleid niederträgt;
Angel! whom to the soul- sick one tender compassion brings downward;
(Angel, whom tender compassion has brought down from heaven to the sick soul,)

deːɐ̯/deːr lɛɐ̯ˈkʰvɪkˈəndə gəˈdaŋkˈən lɪn deːɐ̯ ˈtʰøːnə ˈhʏlə leːkˈtʰ;
der erquickende Gedanken in der Töne Hülle legt;
who refreshing thoughts in the tones' outer wrapping places;
(you, who swathe refreshing thoughts in tones,)

ˈlɪndɐntˈ, ʃtˈat deːɐ̯ ˈdɔrnənraŋkˈən, ˈza͜enən ˈfɪtˈɪç lʊm liːn ʃlɛːkˈtʰ:
lindernd, statt der Dornenranken, seinen Fittich um ihn schlägt:
soothingly, instead of the thorny tendrils, his wing around him wraps:
(you, who soothingly wrap your protective wings around him instead of life's thorny tendrils,)

deːm kʰa͜en ˈleːɐ̯dəntʰroːstˈ gəˈbliːbən, ˈza͜enɐ ˈʃtˈʊmən ˈʃveːɐ̯muːt tʰrɔ͜ø —
dem kein Erdentrost geblieben, seiner stummen Schwermut treu —
for whom no earthly comfort (has) remained, to his silent melancholy loyal —
(him, for whom no earthly comfort has remained, him, who is loyal to his silent melancholy,)

leːr liːn ˈva͜enən, leːr liːn ˈliːbən, lʊntˈ za͜en ˈleːbən blyːtˈ liːm nɔ͜ø.
lehr' ihn weinen, lehr' ihn lieben, und sein Leben blüht ihm neu.
teach him to weep, teach him to love, and his life blooms for him anew.
(teach him how to weep, teach him how to love, and his life will bloom for him anew.)

ˈgaːbə, ˈʃtˈɛrpˈlɪçən fɛɐ̯ˈliːən, t͜saːɐ̯tˈ gəˈfyːltˈəs, ʃɔ͜ø fɛɐ̯ˈheːltʰ,
Gabe, Sterblichen verliehen, zart Gefühltes, scheu verhehlt,
Gift, to mortals lent, delicately felt, shyly hidden,
(A gift, lent to mortals, something delicately felt, shyly hidden,)

t͜suː fɛɐ̯ˈtʰra͜on lan meloˈdiːən — ˈzyːsə maxt, diː niː fɛɐ̯ˈfeːltʰ,
zu vertraun an Melodien — süsse Macht, die nie verfehlt,
to trust in melodies — sweet power, which never fails
(the gift to trust in melody — Harmony, the sweet power that never fails)

zeːl lan ˈzeːlə ˈhɪnt͜sut͜siːən; vas bəˈzeːlɪçtˈ, vas lʊns kʰvɛːltʰ,
Seel' an Seele hinzuziehen; was beseligt, was uns quält,
soul to soul to each other to draw; that which makes happy, that which us torments,
(to draw one soul to another; whatever makes us happy, whatever torments us,)

vas mɪt‘ 'vɔrt‘ən 'la͜ostsudrʏk‘ən 'kʰa͜enɐ 'ʃp‘ra:xə kʰraft‘ gə'laŋ —
was mit Worten auszudrücken keiner Sprache Kraft gelang —
that which with words to express no language's power succeeded —
(whatever no language has had the power to express in words —)

'ze:nzʊxt‘, 'ʃa͜oɐ(r) lʊnt‘ lɛnt'tsʏk‘ən tsu: lɛɐ̯'gi:sən lɪm gə'zaŋ.
Sehnsucht, Schauer und Entzücken zu ergiessen im Gesang.
yearning, horror, and rapture to pour out in the song.
(Harmony never fails to pour out all of that in song, whether yearning, horror, or rapture.)

ʃt‘ɪm la͜os 'je:nən 'lɪçt‘ɐn 'sfɛ:rən, ʃpra:x la͜os 'psy:çəs 'fa:t‘ɐlant‘,
Stimm' aus jenen lichtern Sphären, Sprach' aus Psyches Vaterland,
Voice from those lighter spheres, language from Psyche's fatherland,
(Voice from those more ethereal spheres, language from the homeland of the soul,)
[Psyche is here the personification of the soul (*psyche*, in Greek, = soul)]

mɪt dɛs 'hɪməls 'zy:sən 'tsɛ:rən hi:ɐ̯/hi:r lɪm 'frɛmdən tʰa:l lɛɐ̯'kʰantʰ —
mit des Himmels süssen Zähren hier im fremden Tal erkannt —
with the heaven's sweet tears here in the foreign valley recognized —
(recognized, here in this foreign valley of mortal life, with sweet tears of nostalgia for heaven—)
[*poem:* **mit des Heimelns** ('ha͜eməlns, homelike feeling's) **süssen Zähren...**
("*anheimeln*" = to make a person feel at home, to remind a person of home)]

ax! zi: fy:lt‘ nɔx li:ɐ̯ bə'ge:rən, 'hø:ɐn 'tso:nən 'tsu:gəvantʰ;
ach! sie fühlt noch ihr Begehren, höhern Zonen zugewandt;
ah! she feels still her desire, to higher zones to-turned; [*sie*, here, = Psyche = the soul]
(ah! the soul still feels its desire to return to higher realms;)

kʰɛnt di 'ʃp‘ra:xə, me:ɐ̯/me:r lals 'vɔrt‘ə, lʊnt‘ fɛɐ̯'nɪmt de:ɐ̯ 'ze:lən tʰo:n;
kennt die Sprache, mehr als Worte, und vernimmt der Seelen Ton;
knows the language, more than words, and perceives the souls' tone;
(it knows the language, more than words, and hears in it the tones of souls that speak;)

vɛ:nt‘ zɪç lan dɛs 'hɪməls 'pfɔrt‘ə, de:ɐ̯ fɛɐ̯'banʊŋ kʰlʊft‘ lɛnt‘'flo:n.
wähnt sich an des Himmels Pforte, der Verbannung Kluft entflohn.
imagines herself at the heaven's portals, the banishment's chasm fled from.
(it imagines itself at the gates of heaven, fled from the chasm to which it was banished.)

tʰø:n lɪn 'la͜ezən 'ʃt‘ɛrbəkʰø:rən dʊrç dɛs 'tʰo:dəs naxt‘ lʊns fo:ɐ̯!
Tön' in leisen Sterbechören durch des Todes Nacht uns vor!
Sound in soft requiem choruses through the death's night to us before!
(Sound for us, Harmony, in soft requiems through the dark night of death!)

ba͜e dɛs 'lɔ͜øsɐn zɪns tsɛɐ̯'ʃt‘ø:rən 'va͜elə lɪn dɛs 'ga͜est‘əs lo:ɐ̯!
Bei des äussern Sinns Zerstören weile in des Geistes Ohr!
With the outer sense's destruction linger in the spirit's ear!
(When our outer senses are being destroyed, linger in the ear of our spirit!)

di: de:ɐ̯/de:r 'le:ɐ̯də nɪçt‘ gə'hø:rən, he:p‘ mɪt‘ 'ʃva:nənzaŋ lɛm'pʰo:ɐ̯!
Die der Erde nicht gehören, heb' mit Schwanensang empor!
Those who to the earth (do) not belong, lift with swan- song aloft!
(Lift aloft with a final swan song those who do not belong to this earth!)
[The swan, silent in life, was believed to sing as it swam away to its death.]

ˈløːzə zanft dɛs ˈleːbəns ˈbandə, ˈmɪldrə kʰampf lʊntʻ lagoˈniː,
Löse sanft des Lebens Bande, mildre Kampf und Agonie,
Loosen gently the life's bonds, alleviate battle and agony,
(Loosen gently the bonds of life, alleviate the struggle and the agony,)

lʊntʻ lɛmˈp͡faŋ lɪm ˈzeːlənlandə lʊns, loː ˈzeːraf, harmoˈniː!
und empfang' im Seelenlande uns, o Seraph, Harmonie!
and receive in the souls- land us, O seraph, Harmony!
(and receive us in the land of the soul, O seraph, Harmony!)

[The poet must have written this poem during a time of deep disillusionment with the world, a time without hope for the future, when music offered the only significant solace in his life. His ten verses are too many for Schuberts's strophic setting; the first two or three—before too much pessimistic philosophizing has begun to dampen the hymn-like fervor—make an effective song.]

Gesang see *An Sylvia*

gəˈzaŋ deːɐ̯ ˈgaestʻɐ ˈlyːbɐ den ˈvasɐn
Gesang der Geister über den Wassern
Song of the Spirits over the Waters

Posthumously published fragment [composed 1816] (poem by Johann Wolfgang von Goethe)

[dɛs ˈmɛnʃən ˈzeːlə glaeçt dem ˈvasɐ: fɔm ˈhɪməl kʰɔmtʻ lɛs,
[Des Menschen Seele gleicht dem Wasser: vom Himmel kommt es,
[The human soul is similar to the water: from the heaven comes it,
[(The human soul is like water: it comes from heaven,)

t͡sʊm ˈhɪməl ʃtʻaekʻtʻ lɛs, lʊntʻ ˈviːdɐ ˈniːdɐ t͡sʊr ˈleːɐ̯də mʊs lɛs, ˈleːvɪç ˈvɛksəlntʻ.
zum Himmel steigt es, und wieder nieder zur Erde muss es, ewig wechselnd.
to the heaven climbs it, and again down to the earth must it, eternally alternating.
(it ascends to heaven, and again must come down to earth, eternally alternating.)

ʃtʻrøːmtʻ fɔn deːɐ̯ ˈhoːən, ˈʃtʻaelən ˈfɛlsvant deːɐ̯ ˈraenə ʃtʻraːl,
Strömt von der hohen, steilen Felswand der reine Strahl,
Streams from the high, steep cliff the pure jet,
(The clear cascade streams down from the top of the high, steep cliff;)

dan ʃtʻɔøpʻtʻ leːɐ̯ ˈliːpʻlɪç lɪn ˈvɔlkʻənˌvɛlən t͡sʊm ˈglatʻən fɛls,
dann stäubt er lieblich in Wolkenwellen zum glatten Fels,
then breaks up into droplets it charmingly in cloud- waves to the smooth rock,
(then it breaks up into a spray of droplets in lovely cloud-waves on its way to the smooth rock,)

ʊntʻ laeçtʻ lɛmˈp͡faŋən, valtʻ leːɐ̯ fɛɐ̯ˈʃlaeɐntʻ,] laes ˈraoʃənt
und leicht empfangen, wallt er verschleiernd,] leis rauschend
and, lightly received, undulates it veilingly,] softly murmuring
(and, lightly received there, it undulates like a light veil over the rock,]* softly murmuring)
[*The part of Schubert's song that has survived begins at this point in the poem.]

dan t͡sʊr ˈtʰiːfə ˈniːdɐ. ˈraːgən ˈkʰlɪpʻən dem ʃtʻʊrt͡s lɛntʻˈgeːgən,
dann zur Tiefe nieder. Ragen Klippen dem Sturz entgegen, **[***poem without* **dann]**
then to the depths down. Protrude crags to the plunge toward,
(then down to the depths below. If crags of rock protrude into the course of the plunge,)

ʃɔ͡ømt' leːɐ̯ ʊnˈmuːt'ɪç, ˈʃt'uːfənva͡ezə, t͡suː dem ˈlap'grʊnt'. [t͡sʊm]
schäumt er unmutig, stufenweise, zu dem Abgrund. [*poem:* **zum Abgrund]**
foams it angrily, step- wise, to the abyss. [to the]
(it foams furiously, step by step, down into the abyss.)

ɪm ˈflaxən ˈbɛt'ə ˈʃla͡eçət' leːɐ̯ das ˈviːzəntʰaːl hɪn, [ʃla͡eçt']
Im flachen Bette schleichet er das Wiesental hin, [*poem:* **schleicht]**
In the flat bed creeps it the meadow-valley along, [creeps]
(Then in a flat bed it creeps along through the meadows of the valley,)

ʊnt' ɪn dem ˈglat'ən zeː ˈva͡edən liːɐ̯/liːr ˈlant'lɪt͡s ˈalə gəˈʃt'ɪrnə.
und in dem glatten See weiden ihr Antlitz alle Gestirne.
and in the smooth lake graze their face(s) all stars.
(and in the smooth lake all the stars see their faces reflected.)

vɪnt' ɪst deːɐ̯ ˈvɛlə ˈliːp'lɪçɐ ˈbuːlə; [ˈbuːlɐ]
Wind ist der Welle lieblicher Buhle; [*poem:* **Buhler]**
Wind is the wave's sweet lover;
(The wind is the sweet lover of the wave;)

vɪnt' mɪʃt' fɔm grʊnt' la͡os ˈʃɔ͡øməndə ˈvoːgən.
Wind mischt vom Grund aus schäumende Wogen.
wind mingles from the depths up foaming billows.
(the wind mingles the foaming billows that rise up from the depths.)

ˈzeːlə dɛs ˈmɛnʃən, viː gla͡eçst duː dem ˈvas- [(s)ɐ!
Seele des Menschen, wie gleichst du dem Was- [ser!
Soul of the human being, how resemble you to the wa- [ter!
(Human soul, how you resemble the wa- [ter!)
[Schubert's surviving manuscript ends in the middle of the word "*Wasser*."]

ˈʃɪk'zaːl dɛs ˈmɛnʃən, viː gla͡eçst duː dem vɪnt'!]
Schicksal des Menschen, wie gleichst du dem Wind!]
Fate of the human being, how resemble you to the wind!]
(Human fate, how you resemble the wind!)]

[The first and last parts of Schubert' setting for solo voice are missing from the surviving manuscript. They are indicated above in brackets. There is, however, a completion by Reinhard van Hoorickx, privately printed. Schubert returned to this poem four times, but the other versions are for multiple male voices (the last, in 1821, for eight male voices and string orchestra, a masterpiece). Goethe was inspired by the Staubbach Falls, a sheer drop of about 300 meters, at Lauterbrunnen, in the Bernese Oberland near Interlaken, Switzerland. The opening lines suggest that Goethe was influenced by Eastern thought and the concept of reincarnation.]

gəˈzaŋ deːɐ̯ ˈnɔrna
Gesang der Norna
Norna's Song

Op. 85, No. 2 [1825] (from *The Pirate* by Sir Walter Scott, German by S. H. Spiker)

mɪç fyːɐ̯t' ma͡en veːk' voːl ˈma͡elənlaŋ dʊrç gɔlf ʊnt' ʃt'roːm ʊnt' ˈvasɐgraːp'.
Mich führt mein Weg wohl meilenlang durch Golf und Strom und Wassergrab.
Me leads my way probably miles- long through gulf and stream and water- grave.
(My way leads me for many miles through gulf and stream and watery grave.)

di ˈvɛlə kʰɛnt den ˈruːnənsang lʊntʻ ˈglɛtʻətʻ zɪç ts͜ʊm ˈʃpʻiːgəl lapʻ.
Die Welle kennt den Runensang und glättet sich zum Spiegel ab.
The wave knows the runic song and smooths itself to the mirror down.
(The wave knows the mysterious song written in runes, and becomes as smooth as a mirror.)

di ˈvɛlə kʰɛnt den ˈruːnənsang, deːɐ̯ gɔlf vɪrtʻ glat, deːɐ̯ ʃtʻroːm vɪrtʻ ʃtʻɪl;
Die Welle kennt den Runensang, der Golf wird glatt, der Strom wird still;
The wave knows the runic song, the gulf becomes smooth, the river becomes quiet;
[*Spiker:* **der Strom ist** (lɪstʻ, is) **still**]

dɔx ˈmɛnʃənhɛrts͜ lɪm ˈvɪldən draŋ, lɛs va͜es nɪçtʻ, vas lɛs ˈzɛlbɐ vɪl.
doch Menschenherz im wilden Drang, es weiss nicht, was es selber will.
but human heart in the wild impulse, it knows not what it itself wants.
(but the human heart in its wild impulse does not even know what it wants itself.)

nuːɐ̯/nuːr ˈla͜enə ʃtʻʊntʻ lɪstʻ miːɐ̯ fɛɐ̯ˈgœntʻ lɪn ˈjaːrəsfrɪst ts͜ʊm ˈkʰlaːgətʰoːn;
Nur eine Stund' ist mir vergönnt in Jahresfrist zum Klageton;
Only one hour is to me granted in (the) space of a year for the lamentation-tone;
(Only one hour in each year is granted to me for my lamentations;)

ziː ʃlɛːkʻtʻ, vɛn ˈdiːzə ˈlampʻə brɛntʰ — iːɐ̯ ʃa͜en fɛɐ̯ˈlɪʃtʰ, ziː lɪstʻ lɛntʻˈfloːn.
sie schlägt, wenn diese Lampe brennt — ihr Schein verlischt, sie ist entfloh'n.
it strikes when this lamp is burning — (when) its light dies out, it is fled.
(that hour strikes when this lamp is burning — when its light goes out, that hour is over.)
[*Spiker:* **ihr Schein erlischt** (lɛɐ̯ˈlɪʃtʻ, dies out)]

ha͜el, ˈmagnʊs ˈtʰœçtɐ, fɔrtʻ lʊntʻ fɔrt! di ˈlampʻə brɛntʻ lɪn ˈtʰiːfɐ ruː.
Heil, Magnus Töchter, fort und fort! die Lampe brennt in tiefer Ruh'.
Hail, Magnus's daughters, forth and forth! the lamp is burning in deep calmness.
(Hail, daughters of Magnus, forever hail! The lamp is still burning steadily.)
[*fort und fort* = continually, all the time]

ɔ͜ʏç gœn lɪç ˈdiːzɐ ˈʃtʻʊndə vɔrtʰ, lɛɐ̯ˈvaxtʻ, lɛɐ̯ˈvaxtʻ lɔ͜ʏç, høːɐ̯tʻ miːɐ̯ ts͜uː!
Euch gönn' ich dieser Stunde Wort, erwacht, erwacht euch, hört mir zu!
To you grant I this hour's word; awake, wake yourselves, listen to me ... !
(To you I grant the words of this hour. Awake, wake yourselves, and listen to me!)
[*zuhören* = to listen]

[The poem is from *The Pirate* by Sir Walter Scott. Norna is the pirate's mother. She is under a curse that permits her to pour out her woes for only one hour in the year, while a magic lamp is burning. The original text is as follows:

For leagues along the watery way, / Through gulf and stream my course has been;
The billows know my runic lay / And smooth their crests to silent green.
The billows know my runic lay, / The gulf grows smooth, the stream is still:
The human hearts, more wild than they, / Know but the rule of wayward will.
One hour is mine in all the year, / To tell my woes — and one alone;
When gleams this magic lamp, 'tis here; / When dies the mystic light 'tis gone.
Daughters of northern Magnus, hail! / The lamp is lit, the flame is clear,
To you I come to tell my tale, / Awake, arise, my tale to hear!]

Gesänge aus "Wilhelm Meister" see *Harfenspieler I, II, III* and *Heiss mich nicht reden, Kennst du das Land, Nur wer die Sehnsucht kennt, So lasst mich scheinen*

Gesänge der Harfners aus "Wilhelm Meister" see *Harfenspieler I, II, III*

ˈglɑ͜ɔbə, ˈhɔfnʊŋ |ʊntʻ ˈliːbə
Glaube, Hoffnung und Liebe
Faith, Hope, and Love

Op. 97 [1828] (Christoph Kuffner)

ˈglɑ͜ɔbə, ˈhɔfə, ˈliːbə! hɛlt͜st duː tʰrɔ͜ø |an ˈdiːzən ˈdra͜eən, [fɛstʻ]
Glaube, hoffe, liebe! Hältst du treu an diesen Dreien, [*Schochow:* **Hältst du fest]**
Believe, hope, love! Hold you loyally to these three, [firmly]
(Have faith, have hope, give love! If you hold faithfully to those three precepts,)

vɪrst duː niː dɪç zɛlpstʻ |ɛntˈt͜sva͜eən, vɪrt da͜en ˈhɪməl ˈnɪmɐ ˈtʰryːbə.
wirst du nie dich selbst entzweien, wird dein Himmel nimmer trübe.
will you never you(r) self disunite, becomes your heaven never cloudy.
(you will never feel yourself inwardly divided, your skies will never become cloudy.)
[*poem:* **wirst du dich nie selbst entzweien]**

ˈglɑ͜ɔbə fɛstʻ |an gɔtʻ |ʊntʻ hɛrt͜s! ˈglɑ͜ɔbə ˈʃveːbətʻ ˈhɪməlvɛrt͜s.
Glaube fest an Gott und Herz! Glaube schwebet himmelwärts.
Believe firmly in God and heart! Faith soars heavenwards.
(Have firm faith in God and in your heart! Faith soars up to heaven.)

meːɐ̯ nɔx |als |ɪm ˈʃtʻɛrnreˌviːɐ̯ leːpʻt deːɐ̯ gɔtʻ |ɪm ˈbuːzən diːɐ̯.
Mehr noch als im Sternrevier lebt der Gott im Busen dir.
More yet than in the star- preserve lives the God in the bosom for you.
(But even more than in the starry sky, God lives inside your breast.)

vɛn |ɑ͜ɔx vɛltʻ |ʊntʻ ˈmɛnʃən ˈlyːgən, kʰan das hɛrt͜s dɔx ˈnɪmɐ ˈtʰryːgən.
Wenn auch Welt und Menschen lügen, kann das Herz doch nimmer trügen.
If even world and mankind lie, can the heart nevertheless never deceive.
(Even if the world and mankind may tell lies, your heart can never deceive you.)

ˈhɔfə diːɐ̯/diːr |ʊnˈʃtʻɛrpʻlɪçkʰa͜etʻ |ʊntʻ hiːˈniːdən ˈbɛsrə t͜sa͜etʰ!
Hoffe dir Unsterblichkeit und hienieden bessre Zeit!
Hope for yourself immortality and here below better time!
(Hope for immortality and for better times here on earth!)

ˈhɔfnʊŋ |ɪstʻ |a͜en ˈʃøːnəs |lɪçtʻ |ʊntʻ |ɛɐ̯ˈhɛlt den veːkʻ deːɐ̯ p͜flɪçtʰ.
Hoffnung ist ein schönes Licht und erhellt den Weg der Pflicht.
Hope is a beautiful light and brightens the path of the duty.
(Hope is a beautiful light, and it brightens the path of duty.)

ˈhɔfə, ˈlaːbɐ ˈfɔrdrə ˈnɪmɐ! tʰaːkʻ vɪrtʻ ˈmɛːlɪç, vas leːɐ̯stʻ ˈʃɪmɐ.
Hoffe, aber fordre nimmer! Tag wird mählich, was erst Schimmer.
Hope, but demand never! Day becomes gradually what first shimmer.
(Hope, but never demand! What at first is but a glimmer in the east will gradually become day.)
[*mählich* or *mählig* (both archaic) = *allmählich* = gradually]

ˈeːdəl ˈliːbə, fɛstʻ |ʊntʻ ra͜en! ˈloːnə ˈliːbə bɪst duː ʃtʻa͜en.
Edel liebe, fest und rein! Ohne Liebe bist du Stein.
Nobly love, firmly and purely! Without love are you stone.
(Love nobly, steadfastly and purely! Without love you are like stone.)

ˈliːbə ˈlɔ͜øtʻrə da͜en gəˈfyːl, ˈliːbə ˈla͜etʻə dɪç lans t͜siːl!
Liebe läut're dein Gefühl, Liebe leite dich ans Ziel!
Love purify your feeling, love lead you to the goal!
(May love purify your feelings, may love lead you to your goal!)

zɔl das ˈleːbən ˈglʏkʻlɪç ˈblyːən, mʊs deːɐ̯ ˈliːbə ˈzɔnə ˈglyːən.
Soll das Leben glücklich blühen, muss der Liebe Sonne glühen.
Shall the life happily bloom, must the love's sun glow.
(For your life to bloom happily, the sun of love must be shining.)

vɪlst duː niː dɪç zɛlpstʻ lɛntˈt͜sva͜eən, ˈhaltʻə tʰrɔ͜ø lan ˈdiːzən ˈdra͜eən!
Willst du nie dich selbst entzweien, halte treu an diesen Dreien!
Want you never you(r) self to disunite, hold loyally to these three!
(If you never want to feel yourself inwardly divided, hold faithfully to those three precepts!)
[*Peters & poem:* **Willst du dich nie selbst entzweien**]

das nɪçt͜s ˈda͜enən ˈhɪməl ˈtʰryːbə, ˈgla͜obə, ˈhɔfə, ˈliːbə.
Dass nichts deinen Himmel trübe, glaube, hoffe, liebe.
That nothing your heaven darken, believe, hope, love.
(So that nothing may darken your skies, have faith, have hope, give love.)

[This was the last of Schubert's songs to be published during his lifetime. It is serious, devout, richly harmonized, and effective if sung with simple sincerity. The three middle verses, one each for faith, hope, and love, are set strophically, framed by the slower, more solemn first and last.]

ˈgɔndəlfaːrɐ
Gondelfahrer
Gondolier

Posthumously published [composed 1824] (poem by Johann Mayrhofer)

ɛs ˈtʰant͜sən moːntʻ lʊntʻ ˈʃtʻɛrnə den ˈflʏçtʻgən ˈga͜estʻɐra͜en:
Es tanzen Mond und Sterne den flücht'gen Geisterreih'n:
There dance moon and stars the fleeting spirits- round dances:
(The moon and stars are dancing the fleeting round of the spirits:)

veːɐ̯ vɪrtʻ fɔn ˈleːɐ̯dənzɔrgən bəˈfaŋən ˈlɪmɐ za͜en!
wer wird von Erdensorgen befangen immer sein!
who will with earthly cares preoccupied always be!
(who would want to be always preoccupied with earthly cares?)

duː kʰanstʻ lɪn ˈmoːndəsʃtʻraːlən nuːn, ˈma͜enə ˈbarkʻə, ˈvalən;
Du kannst in Mondesstrahlen nun, meine Barke, wallen;
You can in moonbeams now, my boat, float;
(You can float in moonbeams now, my boat;)

lʊntʻ ˈlalɐ ˈʃraŋkʻən loːs, viːkʻt dɪç dɛs ˈmeːrəs ʃoːs.
und aller Schranken los, wiegt dich des Meeres Schoss.
and of all restraints free, rocks you the sea's lap.
(and, free of all restraints, rock on the lap of the sea.)

fɔm ˈmarkʻʊstʰʊrmə ˈtʰø:ntʻə de:ɐ̯ ʃpʻrʊx de:ɐ̯ ˈmɪtʻɐnaxtʰ:
Vom Markusturme tönte der Spruch der Mitternacht:
From Mark's tower sounded the verdict of the midnight:
(From the bell tower in St. Mark's Square the verdict of midnight has sounded:)

zi: ˈʃlʊmɐn ˈfri:tʻlɪç ˈlalə, lʊntʻ nu:ɐ̯ de:ɐ̯ ˈʃɪfɐ vaxtʰ.
sie schlummern friedlich alle, und nur der Schiffer wacht.
they slumber peacefully all, and only the boatman is awake.
(all are sleeping peacefully, and only the boatman is awake.)

[This is Schubert's last setting of a poem by his friend Mayrhofer. The bell that tolls midnight in Saint Mark's Square in Venice, the barcarolle rhythm, and the darkness of an accompaniment that never leaves the bass cleff set the scene and define the mood. Besides the bell tower—"the *campanile*"—that stands in the square opposite the basilica, there is a clock tower, on top of which two enormous bronze giants strike a correspondingly large bell with their hammers.]

gɔtʻ lɪm ˈfry:lɪŋ(ə)
Gott im Frühlinge / Gott im Frühling
God in the Spring

Posthumously published [composed 1816] (poem by Johann Peter Uz)

ɪn ˈza͜enəm ˈʃɪmɐndən gəˈvantʻ hast du: den ˈfry:lɪŋ lʊns gəˈzantʰ,
In seinem schimmernden Gewand hast Du den Frühling uns gesandt,
In his shimmering garment have You the spring to us sent,
(You have sent us the spring in his shimmering garments,)

ʊntʻ ˈro:zən lʊm za͜en ha͜opʻtʻ gəˈvʊndən. hɔltʻˈlɛçəlntʻ kʰɔmtʻ le:ɐ̯ ʃo:n!
und Rosen um sein Haupt gewunden. Holdlächelnd kommt er schon!
and roses about his head entwined. Graciously smiling comes he already!
(and entwined roses about his head. Graciously smiling, he is already coming!)
[*GA & poem:* **kömmt*** (kʰœmtʻ, comes—obs.)]

ɛs ˈfy:rən li:n di ˈʃtʻʊndən, lo: gɔtʻ, la͜of ˈza͜enən ˈblu:məntʰro:n.
Es führen ihn die Stunden, O Gott, auf seinen Blumenthron.
There lead him the hours, O God, onto his flower- throne.
(The hours are leading him to his throne of flowers, O God.)

e:ɐ̯ ge:tʻ lɪn ˈbʏʃən lʊntʻ zi: ˈbly:ən; den ˈflu:rən kʰɔmtʻ li:ɐ̯ ˈfrɪʃəs gry:n,
Er geht in Büschen und sie blühen; den Fluren kommt ihr frisches Grün,
He goes into bushes and they blossom; to the meadows comes their fresh green,
(He moves among the bushes and they blossom; a fresh green returns to the meadows,)
[*Peters & poem:* **blüh'n** (bly:n, bloom), *GA & poem:* **kömmt*** (kʰœmtʻ, comes—obs.)]

ʊntʻ ˈvɛldɐn vɛkstʻ li:ɐ̯ ˈʃatʻən ˈvi:dɐ, de:ɐ̯ vɛstʻ, li:pʻˈkʰo:zəntʻ,
und Wäldern wächst ihr Schatten wieder, der West, liebkosend,
and for forests grows their shade again, the west (wind), caressingly,
(and shade spreads out again in the forests; the west wind, caressingly,)

ʃvɪŋtʻ za͜en ˈtʰa͜oəndəs gəˈfi:dɐ(r), lʊntʻ ˈje:dɐ ˈfro:ə ˈfo:gəl zɪŋtʰ.
schwingt sein tauendes Gefieder, und jeder frohe Vogel singt.
waves its thawing wings, and every happy bird sings.

mɪt' 'lɔ̯øʁɐ 'liːdɐ 'zyːsəm kʰlaŋ, liːɐ̯ 'føːgəl, zɔl lɑ̯ox maɛ̯n gə'zaŋ
Mit eurer Lieder süssem Klang, ihr Vögel, soll auch mein Gesang
With your songs' sweet sound, you birds, shall also my song
(With the sweet sound of your songs, you birds, my song shall also)

t̯sʊm 'faːt'ɐ deːɐ̯ na'tʰuːɐ̯ zɪç 'ʃvɪŋən, lɛnt't̯sʏk'ən raɛ̯st' mɪç hɪn!
zum Vater der Natur sich schwingen, Entzückung reisst mich hin!
to the Father of the Nature itself swing, rapture tears me hence!
(soar up to the Father of all nature; rapture carries me away!)
[*hinreissen* = to carry away; overcome; delight, transport]

ɪç vɪl dem hɛrn loːp''zɪŋən, dʊrç deːn lɪç 'vʊrdə, vas lɪç bɪn!
Ich will dem Herrn lobsingen, durch den ich wurde, was ich bin!
I want to the Lord praises to sing, through whom I became what I am!
(I want to sing praises to the Lord, through whom I became what I am!)
[note: *lobsingen* is usually accented on the first syllable; the music stresses the second]

[oː 'gyːt'ɪçst'ɐ! dɛn veːɐ̯/veːr lɪst' guːt', viː duː, deːɐ̯/deːr 'lalən 'guːt'əs tʰuːtʰ?
[O Gütigster! Denn wer ist gut, wie Du, der allen Gutes tut?
[O Most Kindly One! For who is kind, like You, who for all good does?
[(O Most Kindly One! For who is as kind as You, You who do good for all?)

duː 'zɔrk't'əst' 'lɑ̯ox fyːɐ̯ maɛ̯n fɛɐ̯'gnyːgən, lals lɑ̯os dem 'groːsən pʰlaːn
Du sorgtest auch für mein Vergnügen, als aus dem grossen Plan
You provided also for *my* pleasure when from the great plan

lɛɐ̯'ʃt'ɑ̯ont'ə 'vɛlt'ən 'ʃt'iːgən, lʊnt' 'zɔnən zɪç gə'ʃafən zaːn.
erstaunte Welten stiegen, und Sonnen sich geschaffen sahn.
astonished worlds arose, and suns themselves created saw.
(astonished worlds arose, and suns beheld themselves created.)

ʃøːn lɪst di 'leːɐ̯də, van ziː blyːt', lʊnt', gant̯s lʊm 'lʊnzrə lʊst' bə'myːt',
Schön ist die Erde, wann sie blüht, und, ganz um unsre Lust bemüht,
Beautiful is the earth when it blooms, and entirely for our delight troubled,
(The earth is beautiful when it is in blossom, and when, entirely concerned for our delight,)

zɪç lɪn dɛs 'fryːlɪŋs 'farbən 'kʰlaɛ̯dət', lʊnt' 'lyːbɐ(r)lal fɔl pʰraxt',
sich in des Frühlings Farben kleidet, und überall voll Pracht,
itself in the spring's colors dresses, and everywhere full of splendor,
(it is dressed in the colors of spring, and when, everywhere full of splendor,)

zɛlpst', voː di 'heːɐ̯də 'vaɛ̯dət', lɪn 'bʊnt'ɐ 't̯siːɐ̯də 'dʏft'ənt' laxtʰ.
selbst, wo die Herde weidet, in bunter Zierde düftend lacht.
itself, where the herd grazes, in bright adornment fragrantly smiles.
(the earth itself smiles, fragrant in bright adornment on the meadow where the herd is grazing.)
[*düftend* (obs.) = *duftend* = being fragrant]

deːɐ̯ 'gɔt'haɛ̯t' 'vʏrdɪgɐ(r) lal'tʰaːɐ̯, vo'rɑ̯of das 'bluːmənraɛ̯çə jaːɐ̯,
Der Gottheit würdiger Altar, worauf das blumenreiche Jahr,
The divinity's worthy altar, upon which the flower- rich year,
(It is an altar worthy of divinity, upon which the flowering year,)

oː hɛr, t͡suː 'd͡aenəm 'voːlgəfalən za͡en 'zyːsəs 'r͡aoxvɛrk' brɪŋt',
O Herr, zu Deinem Wohlgefallen sein süsses Rauchwerk bringt,
O Lord, to Your good will its sweet perfume brings,
(O Lord, brings its sweet perfume as an offering to Your good will,)

ɪn'dɛs fɔn 'naxt'ɪgalən l͡aen 'froːɐ 'loːp'gəzaŋ lɛɐ̯'kʰlɪŋtʰ!
indess von Nachtigallen ein froher Lobgesang erklingt!
while from nightingales a happy song of praise resounds!
(while nightingales sing a joyous song of praise!)

duː hast' mɪt' 'ʃøːnha͡et, diː lɛnt't͡sʏk't, das 'lant'lɪt͡s deːɐ̯ na'tʰuːɐ̯ gə'ʃmʏk't',
Du hast mit Schönheit, die entzückt, das Antlitz der Natur geschmückt,
You have with beauty that enchants the face of the nature adorned,
(You have adorned the face of nature with enchanting beauty,)

oː 'lalɐ 'ʃøːnha͡et' 'ra͡eçə 'kʰvɛlə! diːɐ̯ geːt' kʰa͡en 'veːzən foːɐ̯!
o aller Schönheit reiche Quelle! Dir geht kein Wesen vor!
O all beauty's rich source! To you goes no being before!
(O rich source of all beauty, no other being precedes You!)

di 'ra͡enst'ə 'liːbə 'ʃvɛlə ma͡en 'gant͡səs hɛrt͡s t͡suː diːɐ̯/diːr lɛm'pʰoːɐ̯!]
Die reinste Liebe schwelle mein ganzes Herz zu Dir empor!]
The purest love swell my whole heart to You upwards!]
(May the purest love swell my whole heart up to You!)]

[*During the eighteenth century (the poem was written in 1763) *kömmt* was common usage; by Schubert's day it was superseded by *kommt*, as in modern German. Schubert set the first three of seven verses in an ABA form. It would be *possible* to repeat the entire exquisite song with verses four, six, and seven (the fifth—"Schön ist die Erde"—does not fit the middle section naturally).]

'graːp'liːt'

Grablied

Song at the Grave

Posthumously published [composed 1815] (poem by Josef Kenner)

eːɐ̯ fiːl den tʰoːt' fyːɐ̯s 'faːt'ɐlant, den 'zyːsən deːɐ̯ bə'fra͡eʊŋsʃlaxtʰ;
Er fiel den Tod fürs Vaterland, den süssen der Befreiungsschlacht;
He fell the death for the fatherland, the sweet (death) of the liberation- battle;
(He fell for the fatherland, a sweet death in the battle for freedom;)

viːɐ̯ 'graːbən liːm mɪt 'tʰrɔ͡øɐ hant, tʰiːf, tʰiːf den 'ʃvart͡sən 'ruːəʃaxtʰ.
wir graben ihm mit treuer Hand, tief, tief den schwarzen Ruheschacht.
we dig for him with loyal hand deep, deep the black rest- pit.
(with loyal hands we are digging a deep, deep pit for his dark resting place.)
[*Peters (in error?):* **wir graben ihn** (liːn, him—accusative case)]

[daː ʃlaːf, t͡sɛɐ'h͡aoənəs gə'ba͡en! voː 'ʃmɛrt͡sən la͡enst' gə'vyːlt' lʊnt' lʊstʰ,
[Da schlaf', zerhauenes Gebein! wo Schmerzen einst gewühlt und Lust,
[There sleep, chopped up bones! where pains once (have) stirred and pleasure,
[(Sleep there, poor mangled body! Where pain and pleasure once stirred,)

ʃlu:k‘ vɪlt‘ lae̯n 'tʰø:t‘ənt‘ blae̯ hɪ'nae̯n lʊnt‘ bra:x den tʰrɔt͡s de:ɐ̯ 'hɛldənbrʊstʰ.]
schlug wild ein tötend Blei hinein und brach den Trotz der Heldenbrust.]
struck savagely a killing lead into and broke the defiance of the hero- breast.]
(a deadly bullet entered savagely and broke the defiance of a heroic heart.)]

da: ʃla:f gə'ʃt‘ɪlt, t͡sɛɐ̯'rɪsnəs hɛrt͡s, zo: 'vʊnʃrae̯ç lae̯nst‘, lao̯f 'blu:mən lae̯n,
Da schlaf' gestillt, zerriss'nes Herz, so wunschreich einst, auf Blumen ein,
There sleep stilled, lacerated heart, so wish- rich once, on flowers ... ,
(Lacerated heart, once so rich in wishes, now stilled, fall asleep there on flowers,)
[*einschlafen* = to fall asleep]

di: vi:ɐ̯/vi:r lɪm 'vae̯lçənfɔlən mɛrt͡s di:ɐ̯/di:r lɪn di 'kʰy:lə 'gru:bə ʃt‘rɔø̯n.
die wir im veilchenvollen März dir in die kühle Grube streu'n.
which we in the violet- full March for you into the cool pit scatter.
(which we scatter into the cool pit for you—there are many violets in this month of March.)
[*variant:* in die stille ('ʃt‘ɪlə, quiet) **Grube]**

ae̯n 'hy:gəl he:p‘t‘ zɪç 'ly:bɐ di:ɐ̯, de:n drʏk‘t‘ kʰae̯n ma:l fɔn 'marmo:ɐ̯ʃt‘ae̯n,
Ein Hügel hebt sich über dir, den drückt kein Mal von Marmorstein,
A mound rises itself over you, which presses no monument of marble- stone,
(Over you a mound is raised which is weighed down by no marble monument;)
[*poem & GA:* **Marmelstein** ('marməlʃt‘ae̯n, marble—poetic, archaic)]

fɔn 'ro:smari:n nu:ɐ̯ 'p͡flant͡sən vi:ɐ̯/vi:r lae̯n 'p͡flɛnt͡sçən lao̯f dem 'hy:gəl lae̯n.
von Rosmarin nur pflanzen wir ein Pflänzchen auf dem Hügel ein.
of rosemary only plant we a little plant on the mound .... .
(instead, we plant a little rosemary plant, symbol of fidelity, on the mound.)
[*einpflanzen* = to plant, implant]

das ʃp‘rɔst‘ lʊnt‘ gry:nt‘ zo: 'tʰrao̯rɪç ʃø:n, fɔn 'dae̯nəm 'tʰrɔø̯ən blu:t‘ gə'dʏŋtʰ.
Das sprosst und grünt so traurig schön, von deinem treuen Blut gedüngt.
That sprouts and grows green so sadly beautiful, by your faithful blood fertilized.
(It sprouts and grows green with such mournful beauty, fertilized by your faithful blood.)

man zi:t t͡sʊm gra:p‘ lae̯n 'mɛ:t‘çən ge:n, das 'lae̯zə 'mɪnəli:dɐ zɪŋtʰ.
Man sieht zum Grab ein Mädchen geh'n, das leise Minnelieder singt.
One sees to the grave a girl go, who softly love songs sings.
(One sees a girl going to the grave, softly singing love songs.) [*poem & GA:* **zu** (t͡su:, to) **Grab]**

di: kʰɛnt das gra:p‘ nɪçt‘, vae̯s lɛs nɪçt‘, vi: de:ɐ̯ zi: ʃt‘ɪl lʊnt‘ fɛst‘ gə'li:p‘tʰ,
Die kennt das Grab nicht, weiss es nicht, wie der sie still und fest geliebt,
She knows the grave not, knows it not, how he her quietly and firmly (had) loved,
(She does not know the grave, does not know how much he had quietly and steadfastly loved her,)

de:ɐ̯/de:r li:ɐ̯ t͡sʊm kʰrant͡s, de:n zi: zɪç flɪçt, den 'ro:smari:n lals 'brao̯t‘ʃmʊk‘ gi:p‘tʰ.
der ihr zum Kranz, den sie sich flicht, den Rosmarin als Brautschmuck gibt.
who her for the wreath which she herself twines, the rosemary as bridal finery gives.
(he who gives her the rosemary for the wreath that she is entwining for herself as bridal finery.)
[*Peters:* den Rosmarin zum Brautkranz (t͡sʊm 'brao̯t‘kʰrant͡s, for the bridal wreath) **gibt]**

[The verse in brackets, above, is omitted in the Peters edition. The original editor, Diabelli, added the three-bar prelude, which is not in Schubert's manuscript. The poem was written in July 1813, during the war to defeat Napoleon and free the lands that he had acquired by conquest. The last three verses tell a touching story and must not be omitted if the song is sung.]

'graːp'liːt' |ɑ͜of '|a͜enən zɔl'daːt'ən
Grablied auf einen Soldaten
Dirge for a Soldier

Posthumously published [composed 1816] (poem by Christian Friedrich Schubart)

t͜siː hɪn, duː 'braːfɐ 'kʰriːgɐ duː! viːɐ̯ 'gla͜et'ən dɪç t͜sʊr 'graːbəsruː,
Zieh hin, du braver Krieger du! wir g'leiten dich zur Grabesruh',
Move hence, you worthy warrior you! We escort you to the grave- rest,
(Journey to the other world, worthy warrior! We escort your body to its resting place,)
[*gleiten* (here) = *geleiten* = to accompany, to escort; *brav* = worthy, fine (not "brave")]

|ʊnt' 'ʃra͜et'ən mɪt' gə'zʊŋk'nɐ veːɐ̯,
und schreiten mit gesunk'ner Wehr,
and stride with lowered weapons,

fɔn 'veːmuːt' ʃveːɐ̯/ʃveːr |ʊnt' ʃt'ʊm foːɐ̯ 'da͜enəm 'zargə heːɐ̯.
von Wehmut schwer und stumm vor deinem Sarge her.
with melancholy heavy and silent before your coffin hither.
(heavy with melancholy and silent, before your coffin.)

duː vaːɐ̯st' |a͜en 'biːdrɐ, 'dɔ͜øt͜ʃɐ man, hast' '|ɪmɐhɪn zoː braːf gə'tʰan.
Du warst ein biedrer, deutscher Mann, hast immerhin so brav getan.
You were an upright, German man, (you) have nevertheless so well done.
(You were an upright German man, and, though you fell, you were fighting very well.)

da͜en hɛrt͜s, fɔl '|eːdlɐ 'tʰap͜fɐkʰa͜et',
Dein Herz, voll edler Tapferkeit,
Your heart, full of noble valor,

hat' niː |ɪm ʃt'ra͜et' gə'ʃɔs |ʊnt' 'zɛːbəlhiːp' gə'ʃɔ͜øtʰ.
hat nie im Streit Geschoss und Säbelhieb gescheut.
has never in the fighting bullet and saber-blow shrunk from.
(has never shrunk from bullet or saber-blow in the fighting.)

vaːɐ̯st' |ɑ͜ox |a͜en 'kʰrɪst'lɪçɐ 'zɔl'daːt, deːɐ̯ 'veːnɪç ʃp'raːx |ʊnt' 'fiːləs tʰaːtʰ,
Warst auch ein christlicher Soldat, der wenig sprach und vieles tat,
(You) were also a Christian soldier, who little spoke and much did,
(You were also a Christian soldier who spoke little and accomplished much,)

dem 'fʏrst'ən |ʊnt dem '|andə tʰrɔ͜ø,
dem Fürsten und dem Lande treu,
to the prince and to the country loyal,
(loyal to prince and country,)

|ʊnt' frɔm da'ba͜e fɔn 'hɛrt͜sən, '|oːnə 'hɔ͜øçəla͜e.
und fromm dabei von Herzen, ohne Heuchelei.
and devout at the same time from heart, without hypocrisy.
(and, at the same time, devout from the heart, without hypocrisy.)

duː ʃt'ant͜st' |ɪn 'grɑ͜ozɐ 'mɪt'ɐnaxt', |ɪn frɔst' |ʊnt' 'hɪt͜sə |ɑ͜of deːɐ̯ vaxtʰ,
Du standst in grauser Mitternacht, in Frost und Hitze auf der Wacht,
You stood in grim midnight, in frost and heat on the watch,
(You stood your watch at grim midnight, in frost and heat,)

lɛɐ̯'tʰru:kst' zo: 'ʃt'ant'haft' 'mançə no:tʰ
ertrugst so standhaft manche Not
endured so steadfastly many a hardship

lʊnt' 'daŋk't'əst' gɔt' fy:ɐ̯ 'vasɐ(r) lʊnt' fy:ɐ̯s 'li:bə bro:tʰ.
und danktest Gott für Wasser und fürs liebe Brot.
and thanked God for water and for the dear* bread.
(and gave thanks to God for bread and water.)
[**das liebe Brot* appears in several fixed expressions; here it implies a meager subsistence]

vi: du: gə'le:p't', zo: ʃt'arpst' lɑ͜ox du:, ʃlɔs͜t 'da͜enə 'lɑ͜ogən 'frɔ͜ødıç t͜su:,
Wie du gelebt, so starbst auch du, schloss'st deine Augen freudig zu,
As you lived, so died also you, closed your eyes gladly ... ,
(You died as you lived; you closed your eyes gladly) [*schlossest ... zu; zuschliessen* = to close]

lʊnt 'daxt'əst': lɑ͜os lıst' nu:n de:ɐ̯ ʃt'ra͜et' lʊnt' kʰamp͜f de:ɐ̯ t͜sa͜etʰ.
und dachtest: Aus ist nun der Streit und Kampf der Zeit.
and thought: Finished is now the struggle and battle of the time.
(and thought: "Now the struggle and the battle of time is finished;)

jɛt͜st' kʰɔmt di 'le:vgə 'ze:lıçkʰa͜etʰ.
Jetzt kommt die ew'ge Seligkeit.
Now comes the eternal bliss.
(now comes eternal bliss.")

de:ɐ̯ 'li:bə 'hɛrgɔt' 'kʰant'ə dıç, lın 'hıməl kʰa:mst du: 'zıçɐlıç.
Der liebe Herrgott kannte dich, in Himmel kamst du sicherlich.
The dear Lord God knew you, into heaven came you surely.
(The dear Lord God knew you; you have surely entered heaven.)

du: 'vıt'və lʊnt' li:ɐ̯ 'kʰındɐla͜en, tʰrɑ͜ot' gɔt' la'la͜en:
Du Witwe und ihr Kinderlein, traut Gott allein:
You, widow, and you little children, trust God alone:

le:ɐ̯ vırt' nu:n 'lɔ͜ørə 'ʃt'ʏt͜sə za͜en. di 'ba:rə 'pʰɔlt'ɐt' lın di grʊftʰ;
Er wird nun eure Stütze sein. Die Bahre poltert in die Gruft;
He will now your support be. The bier rattles into the pit;
(He will now be your support. The bier rattles as it is lowered into the grave;)

vi:ɐ̯/vi:r 'la:bɐ 'dɔnɐn lın di lʊft da͜en 'lɛt͜st'əs 'le:bəvo:l dra͜e'ma:l.
wir aber donnern in die Luft dein letztes Lebewohl dreimal.
we however thunder into the air your last farewell three times.
(we, however, fire three thundering salvos into the air as our last farewell to you.)

lım 'hıməlsza:l dɔrt' ze:n vi:ɐ̯ dıç lo:n 'lalə kʰva:l.
Im Himmelssaal dort sehn wir dich ohn' alle Qual.
In the heaven- hall there see we you without all pain.
(We picture you up there in the halls of heaven, free of all pain.)

ne:mt' 'za͜enən 'zɛ:bəl fɔn de:ɐ̯ ba:ɐ̯/ba:r, lʊnt' za͜et' zo: bra:f, vi: le:ɐ/le:r lɛs va:ɐ̯.
Nehmt seinen Säbel von der Bahr, und seid so brav, wie er es war.
Take his saber from the bier, and be as good as he it was.
(Take his saber from the bier, and be as good a soldier as he was.)
[*poem:* **als** (lals, as) **wie er war** (as how he was)]

dan ˈyːbɐvɪndən viːɐ̯, viː leːɐ̯:
Dann überwinden wir, wie er:
Then overcome we, as he:
(Then we shall overcome, as he did,)

ǀʊnt‘ ha̯es ǀʊnt‘ ʃveːɐ̯ drʏk‘t‘ ǀʊns dɛs ˈleːbəns jɔx nɪçt‘ meːɐ̯.
und heiss und schwer drückt uns des Lebens Joch nicht mehr.
and hot and heavy weighs down us the life's yoke not more.
(and life's hot and heavy yoke will no longer weigh us down.)

[The title of the original poem is "*Totenmarsch*" (Funeral March). Eight verses are too many; but the song has some affecting moments, such as the soft major chord on the last syllable of "*Grabesruh*'," the expressiveness of the poignant dissonances, and, in the postlude, the crescendo of emotion, followed by a sudden *piano*. Two, three, or four verses would suffice.]

ˈgraːpˈliːt‘ fyːɐ̯ di ˈmʊt‘ɐ
Grablied für die Mutter
A Mother's Funeral Song

Posthumously published [composed 1818] (author unknown*)

ˈha̯ɔxə ˈmɪldɐ(r), ˈlaːbəntˈlʊftʰ, ˈkʰlaːgə ˈzanft‘ɐ, filoˈmeːlə,
Hauche milder, Abendluft, klage sanfter, Philomele,
Breathe more mildly, evening air, lament more gently, Philomela,
[Philomela is a poetic name for the nightingale, its origin in Greek mythology]

ˈa̯enə ˈʃøːnə, ˈlɛŋəlra̯enə ˈzeːlə ʃlɛːft‘ ǀɪn ˈdiːzɐ grʊftʰ.
eine schöne, engelreine Seele schläft in dieser Gruft.
a beautiful, angel-pure soul sleeps in this grave.

bla̯eç ǀʊnt‘ ʃt‘ʊm ǀam ˈdyːst‘ɐn rant‘ ʃt‘eːt deːɐ̯ ˈfaːt‘ɐ mɪt dem ˈzoːnə,
Bleich und stumm am düstern Rand steht der Vater mit dem Sohne,
Pale and silent at the gloomy edge stands the father with the son,
(Pale and silent at the gloomy graveside, the father stands with his son,)

ˈdeːnən ˈliːrəs ˈleːbəns ˈʃøːnst‘ə ˈkʰroːnə ʃnɛl mɪt‘ liːɐ̯ fɛɐ̯ˈʃvant‘.
denen ihres Lebens schönste Krone schnell mit ihr verschwand.
for whom their life's most beautiful crown quickly with her vanished.
(for both of whom the most beautiful crown of their life quickly vanished with her.)

ʊnt‘ ziː ˈva̯enən ǀɪn di grʊftʰ, ˈlaːbɐ(r) ˈliːrɐ ˈliːbə ˈt̮sɛːrən
Und sie weinen in die Gruft, aber ihrer Liebe Zähren
And they weep into the grave, but their love's tears
(And they weep into the grave; but the tears of their love)

ˈveːɐ̯dən zɪç t̮sʊm ˈpʰɛrlənkʰrant̮s fɛɐ̯ˈkʰlɛːrən, vɛn deːɐ̯/deːr ˈlɛŋəl ruːftʰ.
werden sich zum Perlenkranz verklären, wenn der Engel ruft.
will themselves to the pearl- wreath transfigure, when the angel calls.
(will be transfigured into a wreath of pearls when the angel calls.)

[*Some commentators have assumed that Schubert wrote these verses himself; Josef von Streinsberg, one of his friends since schooldays, claimed that the song was written in memory of his own mother, who died in 1818, whereas Schubert's mother had died several years earlier.

Either man—or someone else—may have written the words; if it was Schubert, he would surely have been moved by the memory of his own mother's death, along with sympathy for his friend.]

ˈgra͜ezəngəzaŋ
Greisengesang
Song of Old Age

Op. 60, No. 1 [1822?] (Friedrich Rückert)

deːɐ̯ frɔstʻ hatʻ miːɐ̯ bəˈra͜efət des ˈha͜ozəs dax;
Der Frost hat mir bereifet des Hauses Dach;
The frost has for me covered with hoar-frost the house's roof;
(Frost has covered the roof of my house;)

dɔx varm ɪstʻ miːɐ̯s gəˈbliːbən ɪm ˈvoːngəmax. [ɪst͜s miːɐ̯]
doch warm ist mir's geblieben im Wohngemach. [*GA:* ist's mir]
but warm is for me it remained in the living-room. [is it for me]
(but it is still warm in my living-room.)

deːɐ̯ ˈvɪntʻɐ hat di ˈʃa͜etʻəl miːɐ̯ va͜es gəˈdekʻtʰ;
Der Winter hat die Scheitel mir weiss gedeckt;
The winter has the crown of the head of me white covered;
(Winter has covered the top of my head with white;)

dɔx fliːst das bluːt, das ˈroːtʻə, dʊrçs ˈhert͜sgəmax.
doch fliesst das Blut, das rote, durchs Herzgemach.
but flows the blood, the red, through the heart-chamber.
(but blood, red blood, flows through the chamber of my heart.)

deːɐ̯ ˈjuːgəntʻfloːɐ̯ deːɐ̯ ˈvaŋən, di ˈroːzən zɪntʻ gəˈgaŋən,
Der Jugendflor der Wangen, die Rosen sind gegangen,
The youth- blossoming of the cheeks, the roses are gone,
(The blossoming of youth has left my cheeks, the roses are gone,)

al gəˈgaŋən la͜eˈnandɐ naːx. voː zɪntʻ ziː ˈhɪngəgaŋən?
all' gegangen einander nach. Wo sind sie hingegangen?
all gone one another after. Where are they gone?
(all gone, one after another. Where have they gone?)

ɪns hert͜s hɪˈnap. daː blyːn ziː naːx fɛɐ̯ˈlaŋən, viː foːɐ̯ zoː naːx.
In's Herz hinab. Da blühn sie nach Verlangen, wie vor so nach.
Into the heart down. There bloom they according to desire, as before so afterwards.
(Down into my heart. There they bloom when I desire them, now as before.)

zɪntʻ ˈlalə ˈfrɔ͜ødənʃtʻrøːmə deːɐ̯ veltʻ fɛɐ̯ˈziːkʻtʰ?
Sind alle Freudenströme der Welt versiegt?
Are all joy- streams of the world dried up?
(Have all the streams of joy in the world run dry?)

nɔx fliːstʻ miːɐ̯ dʊrç den ˈbuːzən la͜en ˈʃtʻɪlɐ bax.
Noch fliesst mir durch den Busen ein stiller Bach.
Still flows for me through the bosom a quiet brook.
(A quiet brook is still flowing through my bosom.)

zɪntʻ ˈlalə ˈnaxtʻɪgalən de:ɐ̯ flu:ɐ̯ fɛɐ̯ˈʃtʻʊmtʰ?
Sind alle Nachtigallen der Flur verstummt?
Are all nightingales of the meadow grown silent?
(Have all the nightingales in the meadow grown silent?)

nɔx lɪstʻ bae̯ mi:ɐ̯/mi:r lɪm ˈʃtʻɪlən hi:ɐ̯/hi:r ˈlae̯nə vax.
Noch ist bei mir im Stillen hier eine wach.
Still is with me in the quiet here one awake.
(Here with me in the quietness one nightingale is still awake.)

zi: ˈzɪŋətʻ: hɛr dɛs ˈhao̯zəs! fɛɐ̯ˈʃlɔø̯s dae̯n tʰo:ɐ̯,
Sie singet: Herr des Hauses! verschleuss dein Tor,
It sings: "Lord of the house, lock your door,
[*verschleuss* (archaic, poetic) = *verschliess'* (modern German)]

das nɪçt di vɛlt, di ˈkʰaltʻə, drɪŋ lɪns gəˈmax.
dass nicht die Welt, die kalte, dring' ins Gemach.
that not the world, the cold one, force a way into the chamber.
(so that the world, the cold world, may not force its way into your room.)

ʃlɔø̯s lao̯s den ˈrao̯ən ˈlo:dəm de:ɐ̯ ˈvɪrkʻlɪçkʰae̯tʰ,
Schleuss aus den rauhen Odem der Wirklichkeit,
Shut out the rough breath of the reality,
(Shut out the rough breath of reality,) [*Odem* (poetic) = *Atem* = breath]

ʊntʻ nu:ɐ̯ dem dʊft de:ɐ̯ ˈtʰrɔø̯mə gi:pʻ dac lʊntʻ fax.
und nur dem Duft der Träume gib Dach und Fach.
and only to the fragrance of the dreams give roof and compartment.
(and give accommodation only to the fragrance of dreams.")
[*Dach und Fach* (a fixed expression) = shelter or accommodation]

[*The nightingale's song continues:*]

[ɪç ˈha:bə vae̯n lʊntʻ ˈro:zən lɪn ˈje:dəm li:tʻ,
[Ich habe Wein und Rosen in jedem Lied,
[I have wine and roses in every song,

ʊntʻ ˈha:bə ˈzɔlçɐ ˈli:dɐ nɔx ˈtʰao̯zəntʻfax.
und habe solcher Lieder noch tausendfach.
and have of such songs still thousandfold.
(and still have thousands of such songs.)

fɔm ˈla:bəntʻ bɪs t͡sʊm ˈmɔrgən lʊntʻ ˈnɛçtʻə dʊrç
Vom Abend bis zum Morgen und Nächte durch
From the evening till to the morning and nights through
(From evening till morning, and whole nights through,)

vɪl lɪç di:ɐ̯ ˈzɪŋən ˈju:gəntʻ lʊntʻ ˈli:bəslax.]
will ich dir singen Jugend und Liebesach.]
will I to you sing youth and love's sighing."]
(I shall sing to you of youth and love's longing.")]

[The title is Schubert's. The poem comes from the collection called *Östliche Rosen* (Oriental Roses). The last two stanzas, in brackets above, were omitted by Schubert (but are included in the setting by Richard Strauss). The introduction and the opening bars seem to offer a harsher view of old age than the poem suggests; but Schubert contrasts the outer frost and the inner warmth with appropriate harmonies, and portrays the consolation of memories and dreams with melismata. A bass singer may descend to the low F# in the phrase "*dass nicht die Welt, die kalte, dring' ins Gemach,*" as the piano does two bars later, imitatively, in the *Gesamtausgabe*.]

ˈgrɛnt͜sən deːɐ̯ ˈmɛnʃhaɐ̯etʰ
Grenzen der Menschheit
Limitations of Humankind

Posthumously published [composed 1821] (poem by Johann Wolfgang von Goethe)

vɛn deːɐ̯/deːr ˈluːɐ̯lalt'ə/ˈluːrlalt'ə, ˈhaɐ̯elɪgə ˈfaːt'ɐ mɪt' gəˈlasənɐ hant'
Wenn der uralte, heilige Vater mit gelassener Hand
When the ancient, holy Father with calm hand
(When the ancient, holy Father with a calm hand)

lɑ͜os ˈrɔləndən ˈvɔlk'ən ˈzeːgnəndə ˈblɪt͜sə ˈlyːbɐ di ˈleːɐ̯də zɛːtʰ,
aus rollenden Wolken segnende Blitze über die Erde sät,
from rolling clouds beneficent lightnings over the earth sows,
(scatters lightning flashes over the earth from rolling clouds,)

kʰʏs lɪç den ˈlɛt͜st'ən zɑ͜om ˈzaɐ̯enəs ˈkʰlaɐ̯edəs,
küss' ich den letzten Saum seines Kleides,
kiss I the last hem of His garment,
(I kiss the lowest hem of His garment,)

ˈkʰɪnt'lɪçə ˈʃɑ͜oɐ tʰiːf lɪn deːɐ̯ brʊstʰ. [tʰrɔ͜ø]
kindliche Schauer tief in der Brust. [*poem:* **treu in der Brust**]
childlike shivers deep in the breast. [sincerely]
(with childlike shivers of awe, deep down in my heart.)

dɛn mɪt' ˈgœt'ɐn zɔl zɪç nɪçt' ˈmɛsən ˈlɪrgənt' laɐ̯en mɛnʃ.
Denn mit Göttern soll sich nicht messen irgend ein Mensch.
For with gods shall himself not measure any ... human being.
(For no human being should attempt to compete with the gods.)
[*irgend ein* = any, some; *sich messen mit* = to compete with]

heːp't' leːɐ̯ zɪç ˈlɑ͜ofvɛrt͜s lʊnt' bəˈryːɐ̯t' mɪt dem ˈʃaɐ̯et'əl di ˈʃt'ɛrnə,
Hebt er sich aufwärts und berührt mit dem Scheitel die Sterne,
Lifts he himself upwards and touches with the crown of his head the stars,
(If he tries to lift himself upwards and touch the stars with the top of his head,)

ˈnɪrgənt͜s ˈhaft'ən dan di ˈlʊnzɪçɐn ˈzoːlən,
nirgends haften dann die unsichern Sohlen,
nowhere adhere then the uncertain soles,
(then nowhere can he find a foothold for the uncertain soles of his feet,)

ʊnt' mɪt' liːm ˈʃp'iːlən ˈvɔlk'ən lʊnt' ˈvɪndə.
und mit ihm spielen Wolken und Winde.
and with him sport clouds and winds.
(and he becomes the sport of clouds and winds.)

ʃt'eːt' leːɐ̯ mɪt' 'fɛst'ən, 'mark'ɪgən 'kʰnɔxən
Steht er mit festen, markigen Knochen
Stands he with firm, well-marrowed bones
(If he stands with firm, vigorous limbs)

ɑo̯f deːɐ̯ voːlgə'grʏndət'ən, 'dɑo̯ɐndən 'leːɐ̯də,
auf der wohlgegründeten, dauernden Erde,
on the well-founded, enduring earth,

ra̯eçt' leːɐ̯ nɪçt' lɑo̯f, nuːɐ̯ mɪt deːɐ̯/deːr 'la̯eçə 'loːdɐ deːɐ̯ 'reːbə zɪç t͡suː fɛɐ̯'gla̯eçən.
reicht er nicht auf, nur mit der Eiche oder der Rebe sich zu vergleichen.
reaches he not up, even with the oak or the vine himself to compare.
(he cannot even reach up to compare himself with the oak or the vine.)

vas lʊnt'ɐ'ʃa̯edət' 'gœt'ɐ fɔn 'mɛnʃən?
Was unterscheidet Götter von Menschen?
What distinguishes gods from human beings?

das 'fiːlə 'vɛlən foːɐ̯ 'jeːnən 'vandəln, la̯en 'leːvɪgɐ ʃt'roːm:
dass viele Wellen vor jenen wandeln, ein ewiger Strom:
that many waves before the former flow onwards, an eternal stream:
(That before the gods many waves flow onwards, an eternal stream;)

ʊns heːp't di 'vɛlə, fɛɐ̯'ʃlɪŋt di 'vɛlə, lʊnt' viːɐ̯ fɛɐ̯'zɪŋk'ən.
uns hebt die Welle, verschlingt die Welle, und wir versinken.
us lifts the wave, swallows the wave, and we sink.
(a wave lifts us up, a wave swallows us, and we sink.)

a̯en 'kʰla̯enɐ rɪŋ bə'grɛnt͡st' 'lʊnzɐ 'leːbən, lʊnt' 'fiːlə gə'ʃlɛçt'ɐ
Ein kleiner Ring begrenzt unser Leben, und viele Geschlechter
A little ring bounds our life, and many generations

'ra̯eən zɪç 'dɑo̯ɐnt' lan 'liːrəs 'daːza̯ens lʊn'lɛnt'lɪçə 'kʰɛt'ə.
reihen sich dauernd an ihres Daseins unendliche Kette.
range themselves constantly in their existence's endless chain.
(are constantly aligning themselves as links in the endless chain of existence.)

[The poet contemplates divine majesty with profound humility. Schubert's remarkable setting for bass voice expresses both the stillness and the depth of such contemplation. The spirit of the poem contrasts stikingly with the rebellious defiance of *Prometheus*, another powerful poem by Goethe, powerfully set by Schubert. Hugo Wolf also created masterly settings of both poems.]

'greːt'çən / 'greːt'çəns 'bɪt'ə / 'greːt'çən lɪm 't͡svɪŋɐ
Gretchen / Gretchens Bitte / Gretchen im Zwinger
Gretchen / Gretchen's Plea / Gretchen at the Ramparts

Posthumously published [composed 1817] (poem from *Faust* by Johann Wolfgang von Goethe)

ax 'na̯egə, duː 'ʃmɛrt͡sənra̯eçə, da̯en 'lant'lɪt͡s 'gnɛːdɪç 'ma̯enɐ noːtʰ!
Ach neige, du Schmerzenreiche, dein Antlitz grädig meiner Not!
Ah incline, you sorrow-laden one, your countenance graciously to my distress!
(Ah, Lady of Sorrows, incline your face graciously to my distress!)

das ʃveːɐ̯t‘ ǀɪm 'hɛrt͡sən, mɪt 't^hɑ͡ozənt‘ 'ʃmɛrt͡sən
Das Schwert im Herzen, mit tausend Schmerzen
The sword in the heart, with (a) thousand pains
(With a sword piercing your heart, with a thousand pains,)

blɪkst‘ ǀɑ͡of t͡suː 'da͡enəs 'zoːnəs tʰoːt‘. t͡sʊm 'faːt‘ɐ blɪkst duː,
blickst auf zu deines Sohnes Tod. Zum Vater blickst du,
(you) look up at your Son's death. To the Father look you,
(you look up at your Son as He dies. You raise your eyes to the Father,)

ǀʊnt‘ 'zɔ͡øft͡sɐ ʃɪkst duː hɪ'nɑ͡of ǀʊm za͡en ǀʊnt 'da͡enə noːtʰ.
und Seufzer schickst du hinauf um sein' und deine Not.
and sighs send you upwards for His and your misery.
(and you send sighs up to heaven for your Son's agony and for your own.)

veːɐ̯ 'fyːlət‘, viː 'vyːlət deːɐ̯ ʃmɛrt͡s miːɐ̯/miːr ǀɪm gə'ba͡en?
Wer fühlet, wie wühlet der Schmerz mir im Gebein?
Who feels how gnaws the pain for me in the bones?
(Who can feel how pain is gnawing at my bones?)

vas ma͡en 'ǀarməs hɛrt͡s hiːɐ̯ 'baŋət‘, vas ǀɛs 't͡sɪt‘ɐt‘,
Was mein armes Herz hier banget, was es zittert,
What my poor heart here fears, what it trembles,
(What my poor heart here fears, how it trembles,)

vas fɛɐ̯'laŋət‘, va͡est‘ nuːɐ̯ duː, nuːɐ̯ duː ǀa'la͡en! vo'hɪn ǀɪç 'ǀɪmɐ 'geːə,
was verlanget, weisst nur du, nur du allein! Wohin ich immer gehe,
what craves, know only you, only you alone! Whither I ever go,
(what it craves, only you know that, you alone! Wherever I go,)

viː veː, viː veː, viː 'veːə vɪrt‘ miːɐ̯/miːr ǀɪm 'buːzən hiːɐ̯!
wie weh, wie weh, wie wehe wird mir im Busen hier!
how aching, how aching, how aching becomes (it) for me in the bosom here!
(what pain, what pain, what pain I feel here in my bosom!)

ɪç bɪn, ǀax, kʰɑ͡om ǀa'la͡enə,
Ich bin, ach, kaum alleine, [*Peters:* **Ich bin, ich bin alleine,**]
I am, ah, scarcely alone, [I am, I am alone,]
(Ah, no sooner am I alone,)

ɪç va͡en, ǀɪç va͡en, ǀɪç 'va͡enə, das hɛrt͡s t͡sɛɐ̯'brɪçt‘ ǀɪn miːɐ̯.
ich wein', ich wein', ich weine, das Herz zerbricht in mir.
I weep, I weep, I weep, the heart breaks in me.
(than I weep, I weep, I weep, and my heart breaks within me.)

[di 'ʃerbən foːɐ̯ 'ma͡enəm 'fɛnst‘ɐ bə'tʰɑ͡ot‘ ǀɪç mɪt 'tʰrɛːnən, ǀax!
[Die Scherben vor meinem Fenster betaut' ich mit Tränen, ach!
[The flower-pots before my window bedewed I with tears, ah!
[(I sprinkled the flower-pots in front of my window with tears—ah!—)

als ǀɪç ǀam 'fryːən 'mɔrgən diːɐ̯ 'diːzə 'bluːmən braːx.
als ich am frühen Morgen dir diese Blumen brach.
when I in the early morning for you these flowers plucked.
(when I was plucking these flowers for you early this morning.)

ʃiːn hɛl lɪn ˈmae̯nə ˈkʰamɐ di ˈzɔnə fryː hɛˈrao̯f,
Schien hell in meine Kammer die Sonne früh herauf,
Shone brightly into my bedroom the sun early up,
(When the rising sun shone up into my bedroom,)

zaːs lɪç lɪn ˈlaləm ˈjamɐ(r) lɪn ˈmae̯nəm bɛtʻ ʃoːn lao̯f.
sass ich in allem Jammer in meinem Bett schon auf.
sat I in all misery in my bed already up.
(I was already sitting up in my bed, in utter misery.)

hɪlf! ˈrɛtʻə mɪç fɔn ʃmaːx lʊnt tʰoːtʻ! lax ˈnae̯gə,
Hilf! Rette mich von Schmach und Tod! Ach neige,
Help! Save me from shame and death! Ah, incline,

duː ˈʃmɛrt͜sənrae̯çə, dae̯n ˈlantʻlɪt͜s ˈgnɛːdɪç ˈmae̯nɐ noːtʰ!]
du Schmerzenreiche, dein Antlitz gnädig meiner Not!]
you sorrow-laden one, your countenance graciously to my distress!]
(Mother of Sorrows, incline your face graciously to my distress!)]

[Schubert's setting is impressive, but incomplete (the remaining verses are in brackets, above). Gretchen, pregnant and abandoned by her lover, has come to a niche in the ramparts of the city, to pray before an image of the Mater Dolorosa and to offer fresh flowers with her desperate prayer. This follows the Scene at the Well, where she was mocked by her former friends.]

ˈgreːtʻçən lam ˈʃpʻinraːdə
Gretchen am Spinnrade
Gretchen at the Spinning Wheel

Op. 2 [1814] (from *Faust* by Johann Wolfgang von Goethe)

ˈmae̯nə ruː lɪstʻ hɪn, mae̯n hɛrt͜s lɪstʻ ʃveːɐ̯;
Meine Ruh ist hin, mein Herz ist schwer;
My peace is gone, my heart is heavy;

ɪç ˈfɪndə ziː ˈnɪmɐ(r) lʊntʻ ˈnɪmɐ meːɐ̯.
ich finde sie nimmer und nimmer mehr.
I find it never and never more. [*sie* is here a feminine pronoun, referring to *Ruh.*]
(I shall never, never find it—my inner peace—any more.)

voː lɪç liːn nɪçtʻ haːpʻ, lɪstʻ miːɐ̯ das graːpʻ,
Wo ich ihn nicht hab, ist mir das Grab,
Where I him not have, is to me the grave,
(Where I do not have *him*, that place is like the *grave* to me,)

di ˈgant͜sə vɛltʻ lɪstʻ miːɐ̯ fɛɐ̯ˈgɛltʰ.
die ganze Welt ist mir vergällt.
the whole world is to me turned into gall.
(the whole world has become a bitter place to me.)

mae̯n ˈlarmɐ kʰɔp͜f lɪstʻ miːɐ̯ fɛɐ̯ˈrʏkʻtʰ, mae̯n ˈlarmɐ zɪn lɪstʻ miːɐ̯ t͜sɛɐ̯ˈʃtʻʏkʻtʰ.
Mein armer Kopf ist mir verrückt, mein armer Sinn ist mir zerstückt.
My poor head is to me crazy, my poor mind is to me torn to pieces.
(My poor head seems crazy to me, my poor mind is torn apart.)

nax ʔi:m nu:ɐ̯ ʃao ʔɪç tsʊm ˈfɛnstʼɐ hɪˈnaos, nax ʔi:m nu:ɐ̯ ge: ʔɪç ʔaos dem haos.
Nach ihm nur schau ich zum Fenster hinaus, nach ihm nur geh ich aus dem Haus.
For him only look I at the window out, for him only go I out of the house.
(I look out the window only for him, searching only for him I go out of the house.)

zaen ˈho:ɐ gaŋ, zaen ˈʔe:dlə gəˈʃtʼalt^h, ˈzaenəs ˈmʊndəs ˈlɛçəln, ˈzaenɐ(r) ˈʔaogən gəˈvalt^h,
Sein hoher Gang, sein edle Gestalt, seines Mundes Lächeln, seiner Augen Gewalt,
His tall walk, his noble figure, his mouth's smile, his eyes' power,
(His tall walk, his noble figure, the smile of his mouth, the power of his eyes,)

ʊntʼ ˈzaenɐ ˈre:də ˈtsaobɐflʊs. zaen ˈhɛndədrʊk^h, ʔʊntʼ ʔax, zaen k^hʊs!
und seiner rede Zauberfluss, sein Händedruck, und ach, sein Kuss!
and his talk's magic flow, his hand-clasp, and ah, his kiss!
(and the magic flow of his talk, the clasp of his hand, and ah, his kiss!)

maen ˈbu:zən drɛŋtʼ zɪç na:x ʔi:m hɪn. ʔax, dʏrftʼ ʔɪç ˈfasən ʔʊntʼ ˈhaltʼən ʔi:n!
Mein Busen drängt sich nach ihm hin, ach, dürft ich fassen und halten ihn!
My bosom urges itself toward him ..., ah, might I grasp and hold him!
(My bosom strains toward him, ah, if I only could grasp and hold him!)

ʊntʼ ˈk^hʏsən ʔi:n, zo: vi: ʔɪç vɔlt^h, ʔan ˈzaenen ˈk^hʏsən fɛɐ̯ˈge:ən zɔlt^h,
und küssen ihn, so wie ich wollt, an seinen Küssen vergehen sollt,
and kiss him, as how I would, at his kisses die (I) should,
(and kiss him, the way I would want to, I should die from his kisses,)

o: k^hœntʼ ʔɪç ʔi:n ˈk^hʏsən, zo: vi: ʔɪç vɔlt^h, ʔan ˈzaenən ˈk^hʏsən fɛɐ̯ˈge:ən zɔlt^h!
o könnt ich ihn küssen, so wie ich wollt, an seinen Küssen vergehen sollt!
oh could I him kiss, as how I would, at his kisses die (I) should!
(oh if I could kiss him as I want to, I should die from his kisses!)

[In Part I of Goethe's *Faust,* Gretchen meets and falls in love with Faust. He enjoys a brief affair with her; then, lured away by the devil, he leaves her, alone, pregnant, and rejected by the community, the church, and her own brother. She sings these words while she is sitting at her spinning wheel, thinking of Faust and trying to spin. When she remembers his kiss, she is too overcome to spin; she makes two feeble attempts to start the wheel again before she is finally able to continue. Again and again she numbly repeats the first two lines as a forlorn refrain. The singer is Gretchen, the accompaniment portrays the spinning wheel. Schubert created this immortal masterpiece when he was only seventeen years old, astonishing the musical world.]

ˈgrʊpʼə ʔaos dem ˈt^hartʼarʊs
Gruppe aus dem Tartarus
Group from Tartarus

Op. 24, No. 1 [1817] (Friedrich von Schiller)

hɔrç — vi: ˈmʊrməln dɛs ʔɛmˈp^hø:ɐ̯tʼən ˈme:rəs,
Horch — wie Murmeln des empörten Meeres,
Hark — like murmuring of the indignant sea,
(Hark — like the murmur of an angry sea,)

vi: dʊrç ˈho:lɐ ˈfɛlzən ˈbɛkʼən vaentʼ ʔaen bax,
wie durch hohler Felsen Becken weint ein Bach,
as through hollow rocks' basin weeps a brook,
(like the sound of a brook that weeps through a basin formed by hollow rocks,)

ʃt'øːnt dɔrt 'dʊmpfɪçˌtʰiːf la͜en 'ʃveːrəs, 'leːrəs, 'kʰvaːllɛɐ̯ˌpʰrɛst'əs lax!
stöhnt dort dumpfigtief ein schweres, leeres, qualerpresstes Ach!
moans there muffled-deep a heavy, empty, torment-wrung moan!
(a heavy, empty moan, wrung from beings in torment, issues there, muffled, from the depths!)

ʃmɛrt͜s fɛɐ̯'t͜sɛrət' liːɐ̯ gə'zɪçt', fɛɐ̯'t͜sva͜eflʊŋ 'ʃp'ɛrət' 'liːrən 'raxən 'fluːxənt' la͜of.
Schmerz verzerret ihr Gesicht, Verzweiflung sperret ihren Rachen fluchend auf.
Pain distorts their face, despair opens their mouths cursing wide.
(Pain distorts their features, in despair their mouths open wide, cursing.)
[*aufsperren* = to unlock, to open wide]

hoːl zɪnt' 'liːrə 'la͜ogən, 'liːrə 'blɪk'ə 'ʃp'ɛːən baŋ naːx dɛs kʰo't͜syːt'ʊs 'brʏk'ə,
Hohl sind ihre Augen, ihre Blicke spähen bang nach des Kozytus Brücke,
Hollow are their eyes, their glances look anxiously toward the Cocytus's bridge,
(Their eyes are hollow, they keep glancing anxiously toward the bridge that crosses the Cocytus,)
[*poem & GA (alternative spelling, same pronunciation):* **Cocytus**]

'fɔlgən 'tʰrɛːnənt' 'za͜enəm 'tʰra͜oɐla͜of.
folgen tränend seinem Trauerlauf.
follow weeping its mournful course.
(their weeping eyes follow the river's mournful course.)

'fraːgən zɪç la͜e'nandɐ(r) 'lɛŋst'lɪç 'la͜ezə, lɔp' nɔx nɪçt' fɔl'lɛndʊŋ/fɔ'lɛndʊŋ za͜e?
Fragen sich einander ängstlich leise, ob noch nicht Vollendung sei?
Ask themselves each other anxiously softly, whether yet not completion (might) be?
(They ask each other anxiously, softly, whether the end of their torment might not yet be near.)

'eːvɪçkʰa͜et' ʃvɪŋt' 'lyːbɐ(r) 'liːnən 'kʰra͜ezə, brɪçt di 'zɛnzə dɛs za'tʰʊrns lɛnt't͜sva͜e.
Ewigkeit schwingt über ihnen Kreise, bricht die Sense des Saturns entzwei.
Eternity swings over them circles, breaks the scythe of the Saturn in two.
(Eternity swings circles above them and breaks Saturn's scythe in two.)

[Tartarus, in Greek legend, is the lowest region of the underworld; it is there that those who have offended the gods are doomed to suffer eternal torments. The Cocytus, according to Vergil, is a river that surrounds Hades, the realm of the dead. Saturn's scythe is a symbol of time that eventually mows down all that exists; for those in Tartarus the scythe of time is broken: their torments will be eternal. This powerful song is one of Schubert's most original creations. An earlier attempt to set the same poem was apparently abandoned after fourteen bars.]

Gute Nacht see *Winterreise*

Guarda che bianca luna see *Vier Canzonen von Metastasio*

'haːgars 'kʰlaːgə
Hagars Klage
Hagar's Lament

Posthumously published [composed 1811] (poem by Clemens August Schücking)

hiːɐ̯/hiːr lam 'hyːgəl 'ha͜esən 'zandəs, [lɪn deːɐ̯ 'mɛnʃənleːrən 'vyːst'ə,]
Hier am Hügel heissen Sandes, [in der menschenleeren Wüste,]
Here on the hill of hot sand, [in the deserted desert,]

zɪts lɪç, lʊnt‘ miːɐ̯ geːgən'lyːbɐ liːk‘t‘ ma͜en 'ʃt‘ɛrbənt‘ kʰɪnt‘,
sitz' ich, und mir gegenüber liegt mein sterbend Kind,
sit I, and to me opposite lies my dying child,
(I sit, and facing me lies my dying child;)

lɛçt͜st‘ naːx 'la͜enəm 'tʰrɔp͜fən 'vasɐ, lɛçt͜st‘ lʊnt‘ rɪŋt‘ ʃoːn mɪt dem 'tʰoːdə,
lechzt nach einem Tropfen Wasser, lechzt und ringt schon mit dem Tode,
thirsts for a drop (of) water, thirsts and wrestles already with the death,
(he is parched with thirst for a drop of water, he thirsts and struggles already with death,)

va͜ent‘, lʊnt‘ blɪk‘t‘ mɪt‘ 'ʃt‘iːrən 'la͜ogən mɪç bə'drɛŋt‘ə 'mʊt‘ɐ(r) lan.
weint, und blickt mit stieren Augen mich bedrängte Mutter an.
weeps, and looks with staring eyes me afflicted mother at.
(he weeps and looks with staring eyes at me, his afflicted mother.)

duː mʊst‘ 'ʃt‘ɛrbən, 'larməs 'vʏrmçən, lax, nɪçt‘ 'la͜enə [la͜enə] 'tʰrɛːnə
Du musst sterben, armes Würmchen, ach, nicht eine [eine] Träne
You must die, poor little mite, ah, not one[, one] tear
(You must die, poor little mite! Ah! Not a single tear)

haːb ɪç lɪn den 'tʰrɔk‘nən 'la͜ogən, voː lɪç dɪç mɪt‘ 'ʃt‘ɪlən kʰan.
hab' ich in den trocknen Augen, wo ich dich mit stillen kann.
have I in the dry eyes, where- I you -with soothe can.
(do I have in my dry eyes with which I might be able to mitigate your thirst.)

[*womit* = wherewith, with which]

haː! zɛː lɪç 'la͜enə 'løːvənmʊt‘ɐ, lɪç 'vɔlt‘ə mɪt‘ liːɐ̯ 'kʰɛmp͜fən.
Ha! säh' ich eine Löwenmutter, ich wollte mit ihr kämpfen,
Ah! saw I a lion- mother, I would with her fight,
(Ah! If I were to see a mother lioness, I would fight with her)

[*poem:* **Säh' ich eine Löwenmutter, ha! ich wollte mit ihr kämpfen**]

['kʰɛmp͜fən mɪt‘ liːɐ̯] lʊm di 'la͜et‘ɐ, [das lɪç 'lœʃt‘ə 'da͜enən dʊrstʰ!]
[kämpfen mit ihr] um die Eiter, [dass ich löschte deinen Durst!]
[fight with her] for the pus, [so that I might quench your thirst!]
(for her milk!) [*Eiter* = (literally) pus; here, according to the sense, it is the lioness's milk]

kʰœnt‘ lɪç la͜os dem 'dʏrən 'zandə nuːɐ̯/nuːr la͜en 'tʰrœp͜fçən 'vasɐ 'za͜ogən!
Könnt' ich aus dem dürren Sande nur ein Tröpfchen Wasser saugen!
Could I out of the arid sand only one little drop (of) water suck!
(If only I could suck even one little drop of water out of the arid sand!)

'aːbɐ(r) lax! [zoː mʊst duː 'ʃt‘ɛrbən, lʊnt‘] lɪç mʊs dɪç 'ʃt‘ɛrbən zeːn!
Aber ach! [so musst du sterben, und] ich muss dich sterben sehn!
But, ah! [like this must you die, and] I must you die see!
(But, ah! [You will have to die like this, and] I will have to see you die!)

kʰa͜om la͜en 'ʃvaxɐ ʃt‘raːl dɛs 'leːbəns 'dɛmɐt‘ la͜of deːɐ̯ 'bla͜eçən 'vaŋə,
Kaum ein schwacher Strahl des Lebens dämmert auf der bleichen Wange,
Scarcely a weak ray of the life glimmers on the pale cheek,
(Scarcely a single faint ray of life is still glimmering on your pale cheeks,)

'dɛmɐt' lɪn den 'mat'ən 'la͜ogən, 'da͜enə brʊst' lɛɐ̯'he:p't' zɪç kʰa͜om
dämmert in den matten Augen, deine Brust erhebt sich kaum.
glimmers in the mat eyes, your chest lifts itself barely.
(or in your lusterless eyes; your chest barely rises when you breathe.)

hi:ɐ̯/hi:r lam 'bu:zən kʰɔm lʊnt' 'vɛlk'ə! kʰœmt' la͜en mɛnʃ dan dʊrç di 'vy:st'ə,
Hier am Busen komm' und welke! Kömmt ein Mensch dann durch die Wüste,
Here at the breast come and wither! Comes a human being then through the desert,
(Come and wither away here at my breast! If someone then should come through the desert,)

zo: vɪrt' le:ɐ̯/le:r lɪn den zant' lʊns 'ʃarən, 'za:gən: das lɪst' va͜ep' lʊnt' kʰɪnt'.
so wird er in den Sand uns scharren, sagen: das ist Weib und Kind.
then will he in the sand us bury hastily, say: "That is woman and child."
(he will hastily bury us in the sand, saying: "That is a woman with her child.") [*poem without* **so**]

[na͜en] ɪç vɪl mɪç fɔn di:ɐ̯ 'vɛndən, das lɪç dɪç nɪçt' 'ʃt'ɛrbən ze:[ə],
[Nein] ich will mich von dir wenden, dass ich dich nicht sterben seh[e],
[No,] I will myself from you turn away, so that I you not die see,
([No,] I shall turn away from you, so that I do not see you die,)

ʊnt' lɪm 'tʰa͜oməl de:ɐ̯ fɛɐ̯'t͜sva͜eflʊŋ 'mʊrə 'vi:dɐ gɔtʰ!
und im Taumel der Verzweiflung murre wider Gott!
and in the delirium of the despair grumble against God!
(so that I may not cry out against God in the delirium of my despair!)

'fɛrnə fɔn di:ɐ̯ vɪl lɪç 'ge:ən, lʊnt' la͜en 'ry:rənt' 'kʰla:k'li:t' 'zɪŋən,
Ferne von dir will ich gehen, und ein rührend Klaglied singen,
Far from you will I go, and a moving lament-song sing,
(I shall go far away from you, and sing a moving lament,)

das du: nɔx lɪm 'tʰo:dəskʰamp͜fə 'tʰrø:st'ʊŋ 'la͜enɐ 'ʃt'ɪmə hø:ɐ̯stʰ.
dass du noch im Todeskampfe Tröstung einer Stimme hörst.
so that you still in the death-struggle comfort of a voice hear.
(so that in your struggle with death you can still hear a comforting voice.)

nu:ɐ̯ t͜sʊm 'lɛt͜st'ən 'kʰla:kgə,be:tə lœf nɪç 'ma͜enə 'dʏrən 'lɪp'ən,
Nur zum letzten Klaggebete öffn' ich meine dürren Lippen,
Only in the last lament-prayer open I my parched lips,
(I shall open my parched lips only to sing that last lamenting prayer,)
[*poem:* **Noch** (nɔx, still/once again) **zum letzten Klaggebete**]

ʊnt dan ʃli:s lɪç zi: la͜of 'lɪmɐ, lʊnt dan 'kʰɔmə balt', lo: tʰo:t'!
und dann schliess' ich sie auf immer, und dann komme bald, o Tod!
and then close I them for ever, and then come soon, O death!
(and then I shall close them forever, and then come soon, O death!)
[*poem:* **und dann komme bald der** (de:ɐ̯, the) **Tod!**]

je'ho:va! blɪk' la͜of lʊns he'rap'! [lax] lɛɐ̯'barmə dɪç dɛs 'kʰna:bən!
Jehova! blick' auf uns herab! [Ach] erbarme dich des Knaben!
Jehovah! look upon us down! [Ah,] move to pity yourself of the boy!
(Jehovah! Look down upon us! [Ah,] take pity on the boy!)

zɛntʻ ǀɑ̯os ˈǀa̯enəm ˈtʰɑ̯ogəvœlkʻə ˈlaːbʊŋ ǀʊns hɛˈrapʻ!
Send' aus einem Taugewölke Labung uns herab!
Send from a dew-cloud refreshment to us down!
(Send refreshing moisture down to us from a dewy cloud!)

ɪstʻ ǀeːɐ̯ nɪçtʻ fɔn ˈǀaːbrams ˈzaːmən? [ax] eːɐ̯ ˈva̯entʻə ˈfrɔ̯ødəntʰrɛːnən,
Ist er nicht von Abrams Samen? [Ach] er weinte Freudentränen,
Is he not of Abraham's seed? [Ah,] he wept tears of joy,

als ǀɪç ǀiːm diːs kʰɪntʻ gəˈboːrən, ǀʊntʻ nuːn vɪrtʻ ǀeːɐ̯/ǀeːr ǀiːm t͡sʊm fluːx!
als ich ihm dies Kind geboren, und nun wird er ihm zum Fluch!
when I for him this child bore, and now becomes he to him to the curse!
(when I bore him this child; and now he has become a curse to him!)

[*poem:* **als ich ihm das** (das, the) **Kind geboren]**

ˈrɛtʻə ˈda̯enəs ˈliːpʻlɪŋs ˈzaːmən! zɛlpstʻ za̯en ˈfaːtʻɐ baːtʻ ǀʊm ˈzeːgən,
Rette deines Lieblings Samen! Selbst sein Vater bat um Segen,
Save your favorite's seed! Even his father asked for (a) blessing,

ʊnt duː ʃpʻraːxstʻ: ǀɛs ˈkʰɔmə ˈzeːgən ˈǀyːbɐ ˈdiːzəs ˈkʰɪndəs hɑ̯opʻtʰ!
und du sprachst: Es komme Segen über dieses Kindes Haupt!
and you spoke: "There come blessing over this child's head!"
(and you spoke: "Let there come a blessing upon this child's head!")

[*poem:* **über dieses Knaben** (ˈkʰnaːbən, boy's) **Haupt]**

haːb ɪç ˈviːdɐ dɪç gəˈzʏndɪçtʻ, haː! zoː ˈtʰrɛfə mɪç di ˈraxə!
Hab' ich wider dich gesündigt, ha! so treffe mich die Rache!
Have I against you sinned, ah! then strike me the vengeance!
(If I have sinned against you, ah, then may your vengeance strike me!)

ˈaːbɐ(r) ǀax! vas tʰaːt deːɐ̯ ˈkʰnaːbə, das ǀeːɐ̯ mɪtʻ miːɐ̯ ˈla̯edən mʊs?
Aber ach! was tat der Knabe, dass er mit mir leiden muss?
But, ah! what did the boy, that he with me suffer must?
(But, ah, what has the boy done, that he should also have to suffer with me?)

vɛːr ɪç dɔx ǀɪn ziːr gəˈʃtʻɔrbən, ǀals ǀɪç ǀɪn deːɐ̯ ˈvyːstʻə ˈǀɪrtʻə,
Wär' ich doch in Sir gestorben, als ich in der Wüste irrte,
Had I at least in Shur died, when I in the desert strayed,
(Would that I had died in Shur, when I was straying in the desert,)

[*poem:* **als ich in den Wüsten** (den ˈvyːstʻən, the deserts) **irrte]**

ʊnt das kʰɪntʻ nɔx ǀʊngəˈboːrən ˈǀʊntʻɐ ˈma̯enəm ˈhɛrt͡sən laːkʻ!
und das Kind noch ungeboren unter meinem Herzen lag!
and the child still unborn beneath my heart lay!
(and the unborn child still lay beneath my heart!)

na̯en, daː kʰaːm ǀa̯en ˈhɔldɐ ˈfrɛmtʻlɪŋ, hiːs mɪç rʏkʻ t͡suː ˈǀaːbram ˈgeːən,
Nein, da kam ein holder Fremdling, hiess mich rück zu Abram gehen,
No, there came a gracious stranger, bid me back to Abraham go,
(No! There a gracious stranger came up to me and bid me go back to Abraham)

ʊnt dɛs 'manəs hɑ͜os bə'tʰreːt'ən, deːɐ̯/deːr lʊns lɪt͜st' fɛɐ̯'ʃt'iːs.
und des Mannes Haus betreten, der uns grausam itzt verstiess.
and the man's house enter, who us cruelly now rejected.
(and enter the house of the man who now has cruelly rejected us.) [*itzt* (archaic) = *jetzt* = now]

vaːɐ̯ deːɐ̯ 'frɛmt'lɪŋ nɪçt' la͜en 'lɛŋəl? dɛn leːɐ̯ ʃp'raːx mɪt' 'hɔldɐ 'miːnə:
War der Fremdling nicht ein Engel? denn er sprach mit holder Miene:
Was the stranger not an angel? For he spoke with gracious mien:
[*poem:* **nicht dein** (da͜en, your) **Engel?...mit hoher** ('hoːɐ, exalted) **Miene]**

'ɪsmalɛl/ɪsmaeːl vɪrt' groːs lɑ͜of 'leːɐ̯dən, [lʊnt'] za͜en 'zaːmən 't͜saːlra͜eç za͜en.
Ismael wird gross auf Erden, [und] sein Samen zahlreich sein.
Ishmael will great on earth, [and] his seed numerous be.
(Ishmael will be great on earth [and] his seed will multiply.)

nuːn 'liːgən viːɐ̯/viːr lʊnt' 'vɛlk'ən; 'lʊnzrə 'la͜eçən 'veːɐ̯dən 'moːdɐn
Nun liegen wir und welken; unsre Leichen werden modern
Now lie we and wilt away; our corpses will molder
(Now we lie here and wilt away; our corpses will molder)
[*poem:* **Ha!** (haː, ah!) **wir liegen nun und welken]**

viː di 'la͜eçən deːɐ̯ fɛɐ̯'fluːxt'ən, diː deːɐ̯/deːr 'leːɐ̯də ʃoːs nɪçt' bɪrk'tʰ.
wie die Leichen der Verfluchten, die der Erde Schoss nicht birgt.
like the corpses of the accursed, which the earth's womb not shelters.
(like the corpses of the accursed, which the womb of the earth does not shelter.)

ʃra͜e t͜sʊm 'hɪməl, 'larmɐ 'kʰnaːbə! 'lœfnə 'da͜enə 'vɛlk'ən 'lɪp'ən!
Schrei' zum Himmel, armer Knabe! öffne deine welken Lippen!
Scream to the heaven, poor boy! Open your parched lips!
(Cry aloud to heaven, poor boy! Open your parched lips!)

gɔt', za͜en hɛr, fɛɐ̯'ʃmɛː das 'fleːən dɛs lʊn'ʃʊlt'gən 'kʰnaːbən nɪçtʰ!
Gott, sein Herr, verschmäh' das Flehen des unschuld'gen Knaben nicht!
God, his Lord, scorn the supplication of the innocent boy not!
(God, his Lord, do not scorn the supplication of this innocent boy!)

[This is the first of Schubert's songs that has survived complete. It is a dramatic scene, a sort of mini-opera for home consumption, modeled on similar marathons by Johann Rudolf Zumsteeg. He was fourteen when he composed it. Someone showed it to Antonio Salieri, whose encouraging reaction prompted the young composer to study with him. Schubert omitted the words of the poem that are in brackets, above. The subject is taken from the Bible, *Genesis*, Chapters 16 and 21. Hagar was an Egyptian, a handmaid to Sarai (as Sarah was then called), the wife of Abram (later Abraham). When Sarai failed to conceive a child, she suggested to her husband that Hagar should bear him a child. When Hagar became pregnant, she began to feel superior to Sarai, who punished her for her scorn. Hagar fled to the wilderness of Shur, where an angel told her to return to her mistress. After her return she gave birth to Ishmael. Some years later, Sarah, at the age of ninety, gave birth to Abraham's second son, Isaac. When she saw Ishmael laughing incredulously that such an old woman could become a mother, Sarah urged Abraham to send Hagar and Ishmael away; after some soul-searching, he gave them a bottle of water and some bread and sent them into the wilderness of Beer-Sheba. Ishmael survived to become the forefather of twelve Arab tribes.]

Halt! see *Die schöne Müllerin*

ˈhɛnflɪŋs ˈliːbəsvɛrbʊŋ
Hänflings Liebeswerbung
The Linnet's Wooing

Op. 20, No. 3 [1817] (Friedrich Kind)

aˈhiːdi! ǀɪç ˈliːbə. mɪlt‘ ˈlɛçəlt di ˈzɔnə, mɪlt‘ ˈveːən di ˈvɛst‘ə,
Ahidi! ich liebe. Mild lächelt die Sonne, mild wehen die Weste,
Twitter! I love. Gently smiles the sun, gently blow the western breezes,
(Twitter! I am in love. The sun is gently smiling, the western breezes blow gently,)

zanft‘ ˈriːzəlt di ˈkʰvɛlə, zyːs ˈdʊft‘ən di ˈbluːmən. ǀɪç ˈliːbə, ǀaˈhiːdi!
sanft rieselt die Quelle, süss duften die Blumen. Ich liebe, Ahidi!
softly ripples the spring, sweet smell the flowers. I love, chirp!
(the water of the spring is softly rippling, the flowers smell sweet. I am in love! Chirp!)

aˈhiːdi! ǀɪç ˈliːbə. dɪç liːb ɪç, duː ˈzanft‘ə, mɪt‘ ˈzaednəm gəˈfiːdɐ,
Ahidi! ich liebe. Dich lieb' ich, du Sanfte, mit seid'nem Gefieder,
Twitter! I love. You love I, you gentle one, with silky feathers,
(Twitter! I am in love. I love you, gentle female with silky feathers,)

mɪt‘ ˈʃt‘raːləndən ˈǀɔøk‘laen, dɪç, ˈʃøːnst‘ə deːɐ ˈʃvɛst‘ɐn! ǀɪç ˈliːbə, ǀaˈhiːdi!
mit strahlenden Äuglein, dich, Schönste der Schwestern! Ich liebe, Ahidi!
with radiant little eyes, you, loveliest of the sisters! I love, chirp!
(with radiant little eyes, you, the loveliest of the sisters! I am in love! Chirp!)

aˈhiːdi! ǀɪç ˈliːbə. ǀoː ziː, viː di ˈbluːmən zɪç ˈliːbəfɔl ˈgryːsən,
Ahidi! ich liebe. O sieh, wie die Blumen sich liebevoll grüssen,
Twitter! I love. Oh look, how the flowers each other lovingly greet,
(Twitter! I am in love. Oh, look how the flowers greet each other lovingly,)

zɪç ˈliːbəfɔl ˈnɪk‘ən! ǀoː ˈliːbə mɪç ˈviːdɐ! ǀɪç ˈliːbə, ǀaˈhiːdi!
sich liebevoll nicken! O liebe mich wieder! Ich liebe, Ahidi!
to each other lovingly nod! Oh, love me in return! I love, chirp!
(how lovingly they nod to each other! Oh, love me in return! I am in love! Chirp!)

aˈhiːdi! ǀɪç ˈliːbə. ǀoː ziː, viː deːɐ/deːr ˈǀeːfɔø mɪt‘ ˈliːbəndən ˈǀarmən
Ahidi! ich liebe. O sieh, wie der Epheu mit liebenden Armen
Twitter! I love. Oh, look, how the ivy with loving arms
(Twitter! I am in love. Oh, look how the ivy with loving arms)

di ˈǀaeçə ǀʊmˈʃlɪŋətʰ. ǀoː ˈliːbə mɪç ˈviːdɐ! ǀɪç ˈliːbə, ǀaˈhiːdi!
die Eiche umschlinget. O liebe mich wieder! Ich liebe, Ahidi!
the oak embraces. Oh, love me in return! I love, chirp!
(embraces the oak. Oh, love me in return! I am in love! Chirp!)

[A charming little song in *Ländler* style, with words by the librettist of Weber's *Der Freischütz*.]

ˈharfənʃpʻiːlɐ. ˈa͜ens. / veːɐ̯ zɪç deːɐ̯ ˈla͜enzaːmkʰa͜etʻ lɛɐ̯ˈgiːpʻtʰ

Harfenspieler. I. / Wer sich der Einsamkeit ergibt

The Harper. I. / He Who Surrenders to Solitude

Op. 12, No. 1 [1816] (poem from *Wilhelm Meister* by Johann Wolfgang von Goethe)

veːɐ̯ zɪç deːɐ̯/deːr ˈla͜enzaːmkʰa͜etʻ lɛɐ̯ˈgiːpʻtʻ, lax! deːɐ̯/deːr lɪstʻ baltʻ laˈla͜en;
Wer sich der Einsamkeit ergibt, ach! der ist bald allein;
He who himself to the solitude gives up, ah! he is soon alone;
(He who gives himself up to solitude, ah, he is soon alone!)

a͜en ˈjeːdɐ leːpʻtʻ, la͜en ˈjeːdɐ liːpʻtʻ, lʊntʻ lɛstʻ liːn ˈza͜enɐ pʰa͜en.
ein jeder lebt, ein jeder liebt, und lässt ihn seiner Pein.
everyone lives, everyone loves, and leaves him to his pain. [*ein jeder* = everyone]
(Others live their own life, love their own loved ones, and leave the solitary man to his pain.)

jaː! lastʻ mɪç ˈma͜enɐ kʰvaːl! lʊntʻ kʰan lɪç nuːɐ̯/nuːr ˈla͜enmaːl
Ja! lasst mich meiner Qual! und kann ich nur einmal
Yes! leave me to my torment! and can I just once
(Yes! Leave me to my torment! And if I can just once)

rɛçtʻ ˈla͜enzaːm za͜en, dan bɪn lɪç nɪçtʻ laˈla͜en.
recht einsam sein, dann bin ich nicht allein.
really solitary be, then am I not alone.
(be truly isolated from others, then I shall still not be alone. Pain is my constant companion.)

ɛs ʃla͜eçtʻ la͜en ˈliːbəndɐ ˈlɑ͜oʃəntʻ zaxtʻ, lɔpʻ ˈza͜enə ˈfrɔ͜ødɪn laˈla͜en?
Es schleicht ein Liebender lauschend sacht, ob seine Freundin allein?
There steals a lover listening softly, whether his lady friend alone?
(A lover steals softly, listening to hear whether his lady friend is alone.)

zoː lyːbɐˈʃla͜eçtʻ ba͜e tʰaːkʻ lʊntʻ naxtʻ mɪç ˈla͜enzaːmən di pʰa͜en,
So überschleicht bei Tag und Nacht mich Einsamen die Pein,
Thus over-steals by day and night me solitary one the pain,
(Thus by day and night pain steals over me, the solitary one,)

mɪç ˈla͜enzaːmən di kʰvaːl. lax veːɐ̯d ɪç leːɐ̯stʻ la͜enˈmaːl
mich Einsamen die Qual. Ach werd' ich erst einmal
me lonesome one the torment. Ah, shall I first once
(torment steals over me, the lonesome one. Ah, when I shall one day)

ˈla͜enzaːm lɪm ˈgraːbə za͜en, daː lɛstʻ ziː mɪç laˈla͜en!
einsam im Grabe sein, da lässt sie mich allein!
lonely in the grave be, then leaves it me alone!
(lie lonely in my grave, then pain will finally leave me alone!)

[The *Harfenspieler* (literally "Harp Player") songs are also known as *Gesänge des Harfners* (Songs of the Harper); each exists in more than one version. The Harper is a poor, half-mad old man, a lonely wanderer, everywhere a stranger, one of the most memorable characters in Goethe's long novel *Wilhelm Meister*. He sings this song, accompanying himself on the harp, in *Wilhelm Meister's Apprenticeship, Part I*, in Chapter 13 of Book II. The Harper songs in their definitive form are among Schubert's finest, most deeply felt inspirations.]

ˈharfənʃpʻiːlɐ. t̮svae̯. / gəˈzɛŋə dɛs ˈharfnɐs. drae̯. / an di ˈtʰyːrən vɪl lɪç ˈʃlae̯çən
Harfenspieler. II. / Gesänge des Harfners. III. / An die Türen will ich schleichen
The Harper. II. / Songs of the Harper. III. / I Shall Steal from Door to Door

Op. 12, No. 3 [1816] (from *Wilhelm Meister* by Johann Wolfgang von Goethe)

an di ˈtʰyːrən vɪl lɪç ˈʃlae̯çən, ʃtʻɪl lʊntʻ ˈzɪtʻzaːm vɪl lɪç ʃteːn;
An die Türen will ich schleichen, still und sittsam will ich stehn;
To the doors will I steal, quietly and modestly will I stand;
(I shall drag my feet from house to house, then quietly and modestly stand there at each door;)
[*GA: Harfenspieler I (Schubert's error):* **fromm** (frɔm, pious) **und sittsam**]

ˈfrɔmə hantʻ vɪrtʻ ˈnaːrʊŋ ˈrae̯çən, lʊntʻ lɪç ˈveːɐ̯də ˈvae̯tʻɐ geːn.
fromme Hand wird Nahrung reichen, und ich werde weiter gehn.
pious hand will nourishment offer, and I shall farther go.
(a pious hand will offer me food, and I shall move on.)

ˈjeːdɐ vɪrtʻ zɪç ˈglʏkʻlɪç ˈʃae̯nən, vɛn mae̯n bɪltʻ foːɐ̯/foːr liːm lɛɐ̯ˈʃae̯ntʰ;
Jeder wird sich glücklich scheinen, wenn mein Bild vor ihm erscheint;
Everyone will to himself fortunate appear, when my image before him appears;
(Everyone will count himself fortunate when he sees my appearance in front of him;)

ˈae̯nə ˈtʰrɛːnə vɪrtʻ leːɐ̯ ˈvae̯nən, lʊntʻ lɪç vae̯s nɪçtʻ vas leːɐ̯ vae̯ntʰ.
eine Träne wird er weinen, und ich weiss nicht was er weint.
a tear will he weep, and I know not why he weeps.
(he will shed a tear, and I shall not know why he weeps.)

[The titles of this song and the next are confusing: in Schubert's manuscript this was the second of the group of three songs; when they were published it became Number Three. There are slight differences; the *Gesamtausgabe* offers both versions, Peters follows the first publication. The poem appears in Book 5, Chapter 14, of *Wilhelm Meister's Apprenticeship, Part II.* The half-mad harper had started a fire that burned down two or three houses, and had threatened a young boy with a knife; he sings this song as he is about to wander away from the town. Wilhelm forcibly prevents him, trying to convince him that his attempt to leave town would seem to confirm the suspicion of guilt. The old man's dragging steps are heard in the piano part of Schubert's song.]

ˈharfənʃpʻiːlɐ. drae̯. / gəˈzɛŋə dɛs ˈharfnɐs. t̮svae̯. / veːɐ̯ niː zae̯n broːtʻ mɪtʻ ˈtʰrɛːnən laːs
Harfenspieler. III. / Gesänge des Harfners. II. / Wer nie sein Brot mit Tränen ass
The Harper. III. / Songs of the Harper. II. / He Who Never Ate His Bread With Tears

Op. 12, No. 2 [1822] (from *Wilhelm Meister* by Johann Wolfgang von Goethe)

veːɐ̯ niː zae̯n broːtʻ mɪtʻ ˈtʰrɛːnən laːs,
Wer nie sein Brot mit Tränen ass,
He who never his bread with tears ate,
(He who never ate his bread with tears,)

veːɐ̯ niː di ˈkʰʊmɐfɔlən ˈnɛçtʻə lao̯f ˈzae̯nəm ˈbɛtʻə ˈvae̯nəntʻ zaːs,
wer nie die kummervollen Nächte auf seinem Bette weinend sass,
who never the sorrowful nights on his bed weeping sat,
(who never sat on his bed weeping through sorrow-filled nights,)

deːɐ̯ kʰɛntʻ lɔ͜øç nɪçtʻ, liːɐ̯ ˈhɪmlɪʃən ˈmɛçtʻə!
der kennt euch nicht, ihr himmlischen Mächte!
he knows you not, you heavenly powers!
(he does not know you, heavenly powers!)

iːɐ̯ fyːɐ̯tʻ lɪns ˈleːbən lʊns hɪˈna͜en, liːɐ̯ last den ˈlarmən ˈʃʊldɪç ˈveːɐ̯dən,
Ihr führt ins Leben uns hinein, ihr lasst den Armen schuldig werden,
You lead into the life us into, you let the poor man guilty become,
(You lead us into life, you let the poor wretch fall into guilt,)

dan lyːbɐˈlastʻ liːɐ̯/liːr liːn deːɐ̯ pʰa͜en: dɛn ˈlalə ʃultʻ rɛçtʻ zɪç la͜of ˈleːɐ̯dən.
dann überlasst ihr ihn der Pein: denn alle Schuld rächt sich auf Erden.
then abandon you him to the pain: for all guilt avenges itself on earth.
(then you abandon him to his pain: for all guilt is avenged on earth.)

[Schubert made three distinctly different settings of this poem, the first two in 1816, the final, definitive version in 1822. The *Gesamtausgabe* includes all three; Peters prints only the third. In Book 2, Chapter 13, of the novel, *Wilhelm Meister's Apprenticeship*, Wilhelm, listening through an upstairs door in a wretched inn, hears the harper half singing, half speaking these words of despair and defiance as he strums on his harp. Now and then the old man seems to be choked with emotion. Wilhelm is moved to tears by the touching lament and cannot resist entering the room to tell the singer that all his own deepest pent-up feelings were released by the song. He finds the poor old man sitting on the straw mattress of a bed in an otherwise totally bare room.]

ˈha͜edənrøːsla͜en
Heidenröslein
Little Rose on the Heath (Rock Rose)

Op. 3, No. 3 [1815] (Johann Wolfgang von Goethe)

zaː la͜en kʰnaːpʻ la͜en ˈrøːsla͜en ʃtʻeːn, ˈrøːsla͜en la͜of deːɐ̯ ˈha͜edən,
Sah ein Knab ein Röslein stehn, Röslein auf der Heiden,
Saw a boy a little rose stand, little rose on the heath,
(A boy saw a little rose, little rose on the heath,)

vaːɐ̯ zoː jʊŋ lʊntʻ ˈmɔrgənʃøːn, liːf leːɐ̯ ʃnɛl lɛs naː t͜suː zeːn,
war so jung und morgenschön, lief er schnell es nah zu sehn,
[it] was so young and morning-beautiful, ran he quickly it near to see,
(it was so young and fresh and beautiful that he quickly ran to see it more closely,)

zaːs mɪtʻ ˈfiːlən ˈfrɔ͜ødən, ˈrøːsla͜en, ˈrøːsla͜en, ˈrøːsla͜en roːtʰ, ˈrøːsla͜en la͜of deːɐ̯ ˈha͜edən.
sah's mit vielen Freuden, Röslein, Röslein, Röslein rot, Röslein auf der Heiden.
saw it with many joys, little rose, little rose, little rose red, little rose on the heath.
(saw it with much delight, *little red rose on the heath.*)

ˈkʰnaːbə ʃpʻraːx : lɪç ˈbrɛçə dɪç, ˈrøːsla͜en la͜of deːɐ̯ ˈha͜edən!
Knabe sprach: ich breche dich, Röslein auf der Heiden!
Boy spoke: I pluck you, little rose on the heath!
(The boy said: "I shall pluck you, little rose on the heath!")

ˈrøːsla͜en ʃpʻraːx : lɪç ˈʃtʻɛçə dɪç, das duː ˈleːvɪç dɛŋkʻstʻ lan mɪç,
Röslein sprach: ich steche dich, dass du ewig denkst an mich,
Little rose spoke: I prick you, so that you forever think of me,
(The little rose said: "I shall prick you, so that you'll forever think of me,)

ʊnt' lɪç vɪls nɪçt' 'laedən. 'rø:slaen ro:tʰ, 'rø:slaen laof de:ɐ 'haedən.
und ich will's nicht leiden. Röslein rot, Röslein auf der Heiden.
and I will it not tolerate. Little rose red, little rose on the heath.
(and I will not tolerate it." *Little red rose on the heath.*)

ʊnt de:ɐ 'vɪldə 'kʰna:bə bra:x 's rø:slaen laof de:ɐ 'haedən;
Und der wilde Knabe brach s' Röslein auf der Heiden;
And the wild boy plucked the little rose on the heath;

'rø:slaen 've:rt'ə zɪç lʊnt' ʃt'a:x, half li:ɐ dɔx kʰaen ve: lʊnt' lax,
Röslein wehrte sich und stach, half ihr doch kein Weh und Ach,
little rose defended herself and pricked, helped her though no woe and alas,
(the little rose defended herself and pricked him; her cry of complaint, though, did not help her;)

mʊst' lɛs 'le:bən 'laedən. 'rø:slaen ro:tʰ, 'rø:slaen laof de:ɐ 'haedən.
musst es eben leiden. Röslein rot, Röslein auf der Heiden.
had to it just suffer. Little rose red, little rose on the heath.
(she just had to suffer it. *Little red rose on the heath.*)

[This poem by Goethe, which in another musical setting has become a familiar folksong in Germany, has more to do with boys and girls than with boys and roses.]

'haemlɪçəs 'li:bən
Heimliches Lieben
Secret Love

Op. 106, No. 1 [1827] (Caroline Louise von Klenke)

o: du:, vɛn 'daenə 'lɪp'ən mɪç bə'ry:rən, [mʏr'tʰɪl]
O du, wenn deine Lippen mich berühren, [*poem:* **Myrtill, wenn deine Lippen...]**
O you, when your lips me touch, [Myrtille (French for blueberry)]
(O you! When your lips touch me,)

zo: vɪl di lʊst di 'ze:lə mi:ɐ/mi:r lɛnt''fy:rən, [dan]
so will die Lust die Seele mir entführen, [*poem:* **dann will die Lust...]**
then wants the pleasure the soul from me to abduct, [then]
(then pleasure wants to carry away my soul,)

ɪç 'fy:lə tʰi:f laen 'na:mənlo:zəs 'be:bən den 'bu:zən 'he:bən. [fy:l] ['zanft'əs,]
ich fühle tief ein namenloses Beben den Busen heben. [*poem:* **ich fühl' ein sanftes,]**
I feel deeply a nameless trembling the bosom lift. [feel] [gentle,]
(I feel, deep within me, a nameless trembling lift my bosom.)

maen 'laogə flamt', glu:t' ʃve:p't' laof 'maenən 'vaŋən,
Mein Auge flammt, Glut schwebt auf meinen Wangen,
My eye flames, fire hovers on my cheeks,
(My eyes are aflame, passion colors my cheeks,)

ɛs ʃlɛ:k't' maen hɛrts laen 'lʊnbəkʰant' fɛɐ'laŋən,
es schlägt mein Herz ein unbekannt Verlangen,
there beats my heart an unknown longing,
(my heart beats with an unknown longing,)

maen gaest', fɛɐ̯'lɪrt'/fɛr'lɪrt' lɪn 'tʰrʊŋk'nɐ 'lɪp'ən 'ʃt'amәln, kʰan kʰaom zɪç 'zamәln.
mein Geist, verirrt in trunkner Lippen Stammeln, kann kaum sich sammeln.
my spirit, gone astray in drunken lips' stammering, can scarcely itself collect.
(my spirit, astray in the stammering of my intoxicated lips, can scarcely compose itself.)

maen 'le:bәn hɛŋt' lɪn 'laenɐ 'zɔlçәn 'ʃt'ʊndә lan 'daenәm 'zy:sәn, 'ro:zәnvaeçәn 'mʊndә,
Mein Leben hängt in einer solchen Stunde an deinem süssen, rosenweichen Munde,
My life hangs in a such hour on your sweet, rose- soft mouth,
(At such an hour my life hangs on your sweet, rose-soft mouth,)

ʊnt' vɪl bae 'daenәm 'tʰraot'әn 'larmlʊm,fasәn mɪç fast' fɛɐ̯'lasәn.
und will bei deinem trauten Armumfassen mich fast verlassen.
and wants at your dear arm-embrace me almost to leave.
(and almost seems to leave me when I am in the embrace of your loving arms.)

o: das lɛs dɔx nɪçt' 'laosɐ zɪç kʰan 'fli:әn, di 'ze:lә gants lɪn 'daenɐ 'ze:lә 'gly:әn,
O dass es doch nicht ausser sich kann fliehen, die Seele ganz in deiner Seele glühen,
Oh, that it really not outside itself can flee, the soul entirely in your soul glow,
(Oh, that my life cannot flee beyond itself, that my entire soul cannot glow within your soul,)
[*poem:* **in deine** ('daenә) **Seele** (into your soul)]

das dɔx di 'lɪp'әn, di: fo:ɐ̯ 'ze:nzʊxt' 'brɛnәn, zɪç 'mʏsәn 'tʰrɛnәn,
dass doch die Lippen, die vor Sehnsucht brennen, sich müssen trennen,
that after all the lips, which with longing burn, themselves must separate,
(that lips that burn with longing cannot remain joined forever,)

das dɔx lɪm kʰʊs maen 've:zәn nɪçt tsɛɐ̯'fli:sәtʰ,
dass doch im Kuss mein Wesen nicht zerfliesset,
that after all in the kiss my being not melts away,
(that my being does not melt away in kisses,)

vɛn lɛs zo: fɛst' lan 'daenәn mʊnt' zɪç 'ʃli:sәtʰ,
wenn es so fest an deinen Mund sich schliesset,
when it so tightly to your mouth itself locks,
(when it is locked so tightly to your mouth,)

ʊnt' lan daen hɛrts, das 'ni:ma:ls laot' darf 'va:gәn, fy:ɐ̯ mɪç tsu: 'ʃla:gәn.
und an dein Herz, das niemals laut darf wagen, für mich zu schlagen.
and to your heart, which never aloud may dare for me to beat.
(and to your heart, which may never dare to beat for me aloud!)
[*poem:* **das nimmer** ('nɪmɐ, never) **laut darf wagen...**]

[This erotic poem is in the form of a Sapphic ode. Its original title is *An Myrtill* (To Myrtille, a female name), so the content can be considered Sapphic as well, considering the feminine authorship and the hints in the poem. The author was the mother of Helmina von Chézy, who wrote the libretto of Weber's *Euryanthe,* the play *Rosamunde*, for which Schubert composed the music, and the verses that he used for the middle section of *Der Hirt auf dem Felsen*. Schubert's setting is beautiful, with a very grateful vocal cantilena and lovely harmonies.]

haes mɪç nɪçt' 're:dən / li:t de:ɐ̯ mɪn'jõ / min'jõ laens
Heiss mich nicht reden / Lied der Mignon / Mignon I
Bid Me Not Speak / Mignon's Song / Mignon I

Op. 62, No. 2 [1826] (poem included in *Wilhelm Meister* by Johann Wolfgang von Goethe)

haes mɪç nɪçt' 're:dən, haes mɪç 'ʃvaegən,
Heiss mich nicht reden, heiss mich schweigen,
Bid me not speak, bid me be silent,

dɛn maen gə'haemnɪs lɪst' mi:ɐ̯ pflɪçtʰ; lɪç 'mœçt'ə di:ɐ̯ maen 'gantsəs 'lɪnrə 'tsaegən,
denn mein Geheimnis ist mir Pflicht; ich möchte dir mein ganzes Innre zeigen,
for my secret is to me duty; I would like to you my whole inside to show,
(for my duty is to keep my secret; I would like to show you all my inner being,)

a'laen das 'ʃɪk'za:l vɪl lɛs nɪçtʰ. tsʊr 'rɛçt'ən tsaet'
allein das Schicksal will es nicht. Zur rechten Zeit
but the fate wants it not. At the right time
(but fate does not allow me to. At the right time)

fɛɐ̯'tʰraep't de:ɐ̯ 'zɔnə laof di 'fɪnst'rə naxt', lʊnt' zi: mʊs zɪç lɛɐ̯'hɛlən;
vertreibt der Sonne Lauf die finstre Nacht, und sie muss sich erhellen;
drives away the sun's course the dark night, and it must itself brighten;
(the sun in its course will drive away the dark night, and night must turn to day;)

de:ɐ̯ 'hart'ə fɛls ʃli:st' 'zaenən 'bu:zən laof,
der harte Fels schliesst seinen Busen auf,
the hard rock opens its bosom up,
(the hard rock will open its bosom)

mɪs'gœnt de:ɐ̯/de:r 'le:ɐ̯də nɪçt di tʰi:f fɛɐ̯'bɔrgnən 'kʰvɛlən.
missgönnt der Erde nicht die tief verborgnen Quellen.
begrudges to the earth not the deep hidden springs.
(and not begrudge the earth its deep, hidden springs.)

aen 'je:dɐ zu:xt' lɪm larm dɛs 'frɔøndəs ru:, dɔrt' kʰan di brʊst'
Ein jeder sucht im Arm des Freundes Ruh, dort kann die Brust
An everyone seeks in the arm of the friend peace, there can the breast
(Everyone seeks peace in the arms of a friend; there the heart can)
[*in the novel:* **des Freundes**; *in the poem as later separately published:* **der Freunde** (de:ɐ 'frɔøndə, of friends—plural)]

lɪn 'kʰla:gən zɪç lɛɐ̯'gi:sən; la'laen laen ʃvu:ɐ̯ drʏk't' mi:ɐ̯ di 'lɪp'ən tsu:,
in Klagen sich ergiessen; allein ein Schwur drückt mir die Lippen zu,
in lamentation itself pour out; but a vow presses to me the lips closed,
(pour itself out in lamentation; but a vow forces my lips to stay closed,)

ʊnt' nu:ɐ̯/nu:r laen gɔt' fɛɐ̯'ma:k' zi: 'laoftsuʃli:sən.
und nur ein Gott vermag sie aufzuschliessen.
and only a god has the power them to unlock.
(and only a god has the power to unlock them.)

[Schubert made two wonderful settings of this haunting poem, the first in 1821 (unpublished until 1870), the second, more famous, in 1826. Both can be found in the *Gesamtausgabe*. The words appear at the end of the Fifth Book of *Wilhelm Meister's Apprenticeship*. Mignon, who recited them "with great expression" on several occasions, is an enigmatic, waif-like young girl, scarred by the trauma of having been kidnapped by gypsies when she was only a small child.]

ˈhɛkʻtʻoːɐ̯s ˈlapʻʃiːtʻ
Hektors Abschied
Hector's Farewell

Op. 58 [1815] (Friedrich von Schiller)

ANDROMACHE:

vɪl zɪç ˈhɛkʻtʻoːɐ̯ ˈleːvɪç fɔn miːɐ̯ ˈvɛndən,
Will sich Hektor ewig von mir wenden,
Wants himself Hector forever from me to turn away,
(Does Hector want to turn away from me forever,)

voː laˈxɪl mɪtʻ ˈlʊnnaːbaːrən ˈhɛndən dem pʰaˈtʰroːkʻlʊs ˈʃrɛkʻlɪç ˈlɔpf̮ɐ brɪŋtʰ?
wo Achill mit unnahbaren Händen dem Patroklus schrecklich Opfer bringt?
where Achilles with inaccessible hands to the Patroklus frightful offering brings?
(to go where Achilles with invulnerable hands is offering a frightful sacrifice to Patroclus*?)
[*poem:* **mit unnahbar'n** (ˈlʊnnaːbaːɐ̯n) **Händen]**

veːɐ̯ vɪrtʻ ˈkʰʏnftʻɪç ˈdaɛ̯nən ˈkʰlaɛ̯nən ˈleːrən, ˈʃpeːrə ˈvɛrfən lʊnt di ˈgœtʻɐ(r) ˈleːrən,
Wer wird künftig deinen Kleinen lehren, Speere werfen und die Götter ehren,
Who will in the future your little one teach spears to throw and the gods to honor,
(In the future who will teach your little son how to throw the javelin and honor the gods,)

vɛn deːɐ̯ ˈfɪnstʻrə ˈlɔrkʻʊs dɪç fɛɐ̯ˈʃlɪŋtʰ?
wenn der finstre Orkus dich verschlingt?
when the dark Orcus you swallows up?
(when dark Orcus, deity of death, has swallowed you?)

HEKTOR:

ˈtʰɔ̯ørəs vaɛ̯pʻ, gəˈbiːtʻə ˈdaɛ̯nə ˈtʰrɛːnən!
Teures Weib, gebiete deine Tränen!
Dear wife, command your tears!
(Dear wife, master your tears!)

naːx deːɐ̯ ˈfɛltʻʃlaxtʻ lɪstʻ maɛ̯n ˈfɔ̯ørɪç ˈzeːnən, ˈdiːzə ˈlarmən ˈʃʏt͡sən ˈpʰɛrgamʊs.
Nach der Feldschlacht ist mein feurig Sehnen, diese Armen schützem Pergamus.
For the pitched battle is my fiery longing, these arms defend Pergamum.
(For I feel an ardent longing for battle; these arms shall defend Troy.)

ˈkʰɛmpf̮əntʻ fyːɐ̯ den ˈhaɛ̯lgən heːɐ̯t deːɐ̯ ˈgœtʻɐ fal lɪç,
Kämpfend für den heil'gen Herd der Götter fall' ich,
Fighting for the holy hearth of the gods fall I,
(I shall fall fighting for the holy hearth of the gods,)

ʊnt dɛs ˈfaːtʻɐlandəs ˈrɛtʻɐ ʃtʻa͜eg ɪç ˈniːdɐ t͜suː dem ˈʃtyːkʃən flʊs.
und des Vaterlandes Retter steig' ich nieder zu dem styg'schen Fluss.
and the fatherland's savior descend I down to the Stygian river.
(and it is as the savior of our fatherland that I shall descend to the river Styx.)
[The shades of the dead must cross the river Styx to enter the underworld domain of Orcus]

ANDROMACHE:

ˈnɪmɐ la͜oʃ lɪç ˈda͜enɐ ˈvafən ˈʃalə, ˈmyːsɪç liːkʻt das ˈla͜ezən lɪn deːɐ̯ ˈhalə,
Nimmer lausch' ich deiner Waffen Schalle, müssig liegt das Eisen in der Halle,
Never listen I (to) your weapon's clang, idle lies the iron in the hall,
(Never again shall I hear the clang of your weapons, your sword will lie idle in the hall,)
[*poem:* **müssig liegt dein** (da͜en, your) **Eisen]**

ˈpʰriːams ˈgroːsɐ ˈhɛldənʃtʻam fɛɐ̯ˈdɪrpʻtʰ. duː vɪrstʻ ˈhɪngeːn,
Priams grosser Heldenstamm verdirbt. Du wirst hingeh'n,
Priam's great heroic race perishes. You will go to that place
(King Priam's great heroic race will perish. You will go to that place)

voː kʰa͜en tʰaːkʻ meːɐ̯ ˈʃa͜enətʰ, deːɐ̯ kʰoˈt͜syːtʻʊs dʊrç di ˈvyːstʻən ˈva͜enətʻ,
wo kein Tag mehr scheinet, der Cocytus durch die Wüsten weinet,
where no day more shines, the Cocytus through the wastelands weeps,
(where no daylight ever shines, where the river Cocytus weeps through the wastelands,)
[The Cocytus was a tributary to the Styx; according to Vergil, it surrounded the underworld.]

ˈda͜enə liːpʻ lɪm ˈleːtʻə ʃtʻɪrpʻtʰ. [ˈliːbə lɪn dem]
deine Lieb' im Lethe stirbt. [*poem:* **deine Liebe in dem Lethe stirbt.]**
your love in the Lethe dies. [love in the]
(your love will die in the waters of Lethe, the river of oblivion.)

HEKTOR:

al ma͜en ˈzeːnən vɪl lɪç, lal ma͜en ˈdɛŋkʻən, lɪn dɛs ˈleːtə ˈʃtʻɪlən ʃtʻroːm fɛɐ̯ˈzɛŋkʻən,
All mein Sehnen will ich, all mein Denken, in des Lethe stillen Strom versenken,
All my longing want I, all my thinking, in the Lethe's quiet stream to sink,
(I shall sink all my longing, all my thinking, in Lethe's quiet stream,)
[*Peters (Schubert's error, corrected in GA):* **in des Lethes** (ˈleːtʻəs) **stillen Strom]**

ˈaːbɐ ˈma͜enə ˈliːbə nɪçtʰ. hɔrç! deːɐ̯ ˈvɪldə tʰoːpʻtʻ ʃoːn lan den ˈma͜oɐn,
aber meine Liebe nicht. Horch! der Wilde tobt schon an den Mauern,
but my love not. Hark! The wild one rages already at the walls,
(but not my love. Hark! Wild Achilles is already raging at the walls;)

ˈgʏrtʻə miːɐ̯ das ʃveːɐ̯tʻ lʊm, las das ˈtʰra͜oɐn!
gürte mir das Schwert um, lass das Trauern!
gird me the sword around, leave the grieving!
(gird on my sword, cease your grieving!)

ˈhɛkʻtʻoːɐ̯s ˈliːbə ʃtʻɪrpʻtʻ lɪm ˈleːtʻə nɪçtʰ.
Hektors Liebe stirbt im Lethe nicht.
Hector's love dies in the Lethe not.
(Hector's love will not die in the Lethe.)

[*Patroclus, in Homer's *Iliad*, fighting on the Greek side in the Trojan War, was slain by Hector, the son of King Priam of Troy. Achilles, the most famous fighter among the Greeks, was determined to avenge his friend's death with all his seemingly invincible might. After terrible slaughter on the battlefield, he killed Hector, and dragged his body behind his chariot three times around the city walls. In Schiller's scene, Andromache, Hector's wife, pleads with him not to answer the summons to single combat with Achilles. Schubert's setting, for two voices, has beautiful and effective moments. It is one of eight songs all dated 19 October 1815. The *Gesamtausgabe* offers two versions that differ only slightly. Peters follows the first publication.]

hɛrpstʰ
Herbst
Autumn

Posthumously published [composed 1828] (poem by Ludwig Rellstab)

ɛs ˈrɑ̯ɔʃən di ˈvɪndə zoː ˈhɛrpstˈlɪç lʊntʼ kʰaltʰ; fɛɐ̯ˈløːdət di ˈfluːrən,
Es rauschen die Winde so herbstlich und kalt; verödet die Fluren,
There roar the winds so autumnal and cold; laid waste the meadows,
(The winds are wailing, autumnal and cold; the meadows are bare,)

lɛntʼˈblɛtʼɐt deːɐ̯ valtʼ. liːɐ̯ ˈbluːmɪgən ˈlɑ̯ɔən! duː ˈzɔnɪgəs gryːn!
entblättert der Wald. Ihr blumigen Auen! du sonniges Grün!
defoliated the woods. You flowery pastures! You sunny green!
(the woods are stripped of leaves. You once flowery pastures! You sunlit greenery!)

zoː ˈvɛlkʼən di ˈblyːtʼən dɛs ˈleːbəns daˈhɪn.
So welken die Blüten des Lebens dahin.
Thus wither the blossoms of the life away.
(Thus must life's blossoms wither away.)

ɛs ˈt̮siːən di ˈvɔlkʼən zoː ˈfɪnstʼɐ(r) lʊntʼ grɑ̯ɔ; fɛɐ̯ˈʃvʊndən di ˈʃtʼɛrnə
Es ziehen die Wolken so finster und grau; verschwunden die Sterne
There move the clouds so dark and grey; vanished the stars
(Clouds pass overhead, so dark and grey; the stars have vanished)

lam ˈhɪmlɪʃən blɑ̯ɔ! lax, viː di gəˈʃtʼɪrnə lam ˈhɪməl lɛntʼˈfliːn,
am himmlischen Blau! Ach, wie die Gestirne am Himmel entfliehn,
in the heavenly blue! Ah, as the stars in the sky flee,
(in the heavenly blue! Ah, as the stars flee from the sky,)

zoː ˈzɪŋkʼət di ˈhɔfnʊŋ dɛs ˈleːbəns daˈhɪn!
so sinket die Hoffnung des Lebens dahin!
thus sinks the hope of the life away!
(thus does hope sink away in our life!)

iːɐ̯ ˈtʰaːgə dɛs ˈlɛnt̮səs mɪtʼ ˈroːsən gəˈʃmʏkʼtʼ,
Ihr Tage des Lenzes mit Rosen geschmückt,
You days of the spring with roses adorned,
(You days of spring, adorned with roses,)

voː lɪç di gəˈliːpʼtʼə lans ˈhɛrt̮sə gəˈdrʏkʼtʼ! [den gəˈliːpʼtʼən]
wo ich die Geliebte ans Herze gedrückt! [*poem:* wo ich den Geliebten*]
when I the beloved (female) to the heart pressed! [the beloved (male)]
(when I pressed my beloved to my heart!)

kʰalt‘ ˈyːbɐ den ˈhyːgəl rɑ͜oʃt‘, ˈvɪndə, daˈhɪn!
Kalt über den Hügel rauscht, Winde, dahin!
Coldly over the hill/grave-mound roar, winds, away!
(Cold winds, wail over that grave! [*or* wail over the hill!])
[in German poetry "*Hügel*" often refers to the mound of earth over a grave]

zoː ˈʃt‘ɛrbən di ˈroːzən deːɐ̯ ˈliːbə daˈhɪn.
So sterben die Rosen der Liebe dahin.
Thus die the roses of the love away.
(Thus do the roses of love die away.)

[Schubert wrote this song for a friend's album, and it remained undiscovered until the 1890s. The winds of autumn rustle the leaves and stir up melancholy thoughts in this strophic song. *A male singer will sing "*die Geliebte*"; a woman may prefer "*den Geliebten*," as in the poem.]

ˈhɛrpst‘liːt‘
Herbstlied
Autumn Song

Posthumously published [composed 1816] (poem by Johann Gaudenz von Salis-Seewis)

bʊnt‘ zɪnt‘ ʃoːn di ˈvɛldɐ, gɛlp‘ di ˈʃt‘ɔp‘əlfɛldɐ(r), lʊnt‘ deːɐ̯ hɛrpst‘ bəˈgɪntʰ.
Bunt sind schon die Wälder, gelb die Stoppelfelder, und der Herbst beginnt.
Multicolored are already the woods, yellow the stubble fields, and the fall begins.
(The woods are already bright with color, the fields of stubble are yellow, and the fall has come.)

ˈroːt‘ə ˈblɛt‘ɐ ˈfalən, ˈgrɑ͜oə ˈneːbəl ˈvalən, ˈkʰyːlɐ veːt deːɐ̯ vɪnt‘.
Rote Blätter fallen, graue Nebel wallen, kühler weht der Wind.
Red leaves fall, grey mists drift about, cooler blows the wind.

viː di ˈfɔlə ˈtʰrɑ͜obə lɑ͜os dem ˈreːbənlɑ͜obə ˈpʰʊrp‘ʊrfarbɪç ʃt‘raːltʰ;
Wie die volle Traube aus dem Rebenlaube purpurfarbig strahlt;
How the full grape out of the vine- foliage purple-color shines;
(How purple the plump grape is gleaming from among the vine leaves!)

am gəˈlɛndɐ ˈra͜efən ˈp͜fɪrzɪçə mɪt‘ ˈʃt‘ra͜efən roːt‘ lʊnt‘ va͜es bəˈmaːltʰ.
am Geländer reifen Pfirsiche mit Striefen rot und weiss bemalt.
on the trellis ripen peaches with streaks red and white painted.
(On the trellis peaches are ripening, looking as if painted with red and white streaks.)

ziː, viː hiːɐ̯ di ˈdɪrnə ˈlɛmzɪç p͜flɑ͜om lʊnt‘ ˈbɪrnə lɪn liːɐ̯ ˈkœrp‘çən leːk‘tʰ;
Sieh, wie hier die Dirne emsig Pflaum' und Birne in ihr Körbchen legt;
See, how here the girl busily plum and pear into her little basket lays;
(See how busily the girl here is putting plums and pears into her little basket,)

dɔrt‘ mɪt‘ ˈla͜eçt‘ən ˈʃrɪt‘ən ˈjeːnə ˈgɔldnə ˈkʰvɪt‘ən lɪn den ˈlant‘hoːf tʰrɛːk‘tʰ!
dort mit leichten Schritten jene goldne Quitten in den Landhof trägt!
there with light steps that one golden quinces into the farmhouse carries!
(while that girl over there is carrying golden quinces into the farmhouse with light steps!)

ˈflɪŋk‘ə ˈtʰrɛːgɐ ˈʃp‘rɪŋən, lʊnt di ˈmɛːt‘çən ˈzɪŋən, ˈlaləs ˈjuːbəlt‘ froː!
Flinke Träger springen, und die Mädchen singen, alles jubelt froh!
Nimble carriers leap, and the girls sing, everyone rejoices happily!

'bʊnt'ə 'bɛndɐ 'ʃve:bən 'tsvɪʃən 'ho:ən 're:bən lɑof dem hu:t' fɔn ʃt'ro:.
Bunte Bänder schweben zwischen hohen Reben auf dem Hut von Stroh.
Colored ribbons float between high grapevines on the hat of straw.
(Colored ribbons on straw hats float among the tall grapevines.)

'gaegə tʰø:nt' lʊnt' 'flø:t'ə bae de:ɐ/de:r 'la:bənt'rø:t'ə lʊnt' lɪm 'mo:ndənglants;
Geige tönt und Flöte bei der Abendröte und im Mondenglanz;
Fiddle sounds and flute at the sunset and in the moon- radiance;
(The fiddle and the flute are heard at sunset and later by the light of the moon;)

'jʊŋə 'vɪntsərɪnən 'vɪŋk'ən lʊnt' bə'gɪnən 'dɔøtʃən 'rɪŋəltʰants.
junge Winzerinnen winken und beginnen deutschen Ringeltanz.
young vintager-girls beckon and begin German round-dance.
(the young women who gather grapes beckon and begin a German round-dance.)

[*Herbstlied* is a simple strophic song in folk-song style.]

'hɛrman lʊnt tʰʊs'nɛlda
Hermann und Thusnelda
Hermann and Thusnelda

Posthumously published [composed 1815] (poem by Friedrich Gottlieb Klopstock)

THUSNELDA:
ha:, dɔrt' kʰɔmt' le:ɐ,
Ha, dort kommt er,
Ah, there comes he,
(Ah, there he comes,)

mɪt' ʃvaes, mɪt' 'rø:mɐblu:t', mɪt dem ʃt'ɑobə de:ɐ ʃlaxt' bə'dɛk'tʰ!
mit Schweiss, mit Römerblut, mit dem Staube der Schlacht bedeckt!
with sweat, with Roman blood, with the dust of the battle covered!
(covered with sweat, with Roman blood, and with the dust of battle!)
[*poem:* **Römerblute** ('rø:mɐblu:t'ə)]

zo: ʃø:n va:ɐ 'hɛrman 'ni:ma:ls! zo: hats li:m ni: fɔn dem 'lɑogə gə'flamtʰ!
So schön war Hermann niemals! So hat's ihm nie von dem Auge geflammt!
So handsome was Hermann never! Thus has it for him never from the eye flamed!
(Hermann was never so handsome! Never have his eyes flamed like that before!)

kʰɔm, lo: kʰɔm, lɪç 'be:bə fo:ɐ lʊstʰ!
Komm, o komm, ich bebe vor Lust! [*poem:* **Komm! ich bebe vor Lust!**]
Come, oh come, I tremble with pleasure!

raeç mi:ɐ den 'la:dlɐ lʊnt das 'tʰri:fəndə ʃve:ɐtʰ! kʰɔm! la:t' mʊnt' ru: hi:ɐ/hi:r lɑos
reich' mir den Adler und das triefende Schwert! Komm! athm' und ruh' hier aus
hand me the eagle and the dripping sword! Come! beathe and rest here ...
[*ausruhen* = to rest thoroughly]

lɪn 'maenɐ(r) lʊm'larmʊŋ fɔn de:ɐ tsu: 'ʃrɛk'lɪçən ʃlaxtʰ! ru: hi:ɐ,
in meiner Umarmung von der zu schrecklichen Schlacht! Ruh' hier,
in my embrace from the too dreadful battle! Rest here,
(in my embrace from the too dreadful battle! Rest here,)

das lɪç den ʃvaes fɔn deːɐ̯ ʃt'ɪrn lap''tʰrɔk'nə lʊnt deːɐ̯ 'vaŋə das bluːtʰ!
dass ich den Schweiss von der Stirn' abtrockne und der Wange das Blut!
that I the sweat from the brow dry and from the cheek the blood!
(so that I may dry the sweat from your brow and the blood from your cheek!)
[*poem:* **dass ich den Schweiss der Stirn' abtrockne** (the sweat *of* your brow)]

viː glyːt di 'vaŋə! 'hɛrman! 'hɛrman! zoː hat dɪç 'niːmaːls tʰʊsnɛlda gə'liːp'tʰ!
wie glüht die Wange! Hermann! Hermann! so hat dich niemals Thusnelda geliebt!
how glows the cheek! Hermann! Hermann! So has you never Thusnelda loved!
(How your cheek is glowing! Hermann! Thusnelda has never loved you as much as now!)

zɛlpst' nɪçt', daː duː tsu'leːɐ̯st' lɪm 'laeçənʃat'ən [lals]
Selbst nicht, da du zuerst im Eichenschatten [*GA:* als du zuerst]
Even not, when you first in the oak- shadow [when]
(Not even then, when in the shadow of the oak tree you first)

mɪt dem 'kʰraft'fɔlən larm mɪç 'vɪldɐ(r) lʊm'fast'əstʰ! 'fliːənt' bliːp' lɪç
mit dem Kraftvollen Arm mich wilder umfasstest! Fliehend blieb ich
with the powerful arm me more wildly embraced! Fleeing stayed I
(embraced me more wildly in your powerful arms! In fleeing, I still stayed near enough)
[*poem:* **mit dem bräunlichen** ('brɔønlɪçən, brown) **Arm mich wilder fasstest** ('fast'əst', seized)]

lʊnt' zaː diːɐ̯ ʃoːn di lʊn'ʃt'ɛrp'lɪçkʰaet' lan, diː nuːn daen lɪstʰ!
und sah dir schon die Unsterblichkeit an, die nun dein ist!
and saw in you already the immortality in, which now yours is!
(to glimpse in you already the immortality that now is fully yours!)

ɛɐ̯'tsɛːlts lɪn 'lalən 'haenən, das laogʊstʊs
Erzählt's in allen Hainen, dass Augustus
Tell (ye) it in all groves, that Augustus
(Let it be told in all our sacred groves that the Roman emperor)

nuːn baŋ mɪt' 'zaenən 'gœt'ɐn 'nɛk't'ar 'tʰrɪŋk'ətʰ.
nun bang' mit seinen Göttern Nektar trinket.
now fearfully with his gods nectar drinks.
(is now drinking nectar with his impotent gods, full of fear.)

ɛɐ̯'tsɛːlt' lɛs, das 'hɛrman lʊn'ʃt'ɛrp'lɪçɐ(r) lɪstʰ!
Erzählt es, dass Hermann unsterblicher ist!
Tell it, that Hermann more immortal is!
(Let it be told that Hermann is more immortal than he!)

HERMANN:
va'rʊm lɔkst duː maen haːɐ̯? liːk't' nɪçt deːɐ̯ 'ʃt'ʊmə 'tʰoːt'ə 'faːt'ɐ foːɐ̯/foːr lʊns?
"Warum lockst du mein Haar? Liegt nicht der stumme tote Vater vor uns?
"Why curl you my hair? Lies not the silent dead father in front of us?
("Why do you curl and bind up my hair? Does not my father lie silent and dead in front of us?)

oː, hɛt' laoˈgʊst'ʊs 'zaenə 'heːrə zɛlpst' gə'fyːɐ̯t', leːɐ̯ 'lɛːgə nɔx 'bluːt'ɪgɐ daː!
O, hätt' Augustus seine Heere selbst geführt, er läge noch blutiger da!"
Oh, had Augustus his armies himself led, he would lie still bloodier there!"
(Oh, if Augustus himself had led his armies, *he* would now be lying there even more bloodied!")

THUSNELDA:
las daen 'zɪŋk'əndəs haːɐ̯ mɪç, 'hɛrman, 'heːbən,
Lass dein sinkendes Haar mich, Hermann, heben,
Let your drooping hair me, Hermann, lift up,
(Let me gather up your drooping hair, Hermann,)

das lɛs 'lyːbɐ den kʰrants ɪn 'lɔk'ən 'droːə!
dass es über den Kranz in Locken drohe!
that it over the wreath in curls threaten!
(so that, in curls above the victor's wreath, it my strike fear into your enemies!)

'ziːk'mar lɪst' bae den 'gœt'ɐn! 'fɔlgə duː, lʊnt' vaen liːm nɪçt' naːx!
Siegmar ist bei den Göttern! Folge du, und wein' ihm nicht nach!
Siegmar is with the gods! Succeed you, and weep for him not after!
(Siegmar is with the gods! Be his successor, and do not weep for him!)
[*Peters:* **Sigmar;** *poem:* **Folg'** (fɔlk') **du]**

[Hermann, an early German hero, was known to the Romans as Arminius (B.C. 18-A.D. 21). He first served in the Roman legions, later led a revolt against them. Thusnelda was his wife. There are several significant musical differences between the *Gesamtausgabe* and the Peters edition.]

Herrn Joseph Spaun see *Epistel von Collin*

'hɪməlsfʊŋk'ən
Himmelsfunken
Sparks from Heaven

Posthumously published [composed 1819] (poem by Johann Petrus Silbert)

deːɐ/deːr 'loːdəm 'gɔt'əs veːtʰ! ʃt'ɪl vɪrt di 'zeːnzʊxt' vax;
Der Odem Gottes weht! Still wird die Sehnsucht wach;
The breath of God wafts! Quietly becomes the longing awake;
(One feels the breath of God! Longing wakens quietly;)

das 'tʰrʊŋk'nə hɛrts fɛɐ̯'geːt' ɪn 'vʊndɐzyːsəm lax!
das trunkne Herz vergeht in wundersüssem Ach!
the intoxicated heart is lost in wondrous-sweet sighing!

viː løːst' zɪç 'leːt'ɐmɪlt deːɐ̯/deːr 'leːɐ̯də 'ʃveːrəs bant',
Wie löst sich äthermild der Erde schweres Band,
How dissolves itself ether-soft the earth's heavy bond,
(How the earth's heavy bonds are dissolved into thin ether,)

di 'haelgə 'tʰrɛːnə kʰvɪlt', lax, naːx dɛs 'hɪməls lant'.
die heil'ge Träne quillt, ach, nach des Himmels Land.
the sacred tear wells up, ah, for the heaven's land.
(sacred tears well up, yearning for the heavenly land.)

viː 'mɛçt'ɪç heːp't das hɛrts zɪç tsuː den 'blɑoən høːn!
Wie mächtig hebt das Herz sich zu den blauen Höh'n!
How mightily lifts the heart itself to the blue heights!
(How mightily the heart is lifted up to the blue heights!)

vas maxt‘ fo:ɐ̯ 'zy:səm ʃmɛrts lɛs lax! zo: tsa:ɐ̯t‘ fɛɐ̯'ge:n?
Was macht vor süssem Schmerz es ach! so zart vergehn?
what makes from sweet pain it ah! so softly swoon?
(What makes it so softly swoon from sweet pain?)

o: 'zy:sɐ 'ho:xgənʊs! mɪlt‘, vi: dɛs 'hɪməls tʰɑo,
O süsser Hochgenuss! mild, wie des Himmels Tau,
O sweet ecstasy! gentle, as the heaven’s dew,
(O sweet ecstasy! Gentle as the dew from heaven,)

vɪŋk‘t‘ 'gɔt‘əs 'faeɐgru:s ho:x lɑos dem 'ʃt‘ɪlən blɑo.
winkt Gottes Feiergruss hoch aus dem stillen Blau.
beckons God’s solemn greeting high from the quiet blue.
(God’s solemn greeting beckons from the quiet blue on high.)

ʊnt das fɛɐ̯'vaest‘ə hɛrts fɛɐ̯'nɪmt den 'ʃt‘ɪlən ru:f,
Und das verwaiste Herz vernimmt den stillen Ruf,
And the orphaned heart perceives the silent call,

ʊnt‘ ze:nt‘ zɪç 'haema:t‘vɛrts tsʊm 'fa:t‘ɐ, de:ɐ̯/de:r lɛs ʃu:f.
und sehnt sich heimatwärts zum Vater, der es schuf.
and yearns itself homelandwards to the Father who it created.
(and yearns for its homeland, and for the Father who created it.)

[The poet longs for heaven. In this strophic song, Schubert’s music sustains a meditative mood, with subtle harmonies that add nuance and depth to the mystical fervor of the words.]

hɪn lʊnt' vi:dɐ 'fli:gən 'pfaelə / a'riet‘ə de:ɐ̯ lu'tsɪndə
Hin und wieder fliegen Pfeile / Ariette der Lucinde
Now and Then Arrows Fly / Lucinda’s Arietta

[composed 1815] (From *Claudine von Villa Bella* by Johann Wolfgang von Goethe)

hɪn lʊnt‘ 'vi:dɐ 'fli:gən 'pfaelə, 'la:mo:ɐs 'laeçt‘ə 'pfaelə 'fli:gən [di]
Hin und wieder fliegen Pfeile, Amors leichte Pfeile fliegen [*GA:* fliegen die Pfeile]
Hence and again fly arrows, Cupid’s light arrows fly [the]
(Now and then the arrows fly, Cupid’s light arrows fly) [*hin und wieder* = now and then]

fɔn dem 'ʃlaŋk‘ən 'gɔldnən 'bo:gən, 'mɛ:t‘çən, zaet‘ li:ɐ̯ nɪçt‘ gə't‘ʰrɔfən?
von dem schlanken goldnen Bogen, Mädchen, seid ihr nicht getroffen?
from the slender golden bow. Girls, are you not smitten?

ɛs lɪst‘ glʏk‘, lɛs lɪst‘ nu:ɐ̯ glʏkʰ. va:'rʊm fli:k‘t‘ le:ɐ̯ zo: lɪn 'laelə?
Es ist Glück, es ist nur Glück. Warum fliegt er so in Eile?
It is luck, it is just luck. Why flies he so in hurry?
(It is luck, just luck. Why is he flying in such a hurry?)

'je:nə dɔrt‘ vɪl le:ɐ̯ bə'zi:gən; ʃo:n lɪst‘ le:ɐ̯ fo:ɐ̯'bae gə'flo:gən,
Jene dort will er besiegen; schon ist er vorbei geflogen,
That one there wants he to conquer; already has he by flown,
(He wants to conquer that young woman over there; he has already flown by her,)

'zɔrk'loːs blaep't deːɐ̯ 'buːzən 'ɔfən. 'geːbət' axt'! eːɐ̯ kʰɔmt tsu'rʏkʰ!
sorglos bleibt der Busen offen. Gebet Acht! Er kommt zurück!
carefree remains the bosom open. Give care! He comes back!
(Her carefree bosom remains open and vulnerable. Take care! He will come back!)

[This is one of the numbers Schubert wrote for Goethe's Singspiel *Claudine von Villa Bella*. Only Act I of his setting has survived. Though this piece was written for the theater, it is sometimes included in a lieder recital. Most of Schubert's numerous stage-works were never performed during his lifetime. In the *Gesamtausgabe* this is found among the theater pieces.]

hɪp'o'liːts liːt'
Hippolits Lied
The Song of Hippolytus

Posthumously published [composed 1826] (poem by Friedrich von Gerstenbergk)

last' mɪç, ɔp' ɪç aox ʃt'ɪl fɛɐ̯'glyː, last' mɪç nuːɐ̯ 'ʃt'ɪlə geːn;
Lasst mich, ob ich auch still vergluh', lasst mich nur stille gehn;
Let me, if I even silently fade away, let me just silently go;
(Let me be, let me just go away silently, even if I must waste away in silence;)

ziː zeː ɪç ʃp'ɛːt', ziː zeː ɪç fryː, ʊnt' 'eːvɪç foːɐ̯ miːɐ̯ ʃt'eːn.
sie seh' ich spät, sie seh' ich früh, und ewig vor mir stehn.
her see I late, her see I early, and forever before me standing.
(I see her standing before me late at night, early in the morning, and forever.)

vas 'laːdət' iːɐ̯ tsʊr ruː mɪç aen? ziː naːm di ruː miːɐ̯ fɔrtʰ,
Was ladet ihr zur Ruh' mich ein? sie nahm die Ruh' mir fort,
Why invite you to the rest me ...? She took the repose from me away,
(Why do you invite me to rest? She has taken away my repose,) [*einladen* = to invite]

ʊnt' voː ziː ɪst, daː mʊs ɪç zaen, hiːɐ̯ zae ɛs 'oːdɐ dɔrtʰ.
und wo sie ist, da muss ich sein, hier sei es oder dort.
and where she is, there must I be, here be it or there.
(and I must be wherever she is, whether it be here or there.)

tsʏrnt 'diːzəm 'armən 'hɛrtsən nɪçt', ɛs hat' nuːɐ̯/nuːr 'aenən feːl:
Zürnt diesem armen Herzen nicht, es hat nur einen Fehl:
Be angry with this poor heart not, it has only one fault:
(Do not be angry with this poor heart; it has only one fault:)

tʰrɔø mʊs ɛs 'ʃlaːgən, bɪs ɛs brɪçt', ʊnt' hat dɛs 'nɪmɐ heːl.
treu muss es schlagen, bis es bricht, und hat dess nimmer Hehl.
faithful must it beat, till it breaks, and has of that never (sought) secrecy/concealment.
(it must beat faithfully till it breaks, and has never made a secret of that.)

last' mɪç, ɪç 'dɛŋk'ə dɔx nuːɐ̯ ziː, ɪn iːɐ̯ nuːɐ̯ 'dɛŋk'ə ɪç;
Lasst mich, ich denke doch nur sie, in ihr nur denke ich;
Let me, I think after all only her, in her only think I;
(Let me be; I think only of her, I think only in her;)

ja:! ˈlo:nə zi: vɛ:r lɪç la͜enstʻ ni: ba͜e ˈlɛŋəln ˈle:vɪkʻlɪç.
ja! ohne sie wär' ich einst nie bei Engeln ewiglich.
yes! without her would be I one day never among angels eternally.
(yes, without her I would have no hope, one day, of an eternal afterlife among the angels.)

ɪm ˈle:bən dɛn lʊntʻ la͜ox lɪm tʰo:tʻ, lɪm ˈhɪməl, zo: vi: hi:ɐ̯,
Im Leben denn und auch im Tod, im Himmel, so wie hier,
In the life then and also in the death, in the heaven, just as here,
(In life, then, and also in death, in heaven just as here,)

ɪm glʏkʻ lʊntʻ lɪn de:ɐ̯ ˈtʰrɛnʊŋ no:tʻ gəˈhø:r lɪç ˈla͜entsɪç li:ɐ̯.
im Glück und in der Trennung Not gehör' ich einzig ihr.
in the happiness and in the separation's distress belong I only to her.
(in happiness and in the pain of separation I belong only to her.)

[Hippolytus was the son of Theseus and Antiope, an Amazon queen. His stepmother Phaedra fell desperately in love with him. That love brought about his death. Euripides, Seneca, and Racine wrote plays on the subject. Hippolytus rejected Phaedra; but in Racine's play he is in love with Aricie. In the *Gesamtausgabe* as well as in the Peters edition the poem is attributed to Johanna Schopenhauer, the mother of the famous philosopher. She included it in her novel *Gabriele*; but the actual author was Friedrich von Gerstenbergk, a member of her literary circle in Weimar.]

ˈhɔxtsa͜etʻli:tʻ
Hochzeitlied
Wedding Song

Posthumously published [composed 1816] (poem by Johann Georg Jacobi)

vɪl ˈzɪŋən lɔ͜øç lɪm ˈaltʻən tʰo:n la͜en li:tʻ fɔn li:pʻ lʊnt tʰrɔ͜ø;
Will singen euch im alten Ton ein Lied von Lieb' und Treu';
(I) want to sing to you in the old tone a song of love and faithfulness;
[*poem:* **ein Lied von alter** (ˈaltʻɐ, old) **Treu'**]

lɛs ˈzaŋəns ˈlʊnzrə ˈfɛ:tʻɐ ʃo:n, dɔx bla͜epʻts de:ɐ̯ ˈli:bə nɔ͜ø.
es sangen's unsre Väter schon, doch bleibt 's der Liebe neu.
there sang it our fathers already, yet remains it for the love new.
(our forefathers have sung it already, yet it remains ever new for love.)

ɪm ˈglʏkʻə maxtʻ lɛs ˈfrɔ͜ødənfɔl, kʰan ˈtʰrø:stʻən lɪn de:ɐ̯ no:tʰ:
Im Glücke macht es freudenvoll, kann trösten in der Not:
In the happiness makes it joyful, can comfort in the distress:
(In happy days it makes you joyful, it can comfort you in times of distress:)

das nɪçts di ˈhɛrtsən ˈʃa͜edən zɔl, nɪçts ˈʃa͜edən, lals de:ɐ̯ tʰo:tʻ;
dass nichts die Herzen scheiden soll, nichts scheiden, als der Tod;
that nothing the hearts part shall, nothing part, but the death;
(that nothing shall part two loving hearts, nothing but death;)

das ˈlɪmɐda:ɐ̯ mɪtʻ ˈfrɪʃəm mu:tʻ de:ɐ̯ man di ˈtʰra͜otʻə ʃʏtstʰ;
dass immerdar mit frischem Mut der Mann die Traute schützt;
that always with fresh courage the man the beloved protects;
(that with fresh courage the man will always protect his beloved;)

ʊnt‘ ˈlaləs ˈɔp͡fɐt‘, guːt‘ lʊnt‘ bluːt‘, vɛns ˈza͜enəm ˈva͜ep‘çən nʏt͡stʰ;
und alles opfert, Gut und Blut, wenn’s seinem Weibchen nützt;
and everything sacrifices, property and blood, if it to his little wife is of use;
(and that he will sacrifice everything, his property and his blood, if that will help his wife;)

das leːɐ̯/leːr la͜of ˈva͜et‘ɐ(r) ˈleːɐ̯də nɪç͡ts lals ziː laˈla͜en bəˈgeːɐ̯tʰ,
dass er auf weiter Erde nichts als sie allein begehrt,
that he on wide earth nothing but her alone desires,
(that he will desire nothing on earth but her alone,)

ziː gɛrn lɪm ʃva͜es dɛs ˈlangəzɪç͡ts fyːɐ̯/fyːr ˈliːrən kʰʊs lɛɐ̯ˈnɛːɐ̯tʰ;
sie gern im Schweiss des Angesichts für ihren Kuss ernährt;
her gladly in the sweat of the countenance for her kiss nourishes;
(that for her kiss he will gladly provide her nourishment with the sweat of his brow;)

das, vɛn di lɛrç lɪm ˈfɛldə ʃlɛːk‘t‘, za͜en va͜ep‘ liːm ˈvɔnə laxtʰ,
dass, wenn die Lerch’ im Felde schlägt, sein Weib ihm Wonne lacht,
that, when the lark in the field sings, his wife for him joy laughs,
(that, when the lark sings in the field, his wife’s smile may give him joy,)

iːm, vɛn deːɐ̯/deːr ˈlak‘ɐ ˈdɔrnən tʰrɛːk‘t, t͡sʊm ʃp‘iːl di ˈlarba͜et‘ maxtʰ,
ihm, wenn der Acker Dornen trägt, zum Spiel die Arbeit macht,
for him, when the farmland thorns bears, to the play the work makes,
(and, when farmland bears only thorns, that she will make the work into play for him,)

ʊnt ˈdɔp‘əlt‘ zyːs deːɐ̯ ˈruːə lʊst‘, lɛɐ̯ˈkʰvɪk‘ənt‘ ˈjeːdəs broːtʰ,
und doppelt süss der Ruhe Lust, erquickend jedes Brot,
and double sweet the rest’s pleasure, refreshing every bread,
(and make the pleasure of rest doubly sweet, and doubly restorative every meal,)

den ˈkʰʊmɐ la͜eçt‘ lan ˈliːrɐ brʊst‘, gəˈlɪndɐ ˈza͜enəm tʰoːt‘.
den Kummer leicht an ihrer Brust, gelinder seinen Tod.
the care light on her breast, more gentle his death.
(and make his cares seem light when he rests on her breast, and make his death more gentle.)

dan fyːlt‘ leːɐ̯ nɔx di ˈkʰalt‘ə hant‘ fɔn ˈliːrɐ hant‘ gəˈdrʏk‘tʰ,
Dann fühlt er noch die kalte Hand von ihrer Hand gedrückt,
Then feels he still the cold hand by her hand pressed,
(Then he will still feel his cold hand being pressed by her hand,)

ʊnt‘ zɪç lɪns ˈnɔ͜øə ˈfaːt‘ɐlant‘ la͜os ˈliːrəm larm lɛntˈ‘rʏk‘tʰ.
und sich ins neue Vaterland aus ihrem Arm entrückt.
and himself into the new fatherland out of her arm carried away.
(and feel himself carried away out of her arms into his new homeland.)

[This simple but delightful strophic song, meant to be sung at weddings, has seven cheerfully touching verses.]

ˈhɔfnʊŋ / di ˈhɔfnʊŋ / ɛs ˈreːdən lʊnt ˈtʰrɔ͜ømən di ˈmɛnʃən

Hoffnung / Die Hoffnung / Es reden und träumen die Menschen

Hope / Men Talk and Dream

Second version: Op. 87, No. 2 [composed between 1815 and 1819] (Friedrich von Schiller)

ɛs ˈreːdən lʊnt ˈtʰrɔ͜ømən di ˈmɛnʃən fiːl fɔn ˈbɛsɐn ˈkʰʏnftˈɪgən ˈtʰaːgən;
Es reden und träumen die Menschen viel von bessern künftigen Tagen;
There talk and dream the human beings much about better future days;
(Men talk and dream a lot about better days in the future;)

naːx ˈla͜enəm ˈglʏkˈlɪçən ˈgɔldənən t͜siːl ziːtˈ man ziː ˈrɛnən lʊntˈ ˈjaːgən.
nach einem glücklichen goldenen Ziel sieht man sie rennen und jagen.
after a happy golden goal sees one them run and chase.
(one sees them running and chasing after a happy, golden goal.)

di vɛltˈ vɪrtˈ laltˈ lʊntˈ vɪrtˈ ˈviːdɐ jʊŋ,
Die Welt wird alt und wird wieder jung,
The world grows old and becomes again young,
(The world grows old, then young again;)

dɔx deːɐ̯ mɛnʃ hɔftˈ ˈlɪmɐ fɛɐ̯ˈbɛsərʊŋ.
doch der Mensch hofft immer Verbesserung.
but the human being hopes always improvement.
(but man keeps hoping for amelioration.)

di ˈhɔfnʊŋ fyːɐ̯tˈ liːn lɪns ˈleːbən la͜en, ziː lʊmˈflatˈɐt den ˈfrøːlɪçən ˈkʰnaːbən,
Die Hoffnung führt ihn ins Leben ein, sie umflattert den fröhlichen Knaben,
The hope leads him into the life in, it flutters about the merry boy,
(Hope leads him into life; it flutters about the merry boy,)

den ˈjʏŋlɪŋ bəˈga͜estˈɐtˈ liːɐ̯ ˈtsa͜obɐʃa͜en, ziː vɪrtˈ mɪt dem gra͜es nɪçtˈ bəˈgraːbən;
den Jüngling begeistert ihr Zauberschein, sie wird mit dem Greis nicht begraben;
the youth (obj.) inspires its magical gleam, it is with the old man not buried;
(its magical gleam inspires the youth, it is not buried with the old man;)
[*first version:* **den Jüngling lockt** (lɔkˈtˈ, lures); *poem:* **den Jüngling locket** (ˈlɔkˈətˈ, lures)]

dɛn bəˈʃliːstˈ leːɐ̯/leːr lɪm ˈgraːbə den ˈmyːdən la͜of,
denn beschliesst er im Grabe den müden Lauf,
for ends he in the grave the weary course,
(for though he ends his weary course in the grave,)

nɔx lam ˈgraːbə p͜flant͜stˈ leːɐ̯ di ˈhɔfnʊŋ la͜of.
noch am Grabe pflanzt er die Hoffnung auf.
still on the grave plants he the hope up.
(yet on that grave he plants the seeds of hope.)

ɛs lɪstˈ kʰa͜en ˈleːrɐ, kʰa͜en ˈʃma͜eçəlndɐ vaːn,
Es ist kein leerer, kein schmeichelnder Wahn, [*1st version & poem without 2nd* **kein**]
it is no empty, no flattering delusion,
(it is no empty, flattering delusion,)

ɛɐ̯ˈtsɔ͜øk‘t‘ lɪm gəˈhɪrnə dɛs ˈtʰoːrən. lɪm ˈhɛrtsən ˈkʰʏndət‘ lɛs la͜ot‘ zɪç lan:
erzeugt im Gehirne des Toren. Im Herzen kündet es laut sich an:
conceived in the brain of the fool. In the heart proclaims it loudly itself ... :
(conceived in the brain of a fool. In the heart it loudly proclaims itself:) [*ankünden* = to proclaim]

t͡suː vas ˈbɛsɐm zɪnt‘ viːɐ̯ gəˈboːrən! lʊnt‘ vas di ˈlɪnərə ˈʃt‘ɪmə ʃp‘rɪçt‘,
zu was Besserm sind wir geboren! Und was die innere Stimme spricht,
for something better are we born! And what the inner voice speaks,
(we are born for something better! And what the inner voice speaks)

das tʰɔ͜øʃt di ˈhɔfəndə ˈzeːlə nɪçtʰ.
das täuscht die hoffende Seele nicht.
that deceives the hoping soul not.
(does not deceive the hopeful soul.)

[Schubert composed a first version in 1815. The date of the second is unknown. It was published in 1827, during Schubert's lifetime. His title, and that of the poem, is *Hoffnung*; but the second version is given the title *Die Hoffnung* in the Peters collection. The editor of the *Gesamtausgabe* changed the vocal line in the ninth bar to correspond to the fifth bar; Peters follows the original publication. The piece loses its character if the tempo is too fast or the accompaniment too loud.]

ˈhɔfnʊŋ / ʃaf, das ˈtʰaːk‘vɛrk‘ ˈma͜enɐ ˈhɛndə
Hoffnung / Schaff', das Tagwerk meiner Hände
Hope / Grant that the Daily Task of My Hands

Posthumously published [composed 1819?] (poem by Johann Wolfgang von Goethe)

ʃaf, das ˈtʰaːk‘vɛrk‘ ˈma͜enɐ ˈhɛndə, ˈhoːəs glʏk‘, das lɪçs fɔlˈlɛndə/fɔˈlɛndə!
Schaff', das Tagwerk meiner Hände, hohes Glück, dass ich's vollende!
Grant, the daily task of my hands, High Fortune, that I it complete!
(O sublime Fortune, grant that I may complete the daily task of my hands!)

las, loː las mɪç nɪçt‘ lɛɐ̯ˈmat‘ən! na͜en, lɛs zɪnt‘ nɪçt‘ ˈleːrə ˈtʰrɔ͜ømə:
Lass, o lass mich nicht ermatten! Nein, es sind nicht leere Träume:
Let, O let me not weaken! No, there are not empty dreams:
(O let me not weaken! No, these are not empty dreams:)

jɛt͡st‘ nuːɐ̯ ˈʃt‘aŋən, ˈdiːzə ˈbɔ͜ømə ˈgeːbən la͜enst‘ nɔx frʊxt‘ lʊnt‘ ˈʃat‘ən.
jetzt nur Stangen, diese Bäume geben einst noch Frucht und Schatten.
now only sticks, these trees (will) give one day yet fruit and shade.
(though only bare trunks as yet, these trees will one day offer fruit and shade.)

[Schubert wrote out the song in two different keys, in F, marked *langsam* (slow), and in E, marked *mässig* (moderate), with the accompaniment raised an octave. Neither manuscript is dated. There is one minor rhythmical variant in the E major version: the first note in the fifteenth bar is dotted for the voice. Both versions are printed in the *Gesamtausgabe*. Schubert set Goethe's short poem in the style of a hymn, with a *staccato* marching bass-line.]

ˈhʊldɪgʊŋ
Huldigung
Homage

Posthumously published [composed 1815] (poem by Ludwig Kosegarten)

gants fɛɐ̯ˈloːrən, gants fɛɐ̯ˈzʊŋkən ɪn daen ˈanʃaon, ˈliːpʻlɪŋɪn, [gaːɐ̯]
Ganz verloren, ganz versunken in dein Anschaun, Lieblingin, [*poem:* **Gar verloren]**
Utterly lost, totally absorbed into your contemplation, darling, [absolutely]
(Utterly lost, totally absorbed in contemplation of you, darling,)

ˈvɔnəbeːbəntʻ, ˈliːbətʰrʊŋkʻən, ʃvɪŋt tsuː diːɐ̯ deːɐ̯ gaestʻ zɪç hɪn.
wonnebebend, liebetrunken, schwingt zu dir der Geist sich hin.
rapture-trembling, love-drunk, soars to you the spirit itself hence.
(trembling with rapture, drunk with love, my spirit soars away to you.)

nɪçts fɛɐ̯ˈmaːkʻ ɪç tsuː bəˈgɪnən, nɪçts tsuː ˈdɛŋkʻən, ˈdɪçtʻən, ˈzɪnən,
Nichts vermag ich zu beginnen, nichts zu denken, dichten, sinnen,
Nothing am able I to undertake, nothing to think, write, reflect,
(Nothing am I able to undertake, nothing can I think, write, or reflect upon,)

nɪçts ɪst, vas das hɛrts miːɐ̯ fʏltʻ, ˈhʊldɪn, als daen ˈhɔldəs bɪltʻ.
nichts ist, was das Herz mir füllt, Huldin, als dein holdes Bild.
nothing is, which the heart for me fills, gracious one, except your lovely image.
(there is nothing that fills my heart, gracious one, except your lovely image.)

ˈzyːsə, ˈraenə, ˈmaːkʻəlloːzə, ˈeːdlə, ˈtʰɔørə, ˈtʰrɛflɪçə,
Süsse, Reine, Makellose, Edle, Teure, Treffliche,
Sweet, pure, spotless, noble, dear, excellent one,
[kʰaltʻ ʊntʻ kʰɔøʃ viː ˈjɛnɐʃneː]
[*poem:* **Süsse, Reine, Makellose, kalt und keusch wie Jennerschnee]**
[cold and chaste as January snow]

ˈʊngəˌʃmɪŋkʻtʻə ˈroːtʻə ˈroːzə, ˈʊnfɛɐ̯ˌzeːɐ̯tʻə ˈliːliə, [ˈʊngəˌzɔntʻə]
ungeschminkte rote Rose, unversehrte Lilie, [*poem:* **ungesonnte Lilie]**
unadorned red rose, undamaged lily, [unsunned (= undamaged by the sun)]

ˈanmuːtsraeçə aneˈmoːnə, ˈalɐ ˈʃøːnən pʰraes ʊntʻ ˈkʰroːnə, [ˈʃøːnhaetʻ]
anmutsreiche Anemone, aller Schönen Preis und Krone, [*poem:* **aller Schönheit]**
grace- rich anemone, of all beautiful things prize and crown, [all beauty's]
(anemone, rich in grace, the prize and crown of all that is beautiful,)

vaest duː aox, gəˈbiːtʻərɪn, viː ɪç gants daen ˈaegən bɪn?
weisst du auch, Gebieterin, wie ich ganz dein eigen bin?
know you also, mistress/commander, how I totally your own am?
(do you really know, mistress of my heart, how totally I am yours to command?)

ˈhʊldɪn, diːɐ̯ haːb ɪç ɛɐ̯ˈgeːbən zeːl ʊntʻ laepʻ ʊntʻ hɛrts ʊntʻ zɪn.
Huldin', dir hab' ich ergeben Seel' und Leib und Herz und Sinn.
Gracious lady, to you have I yielded soul and body and heart and mind.

ˈoːnə dɪç vɛːɐ̯ tʰoːt das ˈleːbən, lʊntʻ mɪt diːɐ̯ deːɐ̯ tʰoːtʻ gəˈvɪn.
Ohne dich wär' Tod das Leben, und mit dir der Tod Gewinn.
Without you were death the life, and with you the death gain.
(Without you life would be death, and by your side death would be a gain.)

ˈzyːsɐ(r) lɪstʻ lɛs, diːɐ̯ t͡suː ˈfroːnən, lals t͡suː ˈtʰraːgən ˈgɔldnə ˈkʰroːnən,
Süsser ist es, dir zu fronen, als zu tragen goldne Kronen,
Sweeter is it, for you to slave, than to wear golden crowns,
(It is sweeter to me to be your slave than to wear a golden crown,)

ˈleːdlɐ, ˈda͜enəm diːnstʻ zɪç va͜en, lals dɛs ˈleːɐ̯tʻbals ˈhɛrʃɐ za͜en.
edler, deinem Dienst sich weihn, als des Erdballs Herrscher sein.
nobler, to your service oneself to consecrate, than the terrestrial globe's ruler to be.
(it is nobler to consecrate oneself to your service than to be ruler of the entire earth.)

vɛn lɪç, ˈtʰra͜otʻə, dɪç lɛɐ̯ˈblɪkʻə, vɪrt di ˈzeːlə miːɐ̯ zoː kʰlaːɐ̯.
Wenn ich, Traute, dich erblicke, wird die Seele mir so klar.
When I, dear one, you behold, becomes the soul for me so clear.
(When I behold you, dearest, my soul becomes clear and bright.)

vɛn lɪç diːɐ̯ di ˈhɛndə ˈdrʏkʻə, t͡sʊkʻt͡s lɪn miːɐ̯ zoː ˈvʊndɐbaːɐ̯.
Wenn ich dir die Hände drücke, zuckt's in mir so wunderbar.
When I to you the hands press, quivers it in me so wondrously.
(When I press your hands, something quivers inside of me so wondrously.)

dɛs lɔˈlʏmpʻɔs ˈhoːə ˈt͡sɛçɐ laːpʻtʻ nɪçtʻ zoː deːɐ̯ ˈnɛkʻtʻar-ˈbɛçɐ, [lɔˈlʏmpʻʊs]
Des Olympos hohe Zecher labt nicht so der Nektar- Becher, [*poem:* Olympus]
The Olympus' sublime drinkers refreshes not so the nectar beaker,
(The cup of nectar does not refresh the sublime drinkers of Mount Olympus as much,)

deːɐ̯/deːr lamˈbroːzia gəˈnʊs, viː mɪç laːpʻt da͜en ˈkʰɔ͜øʃɐ kʰʊs.
der Ambrosia Genuss, wie mich labt dein keuscher Kuss.
(nor) the ambrosia's enjoyment, as me refreshes your chaste kiss.
(nor the enjoyment of ambrosia, as your chaste kiss refreshes me.)

mɪç lʊmˈbeːbən ˈzyːsə ˈʃa͜oɐ, kʰraftʻ lʊntʻ ˈlaːtʻəm ˈmaŋəln miːɐ̯,
Mich umbeben süsse Schauer, Kraft und Atem mangeln mir,
Me around tremble sweet shivers, strength and breath are lacking for me,
(Sweet shivers tremble all around my body, strength and breath fail me,)

ˈfrɔ͜ødə ˈʃytʻəltʻ mɪç lʊnt ˈtʰra͜oɐ, ˈbaŋə ʃɔ͜ø lʊntʻ ˈgluːtʻbəgiːɐ̯,
Freude schüttelt mich und Trauer, bange Scheu und Glutbegier,
joy shakes me and grief, anxious shyness and passionate desire,
(joy and grief, anxious shyness, and passionate desire agitate me,)

vɛn lɪç mɪç dem ˈha͜elɪçtʻuːmə ˈda͜enəs ˈkʰɛlçəs, ˈleːdlə ˈbluːmə, ˈt͡sɪtʻɐntʻ ˈnaːə,
wenn ich mich dem Heligtume deines Kelches, edle Blume, zitternd nahe,
when I myself to the sanctuary of your chalice, noble flower, trembling near,
(when I, trembling, draw near to the sanctuary of your chalice, noble flower,)

ˈnɛlkʻəndʊftʻ mɪç lʊmˈveːtʻ lʊntʻ ˈlambra- lʊftʰ. [ˈnɛlkʻənlʊftʻ ˈlambradʊftʰ]
Nelkenduft mich umweht und Ambra-Luft. [*poem:* Nelkenluft... Ambraduft]
carnation fragrance me wafts about and amber air. [carnation air...amber perfume]
(the fragrance of carnations and amber wafts about me in the air.)

kʰœnt‘ lɪç, lax, dɪç nuːɐ̯/nuːr lʊmˈʃmiːgən ˈlaenən ˈlaŋən ˈzɔmɐtʰaːk‘;
Könnt' ich, ach, dich nur umschmiegen einen langen Sommertag;
Could I, ah, you only nestle around a long summer day;
(Ah, if I could only nestle next to you for a whole long summer day;)
[*poem:* **nur umfangen** (lʊmˈfaŋən, embrace)]

diːɐ̯/diːr lam ˈlɔfnən ˈbuzən ˈliːgən, ˈlaoʃənt ˈdaenəs ˈhɛrtsəns ʃlaːk‘!
dir am offnen Busen liegen, lauschend deines Herzens Schlag!
to you on the open bosom lie, listening (to) your heart's beat!
(if I could only lie upon your open bosom, listening to your beating heart!)
[ˈvaedənt‘ laof den ˈroːzənvaŋən,] [laof dɛs]
[*poem:* **weidend auf den Rosenwangen, lauschend auf des Herzens Schlag!**]
[grazing upon the rosy cheeks] [to the]
[(grazing on your rosy cheeks, listening to the beating of your heart!)]

kʰœnt‘ lɪç, lax, dɪç nuːɐ̯/nuːr lʊmˈflɛçt‘ən lɪn den ˈlɛŋst‘ən ˈvɪnt‘ɐnɛçt‘ən,
Könnt' ich, ach, dich nur umflechten in den längsten Winternächten,
Could I, ah, you only entwine around in the longest winter nights,
(Ah, if I could only entwine around you in the longest winter nights,)

ˈlaengəviːk‘t‘ lɪn ˈzaednən tʰraom laof dɛs ˈbuːzəns ˈʃvaːnənflaom.
eingewiegt in seidnen Traum auf des Busens Schwanenflaum.
lulled to sleep into silken dream on the bosom's swan's- down.
(lulled into a silken dream on the swan's-down of your bosom.)
[laof ˈvaeçəm flaom, diːɐ̯/diːr lɪm larm]
[*poem:* **eingewiegt auf weichem Flaum, dir im Arm, in seidnen Traum.**]
[on soft down, to you in the arm]
[(lulled into a silken dream on soft down, in your arms.)]

kʰœnt‘ lɪç, lax, maen ˈgantsəs ˈleːbən ˈlaentsɪç diːɐ̯/diːr, lɛlˈviːna, vaen!
Könnt' ich, ach, mein ganzes Leben einzig dir, Elwina, weihn!
Could I, ah, my whole life only to you, Elvina, consecrate!
(Ah, if I could consecrate my entire life only to you, Elvina!)
[dʏrft‘ lɪç tsaet‘ lʊnt‘ muːs lʊnt‘ ˈleːbən]
[*poem:* **Dürft' ich Zeit und Muss' und Leben einzig dir, Elwina, weihn!**]
[Might I time and leisure and life...]
[(If I could only dedicate my time, my leisure, and my life to you alone, Elvina!)]

dʏrft‘ lɪç ˈhandəln, ˈdʊldən, ˈʃt‘reːbən fyːɐ̯ dɪç lʊnt‘ mɪt diːɐ̯/diːr laˈlaen!
Dürft' ich handeln, dulden, streben für dich und mit dir allein!
Might I act, endure, strive for you and with you alone!
(If I could act, endure, and strive only for you and with you alone!)

ˈvaːɐ̯lɪç dan vɛːɐ̯ ˈdaːzaen ˈvɔnə! lʊnt‘ vɛn ˈmaenəs ˈleːbəns ˈzɔnə
Wahrlich dann wär' Dasein Wonne! Und wenn meines Lebens Sonne
Truly then were existence rapture! And if my life's sun
(Truly then existence would be rapture! And if the sun of my life)
[*poem:* **Und wenn einst** (laenst‘, one day) **des Daseins** (dɛs ˈdaːzaens, existence's) **Sonne**]

ˈlʊnt‘ɐgɪŋ lɪn ˈfɪnst‘ɐnɪs, loː, zoː vɛːɐ̯/vɛːr laox tʰoːt‘ miːɐ̯ zyːs.
unterging in Finsternis, o, so wär' auch Tod mir süss.
set in darkness, oh, then were even death to me sweet.
(were to set in darkness, oh, then even death would be sweet to me.)
[*poem:* **wär' auch Untergang** (ˈlʊnt‘ɐgaŋ, downfall) **mir süss**]

'zɔlt'ə 'dʊŋk'əl de:n lʊm've:bən, de:m lɛl'vi:nəns 'lɑo̯gə glɛnt͡stʰ?
Sollte Dunkel den umweben, dem Elwinens Auge glänzt?
Should darkness him weave about, (on) whom Elvina's eye shines?
(Would darkness surround the man upon whom Elvina's eyes are shining?)

zɔlt' lɪç fo:ɐ̯ de:ɐ̯/de:r 'lʊrnə 'be:bən, di: lɛl'vi:na 'vae̯nənt' kʰrɛnt͡stʰ?
Sollt' ich vor der Urne beben, die Elwina weinend kränzt?
Should I before the urn tremble, which Elvina weeping garlands?
(Should I tremble at the thought of the funereal urn that Elvina, weeping, adorns with garlands?)
[*poem:* **vor der Urn'** (lʊrn) **erbeben** (lɛɐ̯'be:bən)]

zɔlt' lɪç nɪçt, du: 'kʰy:lə 'kʰamɐ(r), lɪn di:ɐ̯ 'ʃlʊmɐn 'zɔndɐ 'jamɐ?
Sollt' ich nicht, du kühle Kammer, in dir schlummern sonder Jammer?
Should I not, you cool chamber, in you slumber without distress?
(Cool tomb, should I not sleep in you without distress?)

hɔrç! lɛl'vi:na 've:mu:t'fɔl zɔ͡øft͡st': mae̯n 'li:p'lɪŋ, 'ʃlʊmrə vo:l!
Horch! Elwina wehmutvoll seufzt: mein Liebling, schlummre wohl!
Hark! Elvina full of melancholy sighs: my darling, slumber well!
(Listen! Elvina, full of tender melancholy, is sighing: "My darling, sleep well!")
[*poem:* **wehmutsvoll** ('ve:mu:t͡sfɔl)]

ʊnt' vi: balt' lɪst' nɪçt' fɛɐ̯'ʃvʊndən 'je:nəs 'ʃlʊmɐs 'kʰʊrt͡sə naxtʰ!
Und wie bald ist nicht verschwunden jenes Schlummers kurze Nacht!
And how soon is not vanished that slumber's short night!
(And how soon has the short night of that slumber not vanished!)
[*poem:* **ist nicht verronnen** (fɛɐ̯'rɔnən, elapsed) **solches** ('zɔlçəs, such) **Schlummers**]

hɔrç, lɛs 'ju:bəlt': 'ly:bɐvʊndən! ʃɑo̯, de:ɐ̯/de:r 'le:vgə tʰa:k' lɛɐ̯'vaxtʰ!
Horch, es jubelt: Überwunden! Schau, der ew'ge Tag erwacht!
Hark, there rejoices: Overcome! Look, the eternal day awakes!
(Listen, there is rejoicing! Hear the words: "Overcome! Behold, the eternal day has dawned!")
[ʃɑo̯, ʃo:n 'glɛnt͡sən 'landrə 'zɔnən! ʃɑo̯, das 'le:vgə 'fry:ro:t' laxtʰ;]
[*poem:* **Schau, schon glänzen andre Sonnen! Schau, das ew'ge Frührot lacht;**]
[Behold, already shine other suns! Behold, the eternal dawn laughs;]
[(Behold, already other suns are shining! Behold, the eternal dawn is smiling)]

dan du: 'tʰɔ͡ørə, dan du: 'lae̯nə, bɪst du: gant͡s lʊnt' 'le:vɪç 'mae̯nə!
Dann du Teure, dann du Eine, bist du ganz und ewig Meine!
Then you dear one, then you only one, are you entirely and eternally mine!
(Then, dear one, only one, then you will be entirely and eternally mine!)
[vo: lɑo̯f lama'rant'nən 'mat'ən 'ze:lən zɪç t͡su: 'ze:lən 'gat'ən,]
[*poem:* **wo auf amarant'nen Matten Seelen sich zu Seelen gatten.**]
[where on amaranthine meadows souls themselves to souls unite.]
[(where, on meadows of flowers that never fade, souls are united to souls.)]

'tʰrɛnʊŋ lɪst das lo:s de:ɐ̯ t͡sae̯t'! 'le:vɪç 'lae̯nɪçt' 'le:vɪçkʰae̯tʰ!
Trennung ist das Los der Zeit! Ewig einigt Ewigkeit!
Separation is the lot of the time! Eternally unites eternity!
(Separation is the lot of those who live in time! Eternity unites eternally!)

[The poet's title was *Minnesang* (Love Song). The many differences (indicated above in brackets) between the text used by Schubert and the published poem suggest that Schubert had access to a different version. His music is graceful and endearing. Two verses would be enough.]

ˈhʏmnə la͜ens
Hymne I
Hymn I

Posthumously published [composed 1819] (poem by Novalis, Friedrich von Hardenberg)

ˈveːnɪɡə ˈvɪsən das ɡəˈha͜emnɪs deːɐ̯ ˈliːbə, ˈfyːlən ˈʊnlɛɐ̯zɛtˈlɪçkʰa͜etˈ ʊntˈ ˈeːvɪɡən dʊrstʰ.
Wenige wissen das Geheimnis der Liebe, fühlen Unersättlichkeit und ewigen Durst.
Few know the secret of the love, feel insatiableness and eternal thirst.
(Few know the secret of love, few feel its insatiableness and eternal thirst.)

dɛs ˈaːbəntˈmaːls ˈɡœtˈlɪçə bəˈdɔ͜øtˈʊŋ ɪst den ˈɪrdɪʃən ˈzɪnən ˈrɛːtsəl;
Des Abendmahls göttliche Bedeutung ist den irdischen Sinnen Rätsel;
The Lord's Supper's divine significance is to the earthly minds enigma;
(The divine significance of Holy Communion is an enigma to earthbound minds;)

ˈaːbɐ veːɐ̯ ˈjeːmaːls fɔn ˈha͜esən, ɡəˈliːpˈtˈən ˈlɪpˈən ˈaːtˈəm dɛs ˈleːbəns zoːkˈ,
aber wer jemals von heissen, geliebten Lippen Atem des Lebens sog,
but he who ever from hot, beloved lips breath of the life imbibed,
(but whoever has ever imbibed the breath of life from passionate, beloved lips,)

veːm ˈha͜elɪɡə ɡluːtˈ ɪn ˈtsɪtˈɐndə ˈvɛlən das hɛrts ʃmɔlts, [
wem heilige Glut in zitternde Wellen das Herz schmolz,
whom holy ardor into trembling waves the heart melted,
(whoever has felt holy ardor melt his heart into trembling waves,)

veːm das ˈa͜oɡə ˈa͜ofɡɪŋ, das leːɐ̯ dɛs ˈhɪməls ˈʊnlɛɐ̯ɡrʏntˈlɪçə ˈtʰiːfə maːs,
wem das Auge aufging, dass er des Himmels unergründliche Tiefe mass,
whom the eye opened, that he the heaven's unfathomable depths measured,
(whoever has opened his eyes to measure the unfathomable depths of heaven,)

vɪrtˈ ˈɛsən fɔn ˈza͜enəm ˈla͜ebə ʊnt ˈtʰrɪŋkˈən fɔn ˈza͜enəm ˈbluːtˈə ˈeːvɪkˈlɪç.
wird essen von seinem Leibe und trinken von seinem Blute ewiglich.
will eat of His body and drink of His blood eternally.

veːɐ̯ hat dɛs ˈɪrdɪʃən ˈla͜ebəs ˈhoːən zɪn lɛɐ̯ˈraːtˈən? veːɐ̯ kʰan ˈzaːɡən,
Wer hat des irdischen Leibes hohen Sinn erraten? Wer kann sagen,
Who has the earthly body's sublime meaning guessed? Who can say
(Who has guessed the sublime meaning of the earthly body? Who can say)

das leːɐ̯ das bluːtˈ fɛɐ̯ˈʃtˈeːtʰ? la͜enstˈ ɪstˈ ˈaləs la͜epˈ, la͜en la͜epˈ,
dass er das Blut versteht? Einst ist alles Leib, ein Leib,
that he the blood understands? One day is all body, one body,
(that he understands the blood? One day all will be body, *one* body,)

ɪn ˈhɪmlɪʃən ˈbluːtə ʃvɪmt das ˈzeːlɪɡə pʰaːɐ̯.
in himmlischem Blute schwimmt das selige Paar.
in celestial blood swims the blessed pair.
(the blessed pair will float in celestial blood.)

oː! das das ˈvɛltˈmeːɐ̯ ʃoːn lɛɐ̯ˈrøːtˈətˈə, ʊntˈ ɪn ˈdʊftˈɪɡəs fla͜eʃ la͜ofˈkʰvœlə deːɐ̯ fɛls!
O! dass das Weltmeer schon errötete, und in duftiges Fleisch aufquölle der Fels!
O that the ocean already might turn red, and into fragrant flesh might well up the rock!
(O that the ocean might already turn red, and that the rock might spring up as fragrant flesh!)

niː ˈlɛndət das ˈzyːsə maːl, niː ˈzɛtˈɪçt di ˈliːbə zɪç;
Nie endet das süsse Mahl, nie sättigt die Liebe sich;
Never ends the sweet meal, never satisfies the love itself;
(The sweet meal never ends, this love is never sated;)

nɪçtˈ ˈlɪnɪç, nɪçtˈ ˈlaegən gəˈnuːk kʰan ziː ˈhaːbən den gəˈliːpˈtˈən.
nicht innig, nicht eigen genug kann sie haben den Geliebten.
not intimate, not (its) own enough can it have the beloved.
(love can not possess the beloved intimately enough, the beloved cannot be enough one's own.)

fɔn ˈlɪmɐ ˈtsɛːɐtˈərən ˈlɪpˈən fɛɐˈvandəltˈ vɪrt das gəˈnɔsənə
Von immer zärteren Lippen verwandelt wird das Genossene
From ever more tender lips transformed becomes the enjoyed food
(The divine food becomes transformed, through ever more sensitive lips,)

ˈlɪnɪkˈlɪçɐ(r) lʊntˈ ˈnɛːɐ. ˈhaesərə ˈvɔllʊst dʊrçˈbeːpˈt di ˈzeːlə,
inniglicher und näher. Heissere Wollust durchbebt die Seele,
more intimately and nearer. More ardent pleasure trembles through the soul,
(into something more intimate, ever nearer. A more ardent pleasure trembles through the soul,)

ˈdʊrstˈɪgɐ(r) lʊntˈ ˈhʊŋrɪgɐ vɪrt das hɛrts: lʊntˈ zoː vɛːɐt deːɐ ˈliːbə gəˈnʊs
durstiger und hungriger wird das Herz: und so währt der Liebe Genuss
thirstier and hungrier becomes the heart: and thus lasts the love's enjoyment
(the heart grows thirstier and hungrier: and thus love's enjoyment lasts)

[*poem:* **währet** (ˈvɛrət, lasts)]

fɔn ˈleːvɪçkʰaet tsuː ˈleːvɪçkʰaetʰ. ˈhɛtˈən di ˈnʏçtˈɐnən ˈlaenmaːl nuːɐ gəˈkʰɔstˈətˈ,
von Ewigkeit zu Ewigkeit. Hätten die Nüchternen einmal nur gekostet,
from eternity to eternity. Had the abstemious once only tasted,
(from eternity to eternity. If the abstainers had but once tasted such food,)

[*poem:* **Hätten die Nüchternen einmal gekostet**]

ˈlaləs fɛɐˈliːsən ziː, lʊntˈ ˈzɛtstˈən zɪç tsuː lʊns
Alles verliessen sie, und setzten sich zu uns
everything would leave behind they, and seat themselves beside us
(they would leave everything else behind and sit down beside us)

lan den tɪʃ deːɐ ˈzeːnzʊxtˈ, deːɐ niː leːɐ vɪrtˈ. ziː lɛɐˈkʰɛntˈən
an den Tisch der Sehnsucht, der nie leer wird. Sie erkennten
at the table of the longing, which never empty becomes. They would recognize
(at the table of longing, which never becomes empty. They would recognize)

deːɐ ˈliːbə lʊnˈlɛntˈlɪçə ˈfʏlə, lʊntˈ ˈpʰriːzən di ˈnaːrʊŋ fɔn laepˈ lʊntˈ bluːtʰ.
der Liebe unendliche Fülle, und priesen die Nahrung von Leib und Blut.
the love's infinite abundance, and praise the nourishment of body and blood.
(love's infinite abundance and extol the nourishment that derives from Christ's body and blood.)

[The poet responds to the sacrament of the Eucharist with a mystical ecstasy that is notably erotic. Schubert's setting emphasizes rather the solemnity and devoutness. Novalis explains elsewhere that his concept of body includes, especially, the mind, and that the blood represents the life force itself. In the terms of Christian symbolism, he expresses his longing to internalize the union with the beloved, with universal mind. He had been engaged to a girl who died before the tragically young age of fifteen. That love and that loss led to a profound spiritual awakening.]

'hʏmnə t͜sva͜e
Hymne II
Hymn II

Posthumously published [composed 1819] (poem by Novalis, Friedrich von Hardenberg)

vɛn lɪç li:n nu:ɐ̯ 'ha:bə, vɛn le:ɐ̯ ma͜en nu:ɐ̯/nu:r lɪst',
Wenn ich ihn nur habe, wenn er Mein nur ist,
If I Him only have, if He mine only is,
(If only I have Him, if only He is mine,)

vɛn ma͜en hɛrt͜s bɪs hɪn t͜sʊm 'gra:bə 'za͜enə 'tʰrɔ͜ø̯ə ni: fɛɐ̯'gɪstʰ:
wenn mein Herz bis hin zum Grabe seine Treue nie vergisst:
if my heart till hence to the grave its faithfulness never forgets:
(if unto the grave my heart never forgets its faithfulness:)

va͜es lɪç nɪçt͜s fɔn 'la͜edə, 'fy:lə nɪçt͜s, lals 'landaxt', li:p' lʊnt' 'frɔ͜ø̯də.
weiss ich nichts von Leide, fühle nichts, als Andacht, Lieb' und Freude.
know I nothing of sorrow, feel nothing but devotion, love, and joy.
(I shall know nothing of sorrow, shall feel nothing but devotion, love, and joy.)

vɛn lɪç li:n nu:ɐ̯ 'ha:bə, las ɪç 'laləs gɛrn,
Wenn ich ihn nur habe, lass' ich alles gern,
If I Him only have, leave I everything gladly,
(If only I have Him, I gladly leave everything else)

fɔlk' lan 'ma͜enəm 'vandɐʃt'a:bə tʰrɔ͜ø̯gə'zɪnt' nu:ɐ̯ 'ma͜enəm hɛrn;
folg' an meinem Wanderstabe treugesinnt nur meinem Herrn;
follow with my wanderer's staff loyally-minded only my Lord;
(and, with my wanderer's staff at my side, loyally follow only my Lord;)

'lasə ʃt'ɪl di 'landɐn 'bra͜et'ə, 'lɪçt'ə, 'fɔlə 'ʃt'ra:sən 'vandɐn. ['ʃt'ɪlə]
lasse still die Andern breite, lichte, volle Strassen wandern. [*poem:* **lasse stille]**
let quietly the others broad, light, full streets roam.
(quietly let the others roam about on broad, light, crowded roads.)

vɛn lɪç li:n nu:ɐ̯ 'ha:bə, ʃla:f ɪç 'frø:lɪç la͜en,
Wenn ich ihn nur habe, schlaf' ich fröhlich ein,
If I Him only have, fall asleep I cheerfully ... , [*einschlafen* = to fall asleep]
(If only I have Him, I shall fall asleep cheerfully,)

'e:vɪç vɪrt t͜su: 'zy:sɐ 'la:bə 'za͜enəs 'hɛrt͜səns flu:t' mi:ɐ̯ za͜en,
ewig wird zu süsser Labe seines Herzens Flut mir sein,
eternally will as sweet refreshment His heart's flood to me be,
(the flood from His heart will eternally be a sweet refreshment to me,)

di: mɪt' 'zanft'əm 't͜svɪŋən 'laləs vɪrt' lɛɐ̯'va͜eçən lʊnt dʊrç'drɪŋən.
die mit sanftem Zwingen alles wird erweichen und durchdringen.
which with gentle compulsion everything will soften and penetrate.
(that flood which will soften and penetrate everything with gentle compulsion.)

vɛn |ɪç |iːn nuːɐ̯ ˈhaːbə, haːb ɪç |a͜ox di vɛltʰ;
Wenn ich ihn nur habe, hab' ich auch die Welt;
If I Him only have, have I also the world:
(If only I have Him, I shall then also have the whole world:)

ˈzeːlɪç, viː |a͜en ˈhɪməlskʰnaːbə, deːɐ̯ deːɐ̯ ˈjʊŋfra͜o ˈʃla͜eɐ hɛltʰ.
selig, wie ein Himmelsknabe, der der Jungfrau Schleier hält.
blissful, like a heavenly cherub who the Virgin's veil holds.
(I shall be blissful as a heavenly cherub who is holding the Virgin's veil.)

ˈhɪngəzɛŋkʻtʻ |ɪm ˈʃa͜oən kʰan miːɐ̯ foːɐ̯ dem ˈ|ɪrdɪʃən nɪçtʻ ˈgra͜oən.
Hingesenkt im Schauen kann mir vor dem Irdischen nicht grauen.
Sunk in the contemplation can to me before the earthly not shudder.
(Absorbed in the contemplation of holy things I cannot shudder at that which is earthly.)

voː |ɪç |iːn nuːɐ̯ ˈhaːbə, |ɪstʻ ma͜en ˈfaːtʻɐlantʻ;
Wo ich ihn nur habe, ist mein Vaterland;
Where I Him only have, is my fatherland;
(Wherever I have Him, that place is my fatherland;)

ʊntʻ |ɛs fɛltʻ miːɐ̯ ˈjeːdə ˈgaːbə viː |a͜en ˈ|ɛrpʻtʰa͜el |ɪn di hantʻ:
und es fällt mir jede Gabe wie ein Erbteil in die Hand:
and there falls to me every gift like an inheritance into the hand:
(and every gift falls into my hand like an inheritance:)

lɛŋstʻ fɛɐ̯ˈmɪstʻə ˈbryːdɐ fɪnd ɪç nuːn |ɪn ˈza͜enən ˈjʏŋɐn ˈviːdɐ.
längst vermisste Brüder find' ich nun in seinen Jüngern wieder.
long ago missed brothers find I now in His disciples again.
(long-missed brothers I now find again in His disciples.)

[This strophic song, much simpler than Schubert's setting of *Hymne I*, is graceful and appealing. Like the other "hymns" by Novalis (pen name of Friedrich Leopold Freiherr von Hardenberg) this is one of the poems published under the general title *Geistliche Lieder* (Spiritual Songs).]

ˈhʏmnə dra͜e
Hymne III
Hymn III

Posthumously published [composed 1819] (poem by Novalis, Friedrich von Hardenberg)

vɛn ˈ|alə ˈ|ʊntʰrɔ͜ø ˈveːɐ̯dən, zoː bla͜eb ɪç diːɐ̯ dɔx tʰrɔ͜ø;
Wenn alle untreu werden, so bleib' ich dir doch treu;
If all unfaithful become, then remain I to You nevertheless true;
(Though all others should become unfaithful, I shall nevertheless remain true to You,)

das ˈdaŋkʻbaːɐ̯kʰa͜etʻ |a͜of ˈ|eːɐ̯dən nɪçtʻ ˈ|a͜osgəʃtʻɔrbən za͜e.
dass Dankbarkeit auf Erden nicht ausgestorben sei.
that gratitude on earth not died out be.
(so that gratitude shall not have died out on earth.)

fyːɐ̯ mɪç |ʊmˈfɪŋ dɪç ˈla͜edən, fɛɐ̯ˈgɪŋstʻ fyːɐ̯ mɪç |ɪn ʃmɛrt͜s;
Für mich umfing dich Leiden, vergingst für mich in Schmerz;
For me enveloped You suffering, (You) died for me in pain;
(For my sake suffering enveloped You, You died in pain for me;)

drʊm geːb ɪç diːɐ̯ mɪtʻ ˈfrɔ͜ødən la͜of ˈleːvɪç ˈdiːzəs hɛrt͜s.
drum geb' ich dir mit Freuden auf ewig dieses Herz.
therefore give I to You with joys for ever this heart.
(therefore with joy I give You this heart for ever.)

ɔftʻ mʊs lɪç ˈbɪtʻɐ ˈva͜enən, das duː gəˈʃtʻɔrbən bɪstʻ,
Oft muss ich bitter weinen, dass du gestorben bist,
Often must I bitterly weep that You died have,
(Often I must weep bitterly to think that You have died,)

ʊntʻ ˈmançɐ fɔn den ˈda͜enən dɪç ˈleːbənslaŋ fɛɐ̯ˈgɪstʰ.
und mancher von den Deinen dich lebenslang vergisst.
and many a man of the Yours You lifelong forgets.
(and that many a man supposed to be a Christian has forgotten You through most of his life.)

fɔn ˈliːbə nuːɐ̯ dʊrçˈdrʊŋən hast duː zoː fiːl gəˈtʰaːn,
Von Liebe nur durchdrungen hast du so viel getan,
By love only permeated have You so much done,
(Permeated by love alone, You have done so much,)

ʊnt dɔx bɪst duː fɛɐ̯ˈkʰlʊŋən, lʊntʻ ˈkʰa͜enɐ dɛŋkʻt daˈran.
und doch bist du verklungen, und keiner denkt daran.
and yet have You faded away, and no one thinks about it. [*verklungen* refers to sounds]
(and yet the sound of Your voice has faded away, and no one thinks about what You have done.)

duː ʃtʻeːstʻ fɔl ˈtʰrɔ͜øɐ ˈliːbə nɔx ˈɪmɐ ˈjeːdəm ba͜e;
Du stehst voll treuer Liebe noch immer jedem bei;
You stand full of faithful love still always to everyone by;
(You still stand by everyone, always full of faithful love;)

ʊntʻ vɛn diːɐ̯ ˈkʰa͜enɐ ˈbliːbə, zoː bla͜epst duː ˈdɛnɔx tʰrɔ͜ø;
und wenn dir keiner bliebe, so bleibst du dennoch treu;
and if to You no one would remain, then remain You nevertheless faithful;
(and even if no one would remain true to You, You nevertheless remain faithful;)

di ˈtʰrɔ͜østʻə ˈliːbə ˈziːgətʻ, lam ˈlɛndə fyːltʻ man ziː,
die treuste Liebe sieget, am Ende fühlt man sie,
the most faithful love triumphs, in the end feels one it,
(that most faithful love will triumph: eventually one will feel it,)

va͜entʻ ˈbɪtʻɐlɪç lʊntʻ ˈʃmiːgətʻ zɪç ˈkʰɪntʻlɪç lan da͜en kʰniː.
weint bitterlich und schmieget sich kindlich an dein Knie.
weeps bitterly and nestles oneself childlike against Your knee.
(one will weep bitterly, and nestle against Your knee like a child.)

ɪç ˈhaːbə dɪç lɛmˈp͜fʊndən, loː, ˈlasə nɪçtʻ fɔn miːɐ̯!
Ich habe dich empfunden, o, lasse nicht von mir!
I have You felt, oh, leave not from me!
(I have felt Your presence; oh, do not forsake me!)

las ˈlɪnɪç mɪç fɛɐ̯ˈbʊndən la͜of ˈleːvɪç za͜en mɪt diːɐ̯.
Lass innig mich verbunden auf ewig sein mit dir.
Let intimately me bound for ever be with You.
(Let me be intimately bound to You for ever.)

a͜enst‘ ˈʃa͜oən ˈma͜enə ˈbryːdɐ(r) la͜ox ˈviːdɐ ˈhɪməlvɛrt͜s,
Einst schauen meine Brüder auch wieder himmelwärts,
One day look my brothers too again heavenwards,
(One day my brothers too will again look up toward heaven,)

ʊnt‘ ˈzɪŋk‘ən ˈliːbənt‘ ˈniːdɐ(r), lʊnt‘ ˈfalən diːɐ̯/diːr lans hɛrt͜s.
und sinken liebend nieder, und fallen dir ans Herz.
and sink lovingly down, and fall to You upon the heart.
(and will sink down lovingly, and will fall upon Your heart.)

[This hymn is musically similar to *Hymne II*. Christ is here addressed directly.]

ˈhʏmnə fiːɐ̯
Hymne IV
Hymn IV

Posthumously published [composed 1819] (poem by Novalis, Friedrich von Hardenberg)

ɪç zaːg ɛs ˈjeːdəm, das leːɐ̯ leːp‘t‘ lʊnt‘ ˈla͜oflɛɐ̯ʃt‘andən lɪstʰ,
Ich sag' es jedem, dass er lebt und auferstanden ist,
I tell it to everyone, that He lives and risen is,
(I tell it to everyone, that He lives and is risen,)

das leːɐ̯/leːr lɪn ˈlʊnzrɐ ˈmɪt‘ə ʃveːp‘t‘ lʊnt‘ ˈleːvɪç ba͜e lʊns lɪstʰ.
dass er in unsrer Mitte schwebt und ewig bei uns ist.
that He in our midst hovers and eternally with us is.
(that He hovers in our midst and is eternally with us.)

ɪç zaːg ɛs ˈjeːdəm, ˈjeːdɐ zaːk‘t‘ lɛs ˈza͜enən ˈfrɔ͜ødən gla͜eç,
Ich sag' es jedem, jeder sagt es seinen Freunden gleich,
I tell it to everyone, each one tells it to his friends right away,

das balt‘ lan ˈlalən ˈlɔrt‘ən tʰaːk‘t das ˈnɔ͜ø͜ə ˈhɪməlra͜eç.
dass bald an allen Orten tagt das neue Himmelreich.
that soon in all places dawns the new kingdom of heaven.
(that the new kingdom of heaven will soon be dawning everywhere.)

jɛt͜st‘ ʃa͜ent di vɛlt dem ˈnɔ͜øən zɪn leːɐ̯st‘ viː la͜en ˈfaːt‘ɐlant‘;
Jetzt scheint die Welt dem neuen Sinn erst wie ein Vaterland;
Now appears the world to the new sense first like a fatherland;
(Now for the first time the world appears to our new consciousness like a true homeland;)

a͜en ˈnɔ͜øəs ˈleːbən nɪmt‘ man hɪn lɛntˈt͜sʏk‘t‘ la͜os ˈza͜enɐ hant‘.
ein neues Leben nimmt man hin entzückt aus seiner Hand.
a new life accepts one ... enraptured from His hand. [*hinnehmen* = to accept]
(enraptured, we receive from His hand a new life.)

hɪˈnʊnt‘ɐ(r) lɪn das ˈtʰiːfə meːɐ̯ fɛɐ̯ˈzaŋk‘ dɛs ˈtʰoːdəs gra͜on,
Hinunter in das tiefe Meer versank des Todes Graun,
Downwards into the deep sea sank the death's horror,
(The horror of death has sunk down into the deep sea,)

ʊnt‘ 'je:dɐ kʰan nu:n la͜eçt‘ |ʊnt‘ he:ɐ̯/he:r |ɪn 'za͜enə 't͜su:k‘ʊnft‘ ʃa͜on.
und jeder kann nun leicht und hehr in seine Zukunft schaun.
and everyone can now light and exalted into his future look.
(and everyone can now look into the future with a light and exalted heart.)

de:ɐ̯ 'dʊŋk‘lə ve:k‘, de:n le:ɐ̯ bə'tʰra:t‘, ge:t‘ |ɪn den 'hɪməl |a͜os,
Der dunkle Weg, den er betrat, geht in den Himmel aus,
The dark path, that He trod, comes to an end in the heaven ... ,
(The dark path that He trod comes to an end in heaven,) [*ausgehen* (here) = to come to an end]

ʊnt‘ ve:ɐ̯ nu:ɐ̯ hø:ɐ̯t‘ |a͜of 'za͜enən ra:t‘, kʰɔmt‘ |a͜ox |ɪn 'fa:t‘ɐs ha͜os.
und wer nur hört auf seinen Rat, kommt auch in Vaters Haus.
and whoever just listens to His counsel, comes also into Father's house.
(and whoever will just listen to His counsel will also come into the Father's house.)

nu:n va͜ent‘ |a͜ox 'kʰa͜enɐ me:ɐ̯/me:r |al'hi:, vɛn |a͜ens di '|a͜ogən ʃli:st‘,
Nun weint auch keiner mehr allhie, wenn Eins die Augen schliesst,
Now weeps also no one more here (on earth), when one the eyes closes,
(Now no one here on earth need weep any more when someone closes his or her eyes in death,)

fɔm 'vi:dɐze:n, ʃp‘ɛ:t‘ 'lo:dɐ fry:, vɪrt 'di:zɐ ʃmɛrt͜s fɛɐ̯'zy:stʰ.
vom Wiedersehn, spät oder früh, wird dieser Schmerz versüsst.
by the reunion, late or early, will be this pain sweetened.
(sooner or later the pain of loss will be sweetened by the reunion.)

ɛs kʰan t͜su: 'je:dɐ 'gu:t‘ən tʰa:t‘ la͜en 'je:dɐ 'frɪʃɐ gly:n,
Es kann zu jeder guten Tat ein jeder frischer glühn,
There can at every good deed an everyone more freshly glow,
(At every good deed every doer can glow with greater freshness,)

dɛn 'hɛrlɪç vɪrt‘ |i:m 'di:zə za:t‘ |ɪn 'ʃø:nɐn 'flu:rən bly:n.
denn herrlich wird ihm diese Saat in schönern Fluren blühn.
for gloriously will for him this seed in more beautiful meadows bloom.
(for the seed he plants will bloom for him gloriously in more beautiful meadows.)

e:ɐ̯ le:p‘t‘, |ʊnt‘ vɪrt‘ nu:n ba͜e |ʊns za͜en, vɛn '|aləs |ʊns fɛɐ̯'lɛstʰ!
Er lebt, und wird nun bei uns sein, wenn alles uns verlässt!
He lives, and will now with us be, when all (else) us forsakes!
(He lives and will now be with us, even when all else forsakes us!)

ʊnt‘ zo: zɔl 'di:zɐ tʰa:k‘ |ʊns za͜en |a͜en 'vɛlt‘fɛɐ̯jʏŋʊŋsfɛstʰ.
Und so soll dieser Tag uns sein ein Weltverjüngungsfest.
And thus shall this day for us be a world-regeneration-celebration.
(And thus this day shall be for us a celebration of the regeneration of the world.)

[The ecstatic words of the poet inspired Schubert only moderately—to a graceful strophic song.]

Hymne an die Jungfrau see *Ave Maria*

ˈiːdəns ˈnaxtˈgəzaŋ / ˈiːdas ˈnaxtˈgəzaŋ
Idens Nachtgesang / Ida's Nachtgesang
Ida's Song to the Night

Posthumously published [composed 1815] (poem by Ludwig Kosegarten)

fɛɐ̯ˈnɪm lɛs, naxtʻ, vas ˈliːda diːɐ̯ fɛɐ̯ˈtʰrɑ͜oətʻ, diː, zat dɛs tʰaːks,
Vernimm es, Nacht, was Ida dir vertrauet, die, satt des Tags,
Hear it, night, what Ida to you confides, who, satiated (with) the day,
(Hear, night, what Ida is confiding to you, she who, satiated with the day,)

lɪn ˈda͜enə ˈlarmə fliːtʰ. liːɐ̯ ˈʃtɛrnə, diː liːɐ̯ hɔltʻ lʊntʻ ˈliːbəntʻ lɑ͜of mɪç ˈʃɑ͜oətʻ,
in deine Arme flieht. Ihr Sterne, die ihr hold und liebend auf mich schauet,
into your arms flees. You stars, which you graciously and lovingly on me look,
(flees into your arms. You stars, you who graciously and lovingly look down at me,)

fɛɐ̯ˈneːmtʻ zyːs ˈlɑ͜oʃəntʻ ˈliːdəns liːtʻ. deːn lɪç gəˈlaːntʻ lɪn ˈliːbəfɔlən ˈʃtʻʊndən,
vernehmt süss lauschend Idens Lied. Den ich geahnt in liebevollen Stunden,
hear sweetly listening Ida's song. Him whom I surmised in love-full hours,
(listen sweetly to Ida's song. The man whom I imagined in love-filled hours,)
[*Peters:* **Ida's** (ˈliːdas) **Lied**]
[*poem:* **in heil'gen Weihestunden** (ˈha͜elgən ˈva͜eəʃtʻʊndən, holy consecrated hours)]

deːm ˈzeːnzʊxt͡skʰraŋkʻ ma͜en hɛrt͡s lɛntˈgeːgən ʃluːkʻ, loː naxtʻ, loː ˈʃtʻɛrnə, høːɐ̯t͡s,
dem sehnsuchtskrank mein Herz entgegen schlug, o Nacht, o Sterne, hört's,
whom sick with longing my heart towards beat, O night, O stars, hear it,
(for whom my heart, sick with longing, was beating, O night, O stars, hear it,)
[*Peters:* **sehnsuchtsvoll** (ˈzeːnzʊxt͡sfɔl, full of longing)]

ɪç ˈhaːbə liːn gəˈfʊndən, dɛs bɪltʻ lɪç lɛŋstʻ lɪm ˈbuːzən tʰruːkʻ. [ˈlɪnɐn]
ich habe ihn gefunden, dess Bild ich längst im Busen trug. [*poem:* **im Innern**]
I have him found, whose image I long in the bosom carried. [inner self]
(I have found him, the man whose image I have long carried in my bosom.)

ʊm ˈza͜enə ˈviːgə ˈlɛçəltʻən di ˈmuːzən, luˈraːnɪ̯a kʰoːstʻ liːm
Um seine Wiege lächelten die Musen, Urania kos't' ihm
Around his cradle smiled the Muses, Urania caressed him
(The Muses smiled around his cradle, Urania caressed him)

ɑ͜of dem ˈkʰɔ͜øʃən ʃoːs, di ˈʃøːnha͜et ˈtʰrɛŋkʻətʻ liːn lan ˈliːrəm ˈnɛkʻtʻar-ˈbuːzən,
auf dem keuschen Schoss, die Schönheit tränket' ihn an ihrem Nektar- Busen,
on the chaste lap, the beauty gave drink to him at her nectar- bosom,
(on her chaste lap, Beauty suckled him at her nectar-breasts,)

ʊntʻ ˈjeːdə ˈçaːrɪs/çarɪs t͡soːkʻ liːn groːs. lɪn ˈza͜enən ˈlɑ͜ogən blɪt͡stʻ pʰroˈmeːtʻɪʃ ˈfɔ͜øɐ.
und jede Charis zog ihn gross. In seinen Augen blitzt promethisch Feuer.
and each Grace brought him up. In his eyes flashes Prometheanly fire.
(and the Three Graces brought him up. The fire of Prometheus flashes in his eyes.)
[*grossziehen* = to bring up, to rear (children)]

gəˈrɛçtʻ lɛntʻˈbrɛntʻ za͜en hɛrt͡s lɪn liːpʻ lʊnt t͡sɔrn.
Gerecht entbrennt sein Herz in Lieb' und Zorn.
Justly takes fire his heart in love and anger.
(His heart is justly on fire with love or anger.)

ɛs lʏp͡ft dem ˈʃmaxtʼəndən di ˈvaːɐ̯hae̯tʼ ˈliːrən ˈʃlae̯ɐ;
Es lüpft dem Schmachtenden die Wahrheit ihren Schleier;
There lifts for the languishing one the truth her veil;
(Truth lifts her veil for him who yearns for truth;)

iːm ˈʃpʼruːdəltʼ ˈføːbʊs ˈhae̯lgɐ bɔrn. frɔ͡ʏnt, duː bɪstʼ mae̯n,
ihm sprudelt Phöbus' heil'ger Born. Freund, du bist mein,
for him bubbles up Phoebus's sacred spring. Friend, you are mine,
(for him the Castalian Spring, sacred to Phoebus, bubbles up. Friend, you are mine,)
[*poem:* **Phöbos** (føːbɔs) **goldner** (ˈgɔldnɐ, golden) **Born]**

nɪçtʼ fyːɐ̯ di ˈkʰʊrt͡sə ˈrae̯zə, diː dʊrç das labyˈrɪnt dɛs ˈleːbəns fyːɐ̯tʰ;
nicht für die kurze Reise, die durch das Labyrinth des Lebens führt;
not for the short journey, that through the labyrinth of the life leads;
(not for the short journey that leads through life's labyrinth;)

ziː, ziː di ˈsfɛːrən dɔrt, di ˈleːvɪç ˈʃøːnən ˈkʰrae̯zə,
sieh, sieh die Sphären dort, die ewig schönen Kreise,
see, see the spheres there, the eternally beautiful circles,
(see, see those spheres up there, the eternally beautiful circling stars,)
[*poem:* **Siehst du** (ziːst duː, do you see) **die Sphären dort...?]**

voː ˈfɛstʼɐ(r) ˈʊnzɐ bantʼ zɪç ʃnyːɐ̯tʰ. frɔ͡ʏntʼ, lɪç bɪn dae̯n,
wo fester unser Band sich schnürt. Freund, ich bin dein,
where more firmly our bond itself ties. Friend, I am yours,
(where our bond will be tied more firmly. Friend, I am yours,)

nɪçtʼ fyːɐ̯ den zant deːɐ̯ ˈt͡sae̯tʼən, deːɐ̯ ˈʃnɛlfɛɐ̯ˌziːgəntʼ ˈkʰroːnɔs luːɐ̯/luːr lɛntʼˈflɔ͡ʏstʰ,
nicht für den Sand der Zeiten, der schnellversiegend Chronos' Uhr entfleusst,
not for the sand of the times, that quickly running out Chronus' hourglass flows out of,
(not for the sand of time that quickly runs out as it flows through Chronus's hourglass,)

dae̯n fyːɐ̯ den ˈriːzənʃtʼroːm ˈhae̯lfɔlɐ(r) ˈleːvɪçkʰae̯tʼən,
dein für den Riesenstrom heilvoller Ewigkeiten,
yours for the gigantic stream of salvation-full eternities,
(I am yours for the colossal stream of eternities, flowing with salvation,)

deːɐ̯/deːr la͡os dɛs ˈleːvgən ˈʊrnə ʃɔ͡ʏstʰ.
der aus des Ew'gen Urne scheusst.
which from the Eternal One's urn shoots.
(that gushes forth from the urn of the Eternal One.)

[The original title of the poem is *Agnes Nachtgesang*, and wherever the lady's name is mentioned it is as Agnes. Schubert changed the name for reasons of his own. In the Peters edition, the first to have been published, the opening chord is given as D minor, whereas the original manuscript has a B flat major chord, as in the *Gesamtausgabe*. There are some differences in dynamics, and in the punctuation of the text, besides the variant indicated in brackets above. The name Urania can refer to the Muse of astronomy or to Aphrodite, goddess of love (but "her chaste lap" suggests that the former is intended). The Titan Prometheus stole the fire of the gods and gave it to mankind. The Castalian Spring on Mount Parnassus was sacred to Phoebus Apollo and the Muses and has come to symbolize the source of artistic inspiration.]

'iːdəns 'ʃvaːnənliːt'

Idens Schwanenlied

Ida's Swan Song

Posthumously published [composed 1815] (poem by Ludwig Kosegarten)

viː ʃa͡ost duː la͡os dem 'neːbəlfloːɐ̯, loː 'zɔnə, bla͡eç lʊnt' 'myːdə!
Wie schaust du aus dem Nebelflor, o Sonne, bleich und müde!
How look you out of the mist- crêpe, O sun, pale and weary!
(How pale and weary you look through your veil of mist, O sun!)

ɛs ʃvɪrt deːɐ̯ 'ha͡emçən 'ha͡ezrɐ kʰoːɐ̯ t͡suː 'ma͡enəm 'ʃvaːnənliːdə.
Es schwirrt der Heimchen heis'rer Chor zu meinem Schwanenliede.
There chirps the crickets' hoarse chorus to my swan song.
(A hoarse chorus of crickets is chirping an accompaniment to my swan song.)

ɛs gɪrt di 'ʃa͡edəndə na'tʰuːɐ̯/na'tʰuːr liːɐ̯ 'leːbəvoːl zoː 'tʰra͡orɪç;
Es girrt die scheidende Natur ihr Lebewohl so traurig;
There coos the departing nature her farewell so sadly;
(Departing Nature coos her farewell so sadly;)

ɛs 'ʃt'eːən bʊʃ lʊnt' valt' lʊnt' fluːɐ̯ zoː 'tʰroːst'loːs lʊnt' zoː 'ʃa͡orɪç.
es stehen Busch und Wald und Flur so trostlos und so schaurig.
there stand bush and forest and field so desolate and so ghastly.
(Bush and forest and field look so desolate and so ghastly.)

ɛnt''blɛt'ɐt' ʃt'eːt deːɐ̯/deːr 'lɛrlənha͡en, lɛnt''la͡op't deːɐ̯ 'tʰra͡ot'ə 'gart'ən,
Entblättert steht der Erlenhain, entlaubt der traute Garten,
Leafless stands the alder grove, stripped of foliage the beloved garden,
[*poem:* **der graue** ('gra͡oə, grey) **Garten**]

voː leːɐ̯/leːr lʊnt' lɪç lɪm 'moːndənʃa͡en la͡e'nandɐ baŋ lɛɐ̯'hart'ən;
wo er und ich im Mondenschein einander bang' erharrten;
where he and I in the moonlight one another anxiously awaited;
(where he and I used to wait for each other anxiously in the moonlight;)

voː leːɐ̯/leːr lʊnt' lɪç lɪm 'moːndənblɪt͡s lɪm ʃirm deːɐ̯ 'lɪndən 'zaːsən,
wo er und ich im Mondenblitz im Schirm der Linden sassen,
where he and I in the moon- flash in the shelter of the linden trees sat,
(where he and I sat in the shelter of the linden trees as moonlight flashed through the foliage,)
[*poem:* **der Linde** ('lɪndə, linden tree—singular)]

ʊnt' la͡of dɛs 'raːzəns 'va͡eçəm zɪt͡s deːɐ̯/deːr 'løːdən vɛlt' fɛɐ̯'gaːsən;
und auf des Rasens weichem Sitz der öden Welt vergassen;
and on the lawn's soft seat the dreary world forgot;
(and on the soft seat of the lawn we forgot the dreary world;)

voː lɪç, gə'leːnt' lan 'za͡enə brʊst', lɪn 'zyːsə 'tʰrɔ͡ømə 'nɪk't'ə,
wo ich, gelehnt an seine Brust, in süsse Träume nickte,
where I, leaned against his breast, into sweet dreams nodded,
(where I, leaning against his chest, dozed into sweet dreams,)

ʊnt‘ ˈhɔldɐ vaːn ʊnt‘ ˈleːdəns lʊst di ˈtʰrɔ͡ømɛndə dʊrçˈt͡sʏk‘t‘ə.
und holder Wahn und Edens Lust die Träumende durchzückte.
and lovely illusion and Eden's pleasure the dreamer through-seized.
(and lovely illusion and Eden's pleasure thoroughly gripped the dreamer.)

ʊnt‘ ˈʃɪmɐt‘ə dɛs ˈa͡ʊfgaŋs glant͡s dʊrç di fɛɐ̯ˈʃviːgnən ˈlɪndən,
Und schimmerte des Aufgangs Glanz durch die verschwieg'nen Linden,
And shimmered the sunrise's splendor through the discreetly silent linden trees,
(And as the splendor of the sunrise shimmered through the discreetly silent linden trees,)

p͡fleːk‘t‘ ɪç den ˈʃøːnst‘ən ˈroːzənkʰrant͡s iːm ʊm den huːt t͡suː ˈvɪndən.
pflegt' ich den schönsten Rosenkranz ihm um den Hut zu winden.
used I the most beautiful rose- garland for him around the hat to wind.
(I used to wind the most beautiful garland of roses around his hat.)

dɔx, ˈkʰa͡enə ˈkʰrɛnt͡sə vɪrt‘ hɪnˈfɔrt da͡en ˈmɛːt‘çən, frɔ͡ønt, diːɐ̯ ˈvɪndən.
Doch, keine Kränze wird hinfort dein Mädchen, Freund, dir winden.
But, no garlands will henceforth your girl, friend, for you twine.
(But henceforth, my friend, your girl will not be able to twine any garlands for you.)

dɛn ˈʊnzrə ˈbluːmən zɪnt‘ fɛɐ̯ˈdɔrt‘, ɛnt‘ˈla͡ʊp‘t‘ zɪnt‘ ˈʊnzrə ˈlɪndən.
Denn unsre Blumen sind verdorrt, entlaubt sind unsre Linden.
For our flowers are withered, leafless are our linden trees.

iːɐ̯ ˈroːzən, diː deːɐ̯ ˈra͡ʊə ɔst‘ ɪn ˈiːrəm ˈkʰnɔsp‘ən ˈp͡flʏk‘t‘ə;
Ihr Rosen, die der rauhe Ost in ihrem Knospen pflückte;
You roses, which the harsh east wind in their budding plucked;
(You roses, which the harsh east wind plucked in the bud;)
[*poem:* **in ihren** (ˈiːrən, their) **Knospen** (buds)]

iːɐ̯ ˈnɛlk‘ən, diː deːɐ̯ ˈfryːə frɔst‘ ˈhalp‘ˌa͡ʊfgəʃlɔsən ˈkʰnɪk‘t‘ə;
ihr Nelken, die der frühe Frost halbaufgeschlossen knickte;
you carnations, which the early frost half-opened bent;
(you carnations, which the early frost bent and broke when you had only half opened;)

ɪst‘ ˈɔ͡øɐ loːs nɪçt‘ a͡ʊx ma͡en loːs? za͡et‘ iːɐ̯ nɪçt‘, vas ɪç ˈveːɐ̯də?
ist euer Los nicht auch mein Los? Seid ihr nicht, was ich werde?
is your lot not also my lot? Are you not what I am becoming?

ɛnt‘ˈkʰa͡emt‘ ɪç nɪçt‘, viː iːɐ̯, dem ʃoːs deːɐ̯ ˈmʏt‘ɐlɪçən ˈeːɐ̯də?
Entkeimt' ich nicht, wie ihr, dem Schoss der mütterlichen Erde?
Sprouted I not, like you, from the womb of the motherly earth?
(Did I not, like you, sprout from the womb of our mother the earth?)

ɪst‘ nɪçt‘ ma͡en halm zoː ˈjuːgənt‘lɪç, zoː ʃlaŋk‘ ɛmˈpʰoːɐ̯ gəˈʃɔsən?
Ist nicht mein Halm so jugendlich, so schlank empor geschossen?
Has not my stem as youthful, as slender upwards shot?
(Has not my stem shot up as youthful and slender as yours?)

hat‘ ˈma͡enɐ ˈblyːt‘ən ˈkʰnɔsp‘ə zɪç nɪçt ˈdrɛŋənt‘ ˈa͡ʊfgəʃlɔsən?
Hat meiner Blüten Knospe sich nicht drängend aufgeschlossen?
Has my blossoms' bud itself not hurriedly opened?
(Has the bud of my blossoms not hurried to open?)

vɛk'tʻ 'ma͜enɐ(r) 'la͜ogən 'bla͜oəs lɪçt, di 'ro:zən 'ma͜enɐ 'vaŋən,
Weckt meiner Augen blaues Licht, die Rose meiner Wangen,
Wakes my eyes' blue light, the rose of my cheeks,
(Does the blue light of my eyes, the rose of my cheek,)

di 'frɪʃə 'ma͜enɐ 'lɪp'ən nɪçt de:ɐ̯ 'jʏŋlɪŋə fɛɐ̯'laŋən?
die Frische meiner Lippen nicht der Jünglinge Verlangen?
the freshness of my lips not the youths' desire?
(or the freshness of my lips not awaken young men's desire?)

ax, kʰla:k'tʻ lʊm 'lɔ͜ørə 'ʃvɛst'ɐ, kʰla:k'tʻ, li:ɐ̯ 'ro:zən lʊnt' li:ɐ̯ 'nɛlk'ən!
Ach, klagt um eure Schwester, klagt, ihr Rosen und ihr Nelken!
Ah, lament for your sister, lament, you roses and you carnations!

vi: balt', lʊnt' hɪn lɪst' 'ma͜enə pʰraxt', lʊnt' 'ma͜enə 'bly:t'ən 'vɛlk'ən!
Wie bald, und hin ist meine Pracht, und meine Blüten welken!
How soon, and gone is my splendor, and my blossoms wither!

fɛɐ̯'ʃt'rɔ͜øt' lɪst' lal ma͜en 'gry:nəs la͜op', gə'kʰnɪk'tʻ ma͜en 'ʃlaŋk'ɐ 'ʃt'ɛŋəl,
Verstreut ist all mein grünes Laub, geknickt mein schlanker Stengel,
Dispersed is all my green foliage, bent my slender stem,

ma͜en ʃt'a͜op' gə'bɛt'ət' lɪn den ʃt'a͜op', ma͜en ga͜est' gə'ra͜eft t͜sʊm 'lɛŋəl!
mein Staub gebettet in den Staub, mein Geist gereift zum Engel!
my dust (is) bedded into the dust, my spirit matured to the angel!
(my dust bedded into the dust, my spirit matured into the angelic state!)

de:ɐ̯ 'vandrɐ, de:ɐ̯/de:r lɪn 'ma͜enɐ t͜si:ɐ̯/t͜si:r, lɪn 'ma͜enɐ 'ʃø:nha͜et' 'ʃɪmɐ mɪç 'ʃa͜ot'ə,
Der Wandrer, der in meiner Zier, in meiner Schönheit Schimmer mich schaute,
The wanderer, who in my finery, in my beauty's shimmer me saw,
(The wanderer who saw me in my glory, in the shimmer of my beauty,)

kʰɔmt' lʊnt' fɔrʃt' na:x mi:ɐ̯/mi:r, lʊnt' zi:t' mɪç 'nɪmɐ, 'nɪmɐ!
kommt und forscht nach mir, und sieht mich nimmer, nimmer!
comes and searches after me, and sees me never, never!
(will come and look for me, and never, never see me!)

ɛs kʰɔmt de:ɐ̯ 'tʰra͜ot'ə, de:n lɪç mi:ɐ̯/mi:r lɛɐ̯'kʰo:rən 'la͜ent͜sɪç 'ha:bə. —
Es kommt der Traute, den ich mir erkoren einzig habe. —
There comes the dear one, whom I for me chosen uniquely have. —
(My dear one will come, he whom I have uniquely chosen for myself. —)

ax, flɔ͜øç, gə'li:p't'ɐ, flɔ͜øç fɔn hi:ɐ̯; da͜en 'mɛ:t'çən ʃlɛ:ft' lɪm 'gra:bə.
Ach, fleuch, Geliebter, fleuch von hier; dein Mädchen schläft im Grabe.
Ah, fly, beloved, fly from here; your girl sleeps in the grave.
['zy:sɐ frɔ͜ønt'] [ʃnɛl]
[*poem:* **Fleuch, süsser Freund, fleuch schnell von hier!**]
[sweet friend] [quickly]

ax, 'tʰra͜orə, 'tʰɔ͜ørɐ, 'tʰra͜orə nɪçtʰ! dɛs 'gra:bəs 'dʊŋk'əl 'ʃvɪndət',
Ach, traure, Teurer, traure nicht! Des Grabes Dunkel schwindet,
Ah, grieve, dear one, grieve not! The grave's darkness disappears,
(Ah, do not grieve, dearest! The darkness of the grave will disappear,)
[*poem:* **Doch** (dɔx, but) **traure, Trauter** ('tʰra͜ot'ɐ, dear one)**, traure nicht!**]

ʊnt' 'hɪmlɪʃ lʊnt' lʊn'ʃt'ɛrp'lɪç lɪçt' glɛntst de:m, de:ɐ̯/de:r ly:bɐ'vɪndətʰ.
und himmlisch und unsterblich Licht glänzt dem, der überwindet.
and celestial and immortal light shines upon him who overcomes.

tʰri'ʊmf! lɑɔf 'hɛrpst'əsdɛmərʊŋ fɔlk't' 'mɪldɐ 'fry:lɪŋsʃɪmɐ.
Triumph! auf Herbstesdämmerung folgt milder Frühlingsschimmer.
Triumph! Upon autumn- twilight follows gentle spring- shimmer.
(Triumph! After the twilight of autumn comes the gentle shimmer of spring.)
[na:x] [ʃp'ri:st']
[*poem:* **Triumph! Nach Herbstesdämmerung spriesst milder Frühlingsschimmer]**
[After] [sprouts]

ɑɔf 'tʰrɛnʊŋ fɔlk't' fɛɐ̯'laenɪgʊŋ, fɛɐ̯'laenɪgʊŋ lɑɔf 'ɪmɐ!
Auf Trennung folgt Vereinigung, Vereinigung auf immer!
Upon separation follows union, union for ever!
(After separation will come reunion, we shall be united forever!)

[This is one of the seven Kosegarten poems that Schubert set in a single day, on October 19th, 1815, after having already struggled through *Hektors Abschied* by Schiller on the same day. Of course, he only needed to set one of the seventeen verses to create a strophic song. It is the song of a dying woman whose beauty has faded like that of the leafless garden outside her room. She sees herself as already dead and longs only for an eternal reunion with her lover beyond death.]

Ihr Bild see *Schwanengesang*

i:ɐ̯ gra:p'
Ihr Grab
Her Grave

Posthumously published [composed 1822?] (poem by Karl August Engelhardt)

dɔrt' lɪst' li:ɐ̯ gra:p', di: laenst' lɪm ʃmɛlts de:ɐ̯ 'ju:gənt' 'gly:t'ə, ['bly:t'ə]
Dort ist ihr Grab, die einst im Schmelz der Jugend glühte, [*Peters:* blühte]
There is her grave, she who once in the luster of the youth glowed. [bloomed]
(There is her grave—she who once glowed with the luster of youth,)

dɔrt' fi:l zi:, dɔrt, di 'ʃø:nst'ə 'bly:t'ə, fɔm bɑɔm dɛs 'le:bəns lap'.
dort fiel sie, dort, die schönste Blüte, vom Baum des Lebens ab.
there fell she, there, the loveliest blossom, from the tree of the life down.
(there she fell, there, the loveliest blossom, from the tree of life.)

dɔrt' lɪst' li:ɐ̯ gra:p', dɔrt' ʃlɛ:ft' zi' 'ʊnt'ɐ 'je:nɐ 'lɪndə;
Dort ist ihr Grab, dort schläft sie unter jener Linde;
There is her grave, there sleeps she under those linden trees;
(There is her grave, there she sleeps under those linden trees;)

ax, 'nɪmɐ(r) lɪç li:n 'vi:dɐ 'fɪndə, den tʰro:st, de:n zi: mi:ɐ̯ ga:p'.
ach, nimmer ich ihn wieder finde, den Trost, den sie mir gab.
ah, never I it again find, the consolation that she to me gave.
(ah, never will I find it again, the consolation that she gave to me.)

dɔrtʻ lɪstʻ liːɐ̯ graːpʻ, fɔm ˈhɪməl kʰaːm ziː,
Dort ist ihr Grab, vom Himmel kam sie,
There is her grave, from the heaven came she,
(There is her grave; she came from heaven)

das di ˈleːɐ̯də miːɐ̯ ˈglʏkʻlɪçən t͡sʊm ˈhɪməl ˈveːɐ̯də,
dass die Erde mir Glücklichen zum Himmel werde,
that the earth for me happy one to the heaven might become,
(so that the earth might become heaven for me, happy man;)

ʊnt dɔrtʻ ʃtʻiːkʻ ziː hɪˈnapʻ. dɔrtʻ lɪstʻ liːɐ̯ graːpʻ,
und dort stieg sie hinab. Dort ist ihr Grab,
and there descended she .... There is her grave, [*hinabsteigen* = to descend]
(and there, *there*, she descended into the earth. There is her grave,)

ʊnt dɔrtʻ lɪn ˈjeːnən ˈʃtʻɪlən ˈhalən, ba͜e liːɐ̯,
und dort in jenen stillen Hallen, bei ihr,
and there in those quiet halls, beside her,
(and there in those quiet vaults, by her side,)

las lɪç mɪtʻ ˈfrɔ͜ødən ˈfalən la͜ox ˈma͜enən ˈpʰɪlgɐʃtʻaːpʻ.
lass ich mit Freuden fallen auch meinen Pilgerstab.
let I with joys fall also my pilgrim's staff.
(I too shall joyfully lay down my pilgrim's staff.)

[The poet chose the pen name Richard Roos. Schubert's setting is touching and deeply felt.]

il ˈmɔːdo di ˈprɛnder ˈmoʎːʎe / di lart ˈla͜en va͜epʻ t͡suː ˈneːmən
Il modo di prender moglie / Die Art ein Weib zu nehmen
The Way to Choose a Wife

Opus 83, No. 3 [1827] (author unknown, attributed to Metastasio in error)

Italian original:

or su! non t͡ʃi penˈsjaːmo, koˈradːd͡ʒo‿e konkluˈdjaːmo,
Or sù! non ci pensiamo, coraggio e concludiamo, [*GA:* **corraggio** (not standard Ital.)]
Now up! not of it let's think, courage and let us conclude,
(Come on! Let's not think about it! Courage, let's get it over with.)

al fiːn ˈsiːo ˈprɛndo ˈmoʎːʎe, sɔ bːbɛːn perˈke lo fo.
al fin s'io prendo moglie, sò ben perchè lo fò.
at end if I take wife, I know well why it I do.
(If in the end I take a wife, I know well why I am doing it.)

lo fɔ per paˈgaːr i ˈdebiti, la ˈprɛndo per konˈtanti,
Lo fò per pagar i debiti, la prendo per contanti,
It I do to pay the debts, her I take for cash,
(I do it to pay my debts, I take her for cash,)

di ˈdirlo e di riˈpɛːterlo difːfikolˈta non‿ɔ.
di dirlo e di ripeterlo difficoltà non ho. [*GA:* **repeterlo** (not standard Italian)]
to say it and to repeat it difficulty not I have.
(I have no difficulty in saying so and in repeating it.)

fra 'tːtanti 'mɔːdi‿e 'tːtanti di 'prɛnder 'moʎːʎe al 'mondo,
Fra tanti modi e tanti di prender moglie al mondo,
Among so many ways and so many to take wife in the world,
(Among so many, many ways to take a wife in this world,)

un 'mɔːdo pju ʤo'kondo del 'miːo tro'vaːr non sɔ.
un modo più giocondo del mio trovar non sò.
a way more happy than mine to find not I know how.
(I cannot find a happier way than mine.)

si 'prɛnde per 'afːfɛtːto, si 'prɛnde per ri'spɛtːto,
Si prende per affetto, si prende per rispetto,
One takes for affection, one takes for respect,
(One marries out of affection, another out of respect,)

si 'prɛnde per kon'siʎːʎo, si 'prɛnde per pun'tiʎːʎo,
si prende per consiglio, si prende per puntiglio,
one takes for advice, one takes for point of honor,
(another because he was advised to, another as a point of honor,)

si 'prɛnde per ka'pritːʧo, ɛ 'veːro, si o nɔ?
si prende per capriccio, è vero, sì o nò?
one takes for whim, is (it) true, yes or no?
(another for a whim; is that true? Yes or no?)

ed 'iːo per medi'ʧiːna di 'tutːti‿i 'maːli 'mjɛːi
Ed io per medicina di tutti i mali miei
And I as medicine for all the ills of mine
(And I, as medicine for all my ills,)

un 'pɔko di spo'ziːna 'prɛndere non po'trɔ?
un poco di sposina prendere non potrò?
a bit of little wife to take not I shall be able?
(shall I not be able to take a little bit of wife?)

ɔ 'detːto‿el ri'diːco, lo fɔ per li kon'tanti,
Ho detto e'l ridico, lo fò per li contanti,
I have said and it I say again, it I do for the cash,
(I have said it and I say it again: I do it for the money;)

lo 'fanːno 'tanti e tːtanti, an'kiːo lo fa'rɔ.
lo fanno tanti e tanti, anch' io lo farò.
it do so many and so many, also I it shall do.
(so many, many do it for that reason; I too shall do it.)

German translation (translator unknown):

vo'lan! |ʊnt' 'loːnə 'tsaːgən, |ɪç mʊs |ɛs 'laenmaːl 'vaːgən,
Wohlan! und ohne Zagen, ich muss es einmal wagen,
Come on! and without hesitation, I must it once risk,
(Come on! And without hesitation I must risk it once,)

mʊs ʃnɛl laen vaep‘ lɛɐ̯'ja:gən, va'rʊm? das vaes lɪç ʃo:n.
muss schnell ein Weib erjagen, warum? das weiss ich schon.
must quickly a wife hunt for, why? that know I already.
(I must quickly hunt me a wife. Why? I know the reason, all right.)

ɪç tʰu:s, nu:n lɪç tʰu:s lɔp‘ dem 'gɛldə, das lɪsts, vas mi:ɐ̯ nɔx 'fe:lt‘ə,
Ich tu's, nun ich tu's ob dem Gelde, das ist's, was mir noch fehlte,
I do it, well, I do it for the money, that is it, that to me still was lacking,
(I shall do it, well, I shall do it for the money; that's what I am still lacking.)

ɪç za:k‘ lɛs 'lɪmɐ sɑ̃ fa'sõ, ja: sɑ̃ fa'sõ, gɛlt‘ lɪst‘ maen 'ʃutsp‘a,tʰro:n.
ich sag' es immer *sans façon*, ja *sans façon*, Geld ist mein Schutzpatron.
I say it always without ceremony, yes, without fuss, money is my patron saint.
(I say it without beating around the bush: money is my patron saint.)

fɔn lal den 'fa:dən 'lafən, di: na:x den 'vaebɐn 'gafən,
Von all den faden Laffen, die nach den Weibern gaffen,
Of all the insipid dandies who after the women gape,
(Among all the insipid dandies who gape after women,)

de:ɐ̯ 'kʰʊk‘ʊk‘ zɔl mɪç 'ʃt‘ra:fən, lɪst‘ laen 'je:dɐ(r) laen vɪçtʰ.
der Kuckuck soll mich strafen, ist ein jeder ein Wicht.
the cuckoo shall me punish, is an each a wretch or a rogue.
(—may the devil take me!—each one is a poor wretch or a rogue.)

de:ɐ̯ nɪmt‘ laen vaep‘ laos 'li:bə, de:ɐ̯/de:r 'landrə laos 'landrəm 'tʰri:bə,
Der nimmt ein Weib aus Liebe, der Andre aus and'rem Triebe,
This one takes a wife out of love, the other out of another instinct,
(This one takes a wife out of love, the other out of a different instinct,)

de:ɐ̯ vael mans li:m gə'ra:t‘ən, de:ɐ̯ 've:gən p‘atro'na:t‘ən,
der weil man's ihm geraten, der wegen Patronaten,
that one because one it to him (has) advised, that one on account of patronages,
(that one because someone advised him to, another one to curry favor,)

de:ɐ̯ vael zɪçs ʃo:n fɛɐ̯'ra:t‘ən, lɪsts 'lalzo? 'lo:dɐ nɪçtʰ?
der weil sich's schon verraten, ist's also? oder nicht?
that one because itself it already (has) betrayed, is it thus? or not?
(that one because something is already becoming obvious; is it so, or not?)

ʊnt‘ lɪç fy:ɐ̯/fy:r lal di 'ʃmɛrtsən,, lɪm 'bɔøt‘əl lʊnt‘ lɪm 'hɛrtsən,
Und ich für all die Schmerzen, im Beutel und im Herzen,
And I for all the pains in the wallet and in the heart,
(And I, for all the pain in my wallet and in my heart,)

zɔl nɪçt‘ laen 'bɪsçən 'vaep‘çən 'ne:mən lals medi'tsi:n?
soll nicht ein bisschen Weibchen nehmen als Medizin?
shall not a bit of little wife take as medicine?
(should I not take a little bit of wife as medicine?)

fy:ɐ̯ den 'bɔøt‘əl, fy:ɐ̯ maen hɛrts?
für den Beutel, für mein Herz?
For the wallet, for my heart?

ıç zaːk‘ lɛs lao̯t‘ lʊnt‘ ˈlɪmɐ, lıç tʰuː vas ˈmançə ˈtʰaːt‘ən,
Ich sag' es laut und immer, ich tu' was manche taten,
I say it loud and always, I do what many did,
(I say it aloud and again and again: I shall do what many have done:)

ıç ˈhae̯raːt di duˈkaːtən, das ˈvae̯p‘çən las lıç t͡siːn.
ich heirat' die Dukaten, das Weibchen lass ich zieh'n.
I marry the ducats, the little wife let I go.
(I shall marry the ducats; the little wife can do as she likes.)

[This is the third of three Italian songs that Schubert dedicated to the great bass, Luigi Lablache, whom he had met in Vienna. The other two poems are by Metastasio, as this was long assumed to be as well. Here Schubert makes a convincing foray into the style of Rossinian opera buffa.]

il tradiˈtor deˈluːzo / deːɐ̯ gəˈtʰɔø̯ʃt‘ə fɛɐ̯ˈrɛːt‘ɐ
Il traditor deluso / Der getäuschte Verräter
The Traitor Deceived

Op. 83, No. 2 [1827] (Pietro Metastasio)

Italian original:

aiˈmɛ. [kwal ˈfɔrt͡sa iˈɲːɲɔːta ˈaːnima ˈkwelːle ˈvoːt͡ʃi!]
Aimè, [qual forza ignota anima quelle voci!]
Alas, [what force unknown animates those voices!]
(Alas, [what unknown power animates those voices?]) [words in brackets omitted by Schubert]

ˈiːo ˈtrɛːmo! ˈiːo ˈsɛnto ˈtutːto‿inonˈdarmi‿il ˈseːno di ˈd͡ʒɛlido suˈdoːr!
io tremo! io sento tutto inondarmi il seno di gelido sudor!
I tremble! I feel all flood me the breast with cold sweat!
(I am trembling! I feel my breast all flooding over with cold sweat!)

ˈfugːga si — aː ˈkwale? kwal ɛ la ˈviːa? ki me laˈdːdiːta?
Fugga si — Ah quale? qual' è la via? Chi me l'addita?
Flee one — Ah which, which is the way? Who to me it shows?
(One should run away — ah, but which is the way? Who will show it to me?)

ɔ ˈdiːo! ke askolˈtaːi? ke maˈvːvenːne? ˈoːve son ˈiːo?
Oh Dio! Che ascoltai? Che m'avvenne? Ove son io?
Oh God! What did I overhear? What to me happened? Where am I?
(Oh God! What have I overheard? What has happened to me? Where am I?)

aː ˈlaːrja dinˈtorno lamˈpedːd͡ʒa, sfaˈvilːla; onˈdedːd͡ʒa, vaˈt͡ʃilːla linˈfiːdo teˈrːreːn!
Ah l'aria d'intorno lampeggia, sfavilla; ondeggia, vacilla l'infido terren!
Ah, the air all around flashes, flickers; undulates, sways the treacherous ground!
(Ah, the air all around flickers with lightning; the treacherous ground is quaking and swaying!)

kwal ˈnɔtːte proˈfonda doˈrːroːr mi t͡ʃirˈconda! ke ˈlːlarve fuˈnɛste,
Qual notte profonda d'orror mi circonda! Che larve funeste,
What night deep of horror me surrounds! What phantoms fatal,
(What deep night of horror surrounds me? What fatal phantoms,)

ke ˈzmaːnje son ˈkweste, ke ˈfːfjɛːro spaˈvɛnto mi ˈsɛnto nel seːn!
che smanie son queste, che fiero spavento mi sento nel sen!
what agitations are these, what fearful fright me I feel in the breast!
(what agitations are these? What fearful fright do I feel in my breast?)

German translation (translator unknown):

veː miːɐ̯, lɪç ˈbeːbə! lɪç fyːl ɛs, ˈvɪldɐ fɛɐ̯ˈt͜svaɛ̯flʊŋ ˈʃa͜oɐ
Weh mir, ich bebe! Ich fühl' es, wilder Verzweiflung Schauer
Woe to me, I tremble! I feel it, wild desperation's shudder
(Woe is me, I tremble! I feel a shudder of desperation)

lɛɐ̯ˈʃtʻarətʻ ˈma͜enə brʊstʰ! fɔrtʻ fɔn hiːɐ̯ — dɔx, voˈhɪn nuːn?
erstarret meine Brust! Fort von hier — Doch, wohin nun?
benumbs my breast! Away from here — but, whither now?
(that benumbs my breast! Away from here! — But whither now?)

voˈhɪn lɛntʻˈfliːən? voˈhɪn mɪç ˈvɛndən? liːɐ̯ ˈgœtʻɐ, ha! vas høːr ɪç?
wohin entfliehen? wohin mich wenden? Ihr Götter, ha! was hör' ich?
whither to flee? whither myself to turn? You gods, ah! what hear I?
(Whither to flee? Whither to turn? You gods, ah, what do I hear?)

ma͜en fɛɐ̯ˈdɛrbən? veː miːɐ̯! voː bɪn lɪç? voː, lax, voː bɪn lɪç?
Mein Verderben? Weh mir! wo bin ich? Wo, ach, wo bin ich?
My ruin? Woe to me! where am I? Where, ah, where am I?
(My ruin?! Woe is me! Where am I? Where, oh where am I?)

ha! rɪŋs zɪnt di ˈlʏftʻə fɔn ˈblɪt͜sən lɛɐ̯ˈglyːətʻ,
Ha! rings sind die Lüfte von Blitzen erglühet,
Ah! all around are the airs by lightnings kindled,
(Ah! All around me the air is aglow with lightning flashes,)

ɛs ˈvaŋkʻətʻ, lɛs ˈfliːət di leːɐ̯t lʊntʻɐ miːɐ̯.
es wanket, es fliehet die Erd' unter mir.
there sways, there flees the earth beneath me.
(the earth is swaying, is dropping away beneath me.)

vɛlç ˈfʊrçtʻbaːrəs ˈgra͜oən mʊs rɪŋs lɪç lɛɐ̯ˈʃa͜oən,
Welch furchtbares Grauen muss rings ich erschauen,
What frightful horror must all around I behold,
(What frightful horror must I behold all around me,)

vɛlç ˈgra͜ozə gəˈʃtʻaltʻən lʊmˈfaŋən mɪç ˈhaltʻən,
welch grause Gestalten umfangen mich halten,
what horrid shapes captive me hold,
(what horrid creatures hold me captive,)

vɛlç ˈfɪnstʻrə gəˈvaltʻən lʊmˈkʰra͜ezən mɪç hiːɐ̯!
welch finstre Gewalten umkreisen mich hier!
what dark powers encircle me here?

[The Italian text comes from a scene in Metastasio's drama *Gioas, re di Giuda* ("Joab, King of Judah"). Schubert created a dramatic recitative and aria for bass in the idiomatic style of *opera seria*. This is the second of three arias that he dedicated to the famous bass Luigi Lablache.]

ɪm ˈlaːbənt‘roːtʰ
Im Abendrot
In the Glow of Sunset

Posthumously published [composed 1825?] (poem by Carl Lappe)

oː viː ʃøːn lɪst ˈda͜enə vɛlt‘, ˈfaːt‘ɐ, vɛn ziː ˈgɔldən ˈʃt‘raːlətʰ! [ˈla͜enə]
O wie schön ist deine Welt, Vater, wenn sie golden strahlet! [*poem:* **ist eine Welt]**
Oh how beautiful is your world, Father, when it golden gleams! [a]
(Oh how beautiful your world is, Father, when it is bathed in golden light,)

vɛn da͜en glant͜s hɛɐ̯ˈniːdɐfɛlt‘, lʊnt den ʃt‘a͜op‘ mɪt‘ ˈʃɪmɐ ˈmaːlətʰ,
Wenn dein Glanz herniederfällt, und den Staub mit Schimmer malet,
When your radiance falls down, and the dust with shimmer paints,
(when your radiance shines down from heaven and paints the dust so that it shimmers,)

vɛn das roːt, das lɪn deːɐ̯ ˈvɔlk‘ə blɪŋk‘t‘, lɪn ma͜en ˈʃt‘ɪləs ˈfɛnst‘ɐ zɪŋk‘tʰ!
wenn das Rot, das in der Wolke blinkt, in mein stilles Fenster sinkt!
when the red, that in the cloud gleams, into my quiet window sinks!
(when the red light that is gleaming in the clouds shines through my quiet window!)

kʰœnt‘ ɪç ˈkʰlaːgən, kʰœnt‘ ɪç ˈt͜saːgən? ˈlirə za͜en lan diːɐ̯/diːr lʊnt‘ miːɐ̯?
Könnt' ich klagen, könnt' ich zagen? irre sein an dir und mir?
Could I complain, could I be faint-hearted? doubtful be about you and me?
(Could I complain, could I lose heart? Could I have doubts about you and me?)

na͜en, lɪç vɪl lɪm ˈbuːzən ˈt‘raːgən ˈda͜enən ˈhɪməl ʃoːn lalˈhiːɐ̯. [daˈhiːɐ̯]
Nein, ich will im Busen tragen deinen Himmel schon allhier. [*poem:* **schon dahier]**
No, I want in the bosom to carry your heaven already all-here. [here]
(No! In my heart I shall carry your heaven, which is already here all around me.)

ʊnt diːs hɛrt͜s, leː lɛs t͜suˈzamənbrɪçt‘, tʰrɪŋk‘t‘ nɔx gluːt‘ lʊnt‘ ʃlʏrft‘ nɔx lɪçtʰ.
Und dies Herz, eh' es zusammenbricht, trinkt noch Glut und schlürft noch Licht.
And this heart, ere it crumbles, drinks still fire and sips still light.
(And this heart of mine, before it turns to dust, will still be drinking sunset fire and sipping light.)

[This jewel is undoubtedly one of Schubert's most beautiful and deeply moving songs. The magical beauty of the world in the light of the setting sun confirms the poet's faith in God. The *Gesamtausgabe* and the Peters version differ in the way the phrase "*Und dies Herz, eh' es zusammenbricht*" is fit to the notes of the melody. Further, Peters, based upon the first draft, indicates 4/4 time, "*Sehr langsam*"; the *Gesamtausgabe*, based on a fair copy, calls for *alla breve*, "*langsam, feierlich.*" The singer needs excellent breath-control and a beautiful *legato*.]

Im Dorfe see *Winterreise*

ɪm ˈfra͜eən
Im Freien
In the Open

Op. 80, No. 3 [1826] (Johann Gabriel Seidl)

ˈdra͜osən lɪn deːɐ̯ ˈva͜et‘ən naxt‘ ʃt‘eː lɪç ˈviːdɐ nuːn:
Draussen in der weiten Nacht steh’ ich wieder nun:
Outside in the wide night stand I again now:
(Outside in the vast night I am now standing again;)

ˈiːrə ˈhɛlə ˈʃt‘ɛrnənpʰraxt‘ lɛst‘ ma͜en hɛrt͜s nɪçt‘ ruːn!
ihre helle Sternenpracht lässt mein Herz nicht ruh’n!
its bright star- splendor lets my heart not rest!
(the bright splendor of the stars keeps my heart from any rest!)

ˈtʰa͜ozənt‘ ˈlarmə ˈvɪŋk‘ən miːɐ̯ zyːs bəˈgeːrənt t͜suː,
Tausend Arme winken mir süss begehrend zu,
A thousand arms beckon to me sweetly desiringly to,
(A thousand arms beckon me, in sweet longing,)

ˈtʰa͜ozənt‘ ˈʃt‘ɪmən ˈruːfən hiːɐ̯: gryːs dɪç, ˈtʰra͜ot‘ɐ, duː!
tausend Stimmen rufen hier: Grüss dich, Trauter, du!
A thousand voices call here: “Greet you, dear one, you!”
(A thousand voices are calling here: “Greetings to you, dear friend!”)
[*poem:* **“Grüss dich, Schwärmer** (ˈʃvɛrmɐ, enthusiast/dreamer)**, du!”**]

oː lɪç va͜es la͜ox, vas mɪç t͜siːtʰ, va͜es la͜ox, vas mɪç ruːftʰ,
O ich weiss auch, was mich zieht, weiss auch, was mich ruft,
Oh, I know too what me draws, know too what me calls,
(Oh, I know what is drawing me here, I know, too, what is calling me,)

vas viː ˈfrɔ͜øndəs gruːs lʊnt‘ liːt‘ ˈlɔk‘ət‘, ˈlɔk‘ət dʊrç di lʊftʰ.
was wie Freundes Gruss und Lied locket, locket durch die Luft.
what like friend’s greeting and song entices, entices through the air.
(what like a friend’s greeting and song entices through the air.) [*poem: one* **locket** *only*]

ziːst duː dɔrt das ˈhʏt‘çən ʃt‘eːn, dra͜of deːɐ̯ ˈmoːnt‘ʃa͜en ruːtʰ?
Siehst du dort das Hüttchen steh’n, drauf der Mondschein ruht?
See you there the cottage stand, on that the moonshine rests?
(Do you see the cottage there on which the moonlight rests?)

dʊrç di ˈblaŋk‘ən ˈʃa͜ebən zeːn ˈla͜ogən, diː miːɐ̯ guːtʰ!
Durch die blanken Scheiben seh’n Augen, die mir gut!
Through the shining (window)panes look eyes which for me care! [**die mir gut** is an idiom]
(Through the shining windowpanes two eyes that care for me are looking out!)

ziːst duː dɔrt das ha͜os lam bax, das deːɐ̯ moːnt‘ bəˈʃa͜entʰ?
Siehst du dort das Haus am Bach, das der Mond bescheint?
See you there the house at the brook, which the moon shines upon?
(Do you see there by the brook the house on which the moon is shining?)

ˈlʊntʻɐ ˈza͜enəm ˈtʰra͜otʻən dax ʃlɛːftʻ ma͜en ˈliːpstʻɐ frɔ͜øntʻ.
Unter seinem trauten Dach schläft mein liebster Freund.
Under its cozy roof sleeps my dearest friend.

ziːst duː ˈjeːnən ba͜om, deːɐ̯ fɔl ˈzɪlbɐflɔkʻən flɪmtʰ?
Siehst du jenen Baum, der voll Silberflocken flimmt?
See you that tree, which full of silverflakes glitters?
(Do you see that tree that is glittering as if adorned with silver flakes?)

oː viː lɔftʻ ma͜en ˈbuːzən ʃvɔl, ˈfroːɐ dɔrtʻ gəˈʃtʻɪmtʰ!
O wie oft mein Busen schwoll, froher dort gestimmt!
Oh how often my bosom swelled, happier there tuned!
(Oh how often my bosom swelled there, tuned at once to a happier mood!)

ˈjeːdəs ˈpʰlɛt͜sçən, das miːɐ̯ vɪŋkʻtʻ, lɪstʻ la͜en ˈliːbɐ pʰlat͜s;
Jedes Plätzchen, das mir winkt, ist ein lieber Platz;
Each little place, that to me beckons, is a dear place;
(Each little place that is beckoning to me is a place dear to my heart;)
[*Peters (in error):* **ist ein teurer** (tʰɔ͜ørɐ, dear) **Platz**]

ʊntʻ voˈhɪn la͜en ʃtʻraːl nuːɐ̯ zɪŋkʻtʻ, lɔkʻtʻ la͜en ˈtʰɔ͜ørɐ ʃat͜s.
und wohin ein Strahl nur sinkt, lockt ein teurer Schatz.
and wherever a ray just sinks, entices a dear treasure.
(and wherever a moonbeam happens to fall, a dear treasure entices me.)

drʊm la͜ox vɪŋkʻtʻ miːɐ̯s ˈlyːbɐ(r)lal zoː bəˈgeːrəntʻ hiːɐ̯,
Drum auch winkt mir's überall so begehrend hier,
Therefore also beckons to me it everywhere so longingly here,
(That is why everything here beckons to me so longingly,)

drʊm la͜ox ruːftʻ lɛs, viː deːɐ̯ ʃal ˈtʰra͜otʻɐ ˈliːbə miːɐ̯.
drum auch ruft es, wie der Schall trauter Liebe mir.
therefore also calls it, like the sound of dear love to me.
(that is why it calls to me, like the sound of a cherished love.)

[The piano part paints the scene: the twinkling stars, the flecks of silver moonlight that flicker on the quivering leaves. The mood is happy, the man is in love, the song is longish but lovable.]

ɪm ˈfryːlɪŋ
Im Frühling
In the Spring

Posthumously published [composed 1826] (poem by Ernst Schulze)

ʃtʻɪl zɪt͜s ɪç lan dɛs ˈhyːgəls haŋ, deːɐ̯ ˈhɪməl lɪstʻ zoː kʰlaːɐ̯,
Still sitz' ich an des Hügels Hang, der Himmel ist so klar,
Quietly sit I on the hill's slope, the sky is so clear,
(I sit quietly on the slope of the hill. The sky is so clear,)

das ˈlʏftʻçən ʃpʻiːltʻ lɪm ˈgryːnən tʰaːl, voː lɪç ba͜em ˈleːɐ̯stʻən ˈfryːlɪŋsʃtʻraːl
das Lüftchen spielt im grünen Tal, wo ich beim ersten Frühlingsstrahl
the breeze plays in the green valley, where I at the first ray of springtime

laenst‘, lax, zo: 'glʏk‘lɪç va:ɐ̯; vo: lɪç lan 'li:rɐ 'zaet‘ə gɪŋ
einst, ach, so glücklich war; wo ich an ihrer Seite ging
once, ah, so happy was; where I at her side went
(was once, ah, so happy; where I walked by her side)

zo: 'tʰraolɪç lʊnt‘ zo: na:, lʊnt tʰi:f lɪm 'dʊŋk‘əln 'fɛlzənkʰvɛl
so traulich und so nah, und tief im dunkeln Felsenquell
so intimately and so close, and deep in the dark rocky spring

den 'ʃø:nən 'hɪməl blao lʊnt‘ hɛl, lʊnt‘ zi: lɪm 'hɪməl za:.
den schönen Himmel blau und hell, und sie im Himmel sah.
the beautiful sky blue and bright, and her in the sky saw.
(I saw the beautiful sky, blue and bright, reflected in the water, and saw *her* in that heaven.)

zi:, vi: de:ɐ̯ 'bʊnt‘ə 'fry:lɪŋ ʃo:n laos kʰnɔsp‘ lʊnt‘ 'bly:t‘ə blɪk‘tʰ!
Sieh, wie der bunte Frühling schon aus Knosp' und Blüte blickt!
See, how the many-colored springtime already out of bud and blossom looks!
(See how many-colored springtime is already peeking out from bud and blossom!)

nɪçt‘ 'lalə 'bly:t‘ən zɪnt‘ mi:ɐ̯ glaeç, lam 'li:pst‘ən pflʏk‘t‘ ɪç
Nicht alle Blüten sind mir gleich, am liebsten pflückt' ich
Not all blossoms are to me alike, at the most agreeably would pluck I
(Not all blossoms are the same to me; I would most like to pluck)
[*poem:* **pflück'** (pflʏk‘, pluck) **ich**]

fɔn de:m tsvaek‘, fɔn 'vɛlçəm zi: gə'pflʏk‘tʰ. dɛn 'laləs lɪst‘ vi: 'da:ma:ls nɔx,
von dem Zweig, von welchem sie gepflückt. Denn alles ist wie damals noch,
from the branch from which she (had) plucked. For all is as then still,
(from the branch from which *she* had once plucked blossoms. For all is still as it was then,)

di 'blu:mən, das gə'fɪlt‘, di 'zɔnə ʃaent‘ nɪçt‘ 'mɪndɐ hɛl,
die Blumen, das Gefild, die Sonne scheint nicht minder hell,
the flowers, the fields, the sun shines not less brightly,
(the flowers, the fields; the sun shines no less brightly,)

nɪçt‘ 'mɪndɐ 'frɔønt‘lɪç ʃvɪmt‘ lɪm kʰvɛl das 'blaoə 'hɪməlsbɪlt‘.
nicht minder freundlich schwimmt im Quell das blaue Himmelsbild.
not less amiably swims in the spring the blue sky- image.
(the blue image of the sky swims no less amiably in the water of the spring.)

ɛs 'vandəln nu:ɐ̯ zɪç vɪl lʊnt‘ va:n, lɛs 'vɛksəln lʊst‘ lʊnt‘ ʃt‘raetʰ;
Es wandeln nur sich Will' und Wahn, es wechseln Lust und Streit;
There changes but itself will and illusion, there alternates pleasure and strife;
(But will and illusion are changeable, pleasure alternates with strife;)

fo'ry:bɐ fli:t de:ɐ̯ 'li:bə glʏk‘, lʊnt‘ nu:ɐ̯ di 'li:bə blaep‘t tsu'rʏk‘,
vorüber flieht der Liebe Glück, und nur die Liebe bleibt zurück,
past flees the love's happiness, and only the love remains behind,
(love's happiness flies away, and only love itself remains behind,)

di li:p‘ lʊnt‘ lax, das laet‘! o: vɛ:r ɪç dɔx laen 'fø:glaen nu:ɐ̯ [das]
die Lieb' und ach, das Leid! O wär' ich doch ein Vöglein nur [*poem:* **das Vöglein]**
the love and ah, the sorrow! Oh were I but a little bird only [the]
(love and sorrow! Oh, if I could only be a little bird)

dɔrtʻ ǀan dem ˈviːzənhaŋ! dan bliːb ɪç ǀa͜of den ˈt͜sva͜egən hiːɐ̯/hiːr
dort an dem Wiesenhang! Dann blieb' ich auf den Zweigen hier
there on the meadow-slope! Then would stay I on the branches here
(there on the slope of the meadow! Then I would stay here on the branches)

ǀʊntʻ zɛŋ ǀa͜en ˈzyːsəs liːtʻ fɔn liːɐ̯ den ˈgant͜sən ˈzɔmɐ laŋ.
und säng' ein süsses Lied von ihr den ganzen Sommer lang.
and would sing a sweet song about her the whole summer long.

[In this loveliest of spring songs Schubert chose to evoke the fresh beauty of nature, rather than the love that did not return. The delightful piano part is a set of variations on one of the themes. The song appeared one month after the composer's death in a Viennese newspaper supplement.]

ɪm ˈha͜enə
Im Haine
In the Grove

Op. 56, No. 3 [1822?] (Franz von Bruchmann)

ˈzɔnənʃtʻraːlən dʊrç di ˈtʰanən, viː ziː ˈfalən,
Sonnenstrahlen durch die Tannen, wie sie fallen,
Sunbeams through the fir trees, as they fall,
(Sunbeams, as they fall through the fir trees,)

t͜siːn fɔn ˈdanən ˈlalə ˈʃmɛrt͜sən, ǀʊntʻ ǀɪm ˈhɛrt͜sən ˈvoːnətʻ ˈra͜enɐ ˈfriːdə nuːɐ̯.
zieh'n von dannen alle Schmerzen, und im Herzen wohnet reiner Friede nur.
draw from thence all pains, and in the heart dwells pure peace only.
(draw all pain away from here; and only pure peace dwells in one's heart.)

ˈʃtʻɪləs ˈza͜ozən ˈla͜oɐ ˈlʏftʻə, ǀʊntʻ ǀɪm ˈbra͜ozən
Stilles Sausen lauer Lüfte, und im Brausen
Quiet soughing of mild breezes, and in the ferment

ˈt͜saːɐ̯tʻə ˈdʏftʻə, diː zɪç ˈna͜egən ǀa͜os den ˈt͜sva͜egən, ˈlaːtʻmətʻ ǀa͜os di ˈgant͜sə fluːɐ̯.
zarte Düfte, die sich neigen aus den Zweigen, atmet aus die ganze Flur.
delicate scents, which themselves incline from the branches, breathes out the entire field.
(the entire meadow exhales delicate scents, which drift down from the branches.)

vɛn nuːɐ̯/nuːr ˈǀɪmɐ ˈdʊŋkʻlə ˈbɔ͜ømə, ˈzɔnənʃɪmɐ, ˈgryːnə ˈzɔ͜ømə ǀʊns ǀʊmˈblyːtʻən
Wenn nur immer dunkle Bäume, Sonnenschimmer, grüne Säume uns umblühten
If only always dark trees, sun-shimmer, green borders us around bloomed
(If only dark trees and greenery would always blossom around us, and the shimmer of sunlight)

ǀʊntʻ ǀʊmˈglyːtʻən, ˈtʰɪlgəntʻ ˈlalɐ ˈkʰvaːlən ʃpʻuːɐ̯!
und umglühten, tilgend aller Qualen Spur!
and around glowed, erasing all torments' trace!
(would always glow all around us, erasing the traces of all our torments!)

[The poet was one of the "*Schubertianer*," the circle of enthusiastic friends who promoted Schubert's songs in Vienna. This little strophic song is all charm and cheerfulness.]

ɪm 'valdə / ɪç 'vandrə 'ly:bɐ bɛrk' lʊnt tʰa:l

Im Walde / Ich wand're über Berg und Tal

In the Forest / I Wander over Mountain and Valley

Op. 93, No. 1 [1825?] (Ernst Schulze)

ɪç 'vandrə 'ly:bɐ bɛrk' lʊnt tʰa:l lʊnt' 'ly:bɐ 'gry:nə 'haedən,
Ich wand're über Berg und Tal und über grüne Heiden,
I wander over mountain and valley and over green heaths,

ʊnt' mɪt' mi:ɐ 'vandɐt' 'maenə kʰva:l, vɪl 'nɪmɐ fɔn mi:ɐ 'ʃaedən.
und mit mir wandert meine Qual, will nimmer von mir scheiden.
and with me wanders my torment, wants never from me to part.
(and my torment wanders with me, it will never part from me.)

ʊnt' ʃift' ɪç laox dʊrçs 'vaet'ə me:ɐ, zi: kʰɛ:m laox dɔrt' vo:l 'hɪnt'ɐhe:ɐ.
Und schifft' ich auch durchs weite Meer, sie käm' auch dort wohl hinterher.
And sailed I even through the wide sea, it would come too there surely behind.
(And even if I sailed across the wide sea, it would no doubt follow behind me there too.)

vo:l bly:n fi:l 'blu:mən laof de:ɐ flu:ɐ, di: ha:b ɪç nɪçt' gə'ze:ən,
Wohl blüh'n viel Blumen auf der Flur, die hab' ich nicht gesehen,
No doubt bloom many flowers on the meadow, them have I not seen,
(No doubt many flowers are blooming in the meadow; I have not seen them;)

dɛn 'laenə 'blu:mə ze: lɪç nu:ɐ/nu:r laof 'lalən 've:gən 'ʃt'e:ən.
denn e i n e Blume seh' ich nur auf allen Wegen stehen.
for *one* flower see I only on all paths stand.
(for I see only one flower on every path I take.)

na:x li:ɐ ha:b ɪç mɪç lɔft' gə'bʏk't' lʊnt dɔx zi: 'nɪmɐ(r) 'lap'gəpflʏk'tʰ.
Nach ihr hab' ich mich oft gebückt und doch sie nimmer abgepflückt.
Toward it have I myself often stooped and yet it never plucked.
(I have often stooped down toward it, and yet never plucked it.)

di 'bi:nən 'zʊmən dʊrç das gra:s lʊnt' 'hɛŋən lan den 'bly:t'ən; ['zʊmzən]
Die Bienen summen durch das Gras und hängen an den Blüten; [*poem:* sumsen]
The bees hum through the grass and hang on the blossoms; [buzz/hum]

das maxt' maen 'laogə tʰry:p' lʊnt' nas, lɪç kʰan mi:ɐs nɪçt' fɛɐ'bi:t'ən.
das macht mein Auge trüb' und nass, ich kann mir's nicht verbieten.
that makes my eye dim and wet, I can to myself it not forbid.
(that makes my eyes grow dim and moist, I cannot help it.)

i:ɐ 'zy:sən 'lɪp'ən, ro:t' lʊnt' vaeç, vo:l hɪŋ ɪç 'nɪmɐ zo: lan lɔøç!
Ihr süssen Lippen, rot und weich, wohl hing ich nimmer so an euch!
Her sweet lips, red and soft, indeed hung I never thus on you!
(You, her sweet lips, red and soft, indeed I never hung like that on you!)

ga:ɐ 'li:p'lɪç 'zɪŋən na: lʊnt' fɛrn di 'fø:gəl laof den 'tsvaegən;
Gar lieblich singen nah und fern die Vögel auf den Zweigen;
Very sweetly sing near and far the birds on the branches;
(Near and far the birds are singing very sweetly on the branches;)

voːl zɛŋ ɪç mɪt den ˈføːgəln gɛrn, dɔx mʊs ɪç ˈtʰrao̯rɪç ˈʃvae̯gən.
wohl säng' ich mit den Vögeln gern, doch muss ich traurig schweigen.
indeed would sing I with the birds gladly, but must I sadly be silent.
(I would indeed like to sing with the birds, but I must sadly be silent.)

dɛn ˈliːbəslʊst‘ lʊnt‘ ˈliːbəspʰae̯n, diː ˈblae̯bən ˈjeːdəs gɛrn laˈlae̯n.
Denn Liebeslust und Liebespein, die bleiben jedes gern allein.
For love's pleasure and love's pain, they remain each gladly alone.
(For love's pleasure and love's pain both prefer to remain alone.)

am ˈhɪməl zeː lɪç ˈflyːgəlʃnɛl di ˈvɔlk‘ən ˈvae̯t‘ɐ ˈtsiːən,
Am Himmel seh' ich flügelschnell die Wolken weiter ziehen,
In the sky see I wing-fast the clouds farther moving,
(I see the clouds in the sky flying onward as if on fast wings,)

di ˈvɛlə ˈriːzəlt‘ lae̯çt‘ lʊnt‘ hɛl, mʊs ˈlɪmɐ naːn lʊnt‘ ˈfliːən.
die Welle rieselt leicht und hell, muss immer nah'n und fliehen.
the wave ripples lightly and brightly, must always approach and flee.
(the waves ripple lightly and brightly, they must constantly draw near and then go back.)

dɔx ˈhaʃən, vɛns fɔm ˈvɪndə ruːt‘, zɪç vɔlk‘ lʊnt‘ ˈvɔlk‘ə, fluːt‘ lʊnt‘ fluːtʰ.
Doch haschen, wenn's vom Winde ruht, sich Wolk' und Wolke, Flut und Flut.
But snatch, when it from the wind rests, each other cloud and cloud, flood and flood.
(But, when the wind rests, clouds catch up with each other, and so do waves.)

ɪç ˈvandrə hɪn, lɪç ˈvandrə heːɐ̯, bae̯ ʃt‘ʊrm lʊnt‘ ˈhae̯t‘ɐn ˈtʰaːgən,
Ich wand're hin, ich wand're her, bei Sturm und heitern Tagen,
I wander to, I wander fro, by storm and calmer days,
(I wander to and fro, through storm and fairer weather,) [*hin und her* = to and fro]

ʊnt dɔx lɛɐ̯ˈʃao̯ lɪçs ˈnɪmɐmeːɐ̯/-meːr lʊnt‘ kʰan lɛs nɪçt‘ lɛɐ̯ˈjaːgən.
und doch erschau' ich's nimmermehr und kann es nicht erjagen.
and yet behold I it nevermore and can it not chase and capture.
(and yet I never find it again, and cannot chase and capture it.)

oː ˈliːbəszeːnən, ˈliːbəskʰvaːl, van ruːt deːɐ̯ ˈvandərɐ(r) lae̯nˈmaːl?
O Liebessehnen, Liebesqual, wann ruht der Wanderer einmal?
O love's longing, love's torment, when rests the wanderer one time?
(O love's longing, love's torment, when will the wanderer one day finally rest?)

[The title of the original poem, from Schulze's "Poetic Diary," is *Im Walde hinter Falkenhagen* ("In the Forest behind Falkenhagen," a village near Göttingen). The triplets in the accompaniment suggest the unhappy lover's restless, obsessive flight.]

ɪm ˈvaldə / ˈvɪndəs ˈrao̯ʃən, ˈgɔt‘əs ˈflyːgəl / ˈvaldəs-naxtʰ

Im Walde / Windes Rauschen, Gottes Flügel / Waldes-Nacht

In the Forest / The Rushing of the Wind, God's Wings / Forest-Night

Posthumously published [composed 1820] (poem by Friedrich von Schlegel)

ˈvɪndəs ˈrao̯ʃən, ˈgɔt‘əs ˈflyːgəl, tʰiːf lɪn ˈkʰyːlɐ ˈvaldəsnaxtʰ,
Windes Rauschen, Gottes Flügel, tief in kühler Waldesnacht,
Wind's rushing, God's wings, deep in cool forest- night,
(At the rushing of the wind, the wings of God, deep in the cool forest at night,)

viː deːɐ̯ hɛlt‘ ɪn ˈrɔsəs ˈbyːgəl, ʃvɪŋt‘ zɪç dɛs gəˈdaŋk‘əns maxtʰ.
wie der Held in Rosses Bügel, schwingt sich des Gedankens Macht.
like the hero into steed’s stirrups, swings itself the thought’s power.
(the power of thought vaults up, like a hero leaping into the stirrups of his steed.)

[drɪŋt‘ hɛˈran deːɐ̯ ˈʃt‘ʏrmə]
[******Stark:* **... dringt heran der Stürme Macht.**]
[rushes onwards the storms’]
[(like a hero leaping into the stirrups of his steed the power of the storm rushes onwards.)]

viː di ˈalt‘ən ˈtʰanən ˈzaozən, høːɐ̯t‘ man ˈgaest‘əsvoːgən ˈbraozən.
Wie die alten Tannen sausen, hört man Geisteswogen brausen.
As the old fir trees moan, hears one spirit- waves roaring.
(As the old fir trees moan in the wind, one hears the waves of the spirit surging.)

[ˈbraozən, høːɐ̯st di ˈvɪndəsbraot duː ˈzaozən.]
[*Stark:* **... brausen, hörst die Windesbraut du sausen.]**
[roar, hear the bride of the wind you moaning.]
[(As the old fir trees roar, you can hear the bride of the wind moaning.)]

ˈhɛrlɪç ɪst deːɐ̯ ˈflamə ˈlɔøçt‘ən ɪn dɛs ˈmɔrgənglantsəs roːtʰ,
Herrlich ist der Flamme Leuchten in des Morgenglanzes Rot,
Glorious is the flame’s shining in the morning-radiance’s red,
(Glorious is the flame that gleams in the red of the radiant dawn,)

[viː di ˈflamənblɪtsə ˈʃiːsən dʊrç deːɐ̯ ˈtʰanənvɪpfəl gryːn!]
[*Stark:* **Wie die Flammenblitze schiessen durch der Tannenwipfel Grün!]**
[How the flame- flashes shoot through the fir tree crowns’ green!]
[(How the flaming lightning flashes shoot through the green tops of the fir trees!)]

ˈoːdɐ diː das fɛlt‘ bəˈlɔøçt‘ən, ˈblɪtsə, ˈʃvaŋɐ(r) ɔft‘ fɔn tʰoːt‘.
oder die das Feld beleuchten, Blitze, schwanger oft von Tod.
or which the field illumine, lightnings, pregnant often with death.
(or in the flashes of lightning, often pregnant with death, that illumine the field.)
[*Peters & poem:* **befeuchten** (bəˈfɔøçt‘ən, moisten)]

[ʊnt‘ fɔn ˈiːrən ˈfɔøɐkʰʏsən ʃt‘ʏrtst‘ fɛɐ̯ˈzɛŋt di ˈaeçə hɪn.]
[*Stark:* **und von ihren Feuerküssen stürzt versengt die Eiche hin.]**
[and from their fire- kisses plunges singed the oak down.]
[(And from their fire-kisses the singed oak comes crashing down.)]

raʃ di ˈflamə tsʊk‘t‘ ʊnt‘ ˈloːdɐt‘, viː tsuː gɔt‘ hɪˈnaofgəfoːdɐtʰ.
Rasch die Flamme zuckt und lodert, wie zu Gott hinaufgefodert.
Quickly the flame darts and blazes, as (if) to God dispatched up.
(Quickly the flame darts and blazes, as if dispatched upward to God.) [*fodern* (obs.) = *fördern*]

ˈeːvɪks ˈraoʃən ˈzanft‘ɐ ˈkʰvɛlən ˈtsaobɐt‘ ˈbluːmən aos dem ʃmɛrts,
Ewig’s Rauschen sanfter Quellen zaubert Blumen aus dem Schmerz,
Eternal murmuring of gentle springs conjures flowers out of the sorrow,
(The eternal murmur of gentle springs conjures flowers out of sorrow,)

[hɔrç! hɪ'nap' ɪns tʰa:l tsu: 'lɑoʃən vɪls di:ɐ̯ 'vɪŋk'ən 'ni:dɐvɛrts;]
[*Stark:* **Horch! hinab ins Tal zu lauschen will's dir winken niederwärts;]**
[Hark! down into the valley to listen wants it to you to beckon downwards;]
[(Hark! Something wants to lure you downwards into the valley to listen;)]

'tʰrɑoɐ dɔx ɪn 'lɪndən 'vɛlən ʃlɛ:k't' ʊns 'lɔk'ənt' an das hɛrts;
Trauer doch in linden Wellen schlägt uns lockend an das Herz;
grief though in soft waves beats for us enticingly against the heart;
(but grief beats enticingly against our hearts in soft waves;)

[dɔrt' fɛɐ̯'bɔrgnɐ 'kʰvɛlən 'rɑoʃən] [di:ɐ̯]
[*Stark:* **dort verborg'ner Quellen Rauschen schlägt dir...]**
[there hidden springs' murmuring] [for you]
[(there the murmur of hidden springs will beat against your heart in soft waves;)]

'fɛrnap' hɪn de:ɐ̯ gaest' gə'tso:gən, di: ʊns 'lɔk't'ən, dʊrç di 'vo:gən.
fernab hin der Geist gezogen, die uns locken, durch die Wogen.
distant hence the spirit drawn, which us entice, through the waves.
(the spirit is drawn far away, through the waves that entice us.)

['lʊft'ɪç kʰɔmt di ʃa:ɐ̯] [dɪç 'lɔk'ət' ɪn]
[*Stark:* **luftig kommt die Schar gezogen, die dich locket in die Wogen.]**
[airily comes the troop along] [you entices into]
[(the airy troop comes along that entices you into the waves.)]

draŋ dɛs 'le:bəns ɑos de:ɐ̯ 'hʏlə, kʰampf de:ɐ̯ 'ʃt'ark'ən 'tʰri:bə vɪlt',
Drang des Lebens aus der Hülle, Kampf der starken Triebe wild,
Urge of the life out of the sheath (of flesh), battle of the strong instincts wild,
(The urge of life to escape from its mortal sheath, the battle of wild and powerful instincts,)

[fo:ɐ̯ de:ɐ̯/de:r 'ɛlfən las dɪç 'varnən, di: di:ɐ̯ 'vɪŋk'ən ɪn den grʊnt',]
[*Stark:* **Vor den Elfen lass dich warnen, die dir winken in den Grund,]**
[Against the elves let yourself be warned, who to you beckon into the ground,]
[(Let yourself be warned against the elves, who beckon you to your destruction,)]

vɪrt tsʊr 'ʃø:nst'ən 'li:bəsfʏlə, dʊrç dɛs 'gaest'əs hɑox gə'ʃt'ɪltʰ.
wird zur schönsten Liebesfülle, durch des Geistes Hauch gestillt.
becomes to the most beautiful love-fullness, through the spirit's breath stilled.
(turns into the most beautiful fullness of love, stilled by the breath of the spirit.)
[*Peters:* **Liebensfülle** ('li:bənsfʏlə, fullness of loving)]

[dɪç mɪt' 'li:bəsraets ʊm'garnən ʊnt' mɪt' zaŋ ɑos 'zy:səm mʊnt'.]
[*Stark:* **dich mit Liebesreiz umgarnen und mit Sang aus süssem Mund.]**
[you with love- charm ensnare and with song from sweet mouth.]
[(ensnare you with love's allurement and with song from a sweet mouth.)]

'ʃœpfərɪʃɐ 'lʏft'ə 've:ən fy:lt' man dʊrç di 'ze:lə 'ge:ən.
Schöpferischer Lüfte Wehen fühlt man durch die Seele gehen.
More creative breezes' blowing feels one through the soul go.
(One feels more creative breezes stirring through the soul.)

['ʃmae̯çlərɪʃɐ] [fy:lst du:]
[*Stark:* Schmeichlerischer Lüfte Wehen fühlst du...]
[More flattering] [feel you]
[(You feel more flattering breezes stirring through your soul.)]

'vɪndəs 'rao̯ʃən, 'gɔt'əs 'fly:gəl, tʰi:f ɪn 'dʊŋk'lɐ 'valdəsnaxtʰ,
Windes Rauschen, Gottes Flügel, tief in dunkler Waldesnacht,
Wind's rushing, God's wings, deep in dark forest- night,
(At the rushing of the wind, the wings of God, deep in the dark forest at night,)
[*Peters:* in kühler ('kʰy:lɐ, cool)**]**

['gae̯st'ɐʃlɪŋən tsu: ɛnt''ge:ən, hɪlft di:ɐ̯ nu:ɐ̯ dɛs 'ʃt'ʊrməs maxtʰ,]
[*Stark:* Geisterschlingen zu entgehen, hilft dir nur des Sturmes Macht,]
[spirit- snares to avoid, helps you only the storm's power,]
[(The power of the storm can only help you to avoid the snares of the spirits,)

frae̯ gə'ge:bən 'alə 'tsy:gəl ʃvɪŋt' zɪç dɛs gə'daŋk'əns maxtʰ,
frei gegeben alle Zügel schwingt sich des Gedankens Macht,
free given all reins swings itself the thought's power,
(the power of thought vaults up, the reins loosened freely,)

[ʃp'rɛŋst du: mɪt' fɛɐ̯'hɛŋt' 'tsy:gəl dʊrç di 'ʃvartsə 'vɛt'ɐnaxtʰ,]
[*Stark:* sprengst du mit verhängtem Zügel durch die schwarze Wetternacht,]
[burst you with flying reins through the black storm- night,]
[(you speed at a gallop through the dark stormy night,)]

hø:ɐ̯t' ɪn 'lʏft'ən 'o:nə 'grao̯zən den gə'zaŋ de:ɐ̯ 'gae̯st'ɐ 'brao̯zən.
hört in Lüften ohne Grausen den Gesang der Geister brausen.
hears in breezes without horror the song of the spirits roar.
(and hears without horror the song of the spirits roaring in the wind.)

[hø:ɐ̯st'] [du: den zaŋ] ['zao̯zən.]
[*Stark:* hörst in Lüften ohne Grausen du den Sang der Geister sausen.]
[hear] [you the song] [howl.]
[(you hear without horror the song of the spirits howling in the wind.)]

[Schubert's title, like that of the poem itself, is *Im Walde*. It is a wild and wonderful song. Schubert revels in the text, repeating most of the lines, sometimes several times, and making the song much longer (fifteen pages in the *Gesamtausgabe*) than a reading of the poem would suggest. The Peters version, following the first publication, bears the title *Waldes-Nacht*, includes *a variant by Ludwig Stark (above in brackets) of Schlegel's text, and is a half-tone lower than the original draft and manuscript copies, upon which the *Gesamtausgabe* (longer by four bars) is based. The missing four-bar phrase would follow the third bar on Peters' page 170. The alteration of the text by Stark changes the character of the poem into a cautionary tale about dangerously seductive nature-spirits in the woods at night, instead of Schlegel's much more subtle spiritual meditation inspired by the awesome wildness of nature in a storm-swept forest.]

In der Ferne see *Schwanengesang*

ɪn deːɐ̯ ˈmɪtʻɐnaxtʰ

In der Mitternacht

At Midnight

Posthumously published [composed 1816] (poem by Johann Georg Jacobi)

ˈtʰoːdəsʃtʻɪlə dɛkʻt das tʰaːl bae̯ dɛs ˈmoːndəs ˈfalbəm ˈʃtʻraːl; [ˈhalbəm]
Todesstille deckt das Tal bei des Mondes falbem Strahl; [*Schochow:* **halbem**]
Deathly stillness covers the valley by the moon's pale yellow beam; [half]
(A deathly stillness lies over the valley in the pale yellow light of the moon;)

ˈvɪndə ˈflʏstʻɐn dʊmpf lʊntʻ baŋ lɪn dɛs ˈvɛçtʻɐs ˈnaxtʻgəzaŋ.
Winde flüstern dumpf und bang in des Wächters Nachtgesang.
winds whisper dully and anxiously in the watchman's night- song.
(winds are whispering dully and anxiously in the song of the night watchman.)

ˈlae̯zɐ, ˈdʊmpfɐ tʰøːntʻ lɛs hiːɐ̯/hiːr lɪn deːɐ̯ ˈbaŋən ˈzeːlə miːɐ̯,
Leiser, dumpfer tönt es hier in der bangen Seele mir,
More softly, more dully sounds it here in the anxious soul to me,
(Something is sounding more softly and even more dully here in my anxious soul,)

nɪmt den ʃtʻraːl deːɐ̯ ˈhɔfnʊŋ fɔrtʻ, viː den moːnt di ˈvɔlkʻə dɔrtʰ.
nimmt den Strahl der Hoffnung fort, wie den Mond die Wolke dort.
takes the ray of the hope away, as the moon (obj.) the cloud (subj.) there.
(removing the last ray of hope, as that cloud there is removing the moon.)

hʏltʻ, liːɐ̯ ˈvɔlkʻən, hʏlt den ʃae̯n ˈlɪmɐ ˈtʰiːfɐ, ˈtʰiːfɐ(r) lae̯n!
Hüllt, ihr Wolken, hüllt den Schein immer tiefer, tiefer ein!
Cover, you clouds, cover the light ever more deeply, more deeply up!
(You clouds, cover the light ever more fully, ever more densely!) [*einhüllen* = cover]

foːɐ̯/foːr liːm ˈbɛrgən vɪl mae̯n hɛrt͡s ˈzae̯nən ˈtʰiːfən, ˈtʰiːfən ʃmɛrt͡s.
Vor ihm bergen will mein Herz seinen tiefen, tiefen Schmerz.
From it to conceal wants my heart its deep, deep pain.
(My heart wants to hide its deep, deep pain from the light.) [*ihn* here refers to *den Schein*]

ˈnɛnən zɔl liːn nɪçtʻ mae̯n mʊntʻ, ˈkʰae̯nə ˈtʰrɛːnə max liːn ˈkʰʊntʻ;
Nennen soll ihn nicht mein Mund, keine Träne mach' ihn kund;
Name shall it not my mouth, no tear make it known ;
(My mouth shall not name it, no tear shall make it known:) [*ihn* here refers to *seinen Schmerz*]

ˈzɛŋkʻən zɔl man liːn hɪˈnapʻ lae̯nstʻ mɪtʻ miːɐ̯/miːr lɪns ˈkʰyːlə graːpʻ.
senken soll man ihn hinab einst mit mir ins kühle Grab.
sink shall one it down one day with me into the cool grave.
(one day it shall be buried with me in the cool grave.)

oː deːɐ̯ ˈʃøːnən ˈlaŋən naxtʻ, voː nɪçtʻ ˈleːɐ̯dənliːbə laxtʰ,
O der schönen langen Nacht, wo nicht Erdenliebe lacht,
O the beautiful long night, where not earthly love laughs,
(O for that beautiful long night, when no earthly love will smile,)

voː fɛɐ̯ˈlasnə ˈtʰrɔ̯ø̯ə nɪçtʻ ˈiːrən kʰrants fɔn ˈdɔrnən flɪçtʰ!
wo verlass'ne Treue nicht ihren Kranz von Dornen flicht!
where forsaken faithfulness not its wreath of thorns plaits!
(when forsaken faithfulness will not plait its wreath of thorns!)

an dɛs ˈtʰoːdəs ˈmɪldɐ hantʻ geːt deːɐ̯ veːkʻ lɪns ˈfaːtʻɐlantʻ;
An des Todes milder Hand geht der Weg ins Vaterland;
At the death's gentle hand goes the way into the fatherland;
(The gentle hand of death will show the way to the homeland of the spirit;)

dɔrtʻ lɪstʻ ˈliːbə ˈzɔndɐ pʰa͜en: ˈzeːlɪç, ˈzeːlɪç veːɐ̯d ɪç za͜en!
dort ist Liebe sonder Pein: selig, selig werd' ich sein!
there is love without pain: blissful, blissful shall I be!
(there love is without pain: there I shall be blissful, blissful!)

[Here the mood of nature at night has an ominous quality in harmony with the feelings of a betrayed lover who longs for death as a door to a realm where pure love exists without pain.]

Indische Legende see *Der Gott und die Bajadere*

Ins stille Land see *Lied*

ifiˈgeːni̯a
Iphigenia
Iphigenia

Op. 98, No. 3 [1817] (poem by Johann Mayrhofer)

blyːt dɛn hiːɐ̯/hiːr lan ˈtʰa͜orɪs ˈʃtʻrandə, la͜os dem ˈtʰɔ̯ø̯rən ˈfaːtʻɐlandə ˈkʰa͜enə ˈbluːmə?
Blüht denn hier an Tauris Strande, aus dem teuren Vaterlande keine Blume?
Blooms then here on Tauris' shore, from the dear fatherland no flower?
(Does then no flower from my beloved homeland bloom here on the shore of Tauris?)
[*poem:* **...Strande keine Blum'** (bluːm) **aus Hellas** (ˈhɛlas, Greece) **Lande**]

veːtʻ kʰa͜en ha͜ox, la͜os den ˈzeːlɪgən gəˈfɪldən, voː gəˈʃvɪstʻɐ mɪtʻ miːɐ̯ ˈʃpʻiːltʻən?
weht kein Hauch, aus den seligen Gefilden, wo Geschwister mit mir spielten?
blows no breath from the blessed fields where siblings with me played?
(Does no breeze blow from the blessed fields where my sisters and my brother played with me?)
[ˈmɪldɐ ˈzeːgənsha͜ox] [ˈliːpʻlɪçən]
[*poem:* **weht kein milder Segenshauch aus den lieblichen Gefilden]**
[mild breath of blessing] [delightful]

ax, ma͜en ˈleːbən lɪstʻ la͜en ra͜ox! ˈtʰra͜oɐntʻ vaŋkʻ ɪç lɪn dem ˈha͜enə,
ach, mein Leben ist ein Rauch! Trauernd wank' ich in dem Haine,
ah, my life is a smoke! Grieving stagger I in the grove,
(Ah, my life goes up in smoke! Grieving, I stagger about in the grove,)
[*poem:* **durch die Haine** (dʊrç di ˈha͜enə, through the groves)]

ˈkʰa͜enə ˈhɔfnʊŋ nɛːr ɪç, ˈkʰa͜enə, ˈma͜enə ˈha͜emaːt tsuː lɛɐ̯ˈzeːn;
keine Hoffnung nähr' ich, keine, meine Heimat zu erseh'n;
no hope nourish I, none, my homeland to behold;
(I nourish no hope, none at all, that I can ever see my homeland again;)

ʊnt di zeː mɪt‘ ˈhoːən ˈvɛlən, diː ˈan ˈkʰlɪp‘ən zɪç tsɛɐ̯ˈʃɛlən,
und die See mit hohen Wellen, die an Klippen sich zerschellen,
and the sea with high waves that on reefs themselves shatter,
(and the sea, with high waves that shatter against the reefs,)
[*poem:* **die an Klippen kalt** (kʰalt, coldly) **zerschellen]**

ˈyːbɐtʰɔø̯p‘t‘ ma͜en ˈla͜ezəs fleːn. ˈgœt‘ɪn, diː duː mɪç gəˈrɛt‘ət‘,
übertäubt mein leises Fleh'n. Göttin, die du mich gerettet,
drowns out my soft entreating. Goddess, who you me rescued,
(drowns out my soft entreaties. Goddess, you who rescued me once,)
[*poem:* **Göttin, welche** (ˈvɛlçə, which) **mich gerettet]**

an di ˈvɪlt‘nɪs ˈlangəkʰɛt‘ət‘, ˈrɛt‘ə mɪç tsʊm ˈtsva͜et‘ən maːl, ˈgnɛːdɪç ˈlasə mɪç
an die Wildnis angekettet, rette mich zum zweiten Mal, gnädig lasse mich
to the wilderness chained, rescue me for the second time, graciously let me
(rescue me, chained to this wilderness, rescue me a second time! Graciously let me,)
[*poem:* **an die Wildnis mich gekettet** (who chained me to the wilderness)]

den ˈma͜enən, las, loː ˈgœt‘ɪn, mɪç lɛɐ̯ˈʃa͜enən lɪn dɛs ˈgroːsən ˈkʰø̯nɪçs zaːl!
den meinen, lass', o Göttin, mich erscheinen in des grossen Königs Saal!
to my dear ones, let, O goddess, me appear in the great king's hall!
(O goddess, let me appear before my dear ones in the great king's hall!)

[King Agamemnon of Mycenae, leader of the Greeks in the Trojan War, and Clytemnestra (the sister of Helen of Troy), had three daughters, Iphigenia, Electra, and Chrysothemis, and a son, Orestes. When the Greek ships were becalmed at Aulis and unable to set sail for Troy, Agamemnon was ordered to sacrifice Iphigenia in exchange for favorable winds. The goddess Artemis (Diana to the Romans), spirited the victim away to barbaric Tauris (now the Crimean Peninsula) on the Black Sea, where she became a priestess in a temple that held a sacred image of the goddess. Schubert was familiar with the works of Gluck and Goethe that are based on this story. The poet, Johann Mayrhofer, shared a room with Schubert between 1819 and 1821. The composer set many of his poems, a number of them based on Greek mythology, almost as soon as they were written down. Schubert's manuscript of *Iphigenia* is in G flat major, as in the *Gesamtausgabe*; Peters follows the original publication, in F major.]

ˈɪrdɪʃəs glʏkʰ
Irdisches Glück
Earthly Happiness

Op. 95, No. 4 [1828?] (Johann Gabriel Seidl)

zoː ˈmançɐ ziːt‘ mɪt‘ ˈfɪnst‘rɐ ˈmiːnə di ˈva͜et‘ə vɛlt‘ zɪç ˈgrɔlənt‘ lan,
So mancher sieht mit finstrer Miene die weite Welt sich grollend an,
So many a one looks with gloomy mien the wide world for himself resentfully at,
(So many a man looks at the wide world resentfully, with a gloomy expression on his face;)

dɛs ˈleːbəns ˈvʊndɐbaːrə ˈbyːnə liːk‘t‘ liːm fɛɐ̯ˈgeːbəns ˈla͜ofgətʰaːn.
des Lebens wunderbare Bühne liegt ihm vergebens aufgetan.
the life's wonderful stage lies to him in vain opened.
(life's wonderful stage lies open before him in vain.)

daː va͜es ɪç ˈbɛsɐ mɪç t͜suː ˈneːmən, lʊntʻ fɛrn, deːɐ̯ ˈfrɔ͜ødə mɪç t͜suː ˈʃɛːmən,
Da weiss ich besser mich zu nehmen, und fern, der Freude mich zu schämen,
There know I better myself to take, and far of the pleasure myself to be ashamed,
(In that respect I know better how to handle myself; and, far from being ashamed of the pleasure,)

gəˈniːs ɪç froː den ˈla͜ogənblɪk^h: das lɪst dɛn dɔx gəˈvɪs la͜en glʏk^h!
geniess ich froh den Augenblick: das ist denn doch gewiss ein Glück!
enjoy I gladly the moment: that is then after all certainly a happiness!
(I gladly enjoy the moment: that is certainly a good reason to be happy, after all!)

ʊm ˈmançəs hɛrt͜s haːb ɪç gəˈvɔrbən, dɔx ˈvɛːɐ̯tʻə ma͜en t^{h}riˈʊmf nɪçtʻ laŋ,
Um manches Herz hab' ich geworben, doch währte mein Triumph nicht lang,
For many a heart have I courted, but lasted my triumph not long,
(I have courted many a heart, but my triumph never lasted very long,)

dɛn ˈbløːtʻha͜etʻ hatʻ miːɐ̯/miːr lɔftʻ fɛɐ̯ˈdɔrbən,
denn Blödheit hat mir oft verdorben,
for stupidity has for me often ruined
(for my stupidity has often ruined)

vas k^{h}a͜om ma͜en ˈfroːzɪn miːɐ̯/miːr lɛɐ̯ˈraŋ.
was kaum mein Frohsinn mir errang.
what barely my cheerfulness for me won.
(what my cheerfulness had almost won for me.)

drʊm bɪn lɪç la͜ox dem nɛt͜s lɛntʻgaŋən:
Drum bin ich auch dem Netz entgangen:
Therefore have I also the net escaped:
(That is also the reason why I have so far escaped the net:)

dɛn va͜el k^{h}a͜en vaːn mɪç hiːltʻ lʊmˈfaŋən,
denn weil kein Wahn mich hielt umfangen,
for since no illusion me held encircled,
(for since no illusion has held me captive,)

k^{h}aːm lɪç fɔn ˈk^{h}a͜enəm la͜ox t͜suˈrʏk^h: ʊnt das lɪst dɔx gəˈvɪs la͜en glʏk^h!
kam ich von keinem auch zurück: und das ist doch gewiss ein Glück!
came I from none also back: and that is after all certainly a happiness!
(I have had none to retreat from: and that is certainly a good reason to be happy, after all!)

k^{h}a͜en ˈlɔrbeːɐ̯ ˈgryːntʻə ˈma͜enəm ˈʃa͜etʻəl, ma͜en ha͜optʻtʻ lʊmˈʃtʻraːltʻ k^{h}a͜en ˈleːrənglant͜s;
Kein Lorbeer grünte meinem Scheitel, mein Haupt umstrahlt kein Ehrenglanz;
No laurel grew for my top, my head irradiates no honor-luster;
(No laurel has been growing to adorn my brow, no luster of honor shines about my head;)

[*GA:* **Ehrenkranz** (ˈleːrənk^{h}rant͜s,, wreath of honor)]

dɔx lɪst daˈrʊm ma͜en t^{h}uːn nɪçtʻ ˈla͜etʻəl, la͜en ˈʃtʻɪlɐ daŋkʻ lɪstʻ la͜ox la͜en k^{h}rant͜s!
doch ist darum mein Tun nicht eitel, ein stiller Dank ist auch ein Kranz!
but is for that reason my doing not vain, a quiet thanks is also a wreath!
(but that does not mean that all I have done was in vain; a quiet word of thanks is also a wreath!)

veːm, vaet' lɛnt''fɛrnt' fɔn 'kʰɛk'ən 'flyːgən, dɛs 'tʰaːləs 'ʃt'ɪlə 'frɔ̯ødən 'gnyːgən,
Wem, weit entfernt von kecken Flügen, des Tales stille Freuden g'nügen,
For whomever, far removed from bold flights, the valley's quiet joys suffice,
(He for whom the quiet joys of the valley suffice, far removed from bold flights,)

deːm baŋt' lɑ̯ox niː fyːɐ̯ zaen gə'nɪkʰ: ʊnt das lɪst dɔx gə'vɪs laen glʏkʰ!
dem bangt auch nie für sein Genick: und das ist doch gewiss ein Glück!
to him (he) is fearful also never for his nape: and that is after all surely a happiness!
(never needs to be fearful for his neck: and that is certainly a good reason to be happy, after all!)
[*Schochow:* **für sein Geschick** (gə'ʃɪk', fate)]

ʊnt' ruːft deːɐ̯ boːt' lɑ̯os 'jeːnən 'raeçən miːɐ̯/miːr laenst', viː 'lalən, lɛrnst' lʊnt' hoːl,
Und ruft der Bot' aus jenen Reichen mir einst, wie Allen, ernst und hohl,
And calls the messenger from those realms to me one day, as to all, grave and hollow,
(And if one day the messenger from the other world calls to me, as to all, in grave, hollow tones,)

dan zaːg ɪç 'vɪlɪç, lɪm lɛnt''vaeçən, deːɐ̯ 'ʃøːnən 'leːɐ̯də: 'leːbəvoːl!
dann sag' ich willig, im Entweichen, der schönen Erde: "Lebewohl!"
then say I willingly, in the vanishing, to the beautiful earth: "Farewell!"
(then I shall willing say "Farewell!" to the beautiful earth as I vanish.)

zaes dɛn, zoː 'drʏk'ən dɔx lam 'lɛndə di hant' miːɐ̯ 'tʰrɔ̯øə 'frɔ̯øndəshɛndə,
Sei's denn, so drücken doch am Ende die Hand mir treue Freundeshände,
So be it then, thus press after all at the end the hand to me loyal friend- hands,
(So be it then, the hands of loyal friends, after all, will press mine again at the end of my life,)

zoː 'zeːgnət dɔx mɪç 'frɔ̯øndəsblɪkʰ: ʊnt das lɪst', 'bryːdɐ, dɔx voːl glʏkʰ!
so segnet doch mich Freundesblick: und das ist, Brüder, doch wohl Glück!
so blesses surely me friend- gaze: and that is, brothers, after all indeed happiness!
(the eyes of friends will surely bless me: and that, brothers, will indeed be happiness, after all!)
[*Peters (and GA in the repeat):* **doch ein Glück!**]

[There is humor in the *acciaccature* with off-beat accents that characterize the grumblers in this cheerful ditty, one of the "Four Refrain Songs" that were published as a group.]

Irrlicht see *Winterreise*

'jaːk't'liːt'

Jagdlied

Hunting Song

Posthumously published [composed 1817] (poem by Zacharias Werner)

tʰra'raː! tʰra'raː! viːɐ̯ 'kʰeːrən da'haem, viːɐ̯ 'brɪŋən di 'bɔ̯øt'ə deːɐ̯ jaːk't'!
Trarah! Trarah! Wir kehren daheim, wir bringen die Beute der Jagd!
Trarah! Trarah! We return home, we bring the booty of the hunt!
(Trarah! We are coming back home, we bring booty from the hunt!)

ɛs 'zɪŋk'ət di naxt', drʊm 'halt'ən viːɐ̯ vaxtʰ; das lɪçt'
Es sinket die Nacht, drum halten wir Wacht; das Licht
There sinks the night, therefore keep we watch; the light
(The night is falling, therefore we keep watch; light)

hat‘ ˈyːbɐ das ˈdʊŋk‘əl maxtʰ! a͜of, a͜of, a͜of! das ˈfɔ͜øɐ(r) ˈlangəfaxtʰ!
hat über das Dunkel Macht! Auf, auf, auf! Das Feuer angefacht!
has over the darkness power! Up, up, up! The fire (be) fanned!
(has power over darkness! Come, come, come! Fan the fire!)

tʰraˈraː! viːɐ̯ ˈt͜sɛçən ɪm kʰra͜es, viːɐ̯ ˈʃp‘ɔt‘ən dɛs ˈdʊŋk‘əls deːɐ̯ naxtʰ.
Trarah! Wir zechen im Kreis, wir spotten des Dunkels der Nacht.
Trarah! We drink in the circle, we mock the darkness of the night.
(Trarah! We drink in a circle, we mock the darkness of night.)
[*poem:* **wir spotten des Dunkels, der Nacht** (we mock the darkness, the night)]

dɛs ˈmɛnʃən maxt‘ ɪn ˈfrɔ͜ødɪgɐ pʰraxt di kʰvaːl fɛɐ̯ˈhøːnt, dɛs ˈtʰoːdəs laxtʰ.
Des Menschen Macht in freudiger Pracht die Qual verhöhnt, des Todes lacht.
The human's power in joyful splendor the torment scoffs at, at the death laughs.
(The strength of a human being in the splendor of joy scoffs at pain and laughs at death.)
[*poem:* **die Qual verhöhnet** (fɛɐ̯ˈhøːnət‘)]

tʰraˈraː! a͜of! di gluːt‘ ɪst‘ ˈlangəfaxtʰ!
Trarah! Auf! Die Glut ist angefacht!
Trarah! Up! The fire is fanned!
(Trarah! Up! The fire is ablaze!)

[The poem is from *Wanda, Königin der Sarmaten*, "a romantic tragedy in five acts with songs," where it is assigned to a "chorus of knights and mounted warriors." Schubert's song was meant to be sung by a male chorus. With much-changed words, and the time of day altered from nightfall to sunrise, Schubert's song was pressed into service as a substitute for the missing ending of *Die Nacht* when that song was first published after the composer's death.]

Jäger, ruhe von der Jagd see *Ellens Gesang II*

ˈjɛːgɐs ˈlaːbənt‘liːt‘

Jägers Abendlied

Huntsman's Evening Song

Op. 3, No. 4 (second version) [1815, 1816] (Johann Wolfgang von Goethe)

ɪm ˈfɛldə ʃla͜eç ɪç ʃt‘ɪl ʊnt‘ vɪlt‘, gəˈʃp‘ant‘ ma͜en ˈfɔ͜øɐroːɐ̯.
Im Felde schleich' ich still und wild, gespannt mein Feuerrohr.
In the field stalk I silent and wild, cocked my gun.
(I am stalking through the field, silent and wild, my gun cocked and ready.)

daː ʃveːp‘t‘ zoː lɪçt da͜en ˈliːbəs bɪlt‘, da͜en ˈzyːsəs bɪlt‘ miːɐ̯ foːɐ̯.
Da schwebt so licht dein liebes Bild, dein süsses Bild mir vor.
Then hovers so light your dear image, your sweet image to me before.
(Then, all at once, your dear, sweet image hovers before me, so full of light.)

duː ˈvandəlst‘ jɛt͜st‘ voːl ʃt‘ɪl ʊnt‘ mɪlt dʊrç fɛlt‘ ʊnt‘ ˈliːbəs tʰaːl,
Du wandelst jetzt wohl still und mild durch Feld und liebes Tal,
You wander now probably silent and gentle through field and dear valley,
(Right now you are probably wandering through field and beloved valley, silent and gentle,)

ʊnt‘ ax ma͜en ʃnɛl fɛɐ̯ˈra͜oʃənt‘ bɪlt‘, ʃt‘ɛlt‘ zɪç diːɐ̯s nɪçt‘ la͜enˈmaːl?
und ach mein schnell verrauschend Bild, stellt sich dir's nicht einmal?
and ah my quickly dying away image, presents itself to you it not once?
(and, ah, does my quickly fading image not ever present itself to you?)

[dɛs ˈmɛnʃən, deːɐ̯ di vɛlt dʊrçˈʃtʻra͜eftʻ fɔl ˈlʊnmuːtʻ lʊntʻ fɛɐ̯ˈdrʊs,
[Des Menschen, der die Welt durchstreift voll Unmut und Verdruss,
[Of the human being, who the world roams through full of ill humor and vexation,
[(The image of the man who is roaming all over the world full of ill humor and vexation)

naːx ˈlɔstʻən lʊntʻ naːx ˈvɛstʻən ʃva͜eftʻ, va͜el leːɐ̯ dɪç ˈlasən mʊs.]
nach Osten und nach Westen schweift, weil er dich lassen muss.]
to east and to west roves, because he you leave must.]
(because he had to leave your side to rove to the east and to the west.)]

miːɐ̯/miːr lɪstʻ lɛs, dɛŋkʻ ɪç nuːɐ̯/nuːr lan dɪç, lals lɪn den moːnt t͜suː zeːn;
Mir ist es, denk' ich nur an dich, als in den Mond zu seh'n;
To me is it, think I only of you, as if into the moon to look;
(Whenever I am thinking of you, it seems to me as if I am gazing into the moon;)

a͜en ˈʃtʻɪlɐ ˈfriːdə kʰɔmtʻ la͜of mɪç, va͜es nɪçtʻ viː miːɐ̯ gəˈʃeːn.
ein stiller Friede kommt auf mich, weiss nicht wie mir gescheh'n.
a quiet peace comes over me, (I) know not how to me happened.
(a quiet peacefulness comes over me, I don't know how it happens.)

[Schubert set this poem twice. The earlier version was first published in 1907, and is therefore not included in Peters or the *Gesamtausgabe*. It can be found in the *Neue Schubert Ausgabe* (IV, volume 1B, page 198) published by Bärenreiter. The third verse of the more familiar second setting is missing in both of the earlier editions, as it is in the fair copy made for Goethe; other copies, however, include the third verse (in brackets above). The song is printed in B major in the Peters collection, one tone lower than the original key of D flat. The huntsman's stealthy prowl is made audible by the sliding chromatic sixths in the first seven bars of the accompaniment. Goethe asked that the first and third verses of his poem be vigorously and a bit wildly delivered, for the second and fourth he prescribed a gentler, softer expression.]

ˈjɛːgɐs ˈliːbəsliːtʻ
Jägers Liebeslied
Huntsman's Love Song

Op. 96, No. 2 [1827] (Franz von Schober)

ɪç ʃiːs den hɪrʃ lɪm ˈgryːnən fɔrstʻ, lɪm ˈʃtʻɪlən tʰaːl das reː,
Ich schiess den Hirsch im grünen Forst, im stillen Tal das Reh,
I shoot the stag in the green forest, in the quiet valley the roe,
[*poem:* **im dunklen** (ˈdʊŋkʻlən, dark) **Forst]**

den ˈlaːdlɐ(r) la͜of dem ˈkʰlɪpʻənhɔrstʻ, di ˈlɛntʻə la͜of dem zeː.
den Adler auf dem Klippenhorst, die Ente auf dem See.
the eagle on the crag- aerie, the duck on the lake.
(the eagle in his nest on a crag, the duck on the lake.) [*poem:* **in** (lɪn, in) **dem Klippenhorst]**

kʰa͜en lɔrt, deːɐ̯ ʃʊt͜s gəˈvɛːrən kʰan, vɛn ˈma͜enə ˈflɪntʻə t͜siːltʰ;
Kein Ort, der Schutz gewähren kann, wenn meine Flinte zielt;
No place that protection afford can when my flintlock takes aim;
(No place can afford protection when my gun is aimed;)

ʊnt 'dɛnɔx haːb ɪç 'hart'ɐ man di 'liːbə la͜ox gə'fyːltʰ!
und dennoch hab' ich harter Mann die Liebe auch gefühlt!
and yet have I hard man the love also felt!
(and yet I, hard man that I am, have also felt love!)

haːp' lɔft' han'tʰiːɐ̯t' lɪn 'ra͜oɐ tsa͜et', lɪn ʃt'ʊrm lʊnt' 'vɪnt'ɐnaxtʰ,
Hab' oft hantiert in rauher Zeit, in Sturm und Winternacht,
(I) have often been busy in rough time, in storm and winter night,
(I have often been busy in rough weather, in storms and winter nights,)

ʊnt' lyːbɐ(r)'la͜est' lʊnt' 'la͜engəʃna͜et, tsʊm bɛt den ʃt'a͜en gə'maxtʰ.
und übereist und eingeschneit, zum Bett den Stein gemacht.
and iced over and snowed in, to the bed the stone made.
(and, iced over and snowed in, made my bed on hard stones.)

a͜of 'dɔrnən ʃliːf ɪç viː la͜of fla͜om, fɔm 'nɔrt'vɪnt' lʊngə'ryːɐ̯tʰ,
Auf Dornen schlief ich wie auf Flaum, vom Nordwind ungerührt,
On thorns slept I as on down, by the north wind untouched,
(I have slept on thorns as if on down, unaffected by the north wind,)

dɔx hat deːɐ̯ 'liːbə 'tsaɐ̯t'ən tʰra͜om di 'ra͜oə brʊst' gə'ʃp'yːɐ̯tʰ.
doch hat der Liebe zarten Traum die rauhe Brust gespürt.
yet has the love's delicate dream the rough breast felt.
(and yet this rough breast of mine has experienced love's delicate dream.)

deːɐ̯ 'vɪldə falk' vaːɐ̯ ma͜en gə'zɛl, deːɐ̯ vɔlf ma͜en 'kʰampf̮gəʃp'an;
Der wilde Falk war mein Gesell, der Wolf mein Kampfgespann;
The wild hawk was my companion, the wolf my battle-teammate;
(The fierce hawk was my companion, the wolf my teammate in battle;)

miːɐ̯ fɪŋ deːɐ̯ tʰaːk' mɪt' 'hʊnt'gə͵bɛl, di naxt' mɪt' 'hʊsa lan.
mir fing der Tag mit Hundgebell, die Nacht mit Hussa an.
for me began the day with hound-baying, the night with "Tallyho!" .... [*anfangen* = begin]
(for me the day began with the baying of hounds, the night with cries of "Tallyho!")
[*poem:* **es** (ɛs, it/there) **fing der Tag**]

a͜en 'tʰanra͜es vaːɐ̯ di 'bluːməntsiːɐ̯/-tsiːr la͜of 'ʃva͜esbəflɛk't'əm huːtʰ,
Ein Tannreis war die Blumenzier auf schweissbeflecktem Hut,
A fir- twig was the flower- decoration on sweat- stained hat,
(A sprig of fir was the floral decoration on my sweat-stained hat,)

ʊnt 'dɛnɔx ʃluːk' di 'liːbə miːɐ̯/miːr lɪns 'vɪldə 'jɛːgɐbluːtʰ.
und dennoch schlug die Liebe mir ins wilde Jägerblut.
and yet struck the love to me into the wild huntsman-blood.
(and yet love struck me and seeped into my wild huntsman's blood.)

oː 'ʃɛːfɐ(r) la͜of dem 'va͜eçən moːs, deːɐ̯ duː mɪt' 'bluːmən ʃp'iːlstʰ,
O Schäfer auf dem weichen Moos, der du mit Blumen spielst,
O shepherd on the soft moss, who you with flowers play,
(O shepherd on the soft moss, you who play with flowers,)
[*poem:* **mit Blüten** ('blyːt'ən, blossoms) **spielst**]

veːɐ̯ vae̯s, lɔp‘ duː zoː hae̯s, zoː groːs, viː lɪç di ˈliːbə fyːlstʰ.
wer weiss, ob du so heiss, so gross, wie ich die Liebe fühlst.
who knows, whether you so ardently, so greatly, as I the love feel.
(who knows whether you feel love as ardently, as deeply, as I do?)

alˈnɛçt‘lɪç ˈlyːbɐm ˈʃvart͡sən valt‘, fɔm ˈmoːndənʃae̯n lʊmˈʃt‘raːltʰ,
Allnächtlich überm schwarzen Wald, vom Mondenschein umstrahlt,
Every night above the black woods, by the moonlight irradiated,
(Every night, above the dark woods, radiant in the moonlight,)
[*Peters:* **übern** (ˈlyːbɐn, over): the accusative gives the sense of *moving* over the woods]

ʃveːp‘t‘ ˈkʰøːnɪçsheːɐ̯ di ˈlɪçt‘gəʃt‘alt‘, viː ziː kʰae̯n ˈmae̯st‘ɐ maːltʰ.
schwebt königshehr die Lichtgestalt, wie sie kein Meister malt.
floats regally-exalted the light-form, as it no master paints.
(her luminous image, such as no master has ever painted, is floating majestically.)
[*poem:* **königsgross** (ˈkʰøːnɪçsgroːs, regally great)]

vɛn ziː dan lao̯f mɪç ˈniːdɐziːt‘, vɛn mɪç liːɐ̯ blɪk‘ dʊrçˈglyːtʰ,
Wenn sie dann auf mich niedersieht, wenn mich ihr Blick durchglüht,
When she then at me looks down, when me her gaze glows through,
(When she then looks down at me, when her gaze glows through me,)

daː vae̯s ɪç, viː dem vɪlt‘ gəˈʃiːt, das foːɐ̯ dem ˈroːrə fliːtʰ.
da weiss ich, wie dem Wild geschieht, das vor dem Rohre flieht.
then know I, how to the deer happens, that from the gun flees.
(then I know how the deer feels as he flees from the gun.)
[*poem:* **dann fühl'** (dan fyːl, then feel) **ich, wie dem Wild**]

ʊnt dɔx! mɪt‘ ˈlaləm glʏk‘ fɛɐ̯ˈlae̯nt, das nuːɐ̯/nuːr lao̯f ˈleːɐ̯dən lɪstʰ,
Und doch! mit allem Glück vereint, das nur auf Erden ist,
And yet! with all happiness united, that only on earth is,
(And yet that fear is united with all the happiness that can be found on earth,)
[*poem:* **Ich fühl's** (ɪç fyːls, I feel it) **mit allem G1ück vereint**]

als vɛn deːɐ̯/deːr ˈlalɐbɛst‘ə frɔ̯ønt‘ mɪç lɪn di ˈlarmə ʃliːstʰ!
als wenn der allerbeste Freund mich in die Arme schliesst!
as when the very best friend me in the arms closes!
(such as when my very best friend is embracing me in his arms!) [*poem:* **wie** (viː, as) **wenn**]

[The heart of the huntsman is hardened to the suffering of the animals he kills, but as susceptible as any man's to the mixed feelings of love. The piano part supplies the hunting horns.]

joˈhana ˈzeːbʊs
Johanna Sebus
Johanna Sebus

Fragment posthumously published [composed 1821] (ballad by Johann Wolfgang von Goethe)

deːɐ̯ dam t͡sɛɐ̯ˈrae̯stʰ, das fɛlt‘ lɛɐ̯ˈbrao̯stʰ, di ˈfluːt‘ən ˈʃp‘yːlən, di ˈflɛçə zao̯stʰ.
Der Damm zerreisst, das Feld erbraust, die Fluten spülen, die Fläche saust.
The dam is breaking, the field foams up, the waters lap, the plain howls.

— ɪç ˈtʰra:gə dɪç, ˈmʊtʻɐ, dʊrç di flu:tʰ, nɔx ra͜eçtʻ zi: nɪçtʻ ho:x,
—“Ich trage dich, Mutter, durch die Flut, noch reicht sie nicht hoch,
—“I carry you, Mother, through the flood, still reaches it not high,
(—“I’ll carry you through the flood, Mother; it’s not yet high,)

ˈɪç ˈva:tʻə gu:tʰ. — a͜ox ˈʊns bəˈdɛŋkʻə, bəˈdrɛŋtʻ vi: vi:ɐ̯ zɪntʻ,
ich wate gut.” —“Auch uns bedenke, bedrängt wie wir sind,
I wade well.” —“Also us think of, in distress as we are,
(I’ll be able to wade.” —“Think of us too, in distress as we are,)

di ˈha͜osgənɔsɪn, dra͜e ˈarmə kʰɪntʻ! di ˈʃvaxə fra͜o! zi: ˈa͜elt daˈfɔn,
die Hausgenossin, drei arme Kind! Die schwache Frau!” Sie eilt davon,
the house-sharer, three poor child(ren)! The weak woman!” She hurries away,
(the weak woman who shares your house, the three poor children!” The girl hurries away,)

zi: tʰrɛ:kʻt di ˈmʊtʻɐ dʊrçs ˈvasɐ ʃo:n. — t͜sʊm ˈby:lə da: ˈrɛtʻətʻ ˈɔ͜øç!
sie trägt die Mutter durchs Wasser schon. —“Zum Bühle da rettet euch!
she carries the mother through the water already. —“To the hill there save yourselves!
(she is already carrying her mother through the water. —“Head for the hill over there)

ˈharət de:ɐ̯ˈva͜el; gla͜eç kʰe:r ɪç t͜suˈrʏkʰ, ˈʊns ˈalən ˈɪstʻ ha͜el.
harret derweil; gleich kehr’ ich zurück, uns allen ist Heil.
wait meanwhile; right away return I back, for us all is salvation.
(and wait a while; I’ll be right back, we’ll all be saved.)

t͜sʊm by:l ˈɪst͜s nɔx ˈtʰrɔkʻən ˈʊntʻ ˈve:nɪgə ʃrɪtʰ; dɔx ne:mtʻ ˈa͜ox mi:ɐ̯
Zum Bühl ist’s noch trocken und wenige Schritt’; doch nehmt auch mir
To the hill is it still dry and few steps; but take also for me
(The way to the hill is still dry, and it’s only a few steps away; but also, for me, take)

ˈma͜enə ˈt͜si:gə mɪtʰ! de:ɐ̯ dam t͜sɛɐ̯ˈʃmɪlt͜stʰ, das fɛltʻ ˈɛɐ̯ˈbra͜ostʰ,
meine Ziege mit!” Der Damm zerschmilzt, das Feld erbraust,
my goat with (you)!” The dam melts away, the field foams up,
(my goat with you!” The dam melts away, the field foams up,)

di ˈflu:tʻən ˈvy:lən, di ˈflɛçə za͜ostʰ. zi: zɛt͜st di ˈmʊtʻɐ(r) ˈa͜of ˈzɪçrəs lantʻ,
die Fluten wühlen, die Fläche saust. Sie setzt die Mutter auf sichres Land,
the waters slosh about, the plain howls. She sets the mother onto safe land,
(the waters slosh about, the plain howls. She sets her mother down on safe ground,)

ʃø:n ˈzu:sçən, gla͜eç ˈvi:dɐ t͜sʊr flu:tʻ gəˈvantʰ. — voˈhɪn? voˈhɪn?
schön Suschen, gleich wieder zur Flut gewandt. —“Wohin? Wohin?
lovely Susie, right away again to the flood turned. —“Whither? Whither?
(lovely Susie, then right away turning back to the flood. —“Where are you going?)

di ˈbra͜etʻə ʃvɔl; dɛs ˈvasɐs ˈɪst ˈhy:bən ˈʊnt ˈdry:bən fɔl.
die Breite schwoll; des Wassers ist hüben und drüben voll.
the breadth swelled; of the water is on this side and on that side full.
(The flood has swollen to a greater breadth; on all sides every space is full of water.)

fɛɐ̯'veːgən lɪns 'tʰiːfə vɪlst duː hɪ'nae̯n! — ziː 'zɔlən lʊnt' 'mʏsən gə'rɛt'ət' zae̯n!
Verwegen ins Tiefe willst du hinein!" —"Sie sollen und müssen gerettet sein!"
Recklessly into the depths want you into!" —"They shall and must rescued be!"
(Recklessly you want to go back into the depths?!" —"They shall be and *must* be rescued!")

[deːɐ̯ dam fɛɐ̯'ʃvɪndətʰ, di 'vɛlə brao̯stʰ. 'lae̯nə 'meːrəsvoːgə,
[Der Damm verschwindet, die Welle braust. Eine Meereswoge,
[The dam disappears, the wave roars. A billow,]

ziː ʃvaŋk't' lʊnt' zao̯stʰ. ʃøːn 'zuːsçən 'ʃrae̯t'ət' gə'voːnt'ən ʃt'eːk',
sie schwankt und saust. Schön Suschen schreitet gewohnten Steg,
it rolls and howls. Lovely Susie strides accustomed footpath,
(it rolls along and howls. Lovely Susie follows the accustomed footpath,)

ʊm'ʃt'røːmt' lao̯x 'glae̯t'ət' ziː nɪçt' fɔm veːk', lɛɐ̯'rae̯çt den byːl
umströmt auch gleitet sie nicht vom Weg, erreicht den Bühl
around-streamed even slips she not from the path, reaches the hill
(even with the water rushing around her she does not slip from the path; she reaches the hill)

lʊnt di 'naxbarɪn, dɔx deːɐ̯/deːr lʊnt den 'kʰɪndɐn kʰae̯n gə'vɪn! deːɐ̯ dam
und die Nachbarin, doch der und den Kindern kein Gewinn! Der Damm
and the neighbor woman, but for that one and the children no gain! The dam
(and the neighbor, but for that poor woman and her children nothing was gained! The dam)

fɛɐ̯'ʃvant', lae̯n meːɐ̯/meːr lɛɐ̯'brao̯sts, den 'kʰlae̯nən 'hyːgəl lɪm kʰrae̯s lʊm'zao̯sts.
verschwand, ein Meer erbraust's, den kleinen Hügel im Kreis umsaust's.
disappeared, a sea foams up it, the little hill [obj.] in the circle around-howls it.
(has disappeared entirely, a sea is roaring in, it howls around the little hill, totally circling it.)

daː 'gɛːnət' lʊnt' 'vɪrbəlt deːɐ̯ 'ʃɔ̯ømәndə ʃlʊnt' lʊnt 'tsiːət di frao̯
Da gähnet und wirbelt der schäumende Schlund und ziehet die Frau
There yawns and whirls the foaming abyss and draws the woman
(The foaming abyss yawns and whirls about and draws the woman)

mɪt den 'kʰɪndɐn tsuː grʊnt'; das hɔrn deːɐ̯ 'tsiːgə fast das lae̯n,
mit den Kindern zu Grund; das Horn der Ziege fasst das Ein',
with the children to bottom; the horn of the goat grasps the one,
(along with her children down into its depths; one child is still holding onto the horn of the goat,)

zoː 'zɔlt'ən ziː 'lalə fɛɐ̯'loːrən zae̯n! ʃøːn 'zuːsçən
so sollten sie alle verloren sein! Schön Suschen
thus were said they all lost to be! Lovely Susie
(that is, according to reports, how they all perished! Lovely Susie)

ʃt'eːt' nɔx ʃtrak' lʊnt' guːtʰ: veːɐ̯ 'rɛt'ət das 'jʊŋə, das 'leːdəlst'ə bluːtʰ?
steht noch strack und gut: wer rettet das junge, das edelste Blut?
stands still upright and well: who rescues the young, the noblest blood?
(is still standing upright, holding her ground: who will rescue the young, noblest heart?)

ʃøːn 'zuːsçən ʃt'eːt' nɔx viː lae̯n ʃt'ɛrn; dɔx 'lalə 'vɛrbɐ zɪnt' 'lalə fɛrn.
Schön Suschen steht noch wie ein Stern; doch alle Werber sind alle fern.
Lovely Susie stands still like a star; but all suitors are all far.
(Lovely Susie still stands there like a star; but all suitors are far away.)

rɪŋs lʊm ziː heːɐ̯/heːr lɪst‘ 'vasɐbaːn, kʰa͜en 'ʃifla͜en 'ʃvɪmət t͡suː liːɐ̯ hɛ'ran.
Rings um sie her ist Wasserbahn, kein Schifflein schwimmet zu ihr heran.
Around about her hither is water- path, no little boat swims to her up to.
(All around her there is unobstructed access over the water, but no little boat comes up to her.)

nɔx 'la͜enmaːl blɪk‘t‘ ziː t͡sʊm 'hɪməl hɪ'na͜of,
Noch einmal blickt sie zum Himmel hinauf,
Still once looks she to the heaven up,
(One more time she looks up toward heaven,)

daː 'neːmən di 'ʃma͜eçəlndən 'fluːt‘ən ziː la͜of. kʰa͜en dam, kʰa͜en fɛlt‘!
da nehmen die schmeichelnden Fluten sie auf. Kein Damm, kein Feld!
then take the caressing waters her up. No dam, no field!
(then the lapping waters receive her. There is no more dam, no more field!)
[*aufnehmen* = to receive, to take up]

nuːɐ̯ hiːɐ̯/hiːr lʊnt dɔrt‘ bə't͡sa͜eçnət‘ la͜en ba͜om, la͜en tʰʊrn den lɔrtʰ.
Nur hier und dort bezeichnet ein Baum, ein Turn den Ort.
Only here and there designates a tree, a tower the place.
(Only, here and there, the top of a tree or a tower identifies a place.)
[*Turn* = an old form of *Turm* = tower]

bə'dɛk‘t‘ lɪst‘ 'laləs mɪt‘ 'vasɐʃval; dɔx 'zuːsçəns bɪlt‘ ʃveːp‘t‘ 'lyːbɐ(r)lal.
Bedeckt ist alles mit Wasserschwall; doch Suschens Bild schwebt überall.
Covered is everything with water- surge; but Susie's image hovers everywhere.
(Everything is covered with surging water; but Susie's image hovers everywhere.)

das 'vasɐ zɪŋk‘t, das lant‘ lɛɐ̯'ʃa͜ent‘ lʊnt‘ 'lyːbɐ(r)lal
Das Wasser sinkt, das Land erscheint und überall
The water subsides, the land appears, and everywhere

vɪrt‘ ʃøːn 'zuːsçən bə'va͜entʰ. lʊnt deːm za͜e, veːɐ̯s nɪçt‘ zɪŋt‘ lʊnt‘ zaːk‘t‘,
wird schön Suschen beweint. Und dem sei, wer's nicht singt und sagt,
is lovely Susie bewept. And (after) him be, who it not sings and tells,
(lovely Susie is mourned. And may he who does not sing or tell her story)

lɪm 'leːbən lʊnt tʰoːt‘ nɪçt‘ 'langəfraːk‘tʰ!]
im Leben und Tod nicht angefragt!]
in the life and death not asked!]
(be shunned in life and death!)]

[The text that Schubert did not set is in brackets above. The song was completed by Reinhard van Hoorickx and privately printed in 1961. Goethe's subtitle explains the circumstances that inspired his ballad: *Zum Andenken der Siebzehnjährigen Schönen Guten aus dem Dorfe Brienen, die 13. Januar 1809 bei dem Eisgange des Rheins und dem grossen Bruche des Dammes von Cleverham Hülfe reichend unterging* ("In memory of the seventeen-year-old, beautiful, virtuous young woman from the village of Brienen who on January 13, 1809, during the freezing over of the Rhine and the great collapse of the dam at Cleverham, perished as she was offering help").]

ˈjuːli̯ʊs ǀan ˈtʰeˈoːnə
Julius an Theone
Julius to Theone

Posthumously published [composed 1816] (poem by Friedrich von Matthisson)

ˈnɪmɐ, ˈnɪmɐ darf ɪç diːɐ̯ gəˈʃtʻeːən, vas ba͜em ˈleːɐ̯stʻən ˈdrʊkʻə ˈda͜enɐ hantʻ,
Nimmer, nimmer darf ich dir gestehen, was beim ersten Drucke deiner Hand,
Never, never may I to you confess, what at the first press of your hand,
(Never, never may I confess to you what, at the first touch of your hand,)

ˈzyːsə ˈt͡sa͜obərɪn, ma͜en hɛrt͡s ǀɛmˈp͡fantʻ! ˈma͜enɐ(r) ˈǀa͜enzaːmkʰa͜etʻ fɛɐ̯ˈbɔrgnəs ˈfleːən,
süsse Zauberin, mein Herz empfand! Meiner Einsamkeit verborg'nes Flehen,
sweet enchantress, my heart felt! My loneliness's hidden supplication,
(sweet enchantress, my heart felt! The hidden supplication of my loneliness)

ˈma͜enə ˈzɔ͜øft͡sɐ vɪrt deːɐ̯ ʃtʻʊrm fɛɐ̯ˈveːən, ˈma͜enə ˈtʰrɛːnən ˈveːɐ̯dən ˈǀʊngəzeːən
meine Seufzer wird der Sturm verwehen, meine Tränen werden ungesehen
my sighs will the storm blow away, my tears will unseen
(and my sighs the storm will blow away; my tears, unseen, will)

ˈda͜enəm ˈbɪldə ˈrɪnən, bɪs di grʊftʻ mɪç ǀɪn liːɐ̯ fɛɐ̯ˈʃviːgnəs ˈdʊŋkʻəl ruːftʰ.
deinem Bilde rinnen, bis die Gruft mich in ihr verschwieg'nes Dunkel ruft.
for your image flow, till the tomb me into its taciturn darkness calls.
(flow for your image, till the tomb calls me into its taciturn darkness.)

ax! duː ˈʃa͜otʻəstʻ miːɐ̯ zoː ˈǀʊnbəfaŋən, zoː fɔl ˈǀɛŋəlˌǀʊnʃʊltʻ ǀɪns gəˈzɪçtʰ,
Ach! du schautest mir so unbefangen, so voll Engelunschuld ins Gesicht,
Ah! You looked at me so artlessly, so full of angelic innocence in the face,
(Ah! You looked into my face so artlessly, with a look so full of angelic innocence,)

ˈvɛːntʻəst den tʰriˈʊmf deːɐ̯ ˈʃøːnha͜etʻ nɪçtʰ! ǀoː tʰeˈoːnə! zaːst du nɪçtʻ
wähntest den Triumph der Schönheit nicht! O Theone! Sahst du nicht
imagined the triumph of the beauty not! O Theone! Saw you not
(you did not imagine the triumph of your beauty! O Theone! Did you not see)

den ˈbaŋən blɪkʻ deːɐ̯ ˈliːbə ǀan ˈda͜enən ˈblɪkʻən ˈhaŋən? [liːpʻ]
den bangen Blick der Liebe an deinen Blicken hangen? [*poem:* **der Lieb']**
the anxious look of the love on your glances hang? [love]
(my anxious look of love hanging on your every glance?)

ˈʃɪmɐtʻə di ˈrøːtʻə ˈma͜enɐ ˈvaŋən diːɐ̯ nɪçtʻ ˈǀaːnʊŋ deːɐ̯ fɛɐ̯ˈloːrnən ruː
Schimmerte die Röte meiner Wangen dir nicht Ahnung der verlornen Ruh'
Shimmered the flush of my cheeks to you not presentiment of the lost peace
(Did the flush of my cheeks not shimmer to you a presentiment of the lost peace)

ˈma͜enəs ˈhɔfnʊŋsloːzən ˈhɛrt͡səns t͡suː? das ǀʊns ˈmeːrə dɔx gəˈʃiːdən ˈhɛtʻən
meines hoffnungslosen Herzens zu? Dass uns Meere doch geschieden hätten
of my hopeless heart to? That us seas yet separated might have
(of my hopeless heart? Oh, if only seas had separated us)

naːx dem 'leːɐ̯st'ən 'la͜ezən drʊk' deːɐ̯ hant'! 'ʃa͜odɐnt' vaŋk' ɪç nuːn lam rant'
nach dem ersten leisen Druck der Hand! Schaudernd wank' ich nun am Rand
after the first soft press of the hand! Shuddering totter I now on the brink
(after that first soft touch of your hand! Shuddering, I now totter on the brink)
[*poem:* **am jähen** ('jɛːən, precipitous/sudden) **Rand**]

'la͜enəs 'lap'grʊnts,, voː la͜of 'dɔrnənbɛt'ən, 'tʰrɛːnənloːs, mɪt dia'mant'nən 'kʰɛt'ən,
eines Abgrunds, wo auf Dornenbetten, tränenlos, mit diamantnen Ketten,
of an abyss, where on thorn- beds, tearless, with diamond chains,
(of an abyss, where on a bed of thorns, without tears, with diamond chains,)

di fɛɐ̯'tsva͜eflʊŋ la͜oʃt', mɪç tsuː 'rɛt'ən! 'hɔldə 'fa͜endɪn 'ma͜enəs 'friːdəns,
die Verzweiflung lauscht, mich zu retten! Holde Feindin meines Friedens,
the despair lies in wait, me to rescue! Lovely enemy of my peace,
(despair lies in wait to rescue me!* Lovely enemy of my peace,)
[*poem:* **lauscht! Ha!** (haː, ah!/ha!) **mich zu retten**]

bɔ͜øt' miːɐ̯ di 'ʃaːlə deːɐ̯ fɛɐ̯'gɛsənha͜etʰ!
beut mir die Schale der Vergessenheit!
offer to me the cup of the forgetfulness! [*beut* = *biete* = offer, proffer]
(offer me the cup of forgetfulness!)

[*Note: Schubert's punctuation changes the sense of the last lines, which is: ... despair lies in wait! Ah, to save me, lovely enemy of my peace, offer me the cup of forgetfulness! The poem was part of an unfinished novel. The names were originally Theon (the man) and Lyda (the woman). Schubert's Mozartean setting is in the style of an eighteenth-century aria.]

'kʰa͜ezɐ 'fɛrdinant' deɐ̯ 'tsva͜et'ə
Kaiser Ferdinand II
Emperor Ferdinand II

Published in 1853 by Ferdinand Schubert as his own work [composed 1818?] (author unknown)

vas 'reːgət di ʃt'at' zɪç lɪn 'frøːlɪçɐ hastʰ? vas 'rɛnət das fɔlk'
Was reget die Stadt sich in fröhlicher Hast? Was rennet das Volk
Why stirs the city itself in merry haste? Why runs the people
(Why is the city stirring in merry haste? Why do the people run)

dʊrç di 'gasən? lɛs 'ʃt'røːmət' hɪ'na͜en lɪn den 'kʰa͜ezɐp'alastʰ;
durch die Gassen? Es strömet hinein in den Kaiserpalast;
through the streets? It [the people] streams in into the imperial palace;
(through the streets? They stream into the imperial palace;)

fɔn dɔrt dʊrç das tʰoːɐ̯/tʰoːr la͜of di 'ʃt'raːsən; lʊnt' va͜et' hɪn lan 'fɛnst'ɐn,
von dort durch das Tor auf die Strassen; und weit hin an Fenstern,
from there through the gate onto the streets; and far hence at windows,
(from there through the gate onto the streets; and, as far as one can see, at windows,)

la͜of 'vɛlən, la͜of 'veːgən, hart' 'laləs 'kʰɔməndən 'frɔ͜ødən lɛnt''geːgən.
auf Wällen, auf Wegen, harrt alles kommenden Freuden entgegen.
on ramparts, on roads, looks forward impatiently all coming joys toward.
(on ramparts, on roads, all are impatiently looking forward to coming joys.)

hɔrç!   hɔrç!   das |ɪst deːɐ̯ ˈtʰrɔmpʰeːt‘ən hal!   ziːst   duːs   dɔrt‘ ˈblɪŋk‘ən
Horch! horch! das ist der Trompeten Hall! Sieh’st du’s dort blinken
Hark! Hark! That is the trumpets’ sound! See you it there shining
(Listen! Listen! That is the sound of trumpets! Do you see something shining there)

fɔn ˈva͜et‘ən? ziːst   duː den ˈlaŋzaːm ˈnaːəndən   ʃval
von weiten? Sieh’st du den langsam nahenden Schwall
from afar? See you the slowly approaching swell
(in the distance? Do you see the slowly approaching throng)

|ɪn gəˈʃlɔsənən   ˈgliːdɐn   ˈra͜et‘ən? viː t͜siːt‘ |a͜os den ˈvafən,
in geschlossenen Gliedern reiten? Wie zieht aus den Waffen,
in closed ranks ride? How draws from the weapons,
(riding in closed ranks? What blinding sparks the midday sun draws from the weapons)

|ɪn ˈdeːnən ziː ˈpʰrʊŋk‘ən, di ˈmɪt‘aːkszɔnə zoː ˈbləndəndə ˈfʊŋk‘ən!
in denen sie prunken, die Mittagssonne so blendende Funken!
in which they parade, the midday sun such blinding sparks!
(that flash on parade!)

ziː   zɪnt‘ |ɛs—|ɛs |ɪst di ˈtʰap͜fərə ʃaːɐ̯,   diː den ˈʃøːnən   ˈfoːɐ̯t͜suːk‘ |ɛɐ̯ˈrʊŋən,
Sie sind es— es ist die tapfere Schar, die den schönen Vorzug errungen,
They are it— it is the valiant troop, that the handsome prerogative won,
(It is they—it is the valiant troop that won a splendid prerogative,)

diː |a͜enst‘ |ɪm ˈ|a͜ogənblɪk‘ ˈhøːçst‘ɐ   gəˈfaːɐ̯ di ˈfrɛçən   reˈbɛlən bəˈt͜svʊŋən.
die einst im Augenblick höchster Gefahr die frechen Rebellen bezwungen.
that once in the moment of highest danger the insolent rebels overcame.
(that once, at the moment of greatest danger, overcame the insolent rebels.)

daː   vart‘ |iːɐ̯   das ˈkʰœst‘lɪçə rɛçt‘   fɛɐ̯ˈliːən,   dʊrç   di ʃt‘at‘,
Da ward ihr das köstliche Recht verliehen, durch die Stadt,
Then was to it [the troop] the precious right granted through the city,
(At that time they were granted the precious right to move freely through the city)

dʊrç   di bʊrk‘ dɛs   ˈkʰa͜ezɐs t͜suː ˈt͜siːən. |a͜en ˈfʊrçt‘baːrɐ   ˈʃvɪndəl
durch die Burg des Kaisers zu ziehen. Ein furchtbarer Schwindel
through the castle of the emperor to move. A frightful swindel
(and through the palace of the emperor. A frightful fraud)

|ɛnt‘ˈflamt‘ə das lant‘, fɔm   ˈgla͜obən deːɐ̯   ˈfɛːt‘ɐ   gəˈfalən,
entflammte das Land, vom Glauben der Väter gefallen,
inflamed the land, from the faith of the fathers fallen,
(had inflamed the land, which had fallen away from the faith of our fathers;)

dʊrçˈt͜siːən |ɛs   ˈhɔrdən mɪt‘ ra͜op‘ |ʊnt‘ brant‘
durchziehen es Horden mit Raub und Brand
traverse it [the land] hordes with plundering and burning
(hordes move about, plundering and burning,)

bɪs naːx   den ˈfʏrst‘lɪçən ˈhalən; dɛn ˈlyːbɐ(r) |ʊnt‘ ˈ|ʊnt‘ɐ
bis nach den fürstlichen Hallen; denn über und unter
till toward the princely halls; then above and below
(even unto princely halls; then in the territories above and below) [*bis nach* = as far as]

den ˈʃa͜edəndən ˈfluːtʻən deːɐ̯/deːr ˈlɛns lɛntʻˈbrɛnən dɛs ˈla͜ofruːɐ̯s ˈgluːtʻən.
den scheidenden Fluten der Enns entbrennen des Aufruhrs Gluten.
the dividing waters of the Enns burn the insurrection's fires.
(the dividing waters of the Enns River the fires of insurrection are burning.)

jɛt͜stʻ vɛlt͜stʻ leːɐ̯ t͜sʊr ˈkʰa͜ezɐʃtʻatʻ vɪltʻ zɪç hɛˈran la͜of
Jetzt wältzt er zur Kaiserstadt wild sich heran auf
Now rolls it [the insurrection] to the imperial city [Vienna] wildly itself up on
(Now the spirit of revolt is wildly whirling up to the imperial city itself, over)

ˈva͜etʻhɪn fɛɐ̯ˈheːrətʻən ˈflɛçən. deːɐ̯/deːr ˈlyːbɐmuːtʻ ˈbɔrgət di ˈmaskʻə fɔn vaːn,
weithin verheereten Flächen. Der Übermut borget die Maske von Wahn,
far-stretching ravaged expanses. The arrogance borrows the mask of madness,
(wide, ravaged expanses. Arrogance borrows the mask of madness)

di ˈbandə deːɐ̯ p͜flɪçt t͜suː t͜sɛɐˈbrɛçən. leːɐ̯ zɪnt dʊrç gəˈvaltʻ
die Bande der Pflicht zu zerbrechen. Er sinnt durch Gewalt
the bonds of the duty to shatter. It [arrogance] intends through force
(to shatter the bonds of duty. It intends through force)

den ˈkʰa͜ezɐ t͜suː ˈt͜svɪŋən, leːɐ̯ ˈzɪnətʻ zɪç ˈtʰrɔt͜sɪgəs rɛçt t͜suː lɛɐ̯ˈrɪŋən.
den Kaiser zu zwingen, er sinnet sich trotziges Recht zu erringen.
the emperor to compel, it intends for itself (a) defiant right to gain.
(to compel the emperor to do its will, it intends to gain for itself a rebellious privilege.)

ɪn deːɐ̯ ˈfɛːtʻɐ bʊrkʻ fɔn den ˈfa͜endən bəˈlɛŋtʻ, fɔn den ˈla͜egənən ˈʃtɛndən fɛɐ̯ˈraːtʻən,
In der Väter Burg von den Feinden beengt, von den eigenen Ständen verraten,
In the father's castle by the enemies constrained, by the own estates betrayed,
(Constrained by enemies in the castle of his forefathers, betrayed by his own estates of the realm,)

fɔn ˈʃtʻʏntʻlɪç ˈvaksəndəm ˈjamɐ bəˈdrɛŋtʻ, den ˈla͜ofruːɐ̯/-ruːr lɪm ˈhɛrt͜sən deːɐ̯
von stündlich wachsendem Jammer bedrängt, den Aufruhr im Herzen der
by hourly increasing misery hard pressed, the insurrection in the heart of the
(hard pressed by hourly increasing misery, with insurrection in the very heart of the)

ˈʃtʻaːtʻən, lʊntʻ fɛrn di ˈkʰla͜enə ʃaːɐ̯ deːɐ̯ gəˈtʰrɔ͜øən, diː fyːɐ̯ rɛçtʻ lʊntʻ
Staaten, und fern die kleine Schar der Getreuen, die für Recht und
states, and far the small troop of the loyal ones, who for justice and
(states, and with the little troop of loyal soldiers far away, those who for the sake of justice and)

p͜flɪçt dem ˈtʰoːdə zɪç ˈva͜eən, zoː ʃtʻantʻ leːɐ̯, deɐ̯ ˈt͜sva͜etʻə ˈfɛrdinantʻ,
Pflicht dem Tode sich weihen, so stand er, der zweite Ferdinand,
duty to the death themselves consecrate, thus stood he, the second Ferdinand,
(duty consecrate themselves to death, there he stood, Ferdinand II,)

la͜en fɛls lɪm ˈvoːgəngəvɪməl. nɪçtʻ kʰɔntʻ leːɐ̯ fɛɐ̯ˈtʰra͜oən la͜of fɔlkʻ lʊntʻ lantʻ,
ein Fels im Wogengewimmel. Nicht konnt' er vertrauen auf Volk und Land,
a rock in the wave-swarm. Not could he rely upon (the) people and country,
(a rock among surging waves. He could not rely upon the country or its people;)

daː fɛɐ̯ˈtʰra͜otʻə za͜en hɛrt͜s zɪç dem ˈhɪməl; daː varf leːɐ̯ mɪtʻ ˈbrʏnstʻɪç ˈfleːəndɐ
da vertraute sein Herz sich dem Himmel; da warf er mit brünstig flehender
then entrusted his heart itself to the heaven; then threw he with ardently pleading
(at that time he entrusted his heart to heaven: he threw himself down, with an ardently pleading)

gəˈbɛrdə zɪç hɪn foːɐ̯ dem bɪlt dɛs lɛɐ̯ˈløːzɐs deːɐ̯/deːr ˈleːɐ̯də.
Gebärde sich hin vor dem Bild des Erlösers der Erde.
gesture himself down before the image of the Redeemer of the earth.
(gesture, before the image of the Redeemer of the earth.)

iːm ˈleːpʻtʻə ˈhoːəs fɛɐ̯ˈtʰraon lɪn deːɐ̯ brʊstʻ lʊntʻ ˈkʰɪntʻlɪç lɛɐ̯ˈgeːbənəs ˈhɔfən;
Ihm lebte hohes Vertrau'n in der Brust und kindlich ergebenes Hoffen;
For him lived high trust in the breast and childlike submissive hope;
(A great sense of trust and a childlike, submissive hope dwelt in his breast;)

eːɐ̯ vaːɐ̯ zɪç dɛs ˈraenən ˈvɪləns bəˈvʊstʻ, zaen hɛrts dem ˈleːvɪgən ˈlɔfən;
er war sich des reinen Willens bewusst, sein Herz dem Ewigen offen;
he was himself of the pure will conscious, his heart to the Eternal One open;
(he was conscious of a pure will, his heart open to the Eternal One;)

zoː ziːtʻ leːɐ̯ tsuː deːm, deːɐ̯ di ˈʃɪkʻʊŋən ˈlaetʻətʻ, deːɐ̯ ˈʃpɛrlɪŋə tsɛːltʻ lʊntʻ
so sieht er zu dem, der die Schickungen leitet, der Sperlinge zählt und
so looks he to Him who the destinies guides, who sparrows counts and
(thus he looks up to Him who guides our destinies, who counts the sparrows, and)

ˈvɛltʻən bəˈraetʻətʰ. lʊntʻ viː leːɐ̯ mɪtʻ gɔtʻ lɪm gəˈbeːtʻə rɪŋtʻ,
Welten bereitet. Und wie er mit Gott im Gebete ringt,
worlds prepares. And as he with God in the prayer grapples,
(creates worlds. And as he grapples with God in prayer,)

daː ˈʃvaegət deːɐ̯ ˈzɔrgən gəˈtʰʏməl; laen ˈlaezɐ tʰoːn lɪn deːɐ̯ zeːl liːm lɛɐ̯ˈkʰlɪŋtʻ,
da schweiget der Sorgen Getümmel; ein leiser Ton in der Seel' ihm erklingt,
then is silent the cares' tumult; a soft tone in the soul to him sounds,
(the tumult of cares becomes silent; a soft tone sounds in his soul,)

lals ˈkʰɛːmə di ˈʃtʻɪmə fɔm ˈhɪməl. jɛtstʻ glaoptʻ leːɐ̯ deːɐ̯ ˈtʰøːnə zɪn tsuː ˈfasən:
als käme die Stimme vom Himmel. Jetzt glaubt er der Töne Sinn zu fassen:
as if came the voice from the heaven. Now believes he the tones' meaning to grasp:
(as if a voice came from heaven. Now he believes that he grasps the meaning of the tones:)

ɪç ˈveːɐ̯də dɪç ˈfɛrdinantʻ ˈnɪmɐ fɛɐ̯ˈlasən! lɛɐ̯ˈmuːtʻɪgətʻ
"Ich werde dich Ferdinand nimmer verlassen!" Ermutiget
"I shall you, Ferdinand, never forsake!" Encouraged
("I shall never forsake you, Ferdinand!" Encouraged,)

ʃtʻeːtʻ fɔm gəˈbeːtʻ leːɐ̯/leːr laof. daː hɔrç— laen ˈdʊmpfəs gəˈrɔøʃə!
steht vom Gebet er auf. Da horch—ein dumpfes Geräusche!
stands from the prayer he up. Then hark— a dull noise!
(he rises from his prayer. Then hark!—a dull noise!)

dʊrç di ˈzɛːlə ˈʃalət deːɐ̯/deːr ˈlaeləndən laof, lʊntʻ ˈvɪldɐ ˈʃtʻɪmən gəˈkʰraeʃə.
Durch die Säle schallet der eilenden Lauf, und wilder Stimmen Gekreische.
Through the halls sounds the hurrying course, and wild voices' shrieking.
(A rushing course and the shrieking of wild voices sound through the halls.)

di reˈbɛlən zɪnts, diː tsʊm ˈkʰaezɐ ˈdrɪŋən,
Die Rebellen sind's, die zum Kaiser dringen,
The rebels are it, who to the emperor force a way,
(It is the rebels, who are forcing their way to the emperor,)

ǀiːn ˈtʰrɔt͜sɪç t͜sʊm ˈʃmɛːlɪçən ˈvae̯çən t͜suː ˈt͜svɪŋən. ziː ǀʊmˈʃtʻeːn ǀiːn
ihn trotzig zum schmählichen Weichen zu zwingen. Sie umsteh'n ihn
him defiantly to the shameful weakening to compel. They stand around him
(defiantly to compel him to a shameful weakening. They stand all around him,)

ˈdrɛŋəntʻ fɔl ˈvaksəndən grɪms; ǀeːɐ̯ zɔl, vas ziː ˈfɔrdɐn, gəˈvɛːrən.
drängend voll wachsenden Grimm's; er soll, was sie fordern, gewähren.
pressing full of growing rage; he shall what they demand concede.
(pressing, full of growing rage; he is expected to concede what they demand.)

kʰɑ͜om kʰan ǀeːɐ̯ dɛs ˈvyːtʻəndən ˈǀʊngəʃtʻyːms dɛs ˈfrɛçən ʃvarms zɪç ǀɛɐ̯ˈveːrən.
Kaum kann er des wütenden Ungestüms des frechen Schwarms sich erwehren.
Scarcely can he of the furious vehemence of the insolent swarm himself defend.
(He can scarcely defend himself against the furious vehemence of the insolent swarm.)

daː ˈʃalətʻ ǀɑ͜of ˈǀa͜enmaːl tʰrɔmˈpʰeːtʻən-gəˈʃmɛtʻɐ, daː fʏltʻ zɪç deːɐ̯ ˈbʊrkʻhoːf—
Da schallet auf einmal Trompeten- Geschmetter, da füllt sich der Burghof—
Then sounds(all)at once trumpets- blaring, then fills itself the castle court—
(Suddenly at that moment a blare of trumpets sounds and the courtyard of the palace is filled—)

daː zɪnt di ǀɛɐ̯ˈrɛtʻɐ. ziː zɪnt͜s; ǀɛs ǀɪst di gəˈtʰrɔ͜ʏən ʃaːɐ̯,
da sind die Erretter. Sie sind's; es ist der Getreuen Schar,
there are the rescuers. They are it; it is the loyal ones' troop,
(the rescuers are there. It is they, it is the troop of loyal soldiers,)

diː den ˈʃøːnstʻən ˈfoːɐ̯t͜suːkʻ ǀɛɐ̯ˈrʊŋən, deːɐ̯ jɛt͜stʻ ǀɪm ˈǀɑ͜ogənblɪkʻ ˈhøːçstʻɐ gəˈfaːɐ̯
die den schönsten Vorzug errungen, der jetzt im Augenblick höchster Gefahr
who the finest prerogative won, for whom now in the moment of highest danger
(who have won that finest prerogative, through whom now, in the moment of greatest danger,)

di ˈkʰyːnə ˈrɛtʻʊŋ gəˈlʊŋən. drɔpʻ vartʻ ǀiːɐ̯ das ˈkʰœstʻlɪçə rɛçtʻ fɛɐ̯ˈliːən,
die kühne Rettung gelungen. Drob ward ihr das köstliche Recht verliehen,
the bold rescue(has) succeeded. For that was for it[the troop] the precious right granted,
(the bold rescue has succeeded. For that the precious privilege has been granted to the troop)

dʊrç di ʃtʻatʻ, dʊrç di bʊrkʻ dɛs ˈkʰa͜ezɐs t͜suː ˈt͜siːən.
durch die Stadt, durch die Burg des Kaisers zu ziehen.
through the city, through the castle of the emperor to move.
(to move freely through the city and through the emperor's palace.)

ɛs ˈtʰruːgən hɛˈrapʻ ziː fɔm ˈfɛrnən gəˈʃtʻaːt deːɐ̯ ˈdoːnɑ͜o bəˈfrɔ͜ʏndətʻə ˈvɛlən.
Es trugen herab sie vom fernen Gestad' der Donau befreundete Wellen.
There carried down them from the distant shore the Danube's befriended waves.
(The befriended waves of the Danube carried them down from the distant shore.)

ʃtʻɪl ˈdraŋən ziː ǀa͜en ǀɪn di ˈt͜saːgəndə ʃtʻatʻ, fɛɐ̯ˈbɔrgən dem blɪkʻ deːɐ̯ reˈbɛlən,
Still drangen sie ein in die zagende Stadt, verborgen dem Blick der Rebellen,
Quietly rushed they in into the quaking city, hidden from the gaze of the rebels,
(Quietly they rushed into the frightened city, hidden from the gaze of the rebels,)

dɛs ˈkʰa͜ezɐs gəˈha͜elɪçtʻəs hɑ͜optʻ t͜suː bəˈfra͜eən,
des Kaisers geheiligtes Haupt zu befreien,
the emperor's sanctified head to free,
(to free the emperor, annointed by God,)

deːɐ̯/deːr ˈɛmˈpʰøːrɐ ʃaːɐ̯ viː ʃpʻrɔ͜ø t͡suː t͡sɛɐ̯ˈʃtʻrɔ͜øən.
der Empörer Schar wie Spreu zu zerstreuen.
the rebels' band like chaff to scatter.
(and to scatter the band of rebels like chaff.)

zoː ˈgeːətʻ nɪçtʻ ˈʊntʻɐ, veːɐ̯ gɔtʻ fɛɐ̯ˈtʰra͜otʻ, veːɐ̯ mɪtʻ muːtʻ ˈʊntʻ ˈkʰrɛftʻɪgəm ˈvɪlən
So gehet nicht unter, wer Gott vertraut, wer mit Mut und kräftigem Willen
Thus goes not under, (he) who God trusts, who with courage and powerful will
(Thus he who puts his trust in God will not perish, he who with courage and a powerful will)

ˈa͜of ˈa͜en t͡siːl, ˈa͜of das ˈhøːçstʻə nuːɐ̯ ʃa͜otʻ, ˈɛntʻˈʃlɔsən, za͜en loːs t͡suː ˈɛɐ̯ˈfʏlən;
auf ein Ziel, auf das höchste nur schaut, entschlossen, sein Los zu erfüllen;
at a goal, at the highest only looks, determined, his lot to fulfill;
(keeps his eye only on the goal, on the highest goal, determined to fulfill his destiny;)

ˈɛntʻˈʃlɔsən, das ˈɔ͜øsɐstʻə, ˈlɛt͡stʻə t͡suː ˈvaːgən,
entschlossen, das Äusserste, Letzte zu wagen,
determined, the utmost, last to risk,
(determined to risk the utmost, the ultimate,)

ˈʊm den ˈʃøːnən, den ˈkʰœstʻlɪçən pʰra͜es t͡suː ˈɛɐ̯ˈjaːgən. ˈʊnt dɛŋkst duː voːl
um den schönen, den köstlichen Preis zu erjagen. Und denkst du wohl
in order the beautiful, the precious prize to pursue. And think you perhaps
(in order to pursue the beautiful, precious prize. And can you perhaps think)

ˈhøːɐn ˈʊntʻ ˈeːdlɐn diːɐ̯/diːr ˈa͜os, ˈals das ˈfaːtʻɐlantʻ fra͜e t͡suː ˈɛɐ̯ˈhaltʻən?
höhern und edlern dir aus, als das Vaterland frei zu erhalten?
higher and nobler for you out, than the fatherland free to maintain?
(of a loftier or nobler goal than to keep one's fatherland free,)

t͡suː ˈɛɐ̯ˈhaltʻən deːɐ̯ ˈhɛrʃɐ gəˈha͜elɪçtʻəs ha͜os, iːɐ̯ ˈkʰøːnɪkʻlɪç ˈmɪldəs ˈvaltʻən;
zu erhalten der Herrscher geheiligtes Haus, ihr königlich mildes Walten;
to preserve the rulers' sanctified house, their royally mild rule;
(to preserve the sanctified ruling house, their royally mild rule,)

dɛs ˈfla͜esəs, deːɐ̯ kʰʊnstʻ gəˈzamәltʻə ˈʃɛt͡sə, deːɐ̯ ˈfɛːtʻɐ gəˈbra͜ox ˈʊntʻ zɪtʻ
des Fleisses, der Kunst gesammelte Schätze, der Väter Gebrauch und Sitt'
the industry's, the art's assembled treasures, the forefathers' custom and propriety
(the assembled treasures of industry and of art, the custom and propriety)

ˈʊntʻ gəˈzɛt͡sə! ˈdarʊm ˈmuːtʻɪç hɪˈna͜os, vɛn di ˈfa͜endə zɪç naːn,
und Gesetze! Darum mutig hinaus, wenn die Feinde sich nah'n,
and laws? Therefore courageously out, when the enemies themselves approach,
(and laws of our forefathers! Therefore, come out courageously when enemies approach,)

ˈʊntʻ mɪtʻ ˈkʰrɛftʻɪgəm ˈvɪlən gəˈʃtʻrɪtʻən! nɪçtʻ ˈʃtʻraːlət deːɐ̯ kʰrant͡s
und mit kräftigem Willen gestritten! Nicht strahlet der Kranz
and with powerful will fought! Not shines the wreath
(and fight with a powerful will! The wreath of victory does not shine)

ˈɪm bəˈgɪnə deːɐ̯ baːn; ˈeːɐ̯ ˈkʰrøːnətʻ nuːɐ̯ deːn, deːɐ̯ gəˈlɪtʻən. di ˈfaːtʻɐlant͡sliːpʻ
im Beginne der Bahn; er krönet nur den, der gelitten. Die Vaterlandslieb'
in the beginning of the track; it crowns only him who (has) endured. The fatherland- love
(at the beginning of the race; it crowns only one who has endured. The love of one's fatherland)

ɪst' l͜aen 'h͜aelɪgəs 'f͜ɔøɐ, kʰ͜aen 'ɔpfɐ t͜su: gro:s— kʰ͜aen blu:t' i:ɐ̯ t͜su: 'tʰ͜ɔøɐ!
ist ein heiliges Feuer, kein Opfer zu gross—kein Blut ihr zu teuer!
is a sacred fire, no sacrifice too great— no blood for it too precious!
(is a sacred fire; no sacrifice is too great, no blood too precious!)

ʊnt' vi: vi:ɐ̯ jɛt͜st' 'pʰr͜aezən di 'tʰapfərə ʃa:ɐ̯, zo: 'pʰr͜aezən 'kʰɔməndə 't͜s͜aet'ən das fɔlk',
Und wie wir jetzt preisen die tapfere Schar, so preisen kommende Zeiten das Volk,
And as we now praise the valiant troop, so praise coming times the people,
(And as we now praise that valiant troop, so shall future times praise the nation)

das zo: 'kʰrɛft'ɪç, zo: 'ho:xgəzɪnt' va:ɐ̯, zɪç 'fr͜aeh͜aet' lʊnt' ru: t͜su: lɛɐ̯'ʃt'r͜aet'ən. lʊnt
dass so kräftig, so hochgesinnt war, sich Freiheit und Ruh' zu erstreiten. Und
that so strong, so high-minded was, for itself freedom and peace to fight for. And
(that was so strong, so noble, as to fight for its freedom and peace. And)

'daŋk'ba:ɐ̯ ʃ͜aot' ɪm gə'zɪçɐt'ən 'glʏk'ə l͜aof'lʊnzrə gə'fa:rən de:ɐ̯/de:r 'lɛnk'əl t͜su'rʏk'ə.
dankbar schaut im gesicherten Glücke auf unsre Gefahren der Enkel zurücke.
gratefully looks in the secured fortune at our dangers the grandchild back.
(our grandchildren in their secure good fortune will look back at the dangers we had to undergo.)

[This song was published by Ferdinand Schubert as his own work, but was almost certainly composed for him by his brother Franz. The author of the poem may have been Heinrich von Collin, as the style is similar to that of *Kaiser Maximilian auf der Martinswand*, published by Ferdinand Schubert in the same collection, entitled *Der kleine Sänger* ("The Little Singer"). Ferdinand II was Holy Roman emperor from 1619 to 1637. His reign was troubled by revolts in several parts of his realm. The song, arranged for two voices and bass in the original publication, has been restored as a solo song with piano accompaniment by Reinhard Van Hoorickx.]

'kʰ͜aezɐ 'maksi'mi:l͜ia:n l͜aof de:ɐ̯ 'mart'i:nsvant' ɪn tʰi'ro:l
Kaiser Maximilian auf der Martinswand in Tirol
Emperor Maximilian on St. Martin's Cliff in Tirol

Posthumously published [composed 1818?] (poem by Heinrich von Collin)

hɪ'n͜aof! hɪ'n͜aof! lɪn ʃp'rʊŋ lʊnt' l͜aof! vo: di lʊft' zo: l͜aeçt',
"Hinauf! hinauf! in Sprung und Lauf! wo die Luft so leicht,
"Up! up! in leap and run! where the air so light,
("Up! Up! Leap and run! Where the air is so light,)

vo: di 'zɔnə zo: kʰla:ɐ̯, nu:ɐ̯ di 'gɛmzə ʃp'rɪŋt', nu:ɐ̯ 'hɔrst'ət de:ɐ̯/de:r la:ɐ̯;
wo die Sonne so klar, nur die Gemse springt, nur horstet der Aar;
where the sun so clear, only the chamois leaps, only nests the eagle;
(where the sun is so clear, where only the chamois leaps, where only the eagle nests;)

vo: das 'mɛnʃəngəvy:l t͜su: 'fy:sən mi:ɐ̯ rɔlt', vo: das 'dɔnɐgəbrʏl
wo das Menschengewühl zu Füssen mir rollt, wo das Donnergebrüll
where the human tumult at feet of me rolls, where the thunder-roaring
(where the human tumult rolls along far below my feet, where the roar of the thunder)

tʰi:f lʊnt'ən grɔlt'. da: lɪst de:ɐ̯/de:r lɔrt', vo: di majɛs'tʰɛ:t'
tief unten grollt. Da ist der Ort, wo die Majestät
deep below rumbles. There is the place where the majesty
(rumbles deep down beneath me. That is the place where majesty)

zɪç ˈhɛrlɪç den ˈhɛrʃɐtʰroːn ǀɛɐ̯ˈhøːtʰ! di ˈʃtʻa͜elə baːn hɪˈnan!
sich herrlich den Herrscherthron erhöht! Die steile Bahn hinan!
for itself gloriously the ruler's throne raises! The steep course upwards!
(gloriously raises its sovereign throne! The steep climb upwards!)

dɔrtʻ ˈp͜fa͜efət di ˈgɛmzə! haː, ˈʃpʻrɪŋə nuːɐ̯ foːɐ̯;
Dort pfeifet die Gemse! Ha, springe nur vor;
There squeals the chamois! Ah, leap just before;
(There the chamois is calling! Ah, go ahead and leap away before me, chamois!)

ˈnaːxzɛt͜st deːɐ̯ ˈjɛːgɐ(r) ǀʊntʻ fliːkʻtʻ ǀɛmˈpʰoːɐ̯. gɛːntʻ ǀa͜ox di kʰlʊftʻ
nachsetzt der Jäger und fliegt empor. Gähnt auch die Kluft
pursues the hunter and flies up. Yawns even the chasm
(The hunter will pursue and fly up after you. Even if a chasm yawns)

ʃvart͜s viː di grʊftʻ, nuːɐ̯ hɪˈnyːbɐ, hɪˈnyːbɐ(r) ǀɪm ˈla͜eçtʻən ʃvʊŋ,
schwarz wie die Gruft, nur hinüber, hinüber im leichten Schwung,
black as the grave, only over, over in the light swing,
(dark as the grave, just leap over it, leap over it with a light vault!)

veːɐ̯ zɛt͜stʻ miːɐ̯ naːx? ǀa͜en ˈkʰa͜ezɐʃpʻrʊŋ? kʰlɪm, ˈgɛmzə,
wer setzt mir nach? Ein Kaisersprung? Klimm, Gemse,
who sets me after? An emperor-leap? Climb, chamois,
(Who will pursue *me*? An imperial leap? Climb, chamois,)

nuːɐ̯/nuːr ǀa͜of di ˈfɛlzənvantʻ! ǀɪn di ˈlʊftʻɪgə høː, ǀan dɛs ˈǀapʻgrʊnt͜s rantʻ
nur auf die Felsenwand! In die luftige Höh', an des Abgrunds Rand
just onto the cliff wall! In the airy heights, at the abyss's rim
(go ahead and climb onto the face of the cliff! In the airy heights, at the rim of the abyss)

max ɪç mɪtʻ ˈǀa͜ezən miːɐ̯ dɔx di baːn, nuːɐ̯ ˈmuːtʻɪç hɪˈna͜of ǀʊntʻ ˈmuːtʻɪç hɪˈnan!
mach' ich mit Eisen mir doch die Bahn, nur mutig hinauf und mutig hinan!
make I with iron for me yet the track, just bravely up and bravely upwards!
(I shall yet make a way for myself with iron spikes, then bravely up and onwards!)

jɛt͜stʻ ˈǀoːnə rast den ʃtʻra͜ox gəˈfastʻ! vɛn ˈtʰʏkʻɪʃ deːɐ̯ t͜sva͜ekʻ
Jetzt ohne Rast den Strauch gefasst! Wenn tückisch der Zweig
Now without rest the bush grasped! If maliciously the branch
(Now grasp that bush without stopping a moment to rest! If the branch maliciously)

fɔm gəˈʃtʻa͜enə lɛstʻ, zoː hɛltʻ mɪç ǀɪm ˈfalə di ˈkʰlɪpʻə nɔx fɛstʰ.
vom Gesteine lässt, so hält mich im Falle die Klippe noch fest."
from the stone lets go, then holds me in the case the crag still firmly."
(tears away from the stone, then in that case the crag will still hold me firmly.")

deːɐ̯ ʃtʻa͜en nɪçtʻ hɛltʻ; deːɐ̯ ˈkʰa͜ezɐ fɛltʻ ǀɪn di ˈtʰiːfən hɪˈnapʻ, t͜sva͜e ˈkʰlaftʻɐ laŋ;
Der Stein nicht hält; der Kaiser fällt in die Tiefen hinab, zwei Klafter lang;
The stone not holds; the emperor falls into the depths down, two fathoms long;
(The stone does not hold; the emperor falls twelve feet down toward the depths;)

daː vart dem ˈkʰyːnən dɔx ˈǀɛtʻvas baŋ. ǀa͜en ˈfɛlzən hɛɐ̯ˈfoːɐ̯/-foːr ǀa͜en ˈveːnɪç raːkʻtʻ,
da ward dem Kühnen doch etwas bang. Ein Felsen hervor ein wenig ragt,
then became the bold one after all rather afraid. A rock outwards a bit juts,
(then the bold man became rather afraid after all. A rock juts out from the face of the cliff;)

das nɛnt‘ lɛːɐ̯ glʏk‘— gɔt‘ za͜es gəˈkʰlaːk‘t‘! ˈla͜enbraːxən di kʰniː;
das nennt er Glück—Gott sei’s geklagt! Einbrachen die Knie;
that names he luck— God be it lamented! In- broke the knees;
(he calls that luck—but let it be lamented to God! His knees were injured;)

dɔx bliːp‘ lɛːɐ̯ ʃt‘eːn! lʊnt ˈtʰɑ͜oməlt‘ zɪç lɑ͜os; daː mʊst‘ lɛːɐ̯ nuːn zeːn:
doch blieb er steh’n! und taumelt’ sich aus; da musst’ er nun seh’n:
but stayed he standing! and staggered himself out; then had to he now see:
(but he could stand on his feet! He lurched dizzily for a moment; then he had to see his situation:)

hiːɐ̯ ˈhɛlfə kʰa͜en ʃp‘rʊŋ, kʰa͜en ˈladlɐʃvʊŋ; dɛn ˈlʊnt‘ɐ(r) liːm
Hier helfe kein Sprung, kein Adlerschwung; denn unter ihm
Here would help no leap, no eagle-swing; for below him
(Here no leap would help, no eagle-like dive; for below him)

zɛŋk‘t‘ zɪç di ˈmart‘iːnsvant‘, deːɐ̯ ˈʃt‘a͜elst‘ə ˈfɛlzən lɪm ˈgant͜sən lant‘.
senkt sich die Martinswand, der steilste Felsen im ganzen Land.
sinks itself the Martin’s wall, the steepest cliff in the whole land.
(Martin’s wall plunges straight down, the sheerest cliff in the whole land.)

eːɐ̯ ʃt‘art‘ hɪˈnap‘ lɪns ˈvɔlk‘əngraːp‘. lɛːɐ̯ ʃt‘art‘ hɪˈnɑ͜of lɪns ˈvɔlk‘ənmeːɐ̯
Er starrt hinab ins Wolkengrab. Er starrt hinauf ins Wolkenmeer
He stares down into the cloud- grave. He stares up into the cloud sea
(He stares down into a cloud-covered grave. He stares up into a sea of clouds,)

lʊnt‘ ˈʃɑ͜oət t͜suˈrʏk‘ lʊnt‘ ˈʃɑ͜oət‘ lʊmˈheːɐ̯. daː t͜sa͜ek‘t‘ zɪç kʰa͜en flɛk‘
und schauet zurück und schauet umher. Da zeigt sich kein Fleck
and looks back and looks around. There shows itself no spot
(and looks back, and looks around. He sees no projecting bit of rock there)

t͜sʊm ʃp‘rʊŋ ˈhant‘bra͜et‘, kʰa͜en ʃt‘rɑ͜ox, deːɐ̯ den t͜sva͜ek‘ dem ˈkʰlɪməndən bɔ͜øt‘.
zum Sprung handbreit, kein Strauch, der den Zweig dem Klimmenden beut.
to the jump hand-broad, no bush, which the branch to the climbing one offers.
(wide enough to jump to, no bush which might offer a branch to the climber.)

ɑ͜os ˈhart‘əm ˈfɛlzən vœlp‘t‘ zɪç la͜en lɔx ʃrɔf ˈhɪnt‘ɐ(r) liːm,
Aus hartem Felsen wölbt sich ein Loch schroff hinter ihm,
Out of hard rock arches itself a hole roughly behind him
(Behind him there is a hole in the hard rock, a sort of rough vaulted niche,)

viː la͜en doːm zoː hoːx. deːɐ̯ ˈkʰa͜ezɐ ruːft‘ lɪn ˈtʰɑ͜obə lʊft‘: la͜e dɔx, viː
wie ein Dom so hoch. Der Kaiser ruft in taube Luft: “Ei doch, wie
as a dome so high. The emperor calls into deaf air: “Oh indeed, how
(as high as a dome. The emperor calls out into deaf air: “Oh, how)

hat‘ mɪç di ˈgɛmzə fɛɐ̯ˈfyːɐ̯tʰ! kʰa͜en veːk‘ t͜suː den ˈleːbəndən ˈniːdɐfyːɐ̯tʰ.
hat mich die Gemse verführt! Kein Weg zu den Lebenden niederführt.”
has me the chamois led astray! No way to the living leads down.”
(the chamois has led me astray! No way leads down to the living.”)

zoː lɪst‘ lɛs gəˈʃeːn, lɛs ˈmʊst‘ə zoː geːn. voː di lʊft‘ zoː la͜eçt‘,
So ist es gescheh’n, es musste so geh’n. Wo die Luft so leicht,
Thus has it happened, it had to thus go. Where the air so light,
(Thus it has happened, it had to go thus. Where the air is so light,)

vo: di 'zɔnə zo: kʰla:ɐ̯, vo: di 'gɛmzə nu:ɐ̯ ʃp'rɪŋt', nu:ɐ̯ 'hɔrst'ət' de:ɐ̯/de:r la:ɐ̯;
wo die Sonne so klar, wo die Gemse nur springt, nur horstet der Aar;
where the sun so clear, where the chamois only leaps, only nests the eagle;
(where the sun is so clear, where only the chamois leaps, where only the eagle nests;)

vo: das 'mɛnʃəngəvy:l t͡su: 'fy:sən li:m rɔlt', vo: das 'dɔnɐgə'brʏl
wo das Menschengewühl zu Füssen ihm rollt, wo das Donnergebrüll
where the human tumult at feet of him rolls, where the thunder-roaring
(where the human tumult rolls along far below his feet, where the roar of the thunder)

tʰi:f lʊnt'ən grɔltʰ. da: ʃt'e:t dɛs 'kʰa͜ezɐs majɛs'tʰɛ:t', zo: ho:x, dɔx nɪçt
tief unten grollt. Da steht des Kaisers Majestät, so hoch, doch nicht
deep below rumbles. There stands the emperor's majesty, so high, yet not
(rumbles deep down below. There stands his majesty the emperor, so high, yet not)

t͡sʊr 'vɔnə lɛɐ̯'hø:tʰ: la͜en 'jamɐzo:n la͜of 'lʊft'ɪgəm tʰro:n. lɛs 'fɪndət de:ɐ̯ 'ho:ə
zur Wonne erhöht: ein Jammersohn auf luftigem Thron. Es findet der Hohe
to the bliss raised: a misery- son on airy throne. There finds the lofty one
(raised to delight: a son of misery on an airy throne. The lofty one finds)

zɪç 'pʰlœt͡slɪç la'la͜en lʊnt' 'fy:lət' zɪç 'ʃa͜oɐnt' fɛɐ̯'lasən lʊnt' kʰla͜en.
sich plötzlich allein und fühlet sich schauernd verlassen und klein.
himself suddenly alone and feels himself shudderingly forsaken and small.
(himself suddenly alone, and, shuddering, feels forsaken and small.)

ɪm 'tʰa:ləsgrʊnt' la͜en 'hɪrt'ə ʃt'ʊnt' lʊnt' zi:t' la͜of de:ɐ̯ 'pʰlat'ə zɪçs 're:gən
Im Talesgrund ein Hirte stund und sieht auf der Platte sich's regen
In the valley floor a shepherd stood and sees on the rock-slope itself it stir
(On the floor of the valley a shepherd stood and saw something on the slope of rock stirring)

lʊnt' 'bʏk'ən lʊnt' 'he:bən lʊnt' 'ʃra͜et'ənt' bə've:gən.
und bücken und heben und schreitend bewegen.
and stooping and lifting and stridingly moving.
(and stooping and rising and walking about.)

de:n bant' vo:l hɪ'na͜of dɛs 'za:t'ans gə'valt? das lɪst', ba͜e gɔt'!
"Den bannt wohl hinauf des Satans Gewalt? Das ist, bei Gott!
"Him confines perhaps up (there) the Satan's power? That is, by God!
("Does Satan's power perhaps confine him up there? That is—by God!—)

'la͜enə 'mɛnʃəngəʃt'altʰ! zo: ru:ft' le:ɐ̯/le:r lʊnt' 'vɪŋk'ət di 'hɪrt'ən hɛɐ̯'ba͜e
eine Menschengestalt!" So ruft er und winket die Hirten herbei
a human form!" Thus calls he and beckons the shepherds hither
(a human being!" Thus he calls, beckoning the other shepherds to gather round,)

lʊnt' 'je:dɐ ʃt'a͜ont', vɛlç 'vʊndɐ(r) lɛs za͜e. gɔt' za͜e mɪt' li:m! lɪst' 'la͜enə ʃt'ɪm.
und jeder staunt, welch Wunder es sei. "Gott sei mit ihm!" ist eine Stimm.
and each is amazed, what marvel it be. "God be with him!" is one voice.
(and each is amazed at the marvel. "God be with him!" they cry as if with one voice.)

de:ɐ̯ 'ʃt'e:ət dɔrt' 'lo:bən lɪn 'gro:sɐ no:tʰ! mʊs lark' vo:l lɛɐ̯'la͜edən den 'hʊŋɐtʰo:t'.
"Der stehet dort oben in grosser Not! muss arg wohl erleiden den Hungertod."
"He stands there above in great need! must badly probably suffer the hunger-death."
("He stands up there in great need! He is bound to die of hunger.")

a͜of ˈla͜eçtʻəm rɔs   la͜en ˈjɛːɡɐtʰrɔs   kʰɔmtʻ nuːn das tʰaːl hɛˈra͜en ɡəˈʃpʻrɛŋtʻ,
Auf leichtem Ross ein Jägertross kommt nun das Tal herein gesprengt,
On light horse a hunter-follower comes now the valley into sprung,
(On a light horse a follower of the hunt now comes springing into the valley,)

voː zɪç di ˈmɛŋə ʃoːn ˈɡafənt drɛŋtʻ, lʊntʻ ˈruːfət den ˈnɛːçstʻən ˈhɪrtʻən lan:
wo sich die Menge schon gaffend drängt, und rufet den nächsten Hirten an:
where itself the crowd already gaping presses, and calls the nearest shepherd to:
(where already a gaping crowd has gathered, and calls to the nearest shepherd:)

naːm voːl deːɐ̯ ˈkʰa͜ezɐ(r) lanˈheːɐ̯ di baːn? hoːx la͜of den ˈlalpʻən
"Nahm wohl der Kaiser anher die Bahn? Hoch auf den Alpen
"Took perhaps the emperor hither the way? High on the alps
("Did the emperor possibly come by this way? High up on the alps)

kʰlɔm leːɐ̯/leːr lɛmˈpʰoːɐ̯, das liːn dɛs ˈjɛːɡɐs blɪkʻ fɛɐ̯ˈloːɐ̯! deːɐ̯ ˈhɪrtʻə blɪkʻtʻ
klomm er empor, dass ihn des Jägers Blick verlor!" Der Hirte blickt
climbed he up, (so) that him the huntsman's gaze lost!" The shepherd looks
(he was climbing, so high that he became lost to the sight of the huntsmen!" The shepherd looks)

la͜of di vantʻ lɛɐ̯ˈʃrɪkʻtʰ. hɪnˈdɔ͜øtʻəntʻ zaːkʻtʻ leːɐ̯ t͜sʊm ˈjɛːɡɐʃvarm:
auf die Wand erschrickt. Hindeutend sagt er zum Jägerschwarm:
at the cliff, alarmed. Pointing says he to the huntsman-swarm:
(up at the cliff in alarm. Pointing, he says to the group of huntsmen:)

dan ʃa͜otʻ liːn dɔrtʻ ˈloːbən! das ɡɔtʻ lɛɐ̯ˈbarm! deːɐ̯ ˈjɛːɡɐ blɪkʻtʻ
"Dann schaut ihn dort oben! dass Gott erbarm!" Der Jäger blickt
"Then see him there above! that God have mercy!" The huntsman looks
("Then see him up there! May God have mercy!" The huntsman looks)

la͜of di vantʻ lɛɐ̯ˈʃrɪkʻtʻ lʊntʻ ˈheːbətʻ nuːn ʃnɛl za͜en ˈʃpʻrɛçɐroːɐ̯
auf die Wand erschrickt und hebet nun schnell sein Sprecherrohr
at the cliff alarmed and raises now quickly his speaker-tube
(up at the cliff in alarm, and now quickly raises his megaphone)

lʊntʻ ˈruːfətʻ, vas ˈmɛnʃənbrʊstʻ maːkʻ, lɛmˈpʰoːɐ̯: hɛr ˈkʰa͜ezɐ, za͜etʻ liːɐ̯s,
und rufet, was Menschenbrust mag, empor: "Herr Kaiser, seid ihr's,
and calls, what human breast can, aloft: "Sir Emperor, are you it,
(and calls up as loudly as human lungs can shout: "Your imperial majesty, is it you)

deːɐ̯ ʃtʻeːtʻ lɪn deːɐ̯ blɛntʻ? zoː vɛrftʻ hɛˈrapʻ ˈla͜enən ʃtʻa͜en bəˈhɛntʻ!
der steht in der Blend'? So werft herab einen Stein behend!"
who stands in the niche? Then throw down a stone quickly!"
(who are standing in the niche? If so, then quickly throw down a stone!")

ʊntʻ ˈfoːɐ̯vɛrt͜s nuːn ˈvoːɡət das ˈmɛnʃənɡəvyːl, lʊntʻ ˈpʰlœt͜slɪç
Und vorwärts nun woget das Menschengewühl, und plötzlich
And forward now surges the human throng, and suddenly
(And now the crowd surges forward; and suddenly)

vaːɐ̯/vaːr lɛs ˈtʰoːtʻənʃtʻɪl. zoː fɛlt deːɐ̯ ʃtʻa͜en ˈzɛŋkʻrɛçtʻ hɪˈna͜en, voː lʊntʻɐ dem ˈfɛlzən
war es totenstill. So fällt der Stein senkrecht hinein, wo unter dem Felsen
was it deathly still. Then falls the stone vertically into, where under the cliff
(all is deathly still. Then the stone falls vertically down, onto a hut beneath the cliff where)

laen 'hy:t'ɐ vaxt', das tsɛɐ'ʃmɛt'ɐt das dax tsu'zamənkʰraxtʰ.
ein Hüter wacht, dass zerschmettert das Dach zusammenkracht.
a keeper is on watch, (so) that, shattered, the roof together- crashes.
(a game-keeper is on duty, so that the roof, shattered by the stone, collapses with a crash.)

dɛs 'fɔlk'əs gə'hɔøl laof 'laenə mael lɪm 'gantsən 'lʊmkʰraes tsu: 'hø:rən,
Des Volkes Geheul auf eine Meil' im ganzen Umkreis zu hören,
The people's howling for a mile in the whole vicinity to be heard,
(The lamentation of the people, heard for a mile in all directions,)

maxt' rɪŋs das 'lɛço lɛm'pʰø:rən. lʊnt tsʊm 'kʰaezɐ(r) laof 'drɪŋət de:ɐ 'jamɐlaot',
macht rings das Echo empören. Und zum Kaiser auf dringet der Jammerlaut,
makes all around the echo stir up. And to the emperor up penetrates the misery- sound,
(stirs up the echoes all around. And the sound of their misery rises up to the emperor,)

de:ɐ kʰaom me:ɐ 'mɛnʃlɪçɐ 'hɪlfə fɛɐ'tʰraotʰ. le:ɐ 'ʃp'anət das laok',
der kaum mehr menschlicher Hilfe vertraut. Er spannet das Aug,
who scarcely (any) more on human help relies. He strains the eye,
(who scarcely relies upon human help any more. He strains his eyes)

le:ɐ 'ʃt'rɛk'ət das lo:ɐ: vas 'vy:lət dɔrt' lʊnt'ən? vas raoʃt' lɛm'pʰo:ɐ?
er strecket das Ohr: "Was wühlet dort unten? was rauscht empor?"
he stretches the ear: "What roots about there below? what roars aloft?"
(and ears: "What is stirring down there? What comes roaring up to me?")

e:ɐ zi:t' lʊnt' laoʃtʰ; fɔrt' vy:lts lʊnt' raoʃtʰ — zo: 'harət' le:ɐ/le:r laos,
Er sieht und lauscht; fort wühlt's und rauscht — so harret er aus,
He looks and listens; forth is agitated it and roars — so waits he out,
(He looks and listens; the roaring and agitation continues — so he holds out,)

'lo:nə 'mʊrən lʊnt' kʰla:k', de:ɐ/de:r 'le:dlə hɛr bɪs tsu: 'mɪt'a:k'.
ohne Murren und Klag', der edle Herr bis zu Mittag.
without grumbling and lamentation, the noble lord till to midday.
(without grumbling or complaining, the noble lord, until noon.)

dɔx 'zɔnənbrant' di 'fɛlzənvant tsu'rʏk' mɪt' 'gly:əndən 'ʃt'ra:lən pʰraltʰ;
Doch Sonnenbrand die Felsenwand zurück mit glühenden Strahlen prallt;
But sunburn the rock- wall back with burning rays reflects;
(But the cliff reflects back with burning rays the fiery sunlight;)

da vɪrt' lʊn'laet'lɪç de:ɐ 'hɪtsə gə'valtʰ. lɛɐ'ʃœpft' fɔn lɛɐ'my:dəndɐ 'gɛmzənja:k't',
da wird unleidlich der Hitze Gewalt. Erschöpft von ermüdender Gemsenjagd,
then becomes unbearable the heat's power. Exhausted from tiring chamois-hunt,
(then the power of the heat becomes unbearable. Exhausted from the tiring chamois-hunt,)

fɔn dʊrst' gə'kʰvɛ:lt', fɔn dem 'hʊŋɐ gə'pʰla:k't', fy:lt' zɪç de:ɐ 'kʰaezɐ
von Durst gequält, von dem Hunger geplagt, fühlt sich der Kaiser
by thirst tormented, by the hunger plagued, feels himself the emperor
(tormented by thirst, plagued by hunger, the emperor feels)

mat' lʊnt' ʃvax. va:ɐs 'vʊndɐ, das 'lɛnt'lɪç di kʰraft' li:m bra:x?
matt und schwach. War's Wunder, dass endlich die Kraft ihm brach?
faint and weak. Was it (any) wonder that finally the strength for him broke?
(faint and weak. Was it any wonder that his strength finally gave way?)

das vʏnʃt‘ lɛ:ɐ̯/lɛ:r la'la͜en: gə'vɪs t͜su: za͜en, lɛ: di bə'zɪnʊŋ li:m fɛɐ̯'fli:stʰ,
Das wünscht er allein: gewiss zu sein, eh' die Besinnung ihm verfliesst,
That wishes he alone: certain to be, ere the consciousness from him flows away,
(He wishes only this: to know for certain, before he loses consciousness,)

ɔp‘ 'hɪlfə ba͜e 'mɛnʃən nɔx 'mø:k‘lɪç lɪstʰ? balt‘ vʊst‘ le:ɐ̯ ra:tʰ lʊnt‘ ʃrɪt
ob Hilfe bei Menschen noch möglich ist? Bald wusst' er Rat und schritt
whether help by humans still possible is? Soon knew he what to do and proceeded
(whether help from human beings is still possible? Soon he knew what to do and went)

t͜sʊr tʰa:t‘ lʊnt‘ ʃri:p‘ mɪt‘ 'ʃt‘ɪft‘ən la͜ofpʰɛrga'mɛnt di fra:k‘ lans fɔlk‘ lʊnt‘
zur Tat und schrieb mit Stiften auf Pergament die Frag' ans Volk und
to the deed and wrote with markers on parchment the question to the people and
(to work and wrote on a piece of parchment his question to the people, and)

'vɪk‘əlt‘ bə'hɛnt‘ mɪt‘ 'gɔldənəm 'bandə das 'tʰɛ:fəla͜en la͜of 'la͜enən gə'vɪçt‘ɪgən
wickelt behend mit goldenem Bande das Täfelein auf einen gewichtigen
wrapped quickly with golden ribbon the little tablet onto a heavy
(with a gold ribbon he quickly wrapped the little sheet around a heavy)

'marmo:ɐ̯ʃt‘a͜en, li:s 'falən di last‘ lɪn di 'tʰi:fə hɪ'nap‘ lʊnt‘ hɔrçt‘ — kʰa͜en la͜ot
Marmorstein, liess fallen die Last in die Tiefe hinab und horcht — kein Laut,
marble- stone, let fall the load into the depths down and listens — no sound,
(marble stone, let it fall down into the depths, and listened — no sound)

de:ɐ̯/de:r li:m 'lant‘vɔrt‘ ga:p‘. lax gɔt‘ lʊnt‘ hɛr! man li:p‘t‘ li:n zo: ze:ɐ̯; drʊm
der ihm Antwort gab. Ach Gott und Herr! Man liebt ihn so sehr; drum
which to him answer gave. Ah God and Lord! One loves him so very (much); therefore
(gave him an answer. Ah, God and Lord! Everyone loves him so much; therefore)

'fɪndət‘ fɔm 'fɔlk‘ə zɪç 'ni:mant‘ la͜en, dem hɛrn la͜en 'bo:t‘ə dɛs 'tʰo:dəs t͜su: za͜en.
findet vom Volke sich niemand ein, dem Herrn ein Bote des Todes zu sein.
finds from the people himself no one in, to the lord a messager of the death to be.
(no one from among the people volunteers to be a messenger of death to his lord, the emperor.)

de:ɐ̯ 'kʰa͜ezɐ, vi: hartʰ, la͜of 'lant‘vɔrt‘ hart‘ lʊnt‘ 'zɛndət den 'drɪt‘ən lʊnt‘ 'fi:ɐ̯t‘ən ʃt‘a͜en:
Der Kaiser, wie hart, auf Antwort harrt und sendet den dritten und vierten Stein:
The emperor, how hard, for answer waits and sends the third and fourth stone:
(The emperor—how hard!—waits for an answer, and sends down a third and then a fourth stone;)

dɔx 'lɪmɐ vɔlt‘ lɛs fɛɐ̯'ge:p‘lɪç za͜en. bɪs ʃo:n lam 'hɪməl di 'zɔnə zɪç zɛŋk‘t‘
doch immer wollt' es vergeblich sein. Bis schon am Himmel die Sonne sich senkt
but always would it in vain be. Until already in the sky the sun itself sinks
(but each time it would be in vain. Until the sun is already sinking low in the sky,)

lʊnt‘ nu:n lɛɐ̯'zɔ͜øft͜sənt de:ɐ̯ hɛr zɪç dɛŋk‘t‘: vɛ:ɐ̯ 'hɪlfə 'mø:k‘lɪç, zi: 'ri:fən lɛs mi:ɐ̯,
und nun erseufzend der Herr sich denkt: "Wär Hilfe möglich, sie riefen es mir,
and now sighing the lord to himself thinks: "Were help possible, they called it to me,
(and now with a sigh the emperor thinks: "If help were possible they would have called up to me,)

zo: har ɪç nu:n 'zɪçrɐ dɛs 'tʰo:dəs lal'hi:ɐ̯. da: ho:p‘ za͜en zɪn t͜su: gɔt‘ zɪç hɪn;
so harr' ich nun sich'rer des Todes allhier." Da hob sein Sinn zu Gott sich hin;
so wait I now surer for the death here." Then raised his mind to God itself hence;
(so I now even more surely wait here for death." Then he raised his mind up to God;)

iːm lɛnt'ˈflamt das hɛrts deːɐ̯ ˈhaelɪgə gaesth, das leːɐ̯
ihm entflammt das Herz der heilige Geist, dass er
in him inflames the heart the Holy Ghost, (so) that he
(the Holy Ghost inflames his heart, so that he)

zɪç ʃnɛl fɔn dem ˈlɪrdɪʃən raesth, ˈvɛk'ʃt'oːst di vɛlth, tsʊm ˈleːvɪgən hɛlth.
sich schnell von dem Irdischen reisst, wegstosst die Welt, zum Ewigen hält.
himself quickly from the earthly tears, pushes away the world, to the Eternal holds.
(quickly tears himself away from earthly concerns, rejects the world, and holds to the Eternal.)

jɛtst' nɪmt' leːɐ̯/leːr laen ˈtheːfəlaen ˈviːdɐ tsʊr hant', bəˈʃraep't' lɛs ˈlaefrɪç.
Jetzt nimmt er ein Täfelein wieder zur Hand, beschreibt es eifrig.
Now takes he a little tablet again to the hand, writes (on) it avidly.
(Now he again takes out a little sheet of parchment and begins to write on it avidly.)

vael ˈfeːlt'ə das bant', zoː bant' leːɐ̯s lam ʃt'aen mɪt dem ˈgɔldənəm fliːs.
Weil fehlte das Band, so band er's am Stein mit dem goldenem Vlies.
Since was lacking the ribbon, so tied he it to the stone with the golden fleece.
(Since he no longer had an extra ribbon, he tied it to the stone with the order of the golden fleece.)

vas zɔlts liːm? leːɐ̯ vaːɐ̯ jaː dɛs ˈthoːdəs gəˈvɪs.
Was sollt's ihm? Er war ja des Todes gewiss.
What should it to him? He was after all of the death certain.
(What difference should the loss of it make to him now? He was certain of death, after all.)

ʊnt' laos dem lɛɐ̯ˈhøːt'ən ˈlʊft'ɪgən graːp' vɪrft' leːɐ̯ den ʃt'aen lɪn das ˈleːbən hɪˈnap'.
Und aus dem erhöhten luftigen Grab wirft er den Stein in das Leben hinab.
And from the elevated airy grave throws he the stone into the life down.
(And from that elevated, airy grave he throws the stone down into life.)

voːl ˈphaenlɪçɐ ʃmɛrts dʊrçˈvyːlət das hɛrts ˈjeːdəm, deːɐ̯ nuːn,
Wohl peinlicher Schmerz durchwühlet das Herz jedem, der nun,
Probably more painful grief churns up the heart to everyone who now,
(Probably even more painful grief now churns in the heart of everyone who)

vas deːɐ̯ ˈkhaezɐ bəˈgeːɐ̯th, ˈvaenənt' fɔm ˈvaenəndən ˈleːzɐ høːɐ̯th.
was der Kaiser begehrt, weinend vom weinenden Leser hört.
what the emperor desires weeping from the weeping reader hears.
(hears, weeping, from the weeping reader, what the emperor desires.)

deːɐ̯ ˈleːzɐ riːf: zoː haest deːɐ̯ briːf: fiːl daŋk', thiˈroːl, fyːɐ̯ ˈdaenə liːp',
Der Leser rief: "So heisst der Brief: 'Viel Dank, Tirol, für deine Lieb,
The reader called: "Thus bids the letter: 'Much thanks, Tirol, for your love,
(The reader shouted out: "This is what the letter says: 'Many thanks, Tirol, for your love,)

diː thrɔø lɪn ˈjeːdɐ noːt' miːɐ̯ bliːp'. dɔx gɔt' fɛɐ̯ˈzuːxt' ɪç mɪt' ˈlyːbɐmuːth,
die treu in jeder Not mir blieb. Doch Gott versucht' ich mit Übermut,
which loyal in every need to me remained. But God tempted I with presumption,
(which has remained loyal to me in every emergency. But I tempted God with my presumption,)

das zɔl lɪç nuːn ˈbyːsən dʊrç laep' lʊnt' bluːth. bae ˈmɛnʃən
das soll ich nun büssen durch Leib und Blut. Bei Menschen
that shall I now expiate through body and blood. Through humans
(and I shall now expiate that sin with my body and blood. Through human help)

lɪst‘ 'kʰa͜enə 'rɛt‘ʊŋ meːɐ̯; 'gɔt‘əs 'vɪlə gə'ʃeːə! gə'rɛçt‘ lɪst deːɐ̯ hɛr!
ist keine Rettung mehr; Gottes Wille geschehe! Gerecht ist der Herr!
is no rescue more; God's will happen! Just is the Lord!
(I can expect no rescue any more; God's will be done! The Lord is just!)

vɪl 'byːsən di ʃult‘ mɪt‘ muːt‘ lʊnt‘ gə'dʊlt‘. mɪt‘ la͜enəm voːl kʰœnt‘ liːɐ̯
Will büssen die Schuld mit Mut und Geduld. Mit einem wohl könnt ihr
Want to expiate the fault with courage and patience. With one thing perhaps could you
(I want to expiate my fault with courage and patience. With one thing you could perhaps)

ma͜en hɛrt͡s lɛɐ̯'frɔ͜øn, lɪç vɪl lɔ͜øç den daŋk‘ lɪm 'tʰoːdə nɔx va͜en.
mein Herz erfreu'n, ich will euch den Dank im Tode noch weih'n.
my heart gladden, I will to you the thanks in the death yet consecrate.
(comfort my heart; I shall consecrate my thanks to you with my death.)

das lʊnfɛɐ̯'va͜eltʰ naːx 'tsiːɐ̯la͜en la͜elt‘ la͜en boːt‘ lʊm das 'ha͜elɪgə zak‘ra'mɛnt‘,
Dass unverweilt nach Zierlein eilt ein Bot' um das heilige Sakrament,
That without delay to Zierlein hurries a messenger for the Holy Sacrament,
(I ask that without delay a messenger hurry to the town of Zierlein to ask for the Holy Sacrament,)

naːx deːm miːɐ̯ 'dʏrst‘ənt di 'zeːlə brɛntʰ. lʊnt‘ vɛn deːɐ̯ 'pʰriːst‘ɐ
nach dem mir dürstend die Seele brennt. Und wenn der Priester
for which in me thirsting the soul burns. And when the priest
(for which my thirsting soul is burning. And when the priest)

ʃt‘eːt‘ lam flʊs, zoː 'kʰʏndət͡s miːɐ̯, 'ʃʏt͡sən, dʊrç 'la͜enən ʃus. lʊnt‘ vɛn
steht am Fluss, so kündet's mir, Schützen, durch einen Schuss. Und wenn
stands by the river, then announce it to me, marksmen, through a shot. And when
(is standing by the river, then let me know, marksmen, by firing a shot. And when)

lɪç den 'zeːgən nuːn zɔl lɛm'pfaːn, zoː dɔ͜øt‘ lɛs la͜en 't͡sva͜et‘ɐ miːɐ̯ 'viːdɐ(r) lan.
ich den Segen nun soll empfah'n, so deut' es ein zweiter mir wieder an.
I the blessing then shall receive, then indicate it a second to me again … .
(it is time for me to receive the blessing, then let a second shot indicate that to me.)

[*andeuten* = indicate]

zeːɐ̯ bɪt‘ ɪç lɔ͜øç, fleːt dan t͡su'gla͜eç mɪt‘ miːɐ̯ t͡sʊm 'hɛlfɐ(r) lɪn 'lalɐ noːtʰ,
Sehr bitt' ich euch, fleht dann zugleich mit mir zum Helfer in aller Not,
Very much ask I you, entreat then at the same time with me to the Helper in all need,
(I ask you very sincerely to pray then together with me to the Helper in every need,)

das leːɐ̯ mɪç ʃtɛrk‘ lɪn dem 'hʊŋɐtʰoːt‘. deːɐ̯ 'boːt‘ə flɔ͜øk‘tʰ,
dass er mich stärk' in dem Hungertod.'" Der Bote fleugt,
that He me strengthen in the hunger-death.'" The messenger flies,
(that He may strengthen me as I face death by starvation." The messenger flies;)

[*fleugt* (archaic) = *fliegt* = flies]

deːɐ̯ 'pʰriːst‘ɐ kʰɔ͜øçt‘ nuːn ʃoːn hɛɐ̯'ba͜e, nuːn ʃt‘eːt‘ leːɐ̯/leːr lam flʊs;
der Priester keucht nun schon herbei, nun steht er am Fluss;
the priest pants now already hither, now stands he by the river;
(the priest, panting, is already running this way; now he stands by the river;)

ʃnɛl ˈkʰʏndəts dem ˈkʰa͜ezɐ(r) ǀan ǀa͜en ʃus. deːɐ̯ ˈʃa͜oət‘ hɪˈnap‘,
schnell kündet's dem Kaiser an ein Schuss. Der schauet hinab,
quickly announces it to the emperor ... a shot. He looks down,
(a shot quickly announces the arrival of the priest to the emperor. He looks down,)

ǀɛɐ̯ˈblɪk‘t di mɔnˈʃt‘rants, dɛn ˈblɪtsənt‘ ǀɛɐ̯ˈglɛntsət‘ ǀiːɐ̯ ˈdeːmant‘kʰrants,
erblickt die Monstranz, denn blitzend erglänzet ihr Demantkranz,
sees the monstrance, for flashing shines its diamond wreath,
(sees the monstrance with the consecrated host, for the diamonds in its wreath flash brightly,)

ʊnt‘ vɪrft‘ zɪç foːɐ̯/foːr ǀiːɐ̯/ǀiːr ǀa͜of di ˈkʰniːə hɪn mɪt tsɛɐ̯ˈkʰnɪrʃt‘əm ˈhɛrtsən,
und wirft sich vor ihr auf die Kniee hin mit zerknirschtem Herzen,
and throws himself before it on the knees down with crushed heart,
(and throws himself down on his knees before it, with a crushed heart)

mɪt‘ ˈglɔ͜øbɪgəm zɪn. di ˈmɛnʃha͜et‘ rɪŋtʰ ǀʊnt‘ ziːk‘t‘ ǀʊnt‘ ʃvɪŋtʰ
mit gläubigem Sinn. Die Menschheit ringt und siegt und schwingt
with devout mind. The humanity wrestles and triumphs and soars
(and a devout mind. His humanity wrestles with itself, and triumphs, and soars)

a͜of ǀɛntˈˈfɛsəlt‘ən ˈflyːgəln ǀɛmˈpʰoːɐ̯ zɪç ʃnɛl tsuː deːɐ̯/deːr ˈǀeːvɪgən ˈliːbə
auf entfesselten Flügeln empor sich schnell zu der ewigen Liebe
on unfettered wings aloft itself swiftly to the eternal love's
(aloft swiftly on unfettered wings to eternal love's)

hoːxˈha͜elɪgən kʰvɛl. ǀʊnt‘ ǀoː! viː fleːtʰ za͜en ˈha͜esəs gəˈbeːtʰ! ǀoː gɔt, duː ˈfaːt‘ɐ(r),
hochheiligem Quell. Und o! wie fleht sein heisses Gebet! "O Gott, du Vater,
high-holy source. And, oh! how entreats his ardent prayer! "O God, Thou Father,
(most holy source. And, oh! how fervently his ardent prayer entreats: "O God, Thou Father)

ǀalˈmɛçt‘ɪç ǀam ˈhɪməlstʰroːn! duː liːp‘, ǀa͜os liːp‘ ǀɛntˈˈkʰvɔlənɐ ˈgɔt‘əszoːn,
allmächtig am Himmelsthron! Du Lieb', aus Lieb' entquollener Gottessohn,
almighty on the heaven- throne! Thou love, from love flowed forth God's Son,
(Almighty on heaven's throne! Thou who art Love, Son of God who has flowed forth from love,)

ǀʊnt duː hoːxˈha͜elɪgɐ ˈgɔt‘əsga͜est, deːɐ̯ ˈba͜edə fɛɐ̯-/fɛrˈǀa͜ent, das ha͜el ǀʊns va͜estʰ;
und du hochheiliger Gottesgeist, der beide vereint, das Heil uns weist;
and Thou high-holy God- Ghost, who both unites, the salvation to us shows;
(and Thou, most sublime Holy Ghost, who unites both, who shows us the way to salvation;)

ǀoː gɔt, dɛs ˈliːbə ǀa͜of ˈjeːdɐ ʃp‘uːɐ̯ fɛɐ̯ˈkʰʏndət‘ ǀa͜ot di ˈva͜et‘ə naˈtʰuːɐ̯!
o Gott, dess' Liebe auf jeder Spur verkündet laut die weite Natur!
O God, whose love in every trace proclaims loudly the vast Nature!
(O God, whose love is proclaimed by vast Nature in its every trace!)

ǀoː ˈtʰa͜oxt‘ə zɪç ʃnɛl ǀɪm ˈliːbəskʰvɛl ma͜en ˈliːbəndɐ ga͜est‘,
O tauchte sich schnell im Liebesquell mein liebender Geist,
Oh immersed itself quickly in the love- source my loving spirit,
(Oh, if only my loving spirit might immerse itself quickly in the source of love,)

ǀʊmˈfast‘ə di vɛltʰ, diː ˈliːbənt‘ ǀam ˈhɛrtsən da͜en ǀarm ǀɛɐ̯ˈhɛltʰ! foːɐ̯ ˈma͜enəm tʰoːt‘
umfasste die Welt, die liebend am Herzen dein Arm erhält! Vor meinem Tod
embraced the world, which lovingly at the heart Thy arm preserves! Before my death
(might embrace the world, which Thy arm preserves lovingly at Thy heart! Before my death)

da͜en ˈhɪməlsbroːtʻ vʏnʃ ɪç, ǀʊnˈvʏrdɪgɐ(r), ǀoː viː zeːɐ̯! ǀoː ziː ǀa͜of mɪç
dein Himmelsbrot wünsch' ich, Unwürdiger, o wie sehr! O sieh auf mich
Thy heaven's bread wish I, unworthy one, O how much! O look upon me
(I who am unworthy wish for Thy celestial bread, oh! how sincerely! Oh, look upon me)

ǀɛɐ̯ˈbarməntʻ heːɐ̯! ǀoː ˈkʰrɪstʊs liːpʻ, tʰrɪtʻ ba͜e miːɐ̯/miːr ǀa͜en ǀʊntʻ fyːɐ̯ mɪç t͜suˈrʏkʰ
erbarmend her! O Christus Lieb', tritt bei mir ein und führ' mich zurück
compassionately hither! O Christ's love, step by me in and lead me back
(compassionately! O Christ's love, enter into me and lead me back) [*eintreten* = enter]

ǀɪn deːɐ̯ ˈfrɔmən fɛɐ̯-/fɛrˈǀa͜en, diː ˈda͜enə ˈliːbə zoː ˈfɔ͜ørɪç bəˈzeːlt,
in der Frommen Verein, die deine Liebe so feurig beseelt,
into the devout ones' union, which Thy love so ardently animates,
(into the union of the devout, which Thy love so ardently animates)

das ˈǀa͜enəs ziː ˈveːɐ̯dən mɪtʻ gɔtʻ ǀʊntʻ vɛltʰ. ǀʊntʻ va͜el ǀɪç nɪçtʻ veːɐ̯tʰ,
dass eines sie werden mit Gott und Welt. Und weil ich nicht wert,
that one they become with God and world. And since I (am) not worthy, (of)
(that they become one with God and the world. And since I am not worthy of)

vas ǀɪç bəˈgeːɐ̯tʰ, ǀa͜en ˈǀa͜ent͜sɪgəs vɔrtʻ ǀa͜os ˈda͜enəm mʊntʻ maxt ˈda͜enən kʰnɛçtʻ
was ich begehrt, ein einziges Wort aus deinem Mund macht deinen Knecht
what I (have) desired, a single word from Thy mouth makes Thy servant
(that which I desire, a single word from Thy mouth can make Thy servant)

ǀa͜ox ˈviːdɐ gəˈzʊntʻ. zoː vɪl ǀeːɐ̯/ǀeːr ǀɪm fleːn foːɐ̯ ˈliːbə fɛɐ̯ˈgeːn.
auch wieder gesund." So will er im Fleh'n vor Liebe vergeh'n.
also again well." Thus wants he in the entreating of love to die.
(well again." Thus in his entreaty he wants to die of love.)

daː ˈkʰʏndətʻ ǀa͜en ˈt͜sva͜etʻɐ ʃʊs ǀiːm ǀan, das ǀeːɐ̯ den ˈzeːgən nuːn zɔl ǀɛmˈp͜faːn.
Da kündet ein zweiter Schuss ihm an, dass er den Segen nun soll empfah'n.
Then announces a second shot to him ... , that he the blessing now shall receive.
(Then a second shot announces to him that he shall now receive the blessing.)
[*ankünden* = to announce; *empfah'n* (poetic) = *empfangen* = receive]

deːɐ̯ hɛr zoˈgla͜eç ǀa͜of ˈfɛlzəngrʊntʻ vɪrftʻ zɪç di ʃtʻɪrn ǀʊnt di ˈhɛndə vʊntʻ;
Der Herr sogleich auf Felsengrund wirft sich die Stirn und die Hände wund;
The lord at once on rocky ground casts himself the forehead and the hands sore;
(The emperor at once strikes the rocky ground with his forehead and hands, making them sore,)

ʊnt deːɐ̯ ˈjɛːgɐ mɪtʻ ˈla͜otʻəm ˈʃpʻrɛçɐroːɐ̯ zaːkʻtʻ ǀiːm dɛs ˈpʰriːstʻɐs ˈvɔrtʻə foːɐ̯:
und der Jäger mit lautem Sprecherrohr sagt ihm des Priesters Worte vor:
and the huntsman with loud megaphone tells him the priest's words ... :
(and the huntsman repeats the priest's words for him through the loud megaphone:)
[*vorsagen* = to tell, to recite, to rehearse]

dɪç ˈzeːgnə gɔtʰ ǀɪn ˈda͜enɐ noːtʰ, deːɐ̯ ˈfaːtʻɐ, deːɐ̯ zoːn ǀʊnt deːɐ̯ ˈha͜elɪgə ga͜estʰ,
"Dich segne Gott in deiner Not, der Vater, der Sohn und der heilige Geist,
"You [obj.] bless God [subj.] in your need, the Father, the Son, and the Holy Ghost,
("May God bless you in your need, the Father, the Son, and the Holy Ghost,)

deːn ˈhɪməl lʊnt‘ leːɐ̯t‘ ˈloːnə ˈlɛndə pʰraestʰ! nuːn laltsuˈmaːl lɪm ˈgantsən tʰaːl das fɔlk‘
den Himmel und Erd' ohne Ende preist!" Nun allzumal im ganzen Tal das Volk
whom heaven and earth without end praises!" Now altogether in the whole valley the folk
(whom heaven and earth praise without end!" Now all together in the whole valley the people,)

laof den ˈkʰniːən hart‘ lɪm gəˈbeːt‘ lʊnt‘ laot‘ fyːɐ̯ das hael dɛs ˈhɛrən fleːtʰ.
auf den Knieen harrt im Gebet und laut für das Heil des Herren fleht.
on the knees waits in the prayer and loudly for the salvation of the lord entreats.
(on their knees in prayer, are waiting, and loudly pleading for the salvation of their emperor.)

den ˈkʰaezɐ ryːɐ̯ts; deːɐ̯ ˈbeːt‘əndən ʃal brɪŋt‘ liːm tsuː ˈloːrən deːɐ̯ ˈviːdɐhal.
Den Kaiser rührt's; der Betenden Schall bringt ihm zu Ohren der Widerhall.
The emperor [obj.] touches it; the praying ones' sound brings to him to ears the echo.
(It touches the emperor; the echo brings up to his ears the sound of his praying people.)

aox leːɐ̯ blaep‘t‘ ˈkʰniːən lɪm gəˈbeːt‘ lʊnt‘ gɔt‘ fyːɐ̯ das voːl deːɐ̯ ˈfœlk‘ɐ fleːtʰ.
Auch er bleibt knieen im Gebet und Gott für das Wohl der Völker fleht.
Also he stays kneeling in the prayer and God for the welfare of the peoples entreats.
(He too remains kneeling in prayer and prays to God for the welfare of the nations that he rules.)

ʃoːn flamt deːɐ̯ moːnt‘ lam horiˈtsɔntʰ, lʊnt‘ ˈhɛrlɪç das ˈgryːnlɪçə fɪrmaˈmɛntʰ
Schon flammt der Mond am Horizont, und herrlich das grünliche Firmament
Already flames the moon on the horizon, and gloriously the greenish firmament
(Already the moon is flaming on the horizon, and the greenish firmament is gloriously)

fɔn ˈfʊŋk‘əlndən ˈʃt‘ɛrnənheːrən brɛntʰ. dɛs ˈhɪməls pʰraxtʰ lɛɐ̯ˈvɛk‘ət‘ mɪt‘ maxt
von funkelnden Sternenheeren brennt. Des Himmels Pracht erwecket mit Macht
with sparkling star- hosts blazes. The sky's splendor awakens with power
(ablaze with hosts of sparkling stars. The splendor of the sky powerfully awakens)

di ˈzeːnzʊxt tsʊm ˈhɪmlɪʃən ˈfaːt‘ɐlant‘; iːm ˈløːzət‘ zɪç ˈjeːdəs ˈlɪrdɪʃə bant‘.
die Sehnsucht zum himmlischen Vaterland; ihm löset sich jedes irdische Band.
the yearning for the celestial fatherland; for him loosens itself every earthly bond.
(a yearning for the celestial fatherland; for him every earthly bond is loosened.)

voː deːɐ̯ ˈzeːrafiːm ˈharfə ˈjuːbəl lɛɐ̯ˈkʰlɪŋt‘, deːɐ̯ ˈzeːlɪgən kʰoːɐ̯ das ˈhaelɪç zɪŋt‘,
Wo der Seraphim Harfe Jubel erklingt, der Seligen Chor das "Heilig" singt,
Where the seraphim's harp rejoicing sounds, the blessed ones' choir the "*sanctus*" sings,
(Where the harp of the seraphim sounds jubilation, the choir of the blessed sings the "*sanctus*,")

voː das ˈlaedən ʃvaek‘t, di bəˈgiːɐ̯də zɪç brɪçt‘, tsʊr ˈleːvɪgən ˈliːbə,
wo das Leiden schweigt, die Begierde sich bricht, zur ewigen Liebe,
where the suffering becomes silent, the desire itself breaks, to the eternal love,
(where the voice of suffering is silent, where desire is overcome, to eternal love,)

tsʊm ˈleːvɪgən lɪçtʰ, daˈhɪn, daˈhɪn ʃvɪŋt‘ zɪç zaen zɪn; lʊnt‘ mɪt‘
zum ewigen Licht, dahin, dahin schwingt sich sein Sinn; und mit
to the eternal light, thither, thither swings itself his mind; and with
(to eternal light, thither, thither soars his mind; and with)

hoːx lɛmˈpʰoːɐ̯gəhoːbənən ˈhɛndən dɛŋt‘ leːɐ̯/leːr lɛnt‘ˈfliːənt‘ zaen ˈleːlənt tsuː ˈlɛndən.
hoch emporgehobenen Händen denkt er entfliehend sein Elend zu enden.
high up- raised hands thinks he forth-fleeing his misery to end.
(his hands raised on high he imagines that he is about to end his misery, fleeing from earth.)

als ʃlaŋkʻ ʔʊntʻ fa͜en ʔa͜en ˈbɔ͜ʏɐla͜en viː deːɐ̯ blɪt͜s ʔiːn ˈblɛndəntʻ foːɐ̯/foːr ʔiːm ʃtʻʊntʻ
Als schlank und fein ein Bäuerlein wie der Blitz ihn blendend vor ihm stund
When slim and fine a farm boy like the lightning him blinding before him stood
(When a slim, delicate farm boy stood before him like a flash of lightning, blinding him,)

ʔʊntʻ gryːstʻ ʔiːn mɪtʻ ˈliːpʻlɪç ʔɛɐ̯ˈtʰøːnəndəm mʊntʻ: hɛr maks, t͜sʊm ˈʃtʻɛrbən
und grüsst' ihn mit lieblich ertönendem Mund: "Herr Max, zum Sterben
and greeted him with charmingly sounding mouth: "Master Max, for the dying
(and greeted him in a charming tone of voice: "Master Max, for dying)

hat͜s voːl nɔx t͜sa͜etʻ, dɔx ˈfɔlgətʻ miːɐ̯ ʃnɛl, deːɐ̯ veːkʻ ʔɪstʻ va͜etʰ! deːɐ̯ ˈkʰa͜ezɐ(r)
hat's wohl noch Zeit, doch folget mir schnell, der Weg ist weit!" Der Kaiser
has it probably still time, but follow me quickly, the way is far!" The emperor
(there's still time left later; follow me quickly, there's a long way to go yet!" The emperor)

ʔɛntʻˈzɛt͜stʻ zɪç ʔɔpʻ dem gəˈzɪçtʻ ʔʊnt ˈtʰra͜oət den ˈʔa͜ogən ʔʊntʻ ˈʔoːrən nɪçtʰ.
entsetzt sich ob dem Gesicht und trauet den Augen und Ohren nicht.
startles himself over the vision and trusts the eyes and ears not.
(is startled by the vision, and does not trust his eyes and ears.)

ʔʊntʻ viː ʔeːɐ̯ ʃa͜otʰ, ʔiːm ˈha͜emlɪç gra͜otʰ; dɛn
Und wie er schaut, ihm heimlich graut; denn
And as he looks, for him secretly shudders; for
(And as he looks he secretly shudders; for) [*ihm graut* = he shudders]

ʔɛs valtʻ ʔan dem ˈkʰnaːbən gaːɐ̯ ˈzɔndɐlɪç ʔa͜en ˈdɛmɐndɐ ʃa͜en,
es wallt an dem Knaben gar sonderlich ein dämmernder Schein,
there floats about the boy quite strangely a dawning light,
(a dimly glowing light seems to float about the boy quite strangely,)

deːɐ̯ nɪçt͜s ˈʔɪrdɪʃəm glɪç. dɔx deːɐ̯ ˈkʰa͜ezɐ(r) ʔɪn hastʰ zɪç ˈviːdɐ fastʻ
der nichts Irdischem glich. Doch der Kaiser in Hast sich wieder fasst
which nothing earthly was like. But the emperor in haste himself again grasps
(a light unlike anything earthly. But the emperor hastily pulls himself together again)

ʔʊntʻ fraːkʻt das ˈkʰnɛːpʻla͜en: veːɐ̯ bɪst duː? ʃpʻrɪç! —ʔa͜en ˈboːtʻə, gəˈzantʻ,
und fragt das Knäblein: "Wer bist du? Sprich!" —"Ein Bote, gesandt,
and asks the little boy: "Who are you? Speak!" —"A messenger, sent

ʔʊm t͜suː ˈrɛtʻən dɪç. —veːɐ̯ ˈt͜sa͜ekʻtʻə diːɐ̯/diːr ʔan t͜sʊr ˈkʰlɪpʻə den veːkʻ?
um zu retten dich." —"Wer zeigte dir an zur Klippe den Weg?"
for to rescue you." —"Who indicated to you ... to the crag the way?"
(to rescue you." —"Who showed you the way to the crag?")

— voːl kʰɛn ʔɪç den bɛrkʻ ʔʊntʻ ˈjeːkʻlɪçən ʃtʻeːkʻ.
—"Wohl kenn' ich den Berg und jeglichen Steg."
— "Well know I the mountain and every footpath."
(—"I know the mountain well, and every footpath.")

zoː hat dɪç deːɐ̯ ˈhɪməl t͜suː miːɐ̯ gəˈʃɪkʻtʰ? —voːl hatʻ ʔeːɐ̯
"So hat dich der Himmel zu mir geschickt?"—"Wohl hat er
"Then has you the heaven to me sent?" —"Well has it

da͜en ˈrɔ͜øɪgəs hɛrt͜s lɛɐ̯ˈblɪkʻtʰ. dra͜of lɛs zɪç dreːtʰ, t͜sʊr ˈhøːlʊŋ geːtʰ lʊntʻ ˈgla͜etʻətʻ
dein reuiges Herz erblickt." Drauf es sich dreht, zur Höhlung geht und gleitet
your repentant heart seen." Thereupon it itself turns, to the cavity goes and glides
(seen your repentant heart." At that the boy turns, goes into the niche, and glides)

nuːn la͜eçt dʊrç den rɪs lɪn di vantʻ, deːn ˈfoːɐ̯heːɐ̯ za͜en ˈfɔrʃəndəs ˈla͜ogə
nun leicht durch den Riss in die Wand, den vorher sein forschendes Auge
now easily through the cleft in the wall, which previously his investigating eye
(now easily through a cleft in the wall that the emperor's investigating eye previously)

nɪçtʻ fantʻ. dʊrç den rɪs gəˈbʏkʻtʰ deːɐ̯ ˈkʰa͜ezɐ zɪç drʏkʻtʰ; ziː,
nicht fand. Durch den Riss gebückt der Kaiser sich drückt; sieh,
not found. Through the cleft stooped the emperor himself presses; see,
(had not found. The emperor, stooping, squeezes himself through the cleft; look,)

daː ˈhʏp͜fət das ˈkʰnɛːpʻla͜en ˈlɔ͜øçtʻəntʻ foˈran, dʊrç ˈʃtʻa͜elə ˈʃlʊxtʻən
da hüpfet das Knäblein leuchtend voran, durch steile Schluchten
there skips the little boy lighting (the way) ahead, through steep gorges
(there the little boy is skipping ahead, lighting the way, through steep gorges)

tʰiːf lapʻ di baːn. voː ˈfʊŋkʻəlnt das leːɐ̯t͜s lan den ˈvɛndən glɪmtʻ, lɪn deːɐ̯ ˈtʰiːfə
tief ab die Bahn. Wo funkelnd das Erz an den Wänden glimmt, in der Tiefe
deep down the path. Where sparkling the ore on the walls glimmers, in the depths
(deep down goes the path. Where the sparkling ore glimmers on the walls, and in the depths)

deːɐ̯ ˈʃvaːdən ˈla͜ofblɪt͜səntʻ ʃvɪmtʰ. lam gəˈvœlpʻ lɛɐ̯ˈtʰøːnt deːɐ̯ ˈʃrɪtʻə hal;
der Schwaden aufblitzend schwimmt. Am Gewölb ertönt der Schritte Hall;
the firedamp flashing swims. In the vault sounds the steps' reverberation;
(a combustible gas swirls about, flashing flame. The vault echoes the sound of their steps;)

fɛrn ˈdɔnɐt dɛs ˈbɛrkʻʃtʻroːms ˈbra͜ozəndɐ fal. ˈtʰiːfɐ nɔx lapʻ, ˈma͜elən hɪˈnapʻ:
fern donnert des Bergstroms brausender Fall. Tiefer noch ab, Meilen hinab:
afar thunders the mountain-stream's roaring falls. Deeper still down, miles down:
(in the distance the mountain stream's roaring falls thunders. Deeper down, still, miles down:)

daː ˈgla͜etʻət das ˈkʰnɛːpʻla͜en lɪn ˈla͜enə ʃlʊxtʰ; di ˈfakʻəl lɛɐ̯ˈlɔʃ. mɪt den ˈhɛndən
da gleitet das Knäblein in eine Schlucht; die Fackel erlosch. Mit den Händen
then glides the little boy into a gorge; the torch went out. With the hands
(then the little boy slips into a gorge; the torch went out. With his hands)

baŋə nuːn zuːxtʻ maks zɪç den veːkʻ hɪnˈfoːɐ̯ lʊnt drɪŋtʻ lɛmˈpʰoːɐ̯/-pʰoːr lʊntʻ
bange nun sucht Max sich den Weg hinvor und dringt empor und
anxiously now seeks Max for himself the way before and presses on upwards and
(Max now anxiously seeks a way out and presses onwards and upwards; and suddenly,)

ʃa͜otʻ ˈla͜oflaːtʻmənt deːɐ̯ ˈʃtʻɛrnə lɪçtʻ lʊntʻ zuːxt den ˈkʰnaːbən lʊntʻ ˈfɪndətʻ liːn nɪçtʰ.
schaut aufatmend der Sterne Licht und sucht den Knaben und findet ihn nicht.
sees breathing again the stars' light and seeks the boy and finds him not.
(breathing a sigh of relief, he sees starlight; he looks for the boy but does not find him.)

daː fastʻ liːn la͜en ˈʃa͜oɐ. nɪçtʻ hatʻ leːɐ̯ gəˈlɪrtʰ; voːl vaːɐ̯/vaːr lɛs la͜en ˈlɛŋəl,
Da fasst ihn ein Schauer. Nicht hat er geirrt; wohl war es ein Engel,
Then seizes him a shudder. Not has he erred; probably was it an angel,
(Then a shiver runs down his spine. He was not mistaken: it must have been an angel)

deːɐ̯/deːr |iːn gəˈfyːɐ̯tʰ. |ʊnt‘ ʃoːn |ɛɐ̯ˈkʰɛnt‘ |eːɐ̯ ˈtsiːɐ̯la͜ens tʰaːl, høːɐ̯t‘ ˈbra͜ozən deːɐ̯
der ihn geführt. Und schon erkennt er Zierleins Tal, hört brausen der
that him guided. And already recognizes he Zierlein’s valley, hears roaring the
(that guided him. And already he recognizes Zierlein’s valley, hears a roaring, the)

ˈmɛŋə fɛɐ̯ˈvɔrənən ʃal. mɪt‘ ˈbeːbəndəm tʰrɪtʰ |eːɐ̯ ˈva͜et‘ɐ ʃrɪtʰ; viː |ɔft‘
Menge verworrenen Schall. Mit bebendem Tritt er weiter schritt; wie oft
crowd’s confused sound. With trembling step he farther strode; how often
(confused sound of the crowd. With trembling steps he kept walking; how often,)

|ɛɐ̯ˈmat‘ət‘ |eːɐ̯ ˈva͜elən mʊs, bɪs |eːɐ̯ naːt dem va͜et‘ |ɛɐ̯ˈglɛnt͜səndən flʊs.
ermattet er weilen muss, bis er naht dem weit erglänzenden Fluss.
exhausted he linger must, till he nears the broad shining river.
(exhausted, he has to stop to rest, before he approaches the broad, shining river.)

nɔx ʃt‘ant‘ |eːɐ̯ va͜etʰ; dɔx hoːx|ɛɐ̯ˈfrɔ͜øt‘ ʃa͜ot‘ |eːɐ̯ den ˈpʰriːst‘ɐ ba͜e ˈfak‘əlglant͜s ʃt‘eːn,
Noch stand er weit; doch hocherfreut schaut er den Priester bei Fackelglanz steh’n,
Still stood he far; but high-delighted sees he the priest in torchlight stand,
(He is still far away; but, highly delighted, he sees the priest standing in the torchlight)

|ʊn|ɛɐ̯ˈmyːt‘lɪç ba͜e deːɐ̯ mɔnˈʃt‘rant͜s. |ʊnt‘ nɔx di gəˈtʰrɔ͜øən gəˈma͜endən ˈkʰniːn |ʊnt‘
unermüdlich bei der Monstranz. Und noch die getreuen Gemeinden knien und
indefatigably by the monstrance. And still the loyal communities kneel and
(indefatigably by the monstrance. And the loyal communities are still kneeling and)

ha͜es |ɪm gəˈbeːt‘ə fyːɐ̯/fyːr |iːn glyːn. za͜en ˈ|a͜ogə vart‘ nas, za͜en hɛrt͜s hoːx ʃvɔl;
heiss im Gebete für ihn glüh’n. Sein Auge ward nass, sein Herz hoch schwoll;
ardently in the prayer for him glow. His eye grew moist, his heart high swelled;
(glowing ardently in prayer for him. His eyes grew moist, his heart swelled high;)

ɛs vaːɐ̯ jaː fɔn ˈtʰa͜ozənt‘ gəˈfyːlən fɔl. ʃnɛl tʰrɪt‘ |eːɐ̯ hɛɐ̯ˈfoːɐ̯, ruːft‘ la͜ot‘ |ɛmˈpʰoːɐ̯:
es war ja von tausend Gefühlen voll. Schnell tritt er hervor, ruft laut empor:
it was after all of thousand feelings full. Quickly steps he forward, calls loudly up:
(it was after all full of a thousand feelings. Quickly he steps forward and calls out loudly:)

ˈloːbət den hɛrn |ʊnt‘ ˈza͜enə maxtʰ! zeːt‘, mɪç hat‘ |a͜en ˈ|ɛŋəl t͜suˈrʏk‘ gəˈbraxtʰ!
“Lobet den Herrn und seine Macht! Seht, mich hat ein Engel zurück gebracht!”
“Praise the Lord and His power! See, me has an angel back brought!”
(“Praise the Lord and His power! See, an angel has brought me back!”)

[Maximilian I was Holy Roman emperor from 1493 to 1519. This long—26 verses!—but vivid account of his rescue from an unreachable ledge on the side of a steep cliff has a very moving ending. Schubert wrote it for his brother Ferdinand to use at his school. Later Ferdinand published it, uncredited to Franz, in an arrangement for vocal duet with bass accompaniment. The original version as a solo song can be found in Volume 14, Part A, of the *Neue Schubert Ausgabe*, published by Bärenreiter in 1988.]

kʰɛnst duː das lant' / mɪnˈjõ (miˈɲõ) / mɪnˈjõs gəˈzaŋ
Kennst du das Land / Mignon / Mignons Gesang
Do You Know the Land / Mignon / Mignon's Song

Posthumously published [composed 1815] (poem by Johann Wolfgang von Goethe)

kʰɛnst duː das lant', voː di t͡siˈtʰroːnən blyːn, lɪm ˈdʊŋk'lən la͡op'
Kennst du das Land, wo die Zitronen blühn, im dunklen Laub
Know you the land where the lemon trees blossom, in the dark foliage
(Do you know the land where lemon trees blossom, where in dark foliage)

di ˈgɔlt'- loˈrɑ̃ːʒən glyːn, la͡en ˈzanft'ɐ vɪnt' fɔm ˈbla͡oən ˈhɪməl veːtʰ,
die Gold-Orangen glühn, ein sanfter Wind vom blauen Himmel weht,
the gold- oranges glow, a gentle wind from the blue sky blows,
(golden oranges glow, where a gentle breeze blows from the blue sky,)

di ˈmʏrt'ə ʃt'ɪl lʊnt' hoːx deːɐ̯ ˈlɔrbeːɐ̯ ʃt'eːtʰ, kʰɛnst duː lɛs voːl?
die Myrte still und hoch der Lorbeer steht, kennst du es wohl?
the myrtle quietly and high the laurel stands, know you it perhaps?
(where the myrtle grows quietly and the laurel tree stands tall? Do you know it, perhaps?)

daˈhɪn! daˈhɪn mœçt' ɪç mɪt diːɐ̯/diːr, loː ma͡en gəˈliːp't'ɐ, t͡siːn.
Dahin! Dahin möcht' ich mit dir, o mein Geliebter, ziehn.
Thither! Thither would like I with you, O my beloved, to go.
(There! There I would like to go with you, O my beloved.)

kʰɛnst duː das ha͡os? la͡of ˈzɔ͡ølən ruːt' za͡en dax, lɛs glɛnt͡st deːɐ̯ zaːl,
Kennst du das Haus? Auf Säulen ruht sein Dach, es glänzt der Saal,
Know you the house? On columns rests its roof, there gleams the hall,
(Do you know the house? Its roof rests on columns, the great hall gleams,)

lɛs ˈʃimɐt das gəˈmax, lʊnt' ˈmarmoːɐ̯bɪldɐ ʃt'eːn lʊnt' zeːn mɪç lan:
es shimmert das Gemach, und Marmorbilder stehn und sehn mich an:
there shimmers the chamber, and marble statues stand and look me at:
(the chamber shimmers, and marble statues stand and look at me:)

vas hat' man diːɐ̯, duː ˈlarməs kʰɪnt', gəˈtʰaːn? kʰɛnst duː lɛs voːl?
was hat man dir, du armes Kind, getan? Kennst du es wohl?
what has one to you, you poor child, done? Know you it perhaps?
("What have they done to you, you poor child?" they seem to say. Do you know it, perhaps?)

daˈhɪn! daˈhɪn mœçt' ɪç mɪt diːɐ̯/diːr, loː ma͡en bəˈʃʏt͡sɐ, ˈt͡siːn.
Dahin! Dahin möcht' ich mit dir, o mein Beschützer, ziehn.
Thither! Thither would like I with you, O my protector, to go.
(There! There I would like to go with you, O my protector.)

kʰɛnst duː den bɛrk' lʊnt' ˈza͡enən ˈvɔlk'ənʃt'eːk'? das ˈma͡oltʰiːɐ̯
Kennst du den Berg und seinen Wolkensteg? Das Maultier
Know you the mountain and its cloud- footpath? The mule
(Do you know the mountain and its footpath in the clouds? The mule)

zu:xt' lɪm 'ne:bəl 'zaenən ve:k'; lɪn 'hø:lən vo:nt de:ɐ̯ 'draxən 'lalt'ə bru:t;
sucht im Nebel seinen Weg; in Höhlen wohnt der Drachen alte Brut;
seeks in the mist its way; in caves dwells the dragons' ancient brood;
(seeks its way through the mist; the ancient brood of dragons lives in caves there;)

ɛs ʃt'ʏrtst de:ɐ̯ fɛls lʊnt' 'ly:bɐ(r) li:n di flu:tʰ. kʰɛnst du: li:n vo:l?
es stürzt der Fels und über ihn die Flut. Kennst du ihn wohl?
there plunges the rock, and over it the torrent. Know you it well?
(the rock falls away steeply, and over it a torrent plunges downwards. Do you know it, perhaps?)

da'hɪn! da'hɪn ge:t' 'lʊnzɐ ve:k'! lo: 'fa:t'ɐ, las lʊns tsi:n!
Dahin! Dahin geht unser Weg! o Vater, lass uns ziehn!
Thither! Thither goes our way! O father, let us go!
(There! There lies our way! O father, let us go!)

[This poem, one of the most famous in the German language, comes from the beginning of Book III of Goethe's novel, *Wilhelm Meister*. Many composers have set it to music, including Beethoven, Schumann, Liszt, Hugo Wolf, and—in French (as *Connais-tu le pays?*) in the opera *Mignon*—Ambroise Thomas. Schubert's manuscript is in A major, as in the *Gesamtausgabe*; Peters follows the first published version, transposed downward to F. Mignon was a mysterious, rather precocious waif, who expressed her deepest feelings more readily in song than in speech. The first verse expresses her yearning for Italy, where she was born. The second is her memory of a magnificent house with statues that seemed to speak to her sympathetically when she was sad. In the third verse she relives the terrifying night of her abduction, when the kidnappers brought her through thick mist across a dangerous alpine pass on the back of a mule. In the novel, Goethe describes how Mignon sang the song: "She started each verse solemnly and grandly, as if she wanted to draw attention to something out of the ordinary or to communicate something important. At the third line the song became gloomier and darker; she expressed the words 'do you know it, perhaps?' mysteriously and cautiously; there was an irresistible longing in 'there, there!' and she knew how to modify 'let us go!' at each repetition in such a way that the phrase was now pleading and urgent, now forceful and promising."]

'kʰla:gə / 'kʰla:gə lan den mo:nt' / daen 'zɪlbɐ ʃi:n
Klage / Klage an den Mond / Dein Silber schien
Lament / Lament to the Moon / Your Silver Gleamed

Posthumously published [composed 1816] (poem by Ludwig Hölty)

daen 'zɪlbɐ ʃi:n dʊrç 'laeçəngry:n, das 'kʰy:lʊŋ ga:p' laof mɪç hɛ'rap',
Dein Silber schien durch Eichengrün, das Kühlung gab auf mich herab,
Your silver gleamed through oak-green, which coolness gave to me down,
(Your silver light gleamed through the green oak leaves, which sent coolness down to me,)

o: mo:nt', lʊnt' 'laxt'ə ru: mi:ɐ̯ 'fro:əm 'kʰna:bən tsu:. ['fro:ən]
o Mond, und lachte Ruh' mir frohem Knaben zu. [*poem & Peters:* **frohen**]
O moon, and laughed peace to me happy boy to. [happy]
(O moon, and smiled peace down to me, when I was a happy boy.)

vɛn jɛtst daen lɪçt dʊrçs 'fɛnst'ɐ brɪçt', laxts 'kʰaenə ru: mi:ɐ̯ 'jʏŋlɪŋ tsu:,
Wenn jetzt dein Licht durchs Fenster bricht, lacht's keine Ruh' mir Jüngling zu,
When now your light through the window breaks, laughs it no peace to me youth to,
(Now when your light breaks through the window, it brings no peace to me, now a young man,)

ziːts͜ 'maenə 'vaŋə blas, maen 'lɑogə 'tʰrɛːnənnas.
sieht's meine Wange blass, mein Auge tränennass.
sees it my cheek pale, my eye wet with tears.
(it sees that my cheek is pale, my eyes are wet with tears.)

baltʻ, 'liːbɐ frɔøntʻ, lax, baltʻ bəˈʃaent daen 'zɪlbɐʃaen den 'laeçənʃtʻaen,
Bald, lieber Freund, ach, bald bescheint dein Silberschein den Leichenstein,
Soon, dear friend, ah, soon illuminates your silver gleam the gravestone,
(Soon, dear friend, ah, soon your silver gleam will shine upon the gravestone)

deːɐ̯ 'maenə 'laʃə bɪrkʻtʰ, dɛs 'jʏŋlɪŋs 'laʃə bɪrkʻtʰ!
der meine Asche birgt, des Jünglings Asche birgt!
that my ashes hides, the youth's ashes hides!
(that hides my ashes, the ashes of this young man!)

[The young man in the poem senses that he will die young; perhaps Schubert had a similar presentiment as he wrote the touching, eloquent setting of the third and final verse.]

'kʰlaːgə / di 'zɔnə ʃtʻaekʻtʰ
Klage / Die Sonne steigt
Lament / The Sun Rises

Posthumously published [composed 1816] (poem by Friedrich von Matthisson)

di 'zɔnə ʃtʻaekʻt, di 'zɔnə zɪŋkʻtʻ, dɛs 'moːndəs 'vɛksəlʃaebə blɪŋkʻtʻ,
Die Sonne steigt, die Sonne sinkt, des Mondes Wechselscheibe blinkt,
The sun rises, the sun sinks, the moon's ever-changing disk gleams,

dɛs 'lɛːtʻɐs blɑo dʊrçˈveːpʻtʻ mɪtʻ glants͜ deːɐ̯ 'ʃtʻɛrnə 'gɔldnɐ 'raeəntʰants͜:
des Äthers Blau durchwebt mit Glanz der Sterne goldner Reihentanz:
the ether's blue through-weaves with splendor the stars' golden round- dance:
(the golden round dance of the stars weaves in splendor through the blue ether:)

dɔx lɛs dʊrçˈʃtʻrøːmt deːɐ̯ 'zɔnə lɪçt, dɛs 'moːndəs 'lɛçəlndəs gəˈzɪçtʻ,
doch es durchströmt der Sonne Licht, des Mondes lächelndes Gesicht,
but there through-streams the sun's light, the moon's smiling face,
(but the sunlight, the smiling face of the moon,)

deːɐ̯ 'ʃtʻɛrnə 'raegən, ʃtʻɪl lʊntʻ heːɐ̯, mɪtʻ 'hoːxgəfyːl diːs hɛrts͜ nɪçtʻ meːɐ̯!
der Sterne Reigen, still und hehr, mit Hochgefühl dies Herz nicht mehr!
the stars' roundelay, quiet and sublime, with exultation this heart not (any) more!
(the roundelay of the stars, quiet and sublime, no longer stream exultation through this heart!)

di 'viːzə blyːt, deːɐ̯ 'bʏʃə gryːn lɛɐ̯ˈtʰøːntʻ fɔn 'fryːlɪŋsmelodiːn,
Die Wiese blüht, der Büsche Grün ertönt von Frühlingsmelodien,
The meadow blossoms, the bushes' green resounds with spring- melodies,
(The meadow is blossoming; the bushes' greenery is resounding with the melodies of spring,)

ɛs valt deːɐ̯ bax lɪm 'laːbəntʻʃtʻraːl hɪnapʻ lɪns 'haenlʊmˌkʰrɛnts͜tʻə tʰaːl:
es wallt der Bach im Abendstrahl hinab ins hainumkränzte Tal:
there flows the brook in the evening ray down into the grove-garlanded valley:
(the brook is flowing down into the grove-garlanded valley in the glow of the setting sun:)

dɔx lɛs lɛɐ̯'heːp't deːɐ̯ 'ha͜enə liːt, di la͜o, di 't^hɑ͜ozənt'farbɪç blyːt',
doch es erhebt der Haine Lied, die Au, die tausendfarbig blüht,
but there lifts the groves' song, the meadow, which thousand-colored blooms,
(but the song of the groves, the meadow that is blooming with a thousand colors,)

deːɐ̯/deːr 'lɛrlənbax lɪm 'laːbənt'lɪçt' viː 'foːɐ̯maːls 'ma͜enə 'zeːlə nɪçt^h!
der Erlenbach im Abendlicht wie vormals meine Seele nicht!
the alder tree brook in the evening light as formerly my soul not!
(the alder tree brook in the evening light do not lift my soul as in days gone by!)

[oː ʃmɛrts! vɛn 'lʊnzrɐ 'juːgənt' frɔ͜ønt dɛs 'lap'ʃiːts 'bɪt'rə 'tsɛːrə va͜ent^h!
[O Schmerz! wenn unsrer Jugend Freund des Abschieds bittre Zähre weint!
[O pain! when our youth's friend the farewell's bitter tear weeps!
[(Oh the pain, when the friend of our youth weeps bitter tears at our farewell!)

zoː t^hrɪft' ba͜em 'froːən 'lɛrnt'əmaːl dɛs 'lant'mans dax la͜en 'vɛt'ɐʃt'raːl!]
So trifft beim frohen Erntemahl des Landmanns Dach ein Wetterstrahl!]
Thus strikes at the happy harvest feast the farmer's roof a flash of lightning!]
(Thus lightning strikes the farmer's roof during a happy harvest feast!)]

[The two-part form of Schubert's setting did not accommodate the fifth verse, in brackets above.]

Klage / Nimmer länger trag' ich see *Der Leidende*

'k^hlaːgə / 't^hrɑ͜oɐ lʊm'fliːst' ma͜en 'leːbən
Klage / Trauer umfliesst mein Leben
Lament / Sorrow Floods My Life

Posthumously published [composed 1816] (author unknown*)

't^hrɑ͜oɐ(r) lʊm'fliːst' ma͜en 'leːbən, 'hɔfnʊŋsloːs ma͜en 'ʃt'reːbən,
Trauer umfliesst mein Leben, hoffnungslos mein Streben,
Sorrow flows around my life, hopeless my striving,
(Sorrow floods my life, my striving seems hopeless,)

ʃt'eːts lɪn gluːt' lʊnt' 'beːbən ʃla͜eçt' miːɐ̯ hɪn das 'leːbən;
stets in Glut und Beben schleicht mir hin das Leben;
constantly in ardor and trembling steals (from) me away the life;
(constantly in ardor and trembling, my life slips away from me;)

oː 'nɪmɐ t^hraːg ɪçs 'lɛŋɐ! 'la͜edən lʊnt' 'ʃmɛrtsən 'vyːlən
o nimmer trag' ich's länger! Leiden und Schmerzen wühlen
O never endure I it longer! Suffering and pains gnaw
(oh, I cannot endure it any longer! Suffering and pain gnaw)

miːɐ̯/miːr lɪn den gə'fyːlən, 'k^ha͜enə 'lʏft'ə 'k^hyːlən 'baŋɐ(r) 'laːndʊŋ 'ʃvyːlən;
mir in den Gefühlen, keine Lüfte kühlen banger Ahndung Schwülen;
to me in the feelings, no breezes cool anxious foreboding's sultrinesses;
(at my feelings; no breezes cool the sultriness of my anxious foreboding;)

[*Ahndung* (obs. in this sense) = *Ahnung* = presentiment, foreboding]

oː ˈnɪmɐ tʰraːɡ ɪçs ˈlɛŋɐ! nuːɐ̯ ˈfɛrnɐ tʰoːtʻ kʰan ˈhaelən
o nimmer trag' ich's länger! Nur ferner Tod kann heilen
O never endure I it longer! Only distant death can heal
(oh, I cannot endure it any longer! Only distant death can heal)

ˈzɔlçɐ ˈʃmɛrtsən ˈvaelən, voː zɪç di ˈpfɔrtʻən ˈtʰaelən,
solcher Schmerzen Weilen, wo sich die Pforten teilen,
such pains' lingering, where themselves the gates divide,
(such lingering pain; when those gates open)

veːɐ̯d ɪç ˈviːdɐ ˈhaelən; |oː ˈnɪmɐ tʰraːɡ ɪçs ˈlɛŋɐ!
werd' ich wieder heilen; o nimmer trag' ich's länger!
shall I again heal; O never endure I it longer!
(I shall be healed; oh, I cannot endure this pain any longer!)

[*When the song was published, the text was attributed to Ludwig Hölty, and there is a manuscript copy marked *Klage II* by Hölty; but the poem has not been found among the poet's published works. The *Gesamtausgabe* prints two versions of the deeply-felt song, the first a sketch. They were composed at a time when it was becoming clear that Schubert could not hope to marry Therese Grob, his first love.]

ˈkʰlaːɡə deːɐ̯ ˈtseːrɛs
Klage der Ceres
Ceres' Lament

Posthumously published [composed 1815-1816] (poem by Friedrich von Schiller)

ɪst deːɐ̯ ˈhɔldə lɛnts lɛɐ̯ˈʃiːnən? hat di ˈleːɐ̯də zɪç fɛɐ̯ˈjʏŋtʰ?
Ist der holde Lenz erschienen? hat die Erde sich verjüngt?
Has the lovely spring appeared? Has the earth itself rejuvenated?
(Has lovely spring appeared? Has the earth become young again?)

di bəˈzɔntʻən ˈhyːɡəl ˈɡryːnən, |ʊnt dɛs ˈlaezəs ˈrɪndə ʃpʻrɪŋtʰ.
Die besonnten Hügel grünen, und des Eises Rinde springt.
The sunny hills turn green, and the ice's crust cracks.
(The sun-warmed hills turn green, and the crust of ice is breaking up.)

ɑos deːɐ̯ ˈʃtʻrøːmə ˈblɑoəm ˈʃpʻiːɡəl laxt deːɐ̯/deːr ˈ|ʊnbəvœlkʻtʻə tsɔøs;
Aus der Ströme blauem Spiegel lacht der unbewölkte Zeus,
From the rivers' blue mirror laughs the unclouded Zeus,
(The reflection of the unclouded sky-god smiles up from the blue mirror of the rivers,)

ˈmɪldɐ ˈveːən ˈtseːfyːɐ̯s ˈflyːɡəl, ˈlɑoɡən tʰraepʻt das ˈjʊŋə raes.
milder wehen Zephyrs Flügel, Augen treibt das junge Reis.
milder flutter Zephyrus' wings, buds puts forth the young sprig.
(the wings of the west wind flutter more gently, the young sprig puts forth buds.)

ɪn dem haen lɛɐ̯ˈvaxən ˈliːdɐ, |ʊnt di |oreˈaːdə ʃpʻrɪçtʰ:
In dem Hain erwachen Lieder, und die Oreade spricht:
In the grove awaken songs, and the oread* speaks:
(Birdsong wakens in the grove, and the nymph of the echoing hillside speaks:)

'da̯enə 'blu:mən 'kʰe:rən 'vi:dɐ, 'da̯enə 'tʰɔxt'ɐ 'kʰe:rət' nɪçtʰ!
Deine Blumen kehren wieder, deine Tochter kehret nicht!
Your flowers return again, your daughter returns not!
("Your flowers come back again, your daughter does not!")

ax, vi: laŋ lɪsts, das lɪç 'valə, 'zu:xənt dʊrç de:ɐ̯/de:r 'le:ɐ̯də flu:ɐ̯!
Ach, wie lang' ist's, dass ich walle, suchend durch der Erde Flur!
Ah, how long is it, that I wander, searching through the earth's meadow!
(Ah, how long I have been wandering, searching through all the meadows of the earth!)

'tʰi:t'a:n, 'da̯enɐ 'ʃt'ra:lən 'lalə zant' ɪç na:x de:ɐ̯ 'tʰɔ̯ørən ʃp'u:ɐ̯;
Titan, deiner Strahlen alle sandt' ich nach der teuren Spur;
Titan,* your rays' all sent I after the dear trace;
(Sun, I sent all of your rays to find a trace of my dear one;)
[*poem:* **deine** ('da̯enə) **Strahlen alle** = all your rays (**deiner Strahlen alle** = all *of* your rays)]

'kʰa̯enɐ hat' mi:ɐ̯ nɔx fɛɐ̯'kʰʏndət' fɔn dem 'li:bən 'langəzɪçtʰ,
keiner hat mir noch verkündet von dem lieben Angesicht,
none has to me yet brought news of the dear countenance,
(but none as yet has brought me any news of her beloved face,)

ʊnt de:ɐ̯ tʰa:k, de:ɐ̯/de:r 'laləs 'fɪndət, di fɛɐ̯'lo:rnə fant' le:ɐ̯ nɪçtʰ.
und der Tag, der alles findet, die Verlorne fand er nicht.
and the day, which everything finds, the lost one found it not.
(and the day, which discovers all, has not found the lost one.)

hast du:, t͡sɔ̯øs, zi: mi:ɐ̯/mi:r lɛnt''rɪsən? hat', fɔn 'li:rəm ra̯et͡s gə'ry:ɐ̯t',
Hast du, Zeus, sie mir entrissen? Hat, von ihrem Reiz gerührt,
Have you, Zeus, her from me snatched away? Has, by her charm touched,
(Have you, Zeus, snatched her away from me? Has, touched by her charm,)

t͡su: dɛs 'lɔrkʰʊs 'ʃvart͡sən 'flʏsən 'pʰlu:t'o zi: hɪ'nap'gəfy:ɐ̯tʰ?
zu des Orkus schwarzen Flüssen Pluto sie hinabgeführt?
to the Orcus' black rivers Pluto her down lead?
(Pluto lead her down to Orcus'* black rivers?)

ve:ɐ̯ vɪrt' na:x dem 'dy:st'ɐn 'ʃt'randə 'ma̯enəs 'gra:məs 'bo:t'ə za̯en?
Wer wird nach dem düstern Strande meines Grames Bote sein?
Who will toward the dark shore my grief's messenger be?
(Who will be the messenger of my grief to that dark shore?)

'e:vɪç ʃt'ø:st de:ɐ̯ kʰa:n fɔm 'landə, dɔx nu:ɐ̯ 'ʃat'ən nɪmt' le:ɐ̯/le:r la̯en.
Ewig stösst der Kahn vom Lande, doch nur Schatten nimmt er ein.
Eternally shoves the boat (off) from the land, but only shadows takes it into (it).
(Eternally, over and over, the boat shoves off from the land, but it takes only shades on board.)

'je:dəm 'ze:lgən la̯ok' fɛɐ̯'ʃlɔsən bla̯ep't das 'nɛçt'lɪçə gə'fɪlt',
Jedem sel'gen Aug' verschlossen bleibt das nächtliche Gefild,
To every blessed one's eye closed remains the nocturnal field,
(Those fields of night remain closed to the eyes of the immortal gods,)

ʊnt‘ zoː laŋ deːɐ̯ ʃt‘ʏks gəˈflɔsən, tʰruːk leːɐ̯ kʰa̯en leˈbɛndɪç bɪlt‘.
und so lang der Styx geflossen, trug er kein lebendig Bild.
and as long the Styx (has) flowed, bore it no living image.
(and as long as the Styx* has flowed it has borne no living thing.)

ˈniːdɐ ˈfyːrən ˈtʰɑo̯zənt‘ ˈʃt‘a̯egə, ˈkʰa̯enɐ fyːɐ̯t t͡sʊm tʰaːk‘ t͡suˈrʏkʰ;
Nieder führen tausend Steige, keiner führt zum Tag zurück;
Down lead (a) thousand paths, none leads to the day back;
(A thousand paths lead downwards, none leads back up to the daylight;)

ˈiːrə ˈtʰrɛːnən brɪŋt‘ kʰa̯en ˈt͡sɔ̯øgə foːɐ̯ deːɐ̯ ˈbaŋən ˈmʊt‘ɐ blɪkʰ.
ihre Tränen bringt kein Zeuge vor der bangen Mutter Blick.
her tears brings no witness before the anxious mother’s gaze.
(no witness brings her tears before the gaze of her anxious mother.)

ˈmʏt‘ɐ, diː ɑo̯s ˈpʰʏras ˈʃt‘amə ˈʃt‘ɛrp‘lɪçə gəˈboːrən zɪnt‘,
Mütter, die aus Pyrrhas Stamme sterbliche geboren sind,
Mothers, who from Pyrrha’s race mortals born are,
(Mortal mothers, born of Pyrrha’s* race,)

ˈdʏrfən dʊrç dɛs ˈgraːbəs ˈflamə ˈfɔlgən dem gəˈliːp‘t‘ən kʰɪnt‘;
dürfen durch des Grabes Flamme folgen dem geliebten Kind;
may through the grave’s flame follow the beloved child;
(may follow a beloved child through the flames of the pyre;)

nuːɐ vas ˈjoːvɪs hɑo̯s bəˈvoːnət‘, ˈnaːət‘ nɪçt dem ˈdʊŋk‘əln ʃt‘rant‘,
nur was Jovis Haus bewohnet, nahet nicht dem dunkeln Strand,
but what Jove’s house inhabits, nears not to the dark shore,
(but those who dwell in Jove’s* house may not draw near to the dark shore,)

nuːɐ̯ di ˈzeːlɪgən fɛɐ̯ˈʃoːnət‘, ˈpʰart͡sən, ˈlɔ̯ørə ˈʃt‘rɛŋə hant‘.
nur die Seligen verschonet, Parzen, eure strenge Hand.
only the blessed spares, Parcae,* your severe hand.
(Your severe hand, goddesses of fate, spares only the immortals.)

ʃtʏrt͡st‘ mɪç lɪn di naxt deːɐ̯ ˈnɛçt‘ə lɑo̯s dɛs ˈhɪməls ˈgɔldnəm zaːl!
Stürzt mich in die Nacht der Nächte aus des Himmels goldnem Saal!
Hurl me into the night of the nights from the heaven’s golden hall!
(Cast me down from heaven’s golden hall into that night of nights!)

ˈeːrət‘ nɪçt deːɐ̯ ˈgœt‘ɪn ˈrɛçt‘ə, lax! ziː zɪnt deːɐ̯ ˈmʊt‘ɐ kʰvaːl!
Ehret nicht der Göttin Rechte, ach! sie sind der Mutter Qual!
Honor not the goddess’s rights, ah! they are the mother’s torment!
(Do not honor the goddess’s rights! Ah, they are the mother’s torment!)

voː ziː mɪt dem ˈfɪnst‘ɐn ˈgat‘ən ˈfrɔ̯øt‘loːs ˈtʰroːnət‘, ʃt‘iːk‘ lɪç hɪn,
Wo sie mit dem finstern Gatten freudlos thronet, stieg’ ich hin,
Where she with the gloomy husband joyless thrones, would descend I thither,
(I would descend to where she is joylessly enthroned with her gloomy husband,)

ʊnt ˈtʰrɛːt‘ə mɪt den ˈla̯ezən ˈʃat‘ən ˈla̯ezə foːɐ̯ di ˈhɛrʃərɪn.
und träte mit den leisen Schatten leise vor die Herrscherin. [*poem without* **und**]
and would step with the quiet shades softly before the queen.

ax, |iːɐ̯/|iːr ˈ|ɑ͜ogə fɔ͜øçt‘ fɔn ˈt͡sɛːrən, zuːxt‘ |ʊmˈzɔnst das ˈgɔldnə lɪçtʰ,
Ach, ihr Auge feucht von Zähren, sucht umsonst das goldne Licht,
Ah, her eye, moist with tears, seeks in vain the golden light,
(Ah, her eyes, moist with tears, seek in vain the golden light,)

ˈɪrət‘ naːx |ɛnt‘ˈfɛrnt‘ən ˈsfɛːrən, |ɑ͜of di ˈmʊt‘ɐ fɛlt‘ |ɛs nɪçtʰ,
irret nach entfernten Sphären, auf die Mutter fällt es nicht,
strays toward distant spheres, upon the mother falls it not,
(stray toward distant spheres, but do not fall upon her mother,)

bɪs di ˈfrɔ͜ødə ziː |ɛntˈdɛk‘ət‘, bɪs zɪç brʊst‘ mɪt‘ brʊst‘ fɛɐ̯ˈ|a͜entʰ/fɛrˈ|a͜entʰ,
bis die Freude sie entdecket, bis sich Brust mit Brust vereint,
until the joy her discovers, until itself breast with breast unites,
(until joy finds her, until their bosoms are united,)

ʊnt, t͡sʊm ˈmɪt‘gəfyːl |ɛɐ̯ˈvɛk‘ət‘, zɛlpst deːɐ̯ ˈrɑ͜oə ˈ|ɔrk‘ʊs va͜entʰ.
und, zum Mitgefühl erwecket, selbst der rauhe Orkus weint.
and, to the compassion awakened, even the rough Orcus weeps.
(and even rough Orcus, awakened to compassion, weeps.)

ˈa͜et‘lɐ vʊnʃ! fɛɐ̯ˈloːrnə ˈkʰlaːgən! ˈruːɪç |ɪn dem ˈgla͜eçən gla͜es
Eitler Wunsch! verlorne Klagen! Ruhig in dem gleichen Gleis
Vain wish! Lost laments! Calmly in the same course

rɔlt dɛs ˈtʰaːgəs ˈzɪçrɐ ˈvaːgən, ˈ|eːvɪç ʃt‘eːt deːɐ̯ ʃlʊs dɛs t͡sɔ͜øs.
rollt des Tages sichrer Wagen, ewig steht der Schluss des Zeus.
rolls the day's reliable chariot, eternal stands the decree of the Zeus.
(the reliable chariot of the day rolls onward, the decree of Zeus stands for ever.)

vɛk‘ fɔn ˈjeːnən ˈfɪnst‘ɐnɪsən vant‘ |eːɐ̯ za͜en bəˈglʏk‘t‘əs hɑ͜op‘tʰ;
Weg von jenen Finsternissen wandt' er sein beglücktes Haupt;
Away from those darknesses turned he his made-happy head;
(He turned his happy head away from those dark regions;)

ˈa͜enmaːl |ɪn di naxt‘ gəˈrɪsən, bla͜ep‘t‘ ziː ˈ|eːvɪç miːɐ̯ gəˈrɑ͜op‘tʰ,
einmal in die Nacht gerissen, bleibt sie ewig mir geraubt,
once into the night snatched away, remains she eternally to me stolen,
(once snatched away into the night, she remains eternally lost to me,)

bɪs dɛs ˈdʊŋk‘əln ˈʃt‘roːməs ˈvɛlə fɔn |ɑ͜oˈroːrəns ˈfarbən glyːtʰ,
bis des dunkeln Stromes Welle von Aurorens Farben glüht,
until the dark river's wave with Aurora's* colors glows,
(until the waves of the dark river will glow with the colors of the dawn,)

ˈiːrɪs ˈmɪt‘ən dʊrç di ˈhœlə ˈ|iːrən ˈʃøːnən ˈboːgən t͡siːtʰ.
Iris mitten durch die Hölle ihren schönen Bogen zieht.
Iris in the midst through the hell her beautiful bow draws,
(until Iris* draws her beautiful rainbow through the midst of hell,)

ɪst‘ miːɐ̯ nɪçt͡s fɔn |iːɐ̯ gəˈbliːbən? nɪçt‘ |a͜en zyːs |ɛɐ̯ˈ|ɪnɐnt‘/|ɛrˈ|ɪnɐnt‘ p͡fant‘,
Ist mir nichts von ihr geblieben? Nicht ein süss erinnernd Pfand,
Is to me nothing of her left? Not a sweet reminding pledge,
(Is nothing of her left to me? Not a sweet token to remind me)

das di ˈfɛrnən zɪç noχ ˈliːbən, ˈkʰae̯nə ʃp'uːɐ̯ deːɐ̯ ˈtʰɔ͜ørən hant'?
dass die Fernen sich noch lieben, keine Spur der teuren Hand?
that the distant ones each other still love, no trace of the precious hand?
(that, though far apart, we still love each other? No trace of her precious hand?)

ˈkʰnʏpfət' zɪç kʰae̯n ˈliːbəskʰnoːt'ən ˈtsvɪʃən kʰɪnt' lʊnt' ˈmʊt'ɐ(r) lan?
Knüpfet sich kein Liebesknoten zwischen Kind und Mutter an?
Ties together itself no love- knot between child and mother ... ?
(Is no love-knot tied between mother and child?) [*anknüpfen* = to tie, join, fasten with a knot]

ˈtsvɪʃən ˈleːbəndən lʊnt ˈtʰoːt'ən lɪst' kʰae̯n ˈbʏnt'nɪs ˈlao̯fgətʰaːn?
Zwischen Lebenden und Toten ist kein Bündnis aufgetan?
Between living and dead is no alliance opened?
(Is no alliance possible between the living and the dead?)

nae̯n, nɪçt' gants lɪst' ziː lɛnt'ˈfloːn! viːɐ̯ zɪnt' nɪçt' gants gəˈtʰrɛntʰ!
Nein, nicht ganz ist sie entfloh'n! Wir sind nicht ganz getrennt!
No, not entirely has she fled! We are not entirely separated!
(No, she is not entirely lost to me! We are not entirely separated!)
[*poem:* **entflohen** (lɛnt'ˈfloːən)**! Nein, wir sind nicht ganz getrennt!**]

ˈhaːbən lʊns di ˈleːvɪç ˈhoːən ˈlae̯nə ˈʃp'raːχə dɔχ fɛɐ̯ˈgœntʰ!
Haben uns die ewig Hohen eine Sprache doch vergönnt!
Have to us the eternally exalted ones a language after all granted!
(The eternally exalted gods have granted us a language, after all!)

vɛn dɛs ˈfryːlɪŋs ˈkʰɪndɐ ˈʃt'ɛrbən, vɛn fɔn ˈnɔrdəs ˈkʰalt'əm hao̯χ
Wenn des Frühlings Kinder sterben, wenn von Nordes kaltem Hauch
When the spring's children die, when from north wind's cold breath
(When the children of the spring die, when from the cold breath of the north wind)

blat' lʊnt' ˈbluːmə zɪç lɛnt'ˈfɛrbən, ˈtʰrao̯rɪç ʃt'eːt deːɐ̯ ˈnak't'ə ʃt'rao̯χ,
Blatt und Blume sich entfärben, traurig steht der nackte Strauch,
leaf and flower themselves fade, sad stands the naked shrub,
(leaves and flowers fade, and the naked shrub stands there in sorrow,)

neːm ɪç miːɐ̯ das ˈhøːçst'ə ˈleːbən lao̯s vɛrˈtʰʊmnʊs ˈrae̯çəm hɔrn,
nehm' ich mir das höchste Leben aus Vertumnus' reichem Horn,
take I to me the highest life from Vertumnus' rich horn,
(I take the supreme life-force from Vertumnus'* rich cornucopia,)

ˈɔpfɐnt' lɛs dem ʃt'ʏks tsuː ˈgeːbən, miːɐ̯ dɛs ˈzaːməns ˈgɔldnəs kʰɔrn.
opfernd es dem Styx zu geben, mir des Samens goldnes Korn.
sacrificing it to the Styx to give, to me the seed's golden corn.
(to give it to the Styx as a sacrifice, I take the golden corn of seeds.)

ˈtʰrao̯ɐnt' zɛŋk' lɪçs lɪn di ˈleːɐ̯də, leːk' lɛs lan dɛs ˈkʰɪndəs hɛrts, [ˈtʰrao̯rənt']
Trauernd senk' ich's in die Erde, leg' es an des Kindes Herz, [*poem:* **traurend**]
Grieving sink I it into the earth, lay it on the child's heart, [grieving]
(Grieving, I sink the seeds, that golden corn, into the earth, lay them near the heart of my child,)

das lɛs ˈla͜enə ˈʃp'ra:xə ˈve:ɐ̯də ˈma͜enɐ ˈli:bə, ˈma͜enəm ʃmɛrt͜s.
dass es eine Sprache werde meiner Liebe, meinem Schmerz.
that it a language become of my love, my pain.
(that they may become a language to express my love and my pain.)

fy:ɐ̯t de:ɐ̯ ˈgla͜eçə tʰant͜s de:ɐ̯ ˈho:rən ˈfrɔ͜ødɪç nu:n den lɛnt͜s t͜suˈrʏkʰ,
Führt der gleiche Tanz der Horen freudig nun den Lenz zurück,
Leads the same dance of the Horae* joyfully now the spring back,
(Now, when the unchanging dance of the seasons joyfully brings back the spring,)

vɪrt das ˈtʰo:t'ə nɔ͜ø gəˈbo:rən fɔn de:ɐ̯ ˈzɔnə ˈle:bənsblɪkʰ.
wird das Tote neu geboren von der Sonne Lebensblick.
becomes the dead newly born from the sun's life-gaze.
(that which was dead will be born anew from the life-giving gaze of the sun.)

ˈkʰa͜emə, di: dem ˈla͜ogə ˈʃt'arbən lɪn de:ɐ̯/de:r ˈle:ɐ̯də ˈkʰalt'əm ʃo:s,
Keime, die dem Auge starben in der Erde kaltem Schoss,
Seeds, which to the eye died in the earth's cold womb,
(Seeds, which to the eye seemed dead in the earth's cold womb,)

ɪn das ˈha͜et'rə ra͜eç de:ɐ̯ ˈfarbən ˈrɪŋən zi: zɪç ˈfrɔ͜ødɪç lo:s.
in das heitre Reich der Farben ringen sie sich freudig los.
into the cheerful realm of the colors wrest they themselves joyfully free.
(struggle joyfully free into spring's cheerful realm of color.)

vɛn de:ɐ̯ ʃt'am t͜sʊm ˈhɪməl la͜eltʰ, zu:xt di ˈvʊrt͜səl ʃɔ͜ø di naxtʰ;
Wenn der Stamm zum Himmel eilt, sucht die Wurzel scheu die Nacht;
When the stem to the sky hurries, seeks the root shyly the night;
(As the stem hurries toward the sky, the roots shyly seek the night;)

gla͜eç lɪn ˈli:rə ˈp͜fle:gə ˈtʰa͜elət' zɪç dɛs ʃt'ʏks, dɛs ˈlɛ:t'ɐs maxtʰ.
gleich in ihre Pflege teilet sich des Styx, des Äthers Macht.
equal in their care divide themselves the Styx's the ether's power.
(the power of the ether and that of the Styx share equally in the care of those growing things.)

halp bəˈry:rən zi: de:ɐ̯ ˈtʰo:t'ən, halp' de:ɐ̯ ˈle:bəndən gəˈbi:tʰ;
Halb berühren sie der Toten, halb der Lebenden Gebiet;
Half touch they the dead's, half the living's domain;
(They exist half in the domain of the dead, half in that of the living;)

ax, zi: zɪnt' mi:ɐ̯ ˈtʰɔ͜ørə ˈbo:t'ən, ˈzy:sə ˈʃt'ɪmən fɔm kʰoˈt͜sy:tʰ!
ach, sie sind mir teure Boten, süsse Stimmen vom Cocyt!
ah, they are to me dear messengers, sweet voices from the Cocytus!*
(ah, to me they are dear messengers, sweet voices from the other world!)

hɛlt' le:ɐ̯ gla͜eç zi: zɛlpst' fɛɐ̯ˈʃlɔsən lɪn dem ˈʃa͜oɐfɔlən ʃlʊnt',
Hält er gleich sie selbst verschlossen in dem schauervollen Schlund,
Holds it although her herself locked up in the dreadful abyss,
(Though she herself is held captive in the dreadful abyss,)

a͜os dɛs ˈfry:lɪŋs ˈjʊŋən ˈʃp'rɔsən ˈre:dət' mi:ɐ̯ de:ɐ̯ ˈhɔldə mʊnt',
aus des Frühlings jungen Sprossen redet mir der holde Mund,
out of the spring's young sprouts speaks to me the lovely mouth,
(her lovely mouth speaks to me from out of the spring's young sprouts,)

das l̯ɑox fɛrn fɔm ˈgɔldnən ˈtʰaːgə, voː di ˈʃatʻən ˈtʰrɑoriç t͜siːn,
dass auch fern vom goldnen Tage, wo die Schatten traurig zieh'n,
that, even far from the golden day, where the shades mournfully drift about,
(telling me that, even far from the golden day, there where shades drift about mournfully,)

ˈliːbəntʻ nɔx deːɐ̯ ˈbuːzən ˈʃlaːgə, ˈt͜sɛːɐ̯tʻlɪç nɔx di ˈhɛrt͜sən glyːn.
liebend noch der Busen schlage, zärtlich noch die Herzen glüh'n.
lovingly still the bosom beat(s), tenderly still the hearts glow.
(her bosom still beats lovingly, and hearts still glow tenderly.)

oː, zoː lastʻ l̯ɔøç froː bəˈgryːsən, ˈkʰɪndɐ deːɐ̯ fɛɐ̯ˈjʏŋtʻən l̯ɑo!
O, so lasst euch froh begrüssen, Kinder der verjüngten Au!
O, so let yourselves happily be greeted, children of the rejuvenated meadow!
(O, so let me greet you happily, children of the rejuvenated meadow!)

ˈɔøɐ kʰɛlç zɔl ˈyːbɐfliːsən fɔn dɛs ˈnɛkʻtʻars ˈraenstʻəm tʰɑo.
Euer Kelch soll überfliessen von des Nektars reinstem Tau.
Your chalice shall overflow with the nectar's purest dew.
(Your chalices shall overflow with the purest dew of nectar.)

ˈtʰɑoxən vɪl lɪç l̯ɔøç lɪn ˈʃtʻraːlən, mɪt deːɐ̯/deːr ˈliːrɪs ˈʃøːnstʻəm lɪçtʻ
Tauchen will ich euch in Strahlen, mit der Iris schönstem Licht
To dip want I you in rays, with the Iris's most beautiful light
(I want to bathe you in sunbeams, with the rainbow's most beautiful light)

vɪl lɪç ˈl̯ɔørə ˈblɛtʻɐ ˈmaːlən, glaeç l̯ɑoˈroːrəns ˈlangəzɪçtʰ.
will ich eure Blätter malen, gleich Aurorens Angesicht.
want I your petals to paint, like Aurora's* countenance.
(I want to paint your petals, like the face of the dawn.)

ɪn dɛs ˈlɛnt͜səs ˈhaetʻɐm ˈglant͜sə ˈleːzə ˈjeːdə ˈt͜saːɐ̯tʻə brʊstʻ,
In des Lenzes heiterm Glanze lese jede zarte Brust,
In the spring's cheerful splendor may read every tender breast,
(May every tender breast read in the spring's cheerful splendor)

ɪn dɛs ˈhɛrpstʻəs ˈvɛlkʻəm ˈkʰrant͜sə ˈmaenən ʃmɛrt͜s l̯ʊntʻ ˈmaenə lʊstʰ.
in des Herbstes welkem Kranze meinen Schmerz und meine Lust.
in the autumn's withered garland my pain and my happiness.
(my happiness and in the autumn's withered garland my pain.)

[Ceres is the Roman name of the Greek Demeter, goddess of the fruitful soil. Her beautiful daughter Persephone was abducted by Pluto, god of the underworld, and became his queen in the realm of the dead. Disconsolate, Demeter roamed the earth, searching for her daughter. She forbade the trees and fields to bear fruit or herbs or grain until Persephone would be restored to her. Mankind was in danger of extinction. Finally Pluto agreed to a compromise: Persephone would spend part of each year with him and the rest with her mother. That is how the seasons began. Schiller's moving poem has eleven stanzas. Schubert's song, actually a solo cantata, is sixteen pages long in the *Gesamtausgabe* and includes some lovely music. *The oreads were nymphs of the hills and mountains. Helios, the sun god, who was called "Titan" by Latin poets. Pyrra, the wife of Deucalion, helped to repopulate the earth after Zeus had sent a great flood to destroy the human race. She and her husband had survived in an ark. Jove (Jovis is the Latin genitive form of Jupiter) was the Roman sky-god, corresponding to the Zeus of the Greeks. The Parcae were the Fates, the three sister-goddesses who spun the thread of each human life, determined its length, and cut it off. Orcus was a Greek death-god, Styx the river that separated the living from the dead, Cocytus a river that encircled the realm of the dead; Vertumnus was the Roman god of the changing seasons and the developing vegetation, Aurora was the goddess of the dawn, Iris of the rainbow; the Horae were goddesses of the seasons.]

ˈkʰlaːgə lʊm ˈaːli bae̯
Klage um Ali Bey
Lament for Ali Bey

Posthumously published [composed 1815/1816?] (poem by Matthias Claudius)

last mɪç! last mɪç! lɪç vɪl ˈkʰlaːgən, ˈfrøːlɪç zae̯n nɪçt‘ meːɐ̯!
Lasst mich! lasst mich! ich will klagen, fröhlich sein nicht mehr!
Let me! Let me! I want to lament, merry to be never more!
(Let me, let me weep! I want to lament, I do not ever want to be merry again!)

ˈaːbu ˈdaːhab hat‘ gəˈʃlaːgən ˈlaːli lʊnt‘ zae̯n heːɐ̯.
Aboudahab hat geschlagen Ali und sein Heer.
Abu Dahab has slain Ali and his army.

zoː lae̯n ˈmʊnt‘rɐ ˈkʰyːnɐ ˈkʰriːgɐ vɪrt‘ nɪçt‘ ˈviːdɐ zae̯n;
So ein muntrer kühner Krieger wird nicht wieder sein;
Such a cheerful, bold warrior will not again be;
(Such a cheerful, bold warrior will never be again;)

ˈyːbɐ(r) ˈlaləs vart‘ leːɐ̯ ˈziːgɐ, hao̯t‘ lɛs kʰʊrts lʊnt‘ kʰlae̯n.
über alles ward er Sieger, haut' es kurz und klein.
over all was he victor, hacked it short and small.
(he was victorious over everyone, hacked them into little pieces.)

eːɐ̯ fɛɐ̯ˈʃmɛːt‘ə vae̯n lʊnt‘ ˈvae̯bɐ, gɪŋ nuːɐ̯ ˈkʰriːgəsbaːn,
Er verschmähte Wein und Weiber, ging nur Kriegesbahn,
He scorned wine and women, went only warpath,
(He scorned wine and spurned women, trod only the path of war,)

ʊnt‘ vaːɐ̯ fyːɐ̯ di ˈtsae̯t‘ʊŋsʃrae̯bɐ gaːɐ̯/gaːr lae̯n ˈliːbɐ man.
und war für die Zeitungsschreiber gar ein lieber Mann.
and was for the newspaper-writers quite a dear man.
(and was the darling of the journalists.)

ˈaːbɐ, nuːn lɪst‘ leːɐ̯ gəˈfalən. das leːɐ̯s dɔx nɪçt‘ vɛːɐ̯!
Aber, nun ist er gefallen. Dass er's doch nicht wär!
But, now is he fallen. That he it though not were!
(But now he has fallen. Oh, that he had not!)

ax, fɔn ˈlalən bae̯s, fɔn ˈlalən vaːɐ̯ kʰae̯n bae̯ viː leːɐ̯.
Ach, von allen Bey's, von allen war kein Bey wie er.
Ah, of all beys, of all was no bey as he.
(Ah, of all the beys there was no bey like him.)

ˈjeːdɐman lɪn ˈziːrʊs ˈzaːgət‘: ˈʃaːdə, das leːɐ̯ fiːl! [ˈzyːri̯ən]
Jedermann in Sirus saget: "Schade, dass er fiel!" [*modern German:* **Syrien**]
Everyone in Syria says: "Too bad that he fell!"

ʊnt‘ lɪn gan͡ts lɛˈgʏp‘t‘ən ˈkʰlaːgət‘ mɛnʃ lʊnt‘ kʰrokʰoˈdiːl.
und in ganz Ägypten klaget Mensch und Krokodil.
and in all Egypt laments human being and crocodile.
(and men, women, and crocodiles are weeping all over Egypt.)

ˈdaːheːr ziːt‘ lɪm ga͜est‘, viːs ˈʃa͜enət‘, lam zeˈra͜el mɪt‘ gra͜os
Daher sieht im Geist, wie's scheinet, am Serail mit Graus
Daher sees in the spirit, as it seems, in the seraglio with horror
(In his harem, Daher pictures with horror—so it seems—)

ˈza͜enəs ˈfrɔ͜øndəs kʰɔp͡f, lʊnt‘ ˈva͜enət‘ zɪç di ˈla͜ogən la͜os. [lɛt‘ ˈt͡seːt‘era. da ˈkaːpo]
seines Freundes Kopf, und weinet sich die Augen aus. [etc. Da Capo]
his friend's head, and weeps himself the eyes out. [etc., from top.]
(his friend's head, and weeps his eyes out. [Etc., from the top.])

[The poem is meant to be humorous, hence the crocodile tears and the "etc. Da Capo." It was inspired by a newspaper report in 1773, after Ali Bey, Prince of the Mamelukes, was murdered by his favorite, Abu Dahab. Daher, a friend of Ali Bey's, was an independent Bedouin sheik in Syria. Schubert first set the poem as an unaccompanied trio for male voices; there exists also a version for solo voice with piano accompaniment, not in Schubert's handwriting. Diabelli published the song in 1848 as a trio for female voices, adding a prelude and postlude.]

ˈkʰlaːk‘liːt‘
Klaglied
Lament

Op. 131, No. 3 [1812] (Johann Friedrich Rochlitz)

ˈma͜enə ruː lɪst daˈhɪn, ˈma͜enə ˈfrɔ͜øt‘ lɪst‘ lɛnt‘ˈfloːn,
Meine Ruh' ist dahin, meine Freud' ist entfloh'n,
My peace is gone, my joy has vanished,

ˈma͜enə frɔ͜øt‘ lɪst daˈhɪn, ˈma͜enə ruː lɪst‘ lɛnt‘ˈfloːn,
meine Freud' ist dahin, meine Ruh' ist entfloh'n, [*phrase added by Schubert*]
my joy is gone, my peace has vanished,

ɪn dem ˈzɔ͜øzəln deːɐ̯ ˈlʏft‘ə, lɪn dem ˈmʊrməln dɛs baxs
in dem Säuseln der Lüfte, in dem Murmeln des Bach's
in the whispering of the breezes, in the murmur of the brook

høːr ɪç ˈbeːbənt‘ nuːɐ̯ ˈkʰlaːgətʰoːn. [ˈza͜enəm ˈʃma͜eçəlndən vɔrtʰ,
hör' ich bebend nur Klageton. [Seinem schmeichelnden Wort,
hear I trembling only lament-tone. [To his flattering word,
(I, trembling, hear only the tone of lamentation. [To his flattering word,)

ʊnt dem drʊk‘ ˈza͜enɐ hant‘, ˈza͜enəm ˈha͜esən fɛɐ̯ˈlaŋən,
und dem Druck seiner Hand, seinem heissen Verlangen,
and to the press of his hand, to his ardent desire,

ˈza͜enəm ˈglyːəndən kʰʊs, veː miːɐ̯, das lɪç nɪçt‘ ˈviːdɐʃt‘ant‘!
seinem glühenden Kuss, weh' mir, dass ich nicht widerstand!
to his burning kiss, woe to me, that I not resisted!
(to his burning kiss—alas, that I offered no resistance!)

vɛn lɪç fɔn fɛrn liːn zeː, vɪl lɪç liːn tsuː miːɐ̯ tsiːn,
Wenn ich von fern ihn seh', will ich ihn zu mir zieh'n,
When I from afar him see, want I him to me to draw,
(When I see him from afar, I want to draw him to me,)

kʰɑɔ̯m lɛntˈdɛkʻtʻ mɪç zaen ˈlɑɔ̯gə, kʰɑɔ̯m tʰrɪtʻ ˈnɛːɐ(r) leːɐ̯ miːɐ̯,
kaum entdeckt mich sein Auge, kaum tritt näher er mir,
scarcely discovers me his eye, scarcely steps nearer he to me,
(but as soon as he sees me, as soon as he steps nearer to me,)

mœçtʻ ɪç gɛrn lɪn maen graːpʻ lɛntʻˈfliːn. ˈlaenmaːl, lax ˈlaenmaːl nuːɐ̯
möcht' ich gern in mein Grab entflieh'n. Einmal, ach einmal nur
would like I gladly into my grave to escape. Once, ah once only
(I would like to escape into my grave. Once, ah, once only)

mœçtʻ ɪç liːn ˈglʏkʻlɪç zeːn hiːɐ̯/hiːr lam ˈkʰlɔpfəndən ˈhɛrtsən,
möcht' ich ihn glücklich seh'n hier am klopfenden Herzen,
would like I him happy to see here on the beating heart,
(I would like to see him happy here on my beating heart,)

an deːɐ̯ ˈzeːnəndən brʊstʰ: ˈvɔltʻə dan ˈlɛçəlntʻ ˈlʊntʻɐgeːn!]
an der sehnenden Brust: wollte dann lächelnd untergeh'n!]
on the yearning breast: would then smiling perish!]
(on my yearning breast: then I would die with a smile!)]

[Schubert set only the first of the four verses; the rest (in brackets) are included in the *Gesamtausgabe*, but the notes and the rhythms need to be adjusted to accommodate them. Schubert's friends considered this song to be his first true *Lied.* The poem is an obvious near-paraphrase of Gretchen's famous lament in Goethe's *Faust.* The music is surprisingly mature.]

Klärchens Lied see *Die Liebe (Freudvoll und leidvoll)*

ˈkʰɔlmas ˈkʰlaːgə
Kolmas Klage
Colma's Lament

Posthumously published [composed 1815] (poem by James Macpherson—"Ossian")
(German verses by Franz von Hummelauer, based on a prose translation by Edmund von Harold)

rʊntʻ lʊm mɪç naxtʻ, lɪç lɪr laˈlaen, fɛɐ̯ˈloːrən lam ˈʃtʻʏrmɪʃən ˈhyːgəl,
Rund um mich Nacht, ich irr' allein, verloren am stürmischen Hügel,
Round about me night, I stray alone, lost on the stormy hill,
(*Macpherson's original:* It is night; I am alone, forlorn on the hill of storms.)

deːɐ̯ ʃtʻʊrm brɑɔ̯stʻ fɔm gəˈbɪrkʻ, deːɐ̯ ʃtʻroːm di ˈfɛlzən hɪˈnapʻ, [hɛˈrapʻ]
der Sturm braust vom Gebirg, der Strom die Felsen hinab, [*Peters:* herab]
the storm roars from the mountains, the torrent the rocks down (hence), [down (hither)]
(The wind is heard in the mountain. The torrent pours down the rock.)

mɪç ʃʏtstʻ kʰaen dax foːɐ̯ ˈreːgən, fɛɐ̯ˈloːrən lam ˈʃtʏrmɪʃən ˈhyːgəl, lɪr lɪç laˈlaen.
mich schützt kein Dach vor Regen, verloren am stürmischen Hügel, irr' ich allein.
me protects no roof from rain, lost on the stormy hill, stray I alone.
(No hut receives me from the rain; forlorn on the hill of winds!)

ɛɐ̯ˈʃa͜en, lo: mo:nt, drɪŋ dʊrçs gəˈvœlk‘, lɛɐ̯ˈʃa͜enət‘, li:ɐ̯ ˈnɛçt‘lɪçən ˈʃt‘ɛrnə,
Erschein', o Mond, dring' durchs Gewölk, erscheinet, ihr nächtlichen Sterne,
Appear, O moon, pierce through the clouds, appear, you nocturnal stars,
(Rise, moon! from behind thy clouds. Stars of the night arise.)

gəˈla͜et‘ət‘ ˈfrɔ͜ønt‘lɪç mɪç, vo: ma͜en gəˈli:p‘t‘ɐ ru:tʰ. mɪt‘ li:m
geleitet freundlich mich, wo mein Geliebter ruht. Mit ihm
lead friendlily me, where my beloved rests. With him
(Lead me, some light, to the place, where my love rests from the chase alone!... With thee)

fli: lɪç den ˈfa:t‘ɐ, mɪt‘ li:m ˈma͜enən ˈhɛrɪʃən ˈbru:dɐ(r), lɛɐ̯ˈʃa͜en, lo: mo:nt‘.
flieh' ich den Vater, mit ihm meinen herrischen Bruder, erschein', o Mond.
flee I the father, with him my domineering brother, appear, O moon.
(I would fly, from my father; with thee, from my brother of pride.)

i:ɐ̯ ˈʃt‘ʏrmə. ˈʃva͜ek‘t‘, lo: ˈʃva͜egə, ʃt‘ro:m,
Ihr Stürme, schweigt, o schweige, Strom,
You storms, be silent, O be silent, stream,
(Cease a little while, O wind! Stream, be thou silent a while!)

mɪç ˈhø:rə, ma͜en ˈli:bəndɐ ˈvandərɐ, zalˈga:r! lɪç bɪns, di: ru:ftʰ. [ˈvandrɐ]
mich höre, mein liebender Wanderer, Salgar! Ich bin's, die ruft. [*Peters:* Wandrer]
me hear, my loving wanderer, Salgar! I am it, who calls. [wanderer]
(Let my voice be heard around. Let my wanderer hear me! Salgar! It is Colma who calls.)

hi:ɐ̯/hi:r lɪst de:ɐ̯ ba͜om, hi:ɐ̯ de:ɐ̯ fɛls, vaˈrʊm fɛɐ̯ˈva͜elst du: ˈlɛŋɐ?
Hier ist der Baum, hier der Fels, warum verweilst du länger?
Here is the tree, here the rock, why linger you longer?
(Here is the tree, and the rock. Salgar, my love! I am here. Why delayest thou thy coming?)

vi: hø:r ɪç den ru:f ˈza͜enɐ ˈʃt‘ɪmə? li:ɐ̯ ˈʃt‘ʏrmə, ʃva͜ek‘tʰ!
Wie hör' ich den Ruf seiner Stimme? Ihr Stürme, schweigt!
How hear I the call of his voice? You storms, be silent!
[*this line not in Macpherson*] (How can I hear his voice calling me? Be silent, you storms!)

dɔx zi:, de:ɐ̯ mo:nt‘ lɛɐ̯ˈʃa͜entʰ, de:ɐ̯ ˈhy:gəl ha͜op‘t‘ lɛɐ̯ˈhɛlətʰ, di flu:t‘ lɪm ˈtʰa:lə glɛnt͜stʰ,
Doch sieh, der Mond erscheint, der Hügel Haupt erhellet, die Flut im Tale glänzt,
But see, the moon appears, the hill's crest brightens, the water in the valley gleams,
(Lo! the calm moon comes forth. The flood is bright in the vale.)

ɪm ˈmo:nt‘lɪçt‘ valt di ˈha͜edə.
im Mondlicht wallt die Heide.
in the moonlight floats the heath.
(The rocks are grey on the steep.)

li:n ze: lɪç nɪçt‘ lɪm ˈtʰa:lə, li:n nɪçt‘ lam ˈhɛlən ˈhy:gəl,
Ihn seh' ich nicht im Tale, ihn nicht am hellen Hügel,
Him see I not in the valley, him not on the bright hill,
(I see him not on the brow.)

kʰa͜en la͜ot‘ fɛɐ̯ˈkʰʏndət‘ li:n, lɪç ˈvandlə ˈla͜enza:m hi:ɐ̯.
kein Laut verkündet ihn, ich wand'le einsam hier.
no sound announces him, I wander alone here.
(His dogs come not before him, with tidings of his near approach. Here I must sit alone!)

dɔx veːɐ̯ zɪntʻ ˈjeːnə dɔrtʰ, gəˈʃtʻrɛkʻtʻ laofˈdʏrɐ ˈhaedə?
Doch wer sind jene dort, gestreckt auf dürrer Heide?
But who are those there, stretched out on arid heath?
(Who lie on the heath beside me?)

ɪsts maen gəˈliːpʻtʻɐ(r), leːɐ̯! lʊntʻ ˈneːbən liːm maen ˈbruːdɐ!
Ist's mein Geliebter, Er! und neben ihm mein Bruder!
Is it my beloved, he! and beside him my brother!
(Are they my love and my brother?...)

ax, baetʻ lɪn ˈliːrəm ˈbluːtʻə, lɛntʻˈbløːst di ˈvɪldən ˈʃveːɐ̯tʻɐ!
Ach, beid' in ihrem Blute, entblösst die wilden Schwerter!
Ah, both in their blood, bared the savage swords!
(Ah, they are dead! Their swords are red from the fight.)

vaˈrʊm lɛɐ̯ˈʃluːkst duː liːn? lʊnt duː, zalˈgaːr, vaˈrʊm?
Warum erschlugst du ihn? und du, Salgar, warum?
Why slayed you him? and you, Salgar, why?
(O my brother! why hast thou slain my Salgar? O Salgar, why hast thou slain my brother?...)

[duː vaːɐ̯st deːɐ̯ ˈʃøːnstʻə miːɐ̯ lʊntʻ leːɐ̯/eːr lɪm ˈkʰampfə ˈʃrɛkʻlɪç.
[Du warst der Schönste mir und er im Kampfe schrecklich.
[You were the handsomest to me and he in the battle terrible.
[(Thou wert fair on the hill among thousands! He was terrible in fight.)

viː liːpʻtʻ ɪç ˈbaedə lɔøç, liːɐ̯ ˈzøːnə ˈmaenɐ ˈliːbə!
Wie liebt' ich beide Euch, ihr Söhne meiner Liebe!
How loved I both you, you sons of my love!
(Dear were ye both to me! ... sons, of my love!)

ax ʃpʻrɛçtʻ nɔx ˈhɔldə ˈvɔrtʻə, lax ˈhøːrətʻ ˈmaenə ˈkʰlaːgən!
Ach sprecht noch holde Worte, ach höret meine Klagen!
Ah speak still gracious words, ah hear my lamentations!
(Speak to me; hear my voice....)

dɔx ˈleːvɪç ʃvaekʻtʻ liːɐ̯ mʊntʻ! ˈlaeskʰaltʻ lɪstʻ ˈliːrə brʊstʰ!]
Doch ewig schweigt ihr Mund! Eiskalt ist ihre Brust!]
But forever is silent their mouth! Ice-cold is their breast!]
(They are silent; silent for ever! Cold, cold are their breasts of clay!)]

ˈgaestʻɐ ˈmaenɐ ˈtʰoːtʻən, ʃpʻrɛçtʻ fɔm ˈfɛlzənhyːgəl, fɔn dɛs ˈbɛrgəs ˈgɪpfəl,
Geister meiner Toten, sprecht vom Felsenhügel, von des Berges Gipfel,
Ghosts of my dead, speak from the rocky hill, from the mountain's summit,
(Oh! from the rock on the hill; from the top of the windy steep, speak, ye ghosts of the dead!)

ˈnɪmɐ ʃrɛkʻtʻ liːɐ̯ mɪç! voː gɪŋtʻ liːɐ̯ tsʊr ˈruːə,
nimmer schreckt ihr mich! Wo gingt ihr zur Ruhe,
never frighten you me! Where went you to the rest,
(Speak, I will not be afraid. Whither are ye gone to rest?)

ax, lɪn ˈvɛlçɐ ˈhølə zɔl lɪç lɔøç nuːn ˈfɪndən? dɔx lɛs tʰøːntʻ kʰaen haox.
ach, in welcher Höhle soll ich euch nun finden? Doch es tönt kein Hauch.
ah, in what cave shall I you now find? But there sounds no breath.
(In what cave of the hill shall I find the departed? No feeble voice is on the gale....)

hiːɐ̯/hiːr ǀɪn ˈtʰiːfəm ˈgraːmə va͜en ɪç bɪs ǀam ˈmɔrgən,
Hier in tiefem Grame wein' ich bis am Morgen,
Here in deep grief weep I until in the morning;
(I sit in my grief! I wait for morning in my tears!)

ba͜ot das graːp', liːɐ̯ ˈfrɔ͜øndə, ʃliːsts nɪçt' ˈloːnə mɪç.
baut das Grab, ihr Freunde, schliesst's nicht ohne mich.
build the tomb, you friends; close it not without me.
(Rear the tomb, ye friends of the dead. Close it not till Colma come....)

viː zɔlt' ɪç hiːɐ̯ ˈva͜elən?
Wie sollt' ich hier weilen?
Why should I here linger?
(Why should I stay behind?)

ǀan dɛs ˈbɛrk'ʃt'roːms ˈluːfɐ mɪt den ˈliːbən ˈfrɔ͜øndən vɪl ǀɪç ˈleːvɪç ruːn.
An des Bergstroms Ufer mit den lieben Freunden will ich ewig ruh'n.
On the mountain stream's bank with the dear friends want I eternally to rest.
(Here shall I rest with my friends, by the stream of the sounding rock.)

[dɛk't di naxt den ˈhyːgəl, ˈʃyt'əlt' vɪnt di ˈha͜edə,
[Deckt die Nacht den Hügel, schüttelt Wind die Heide,
[Covers the night the hill, shakes wind the heath,
[(When night comes on the hill; when the loud winds arise;)

kʰlaːk't' ma͜en ga͜est' ǀɪm ˈvɪndə ˈma͜enɐ ˈfrɔ͜øndə tʰoːt'.
klagt mein Geist im Winde meiner Freunde Tod.
laments my ghost in the wind my friends' death.
(my ghost shall stand in the blast, and mourn the death of my friends.)

ˈla͜enzaːm høːɐ̯ts deːɐ̯ ˈjɛːgɐ, liːp't' ǀʊnt' ʃɔ͜øt di ˈʃt'ɪmə,
Einsam hört's der Jäger, liebt und scheut die Stimme,
Lonely hears it the huntsman, loves and fears the voice,
(The hunter shall hear from his booth. He shall fear but love my voice!)

zyːs di ˈfrɔ͜øndə ˈkʰlaːgənt', ˈba͜edə liːp't' ɪç ziː.]
süss die Freunde klagend, beide liebt' ich sie.]
sweetly the friends lamenting, both loved I them.]
(For sweet shall my voice be for my friends: pleasant were her friends to Colma!)]

[The two stanzas in brackets, above, are missing in Schubert's setting, but they fit the rhythm of his music. The English original comes from *The Songs of Selma*. Colma loves Salgar, the son of her father's enemy. On this stormy night she finds his body and that of her brother, each loved one slain by the other. Schubert's song is the first of his "Ossian" settings—and one of the best.]

Kriegers Ahnung see *Schwanengesang*

ˈlaːbətʰraŋkʻ deːɐ̯ ˈliːbə
Labetrank der Liebe
The Restorative Drink of Love

Posthumously published [composed 1815] (poem by Joseph Ludwig Stoll)

vɛn ǀɪm ˈʃpʻiːlə ˈlaezɐ ˈtʰøːnə ˈmaenə ˈkʰraŋkʻə ˈzeːlə ʃveːpʻtʰ,
Wenn im Spiele leiser Töne meine kranke Seele schwebt,
When in the play of soft tones my sick soul hovers,
(When my sick soul hovers amid the play of soft tones,)

ʊnt deːɐ̯ ˈveːmuːtʻ ˈzyːsə ˈtʰrɛːnə ˈdaenəm ˈvarmən blɪkʻ ǀɛntʻˈʃveːpʻtʰ:
und der Wehmut süsse Träne deinem warmen Blick entschwebt:
and the melancholy's sweet tear at your warm gaze floats away:
(and a sweet tear of melancholy evaporates under your warm gaze:)

zɪŋkʻ ɪç diːɐ̯ bae ˈzanftʻəm ˈvalən ˈdaenəs ˈbuːzəns ˈʃpʻraːxloːs hɪn;
sink' ich dir bei sanftem Wallen deines Busens sprachlos hin;
sink I to you at gentle undulating of your bosom speechlessly down;
(I sink down, speechless, onto your gently undulating bosom;)

ˈɛŋəlmeloˌdiːən ˈʃalən, ǀʊnt deːɐ̯/deːr ˈleːɐ̯də ˈʃatʻən fliːn.
Engelmelodien schallen, und der Erde Schatten fliehn.
angel-melodies sound, and the earth's shadows flee.
(angelic melodies sound, and earth's shadows flee.)

zoː ǀɪn ˈleːdən ˈhɪngəzʊŋkʻən, liːpʻ mɪtʻ ˈliːbə ˈǀʊmgətʰaoʃtʰ,
So in Eden hingesunken, Lieb' mit Liebe umgetauscht,
Thus in Eden sunk down, love with love exchanged,
(Thus, immersed in Eden, love exchanged with love,)

ˈkʰʏsə ˈlɪspʻəlntʻ ˈvɔnətʰrʊŋkʻən, viː fɔn ˈzeːrafiːm ǀʊmˈraoʃtʰ:
Küsse lispelnd wonnetrunken, wie von Seraphim umrauscht:
kisses whispering drunk with rapture, as by seraphim around-rustled:
(whispering kisses, drunk with rapture, as if surrounded by the rustling wings of seraphim:)

raeçst duː miːɐ̯/miːr ǀɪm ˈǀɛŋəlbɪldə ˈliːbəvarmən ˈlaːbətʰraŋkʰ,
reichst du mir im Engelbilde liebewarmen Labetrank,
offer you to me in the angel-image love-warm restorative drink,
(you, in your angelic form, offer me a restorative drink, warm as love,)

vɛn ǀɪm ˈʃnøːdən ˈʃtʻaopʻgəfɪldə ˈʃmaxtʻəntʻ ˈmaenə ˈzeːlə zaŋkʰ.
wenn im schnöden Staubgefilde schmachtend meine Seele sank.
when in the vile dust- field languishing my soul sank.
(just as my languishing soul was sinking back into the vile dust of the fields.)

[Thanks to the music alone, this graceful, unpretentious song is a little jewel, unjustly ignored.]

ˈlaxən lʊntʻ ˈva͜enən
Lachen und Weinen
Laughing and Crying

Op. 59, No. 4 [1822-3?] (Friedrich Rückert)

ˈlaxən lʊntʻ ˈva͜enən t͜suː ˈjeːkʻlɪçɐ ˈʃtʻʊndə ruːtʻ ba͜e deːɐ̯ liːpʻ
Lachen und Weinen zu jeglicher Stunde ruht bei der Lieb'
Laughing and crying at every hour rests in the love
(In love, laughing and crying at any odd hour depends)

la͜of zoː ˈmançɐla͜e ˈgrʊndə. ˈmɔrgəns laxtʻ ɪç foːɐ̯ lʊstʰ;
auf so mancherlei Grunde. Morgens lacht' ich vor Lust;
on so many a different cause. In the morning laughed I for pleasure;
(upon so many different causes. In the morning I laughed for joy;)

ʊntʻ vaˈrʊm lɪç nuːn ˈva͜enə ba͜e dɛs ˈlaːbəndəs ˈʃa͜enə, ɪstʻ miːɐ̯ zɛlpʻ nɪçtʻ bəˈvʊstʰ.
und warum ich nun weine bei des Abendes Scheine, ist mir selb' nicht bewusst.
and why I now weep in the evening's gleam, is to me myself not known.
(and why I should be weeping now in the glow of evening I myself don't even know.)

ˈva͜enən lʊntʻ ˈlaxən t͜suː ˈjeːkʻlɪçɐ ˈʃtʻʊndə ruːtʻ ba͜e deːɐ̯ liːpʻ
Weinen und Lachen zu jeglicher Stunde ruht bei der Lieb'
Crying and laughing at every hour rests in the love
(In love, crying and laughing at any odd hour depends)

la͜of zoː ˈmançɐla͜e ˈgrʊndə. ˈlaːbənt͜s va͜entʻ ɪç foːɐ̯ ʃmɛrt͜s;
auf so mancherlei Grunde. Abends weint' ich vor Schmerz;
on so many a different cause. In the evening wept I for pain;
(upon so many different causes. In the evening I wept with pain;)

ʊntʻ vaˈrʊm duː lɛɐ̯ˈvaxən kʰanstʻ lam ˈmɔrgən mɪtʻ ˈlaxən,
und warum du erwachen kannst am Morgen mit Lachen,
and why you awaken can in the morning with laughing,
(and how you can wake up in the morning laughing)

mʊs lɪç dɪç ˈfraːgən, loː hɛrt͜s.
muss ich dich fragen, o Herz.
must I you ask, O heart.
(I have to ask you, my heart.)

[The changes from major to minor and back again, so typical of Schubert, make the point very effectively in this well-known and humorous song.]

lambɛrˈtʰiːnə
Lambertine
Lambertine

Posthumously published [composed 1815] (poem by Joseph Ludwig Stoll)

oː ˈliːbə, diː ma͜en hɛrt͜s lɛɐ̯ˈfʏlətʻ, viː ˈvɔnəfɔl lɪst ˈda͜enə ˈzeːlɪçkʰa͜etʰ,
O Liebe, die mein Herz erfüllet, wie wonnevoll ist deine Seligkeit,
O love, that my heart fills, how ecstasy-full is your bliss,
(O love that fills my heart, how ecstatic is your bliss,)

dɔx lax! viː 'grɑ͜ozaːm 'pʰa͜enɪgənt dʊrç'vyːlət' mɪç 'hɔfnʊŋsloːzɪçkʰa͜etʰ.
doch ach! wie grausam peinigend durchwühlet mich Hoffnungslosigkeit.
but ah! how cruelly tormentingly churns up me hopelessness.
(but ah, how cruelly, how tormentingly hopelessness gnaws at me!)

eːɐ̯ liːp't' mɪç nɪçt', fɛɐ̯'loːrən lɪst' 'loːnə liːn dɛs 'leːbəns 'zyːsə lʊstʰ.
Er liebt mich nicht, verloren ist ohne ihn des Lebens süsse Lust.
He loves me not, lost is without him the life's sweet pleasure.
(He does not love me, without him life's sweet pleasure is lost.)

ɪç bɪn t͜suː 'bɪt'ɐn 'la͜edən nuːɐ̯ gə'boːrən, nuːɐ̯ ʃmɛrt͜s drʏk't' 'ma͜enə brʊstʰ.
Ich bin zu bittern Leiden nur geboren, nur Schmerz drückt meine Brust.
I am to bitter sufferings only born, only pain presses my breast.
(I was born only for bitter suffering, only pain presses my breast.)

dɔx na͜en, lɪç vɪl nɪçt' 'lɛŋɐ 'tʰroːst'loːs 'kʰlaːgən,
Doch nein, ich will nicht länger trostlos klagen,
But no, I want no longer inconsolably to lament,
(But no, I do not want to lament inconsolably any longer,)

t͜suː 'zeːən liːn gœnt' miːɐ̯ das 'ʃɪk'zaːl nɔx,
zu sehen ihn gönnt mir das Schicksal noch,
to see him grants to me the fate still,
(fate still allows me to see him,)

darf lɪç liːm lɑ͜ox nɪçt' 'ma͜enə 'liːbə 'zaːgən, gnyːk't' miːɐ̯ za͜en 'lanblɪk' dɔx.
darf ich ihm auch nicht meine Liebe sagen, g'nügt mir sein Anblick doch.
may I him even not my love tell, is enough to me his sight nevertheless.
(even if I may not tell him my love, the sight of him is nevertheless enough for me.)

za͜en bɪlt' lɪst tʰroːst' lɪn 'ma͜enəm 'ʃt'ɪlən 'kʰʊmɐ,
Sein Bild ist Trost in meinem stillen Kummer,
His picture is comfort in my quiet grief,
(His picture is a comfort in my quiet grief,)

hiːɐ̯ haːb ɪçs miːɐ̯ t͜sʊr 'vɔnə 'lɑ͜ofgəʃt'ɛltʰ,
hier hab' ich's mir zur Wonne aufgestellt,
here have I it for me to the delight set up,
(I have set it up here for my delight,)

diːs zɔl mɪç 'laːbən, bɪs das 'lɛvgɐ 'ʃlʊmɐ ma͜en 'mat'əs hɛrt͜s bə'fɛltʰ.
dies soll mich laben, bis dass ew'ger Schlummer mein mattes Herz befällt.
this shall me comfort, until that eternal slumber my lifeless heart befalls.
(that shall comfort me, until eternal slumber overcomes my lifeless heart.)

[Lambertine is the name of the girl who pours out her troubled heart in the poem. The song has three distinct parts, slow, fast, slow; the very expressive prelude and first vocal melody promise much, but the last section seems less inspired and the closing bars are disappointingly weak.]

la pasto'rɛl:la
La pastorella
The Shepherdess

Posthumously published [composed 1817] (poem by Carlo Goldoni)

la pasto'rɛl:la‿al 'pra:to kon'tɛnta se ne va, [kol 'gred:dʒe]
La pastorella al prato contenta se ne va, [*poem:* **col gregge se ne va]**
The shepherdess to the meadow happily ... ... goes, [with the flock]
(The shepherdess goes happily to the meadow,)

kol:l‿ aɲ:ɲel:li:no a 'l:la:to kan'tando‿in liber'ta. [kon aɲ:ɲel:li:ne a'l:la:to]
coll' agnellino a lato cantando in libertà. [*poem:* **con agnelline allato]**
with the little lamb at (her) side singing in freedom. [with little lambs at (her) side]
(singing in freedom, with a little lamb at her side.)

se lin:no'tʃɛnte‿a'mo:re gra'di:ʃ:ʃe‿ il 'suo pas'to:re,
Se l'innocente amore gradisce il suo pastore, [*GA (in error):* **grandisce]**
If the innocent love is pleasing to the her shepherd,
(If innocent love is pleasing to her shepherd,) [*poem:* **se l'innocente amante** (a'mante, lover)]

la 'bɛl:la pasto'rɛl:la kon'tɛnta‿oɲ:ɲo:r sa'ra.
la bella pastorella contenta ognor sarà.
the beautiful shepherdess happy always will be.
(the beautiful shepherdess will always be happy.)

[The poem comes from *Il filosofo di campagna* ("The Country Philospher"), a play by Goldoni originally set to music by Galuppi. Schubert was inspired by the current popularity of Rossini, then all the rage in Vienna, to write an arietta in *bel canto* style.]

'lao̯ra lam kʰla'vi:ɐ̯
Laura am Klavier
Laura at the Piano

Posthumously published [two versions, both composed 1816] (poem by Friedrich von Schiller)

vɛn dae̯n 'fɪŋɐ dʊrç di 'zae̯t'ən 'mae̯st'ɐt', 'lao̯ra,
Wenn dein Finger durch die Saiten meistert, Laura,
When your finger through the strings masters, Laura,
(When your fingers master the strings, Laura,)

ɪt̯st t̯sʊr 'ʃt'a:t'uə/st'a:t'uə lɛnt''gae̯st'ɐt', lɪt̯st' lɛnt''kʰœrp'ɐt' ʃt'e: ɪç da.
itzt zur Statue entgeistert, itzt entkörpert steh' ich da.
now to the statue de- souled, now disembodied stand I there. [*itzt = jetzt*]
(I stand there, one moment like a soulless statue, the next as if disembodied altogether.)

du: gə'bi:t'əst' 'y:bɐ tʰo:t' lʊnt' 'le:bən, 'mɛçt'ɪç,
Du gebietest über Tod und Leben, mächtig,
You have command over death and life, powerful,

vi: fɔn 'tʰao̯zənt' 'nɛrfgəve:bən 'ze:lən 'fɔrdɐt' fila'dɛlfia.
wie von tausend Nervgeweben Seelen fordert Philadelphia.
as from a thousand nerve-tissues souls demands Philadelphia.
(like Philadelphia, who exacts souls from a thousand nerve-endings.)

ˈeːrlɛɐ̯biːtʻɪç ˈlɑ̯ezɐ ˈrɑɔ̯ʃən dan di ˈlʏftʻə, diːɐ̯ t͡suː ˈlɑɔ̯ʃən;
Ehrerbietig leiser rauschen dann die Lüfte, dir zu lauschen;
Honor-offering more softly murmur then the breezes, to you to listen;
(The breezes, offering homage, murmur more softly in order to listen to you;)

ˈhɪngəʃmiːdət t͡sʊm gəˈzaŋ ʃtʻeːn ɪm ˈleːvgən ˈvɪrbəlgaŋ,
hingeschmiedet zum Gesang steh'n im ew'gen Wirbelgang,
hammered and shaped to the song stand in the eternal turmoil-motion,
(In the midst of eternal turmoil, listening natures, molded and shaped to the contours of the song,)

ˈɑ̯ent͡suˌt͡siːn di ˈvɔnəfʏlə, ˈlɑɔ̯ʃəndə naˈtʰuːrən ˈʃtʻɪlə.
einzuzieh'n die Wonnefülle, lauschende Naturen stille.
to take in the bliss- abundance, listening natures still.
(stand still to imbibe the abundance of bliss.)

ˈt͡sɑɔ̯bərɪn! mɪt ˈtʰøːnən, viː mɪç mɪtʻ ˈblɪkʻən, t͡svɪŋst duː ziː.
Zauberin! mit Tönen, wie mich mit Blicken, zwingst du sie.
Enchantress! with tones, as me with glances, compel you them.
(Enchantress! You master them with tones as you do me with glances.)

ˈzeːlənfɔlə harmoˈniːən ˈvɪməln, ˈlɑ̯en ˈvɔlʏstʻɪç ˈʊngəʃtʻyːm,
Seelenvolle Harmonien wimmeln, ein wollüstig Ungestüm,
Soulful harmonies swarm, a voluptuous vehemence,
(Soulful harmonies, in voluptuous vehemence, swarm)

ɑɔ̯s den ˈzɑ̯etʻən, viː ɪɑɔ̯s ˈiːrən ˈhɪməln ˈnɔ̯øgəboːrnə ˈzeːrafɪːm;
aus den Saiten, wie aus ihren Himmeln neugeborne Seraphim;
from the strings, as from their heavens newborn seraphim;
(from the strings, like newborn seraphim that swarm down from their heavens;)

[*2nd version:* **aus ihren** (ˈiːrən, their) **Saiten]**

viː, dɛs ˈkʰaːɔs ˈriːzənlarm lɛntʻˈrɔnən, ˈlɑɔ̯fgəjaːkʻtʻ fɔm ˈʃœp͡fʊŋsʃtʻʊrm,
wie, des Chaos Riesenarm entronnen, aufgejagt vom Schöpfungssturm,
as, the Chaos's giant arm escaped from, chased up by the creation- storm,
(as, freed from the giant arms of Chaos and raised up by the storm of creation,)

di ˈzɔnən ˈfʊŋkʻəlntʻ ˈfuːrən lɑɔ̯s deːɐ̯ naxtʻ, ʃtʻrøːmt deːɐ̯ ˈtʰøːnə ˈt͡sɑɔ̯bɐmaxtʰ.
die Sonnen funkelnd fuhren aus der Nacht, strömt der Töne Zaubermacht.
the suns flashing emerged out of the night, streams the tones' magic- power.
(suns emerged flashing out of night, so does the magic power of your tones stream forth.)

ˈliːpʻlɪç lɪt͡stʻ, viː ˈlyːbɐ ˈglatʻən ˈkʰiːzəln ˈzɪlbɐhɛlə ˈfluːtʻən ˈriːzəln,
Lieblich itzt, wie über glatten Kieseln silberhelle Fluten rieseln,
Sweetly now, as over smooth pebbles silver-bright waters ripple,
(Now sweetly, like silver-bright water rippling over smooth pebbles;)

majɛsˈtʰɛːtʻɪʃ ˈpʰrɛçtʻɪç nuːn, viː dɛs ˈdɔnɐs ˈlɔrgəltʰoːn, ˈʃtʻʏrməntʻ fɔn ˈhɪnən lɪt͡stʻ,
Majestätisch prächtig nun, wie des Donners Orgelton, stürmend von hinnen itzt,
majestically splendid now, like the thunder's organ-tone, storming from hence now,
(now majestically, magnificently, like the organ-tone of the thunder; now storming away,)

vi: zɪç fɔn ˈfɛlzən ˈrɑo̯ʃəndə ˈʃɔ̯ø̯məndə ˈgi:sbɛçə ˈvɛlt̮sən,
wie sich von Felsen rauschende schäumende Giessbäche wälzen,
as themselves from cliffs roaring, foaming mountain torrents roll,
(like roaring, foaming mountain torrents that plunge down from rocky cliffs;)

ˈhɔldəs gəˈzɔ̯ø̯zəl balt', ˈʃmae̯çlərɪʃ ˈlɪndə,
holdes Gesäusel bald, schmeichlerisch linde,
lovely rustling soon, caressingly gentle,
(one moment a lovely rustling, caressingly gentle,)

vi: dʊrç den ˈlɛsp'ənvalt' ˈbu:ləndə ˈvɪndə, ˈʃve:rɐ nu:n
wie durch den Espenwald buhlende Winde, schwerer nun
as through the aspen woods wooing winds, heavier now
(like amorous winds what woo aspen trees in the woods; then heavier)

lʊnt' melaŋˈkʰo:lɪʃ ˈdy:st'ɐ, vi: dʊrç ˈtʰo:t'ɐ ˈvy:st'ən ˈʃɑo̯ɐnaxt'gəˌflʏst'ɐ,
und melancholisch düster, wie durch toter Wüsten Schauernachtgeflüster,
and melancholically gloomy, like through dead wastes horror- night-whispering,
(and darkly melancholy, like horrifying whispers at night, through dead wastes,)

vo: fɛɐ̯ˈlo:rnəs ˈhɔ̯ø̯lən ʃvae̯ft', ˈtʰrɛ:nənvɛlən de:ɐ̯ kʰoˈt̮sy:t'ʊs ʃlae̯ftʰ.
wo verlornes Heulen schweift, Tränenwellen der Cocytus schleift.
where lost howling roams, tear- waves the Cocytus trails.
(where howling, lost souls roam about, where Cocytus, river of death, trails waves of tears.)

ˈmɛ:t'çən, ʃp'rɪç! lɪç ˈfra:gə, gi:p' mi:ɐ̯ ˈkʰʊndə:
Mädchen, sprich! Ich frage, gib mir Kunde:
Girl, speak! I ask, give to me information:
(Girl, speak! I ask you, tell me:)

ʃt'e:st' mɪt' ˈhø:ɐn ˈgae̯st'ɐn du: lɪm ˈbʊndə?
stehst mit höhern Geistern du im Bunde?
stand with higher spirits you in the league?
(are you in league with higher spirits?)

ɪst̮s di ˈʃp'ra:xə, ly:k' mi:ɐ̯ nɪçt', di: man lɪn leˈly:zən ʃp'rɪçtʰ?
Ist's die Sprache, lüg' mir nicht, die man in Elysen spricht?
Is it the language, lie to me not, that one in Elysium speaks? [*Elysen* = *Elysium*]
(Is this the language—do not lie to me!—that they speak in Elysium?)
[*1st version:* **im** (lɪm, in the) **Elysen]**

[Schubert wrote two different versions in the same month of March 1816. Both are included in the *Gesamtausgabe*. Both feature the same melody, first sounded in the prelude. The first version has some lovely vocal phrases that do not appear in the second; but the latter is more unified in its structure. Both use recitative style in the beginning, the middle, and the end. Both illustrate the varying moods invoked by the poem, serene, stormy, or sinister. "Philadelphia" refers not to the city in America but to a conjuror who had amused Frederick the Great with his tricks.]

'leːbənsliːt'
Lebenslied
Song of Life

Posthumously published [composed 1816] (poem by Friedrich von Matthisson)

'kʰɔmən lʊnt' 'ʃaedən, 'zuːxən lʊnt' 'maedən, 'fʏrçt'ən lʊnt' 'zeːnən,
Kommen und Scheiden, Suchen und Meiden, Fürchten und Sehnen,
Coming and departing, seeking and avoiding, fearing and longing,

'tsvaefəln lʊnt' 'vɛːnən, 'larmuːt' lʊnt' 'fʏlə, fɛɐ'løːdʊŋ/fɛr'løːdʊŋ lʊnt' pʰraxt'
Zweifeln und Wähnen, Armut und Fülle, Verödung und Pracht
Doubting and surmising, poverty and abundance, desolation and splendor

'vɛksəln laof 'leːɐdən viː 'dɛmrʊŋ lʊnt' naxtʰ! ['vɛksəlt']
wechseln auf Erden wie Dämmrung und Nacht! [*Peters:* **wechselt** (less good)]
alternate on earth like twilight and night! [alternates]

['frʊxt'loːs hiː'niːdən rɪŋst duː naːx 'friːdən! 'tʰɔøʃəndə 'ʃɪmɐ
[Fruchtlos hienieden ringst du nach Frieden! Täuschende Schimmer
[Fruitlessly here below strive you after peace! Deceptive shimmers
[(Fruitlessly here on earth you strive for peace! Deceptive shimmers)

'vɪŋk'ən diːɐ/diːr 'lɪmɐ; dɔx, viː di 'fʊrçən dɛs 'glaet'əndən kʰaːns,
winken dir immer; doch, wie die Furchen des gleitenden Kahns,
beckon to you always; but, like the furrows of the gliding boat,

'ʃvɪndən di 'tsaobɐgəbɪldə dɛs vaːns!]
schwinden die Zaubergebilde des Wahns!]
vanish the magic creations of the illusion!]
(the magical creations of illusion vanish!)]

aof tsuː deːɐ 'ʃt'ɛrnə 'lɔøçt'əndɐ 'fɛrnə 'blɪk'ə fɔm 'ʃt'aobə 'muːt'ɪç deːɐ 'glaobəː
Auf zu der Sterne leuchtender Ferne blicke vom Staube mutig der Glaube:
Up to the stars' radiant distance gaze from the dust bravely the faith:
(Let faith lift your gaze bravely up from the dust to the radiant distance of the stars:)

dɔrt' nuːɐ fɛɐ'kʰnʏpft' laen lʊn'ʃt'ɛrp'lɪçəs bant' 'vaːɐhaet' lʊnt' 'friːdən,
dort nur verknüpft ein unsterbliches Band Wahrheit und Frieden,
there only joins an immortal bond truth and peace,
(only there does an immortal bond join together truth and peace,)

fɛɐlaen/fɛrlaen lʊnt' bə'ʃt'ant'! ['gʏnst'ɪgə 'fluːt'ən 'tʰraːgən di 'guːtən,
Verein und Bestand! [Günstige Fluten tragen die Guten,
union and permanency! [Favorable tides carry the good,

'fœrdɐn di 'braːfən 'zɪçɐ tsʊm 'haːfən, lʊnt', laen har'moːnɪʃ fɛɐ'kʰlɪŋəndəs liːt',
fördern die Braven sicher zum Hafen, und, ein harmonisch verklingendes Lied,
advance the upright safely to the harbor, and, a harmoniously dying away song,
(advance the upright safely to the harbor; and, like a song that dies away,)

ʃli:st‘ zɪç das 'le:bən dem 'le:dlən gə'my:tʰ!] 'mɛnlɪç tsu: 'laedən,
schliesst sich das Leben dem edlen Gemüt!] Männlich zu leiden,
closes itself the life for the noble spirit!] Manfully to endure,
(life ends with harmony for the noble spirit!] Manfully to endure,)

'kʰraft‘fɔl tsu: 'maedən, kʰy:n tsu: fɛɐ̯'laxt‘ən/fɛr'laxt‘ən, blaep‘ 'ʊnzɐ 'tʰraxt‘ən!
kraftvoll zu meiden, kühn zu verachten, bleib' unser Trachten!
vigorously to avoid, boldly to despise, remain our aim!
(vigorously to avoid, boldly to despise: let that remain our aim,)

blaep‘ 'ʊnzɐ 'kʰɛmpfən! ɪn 'le:ɐnɐ brʊst‘ ʊns dɛs ʊn'ʃt‘rɛ:flɪçən 'vɪləns bə'vʊstʰ!
bleib' unser Kämpfen! in eherner Brust uns des unsträflichen Willens bewusst!
remain our struggle! in brazen breast ourself of the irreproachable will conscious!
(let that remain our struggle, conscious of an irreproachable will in our unflinching breast!)
[*Peters:* **und** (ʊnt, and) **des unsträflichen Willens bewusst!** (less good)]

[Of the five verses, the Peters edition omits the second and fourth, in brackets above. Schubert's setting has depth and poignancy, the pessimism balanced with courage and faith, as in the poem.]

'le:bənsmelo,di:ən
Lebensmelodien
Melodies of Life

Op. 111, No. 2 [1816] (August Wilhelm von Schlegel)

DER SCHWAN (de:ɐ̯ ʃva:n, the swan):

aof den 'vasɐn vo:nt‘ maen 'ʃt‘ɪləs 'le:bən,
Auf den Wassern wohnt mein stilles Leben,
On the waters dwells my quiet life,
(My quiet life is spent on the waters,)

tsi:t‘ nu:ɐ̯ 'glaeçə 'kʰraezə, di: fɛɐ̯'ʃve:bən,
zieht nur gleiche Kreise, die verschweben,
draws only same circles, which float away,
(it draws equal circles, which float away to nothing,)

ʊnt‘ mi:ɐ̯ 'ʃvɪndət‘ ni: ɪm 'fɔøçt‘ən 'ʃp‘i:gəl de:ɐ̯ gə'bo:gnə hals ʊnt di gə'ʃt‘altʰ.
und mir schwindet nie im feuchten Spiegel der gebogne Hals und die Gestalt.
and for me disappears never in the moist mirror the curved neck and the figure.
(my curved neck and my figure never disappear from the moist mirror.)

DER ADLER (de:ɐ̯ 'adlɐ, the eagle):

ɪç haos ɪn den 'fɛlzɪgən 'kʰlʏft‘ən, ɪç braos ɪn den 'ʃt‘ʏrməndən 'lʏft‘ən,
Ich haus' in den felsigen Klüften, ich braus' in den stürmenden Lüften,
I dwell in the rocky clefts, I rage in the storming airs,
(I dwell in rocky crevasses, I rush through storm-winds,)

fɛɐ̯ˈtʰrɑo̯ənt dem ˈʃlaːɡəndən ˈflyːɡəl bae̯ jaːkʻtʻ lʊntʻ kʰampf lʊntʻ ɡəˈvaltʰ.
vertrauend dem schlagenden Flügel bei Jagd und Kampf und Gewalt.
trusting in the beating wing in hunt and battle and violence.
(trusting in my beating wings when I hunt, do battle, and perpetrate violence.)

[*Peters:* **bei Jagd, bei Kampf und Gewalt.**]

DER SCHWAN:

mɪç lɛɐ̯ˈkʰvɪkʻt das blɑo̯ deːɐ̯ ˈhae̯tʻɐn ˈlʏftʻə,
Mich erquickt das Blau der heitern Lüfte,
Me refreshes the blue of the serene airs,
(The blue of the serene air refreshes me,)

mɪç bəˈrɑo̯ʃən zyːs deːɐ̯ ˈkʰalmʊs ˈdʏftʻə,
mich berauschen süss der Kalmus Düfte,
me intoxicates sweetly the calami's fragrances,
(the fragrance of the calamus reeds intoxicates me,)

vɛn lɪç lɪn dem glants deːɐ̯/deːr ˈlaːbəntʻrøːtʻə vae̯ç bəˈfiːdɐtʻ ˈviːɡə ˈmae̯nə brʊstʰ.
wenn ich in dem Glanz der Abendröte weich befiedert wiege meine Brust.
when I in the gleam of the sunset softly feathered rock my breast.
(when in the gleam of the sunset I rock my softly feathered breast in the cradle of the water.)

DER ADLER:

ɪç ˈjɑo̯xtsə daˈheːɐ̯/daˈheːr lɪn ɡəˈvɪtʻɐn, vɛn ˈlʊntʻən den valtʻ ziː tsɛɐ̯ˈʃpʻlɪtʻɐn,
Ich jauchze daher in Gewittern, wenn unten den Wald sie zersplittern,
I exult from there in storms, when below the forest they splinter,
(From my crag I exult in storms, when they are splintering the forests down below,)

ɪç ˈfraːɡə den blɪts, lɔpʻ leːɐ̯ ˈtʰøːtʻə, mɪtʻ ˈfrøːlɪç fɛɐ̯ˈnɪçtʻəndɐ lʊstʰ.
ich frage den Blitz, ob er töte, mit fröhlich vernichtender Lust.
I ask the lightning, whether it kills with merry annihilating pleasure.

DER SCHWAN:

fɔn laˈpʰɔlos ˈvɪŋkʻən ˈlae̯ŋɡəlaːdən, darf lɪç mɪç lɪn ˈvoːllɑo̯tʻʃtʻrøːmən ˈbaːdən,
Von Apollos Winken eingeladen, darf ich mich in Wohllautströmen baden,
By Apollo's beckoning invited, may I myself in euphony-streams bathe,
(Invited by the beckoning of Apollo,[1] I am allowed to bathe in streams of harmony,)

iːm ɡəˈʃmiːkʻt tsuː ˈfyːsən, vɛn di ˈliːdɐ ˈtʰøːnəntʻ veːn lɪn ˈtʰɛmpəs mae̯ hɪˈnapʻ.
ihm geschmiegt zu Füssen, wenn die Lieder tönend wehn in Tempes Mai hinab.
to him pressed close at feet, when the songs sounding waft in Tempe's May down.
(nestled close against his feet, when his songs waft down into the Vale of Tempe[2] in May.)

DER ADLER:

ɪç ˈtʰroːnə bae̯ ˈjuːpitʻɐs ˈzɪtsə; leːɐ̯ vɪŋkʻtʻ lʊntʻ lɪç hoːl lɪːm di ˈblɪtsə,
Ich throne bei Jupiters Sitze; er winkt und ich hol' ihm die Blitze,
I throne by Jupiter's[3] seat; he gives a sign and I fetch him the lightnings,

dan zɛŋk' ɪç ɪm ʃla:f das gəˈfi:dɐ(r) ɪaof ˈzaenən gəˈbi:t'əndən ʃt'a:p'.
dann senk' ich im Schlaf das Gefieder auf seinen gebietenden Stab.
then sink I in the sleep the feathers onto his commanding staff.
(then I lower my feathers in sleep and perch on his staff of command.)

DER SCHWAN:

fɔn de:ɐ ˈze:lgən ˈgœt'ɐkʰraft dʊrçˈdrʊŋən,
Von der sel'gen Götterkraft durchdrungen,
By the blissful divine power penetrated,
(Penetrated by blissful divine power,)

ha:b ɪç mɪç ɪʊm ˈle:das ʃo:s gəˈʃlʊŋən;
hab' ich mich um Ledas Schoss geschlungen;
have I myself around Leda's lap wound;
(I have twined myself about Leda's[4] lap;)

ˈʃmaeçəlnt ˈdrʏk't'ən mɪç di ˈtsa:ɐt'ən ˈhɛndə, ɪals li:ɐ zɪn ɪɪn ˈvɔnə zi: fɛɐˈlo:ɐ.
schmeichelnd drückten mich die zarten Hände, als ihr Sinn in Wonne sie verlor.
caressingly pressed me the delicate hands, as her sense in ecstasy she lost.
(caressingly her delicate hands pressed me, as she lost her senses in ecstasy.)

DER ADLER:

ɪç kʰam ɪaos den ˈvɔlk'ən gəˈʃɔsən, ɪɛnt'ˈrɪs li:ɐ den ˈblø:dən gəˈnɔsən:
Ich kam aus den Wolken geschossen, entriss ihr den blöden Genossen:
I came out of the clouds shot, tore from her the bashful companion:
(I shot out of the clouds, and tore from her her bashful companion:)

ɪç tʰru:k' ɪɪn den ˈkʰlaoən bəˈhɛndə tsʊm ɪoˈlʏmp' ganyˈme:dən ɪɛmˈpʰo:ɐ.
ich trug in den Klauen behende zum Olymp Ganymeden empor.
I carried in the claws nimbly to the Olympus Ganymede up.
(in my claws I nimbly carried Ganymede[5] up to Olympus.)

DER SCHWAN:

zo: gəˈba:ɐ zi: ˈfrɔøntˈlɪçə naˈtʰu:rən, ˈhe:lena ɪʊnt' ɪɔøç, li:ɐ diɔsˈkʰu:rən,
So gebar sie freundliche Naturen, Helena und euch, ihr Dioskuren,
Thus bore she friendly natures, Helen and you, you Dioscuri,
(Thus she gave birth to those amiable natures, Helen[6] and you, Dioscuri,[7])

ˈmɪldə ʃt'ɛrnə, ˈde:rən ˈbry:dɐtʰu:gənt' ˈvɛksəlnt' ˈʃat'ənvɛlt' ɪʊnt' ˈhɪməl tʰaeltʰ.
milde Sterne, deren Brüdertugend wechselnd Schattenwelt und Himmel teilt.
gentle stars, whose brotherly virtue alternately shadow- world and heaven shares.
(kindly stars, you whose brotherly virtue alternately shares the world of shadows and the sky.)

DER ADLER:

nu:n tʰrɛŋk't' ɪaos nɛk'ˈtʰa:rɪʃəm ˈbɛçɐ de:ɐ ˈjʏŋlɪŋ di ˈle:vɪgən ˈtsɛçɐ;
Nun tränkt aus nektarischem Becher der Jüngling die ewigen Zecher;
Now gives to drink from nectarean goblet the youth the eternal drinkers;
(Now the young man serves the immortal drinkers from the goblet of nectar;)

niː brɔ͜ønt‘ zɪç di ˈvaŋə deːɐ̯ ˈjuːgənt‘, viː ˈlɛnt‘loːs di t͜sa͜et‘ la͜ox lɛnt‘ˈla͜elth.
nie bräunt sich die Wange der Jugend, wie endlos die Zeit auch enteilt.
never browns itself the cheek of the youth, however endlessly the time even hurries by.
(his cheek keeps the clear glow of youth, no matter how endlessly time hurries by.)

DER SCHWAN:

ˈaːndəfɔl bəˈtʰraxt‘ ɪç lɔft di ˈʃt‘ɛrnə, lɪn deːɐ̯ fluːt di ˈtʰiːfgəvœlp‘t‘ə ˈfɛrnə,
Ahndevoll betracht' ich oft die Sterne, in der Flut die tiefgewölbte Ferne,
Full of presentiment observe I often the stars, in the water the deep-vaulted distance,
(Full of presentiment, I often observe the stars, the deep-vaulted distance reflected in the water,)

ʊnt‘ mɪç t͜siːt‘ la͜en ˈlɪnɪç ˈryːrənt‘ ˈzeːnən la͜os deːɐ̯ ˈha͜emaːt‘ lɪn la͜en ˈhɪmlɪʃ lant‘.
und mich zieht ein innig rührend Sehnen aus der Heimat in ein himmlisch Land.
and me draws a fervent moving longing from the homeland into a heavenly land.
(and a fervent, moving longing draws me from my native place into a heavenly land.)

DER ADLER:

ɪç ˈvant‘ə di ˈflyːgə mɪt‘ ˈvɔnə ʃoːn fryː t͜sʊr lʊnˈʃt‘ɛrp‘lɪçən ˈzɔnə,
Ich wandte die Flüge mit Wonne schon früh zur unsterblichen Sonne,
I turned the flights with joy already early to the immortal sun,
(With joy I have already early on turned my flights toward the immortal sun,)

[*Peters:* **Flügel** (ˈflyːgəl, wings)]

kʰan niː lan den ʃt‘a͜op‘ mɪç gəˈvøːnən, lɪç bɪn mɪt den ˈgœt‘ɐn fɛɐ̯ˈvanth.
kann nie an den Staub mich gewöhnen, ich bin mit den Göttern verwandt.
can never to the dust myself accustom, I am with the gods related.
(I can never accustom myself to the dust; I am related to the gods.)

DER SCHWAN:

ˈvɪlɪç va͜eçt dem tʰoːt‘ la͜en ˈzanft‘əs ˈleːbən;
Willig weicht dem Tod ein sanftes Leben;
Willingly yields to the death a gentle life;
(A gentle life yields willingly to death;)

vɛn zɪç ˈma͜enɐ ˈgliːdɐ bant‘ lɛnt‘ˈveːbən,
wenn sich meiner Glieder Band' entweben,
when themselves my limbs' bonds unravel,
(when the bonds of my body unravel,)

løːst di ˈt͜sʊŋə zɪç: meˈloːdɪʃ ˈfa͜eɐt‘ ˈjeːdɐ ha͜ox den ˈha͜elgən ˈla͜ogənblɪkh.
löst die Zunge sich: melodisch feiert jeder Hauch den heil'gen Augenblick.
loosens the tongue itself: melodically celebrates each breath the holy moment.
(my tongue is freed: each breath celebrates the holy moment with melody.[8])

DER ADLER:

di ˈfak‘əl deːɐ̯ ˈtʰoːt‘ən fɛɐ̯ˈjʏŋət‘, la͜en ˈblyːəndɐ ˈføːnɪks, lɛnt‘ˈʃvɪŋət di ˈzeːlə
Die Fackel der Toten verjünget, ein blühender Phönix, entschwinget die Seele
The torch of the dead rejuvenates, a blossoming phoenix, soars away the soul
(The torch of the dead rejuvenates; the soul soars up, a blossoming phoenix,[9])

zɪç fra͜e lʊnt' lɛnt''ʃla͜eɐt', lʊnt' 'gry:sət' li:ɐ̯ 'gœt'lɪçəs glʏkʰ.
sich frei und entschleiert, und grüsset ihr göttliches Glück.
itself free and unveiled, and greets its divine good fortune.
(free and unveiled, and greets its divine good fortune.)

DIE TAUBEN (di 'tʰɑ͜obən, the doves):

ɪn de:ɐ̯ 'mʏrt'ən 'ʃat'ən, 'gat'ə tʰrɔ͜ø dem 'gat'ən, 'flat'ɐn vi:ɐ̯/vi:r lʊnt 'tʰɑ͜oʃən
In der Myrten Schatten, Gatte treu dem Gatten, flattern wir und tauschen
In the myrtles' shadow, spouse true to the spouse, flutter we and exchange
(In the shadow of the myrtle bushes, each spouse faithful to the other, we flutter and exchange)

'mançən 'laŋən kʰʊs. 'zu:xən lʊnt' 'lɪrən, 'fɪndən lʊnt' 'gɪrən,
manchen langen Kuss. Suchen und irren, finden und girren,
many a long kiss. Seeking and straying, finding and cooing,

'ʃmaxt'ən lʊnt' 'lɑ͜oʃən, vʊnʃ lʊnt' gə'nʊs.
schmachten und lauschen, Wunsch und Genuss.
languishing and listening, wish and gratification.

've:nʊs 'va:gən 'tsi:ən 'ʃnɛ:bəlnt' vi:ɐ̯/vi:r lɪm 'fli:ən;
Venus' Wagen ziehen schnäbelnd wir im Fliehen;
Venus's chariot draw billing and cooing we in the fleeing;
(We draw Venus's chariot,[10] billing and cooing as we fly;)

'ʊnzrə 'blɑ͜oən 'ʃvɪŋən zɔ͜ømt de:ɐ̯ 'zɔnə gɔlt'. lo: vi: lɛs 'fɛçəlt',
unsre blauen Schwingen säumt der Sonne Gold. O wie es fächelt,
our blue wings rims the sun's gold. O how it fans,
(the gold of the sun rims our blue wings. Oh, what a flurry of fluttering wings)

vɛn zi: lʊns 'lɛçəlt'! 'la͜eçt'əs gə'lɪŋən! 'li:p'lɪçɐ zɔlt'!
wenn sie uns lächelt! Leichtes Gelingen! Lieblicher Sold!
when she at us smiles! Easy success! Lovely pay!
(when she smiles at us! Easy success! Lovely wages!)

'vɛndə dɛn di 'ʃt'ʏrmə, 'ʃø:nə 'gœt'ɪn!
Wende denn die Stürme, schöne Göttin!
Turn away then the storms, beautiful goddess!

'ʃirmə ba͜e bə'ʃa͜ednɐ 'frɔ͜ødə 'da͜enɐ 'tʰɑ͜obən pʰa:ɐ̯!
Schirme bei bescheidner Freude deiner Tauben Paar!
Shelter in unassuming joy your doves' pair!
(Shelter your pair of doves in their unassuming joy!)

las lʊns ba͜e'zamən! 'lo:dɐ(r) lɪn 'flamən 'lɔpfrə lʊns 'ba͜edə 'da͜enəm lal'tʰa:ɐ̯!
Lass uns beisammen! Oder in Flammen opfre uns beide deinem Altar!
Leave us together! Or in flames sacrifice us both to your altar!
(Let us stay together! Or else offer us both in flames as a sacrifice to your altar!)

[Schubert provided three separate, contrasting melodies, one each for the swan, the eagle, and the pair of doves. Since his manuscript has not survived, there is no way of knowing how many of the seventeen verses he meant to be sung. Peters offers a selection of seven; the *Gesamtausgabe* prints them all. [1]Apollo was the great musician among the gods. [2]Tempe is a beautiful valley in Thessaly. [3]The eagle and the thunderbolt were attributes of Jupiter (Zeus), as doves and myrtle were of Venus. [4]In the form of a swan, Jupiter made love to Leda, a beautiful mortal who bore him two daughters, [6]Helen—later famous as "Helen of Troy"—and Clytemnestra, and two sons, the "heavenly twins" Castor and Pollux (or Polydeuces), who were also known as the [7]Dioscuri (sons of Zeus). When Castor died, Pollux refused immortality unless he could share it with his brother. Zeus therefore allowed them both to spend half their time in the heavens, as the constellation called Gemini, and half in the shadow-land of the dead. Poseidon, god of the sea, made them saviors of ship-wrecked sailors and gave them the power to command favorable winds. [5]In another myth, Zeus assumed the form of an eagle to carry Ganymede, handsome son of the first king of Troy, up to heaven, where he became cup-bearer to the gods. His image was set among the stars as Aquarius. [8]The swan, according to legend, sings a haunting song before it dies. [9]The Phoenix is a mythical bird that immolates itself in fire, then rises reborn from its own ashes. [10]The chariot of Venus, the goddess of love, was drawn by a pair of doves.]

ˈleːbənsmuːtʰ / ˈfrøːlɪçɐ ˈleːbənsmuːtʰ
Lebensmut / Fröhlicher Lebensmut
Courage for Living / Joyful Courage

Posthumously published [composed 1827?] (poem by Ludwig Rellstab)

ˈfrøːlɪçɐ ˈleːbənsmuːtʻ bra͜ostʻ |ɪn dem ˈraʃən bluːtʰ;
Fröhlicher Lebensmut braust in dem raschen Blut;
Joyful courage for living surges in the impetuous blood;

ˈʃpʻruːdəlntʻ |ʊntʻ ˈzɪlbɐhɛl ˈra͜oʃət deːɐ̯ ˈleːbənskʰvɛl.
sprudelnd und silberhell rauschet der Lebensquell.
effervescent and silver-bright rushes the fountainhead of life.
(the fountainhead of life is flowing, effervescent and silver-bright.)

dɔx |eː di ˈʃtʻʊndə fliːtʻ, ˈ|eːə deːɐ̯ ga͜estʻ fɛɐ̯ˈglyːtʰ,
Doch eh' die Stunde flieht, ehe der Geist verglüht,
But before the hour flees, before the spirit fades,

ʃœpftʻ |a͜os deːɐ̯ ˈkʰlaːrən fluːtʻ ˈfrøːlɪçən ˈleːbənsmuːtʰ!
schöpft aus der klaren Flut fröhlichen Lebensmut!
draw from the clear water joyful courage for living!

[ˈmuːtʻɪgən ʃpʻrʊŋ gəˈvaːkʻtʻ; ˈnɪmɐ gəˈvɪntʻ, veːɐ̯ t͜saːkʻtʰ;
[Mutigen Sprung gewagt; nimmer gewinnt, wer zagt;
[Courageous leap (be) dared; never wins, (he) who hesitates;
[(Dare the courageous leap: he who hesitates never wins;)

ʃnɛl |ɪst das ˈvɛksəlglʏkʻ, da͜en |ɪst deːɐ̯/deːr ˈ|a͜ogənblɪkʰ.
schnell ist das Wechselglück, dein ist der Augenblick.
quick is the changeable fortune, yours is the moment.
(fortune can change quickly: yours is the moment.)

veːɐ̯ ˈkʰa͜enən ʃpʻrʊŋ fɛɐ̯ˈzuːxtʻ, brɪçtʻ ˈkʰa͜enə ˈzyːsə frʊxtʰ.
Wer keinen Sprung versucht, bricht keine süsse Frucht.
He who no leap attempts, plucks no sweet fruit.
(He who attempts no leap plucks no sweet fruit.)

ɑ͜of! veːɐ̯ das glʏk‘ lɛɐ̯'jaːk‘t‘, 'muːt‘ɪgən ʃp‘rʊŋ gə'vaːk‘tʰ.
Auf! Wer das Glück erjagt, mutigen Sprung gewagt.
Up! He who the fortune pursues, courageous leap (be) dared.
(Come! He who pursues fortune must dare the courageous leap.)

'muːt‘ɪç lʊm'larmt den tʰoːt‘! trɪft‘ lɔ͜øç za͜en 'maxt‘gəboːtʰ.
Mutig umarmt den Tod! trifft euch sein Machtgebot.
Bravely embrace the death! strikes you his power-command.
(Embrace death bravely, if his powerful command chooses you.)

neːmt‘ 'lɔ͜øɐ 'fɔləs glaːs, ʃt‘oːst‘ lan za͜en 'ʃt‘ʊndənglaːs;
Nehmt euer volles Glas, stosst an sein Stundenglas;
Take your full glass, clink (it) against his hourglass;

'tʰaːnat‘ɔs 'bryːdɐʃaft‘ 'lœfnət dɛs 'leːbəns haftʰ.
Thanatos' Brüderschaft öffnet des Lebens Haft.
Thanatos's brotherhood opens the life's confinement.
(The fellowship of Thanatos frees us from the confinement of life.)
[*poem:* **des Todes** (dɛs 'tʰoːdəs, death's) **Brüderschaft** (changed to fit the rhythm)]

nɔ͜ø glɛnt͡st‘ la͜en 'mɔrgənroːt‘; 'muːt‘ɪç lʊm'larmt den tʰoːt‘!]
Neu glänzt ein Morgenrot; mutig umarmt den Tod!]
New gleams a dawn; bravely embrace the death!]
(A new dawn is gleaming; embrace death bravely!)]

[Schubert's manuscript breaks off at the end of the first verse, but it is essentially complete, missing only a postlude. The *Gesamtausgabe* presents this spirited song as a fragment; Peters repeats the prelude as an appropriate postlude and prints all three verses. The music is irresistibly energetic, carrying the voice up to a climactic B flat. Some commentators find such music unsuitable for the last verse; but the poet's view is anything but solemn or lugubrious: Thanatos, the personification of death, is seen here as a brother to be embraced, even as a drinking buddy.]

'leːbənsmuːtʰ / oː viː drɪŋt das 'jʊŋə 'leːbən
Lebensmut / O wie dringt das junge Leben
Courage for Living / Oh, How Powerfully Young Life Surges

Posthumously published [composed 1826] (poem by Ernst Schulze)

oː viː drɪŋt das 'jʊŋə 'leːbən 'kʰrɛft‘ɪç miːɐ̯ dʊrç zɪn lʊnt‘ hɛrt͡s!
O wie dringt das junge Leben kräftig mir durch Sinn und Herz!
Oh, how surges the young life powerfully in me through mind and heart!
(Oh, how powerfully young life surges through my mind and heart!)

'aləs fyːl ɪç glyːn lʊnt‘ 'ʃt‘reːbən, 'fyːlə 'dɔp‘əlt‘ lʊst‘ lʊnt‘ ʃmɛrt͡s.
Alles fühl' ich glühn und streben, fühle doppelt Lust und Schmerz.
Everything feel I glow and strive, feel double pleasure and pain.
(I feel everything glowing and striving, I feel doubled pleasure and pain.)

'frʊxt‘loːs zuːx ɪç lɔ͜øç t͡suː 'halt‘ən, 'ga͜est‘ɐ 'ma͜enɐ 'reːgən brʊstʰ!
Fruchtlos such' ich euch zu halten, Geister meiner regen Brust!
Fruitlessly seek I you to hold, spirits of my excited breast!
(In vain I seek to hold you, spirits of my excited breast!)

naːx gəˈfalən møːkʼtʼ liːɐ̯ ˈvaltʼən, za͜es t͜sʊm ˈla͜edə, za͜es t͜sʊr lʊstʰ.
Nach Gefallen mögt ihr walten, sei's zum Leide, sei's zur Lust.
According to pleasure may you rule, be it to the sorrow, be it to the delight.
(You may rule according to your pleasure, whether it bring sorrow or delight.)

ˈloːdrə nuːɐ̯, gəˈvaltʼgə ˈliːbə, ˈhøːɐ ˈloːdrə nuːɐ̯/nuːr lɛmˈpʰoːɐ̯!
Lodre nur, gewalt'ge Liebe, höher lodre nur empor!
Blaze only, powerful love, higher blaze only up!
(So blaze away, powerful love, blaze even higher!)

brɛçtʼ, liːɐ̯ ˈfɔlən ˈblyːtʼəntʰriːbə, ˈmɛçtʼɪç ˈʃvɛləntʼ nuːɐ̯ hɛɐ̯ˈfoːɐ̯!
Brecht, ihr vollen Blütentriebe, mächtig schwellend nur hervor!
Break, you full blossom-sprouts, mightily swelling only through!
(Burst into blossom, you full, mightily swelling sprouts!)
[*hervorbrechen* = to break through, sally forth]

maːkʼ das hɛrt͜s zɪç ˈbluːtʼɪç ˈfɛrbən, maːks fɛɐ̯ˈgeːn ɪn ˈraʃɐ pʰa͜en;
Mag das Herz sich blutig färben, mag's vergehn in rascher Pein;
May the heart itself bloody color, may it perish in swift pain;
(Let my heart bleed, let it perish in swift pain;)

ˈliːbɐ vɪl lɪç gant͜s fɛɐ̯ˈdɛrbən, lals nuːɐ̯ halpʼ leˈbɛndɪç za͜en.
lieber will ich ganz verderben, als nur halb lebendig sein.
rather want I totally to be ruined, than only half alive to be.
(I would rather be totally ruined than be only half alive.)

ˈdiːzəs ˈt͜saːgən, ˈdiːzəs ˈzeːnən, das di brʊstʼ fɛɐ̯ˈgeːpʼlɪç ʃvɛltʰ,
Dieses Zagen, dieses Sehnen, das die Brust vergeblich schwellt,
This timorousness, this yearning, which the breast in vain swells,
(This timorousness, this yearning that swells my breast in vain,)

ˈdiːzə ˈzɔ͜øft͜sɐ, ˈdiːzə ˈtʰrɛːnən, diː deːɐ̯ ʃtʼɔlt͜s gəˈfaŋən hɛltʰ,
diese Seufzer, diese Tränen, die der Stolz gefangen hält,
these sighs, these tears, which the pride captive holds,
(these sighs, these tears, which pride holds back,)

ˈdiːzəs ˈʃmɛrt͜slɪç ˈla͜etʼlə ˈrɪŋən, ˈdiːzəs ˈkʰɛmp͜fən ˈloːnə kʰraftʼ,
dieses schmerzlich eitle Ringen, dieses Kämpfen ohne Kraft,
this painfully vain wrestling, this struggling without strength,

ˈloːnə ˈhɔfnʊŋ lʊntʼ fɔlˈbrɪŋən, hatʼ ma͜en ˈbɛstʼəs mark lɛɐ̯ˈʃlaftʰ.
ohne Hoffnung und Vollbringen, hat mein bestes Mark erschlafft.
without hope and consummation, has my best marrow enervated.
(without hope and without consummation, has enervated me to my very marrow.)

ˈliːbɐ ˈvɛkʼə raʃ lʊntʼ ˈmuːtʼɪç, ˈʃlaxtʼruːf, den lɛntʼˈʃlafnən zɪn!
Lieber wecke rasch und mutig, Schlachtruf, den entschlaf'nen Sinn!
Rather waken quickly and bravely, war- cry, the disenfeebled mind!
(Rather, war cry, waken quickly and bravely a disenfeebled mind!)

ˈlaŋə tʰrɔ͜ømtʼ ɪç, ˈlaŋə ruːtʼ ɪç, gaːpʼ deːɐ̯ ˈkʰɛtʼə laŋ mɪç hɪn.
Lange träumt' ich, lange ruht' ich, gab der Kette lang mich hin.
Long dreamed I, long rested I, gave to the chain long myself up.
(Long have I dreamed, long have I rested, long have I given myself up to the chains.)

hiːɐ̯/hiːr lɪstʻ 'hœlə nɪçtʻ, nɔx 'hɪməl, 'veːdɐ frɔstʻ lɪstʻ hiːɐ̯, nɔx gluːtʰ;
Hier ist Hölle nicht, noch Himmel, weder Frost ist hier, noch Glut;
Here is hell not, nor heaven, neither frost is here, nor fire;
(Here it is neither hell nor heaven, neither frost is here nor fire;)

a͜ofl ɪns 'fa͜entʻlɪçə gəʻtʰʏməl, 'rʏstʻɪç 'va͜etʻɐ dʊrç di fluːtʰ!
Auf ins feindliche Getümmel, rüstig weiter durch die Flut!
Up into the hostile tumult, vigorously farther through the flood!

das nɔx 'la͜enmaːl vʊnʃ lʊntʻ 'vaːgən, tsɔrn lʊntʻ 'liːbə, voːl lʊntʻ veː
Dass noch einmal Wunsch und Wagen, Zorn und Liebe, Wohl und Weh
That still once wish and daring, anger and love, weal and woe
(So that once more desire and daring, anger and love, well-being and wretchedness)
[*noch einmal* = once more]

'iːrə 'vɛlən lʊm mɪç 'ʃlaːgən la͜of dɛs 'leːbəns 'vɪldɐ zeː,
ihre Wellen um mich schlagen auf des Lebens wilder See,
their waves around me beat on the life's wild sea,
(may pound me on life's wild sea with their waves,)

ʊntʻ lɪç kʰyːn lɪm 'tʰapfɐn 'ʃtʻra͜etʻə mɪt dem ʃtʻroːm, deːɐ̯ mɪç lɛntʻ'raftʻ,
und ich kühn im tapfern Streite mit dem Strom, der mich entrafft,
and I boldly in the valiant struggle with the current, which me carries off (course),
(and I, in valiant struggle with the current that is carrying me off course, may boldly)

'zɛlbɐ 'ma͜enən 'naxən 'la͜etʻə, 'frɔ͜ødɪç lɪn gəʻpʰryːftʻɐ kʰraftʰ.
selber meinen Nachen leite, freudig in geprüfter Kraft.
myself my small boat steer, joyfully in tested strength.
(steer my little boat by myself, rejoicing in strength that has been put to the test.)

[Schubert gave the song its title; the poet simply labled his poem "*Am 1sten April 1815*" (On April 1st, 1815). The third stanza is appropriately set in a minor key; the melody is modified as well, and altered again for the last two verses.]

'leːbənstʰra͜om / ɪç zaːs lan 'la͜enɐ 'tʰɛmpʻəlˌhalə
Lebenstraum / Ich sass an einer Tempelhalle
Dream of Life / I Sat at the Entrance to a Temple

Recently published in incomplete form [composed 1809-10?] (poem by Gabriele von Baumberg)

ɪç zaːs lan 'la͜enɐ 'tʰɛmpʻəlhalə, lam 'muːzənha͜en, lʊm'ra͜oʃtʻ
Ich sass an einer Tempelhalle, am Musenhain, umrauscht
I sat at a temple hall, in the Muses-grove, around-murmured
(I sat at the entrance of a temple in the grove of the Muses, surrounded by the murmur)
[*poem:* **Ich sass vor** (foːɐ̯, in front of) **eines Tempels** ('la͜enəs 'tʰɛmpʻəls, a temple's) **Halle**]

[*one repeat only*] [*bar 23*]
fɔm 'naːən 'vasɐfalə lɪm 'zanftʻən 'laːbəntʻʃa͜en. kʰa͜en 'lʏftʻçən 'veːtʻə;
vom nahen Wasserfalle im sanften Abendschein. Kein Lüftchen wehte;
by the near waterfall in the gentle evening-glow. No breeze blew;
(of the near-by waterfall in the gentle glow of sunset. No breeze was blowing;)

[bar 26] *[bar 32]*
[ʊnt] di zɔn ɪm ˈʃaedən fɛɐ̯ˈgʏldətʻə di ˈmatʻən ˈtʰraoɐvaedən.
[und] die Sonn' im Scheiden vergüldete die matten Trauerweiden.
[and] the sun in the departing gilded the languid weeping willows.
([and] the departing sun gilded the languid weeping willows.)

[bar 38] *[repeat]*
ʃtʻɪl ˈzɪnəntʻ zaːs lɪç ˈlaŋə daː, das haoptʻtʻ gəˈʃtʻʏtstʻ laof ˈmaenə ˈrɛçtʻə.
Still sinnend sass ich lange da, das Haupt gestützt auf meine Rechte.
Quietly musing sat I long there, the head supported on my right hand.
(Quietly musing, I sat there a long time, my head resting on my right hand.)

[bar 52] *[upbeat to 55; various repeats]*
ɪç ˈdaxtʻə ˈtsuːkʻʊnftʻ lʊntʻ fɛɐ̯ˈgaŋənhaetʰ; lʊntʻ zaː laof ˈlaenəm bɛrkʻ,
Ich dachte Zukunft und Vergangenheit; und sah auf einem Berg,
I thought future and past; and saw on a mountain,
(I thought about the future and the past; and I saw on a mountain,)

[upbeat to 69, 2 repeats] *[101, repeat]* *[119, repeat]*
dem tʰroːn deːɐ̯ ˈgœtʻɐ naː, den ˈlaofləntʻhaltʻ fɔm ˈhaelɪgən gəˈʃlɛçtʻə deːɐ̯ ˈzɛŋɐ
dem Thron der Götter nah, den Aufenthalt vom heiligen Geschlechte der Sänger
to the throne of the gods near, the abode of the holy race of the singers
(near to the throne of the gods, the abode of the holy race of the singers)

[131, repeat]
laltʻ lʊntʻ ˈnɔøɐ tsaetʻ, lan ˈdeːrən ˈliːdə zɪç di ˈnaːxvɛltʻ nɔx lɛɐ̯ˈfrɔøtʰ.
alt' und neuer Zeit, an deren Liede sich die Nachwelt noch erfreut.
of old and new time, in whose song itself the posterity still delights.
(of olden and newer times, in whose song their posterity still finds delight.)

[recit.]
tʰoːtʰ, ˈlʊnbəmɛrkʻtʰ, lʊntʻ lɛŋstʻ fɛɐ̯ˈgɛsən
Tot, unbemerkt, und längst vergessen
Dead, unnoticed, and long since forgotten

[andante, repeat]
ˈʃliːfən fɛrn lɪn dɛs ˈtʰaːləs ˈdʊŋkʻəln ˈtʰiːfən di ˈgœtʻɐ(r) ˈliːrɐ tsaetʰ,
schliefen fern in des Tales dunkeln Tiefen die Götter ihrer Zeit,
sleep far in the valley's dark depths the gods of their time,
(the gods of their time are sleeping far below in the depths of the valley,)

[adagio, upbeat to 168] *[adagio, 178]*
ɪm ˈriːzənʃatʻən deːɐ̯ fɛɐ̯ˈgɛŋlɪçkʰaetʰ. lʊntʻ ˈlaŋzaːm ˈʃveːbəntʻ
im Riesenschatten der Vergänglichkeit. Und langsam schwebend
in the giant shadow of the transitoriness. And slowly floating
(in the giant shadow of transitoriness. And, slowly floating,)

[word repeated] *[word repeated]*
kʰaːm laos ˈjeːnəm ˈdʊŋkʻəln ˈtʰaːlə, lɛntʻˈʃtʻiːgən ˈlaenəm ˈmɔrʃən ˈhɛldənmaːlə,
kam aus jenem dunkeln Tale, entstiegen einem morschen Heldenmale,
came from that dark valley, risen from a decayed hero- monument,
(there came out of that dark valley, risen from a crumbling monument to some hero,)

[*189*] [*repeat "und bot"*]
[jɛt͡st'] ˈla͜enə ˈdyːst'ərə gəˈʃt'alt daˈheːɐ̯, lʊnt' boːtʰ (lɪnˈdeːm ziː viː fɔn ˈloːngəfɛːɐ̯
[jetzt] eine düstere Gestalt daher, und bot (indem sie wie von ohngefähr
[now] a dim figure hither, and offered (as it as if by chance
([now] a dim figure toward me, and it offered me in passing, as if by chance,)
[*von ohngefähr* (archaic) = *von ungefähr* = by chance]

[*196, allegro, dolce*] [*209*]
foˈryːbɐt͡soːk') lɪn ˈla͜enɐ ˈmoːnbəkʰrɛnt͡st'ən ˈʃaːlə la͜os ˈleːt'əs ˈkʰvɛlə miːɐ̯ fɛɐ̯ˈgɛsənha͜etʰ.
vorüberzog) in einer mohnbekränzten Schale aus Lethes Quelle mir Vergessenheit.
passed by) in a poppy-wreathed bowl from Lethe's spring to me oblivion.
(in a bowl wreathed with poppies, oblivion from Lethe's spring.)

[*recit., 213*] [*216*]
bəˈtʰrɔfən, vɔlt' ɪç di lɛɐ̯ˈʃa͜enʊŋ ˈfraːgən: vas ˈdiːzɐ tʰraŋk' miːɐ̯ ˈnʏt͡sən zɔl?
Betroffen, wollt' ich die Erscheinung fragen: was dieser Trank mir nützen soll?
Taken aback, wanted I the apparition to ask: what this drink to me be of use shall?
(Taken aback, I wanted to ask the apparition what use that drink should be to me.)

[*225*]
dɔx ʃoːn vaːɐ̯ ziː lɛnt'ˈfloːən: lɪç zaːs mɪt' ˈʃt'ɪləm grɔl; [lɛnt'ˈfloːn]
Doch schon war sie entflohen: ich sah's mit stillem Groll; [*poem:* entfloh'n]
But already was it fled: I saw it with quiet resentment; [fled]
(But it had already fled: I saw that with quiet resentment;)

[*here Schubert's setting breaks off*]
dɛn ˈma͜enən ˈvʏnʃən kʰɔnt' ɪç [nɪçt' lɛnt'ˈzaːgən.
denn meinen Wünschen konnt' ich [nicht entsagen.
for my wishes could I [not renounce.
(for I could [not give up] my wishes.)

[Schubert's manuscript breaks off after 231 bars (in the 28th line of a 222-line poem). The form is that of a solo cantata. It was Schubert's earliest effort in that form. Only the first fourteen words were written in by the composer, although the voice part was notated as far as it went. The words that follow can be made to fit, as indicated above (with numerous repetitions). The music, up to the end of bar 231, is printed in Volume 6 of Bärenreiter's *Neue Schubert Ausgabe*. For a long time the title and authorship of the poem were unknown; it was listed among Schubert's works by its first line. The authoress seems to sense that oblivion would be the fate of her song.]

ˈla͜edən deːɐ̯ ˈtʰrɛnʊŋ
Leiden der Trennung
The Sorrows of Separation

Posthumously published [composed 1816] (poem by Heinrich von Collin, after Metastasio)

fɔm ˈmeːrə tʰrɛnt' zɪç di ˈvɛlə, lʊnt' ˈzɔ͜øft͡sət dʊrç ˈbluːmən lɪm tʰaːl,
Vom Meere trennt sich die Welle, und seufzet durch Blumen im Tal,
From the sea separates itself the wave, and sighs through flowers in the valley,
(The wave is separated from the sea, and sighs through flowers in the valley,)

ʊnt' ˈfyːlət', gəˈviːk't' lɪn deːɐ̯ ˈkʰvɛlə, gəˈbant' lɪn dem ˈbrʊnən, nuːɐ̯ kʰvaːl!
und fühlet, gewiegt in der Quelle, gebannt in dem Brunnen, nur Qual!
and feels, cradled in the spring, confined in the well, only torment!

ɛs zeːntʻ zɪç di ˈvɛlə ɪn ˈlɪspʻəlndɐ ˈkʰvɛlə, [ziː]
Es sehnt sich die Welle in lispelnder Quelle, [*poem:* **Sie sehnt sich, die Welle,]**
There longs itself the wave in whispering spring, [It longs, the wave,]
(The wave in the whispering spring,)

ɪm ˈmʊrməlndən ˈbaxə, ɪm ˈbrʊnəngəmaxə, t͜sʊm meːɐ̯,
im murmelnden Bache, im Brunnengemache, zum Meer,
in the murmuring brook, in the well- chamber, to the sea,
(in the murmuring brook, in the casing of the well, is longing to go back to the sea)

fɔn deːm ziː kʰaːm, fɔn deːm ziː ˈleːbən naːm, [la͜os]
von dem sie kam, von dem sie Leben nahm, [*poem:* **aus dem sie Leben nahm]**
from which it came, from which it life took, [out of which it life took]
(from which it came, from which it derived its life,)

fɔn deːm, dɛs ˈɪrəns matʻ ʊntʻ ˈmyːdə, ziː ˈzyːsə ruː fɛɐ̯ˈhɔftʻ ʊntʻ ˈfriːdə.
von dem, des Irrens matt und müde, sie süsse Ruh' verhofft und Friede.
from which, of the straying weak and weary, it sweet rest hoped and peace.
(from which, weak and weary of straying, it hoped to receive sweet rest and peace.)

[The poem is a rather free translation of an aria for Arbace in Act III, Scene 1, of Metastasio's *Artaserse*. Schubert's lovely setting is Mozartean in its surface grace and underlying depth.]

Letzte Hoffnung see *Winterreise*

ˈli̯aːnə
Liane
Liane

Posthumously published [composed 1815] (poem by Johann Mayrhofer)

hast duː liˈaːnən nɪçtʻ gəˈzeːən? —ɪç zaː ziː t͜suː dem ˈtʰa͜eçə geːn. [gəˈzeːn]
"Hast du Lianen nicht gesehen?" —"Ich sah sie zu dem Teiche geh'n." [*poem:* **geseh'n]**
"Have you Liane not seen?" —"I saw her to the pond go."
("Haven't you seen Liane?" —"I saw her going to the pond.")

dʊrç bʊʃ ʊntʻ ˈhɛkʻə rɛntʻ leːɐ̯ fɔrtʻ, ʊntʻ kʰɔmtʻ an ˈiːrən ˈliːpʻlɪŋslɔrtʰ.
Durch Busch und Hecke rennt er fort, und kommt an ihren Lieblingsort.
Through bush and hedge runs he forth, and comes to her favorite place.
(He runs off through bush and hedgerow, and comes to her favorite place.)
[*poem:* **Hecken** (ˈhɛkʻən, hedges)**.... zu ihrem** (t͜suː ˈiːrəm, to her) **Lieblingsort]**

di ˈlɪndə ʃpʻantʻ liːɐ̯ ˈgryːnəs nɛt͜s, la͜os ˈroːzən tʰøːnt dɛs baxs gəˈʃvɛt͜s;
Die Linde spannt ihr grünes Netz, aus Rosen tönt des Bachs Geschwätz;
The linden spreads its green net, from roses sounds the brook's chatter;
(The linden spreads its green netting, the babbling of the brook is heard among the roses;)

di ˈblɛtʻɐ ˈrøːtʻətʻ ˈzɔnəngɔltʻ, ʊntʻ ˈaləs ɪst deːɐ̯ ˈfrɔ͜ødə hɔltʻ.
die Blätter rötet Sonnengold, und alles ist der Freude hold.
the leaves reddens sun- gold, and everything is to the joy favorable.
(the gold of the sun tinges the leaves, and everything is conducive to joy.)

li'a:nə fɛ:ɐ̯t' laof 'laenəm kʰa:n, fɛɐ̯'tʰraot'ə 'ʃvɛ:nə ne:bən'lan.
Liane fährt auf einem Kahn, vertraute Schwäne nebenan.
Liane sails on a boat, familiar swans alongside.
(Liane is in a boat, with friendly swans swimming alongside.)

zi: ʃp'i:lt di 'laot'ə, zɪŋt' laen li:t', vi: 'li:bə lɪn li:ɐ̯ 'ze:lɪç bly:tʰ.
Sie spielt die Laute, singt ein Lied, wie Liebe in ihr selig blüht.
She plays the lute, sings a song, as love in her blissfully blooms.
(She plays the lute and sings a song, as love blissfully blooms in her heart.)

das 'ʃiflaen 'ʃvaŋk'ət', vi: lɛs vɪl, zi: zɛŋk't das haop't' lʊnt 'dɛŋk'ət' ʃt'ɪl
Das Schifflein schwanket, wie es will, sie senkt das Haupt und denket still
The little boat rocks, as it will, she sinks the head and thinks quietly
(The little boat rocks, drifts where it will; she lowers her head and is quietly thinking)

lan li:n, de:ɐ̯/de:r lɪm gə'bʏʃə lɪst', zi: balt' lɪn 'zaenə 'larmə ʃli:stʰ. [nu:ɐ̯/nu:r li:n]
an ihn, der im Gebüsche ist, sie bald in seine Arme schliest. [*poem:* **nur ihn]**
of him, who in the bushes is, she soon in his arms encloses. [only (of) him]
(of him, who is there in the bushes, and who will soon enclose her in his arms.)

[The song is a pleasant trifle, with some typical water-music in the piano part.]

lɪçt' lʊnt' 'li:bə
Licht und Liebe
Light and Love

Posthumously published [composed 1822?] (poem by Matthäus von Collin)

Tenor:
'li:bə lɪst' laen 'zy:səs lɪçtʰ. vi: di 'le:ɐ̯də ʃt're:p't tsʊr 'zɔnə,
Liebe ist ein süsses Licht. Wie die Erde strebt zur Sonne,
Love is a sweet light. As the earth strives for the sun,

lʊnt tsu: 'je:nən 'hɛlən 'ʃt'ɛrnən lɪn den 'vaet'ən 'blaoən 'fɛrnən,
und zu jenen hellen Sternen in den weiten blauen Fernen,
and for those bright stars in the broad blue distances,

ʃt're:p't das hɛrts na:x 'li:bəsvɔnə; dɛn zi: lɪst' laen 'zy:səs lɪçtʰ.
strebt das Herz nach Liebeswonne; denn sie ist ein süsses Licht.
strives the heart for love's ecstasy; for it is a sweet light.
(the heart strives for the ecstasy of love, for love is a sweet light.)

Soprano:
zi:, vi: ho:x lɪn 'ʃt'ɪlɐ 'faeɐ 'dro:bən 'hɛlə 'ʃt'ɛrnə 'fʊŋk'əln,
Sieh, wie hoch in stiller Feier droben helle Sterne funkeln,
See, how high in quiet celebration up there bright stars sparkle,
(See how the bright stars are sparkling, high above us, in quiet celebration,)

fɔn de:ɐ̯/de:r 'le:ɐ̯də fli:n di 'dʊŋk'əln, 'ʃve:ɐ̯mu:tsfɔlən 'tʰry:bən 'ʃlaeɐ.
von der Erde fliehn die dunkeln, schwermutsvollen trüben Schleier.
from the earth flee the dark, melancholy, gloomy veils.
(as the dark, gloomy veils of melancholy flee from the earth.)

ˈveːə miːɐ̯, viː zoː ˈtʰryːbə fyːl ɪç tʰiːf mɪç ɪm gəˈmyːt‘ə, [dɔx]
Wehe mir, wie so trübe fühl' ich tief mich im Gemüte, [*poem:* **doch wie so trübe]**
Woe to me, how so gloomy feel I deep myself in the feeling, [but]
(Woe is me, how depressed I feel, deep in my heart,)

das ɪn ˈfrɔ͜ødən zɔnst‘ ɛɐ̯ˈblyːt‘ə, nuːn fɛɐ̯ˈla͜enzaːmt‘/fɛrˈla͜enzaːmt‘ ˈloːnə ˈliːbə.
das in Freuden sonst erblühte, nun vereinsamt ohne Liebe.
which in joys formerly blossomed, now grown lonely without love.
(which formerly blossomed with joy, but now has grown lonely without love.)

Soprano and tenor, alternately or together:
ˈliːbə ɪst‘ la͜en ˈzyːsəs lɪçtʰ... naːx ˈliːbəsvɔnə. ˈliːbə ɪst‘ la͜en ˈzyːsəs lɪçtʰ.
Liebe ist ein süsses Licht... [etc., as above] **nach Liebeswonne. Liebe ist ein süsses Licht.**
Love is a sweet light... for love's ecstasy. Love is a sweet light.
[*poem:* **Liebeswonne: denn sie** (dɛn ziː, for it) **ist ein süsses Licht.]**

[The music is beautiful, even if the words are banal. The text is taken from the fourth act of a play, *Der Tod Friedrichs des Streitbaren* ("The Death of Frederick the Valiant"). Duke Frederick has returned to a valley where once he was happy with his lost love. He hears distant voices singing of love. Schubert omitted the lines of the Duke, which twice interrupt the song.]

Liebesbotschaft see *Schwanengesang*

ˈliːbə ʃvɛrmt‘ ɑ͜of ˈalən ˈveːgən / aˈri̯ɛt‘ə deːɐ̯ ˈkʰlɑ͜odiːnə
Liebe schwärmt auf allen Wegen / Ariette der Claudine
Love Roves Everywhere / The Arietta of Claudine

Posthumously published [composed 1815] (poem by Johann Wolfgang von Goethe)

ˈliːbə ʃvɛrmt‘ ɑ͜of ˈalən ˈveːgən; ˈtʰrɔ͜øə voːnt‘ fyːɐ̯ zɪç laˈla͜en.
Liebe schwärmt auf allen Wegen; Treue wohnt für sich allein.
Love roves on all roads; faithfulness dwells for itself alone.
(Love can be found everywhere; faithfulness keeps to itself, alone.)

ˈliːbə kʰɔmt‘ lɔ͜øç raʃ lɛntˈ‘geːgən; ˈlɑ͜ofgəzuːxt‘ vɪl ˈtʰrɔ͜øə za͜en.
Liebe kommt euch rasch entgegen; aufgesucht will Treue sein.
Love comes to you quickly towards; sought out wants faithfulness to be.
(Love comes to meet you quickly, obligingly; faithfulness needs to be sought out.)
[*entgegenkommen* = to come to meet, to meet half-way]

[The words are from Goethe's play *Claudine von Villa Bella*. The song was labeled "*Ariette*" in Schubert's unfinished score. Although written for the stage, it is often sung in recitals.]

ˈliːbəslɑo̯ʃən

Liebeslauschen

Eavesdropping Love / A Serenade Overheard

Posthumously published [composed 1820] (poem by Franz Xaver von Schlechta)

hiːɐ̯/hiːr ˈʊntʻən ʃtʻeːtʻ lae̯n ˈrɪtʻɐ ǀɪm ˈhɛlən ˈmoːndənʃtʻraːl, [deːɐ̯]
Hier unten steht ein Ritter im hellen Mondenstrahl, [*poem:* **der Ritter]**
Here below stands a knight in the bright ray of moonlight, [the knight]

ʊntʻ zɪŋt t͡suː ˈzae̯nəm ˈt͡sɪtʻɐ(r) lae̯n liːtʻ fɔn ˈzyːsɐ kʰvaːl:
und singt zu seinem Zither ein Lied von süsser Qual:
and sings to the accompaniment of his zither, a song of sweet torment:

[ɛs ˈtʰøːnətʻ ˈzae̯nə ˈt͡sɪtʻɐ fɔn ˈtʰrɔø̯ɐ ˈliːbə kʰvaːl]
[*poem:* **Es tönet seine Zither von treuer Liebe Qual]**
[there sounds his zither of true love's torment]
[(his zither gives out sounds that express the torment of true love)]

ˈlʏftʻə, ʃpʻant di ˈblɑo̯ən ˈʃvɪŋən zanftʻ fyːɐ̯ ˈmae̯nə ˈboːtʻʃaftʻ lɑo̯s,
"Lüfte, spannt die blauen Schwingen sanft für meine Botschaft aus,
"Breezes, spread the blue wings gently for my message out,
("Breezes, spread out your blue wings gently for my message,)

ˈruːfətʻ ziː mɪtʻ ˈlae̯zəm ˈkʰlɪŋən ǀan diːs ˈfɛnstʻɐlae̯n hɛˈrɑo̯s. [ˈfɛnstʻɐçən]
rufet sie mit leisem Klingen an dies Fensterlein heraus. [*poem:* **Fensterchen]**
call her with soft sounding to this little window out. [little window]
(call her with soft music to come to that little window.)

zaːkʻtʻ liːɐ̯, das ǀɪm ˈblɛtʻɐdaxə zɔø̯ft͡s lae̯n ˈvoːlbəkʰantʻɐ lɑo̯tʰ,
Sagt ihr, dass im Blätterdache seufz' ein wohlbekannter Laut,
Tell her that in the leaves- roof sighs a well-known sound,
(Tell her that in the shelter of foliage a well-known voice—that of the nightingale—is sighing,)

zaːkʻtʻ liːɐ̯, das nɔx ˈlae̯nɐ ˈvaxə, ǀʊnt di naxtʻ zae̯ kʰyːl ǀʊnt tʰrɑo̯tʰ.
sagt ihr, dass noch einer wache, und die Nacht sei kühl und traut.
tell her that still one is awake, and the night is cool and cozy.
(tell her that another being is also awake, and that the night is cool and cozy.)
[*noch einer* = another one]

zaːkʻtʻ liːɐ̯, viː dɛs ˈmoːndəs ˈvɛlə zɪç ǀan ˈliːrəm ˈfɛnstʻɐ brɪçtʰ,
Sagt ihr, wie des Mondes Welle sich an ihrem Fenster bricht,
Tell her how the moon's wave itself at her window breaks,
(Tell her how a wave of moonlight breaks at her window,)

zaːkʻtʻ liːɐ̯, viː deːɐ̯ valt, di ˈkʰvɛlə, ˈhae̯mlɪç ǀʊntʻ fɔn ˈliːbə ʃpʻrɪçtʰ!
sagt ihr, wie der Wald, die Quelle, heimlich und von Liebe spricht!
tell her how the forest, the fountain, secretly and of love speaks!
(tell her how the forest and the fountain secretly speak of love!)

[*The next stanza is not in the published poem; suddenly the lady is addressed directly:*]

las liːn 'lɔ͡ʏçt'ən dʊrç di 'bɔ͡ʏmə, 'da͡enəs 'bɪldəs 'zyːsən ʃa͡en,
Lass' ihn leuchten durch die Bäume, deines Bildes süssen Schein,
Let it shine through the trees, your image's sweet light,
(Let the sweet radiance of your image shine through the trees,)

das zɪç hɔlt' lɪn 'ma͡enə 'tʰrɔ͡ʏmə lʊnt' ma͡en 'vaxən 've:bət' la͡en.
das sich hold in meine Träume und mein Wachen webet ein."
which itself charmingly into my dreams and my waking weaves into."
(that image that weaves itself so charmingly into my dreams and my waking thoughts.")

dɔx draŋ di 'tsa:ɐt'ə 'va͡ezə vo:l nɪçt tsu: 'li:p'çəns lo:ɐ̯,
Doch drang die zarte Weise wohl nicht zu Liebchens Ohr,
But penetrated the delicate melody perhaps not to sweetheart's ear
(But the soft melody seemed not to have reached his sweetheart's ear;)
[*poem:* **zu ihrem** ('li:rəm, her) **Ohr**]

de:ɐ̯ 'zɛŋɐ ʃvaŋ zɪç 'la͡ezə tsʊm 'fɛnst'ɐla͡en lɛm'pʰo:ɐ̯.
der Sänger schwang sich leise zum Fensterlein empor.
the singer swung himself softly to the little window up.
(the singer swung himself softly up to the little window.)

ʊnt' 'lo:bən tso:k' de:ɐ̯ 'rɪt'ɐ(r) la͡en 'kʰrɛntsçən la͡os de:ɐ̯ brʊst',
Und oben zog der Ritter ein Kränzchen aus der Brust,
And up there drew the knight a little garland from the breast,
(And up there the knight drew a little garland from his breast,)

das bant' le:ɐ̯ fɛst' lam 'gɪt'ɐ(r) lʊnt' 'zɔ͡ʏftst'ə: bly:t' lɪn lʊstʰ!
das band er fest am Gitter und seufzte: "Blüht in Lust! [*Peters ends the quote*]
that tied he firmly to the lattice and sighed: "Bloom in joy!
(which he tied firmly to the lattice, sighing: "Bloom in joy!)

ʊnt' fra:k't' zi:, ve:ɐ̯/ve:r lɔ͡ʏç 'braxt'ə, dan, 'blu:mən, tʰu:t' li:ɐ̯ kʰʊnt'—
und fragt sie, wer euch brachte, dann, Blumen, tut ihr kund"— [*Peters: colon only*]
and asks she who you brought, then, flowers, let her know"—
(and if she asks you who brought you, then, flowers, tell her..."—)

[*Apparently the lady for whom the serenade was intended was not at her window, but in the garden, unseen and listening!*]

a͡en 'ʃt'ɪmçən 'lʊnt'ən 'laxt'ə: da͡en 'rɪt'ɐ 'li:bəmʊnt'.
Ein Stimmchen unten lachte: "Dein Ritter Liebemund."
A little voice down below laughed: "Your Knight Liebemund, [= "Love-Mouth"]
(A feminine voice from below laughed and finished his sentence: "Your Knight Liebemund,)

[*This is Schubert's delightful idea, not in the poem:*]
da͡en 'rɪt'ɐ 'li:bə-, 'li:bə-, 'li:bəmʊnt'!
dein Ritter Liebe-, Liebe-, Liebemund!"
your Knight Liebe- Liebe- Liebemund!" [= "Love-love-love-mouth"]

[The poem is the second of "Two Romances," inspired by paintings by Ludwig Schnorr von Carolsfeld (the father of Wagner's first Tristan). Schubert's text includes a fifth stanza that does not appear in the published poem ("*Lass ihn leuchten*"). The painter and the poet both belonged to Schubert's circle of friends. The painting behind this poem shows a knight plucking a zither in the moonlight beneath his lady's window. The song is a charming precursor, in accompaniment and interludes, of the later *Ständchen* familiar to almost everyone as "Schubert's Serenade."]

ˈliːbəsrɑ͜oʃ
Liebesrausch
Love's Intoxication

Posthumously published [composed 1815] (poem by Theodor Körner)

diːɐ̯, ˈmɛːtʻçən, ʃlɛːkʻtʻ mɪtʻ ˈla͜ezəm ˈbeːbən ma͜en hɛrt͜s fɔl tʰrɔ͜ø lʊntʻ ˈliːbə t͜suː;
Dir, Mädchen, schlägt mit leisem Beben mein Herz voll Treu' und Liebe zu;
For you, girl, beats with soft trembling my heart full of loyalty and love to;
(My heart, softly trembling, full of faithfulness and love, beats for you, dear girl!)

ɪn diːɐ̯/diːr, lɪn diːɐ̯ fɛɐ̯ˈzɪŋkʻtʻ ma͜en ˈʃtʻreːbən, ma͜en ˈʃøːnstʻəs t͜siːl bɪst duː!
in dir, in dir versinkt mein Streben, mein schönstes Ziel bist du!
in you, in you sinks my striving, my most beautiful goal are you!
(In you, in you my striving ceases: you are my most beautiful goal!)

da͜en ˈnaːmə nuːɐ̯/nuːr lɪn ˈha͜elgən ˈtʰøːnən hatʻ ˈma͜enə ˈkʰyːnə brʊstʻ gəˈfʏltʰ;
Dein Name nur in heil'gen Tönen hat meine kühne Brust gefüllt;
Your name alone in holy tones has my bold breast filled;
(Your name alone has filled my bold breast with holy music;)

ɪm glant͜s dɛs ˈguːtʻən lʊnt dɛs ˈʃøːnən ʃtʻraːltʻ miːɐ̯ da͜en ˈhoːəs bɪltʻ.
im Glanz des Guten und des Schönen strahlt mir dein hohes Bild.
in the radiance of the Good and the Beautiful shines for me your lofty image.
(Your lofty image shines upon me with the radiance of goodness and beauty.)

di ˈliːbə ʃpʻrɔstʻ lɑ͜os ˈt͜saːɐ̯tʻən ˈkʰa͜emən, lʊntʻ ˈliːrə ˈblyːtʻən ˈvɛlkʻən niː!
Die Liebe sprosst aus zarten Keimen, und ihre Blüten welken nie!
The love sprouts from tender buds, and its blossoms fade never!
(Love sprouts from tender buds, and its blossoms never fade!)

duː, ˈmɛːtʻçən, leːpstʻ lɪn ˈma͜enən ˈtʰrɔ͜ømən mɪtʻ ˈzyːsɐ harmoˈniː.
Du, Mädchen, lebst in meinen Träumen mit süsser Harmonie.
You, girl, live in my dreams with sweet harmony.

bəˈga͜estʻrʊŋ rɑ͜oʃtʻ lɑ͜of mɪç hɛɐ̯ˈniːdɐ, kʰyːn gra͜ef ɪç lɪn di ˈza͜etʻən la͜en,
Begeist'rung rauscht auf mich hernieder, kühn greif' ich in die Saiten ein,
Inspiration rushes upon me down, boldly grasp I into the strings into,
(Inspiration pours down upon me, I boldly strike the strings,)

ʊntʻ ˈlalə ˈma͜enə ˈʃøːnstʻən ˈliːdɐ, ziː ˈnɛnən dɪç laˈla͜en.
und alle meine schönsten Lieder, sie nennen dich allein.
and all my loveliest songs, they name you alone.

ma͜en ˈhɪməl glyːtʻ lɪn ˈda͜enən ˈblɪkʻən, lan ˈda͜enɐ brʊstʻ ma͜en pʰaraˈdiːs.
Mein Himmel glüht in deinen Blicken, an deiner Brust mein Paradies.
My heaven glows in your glances, at your breast (is) my paradise.
(My heaven glows in your glances, my paradise is at your breast.)

ax! 'lalə 'raetsə, di: dɪç 'ʃmʏk'ən, zi: zɪnt' zo: hɔlt', zo: zy:s.
Ach! alle Reize, die dich schmücken, sie sind so hold, so süss.
Ah! all charms that you adorn, they are so lovely, so sweet.
(Ah! All of the charms that adorn you are so lovely, so sweet!)

ɛs vo:k't di brʊst' ɪn frɔøt' ʊnt' 'ʃmɛrtsən, nu:ɐ̯/nu:r 'laenə 'ze:nzʊxt' le:p't' ɪn mi:ɐ̯,
Es wogt die Brust in Freud' und Schmerzen, nur eine Sehnsucht lebt in mir,
There swells the breast in joy and pains, only *one* longing lives in me,
(My breast swells with joy and pain, only *one* longing is alive in me,)

nu:ɐ̯/nu:r laen gə'daŋk'ə hi:ɐ̯/hi:r ɪm 'hɛrtsən: de:ɐ̯/de:r 'le:vgə draŋ na:x di:ɐ̯.
nur ein Gedanke hier im Herzen: der ew'ge Drang nach dir.
only *one* thought here in the heart: the eternal craving for you.
(only *one* thought here in my heart: the eternal craving for you.)

[This beautiful song captures the poet's rapture to perfection. Schubert attempted an earlier setting of the poem, a promising six-bar fragment (which has been completed by Reinhard van Hoorickx, recorded with other "Unknown Schubert Songs," and privately published).]

'li:bəstʰɛndəˌlae
Liebeständelei
Amorous Dalliance

Posthumously published [composed 1815] (poem by Theodor Körner)

'zy:səs 'li:p'çən! kʰɔm tsu: mi:ɐ̯! 'tʰaozənt' 'kʰʏsə ge:b ɪç di:ɐ̯.
Süsses Liebchen! Komm zu mir! Tausend Küsse geb' ich dir.
Sweet darling! Come to me! (A) thousand kisses give I to you.
(Sweet darling, come to me! I'll give you a thousand kisses.)

zi: mɪç hi:ɐ̯ tsu: 'daenən 'fy:sən. 'mɛ:t'çən, 'daenɐ 'lɪp'ən glu:t'
Sieh mich hier zu deinen Füssen. Mädchen, deiner Lippen Glut
See me here at your feet. Girl, your lips' fire
(See me here at your feet. Girl, the fire of your lips)

gi:p't' mi:ɐ̯ kʰraft' ʊnt' 'le:bənsmu:tʰ. las dɪç 'kʰʏsən!
gibt mir Kraft und Lebensmut. Lass dich küssen!
gives to me strength and life- courage. Let yourself (be) kissed!
(will give me strength and high spirits. Let yourself be kissed!)

'mɛ:t'çən, 've:ɐ̯də dɔx nɪçt' ro:t'! vens di 'mʊt'ɐ(r) aox fɛɐ̯'bo:tʰ.
Mädchen, werde doch nicht rot! Wenn's die Mutter auch verbot.
Girl, become by all means not red! If it the mother even forbade.
(Girl, don't blush! Even if your mother did forbid it,)

zɔlst du: 'lalə 'frɔødən 'mɪsən? nu:ɐ̯/nu:r lan dɛs gə'li:p't'ən brʊst'
Sollst du alle Freuden missen? Nur an des Geliebten Brust
Shall you all joys miss? Only on the lover's breast
(do you have to miss all the pleasures? Only on your lover's breast)

bly:t dɛs 'le:bəns 'ʃø:nst'ə lʊstʰ. las dɪç 'kʰʏsən!
blüht des Lebens schönste Lust. Lass dich küssen!
blooms the life's most beautiful pleasure. Let yourself (be) kissed!
(does life's most beautiful pleasure bloom. Let yourself be kissed!)

'li:p'çən, 'va:rum tsi:ɐst du: dıç? 'hø:rə dɔx ꞁʊnt' 'kʰʏsə mıç.
Liebchen, warum zierst du dich? Höre doch und küsse mich.
Sweetheart, why give airs you yourself? Hear by all means and kiss me.
(Sweetheart, why do you give yourself airs? Hear me, for heaven's sake, and kiss me.)

vılst du: nıçts fɔn 'li:bə 'vısən?
Willst du nichts von Liebe wissen?
Want you nothing of love to know?
(Don't you want to know anything about love?)

vo:k't di:ɐ nıçt daen 'kʰlaenəs hɛrts balt' ꞁın 'frɔødən, balt' ꞁın ʃmɛrts?
Wogt dir nicht dein kleines Herz bald in Freuden, bald in Schmerz?
Surges for you not your little heart now in joys, now in pain?
(Does your little heart not sometimes surge with joy, sometimes with pain?)

las dıç 'kʰʏsən! zi:, daen 'ʃt'rɔøbən hılft di:ɐ nıçt';
Lass dich küssen! Sieh', dein Sträuben hilft dir nicht;
Let yourself (be) kissed! See, your resistance helps you not;
(Let yourself be kissed! See, your resistance doesn't help you;)

ʃo:n ha:b ıç na:x 'zɛŋɐs pflıçt di:ɐ den 'le:ɐst'ən kʰʊs ꞁɛnt''rısən!
schon hab' ich nach Sängers Pflicht dir den ersten Kuss entrissen!
already have I according to singer's duty from you the first kiss snatched away!
(already I have done my duty as a singer and snatched the first kiss from you!)

ʊnt' nu:n zıŋkst du:, 'li:bəvarm, 'vılıç zɛlpst' ꞁın 'maenən ꞁarm.
Und nun sinkst du, liebewarm, willig selbst in meinen Arm.
And now sink you, love-warm, willingly yourself into my arm.
(And now, warm with love, you sink willingly into my arms,)

lɛst dıç 'kʰʏsən!
Läss'st dich küssen!
(You) let yourself (be) kissed!
(You let me kiss you after all!)

[This song about the technique of seduction, sweetened by attractive music and the singer's charm, would endanger public morality if such tips were not already familiar to the male libido!]

'li:p'ha:bɐ ꞁın 'ꞁalən gə'ʃt'alt'ən
Liebhaber in allen Gestalten
A Lover in All Forms

Posthumously published [composed 1817] (poem by Johann Wolfgang von Goethe)

ıç vɔlt' ꞁıç vɛ:ɐ/vɛ:r ꞁaen fıʃ, zo: 'hʊrt'ıç ꞁʊnt' frıʃ;
Ich wollt' ich wär' ein Fisch, so hurtig und frisch;
I would I were a fish, so agile and fresh;
(I wish I were a fish, so agile and fresh;)

ʊnt' kʰɛ:mst du: tsu: 'ꞁaŋəln, ꞁıç 'vʏrdə nıçt' 'maŋəln.
und kämst du zu angeln, ich würde nicht mangeln.
and came you to fish, I would not be lacking.
(and if you came to fish I would not fail you.)

ɪç vɔlt‘ lɪç vɛːɐ̯/vɛːr la͜en pfeːɐ̯t‘, daː vɛːr ɪç diːɐ̯ veːɐ̯tʰ.
Ich wollt' ich wär' ein Pferd, da wär' ich dir wert.
I would I were a horse, then were I to you worth.
(I wish I were a horse, then I would be worth something to you.)

oː vɛːr ɪç la͜en 'vaːgən, bə'kʰveːm dɪç tsuː 'tʰraːgən.
O wär' ich ein Wagen, bequem dich zu tragen.
Oh were I a carriage, comfortably you to carry.
(Oh, if I were only a carriage, to carry you in comfort!)

ɪç vɔlt‘ lɪç 'vɛːrə gɔlt‘, diːɐ̯/diːr 'lɪmɐ(r) lɪm zɔlt‘;
Ich wollt' ich wäre Gold, dir immer im Sold;
I would I were gold, of you always in the pay;
(I wish I were money, always at your service;) [*dir im Sold* = in your pay = in your employment]

ʊnt tʰɛːtst duː vas 'kʰa͜ofən, kʰɛːm ɪç gə'la͜ofən. ['viːdɐ]
und tät'st du was kaufen, käm' ich gelaufen. [*poem:* **käm' ich wieder gelaufen**]
and would do you something buy, came I running (back). [back]
(and if you bought something, I would come running back to you.)

[ɪç vɔlt‘ lɪç vɛːɐ̯ tʰrɔ͜ø, ma͜en 'liːp‘çən ʃt‘eːts nɔ͜ø; ['vɛːrə]
[Ich wollt' ich wär' treu, mein Liebchen stets neu; [*to fit the music:* **wäre treu**]
[I wish I were faithful, my sweetheart ever new;

ɪç vɔlt‘ mɪç fɛɐ̯'ha͜esən, vɔlt‘ 'nɪmɐ fɛɐ̯'ra͜ezən.
ich wollt' mich verheissen, wollt' nimmer verreisen.
I would myself promise, would never travel away from home.
(I would promise myself, would never leave home.)

ɪç vɔlt‘ lɪç vɛːɐ̯/vɛːr laltʰ lʊnt‘ 'rʊntslɪç lʊnt‘ kʰaltʰ; ['vɛːrə]
Ich wollt' ich wär' alt und runzlig und kalt; [*to fit the music:* **wäre alt]**
I wish I were old and wrinkled and cold;

tʰɛːtst duː miːɐ̯s fɛɐ̯'zaːgən, daː kʰœnt‘ mɪçs nɪçt‘ 'pʰlaːgən.
tät'st du mir's versagen, da könnt' mich's nicht plagen.
did you to me it refuse, then could me it not bother.
(if you refused to give it to me, then it could not bother me any more.)

vɛːr ɪç 'lafə zo'gla͜eç, fɔl 'nɛk‘əndɐ ʃt‘ra͜eç;
Wär' ich Affe sogleich, voll neckender Streich'; [*to fit the music:* **wär' Affe ich sogleich]**
Were I monkey at once, full of teasing pranks;
(I wish I were a monkey right away, full of teasing pranks!)

hɛt‘ vas dɪç fɛɐ̯'drɔsən, zoː maxt‘ ɪç diːɐ̯ 'pʰɔsən.
hätt' was dich verdrossen, so macht' ich dir Possen.
had something you upset, then made I for you fooleries.
(If something upset you, then I would amuse you with funny tricks.)

vɛːr ɪç guːt‘ viː la͜en ʃaːf, viː deːɐ̯ 'løːvə zoː braːf;
Wär' ich gut wie ein Schaf, wie der Löwe so brav; [*to fit the music: need to add a note*]
Were I good as a sheep, as the lion so upright;
(I wish I were as docile as a sheep, as brave as a lion!)

hɛt‘ ˈlɑ͜ogən viːs ˈlʏksçən, lʊnt‘ ˈlɪst‘ən viːs ˈfʏksçən.
hätt' Augen wie's Lüchschen, und Listen wie's Füchschen.
had (I) eyes like the little lynx, and cunning ruses like the little fox.
(I wish I had sharp eyes like the lynx, and the cunning of the fox.)

vas ˈlaləs lɪç vɛːɐ̯, das gœnt‘ ɪç diːɐ̯ zeːɐ̯;
Was alles ich wär', das gönnt' ich dir sehr; [*to fit the music:* **was alles ich dann wär'**]
Whatever all I were, that grant I to you very well;
(You are very welcome to whatever I would be, to all of those things;)

mɪt‘ ˈfʏrst‘lɪçən ˈgaːbən duː ˈzɔlt‘əst‘ mɪç ˈhaːbən.]
mit fürstlichen Gaben du solltest mich haben.]
with princely gifts you should me have.]
(you should have me with princely gifts.)]

dɔx bɪn lɪç viː lɪç bɪn, lʊnt‘ nɪm mɪç nuːɐ̯ hɪn!
Doch bin ich wie ich bin, und nimm mich nur hin!
But am I as I am, and accept me just ...! [*hinnehmen* = accept, put up with]
(But I am as I am, and just accept me that way!)

vɪlst‘ ˈbɛsrə bəˈzɪt͡sən, zoː las diːɐ̯ ziː ˈʃnɪt͡sən. [duː]
willst bess're besitzen, so lass dir sie schnitzen. [*poem:* **willst du bess're**]
want (you) better ones to possess, then let for you them (be) carved. [you]
(If you want lovers in better shapes, then order some craftsman to carve them for you.)

ɪç bɪn nuːn viː lɪç bɪn, zoː nɪm mɪç nuːɐ̯ hɪn!
Ich bin nun wie ich bin, so nimm' mich nur hin!
I am now as I am, so accept me just ...!
(I am now as I am, so just accept me that way!)

[It seems that Schubert intended that the first three and the last verse be sung. The others are in brackets, above. The *Gesamtausgabe* prints all nine verses, but only the first two under the vocal line. Peters offers the first, the third, and the ninth. The song has humor and playful charm.]

liːp‘ ˈmɪna
Lieb Minna
Sweet Minna

Posthumously published [composed 1815] (poem by Albert Stadler)

ˈʃvyːlɐ hɑ͜ox veːt‘ miːɐ̯ hɛˈryːbɐ, vɛlk‘t di bluːm lan ˈma͜enɐ brʊstʰ.
"Schwüler Hauch weht mir herüber, welkt die Blum' an meiner Brust.
"Sultry breeze wafts to me over, withers the flower at my breast.
("A sultry breeze is wafting over to me; it withers the flower at my breast.)

ax, voː va͜elst duː, ˈvɪlhɛlm, ˈliːbɐ? ˈma͜enɐ ˈzeːlə ˈzyːsə lʊstʰ!
Ach, wo weilst du, Wilhelm, Lieber? Meiner Seele süsse Lust!
Ah, where linger you, William, dear one? My soul's sweet joy!
(Ah, where are you lingering, William, my dear one, sweet joy of my soul?)

ˈeːvɪç ˈva͜enən, niː lɛɐ̯ˈʃa͜enən! ʃlɛːfst‘ voːl ʃoːn lɪm ˈkʰyːlən ˈʃoːsə,
Ewig Weinen, nie Erscheinen! Schläfst wohl schon im kühlen Schosse,
Eternal weeping, never appearing! (You) sleep perhaps already in the cool womb,
(I weep forever, you never appear! Perhaps you are already sleeping in earth's cool womb;)

dɛŋkst‘ l̯aox ma̯en nɔx ˈlʊnt‘ɐm ˈmoːzə?
denkst auch mein noch unterm Moose?"
think (you) also of me still, beneath the moss?"
(do you also still think of me, as you lie there beneath the moss?)

ˈmɪna ˈva̯enət‘, lɛs fɛɐ̯ˈfloːgən ˈmɛːlɪç vaŋ- lʊnt‘ ˈlɪp‘ənroːtʰ.
Minna weinet, es verflogen mählig Wang- und Lippenrot.
Minna weeps, there fly away gradually cheek- and lip- red.
(Minna weeps, and gradually the color leaves her cheeks and her lips.)

ˈvɪlhɛlm vaːɐ̯ hɪˈna̯osgə͡tsoːgən mɪt den ra̯en ͡tsʊm ˈʃlaxt‘əntʰoːt‘.
Wilhelm war hinausgezogen mit den Reih'n zum Schlachtentod.
William had marched out with the ranks to the battle- death.
(William had marched out with the ranks to face death on the battlefield.)

fɔn deːɐ̯ ˈʃt‘ʊndə ˈkʰa̯enə ˈkʰʊndə! ʃlɛːfst‘ voːl lɛŋst‘ lɪm ˈkʰyːlən ˈʃoːsə,
Von der Stunde keine Kunde! Schläfst wohl längst im kühlen Schosse,
From that hour no news! (You) sleep perhaps long since in the cool womb,
(Since that hour no news! You have perhaps long since been sleeping in that cool womb,)

dɛŋk‘t da̯en, ˈmɪna, ˈlʊnt‘ɐm ˈmoːzə.
denkt dein, Minna, unterm Moose.
thinks of you, Minna, beneath the moss.
(Minna is thinking of you, there under the moss.)

ˈliːp‘çən zɪ͡tst‘ lɪm ˈʃt‘ɪlən ˈharmə, ziːt di ˈgɔldnən ˈʃt‘ɛrnla̯en ͡tsiːn,
Liebchen sitzt im stillen Harme, sieht die goldnen Sternlein ziehn,
Sweetheart sits in the quiet grief, sees the golden little stars pass by,
(Your sweetheart sits there in quiet grief, sees the golden stars passing by,)

ʊnt deːɐ̯ moːnt‘ ʃa̯ot‘ la̯of di ˈlarmə ˈmɪt‘la̯e͡tsfɔlən ˈblɪk‘əs hɪn.
und der Mond schaut auf die Arme mitleidsvollen Blickes hin.
and the moon looks at the poor girl (with) compassionate gaze down.
(and the moon looks down at the poor girl with a compassionate gaze.)

hɔrç, daː ˈveːən la̯os den ˈhøːən ˈlaːbənt‘lʏft‘çən liːɐ̯ hɛˈryːbɐ:
Horch, da wehen aus den Höhen Abendlüftchen ihr herüber:
Hark, there waft from the heights evening breezes to her over:
(Hark, from the heights there evening breezes are wafting over to her:)

dɔrt‘ lam ˈfɛlzən hart da̯en ˈliːbɐ.
"Dort am Felsen harrt dein Lieber."
"There by the cliff waits your dear one."
("There by the cliff your dear one is waiting," they whisper to her.)

ˈmɪna la̯elt‘ lɪm ˈmoːndənflɪmɐ bla̯eç lʊnt‘ ˈlaːnənt dʊrç di fluːɐ̯,
Minna eilt im Mondenflimmer bleich und ahnend durch die Flur,
Minna hurries in the moon- glimmer pale and full of foreboding through the meadow,
(Minna, pale and full of foreboding, hurries across the meadow in the moonlight,)

ˈfɪndət‘ ˈliːrən ˈvɪlhɛlm ˈnɪmɐ, ˈfɪndət‘ ˈza̯enən ˈhyːgəl nuːɐ̯.
findet ihren Wilhelm nimmer, findet seinen Hügel nur.
finds her William never, finds his (grave-) mound only.
(but she does not find her William, she only finds his grave.)

bɪn balt 'dry:bən bae̯ di:ɐ̯, 'li:bən, za:kst' mi:ɐ̯/mi:r ǀao̯s dem 'kʰy:lən 'ʃo:sə:
"Bin bald drüben bei dir, Lieben, sagst mir aus dem kühlen Schosse:
"Am soon over there with you, dear one, (you) say to me from the cool womb:
("Soon I shall be with you in the other world, dear one; from the cool earth you say to me:)

dɛŋk' dae̯n, 'mɪna, 'ǀʊnt'ɐm 'mo:zə.
'Denk' dein, Minna, unterm Moose.'"
'(I) think of you, Minna, beneath the moss.'"
('Beneath the moss I am thinking of you, Minna.'")

ʊnt' fi:l 'tʰao̯zənt' 'bly:mçən 'ʃt'ae̯gən 'frɔø̯nt'lɪç ǀao̯s dem gra:p' hɛ'rao̯f.
Und viel tausend Blümchen steigen freundlich aus dem Grab herauf.
And many thousand little flowers rise kindly from the grave up.
(And many thousands of little flowers rise up kindly from the grave.)

'mɪna kʰɛnt di 'li:bəstso̯ø̯gən, 'bɛt'ət' zɪç ǀae̯n 'pʰlɛtsçən drao̯f.
Minna kennt die Liebeszeugen, bettet sich ein Plätzchen drauf.
Minna recognizes the love- witnesses, beds herself a little place upon them.
(Minna recognizes the witnesses of love; she makes herself a little place upon them as a bed.)

bɪn glae̯ç 'dry:bən bae̯ di:ɐ̯, 'li:bən! le:k't' zɪç ǀao̯f di 'bly:mçən 'ni:dər,
"Bin gleich drüben bei dir, Lieben!" Legt sich auf die Blümchen nieder,
"Am at once over there with you, dear one!" Lays herself upon the little flowers down,
("At once I shall be with you yonder, dear one!" She lies down upon the little flowers,)

'fɪndət' 'ǀi:rən 'vɪlhɛlm 'vi:dɐ.
findet ihren Wilhelm wieder.
finds her William again.
(and finds her William again.)

[The poet was one of Schubert's schoolmates at the imperial *Stadtkonvikt*, a conservatory for the training of the boys who sang in the court choir. Schubert's lovely, touching music transfigures the naïve amd rather banal sentimentality of his friend's poem.]

li:t' / 'bry:dɐ, 'ʃrɛk'lɪç brɛnt di 'tʰrɛ:nə
Lied / Brüder, schrecklich brennt die Träne
Song / Brothers, the Tears Burn Terribly

Posthumously published [composed 1817] (author unknown)

'bry:dɐ, 'ʃrɛk'lɪç brɛnt di 'tʰrɛ:nə, di: fɛɐ̯'ʃɛ:mt'ə 'ǀarmu:t' vae̯ntʰ;
Brüder, schrecklich brennt die Träne, die verschämte Armut weint;
Brothers, terribly burns the tear, which abashed Poverty weeps;
(Brothers, the tears that abashed Poverty weeps burn terribly;)

'fɪndət 'di:zə 'jamɐstse:nə ǀʊnt'ɐ(r) ǀʊns vo:l 'kʰae̯nən frɔø̯nt'?
findet diese Jammerszene unter uns wohl keinen Freund?
finds this scene of misery among us perhaps no friend?
(is it possible that this scene of misery cannot find a friend among us?)

de:ɐ̯ fɛɐ̯'tsvae̯flʊŋ 'pʰrae̯sgəge:bən rɪŋt' di 'vɛlk'ən 'hɛndə zi:;
Der Verzweiflung preisgegeben ringt die welken Hände sie;
To the despair abandoned wrings the withered hands she;
(Abandoned to despair, she wrings her withered hands;)

kʰɔmt', lɛɐ̯'lae̯çt'ɐt' hɔø̯t' li:ɐ̯ 'le:bən dʊrç dɛs 'mɪt'lae̯ts zʏmp'atʰi:.
kommt, erleichtert heut' ihr Leben durch des Mitleids Sympathie.
come, ease today her life through the compassion's fellow feeling.
(come, ease her life today through compassionate sympathy.)

[This song was composed as a soprano solo with orchestral accompaniment. It seems to have been written for the benefit of an orphanage, where Schubert's brother—who later published an arrangement under his own name—was employed as a teacher.]

Lied (Des Lebens Tag ist schwer) see *Die Mutter Erde*

li:t' / ɛs lɪst' zo: 'langəne:m
Lied / Es ist so angenehm
Song / It Is So Pleasant

Posthumously published [composed 1815] (poem attributed to Friedrich von Schiller)

ɛs lɪst' zo: 'langəne:m, zo: zy:s, lʊm 'lae̯nən 'li:bən man t͡su: 'ʃp'i:lən,
Es ist so angenehm, so süss, um einen lieben Mann zu spielen,
It is so pleasant, so sweet, around a dear man to play,
(It is so pleasant, so sweet, to dally with a man you love,)

ɛnt't͡sʏk'ənt', vi: lae̯n pʰara'di:s, dɛs 'manəs 'fɔø̯ɐkʰʊs t͡su: 'fy:lən.
entzückend, wie ein Paradies, des Mannes Feuerkuss zu fühlen.
delightful, like a paradise, the man's fire- kiss to feel.
(delightful, like paradise, to feel the man's fiery kiss.)

jɛt͡st' vae̯s lɪç, vas mae̯n 'tʰɑo̯bənpʰa:ɐ̯ mɪt' 'zae̯nəm 'zanft'ən 'gɪrən 'za:k't'ə,
Jetzt weiss ich, was mein Taubenpaar mit seinem sanften Girren sagte,
Now know I, what my pair of doves with its gentle cooing said,
(Now I know what my pair of doves was saying with its gentle cooing,)

ʊnt' vas de:ɐ̯ 'naxt'ɪgalən ʃa:ɐ̯ zo: 't͡sɛ:ɐ̯t'lɪç zɪç lɪn 'li:dɐn 'kʰla:k't'ə.
und was der Nachtigallen Schar so zärtlich sich in Liedern klagte.
and what the nightingales' flock so tenderly itself in songs lamented.
(and what the flock of nightingales was lamenting so tenderly in song.)

jɛt͡st' vae̯s lɪç, vas mae̯n 'fɔləs hɛrt͡s lɪn 'le:vɪç 'laŋən 'nɛçt'ən 'lɛŋt'ə;
Jetzt weiss ich, was mein volles Herz in ewig langen Nächten engte;
Now know I, what my full heart in eternally long nights constricted;
(Now I know what was constricting my full heart in those long, never-ending nights;)

jɛt͡st' vae̯s lɪç, 'vɛlçɐ 'zy:sə ʃmɛrt͡s lɔft' 'zɔø̯ft͡sənt' 'mae̯nən 'bu:zən 'drɛŋt'ə;
jetzt weiss ich, welcher süsse Schmerz oft seufzend meinen Busen drängte;
now know I, which sweet pain often sighing my bosom afflicted;
(now I know which sweet pain so often afflicted my sighing bosom;)

va'rʊm kʰae̯n 'bly:mçən mi:ɐ̯ gə'fi:l, va'rʊm de:ɐ̯ mae̯ mi:ɐ̯ 'nɪmɐ 'laxt'ə,
warum kein Blümchen mir gefiel, warum der Mai mir nimmer lachte,
why no little flower me pleased, why the May for me never laughed,
(I know why no little flower ever pleased me, why May never smiled for me,)

va'rʊm de:ɐ̯ 'fø:gəl 'li:dɐʃp'i:l mɪç 'nɪmɐme:ɐ̯ tsʊr 'frɔ͜ødə 'faxt'ə.
warum der Vögel Liederspiel mich nimmermehr zur Freude fachte.
why the birds' song- play me nevermore to the joy fanned.
(why the songful play of the birds never fanned the flame of joy in me.)

mi:ɐ̯ 'tʰrɑ͜oɐt'ə di 'gantsə vɛlt', lɪç 'kʰant'ə nɪçt di 'ʃø:nst'ən 'tʰri:bə.
Mir trauerte die ganze Welt, ich kannte nicht die schönsten Triebe.
To me mourned the whole world, I knew not the most beautiful desires.
(To me the whole seemed in mourning, I did not know the most beautiful desires.)

nu:n ha:b ɪç, vas mi:ɐ̯ lɛŋst' gə'fe:lt', bə'na͜edə mɪç, na'tʰu:ɐ̯/na'tʰu:r — lɪç 'li:bə!
Nun hab' ich, was mir längst gefehlt, beneide mich, Natur — ich liebe!
Now have I, what to me so long was lacking, envy me, Nature — I love!
(Now I have what I lacked so long: envy me, Nature! — I am in love!)

[The poem was first printed in a "Ladies' Pocket-book" several years after Schiller's death. It does not appear in recent collected editions of his poetry. Schubert's strophic setting is graceful.]

li:t' / 'fɛrnə fɔn de:ɐ̯ 'gro:sn̩ ʃt'atʰ
Lied / Ferne von der grossen Stadt
Song / Far from the Big City

Posthumously published [composed 1816] (poem by Karoline Pichler)

'fɛrnə fɔn de:ɐ̯ 'gro:sən ʃt'at', nɪm mɪç lɑ͜of lɪn 'da͜enə 'ʃt'ɪlə,
Ferne von der grossen Stadt, nimm mich auf in deine Stille,
Far from the big city, take me up into your stillness,
(Far from the big city, receive me into your stillness,) [*aufnehmen* = take up, receive]

tʰa:l, das mɪt dɛs 'fry:lɪŋs 'fʏlə di na'tʰu:ɐ̯ gə'ʃmʏk't' hatʰ;
Tal, das mit des Frühlings Fülle die Natur geschmücket hat;
valley, that with the spring's abundance the nature adorned has;
(valley, that nature has adorned with spring's abundance;)
[*poem:* **mit der** (de:ɐ̯, the) **Frühlingsfülle** ('fry:lɪŋsfʏlə, spring-abundance)]

vo: kʰa͜en 'lɛrmən, kʰa͜en gə'tʰʏməl 'ma͜enən 'ʃlʊmɐ 'kʰʏrtsɐ maxt',
wo kein Lärmen, kein Getümmel meinen Schlummer kürzer macht,
where no noise-making, no tumult my slumber shorter makes,
(where no noise, no tumult shortens my sleep,)

ʊnt' la͜en 'le:vɪç 'ha͜et'rɐ 'hɪməl 'ly:bɐ 'ze:lgən 'flu:rən laxtʰ.
und ein ewig heit'rer Himmel über sel'gen Fluren lacht.
and an eternally serene sky above blissful meadows laughs.
(and an eternally serene sky is smiling above blissful meadows.)

'frɔ͜ødən, di: di 'ru:ə bɔ͜øt', vɪl lɪç 'lʊngəʃt'ø:ɐt' hi:ɐ̯ 'ʃmɛk'ən,
Freuden, die die Ruhe beut, will ich ungestört hier schmecken,
Joys, that the peace offers, want I undisturbed here to taste,
(Undisturbed I want to taste here the joys that peace and quiet offer,)

hi:ɐ̯, vo: 'bɔ͜ømə mɪç bə'dɛk'ən, lʊnt di 'lɪndə dʊft' fɛɐ̯'ʃt'rɔ͜øtʰ.
hier, wo Bäume mich bedecken, und die Linde Duft verstreut.
here, where trees me shelter, and the linden fragrance scatters.
(here, where trees give me shelter and where the linden sheds fragrance all around.)

'di:zə 'kʰvɛlə za͜e ma͜en 'ʃp'i:gəl, ma͜en pʰar'kʰɛt de:ɐ̯ 'jʊŋə kʰle:,
Diese Quelle sei mein Spiegel, mein Parkett der junge Klee,
This spring be my mirror, my parquet the young clover,
(Let this spring be my mirror, the young clover be my parquet floor,)

ʊnt de:ɐ̯ frɪʃ bə'ra:st'ə 'hy:gəl za͜e ma͜en 'gry:nəs kʰana'pʰe:.
und der frisch beras'te Hügel sei mein grünes Kanapee.
and the freshly grassed hill be my green settee.

'da͜enɐ 'mʏt'ɐlɪçən ʃp'u:ɐ̯, dem gə'zɛt͜s,
Deiner mütterlichen Spur, dem Gesetz,
Your motherly footprint, the law,
(Your motherly footprints, the law)

das 'ʔʊngərɔxən nɔx kʰa͜en 'ʃt'ɛrp'lɪçɐ gə'brɔxən, vɪl ʔɪç 'fɔlgən, ʔo: na't'u:ɐ̯!
das ungerochen noch kein Sterblicher gebrochen, will ich folgen, o Natur!
that unavenged yet no mortal (has) broken, want I to follow, O Nature!
(that, unavenged, no mortal has as yet ever broken, I want to follow, O Nature!)

a͜os dem 'dʊŋk'əln ʃo:s de:ɐ̯/de:r 'ʔe:ɐ̯dən vɪl ʔɪç 'frɔ͜ødən mi:ɐ̯/mi:r ʔɛɐ̯'t͜si:n,
Aus dem dunkeln Schoss der Erden will ich Freuden mir erziehn,
Out of the dark womb of the earth want I joys for me to raise,
(Out of the dark womb of the earth I want to raise my joys,)

ʊnt' ʔa͜os ba͜om ʔʊnt' 'blu:mə 've:ɐ̯dən 'ze:lɪçkʰa͜et'ən mi:ɐ̯/mi:r ʔɛɐ̯'bly:n.
und aus Baum und Blume werden Seligkeiten mir erblühn.
and from tree and flower will blisses for me bloom.
(and bliss will bloom for me from tree and flower.)

ma͜en t͜su'fri:dnəs hɛrt͜s ʔɛɐ̯'frɔ͜øt' ʔan den 'zɛlpst'gəp͜fle:k't'ən 'kʰa͜emən,
Mein zufried'nes Herz erfreut an den selbstgepflegten Keimen,
My contented heart rejoices in the self- tended buds,
(My contented heart rejoices in the buds that I tended myself,)

an den 'hɔfnʊŋsfɔlən 'bɔ͜ømən zɪç mɪt' 'mʊt'ɐt͜sɛ:ɐ̯t'lɪçkʰa͜etʰ.
an den hoffnungsvollen Bäumen sich mit Mutterzärtlichkeit.
in the hopeful trees itself with motherly tenderness. [*erfreut sich an* = rejoices in]
(in the trees, so full of promise, that I tended myself with motherly tenderness.)
[*poem:* **Vaterzärtlichkeit** ('fa:t'ɐt͜sɛ:ɐ̯t'lɪçkʰa͜etʰ, fatherly tenderness)]

vɛn di 'blu:mən zɪç fɛɐ̯'mɛ:lən ʔɪn de:ɐ̯ 'zɔnə 'mɪldəm lɪçt',
Wenn die Blumen sich vermählen in der Sonne mildem Licht,
When the flowers each other wed in the sun's mild light,
(When the flowers wed each other in the sun's gentle light,)

vɪl ʔɪç 'je:də 'bly:t'ə 't͜sɛ:lən, di: mi:ɐ̯ 'zy:sə frʊxt' fɛɐ̯'ʃp'rɪçtʰ.
will ich jede Blüte zählen, die mir süsse Frucht verspricht.
want I each blossom to count, which to me sweet fruit promises.
(I want to count each blossom that promises me sweet fruit.)

'ma͜enə 'bi:nənrep'u͵bli:k' 'zʊmət dɔrt' ʔɪm 'lɪndənʃat'ən,
Meine Bienenrepublik summet dort im Lindenschatten,
My bee- republic hums there in the linden-shadow,
(My republic of bees hums there in the shadow of the linden,)

brɪŋt‘ fɔn ˈbluːmənfɔlən ˈmat‘ən miːɐ̯ dɛs ˈhoːnɪçs gɔlt t͡suˈrʏkʰ;
bringt von blumenvollen Matten mir des Honigs Gold zurück;
brings from flower- full meadows to me the honey's gold back;
(brings back to me from flower-filled meadows the gold of their honey;)

a͜ɔf dɛs ˈhyːgəls ˈtʰrɔk‘nəm ˈraːzən halp‘ |ɪm ˈʃat‘ən ˈhɪngəʃt‘rɛk‘t‘,
auf des Hügels trocknem Rasen halb im Schatten hingestreckt,
on the hill's dry grass half in the shadow stretched out,
(stretched out on the dry grass of the hill, half in the shadow,)

seː ɪç ˈma͜enə ˈlɛmɐ ˈgraːzən, diː das ˈfa͜enst‘ə fliːs bəˈdɛk‘tʰ.
seh' ich meine Lämmer grasen, die das feinste Vlies bedeckt.
see I my lambs grazing, which the finest fleece covers.
(I see my lambs grazing, covered with the finest fleece.)

vɛn dʊrç fla͜es |ʊnt‘ ˈzɔnənbrant‘ fryː di ˈʃvɛçɐn ˈkʰrɛft‘ə ˈʃvɪndən,
Wenn durch Fleiss und Sonnenbrand früh die schwächern Kräfte schwinden,
When through industry and sunburn early the weaker powers disappear,
(When from hard work and sunburn my energy begins to give out,)

ruː ɪç |ɪn dɛs ˈtʰaːləs ˈgrʏndən, |an deːɐ̯ ˈfɛlzənkʰvɛlə rant‘.
ruh' ich in des Tales Gründen, an der Felsenquelle Rand.
rest I in the valley's depths, at the rocky spring's edge.
(I rest in the depths of the valley, by the edge of the rocky spring.)

ˈiːrə liːp‘ |ʊnt‘ ˈiːrən ˈkʰʊmɐ zɪŋt di ˈtʰʊrt‘əltʰa͜ɔp‘ |ɪm ha͜en,
Ihre Lieb' und ihren Kummer singt die Turteltaub' im Hain,
Her love and her sorrow sings the turtledove in the grove,
(The turtledove in the grove is singing of her love and her sorrow,)

ʊnt‘ |ɛs viːk‘t‘ |ɪn ˈzanft‘ən ˈʃlʊmɐ mɪç deːɐ̯ ˈkʰvɛlə ˈmʊrməln |a͜en.
und es wiegt in sanften Schlummer mich der Quelle Murmeln ein.
and there lulls into gentle slumber me the spring's murmuring ... .
(and the murmur of the spring lulls me into gentle slumber.) [*einwiegen* = to rock to sleep]

heːp‘t deːɐ̯ ˈmɪldə hɛrpst‘ za͜en ha͜ɔp‘t‘, mɪt dem ˈfrʏçt‘ənkʰrant͡s gəˈʃmʏk‘ət‘,
Hebt der milde Herbst sein Haupt, mit dem Früchtenkranz geschmücket,
Raises the mild autumn his head, with the fruit- wreath adorned,
(The mild Autumn raises his head, adorned with a wreath of fruits,)

a͜ɔs den ˈfluːrən, |ʊnt‘ |ɛɐ̯ˈblɪk‘ət‘ rɪŋs di ˈgɛrt‘ən, halp‘ |ɛntˈ|la͜ɔp‘tʰ:
aus den Fluren, und erblicket rings die Gärten, halb entlaubt:
from the fields, and looks at all around the gardens, half defoliated:
(raises his head from the fields and looks about at the gardens, stripped of half their leaves:)

oː viː ˈlaːbən dan den ˈga͜ɔmən ˈtʰra͜ɔbən, diː ma͜en ˈva͜enʃt‘ɔk‘ tʰrɛːk‘t‘,
o wie laben dann den Gaumen Trauben, die mein Weinstock trägt,
oh, how refresh then the palate grapes, which my grapevine bears,
(oh, how the grapes that my grapevine bears then refresh the palate,)

ˈoːdɐ bla͜ɔ bəˈra͜eft‘ə ˈp͡fla͜ɔmən fɔn dem ba͜ɔm, deːn |ɪç gəˈp͡fleːk‘tʰ!
oder blau bereifte Pflaumen von dem Baum, den ich gepflegt!
or blue-ripened plums from the tree, which I tended!

ɛntʻlɪç, vɛn deːɐ̯ ˈnɔrtʻvɪntʻ ʃtʻʏrmt dʊrç di ˈblɛtʻɐloːzən ˈvɛldɐ
Endlich, wenn der Nordwind stürmt durch die blätterlosen Wälder
Finally, when the north wind storms through the leafless woods

ʊntʻ l͜aʊf di lɛɐ̯ˈʃtʻartʻən ˈfɛldɐ ˈgant͜sə ˈʃneːgəbɪrgə tʰʏrmtʰ,
und auf die erstarrten Felder ganze Schneegebirge türmt,
and upon the torpid fields entire snow- mountains piles up,
(and piles up entire mountains of snow upon the frozen fields,)

dan fɛɐ̯ˈkʰʏrt͜sətʻ lam kʰaˈmiːnə ˈfrɔ͜øntʻʃaftʻ miːɐ̯ di ˈvɪntʻɐnaxtʻ,
dann verkürzet am Kamine Freundschaft mir die Winternacht,
then shortens at the fireplace friendship for me the winter night,
(then friends by the fireplace shorten the winter night for me,)

bɪs, gəˈʃmʏkʻtʻ mɪtʻ ˈfrɪʃəm ˈgryːnə, nɔ͜ø deːɐ̯ ˈjʊŋə lɛnt͜s lɛɐ̯ˈvaxtʰ.
bis, geschmückt mit frischem Grüne, neu der junge Lenz erwacht.
till, adorned with fresh green, anew the young spring awakens.
(until the young Spring, adorned with fresh greenery, awakens anew.)

[Karoline Pichler was known for her literary salon in Vienna. Schubert set three of her poems. This attractive strophic song extols the joys of country living, where “an eternally serene sky smiles above blissful meadows” (perhaps Austria’s notorious “*Schnürlregen*”—continuous drizzle—was less prevalent in those days). The first and last phrases echo Mozart’s “Alleluja,” and the last also recalls Haydn’s hymn to the emperor. Eight verses are obviously too many.]

liːtʻ / ɪç bɪn fɛɐ̯ˈgnyːkʻtʰ / t͜suˈfriːdənha͜etʰ
Lied / Ich bin vergnügt / Zufriedenheit
Song / I Am Happy / Contentment

Posthumously published [two versions composed 1816] (poem by Matthias Claudius)

ɪç bɪn fɛɐ̯ˈgnyːkʻtʻ, lɪm ˈziːgəstʰoːn fɛɐ̯ˈkʰʏntʻ lɛs ma͜en gəˈdɪçtʰ,
Ich bin vergnügt, im Siegeston verkünd’ es mein Gedicht,
I am happy, in the triumph-tone proclaim it my poem,
(I am happy, let my poem proclaim that in a tone of triumph,)

ʊntʻ ˈmançɐ man mɪtʻ ˈza͜enɐ kʰroːn lʊntʻ ˈst͜sɛpʻtʻɐ(r) lɪstʻ lɛs nɪçtʰ.
und mancher Mann mit seiner Kron’ und Szepter ist es nicht.
and many a man with his crown and scepter is it not.
(and many a man with his crown and scepter is not.)

ʊntʻ vɛːɐ̯/vɛːr leːɐ̯s l͜aʊx; nuːn, ˈlɪmɐhɪn! maːkʻ leːɐ̯s! zoː lɪstʻ leːɐ̯, vas lɪç bɪn.
Und wär’ er’s auch; nun, immerhin! mag er’s! so ist er, was ich bin.
And were he it even; well, no matter! May he it (be)! then is he what I am.
(And even if he were: well, why not? Let him be happy! Then he will be as I am.)
[*first version:* **mag er’s doch** (dɔx, after all)**! so ist er was ich bin**]

dɛs ˈzʊltʻaːns pʰraxt, dɛs ˈmoːgʊls gɛlt, dɛs glʏkʻ, viː hiːs leːɐ̯ dɔx,
Des Sultans Pracht, des Moguls Geld, des Glück, wie hiess er doch,
The sultan’s splendor, the mogul’s money, his luck, how is called he however,
(The sultan’s splendor, the mogul’s money, his luck—oh, what was his name?—)

de:ɐ̯/de:r, ǀals ǀe:ɐ̯ hɛr va:ɐ̯ fɔn de:ɐ̯ vɛlt, t͡sʊm mo:nt‘ hɪ'na͡of za: nɔx?
der, als er Herr war von der Welt, zum Mond hinauf sah noch?
who, when he lord was of the world, to the moon up looked still?
(the one who, when he was master of the earth, still looked up covetously at the moon?)

ɪç 'vʏnʃə nɪçt͡s fɔn 'ǀalə de:m, t͡su: 'lɛçəln drɔp‘ fɛlt‘ mi:ɐ̯ bə'kʰve:m.
Ich wünsche nichts von alle dem, zu lächeln drob fällt mir bequem.
I wish nothing of all that, to smile at it falls to me comfortably.
(I wish for none of all that; to smile at it comes easily to me.)

[t͡su'fri:dən za͡en, das ǀɪst‘ ma͡en ʃp‘rʊx! vas hʏlf mi:ɐ̯ gɛlt‘ ǀʊnt‘ ǀe:ɐ̯?
[Zufrieden sein, das ist mein Spruch! Was hülf' mir Geld und Ehr'?
[Contented to be, that is my motto! What would help me money and honor?
[(To be contented, that is my motto! What help would money and honor be to me?)

das, vas ǀɪç ha:p‘, ǀɪst‘ mi:ɐ̯ gə'nu:k‘, ve:ɐ̯ kʰlu:k‘ ǀɪst‘, vʏnʃt‘ nɪçt‘ ze:ɐ̯;
Das, was ich hab', ist mir genug, wer klug ist, wünscht nicht sehr;
That which I have is for me enough; (he) who wise is, wishes not very (much);
(What I have is enough for me; the wise man does not wish for very much;)

dɛn, vas man 'vʏnʃət‘, vɛn mans hat‘, zo: ǀɪst‘ man 'da:rʊm dɔx nɪçt‘ zatʰ.
denn, was man wünschet, wenn man's hat, so ist man darum doch nicht satt.
for what one wishes, when one it has, then is one for that yet not satisfied.
(for when one has what one wished for, one is nevertheless still not satisfied.)

ʊnt‘ gɛlt‘ ǀʊnt‘ ǀe:ɐ̯/ǀe:r ǀɪst‘ 'ǀo:bəndra͡of ǀa͡en ze:ɐ̯ t͡sɛɐ̯'brɛçlɪç gla:s.
Und Geld und Ehr' ist obendrauf ein sehr zerbrechlich Glas.
And money and honor is furthermore a very fragile glass.
(And, furthermore, money and honor are like a very fragile piece of glass.)

de:ɐ̯ 'dɪŋə 'vʊndɐba:rɐ la͡of, (ǀɛɐ̯'fa:rʊŋ 'le:rət das)
Der Dinge wunderbarer Lauf, (Erfahrung lehret das)
The things' amazing course (experience teaches that)
(The surprising course of events—experience teaches us this—)

fɛɐ̯-/fɛr'ǀɛndɐt‘ 've:nɪç ǀɔft‘ ǀɪn fi:l, ǀʊnt‘ zɛt͡st dem 'ra͡eçən man za͡en t͡si:l.
verändert wenig oft in viel, und setzt dem reichen Mann sein Ziel.
changes little often into much, and sets for the rich man his limit.
(often changes little into much, and curbs the rich man.)

[*einem ein Ziel setzen* = to curb someone]

rɛçt tʰu:n ǀʊnt‘ 'ǀe:dəl za͡en ǀʊnt‘ gu:t‘, ǀɪst‘ me:ɐ̯/me:r ǀals gɛlt‘ ǀʊnt‘ ǀe:ɐ̯;
Recht tun und edel sein und gut, ist mehr als Geld und Ehr';
Right to do and noble to be and good, is more than money and honor;
(To do the right thing, to be noble and good, that is worth more than money and honor;)

da: hat‘ man 'ǀɪmɐ 'gu:t‘ən mu:t‘ ǀʊnt‘ 'frɔ͡ødə ǀʊm zɪç he:ɐ̯,
da hat man immer guten Mut und Freude um sich her,
then has one always good courage and joy around oneself hither,
(then one has always good humor and joy all around one,)

ʊnt' man |ɪst' ʃt'ɔlts, |ʊnt' mɪt' zɪç |a͜ens, ʃɔ͜øt' kʰa͜en gəˈʃœpf |ʊnt' ˈfʏrçt'ət' kʰa͜ens.
und man ist stolz, und mit sich eins, scheut kein Geschöpf und fürchtet keins.
and one is proud and with oneself one, shuns no creature and fears none.
(and one is proud and at one with oneself, shuns no creature and fears none.)

ɪç bɪn fɛɐˈgny:k't'... mɪt' |a͜enɐ kʰro:n...]
Ich bin vergnügt... (same as first stanza except:) **mit einer Kron...]**
I am happy... with a crown...]

[The text is a paraphrase in German of the English poem by Sir Edward Dyer, "My mind to me a kingdom is." Schubert made two settings, both in the *Gesamtausgabe*, which prints all six verses with the later version, but only the first two with the earlier (since the last lines of the third, fourth, and fifth stanzas do not fit the music). If two verses suffice, the first version is the better.]

li:t' / ɪns ˈʃt'ɪlə lant'
Lied / Ins stille Land
Song / Into the Quiet Land

Posthumously published [composed 1816] (poem by Johann Gaudenz von Salis-Seewis)

ɪns ˈʃt'ɪlə lant'! ve:ɐ̯ ˈla͜et'ət' |ʊns hɪˈny:bɐ?
Ins stille Land! Wer leitet uns hinüber?
Into the quiet land! Who leads us over to the other side?
(Into the quiet land! Who will lead us over into it?)

ʃo:n vœlk't' zɪç |ʊns de:ɐ̯/de:r |a:bənt'hɪməl ˈtʰry:bɐ,
Schon wölkt sich uns der Abendhimmel trüber,
Already clouds itself for us the evening sky more gloomily,
(Already the evening sky is clouding over and growing more gloomy for us,)

ʊnt' |ɪmɐ ˈtʰrʏmɐfɔlɐ vɪrt de:ɐ̯ ʃt'rant'.
und immer trümmervoller wird der Strand.
and ever wreakage-fuller becomes the shore.
(and the shore is ever more littered with wreakage.)

ve:ɐ̯ ˈla͜et'ət' |ʊns mɪt' ˈzanft'ɐ hant' hɪˈny:bɐ(r), |ax! hɪˈny:bɐ(r) |ɪns ˈʃt'ɪlə lant'?
Wer leitet uns mit sanfter Hand hinüber, ach! hinüber ins stille Land?
Who leads us with gentle hand over, ah! over into the quiet land?
(Ah, whose gentle hand will lead us over, over into the quiet land?)

ɪns ˈʃt'ɪlə lant'! t͜su: |ɔ͜øç, |i:ɐ̯ ˈfra͜eən ˈrɔ͜ømə fy:ɐ̯ di fɛɐ̯-/fɛrˈle:dlʊŋ!
Ins stille Land! zu euch, ihr freien Räume für die Veredlung!
Into the quiet land! to you, you free spaces for the ennobling!
(Into the quiet land! Onward to you, free spaces where the soul can strive toward ennoblement!)

ˈt͜sa:ɐ̯t'ə ˈmɔrgəntʰrɔ͜ømə de:ɐ̯ ˈʃø:nən ˈze:lən! ˈkʰʏnft'gən ˈda:za͜ens p͜fant'.
zarte Morgenträume der schönen Seelen! Künft'gen Daseins Pfand.
delicate morning dreams of the beautiful souls! Future existence's pledge.
(Tender morning dreams of beautiful souls! Pledge of a future existence.
[*Peters:* **zarte Morgenträume, der schönen Seelen künft'gen Daseins Pfand]**
[(Tender morning dreams, the beautiful souls' pledge of a future existence)]

veːɐ̯ tʰrɔ͜ø dɛs ˈleːbəns kʰampf̮ bəˈʃtant, tʰrɛːkʻtʻ ˈza͜enɐ ˈhɔfnʊŋ ˈkʰa͜emə
Wer treu des Lebens Kampf bestand, trägt seiner Hoffnung Keime
(He) who staunchly the life's battle endured, bears his hope's buds
(He who has staunchly endured life's battle bears the buds of hope)

lɪns ˈʃtʻɪlə lantʻ. ax lantʻ! lax lantʻ fyːɐ̯/fyːr ˈlalə ˈʃtʻʊrmbədroːtʻən!
ins stille Land. Ach Land! ach Land für alle Sturmbedrohten!
into the quiet land. Ah land! ah land for all storm-threatened!
(into the quiet land. Ah, land! Ah, land for all who are threatened by storms!)

deːɐ̯ ˈmɪldəstʻə fɔn ˈlʊnzɐs ˈʃɪkʻzaːls ˈboːtʻən vɪŋkʻtʻ lʊns,
Der mildeste von unsers Schicksals Boten winkt uns,
The mildest of our fate's messengers beckons us,

di ˈfakʻəl ˈlʊmgəvantʻ, lʊntʻ ˈla͜etʻətʻ lʊns mɪtʻ ˈzanftʻɐ hantʻ
die Fackel umgewandt, und leitet uns mit sanfter Hand
the torch inverted, and leads us with gentle hand
(his torch inverted,* and leads us with his gentle hand)
[*the annunciator of death is often depicted in art with an inverted (extinguished) torch]

lɪns lant deːɐ̯ ˈgroːsən ˈtʰoːtʻən, lɪns ˈʃtʻɪlə lantʻ.
ins Land der grossen Toten, ins stille Land.
into the land of the great dead, into the quiet land.

[Schubert made two very similar versions of this strophic song, the second a tone higher, both haunting. He used the melody again in his best-known setting of "*Nur wer die Sehnsucht kennt.*"]

liːtʻ / ˈmʊtʻɐ geːt dʊrç ˈliːrə ˈkʰamɐn / liːtʻ la͜os lʊnˈdiːnə
Lied / Mutter geht durch ihre Kammern / Lied aus "Undine"
Song / Mother Goes Through Her Rooms / Song from *Undine*

Posthumously published [composed 1816] (poem by Friedrich de la Motte Fouqué)

ˈmʊtʻɐ geːt dʊrç ˈliːrə ˈkʰamɐn, rɔ͜ømt di ˈʃrɛŋkʻə la͜en lʊntʻ la͜os, zuːxtʻ,
Mutter geht durch ihre Kammern, räumt die Schränke ein und aus, sucht,
Mother goes through her rooms, clears the cupboards in and out, seeks,
(Mother goes through her rooms, clearing out the cupboards and putting things back; searching)

lʊntʻ va͜es nɪçtʻ vas, mɪtʻ ˈjamɐn, ˈfɪndətʻ nɪçts lals ˈleːrəs ha͜os.
und weiss nicht was, mit Jammern, findet nichts als leeres Haus.
and knows not what, with misery, finds nothing but empty house.
(in misery, not knowing for what, and finding nothing but an empty house.)

ˈleːrəs ha͜os! loː vɔrt deːɐ̯ ˈkʰlaːgə, deːm, deːɐ̯/deːɐ̯ la͜enstʻ
Leeres Haus! O Wort der Klage, dem, der einst
Empty house! O word of the lament, for whom, who once
Empty house! O word of lamentation for one who once)

la͜en ˈhɔldəs kʰɪntʻ drɪn gəˈgɛŋəltʻ hatʻ lam ˈtʰaːgə,
ein holdes Kind drin gegängelt hat am Tage,
a dear child inside led by the hand has in the day, [*gängeln* = toddle; lead by the hand]
(inside that house in the daytime has led by the hand a dear child that was learning to walk,)

drɪn gəˈviːk‘t‘ ɪn ˈnɛçt‘ən lɪnt‘. ˈviːdɐ ˈgryːnən voːl di ˈbuːxən,
drin gewiegt in Nächten lind. Wieder grünen wohl die Buchen,
inside rocked in nights gently. Again grow green probably the beech trees,
(at night has gently rocked it. Once again the beech trees will probably grow green;)

ˈviːdɐ kʰɔmt deːɐ̯ ˈzɔnə lɪçt‘, ˈlaːbɐ, ˈmʊt‘ɐ, las da͜en ˈzuːxən,
wieder kommt der Sonne Licht, aber, Mutter, lass dein Suchen,
again comes the sun's light, but, mother, leave your searching,
(the light of the sun will return; but, mother, stop your searching:)

ˈviːdɐ kʰɔmt da͜en ˈliːbəs nɪçtʰ.
wieder kommt dein Liebes nicht.
again comes your dear not.
(your dear child will not come back again.)

ʊnt‘ vɛn ˈlaːbənt‘lʏft‘ə ˈfɛçəln, ˈfaːt‘ɐ ha͜em t͜sʊm ˈheːɐ̯də kʰeːɐ̯t‘,
Und wenn Abendlüfte fächeln, Vater heim zum Herde Kehrt,
And when evening breezes fan, father home to the hearth returns,
(And when the evening breezes blow and father returns home to the hearth,)

reːk‘t‘ sɪçs fast‘ ɪn liːm, viː ˈlɛçəln, dran dɔx gla͜eç di ˈtʰrɛːnə t͜seːɐ̯tʰ.
regt sich's fast in ihm, wie Lächeln, dran doch gleich die Träne zehrt.
stirs itself it almost in him like smiling, thereat though at once the tear consumes.
(something almost like a smile starts to stir in him, followed at once by a burning tear.)

ˈfaːt‘ɐ va͜es, ɪn ˈza͜enən ˈt͜sɪmɐn ˈfɪndət‘ leːɐ̯ di ˈtʰoːdəsruː,
Vater weiss, in seinen Zimmern findet er die Todesruh,
Father knows, in his rooms finds he the stillness of death,
(Father knows that in his rooms he will find the stillness of death,)

høːɐ̯t‘ nuːɐ̯ ˈbla͜eçɐ ˈmʊt‘ɐ ˈvɪmɐn lʊnt‘ kʰa͜en ˈkʰɪnt‘la͜en laxt‘ liːm t͜suː.
hört nur bleicher Mutter Wimmern und kein Kindlein lacht ihm zu.
hears only pale mother's whimpering and no little child laughs to him at.
(he will hear only the whimpering of a pale mother, and no little child will be smiling at him.)

[The text of this plaintive strophic song is taken from *Undine*, a famous romantic fairy tale.]

liːt‘ la͜os deːɐ̯ ˈfɛrnə

Lied aus der Ferne

Song From Afar

Posthumously published [composed 1814] (poem by Friedrich von Matthisson)

vɛn ɪn dɛs ˈlaːbənt͜s ˈlɛt͜st‘əm ˈʃa͜enə diːɐ̯/diːr ˈla͜enə ˈlɛçəlndə gəˈʃt‘alt‘,
Wenn in des Abends letztem Scheine dir eine lächelnde Gestalt,
When in the evening's last gleam to you a smiling form,
(When in the last glow of evening a smiling form)

lam ˈraːzənzɪt͜s lɪm ˈla͜eçənha͜enə, mɪt‘ vɪŋk‘ lʊnt‘ gruːs foˈryːbɐ valtʰ,
am Rasensitz im Eichenhaine, mit Wink und Gruss vorüber wallt,
at the grassy seat in the oak grove, with wave and greeting past floats,
(floats past you with a wave and a greeting, by the grassy seat in the oak grove,)

das lɪst dɛs ˈfrɔ͜øndəs ˈtʰrɔ͜øɐ ga͜est, deːɐ̯ frɔ͜øtʻ lʊntʻ ˈfriːdən diːɐ̯ fɛɐ̯ˈha͜estʰ.
das ist des Freundes treuer Geist, der Freud' und Frieden dir verheisst.
that is the friend's faithful spirit, who joy and peace to you promises.
(that is the faithful spirit of your friend, who promises you joy and peace.)

vɛn lɪn dɛs ˈmoːndəs ˈdɛmɐlɪçtʻə zɪç ˈda͜enɐ ˈliːbə tʰra͜om fɛɐ̯ˈʃøːnt,
Wenn in des Mondes Dämmerlichte sich deiner Liebe Traum verschönt,
When in the moon's dim light itself your love's dream beautifies,
(When in the dim moonlight your dream of love becomes more beautiful,)

dʊrç ˈt͜syːtʻizʊs lʊntʻ ˈveːmuːt͜sfɪçtʻə meˈloːdɪʃəs gəˈzɔ͜øzəl tʰøːntʰ,
durch Zytisus und Wehmutsfichte melodisches Gesäusel tönt,
through cytisus and melancholy spruce melodious murmuring sounds,
(when a melodious murmur sounds through the broom shrubs and the melancholy spruce,)

ʊntʻ ˈlaːnʊŋ diːɐ̯ den ˈbuːzən heːpʻtʰ: das lɪstʻ ma͜en ga͜est, deːɐ̯ dɪç lʊmˈʃveːpʻtʰ.
und Ahnung dir den Busen hebt: das ist mein Geist, der dich umschwebt.
and presentiment in you the bosom lifts: that is my spirit, that you about-hovers.
(and a presentiment lifts your bosom: that will be my spirit, that hovers about you.)

fyːlst duː, ba͜em ˈzeːlɪgən fɛɐ̯ˈliːrən lɪn dɛs fɛɐ̯ˈgaŋnən ˈt͜sa͜obɐlantʻ,
Fühlst du, beim seligen Verlieren in des Vergangnen Zauberland,
Feel you, in the blissful being lost in the past's magic- land,
(If you feel, when you are blissfully lost in memories of the enchanted land of the past,)

la͜en ˈlɪndəs, ˈga͜estʻɪgəs bəˈryːrən, viː ˈt͜seːfyːɐ̯s kʰʊs lan lɪpʻ lʊntʻ hantʻ,
ein lindes, geistiges Berühren, wie Zephyrs Kuss an Lipp' und Hand,
a gentle, spiritual touching, like Zephyrus' kiss on lip and hand,
(a gentle, spiritual touch, like the kiss of the west wind on your lips and on your hand,)

ʊntʻ vaŋkʻt deːɐ̯ ˈkʰɛrt͜sə ˈflatʻɐntʻ lɪçtʰ: das lɪstʻ ma͜en ga͜estʻ, loː ˈt͜sva͜eflə nɪçtʰ!
und wankt der Kerze flatternd Licht: das ist mein Geist, o zweifle nicht!
and wavers the candle's fluttering light: that is my spirit, oh doubt not!
(and if the candle flame flickers: that will be my spirit, oh, do not doubt that!)

høːɐ̯st duː, ba͜em ˈzɪlbɐglant͜s deːɐ̯ ˈʃtʻɛrnə, la͜es lɪm fɛɐ̯ˈʃviːgnən ˈkʰɛmɐla͜en,
Hörst du, beim Silberglanz der Sterne, leis' im verschwiegnen Kämmerlein,
Hear you, in the silvery splendor of the stars, softly in the discreet little chamber,
(If you hear, in your discreet bed-chamber, softly, when the stars are shining in silvery splendor,)

gla͜eç ˈlɛːɔlsharfən la͜os deːɐ̯ ˈfɛrnə, das ˈbʊndəsvɔrtʻ: la͜of ˈleːvɪç da͜en!
gleich Äolsharfen aus der Ferne, das Bundeswort: Auf ewig dein!
like aeolian harps from the distance, the word of union: "For ever yours!"
(like the sound from afar of aeolian harps, the words that seal our union, "Forever yours,")

dan ˈʃlʊmrə zanftʻ; lɛs lɪstʻ ma͜en ga͜est, deːɐ̯ frɔ͜øtʻ lʊntʻ ˈfriːdən diːɐ̯ fɛɐ̯ˈha͜estʰ.
Dann schlummre sanft; es ist mein Geist, der Freud' und Frieden dir verheisst.
Then sleep sweetly; it is my spirit that joy and peace to you promises.
(then sleep sweetly; it is my spirit that promises you joy and peace.)

[Schubert made two settings of this poem; the *Gesamtausgabe* prints only the first, the *Neue Schubert Ausgabe*, Volume 7, offers both. The second version is one tone lower, and simpler, omitting the variants among the verses (two added bars, with sixteenth-note figurations for the piano, in the second and third verses, three different notes before the *fermata* in the fourth, and a variation in the interludes and postlude). The tone is cheerful, cozy, and far from supernatural.]

liːt deːɐ̯ ˈlanə la͜el / liːt deːɐ̯ ˈlana la͜el
Lied der Anne Lyle / Lied der Anna Lyle
The Song of Annot Lyle

Op. 85, No. 1 [1825?] (poem by Andrew MacDonald, used by Sir Walter Scott)

vɛːɐ̯st duː ba͜e miːɐ̯/miːr ɪm ˈleːbənstʰaːl, gɛrn vɔltʻ ɪç ˈaləs mɪt diːɐ̯ ˈtʰa͜elən;
Wärst du bei mir im Lebenstal, gern wollt' ich alles mit dir teilen;
Were you with me in the life- valley, gladly would I all with you share;
(If you were with me here in life's valley, I would gladly share everything with you;)
[*MacDonald:* Wert thou, like, me, in life's low vale, with thee how blest, that lot I share;]

mɪt diːɐ̯ t͜suː fliːn vɛːɐ̯ ˈla͜eçtʻə vaːl, ba͜e ˈmɪldəm vɪntʻ, ba͜e ˈʃtʻʊrməs ˈhɔ͜ølən.
mit dir zu flieh'n wär' leichte Wahl, bei mildem Wind, bei Sturmes Heulen.
with you to flee were easy choice, by mild wind, by storm's howling.
(to fly with you would be an easy choice, whether by mild wind or in a raging gale.)
[*M:* with thee I'd fly wherever gale could waft, or bounding galley bear.]

dɔx tʰrɛntʻ lʊns ˈhartʻə ˈʃɪkʻzaːlsmaxtʻ, lʊns lɪstʻ nɪçtʻ ˈgla͜eçəs loːs gəˈʃriːbən,
Doch trennt uns harte Schicksalsmacht, uns ist nicht gleiches Los geschrieben,
But separates us hard fate's power, for us is not same lot written,
(But the power of severe Fate parted us; the same lot was not decreed for both of us:)
[*M:* But parted by severe decree, far different must our fortunes prove;]

ma͜en glʏkʻ lɪstʰ, vɛn diːɐ̯ ˈfrɔ͜ødə laxtʰ, lɪç va͜en lʊntʻ ˈbeːtʻə fyːɐ̯ den ˈleːbən.
mein Glück ist, wenn dir Freude lacht, ich wein' und bete für den Lieben.
my happiness is, when for you joy laughs, I weep and pray for the dear one.
(my happiness is when joy smiles upon you; I weep and pray for my dear one.)
[*M:* may thine by joy — enough for me to weep and pray for him I love.]

ɛs vɪrtʻ ma͜en ˈtʰøːrɪçtʻ hɛrt͜s fɛɐ̯ˈgeːn, vɛns ˈlalə ˈhɔfnʊŋ ziːtʻ fɛɐ̯ˈʃvɪndən,
Es wird mein Töricht' Herz vergeh'n, wenn's alle Hoffnung sieht verschwinden,
There will my foolish heart perish, when it all hope sees disappear,
(My foolish heart will die when it sees all hope disappear,)
[*M:* The pangs this foolish heart must feel, when hope shall be for ever flown,]

dɔx zɔls niː ˈza͜enən graːm gəˈʃtʻeːn, niː ˈmʏrɪʃ ˈkʰlaːgəntʻ liːn fɛɐ̯ˈkʰʏndən.
doch soll's nie seinen Gram gesteh'n, nie mürrisch klagend ihn verkünden.
but shall it never its grief confess, never sullenly lamenting it make known.
(but it shall never confess its grief, never sullenly lamenting make it known.)
[*M:* no sullen murmur shall reveal, no selfish murmurs ever own.]

ʊnt drʏkʻt dɛs ˈleːbəns last das hɛrt͜s, zɔl niː den ˈmatʻən blɪkʻ ziː ˈtʰryːbən,
Und drückt des Lebens Last das Herz, soll nie den matten Blick sie trüben,
And oppresses the life's burden the heart, shall never the lifeless look it dim,
(And if the burden of life weighs down my heart, it shall never dim my look or make it lifeless,)
[*M:* Nor will I through life's weary years, like a pale drooping mourner move,]

zoː ˈlaŋə maen ɡəˈhaemɐ ʃmɛrts, laen ˈkʰʊmɐ ˈvɛːrə fyːɐ̯ den ˈliːbən.
so lange mein geheimer Schmerz, ein Kummer wäre für den Lieben.
as long (as) my secret pain, a sorrow were for the dear one.
(as long as my secret pain would be a sorrow to my dear one.)
[*M:* While I can think my secret tears may wound the heart of him I love.]

[Sir Walter Scott took the poem from *Love and Loyalty*, a comedy by Andrew MacDonald, and gave it to his character Annot Lyle, the lost daughter of the Knight of Ardenvohr in *A Legend of Montrose*, since, according to Scott, "it expressed her feelings." The German translation has been attributed to Sofie May, but no copy has been found in any German or Austrian library.]

liːt deːɐ̯ ˈliːbə
Lied der Liebe
Song of Love

Posthumously published [composed 1814] (poem by Friedrich von Matthisson)

dʊrç ˈfɪçtʻən lam ˈhyːɡəl, dʊrç ˈlɛrlən lam bax,
Durch Fichten am Hügel, durch Erlen am Bach,
Through fir trees on the hill, through alders by the brook,

fɔlkʻtʻ ˈlɪmɐ daen ˈbɪltʻnɪs, duː ˈtʰrɑotʻə! miːɐ̯ naːx; lɛs ˈlɛçəltʻ baltʻ ˈliːbə,
folgt immer dein Bildnis, du Traute! mir nach; es lächelt bald Liebe,
follows always your image, you dear one! me after; it smiles now love,
(your image always follows after me, dear one! It smiles at me, now a look of love,)
[*poem:* **bald Wehmut** (ˈveːmuːtʻ, melancholy)]

lɛs ˈlɛçəltʻ baltʻ ruː, lɪm ˈfrɔ͜øntʻlɪçən ˈʃɪmɐ dɛs ˈmoːndəs miːɐ̯ tsuː.
es lächelt bald Ruh', im freundlichen Schimmer des Mondes mir zu.
it smiles now peace, in the friendly shimmer of the moon to me at.
(now a look of peace, in the friendly shimmer of the moon.) [*zulächeln* = to smile at]

den ˈroːzənʃtʻrɔ͜øçən dɛs ˈɡartʻəns
Den Rosengesträuchen des Gartens
From the rose bushes of the garden

lɛntʻˈvaltʻ lɪm ˈɡlantsə deːɐ̯ ˈfryːə di ˈhɔldə ɡəˈʃtʻaltʰ; ziː ʃveːpʻtʻ
entwallt im Glanze der Frühe die holde Gestalt; sie schwebt
floats out in the radiance of the early morning the lovely form; it hovers
(the lovely form floats out in the radiance of the early morning; it floats)

lɑos deːɐ̯ ˈbɛrɡə bəˈpʰʊrpʻʊrtʻən floːɐ̯ ɡlaeç ˈlaenəm leˈlyːzɪʃən ˈʃatʻən hɛɐ̯ˈfoːɐ̯.
aus der Berge bepurpurtem Flor gleich einem elysischen Schatten hervor.
out of the mountains' purpled crepe like an Elysian shade forth.
(like an Elysian shade out of the purple that veils the distant mountains,)

ɔftʻ haːb lɪç lɪm ˈtʰrɑomə, lals ˈʃøːnstʻə deːɐ̯ ˈfeːən, [tʰrɑom] [di]
Oft hab' ich im Traume, als schönste der Feen, [*poem:* **im Traum, als die schönste]**
Often have I in the dream, as loveliest of the fairies, [dream] [the]
(I have often seen you in my dreams as the loveliest of the fairies,)

lɑ͜of ˈgɔldənəm ˈtʰroːnə dɪç ˈʃt‘raːlən gəˈzeːn; lɔft‘ hab ɪç,
auf goldenem Throne dich strahlen geseh'n; oft hab' ich,
on golden throne you radiating seen; often have I,
(seen you radiant on a golden throne; often I have)

t͜sʊm ˈhoːən loˈlʏmp‘ʊs lɛntˈt͜sʏk‘t‘, lals ˈheːbə dɪç ˈlʊnt‘ɐ den ˈgœt‘ɐn lɛɐ̯ˈblɪk‘tʰ.
zum hohen Olympus entzückt, als Hebe dich unter den Göttern erblickt.
to the high Olympus transported, as Hebe you among the gods glimpsed.
(glimpsed you, transported to high Olympus, as Hebe, goddess of youth, among the gods.)

miːɐ̯ halt‘ lɑ͜os den ˈtʰiːfən, miːɐ̯ halt‘ fɔn den høːn, da͜en ˈhɪmlɪʃɐ ˈnaːmə
Mir hallt aus den Tiefen, mir hallt von den Höh'n, dein himmlischer Name
To me sounds from the depths, to me sounds from the heights, your heavenly name
(Your heavenly name comes resounding to me from the depths and from the heights,)

viː ˈsfɛːrəngətʰøːn. lɪç ˈvɛːnə den hɑ͜ox, deːɐ̯ di ˈblyːt‘ən lʊmˈveːp‘t‘,
wie Sphärengetön. Ich wähne den Hauch, der die Blüten umwebt,
like music of the spheres. I imagine the breath, which the blossoms around-weaves,
(like the music of the spheres. I imagine the breeze that stirs the blossoms)

fɔn ˈda͜enɐ meˈloːdɪʃən ˈʃt‘ɪmə dʊrçˈbeːp‘tʰ. lɪn ˈha͜elɪgɐ ˈmɪt‘ɐnaxt͜sʃt‘ʊndə
von deiner melodischen Stimme durchbebt. In heiliger Mitternachtsstunde
by your melodious voice through-trembled. In holy midnight- hour
(to be trembling with the vibrations of your melodious voice. At the sacred hour of midnight)

dʊrçˈkʰra͜est dɛs ˈlɛːt‘ɐs gəˈfɪldə ma͜en ˈlaːnəndɐ ga͜estʰ.
durchkreist des Äthers Gefilde mein ahnender Geist.
through-circles the ether's fields my intuiting spirit.
(my intuitive spirit circles through ethereal domains.)

gəˈliːp‘t‘ə! dɔrt‘ vɪŋk‘t‘ lʊns la͜en lant‘,
Geliebte! dort winkt uns ein Land,
Beloved! there beckons to us a land,
(Beloved, there a land is beckoning to us)

voː deːɐ̯ frɔ͜ønt‘ lɑ͜of ˈleːvɪç deːɐ̯ ˈfrɔ͜øndɪn zɪç ˈviːdɐ fɛɐ̯-/fɛrˈla͜entʰ.
wo der Freund auf ewig der Freundin sich wieder vereint.
where the (male) friend for ever to the (female) friend himself again unites.
(where the lover will be forever united again with his beloved.)

di ˈfrɔ͜ødə, ziː ˈʃvɪndət‘, lɛs ˈdɑ͜oɐt‘ kʰa͜en la͜et‘; di ˈjaːrə fɛɐ̯ˈrɑ͜oʃən
Die Freude, sie schwindet, es dauert kein Leid; die Jahre verrauschen
The joy, it disappears, there lasts no sorrow; the years pass away
(Joy disappears, no sorrow is lasting; the years pass away)

lɪm ˈʃt‘roːmə deːɐ̯ t͜sa͜et‘; di ˈzɔnə vɪrt‘ ˈʃt‘ɛrbən, di ˈleːɐ̯də fɛɐ̯ˈgeːn:
im Strome der Zeit; die Sonne wird sterben, die Erde vergeh'n:
in the stream of the time; the sun will die, the earth perish:
(in the stream of time; the sun will die, the earth will perish:)

dɔx ˈliːbə mʊs ˈleːvɪç lʊnt‘ ˈleːvɪç bəˈʃt‘eːn.
doch Liebe muss ewig und ewig besteh'n.
but love must ever and ever endure.
(but love must endure for ever and ever.)

[The first four verses of Schubert's setting are identical; the fifth, in total contrast, is treated as recitative; and the last returns to the charming earlier melody, with a flatted note on the word "*sterben*" for a touch of pathos, and a more elaborate accompaniment. Hebe was the cup-bearer of the gods on Mount Olympus. Elysium was the home of happy spirits—"shades"—after death.]

Lied der Mignon see *Heiss mich nicht reden,*
Nur wer die Sehnsucht kennt,
So lass mich scheinen

li:t dɛs gəˈfaŋənən ˈjɛ:gɐs
Lied des gefangenen Jägers
The Lay of the Imprisoned Huntsman
(From Sir Walter Scott's *The Lady of the Lake*)

Op. 52, No. 7 [1825] (German translation by Adam Storck)

maen rɔs zo: my:tʻ ǀɪn dem ˈʃtʻalə zɪç ˈʃtʻe:tʻ, maen falkʻ
Mein Ross so müd' in dem Stalle sich steht, mein Falk'
My horse so weary in the stall itself stands, my falcon
(My horse is so weary of standing in the stall, my falcon)
[*sich müde stehen* = to tire oneself out with standing]

ǀɪst de:ɐ̯ kʰapʻ ǀʊnt de:ɐ̯ ˈʃtʻaŋə zo: laetʻ, maen ˈmy:sɪgəs ˈvɪntʻʃpʻi:l
ist der Kapp' und der Stange so leid, mein müssiges Windspiel
is of the hood and the perch so sorry, my idle greyhound
(is so sick of hood and perch, my idle greyhound)

zaen ˈfʊtʻɐ fɛɐ̯ˈʃmɛ:tʻ, ǀʊntʻ mɪç kʰrɛŋkʻt dɛs ˈtʰʊrməs ˈǀaenza:mkʰaetʰ.
sein Futter verschmäht, und mich kränkt des Turmes Einsamkeit.
his food disdains, and me offends the tower's solitude.
(disdains his food, and the solitude of this tower offends me.)

ax, vɛ:r ɪç nu:ɐ̯, vo: ǀɪç tsuˈfo:ɐ̯ bɪn gəˈve:zən, di ˈhɪrʃja:kʻtʻ ˈvɛ:rə
Ach, wär' ich nur, wo ich zuvor bin gewesen, die Hirschjagd wäre
Ah, were I only where I before have been, the stag hunt would be
(Ah, if only I were where I was before, the stag hunt would be)

zo: rɛçtʻ maen ˈve:zən, den ˈblu:tʻhʊntʻ lo:s, gəˈʃpʻant den ˈbo:gən:
so recht mein Wesen, den Bluthund los, gespannt den Bogen:
so fittingly my nature, the bloodhound free, bent the bow:
(so fitting to my nature, the bloodhound running free, the bow bent and ready:)

ja:, ˈzɔlçəm ˈle:bən bɪn ǀɪç gəˈvo:gən! ǀɪç ˈhasə de:ɐ̯ ˈtʰʊrmǀu:ɐ̯ ˈʃlɛ:frɪgən kʰlaŋ,
ja, solchem Leben bin ich gewogen! Ich hasse der Turmuhr schläfrigen Klang,
yes, for such a life am I well disposed! I hate the steeple clock's drowsy chime,
(yes, I am well disposed toward such a life! I hate the drowsy chime of the steeple clock,)

ɪç ma:kʻ nɪçtʻ ze:n, vi: di tsaetʻ fɛɐ̯ˈʃtʻraeçtʻ, vɛn tsɔl ǀʊm tsɔl
ich mag nicht seh'n, wie die Zeit verstreicht, wenn Zoll um Zoll
I like not to see how the time elapses, when inch by inch
(I do not like to see how time slips by, when inch by inch)

di 'mɑ̯oɐ(r) lɛnt''laŋ de:ɐ̯ 'zɔnənʃt'ra:l zo: 'laŋza:m ʃlɑ̯eçtʰ.
die Mauer entlang der Sonnenstrahl so langsam schleicht.
the wall along the sunbeam so slowly crawls.
(the sunbeam crawls so slowly along the wall.)

zɔnst' 'pfle:k't'ə di 'lɛrçə den 'mɔrgən t̯su: 'brɪŋən,
Sonst pflegte die Lerche den Morgen zu bringen,
At other times used the lark the morning to bring,
(At other times the lark used to bring the morning,)

di 'dʊŋk'lə 'do:lə t̯sʊr ru: mɪç t̯su: 'zɪŋən;
die dunkle Dohle zur Ruh' mich zu singen;
the dark jackdaw to the rest me to sing;
(the dark jackdaw used to sing me to my rest;)

ɪn 'di:zəs 'ʃlɔsəs 'kʰø:nɪçshalən, da: kʰan kʰɑ̯en lɔrt' mi:ɐ̯ je: gə'falən.
in dieses Schlosses Königshallen, da kann kein Ort mir je gefallen.
in this castle's royal halls, here can no place to me ever be pleasing.
(no place in this castle's royal halls can ever be pleasing to me.)

[*poem:* **-hallen ist** (lɪst', is) **kein Ort, der** (de:ɐ̯, that) **mir kann gefallen** (kʰan gə'falən, can please)]

fry:, vɛn de:ɐ̯ 'lɛrçə li:t' lɛɐ̯'ʃalt', zɔn ɪç mɪç nɪçt' lɪn 'lɛləns blɪk',
Früh, wenn der Lerche Lied erschallt, sonn' ich mich nicht in Ellens Blick,
Early, when the lark's song sounds, sun I myself not in Ellen's gaze,
(Early in the morning, when the lark's song is sounding, I cannot sun myself in Ellen's gaze,)

nɪçt' fɔlg ɪç dem 'flʏçt'ɪgən hɪrʃ dʊrç den valt', lʊnt' 'kʰe:rə, vɛn
nicht folg' ich dem flüchtigen Hirsch durch den Wald, und kehre, wenn
not follow I the fleeting stag through the forest, and return, when
(I cannot follow the fleet stag through the forest, and return home when)

'la:bənt tʰɑ̯ot, t̯su'rʏkʰ; nɪçt' ʃalt' mi:ɐ̯/mi:r li:ɐ̯ 'fro:əs vɪl'kʰɔmən lɛnt''ge:gən,
Abend taut, zurück; nicht schallt mir ihr frohes Willkommen entgegen,
evening dews, back; not sounds to me her glad welcome towards,
(the evening dew is falling; the sound of her glad welcome does not come to meet me,)

nɪçt' kʰan lɪç das vɪlt' li:ɐ̯ t̯su: 'fy:sən me:ɐ̯ 'le:gən, nɪçt' me:ɐ̯ vɪrt de:ɐ̯/de:r 'la:bənt'
nicht kann ich das Wild ihr zu Füssen mehr legen, nicht mehr wird der Abend
not can I the game for her at feet more lay, not more will the evening
(I cannot lay the game at her feet any more, no more will the evening)

lʊns 'ze:lɪç lɛnt''ʃve:bən: da'hɪn, da'hɪn lɪst' 'li:bən lʊnt' 'le:bən!
uns selig entschweben: dahin, dahin ist Lieben und Leben!
for us blissfully float away: gone, gone is loving and living!
(float blissfully away for us: gone, gone is loving and living!)

[Scubert set the poem to a virile polonaise rhythm that is not uncharacteristic of some Scottish music. The lack of modulation gives a certain monotony to the song—but the monotony of imprisonment is implicit in the words. In *The Lady of the Lake*, Canto VI, Ellen overhears Malcolm Graeme, her lover, singing this song from a tower of Stirling Castle, where he is held prisoner:

My hawk is tired of perch and hood, / My idle greyhound loathes his food,
My horse is weary of his stall, / And I am sick of captive thrall.

I wish I were, as I have been, / Hunting the hart in forest green,
With benden bow and bloodhound free. / For that's the life is meet for me.
I hate to learn the ebb of time, / From yon dull steeple's drowsy chime,
Or mark it as the sunbeams crawl, / Inch after inch, along the wall.
The lark was wont my matins ring, / The sable rook my vespers sing;
Those towers, although a king's they be, / Have not a hall of joy for me.
No more at dawning morn I rise, / And sun myself in Ellen's eyes,
Drive the fleet deer the forest through, / And homeward wend with evening dew;
A blithesome welcome blithely meet, / And lay my trophies at her feet,
While fled the eve on wing of glee — / That life is lost to love and me!]

liːt dɛs ˈ|ɔrfɔ͜øs, |als |eːɐ̯ |ɪn di ˈhœlə gɪŋ / ˈɔrfɔ͜øs

Lied des Orpheus, als er in die Hölle ging / Orpheus

The Song of Orpheus As He Entered The Underworld / Orpheus

Posthumously published [composed 1816] (poem by Johann Georg Jacobi)

ˈvɛlt͡sə dɪç hɪnˈvɛk‘, duː ˈvɪldəs ˈfɔ͜øɐ! ˈdiːzə ˈza͜et‘ən hat‘ |a͜en gɔt‘ gəˈkʰrøːnt‘;
Wälze dich hinweg, du wildes Feuer! diese Saiten hat ein Gott gekrönt;
Roll yourself away, you wild fire! These strings has a god crowned;
(Roll away from me, wild fire! A god has crowned the strings of this lyre;)

ˈeːɐ̯, mɪt‘ ˈvɛlçəm ˈjeːdəs ˈ|ʊngəhɔ͜øɐ(r), |ʊnt‘ fiˈla͜eçt di hœlə zɪç fɛɐ̯ˈzøːntʰ.
er, mit welchem jedes Ungeheuer, und vielleicht die Hölle sich versöhnt.
he, with whom every monster, and perhaps the hell itself reconciles.
(he, with whom every monster and perhaps even hell itself makes its peace.)

ˈdiːzə ˈza͜et‘ən ˈʃt‘ɪmt‘ə ˈza͜enə ˈrɛçt‘ə: ˈfʏrçt‘ɐlɪçə ˈʃat‘ən, fliːtʰ!
Diese Saiten stimmte seine Rechte: fürchterliche Schatten, flieht!
These strings tuned his right hand: fearful shadows, flee!
(His right hand tuned these strings: fearful shadows, flee!)

ʊnt‘ |iːɐ̯ ˈvɪnzəlndən bəˈvoːnɐ ˈdiːzɐ ˈnɛçt‘ə, ˈhɔrçət‘ |ɑ͜of ma͜en liːt‘!
Und ihr winselnden Bewohner dieser Nächte, horchet auf mein Lied!
And you whimpering inhabitants of these nights, harken to my song!
(And you, whimpering inhabitants of this darkness, listen to my song!)

fɔn deːɐ̯/deːɐ̯ ˈ|eːɐ̯də, voː di ˈzɔnə ˈlɔ͜øçt‘ət‘, |ʊnt deːɐ̯ ˈʃt‘ɪlə moːnt‘,
Von der Erde, wo die Sonne leuchtet, und der stille Mond,
From the earth, where the sun shines and the quiet moon,

voː deːɐ̯ tʰɑ͜o das ˈjʊŋə moːs bəˈfɔ͜øçt‘ət‘, voː gəˈzaŋ |ɪm ˈgryːnən ˈfɛldə voːntʰ;
wo der Tau das junge Moos befeuchtet, wo Gesang im grünen Felde wohnt;
where the dew the young moss moistens, where song in the green fields dwells;
(where the dew moistens the young moss, where song dwells in the green fields,)

ɑ͜os deːɐ̯ ˈmɛnʃən ˈzyːsəm ˈfaːt‘ɐlandə, voː deːɐ̯ ˈhɪməl |ɔ͜øç zoː ˈfroːə ˈblɪk‘ə gaːp‘,
aus der Menschen süssem Vaterlande, wo der Himmel euch so frohe Blicke gab,
from the humans' sweet fatherland, where the sky to you so happy glances gave,
(from the sweet homeland of mankind, where the sky once gave you such happy glances,)

'ts͡iːən mɪç di 'ʃøːnstʻən 'bandə, 'ts͡iːətʻ mɪç di 'liːbə zɛlpstʻ hɛ'rapʻ.
ziehen mich die schönsten Bande, ziehet mich die Liebe selbst herab.
draw me the most beautiful bonds, draws me the love itself down.
(the most beautiful bonds and love itself draw me down here.)

'ma͜enə 'kʰlaːgə tʰøːntʻ |ɪn '|ɔ͜ørə 'kʰlaːgə; va͜etʻ fɔn hiːɐ̯ gə'floːən |ɪst das glʏkʰ;
Meine Klage tönt in eure Klage; weit von hier geflohen ist das Glück;
My lament sounds in your lament; far from here flown has the happiness;
(My lament sounds in your own lament: happiness has flown far away from here;)
[*2nd version & Peters:* **weit von ihr** (|iːɐ̯, it—your lament)]

'|aːbɐ dɛŋkʻtʻ |an 'jeːnə 'tʰaːgə, ʃa͜otʻ |ɪn 'jeːnə vɛlt ts͡u'rʏkʰ!
aber denkt an jene Tage, schaut in jene Welt zurück!
but think of those days, look into that world back!
(but think of those days of the past, look back at that world!)

vɛn |iːɐ̯ daː nuːɐ̯/nuːr '|a͜enən '|a͜edəndən |ʊm'|armtʻətʻ, [|ʊm'|armətʻ]
Wenn ihr da nur einen Leidenden umarmtet, [*Peters (in error):* **umarmet**]
If you then even one sufferer embraced, [embrace]
(If you ever embraced even one suffering soul then,)

oː zoː fyːlt di 'vɔlʊstʻ nɔx '|a͜enmaːl, |ʊnt deːɐ̯/deːr '|a͜ogənblɪkʻ,
o so fühlt die Wollust noch einmal, und der Augenblick,
oh, then feel the pleasure still once, and the moment
(oh, then feel that pleasure once more, and may the moment)

|ɪn deːm |iːɐ̯/|iːr |ɔ͜øç |ɛɐ̯'barmtʻətʻ, '|ɪndrə 'diːzə '|aŋə kʰvaːl! |oː |ɪç 'zeːə
in dem ihr euch erbarmtet, lindre diese lange Qual! O ich sehe
in which you yourselves move to pity, (may) ease this long torment! Oh, I see
(in which you are moved to compassion ease this long torment!)

'tʰrɛːnən 'fliːsən! dʊrç di 'fɪnstʻɐnɪsə brɪçtʻ |a͜en ʃtʻraːl fɔn 'hɔfnʊŋ;
Tränen fliessen! durch die Finsternisse bricht ein Strahl von Hoffnung;
tears flowing! Through the darknesses breaks a ray of hope;
(tears flowing! A ray of hope is breaking through the darkness:)
[*poem:* **bricht nun** (nuːn, now) **ein Strahl**]

'|eːvɪç 'byːsən '|asən |ɔ͜øç di 'guːtʻən 'gœtʻɐ nɪçtʰ! 'gœtʻɐ, diː fyːɐ̯/fyːr |ɔ͜øç
ewig büssen lassen euch die guten Götter nicht! Götter, die für euch
eternally to expiate let you the kind gods not! Gods who for you
(the kindly gods will not make you do penance forever! Gods who for you)

di '|eːɐ̯də 'ʃuːfən, 'veːɐ̯dən |a͜os deːɐ̯ 'tʰiːfən naxtʻ |ɔ͜øç |ɪn 'zeːlɪgə gə'fɪldə 'ruːfən,
die Erde schufen, werden aus der tiefen Nacht euch in selige Gefilde rufen,
the earth created will out of the deep night you into blessed fields call,
(created the earth will call you out of this deep night into the fields of the blest,)

voː di 'tʰuːgəntʻ '|ʊntʻɐ 'roːzən laxtʰ.
wo die Tugend unter Rosen lacht.
where the virtue among roses laughs.
(where Virtue smiles among the roses.)

[Schubert made two versions of this magnificent song: the first called for a range of over two octaves, from low A flat to high A natural; his revision altered some high-lying phrases and transposed the last section downward, making the piece more accessible to most singers, and it is that second version, called simply "Orpheus," that is found in the Peters edition. The *Gesamtausgabe* prints both. In the famous myth, Orpheus, disconsolate over the loss of his young bride Eurydice, journeys to the land of the dead to plead for her return. He succeeds in moving the infernal powers with the eloquence of his singing. Orpheus was the son of a Thracian king and the muse Calliope. The god referred to is Apollo, lord of the muses, who gave the lyre to Orpheus. The "monster" may be Cerberus, the three-headed dog that guards the entrance to Hades. In this poem the author alters certain elements of the familiar story: here the singer addresses not the rulers of the underworld and not the Furies, but wretched souls in darkness, bringing them a ray of hope that through the experience of compassion they may eventually be freed from purgatory and enter a realm of peace. There is perhaps a Christian overtone there, a reminder of Christ's descent into hell after his death on the cross.]

li:t' 'lae̯nəs 'kʰɪndəs
Lied eines Kindes
The Song of a Child

Posthumously published as a fragment [composed 1817] (author unknown)

'lao̯t'ɐ 'frɔø̯də fy:l ɪç, 'lao̯t'ɐ 'li:bə hø:r ɪç,
Lauter Freude fühl' ich, lauter Liebe hör' ich,
Nothing but joy feel I, nothing but love hear I,
(I feel nothing but joy, I hear nothing but words of love,)

ɪç zo: 'ly:bɐglʏk'lɪç 'frø:lɪç 'ʃp'i:lənt' kʰɪnt'.
ich so überglücklich fröhlich spielend Kind.
I so more-than-happily merrily playing child.
(I am so exceedingly happy, a merry child at play.)

dɔrt de:ɐ̯ 'gu:t'ə 'fa:t'ɐ, hi:ɐ̯ di 'li:bə 'mʊt'ɐ, rʊnt' hɛ'rʊm vi:ɐ̯ 'kʰɪndɐ.
Dort der gute Vater, hier die liebe Mutter, rund herum wir Kinder.
There the kind father, here the dear mother, round about we children.
(There is our kind father, here is our dear mother, and we children are all around them.)

[The song is a pretty fragment that breaks off after only twenty-four bars. It has been completed and privately printed by Reinhard van Hoorickx. The accompaniment is notated throughout in the treble cleff. The poet is unknown, and therefore also the rest of the poem.]

li:t' 'lae̯nəs 'kʰri:gɐs
Lied eines Kriegers
The Song of a Soldier

Posthumously published [composed 1824] (author unknown)

dɛs 'ʃt'ɔlt͡sən 'mɛnɐle:bəns 'ʃø:nst'ə 't͡sae̯çən zɪnt' 'flamə, 'dɔnɐ(r)
Des stolzen Männerlebens schönste Zeichen sind Flamme, Donner
The proud masculine life's finest emblems are flame, thunder
(The finest emblems of the proud, masculine life are flame, thunder,)

ʊnt di kʰraft de:ɐ̯/de:r 'lae̯çən. dɔx nɪçt͡s me:ɐ̯ fɔm 'lae̯zənʃp'i:l
und die Kraft der Eichen. Doch nichts mehr vom Eisenspiel
and the strength of the oaks. But nothing more of the iron game
(and the strength of the oak. But no more of the iron game)

ʊnt' nɪçt͡s fɔm blɪt͡s deːɐ̯ 'vafən, deːɐ̯/deːr 'leːvgə 'friːdə
und nichts vom Blitz der Waffen, der ew'ge Friede
and nothing of the lightning of the weapons, the eternal peace
(and no more of the flash of weapons; eternal peace)

[*Peters:* **vom Spiel** (ʃp'iːl, play) **der Waffen]**

vart' lʊns 't͡suːgəvɛndət, dem 'ʃlaːfə vart di kʰraft deːɐ̯ faost' fɛɐ̯'p͡fɛndətʰ.
ward uns zugewendet, Dem Schlafe ward die Kraft der Faust verpfändet.
was us bestowed upon, for the sleep was the strength of the fist pawned.
(was bestowed upon us, the strength of the fist was pawned in exchange for sleep.)

t͡svaːɐ̯ jʏŋst' nɔx 'haːbən viːɐ̯ das ʃveːɐ̯t' gə'ʃvʊŋən lʊnt' kʰyːn
Zwar jüngst noch haben wir das Schwert geschwungen und kühn
To be sure, recently still have we the sword brandished and boldly
(To be sure, until recently we still brandished our swords and boldly)

laof 'leːbən 'loːdɐ tʰoːt' gə'rʊŋən. jɛt͡st' 'laːbɐ zɪnt di 'tʰaːgə 'hoːən kʰamp͡fs
auf Leben oder Tod gerungen. Jetzt aber sind die Tage hohen Kampfs
for life or death struggled. Now however are the days of high battle
(fought for life or death. Now, however, those days of noble battle have)

fɛɐ̯'kʰlʊŋən, lʊnt' vas lʊns bliːp' laos 'jeːnən 'tʰaːgən, lɛs lɪst' foːɐ̯'bae,
verklungen, und was uns blieb aus jenen Tagen, es ist vorbei,
faded away, and what to us remained from those days, it is past,
(faded away, and whatever glory remained for us from those days, that is over now;)

balt' zɪnt͡s, lax, nuːɐ̯ nɔx 'zaːgən.
bald sind's, ach, nur noch Sagen.
soon are there, ah, only still legends.
(soon, alas, there will only be old legends left.)

[The *Gesamtausgabe* offers the piece in its original form, "for a bass voice and chorus (unison) with accompaniment of the pianoforte," with solos and chorus in the bass cleff. Peters reproduces the first edition, with the voice parts in the treble cleff and with minor rhythmic variants in the second verse. There may be two ways of looking at this song: from the viewpoint of the sabre-rattling Teuton, swaggering masculinity regrets the coming of peace after the challenging violence of war, the excitement is over and soon stale war stories will be all that's left of our heroics; or—for those disillusioned with the search for glory on the battlefield—these may be the voices of those soldiers for whom "eternal peace" was the "sleep" of the grave. Do the shifts from major to minor and the solemn starkness of the choral contributions express dissatisfaction with a dishonorable peace treaty, or merely disappointment that the test of battle is over, and glumness at the prospect of peaceful boredom? In any case, each of the two verses starts with virile vigor in the major key and ends with an ominous near-monotone in the minor.]

liːt' 'laenəs 'ʃɪfɐs lan di diɔs'kʰuːrən

Lied eines Schiffers an die Dioskuren

The Song of a Seaman to the Dioscuri

Op. 65, No. 1 [1822?] (Johann Mayrhofer)

diɔs'kʰuːrən, 't͡svɪlɪŋsʃt'ɛrnə, diː liːɐ̯ 'lɔøçt'ət' 'maenəm 'naxən,
Dioskuren, Zwillingssterne, die ihr leuchtet meinem Nachen,
Dioscuri, twin stars, who you shine upon my boat,
(Dioscuri, twin stars, you who shine upon my boat,)

mıç bəˈruːıçtʻ lɑ͜ofdem ˈmeːrə ˈlɔ͜ørə ˈmıldə, ˈlɔ͜øɐ ˈvaxən.
mich beruhigt auf dem Meere eure Milde, euer Wachen.
me calms on the sea your mildness, your watchfulness.
(your mildness and your watchfulness calm me on the sea.)

veːɐ̯/veːr lɑ͜ox, fɛstʻ lın zıç bəˈgrʏndətʻ, lʊnfɛɐ̯ˈt͜saːkʻt dem ʃtʻʊrm bəˈgeːgnətʰ,
Wer auch, fest in sich begründet, unverzagt dem Sturm begegnet,
(He) who even, firmly in himself based, intrepidly the storm meets,
(Even he who, firmly confident in himself, intrepidly meets the storm)

fyːltʻ zıç dɔx lın ˈlɔ͜ørən ˈʃtʻraːlən ˈdɔpʻəltʻ ˈmuːtʻıç lʊntʻ gəˈzeːgnətʰ.
fühlt sich doch in euren Strahlen doppelt mutig und gesegnet.
feels himself nevertheless in your rays doubly brave and blest.
(feels nevertheless doubly brave and blest in your rays.)

ˈdiːzəs ˈruːdɐ, das lıç ˈʃvıŋə, ˈmeːrəsfluːtʻən t͜suː t͜sɛɐ̯ˈtʰa͜elən,
Dieses Ruder, das ich schwinge, Meeresfluten zu zerteilen,
This oar that I wield sea- waters to split,
(This oar that I wield to cleave the waves of the sea)

ˈhɛŋə lıç, zoː lıç gəˈbɔrgən, lɑ͜of lan ˈlɔ͜ørəs ˈtʰɛmpʻəls ˈzɔ͜ølən.
hänge ich, so ich geborgen, auf an eures Tempels Säulen.
hang I, so I in safety, up on your temple's columns.
(I shall hang up on a column of your temple if I reach land in safety.)

[The Dioscuri (*Dios* + *kouroi* = sons of Zeus), Castor and Pollux, became the constellation Gemini, the "heavenly twins," its two principal stars being both of the first magnitude. Since ancient times they were believed to have the power to protect mariners from the dangers of the sea. The title of the original poem is "*Schiffers Nachtlied*" (A Seaman's Night-song). Schubert's setting is nobly beautiful, serene and deep, a masterpiece in forty bars.]

liːtʻ lın deːɐ̯ ˈlapʻveːzənha͜etʰ
Lied in der Abwesenheit
Song of Absence

Ending lost, posthumously published [composed 1816] (Friedrich Leopold, Graf zu Stolberg)

ax, miːɐ̯/miːr lıst das hɛrt͜s zoː ʃveːɐ̯! ˈtʰrɑ͜orıç lır ıç hın lʊntʻ heːɐ̯.
Ach, mir ist das Herz so schwer! Traurig irr' ich hin und her.
Ah, to me is the heart so heavy! Sadly wander I to and fro.
(Ah, my heart is so heavy! Sadly I wander to and fro.)

ˈzuːxə ˈruːə, ˈfındə ˈkʰa͜enə, geː lans ˈfɛnstʻɐ hın, lʊntʻ ˈva͜enə!
Suche Ruhe, finde keine, geh' ans Fenster hin, und weine!
Seek peace, find none, go to the window hence, and weep!
(I search for peace, find none, go to the window, and weep!)
[*poem:* **Suche Ruh'** (ruː, peace) **und** (lʊntʻ, and) **finde keine]**

ˈzɛːsəst duː lɑ͜of ˈma͜enəm ʃoːs, vʏrd ıç ˈlalɐ ˈzɔrgən loːs,
Sässest du auf meinem Schoss, würd' ich aller Sorgen los,
Were sitting you on my lap, would I of all cares (be) free,
(If you were sitting on my lap, I would be free of all cares,)

ʊnt' lɑos 'daenən 'blɑoən 'lɑogən vʏrd ɪç li:p' lʊnt' 'vɔnə 'zɑogən!
und aus deinen blauen Augen würd' ich Lieb' und Wonne saugen!
and out of your blue eyes would I love and rapture imbibe!
(and out of your blue eyes I would imbibe love and rapture!)

kʰœnt' ɪç glaeç, du: 'zy:səs kʰɪnt', 'fli:gən hɪn tsu: di:ɐ̯ gə'ʃvɪnt'!
Könnt' ich gleich, du süsses Kind, fliegen hin zu dir geschwind!
Could I right now, you sweet child, fly away to you quickly!
(Oh, you sweet child, if I could only fly away to you quickly, right now!)
[*poem:* **Könnt' ich doch** (dɔx, but—if I could but...)]

kʰœnt' ɪç 'le:vɪç dɪç lʊm'faŋən, lʊnt' lan 'daenən 'lɪp'ən 'haŋən!
Könnt' ich ewig dich umfangen, und an deinen Lippen hangen!
Could I eternally you embrace, and on your lips hang!
(If I could only embrace you and hang on your lips forever!)

[The last page of Schubert's manuscript is lost. Attempts to supply the missing ending have been made by Eusebius Mandyczewski, Reinhard van Hoorickx, and Karl Pils. The version by van Hoorickx is included in a recording of "Unknown Schubert Songs."]

'li:dəslɛnt'
Liedesend
Song's End

Posthumously published [composed 1816] (poem by Johann Mayrhofer)

ɑof 'zaenəm 'gɔldnən 'tʰro:nə de:ɐ̯ 'grɑoə 'kʰø:nɪç zɪtstʰ,
Auf seinem goldnen Throne der graue König sitzt,
Upon his golden throne the grey king sits,

e:ɐ̯ 'ʃt'arət' lɪn di 'zɔnə, di: ro:t' lɪm 'vɛst'ən blɪtstʰ.
er starret in die Sonne, die rot im Westen blitzt.
he stares into the sun, which red in the west flashes.
(he stares into the sun, which blazes red in the west.)
[*1st version:* **und** (ʊnt', and) **starret...** *both versions (in GA):* **in** (lɪn, in) **Westen**]

de:ɐ̯ 'zɛŋɐ ry:ɐ̯t di 'harfə, zi: 'rɑoʃət' 'zi:gəszaŋ;
Der Sänger rührt die Harfe, sie rauschet Siegessang;
The singer touches the harp, which murmurs triumphant song;
[*1st version:* **Der Barde** ('bardə, bard)]

de:ɐ̯/de:r lɛrnst' je'dɔx, de:ɐ̯ 'ʃarfə, le:ɐ̯ tʰrɔtst dem 'fɔlən kʰlaŋ.
der Ernst jedoch, der scharfe, er trotzt dem vollen Klang.
the seriousness however, the sharp, it defies the full sound.
(but the severe seriousness of the king's mood does not yield to the full sound.)

nu:n ʃt'ɪmt' le:ɐ̯ 'zy:sə 'vaezən, lans hɛrts zɪç 'kʰlamɐnt' lan;
Nun stimmt er süsse Weisen, ans Herz sich klammernd an;
Now tunes he sweet melodies, to the heart themselves clinging to;
(Now the bard tunes his harp to sweet melodies that cling to the heart,)

ɔp‘ leːɐ̯/leːr liːn nɪçt‘ mɪt‘ 'laezən fɛɐ̯'zuːxən 'mɪldɐn kʰan.
ob er ihn nicht mit leisen Versuchen mildern kann.
whether he him not with gentle attempts soften can.
(to see whether he can soften the king with gentler attempts.)

fɛɐ̯'geːp‘lɪç lɪst‘ zaen 'myːən, lɛɐ̯'ʃœpft dɛs 'liːdəs raeç,
Vergeblich ist sein Mühen, erschöpft des Liedes Reich,
In vain is his effort, exhausted the song's realm,
(His efforts are in vain, the realm of song is exhausted,)

ʊnt‘ laof deːɐ̯ 'ʃt‘ɪrnə 'tsiːən di 'zɔrgən 'vɛt‘ɐglaeç.
und auf der Stirne ziehen die Sorgen wettergleich.
and on the forehead gather the cares storm- like.
(and cares start to cloud the king's forehead as if a storm were brewing there.)

deːɐ̯ 'bardə, tʰiːf lɛɐ̯'bɪt‘ɐt‘, ʃlɛːk‘t di harf lɛnt'tsvae,
Der Barde, tief erbittert, schlägt die Harf' entzwei,
The bard, deeply embittered, smashes the harp to pieces,
[*poem & 1st version:* **schlägt seine** ('zaenə, his) **Harf'**]

ʊnt dʊrç di 'lʏft‘ə 'tsɪt‘ɐt deːɐ̯ 'zɪlbɐzaet‘ən ʃrae.
und durch die Lüfte zittert der Silbersaiten Schrei.
and through the airs trembles the silver strings' cry.
(and the cry of the silver strings trembles through the air.)
[*poem:* **durch die Halle** ('halə, hall)]

dɔx viː laox 'lalə 'beːbən, deːɐ̯ 'hɛrʃɐ 'tsʏrnət‘ nɪçt‘;
Doch wie auch alle beben, der Herrscher zürnet nicht;
But as even all quake, the ruler is angry not;
(But even though everyone else is quaking, the ruler is not angry;)
[*GA, both versions:* **Und** (ʊnt‘, and) **wie auch**]

deːɐ̯ 'gnaːdən 'ʃt‘raːlən 'ʃveːbən laof 'zaenən 'langəzɪçtʰ.
der Gnaden Strahlen schweben auf seinem Angesicht.
the mercy's rays hover on his countenance.
(the light of mercy illumines his countenance.)

duː 'vɔlə mɪç nɪçt 'tsaeən deːɐ̯ 'lʊnlɛmpfɪnt‘lɪçkʰaetʰ:
"Du wolle mich nicht zeihen der Unempfindlichkeit:
"You want [*imperitive*] me not to accuse of the insensitivity:
("Do not want to accuse me of insensitivity:)
[*GA, both versions:* **Du wollest** ('vɔləst‘, want—you do not want)]

ɪn laŋ fɛɐ̯'blyːt‘ən 'maeən, viː hast duː mɪç lɛɐ̯'frɔøtʰ!
in lang verblühten Maien, wie hast du mich erfreut!
in long since faded Mays, how have you me gladdened!
(how happy you made me in months of May, long since faded!)

viː 'jeːdə lʊst‘ gə'ʃt‘aegɐtʰ, diː laos deːɐ̯/deːr 'lʊrnə fiːl!
Wie jede Lust gesteigert, die aus der Urne fiel!
How every pleasure intensified, that from the urn fell!
(How you intensified every pleasure that fell to my lot from the urn of destiny!)

vas miːɐ̯/miːr la͡en gɔt' fɛɐ̯'va͡egɐt', lɛɐ̯'ʃt'at'ət'ə da͡en ʃp'iːl.
Was mir ein Gott verweigert, erstattete dein Spiel.
What to me a god refused, restored your playing.
(Whatever a god refused to me, your playing restored.)

fɔm 'kʰalt'ən 'hɛrt͡sən 'gla͡et'ət' nuːn 'liːdəst͡sa͡obɐ(r) lap';
Vom kalten Herzen gleitet nun Liedeszauber ab;
From the cold heart glides now song's magic off;
(Now the magic of song glides off my cold heart;)

ʊnt' 'ɪmɐ 'nɛːɐ 'ʃra͡et'ət' nuːn fɛɐ̯'gɛŋlɪçkʰa͡et' lʊnt' graːp'.
und immer näher schreitet nun Vergänglichkeit und Grab."
and ever nearer strides now transitoriness and grave.
(and ever nearer now stride transience and the grave.")
[*poem & 1st version:* **und immer näher schreitet Vergänglichkeit und Grab**]

[Schubert made two versions, both in the *Gesamtausgabe*; Peters offers the second, with some verbal modifications based on the original poem and a shortened postlude. The king's lines are in the bass clef in the first version. In both versions Schubert brings his friend's poem to vivid life.]

'lɪla lan di 'mɔrgənrøːt'ə
Lilla an die Morgenröte
Lilla to the Dawn

Posthumously published [composed 1815] (author unknown)

viː ʃøːn bɪst duː, duː 'gʏldnə 'mɔrgənrøːt'ə, viː 'fa͡eɐlɪç bɪst duː!
Wie schön bist du, du güldne Morgenröte, wie feierlich bist du!
How beautiful are you, you golden dawn, how majestic are you!
(How beautiful you are, golden dawn, how majestic you are!)

diːɐ̯ ja͡oxt͡st' lɪm 'fɛst'lɪçən gə'zaŋ deːɐ̯ 'fløːt'ə deːɐ̯ 'ʃɛːfɐ 'daŋk'baːɐ̯ t͡suː.
Dir jauchzt im festlichen Gesang der Flöte der Schäfer dankbar zu.
To you exults in the festive song of the flute the shepherd gratefully to.
(The shepherd gratefully exults to you in the festive song of the flute.)

dɪç gryːst dɛs 'valdəs kʰoːɐ̯, me'loːdɪʃ 'zɪŋət di lɛrç lʊnt' 'naxt'ɪgal,
Dich grüsst des Waldes Chor, melodisch singet die Lerch' und Nachtigall,
You greets the forest's choir, melodiously sings the lark and nightingale,
(The forest choir greets you, the lark and nightingale sing melodiously,)

ʊnt' rɪŋs lʊm'heːɐ̯ fɔn bɛrk' lʊnt tʰaːl lɛɐ̯'kʰlɪŋət deːɐ̯ 'frɔ͡ødə 'viːdɐhal.
und rings umher von Berg und Tal erklinget der Freude Widerhall.
and round about from mountain and valley sounds the joy's echo.
(and all around from mountain and valley the echo of that joy is sounding.)

[A short and simple, pretty song, with shepherd's flutes and twittering birds at the end.]

lin'kanto 'deʎːʎi 'ɔkːki / di maxt deːɐ̯ 'laoɡən

L'incanto degli occhi / Die Macht der Augen

The Enchantment of Eyes / The Power of Eyes

Op. 83 [1827] (Pietro Metastasio)

da 'vːvoːi, 'kaːri 'luːmi, di'pɛnde‿il 'mio 'staːto; 'voːi 'sjɛːte‿i 'mjɛːi 'nuːmi,
Da voi, cari lumi, dipende il mio stato; voi siete i miei numi,
Upon you, dear eyes, depends the my condition; you are the my gods,
(My condition depends upon you, dear eyes; you are my gods,) [*lumi* = lights = eyes (poetic)]

'voːi 'sjɛːte‿il 'miːo 'faːto. a 'vːvɔstro ta'lɛnto mi 'sɛnto kan'dʒaːr.
voi siete il mio fato. A vostro talento mi sento cangiar.
you are the my fate. According to your will myself I feel change.
(you are my destiny. I feel myself change according to your will.)

ar'diːr minspi'raːte, se 'lːljɛːti splen'dete; se 'tːtorbidi 'sjɛːtə, mi 'faːte tre'maːr.
Ardir m'inspirate, se lieti splendete; se torbidi siete, mi fate tremar.
To dare me you inspire, if happy you shine; if turbid you are, me you make tremble.
(If you shine brightly you inspire me to boldness; if you are cloudy, you make me tremble.)

German translation (translator unknown):

nuːɐ̯/nuːr lɔ͜øç, 'ʃøːnə 'ʃtʻɛrnə, gə'høːɐ̯tʻ lal ma͜en 'leːbən, viː 'gœtʻɐ zoː 'fɛrnə,
Nur euch, schöne Sterne, gehört all mein Leben, wie Götter so ferne,
Only to you, lovely stars, belongs all my life, as gods so distant,
(All my life belongs only to you, lovely stars, as distant as gods,)

bə'zeːltʻ liːɐ̯ ma͜en 'ʃtʻreːbən. naːx 'lɔ͜øərəm 'vɪŋkʻə bə'veːkʻtʻ zɪç ma͜en zɪn.
beseelt ihr mein Streben. Nach euerem Winke bewegt sich mein Sinn.
animate you my striving. According to your signal moves itself my mind,
(you inspire my striving. My feelings shift according to your signals.)

iːɐ̯ zeːtʻ mɪç fɛɐ̯'veːgən, vɛn 'frøːlɪç liːɐ̯ 'ʃtʻraːlətʻ,
Ihr seht mich verwegen, wenn fröhlich ihr strahlet,
You see me bold when merrily you shine,
(When you shine merrily, you will see me bold;)

vɛn 'tʰryːpʻzɪn lɔ͜øç 'maːlətʻ, kʰvɛːltʻ laŋstʻ mɪç da'hɪn.
wenn Trübsinn euch malet, quält Angst mich dahin.
when gloom you paints, torments fear me away.
(when gloom tints your eyes, fear torments me horribly.)

[The Italian text is the aria of Licinio from Act II, Scene 5, of *Attilio Regolo*. The song is one of three that Schubert composed for the famous basso Luigi Lablache, whom he met in Vienna.]

lit'a'na͜e la͜of das fɛst' 'lalɐ 'ze:lən
Litanei auf das Fest aller Seelen
Litany for the Feast of All Souls

Posthumously published [composed 1816] (poem by Johann Georg Jacobi)

ru:n lɪn 'fri:dən 'lalə 'ze:lən, di: fɔl'braxt' la͜en 'baŋəs 'kʰvɛ:lən,
Ruh'n in Frieden alle Seelen, die vollbracht ein banges Quälen,
Rest in peace all souls, who finished a fearful tormenting,
(May all souls rest in peace, those who have finished a fearful torment,)

di: fɔl'lɛndət' 'zy:sən tʰra͜om, 'le:bənszat', gə'bo:rən kʰa͜om,
die vollendet süssen Traum, lebenssatt, geboren kaum,
who (have) ended sweet dream, weary of life, born barely,
(those who have ended a sweet dream, whether weary of life, or barely born,)

a͜os de:ɐ̯ vɛlt' hɪ'ny:bɐ 'ʃi:dən: 'lalə 'ze:lən ru:n lɪn 'fri:dən!
aus der Welt hinüber schieden: alle Seelen ruh'n in Frieden!
from the world to the other side departed: all souls rest in peace!
(departed from this world to the other: may all souls rest in peace!)

[di: zɪç hi:ɐ̯ gə'ʃp'i:lən 'zu:xt'ən, 'lœft'ɐ 'va͜ent'ən, 'nɪmɐ 'flu:xt'ən,
[Die sich hier Gespielen suchten, öfter weinten, nimmer fluchten,
[Who for themselves here playmates sought, oftener wept, never cursed,
[(Those who sought playmates here, who more often wept, and never cursed)

vɛn fɔn 'li:rɐ 'tʰrɔ͜øən hant' 'kʰa͜enɐ je: den drʊk' fɛɐ̯'ʃt'ant';
wenn von ihrer treuen Hand Keiner je den Druck verstand;
when of their loyal hand no one ever the pressure understood;
(when no one ever understood the pressure of their loyal hand;)

'lalə, di: fɔn 'hɪnən 'ʃi:dən, 'lalə 'ze:lən ru:n lɪn 'fri:dən!
alle, die von hinnen schieden, alle Seelen ruh'n in Frieden!]
all, who from hence departed, all souls rest in peace!]
(may all who have departed from this world, may all souls rest in peace!)]

'li:bəfɔlɐ 'mɛ:t'çən 'ze:lən, 'de:rən 'tʰrɛ:nən nɪçt t͜su: 't͜sɛ:lən,
Liebevoller Mädchen Seelen, deren Tränen nicht zu zählen,
Love-full girls' souls, whose tears not to be counted,
(The souls of loving girls whose tears are too many to be counted,)

di: la͜en 'falʃɐ frɔ͜ønt' fɛɐ̯'li:s, lʊnt di 'blɪndə vɛlt' fɛɐ̯'ʃt'i:s:
die ein falscher Freund verliess, und die blinde Welt verstiess:
whom a false friend deserted, and the blind world rejected:

'lalə, di: fɔn 'hɪnən 'ʃi:dən, 'lalə 'ze:lən ru:n lɪn 'fri:dən!
alle, die von hinnen schieden, alle Seelen ruh'n in Frieden!
all, who from hence departed, all souls rest in peace!
(may all who have departed from this world, may all souls rest in peace!)

[ʊnt de:ɐ̯ 'jʏŋlɪŋ, de:m, fɛɐ̯'bɔrgən, 'za͜enə bra͜ot' lam 'fry:ən 'mɔrgən,
[Und der Jüngling, dem, verborgen, seine Braut am frühen Morgen,
[And the youth, for whom, secretly, his bride in the early morning,
[(And the young man for whom, secretly, in the early morning, his intended bride)

va͜el lɪːn liːpʻ lɪns graːpʻ gəˈleːkʻtʻ, la͜of za͜en graːpʻ di ˈkʰɛrt͜sə tʰrɛːkʻtʰ...
weil ihn Lieb' ins Grab gelegt, auf sein Grab die Kerze trägt...
because him love into the grave laid, onto his grave the candle carries...
(brings a candle to place on his grave, because love had laid him into the grave,..)

ˈalə ˈga͜estʻɐ, diː fɔl ˈkʰlaːɐ̯ha͜etʻ, ˈvʊrdən ˈmɛrtʻyrɐ deːɐ̯ ˈvaːɐ̯ha͜etʻ,
Alle Geister, die, voll Klarheit, wurden Märtyrer der Wahrheit,
All spirits, which, full of clarity, became martyrs of the truth,
(All those spirits that became clear-sighted martyrs in the cause of truth,

ˈkʰɛmp͜ftʻən fyːɐ̯ das ˈha͜elɪçtʻuːm, ˈzuːxtʻən nɪçt deːɐ̯ ˈmartʻɐ ruːm...]
kämpften für das Heiligtum, suchten nicht der Marter Ruhm...]
fought for the holy shrine, sought not the torture's fame...]
(who fought for the holy shrine, who did not seek fame through torment...)]

ʊnt diː niː deːɐ̯ ˈzɔnə ˈlaxtʻən, ˈlʊntʻɐm moːntʻ la͜of ˈdɔrnən ˈvaxtʻən,
Und die nie der Sonne lachten, unterm Mond auf Dornen wachten,
And who never to the sun laughed, under the moon on thorns were sleepless,
(And those who never smiled at the sun, who were sleepless under the moon on a bed of thorns,)

gɔtʻ, lɪm ˈra͜enən ˈhɪməlslɪçtʻ, la͜enst t͜suː zeːn fɔn ˈlangəzɪçtʰ...
Gott, im reinen Himmelslicht, einst zu sehn von Angesicht...
God, in the pure light of heaven, one day to see by countenance...
(one day to see God face to face in the pure light of heaven...)

[ʊnt diː gɛrn lɪm ˈroːzəngartʻən ba͜e dem ˈfrɔ͜ødənbɛçɐ ˈhartʻən,
[Und die gern im Rosengarten bei dem Freudenbecher harrten,
[And who gladly in the rose- garden at the joy- goblet tarried,
[(And those who liked to tarry in the rose garden with the cup of pleasure,)

ˈlaːbɐ dan, t͜sʊr ˈbøːzən t͜sa͜etʻ, ˈʃmɛkʻtʻən ˈza͜enə ˈbɪtʻɐkʰa͜etʰ...
aber dann, zur bösen Zeit, schmeckten seine Bitterkeit...
but then, at the bad time, tasted its bitterness...
(but then, when times turned hard, tasted its bitterness...)

a͜ox diː ˈkʰa͜enən ˈfriːdən ˈkʰantʻən, ˈlaːbɐ muːtʻ lʊntʻ ˈʃtʻɛrkʻə ˈzantʻən
Auch die keinen Frieden kannten, aber Mut und Stärke sandten
Also who no peace knew, but courage and strength sent
(Those too who knew no peace, but who sent courage and strength)

ˈlyːbɐ ˈla͜eçənfɔləs fɛltʻ lɪn di halpʻlɛntʻˈʃlaːfnə vɛltʰ:
über leichenvolles Feld in die halbentschlaf'ne Welt:
over corpse-filled field into the half-deceased world:
(into the half-dead world over a battlefield strewn with corpses:)

ˈlalə, diː fɔn ˈhɪnən ˈʃiːdən, ˈlalə ˈzeːlən ruːn lɪn ˈfriːdən!
alle, die von hinnen schieden, alle Seelen ruh'n in Frieden!]
all, who from hence departed, all souls rest in peace!]
(may all who have departed from this world, may all souls rest in peace!)]

[*last verse same as the first*]

[Schubert's manuscript gives the first verse, with repeat marks. The first edition offered verses 1, 3, and 6, as in Peters. The *Gesamtausgabe* prints all nine. On All Souls' Day, November 2nd, many Germans place candles on the graves of their loved ones. In this exquisite and infinitely touching song there is tender compassion, heart-breaking sadness, and peaceful consolation; to do it justice, the singer needs a beautiful *legato*, endless breath, and deep feeling for the words.]

loːp‘ deːɐ̯ ˈtʰrɛːnən
Lob der Tränen
In Praise of Tears

Op. 13, No. 2 [1818?] (August Wilhelm von Schlegel)

ˈla͜oə ˈlʏft‘ə, ˈbluːməndʏft‘ə, ˈlalə lɛnt͜s- lʊnt‘ ˈjuːgənt‘lʊstʰ;
Laue Lüfte, Blumendüfte, alle Lenz- und Jugendlust;
Warm breezes, flower fragrances, all spring and youth pleasure;
(Warm breezes, fragrant flowers, all the pleasures of spring and of youth;)

ˈfrɪʃɐ ˈlɪp‘ən ˈkʰʏsə ˈnɪp‘ən, zanft‘ gəˈviːk‘t‘ lan ˈt͜saːɐ̯t‘ɐ brʊstʰ;
frischer Lippen Küsse nippen, sanft gewiegt an zarter Brust;
fresh lips' kisses to sip, gently lulled on tender breast;
(to sip kisses from fresh lips, gently lulled on a tender breast;)

dan deːɐ̯ ˈtʰra͜obən ˈnɛk‘t‘ar ˈra͜obən; ˈra͜eəntʰant͜s | lʊnt‘ ʃp‘iːl lʊnt‘ ʃɛrt͜s:
dann der Trauben Nektar rauben; Reihentanz und Spiel und Scherz:
then the grapes' nectar to steal; round dance and play and jest:
(then to steal nectar from the grapes; round dances and games and jests:)

vas di ˈzɪnən nuːɐ̯ gəˈvɪnən: lax, lɛɐ̯ˈfʏlt‘ lɛs jeː das hɛrt͜s?
was die Sinnen nur gewinnen: ach, erfüllt es je das Herz?
what the senses only win: ah, fulfills it ever the heart?
(that which only the senses gain: ah, can that ever fulfill the heart?)

vɛn di ˈfɔ͜øçt‘ən ˈla͜ogən ˈlɔ͜øçt‘ən fɔn deːɐ̯ ˈveːmuːt‘ ˈlɪndəm tʰa͜o,
Wenn die feuchten Augen leuchten von der Wehmut lindem Tau,
When the moist eyes shine from the melancholy's gentle dew,
(When moist eyes shine with the gentle dew of melancholy,)

dan lɛnt‘ˈziːgəlt, drɪn gəˈʃp‘iːgəlt‘, zɪç dem blɪk‘ di ˈhɪməlsla͜o.
dann entsiegelt, drin gespiegelt, sich dem Blick die Himmels-Au.
then unseals, within mirrored, itself to the gaze the heaven- meadow.
(then the fields of heaven, mirrored in those eyes, are revealed to the gaze.)

viː lɛɐ̯ˈkʰvɪk‘lɪç la͜ogənˈblɪk‘lɪç lœʃt‘ lɛs ˈjeːdə ˈvɪldə gluːtʰ!
Wie erquicklich augenblicklich löscht es jede wilde Glut!
How refreshingly in a moment extinguishes it every wild fire!
(How refreshingly, in one moment, that extinguishes every savage passion!)

viː fɔm ˈreːgən ˈbluːmən ˈp͜fleːgən, ˈheːbət‘ zɪç deːɐ̯ ˈmat‘ə muːtʰ.
Wie vom Regen Blumen pflegen, hebet sich der matte Mut.
As from the rain flowers are accustomed (to do), lifts itself the exhausted courage.
(Like flowers in the rain, exhausted courage is revived again.)

nıçt‘ mıt‘ ˈzyːsən ˈvasɐflʏsən t͡svaŋ pʰroˈmeːt‘ɔ͜øs ˈʊnzɐn la͜em.
Nicht mit süssen Wasserflüssen zwang Prometheus unsern Leim.
Not with sweet water- rivers forced Prometheus our loam.
(Prometheus did not mold our clay into human shape with rivers of sweet water.)
[*Leim* = glue, but is related to *Lehm* = loam or clay, the obvious meaning here]

na͜en, mıt ˈtʰrɛːnən; drʊm ˈım ˈzeːnən ˈʊnt‘ ˈım ʃmɛrt͡s zınt‘ viːɐ̯ daˈha͜em.
Nein, mit Tränen; drum im Sehnen und im Schmerz sind wir daheim.
No, with tears; therefore in the longing and in the pain are we at home.
(No, with tears; therefore we are at home in longing and in pain.)

ˈbıt‘ɐ ˈʃvɛlən ˈdiːzə ˈkʰvɛlən fyːɐ̯ den ˈleːɐ̯t‘ˈʊmfaŋnən zın,
Bitter schwellen diese Quellen für den erdumfangnen Sinn,
Bitter swell these springs for the earthbound mind,
(For the earthbound mind, the water from those springs is bitter,)

dɔx ziː ˈdrɛŋən ˈa͜os den ˈɛŋən ˈın das meːɐ̯ deːɐ̯ ˈliːbə hın.
doch sie drängen aus den Engen in das Meer der Liebe hin.
but they surge out of the narrows into the sea of the love hence.
(but they surge out of narrow straits into the open sea of love.)

ˈeːvgəs ˈzeːnən flɔs ˈın ˈtʰrɛːnən, ˈʊnt‘ ˈʊmˈgaːp‘ di ˈʃt‘arə vɛltʰ,
Ew'ges Sehnen floss in Tränen, und umgab die starre Welt,
Eternal longing flowed in tears, and encircled the rigid world,

diː ˈın ˈarmən za͜en ˈɛɐ̯ˈbarmən ˈımɐˈdaːɐ̯/-ˈdaːr ˈʊmˈfluːt‘ənt‘ hɛltʰ.
die in Armen sein Erbarmen immerdar umflutend hält.
which (obj.) in arms His mercy (subj.) forever around-flowing holds.
(which divine mercy, forever flowing all around it, holds in its arms.)

zɔl da͜en ˈveːzən dɛn gəˈneːzən, fɔn dem ˈleːɐ̯dənʃt‘a͜obə loːs,
Soll dein Wesen denn genesen, von dem Erdenstaube los,
Shall your being then be healed, from the earth- dust free,
(If your being is then to be healed, and freed from the dust of earth,)

mʊst‘ ˈım ˈva͜enən dıç fɛɐ̯-/fɛrˈla͜enən ˈjeːnɐ ˈvasɐ ˈha͜elgəm ʃoːs.
musst im Weinen dich vereinen jener Wasser heilgem Schoss.
(you) must in the weeping yourself unite (with) that water's holy womb.
(you must be united through weeping with the holy source of that water.)

[In the last two stanzas, at least, the serious message of the poem, in counterpoint with its sing-song inner rhymes, is that humankind grows spiritually only through suffering. Schubert's melodically and harmonically enchanting music seems most appropriate to the first two verses, where the tears are those of gentle melancholy only. The reference to Prometheus, best known as the titan who stole the fire of the gods and brought it to mankind, is based upon a version of the myth in which he creates man anew out of clay and tears, after the flood that destroyed Atlantis (discussed in *The Greek Myths*, Volume I, Chapter 39, by Robert Graves).]

lo:p‘ dɛs t^{h}o'k^{h}a͜eɐs
Lob des Tokayers
In Praise of Tokay

Op. 118, No. 4 [1815] (Gabriele von Baumberg)

o: 'k^{h}œst‘lɪçɐ t^{h}o'k^{h}a͜eɐ! lo: 'k^{h}ø:nɪk‘lɪçɐ va͜en, [du:]
O köstlicher Tokayer! o königlicher Wein, [*Peters:* **du königlicher Wein!]**
O delicious Tokay! O kingly wine, [you]

du: 'ʃt‘ɪmt‘əst‘ 'ma͜enə 'la͜eɐ t͜su: 'zɛlt‘nən ra͜emə'ra͜en.
du stimmest meine Leier zu seltnen Reimerei'n.
you tune my lyre to rare doggerel rhymes.

mɪt‘ laŋ lɛnt‘'be:ɐ̯t‘ɐ 'vɔnə lʊnt‘ 'nɔ͜ølɛɐ̯vaxt‘əm ʃɛrt͜s
Mit lang' entbehrter Wonne und neuerwachtem Scherz
With long- missed joy and newly awakened jest

ɛɐ̯'vɛrmst du:, gla͜eç de:ɐ̯ 'zɔnə, ma͜en 'halp‘lɛɐ̯ʃt‘ɔrbnəs hɛrt͜s.
erwärmst du, gleich der Sonne, mein halberstorb'nes Herz.
warm you, like the sun, my half-dead heart.
(you warm, like the sun, my half-dead heart.)

du: 'gi:səst‘ k^{h}raft‘ lʊnt‘ 'fɔ͜øɐ dʊrç mark‘ lʊnt dʊrç gə'ba͜en.
Du giessest Kraft und Feuer durch Mark und durch Gebein.
You pour strength and fire through marrow and through bone.

ɪç 'fy:lə 'nɔ͜øəs 'le:bən dʊrç 'ma͜enə 'la:dɐrn ʃp‘ry:n,
Ich fühle neues Leben durch meine Adern sprüh'n,
I feel new life through my veins spraying,
(I feel new life spraying through my veins,)

ʊnt 'da͜enə 'nɛk‘t‘ar,re:bən lɪn 'ma͜enəm 'bu:zən gly:n.
und deine Nektarreben in meinem Busen glüh'n.
and your nectar vines in my bosom glowing.
(and your nectar grapes glowing in my bosom.)

di:ɐ̯ zɔl, lals 'gra:mt͜sɛɐ̯ʃt‘rɔ͜øɐ, di:s li:t‘ gə'va͜eət‘ za͜en!
Dir soll, als Gramzerstreuer, dies Lied geweihet sein!
To you shall, as grief- dispeller, this song dedicated be!
(This song shall be dedicated to you, as the dispeller of grief!)

ɪn 'ʃve:ɐ̯mu:t͜sfɔlən 'la͜ɔnən bə'fly:gəlst du: das blu:t^h;
In schwermutsvollen Launen beflügelst du das Blut;
In melancholy-full moods be-wing you the blood;
(In melancholy moods you give wings to the blood;)

ba͜e 'blɔndən lʊnt‘ ba͜e 'bra͜ɔnən gi:pst du: dem 'blø:t‘zɪn mu:t^h.
bei Blonden und bei Braunen gibst du dem Blödsinn Mut.
in blondes and in brunettes give you to the bashfulness courage.
(you give courage to bashfulness in blondes and brunettes.)

[The words to this jolly drinking song were by a woman, "the Sappho of Vienna."]

'loːdas gə'ʃp'ɛnstʰ
Lodas Gespenst
Loda's Ghost

Posthumously published [composed 1816] (prose poem by James Macpherson—"Ossian")
(German translation by Edmund von Harold)

deːɐ̯ 'blaeçə, 'kʰalt'ə moːnt' lɛɐ̯'hoːp' zɪç ɪn 'ɔst'ən. deːɐ̯ ʃlaːf
Der bleiche, kalte Mond erhob sich in Osten. Der Schlaf
The pale, cold moon raised itself in east. The sleep
(*Macpherson:* The wan, cold moon rose, in the east. Sleep)
[*Peters:* **im** (ɪm, in the) **Osten;** *Harold:* **Der bleiche und** (ʊnt', and) **kalte Mond]**

ʃt'iːk' laof di 'jʏŋlɪŋə 'niːdɐ, 'iːrə 'blaoən 'hɛlmə 'ʃɪmɐn tsʊm ʃt'raːl;
stieg auf die Jünglinge nieder, ihre blauen Helme schimmern zum Strahl;
descended onto the youths down, their blue helmets shimmer to the beam;
(descended on the youths! Their blue helmets glitter to the beam;)
[*Peters:* **sank** (zaŋk', sank) **auf die Jünglinge nieder... im** (ɪm, in the) **Strahl]**

das 'ʃt'ɛrbəndə 'fɔøɐ fɛɐ̯'geːtʰ. deːɐ̯ ʃlaːf 'laːbɐ 'ruːt'ə nɪçt' laof dem 'kʰøːnɪç:
das sterbende Feuer vergeht. Der Schlaf aber ruhte nicht auf dem König:
the dying fire wastes away. The sleep however rested not on the king:
(the fading fire decays. But sleep did not rest on the king;)

eːɐ̯ hoːp' zɪç 'mɪt'ən ɪn 'zaenən 'vafən, ʊnt' ʃt'iːk' 'laŋzaːm den 'hyːgəl hɪ'naof,
er hob sich mitten in seinen Waffen, und stieg langsam den Hügel hinauf,
he raised himself in the midst of his weapons, and climbed slowly the hill up,
(he rose in the midst of his arms, and slowly ascended the hill)
[ɪm 'glantsə 'zaenɐ] [leːɐ̯] [hɪ'nan]
[*Peters:* **im Glanze seiner Waffen, und langsam stieg er den Hügel hinan]**
[in the splendor of his] [he] [upward]

di 'flamə dɛs tʰʊrms fɔn 'zarno tsuː zeːn. di 'flamə vaːɐ̯ 'dyːst'ɐ(r) ʊnt' fɛrn;
die Flamme des Turms von Sarno zu sehn. Die Flamme war düster und fern;
the flame of the tower of Sarno to see. The flame was dim and distant;
(to behold the flame of Sarno's tower. The flame was dim and distant;)
[*Peters (in error):* **Saruo;** *Harold:* **Turns** (tʰʊrns, tower's—archaic form)]

deːɐ̯ moːnt' fɛɐ̯'bark' ɪn 'ɔst'ən zaen 'roːt'əs gə'zɪçtʰ;
der Mond verbarg in Osten sein rotes Gesicht;
the moon hid in east its red face;
(the moon hid her red face in the east.)
[*Peters:* **im** (ɪm, in the) **Osten sein Antlitz** ('lant'lɪts, face) **blutig rot** ('bluːt'ɪç roːtʰ, bloody red)]

ɛs ʃt'iːk' laen 'vɪnt'ʃt'oːs fɔm 'hyːgəl hɛ'rap', laof 'zaenə 'ʃvɪŋən
es stieg ein Windstoss vom Hügel herab, auf seinen Schwingen
there descended a gust of wind from the hill down, on its wings
(A blast came from the mountain; on its wings)
[*Peters:* **es braust** (braost', roared) **ein Windstoss]**

va:ɐ̯ 'lo:das gə'ʃp'ɛnstʰ. lɛs kʰa:m tsu: 'zaenɐ 'haema:t', lʊm'rɪŋt' fɔn 'zaenən 'ʃrɛk'ən,
war Lodas Gespenst. Es kam zu seiner Heimat, umringt von seinen Schrecken,
was Loda's ghost. It came to his homeland, surrounded by his terrors,
(was the spirit of Loda. He came to his place in his terrors,)

[*Peters:* **fuhr** (fu:ɐ̯, rode) **Lodas Gespenst....von düstern** ('dy:st'ɐn, dark) **Schrecken;**
Harold: **mit** (mɪt', with) **seinen Schrecken]**

ʊnt' 'ʃyt'əlt' 'zaenən 'dy:st'ɐn ʃp'e:ɐ̯.
und schüttelt' seinen düstern Speer.
and shook his dark spear.
(and shook his dusky spear.)

[*Peters:* **den gewalt'gen** (den gə'valt'gən, the powerful) **Speer;** *Harold:* **schüttelte** ('ʃyt'əlt'ə)]

ɪn 'zaenəm 'dʊŋk'əln gə'zɪçt' gly:n 'zaenə 'laogən vi: 'flamən; 'zaenə 'ʃt'ɪmə glaeçt'
In seinem dunkeln Gesicht glühn seine Augen wie Flammen; seine Stimme gleicht
In his dark face glow his eyes like flames; his voice is like
(His eyes appeared like flames in his dark face; his voice is like)

[*Peters:* **erglühn** (lɛɐ̯'gly:n, glow) **die** (di, the) **Augen]**

lɛnt''fɛrnt'əm 'dɔnɐ. 'fɪŋgal ʃt'i:s 'zaenən ʃp'e:ɐ̯/ʃp'e:r lɪn di naxt' lʊnt' ho:p' 'zaenə
entferntem Donner. Fingal stiess seinen Speer in die Nacht und hob seine
distant thunder. Fingal thrust his spear into the night and raised his
(distant thunder. Fingal advanced his spear in night, and raised his)

[*Peters:* **und erhob** (lɛɐ̯'ho:p', raised)]

'mɛçt'ɪgə 'ʃt'ɪmə: tsi: dɪç tsu'rʏk', du: 'naxt'zo:n, ru:f 'daenə 'vɪndə lʊnt' flɔøç!
mächtige Stimme: Zieh dich zurück, du Nachtsohn, ruf deine Winde und fleuch!
mighty voice: "Draw yourself back, you night-son, call your winds and flee!
(voice on high. "Son of night, retire: call thy winds, and fly!)

va'rʊm lɛɐ̯'ʃaenst du: fo:ɐ̯ mi:ɐ̯ mɪt 'daenən 'ʃat'ɪçt'ən 'vafən? ['ʃat'ɪgən]
Warum erscheinst du vor mir mit deinen schattigten Waffen? [*Peters:* **schattigen]**
Why appear you before me with your shadow-made weapons? [shadowy]
(Why dost thou come to my presence, with thy shadowy arms?)

fʏrçt' ɪç 'daenə 'dy:st'rə 'bɪldʊŋ, du: gaest dɛs 'laedɪgən 'lo:da?
Fürcht' ich deine düstre Bildung, du Geist des leidigen Loda?
Fear I your gloomy form, you ghost of the disagreeable Loda?
(Do I fear your gloomy form, spirit of dismal Loda?)

[*Peters:* **riesigen** ('ri:zɪgən, gigantic) **Loda;** *Harold:* **düstere** ('dy:st'ərə)]

ʃvax lɪst daen ʃilt', 'kʰraft'lo:s daen 'lʊft'bɪlt' lʊnt daen ʃve:ɐ̯tʰ;
Schwach ist dein Schild, kraftlos dein Luftbild und dein Schwert;
Weak is your shield, powerless your apparition and your sword;
(Weak is thy shield of clouds: feeble ist that meteor, thy sword!) [meteor = airy phenomenon]

[fɔn 'vɔlk'ən] [das]
[*Harold:* **dein Schild von Wolken: kraftlos das Luftbild, dein Schwert]**
[of clouds] [the]

de:ɐ̯ 'vɪnt'ʃt'o:s rɔlt' zi: tsu'zamən, lʊnt du: 'zɛlbɐ bɪst' fɛɐ̯'lo:rən:
der Windstoss rollt sie zusammen, und du selber bist verloren:
the gust of wind rolls them together, and you yourself are lost:
(The blast rolls them together; and thou thyself art lost.)

[vɪnt t͡sɛɐ̯ˈʃtʻɔ͡øpʻt ˈda͡enə ˈvafən] [zɛlpstʻ]
[*Peters:* **der Wind zerstäubt deine Waffen, und du selbst bist verloren]**
[wind disperses your weapons] [yourself]

flɔ͡øç fɔn ˈma͡enən ˈla͡ogən, du: ˈnaxtʻzo:n! ru:f ˈda͡enə ˈvɪndə lʊntʻ flɔ͡øç!
Fleuch von meinen Augen, du Nachtsohn! ruf' deine Winde und fleuch!
Flee from my eyes, you night-son! call your winds and flee!"
(Fly from my presence, son of night! call thy winds and fly!")

mɪtʻ ˈho:lɐ ˈʃtʻɪmə fɛɐ̯ˈzɛt͡stʻə de:ɐ̯ ga͡estʰ: vɪlst du: la͡os ˈma͡enɐ ˈha͡ema:tʻ mɪç ˈtʰra͡ebən?
Mit hohler Stimme versetzte der Geist: Willst du aus meiner Heimat mich treiben?
With hollow voice answered the ghost: "Will you from my homeland me drive?
("Dost thou force me from my place?" replied the hollow voice.)

fo:ɐ̯ mi:ɐ̯ bɔ͡økʻtʻ zɪç das fɔlkʰ; lɪç dre: di ʃlaxtʻ lɪm ˈfɛldə de:ɐ̯ ˈtʰap͡fɐn.
Vor mir beugt sich das Volk; ich dreh' die Schlacht im Felde der Tapfern.
Before me bend themselves the people; I turn the battle in the field of the valiant.
("The people bend before me. I turn the battle in the field of the brave.)
[*Peters:* **ich lenke** (ˈlɛŋkʻə, direct/control) **die Schlacht]**

la͡of ˈfœlkʻɐ vɛrf ɪç den blɪkʰ, lʊntʻ zi: fɛɐ̯ˈʃvɪndən.
Auf Völker werf' ich den Blick, und sie verschwinden.
On nations cast I the gaze, and they disappear.
(I look on the nations and they vanish:)
[*Harold:* **Auf Völker werf' ich mein** (ma͡en, my) **Aug** (la͡okʻ, eye)]

ma͡en ˈlo:dəm fɛɐ̯ˈbra͡etʻət den tʰo:tʻ. la͡of den ˈrʏkʻən de:ɐ̯ ˈvɪndə ʃra͡etʻ ɪç foˈran,
Mein Odem verbreitet den Tod. Auf den Rücken der Winde schreit' ich voran,
My breath spreads the death. On the backs of the winds stride I onward,
(my nostrils pour the blast of death. I come abroad on the winds:)
[*Peters:* **verbreitet Tod. Auf dem** (dem) **Rücken** (on the back—singular)]

fo:ɐ̯ ˈma͡enəm gəˈzɪçtʻə ˈbra͡ozən lɔrˈkʰa:nə. ˈla:bɐ ma͡en zɪt͡s lɪstʻ ˈly:bɐ den ˈvɔlkʻən,
vor meinem Gesichte brausen Orkane. Aber mein Sitz ist über den Wolken,
before my face roar hurricanes. But my seat is above the clouds,
(the tempests are before my face. But my dwelling is calm, above the clouds;)
[ma͡en ˈfʊrxtʻba:rəs na:n fɛɐ̯ˈkʰʏndən]
[*Peters:* **mein furchtbares Nah'n verkünden Orkane;]**
[my fearful approach announce]
[(hurricanes announce my fearful approach)]
[*Harold:* **Aber mein Sitz ist ruhig** (ˈru:ɪç, calm) **über den Wolken]**

ˈangəne:m di gəˈfɪldə ˈma͡enɐ ru:!
angenehm die Gefilde meiner Ruh'!
pleasant the fields of my rest!"
(the fields of my rest are pleasant.") [*Peters:* **lieblich sind** (ˈli:pʻlɪç zɪntʻ, lovely are) **die Gefilde]**

bəˈvo:n ˈda͡enə ˈlangəne:mən gəˈfɪldə, ˈza:kʻtʻə de:ɐ̯ ˈkʰø:nɪç,
Bewohn' deine angenehmen Gefilde, sagte der König,
"Inhabit your pleasant fields," said the king,
("Dwell in thy pleasant fields," said the king;)
[*Peters:* **deine lieblichen** (ˈli:pʻlɪçən, lovely) **Gefilde, sprach** (ʃpʻra:x, spoke) **der König]**

dɛŋk‘ nɪçt‘ lan 'kʰɔmhals lɛɐ̯'tsɔ̯økʼt‘ən.
denk' nicht an Comhals Erzeugten.
think not of Comhal's begotten (son).
(let Comhal's son be forgot.)

[dox lɛnt‘'vaeç foːɐ̯ 'kʰoːmals lɛɐ̯'tsɔ̯øk‘t‘əm!]
[*Peters:* **doch entweich' vor Comals Erzeugtem!]**
[but vanish before Com(h)al's begotten (son)!]

'ʃt‘aegən 'maenə 'ʃrɪt‘ə laos 'maenən 'hyːgəln lɪn 'daenə 'friːt‘lɪçə 'leːbnə hɪ'naof?
Steigen meine Schritte aus meinen Hügeln in deine friedliche Eb'ne hinauf?
Ascend my steps from my hills into your peaceful plain up?
(Do my steps ascend from my hills into thy peaceful plains?)

[fɔn] [tsuː 'daenɐ 'friːt‘lɪçən 'voːnʊŋ lɛm'pʰoːɐ̯?]
[*Peters:* **von meinen Hügeln zu deiner friedlichen Wohnung empor?]**
[from] [to your peaceful dwelling aloft?]

bə'geːg nɪç diːɐ̯ mɪt‘ 'laenəm ʃp‘eːɐ̯ (r) laof 'daenɐ 'vɔlk‘ə, duː gaest dɛs 'laedɪgən 'loːda?
Begegn' ich dir mit einem Speer, auf deiner Wolke, du Geist des leidigen Loda?
Meet I you with a spear, on your cloud, you ghost of the dreadful Loda?
(Do I meet thee with a spear, on thy cloud, spirit of dismal Loda?)

[bə'geːgnət‘] [gə'hoːbnəm] ['riːzɪgən]
[*Peters:* **Begegnet' ich dir mit gehob'nem Speer...du Geist des riesigen Loda?]**
[met] [raised] [gigantic]

va'rʊm 'rʊntsəlst duː dɛn 'daenə ʃt‘ɪrn laof mɪç? va'rʊm 'ʃʏt‘əlst‘ duː 'daenən
Warum runzelst du denn deine Stirn' auf mich? Warum schüttelst du deinen
Why wrinkle you then your forehead at me? Why shake you your
(Why then dost thou frown on me? why shake thine)

[blɪkst] [mɪt‘ 'droːəndəm 'laogə] [ʃvɪŋst]
[*P:* **Warum blickst du mit drohendem Auge auf mich? Warum schwingst du deinen]**
[look] [with threatening eye] [brandish]

'lʊft‘ɪgən ʃp‘eːɐ̯? duː 'rʊntsəlst 'daenə ʃt‘ɪrn fɛɐ̯'geːbəns: niː floː lɪç foːɐ̯ den 'mɛçt‘ɪgən
luftigen Speer? Du runzelst deine Stirn' vergebens: nie floh ich vor den Mächtigen
airy spear? You wrinkle your brow in vain: never fled I before the mighty
(airy spear? Thou frownest in vain: I never fled from the mighty)

[ɛs 'droːət‘ miːɐ̯ daen 'flamənlaok‘] [dem 'hɛldən]
[*P:* **Es drohet mir dein Flammenaug' vergebens, nie floh ich vor dem Helden]**
[There threatens me your flame- eye] [the hero]

lɪm kʰriːk‘. lʊnt‘ 'zɔlən di 'zøːnə dɛs vɪnts den 'kʰøːnɪç fɔn 'mɔrvən lɛɐ̯'ʃrɛk‘ən?
im Krieg. Und sollen die Söhne des Winds den König von Morven erschrecken?
in the war. And shall the suns of the wind the king of Morven frighten?
(in war. And shall the sons of the wind frighten the king of Morven?)

['kʰriːgə. nuːn zɔl laen gə'bɪldə fɔn 'vɔlk‘ən]
[*Peters:* **im Kriege. Nun soll ein Gebilde von Wolken]**
[war. Now shall a form (made) of clouds]

naen, naen! leːɐ̯ kʰɛnt di 'ʃvɛçə 'liːrɐ 'vafən! flɔ̯øç tsuː 'daenəm lant‘,
Nein, nein! er kennt die Schwäche ihrer Waffen! Fleuch zu deinem Land,
No, no! He knows the weakness of their weapons!"—"Flee to your land,
(No: he knows the weakness of their arms!" "Fly to thy land,") [*Harold:* only one **Nein]**

[*Peters:* **die Schwächen** ('ʃvɛçən, weaknesses) **solcher** ('zɔlçɐ, of such) **Waffen]**

fɛɐ̯ˈzɛt͡stʻə di ˈbɪldʊŋ, fas di ˈvɪndə lʊntʻ flɔ͡øç! lɪç halt di ˈvɪndə lɪn deːɐ̯ ˈhøːlə
versetzte die Bildung, fass' die Winde und fleuch! Ich halt' die Winde in der Höhle
answered the form, "seize the winds and flee! I hold the winds in the hollow
(replied the form: "receive the wind and fly! The blasts are in the hollow)

[das gəˈbɪldə, nɪm hɪn di ˈvʊndə]
[*Peters:* **versetzte das Gebilde, nimm hin die Wunde und fleuch!**]
[the apparition, "take hence the wound (misprint?)]

ˈma͡enɐ hantʻ; lɪç bəˈʃtʻɪm den la͡oføf dɛs ʃtʻʊrms. deːɐ̯ ˈkʰøːnɪç fɔn ˈzoːra lɪstʻ ma͡en zoːn,
meiner Hand; ich bestimm' den Lauf des Sturms. Der König von Sora ist mein Sohn,
of my hand; I determine the course of the storm. The king of Sora is my son,
(of my hand: the course of the storm is mine. The king of Sora is my son,)

[*P:* **mir gehört die Macht** (miːɐ̯ gəˈhøːɐ̯t di maxt, to me belongs the might) **des Sturms**]

eːɐ̯ na͡ekʻtʻ zɪç foːɐ̯ dem ˈʃtʻa͡enə ˈma͡enɐ kʰraftʰ. za͡en heːɐ̯ lʊmˈrɪŋtʻ ˈkʰarɪk- ˈtuːra,
er neigt sich vor dem Steine meiner Kraft. Sein Heer umringt Carric-Thura,
he bends himself before the stone of my power. His army surrounds Carric- thura,
(he bends at the stone of my power. His battle is around Carric-thura;)

[iːn lʊmˈʃtʻraːlt deːɐ̯ glant͡s ˈma͡enəs ruːms]
[*Peters:* **ihn umstrahlt der Glanz meines Ruhms**]
[him around-shines the splendor of my fame]
[(the splendor of my fame shines around him)]

ʊntʻ leːɐ̯ vɪrtʻ ˈziːgən! flɔ͡øç t͡suː ˈda͡enəm lantʻ, lɛɐ̯ˈt͡sɔ͡økʻtʻɐ fɔn ˈkʰɔmhal,
und er wird siegen! Fleuch zu deinem Land, Erzeugter von Comhal,
and he will conquer! Flee to your land, begotten (son) of Comhal,
(and he will prevail! Fly to thy land, son of Comhal,) [*Peters:* **von Comal** (ˈkʰoːmal)]

ˈloːdɐ ˈʃpʻyːrə ˈma͡enə vuːtʻ, ˈma͡enə ˈflaməndə vuːtʰ! leːɐ̯ hoːpʻ
oder spüre meine Wut, meine flammende Wut! Er hob
or feel my wrath, my flaming wrath!" He lifted
(or feel my flaming wrath!" He lifted) [*Harold:* **oder spüre meine flammende Wut!**]

[ˈloːdɐ ˈfalə ˈma͡enɐ] [ˈma͡enɐ ˈflaməndɐ]
[*Peters:* **oder falle meiner Wut, meiner flammender Wut**]
[or fall to my] [to my flaming]

ˈza͡enən ˈʃatʻɪçtʻən ʃpʻeːɐ̯ lɪn di ˈhøːə, leːɐ̯ ˈna͡ekʻtʻə ˈfoːɐ̯vɛrt͡s ˈza͡enə ˈʃrɛkʻbaːrə ˈlɛŋə.
seinen schattigten Speer in die Höhe, er neigte vorwärts seine schreckbare Länge.
his shadowed spear into the heights, he bent forwards his dreadful length.
(high his shadowy spear! He bent forward his dreadful height.)

[ˈʃatʻɪgən] [ˈzɛŋkʻtʻə] [ˈfʊrçtʻbaːrə]
[*Peters:* **schattigen... er senkte vorwärts seine furchtbare Länge**]
[shadowy] [sank] [frightful]

ˈfɪŋgal gɪŋ liːm lɛntʻˈgeːgən lʊnt ˈt͡sʏkʻtʻə za͡en ʃveːɐ̯tʰ. deːɐ̯ ˈblɪt͡səndə p͡faːt dɛs ʃtʻaːls
Fingal ging ihm entgegen und zückte sein Schwert. Der blitzende Pfad des Stahls
Fingal went him toward and drew his sword. The flashing path of the steel
(Fingal, advancing, drew his sword....The gleaming path of the steel)

[*Peters:* **und zuckte** (ˈt͡sʊkʻtʻə, jerked) **sein Schwert**]
[di ˈklɪŋə dɛs ˈdʊŋkʻəlbra͡onən ˈluːno]
[*Harold (& Macpherson), cut by Schubert:* **(Schwert), die Klinge des dunkelbraunen Luno.**]
[*Macpherson:* (the blade of dark- brown Luno.)]

dʊrç'draŋ den 'dy:st'ɐn gaesth. di 'bɪldʊŋ tsɛɐ̯'flɔs gə'ʃt'alt'lo:s ɪn lʊfth,
durchdrang den düstern Geist. Die Bildung zerfloss gestaltlos in Luft,
pierced the gloomy ghost. The form melted shapelessly into air,
(winds through the gloomy ghost. The form fell shapeless into air,)

[*Peters:* **Das Gebilde** (das gə'bɪldə, the apparition) **zerfloss**]

vi: 'laenə 'zɔøːlə fɔn raox, 'vɛlçə de:ɐ̯ ʃt'a:p' dɛs 'jʏŋlɪŋs bə'ry:ɐ̯t',
wie eine Säule von Rauch, welche der Stab des Jünglings berührt,
like a column of smoke, which the staff of the youth touches,
(like a column of smoke, which the staff of the boy disturbs,)

[tsɛɐ̯'ʃt'ɔøp't' fɔm 'haoxə dɛs 'vɪndəs]
[*Peters:* **Rauch, zerstäubt vom Hauche des Windes**]
[dispersed by the breath of the wind]

vi: le:ɐ̯/le:r laos de:ɐ̯ 'ʃt'ɛrbəndən 'ʃmi:də 'laofʃt'aek'th. laot' ʃri: 'lo:das gə'ʃp'ɛnst',
wie er aus der sterbenden Schmiede aufsteigt. Laut schrie Lodas Gespenst,
as it from the dying forge rises. Loudly shrieked Loda's ghost,
(as it rises from the half-extinguished furnace. The spirit of Loda shrieked,)

[vɛn zi:] ['glu:t'hɛlən]
[*Peters:* **wenn sie aus der gluthellen Schmiede aufsteigt**]
[when it (the column)] [fire-bright]

lals lɛs, lɪn zɪç 'zɛlbɐ gə'rɔlt', laof dem 'vɪndə zɪç ho:p'. lɪnɪs'tho:rə 'be:p't'ə baem khlaŋ.
als es, in sich selber gerollt, auf dem Winde sich hob. Inistore bebte beim Klang.
as it, in itself itself rolled, on the wind itself lifted. Inistore shook at the sound.
(as, rolled into himself, he rose on the wind. Inistore shook at the sound.)

['ne:bəl tsɛɐ̯'fli:sənt'] [be:p't' bae dem]
[*Peters:* **als es in Nebel zerfliessend,.. bebt bei dem Klang**]
[mist dissolving] [shakes at the]

aof dem 'lap'grʊnt' 'hø:ɐ̯t'əns di 'vɛlən; zi: 'ʃt'andən
Auf dem Abgrund hörten's die Wellen; sie standen
In the abyss heard it the waves; they stood (still)
(The waves heard it on the deep. They stopped)

[*Peters:* **tief im** (thi:f lɪm, deep in the) **Abgrund... sie starrten** ('ʃt'art'ən, became rigid)]

fo:ɐ̯ 'ʃrɛk'ən lɪn de:ɐ̯ 'mɪt'ə 'li:rəs laofs. di 'frɔøndə 'fɪŋals 'ʃp'raŋən 'phlœtslɪç
vor Schrecken in der Mitte ihres Laufs. Die Freunde Fingals sprangen plötzlich
for fright in the midst of their course. The friends of Fingal sprang suddenly
(in their course with fear: the friends of Fingal started, at once;)

[*Peters:* **in Mitten** (lɪn 'mɪt'ən, in the middle) **ihres Laufs**]

lɛm'pho:ɐ̯, zi: 'grɪfən 'li:rə gə'vɪçt'ɪgən 'ʃp'e:rə; zi: 'mɪst'ən den 'khø:nɪç:
empor, sie griffen ihre gewichtigen Speere; sie missten den König:
up, they grasped their weighty spears; they missed the king:
(they took their heavy spears. They missed the king;)

[*Peters:* **sie fassten** ('fast'ən, seized) **ihre gewichtigen Speere**]

'tsɔrnɪç 'fu:rən zi: laof; lal 'li:rə 'vafən lɛɐ̯'ʃɔlən! de:ɐ̯ mo:nt' rʏk't' lɪm 'lɔst'ən fo'ran.
zornig fuhren sie auf; all' ihre Waffen erschollen! Der Mond rückt' im Osten voran.
angrily rose they up; all their weapons resounded! The moon came in the east forth.
(they rose in rage; all their arms resound! The moon came forth in the east.)

[*Peters:* (*missing:* **zornig fuhren sie auf;**) **all' ihre Waffen ertönten** (lɛɐ̯'thø:nt'ən, sounded)]

ˈfɪŋgal kʰeːɐ̯tʻ |ɪm kʰlaŋ ˈzaenɐ ˈvafən tsuˈrʏkʰ. groːs vaːɐ̯ deːɐ̯ ˈjʏŋlɪŋə ˈfrɔødə,
Fingal kehrt' im Klang seiner Waffen zurück. Gross war der Jünglinge Freude,
Fingal returned in the clang of his weapons back. Great was the youths' joy,
(Fingal returned in the gleam of his arms. The joy of his youth was great,)
[*Harold:* **kehrte** (ˈkʰeːɐ̯tʻə, returned)]

ˈiːrə ˈzeːlən ˈruːɪç, viː das meːɐ̯ naːx dem ʃtʻʊrm. |ʊˈliːn hoːpʻ den ˈfrɔødəngəzaŋ;
ihre Seelen ruhig, wie das Meer nach dem Sturm. Ullin hob den Freudengesang;
their souls calm, like the sea after the storm. Ullin raised the joy- song;
(their souls settled, as a sea from a storm. Ullin raised the song of gladness.)
[ˈzeːlə] [ˈ|ʊlɪn |ɛɐ̯ˈhoːpʻ] [ˈjuːbəlgəzaŋ]
[*Peters:* **ihre Seele ruhig... Ullin erhob den Jubelgesang]**
[soul] [Ullin raised] [song of rejoicing]

di ˈhyːgəl |ɪnɪsˈtʰoːrəs froˈlɔkʻtʻən. hoːx ʃtʻiːkʻ di ˈflamə deːɐ̯/deːr ˈ|aeçə;
die Hügel Inistores frohlockten. Hoch stieg die Flamme der Eiche;
the hills of Inistore rejoiced. High rose the flame of the oak;
(The hills of Inistore rejoiced. The flame of the oak arose;)

ˈhɛldəngəʃɪçtʻən ˈvʊrdən |ɛɐ̯ˈtseːltʰ. [ˈhɛldəngəzɛŋə |ɛɐ̯ˈfrɔøtʻən den kʰraes.]
Heldengeschichten wurden erzählt. [*Peters:* **Heldengesänge erfreuten den Kreis.**
hero- stories were told. [Songs of heroes gladdened the circle.]
(and the tales of heroes are told.)

[*Peters adds the following, the music taken from Schubert's trio* "Punschlied"*:*]

[hael ˈ|ʊnzɐm ˈkʰøːnɪç, ˈtʰapfɐ(r) |ʊntʻ ʃtʻarkʻ, |iːm bɔøkʻtʻ zɪç ˈjeːdɐ ˈviːdɐʃtʻantʻ
[Heil unserm König, tapfer und stark, ihm beugt sich jeder Widerstand
[Hail to our king, valiant and strong, (before) him bends itself every opposition
[(Hail to our king, valiant and strong! Every opposition bends before him,)

|ʊntʻ zɛlpst deːɐ̯ ˈgaestʻɐ ˈʃrɛkʻlɪçə maxtʻ! hael |iːm, deːɐ̯ ˈmɔrvəns ˈkʰøːnɪç |ɪstʰ!]
und selbst der Geister schreckliche Macht! Heil ihm, der Morvens König ist!]
and even the ghosts' fearful power! Hail to him, who Morven's king is!]
(and even the fearful power of ghosts! Hail to him who is Morven's king!)]

[The text is from "Carric-thura," supposedly one of the poetic lays of the ancient Celtic bard Ossian, actually the work of James Macpherson, who in his notes to this story identifies Loda's ghost with the spirit of Odin, chief of the Nordic gods, who is still believed to fly through stormy night skies, even in present-day Switzerland, as described by Carl Jung in his memoirs. Schubert based his musically rather conventional setting on Harold's translation, and that is the version offered by the *Gesamtausgabe*; but when the song was originally published by Anton Diabelli in 1830 the text was altered in nearly every line, and the music adjusted to fit the changes; furthermore two bars and the original postlude were cut and an interlude was added to introduce the music of Schubert's trio for male voices "*Punschlied,*" with new words by Leopold von Sonnleithner (this "Punch-Song" is not the same as the solo *Lied* with the identical title). The Peters edition follows the Diabelli version, which is true neither to Schubert nor to Macpherson.]

ˈlɔrma
Lorma
Lorma

Posthumously published [composed 1816] (prose poem by James Macpherson— "Ossian")
(German translation by Edmund von Harold)

ˈlɔrma zaːs ǀɪn deːɐ̯ ˈhalə fɔn ˈǀaldo. ziː zaːs bae̯m lɪçtʻ ˈǀae̯nɐ ˈflaməndən ˈǀae̯çə.
Lorma sass in der Halle von Aldo. Sie sass beim Licht einer flammenden Eiche.
Lorma sat in the hall of Aldo. She sat by the light of a flaming oak.
(*Macpherson:* Lorma sat in Aldo's hall. She sat at the light of a flaming oak.)

di naxtʻ ʃtʻiːkʻ hɛˈrapʻ, ˈǀaːb reːɐ̯ ˈkʰeːɐ̯tʻə nɪçtʻ ˈviːdɐ t͡suˈrʏkʰ. ˈlɔrmas ˈzeːlə
Die Nacht stieg herab, ab'r er kehrte nicht wieder zurück. Lormas Seele
The night descended down, but he came not again back. Lorma's soul
(The night came down; but he did not return. The soul of Lorma) [*Harold:* **aber** (ˈǀaːbɐ, but)]

vaːɐ̯ tʰryːpʻ. vas hɛlt dɪç, duː ˈjɛːgɐ fɔn ˈkʰoːna, t͡suˈrʏkʻ? duː hastʻ jaː fɛɐ̯ˈʃpʻrɔxən
war trüb. "Was hält dich, du Jäger von Cona, zurück? du hast ja versprochen
was sad. "What holds you, you hunter of Cona, back? You have after all promised
(is sad! "What detains thee, hunter of Cona? Thou didst promise) [*Harold: without* **ja**]

ˈviːdɐ t͡su ˈkʰeːrən! ˈvaːrən di ˈhɪrʃə vae̯tʻ ǀɪn deːɐ̯ ˈfɛrnə?
wider zu kehren! Waren die Hirsche weit in der Ferne?
again to return! Were the stags far in the distance?
(to return. Has the deer been distant far?)

ˈbrao̯zən ǀan deːɐ̯ ˈhae̯də di ˈdyːstʻɐn ˈvɪndə ǀʊm dɪç? ǀɪç bɪn ǀɪm ˈlandə
Brausen an der Heide die düstern Winde um dich? Ich bin im Lande
Roar on the heath the gloomy winds around you? I am in the land
(Do the dark winds sigh round thee on the heath? I am in the land)

deːɐ̯ ˈfrɛmdən. veːɐ̯/veːr ǀɪstʻ mae̯n frɔ͡ø̯ntʻ, ǀals ˈǀaldo? ˈkʰɔmə fɔn ˈdae̯nən
der Fremden. Wer ist mein Freund, als Aldo? Komme von deinen
of the strangers. Who is my friend, but Aldo? Come from your
(of strangers; where is my friend, but Aldo? Come from thy) [*Harold:* **komm** (kʰɔm, come)]

ǀɛɐ̯ˈʃaləndən ˈhyːgəln, ǀoː mae̯n ˈbɛstʻɐ gəˈliːpʻtʻɐ! ziː vantʻ ˈǀiːrə ˈǀao̯gən
erschallenden Hügeln, o mein bester Geliebter!" Sie wandt' ihre Augen
sounding hills, O my best beloved!" She turned her eyes
(sounding hills, O my best beloved!" Her eyes are turned)

ˈgeːgən das tʰoːɐ̯. ziː lao̯ʃt t͡sʊm ˈbrao̯zəndən vɪntʻ. ziː dɛŋkʻtʻ,
gegen das Tor. Sie lauscht zum brausenden Wind. Sie denkt,
toward the gate. She listened to the roaring wind. She thinks,
(toward the gate. She listens to the rustling blast. She thinks)

ǀɛs ˈzae̯ən di ˈtʰrɪtʻə fɔn ˈǀaldo. frɔ͡ø̯tʻ ʃtʻae̯kʻtʻ ǀɪn ˈǀiːrəm ˈǀantʻlɪt͡s,
es seien die Tritte von Aldo. Freud' steigt in ihrem Antlitz,
it may be the steps of Aldo. Joy rises in her countenance,
(it is Aldo's tread. Joy rises in her face!) [*Harold:* **dies'** (diːs, these) **seien die Tritte**]

'a:bɐ 've:mu:t' kʰe:ɐ̯t' 'vi:dɐ, vi: lam mo:nt' 'la͜enə 'dʏnə 'vɔlk'ə, t͡su'rʏkʰ.
aber Wehmut kehrt wieder, wie am Mond eine dünne Wolke, zurück.
but melancholy returns again, as on the moon a thin cloud, back.
(But sorrow returns again, like a thin cloud on the moon.)

[Schubert left this song, as well as an earlier attempt, unfinished. It is from "The Battle of Lora," one of the "Ossian" songs. Lorna was the beautiful wife of the Scandinavian king of Sora; she fell in love with Aldo, a brave Celtic chieftain, and ran away with him to Scotland. Her husband pursued the lovers, and slew Aldo in single combat. Lorna afterwards died of grief. Schubert's first version has been completed and privately published by Reinhard van Hoorickx.]

lu'i:zəns 'lant'vɔrtʰ
Luisens Antwort
Louisa's Answer

Posthumously published [composed 1815] (poem by Ludwig Kosegarten)

vo:l 'va͜enən 'gɔt'əs 'lɛŋəl, vɛn 'li:bəndə zɪç 'tʰrɛnən,
Wohl weinen Gottes Engel, wenn Liebende sich trennen,
No doubt weep God's angels, when lovers from each other part,
(No doubt God's angels weep when lovers are parted;)

vi: ve:ɐ̯d ɪç 'le:bən 'kʰœnən, gə'li:p't'ɐ(r), 'lo:nə dɪç!
wie werd' ich leben können, Geliebter, ohne dich!
how shall I to live be able, beloved, without you!
(How shall I be able to live without you, beloved?)

gə'ʃt'ɔrbən 'lalən 'frɔ͜ødən, le:b ɪç fɔrt''lan den 'la͜edən,
Gestorben allen Freuden, leb' ich fortan den Leiden,
Dead to all joys, live I henceforth for the sorrows,
(Dead to all joys, I live from now on for my sorrows,)

ʊnt' 'nɪmɐ, 'vɪlhɛlm, 'nɪmɐ fɛɐ̯'gɪst' lu'i:za dɪç.
und nimmer, Wilhelm, nimmer vergisst Luisa dich.
and never, William, never forgets Louisa you.
(and Luisa will never, never forget you, William.)

vi: kʰœnt' ɪç da͜en fɛɐ̯'gɛsən! vo'hɪn lɪç, frɔ͜ønt', mɪç 'vɛndə,
Wie könnt' ich dein vergessen! Wohin ich, Freund, mich wende,
How could I you forget! Wherever I, friend, myself turn,
(How could I forget you? Wherever I turn, my friend,)

vo'hɪn den blɪk' nu:ɐ̯ 'zɛndə, lʊm'ʃt'ra:lt da͜en 'bɪlt'nɪs mɪç.
wohin den Blick nur sende, umstrahlt dein Bildnis mich.
wherever the gaze only send, around-shines your image me.
(wherever I chance to look, your image shines all around me.)

mɪt 'tʰrʊŋk'ənəm lɛnt'tsʏk'ən ze: ɪç lɛs la͜of mɪç 'blɪk'ən.
Mit trunkenem Entzücken seh' ich es auf mich blicken.
With intoxicated rapture see I it at me look.
(Drunk with rapture I see it looking at me.)

na͜en, ˈnɪmɐ, ˈvɪlhɛlm, ˈnɪmɐ fɛɐ̯ˈgɪst‘ luˈiːza dɪç.
Nein, nimmer, Wilhelm, nimmer vergisst Luisa dich.
No, never, William, never forgets Louisa you.
(No, Luisa will never, never forget you, William.)

viː kʰœnt‘ ɪç da͜en fɛɐ̯ˈgɛsən! gəˈrøːt‘ət‘ fɔn fɛɐ̯ˈlaŋən,
Wie könnt' ich dein vergessen! Gerötet von Verlangen,
How could I you forget! Flushed from desire,
(How could I forget you? Flushed with desire,)

viː ˈflamt‘ən ˈda͜enə ˈvaŋən, fɔn ˈɪnbrʊnst‘ nas, |ʊm mɪç!
wie flammten deine Wangen, von Inbrunst nass, um mich!
how flamed your cheeks, from ardor wet, for me!
(how your cheeks were on fire, moist with ardor, for me!)

ɪm ˈviːdɐʃa͜en deːɐ̯ ˈda͜enən, viː ˈlɔ͜øçt‘ət‘ən di ˈma͜enən!
Im Widerschein der Deinen, wie leuchteten die Meinen!
In the reflection of the yours, how shone the mine!
(As reflected in yours, how mine also shone!)

na͜en, ˈnɪmɐ, ˈvɪlhɛlm, ˈnɪmɐ fɛɐ̯ˈgɪst‘ luˈiːza dɪç.
Nein, nimmer, Wilhelm, nimmer vergisst Luisa dich.
No, never, William, never forgets Louisa you.
(No, Luisa will never, never forget you, William.)

viː kʰœnt‘ ɪç da͜en fɛɐ̯ˈgɛsən! fɛɐ̯ˈgɛsən,
Wie könnt' ich dein vergessen! Vergessen,
How could I you forget! Forget,
(How could I forget you? How could I forget)

viː di ˈbløːdə ɪn blɪk‘ |ʊnt‘ nɪk‘ |ʊnt‘ ˈreːdə di ˈliːbə zyːs bəˈʃlɪç.
wie die Blöde in Blick und Nick und Rede die Liebe süss beschlich.
how the shy girl [obj.] in glance and nod and speech the love [subj.] sweetly stole upon.
(how sweetly love stole upon the shy girl with a glance and a nod and a word.)

da͜en ˈt͜saːɐ̯t‘əs ˈliːbəsfleːən, ma͜en ˈʃt‘aməlndəs gəˈʃt‘eːən zɔlt‘ ɪç fɛɐ̯ˈgɛsən?
Dein zartes Liebeflehen, mein stammelndes Gestehen sollt' ich vergessen?
Your tender love- pleading, my stammering confession should I forget?
(Should I forget your tender pleading, my stammering confession of love?)

ˈnɪmɐ fɛɐ̯ˈgɪst‘ luˈiːza dɪç. viː kʰœnt‘ ɪç da͜en fɛɐ̯ˈgɛsən!
Nimmer vergisst Luisa dich. Wie könnt' ich dein vergessen!
Never forgets Louisa you. How could I you forget!
(Louisa will never forget you. How could I forget you?)

di ˈtʰøːnə jeː fɛɐ̯ˈlɛrnən, voˈrɪn bɪs t͜suː den ˈʃt‘ɛrnən duː mɪç |ɛɐ̯ˈhoːbəst‘, mɪç!
Die Töne je verlernen, worin bis zu den Sternen du mich erhobest, mich!
The tones ever unlearn, in which till to the stars you me lifted up, me!
(How could I ever forget the tones in which you lifted me up to the stars? Me!)

ax, |ʊnla͜osˈlœʃlɪç ˈkʰlɪŋən ziː miːɐ̯/miːr |ɪn ˈloːrən, ˈzɪŋən miːɐ̯/miːr |ɪm ˈhɛrt͜sən.
Ach, unauslöschlich klingen sie mir in Ohren, singen mir im Herzen.
Ah, inextinguishable sound they to me in ears, sing to me in the heart.
(Ah, inextinguishably they still sound in my ears, they sing in my heart.)

ˈnɪmɐ fɛɐ̯ˈgɪstʻ luˈiːza dɪç. viː kʰœntʻ ɪç da͜en fɛɐ̯ˈgɛsən! fɛɐ̯ˈgɛsən ˈda͜enɐ ˈbriːfə
Nimmer vergisst Luisa dich. Wie könnt' ich dein vergessen! Vergessen deiner Briefe
Never forgets Louisa you. How could I you forget! Forget your letters
(Louisa will never forget you. How could I forget you? How could I forget your letters)

fɔl ˈtsaːɐ̯tʻɐ, ˈtʰrɔ͜øɐ ˈliːbə, fɔl ˈhɛrbən graːms lʊm mɪç!
voll zarter, treuer Liebe, voll herben Grams um mich!
full of tender, true love, full of bitter sadness for me!

ɪç vɪl ziː ˈzɔrkʻzaːm ˈvaːrən, fyːɐ̯ ˈma͜enən zarkʻ ziː ˈʃpʻaːrən.
Ich will sie sorgsam wahren, für meinen Sarg sie sparen.
I want them carefully to preserve, for my coffin them to save.
(I want to preserve them carefully, I want to save them to be placed in my coffin.)

gəˈliːpʻtʻɐ, ˈnɪmɐ, ˈnɪmɐ fɛɐ̯ˈgɪstʻ luˈiːza dɪç.
Geliebter, nimmer, nimmer vergisst Luisa dich. [*poem:* **Nein, Wilhelm, nimmer, nimmer**]
Beloved, never, never forgets Louisa you.
(Beloved, Louisa will never, never forget you.)

viː kʰœntʻ ɪç da͜en fɛɐ̯ˈgɛsən! fɛɐ̯ˈgɛsən ˈjeːnɐ ˈʃtʻʊndən,
Wie könnt' ich dein vergessen! Vergessen jener Stunden,
How could I you forget! Forget those hours,
(How could I forget you? How could I forget those hours)

voː lɪç fɔn diːɐ̯/diːr lʊmˈvʊndən, lʊmˈflɛçtʻəntʻ ˈlɪnɪçst dɪç, [ˈlɪnɪç]
wo ich von dir umwunden, umflechtend innigst dich, [*poem:* **innig**]
when I by you around-wound, around-weaving most intimately you, [intimately]
(when I, wrapped in your arms, entwining my arms most intimately about you,)

an ˈda͜enə brʊstʻ mɪç ˈleːntʻə, gants da͜en tsuː za͜en mɪç ˈzeːntʻə!
an deine Brust mich lehnte, ganz dein zu sein mich sehnte!
on your breast myself leaned, completely yours to be myself yearned!
(leaned against your chest and yearned to be yours completely!) [*sich sehnen* = to yearn]

gəˈliːpʻtʻɐ, ˈnɪmɐ, ˈnɪmɐ fɛɐ̯ˈgɪstʻ luˈiːza dɪç. viː kʰœntʻ ɪç da͜en fɛɐ̯ˈgɛsən!
Geliebter, nimmer, nimmer vergisst Luisa dich. Wie könnt' ich dein vergessen!
Beloved, never, never forgets Louisa you. How could I you forget!
(Beloved, Louisa will never, never forget you. How could I forget you?)

fɛɐ̯ˈgɛsən jeː deːɐ̯ ˈfraːgən, diː duː lɪn ˈʃøːnɐn ˈtʰaːgən loːn ˈlɛndə ˈfraːkʻtʻəstʻ:
Vergessen je der Fragen, die du in schönern Tagen ohn' Ende fragtest:
Forget ever the questions, which you in fairer days without end asked:
(How could I ever forget the questions which in fairer days you used to ask me unceasingly:)

ʃpʻrɪç, luˈiːza, bɪst duː ˈma͜enə? jaː, ˈtʰra͜otʻɐ, jaː di ˈda͜enə bɪn lɪç la͜of ˈleːvɪç.
"Sprich, Luisa, bist du meine?" Ja, Trauter, ja die Deine bin ich auf ewig.
"Speak, Louisa, are you mine?" Yes, dear one, yes the yours am I for ever.
("Speak, Louisa, are you mine?" Yes, dear one, yes! I am yours forever.)

ˈnɪmɐ fɛɐ̯ˈgɪstʻ luˈiːza dɪç. viː kʰœntʻ ɪç da͜en fɛɐ̯ˈgɛsən!
Nimmer vergisst Luisa dich. Wie könnt' ich dein vergessen!
Never forgets Louisa you. How could I you forget!
(Louisa will never forget you. How could I forget you?)

fɛɐ̯'gɛsən je: de:ɐ̯ 'ʃa͜oɐ fɔn 'ze:lɪçkʰa͜etʻ lʊnt 'tʰra͜oɐ, di: 'lalgəvaltʻɪç
Vergessen je der Schauer von Seligkeit und Trauer, die allgewaltig
Forget ever the shudders of bliss and grief, which all-powerfully
(How could I ever forget the shivers of bliss and grief that all-powerfully)

mɪç lan 'da͜enɐ brʊst dʊrç't͜sʏkʻtʻən, la͜os 'da͜enəm larm lɛntʻ'rʏkʻtʻən t͜su: 'hø:ɐn 'sfɛ:rən!
mich an deiner Brust durchzückten, aus deinem Arm entrückten zu höhern Sphären!
me at your breast through-flashed, from your arm carried away to higher spheres!
(ran through me at your breast, that carried me away out of your arms to higher spheres?)

'nɪmɐ fɛɐ̯'gɪstʻ lu'i:za dɪç. vi: kʰœntʻ ɪç da͜en fɛɐ̯'gɛsən!
Nimmer vergisst Luisa dich. Wie könnt' ich dein vergessen!
Never forgets Louisa you. How could I you forget!
(Louisa will never forget you. How could I forget you?)

fɛɐ̯'gɛsən je: de:ɐ̯ 'kʰva:lən, vo'mɪtʻ la͜os 'gɔldnən 'ʃa:lən di 'li:bə 'tʰrɛŋkʻtʻə mɪç!
Vergessen je der Qualen, womit aus gold'nen Schalen die Liebe tränkte mich!
Forget ever the torments with which from golden goblets the love gave to drink me!
(Can I ever forget the torments that love gave me to drink out of golden goblets?)

vas lɪç lʊm dɪç gə'lɪtʻən, vas lɪç lʊm dɪç gə'ʃtʻrɪtʻən, zɔltʻ ɪç fɛɐ̯'gɛsən?
Was ich um dich gelitten, was ich um dich gestritten, sollt' ich vergessen?
What I for you (have) suffered, what I for you (have) fought, should I forget?
(Should I forget what I have suffered for your sake, the battles I have fought on your account?)

'nɪmɐ fɛɐ̯'gɪstʻ lu'i:za dɪç. lɪç kʰan dɪç nɪçtʻ fɛɐ̯'gɛsən!
Nimmer vergisst Luisa dich. Ich kann dich nicht vergessen!
Never forgets Louisa you. I can you not forget!
(Louisa will never forget you. I can not forget you!)

la͜of 'je:dəm 'ma͜enɐ 'tʰrɪtʻə, ɪn 'ma͜enɐ 'li:bən 'mɪtʻə, lʊm'ʃve:pʻt da͜en 'bɪltʻnɪs mɪç.
Auf jedem meiner Tritte, in meiner Lieben Mitte, umschwebt dein Bildnis mich.
At each of my steps, in my dear ones' midst, around-hovers your image me.
(Your image hovers about me at every step I take, and in the midst of my loved ones.)

a͜of 'ma͜enɐ 'la͜envantʻ 'ʃɪmɐt͜s, lan 'ma͜enəm 'fo:ɐ̯haŋ 'flɪmɐt͜s.
Auf meiner Leinwand schimmert's, an meinem Vorhang flimmert's.
On my canvas shimmers it, on my curtain glimmers it.
(It shimmers on my canvas when I paint, it glimmers on my curtain.)

gə'li:pʻtʻɐ, 'nɪmɐ, 'nɪmɐ fɛɐ̯'gɪstʻ lu'i:za dɪç.
Geliebter, nimmer, nimmer vergisst Luisa dich. [*poem:* **Nein, Wilhelm, nimmer, nimmer**]
Beloved, never, never forgets Louisa you.
(Beloved, Louisa will never, never forget you.)

ɪç kʰan dɪç nɪçtʻ fɛɐ̯'gɛsən! mɪtʻ 'je:dəm 'gɔldnən 'mɔrgən
Ich kann dich nicht vergessen! Mit jedem gold'nen Morgen
I can you not forget! With every golden morning
(I can't forget you! With every golden morning)

ɛɐ̯'vaxtʻ ma͜en 't͜sɛ:ɐ̯tʻlɪç 'zɔrgən, ma͜en 'zɔ͜øft͜sən, lax, lʊm dɪç!
erwacht mein zärtlich Sorgen, mein Seufzen, ach, um dich!
wakes my tender worrying, my sighing, ah, for you!
(my tender concern awakens, my sighing, ah, for you!)

vo: va͜elst du: ˈlɪt͜st, du: ˈla͜enɐ? vas dɛŋkst du: ˈlɪt͜st, du: ˈma͜enɐ?
"Wo weilst du itzt, du Einer? was denkst du itzt, du Meiner?
"Where linger you now, you one? what think you now, you mine? [*itzt* = *jetzt* = now]
("Where are you now, my one-and-only one? What are you thinking about, you who are mine?)

dɛŋkst du: ˈla͜ox ˈlan luˈi:zən? luˈi:za dɛŋk'tʻ ˈlan dɪç! ˈlɪç kʰan dɪç nɪçtʻ fɛɐ̯ˈgɛsən!
Denkst du auch an Luisen? Luisa denkt an dich!" Ich kann dich nicht vergessen!
Think you also of Louisa? Louisa thinks of you!" I can you not forget!
(Are you thinking about Louisa? Louisa is thinking about you!" I can't forget you!)

dɛs naxt͜s ˈla͜of ˈma͜enəm ˈbɛtʻə gəˈma:ntʻ mɪçs ˈlɔftʻ,
Des Nachts auf meinem Bette gemahnt mich's oft,
At night on my bed reminds me it often,
(At night, lying on my bed, I often feel)

ˈlals ˈhɛtʻə da͜en ˈlarm ˈlʊmˈʃlʊŋən mɪç. dɛs ˈpʰɛndəls ˈʃvɪŋʊŋ vɛkʻtʻ mɪç,
als hätte dein Arm umschlungen mich. Des Pendels Schwingung weckt mich,
as if had your arm embraced me. The pendulum's swinging wakes me,
(as if your arms had just embraced me. The swinging of the pendulum awakens me,)

das hɔrn dɛs ˈvɛçtʻɐs ʃrɛkʻtʻ mɪç, ˈlaˈla͜en bɪn ˈlɪç ˈlɪm ˈdʊŋkʻəl [ˈdʊŋkʻəln]
das Horn des Wächters schreckt mich, allein bin ich im Dunkel [*poem:* Dunkeln]
the horn of the watchman alarms me, alone am I in the dark [darkening]
(the night watchman's horn alarms me; I am alone in the dark)

ˈlʊntʻ ˈva͜enə ʃtʻɪl ˈlʊm dɪç. ˈlɪç kʰan dɪç nɪçtʻ fɛɐ̯ˈgɛsən!
und weine still um dich. Ich kann dich nicht vergessen!
and weep quietly for you. I can you not forget!
(and quietly weep for you. I can't forget you!)

nɪçtʻ ˈfrɛmdə ˈhʊldɪgʊŋən, nɪçtʻ ˈskʻla:fənˌlanbe:tʻʊŋən, ˈlo: frɔ͜ønt', fɛɐ̯ˈdrɛŋən dɪç.
Nicht fremde Huldigungen, nicht Sklavenanbetungen, o Freund, verdrängen dich.
Not strange homages, not slave- worships, O friend, displace you.
(You cannot be dislodged from my heart by the homage or slavish worship of others.)

luˈi:za li:pʻtʻ nu:ɐ̯/nu:r ˈla͜enən, nu:ɐ̯/nu:r ˈla͜enən kʰan zi: ˈma͜enən,
Louisa liebt nur Einen, nur Einen kann sie meinen,
Louisa loves only one man, only one can she love, [*meinen* (poetical) = love]

nu:ɐ̯/nu:r ˈla͜enən ni: fɛɐ̯ˈgɛsən, fɛɐ̯ˈgɛsən ˈnɪmɐ dɪç.
nur Einen nie vergessen, vergessen nimmer dich.
only one never forget, forget never you.
(only one can she never forget: she can never forget you.)

luˈi:za li:pʻtʻ nu:ɐ̯/nu:r ˈla͜enən, fɛɐ̯ˈʃmɛ:t dɛs ˈʃtʻʊt͜sɐs ˈʃma͜eçəln,
Louisa liebt nur Einen, verschmäht des Stutzers Schmeicheln,
Louisa loves only one man, disdains the dandy's flattering,

fɛɐ̯ˈhø:ntʻ za͜en ˈzy:slɪç ˈhɔ͜øçəln, gəˈdɛŋkʻtʻ, ˈlo: ˈvɪlhɛlm, da͜en;
verhöhnt sein süsslich Heucheln, gedenkt, o Wilhelm, dein;
mocks his mawkish sham, thinks, O William, of you;

dɛŋk'‘t 'daenəs 'gaest‘əs 'la:dəl, daen 'li:bən 'zɔndɐ 'tʰa:dəl,
denkt deines Geistes Adel, dein Lieben sonder Tadel,
thinks of your spirit's nobility, your loving without fault,
(thinks of the nobility of your spirit, your irreproachable loving,)

daen hɛrts zo: tʰrɔø, zo: 'bi:dɐ(r), lʊnt‘ brɛnt‘ fy:ɐ dɪç la'laen.
dein Herz so treu, so bieder, und brennt für dich allein.
your heart so true, so upright, and burns for you alone.

fy:ɐ dɪç nu:ɐ ma:k‘ lɪç 'brɛnən, fy:ɐ dɪç, fy:ɐ dɪç nu:ɐ 'fy:lən.
Für dich nur mag ich brennen, für dich, für dich nur fühlen.
For you only may I burn, for you, for you only feel.
(Only for you may I burn; only for you, for you may I feel what I feel.)

di:s 'fɔøɐ(r) lɪn mi:ɐ 'kʰy:lən ma:k‘ tsaet‘, ma:k‘ 'fɛrnə nɪçtʰ.
Dies Feuer in mir kühlen mag Zeit, mag Ferne nicht.
This fire in me cool may time, may distance not.
(Neither time nor distance can cool this fire in me.)

fɔn di:ɐ, fɔn di:ɐ mɪç 'ʃaedən ma:k‘ 'frɔødə nɪçt‘, nɪçt‘ 'laedən,
Von dir, von dir mich scheiden mag Freude nicht, nicht Leiden,
From you, from you me separate may joy not, not suffering,
(Neither joy nor suffering can separate me from you,)

ma:k‘ nɪçt di hant dɛs 'tʰo:dəs, zɛlpst daen fɛɐ'gɛsən nɪçtʰ.
mag nicht die Hand des Todes, selbst dein Vergessen nicht.
may not the hand of the death, even your forgetting not.
(nor the hand of death, nor even your forgetting me.)

zɛlpst‘ vɛn du: falʃ lʊnt 'tʰrɔølo:s lan 'frɛmdə brʊst dɪç 'ʃmi:k‘t‘əstʰ,
Selbst wenn du falsch und treulos an fremde Brust dich schmiegtest,
Even if you false and unfaithful at foreign breast yourself nestled,
(Even if you became false and unfaithful, if you nestled against another woman's breast,)

ɪn 'frɛmdəm larm dɪç 'vi:k‘t‘əst‘, fɛɐ'gɛsənt‘ ʃvu:ɐ/ʃvu:r lʊnt‘ pflɪçtʰ,
in fremdem Arm dich wiegtest, vergessend Schwur und Pflicht,
in foreign arm yourself lulled, forgetting vow and duty,
(if you lulled yourself in another's arms, forgetting your vows and your duty,)

ɪn 'frɛmdən 'flamən 'brɛnt‘əst‘, lu'i:zən ga:ɐ fɛɐ'kʰɛnt‘əstʰ,
in fremden Flammen brenntest, Luisen gar verkenntest,
in foreign fires burned, Luisa even misjudged,
(if you burned with another flame, even misjudged your Louisa,)

lu'i:zən ga:ɐ fɛɐ'gɛ:səst‘— lɪç, lax! fɛɐ'gɛ:s dɪç nɪçtʰ!
Louisen gar vergässest — ich, ach! vergäss' dich nicht!
Louisa even would forget — I, ah! would forget you not!
(if you would even *forget* Louisa — I would not forget you!)

fɛɐ-/fɛr'laxt‘ət‘ lʊnt‘ fɛɐ'gɛsən, fɛɐ'lo:rən lʊnt‘ fɛɐ'lasən,
Verachtet und vergessen, verloren und verlassen,
Despised and forgotten, lost and forsaken,

kʰœnt‘ lɪç dɪç dɔx nɪçt‘ 'hasən; ʃt‘ɪl 'grɛ:mən vʏrd ɪç mɪç,
könnt' ich dich doch nicht hassen; still grämen würd' ich mich,
could I you yet not hate; quietly grieve would I myself,
(I could nevertheless not hate you; I would quietly grieve) [*sich grämen* = to grieve]

bɪs tʰo:t‘ zɪç ma͜en lɛɐ̯'barmt‘ə, das gra:p‘ mɪç kʰy:l lʊm'larmt‘ə —
bis Tod sich mein erbarmte, das Grab mich kühl umarmte —
till death itself on me took pity, the grave me coolly embraced —
(until death took pity on me and the grave took me into its cool embrace —)

dɔx la͜ox lɪm gra:p‘, lɪm 'hɪməl, lo: 'vɪlhɛlm, li:p‘t‘ ɪç dɪç!
doch auch im Grab, im Himmel, o Wilhelm, liebt' ich dich!
but even in the grave, in the heaven, O William, would love I you!
(but even in the grave, even in heaven, O William, I would love you!)

ɪn 'mɪldəm 'lɛŋəlglant͜sə vʏrd ɪç da͜en bɛt‘ lʊm'ʃɪmɐn,
In mildem Engelglanze würd' ich dein Bett umschimmern,
In mild angel-glow would I your bed around-shimmer,
(I would shimmer about your bed in a soft angel-glow,)
[*poem:* **Im Grau'n der Mitternächte** (ɪm gra͜on de:ɐ̯ 'mɪt‘ɐnɛçt‘ə, In the dread of midnight)]

ʊnt 'tsɛ:ɐ̯t‘lɪç dɪç lʊm'vɪmɐn: lɪç bɪn lu'i:za, lɪç!
und zärtlich dich umwimmern: "Ich bin Luisa, ich!
and tenderly you around-whimper: "I am Louisa, I!
(and tenderly whisper to you: "I am Louisa, it is I!)
[*poem:* **und leis' ins Ohr dir wimmern** (la͜es lɪns lo:ɐ̯ di:ɐ̯ 'vɪmɐn, softly in your ear whimper)]

lu'i:za kʰan nɪçt‘ 'hasən, lu'i:za dɪç nɪçt‘ 'lasən,
Luisa kann nicht hassen, Luisa dich nicht lassen,
Louisa can not hate, Louisa you not leave,
(Louisa can not hate; Louisa can not leave you,)

lu'i:za kʰɔmt, t͜su: 'ze:gnən, lʊnt‘ li:p‘t‘ la͜ox 'dro:bən dɪç!
Luisa kommt, zu segnen, und liebt auch droben dich!"
Louisa comes to bless, and loves too up there you!"
(Louisa will come to bless you, for she will love you in the other world as well as here!")

[Schubert composed eight of Kosegarten's poems, including the above, in one day, October 19, 1815. No one expects the singer to sing all nineteen verses; but the song is beautiful.]

'ma:homɛt͜s gə'zaŋ
Mahomets Gesang
Mohammed's Song

Two fragments posthumously published [composed 1817, 1821] (Johann Wolfgang von Goethe)

ze:t den 'fɛlzənkʰvɛl, 'frɔ͜ødəhɛl, vi: la͜en 'ʃt‘ɛrnənblɪkʰ. 'ly:bɐ 'vɔlk‘ən
Seht den Felsenquell, freudehell, wie ein Sternenblick. Über Wolken
See the rocky spring, joy- bright, like a star- glance. Above clouds
(See the spring among the rocks, joyous and bright, like the glance of a star. Above the clouds)

ˈnɛːɐ̯tʻən ˈzaenə ˈjuːgənt ˈguːtʻə ˈgaestʻɐ ˈtsvɪʃən ˈkʰlɪpʻən ʔɪm gəˈbʏʃ.
nährten seine Jugend gute Geister zwischen Klippen im Gebüsch.
nourished his youth good spirits between crags in the bushes.
(kindly spirits nourished his youth in the bushes between the crags.)

ˈjʏŋlɪŋfrɪʃ tʰantstʻ ʔeːɐ̯/ʔeːr ʔaos deːɐ̯ ˈvɔlkʻə ʔaof di ˈmarmoːɐ̯fɛlzən ˈniːdɐ,
Jünglingfrisch tanzt er aus der Wolke auf die Marmorfelsen nieder,
young-man-fresh dances he from the cloud onto the marble rocks down,
(With the freshness of young manhood he dances down from the cloud onto the marble rocks,)

ˈjaoxtsətʻ ˈviːdɐ naːx dem ˈhɪməl. dʊrç di ˈgɪpfəlgɛŋə
Jauchzet wieder nach dem Himmel. Durch die Gipfelgänge
exults again toward the sky. Through the summit-passages
(leaping up again exultantly toward the sky. Through channels near the summit)

jaːkʻtʻ ʔeːɐ̯ ˈbʊntʻən ˈkʰiːzəln naːx, ʔʊntʻ mɪtʻ ˈfryːəm ˈfyːrɐtʰrɪtʻ
jagt er bunten Kieseln nach, und mit frühem Führertritt
chases he brightly colored pebbles after, and with early leader- step
(he chases after brightly colored pebbles; and with the confident step of early leadership)

raestʻ ʔeːɐ̯ ˈzaenə ˈbruːdɐkʰvɛlən mɪtʻ zɪç fɔrtʰ.
reisst er seine Bruderquellen mit sich fort.
carries he his brother-springs with himself away.
(he carries his brother springs along with him on his way.)

ˈdrʊntʻən ʔɪn dem tʰaːl ˈʔʊntʻɐ ˈzaenəm ˈfuːstʰrɪtʻ ˈveːɐ̯dən ˈbluːmən,
Drunten in dem Tal unter seinem Fusstritt werden Blumen,
Below in the valley beneath his footstep become flowers,
(Down in the valley flowers rise where he has trod,)
[*Goethe's order of the words:* **Drunten werden in dem Tal unter seinem Fusstritt Blumen**]

ʊnt di ˈviːzə leːpʻtʻ fɔn ˈzaenəm haox. dɔx ʔiːn hɛltʻ kʰaen ˈʃatʻəntʰaːl,
und die Wiese lebt von seinem Hauch. Doch ihn hält kein Schattental,
and the meadow lives from his breath. But him holds no shadow- valley,
(and the meadow lives from his breath. But no shady valley can hold him for long,)

ˈkʰaenə ˈbluːmən, diː ʔiːm ˈzaenə kʰniː ʔʊmˈʃlɪŋən,
keine Blumen, die ihm seine Knie' umschlingen,
no flowers, which to him his knees embrace,
(nor the flowers that embrace his knees,)

iːm mɪtʻ ˈliːbəsʔaogən ˈʃmaeçəln: naːx deːɐ̯/deːr ˈʔeːbnə drɪŋtʻ zaen laof
ihm mit Liebesaugen schmeicheln: nach der Ebne dringt sein Lauf
him with love- eyes flatter: toward the plain surges his course
(and flatter him with amorous eyes: his course presses on toward the plain,)

ˈʃlaŋənvandəlntʻ. ˈbɛçə ˈʃmiːgən zɪç gəˈzɛlɪç ʔan. nuːn tʰrɪtʻ ʔeːɐ̯/ʔeːr
schlangenwandelnd. Bäche schmiegen sich gesellig an. Nun tritt er
snake- wending. Brooks join themselves sociably up (with him). Now steps he
(winding about like a snake. Brooks join up with him sociably. Now he steps)

ɪn di ˈleːbnə ˈzɪlbɐpʰraŋənt', ǀʊnt di ˈleːbnə pʰraŋt' mɪt' ǀiːm,
in die Ebne silberprangend, und die Ebne prangt mit ihm,
into the plain silver-resplendent, and the plain is resplendent with him,
(into the plain, resplendent in silver, and the plain becomes resplendent with his presence,)

ʊnt di ˈflʏsə fɔn deːɐ̯/deːr ˈleːbnə, ǀʊnt di ˈbɛçə fɔn den ˈbɛrgən,
und die Flüsse von der Ebne, und die Bäche von den Bergen,
and the rivers of the plain, and the brooks from the mountains,

ˈjaoxtsən ǀiːm ǀʊnt' ˈruːfən: ˈbruːdɐ! ˈbruːdɐ, nɪm di ˈbryːdɐ mɪt',
jauchzen ihm und rufen: Bruder! Bruder, nimm die Brüder mit,
shout with joy to him and call: "Brother! Brother, take the brothers with (you),
(shout with joy and call to him: "Brother! Brother, take your brothers with you,)

mɪt tsuː ˈdaenəm ˈǀalt'ən [ˈfaːt'ɐ, tsuː dem ˈleːvgən ˈǀoːtseaːn....]
mit zu deinem alten [Vater, zu dem ew'gen Ozean....]
with (you) to your old [father, to the eternal ocean....]

[Schubert made two attempts to set this poem, the first (which rearranges several of Goethe's lines) in 1817, the second—for a bass voice—in 1821; but both versions remained fragments (both are published in the *Gesamtausgabe*). The poem continues for another thirty-two lines. It was intended for a play *about* Mohammed, and would have been sung by his cousin Ali and his daughter Fatima in his honor. The title is misleading. The play was never finished. Goethe personifies the river as an exuberant young man, a leader. In the first fragment, Schubert characterizes the spring that becomes a river with a perpetual motion of bubbling triplets.]

ˈmaeliːt'
Mailied
May Song

Privately published [composed 1816] (poem by Ludwig Hölty)

ˈgryːnɐ vɪrt di ǀao, ǀʊnt deːɐ̯ ˈhɪməl blao; ˈʃvalbən ˈkʰeːrən ˈviːdɐ,
Grüner wird die Au, und der Himmel blau; Schwalben kehren wieder,
Greener becomes the meadow, and the sky blue; swallows return again,
(The meadow grows greener, and the sky becomes blue; the swallows are returning,)

ʊnt di ˈǀeːɐ̯st'lɪŋsliːdɐ ˈkʰlaenɐ ˈføːgəlaen ˈtsvɪtʃɐn dʊrç den haen.
und die Erstlingslieder kleiner Vögelein zwitschern durch den Hain.
and the first songs of small little birds twitter through the grove.
(and little birds are twittering their first songs through the grove.)

ǀaos dem ˈblyːt'ənʃt'raox veːt deːɐ̯ ˈliːbə haox: zaet deːɐ̯ lɛnts ǀɛɐ̯ˈʃiːnən,
Aus dem Blütenstrauch weht der Liebe Hauch: seit der Lenz erschienen,
From the blossoming bush wafts the love's breath: since the spring (has) appeared,
(The breath of love wafts from the blossoming bush: since spring appeared)

ˈvalt'ət' ziː ǀɪm ˈgryːnən, maːlt di ˈbluːmən bʊnt', roːt dɛs ˈmɛːt'çəns mʊnt'.
waltet sie im Grünen, malt die Blumen bunt, rot des Mädchens Mund.
rules it [love] in the greenery, paints the flowers colored, red the girl's mouth.
(love rules in the greenery, love colors the flowers, and paints a girl's mouth red.)

'bry:dɐ, 'kʰʏsət' li:n! dɛn di 'ja:rə fli:n! 'la͜enən kʰʊs ɪn 'le:rən
Brüder, küsset ihn! denn die Jahre fliehn! Einen Kuss in Ehren
Brothers, kiss it! for the years flee! A kiss in honor [= in good faith]
(Brothers, kiss that mouth! For the years fly by! A kiss in good faith)

kʰan lɔ͜øç 'ni:mant' 've:rən! kʰʏst' li:n, 'bry:dɐ, kʰʏst', va͜el le:ɐ̯ 'kʰʏslɪç lɪstʰ!
kann euch niemand wehren! Küsst ihn, Brüder, küsst, weil er küsslich ist!
can to you no one forbid! Kiss it, brothers, kiss, because it kissable is!
(no one can deny you! Kiss that mouth, brothers, kiss it, because it is kissable!)

ze:t, de:ɐ̯ 'tʰa͜obɐ gɪrt', ze:t, de:ɐ̯ 'tʰa͜obə ʃvɪrt' lʊm za͜en 'li:bəs 'tʰɔ͜øp'çən!
Seht, der Tauber girrt, seht, der Tauber schwirrt um sein liebes Täubchen!
See, the male dove coos, see, the male dove buzzes about his dear little dove!
(See, the male dove coos and hovers about his dear little mate!)

ne:mt' lɔ͜øç la͜ox la͜en 'va͜ep'çən, vi: de:ɐ̯ 'tʰa͜obɐ tʰu:t', lʊnt' za͜et' 'vo:lgəmu:tʰ!
Nehmt euch auch ein Weibchen, wie der Tauber tut, und seid wohlgemut!
Take yourself also a little wife, as the male dove does, and be cheerful!
(Take yourself a little wife too, as the male dove does, and be happy!)

[Schubert set this text three times, as a trio for male voices, as a duet, and as a solo song, which has survived in the songbook of his first love, Therese Grob. There he wrote out the words of the first verse with the music, with repeat marks. The song remained unpublished until privately printed by Reinhard Van Hoorickx.]

ma'ri
Marie
Marie

Posthumously published [composed 1819?] (poem by Novalis)

ɪç 'ze:ə dɪç lɪn 'tʰa͜ozənt' 'bɪldɐn, ma'ri:a, 'li:p'lɪç 'la͜osgədrʏk't',
Ich sehe dich in tausend Bildern, Maria, lieblich ausgedrückt,
I see you in (a) thousand pictures, Mary, sweetly expressed,
(I see you sweetly expressed in a thousand pictures, Mary,)

dɔx kʰa͜ens fɔn 'lalən kʰan dɪç 'ʃɪldɐn, vi: 'ma͜enə 'ze:lə dɪç lɛɐ̯'blɪk'tʰ.
doch keins von allen kann dich schildern, wie meine Seele dich erblickt.
but none of all can you (obj.) depict as my soul you sees.
(but none of them can depict you as my soul sees you.)

ɪç va͜es nu:ɐ̯, das de:ɐ̯ vɛlt' gə'tʰʏməl za͜et'de:m mi:ɐ̯ vi: la͜en tʰra͜om fɛɐ̯'ve:tʰ;
Ich weiss nur, dass der Welt Getümmel seitdem mir wie ein Traum verweht;
I know only that the world's tumult since then for me as a dream fades away;
(I only know that the tumult of the world has ever since faded away for me like a dream;)

ʊnt' la͜en lʊn'nɛnba:ɐ̯ 'zy:sɐ 'hɪməl mi:ɐ̯/mi:r 'le:vɪç lɪm gə'my:t'ə ʃt'e:tʰ.
und ein unnennbar süsser Himmel mir ewig im Gemüte steht.
and an inexpressibly sweet heaven for me eternally in the spirit stands.
(and an inexpressibly sweet heaven stays eternally in my spirit.)

[Novalis was the pen name of Friedrich Leopold von Hardenberg. The poem is addressed to the Virgin Mary; Schubert gave his graceful song the title "Marie."]

ˈmeːrəs ˈʃtʻɪlə

Meeres Stille

Calm Sea

Op. 3, No. 2 [1815] (Johann Wolfgang von Goethe)

ˈtʰiːfə ˈʃtʻɪlə hɛrʃtʻ ǀɪm ˈvasɐ(r), ˈloːnə ˈreːgʊŋ ruːt das meːɐ̯,
Tiefe Stille herrscht im Wasser, ohne Regung ruht das Meer,
Deep stillness reigns in the water, without motion rests the sea,
(Deep stillness reigns in the water; the sea is at rest, without motion,)

ʊntʻ bəˈkʰʏmɐtʻ ziːt deːɐ̯ ˈʃɪfɐ ˈglatʻə ˈflɛçə rɪŋs ǀʊmˈheːɐ̯.
und bekümmert sieht der Schiffer glatte Fläche rings umher.
and troubled sees the seaman smooth surface round about.
(and the seaman, troubled, sees a smooth surface all around.)

ˈkʰae̯nə lʊftʻ fɔn ˈkʰae̯nɐ ˈzae̯tʻə! ˈtʰoːdəsʃtʻɪlə ˈfʏrçtʻɐlɪç!
Keine Luft von keiner Seite! Todesstille fürchterlich!
No air from no side! Deathly stillness frightful!
(No wind from any direction! A frightful deathly stillness!)

ɪn deːɐ̯/deːr ǀʊngəˈhɔ͜øɐn ˈvae̯tʻə ˈreːgətʻ ˈkʰae̯nə ˈvɛlə zɪç.
In der ungeheuern Weite reget keine Welle sich.
In the enormous breadth stirs no wave itself.
(No wave is stirring in the enormous vastness.)

[Schubert effectively captures the quietly ominous mood of Goethe's poem with a series of thirty-two slow *pianissimo* arpeggios, one to a bar. The boat is becalmed, motionless in the water, far from land. An earlier version is included in the *Neue Schubert Ausgabe IV*, volume 1.]

Mein! see *Die schöne Müllerin*

mae̯n ˈfriːdən

Mein Frieden

My Peace

Published 1980 [date of composition unknown] (poem by C. Heine)

ˈfɛrnə, ˈfɛrnə ˈflamən ˈhɛlə ˈʃtʻɛrnə, geːən ˈniːdɐ, ˈkʰɔmən ˈviːdɐ,
Ferne, ferne flammen helle Sterne, gehen nieder, kommen wieder,
Far, far flame bright stars, go down, come again,
(Far, far distant bright stars are blazing; they set, they rise again,)

ˈblɪkʻən ǀɑo̯f mɪç ˈtʰrɑo̯lɪç ˈniːdɐ. vae̯tʻ ǀɑo̯s ˈblɑo̯ɐ ˈfɛrnə
blicken auf mich traulich nieder. Weit aus blauer Ferne
look at me cordially down. Afar from blue distance
(they look down at me in a friendly way. Far away, in the blue distance

ˈʃɪmɐn nuːɐ̯ di ˈʃtʻɛrnə. ˈfɛrnə, ˈfɛrnə ˈflamən ˈhɛlə ˈʃtʻɛrnə,
schimmern nur die Sterne. Ferne, ferne flammen helle Sterne,
shimmer only the stars. Far, far flame bright stars,
(the stars only shimmer. Far, far distant bright stars are blazing,)

ˈʃtʻa͜egən ˈnɪmɐ t͡suː miːɐ̯ ˈniːdɐ, ˈbrɪŋən ˈnɪmɐ ˈfriːdən ˈviːdɐ;
steigen nimmer zu mir nieder, bringen nimmer Frieden wieder;
descend never to me down, bring never peace again;
(they never descend to me, they never bring back lost peace;)

va͜etʻ ǀa͜os ˈbla͜oɐ ˈfɛrnə ˈʃɪmɐn nuːɐ̯ di ˈʃtʻɛrnə.
weit aus blauer Ferne schimmern nur die Sterne.
afar from blue distance shimmer only the stars.
(Far away, the stars only shimmer in the blue distance.)

ˈfɛrnə, ˈfɛrnə ˈflamən ˈhɛlə ˈʃtʻɛrnə, ˈɪmɐ ˈhɛlɐ vɪrtʻ ǀiːɐ̯ ˈblɪŋkʻən,
Ferne, ferne flammen helle Sterne, immer heller wird ihr Blinken,
Far, far flame bright stars, ever brighter grows their twinkling,
(Far, far distant bright stars are blazing; their twinkling grows brighter and brighter,)

ˈvɔlən ʃtʻɪl hɪˈna͜of mɪç ˈvɪŋkʻən; ˈfriːdən ǀɪstʻ nɪçtʻ ˈfɛrnə,
wollen still hinauf mich winken; Frieden ist nicht ferne,
want quietly up to there me to beckon; peace is not far,
(they seem to want to beckon me quietly to come up to them; peace is not far away after all,)

voːntʻ ǀa͜of ˈjeːnəm ˈʃtʻɛrnə.
wohnt auf jenem Sterne.
dwells on that star.
(for it dwells on that star.)

[In 1865 a biography of Schubert listed one of his songs as "*Mein Finden*"; the song seemed to have disappeared. Then the above song was discovered in the Seitenstetten monastery in Austria. It was finally published in facsimile in *The Musical Times, CXXI,* 1980 (on page 98), in an article by Reinhard Van Hoorickx. Evidently *Mein Finden* was a hasty misreading of an unclear manuscript copy of "*Mein Frieden.*" In any case, the music is lovely, even if the poem is doggerel.]

ma͜en gruːs ǀan den ma͜e
Mein Gruss an den Mai
My Greeting to May

Posthumously published [composed 1815] (poem by Johann Gottfried Kumpf)

za͜e miːɐ̯ geˈgryːstʻ, ǀoː ma͜e, mɪt ˈda͜enəm ˈblyːtʻənhɪməl, mɪt ˈda͜enəm lɛnt͡s,
Sei mir gegrüsst, o Mai, mit deinem Blütenhimmel, mit deinem Lenz,
Be by me greeted, O May, with your blossom-heaven, with your spring,
(I greet you, May, with your heaven of blossoms, and your springtime,)

mɪt ˈda͜enəm ˈfrɔ͜ødənmeːr. za͜e miːɐ̯ gəˈgryːstʻ mɪt ˈda͜enəm ˈfrøːlɪçən gəˈvɪməl
mit deinem Freudenmeer. Sei mir gegrüsst mit deinem fröhlichen Gewimmel
with your joys- sea. Be by me greeted with your merry swarm
(with your sea of joy. I greet you and your merry swarm)
[*poem:* **Sei mir gegrüsst, du fröhliches** (duː ˈfrøːlɪçəs, you merry) **Gewimmel**]

deːɐ̯ nɔ͜ø bəˈleːpʻtʻən ˈveːzən ǀʊm mɪç heːɐ̯. da͜en ˈgœtʻɐha͜ox dʊrçˈʃtʻrøːmt das
der neu belebten Wesen um mich her. Dein Götterhauch durchströmt das
of the newly brought to life beings around me hither. Your divine breath through-streams the
(of creatures newly brought to life all around me. Your divine breath streams through the)

'dy:st'rə grɑo de:ɐ̯ 'lʏft'ə, lʊnt' ʃnɛl bə'gry:nt' zɪç bɛrk' lʊnt tʰa:l lʊnt' lɑo,
düstre Grau der Lüfte, und schnell begrünt sich Berg und Tal und Au,
gloomy grey of the airs, and quickly greens itself mountain and valley and meadow,
(gloomy grey air, and quickly mountain, valley, and meadow become green;)

ɛs 've:ən 'ʃmaeçəlnt' 'lɪndə 'balza:mdʏft'ə, lɛs 'laxət' hɛl dɛs 'lɛ:t'ɐs 'kʰla:rəs blɑo.
es wehen schmeichelnd linde Balsamdüfte, es lachet hell des Äthers klares Blau.
there blow caressingly mild balm- scents, there laughs brightly the ether's clear blue.
(mild, balmy scents waft caressingly, and the clear blue of the ether smiles brightly.)

de:ɐ̯/de:r 'le:ɐ̯də pʰʊls lɛɐ̯'vaxt, dɛs 'le:bəns 'lø:də 'halən bə'kʰlaedən zɪç mɪt'
Der Erde Puls erwacht, des Lebens öde Hallen bekleiden sich mit
The earth's pulse awakes, the life's bare halls dress themselves with
(Earth's pulse awakens, life's bare halls are dressed in)

'frɪʃəm 'zɪlbɐglants; tsu: di:ɐ̯, tsu: 'daenəm 'frɔødəntʰɛmp'əl
frischem Silberglanz; zu dir, zu deinem Freudentempel
fresh silver-splendor; to you, to your joys- temple
(fresh, silvery splendor; to you, to your temple of joy)

'valən di 'jʏŋst'ən 'ho:rən mɪt dem 'bly:t'ənkʰrants. di 'ʃvalbə kʰɔmt,
wallen die jüngsten Horen mit dem Blütenkranz. Die Schwalbe kommt,
wander the youngest Horae with the blossom-wreath. The swallow comes,
(the youngest goddesses of the seasons bring their wreath of blossoms. The swallow comes,)

di 'lɛrçə 'vɪrbəlt' 'zy:sə 'li:dɐ, de:ɐ̯ 'valt'ʃt'ro:m rɑoʃt' lɑos 'gry:nɐ naxt' hɛɐ̯'fo:ɐ̯:
die Lerche wirbelt süsse Lieder, der Waldstrom rauscht aus grüner Nacht hervor:
the lark warbles sweet songs, the forest stream rushes from green night forth:
(the lark warbles sweet songs, the forest stream rushes forth out of green darkness:)

ʊnt' 'je:dɐ tʰo:n lʊnt' 'je:dɐ kʰlaŋ kʰe:ɐ̯t' 'vi:dɐ tsʊm 'ju:bəllɑot' lɪm harmo'ni:ənkʰo:ɐ̯.
und jeder Ton und jeder Klang kehrt wieder zum Jubellaut im Harmonienchor.
and each tone and each sound returns again to the rejoice-sound in the harmonies-chorus.
(and each tone and each sound joins the jubilation in a harmonious chorus.)

ax, 'laŋə va:ɐ̯/va:r lɪç fɛrn fɔm 'ʃt'ɪlən 'haema:tstʰa:lə, vo:
Ach, lange war ich fern vom stillen Heimatstale, wo
Ah, long was I far from the quiet homeland-valley, where
(Ah, for a long time I was far away from the quiet valley of my homeland; I was where)

zɪç zo: ʃø:n daen 'lʏp'gɐ ʃt'ro:m lɛɐ̯'gi:stʰ; dɔx 'ʃœpfən vɪl lɪç jɛtst
sich so schön dein üpp'ger Strom ergiesst; doch schöpfen will ich jetzt
itself so beautifully your abundant stream pours; but to draw want I now
(your abundant stream gushes forth most opulently; but I now want to draw)

di 'fɔlə 'ʃa:lə fɔm 'bɔrnə, de:ɐ̯/de:r lɪn 'zaenəm 'ʃo:sə fli:stʰ.
die volle Schale vom Borne, der in seinem Schosse fliesst.
the full vessel from the spring that into its lap flows.
(a full bowl of water from the spring that flows into the lap of the valley where I grew up.)

tsva:ɐ̯ bly:t de:ɐ̯/de:r 'lø:lbɑom dɔrt, di 'mandəl, pʰomə'rantsə;;
Zwar blüht der Ölbaum dort, die Mandel, Pomeranze;
To be sure blooms the olive-tree there, the almond, orange;
(To be sure, the olive-tree, the almond, and the orange bloom there where I was for so long;)

di 'tʰraobə ʃmɛk't' zo: zy:s lam 'me:rəsʃt'rant'; das 'le:bən 'glaet'ət' zanft'
die Traube schmeckt so süss am Meeresstrand; das Leben gleitet sanft
the grape tastes so sweet at the seashore; the life glides gently
(the grape tastes so sweet at the seashore; life glides gently by)

lɪm 'laeçt'əm 'tʰantsə, lʊnt' 'fraeɐ ʃlɛ:k't das hɛrts lɪm 'vɛrmɐn lant'.
im leichtem Tanze, und freier schlägt das Herz im wärmern Land.
in the light dance, and more freely beats the heart in the warmer land.
(in a light dance, and one's heart beats more freely in that warmer land;)

dɔx 'li:p'lɪç bly:t' laox lʊns di 'tsa:ɐt'ə lap'ri'kʰo:zə,
Doch lieblich blüht auch uns die zarte Aprikose,
But sweetly blooms also for us the tender apricot,
(but the tender apricot blooms sweetly for *us* too,)

ʊnt' 'varmə 'hɛrtsən tsɔøk't' maen 'fa:t'ɐlant', lʊnt'
und warme Herzen zeugt mein Vaterland, und
and warm hearts engenders my fatherland, and
(and my fatherland engenders warm hearts, and)

ho:x lɛnt'tsʏk't' mɪç 'lʊnzrə 'ʃp'ɛ:t'rə 'ro:zə, gə'pflʏk't' fɔn 'zɪlis 'tʰrɔøɐ 'li:liənhant'.
hoch entzückt mich unsre spät're Rose, gepflückt von Sillis treuer Lilienhand.
highly delights me our later rose, plucked by Silli's loyal lily-hand.
(the rose that blooms later here highly delights me when plucked by Silli's loyal lily-white hand.)

an 'daenə brʊst', na'tʰu:ɐ! las mɪç fɛɐ'tʰraoənt' 'zɪŋk'ən, lɛɐ'halt'ə mi:ɐ
An deine Brust, Natur! lass mich vertrauend sinken, erhalte mir
At your breast, Nature, let me trustingly sink, keep for me
(Upon your breast, Nature, let me trustingly sink down; preserve in me)

den 'raenən 'le:bənsmu:tʰ; lɪn 'fɔlən 'tsy:gən vɪl lɪç 'fro:zɪn 'tʰrɪŋk'ən,
den reinen Lebensmut; in vollen Zügen will ich Frohsinn trinken,
the pure life- courage; in full draughts want I cheerfulness to drink,
(pure high spirits; I want to drink cheerfulness in full draughts,)

ʊnt' nɔø dʊrç'ʃt'rø:mə mɪç de:ɐ 'frɔødə glu:tʰ. zae mi:ɐ gə'gry:st', lo: mae!
und neu durchströme mich der Freude Glut. Sei mir gegrüsst, o Mai!
and anew through-stream me the joy's fire. Be by me greeted, O May!
(and may the fire of joy stream through me anew. I greet you, May,)

mɪt 'daenəm 'frɔødənme:rə, mɪt 'daenɐ lʊst', mɪt 'daenɐ 'blu:mənpʰraxtʰ;
mit deinem Freudenmeere, mit deiner Lust, mit deiner Blumenpracht;
with your joys- sea, with your pleasure, with your flower- splendor;
(with your sea of joy, with your pleasure, with the splendor of your flowers;)

du: 'ʃø:nɐ 'jʏŋlɪŋ, 'tʰrɔk'nə 'je:də 'tsɛ:rə, lɛɐ'hɛlə 'je:də 'dʊŋk'lə 'ʃɪk'za:lsnaxtʰ!
du schöner Jüngling, trockne jede Zähre, erhelle jede dunkle Schicksalsnacht!
you beautiful youth, dry every tear, brighten every dark destiny- night!
(May, beautiful youth, dry every tear, brighten every night made dark by destiny!)

[A charming little strophic song in praise of spring. Schubert wrote out the first verse, put repeat signs at the end, and noted: "Eight more verses." Since he added two extra syllables in setting the third line, the corresponding line of each following verse will also need some modification, some repetition of a word or two, which he did not indicate. In the third verse, for example, to make the poem fit the music, the singer could sing: *“zu dir, zu dir, zu deinem Freudentempel wallen.”* The poet has returned happily to his homeland after a sojourn in a warm, southern country.]

ˈmɛmnɔn
Memnon
Memnon

Op. 6, No. 1 [1817] (Johann Mayrhofer)

den tʰaːk hɪnˈdʊrç nuːɐ̯/nuːr ˈla̯enmaːl maːkʻ |ɪç ˈʃpʻrɛçən, gəˈvoːnt t͜suː ˈʃva̯egən ˈ|ɪmɐ
Den Tag hindurch nur einmal mag ich sprechen, gewohnt zu schweigen immer
The day throughout only once may I speak, used to be silent always
(During the day only *once* may I speak, accustomed as I am to keeping always silent)

|ʊnt t͜suː ˈtʰra̯oɐn: vɛn dʊrç di ˈnaxtʻgəboːrnən ˈneːbəlma̯oɐn [van]
und zu trauern: wenn durch die nachtgebor’nen Nebelmauern [*poem:* **wann]**
and to grieve: when through the night-born mist- walls [when]
(and to grieving: when through walls of mist born of the night)

|a̯oˈroːrəns ˈpʰʊrpʻʊrʃtʻraːlən ˈliːbəntʻ ˈbrɛçən. fyːɐ̯ ˈmɛnʃən|oːrən zɪntʻ |ɛs
Aurorens Purpurstrahlen liebend brechen. Für Menschenohren sind es
Aurora’s purple rays lovingly break. For human ears are it
(Aurora’s purple rays lovingly break at dawn. For human ears the sounds I make are)

harmoˈniːən. va̯el |ɪç di ˈkʰlaːgə zɛlpstʻ meˈloːdɪʃ ˈkʰʏndə, |ʊnt dʊrç
Harmonien. Weil ich die Klage selbst melodisch künde, und durch
harmonies. Because I the lament myself melodically announce, and through
(harmonious. Because I intone my lament in melody, and because through)

deːɐ̯ ˈdɪçtʻʊŋ gluːt das ˈra̯oə ˈrʏndə, fɛɐ̯ˈmuːtʻən ziː |ɪn miːɐ̯/miːr |a̯en ˈzeːlɪç ˈblyːən.
der Dichtung Glut das Rauhe ründe, vermuten sie in mir ein selig Blühen.
the poetry’s fire the roughness round, assume they in me a blissful blooming.
(the fire of poetry I round off all roughness, they assume in me a blissful blossoming.)

ɪn miːɐ̯, naːx deːm dɛs ˈtʰoːdəs ˈ|armə ˈlaŋən, |ɪn ˈdɛsən ˈtʰiːfstʻəm ˈhɛrt͜sən
In mir, nach dem des Todes Arme langen, in dessen tiefstem Herzen
In me, toward whom the death’s arms reach, in whose deepest heart
(In *me*, toward whom the arms of death are reaching, in *me*, in whose deepest heart)

ˈʃlaŋən ˈvyːlən, gəˈnɛːɐ̯tʻ fɔn ˈma̯enən ˈʃmɛrt͜slɪçən gəˈfyːlən,
Schlangen wühlen, genährt von meinen schmerzlichen Gefühlen,
serpents burrow, nourished by my painful feelings,
(serpents are burrowing, nourished by my painful emotions, in *me*,)

fastʻ ˈvyːtʻənt dʊrç |a̯en ˈ|ʊngəʃtʻɪltʻ fɛɐ̯ˈlaŋən: mɪt diːɐ̯, dɛs ˈmɔrgəns ˈgœtʻɪn,
fast wütend durch ein ungestillt Verlangen: mit dir, des Morgens Göttin,
almost frantic through an unstilled longing: with you, the morning’s goddess,
(almost frantic with an unsatisfied longing: with you, goddess of the dawn,)

mɪç t͜suː ˈ|a̯enən, |ʊntʻ va̯etʻ fɔn ˈdiːzəm ˈnɪçtʻɪgən gəˈtʰriːbə,
mich zu einen, und weit von diesem nichtigen Getriebe,
myself to unite, and far from this futile bustle,
(to unite myself, and, far from the futile activity of this world,)

ɑ͜os 'sfɛːrən 'leːdlɐ 'fra͜ehaeta͜et', |ɑ͜os 'sfɛːrən 'ra͜enɐ 'liːbə,
aus Sphären edler Freiheit, aus Sphären reiner Liebe, [*poem without 2nd* **aus Sphären**]
from spheres of noble freedom, from spheres of pure love,

a͜en 'ʃt'ɪlɐ, 'bla͜eçɐ ʃt'ɛrn hɛ'rap' t͜suː 'ʃa͜enən.
ein stiller, bleicher Stern herab zu scheinen. [*poem:* **ein bleicher stiller Stern**]
a quiet, pale star down to shine.
(to shine down as a quiet, pale star.)

[Schubert made a very noble and richly beautiful song out of this most moving poem by his melancholy friend (who committed suicide a few years later). Memnon was the son of Aurora, goddess of the dawn. The statue in Egypt that was given his name sounds a musical tone when struck by the first rays of daybreak. The poet laments that his music—his poetry—is interpreted according to its aesthetic component, the melody and harmony of its surface, and that the deep, underlying torment of his heart is unperceived and misunderstood. His longing for a nobler world, beyond the meaningless turmoil of everyday life, is eloquently expressed by Schubert.]

Mignon / Mignons Gesang see *Kennst du das Land*
Mignon I see *Heiss mich nicht reden*
Mignon II see *So lasst mich scheinen*
Mignon und der Harfner see *Nur wer die Sehnsucht kennt*

'mɪnəliːt'
Minnelied
Love Song

Posthumously published [composed 1816] (poem by Ludwig Hölty)

'hɔldɐ kʰlɪŋt deːɐ̯ 'foːgəlzaŋ, vɛn di 'lɛŋəlra͜enə,
Holder klingt der Vogelsang, wenn die Engelreine,
Lovelier sounds the bird- song, when the angel-pure one,
(Bird song sounds lovelier when the angelic woman)

diː ma͜en 'jʏŋlɪŋshɛrt͜s bə't͜svaŋ, 'vandəlt dʊrç di 'ha͜enə.
die mein Jünglingsherz bezwang, wandelt durch die Haine.
who my young man's heart conquered, wanders through the grove.
(who conquered my heart when I was still very young wanders through the grove.)

'rø:t'ɐ 'blyːət tʰaːl |ʊnt' |ɑ͜o, 'gryːnɐ vɪrt deːɐ̯ 'vaːzən, ['blyːən]
Röter blühet Tal und Au, grüner wird der Wasen, [*poem:* **blühen**]
Redder blooms valley and meadow, greener becomes the grass, [bloom]
(Valley and meadow bloom redder and the grass grows greener)

voː miːɐ̯ 'bluːmən roːt' |ʊnt' blɑ͜o 'iːrə 'hɛndə 'laːzən.
wo mir Blumen rot und blau ihre Hände lasen.
where for me flowers red and blue her hands gather.
(where her hands gather red and blue flowers for me.)

[di 'fɪŋɐ 'ma͜enɐ frɑ͜o 'ma͜eənbluːmən]
[*poem:* **wo die Finger meiner Frau Maienblumen lasen**]
[the fingers of my wife May flowers]
[(where the fingers of my wife gather May flowers)]

oːnə ziː lɪstʼ ˈlaləs tʰoːtʰ, vɛlkʼ zɪntʼ blyːtʼ lʊntʼ ˈkʰrɔ͜øtʼɐ;
Ohne sie ist alles tot, welk sind Blüt' und Kräuter;
Without her is everything dead, faded are blossom and herbs;
(Without her everything is dead, blossoms fade, herbs are withered,)

ʊntʼ kʰa͜en ˈfryːlɪŋslaːbəntʼroːt dʏŋkʼtʼ miːɐ̯ ʃøːn lʊntʼ ˈha͜etʼɐ.
und kein Frühlingsabendrot dünkt mir schön und heiter.
and no spring sunset seems to me beautiful and serene.
(and no spring sunset seems beautiful and serene to me.)

ˈtʰra͜otʼə, ˈmɪnɪkʼlɪçə fra͜o, ˈvɔləstʼ ˈnɪmɐ ˈfliːən;
Traute, minnigliche Frau, wollest nimmer fliehen;
Dear, lovable wife/lady, want never to flee:
(Dear, lovable wife [or lady], do not ever want to flee,)

das ma͜en hɛrt͜s gla͜eç ˈdiːzɐ(r) la͜o møːkʼ lɪn ˈvɔnə ˈblyːən!
dass mein Herz gleich dieser Au mög' in Wonne blühen!
that my heart like this meadow may in bliss bloom!
(stay beside me, so that my heart may bloom in bliss like this meadow!)

[Brahms (though a lifelong bachelor) made a well-known setting of this same poem, the love song of a married man to his wife. Schubert may have changed the words to make his song suitable for an *unmarried* lover as well, since "*Frau*" can mean either "wife" or "lady."]

Minnesang see *Huldigung*

miˈnoːna
Minona
Minona

Posthumously published [composed 1815] (ballad by Friedrich Anton Bertrand)

viː ˈtʰra͜ebən di ˈvɔlkʼən zoː ˈfɪnstʼɐ(r) lʊntʼ ʃveːɐ̯
Wie treiben die Wolken so finster und schwer
How scud the clouds so dark and heavy
(How dark and heavy are the clouds that are scudding)

ˈyːbɐ di ˈliːpʼlɪçə ˈlɔ͜øçtʼə daˈheːɐ̯! [dɔrtʼ]
über die liebliche Leuchte daher! [*poem:* **dort über die liebliche Leuchte daher]**
over the lovely shining light thence! [there]
(over the lovely face of the sun and coming this way!)

viː ˈrasəln di ˈtʰrɔpfən la͜of ˈfɛnstʼɐ(r) lʊnt dax! viː ˈtʰra͜ebət͜s daː ˈdra͜osən
Wie rasseln die Tropfen auf Fenster und Dach! Wie treibet's da draussen
How rattle the drops on window and roof! How sets in motion it there outside
(How the raindrops rattle against the windows and the roof! How everything outside is agitated)

zoː ˈvyːtʼɪç lʊntʼ jax, lals ˈtʰriːbən zɪç ˈga͜estʼɐ(r) lɪn ˈʃlaxtʼən!
so wütig und jach, als trieben sich Geister in Schlachten!
so furious and fast, as if propel each other ghosts into battles! [*jach = jäh* = sudden, quick]
(so furiously and fast, as if ghosts were propelling each other into battle!)

ʊntʻ ˈvʊndɐ! viː ˈpʰlœt͜slɪç di ˈkʰɛmp͜fəndən ruːn,
Und Wunder! Wie plötzlich die Kämpfenden ruh'n,
And marvel! How suddenly the combatants rest,

als ˈbantʻən jɛt͜stʻ ˈgrɛːbɐ(r) liːɐ̯ ˈtʰra͜ebən lʊnt tʰuːn! [lɪt͜stʻ]
als bannten jetzt Gräber ihr Treiben und Tun! [*poem:* **als bannten itzt Gräber**]
as if banished now graves their driving and doing! [now]
(as if the grave put an end to their strenuous activity!)

ʊntʻ ˈlyːbɐ di ˈha͜edə, lʊntʻ ˈlyːbɐ den valtʻ, viː veːtʻ lɛs zoː ˈløːdə,
Und über die Heide, und über den Wald, wie weht es so öde,
And over the heath, and over the woods, how blows it so desolately,
(And over the heath, and over the woods, how desolately the wind blows,)
[*poem:* **wie weht es herüber** (hɛˈryːbɐ, over this way) **so öde**]

viː veːtʻ lɛs zoː kʰaltʻ, zoː ˈʃa͜orɪç fɔm ˈʃɪmɐndən ˈfɛlzən!
wie weht es so kalt, so schaurig vom schimmernden Felsen!
how blows it so cold, so horribly from the shimmering crag!
(how cold it blows, how horribly, from the shimmering crag!) [*poem: no repeat of* **wie weht es**]

oː ˈlɛtʻgar! voː ˈʃvɪrət da͜en ˈboːgəngəʃɔs, voː ˈflatʻɐt da͜en ˈhaːɐ̯bʊʃ?
O Edgar! Wo schwirret dein Bogengeschoss, wo flattert dein Haarbusch?
O Edgar! Where whirs your bow- shot, where flutters your hair- bush?
(O Edgar! Where is your arrow whirring, where is your shock of hair fluttering in the wind?)

voː ˈtʰʊməlt da͜en rɔs? voː ˈʃna͜obən di ˈʃvɛrt͜slɪçən ˈdɔgən lʊm dɪç?
Wo tummelt dein Ross? Wo schnauben die schwärzlichen Doggen um dich?
Where hurries your horse? Where pant the blackish mastiffs around you?
(Where is your horse hurrying? Where are the black mastiffs panting about you?)

voː ʃpʻɛːst duː lam ˈfɛlzən ˈbɔ͜øtʻə fyːɐ̯ mɪç? da͜en ˈharət das ˈliːbəndə ˈmɛːtʻçən,
Wo spähst du am Felsen Beute für mich? Dein harret das liebende Mädchen,
Where scout you by the crag game for me? For you waits the loving girl,
(Near the crag, where are you scouting out game for me? Your loving girl is waiting for you,)
[*poem:* **Wo spähst du am Felsen der** (deːɐ̯, for the) **Beute für mich?**]

da͜en ˈharətʻ, loː ˈjʏŋlɪŋ, lɪm ˈjeːkʻlɪçən la͜otʻ, [lɪn ˈjeːkʻlɪçəm]
dein harret, o Jüngling, im jeglichen Laut, [*poem:* **in jeglichem Laut**]
for you waits, O youth, in the every sound, [in every]
(is waiting for you, dear young man, in every sound,)

da͜en ˈharətʻ zoː ˈʃmaxtʻənt di ˈt͜saːgəndə bra͜otʰ. lɛs dʏŋkʻtʻ liːɐ̯
dein harret so schmachtend die zagende Braut. Es dünkt ihr
for you waits so piningly the timorous bride. It seems to her
(your frightened bride is waiting and pining so for you. She imagines that)

t͜sɛɐ̯ˈrɪsən das ˈliːbəndə bantʻ, lɛs dʏŋkʻtʻ liːɐ̯ zoː ˈbluːtʻɪç das ˈjɛːgɐgəvantʻ.
zerrissen das liebliche Band, es dünkt ihr so blutig das Jägergewand.
torn apart the lovely bond, it seems to her so bloody the hunter-garment.
(the lovely bond has been broken, she imagines your hunting garment to be all bloody.)
[*poem:* **dein** (da͜en, your) **Jägergewand**]

voːl 'mɪnən di 'tʰoːt'ən lʊns 'nɪmɐ. nɔx 'halət den 'moːzɪgən 'hyːgəl lɛnt''laŋ
Wohl minnen die Toten uns nimmer. Noch hallet den moosigen Hügel entlang
Probably love the dead us never. Still echoes the mossy hill along
(The dead probably never love us. Along the mossy hill, she imagines, there is still echoing)

viː 'harfəngəlɪsp'əl liːɐ̯ 'mɪnəgəzaŋ. [deːɐ̯]
wie Harfengelispel ihr Minnegesang. [*poem:* **der Minnegesang]**
like harp- whispering their love song. [the]
(their love song, a sound like the whispering of harps.)

vas frɔmt' lɛs? ʃoːn 'blɪk'ən di 'ʃt'ɛrnə deːɐ̯ naxt' ['blɪŋk'ən]
Was frommt es? Schon blicken die Sterne der Nacht [*poem:* **Schon blinken]**
What avails it? Already look the stars of the night [gleam]
(To what avail? She imagines the stars of the night already looking)

hɪ'nʊnt'ɐ t͜sʊm 'bɛt'ə fɔn 'leːɐ̯də gə'maxtʰ, voː 'la͜ezɐn di 'mɪnəndən 'ʃlaːfən.
hinunter zum Bette von Erde gemacht, wo eisern die Minnenden schlafen.
down to the bed of earth made, where iron the loving ones sleep.
(down at the bed made of earth in which the lovers are sleeping, rigid as iron.)

zoː kʰlaːk't' ziː; lʊnt' 'la͜ezə tʰap't͜s 'dra͜osən lʊm'heːɐ̯/-'heːr, lɛs 'vɪnzəlt' zoː 'lɪnɪç,
So klagt sie; und leise tappt's draussen umher, es winselt so innig,
Thus laments she; and softly gropes it outside around, it whimpers so earnestly,
(Thus she laments; and there is a soft groping about outside, a heartfelt whimpering,)

zoː 'ʃa͜odɐnt' lʊnt' ʃveːɐ̯. lɛs fast' ziː lɛnt''zɛt͜sən, [gra͜eft']
so schaudernd und schwer. Es fasst sie Entsetzen, [*poem:* **Es greift sie]**
so shiveringly and heavily. There seizes her horror, [seizes]
(so fearful and heavy. Horror seizes her,)

ziː 'vaŋk'ət t͜sʊr tʰyːɐ̯, balt' ʃmiːk't' zɪç di 'ʃøːnst'ə deːɐ̯ 'dɔgən foːɐ̯/foːr liːɐ̯,
sie wanket zur Tür, bald schmiegt sich die schönste der Doggen vor ihr,
she staggers to the door, soon cringes itself the finest of the mastiffs before her,
(she staggers to the door; soon the finest of the mastiffs is cringing before her,)

deːɐ̯ 'liːp'lɪŋ dɛs 'harəndən 'mɛːt'çəns; nɪçt' viː ziː nɔx 'gɛst'ɐn,
der Liebling des harrenden Mädchens; nicht wie sie noch gestern,
the favorite of the waiting girl; not as it still yesterday,
(the waiting girl's favorite; but how different from yesterday, when it)

mɪt' 'kʰoːzəndəm draŋ, la͜en 'boːt'ə dɛs 'liːbən, t͜sʊm 'buːzən liːɐ̯ ʃp'raŋ —
mit kosendem Drang, ein Bote des Lieben, zum Busen ihr sprang —
with caressing impulse, a messenger of the dear one, to the bosom of her leaped —
(had leaped up to her breast with a caressing impulse, a messenger from her dear one, —)

kʰa͜om heːp't' ziː fɔm 'boːdən den 'tʰra͜oɐndən blɪk',
kaum hebt sie vom Boden den trauernden Blick,
scarcely lifts it from the ground the grieving gaze,
(it scarcely lifts its mournful eyes from the ground,)

ʃla͜eçt' 'niːdɐ t͜sʊm 'p͜fœrt'çən, lʊnt' 'kʰeːrət t͜su'rʏk', ['viːdɐ]
schleicht nieder zum Pförtchen, und kehret zurück, [*poem:* **schleicht wieder]**
creeps down to the little gate, and returns back, [again]
(it creeps down to the little gate and comes back again)

di 'ʃrɛk'lıçə 'kʰʊndə tsu: 'dɔøt'ən. mi'no:na fɔlk't' 'ʃvaegənt'
die schreckliche Kunde zu deuten. Minona folgt schweigend
the frightful tidings to indicate. Minona follows keeping silent
(to indicate the frightful tidings. Minona follows silently)

mıt' 'blaeçəm gə'zıçtʰ, lals ru:ft' lɛs di 'larmə fo:ɐ̯s 'ho:ə gə'rıçtʰ;
mit bleichem Gesicht, als ruft es die Arme vors hohe Gericht;
with pale face, as if calls it the poor one before the high court of justice;
(with a pale face, as if the poor girl were called before the high court;)

ɛs 'lɔøçt'ət' zo: 'dy:st'ɐ de:ɐ̯ 'nɛçt'lıçə ʃt'ra:l, zi: fɔlk't' li:ɐ̯ dʊrç 'mo:rə,
es leuchtet so düster der nächtliche Strahl, sie folgt ihr durch Moore,
there shines so dimly the nocturnal ray, she follows it (the dog) through fen,
(the rays of moonlight are dim tonight; she follows the dog through fen,)

dʊrç 'haedən lʊnt tʰa:l tsʊm 'fu:sə dɛs 'ʃımɐndən 'fɛlzən.
durch Heiden und Tal zum Fusse des schimmernden Felsen.
through heath and valley to the foot of the shimmering crag.

vo: 'vaelət', lo: 'ʃımɐndɐ 'fɛlzən, de:ɐ̯ tʰo:t'?
"Wo weilet, o schimmernder Felsen, der Tod?
"Where lingers, O shimmering crag, the death?
("Where is death lurking, you shimmering crag?)

vo: 'ʃlʊmɐt de:ɐ̯ 'ʃlɛ:fɐ fɔm 'blu:t'ə nɔx ro:tʰ? [fɔn] [zo:]
wo schlummert der Schläfer vom Blute noch rot?" [*poem:* von Blute so rot?]
where slumbers the sleeper from the blood still red?" [from blood so red?]
(Where is the sleeper slumbering, still red with blood?")

vo:l va:ɐ̯/va:r lɛs tsɛɐ̯'rısən das 'li:p'lıçə bant', vo:l
Wohl war es zerrissen das liebliche Band, wohl
Perhaps was it torn apart the lovely bond, perhaps
(Perhaps the bond of love has been torn apart, perhaps)

hat' li:m, gə'ʃlɔødɐt' fɔn 'tʰʏk'ıʃɐ hant', laen 'mɔrt'pfael den 'bu:zən dʊrç'ʃnıt'ən.
hatt' ihm, geschleudert von tückischer Hand, ein Mordpfeil den Busen durchschnitten.
had him, shot by malicious hand, a murder-arrow the bosom through-cut.
(a murderous arrow, shot by a malicious hand, had pierced his breast.)

ʊnt' lals zi: nu:n 'na:ət' mıt' 'lɛŋst'lıçəm ʃrae, gə'va:ɐ̯t' zi:
Und als sie nun nahet mit ängstlichem Schrei, gewahrt sie
And as she now nears with frightened scream, perceives she
(And now, as she approaches with a frightened scream, she notices)

den 'bo:gən dɛs 'fa:t'ɐs da'bae. lo: 'fa:t'ɐ, lo: 'fa:t'ɐ, fɛɐ̯'tsae lɛs di:ɐ̯ gɔtʰ, vo:l
den Bogen des Vaters dabei. "O Vater, o Vater, verzeih' es dir Gott, wohl
the bow of the father close by. "O father, O father, may forgive it to you God, probably
(her father's bow close by. "O father, O father, may God forgive you for this! Probably)

hast du: mi:ɐ̯ 'hɔøt'ə mıt' 'fre:fəlndəm ʃp'ɔt' zo: 'ʃrɛk'lıç den 'drɔøʃvu:ɐ̯/-ʃvu:r lɛɐ̯'fʏlətʰ!
hast du mir heute mit frevelndem Spott so schrecklich den Dräuschwur erfüllet!
have you to me today with criminal scorn so frightfully the threat-vow fulfilled!
(with wicked scorn you have so cruelly fulfilled today the vow with which you threatened me!)

dɔx, zɔl lɪç tsɛɐ̯ˈmalmətʻ fɔn ˈhɪnən nuːn geːn? [lɪtstʻ]
Doch, soll ich zermalmet von hinnen nun gehn? [*poem:* **itzt gehn**]
But, shall I crushed from here now go? [now (obs.)]
(But shall I now go away from here, crushed?)

eːɐ̯ ʃlɛːftʻ jaː zoː ˈlɔkʻəntʻ, zoː ˈvɔnɪç, zoː ʃøːn! [lʊntʻ]
Er schläft ja so lockend, so wonnig, so schön! [*poem:* **so wonnig und schön**]
He sleeps after all so alluringly, so blissfully, so beautifully! [and]

gəˈkʰnʏpftʻ lɪstʻ laof ˈleːvɪç das ˈleːɐnə bantʻ lʊntʻ ˈgaestʻɐ [nuːn]
Geknüpft ist auf ewig das eherne Band und Geister [*poem:* **Geknüpft ist nun ewig**]
Tied is for ever the bronze bond and spirits [now]
(A firm, imperishable bond is now tied forever, and the spirits)

deːɐ̯ ˈfɛːtʻɐ(r) lɪm ˈneːbəlgəvantʻ lɛɐ̯ˈgraefən di ˈzɪlbɐnən ˈharfən. lʊntʻ ˈpʰlœtslɪç
der Väter im Nebelgewand ergreifen die silbernen Harfen." Und plötzlich
of the fathers in the mist- garment grasp the silver harps." And suddenly
(of our forefathers in garments of mist will play on silver harps." And suddenly)
[*poem:* **die silberne** (ˈzɪlbɐnə ˈharfə, silver harp) **Harfe**]

lɛntʻˈraestʻ ziː mɪtʻ ˈzeːnəndɐ(r) lael deːɐ̯ ˈvʊndə dɛs ˈliːbən den ˈtʰøːtʻəndən pfael,
entreisst sie mit sehnender Eil' der Wunde des Lieben den tötenden Pfeil,
tears out she with longing haste from the wound of the dear one the killing arrow,
(with yearning haste she tears the deadly arrow from the wound of her dear one)

ʊntʻ ʃtʻøːstʻ liːn, lɛɐ̯ˈgrɪfən fɔn ˈlɪnɪgəm veː, mɪtʻ hastʻ lɪn den ˈbuːzən
und stösst ihn, ergriffen von innigem Weh, mit Hast in den Busen
and plunges it, deeply stirred by fervent grief, with haste into the bosom
(and, deeply stirred by fervent grief, she hurriedly plunges it into her bosom)
[*poem:* **sie** (ziː, she) **stösst ihn, ergriffen von Freuden und** (ˈfrɔødən lʊntʻ, joys and) **Weh**]

zoː ˈblɛndəntʻ viː ʃneː, lʊntʻ zɪŋkʻtʻ lam ˈʃɪmɐndən ˈfɛlzən. [ˈzɪŋkʻətʻ]
so blendend wie Schnee, und sinkt am schimmernden Felsen. [*poem:* **sinket**]
as dazzling as snow, and sinks by the shimmering crag. [sinks]
(as dazzlingly white as snow, and sinks down by the shimmering crag.)

[The full title of the ballad is "*Minona, oder die Kunde der Dogge*" (Minona, or The Mastiff's Message). Most of the song is recitative; the climax calls for a high B natural from the soprano. As a postlude to the heroine's suicide, the piano repeats *pianissimo* the phrase "*Wohl minnen die Toten uns nimmer*" ("The dead probably never love us")—irony, or uncharacteristic cynicism?]

Mio ben, ricordati see *Vier Canzonen von Metastasio*

ˈmiːzero pargoˈletːto
Misero Pargoletto
Poor Little Child

Posthumously published [composed 1813] (from *Demofoönte* by Pietro Metastasio)

ˈmiːzero pargoˈletːto, il ˈtuːo deˈstiːn non ˈsaːi. aː! non ʎːʎi ˈdiːte ˈmaːi
Misero pargoletto, il tuo destin non sai. Ah! non gli dite mai
Poor little child, the your destiny not you know. Ah! not to him tell ever
(Poor little child, you do not know your destiny. Ah! Do not ever tell him)

kwal 'ɛːra‿il dʒeni'toːr. 'koːme‿in un 'punto, o 'diːo, 'tutːto kan'dʒɔ das'pɛtːto!
qual era il genitor. Come in un punto, oh Dio, tutto cangiò d'aspetto!
what was the father. How in one point, oh God, all changed of aspect!
(what his father was. Oh God, how in one moment everything changed its aspect!)
[*poem:* **cambiò** (kam'bjɔ, changed)]

'voːi 'fɔste‿il 'miːo di'lɛtːto, 'voːi 'sjɛːte‿il 'miːo te'rːroːr.
Voi foste il mio diletto, voi siete il mio terror.
You were the my delight, you are the my terror.
(You were my delight; now you are my terror.)

[This is a *da capo* aria for soprano, without the recitative. The text is from Act III, Scene 5, of Metastasio's *Demofoönte*. Schubert was a student of Salieri's at the time of composition; two of his sketches for an earlier version have survived and are printed in the *Neue Schubert Ausgabe*.]

Mit dem grünen Lautenbande see *Die schöne Müllerin*

Morgengruss see *Die schöne Müllerin*

'mɔrgənliːt' / di 'froːə nɔ͜øbə'leːp't'ə fluːɐ̯
Morgenlied / Die frohe neubelebte Flur
Morning Song / The Joyful, Newly Revived Meadow

Posthumously published [composed 1816] (author unknown)

di 'froːə nɔ͜øbə'leːp't'ə fluːɐ̯ zɪŋk't' 'iːrəm 'ʃœpfɐ daŋkʰ.
Die frohe neubelebte Flur singt ihrem Schöpfer Dank.
The joyful new-revived meadow sings to its Creator thank(s).
(The joyful, newly revived meadow sings thanks to its Creator.)

oː hɛr ʊnt' 'faːt'ɐ deːɐ̯ na'tʰuːɐ̯, diːɐ̯ tʰøːn a͜ox ma͜en gə'zaŋ!
O Herr und Vater der Natur, dir tön' auch mein Gesang!
O Lord and Father of the Nature, to you sound also my song!
(O Lord and Father of Nature, may my song also resound to you!)

deːɐ̯ 'leːbənsfrɔ͜ødən ʃɛŋkst duː fiːl deːm, deːɐ̯ zɪç 'va͜eslɪç frɔ͜øtʰ.
Der Lebensfreuden schenkst du viel dem, der sich weislich freut.
Of the life- joys bestow you many upon him, who himself wisely gladdens.
(You bestow many of life's pleasures upon him who enjoys them wisely.)

diːs za͜e, oː 'faːt'ɐ, ʃt'eːt͜s das t͜siːl ba͜e 'ma͜enɐ 'frøːlɪçkʰa͜etʰ.
Dies sei, o Vater, stets das Ziel bei meiner Fröhlichkeit.
This be, O Father, always the goal in my cheerfulness.
(May that always be, O Father, the goal of my cheerfulness.)

ɪç kʰan mɪç nɔx dɛs 'leːbəns frɔ͜øn ɪn 'diːzɐ 'ʃøːnən vɛltʰ;
Ich kann mich noch des Lebens freu'n in dieser schönen Welt;
I can myself still of the life gladden in this beautiful world;
(I can still rejoice in life in this beautiful world;)

ma͜en hɛrt͜s zɔl deːm gə'ha͜elɪçt' za͜en, deːɐ̯ 'va͜eslɪç ziː ɛɐ̯'hɛltʰ.
mein Herz soll dem geheiligt sein, der weislich sie erhält.
my heart shall to Him consecrated be, who wisely it (the world) keeps.
(my heart shall be consecrated to Him who wisely sustains it.)

vɛn dan miːɐ̯ ˈmyːdən vɪŋk‘t deːɐ̯ tʰoːt t͡sʊr ˈbɛsɐn vɛlt t͡suː geːn,
Wenn dann mir Müden winkt der Tod zur bessern Welt zu geh'n,
When then to me weary one beckons the death to the better world to go,
(When one day death beckons me, weary one, to go to the better world,)

zoː brɪçt‘ la͜en ˈʃøːnrəs ˈmɔrgənroːt‘ miːɐ̯/miːr lan ba͜em ˈla͜ofleːɐ̯ʃt‘eːn.
so bricht ein schön'res Morgenrot mir an beim Aufersteh'n.
then breaks a more beautiful dawn for me ... at the resurrection.
(then a more beautiful day will dawn for me at the resurrection.) [*anbrechen* = dawn, start]

[This little song celebrates a cheerful view of life, and offers thanks to its Creator.]

ˈmɔrgənliːt‘ / eː di ˈzɔnə fryː ˈla͜ofleːɐ̯ʃt‘eːtʰ

Morgenlied / Eh' die Sonne früh aufersteht

Morning Song / Before the Sun Rises in the Morning

Op. 4, No. 2 [1820] (Zacharias Werner)

eː di ˈzɔnə fryː ˈla͜ofleːɐ̯ʃt‘eːt‘, vɛn la͜os dem ˈdamp͡fəndən meːɐ̯
Eh' die Sonne früh aufersteht, wenn aus dem dampfenden Meer
Before the sun early rises, when from the steaming sea
(Before the sun rises in the morning, when from the misty sea)

hɛˈra͜of lʊnt‘ hɛˈrʊnt‘ɐ das ˈmɔrgənroːt‘ veːt‘, foˈran fɛːɐ̯t‘ mɪt dem
herauf und herunter das Morgenrot weht, voran fährt mit dem
up and down the dawn blows, onward fares with the
(the red light of dawn wavers up and down, when it advances onwards with its)

ˈlɔ͜øçt‘əndən ʃp‘eːɐ̯: ˈflat‘ɐn ˈføːgla͜en daˈhɪn lʊnt daˈheːɐ̯, ˈzɪŋən ˈfrøːlɪç
leuchtenden Speer: flattern Vöglein dahin und daher, singen fröhlich
shining spear: flutter little birds hence and hither, sing merrily
(spear of light: little birds flutter here and there, singing merrily)

di kʰrɔ͜øt͡s lʊnt di kʰveːɐ̯/kʰveːr la͜en liːt‘, la͜en ˈjuːbəlndəs liːt‘. vas
die Kreuz und die Quer ein Lied, ein jubelndes Lied. "Was
the cross(wise) and the oblique a song, an exulting song. "Why
(in all directions their exultant song. "Why) [*die Kreuz und die Quer* = in all directions]

frɔ͜øt‘ liːɐ̯ ˈføːgla͜en lɔ͜øç ˈlalt͡suˌmaːl zoː ˈhɛrt͡sɪç lɪm ˈvɛrməndən ˈzɔnənʃt‘raːl?
freut ihr Vöglein euch allzumal so herzig im wärmenden Sonnenstrahl?"
gladden you birds yourselves all at once so charmingly in the warming sunbeam?"
(are you birds rejoicing all at once so charmingly in the warming rays of the sun?")
[*ihr freut euch* = you are rejoicing, you are delighted]

viːɐ̯ frɔ͜øn lʊns, das viːɐ̯ ˈleːbən lʊnt‘ zɪnt‘, lʊnt das viːɐ̯ ˈlʊft‘gə gəˈzɛlən zɪnt‘,
"Wir freu'n uns, dass wir leben und sind, und dass wir luft'ge Gesellen sind,
"We gladden ourselves that we live and are, and that we airy fellows are,
("We rejoice that we are alive, that we exist, and that we are airy fellows;)

naːx ˈløːp‘lɪçəm bra͜ox dʊrçˈflat‘ɐn viːɐ̯ ˈfrøːlɪç den ʃt‘ra͜ox,
nach löblichem Brauch durchflattern wir fröhlich den Strauch,
according to laudable custom through-flutter we merrily the bush,
(in accordance with a laudable custom we flutter merrily through the bushes;)

lʊmˈveːtʻ fɔm ˈliːpʻlɪçən ˈmɔrgənvɪntʻ, lɛɐ̯ˈgœt͡sət di ˈzɔnə zɪç lɑ͡ɔx.
umweht vom lieblichen Morgenwind, ergötzet die Sonne sich auch."
around-blown by the lovely morning wind, enjoys the sun itself also."
(with the lovely morning wind blowing all around, the sun also enjoys itself.")

vas zɪt͡stʻ liːɐ̯ ˈføːgla͡en zoː ʃtʻʊm lʊntʻ gəˈdʊkʻtʻ lam dax lɪm ˈmoːzɪgən nɛstʰ?
"Was sitzt ihr Vöglein so stumm und geduckt am Dach im moosigen Nest?"
"Why sit you birds so mute and ducked down on the roof in the mossy nest?"
("Why do you birds sit in your mossy nest on the roof, so mute and so ducked down?")
[*poem without* **so**]

viːɐ̯ ˈzɪt͡sən, va͡el lʊns di zɔn nɪçtʻ bəˈgʊkʻtʻ, [bəˈkʰʊkʻtʻ]
"Wir sitzen, weil uns die Sonn' nicht beguckt, [*poem:* **bekuckt]**
"We sit, because us the sun not looks at, [looks at (dialect)]
("We are sitting here because the sun is not looking at us,)

ʃoːn hatʻ ziː di naxtʻ lɪn di ˈvɛlən gəˈdʊkʻtʰ; deːɐ̯ moːntʻ laˈla͡en,
schon hat sie die Nacht in die Wellen geduckt; der Mond allein,
already has it [obj.] the night [subj.] into the waves ducked down; the moon alone,
(already night has dunked it into the waves; only the moon,)

deːɐ̯ ˈliːpʻlɪçə ʃa͡en, deːɐ̯ ˈzɔnə ˈliːpʻlɪçɐ ˈviːdɐʃa͡en
der liebliche Schein, der Sonne lieblicher Widerschein
the lovely light, the sun's lovely reflection

lʊns lɪn deːɐ̯ ˈdʊŋkʻəlha͡etʻ nɪçtʻ fɛɐ̯ˈlɛstʻ, daˈrɔpʻ viːɐ̯/viːr lɪm ˈʃtʻɪlən lʊns frɔ͡øn.
uns in der Dunkelheit nicht verlässt, darob wir im Stillen uns freu'n."
us in the darkness not forsakes, over that we in the quiet ourselves gladden."
(does not forsake us in the darkness; we are glad about that, in the stillness.")
[*GA:* **nie** (niː, never) **verlässt** (*never* forsakes us—*but the moon is not out every night!*)]

oː ˈjuːgəntʻ, ˈkʰyːlɪgə ˈmɔrgənt͡sa͡etʻ, voː viːɐ̯ di ˈhɛrt͡sən gəˈlœfnətʻ lʊntʻ va͡etʻ,
O Jugend, kühlige Morgenzeit, wo wir, die Herzen geöffnet und weit,
O youth, cool morning-time, when we, the hearts opened and wide,
(O youth, cool morning of life, when we, our hearts opened wide,)

mɪtʻ ˈraʃəm lʊntʻ lɛɐ̯ˈvaxəndəm zɪn, deːɐ̯ ˈleːbənsfrɪʃə lʊns lɛɐ̯ˈfrɔ͡øtʻ,
mit raschem und erwachendem Sinn, der Lebensfrische uns erfreut,
with lively and awakening mind, in the life- freshness ourselves (have) delighted,
(with a lively and awakening mind, have delighted in life's freshness,)
[*Peters:* **des** (dɛs, of the— genetive article for "*Lebens,*" life's) **Lebens Frische]**

voːl floːst duː daˈhɪn! daˈhɪn! viːɐ̯/viːr ˈlaltʻən ˈzɪt͡sən gəˈdʊkʻtʻ lɪm nɛstʰ!
wohl flohst du dahin! dahin! Wir Alten sitzen geduckt im Nest!
to be sure fled you away! away! We old ones sit ducked down in the nest!
(O youth, you have fled away, to be sure! We old ones are now sitting ducked down in the nest!)
[*Peters:* **fliehst** (fliːst, flee)]

aˈla͡en deːɐ̯ ˈliːpʻlɪçə ˈviːdɐʃa͡en deːɐ̯ ˈjuːgəntt͡sa͡etʰ, voː viːɐ̯/viːr
Allein der liebliche Widerschein der Jugendzeit, wo wir
Only the lovely reflection of the youth- time, when we
(Only the lovely reflection of that time of youth, when we)

ɪm ˈfry:ro:t‘ ʊns ɛɐ̯ˈfrɔ͜øt‘, ʊns a͜ox ɪm ˈalt‘ɐ ni: fɛɐ̯ˈlɛst‘,
im Frührot uns erfreut, uns auch im Alter nie verlässt,
in the dawn ourselves (have) gladdened, us even in the old age never forsakes,
(once rejoiced in the dawn, only *that* never forsakes us, even in our old age,)

[*poem:* **nicht** (nɪçt‘, not) **verlässt]**

di ˈʃt‘ɪlə, ˈzɪnɪgə ˈfrø:lɪçkʰa͜etʰ!
die stille, sinnige Fröhlichkeit!
the quiet, thoughtful cheerfulness!
(the reflection of that quiet, thoughtful cheerfulness!)

[The key is A minor for age and for the questions, A major for youth and the cheerful answers of the birds with their jolly interludes (except, momentarily, when they mention the departure of the sun). The poem comes from a drama by Werner, *Die Söhne des Tales* ("The Sons of the Valley"), Part I (*Die Templer auf Cypern*—"The Templers in Cyprus"), Act I, Scene 5.]

ˈmɔrgənli:t‘ / vɪlˈkʰɔmən, ˈro:t‘əs ˈmɔrgənlɪçtʰ

Morgenlied / Willkommen, rotes Morgenlicht

Morning Song / Welcome, Rosy Light of Dawn

Posthumously published [composed 1815] (poem by Friedrich Leopold Graf zu Stolberg)

vɪlˈkʰɔmən, ˈro:t‘əs ˈmɔrgənlɪçt‘! ˈɛs ˈgry:sət dɪç ma͜en ga͜estʰ,
Willkommen, rotes Morgenlicht! es grüsset dich mein Geist,
Welcome, red morning light! There greets you my spirit,
(Welcome, rosy light of dawn! My spirit greets you,)

de:ɐ̯ dʊrç dɛs ˈʃla:fəs ˈhʏlə brɪçt‘, ʊnt‘ ˈza͜enən ˈʃœpfɐ pʰra͜estʰ.
der durch des Schlafes Hülle bricht, und seinen Schöpfer preist.
which through the sleep's cover breaks, and its Creator praises.
(as it breaks through the veil of sleep and praises its Creator.)

vɪlˈkʰɔmən, ˈgɔldnɐ ˈmɔrgənʃt‘ra:l, de:ɐ̯ ʃo:n den bɛrk‘ bəˈgry:stʰ,
Willkommen, goldner Morgenstrahl, der schon den Berg begrüsst,
Welcome, golden morning ray, which already the mountain [obj.] greets,
(Welcome, golden ray of morning that already greets the mountain,)

ʊnt‘ balt‘ ɪm ˈʃt‘ɪlən ˈkʰvɛləntʰa:l di ˈkʰla͜enə ˈblu:mə kʰʏstʰ!
und bald im stillen Quellental die kleine Blume küsst!
and soon in the quiet stream- valley the little flower kisses!
(and will soon kiss the little flower in the quiet valley where the stream is flowing!)

o: ˈzɔnə, za͜e mi:ɐ̯ ˈgɔt‘əs bɪlt‘, de:ɐ̯ ˈtʰɛ:k‘lɪç dɪç ɛɐ̯ˈnɔ͜øtʰ,
O Sonne, sei mir Gottes Bild, der täglich dich erneut,
O sun, be for me God's image, who daily you renews,
(O sun, be for me the image of God, who daily renews you,)

de:ɐ̯/de:r ˈɪmɐ he:ɐ̯/he:r, ʊnt‘ ˈɪmɐ mɪlt, di ˈgantsə vɛlt‘ ɛɐ̯ˈfrɔ͜øtʰ!
der immer hehr, und immer mild, die ganze Welt erfreut!
who ever sublime, and ever gentle, the whole world makes glad!
(who, ever sublime and ever gentle, gives joy to the whole world,)

deːɐ̯, viː di bluːm lɪm ˈkʰvɛləntʰaːl, loː ˈzɔnə, dɪç lɛɐ̯ˈʃuːf,
Der, wie die Blum' im Quellental, o Sonne, dich erschuf,
Who, like the flower in the stream-valley, O sun, you [obj.] created,
(who, as He did the flower in the valley of the stream, created you, O sun,)

als ˈda͜enə ˈʃvɛstʻɐn ˈlalt͜suːˌmaːl lɛntʻˈflamtʻən ˈza͜enəm ruːf.
als deine Schwestern allzumal entflammten seinem Ruf.
when your sisters all at once flamed forth at His call.
(when you and your sister suns, the stars, all flamed forth together at His call.)

iːɐ̯ ˈvandəltʻ la͜of bəˈʃtʻɪmtʻɐ baːn la͜enˈheːɐ̯/-heːr lʊntʻ ˈʃtʻra͜oxəltʻ nɪçtʰ;
Ihr wandelt auf bestimmter Bahn einher und strauchelt nicht;
You [plural] wander on determined course along and stumble not;
(You suns and stars move in fixed orbits and do not stray or stumble;)

dɛn ˈgɔtʻəs ˈloːdəm ha͜oxtʻ lɔ͜øç lan, za͜en la͜okʻ lɪstʻ ˈlɔ͜øɐ lɪçtʰ.
denn Gottes Odem haucht euch an, sein Aug' ist euer Licht.
for God's breath breathes you upon, His eye is your light.
(for God's breath wafts about you, and His eye is your light.)

eːɐ̯ ˈla͜etʻətʻ lɔ͜øç lam ˈgɛŋəlbantʻ, ha͜el miːɐ̯!/miːr! leːɐ̯ fyːɐ̯tʻ la͜ox mɪç!
Er leitet euch am Gängelband, heil mir! Er führt auch mich!
He guides you at the leading-string, good luck for me! He leads also me!
(He guides you as a parent guides a toddler; how fortunate I am: He leads me too!)
[*gängeln* = to toddle; *Gängelband* = leading-strings to guide a toddler]

eːɐ̯, deːɐ̯/deːr loˈriːɔns ˈgʏrtʻəl bantʻ, fɛɐ̯ˈbantʻ la͜ox mɪç mɪtʻ zɪç!
Er, der Orions Gürtel band, verband auch mich mit sich!
He, who Orion's belt bound, bound also me with Himself!
(He who bound Orion's belt* bound me to Himself!)

eːɐ̯ ˈla͜etʻətʻ ˈjeːdən, deːɐ̯/deːr liːm tʰra͜otʻ, mɪtʻ ˈlʊnzɪçtʻbaːrɐ hantʻ,
Er leitet jeden, der ihm traut, mit unsichtbarer Hand,
He guides everyone who Him trusts with invisible hand,
(With an invisible hand, He guides everyone who trusts in Him,)

als vɛːr leːɐ̯ nuːɐ̯/nuːr liːm ˈlanfɛɐ̯tʰra͜otʻ, lan ˈza͜enəm ˈgɛŋəlbantʻ!
als wär' er nur ihm anvertraut, an seinem Gängelband!
as if were he only to Him entrusted, on his leading-string!
(as if each person were entrusted only to Him, to His guidance!)

di ˈzɔnə ˈʃtʻa͜egətʻ! va͜epʻ lʊntʻ kʰɪntʻ, lɛɐ̯ˈvaxtʻ! lɛɐ̯ˈvaxtʻ viː ziː!
Die Sonne steiget! Weib und Kind, erwacht! Erwacht wie sie!
The sun rises! Wife and child, wake up! Wake up like it!
(The sun is rising! Wife and child, wake up! Wake up like the sun!)

ɛɐ̯ˈvaxətʻ! ˈvɛrfən viːɐ̯ gəˈʃvɪntʻ lʊns ˈlalə hɪn la͜ofs kʰniː!
Erwachet! Werfen wir geschwind uns alle hin aufs Knie!
Wake up! Throw we quickly ourselves all down on the knee!
(Wake up! Let us all throw ourselves down on our knees!)

ʊnt dan t͜sʊr 'tʰa:gəslarba͜et', frɪʃ, za͜en 'ze:gən 'lɔ͜øçt'ət' hɛl!
Und dann zur Tagesarbeit, frisch, sein Segen leuchtet hell!
And then to the daily work, fresh, His blessing shines brightly!
(And then to our daily work, fresh! His blessing, through the sun, is shining brightly!)

de:ɐ̯ hɛr bə'ra͜et'ət' 'lʊnzɐn tʰɪʃ. lʊns kʰvɪlt de:ɐ̯ 'frɔ͜ødə kʰvɛl!
Der Herr bereitet unsern Tisch. Uns quillt der Freude Quell!
The Lord prepares our table. For us wells up the joy's spring!
(The Lord prepares our table. For us the spring of joy wells up!)

ʊns 'ʃt'ra:lət' 'gɔt'əs 'hɛrlɪçkʰa͜et' la͜ox la͜os de:ɐ̯/de:r 'lʊnzɐn grʊftʰ;
Uns strahlet Gottes Herrlichkeit auch aus der Unsern Gruft;
For us radiates God's glory even from of the ours tomb;
(For us God's glory even radiates from the tomb of our loved ones;)

vi:ɐ̯ 'vɪsən, ve:ɐ̯ t͜sʊr 'ze:lɪçkʰa͜et' zi: ri:f, lʊnt' balt' lʊns ru:ftʰ!
wir wissen, wer zur Seligkeit sie rief, und bald uns ruft!
we know who to the bliss them called and soon us calls!
(we know who called them to bliss, and will soon call us!)

de:m zɪnt' la͜ox 'za͜enə 'tʰo:t'ən na:, ve:ɐ̯ gɔt, den 'hɛrən, pʰra͜estʰ,
Dem sind auch seine Toten nah', wer Gott, den Herren, preist,
To him are also his dead near, who God [obj.], the Lord, praises,
(To him who praises God, the Lord, his beloved dead are also near;)

ʊnt' 'frɔ͜ødɪç lɪm ha'le:luja zɪç 'di:zɐ vɛlt' lɛnt''ra͜estʰ. [*normally* hale'lu:ja]
und freudig im Halleluja sich dieser Welt entreisst.
and joyfully in the hallelujah himself from this world tears away.
(he joyfully tears himself away from this world to join in the great cry of "hallelujah.")

[Only the first two verses are printed with the music, which is appropriate to their cheerful tone, but would not be to the poem as a whole. Schubert's strophic setting is a graceful trifle, but a perfect one, in the style of a German folk song, similar to Mozart's "*Komm, lieber Mai.*" *Orion's "belt" is formed by three stars in a row, three jewels of the evening sky in winter.]

Mut see *Winterreise*

na:x 'la͜enəm gə'vɪt'ɐ
Nach einem Gewitter
After a Storm

Posthumously published [composed 1817] (poem by Johann Mayrhofer)

a͜of den 'blu:mən 'flɪmɐn 'pʰɛrlən, filo'me:ləns 'kʰla:gən 'fli:sən,
Auf den Blumen flimmern Perlen, Philomelens Klagen fliessen,
On the flowers glisten pearls, Philomela's* laments flow,
(Pearls are glistening on the flowers, the laments of the nightingale flow from her throat,)

'mu:t'ɪgɐ nu:n 'dʊŋk'lə 'lɛrlən lɪn di 'ra͜enən 'lʏft'ə 'ʃp'ri:sən. ['bla͜oən]
mutiger nun dunkle Erlen in die reinen Lüfte spriessen. [*poem:* in die blauen Lüfte]
more bravely now dark alders into the pure airs sprout. [blue]
(the dark alder trees send forth sprouts more bravely now into the pure air.)

ʊnt dem ˈtʰaːlə, zoː lɛɐ̯ˈblɪçən, ˈkeːrət‘ ˈhɔldə ˈrøːt‘ə ˈviːdɐ,
Und dem Tale, so erblichen, kehret holde Röte wieder,
And to the valley, so faded, returns lovely redness again,
(And to the valley, so pale during the storm, a lovely blush returns;)

ɪn deːɐ̯ ˈblyːt‘ən ˈvoːlgərʏçən ˈbaːdən ˈføːgəl liːɐ̯ gəˈfiːdɐ.
in der Blüten Wohlgerüchen baden Vögel ihr Gefieder.
in the blossoms' pleasant scents bathe birds their feathers.
(birds bathe their feathers in the sweet fragrance of the blossoms.)
[*poem:* **und** (ʊnt‘, and) **in duftigen** (ˈdʊft‘ɪgən, fragrant) **Gerüchen** (gəˈrʏçən, scents)]

hat di brʊst‘ zɪç ˈlɑ͜osgəvɪt‘ɐt‘, ˈza͜et‘vɛrt͜s leːnt deːɐ̯ gɔt den ˈboːgən,
Hat die Brust sich ausgewittert, seitwärts lehnt der Gott den Bogen,
Has the breast itself out-stormed, sideways leans the god the bow,
(When his breast has stormed itself out, the sun-god puts up his bow, leans it on his shoulder,)

ʊnt‘ za͜en ˈgɔldən ˈlant‘lɪt͜s ˈt͜sɪt‘ɐt‘ ˈra͜enɐ(r) lɑ͜of fɛɐ̯ˈzøːnt‘ən ˈvoːgən.
und sein golden Antlitz zittert reiner auf versöhnten Wogen.
and his golden countenance trembles more purely on reconciled waves.
(and his golden reflection trembles more pristinely on conciliated waves.)

[This song, exquisite in its musical charm, deserves to be better known. *Philomela, daughter of a king of Athens, was transformed into a nightingale in Ovid's version of the ancient myth.]

ˈnaxt‘gəzaŋ / oː giːp‘, fɔm ˈva͜eçən ˈp͜fyːlə
Nachtgesang / O gib, vom weichen Pfühle
Night Song / O Give, from the Soft Pillow

Posthumously published [composed 1814] (poem by Johann Wolfgang von Goethe)

oː giːp‘, fɔm ˈva͜eçən ˈp͜fyːlə, ˈtʰrɔ͜ømənt‘, la͜en halp‘ gəˈhøːɐ̯!
O gib, vom weichen Pfühle, träumend, ein halb Gehör!
O give, from the soft pillow, dreaming, a half hearing!
(O give me half a hearing, from your soft pillow, dreaming!)

ba͜e ˈma͜enəm ˈza͜et‘ənʃp‘iːlə ˈʃlaːfə! vas vɪlst duː meːɐ̯?
Bei meinem Saitenspiele schlafe! was willst du mehr?
To my lyre sleep! What want you more?
(Sleep to the sound of my strings! What more do you wish?)

ba͜e ˈma͜enəm ˈza͜et‘ənʃp‘iːlə ˈzeːgnət deːɐ̯ ˈʃt‘ɛrnə heːɐ̯ di ˈleːvɪgən gəˈfyːlə;
Bei meinem Saitenspiele segnet der Sterne Heer die ewigen Gefühle;
To my lyre blesses the stars' host the eternal feelings;
(With the sound of my strings the host of stars blesses eternal feelings;)

ˈʃlaːfə! vas vɪlst duː meːɐ̯? di ˈleːvɪgən gəˈfyːlə ˈheːbən mɪç,
schlafe! was willst du mehr? Die ewigen Gefühle heben mich,
sleep! What want you more? The eternal feelings lift me,
(sleep! What more do you wish? These eternal feelings raise me,)

hoːx lʊnt‘ heːɐ̯, lɑ͜os ˈlɪrdɪʃəm gəˈvyːlə; ˈʃlaːfə! vas vɪlst duː meːɐ̯?
hoch und hehr, aus irdischem Gewühle; schlafe! was willst du mehr?
high and exalted, out of earthly turmoil; sleep! What want you more?
(high and exalted, above all earthly turmoil; sleep! What more do you wish?)

fɔm 'ɪrdɪʃən gə'vy:lə tʰrɛnst du: mɪç nu:ɐ̯ t͡su: ze:ɐ̯,
Vom irdischen Gewühle trennst du mich nur zu sehr,
From the earthly tumult separate you me only too much,
(You separate me only too *well* from earthly tumult,)

banst' mɪç ɪn 'di:zə 'kʰy:lə; 'ʃla:fə! vas vɪlst du: me:ɐ̯?
bannst mich in diese Kühle; schlafe! was willst du mehr?
banish me into this coolness; sleep! What want you more?
(you banish me into this coolness; sleep! What more do you wish?)

banst' mɪç ɪn 'di:zə 'kʰy:lə, gi:pst' nu:ɐ̯/nu:r ɪm tʰrɑ͜om gə'hø:ɐ̯.
Bannst mich in diese Kühle, gibst nur im Traum Gehör.
(You) banish me into this coolness, give only in the dream hearing.
(You banish me into this coolness, you listen to me only in your dream.)

ax, ɑ͜of dem 'vae̯çən 'p͡fy:lə 'ʃla:fə! vas vɪlst du: me:ɐ̯?
Ach, auf dem weichen Pfühle schlafe! was willst du mehr?
Ah, on the soft pillow sleep! What want you more?
(Ah, sleep on your soft pillow! What more do you wish?)

[It is the voice of the lover, singing to his lady as she sleeps. Peters follows the first published edition (1850); the *Gesamtausgabe* follows Schubert's original version (which was a half-tone higher and had no prelude or postlude). Peters prints only the first three of the five verses.]

'naxt'gəzaŋ / 'tʰi:fə 'fae̯ɐ
Nachtgesang / Tiefe Feier
Night Song / Deep Solemnity

Posthumously published [composed 1815] (poem by Ludwig Kosegarten)

'tʰi:fə 'fae̯ɐ 'ʃɑ͜oɐt ʊm di vɛltʰ. 'brɑ͜onə 'ʃlae̯ɐ 'hʏlən valt' ʊnt' fɛlt'.
Tiefe Feier schauert um die Welt. Braune Schleier hüllen Wald und Feld.
Deep solemnity showers around the world. Brown veils cover forest and field.
(Deep solemnity descends upon the world. Dark veils cover forest and field.)
[*later edition of poem:* **Ernste** ('ɛrnst'ə, serious) **Feier; Trauerschleier** ('tʰrɑ͜oɐʃlae̯ɐ, mourning veils)]

tʰry:p' ʊnt' mat' ʊnt' 'my:də nɪk't' 'je:dəs 'le:bən lae̯n, ʊnt' 'na:mənlo:zɐ 'fri:də
Trüb' und matt und müde nickt jedes Leben ein, und namenloser Friede
Dreary and dull and tired drops every life asleep, and nameless peace
(Sad and dull and tired, all living things drop off into sleep, and an ineffable peace)

ʊm'zɔ͜øzəlt' 'aləs zae̯n. 'vaxɐ 'kʰʊmɐ, fɛɐ̯'las lae̯n 'vae̯lçən mɪç!
umsäuselt alles Sein. Wacher Kummer, verlass ein Weilchen mich!
around-murmurs all being. Wakeful care, leave a little while me!
(envelops all beings in a soft murmur. Wakeful care, leave me for a little while!)
[*GA:* **Wahrer** ('va:rɐ, true) **Kummer;** *Peters (to fit the music):* **lass** (las, leave)]

'gɔldnɐ 'ʃlʊmɐ, kʰɔm, ʊm'fly:glə mɪç!
Goldner Schlummer, komm', umflügle mich!
Golden slumber, come, around-wing me!
(Golden slumber, come, spread your wings about me!)

[ʊnt']
[*GA & poem:* **komm', und umflügle**]
[and]

ˈtʰrɔkʻnə ˈmaenə ˈtʰrɛːnən mɪt ˈdaenəs ˈʃlaeɐs zaom, [ˈfɪtʻɪçs]
Trockne meine Tränen mit deines Schleiers Saum, [*later edition of poem:* **deines Fittichs]**
Dry my tears with your veil's edge, [wing's]
(Dry my tears with the hem of your veil,)

ʊnt ˈtʰɔøʃə, frɔønt', maen ˈzeːnən mɪt ˈdaenəm ˈʃøːnstʻən tʰraom.
und täusche, Freund, mein Sehnen mit deinem schönsten Traum.
and delude, friend, my yearning with your most beautiful dream.

ˈblaoə ˈfɛrnə, hoːx ˈyːbɐ mɪç lɛɐ̯ˈhøːtʻ, ˈhaelgə ˈʃtʻɛrnə lɪn ˈheːrɐ majɛsˈtʰɛːtʰ!
Blaue Ferne, hoch über mich erhöht, heil'ge Sterne in hehrer Majestät!
Blue distance, high above me raised, holy stars in sublime majesty!
(Blue distance, raised high above me, holy stars in your sublime majesty,)

[rɪŋs lɪn di naxtʻ fɛɐ̯ˈzɛːtʰ!]
[*later edition of poem:* **heil'ge Sterne, rings in die Nacht versä't!]**
[all around in the night sown]
[(holy stars, sown all around in the night)]

zaːkʻtʻ miːɐ̯/miːr, lɪstʻ lɛs ˈʃtʻɪlɐ, liːɐ̯ ˈfʊŋkʻəlndən, bae lɔøç,
Sagt mir, ist es stiller, ihr Funkelnden, bei euch,
Tell me, is it quieter, you sparkling ones, by you,
(Tell me, you sparkling stars, is it quieter up there where you are,)
[*later edition of poem:* **ihr Schweigenden** (ˈʃvaegəndən, silent ones)]

als lɪn deːɐ̯/deːr ˈlaetʻəlkʰaetʻən ˈlaofruːɐ̯fɔləm raeç?
als in der Eitelkeiten aufruhrvollem Reich?
than in the vanities' tumult- full realm?
(than in this tumultuous realm of the vanities?)

[ˈdrʊntʻən] [dɛs ˈlaetʻlən]
[*later edition of poem:* **als drunten in des Eitlen]**
[below] [the vain's]
[(than down below, in the tumultuous realm of vanity?)]

[The second and third verses of this solemn hymn to the night will fit the music only if a note is added here and there (or in two cases subtracted). Peters prints the first two of the three verses.]

Nachtgesang (by Collin) see *Licht und Liebe*

ˈnaxtʻhʏmnə
Nachthymne
Hymn in Praise of Night

Posthumously published [composed 1820] (poem by Novalis)

hɪˈnyːbɐ val ɪç, lʊntʻ ˈjeːdə pʰaen vɪrtʻ laenstʻ laen ˈʃtʻaxəl deːɐ̯ ˈvɔlʊstʻ zaen.
Hinüber wall' ich, und jede Pein wird einst ein Stachel der Wollust sein.
To the other side float I, and every pain will one day a sting of the pleasure be.
(I float into the other world, and every pain will one day become a sting of pleasure.)

nɔx ˈveːnɪç ˈtsaetʻən, zoː bɪn lɪç loːs, lʊntʻ ˈliːgə ˈtʰrʊŋkʻən deːɐ̯ liːpʻ lɪm ʃoːs.
Noch wenig Zeiten, so bin ich los, und liege trunken der Lieb' im Schoss.
Still little times, then am I free, and lie intoxicated of the love in the lap.
(A little time more, and then I shall be free and lie intoxicated in the lap of love.)

ʊnˈlɛntʻlɪçəs ˈleːbən voːkʻtʻ ˈmɛçtʻɪç lɪn miːɐ̯, lɪç ˈʃɑo̯ə fɔn ˈloːbən hɛˈrʊntʻɐ naːx diːɐ̯.
Unendliches Leben wogt mächtig in mir, ich schaue von oben herunter nach dir.
Infinite life surges mightily in me, I look from above down toward you.

an ˈjeːnəm ˈhyːgəl fɛɐ̯ˈlɪʃt dae̯n glants; lae̯n ˈʃatʻən ˈbrɪŋət den ˈkʰyːləndən kʰrants.
An jenem Hügel verlischt dein Glanz; ein Schatten bringet den kühlenden Kranz.
On that hill is extinguished your luster; a shadow brings the cooling wreath.
(Your luster, Light, is extinguished upon that hill; a shadow brings the cooling funereal wreath.)

oː ˈzɑo̯gə, gəˈliːpʻtʻɐ, gəˈvaltʻɪç mɪç lan, das lɪç lɛntʻˈʃlʊmɐn lʊntʻ ˈliːbən kʰan!
O, sauge, Geliebter, gewaltig mich an, dass ich entschlummern und lieben kann!
O, suck, beloved, powerfully me in, that I fall asleep/pass away and love can!
(O beloved, Death, draw me powerfully to you, so that I can fall asleep and love!)

ɪç ˈfyːlə dɛs ˈtʰoːdəs fɛɐ̯ˈjʏŋəndə fluːtʻ, tsuː ˈbalzaːm lʊntʻ ˈlɛːtʻɐ fɛɐ̯ˈvandəltʻ mae̯n bluːtʰ;
Ich fühle des Todes verjüngende Flut, zu Balsam und Äther verwandelt mein Blut;
I feel the death's rejuvenating flood, to balm and ether is transformed my blood;
(I feel rejuvenating death flood over me: my blood is transformed into balm and ether;)

ɪç ˈleːbə bae̯ ˈtʰaːgə fɔl ˈglɑo̯bən lʊntʻ muːtʰ, lʊntʻ ˈʃtʻɛrbə di ˈnɛçtʻə lɪn ˈhae̯lɪgɐ gluːtʰ.
ich lebe bei Tage voll Glauben und Mut, und sterbe die Nächte in heiliger Glut.
I live by day full of faith and courage, and die the nights in holy fire.
(By day I live full of faith and courage, and at night I die in holy fire.)

[The title is often translated as "Hymn to the Night"; but, strictly speaking, it is Light, not Night, that is first addressed, and then Death, as "Geliebter" ("beloved"). Novalis prefaced the poem with a long introduction in prose, in which he addresses Light, which was born from Darkness and will one day die; whereas the Night is the eternal mother of all things. The hymn continues to address Light, then to call upon Death. Without the preceding words in prose, none of that is absolutely clear to the reader or to the listener. Schubert's song is in four contrasting sections: the first sustained and darkly colored, hymnlike; the second, surging with the energy of "infinite life"; the third, addressed to Death, with a sense of anticipation and hope; the last with a flickering of "holy fire" in the piano part, that dissolves into ether at the end. In an effort to stretch the impressive poem over a broader musical canvas, Schubert repeated many of the lines. The song was first published in 1872 in a version transposed down one tone to C major.]

ˈnaxtʻʃtʻʏkʰ
Nachtstück
Night Piece / Nocturne

Op. 36, No. 2 [1819] (Johann Mayrhofer)

vɛn ˈlyːbɐ ˈbɛrgə zɪç deːɐ̯ ˈneːbəl ˈbrae̯tʻətʰ, lʊntʻ ˈluːna mɪtʻ gəˈvœlkʻən kʰɛmpftʰ,
Wenn über Berge sich der Nebel breitet, und Luna mit Gewölken kämpft,
When over mountains itself the mist spreads, and Luna with clouds battles,
(When the mist spreads over the mountains, and the moon battles with the clouds,)
[*poem:* **Wann** (van, when)]

zoː nɪmt deːɐ̯/deːr ˈlaltʻə ˈzae̯nə ˈharfə, lʊntʻ ˈʃrae̯tʻətʻ, lʊntʻ zɪŋtʻ
so nimmt der Alte seine Harfe, und schreitet, und singt
then takes the old man his harp, and strides, and sings
(then the old man takes his harp, and walks, and sings) [*poem:* **Harf'** (harf, harp)]

valt'ˈla͜envɛrts ǀʊnt' gəˈdɛmpftʰ: du: ˈha͜elgə naxtʰ! balt' ǀɪsts fɔlˈbraxtʰ.
waldeinwärts und gedämpft: "Du heilge Nacht! Bald ist's vollbracht.
woods-inwards and subdued: "You holy night! Soon is it completed.
(softly as he enters the woods: "You holy night! Soon it will be over.)

balt' ʃla:f ɪç ǀi:n, den ˈlaŋən ˈʃlʊmɐ, de:ɐ̯ mɪç ǀɛɐ̯ˈlø:st' fɔn ˈǀaləm ˈkʰʊmɐ.
Bald schlaf' ich ihn, den langen Schlummer, der mich erlöst von allem Kummer.
Soon sleep I it, the long slumber, which me releases from all care.
(Soon I shall sleep that long slumber that will free me from all care.)

[*poem:* **von jedem** (ˈje:dəm, every) **Kummer**]

di ˈgry:nən ˈbɔ͜ømə ˈra͜oʃən dan: ʃla:f zy:s, du: ˈgu:t'ɐ(r) ˈǀalt'ɐ man;
Die grünen Bäume rauschen dann: 'Schlaf süss, du guter alter Mann';
The green trees murmur then: 'Sleep sweetly, you good old man';

di ˈgrɛ:zɐ ˈlɪsp'əln ˈvaŋk'ənt' fɔrt': vi:ɐ̯ ˈdɛk'ən ˈza͜enən ˈru:əǀɔrtʰ;
die Gräser lispeln wankend fort: 'Wir decken seinen Ruheort';
the grasses whisper wavering forth: 'We cover his resting place';
(the rippling grasses keep on whispering: 'We shall cover his resting place';)

ʊnt' ˈmançɐ ˈli:bə ˈfo:gəl ru:ft': ǀo: last' ǀi:n ru:n ǀɪn ˈra:zəngrʊftʰ! [ˈtʰra͜ot'ə]
und mancher liebe Vogel ruft: 'O lasst ihn ruh'n in Rasengruft!'" [*poem:* **traute Vogel**]
and many a dear bird calls: 'O let him rest in turf- tomb!' [dear]
(and many a dear bird calls: 'O let him rest in his tomb of grass!')

[*GA:* **O lass** (las, let—addressing one only) **ihn** (*lasst*—addressing more than one)]

de:ɐ̯/de:r ˈǀalt'ə hɔrçtʰ, de:ɐ̯/de:r ˈǀalt'ə ʃva͜ek'tʰ— de:ɐ̯ tʰo:t' hat' zɪç tsu: ǀi:m gəˈna͜ek'tʰ.
Der Alte horcht, der Alte schweigt—der Tod hat sich zu ihm geneigt.
The old man listens, the old man is silent— the death has itself to him inclined.
(The old man listens, the old man is silent.... Death has heard, and has granted his wish.)

[This poem inspired Schubert to some very beautiful music. The descending thirds in the introduction suggest the descent of the misty night and the approach of a welcome death; little stabs of pain in the treble give a hint of the cares from which the old man seeks release. In the accompaniment we hear his footsteps toward the woods, then the sound of his harp as he sings his moving hymn to the night, then the rustling of the leaves and grasses, as he dies in the bosom of nature. Schubert's sketch is in C# minor (as in the *Gesamtausgabe*); the version published during his lifetime, presumably reflecting his own decision, is a half tone lower (as in Peters).]

naxt' ǀʊnt ˈtʰrɔ͜ømə
Nacht und Träume
Night and Dreams

Op. 43, No. 2 [1822?] (Matthäus von Collin)

ˈha͜elgə naxt, du: ˈzɪŋk'əst' ˈni:dɐ; ˈni:dɐ ˈvalən ǀa͜ox di ˈtʰrɔ͜ømə,
Heil'ge Nacht, du sinkest nieder; nieder wallen auch die Träume,
Holy night, you sink down; down float also the dreams,
(Holy night, you sink down; dreams, too, come floating down,)

vi: da͜en ˈmo:nt'lɪçt dʊrç di ˈrɔ͜ømə, dʊrç de:ɐ̯ ˈmɛnʃən ˈʃt'ɪlə brʊstʰ.
wie dein Mondlicht durch die Räume, durch der Menschen stille Brust.
like your moonlight through the spaces, through the humans' quiet breast.
(like your moonlight through space, through the quiet hearts of human beings.)

diː bəˈlɑ͜oʃən ziː mɪtʻ lʊstʰ, ˈruːfən, vɛn deːɐ̯ tʰaːkʻ lɛɐ̯ˈvaxtʻ:
Die belauschen sie mit Lust, rufen, wenn der Tag erwacht:
Them listen to they with pleasure, call, when the day awakes:
(they listen to those dreams with pleasure; they cry out when day awakes:)

ˈkʰeːrə ˈviːdɐ, ˈha͜elgə naxtʰ! ˈhɔldə ˈtʰrɔ͜ømə, ˈkʰeːrətʻ ˈviːdɐ!
"Kehre wieder, heil'ge Nacht! holde Träume, kehret wieder!"
"Return again, holy night! Lovely dreams, return again!"
("Come back, holy night! Lovely dreams, come back!")

[The text of this famous song was used by Collin as the "Song of the Count" in his play, *Fortunats Abfahrt von Cypern* (*Fortunato's Departure from Cyprus*). Schubert's setting calls for a perfect *legato* and exceptional breath control. With the right singer the effect is magical.]

ˈnaxtʻvi̯oːlən
Nachtviolen
Night Violets / Dame's Violets

Posthumously published [composed 1822] (poem by Johann Mayrhofer)

ˈnaxtʻvioːlən, ˈnaxtʻvioːlən! ˈdʊŋkʻlə ˈlɑ͜ogən, ˈzeːlənfɔlə, ˈzeːlɪç lɪstʻ lɛs,
Nachtviolen, Nachtviolen! dunkle Augen, seelenvolle, selig ist es,
Night violets, night violets! dark eyes, soulful, blissful is it,
(Night violets, night violets! Dark, soulful eyes, it is blissful)

zɪç fɛɐ̯ˈzɛŋkʻən lɪn dem ˈzamtʻnən blɑ͜o. [fɛɐ̯ˈtʰiːfən lɪn das ˈzamtʻnə]
sich versenken in dem sammtnen Blau. [*poem:* **sich vertiefen in das sammtne Blau**]
oneself to sink in the velvety blue. [sink deeper into the velvety]
(to sink down in that velvety blue.) [(to sink deeper into that velvety blue)]

ˈgryːnə ˈblɛtʻɐ ˈʃtʻreːbən ˈfrɔ͜ødɪç lɔ͜øç t͜suː ˈhɛlən, lɔ͜øç t͜suː ˈʃmʏkʻən;
Grüne Blätter streben freudig euch zu hellen, euch zu schmücken;
Green leaves strive cheerfully you to brighten, you to adorn;
(Green leaves strive cheerfully to brighten you, to adorn you;)
[*Peters (in error):* **euch zu helfen** (ˈhɛlfən, help)**, euch zu schmücken**]

dɔx liːɐ̯ ˈblɪkʻətʻ lɛrnstʻ lʊntʻ ˈʃva͜egəntʻ lɪn di ˈlɑ͜oə ˈfryːlɪŋslʊftʰ.
doch ihr blicket ernst und schweigend in die laue Frühlingsluft.
but you gaze seriously and silently into the mild spring air.
[ˈʃɑ͜oətʻ] [ˈlaːnəntʻ] [ˈzɔmɐlʊftʰ]
[*later version of poem:* **doch ihr schauet ernst und ahnend in die laue Sommerluft**]
[look] [surmising] [summer air]

[jaː, zoː ˈfɛsəltʻ liːɐ̯ den ˈdɪçtʻɐː]
[Ja, so fesselt ihr den Dichter:]
[Yes, thus captivate you the poet:]
[(Yes, thus you captivate the poet:)]

mɪtʻ lɛɐ̯ˈhaːbnən ˈveːmuːt͜sʃtʻraːlən ˈtʰraːfətʻ liːɐ̯ ma͜en ˈtʰrɔ͜øəs hɛrt͜s, [za͜en]
mit erhabnen Wehmutsstrahlen trafet ihr mein treues Herz, [*poem:* **sein treues Herz**]
with sublime melancholy-rays struck you my loyal heart, [his]
(with sublime beams of melancholy you have pierced my loyal heart;)

ʊnt‘ nuːn blyːt‘ lɪn 'ʃt‘ʊmən 'nɛçt‘ən fɔrt di 'haelɪgə fɛɐ'bɪndʊŋ... [zoː]
und nun blüht in stummen Nächten fort die heilige Verbindung... [*poem:* **und so blüht**]
and now blooms in mute nights forth the holy bond... [so]
(and now in silent nights our holy bond continues to blossom...)

[ʊnlaos'ʃp‘rɛçlɪç, lʊnbə'grɪfən, — lʊnt di vɛlt‘ lɛɐ'raeçt‘ ziː nɪçtʰ.]
[Unaussprechlich, unbegriffen, — und die Welt erreicht sie nicht.]
[Inexpressible, uncomprehended, — and the world reaches it not.]
[(a bond that is inexpressible, uncomprehended, — and inaccessible to the world.)]

[Schubert left out the lines in brackets, above. The text he used was still in manuscript and differed from the later published version of his friend's poem. The song was composed eleven months after Schubert and Mayrhofer had stopped rooming together, after a turbulent friendship.]

'nɛːə dɛs gə'liːp‘t‘ən
Nähe des Geliebten
Nearness of the Beloved

Op. 5, No. 2 [1815] (Johann Wolfgang von Goethe)

ɪç 'dɛŋk‘ə daen, vɛn miːɐ deːɐ 'zɔnə 'ʃɪmɐ fɔm 'meːrə ʃt‘raːltʰ;
Ich denke dein, wenn mir der Sonne Schimmer vom Meere strahlt;
I think of you, when to me the sun's shimmer from the sea shines;
(I think of you when the shimmer of the sun shines to me from the sea;)

ɪç 'dɛŋk‘ə daen, vɛn zɪç dɛs 'moːndəs 'flɪmɐ(r) lɪn 'kʰvɛlən maːltʰ.
ich denke dein, wenn sich des Mondes Flimmer in Quellen malt.
I think of you, when itself the moon's glitter in springs paints.
(I think of you when the reflection of the moon glitters in fresh spring waters.)

ɪç 'zeːə dɪç, vɛn laof dem 'fɛrnən 'veːgə deːɐ ʃt‘aop‘ zɪç heːp‘tʰ;
Ich sehe dich, wenn auf dem fernen Wege der Staub sich hebt;
I see you, when on the distant road the dust itself raises;
(I see you when the dust rises on the distant road;)

ɪn 'tʰiːfɐ naxt‘, vɛn laof dem 'ʃmaːlən 'ʃt‘eːgə deːɐ 'vandrɐ beːp‘tʰ.
in tiefer Nacht, wenn auf dem schmalen Stege der Wandrer bebt.
in deep night, when on the narrow footpath the wanderer trembles.
(I see you in the depths of night, when the wanderer trembles on the narrow footpath.)

ɪç 'høːrə dɪç, vɛn dɔrt‘ mɪt 'dʊmpfəm 'raoʃən di 'vɛlə ʃt‘aek‘tʰ.
Ich höre dich, wenn dort mit dumpfem Rauschen die Welle steigt.
I hear you, when there with dull roar the wave rises.
(I hear you when the waves swell with a muffled roar.)

ɪm 'ʃt‘ɪlən 'haen, daː geː ɪç lɔft tsuː 'laoʃən, vɛn 'laləs ʃvaek‘tʰ.
Im stillen Hain, da geh' ich oft zu lauschen, wenn alles schweigt.
In the quiet grove, there go I often to listen, when all is silent.
(I hear you in the quiet grove, where I often go to listen, when all is silent.)
[*poem:* **Im stillen Haine** ('haenə, grove) **geh' ich** (*without "da"*)]

ɪç bɪn ba͡e diːɐ̯, duː za͡estʻ la͡ox nɔx zoː ˈfɛrnə, duː bɪstʻ miːɐ̯ naː!
Ich bin bei dir, du seist auch noch so ferne, du bist mir nah!
I am with you, you be even still so far, you are to me near!
(I am with you; however far you may be, you are near to me!)

di ˈzɔnə zɪŋkʻtʻ, baltʻ ˈlɔ͡øçtʻən miːɐ̯ di ˈʃtʻɛrnə. loː vɛːɐ̯st duː daː!
Die Sonne sinkt, bald leuchten mir die Sterne. O wärst du da!
The sun sinks, soon shine for me the stars. O were you here!
(The sun is setting; soon the stars will be shining for me. Oh, if you were only here!)

[I think of you whether nature is beautiful or harsh; I hear you in the sounds of nature, and in its silence; I see you before me wherever I travel. That is the thought; though some women might not find it flattering to be seen in the dust of the road or heard in the dull roar of the waves, they would surely be mollified by Schubert's enchanting music. The *Gesamtausgabe* and the *Neue Schubert Ausgabe* both include Schubert's first draft, which he discarded with the notation "*Gilt nicht*" ("No good"). Goethe wrote the poem to fit a melody that had delighted him at a party.]

ˈnaːmənstʰaːksliːtʻ
Namenstagslied
Name-Day Song

Posthumously published [composed 1820] (poem by Albert Stadler)

ˈfaːtʻɐ, ʃɛŋkʻ miːɐ̯ ˈdiːzə ˈʃtʻʊndə, høːr la͡en liːtʻ la͡os ˈma͡enəm ˈmʊndə!
Vater, schenk' mir diese Stunde, hör' ein Lied aus meinem Munde!
Father, grant me this hour, hear a song from my mouth!

diːɐ̯ fɛɐ̯ˈdaŋkʻ ɪç das gəˈlɪŋən ˈma͡enə ˈvʏnʃə hɔ͡øt t͡suː ˈzɪŋən,
Dir verdank' ich das Gelingen meine Wünsche heut' zu singen,
To you owe I the success, my wishes today to sing,
(I owe to you the success of my plan to sing my congratulations to you today,)

dɛn duː hastʻ mɪtʻ ˈgyːtʻgɐ hantʻ miːɐ̯ den veːkʻ daˈt͡suː gəˈbaːntʰ.
denn du hast mit güt'ger Hand mir den Weg dazu gebahnt.
for you have with kindly hand for me the way to that prepared.
(for with a kindly hand you have prepared the way to that for me.)

oː, las ˈdiːzə hantʻ mɪç ˈkʰʏsən! ziː dɛs ˈdaŋkʻəs ˈtʰrɛːnə ˈfliːsən!
O, lass diese Hand mich küssen! Sieh' des Dankes Träne fliessen!
Oh, let this hand me kiss! See the gratitude's tear flow!
(Oh, let me kiss that hand! See my tears of gratitude flowing!)

dɛn ziː hatʻ miːɐ̯ meːɐ̯ gəˈgeːbən lals gəˈzaŋ: la͡en ˈʃøːnəs ˈleːbən;
Denn sie hat mir mehr gegeben als Gesang: ein schönes Leben;
For it has to me more given than song: a beautiful life;
(For your hand has given more to me than song: it has given me a beautiful life;)

ʊntʻ mɪtʻ ˈkʰɪntʻlɪç ˈfroːəm blɪkʻ daŋkʻ ɪç liːɐ̯ dɛs ˈleːbəns glʏkʰ.
und mit kindlich frohem Blick dank' ich ihr des Lebens Glück.
and with childlike happy gaze thank I it (for) the life's happiness.
(and, with a childlike, happy look in my eyes, I thank that hand for the happiness of my life.)

'hɪməl, 'zɛndə 'dae̯nən 'ze:gən dem fɛɐ̯-/fɛr'le:ɐ̯t'ən man lɛnt''ge:gən!
Himmel, sende deinen Segen dem verehrten Mann entgegen!
Heaven, send your blessing to the revered man toward!
(Heaven, send your blessing down upon this venerated man!)

'ʃt'ra:lə li:m, dɛs 'glʏk'əs 'zɔnə! ʃɔ̯ø̯m li:m 'ly:bɐ, kʰɛlç de:ɐ̯ 'vɔnə!
Strahle ihm, des Glückes Sonne! Schäum' ihm über, Kelch der Wonne!
Beam for him, the happiness's sun! Foam for him over, goblet of joy!
(Beam upon him, sun of happiness! Foam over for him, goblet of joy!)

ʊnt' fɔn 'blu:mən fɔl de:ɐ̯ pʰraxtʰ zae̯ lae̯n kʰrant͡s li:m 'da:ɐ̯gəbraxtʰ.
Und von Blumen voll der Pracht sei ein Kranz ihm dargebracht.
And of flowers full of the splendor be a wreath to him presented.
(And let a magnificent wreath of flowers be presented to him.)

'di:zən kʰrant͡s lɪn 'dae̯nən 'ha:rən 'mø:gə gɔt' lʊns ʃt'e:t͡s bə'va:rən,
Diesen Kranz in deinen Haaren möge Gott uns stets bewahren,
This wreath in your hairs may God for us always preserve,
(May God always keep for us this wreath in your hair,)

ʊnt' lɪç fle:s mɪt' 'nasən 'blɪk'ən: nɔx lae̯n 't͡svae̯t'ɐ zɔl dɪç 'ʃmʏk'ən,
und ich fleh's mit nassen Blicken: noch ein zweiter soll dich schmücken,
and I entreat it with moist glances: still a second one shall you adorn,
(and with moist eyes I entreat this: still another, a second wreath, shall adorn you,)

blao̯ lʊnt' 'gɔldən, dɛn hi:ɐ̯ ʃp'rɪçt' 'je:dɐ mʊnt': fɛɐ̯'gɪs mae̯n nɪçtʰ!
blau und golden, denn hier spricht jeder Mund: Vergiss mein nicht!
blue and gold, for here speaks every mouth: "Forget me not!"
(one all blue and gold, for here every mouth is saying: "Forget me not!")

[The poet asked Schubert to set this poem to music so that Fräulein Josefine von Koller could sing it to her father on the occasion of his name-day (which happened to be March 19). The composer graciously complied, with a rather lovely song that the young lady sang with great feeling. Schubert had met her the summer before, and had enjoyed making music with her.]

na'tʰu:ɐ̯gənʊs

Naturgenuss

The Enjoyment of Nature

Posthumously published [composed 1815?] (poem by Friedrich von Matthisson)

ɪm 'la:bənt'ʃɪmɐ valt de:ɐ̯ kʰvɛl dʊrç 'vi:zənblu:mən 'pʰʊrp'ʊrhɛl,
Im Abendschimmer wallt der Quell durch Wiesenblumen purpurhell,
In the evening shimmer flows the spring through meadow-flowers purple-bright,
(In the shimmer of evening the brook flows among the purple-bright flowers of the meadow,)

de:ɐ̯ 'pʰap'əlvae̯də 'vɛksəlnt' gry:n ve:t' 'ru:əlɪsp'əlnt 'dry:bɐ hɪn.
der Pappelweide wechselnd Grün weht ruhelispelnd drüber hin.
the poplar-willow's changing green blows peace-whispering over it hence.
(the changing green of the poplars flutters above it, whispering peace.)

ɪm ˈlɛntsʰaox veːpʻt deːɐ̯ gaest dɛs hɛrn! ziː! ˈlaoflɛɐ̯ʃtʻeːʊŋ naː lʊntʻ fɛrn,
Im Lenzhauch webt der Geist des Herrn! Sieh! Auferstehung nah und fern,
In the spring-breath weaves the spirit of the Lord! Look! Resurrection near and far,
(The spirit of the Lord is active in the breath of spring! Look! There is resurrection, near and far!)
[*Peters:* **weht** (veːt, blows/wafts) **der Geist**]

ziː! ˈjuːgəntʻfʏlə, ˈʃøːnhaetsmeːɐ̯(r), lʊntʻ ˈvɔnətʰaoməl rɪŋs lʊmˈheːɐ̯.
sieh! Jugendfülle, Schönheitsmeer, und Wonnetaumel rings umher.
see! youth- profusion, beauty- sea, and rapture-reeling round about.
(Look! The profusion of youth, a sea of beauty, and everything all around reeling with rapture.)

ɪç ˈblɪkʻə heːɐ̯/heːr, lɪç ˈblɪkʻə hɪn, lʊntʻ ˈlɪmɐ ˈhøːɐ ʃveːpʻtʻ maen zɪn.
Ich blicke her, ich blicke hin, und immer höher schwebt mein Sinn.
I look here, I look there, and ever higher soars my mind.
(I look here, I look there, and my mind soars higher and higher.)

nuːɐ̯ tʰantʻ zɪntʻ pʰraxtʻ lʊntʻ gɔltʻ lʊntʻ ruːm, naˈtʰuːɐ̯/-tʰuːr, lɪn ˈdaenəm ˈhaelɪçtʻuːm!
Nur Tand sind Pracht und Gold und Ruhm, Natur, in deinem Heiligtum!
Only bauble are splendor and gold and fame, Nature, in your sanctuary!
(Nature, in your sanctuary worldly splendor, gold, and fame are merely baubles!)

dɛs ˈhɪməls ˈlaːnʊŋ deːn lʊmˈveːtʻ, deːɐ̯ ˈdaenən ˈliːbəstʰoːn fɛɐ̯ˈʃtʻeːtʰ;
Des Himmels Ahnung den umweht, der deinen Liebeston versteht;
The heaven's presentiment him blows about, who your love- tone understands;
(An intimation of heaven wafts around him who understands your tones of love;)

dɔx, lan daen ˈmʊtʻɐhɛrts gəˈdrʏkʻtʻ, vɪrtʻ leːɐ̯ tsʊm ˈhɪməl zɛlpstʻ lɛntˈtsʏkʻtʰ!
doch, an dein Mutterherz gedrückt, wird er zum Himmel selbst entzückt!
but, to your mother-heart pressed, becomes he to the heaven itself transported!
(but, pressed to your motherly heart, he is transported to heaven itself!)

[The poet revels in nature. An agreeable little strophic song with some nice turns of phrase.]

Non t'accostar all' urna see *Vier Canzonen von Metastasio*

ˈnɔrmans gəˈzaŋ
Normanns Gesang (Peters) / **Norman's Gesang** (*Gesamtausgabe*)
Norman's Song
(from *The Lady of the Lake* by Sir Walter Scott)

Op. 52, No. 5 [1825] (German translation by Adam Storck)

di naxtʻ brɪçtʻ baltʻ hɛˈraen, dan leːg ɪç mɪç tsʊr ruː,
Die Nacht bricht bald herein, dann leg' ich mich zur Ruh,
The night breaks soon in here, then lay I myself to the rest,
(Night will soon be falling; then I shall lie down to rest,) [*hereinbrechen* = fall, set in, overtake]

di ˈhaedə lɪstʻ maen ˈlaːgɐ, das ˈfarnkʰraot dɛkʻtʻ mɪç tsuː.
die Heide ist mein Lager, das Farnkraut deckt mich zu.
the heath is my couch, the fern covers me up.
(the heath will be my bed, and ferns will be my covers.)

mɪç lʊlt deːɐ̯ ˈvaxə tʰrɪt‘ voːl lɪn den ʃlaːf hɪˈnae̯n.
Mich lullt der Wache Tritt wohl in den Schlaf hinein.
Me lulls the sentinel's step probably into the sleep in.
(The sentinel's steps will probably lull me into sleep.)

ax, mʊs zoː vae̯t‘ fɔn diːɐ̯, maˈriːa, ˈhɔldə, zae̯n!
Ach, muss so weit von dir, Maria, Holde, sein!
Ah, (I) must so far from you, Mary, lovely one, be!
(Ah, I have to be so far from you, Mary, my lovely one!)

ʊnt‘ vɪrt‘ lɛs ˈmɔrgən ˈlaːbənt‘, lʊnt‘ kʰɔmt di ˈtʰryːbə tsae̯t‘,
Und wird es morgen Abend, und kommt die trübe Zeit,
And becomes it tomorrow evening, and comes the gloomy time,
(And when tomorrow evening has come, and when the gloomy time has come,)

dan lɪst‘ fiˈlae̯çt‘ mae̯n ˈlaːgɐ deːɐ̯ ˈbluːtʼɪç ˈroːt‘ə pʰlae̯t‘,
dann ist vielleicht mein Lager der blutig rote Plaid,
then is perhaps my couch the bloody red plaid,
(then perhaps my couch will be my plaid, red with my blood;)

mae̯n‿ˈlaːbənt‘liːt‘ fɛɐ̯ˈʃt‘ʊmət, duː ʃlae̯çst dan tʰryːp‘ lʊnt‘ baŋ,
mein Abendlied verstummet, du schleichst dann trüb' und bang,
my evening song grows silent, you creep then gloomy and afraid,
(my evening song grows silent; gloomy and afraid, you will creep over to me;)

maˈriːa, mɪç ˈvɛk‘ən kʰan nɪçt dae̯n ˈtʰoːt‘ənzaŋ. [lax]
Maria, mich wecken kann nicht dein Totensang. [*Storck:* **Maria, ach mich wecken**]
Mary, me waken can not your song for the dead. [ah]
(Mary, your song of death cannot waken me.)

zoː mʊst‘ ɪç fɔn diːɐ̯ ˈʃae̯dən, duː ˈhɔldə, ˈzyːsə brao̯tʰ?
So musst' ich von dir scheiden, du holde, süsse Braut?
Thus had I from you to part, you lovely, sweet bride?
(Did I have to part from you like that, my lovely, sweet bride?)

viː maːkst duː naːx miːɐ̯ ˈruːfən, viː maːkst duː ˈvae̯nən lao̯tʰ! [ˈnaːxruːfən]
Wie magst du nach mir rufen, wie magst du weinen laut! [*Storck:* **du mir nachrufen**]
How may you after me call, how may you weep loudly! [call after]
(How you may be calling for me, how loudly you may be weeping!)

ax, ˈdɛŋk‘ən darf lɪç nɪçt‘ lan ˈdae̯nən ˈhɛrbən ʃmɛrts,
Ach, denken darf ich nicht an deinen herben Schmerz,
Ah, think may I not of your bitter pain,
(Ah, I must not think about your bitter pain,)

ax, ˈdɛŋk‘ən darf lɪç nɪçt‘ lan dae̯n gəˈtʰrɔø̯əs hɛrts.
ach, denken darf ich nicht an dein getreues Herz.
ah, think may I not of your faithful heart.
(ah, I must not think about your faithful heart.)

nae̯n, ˈtsɛːɐ̯t‘lɪç ˈtʰrɔø̯əs ˈzeːnən darf ˈheːgən ˈnɔrman nɪçt‘, [ˈnɔrman]
Nein, zärtlich treues Sehnen darf hegen Norman nicht, [*Peters:* **Normann**]
No, tender faithful yearning may shelter Norman not, [*variant spelling*]
(No, Norman must not harbor such feelings as tender, faithful yearning)

vɛn lɪn den fa͜ent‘ kʰlan-'lalp‘in vi: ʃt‘ʊtm lʊnt‘ 'ha:gəl brɪçt‘, ['lalp‘in]
wenn in den Feind Clan-Alpine wie Sturm und Hagel bricht, [*GA:* **Clan Alpin]**
when into the enemy Clan Alpine like storm and hail breaks, [Alpine]
(when Clan Alpine tears into the enemy like a hail storm;)

vi: la͜en gə'ʃp‘ant‘ɐ 'bo:gən za͜en 'mu:t‘ɪç hɛrt͜s dan za͜e,
wie ein gespannter Bogen sein mutig Herz dann sei,
like a drawn bow his brave heart then be,
(may his brave heart then be like a drawn bow,)

za͜en fu:s, ma'ri:a, vi: de:ɐ̯ p͜fa͜el zo: raʃ lʊnt‘ fra͜e!
sein Fuss, Maria, wie der Pfeil so rasch und frei!
his foot, Mary, like the arrow so rapid and free!
(his foot, Mary, as rapid and free as an arrow!)

vo:l vɪrt di 'ʃt‘ʊndə 'kʰɔmən, vo: nɪçt di 'zɔnə ʃa͜ent‘,
Wohl wird die Stunde kommen, wo nicht die Sonne scheint,
Probably will the hour come when not the sun shines,
(That hour well may come, when the sun no longer shines,)

du: vaŋkst t͜su: 'da͜enəm 'nɔrman, da͜en 'hɔldəs 'la͜ogə va͜entʰ.
du wankst zu deinem Norman, dein holdes Auge weint.
you stagger to your Norman, your lovely eye weeps.
(you stagger over to your Norman, your lovely eyes are weeping.)

dɔx fal ɪç lɪn de:ɐ̯ ʃlaxtʰ, hʏlt 'tʰo:dəsʃa͜oɐ mɪç,
Doch fall' ich in der Schlacht, hüllt Todesschauer mich,
But fall I in the battle, envelops death-horror me,
(But if I fall in the battle, if the horror that is death shrouds me,)

o: gla͜op‘, ma͜en 'lɛtst‘ɐ 'zɔ͜øftsɐ, ma'ri:a, lɪst‘ fy:ɐ̯ dɪç.
o glaub', mein letzter Seufzer, Maria, ist für dich.
O believe, my last sigh, Mary, is for you.
(O believe me, my last sigh, Mary, will be for you.)

dɔx kʰe:r ɪç 'zi:k‘ra͜eç 'vi:dɐ(r) la͜os 'kʰy:nɐ 'mɛnɐʃlaxt‘.
Doch kehr' ich siegreich wieder aus kühner Männerschlacht,
But return I victorious again from bold men's battle,
(But if I return from the battle of bold men as one of the victors,)

dan 'gry:sən vi:ɐ̯ zo: 'frɔ͜ødɪç das na:n de:ɐ̯ 'ʃt‘ɪlən naxtʰ,
dann grüssen wir so freudig das Nah'n der stillen Nacht,
then greet we so joyfully the approach of the quiet night,
(then we shall greet the approach of the quiet night so joyfully:)

das 'la:gɐ(r) lɪst‘ bə'ra͜et‘ət‘, lʊns vɪŋk‘t di 'zy:sə ru:,
das Lager ist bereitet, uns winkt die süsse Ruh',
the couch is prepared, us beckons the sweet rest,
(our nuptial couch is ready, sweet rest will beckon to us,)

de:ɐ̯ 'hɛnflɪŋ zɪŋt‘ 'bra͜ot‘li:dɐ, ma'ri:a, hɔlt‘ lʊns t͜su:.
der Hänfling singt Brautlieder, Maria, hold uns zu.
the linnet sings bridal songs, Maria, graciously us to.
(and the linnet will sing lovely bridal songs to us, Maria.)

[ɛs vɪŋk't di 'zy:sə ru:, ma'ri:a, hɔlt' lʊns t͡su:.]
[*Schubert's coda:* **Es winkt die süsse Ruh', Maria, hold uns zu.]**
[There beckons the sweet rest, Maria, graciously us to.]
[(Sweet rest beckons graciously to us, Maria.)]

[The relentless rhythm portrays the galloping horse, the final shift to the major key the hope of victory and a happy consummation of the marriage that was interrupted at the church door by the rallying of Clan Alpine to meet the foe. The incident occurs in Canto III of *The Lady of the Lake*; Norman is riding toward the place of battle and he sings to vent his feelings of fear and of hope:

The heath this night must be my bed, / The bracken curtain for my head,
My lullaby the warder's tread, / Far, far from love and thee, Mary.
Tomorrow eve, more stilly laid, / My couch may be my bloody plaid,
My vesper song thy wail, sweet maid! / It will not waken me, Mary!
I may not, dare not, fancy now / The grief that clouds thy lovely brow,
I dare not think upon thy vow / And all it promised me, Mary.
No fond regret must Norman know: / When bursts Clan Alpine on the foe,
His heart must be like bended bow, / His foot like arrow free, Mary.
A time will come with feeling fraught, / For if I fall in battle fought,
Thy hapless lover's dying thought / Shall be a thought on thee, Mary.
And if returned from conquered foes, / How blithely will the evening close,
How sweet the linnet sing repose / To my young bride and me, Mary!]

nu:ɐ̯ ve:ɐ̯ di 'li:bə kʰɛntʰ

Nur wer die Liebe kennt

Only Someone Who Knows Love

Fragment (D 513 A) [date unknown—1817?] (poem by Zacharias Werner)

nu:ɐ̯ ve:ɐ̯ di 'li:bə kʰɛnt', fɛɐ̯'ʃt'e:t das 'ze:nən,
Nur wer die Liebe kennt, versteht das Sehnen,
Only who the love knows, understands the longing,
(Only someone who knows love can understand the longing)

an den gə'li:p't'ən 'le:vɪç fɛst t͡su: 'haŋən,
an den Geliebten ewig fest zu hangen,
to the beloved eternally firmly to cling,
(forever to cling firmly to one's beloved,)

lʊnt' 'le:bənsmu:t' la͡os 'za͡enəm la͡ok' t͡su: 'tʰrɪŋk'ən.
und Lebensmut aus seinem Aug zu trinken.
and life- courage from his eye to drink.
(and to drink exhilaration from his or her eyes.)

de:ɐ̯ kʰɛnt das 'ʃmɛrt͡slɪç 'ze:lɪgə fɛɐ̯'laŋən, da'hɪn t͡su: 'ʃmɛlt͡sən
Der kennt das schmerzlich selige Verlangen, dahin zu schmelzen
He knows the painfully blissful desire away to melt
(Someone who knows love knows the painfully blissful desire to melt away)

lɪn la͡en me:ɐ̯ fɔn 'tʰrɛ:nən, lʊnt' 'la͡ofgəlø:st' lɪn 'li:bə t͡su: fɛɐ̯'zɪŋk'ən.
in ein Meer von Tränen, und aufgelöst in Liebe zu versinken.
into a sea of tears, and dissolved in love to sink.
(in a sea of tears and, dissolved, to drown in love.)

[Schubert composed music for the first six verses (above) of a thirteen-line poem, inspired by "*Nur wer die Sehnsucht kennt*" from Goethe's *Wilhelm Meister*. Reinhard Van Hoorickx has completed a performing version, published in *Mitteilungen des Steirischen Tonkünstlerbundes*, July 1974. The poem appeared under the title "*Impromptu*" in *Die Harfe*, a periodical, in 1815.]

nuːɐ̯ veːɐ̯ di ˈzeːnzʊxtʻ kʰɛntʰ / liːt deːɐ̯ mɪnˈjõ / ˈzeːnzʊxtʰ / mɪnˈjõ lʊnt deːɐ ˈharfnɐ
Nur wer die Sehnsucht kennt / Lied der Mignon / Sehnsucht / Mignon und der Harfner
Only Someone Who Knows Longing / Mignon's Song / Longing / Mignon and the Harper

Op. 62, Nos. 1 & 4 [1826] (poem included in *Wilhelm Meister* by Johann Wolfgang von Goethe)

nuːɐ̯ veːɐ̯ di ˈzeːnzʊxtʻ kʰɛntʻ, va͜es, vas lɪç ˈla͜edə!
Nur wer die Sehnsucht kennt, weiss, was ich leide!
Only who the longing knows, knows what I suffer!
(Only someone who knows longing can know what I am suffering!)

aˈla͜en lʊntʻ ˈlapʻgətʰrɛntʻ fɔn ˈlalɐ ˈfrɔ͜ødə,
Allein und abgetrennt von aller Freude,
Alone and separated from all joy,

zeː ɪç lans fɪrmaˈmɛntʻ naːx ˈjeːnɐ ˈza͜etʻə.
seh' ich ans Firmament nach jener Seite.
look I at the firmament toward that side.
(I look at the sky in that direction.)

ax! deːɐ̯ mɪç liːpʻtʻ lʊntʻ kʰɛntʻ lɪstʻ lɪn deːɐ̯ ˈva͜etʻə.
Ach! der mich liebt und kennt ist in der Weite.
Ah! who me loves and knows is in the distance.
(Ah! The one who loves me and *knows* me is far away.)

ɛs ˈʃvɪndəltʻ miːɐ̯, lɛs brɛntʻ ma͜en ˈla͜engəva͜edə.
Es schwindelt mir, es brennt mein Eingeweide.
It is dizzy to me, it burns my entrails.
(My head is reeling, my vitals are burning.)

nuːɐ̯ veːɐ̯ di ˈzeːnzʊxtʻ kʰɛntʻ, va͜es, vas lɪç ˈla͜edə!
Nur wer die Sehnsucht kennt, weiss, was ich leide!
Only who the longing knows, knows what I suffer!
(Only someone who knows longing can know what I am suffering!)

[Schubert made six settings of this famous poem (familiar to almost everyone as Tchaikovsky's "None But The Lonely Heart"), four times as a solo song (the first in *two* versions!), once each as a duet (op. 62, no. 1) and as a male quintet. He used various titles, listed above. The first three versions for solo voice were not published during his lifetime, but are included in the *Gesamtausgabe*. Peters prints only the well-known fourth. In *Wilhelm Meister* the poem occurs at the end of Book IV, Chapter 11: Wilhelm feels "a dreamy yearning," and, "as if tuning into his sentiments," at that very moment Mignon and the old harper are singing a song "as an irregular duet" and "with the most heartfelt expression." Both poem and song express a deep loneliness, a sense of alienation from present surroundings, and a poignant yearning for the one who loves and understands you—but is far away.]

ɔː kʰvɛl, vas ʃtʻrøːmst duː raʃ lʊntʻ vɪltʻ / di ˈbluːmə lʊnt deːɐ̯ kʰvɛl

O Quell, was strömst du rasch und wild / Die Blume und der Quell

O Spring, Why Do You Flow So Fast and Wild / The Flower and the Spring

Fragment (D 874) [1826] (Ernst Schulze)

DIE BLUME (di ˈbluːmə, the flower):

ɔː kʰvɛl, vas ʃtʻrøːmst duː raʃ lʊntʻ vɪltʻ lʊntʻ vyːlstʻ lɪn ˈdaɐ̯nəm ˈzɪlbɐzandə lʊnt
O Quell, was strömst du rasch und wild und wühlst in deinem Silbersande und
O spring, why stream you fast and wild and burrow in your silver sand and
(O spring, why do you flow so fast and so wildly, and burrow about in your silvery sand, and)

drɛŋstʻ, fɔn ˈvaɐ̯çəm ʃaɔ̯m fɛɐ̯ˈhʏlt, dɪç ˈʃvɛləntʻ laɔ̯f lam ˈgryːnən ˈrandə?
drängst, von weichem Schaum verhüllt, dich schwellend auf am grünen Rande?
push, by soft foam veiled, yourself swellingly up on the green rim?
(push yourself up, swelling, and veiled in soft foam, on the grassy rim?)

oː ˈriːzlə, kʰvɛl, dɔx glatʻ lʊntʻ hɛl, das lɪç, fɛɐ̯ˈkʰlɛːɐ̯tʻ fɔn ˈt͡saːɐ̯tʻəm ˈtʰaɔ̯ə,
O riesle, Quell, doch glatt und hell, dass ich, verklärt von zartem Taue,
O ripple, spring, but smooth and clear, that I, transfigured by delicate dew,
(But, spring, let your rippling be smooth and clear, so that I, transfigured by delicate dewdrops,)

maɐ̯n ˈt͡sɪtʻɐntʻ bɪltʻ lɪn diːɐ̯/diːr lɛɐ̯ˈʃaɔ̯ə!
mein zitternd Bild in dir erschaue!
my trembling image in you behold!
(may see my trembling reflection!)

[DER QUELL (deːɐ̯ kʰvɛl, the spring):

oː ˈbluːmə, kʰan lɪç ˈruːɪç zaɐ̯n, vɛn zɪç daɐ̯n bɪltʻ lɪn miːɐ̯ bəˈʃpʻiːgəltʰ,
O Blume, kann ich ruhig sein, wenn sich dein Bild in mir bespiegelt,
O flower, can I calm be, when itself your image in me mirrors,
(O flower, can I be calm when your image is mirrored in me,)

ʊntʻ ˈvʊndɐbaːrə ˈliːbəspʰaɐ̯n mɪç baltʻ t͡suˈrʏkʻhɛltʻ, baltʻ bəˈflyːgəltʰ?
und wunderbare Liebespein mich bald zurückhält, bald beflügelt?
and wondrous love- pain me now holds back, now gives wings to?
(and the wondrous pain of love at one moment holds me back, at the next gives me wings?)

drʊm ʃtʻreːb ɪç laɔ̯f mɪtʻ ˈlɪrəm laɔ̯f
Drum streb' ich auf mit irrem Lauf
Therefore strive I on with mad course
(Therefore I struggle on in this mad course,)

lʊntʻ vɪl mɪtʻ ˈʃmaxtʻəndəm fɛɐ̯ˈlaŋən, duː ˈt͡saːɐ̯tʻə, ˈdaɐ̯nən kʰɛlç lʊmˈfaŋən.
und will mit schmachtendem Verlangen, du Zarte, deinen Kelch umfangen.
and want with languishing desire, you delicate one, your chalice to embrace.
(and, with languishing desire, I long to embrace your chalice, delicate one.)

DIE BLUME:

oː kʰvɛl, lɪç 'ʃt'eːə fiːl t͜suː fɛrn, duː kʰanst dɪç niː t͜suː miːɐ̯/miːr lɛɐ̯'heːbən;
O Quell, ich stehe viel zu fern, du kannst dich nie zu mir erheben;
O spring, I stand much too far, you can yourself never to me raise;
(O spring, I am much too far above you, you can never raise yourself up to me;)

dɔx 'frɔ͜ønt'lɪç zɔl ma͜en 'blyːt'ənʃt'ɛrn la͜of 'da͜enɐ 'ha͜et'ɐn 'flɛçə 'beːbən.
doch freundlich soll mein Blütenstern auf deiner heitern Fläche beben.
but amiably shall my blossom-star on your serene surface tremble.
(but my star-shaped, blossoming image ought to be trembling amiably on your serene surface.)

drʊm 'riːzlə hɪn mɪt' 'ʃt'ɪləm zɪn! zyːs lɪst͜s,
Drum riesle hin mit stillem Sinn! Süss ist's,
Therefore ripple away with quiet mind! Sweet is it,
(Therefore ripple away with a quiet mind! It is sweet)

lɪm 'buːzən 'loːnə 'kʰlaːgən deːɐ̯ 'liːpst'ən 'kʰɔ͜ øʃəs bɪlt t͜suː 'tʰraːgən.
im Busen ohne Klagen der Liebsten keusches Bild zu tragen.
in the bosom without complaint the dearest's chaste image to bear.
(to bear in your bosom, without complaint, the chaste image of your dearest one.)

DER QUELL:

oː 'bluːmə, raːt' lʊnt tʰroːst' lɪst' la͜eçt', dɔx ʃveːɐ̯/ʃveːr lɪst͜s, 'hɔfnʊŋsloːs t͜suː 'glyːən;
O Blume, Rat und Trost ist leicht, doch schwer ist's, hoffnungslos zu glühen;
O flower, advice and comfort is easy, but hard is it, hopelessly to burn;
(O flower, it is easy to give advice and comfort, but it is hard to burn without hope;)

vɛn la͜ox ma͜en kʰʊs dɪç nɪçt' lɛɐ̯'ra͜eçt', zoː mʊs lɪç 'leːvɪç dɔx mɪç 'myːən.
wenn auch mein Kuss dich nicht erreicht, so muss ich ewig doch mich mühen.
if even my kiss you not reaches, so must I forever though myself take pains.
(even if my kiss does not reach you, I nevertheless must forever be trying.)

a͜en blat' la'la͜en las duː hɪ'na͜en lɪn 'ma͜enə 'vɪldə 'tʰiːfə 'falən!
Ein Blatt allein lass du hinein in meine wilde Tiefe fallen!
One petal alone let you in into my wild depths fall!
(Let just one petal fall into my wild depths!)

dan vɪl lɪç ʃt'ɪl fo'ryːbɐvalən.]
Dann will ich still vorüberwallen.]
Then want I quietly past to flow.]
(Then I shall try to flow past you quietly.)]

[Schubert left a sketch of the first verse, with an introduction, the vocal line, and indications of the accompaniment. A performing version has been completed and privately printed by Reinhard Van Hoorickx, with the title "*Die Blume und der Quell.*"]

o'rɛst' lɑo̯f 'tʰɑo̯rɪs
Orest auf Tauris
Orestes on Tauris

Posthumously published [composed 1817] (poem by Johann Mayrhofer)

ɪst di:s 'tʰɑo̯rɪs? vo: de:ɐ̯/de:r lɔ̯ø̯me'ni:dən vu:t t͡su: 'ʃt'ɪlən, 'pʰy:t'i̯a fɛɐ̯'ʃp'ra:x?
Ist dies Tauris? wo der Eumeniden Wut zu stillen, Pythia versprach?
Is this Tauris? where the Eumenides' fury to appease, Pythia promised?
(Can this be Tauris, where Pythia promised to appease the fury of the Eumenides?)
[*poem:* **Dieses** ('di:zəs, this) **Tauris?...Pythius** ('pʰy:t'i̯ʊs,, Pithios = Delphi)]

ve:! di 'ʃvɛst'ɐn mɪt den 'ʃlaŋənha:rən 'fɔlgən mi:ɐ̯
Weh! die Schwestern mit den Schlangenhaaren folgen mir
Woe! the sisters with the snake- hairs follow me
(Alas, the snake-haired sisters follow me)

fɔm lant de:ɐ̯ 'gri:çən na:x! 'rɑo̯əs 'la̯elant', 'kʰʏndəst' 'kʰa̯enən 'ze:gən:
vom Land der Griechen nach! Rauhes Eiland, kündest keinen Segen:
from the land of the Greeks after! Rough island, (you) announce no blessing:
(from the land of the Greeks! Rough Island, you give no hint of any blessing:)

'nɪrgənt͡s ʃp'rɔst de:ɐ̯ 't͡se:rɛs 'mɪldə frʊxtʰ; 'ka̯enə 're:bən bly:n, ['gɔldnə]
nirgends sprosst der Ceres milde Frucht; keine Reben blüh'n, [*poem:* **goldne Frucht**]
nowhere sprouts the Ceres's mild fruit; no grapevines bloom, [golden]
(nowhere here does Ceres' tender fruit grow; no grapevines are blooming,)

de:ɐ̯ 'lʏft'ə 'zɛŋɐ, vi: di: 'ʃifə, 'ma̯edən 'di:zə bʊxtʰ.
der Lüfte Sänger, wie die Schiffe, meiden diese Bucht.
the airs' singers, like the ships, avoid this bay.
(the birds, like the ships, avoid this bay.)

'ʃt'a̯enə fy:k't di kʰʊnst' nɪçt t͡su: gə'bɔ̯ø̯dən, 't͡sɛlt'ə ʃp'ant dɛs 'skʰy:t'ən 'larmu:t' zɪç;
Steine fügt die Kunst nicht zu Gebäuden, Zelte spannt des Skythen Armut sich;
Stones joins the art not to buildings, tents stretches the Scythian's poverty for itself;
(Here art does not join stones together into buildings; the Scythian in his poverty sets up tents;)

'ʊnt'ɐ 'ʃt'arən 'fɛlzən, 'rɑo̯ən 'vɛldɐn lɪst das 'le:bən 'la̯enza:m, 'ʃɑo̯ɐlɪç! lʊnt' hi:ɐ̯ zɔl,
unter starren Felsen, rauhen Wäldern ist das Leben einsam, schauerlich! Und hier soll,
beneath rigid crags, rough forests is the life lonely, terrible! And here shall,
(beneath rigid cliffs, in savage forests life is lonely, terrible! And here—)
[*poem:* **"Allhier** (al'hi:ɐ̯, here) **soll,"... heil'ge** ('ha̯elgə, holy)]

zo: lɪst'ja: dɔx lɛɐ̯'gaŋən lan den 'fle:əndən de:ɐ̯ 'ha̯elɪgə ʃp'rʊx,
so ist ja doch ergangen an den Flehenden der heilige Spruch,
thus is you know after all promulgated to the pleading one the holy decree,
(thus, after all, was the holy decree promulgated to the suppliant—)

'a̯enə 'ho:ə 'pʰri:st'ərɪn di'a:nəns 'lø:zən 'ma̯enən lʊnt de:ɐ̯ 'fɛ:t'ɐ flu:x.
eine hohe Priesterin Dianens lösen meinen und der Väter Fluch.
a high priestess of Diana annul my and the fathers' curse.
(a high priestess of Diana shall annul the curse on me and on my forefathers.)

[zɔl di ˈboːgənʃp‘anərɪn diˈaːna ˈløːzən ˈdaenən]
[*poem:* **"soll die Bogenspannerin Diana lösen deinen..."**]
[shall the archeress Diana annul your]
[("The archeress Diana shall annul your curse...")]

[Greek antiquity and its legends were one of the poet's passions, and his friend and sometime roommate set many of such pieces to music. The subject of this song—and of its companion, *Der entsühnte Orest,*—is one of the most famous in all Greek literature, and has inspired many later dramas. Orestes killed his mother Clytemnestra because she had murdered his father, her husband, King Agamemnon. Thus two laws came into irreconcilable conflict: matricide is a heinous crime; but it was the duty of a son to avenge his father's murder. Orestes, in punishment, was pursued night and day by the snake-haired Furies (piously called the Eumenides—"gracious ones"—to placate them); in despair he threatened to take his own life unless Apollo would free him from their ceaseless scourging. The Pythian priestess at Delphi, who interpreted the decrees of the god, told Orestes that his torment would end if he would sail to the "island" of Tauris (usually identified as the Crimean peninsula), home of the Scythians, and bring back a sacred statue of Diana (Artemis to the Greeks). He did not know that the high priestess of Diana was his own sister, Iphigenia. Both were of the House of Atreus, long under a curse because of the crimes of succeeding generations. Ceres, incidentally, was the goddess of the fruitful soil.]

Orpheus see *Lied des Orpheus*

ˈɔsi̯ans liːt‘ naːx dem ˈfalə ˈnaːt‘ɔs
Ossians Lied nach dem Falle Nathos'
Ossian's Song after the Death of Nathos

Posthumously published [composed 1815] (prose poem by James Macpherson— "Ossian")
(German translation by Edmund von Harold)

bɔ̯økʼt‘ lɔ̯øç ɑ̯ɔs ˈlɔ̯ørən ˈvɔlk‘ən ˈniːdɐ(r), liːɐ̯ ˈgaest‘ɐ ˈmaenɐ ˈfɛːt‘ɐ, ˈbɔ̯øgət‘ lɔ̯øç!
Beugt euch aus euren Wolken nieder, ihr Geister meiner Väter, beuget euch!
Bend yourselves from your clouds down, you ghosts of my fathers, bend yourselves!
(*Macpherson's original:* Bend forward from your clouds, ghosts of my fathers! bend.)
[*Harold:* **beugt euch** *both times* (*not* **beuget euch**)]

leːk‘t‘ lap‘ das ˈroːt‘ə ˈʃrɛk‘ən ˈlɔ̯ørəs lɑ̯ofs! lɛmˈp̯fanʈ den ˈfaləndən ˈfyːrɐ,
Legt ab das rote Schrecken eures Laufs! Empfangt den fallenden Führer,
Lay down the red terror of your course! Receive the falling leader,
(Lay by the red terror of your course. Receive the falling chief;)
[*Peters:* **die grausen** (di ˈgrɑ̯ozən, the horrid) **Schrecken eures Flugs** (fluːks, flight)]

eːɐ̯ ˈkʰɔmə lɑ̯os ˈlaenəm lɛntʼˈfɛrnt‘ən lant‘, ˈloːdɐ(r) leːɐ̯ ʃt‘aek‘ lɑ̯os dem ˈtʰoːbəndən meːɐ̯!
er komme aus einem entfernten Land, oder er steig' aus dem tobenden Meer!
he come from a distant land, or he rise from the raging sea!
{whether he comes from a distant land, or rises from the rolling sea.)
[*Harold:* **oder steig** (*without* **er**)]

zaen kʰlaet‘ fɔn ˈneːbəl zae naː, zaen ʃp‘eːɐ̯/ʃp‘eːr lɑ̯os ˈlaenɐ ˈvɔlk‘ə gəˈʃt‘alt‘ətʰ,
Sein Kleid von Nebel sei nah', sein Speer aus einer Wolke gestaltet,
His robe of mist be near, his spear out of a cloud formed,
(Let his robe of mist be near; his spear that is formed of a cloud.)
[*Peters:* **Es** (ɛs, it) **sei sein Kleid aus** (lɑ̯os, out of) **Nebel**]

zaen ʃveːɐ̯t‘ laen lɛɐ̯'lɔʃnəs 'lʊft‘bɪlt‘,
sein Schwert ein erlosch'nes Luftbild, [Schubert has shortened the original line:]
his sword an extinguished vision,*

[ʃt‘ɛl laen halp‘ lɛɐ̯'lɔʃənəs 'lʊft‘bɪlt‘ lan 'zaenə 'zaet‘ə, lɪn gə'ʃt‘alt dɛs 'hɛldən- ʃveːɐ̯ts.]
[Stell ein halb erloschenes Luftbild an seine Seite, in Gestalt des Helden-Schwerts.]
[Place a half- extinguished vision by his side, in form of the hero- sword.]
(Place an half-extinguished meteor* by his side, in the form of the hero's sword.)

[**Harold translates Macpherson's "meteor" as "Luftbild" (= vision); sometimes it is indeed used in its general sense of some special phenomenon in the atmosphere; but here it seems to mean a "shooting star," as in modern English usage.*]

ʊnt‘ lax, zaen gə'zɪçt‘ zae 'liːp‘lɪç, das 'zaenə 'frɔøndə fro'lɔk‘ən lɪn 'zaenɐ 'geːgənvartʰ. loː
und ach, sein Gesicht sei lieblich, dass seine Freunde frohlocken in seiner Gegenwart. O
and ah, his face be lovely, that his friends rejoice in his presence. O
(And, oh! let his countenance be lovely, that his friends may delight in his presence.)
[*Peters:* **sein Antlitz** ('lant‘lɪts, countenance) **aber** ('laːbɐ, however) **sei lieblich]**

bɔøk‘t‘ lɔøç laos 'lɔørən 'vɔlk‘ən 'niːdɐ(r), liːɐ̯ 'gaest‘ɐ 'maenɐ 'fɛːt‘ɐ, 'bɔøgət‘ lɔøç!
beugt euch aus euren Wolken nieder, ihr Geister meiner Väter, beuget euch!
bend yourselves from your clouds down, you ghosts of my fathers, bend yourselves!
(Bend from your clouds, ghosts of my fathers! bend!)

[The text comes from *Dar-Thula*, in *The Poems of Ossian*. The excerpt above is preceded by these words: "Some of my heroes are low," said the grey-haired king of Morven. "I hear the sound of death on the harp. Ossian, touch the trembling string. Bid the sorrow rise; that their spirits may fly with joy, to Morven's woody hills!" I touched the harp before the king; the sound was mournful and low." Schubert's title is misleading; Nathos, soon to die, is still alive. The king has felt a premonition. For Schubert's other "Ossian" songs, see the following titles: *Cronnan, Das Mädchen von Inistore, Der Tod Oscars, Die Nacht, Kolmas Klage, Lodas Gespenst, Lorma*, and *Shilrik und Vinvela.*]

Pause see *Die schöne Müllerin*

paks vo'bɪskʊm
Pax vobiscum
Peace Be With You

Posthumously published [composed 1817] (poem by Franz von Schober)

deːɐ 'friːdə zae mɪt‘ lɔøç! das vaːɐ̯ daen 'lap‘ʃiːtszeːgən. lʊnt‘ zoː
"Der Friede sei mit euch!" das war dein Abschiedssegen. Und so
"The peace be with you!" that was your farewell blessing. And so
("Peace be with you!" That was your farewell blessing. And then,)

fɔm kʰraes deːɐ̯ 'glɔøbɪgən lʊm'kʰniːt‘, fɔm 'ziːgəsʃt‘raːl deːɐ̯ 'gɔt‘haet‘ 'langəglyːtʰ,
vom Kreis der Gläubigen umkniet, vom Siegesstrahl der Gottheit angeglüht,
by the circle of the believers about-kneeled, by the triumph-ray of the divinity illumined,
(encircled by kneeling believers, illumined by rays of victorious divinity,)

flo:kst du: dem ˈle:vgən ˈhaemaːtlantʻ lɛntʻˈge:gən. lʊntʻ ˈfri:də kʰa:m lɪn ˈli:rə ˈtʰrɔøən ˈhɛrtsən,
flogst du dem ew'gen Heimatland entgegen. Und Friede kam in ihre treuen Herzen,
flew you to the eternal homeland toward. And peace came into their faithful hearts,
(you ascended to your eternal homeland. And peace entered their faithful hearts,)

ʊntʻ ˈlo:ntʻə zi: lɪn ˈli:rən ˈgrø:stʻən ˈʃmɛrtsən, [ˈhø:çstʻən]
und lohnte sie in ihren grössten Schmerzen, [*poem:* **höchsten Schmerzen**]
and rewarded them in their greatest sorrows, [highest/loftiest]

ʊntʻ ˈʃtʻɛrkʻtʻə zi: lɪn ˈli:rəm ˈmartʻɐtʰo:tʻ. lɪç ˈglaobə dɪç, du: ˈgro:sɐ gɔtʰ!
und stärkte sie in ihrem Martertod. Ich glaube dich, du grosser Gott!
and strengthened them in their torture-death. I believe (in) you, you great God!
(and strengthened them in their death by torture. I believe in you, great God!)

de:ɐ ˈfri:də zae mɪtʻ lɔøç!
"Der Friede sei mit euch!"
"The peace be with you!"
("Peace be with you!")

zo: laxt di ˈle:ɐstʻə ˈblu:mə dɛs ˈjʊŋən ˈfry:lɪŋs lʊns fɛɐˈtʰraolɪç lan,
so lacht die erste Blume des jungen Frühlings uns vertraulich an,
thus laughs the first flower of the young spring us familiarly at,
(thus the first flower of the young spring smiles at us familiarly,)

vɛn zi:, mɪtʻ ˈlalən ˈraetsən ˈlangətʰa:n, zɪç ˈbɪldətʻ lɪn de:ɐ ˈʃœpfʊŋ ˈhaelɪçtʻu:mə.
wenn sie, mit allen Reizen angetan, sich bildet in der Schöpfung Heiligtume.
when it, with all charms attired, itself forms in the creation's sanctuary.
(when, adorned with all charms, it is formed in the sanctuary of creation.)

ve:n ˈzɔltʻə laox nɪçtʻ ˈfri:də da: lʊmˈʃve:bən, vo: le:ɐtʻ lʊntʻ ˈhɪməl
Wen sollte auch nicht Friede da umschweben, wo Erd' und Himmel
Whom should also not peace then about-hover, when earth and heaven
(About whom should peace not also hover then, when earth and heaven)

ˈrɪŋsˌlʊm zɪç bəˈle:bən, lʊntʻ ˈlaləs ˈlaofʃtʻe:tʻ laos dɛs ˈvɪntʻɐs tʰo:tʻ?
ringsum sich beleben, und alles aufsteht aus des Winters Tod?
all around themselves revive, and all is resurrected from the winter's death?
(are coming back to life all around us, and everything is resurrected from its death in winter?)
[*Peters:* **wonnig** (ˈvɔnɪç, blissfully) **sich beleben**]

ɪç hɔf laof dɪç, du: ˈʃtʻarkʻɐ gɔtʰ! de:ɐ ˈfri:də zae mɪtʻ lɔøç!
Ich hoff' auf dich, du starker Gott! "Der Friede sei mit euch!"
I hope for you, you strong God! "The peace be with you!"
(I place my hope in you, strong God! "Peace be with you!")

ru:fst du: lɪm ˈro:zənglyːən dɛs ˈhɪməls lʊns lan ˈje:dəm ˈla:bənt tsu:, vɛn ˈlalə ˈve:sən
rufst du im Rosenglühen des Himmels uns an jedem Abend zu, wenn alle Wesen
call you in the rose- glowing of the sky us at every evening to, when all beings
(you call to us every evening in the rosy glow of the sunset sky, when all creatures)

ʦʊr lɛɐ̯ˈzeːntʻən ruː fɔm ˈhartʻən gaŋ dɛs ˈʃvyːlən ˈtʰaːgəs ˈʦiːən;
zur ersehnten Ruh' vom harten Gang des schwülen Tages ziehen;
to the longed for rest from the hard course of the sultry day move;
(move toward their longed-for rest after the hard activity of the sultry day;)

[*poem:* **zur erwünschten** (lɛɐ̯ˈvʏnʃtʻən, desired) **Ruh'**]

ʊntʻ bɛrkʻ lʊnt tʰaːl lʊntʻ ʃtʻroːm lʊntʻ ˈmeːrəsvoːgən,
und Berg und Tal und Strom und Meereswogen,
and mountain and valley and stream and sea- waves,
(and mountain and valley and stream and the waves of the sea,)

[ˈzeːəsvoːgən]
[*Peters:* **Seeswogen]**
[sea- waves]

fɔm ˈva̯eçən hɑ̯ɔx dɛs ˈneːbəls lyːbɐˈfloːgən, nɔx ˈʃøːnɐ ˈveːɐ̯dən
vom weichen Hauch des Nebels überflogen, noch schöner werden
from the soft breath of the mist overflown, still more beautiful become
(with the soft breath of the mist drifting over them, become even more beautiful)

ˈlʊntʻɐm ˈmɪldən roːtʰ; lɪç ˈliːbə dɪç, duː ˈguːtʻɐ gɔtʰ!
unterm milden Rot; ich liebe dich, du guter Gott!
beneath the gentle red; I love you, you kind God!
(in the gentle red glow; I love you, kindly God!)

[Schubert reversed the last two stanzas of the poem, to end with "love" instead of "hope." This hymn-like song, with different words from the same poet, was played at Schubert's funeral.]

ˈpɛnsa, ke ˈkːkwesto iˈstante
Pensa, che questo istante
Bear In Mind That This Moment

Posthumously published [composed 1813] (poem by Pietro Metastasio)

ˈpɛnsa, ke ˈkːkwesto iˈstante del tuːo deˈstiːn deˈʧiːdə,
Pensa, che questo istante del tuo destin decide,
Think, that this instant of the your destiny decides,
(Bear in mind that this moment decides your destiny,)

ˈkɔdːʤi riˈnaʃːʃe‿alˈʧiːde per la fuˈtuːra‿eˈta! ˈpɛnsa ke‿aˈdulto ˈsɛːi,
ch'oggi rinasce Alcide per la futura età! Pensa che adulto sei,
that today is reborn Alcides for the future age! Think that adult you are,
(that today Alcides is reborn for future ages! Bear in mind that you are now an adult,)

ke ˈsɛːi di ˈʤɔːve‿un ˈfiʎːʎo, ke ˈmːmɛrto‿ɛ non konˈsiːʎːʎo, la ˈʃelta ˈtuːa saˈra!
che sei di Giove un figlio, che merto e non consiglio la scelta tua sarà!
that you are of Jove a son, that merit and not advice the choice yours will be!
(that you are a son of Jove, that merit and not my advice will determine your choice!)

[Schubert wrote this nobly beautiful song—"*arietta* for a bass voice"—while he was a pupil of Antonio Salieri. It shows a perfect mastery of Italian style. The *Neue Schubert Ausgabe*, Songs, Book 6, prints two versions and a facsimile of the manuscript, which clearly shows that the g# in the eighth bar of the *Gesamtausgabe* version is a misprint and should be an e. The text comes from an aria for Fronimo, Hercules' tutor, in Act I of Metastasio's libretto, *Alcide al Bivio* ("Alcides at the Crossroads"). Alcides is another name for Hercules, Jove is Jupiter or Zeus, king of the gods. Hercules must now choose his future path without the help of his tutor's advice.]

p͜flɪçt‘ |ʊnt‘ ˈliːbə
Pflicht und Liebe
Duty and Love

Posthumously published [composed 1816] (poem by Friedrich Wilhelm Gotter)

duː, deːɐ̯/deːr ˈleːvɪç |ʊm mɪç ˈtʰʀɑ͜oɐtʰ, nɪçt‘ |aˈla͜en, nɪçt‘ ˈ|ʊnbədɑ͜oɐt‘, ˈjʏŋlɪŋ,
Du, der ewig um mich trauert, nicht allein, nicht unbedauert, Jüngling,
You, who eternally for me grieve, not alone, not unpitied, young man,
(You, who grieve for me eternally, — not *alone*, not *unpitied*, young friend,)

ˈzɔ͜øft͜səst duː; vɛn foːɐ̯ ʃmɛrt͜s di ˈzeːlə ˈʃɑ͜oɐt‘, ˈlyːgət‘ ˈma͜enə ˈʃt‘ɪrnə ruː.
seufzest du; wenn vor Schmerz die Seele schauert, lüget meine Stirne Ruh’.
sigh you; when for pain the soul shudders, lies my brow calm.
(do you sigh; when my soul is shuddering with pain, my brow lies that I am calm.)

ˈda͜enəs ˈnasən ˈblɪk‘əs ˈfleːən vɪl |ɪç, darf |ɪç nɪçt‘ fɛɐ̯ˈʃt‘eːn; [fɛɐ̯ˈʃt‘eːən]
Deines nassen Blickes Flehen will ich, darf ich nicht versteh’n; [*poem:* verstehen]
Your moist look’s pleading want I, may I not understand; [understand]
(I do not want to understand, I *may* not understand the pleading in your tear-drenched eyes;)

ˈaːbɐ ˈt͜sʏrnə nɪçtʰ! vas |ɪç ˈfyːlə, t͜suː gəˈʃt‘eːən, |ʊnt‘ɐˈzaːk‘t‘ miːɐ̯ ˈma͜enə p͜flɪçtʰ.
aber zürne nicht! was ich fühle, zu gestehen, untersagt mir meine Pflicht.
but be angry not! what I feel, to confess, forbids me my duty.
(but do not be angry! My duty forbids me to confess what I am feeling.)

[ˈʊnbəkʰant‘ mɪt‘ ʀɔ͜ø |ʊnt‘ ˈla͜edə, viː di ˈlɛmçən |ɑ͜of deːɐ̯ ˈva͜edə,
[Unbekannt mit Reu’ und Leide, wie die Lämmchen auf der Weide,
[Unfamiliar with regret and suffering, like the little lambs on the pasture,
[(Unfamiliar with regret and suffering, like little lambs on the pasture,)

ˈʃp‘iːlt‘ən |ɪç |ʊnt duː. ˈjeːdɐ tʰaːk‘ riːf |ʊns t͜sʊr ˈfrɔ͜ødə, ˈjeːdə naxt t͜suː ˈzanft‘ɐ ruː.
spielten ich und du. Jeder Tag rief uns zur Freude, jede Nacht zu sanfter Ruh.
played I and you. Each day called us to the joy, each night to gentle rest.
(you and I used to play. Each day called us to new joy, each night to gentle rest.)

ˈeːvɪç zɪnt‘ viːɐ̯ nuːn gəˈʃiːdən! ˈdɛnɔx, liːpst duː filaˈiːdən, flɔ͜øç |iːɐ̯/iːr
Ewig sind wir nun geschieden! Dennoch, liebst du Philaiden, fleuch ihr
Forever are we now separated! Nevertheless, love you Phillida, flee her
(Now we are separated forever! Nevertheless, if you love me, avoid the sight of my)

ˈ|angəzɪçtʰ! nɪm |iːɐ̯ nɪçt deːɐ̯ ˈtʰaːgə ˈfriːdən, |ʊnt deːɐ̯ ˈnɛçt‘ə ˈʃlʊmɐ nɪçtʰ!]
Angesicht! Nimm ihr nicht der Tage Frieden, und der Nächte Schlummer nicht!]
countenance! Take from her not the days’ peace, and the nights’ slumber not!]
(face! Do not rob my days of peace, nor my nights of sleep!)]

frɔ͜ønt‘, ʃva͜ef |ɑ͜os mɪt ˈda͜enən ˈblɪk‘ən! las dɪç di naˈtʰuːɐ̯/-ˈtʰuːr |ɛntˈt͜sʏk‘ən,
Freund, schweif’ aus mit deinen Blicken! lass dich die Natur entzücken,
Friend, roam about with your glances! let you the nature delight,
(My friend, let your eyes roam about, let nature delight you,)

diː diːɐ̯ zɔnst‘ gəˈlaxtʰ! ǀax, ziː vɪrt‘ ǀɑ͜ox mɪç bəˈglʏk‘ən,
die dir sonst gelacht! Ach, sie wird auch mich beglücken,
which for you formerly laughed! Ah, it will also me make happy,
(which used to smile upon you! Ah, Nature will make me happy too,)

vɛn ziː dɪç ǀeːɐ̯st‘ ˈglʏk‘lɪç maxtʰ. ˈtʰrɑ͜ot‘ɐ ˈjʏŋlɪŋ, ˈǀɛçlə ˈviːdɐ!
wenn sie dich erst glücklich macht. Trauter Jüngling, lächle wieder!
if it you first happy makes. Dear young man, smile again!
(if she first makes you happy. Dear young man, smile again!)

ziː, ba͜em ˈgruːsə ˈfroːən zaŋs ʃt‘a͜ek‘t di zɔn ǀɛmˈpʰoːɐ̯! [ˈfroːɐ ˈliːdɐ]
Sieh', beim Grusse frohen Sangs steigt die Sonn' empor! [*poem:* **froher Lieder**]
See, at the greeting of happy song rises the sun aloft! [of happy songs]
(See, the sun is rising, greeted by happy birdsong!)

ˈtʰryːbə zaŋk‘ ziː ˈgɛst‘ɐn ˈniːdɐ; ˈhɛrlɪç geːt‘ ziː hɔ͜øt‘ hɛɐ̯ˈfoːɐ̯. [ˈtʰryːbɐ]
Trübe sank sie gestern nieder; herrlich geht sie heut' hervor. [*poem:* **Trüber**]
Gloomily sank it yesterday down; gloriously goes it today forth. [more gloomily]
(Yesterday it set in gloom; today it comes forth gloriously.)

[Schubert set this poem to music at the time when he was losing his sweetheart Therese Grob to her father's will. The words suggest a situation painfully close to his own. His composition breaks off just before the last bar of the voice part; Max Friedländer completed the phrase and supplied a postlude for the Peters edition. Schubert omitted the middle verses, in brackets above. This beautiful song would no doubt be much better known if Schubert himself had finished it.]

ˈp͜flyːgɐliːt‘
Pflügerlied
Plowman's Song

Posthumously published [composed 1816] (poem by Johann Gaudenz von Salis-Seewis)

ˈǀarba͜et‘zaːm ǀʊnt‘ ˈvak‘ɐ, ˈp͜flyːgən viːɐ̯ den ˈǀak‘ɐ, ˈzɪŋənt‘ ǀɑ͜of ǀʊnt‘ ǀap‘.
Arbeitsam und wacker, pflügen wir den Acker, singend auf und ab.
Industrious and stouthearted, plow we the field, singing up and down.
(Industrious and stouthearted, we plow the field, singing as we go to and fro.)

ˈzɔrk‘zaːm ˈtʰrɛnən ˈvɔlən viːɐ̯ di ˈlɔk‘ɐn ˈʃɔlən, ˈǀʊnzrɐ ˈzaːt‘ən graːp‘.
Sorgsam trennen wollen wir die lockern Schollen, unsrer Saaten Grab.
Carefully to part want we the loose clods, our seeds' grave.
(Let us carefully part the loose clods, the grave of our seeds.)

ɑ͜of ǀʊnt‘ ˈǀap‘vɛrt͜s ˈt͜siːənt‘ ˈfʊrçən viːɐ̯, ʃt‘eːt͜s ˈ fliːənt das ǀɛɐ̯ˈra͜eçt‘ə t͜siːl.
Auf- und abwärts ziehend furchen wir, stets fliehend das erreichte Ziel.
Up and downwards drawing furrow we, always fleeing the reached goal.
(Plowing up and down, we cut furrows, always away from the goal we have already reached.)

vyːl, ǀoː ˈp͜flyːk‘ʃaːɐ̯, ˈvyːlə! ˈǀɑ͜osən drʏk‘t di ˈʃvyːlə, tʰiːf ǀɪm grʊnt‘ ǀɪst͜s kʰyːl.
Wühl', o Pflugschar, wühle! Aussen drückt die Schwüle, tief im Grund ist's kühl.
Dig, O plowshare, burrow! Outside oppresses the sultriness, deep in the ground is it cool.
(Dig, plowshare, burrow! Outside the heat is oppressive, but deep in the ground it's cool.)

na͜ek't den blɪk' t͜sʊr 'le:ɐ̯də, li:p' lʊnt' 'ha͜emlɪç 've:ɐ̯də lʊns li:ɐ̯ 'dʊŋk'lɐ ʃo:s:
Neigt den Blick zur Erde, lieb und heimlich werde uns ihr dunkler Schoss:
Bend the gaze to the earth, dear and comfortable become to us its dark womb:
(Bend your gaze to the earth: may its dark womb become dear and comfortable to us:)

hi:ɐ̯/hi:r lɪst dɔx kʰa͜en 'bla͜ebən; 'la͜osgəzɛ:t t͜sɛɐ̯'ʃt'ɔ͜øbən lɪst' la͜ox 'lʊnzɐ lo:s.
hier ist doch kein Bleiben; ausgesä't zerstäuben ist auch unser Los.
here is after all no staying; sown become dust is also our lot.
(after all there is no staying here; sown, turned to dust—that is also *our* lot.)

'zɛ:ət', fro: lɪm 'hɔfən, 'grɛ:bɐ 'harən lɔfən, 'flu:rən zɪnt' bə'ba͜otʰ;
Säet, froh im Hoffen, Gräber harren offen, Fluren sind bebaut;
Sow, happy in the hoping, graves wait open, fields are tilled;
(Sow, happy in your hopes: graves are waiting, open; fields are tilled;)

dɛk't' mɪt' lɛk' lʊnt' 'ʃp'a:t'ən di fɛɐ̯'zɛŋk't'ən 'za:t'ən, lʊnt dan: gɔt' fɛɐ̯'tʰra͜otʰ!
deckt mit Egg' und Spaten die versenkten Saaten, und dann: Gott vertraut!
cover with harrow and spade the sunken seeds, and then: God trust!
(cover the sown seeds, using the harrow and the spade, and then: trust in God!)

'gɔt'əs 'zɔnə 'lɔ͜øçt'ət', 'la͜oɐ 're:gən 'fɔ͜øçt'ət das lɛnt''kʰa͜emt'ə gry:n.
Gottes Sonne leuchtet, Lauer Regen feuchtet das entkeimte Grün.
God's sun shines, tepid rain moistens the sprouted green.
(God's sun will shine, and warm rain will moisten the green sprouts.)

flɔk', lo: ʃne:, lʊnt' 'ʃt'rɛk'ə 'da͜enə 'zɪlbɐdɛk'ə 'ʃirmənt 'dry:bɐ hɪn!
Flock', o Schnee, und strecke deine Silberdecke schirmend drüber hin!
Flake, O snow, and stretch your silver cover shelteringly over it out!
(Come down in flakes, snow, and spread your silver cover over the sown seeds to shelter them!)

'ɛrnt'ən 've:ɐ̯dən 'vaŋk'ən, vo: nu:ɐ̯ 'kʰœrnɐ 'zaŋk'ən; 'mʊt'ɐ(r) le:ɐ̯t' lɪst tʰrɔ͜ø.
Ernten werden wanken, wo nur Körner sanken; Mutter Erd' ist treu.
Crops will sway, where only grains sank; Mother Earth is faithful.
(Crops will be swaying where only seeds had sunk into the ground; Mother Earth is faithful.)

nɪçt͜s vɪrt' hi:ɐ̯ fɛɐ̯'nɪçt'ət', lʊnt' fɛɐ̯'ve:zʊŋ 'zɪçt'ət' nu:ɐ̯ fɔm kʰa͜em di ʃp'rɔ͜ø.
Nichts wird hier vernichtet, und Verwesung sichtet nur vom Keim die Spreu.
Nothing is here destroyed, and decay sights only from the germ the chaff.
(Nothing is destroyed here, and only the chaff, separated from the seed, will be left to decay.)

di: fo:ɐ̯/fo:r lʊns lɛnt''ʃli:fən, 'ʃlʊmɐn, lɪn di 'tʰi:fən 'li:rɐ grʊft' gə'zɛ:tʰ;
Die vor uns entschliefen, schlummern, in die Tiefen ihrer Gruft gesä't;
Those who before us passed away, slumber, into the depths of their grave sown;
(Those who have passed away before us are sleeping in their graves, like seeds sown in earth;)

'lɛŋɐ vɪrt' lɛs 'zɔ͜ømən, bɪs di 'grɛ:bɐ 'kʰa͜emən, 'gɔt'əs za:t' lɛɐ̯'ʃt'e:tʰ!
länger wird es säumen, bis die Gräber keimen, Gottes Saat ersteht!
longer will it delay, till the graves sprout, God's seed rises!
(it will take longer for the graves to germinate; but then God's seed will rise!)

ve:ɐ̯/ve:r lʊm 'tʰo:t'ə 'tʰra͜orət', gla͜op' lɛs, 'le:vɪç 'da͜orət' nɪçt de:ɐ̯/de:r 'la͜osza:t t͜sa͜etʰ.
Wer um Tote trauret, glaub' es, ewig dauret nicht der Aussaat Zeit.
Whoever for dead mourns, believe it, forever lasts not the sowing time.
(Whoever mourns for dead loved ones, believe this: the sowing time does not last forever.)

ɑos ʔɛntˈʔhʏlstʻɐ ˈʃaːlə kʰɑemtʻ ʔɪm ˈtʰoːdəstʰaːlə frʊçt deːɐ̯/deːr ˈʔeːvɪçkʰɑetʰ.
Aus enthüls'ter Schale keimt im Todestale Frucht der Ewigkeit!
From husked shell buds in the death-valley fruit of the eternity!
(Out of the husked shells in the valley of death the fruit of eternity will sprout!)

[Schubert set this poem as a simple strophic song with a touch of rural charm.]

ˈfiːdilə
Phidile
Phidile

Posthumously published [composed 1816] (poem by Matthias Claudius)

ɪç vaːɐ̯/vaːr ʔeːɐ̯stʻ ˈzɛçtseːn ˈzɔmɐ(r) ʔaltʻ, ʔʊnˈʃʊldɪç ʔʊntʻ nɪçts ˈvɑetʻɐ,
Ich war erst sechzehn Sommer alt, unschuldig und nichts weiter,
I was just sixteen summers old, innocent and nothing further,
(I was just sixteen summers old, innocent and nothing else,)

ʊntʻ ˈkʰantʻə nɪçts ʔals ˈʔʊnzɐn valtʻ, ʔals ˈbluːmən, graːs ʔʊntʻ ˈkʰrɔøtʻɐ.
und kannte nichts als unsern Wald, als Blumen, Gras und Kräuter.
and knew nothing but our woods, but flowers, grass, and herbs.
(and knew nothing but our woods, nothing but flowers, grass, and herbs.)

daː kʰaːm ʔɑen ˈfrɛmdɐ ˈjʏŋlɪŋ heːɐ̯; ʔɪç hatʻ ʔiːn nɪçtʻ fɛɐ̯ˈʃriːbən,
Da kam ein fremder Jüngling her; ich hatt' ihn nicht verschrieben,
Then came a stranger youth hither; I had him not written for,
(Then along came a young stranger; I had not invited him,)

ʊntʻ ˈvʊstʻə nɪçtʻ, voˈhɪn nɔx heːɐ̯; deːɐ̯ kʰaːm ʔʊntʻ ʃpʻraːx fɔn ˈliːbən.
und wusste nicht, wohin noch her; der kam und sprach von Lieben.
and knew not, whither nor whence; he came and spoke of loving.
(and did not know where he came from or where he was going; he came and spoke of love.)

eːɐ̯ ˈhatʻə ˈʃøːnəs ˈlaŋəs haːɐ̯/haːr ʔʊm ˈzɑenən ˈnakʻən ˈveːən;
Er hatte schönes langes Haar um seinen Nacken wehen;
He had beautiful long hair around his nape of the neck blowing;
(He had beautiful long hair blowing about the nape of his neck;)

ʊntʻ ˈʔɑenən ˈnakʻən, ʔals das vaːɐ̯, haːb ɪç nɔx niː gəˈzeːən.
und einen Nacken, als das war, hab' ich noch nie gesehen.
and a neck, as that was, have I yet not seen.
(and I had not yet seen a neck such as that was.)

zɑen ˈʔɑogə, ˈhɪməlblɑo ʔʊntʻ kʰlaːɐ̯! ʃiːn ˈfrɔøntʻlɪç vas tsuː ˈfleːən;
Sein Auge, himmelblau und klar! schien freundlich was zu flehen;
His eye, sky- blue and clear! seemed amicably (for) something to plead;
(His eyes, sky blue and clear, seemed to be pleading for something in a friendly way;)

zoː blɑo ʔʊntʻ ˈfrɔøntʻlɪç, ʔals das vaːɐ̯, haːb ɪç nɔx kʰɑens gəˈzeːən.
so blau und freundlich, als das war, hab' ich noch kein's gesehen.
so blue and friendly, as that was, have I yet none seen.
(I had not yet seen eyes as blue and friendly as those were.)

ʊnt‘ zaen gəˈzɪçt‘, viː mɪlç lʊnt‘ bluːt‘! lɪç haːps niː zoː gəˈzeːən;
Und sein Gesicht, wie Milch und Blut! ich hab's nie so gesehen;
And his face, like milk and blood! I have it never so seen;
(And his face, like peaches and cream! I had never seen one like it;)
[*wie Milch und Blut* = like cream and roses, like peaches and cream]

ɑox vas leːɐ̯ ˈzaːk‘t‘ə, vaːɐ̯ zeːɐ̯ guːt‘, nuːɐ̯ kʰɔnt‘ ɪç nɪçt‘ fɛɐ̯ˈʃt‘eːən.
auch was er sagte, war sehr gut, nur konnt' ich nicht verstehen.
also what he said, was very good, only could I not understand.
(what he said was also very good, except that I could not understand it.)

eːɐ̯ gɪŋ miːɐ̯/miːr ˈlalənt‘ˌhalbən naːx, lʊnt ˈdrʏk‘t‘ə miːɐ̯ di ˈhɛndə,
Er ging mir allenthalben nach, und drückte mir die Hände,
He went me everywhere after, and pressed for me the hands,
(He followed me everywhere, and pressed my hands,)

ʊnt‘ ˈzaːk‘t‘ə ˈlɪmɐ(r) loː lʊnt‘ lax, lʊnt‘ ˈkʰʏst‘ə ziː bəˈhɛndə.
und sagte immer O und Ach, und küsste sie behende.
and said always Oh and Ah, and kissed them adroitly.
(and kept saying "Ooh!" and "Ah!" and kissing them adroitly.)

ɪç zaː liːn ˈlaenmaːl ˈfrɔøntˈlɪç lan, lʊnt‘ ˈfraːk‘t‘ə, vas leːɐ̯ ˈmaent‘ə;
Ich sah' ihn einmal freundlich an, und fragte, was er meinte;
I looked him once friendly at, and asked, what he meant;
(I looked at him once, in a friendly way, and asked him what he meant;)

daː fiːl deːɐ̯ ˈjʊŋə ˈʃøːnə man miːɐ̯/miːr lʊm den hals lʊnt‘ ˈvaent‘ə.
da fiel der junge schöne Mann mir um den Hals und weinte.
at that fell the young handsome man to me around the neck and wept.
(at that the handsome young man fell on my neck and wept.)

das ˈhat‘ə ˈniːmant‘ nɔx gəˈtʰaːn; dɔx vaːɐ̯s miːɐ̯ nɪçt t͡suˈviːdɐ
Das hatte niemand noch getan; doch war's mir nicht zuwider
That had no one yet done; but was it to me not offensive
(No one had ever done that to me before; but it was not offensive to me)

ʊnt‘ ˈmaenə ˈbaedə ˈlɑogən zaːn lɪn ˈmaenən ˈbuːzən ˈniːdɐ.
und meine beide Augen sah'n in meinen Busen nieder.
and my both eyes looked into my bosom down.
(and both my eyes looked down toward my bosom.)

ɪç zaːk‘t‘ liːm nɪçt‘ laen ˈlaent͡sɪç vɔrt‘, lals lɔp‘ lɪçs ˈlyːbəl ˈnɛːmə,
Ich sagt' ihm nicht ein einzig Wort, als ob ich's übel nähme,
I said to him not a single word, as if I it amiss would take,
(I did not say a single word to him that might have made him think I took it amiss,)

kʰaen ˈlaent͡sɪks, lʊnt‘ — leːɐ̯ ˈfloːə fɔrt‘; vɛn leːɐ̯ dɔx ˈviːdɐ ˈkʰɛːmə!
kein einzig's, und — er flohe fort'; wenn er doch wieder käme!
not single, and — he fled away; if he only again would come!
(not a single word, and — he ran away; oh, if only he would come back again!)

[The music is charming, and marked "innocently." Phidile is a rather fancy name for the simple, unsophisticated country girl who is telling the story of her first contact with love.]

filɔk‘ˈtʰeːtʰ
Philoktet
Philoctetes

Posthumously published [composed 1817] (poem by Johann Mayrhofer)

daː zɪt͡s ɪç ˈloːnə ˈboːgən, lʊnt‘ ˈʃt‘arə lɪn den zant‘. vas tʰaːt‘ lɪç diːɐ̯/diːr, luˈlʏsɛs?
Da sitz' ich ohne Bogen, und starre in den Sand. Was tat ich dir, Ulysses?
Here sit I without bow, and stare into the sand. What did I to you, Ulysses?
(Here I sit without a bow, and stare into the sand. What have I done to you, Ulysses,)
[*note: question mark placed as in the poem (and in Peters)*]

das duː ziː miːɐ̯/miːr lɛnt‘ˈvant, di ˈvafə, diː den ˈtʰroːjɐn dɛs ˈtʰoːdəs ˈboːt‘ə vaːɐ̯,
dass du sie mir entwandt, die Waffe, die den Trojern des Todes Bote war,
that you it from me stole, the weapon, which to the Trojans the death's messenger was,
(that you should steal from me the weapon that was a messenger of death to the Trojans,)
[*poem:* **die dem Feinde** (dem ˈfa͜endə, for the enemy)]

diː la͜of deːɐ̯ ˈvyːst‘ən ˈlɪnzəl miːɐ̯/miːr lˈʊnt‘ɐhalt‘ gəˈbaːɐ̯. lɛs ˈra͜oʃən ˈføːgəlʃvɛrmə
die auf der wüsten Insel mir Unterhalt gebar. Es rauschen Vögelschwärme
which on the desert island for me sustenance bore. There murmur birds-swarms
(that provided my sustenance on this deserted island? Flocks of birds murmur)

miːɐ̯/miːr ˈlyːbɐm ˈgra͜ezən ha͜op‘tʰ; lɪç ˈgra͜efə naːx dem ˈboːgən, — lʊmˈzɔnstʰ —
mir überm greisen Haupt; ich greife nach dem Bogen, — umsonst —
to me over the old man's head; I grasp for the bow, — in vain —
(above my old head; I reach for the bow — but in vain:)
[*poem:* **mir übers greise** (ˈlyːbɐs ˈgra͜ezə, over the grey—movement over and *past*) **Haupt**]

eːɐ̯/eːr lɪst‘ gəˈra͜op‘tʰ! la͜os ˈdɪçt‘əm ˈbʊʃə ˈraʃəlt deːɐ̯ ˈbra͜onə hɪrʃ hɛɐ̯ˈfoːɐ̯;
er ist geraubt! Aus dichtem Busche raschelt der braune Hirsch hervor;
it is stolen! Out of thick bush crackles the brown stag forth;
(it has been stolen! The brown stag comes out from the thick, crackling bushes;)

ɪç ˈʃt‘rɛk‘ə ˈleːrə ˈlarmə t͡sʊr ˈneːmezɪs lɛmˈpʰoːɐ̯. duː ˈʃla͜oɐ ˈkʰøːnɪç, ˈʃɔ͜øə
ich strecke leere Arme zur Nemesis empor. Du schlauer König, scheue
I stretch empty arms to the Nemesis up. You sly king, shun
(I stretch my empty arms toward Nemesis, goddess of retribution. Ulysses, you sly king, beware)

deːɐ̯ ˈgœt‘ɪn ˈrɛçɐblɪkʰ! lɛɐ̯ˈbarmə dɪç lʊnt‘ ˈʃt‘ɛlə den ˈboːgən miːɐ̯ t͡suˈrʏkʰ.
der Göttin Rächerblick! erbarme dich und stelle den Bogen mir zurück.
the goddess's avenger-gaze! have mercy yourself and put the bow for me back.
(the avenging gaze of the goddess! Have mercy and give me back my bow.)
[*erbarme dich* = have mercy]

[When Hercules (Heracles) ordered that his own funeral pyre be kindled, only Philoctetes, son of a shepherd, was willing to obey him. In return, Hercules gave him his quiver, bow, and arrows. After the Greek hero Achilles was slain by treachery near the end of the Trojan War, an oracle prophesied that Troy could be taken only with the help of Hercules' bow and arrows. Ulysses (Odysseus), the wiliest of the Greek kings, was sent to the island of Lemnos to get them away from Philoctetes, which he managed to do by trickery. (Later, it was Philoctetes whose arrow brought about the death of Paris, the prince of Troy who had started the Trojan War by stealing the beautiful queen of Sparta from her husband.) Philoctetes is the hero of a play by Sophocles.]

ˈpʰɪlgɐvaezə
Pilgerweise
Pilgrim's Song

Posthumously published [composed 1823] (poem by Franz von Schober)

ɪç bɪn laen ˈvalɐ(r) laof deːɐ/deːr ˈleːɐdə lʊntʻ ˈgeːə ʃtʻɪl fɔn haos tsuː haos,
Ich bin ein Waller auf der Erde und gehe still von Haus zu Haus,
I am a pilgrim on the earth and go quietly from house to house,

oː raeçtʻ mɪtʻ ˈfrɔøntʻlɪçɐ gəˈbɛːɐdə deːɐ ˈliːbə ˈgaːbən miːɐ hɛˈraos!
o reicht mit freundlicher Gebärde der Liebe Gaben mir heraus!
O reach with friendly gesture the love's gifts to me out!
(O give me gifts of love with a friendly gesture!)

mɪtʻ ˈlɔfnən, ˈtʰaelnaːmsfɔlən ˈblɪkʻən, mɪtʻ ˈlaenəm ˈvarmən ˈhɛndədrʊk
Mit off'nen, teilnahmsvollen Blicken, mit einem warmen Händedruck
With open, sympathetic glances, with a warm clasp of the hand

kʰœntʻ liːɐ diːs ˈlarmə hɛrts lɛɐˈkʰvɪkʻən, lʊntʻ lɛs bəˈfraen fɔn ˈlaŋəm drʊkʰ.
könnt ihr dies arme Herz erquicken, und es befrei'n von langem Druck.
could you this poor heart refresh, and it free from long pressure.
(you could refresh this poor heart of mine, and free it from long oppression.)

dɔx ˈrɛçnətʻ nɪçt, das lɪç lɔøçs ˈloːnən, mɪtʻ ˈgeːgəndiːnstʻ fɛɐˈgɛltʻən zɔl;
Doch rechnet nicht, dass ich euch's lohnen, mit Gegendienst vergelten soll;
But reckon not, that I you (for) it reward, with service in return repay shall;
(But do not reckon that I shall reward you for that, or shall repay you with service in return;)

ɪç ˈʃtʻrɔøə nuːɐ mɪtʻ ˈbluːmənkʰroːnən, mɪtʻ ˈblaoən, ˈlɔørə ˈʃvɛlə fɔl;
ich streue nur mit Blumenkronen, mit blauen, eure Schwelle voll;
I strew only with flower corollas, with blue ones, your threshold full;
(I shall only strew the petals of blue flowers copiously over your threshold,)

ʊntʻ geːpʻ laen liːtʻ lɔøç nɔx tsʊr ˈtsɪtʻɐ, mɪtʻ flaes gəˈzʊŋən lʊntʻ gəˈʃpʻiːltʰ,
und geb' ein Lied euch noch zur Zither, mit Fleiss gesungen und gespielt,
and give a song to you besides to the zither, with diligence sung and played,
(and sing you a song besides, accompanied by the zither, singing and playing with diligence,)
[zɪŋ] [ˈʃtʻɪləs] [das ˈʃtʻaməlntʻ mɪt dem ˈzɔøftsɐ rɪŋtʰ,]
[*poem:* und sing' ein stilles Lied zur Zither, das stammelnd mit dem Seufzer ringt,]
[sing] [quiet] [that stammering with the sigh struggles,]
[(and sing a quiet song, to the zither, a stammering song that wrestles with a sigh,]

das lɔøç fiˈlaeçtʻ nuːɐ ˈlaeçtʻɐ ˈflɪtʻɐ(r), laen laeçtʻ lɛntʻˈbeːɐlɪç guːtʻ lɔøç gɪltʰ.
das euch vielleicht nur leichter Flitter, ein leicht entbehrlich Gut euch gilt.
that to you perhaps only light tinsel, an easily dispensable commodity to you means.
(a song that to you perhaps seems only flimsy tinsel, an easily dispensable commodity.)
[voːl gaːɐ viː] [viː ˈlyːbɐflʏsgəs ˈʃpʻiːlvɛrk kʰlɪŋtʰ]
[*poem:* das euch wohl gar wie leichter Flitter, wie überflüss'ges Spielwerk klingt]
[perhaps even like] [like superfluous chiming sounds]
[(that perhaps even sounds to you like flimsy tinsel, like superfluous chiming)]

miːɐ̯ gɪlt‘ lɛs fiːl, lɪç kʰans nɪçt‘ 'mɪsən, lʊnt‘ 'lalən 'pʰɪlgɐn lɪst‘ lɛs veːɐ̯tʰ;
Mir gilt es viel, ich kann's nicht missen, und allen Pilgern ist es wert;
To me means it much, I can it not miss, and to all pilgrims is it of value;
(To me it means much, I cannot be without it, and it is of value to all pilgrims;)

[kʰlɪŋt‘ lɛs zyːs] ['jeːdəm 'pʰɪlgɐ]
[*poem:* **Mir klingt es süss... und jedem Pilger]**
[sounds it sweet] [to each pilgrim]
[(It sounds sweet to me... and it is of value to each pilgrim)]

dɔx 'fraelɪç liːɐ̯, liːɐ̯ kʰœnt‘ nɪçt‘ 'vɪsən, vas deːn bə'zeːlɪçt, deːɐ̯/deːr lɛnt‘'beːɐ̯tʰ.
doch freilich ihr, ihr könnt nicht wissen, was den beseligt, der entbehrt.
but of course you, you could not know, what him makes happy, who does without.
(But of course you could not know what makes *him* happy who does without so many things.)

fɔm 'lyːbɐflʊs zaet‘ liːɐ̯/liːr lɛɐ̯'frɔøətʰ, lʊnt‘ 'fɪndət 'tʰaozənt‘fax lɛɐ̯'zats;
Vom Überfluss seid ihr erfreuet, und findet tausendfach Ersatz;
By the abundance are you gladdened, and (you) find thousandfold replenishment;
(You rejoice in abundance, and you can find a thousandfold replenishment;)

aen tʰaːk‘ dem 'landɐn 'langəraeət‘ fɛɐ̯'grøːsət‘ 'lɔørən 'liːbəsʃats.
ein Tag dem andern angereihet vergrösset euren Liebesschatz.
one day to the others ranged increases your love- treasure.
(day by day your wealth of love increases.)

dɔx miːɐ̯, zoː viː lɪç 'vaet‘ɐ 'ʃt‘reːbə lan 'maenəm 'hart‘ən 'vandɐʃt‘aːbə,
Doch mir, so wie ich weiter strebe an meinem harten Wanderstabe,
But for me, so as I farther strive with my hard wanderer's staff,
(But for me, as I strive onwards with my sturdy staff in my hand,)

[*poem:* **Wanderstab** ('vandɐʃt‘aːp‘, wanderer's staff)]

raest‘ lɪn dɛs 'glʏk‘əs 'lʊst‘gəveːbə laen 'faːdən naːx dem 'landɐn lap‘. ['lʊft‘gəveːbə]
reisst in des Glückes Lustgewebe ein Faden nach dem andern ab. [*poem:* **Luftgewebe]**
tears in the fortune's pleasure-fabric one thread after the others off. [airy-tissue]
(one thread after another tears off in fortune's fabric of pleasures.)

drʊm kʰan lɪç nuːɐ̯ fɔn 'gaːbən 'leːbən, fɔn 'laogənblɪk‘ tsuː 'laogənblɪkʰ,
Drum kann ich nur von Gaben leben, von Augenblick zu Augenblick,
Therefore can I only from gifts live, from moment to moment,
(Therefore I can only live on charity, from moment to moment,)

oː 'vɔlət‘ 'foːɐ̯vʊrfsloːs ziː 'geːbən! tsuː 'lɔørɐ lʊst, tsuː 'maenəm glʏkʰ.
o wollet vorwurfslos sie geben! zu eurer Lust, zu meinem Glück.
O want reproachless them to give! at your pleasure, to my good fortune.
(O may you want to give without reproaches, at your pleasure, and to my good fortune!)

ɪç bɪn laen 'valɐ(r) laof deːɐ̯/deːr 'leːɐ̯də lʊnt‘ 'geːə ʃt‘ɪl fɔn haos tsuː haos,
Ich bin ein Waller auf der Erde und gehe still von Haus zu Haus,
I am a pilgrim on the earth and go quietly from house to house,

oː raeçt‘ mɪt‘ 'frɔønt‘lɪçɐ gə'bɛːɐ̯də deːɐ̯ 'liːbə 'gaːbən miːɐ̯ hɛ'raos!
o reicht mit freundlicher Gebärde der Liebe Gaben mir heraus!
O reach with friendly gesture the love's gifts to me out!
(O give me gifts of love with a friendly gesture!)

[The *Gesamtausgabe* follow the original manuscript, in F# minor; Peters reproduces the first edition, in E minor (Schubert also left a copy in D minor). The poet was a close friend, and Schubert's setting of his sometimes ungracious poem bathes it in haunting beauty.]

pʰroˈmeːtʻɔ͜øs
Prometheus
Prometheus

Posthumously published [composed 1819] (poem by Johann Wolfgang von Goethe)

bəˈdɛkʻə ˈda͜enən ˈhɪməl, tsɔ͜øs, mɪtʻ ˈvɔlkʻəndʊnstʰ, lʊntʻ ˈlyːbə,
Bedecke deinen Himmel, Zeus, mit Wolkendunst, und übe,
Cover your heaven, Zeus, with cloud- haze, and exercise,
(Cover your heaven, Zeus, with clouds and haze, and practice,)

dem ˈkʰnaːbən gla͜eç, deːɐ̯ ˈdɪstʻəln kʰœɐ̯pftʰ, lan ˈla͜eçən dɪç lʊntʻ ˈbɛrgəshøːn;
dem Knaben gleich, der Disteln köpft, an Eichen dich und Bergeshöh'n;
to the boy like, who thistles beheads, on oaks yourself and mountain heights;
(like a boy who tears the heads off thistles, on oak trees and mountain tops;)
[*übe dich* = exercise yourself, practice]

mʊstʻ miːɐ̯ ˈma͜enə ˈleːɐ̯də dɔx ˈlasən ʃtʻeːn, lʊntʻ ˈma͜enə ˈhʏtʻə,
musst mir meine Erde doch lassen steh'n, und meine Hütte,
(you) must to me my earth though leave stand, and my hut,
(you have to leave my earth alone, though, and my hut,)

diː duː nɪçtʻ gəˈba͜otʰ, lʊntʻ ˈma͜enən heːɐ̯tʻ, lʊm ˈdɛsən gluːt duː mɪç bəˈna͜edəstʰ.
die du nicht gebaut, und meinen Herd, um dessen Glut du mich beneidest.
which you not built, and my hearth, for whose heat you me envy.
(which you did not build, and my hearth, whose heat you envy me.)

ɪç ˈkʰɛnə nɪçts ˈlɛrmərəs ˈlʊntʻɐ deːɐ̯ zɔn lals lɔ͜øç, ˈgœtʻɐ!
Ich kenne nichts Ärmeres unter der Sonn' als euch, Götter!
I know nothing poorer beneath the sun than you, gods!

iːɐ̯ nɛːɐ̯tʻ ˈkʰʏmɐlɪç fɔm ˈlɔpfɐʃtʻɔ͜øɐn lʊntʻ gəˈbeːtsha͜ox ˈlɔ͜ørə majɛsˈtʰɛːtʰ,
Ihr nährt kümmerlich vom Opfersteuern und Gebetshauch eure Majestät,
You nourish scantily from the sacrifice-taxes and prayer-breath your majesty,
(You nourish your majesty scantily on levies of sacrifice and the breath of prayer,)
[*poem:* **nähret** (ˈnɛːrətʻ, nourish)**... von** (fɔn, with) **Opfersteuern]**

ʊnt ˈdarpʻtʻətʻ, ˈvɛːrən nɪçtʻ ˈkʰɪndɐ lʊntʻ ˈbɛtʻlɐ ˈhɔfnʊŋsfɔlə ˈtʰoːrən.
und darbtet, wären nicht Kinder und Bettler hoffnungsvolle Toren.
and starved, were not children and beggars hopeful fools.
(and would starve if children and beggars were not hopeful fools.)

daː lɪç la͜en kʰɪntʻ vaːɐ̯, nɪçtʻ ˈvʊstʻə, voː la͜os nɔx la͜en, kʰeːɐ̯tʻ ɪç
Da ich ein Kind war, nicht wusste, wo aus noch ein, kehrt' ich
When I a child was, not knew, where out nor in, turned I
(When I was a child and did not know which way to turn, I lifted)
[*nicht aus noch ein wissen* = not know which way to turn]

ma͜en fɛɐ̯-/fɛrˈ|ɪrtʻəs ˈ|ɑ͜ogə t͡sʊr ˈzɔnə, |als vɛn ˈdryːbɐ vɛːɐ̯/vɛːr |a͜en |oːɐ̯,
mein verirrtes Auge zur Sonne, als wenn drüber wär' ein Ohr,
my gone astray eye to the sun, as if above that were an ear,
(my misled eyes to the sun, as if there were an ear above it somewhere)

t͡suː ˈhøːrən ˈma͜enə ˈkʰlaːgə, |a͜en hɛrt͡s, viː ma͜ens,
zu hören meine Klage, ein Herz, wie mein's,
to hear my complaint, a heart, like mine,

zɪç dɛs bəˈdrɛŋtʻən t͡suː |ɛɐ̯ˈbarmən. veːɐ̯ half miːɐ̯ ˈviːdɐ deːɐ̯ tʰiˈtʰaːnən ˈ|yːbɐmuːtʰ?
sich des Bedrängten zu erbarmen. Wer half mir wider der Titanen Übermut?
itself of the oppressed to feel pity. Who helped me against the Titans' arrogance?
(to feel compassion for the oppressed. Who helped me against the arrogance of the Titans?)

veːɐ̯ ˈrɛtʻətʻə fɔm ˈtʰoːdə mɪç, fɔn skʻlaːvəˈra͜e? hast duː nɪçtʻ
Wer rettete vom Tode mich, von Sklaverei? Hast du nicht
Who saved from the death me, from slavery? Have you not
(Who saved me from death or from slavery? Have you not)

ˈ|aləs zɛlpstʻ fɔlˈ|ɛndətʰ, ˈha͜elɪç ˈglyːəntʻ hɛrt͡s? |ʊntʻ ˈglyːtʻəstʻ jʊŋ |ʊntʻ guːtʰ,
alles selbst vollendet, heilig glühend Herz? Und glühtest jung und gut,
all yourself accomplished, sacredly glowing heart? And (you) glowed young and good,
(achieved all that by yourself, holy, glowing heart? And, young and good, did you not glow,)

bəˈtʰroːgən, ˈrɛtʻʊŋsdaŋkʻ dem ˈʃlaːfəndən daː ˈdroːbən? |ɪç dɪç ˈ|eːrən?
betrogen, Rettungsdank dem Schlafenden da droben? Ich dich ehren?
deceived, (with) rescue- thanks for the sleeping one there above? I you honor?
(deceived, with misplaced gratitude to that sleeper up there for your rescue? I should honor you?)

voˈfyːɐ̯? hast duː di ˈʃmɛrt͡sən gəˈ|ɪndɐtʻ jeː dɛs bəˈlaːdənən?
Wofür? Hast du die Schmerzen gelindert je des Beladenen?
For what? Have you the pains relieved ever of the burdened?
(For what? Have you ever relieved the pains of the overburdened?)

hast duː di ˈtʰrɛːnən gəˈʃtʻɪltʻ jeː dɛs gəˈ|ɛŋstʻətʻən?
Hast du die Tränen gestillet je des Geängsteten?
Have you the tears quenched ever of the frightened?
(Have you ever dried the tears of the frightened?)

hatʻ nɪçtʻ mɪç t͡sʊm ˈmanə gəˈʃmiːdət di |alˈmɛçtʻɪgə t͡sa͜etʻ
Hat nicht mich zum Manne geschmiedet die allmächtige Zeit [*GA:* **Hat mich nicht**]
Has not me to the man forged the almighty time
(Have I not been forged into manhood by all-powerful Time)

|ʊnt das ˈ|eːvɪgə ˈʃɪkʻzaːl, ˈma͜enə hɛrn |ʊnt ˈda͜enə?
und das ewige Schicksal, meine Herrn und deine?
and the eternal fate, my lords and yours?
(and eternal Fate, my masters and yours?)

ˈvɛːntʻəst duː ˈ|ɛtʻva, |ɪç ˈzɔltʻə das ˈleːbən ˈhasən, |ɪn ˈvyːstʻən ˈfliːən,
Wähntest du etwa, ich sollte das Leben hassen, in Wüsten fliehen,
Imagine you perhaps, I should the life hate, into deserts flee,
(Do you perhaps imagine that I should hate life and flee into the desert)

vae̯l nɪçt‘ 'lalə 'bly:t‘ənt^hrɔ̯ømə 'rae̯ft‘ən? hi:ɐ̯ zɪts lɪç,
weil nicht alle Blütenträume reiften? Hier sitz' ich,
because not all blossom-dreams ripened? Here sit I,
(because not all of my dream-blossoms ripened into fruit? Here I sit,)

'fɔrmə 'mɛnʃən na:x 'mae̯nəm 'bɪldə, lae̯n gə'ʃlɛçt, das mi:ɐ̯ glae̯ç zae̯,
forme Menschen nach meinem Bilde, ein Geschlecht, das mir gleich sei,
form human beings according to my image, a race, that to me like be,
(forming human beings in my own image, creating a race that shall be like me,)

t͡su: 'lae̯dən, t͡su: 'vae̯nən, t͡su: gə'ni:sən lʊnt t͡su: 'frɔ̯øən zɪç,
zu leiden, zu weinen, zu geniessen und zu freuen sich,
to suffer, to weep, to enjoy and to gladden itself,
(to suffer, to weep, to find enjoyment and be glad,)

ʊnt dae̯n nɪçt t͡su: 'laxt‘ən, vi: lɪç!
und dein nicht zu achten, wie ich!
and of you not to take notice, as I!
(and to ignore you, as I do!)

[The text of this powerful song is a monologue from the third scene of an unfinished drama. Prometheus dared to defy the will of the Olympian gods; he brought the gift of divine fire to mankind, and for that he was cruelly punished by Zeus. After a mighty flood, Prometheus formed a new race, independent of the old. Here he is a symbol of the artist, among other things, who gives immortal life to creations of the imagination. Also, this Prometheus represents a revolt against the stagnation of religion and the indifference to suffering that seemed to have permeated the church at the time Goethe wrote those stinging words. Yet the same year, 1774, that brought forth such vehemence against "Zeus" also brought the lyrical ecstasy of union with the "All-loving Father" in Goethe's beautiful *Ganymed*! The song was composed for bass voice, as printed in the *Gesamtausgabe*, and it expanded the boundaries of what an art song can express.]

Psalm XIII see *Der XIII. Psalm*

p^hʊnʃli:t‘ (im 'nɔrdən t͡su: 'zɪŋən)

Punschlied (im Norden zu singen)

Song in Praise of Punch (To be Sung in the North)

Posthumously published [composed 1815] (poem by Friedrich von Schiller)

ɑ͡ʊf de:ɐ̯ 'bɛrgə 'frae̯ən 'hø:ən, lɪn de:ɐ̯ 'mɪt‘a:kszɔnə ʃae̯n,
Auf der Berge freien Höhen, in der Mittagssonne Schein,
On the mountains' free heights, in the midday sun's shine,
(On the free heights of the mountains, in the brightness of the midday sun,)

an dɛs 'varmən 'ʃt‘ra:ləs 'k^hrɛft‘ən t͡sɔ̯øk‘t‘ na't^hu:ɐ̯ den 'gɔldnən vae̯n.
an des warmen Strahles Kräften zeugt Natur den goldnen Wein.
from the warm ray's powers begets Nature the golden wine.
(through the power of its warm rays, Nature produces golden wine.)

ʊnt‘ nɔx 'ni:mant‘ hat͡s lɛɐ̯'k^hʊndət‘, vi: di 'gro:sə 'mʊt‘ɐ ʃaft^h;
Und noch niemand hat's erkundet, wie die grosse Mutter schafft;
And still no one has it ascertained, how the great mother creates;
(And no one has as yet ascertained how the great Mother creates;)

ʊnlɛɐ̯ˈgrʏntˈlɪç lɪst das ˈvɪrkˈən, lʊnlɛɐ̯ˈfɔrʃlɪç lɪst di kʰraftʰ.
unergründlich ist das Wirken, unerforschlich ist die Kraft.
unfathomable is the operation, inscrutable is the power.
(her operation is unfathomable, her power inscrutable.)

ˈfʊŋkˈəlntˈ viː la͜en zoːn deːɐ̯ ˈzɔnə, viː dɛs ˈlɪçtˈəs ˈfɔ͜økʰvɛl,
Funkelnd wie ein Sohn der Sonne, wie des Lichtes Feuerquell,
Sparkling like a son of the sun, like the light's fire- source,
(Sparkling like a son of the sun, like the fiery source of light,)

ʃpˈrɪŋtˈ leːɐ̯ ˈpʰɛrləntˈ la͜os deːɐ̯ ˈtʰɔnə, ˈpʰʊrpˈʊrn lʊntˈ kʰrɪsˈtʰalənhɛl. lʊntˈ lɛɐ̯ˈfrɔ͜øətˈ
springt er perlend aus der Tonne, purpurn und kristallenhell. Und erfreuet
springs it bubbling from the cask, purple and crystal clear. And gladdens
(it springs bubbling from the cask, purple and crystal clear. And it gladdens)

ˈlalə ˈzɪnən, lʊntˈ lɪn ˈjeːdə ˈbaŋə brʊstˈ giːstˈ leːɐ̯/leːr la͜en balˈzaːmɪʃ ˈhɔfən
alle Sinnen, und in jede bange Brust giesst er ein balsamisch Hoffen
all senses, and into every anxious breast pours it in balsamically hope
(all our senses, and into every anxious breast it pours hope, like balm,) [*eingiessen* = pour in]

lʊnt dɛs ˈleːbəns ˈnɔ͜øə lʊstˈ [lʊnt dɛs ˈleːbəns ˈhøːçstˈə lʊstʰ].
und des Lebens neue Lust [*Peters (in the repeat)*: und des Lebens höchste Lust].
and the life's new pleasure [and the life's highest pleasure].
(and new pleasure in life.) [(and life's highest pleasure.)]

ˈaːbɐ matˈ la͜of ˈlʊnzrə ˈt͜soːnən fɛlt deːɐ̯ ˈzɔnə ˈʃrɛːgəs lɪçtʰ;
Aber matt auf unsre Zonen fällt der Sonne schräges Licht;
But dully upon our zones falls the sun's slanting light;
(But the sun's light falls slanting and dull upon our northern zones;)

nuːɐ̯ di ˈblɛtˈɐ kʰan ziː ˈfɛrbən, ˈlaːbɐ ˈfrʏçtˈə ra͜eftˈ ziː nɪçtʰ.
nur die Blätter kann sie färben, aber Früchte reift sie nicht.
only the leaves can it color, but fruits ripens it not.
(it can only color the leaves; it does not ripen fruit.)

dɔx deːɐ̯ ˈnɔrdən la͜ox vɪl ˈleːbən, lʊntˈ vas leːpˈtˈ, vɪl zɪç lɛɐ̯ˈfrɔ͜øn;
Doch der Norden auch will leben, und was lebt, will sich erfreu'n;
But the North also wants to live, and what lives, wants itself to gladden;
(But the North also wants to live; and whatever lives wants to be happy;)

ˈdarʊm ʃafən viːɐ̯/viːr lɛɐ̯ˈfɪndəntˈ ˈloːnə ˈva͜enʃtˈɔkˈ lʊns den va͜en.
darum schaffen wir erfindend ohne Weinstock uns den Wein.
therefore create we inventively without grape vines for ourselves the wine.
(therefore we inventively create wine for ourselves without grape vines.)

bla͜eç nuːɐ̯/nuːr lɪst͜s, vas viːɐ̯ bəˈra͜etˈən la͜of dem ˈhɔ͜øslɪçən lalˈtʰaːɐ̯;
Bleich nur ist's, was wir bereiten auf dem häuslichen Altar;
Pale only is it, what we prepare on the domestic altar;
(But what we prepare on our domestic altar is only pale;)

vas naˈtʰuːɐ̯ leˈbɛndɪç ˈbɪldətˈ, ˈglɛnt͜səntˈ lɪst͜s lʊntˈ ˈleːvɪç kʰlaːɐ̯.
was Natur lebendig bildet, glänzend ist's und ewig klar.
what Nature alive forms, gleaming is it and eternally clear.
(what Nature forms alive is gleaming and eternally clear.)

'a:bɐ 'frɔ͜ødɪç |a͜os de:ɐ̯ 'ʃa:lə 'ʃœpfən vi:ɐ̯ di 'tʰry:bə flu:tʰ;
Aber freudig aus der Schale schöpfen wir die trübe Flut;
But joyfully from the bowl ladle we the murky flood;
(But we joyfully ladle the murky fluid from the bowl;)

a͜ox di kʰʊnst' |ɪst' 'hɪməlsga:bə, bɔrk't' zi: gla͜eç fɔn '|ɪrdʃɐ glu:tʰ.
auch die Kunst ist Himmelsgabe, borgt sie gleich von ird'scher Glut.
also the art is heaven- gift, borrows it though from earthly fire.
(art, too, is a gift from heaven, though it borrows from earthly ardor.)
[*note: "art," here, means artful creativity, skill, inventiveness*]

'i:rəm 'vɪrk'ən 'fra͜egəge:bən |ɪst de:ɐ̯ 'kʰrɛft'ə 'gro:səs ra͜eç;
Ihrem Wirken freigegeben ist der Kräfte grosses Reich;
To its operation free given is the powers' great realm;
(The great realm of its powers is set free for its operation;) [*freigeben* = set free, release]

'nɔ͜øəs 'bɪldənt' |a͜os dem '|alt'ən, ʃt'ɛlt' zi: zɪç dem 'ʃœpfɐ gla͜eç.
Neues bildend aus dem Alten, stellt sie sich dem Schöpfer gleich.
new forming out of the old, puts it itself to the Creator equal.
(forming the new out of the old, art aspires to put itself on a par with the Creator.)

zɛlpst das bant de:ɐ̯/de:r |ele'mɛnt'ə tʰrɛnt' |i:ɐ̯ 'hɛrʃəndəs gə'bo:tʰ,
Selbst das Band der Elemente trennt ihr herrschendes Gebot,
Even the bond of the elements severs its governing command,
(Its governing command can even sever the bond of the elements,)

ʊnt' zi: |a:mt' mɪt' 'he:ɐ̯dəsflamən na:x den 'ho:ən 'zɔnəngɔtʰ.
und sie ahmt mit Herdesflammen nach den hohen Sonnengott.
and it imitates with hearth flames ... the high sun- god.
(and with flames from the hearth it imitates the sublime sun-god.) [*nachahmen* = imitate]

'fɛrnhɪn tsu: den 'ze:lgən '|ɪnzəln 'rɪçt'ət' zi: de:ɐ̯ 'ʃifə |a͜of,
Fernhin zu den sel'gen Inseln richtet sie der Schiffe Lauf,
Far away to the blessed islands directs it the ship's course,
(Far away to the isles of the blessed it directs the ship's course,)

ʊnt dɛs 'zy:dəns 'gɔldnə 'frʏçt'ə 'ʃʏt'ət' zi: |ɪm 'nɔrdən |a͜of.
und des Südens goldne Früchte schüttet sie im Norden auf.
and the South's golden fruits heaps it in the North up.
(and in the North it heaps up the golden fruit of the South.)

drʊm |a͜en 'zɪnbɪlt' |ʊnt' |a͜en 'tsa͜eçən za͜e |ʊns 'di:zɐ 'fɔ͜øɐzaftʰ,
Drum ein Sinnbild und ein Zeichen sei uns dieser Feuersaft,
Therefore a symbol and a sign be to us this fire- juice,
(Therefore let this fiery juice be to us a symbol and a sign)

vas de:ɐ̯ mɛnʃ zɪç kʰan |ɛɐ̯'laŋən mɪt dem 'vɪlən |ʊnt de:ɐ̯ kʰraftʰ.
was der Mensch sich kann erlangen mit dem Willen und der Kraft.
what the human being for him-/herself can procure with the will and the power.
(of what we humans can procure for ourselves with enough will power and skill.)

[This energetic drinking song is notated as a vocal duet, with or without accompaniment. The *Gesamtausgabe* prints all twelve verses; Peters has chosen the first, third, and fourth. Not many drinkers would get beyond them, certainly not to the more philosphical verses near the end!]

kwelːlinːnoˈʧɛnte ˈfiʎːʎo / ˈarja del‿ˈlanʤelo
Quell' innocente figlio / Aria dell' angelo
That Innocent Son / Aria of the Angel

Posthumously published [composed 1812] (poem by Pietro Metastasio)

kwelːlinːnoˈʧɛnte ˈfiʎːʎo, ˈdoːno del ʧɛl siː ˈrːraːro, kwel ˈfiʎːʎo‿a tːte si kːkaːro,
Quell' innocente figlio, dono del Ciel sì raro, quel figlio a te sì caro,
That innocent son, gift of the heaven so rare, that son to you so dear,
(That innocent son, so rare a gift from heaven, that son so dear to you,)

ˈkwelːlo vwɔl ˈdiːo da tːte. vwɔl ke riˈmaŋga eˈzaŋgwe ˈsotːto‿al
quello vuol Dio da te. Vuol che rimanga esangue sotto al
that wants God from you. (He) wants that (he) remain dead beneath the
(God wants that son from you. He wants him to be dead before his)

paˈtɛrno ˈʧiʎːʎo, vwɔl ke ne ˈsparga‿il ˈsaŋgwe ki ˈvːviːta ʤa ʎːʎi djɛ.
paterno ciglio, vuol che ne sparga il sangue chi vita già gli diè.
paternal brow, wants that of him shed the blood who life formerly to him gave.
(father's eyes, wants that his blood be shed by the man who once gave him life.)

[Schubert set this text from the oratorio *Isacco* ("Isaac") while he was studying composition with Antonio Salieri. Only the original melody line has survived, with the teacher's corrections. An accompaniment has been provided and privately published by Reinhard Van Hoorickx.]

Rast see *Winterreise*

Raste Krieger see *Ellens Gesang I*

ˈrastʻ loːzə ˈliːbə
Rastlose Liebe
Love Without Rest

Op. 5, No. 1 [1815] (Johann Wolfgang von Goethe)

dem ʃneː, dem ˈreːgən, dem vɪntʻ lɛntʻˈgeːgən, lɪm dampf deːɐ̯ ˈkʰlʏftʻə,
Dem Schnee, dem Regen, dem Wind entgegen, im Dampf der Klüfte,
To the snow, to the rain, to the wind opposed, in the mist of the ravines,
(Against the snow, against the rain, against the wind, in the misty ravines,)

dʊrç ˈneːbəldʏftʻə, ˈlɪmɐ tsuː! ˈlɪmɐ tsuː! ˈloːnə rastʻ lʊntʻ ruː!
durch Nebeldüfte, immer zu! Immer zu! ohne Rast und Ruh'!
through fog- scents, always to! Always to! without rest and peace!
(through the smell of the fog, keep on! Keep on, without rest or peace!) [*immer zu!* = keep on!]

ˈliːbɐ dʊrç ˈlaedən vɔltʻ ɪç mɪç ˈʃlaːgən, [mœçtʻ]
Lieber durch Leiden wollt' ich mich schlagen, [*poem:* **möcht' ich mich schlagen]**
Rather through suffering would I myself fight, [would like]
(I would rather fight my way through suffering) [(would I like to fight my way)]

ˈals zoː fiːl ˈfrɔ̯ødən dɛs ˈleːbəns lɛɐ̯ˈtʰraːgən. ˈalə das ˈna̯egən fɔn ˈhɛrt͡sən t͡suː ˈhɛrt͡sən,
als so viel Freuden des Lebens ertragen. Alle das Neigen von Herzen zu Herzen,
than so many joys of the life endure. All the inclining of heart to heart,
(than endure so many of life's joys. All this inclination of one heart to another,)

ax, viː zoː ˈla̯egən ˈʃafət das ˈʃmɛrt͡sən! [lɛs]
ach, wie so eigen schaffet das Schmerzen! [*GA:* **schaffet es**]
ah, how so curiously creates that pains! [it]
(ah, how curiously that creates pain!)

viː, zɔl lɪç fliːn? ˈvɛldɐvɛrt͡s t͡siːn? ˈaləs fɛɐ̯ˈgeːbəns! [ˈfliːən... ˈt͡siːən]
Wie, soll ich flieh'n? Wälderwärts zieh'n? Alles vergebens! [*poem:* **fliehen... ziehen**]
What, shall I flee? Forestward move? All in vain! [flee... move]
(What? Shall I flee? Run to the woods? All in vain!)

[*GA:* **Wie soll ich flieh'n?** (How shall I flee?)]
[*note: some editions of the poem have a comma, some not.*]

ˈkʰroːnə dɛs ˈleːbəns, glʏk ˈloːnə ruː, ˈliːbə, bɪst duː.
Krone des Lebens, Glück ohne Ruh', Liebe, bist du.
Crown of the life, happiness without peace, love, are you.
(Love, you are the crown of life, you are happiness without peace!)

[The poem was written after a snowstorm in 1776, as Goethe was falling in love with Charlotte von Stein. Schubert captures all the impetuosity and passion, the struggle with mixed feelings.]

ˈrɪtʼɐ ˈtʰɔgn̩bʊrk'
Ritter Toggenburg
The Knight of Toggenburg

Posthumously published [composed 1816] (poem by Friedrich von Schiller)

ˈrɪtʼɐ, ˈtʰrɔ̯øə ˈʃvɛstʼɐliːbə ˈvɪtʼmətʼ lɔ̯øç diːs hɛrt͡s;
"Ritter, treue Schwesterliebe widmet euch dies Herz;
"Knight, faithful sister- love dedicates to you this heart;
("Sir Knight, my heart dedicates to you a faithful, sisterly kind of love;

ˈfɔrdɐtʼ ˈkʰa̯enə ˈlandrə ˈliːbə, dɛn lɛs maxtʼ miːɐ̯ ʃmɛrt͡s. [ˈfoːdɐtʼ]
fordert keine andre Liebe, denn es macht mir Schmerz. [*poem:* **fodert** (obs.)]
demand no other love, for it makes for me pain. [demand]
(ask of me no other kind, for that would be painful to me.)

ˈruːɪç maːk lɪç lɔ̯øç lɛɐ̯ˈʃa̯enən, ˈruːɪç ˈgeːən zeːn.
Ruhig mag ich euch erscheinen, ruhig gehen seh'n.
Calmly like I you appear, calmly go to see.
(Calmly I would like to see you appear, calmly see you go.)

ˈlɔ̯ørɐ(r) ˈla̯ogən ˈʃtʼɪləs ˈva̯enən kʰan lɪç nɪçtʼ fɛɐ̯ˈʃtʼeːn.
Eurer Augen stilles Weinen kann ich nicht versteh'n."
Your eyes' quiet weeping can I not understand."
(I cannot understand the silent tears in your eyes.")

ʊnt‘ leːɐ̯ høːɐ̯ts mɪt‘ ˈʃt‘ʊməm ˈharmə, raest‘ zɪç ˈbluːt‘ənt‘ loːs, [ˈʃt‘ʊmən]
Und er hört's mit stummem Harme, reisst sich blutend los, [*Peters:* **stummen** (error)]
And he hears it with mute sorrow, tears himself bleeding away, [mute]
(And he hears that with mute sorrow, tears himself away with a bleeding heart,)

pʰrɛst‘ ziː ˈhɛft‘ɪç lɪn di ˈlarmə, ʃvɪŋt‘ zɪç laof zaen rɔs,
presst sie heftig in die Arme, schwingt sich auf sein Ross,
presses her vehemently into the arms, swings himself onto his steed,
(presses her vehemently in his arms, leaps onto his steed,)

ʃik‘t tsuː ˈzaenən ˈmanən ˈlalən lɪn dem ˈlandə ʃvaets;
schickt zu seinen Mannen allen in dem Lande Schweiz;
sends to his vassals all in the land Schwyz;
(sends orders to all his male vassals in the land of Schwyz;)
[*note: Switzerland was not yet a country at the time of the crusades.*]

naːx dem ˈhaelgən graːp‘ ziː ˈvalən, laof deːɐ̯ brʊst das kʰrɔøts.
nach dem heil'gen Grab sie wallen, auf der Brust das Kreuz.
toward the holy grave they go on pilgrimage, on the breast the cross.
(to the holy sepulchre they go on pilgrimage, the cross on their breasts.)

ˈgroːsə ˈtʰaːt‘ən dɔrt‘ gəˈʃeːən dʊrç deːɐ̯ ˈhɛldən larm,
Grosse Taten dort geschehen durch der Helden Arm,
Great deeds there happen through the heroes' arm,
(Great deeds are accomplished there through the heroes' strength and valor,)

ˈiːrəs ˈhɛlməs ˈbʏʃə ˈveːən lɪn deːɐ̯ ˈfaendə ʃvarm;
ihres Helmes Büsche wehen in der Feinde Schwarm;
their helmet's bushes blow in the enemies' swarm;
(the plumes on their helmets flutter in the midst of swarming enemies;)

ʊnt des ˈtʰɔgənbʊrgɐs ˈnaːmə ʃrɛk‘t den ˈmuːzəlman;
und des Toggenburgers Name schreckt den Muselmann;
and the Toggenburger's name frightens the Mussulman;

dɔx das hɛrts fɔn ˈzaenəm ˈgraːmə nɪçt‘ gəˈneːzən kʰan.
doch das Herz von seinem Grame nicht genesen kann.
yet the heart from its sorrow not recover can.
(yet his heart cannot recover from its sorrow.)

ʊnt‘ laen jaːɐ̯ hat‘ leːɐ̯s gəˈtʰraːgən, tʰrɛːk‘ts nɪçt‘ ˈlɛŋɐ meːɐ̯,
Und ein Jahr hat er's getragen, trägt's nicht länger mehr,
And a year has he it borne, bears it not longer more,
(And he has borne that burden for a year; he can bear it no longer,)

ˈruːə kʰan leːɐ̯ nɪçt‘ lɛɐ̯ˈjaːgən lʊnt‘ fɛɐ̯ˈlɛst das heːɐ̯,
Ruhe kann er nicht erjagen und verlässt das Heer,
Peace can he not gain and leaves the army,
(he can gain no peace of mind, and he leaves his army,)

ziːt‘ laen ʃif lan ˈjɔpəs ˈʃt‘randə, das di ˈzeːgəl blɛːtʰ,
sieht ein Schiff an Joppes Strande, das die Segel bläht,
sees a ship at Joppa's shore, that the sails swells,
(sees a ship with swelling sails by the shore at Joppa,) [*note: Joppa is the ancient name of Jaffa*]

'ʃifət' ha͜em tsʊm 'tʰɔ͜øʁən 'landə, vo: li:ɐ̯/li:r 'la:t'əm ve:tʰ.
schiffet heim zum teuren Lande, wo ihr Atem weht.
sails home to the dear land, where her breath blows.
(sails home to the dear land where her breath is borne on the air.)

ʊnt' lan 'li:rəs 'ʃlɔsəs 'p͜fɔrt'ə kʰlɔp͜ft de:ɐ̯ 'pʰɪlgɐ(r) lan,
Und an ihres Schlosses Pforte klopft der Pilger an,
And at her castle's gate knocks the pilgrim at,
(And the pilgrim knocks at the gate of her castle,) [*anklopfen* = to knock (at a door, etc.)]

ax, lʊnt' mɪt dem 'dɔnɐvɔrt'ə vɪrt' zi: 'la͜ofgətʰa:n:
ach, und mit dem Donnerworte wird sie aufgetan:
ah, and with the thunder word is it opened:
(ah, and it is opened with these words that stunned like a thunderbolt:)

di: li:ɐ̯ 'zu:xət, tʰrɛ:k't den 'ʃla͜eɐ(r), lɪst dɛs 'hɪməls bra͜ot',
"Die ihr suchet, trägt den Schleier, ist des Himmels Braut,
"(She) whom you seek, wears the veil, is the heaven's bride,
("She whom you seek wears the veil, she is a bride of heaven,)

'gɛst'ɐn va:ɐ̯ dɛs 'tʰa:gəs 'fa͜eɐ, de:ɐ̯ zi: gɔt' gə'tʰra͜otʰ. [de:ɐ̯ tʰa:k' de:ɐ̯]
gestern war des Tages Feier, der sie Gott getraut." **[*P.:* der Tag der Feier]**
yesterday was the day's celebration, which her (to) God wedded." [the day of the]
(yesterday was the celebration of the day that wedded her to God.")

da: fɛɐ̯'lɛsət' le:ɐ̯/le:r la͜of 'lɪmɐ 'za͜enɐ 'fɛ:t'ɐ ʃlɔs,
Da verlässet er auf immer seiner Väter Schloss,
Thereupon leaves he for ever his fathers' castle,
(Thereupon he leaves the castle of his forefathers for ever,)

'za͜enə 'vafən zi:t' le:ɐ̯ 'nɪmɐ, nɔx za͜en 'tʰrɔ͜øəs rɔs,
seine Waffen sieht er nimmer, noch sein treues Ross,
his weapons sees he never, nor his faithful charger,
(he never again sees his weapons or his faithful horse,)

fɔn de:ɐ̯ 'tʰɔgənbʊrk' hɛɐ̯'ni:dɐ ʃt'a͜ek't' le:ɐ̯/le:r lʊnbə'kʰant',
von der Toggenburg hernieder steigt er unbekannt,
from the Toggenburg down climbs he unrecognized,
(he descends unrecognized from Toggenburg Castle,)

dɛn lɛs dɛk't di 'le:dəln 'gli:dɐ 'hɛ:rənəs gə'vant'. ['le:dlən]
denn es deckt die edeln Glieder härenes Gewand. **[*Peters:* edlen]**
for there covers the noble limbs hair garment. [noble]
(for a hair shirt covers his noble limbs.)

ʊnt' lɛɐ̯'ba͜ot' zɪç 'la͜enə 'hʏt'ə 'je:nɐ 'ge:gənt' na:, [le:ɐ̯ ba͜ot']
Und erbaut sich eine Hütte jener Gegend nah, **[*Peters:* er baut]**
And builds himself a hut to that region near, [he builds]
(And he builds himself a hut near that neighborhood)

vo: das 'kʰlo:st'ɐ(r) la͜os de:ɐ̯ 'mɪt'ə 'dy:st'rɐ 'lɪndən za:;
wo das Kloster aus der Mitte düstrer Linden sah;
where the convent out from the midst of dark lindens looked;
(where the convent looked out from among dark linden trees;)

'harənt' fɔn dɛs 'mɔrgəns 'lɪçt'ə bɪs tsu: 'la:bənts ʃaen, 'ʃt'ɪlə 'hɔfnʊŋ ɪm gə'zɪçt'ə,
harrend von des Morgens Lichte bis zu Abends Schein, stille Hoffnung im Gesichte,
waiting from the morning's light till to evening's shine, silent hope in the face,
(waiting from the first light of the morning until the glow of evening, silent hope in his face,)

za:s le:ɐ da: la'laen. 'blɪk't'ə na:x dem 'kʰlo:st'ɐ 'dry:bən, 'blɪk't'ə 'ʃt'ʊndənlaŋ
sass er da allein. Blickte nach dem Kloster drüben, blickte stundenlang
sat he there alone. Looked toward the convent yonder, looked hours- long
(he sat there alone. He looked toward the convent opposite him, looked for hour after hour)

na:x dem 'fɛnst'ɐ 'zaenɐ 'li:bən, bɪs das 'fɛnst'ɐ kʰlaŋ, bɪs di 'li:p'lɪçə
nach dem Fenster seiner Lieben, bis das Fenster klang, bis die Liebliche
toward the window of his dear one, till the window rattled, till the lovely one

zɪç 'tsaek't'ə,, bɪs das 'tʰɔøʀə bɪlt' zɪç ɪns tʰa:l hɛ'rʊnt'ɐ 'naek't'ə, 'ru:ɪç, 'lɛŋəlmɪlt'.
sich zeigte, bis das teure Bild sich ins Tal herunter neigte, ruhig, engelmild.
herself showed, till the dear image itself into the valley down bent, calm, angel-mild.
(showed herself, till the dear figure bent down toward the valley, calm, angelically gentle.)

ʊnt dan le:k't' e:ɐ fro: zɪç 'ni:dɐ, ʃli:f gə'tʰrø:st'ət' laen, ʃt'ɪl zɪç 'frɔøənt',
Und dann legt' er froh sich nieder, schlief getröstet ein, still sich freuend,
And then laid he happy himself down, slept comforted ..., quietly himself gladdening,
(And then he lay down happily and fell asleep comforted, quietly rejoicing)

[*schlief ein* = fell asleep]

vɛn lɛs 'vi:dɐ 'mɔrgən 'vʏrdə zaen. lʊnt' zo: za:s le:ɐ 'fi:lə 'tʰa:gə, za:s fi:l 'ja:rə laŋ,
wenn es wieder Morgen würde sein. Und so sass er viele Tage, sass viel Jahre lang,
when it again morning would be. And thus sat he many days, sat many years long,
(when it would be morning again. And he sat thus for many days, for many long years,)

'harənt' 'lo:nə ʃmɛrts lʊnt' 'kʰla:gə, bɪs das 'fɛnst'ɐ kʰlaŋ, bɪs di 'li:p'lɪçə
harrend ohne Schmerz und Klage, bis das Fenster klang, bis die Liebliche
waiting without pain and complaint, till the window rattled, till the lovely one
(waiting without pain or complaint, till the window rattled, till the lovely one

zɪç 'tsaek't'ə,, bɪs das 'tʰɔøʀə bɪlt' zɪç ɪns tʰa:l hɛ'rʊnt'ɐ 'naek't'ə, 'ru:ɪç, 'lɛŋəlmɪlt'.
sich zeigte, bis das teure Bild sich ins Tal herunter neigte, ruhig, engelmild.
herself showed, till the dear image itself into the valley down bent, calm, angel-mild.
(showed herself, till the dear figure bent down toward the valley, calm, angelically gentle.)

ʊnt' zo: za:s le:ɐ/le:r, 'laenə 'laeçə, 'laenəs 'mɔrgəns da:;
Und so sass er, eine Leiche, eines Morgens da;
And thus sat he, a corpse, one morning there;
(And one morning he was sitting there like that, but now a corpse;)

na:x dem 'fɛnst'ɐ nɔx das 'blaeçə, 'ʃt'ɪlə 'lant'lɪts za:.
nach dem Fenster noch das bleiche, stille Antlitz sah.
toward the window still the pale, silent countenance looked.
(his pale, silent face was still looking toward her window.)

[Besides the fact that they are in different keys, there is a major difference between the versions found in the *Gesamtausgabe* and in Peters: in the latter, the last verse shifts to the major mode, with a different accompaniment and a partly different melody, giving the poor knight a sort of transfiguration as he dies. Apparently the Peters version is based upon a lost original variant.]

roˈmant͡sə / a͜en ˈfrɔ͜ølaen kʰlaːkʻtʻ lɪm ˈfɪnstʻɐn tʰʊrm
Romanze / Ein Fräulein klagt' im finstern Turm
Romance / A Damsel Lamented in the Dark Tower

Posthumously published [composed 1814] (poem by Friedrich von Matthisson)

a͜en ˈfrɔ͜øla͜en kʰlaːkʻtʻ lɪm ˈfɪnstʻɐn tʰʊrm lam ˈzeːgəʃtʻaːtʻ lɛɐ̯ˈba͜otʰ.
Ein Fräulein klagt' im finstern Turm, am Seegestad' erbaut.
A damsel lamented in the dark tower, by the seashore built.
(A damsel lamented in the dark tower that was built by the seashore.)

ɛs ra͜oʃtʻ lʊntʻ ˈhɔ͜øltʻə voːkʻ lʊntʻ ʃtʻʊrm lɪn ˈliːrəs ˈjamɐs la͜otʰ.
Es rauscht' und heulte Wog' und Sturm in ihres Jammers Laut.
There roared and howled wave and storm in her distress's sound.
(The roaring of the waves and the howling of the storm mingled with her cries of distress.)

roˈzaːlia fɔn mõtɑ̃ˈvɛːɐ̯ hiːs ˈmançəm ˈtʰruːbaduːɐ̯
Rosalia von Montanvert hiess manchem Troubadour
Rosalia of Montanvert meant to many a troubadour

lʊntʻ ˈla͜enəm ˈgant͡sən ˈrɪtʻɐheːɐ̯ di ˈkʰroːnə deːɐ̯ naˈtʰuːɐ̯.
und einem ganzen Ritterheer die Krone der Natur.
and to a whole knight-army the crown of the nature.
(and to a whole army of knights the crowning achievement of Nature.)

dɔx ˈleːə nɔx liːɐ̯ hɛrt͡s di maxt deːɐ̯ ˈzyːsən mɪn lɛmˈp͡fantʻ,
Doch ehe noch ihr Herz die Macht der süssen Minn' empfand,
But before still her heart the power of the sweet courtly love felt,
(But before her heart had felt the power of sweet love) [*Minne* = courtly love]

ɛɐ̯ˈlaːkʻ deːɐ̯ ˈfaːtʻɐ(r) lɪn deːɐ̯ ʃlaxtʻ lam zaraˈt͡seːnənʃtʻrantʻ.
erlag der Vater in der Schlacht am Sarazenenstrand.
fell her father in the battle by the Saracens- shore.
(her father fell in battle by the Saracen shore.)

deːɐ̯/deːr loːm, la͜en ˈrɪtʻɐ ˈmanfry, vart t͡sʊm ˈʃɪrmfoːkʻtʻ liːɐ̯ bəˈʃtʻɛltʰ; [iːɐ̯]
Der Ohm, ein Ritter Manfry, ward zum Schirmvogt ihr bestellt; [*poem:* **Ihr Ohm**]
The uncle, a Knight Manfrey, was as the guardian for her appointed; [her]
(Her uncle, a knight named Manfrey, was appointed as her guardian;)

deːm laxtʻ lɪns hɛrt͡s, viː ˈfɛlzən hartʰ, dɛs ˈfrɔ͜øla͜ens guːtʻ lʊntʻ gɛltʻ.
dem lacht' ins Herz, wie Felsen hart, des Fräuleins Gut und Geld.
to him laughed (= smiled) into the heart, as rock hard, the damsel's goods and money.
(the damsel's property and money enticed his heart, as hard as stone.)

baltʻ ˈlyːbɐ(r)lal lɪm ˈlandə gɪŋ di ˈtʰra͜oɐkʰʊntʻ lʊmˈheːɐ̯:
Bald überall im Lande ging die Trauerkund' umher:
Soon everywhere in the land went the mournful tidings around:
(Soon the mournful tidings circulated throughout the land:)

dɛs ˈtʰoːdəs ˈkʰaltʻə naxtʻ lʊmfɪŋ di ˈroːzə mõtɑ̃ˈvɛːɐ̯!
"Des Todes kalte Nacht umfing die Rose Montanvert!"
"The death's cold night encircled the Rose Montanvert!"
("The cold night of death has enveloped Rose Montanvert!")

a͜en 'ʃvart͜səs 'tʰoːt'ənfɛːnla͜en valt' hoːx la͜of dɛs 'frɔ͜ølaens bʊrk';
Ein schwarzes Totenfähnlein wallt hoch auf des Fräuleins Burg;
A black funeral little flag flutters high on the damsel's castle;
(A little black funeral flag flutters high above the damsel's castle;)

di 'dʊmp͜fə 'la͜eçənglɔk'ə ʃalt dra͜e tʰaːk' lʊnt' nɛçt' hɪn'dʊrç.
die dumpfe Leichenglocke schallt drei Tag' und Nächt' hindurch.
the hollow corpse- bell rang three days and nights throughout.
(the hollow death-knell was sounded throughout three days and nights.)

a͜of 'leːvɪç hɪn, la͜of 'leːvɪç tʰoːt', loː 'roːzə mõtɑ̃'veːɐ̯!
Auf ewig hin, auf ewig tot, o Rose Montanvert!
For ever gone, for ever dead, O Rose Montanvert!

nuːn 'mɪldɐst duː deːɐ̯ 'vɪt'və noːt, deːɐ̯ 'va͜ezə ʃmɛrt͜s nɪçt' meːɐ̯!
Nun milderst du der Witwe Not, der Waise Schmerz nicht mehr!
Now alleviate you the widow's need, the orphan's pain not (any) more!
(Now you will no longer be there to alleviate the widow's need, the orphan's pain!)

zoː kʰlaːk't' la͜en'myːt'ɪç* lalt' lʊnt' jʊŋ, den blɪk' fɔn 'tʰrɛːnən ʃveːɐ̯,
So klagt' einmütig Alt und Jung, den Blick von Tränen schwer,
Thus lamented of one mind old and young, the gaze with tears heavy,
(Thus, as if with one voice, their eyes brimming with tears, both old and young bemoaned)
[**normally:* 'la͜enmyːt'ɪç]

fɔm 'fryːroːt' bɪs t͜sʊr 'dɛmərʊŋ, di 'roːzə mõtɑ̃'veːɐ̯.
vom Frührot bis zur Dämmerung, die Rose Montanvert.
from the dawn till to the twilight, the Rose Montanvert.
(Rose Montanvert from dawn till twilight.)

deːɐ̯/deːr loːm lɪn 'la͜enəm tʰʊrm ziː bark', lɛɐ̯'fʏlt' mɪt' 'moːdɐdʊftʰ!
Der Ohm in einem Turm sie barg, erfüllt mit Moderduft!
The uncle in a tower her concealed, filled with mold- scent!
(Her uncle concealed her in a tower that smelled of mold and decay!)

dra͜of 'zɛŋk't'ə man den 'leːrən zark' voːl lɪn deːɐ̯ 'fɛːt'ɐ grʊftʰ.
Drauf senkte man den leeren Sarg wohl in der Väter Gruft.
Thereupon lowered one the empty coffin probably into the (fore)fathers' vault.
(Then the empty coffin was brought down into the vaulted tomb of her forefathers.)

das 'frɔ͜øla͜en 'hɔrçt'ə, ʃt'ɪl lʊnt' baŋ, deːɐ̯ 'pʰriːst'ɐ lit'a'na͜en;
Das Fräulein horchte, still und bang, der Priester Litanei'n;
The damsel listened to, silent and afraid, the priests' litany;
(The damsel, silent and frightened, could hear the litany of the priests;)

tʰryːp' lɪn dɛs 'kʰɛrk'ɐs 'gɪt'ɐ draŋ deːɐ̯ 'fak'əln 'roːt'ɐ ʃa͜en.
trüb' in des Kerkers Gitter drang der Fackeln roter Schein.
cheerlessly into the dungeon's bars penetrated the torches' red shine,
(the red gleam of the torches penetrated cheerlessly into her dungeon.)

ziː 'laːnt'ə 'ʃa͜odɐnt' liːɐ̯ gə'ʃɪk'; liːɐ̯ vart' zoː dʊmp͜f, liːɐ̯ vart' zoː ʃveːɐ̯,
Sie ahnte schaudernd ihr Geschick; ihr ward so dumpf, ihr ward so schwer,
She surmised shuddering her fate; to her became so dull, to her became so heavy,
(Shuddering, she surmised her fate; her senses became dull and heavy,)
[*poem:* **ihr ward so dumpf und** (lʊnt', and) **schwer**]

ɪn ˈtʰoːdəsnaxtˈ lɛɐ̯ˈʃtˈarpˈ liːɐ̯ blɪkʰ; ziː zaŋkˈ lʊntˈ vaːɐ̯ nɪçtˈ meːɐ̯. [ˈtʰoːdəsgrɑo̯n]
in Todesnacht erstarb ihr Blick; sie sank und war nicht mehr. [*poem:* Todesgraun]
into death-night died away her gaze; she sank and was not (any) more. [death-horror]
(the light in her eyes died away into the dark night of death; she sank down and ceased to exist.)

dɛs tʰʊrms ruˈiːnən lan deːɐ̯ zeː zɪntˈ ˈhɔ͜øtˈə nɔx t͡suː ʃɑo̯n;
Des Turms Ruinen an der See sind heute noch zu schaun;
The tower's ruins by the sea are today still to see;
(The ruins of that tower by the sea can still be seen today;)

den ˈvandrɐ fastˈ lɪn ˈliːrɐ nɛː la͜en ˈvʊndɐzaːməs grɑo̯n.
den Wandrer fasst in ihrer Näh' ein wundersames Graun.
the wanderer (obj.) seizes in their vicinity a wondrous horror (subj.).
(a strange horror seizes the traveler who happens to be in their vicinity.)

ɑo̯x ˈmançɐ hɪrtˈ fɛɐ̯ˈkʰʏndətˈ lɔ͜øç, das leːɐ̯ ba͜e naxtˈ lalˈdaː
Auch mancher Hirt verkündet euch, dass er bei Nacht allda
Also many a shepherd informs you, that he by night there
(Also, many a shepherd will inform you that at night there he)

lɔftˈ, ˈla͜enɐ ˈzɪlbɐvɔlkˈə gla͜eç, das ˈfrɔ͜øla͜en ˈʃveːbən zaː.
oft, einer Silverwolke gleich, das Fräulein schweben sah.
often, to a silver cloud like, the damsel hover saw.
(has often seen the damsel hovering in the air like a silver cloud.)

[The *Neue Schubert Ausgabe* offers two versions of the song, as well as a probable first draft. It is one of the young composer's more successful efforts in this ghostly genre.]

roˈmant͡sə / ɪn deːɐ̯ ˈfɛːtˈɐ ˈhalən
Romanze / In der Väter Hallen
Romance / In the Halls of His Fathers

Unpublished fragment [composed 1816] (poem by Friedrich Leopold Graf zu Stolberg)

ɪn deːɐ̯ ˈfɛːtˈɐ ˈhalən ˈruːtˈə ˈrɪtˈɐ ˈruːdɔlfs ˈhɛldənlarm,
In der Väter Hallen ruhte Ritter Rudolfs Heldenarm,
In the fathers' halls rested Knight Rudolf's hero- arm,
(In the halls of his forefathers Sir Rudolf rested his heroic arm,)

ˈruːdɔlfs, deːn di ʃlaxtˈ lɛɐ̯ˈfrɔ͜øtˈə, ˈruːdɔlfs,
Rudolfs, den die Schlacht erfreute, Rudolfs,
Rudolf's, whom the battle delighted, Rudolf's,
(Rudolf, who delighted in battle, Rudolf,)

ˈvɛlçən ˈfraŋkˈra͜eç ˈʃɔ͜øtˈə lʊnt deːɐ̯ zaraˈt͡seːnən ʃvarm.
welchen Frankreich scheute und der Sarazenen Schwarm.
whom France feared and the Saracens' swarm.
(who was feared by France and the Saracen hordes.)

[Schubert wrote only seven bars; the fragment can be found in the *Neue Schubert Ausgabe*, Volume 7 of the songs. The poem has thirteen verses. Reinhard Van Hoorickx has completed Schubert's setting of the first verse and published it privately.]

roˈmantsə laos: deːɐ̯ ˈhɔøslɪçə kʰriːkʿ (di fɛɐ̯ˈʃvoːrənən) / ɪç ˈʃlaeçə baŋ

Romanze aus: "Der häusliche Krieg" ("Die Verschworenen") / Ich schleiche bang

Romance from *The Domestic War* (*The Conspirators*) / I Creep About Anxiously

Posthumously published [composed 1823] (text by Ignaz Franz Castelli)

ɪç ˈʃlaeçə baŋ lʊntʿ ʃtʿɪl hɛˈrʊm, das hɛrts pʰɔxtʿ miːɐ̯ zoː ʃveːɐ̯,
Ich schleiche bang und still herum, das Herz pocht mir so schwer,
I creep anxiously and quietly about, the heart beats in me so heavy,
(I creep about anxiously and quietly, my heart is beating so hard,)

das ˈleːbən dɔøçtʿ miːɐ̯/miːr løːtʿ lʊntʿ ʃtʿʊm, lʊntʿ fluːɐ̯/fluːr lʊntʿ bʊrkʿ zoː leːɐ̯.
das Leben däucht mir öd' und stumm, und Flur und Burg so leer.
the life seems to me bleak and silent, and field and castle so empty.
(life seems to me to be bleak and silent, and the fields and the castle seem so empty.)
[*däuchten* (obs.) = *deuchten* (poetic) = *dünken* = to seem]

ʊntʿ ˈjeːdə ˈfrɔødə ʃpʿrɪçtʿ miːɐ̯ hoːn, lʊntʿ ˈjeːdɐ tʰoːn lɪstʿ ˈkʰlaːgətʰoːn,
Und jede Freude spricht mir Hohn, und jeder Ton ist Klageton,
And every joy speaks to me mockery, and every tone is lament-tone,
(And every joy is a mockery to me, and every sound has a tone of lamentation,)

jaː ˈkʰlaːgətʰoːn, lɪst deːɐ̯ gəˈliːpʿtʿə fɛrn, tʰryːpʿtʿ zɪç dɛs ˈlaogəs ʃtʿɛrn.
ja Klageton, ist der Geliebte fern, trübt sich des Auges Stern.
yes lament-tone, is the beloved man far, dims itself the eye's star.
(yes, a tone of lamentation, if my beloved is far away, the stars in my eyes grow dim.)

ax, vas di ˈliːbə ˈlaenmaːl bantʿ, zɔl niː zɪç ˈtʰrɛnən meːɐ̯.
Ach, was die Liebe einmal band, soll nie sich trennen mehr.
Ah, what the love once bound, shall never itself part (any) more.
(Ah, what love has joined together should never be parted again.)

vas zuːxst duː lɪn dem ˈfrɛmdən lantʿ, lʊntʿ vaetʿ dɔrtʿ ˈlyːbɐm meːɐ̯?
Was suchst du in dem fremden Land, und weit dort überm Meer?
What seek you in the foreign land, and far there over the sea?
(What are you looking for in that foreign land, far across the sea?)

vɛn dɔrtʿ laox ˈbʊntʿrə ˈbluːmən blyːn, kʰaen hɛrts vɪrtʿ ˈhaesɐ fyːɐ̯ dɪç glyːn,
Wenn dort auch bunt're Blumen blüh'n, kein Herz wird heisser für dich glüh'n,
If there even more colorful flowers bloom, no heart will hotter for you glow,
(Even if more colorful flowers are blooming there, no heart will glow for you more ardently,)

jaː ˈkʰaenəs! loː blaepʿ nɪçtʿ ˈlɛŋɐ fɛrn, duː ˈmaenəs ˈleːbəns ʃtʿɛrn!
ja keines! O bleib' nicht länger fern, du meines Lebens Stern!
yes none! O stay not longer far, you my life's star!
(no, none! O stay no longer far away, you who are the star of my life!)

[This "romance" is an absolute gem; though intended for the stage, the piece deserves a place among Schubert's lieder. The plot of the one-act *Singspiel* is based on the Lysistrata theme, transferred to the Age of Chivalry. The wives of the crusaders, disgusted that their men are always away, fighting, conspire to teach them a lesson when they come home from war. The original title, *The Conspirators*, was considered dangerously subversive by the Viennese censors.]

roˈmantsə laos ˈroːzamʊndə / deːɐ̯ ˈfɔlmoːntʻ ʃtʻraːltʰ

Romanze aud "Rosamunde" / Der Vollmond strahlt

Romance from *Rosamunde* / The Full Moon Beams

Op. 26 [1823] (Wilhelmine von Chézy)

deːɐ̯ ˈfɔlmoːntʻ ʃtʻraːltʻ laof ˈbɛrgəshøːn — viː haːb ɪç dɪç fɛɐ̯ˈmɪstʰ!
Der Vollmond strahlt auf Bergeshöh'n — wie hab' ich dich vermisst!
The full moon beams on mountain heights — how have I you missed!
(The full moon is beaming on mountain heights — how I have missed you!)

duː ˈzyːsəs hɛrts! lɛs lɪstʻ zoː ʃøːn, vɛn tʰrɔø di ˈtʰrɔø kʰʏstʰ!
Du süsses Herz! es ist so schön, wenn treu die Treue küsst!
You sweet heart! It is so beautiful, when faithfully the fidelity/faithful woman* kisses!
(You sweet heart! It is so beautiful when faithful lovers kiss!)
[**die Treue* can mean either "fidelity" itself or "the faithful one" (female)]

vas frɔmt dɛs ˈmaeən ˈhɔldə tsiːɐ̯? duː vaːɐ̯stʻ maen ˈfryːlɪŋsʃtʻraːl!
Was frommt des Maien holde Zier? Du warst mein Frühlingsstrahl!
What avails the May's lovely ornament? You were my spring- ray!
(Of what use, now, is the lovely blossoming of May? You were my ray of spring sunshine!)

lɪçtʻ ˈmaenɐ naxtʻ, loː ˈlɛçlə miːɐ̯/miːr lɪm ˈtʰoːdə nɔx laenˈmaːl!
Licht meiner Nacht, o lächle mir im Tode noch einmal!
Light of my night, O smile to me in the death still once! [*noch einmal* = once more]
(Light of my night, O smile at me once more in death—come to me from the other world!)

ziː tʰraːtʻ hɪˈnaen baem ˈfɔlmoːntʻʃaen, ziː ˈblɪkʻtʻə ˈhɪməlvɛrts:
Sie trat hinein beim Vollmondschein, sie blickte himmelwärts:
She stepped in by the full-moon-shine, she gazed heavenward:
(She entered the room in the light of the full moon and gazed up toward heaven:)

ɪm ˈleːbən fɛrn, lɪm ˈtʰoːdə daen! lʊntʻ zanftʻ braːx hɛrts lan hɛrts.
"Im Leben fern, im Tode dein!" und sanft brach Herz an Herz.
"In the life far, in the death yours!" and gently broke heart on heart.
("Far away in life, in death I am yours!" and his heart gently broke against hers as he died.)

[This "Romance" is one of the pieces that Schubert wrote for *Rosamunde, Fürstin von Cypern* ("Rosamund, Princess of Cyprus"), a romantic drama in four acts by Wilhelmine ("Helmina") von Chézy (who was also responsible for the disastrous libretto of Weber's *Euryanthe*). The play was produced in Vienna in December 1823 and failed after ten performances, but the music was well received and several numbers remain popular. Peters includes this song among the lieder.]

Romanze aus dem Melodram: Die Zauberharfe see *Was belebt die schöne Welt*

roˈmantsə dɛs ˈrɪçart‘ ˈløːvənhɛrts
Romanze des Richard Löwenherz
The Romance of Richard the Lionhearted

Op. 86 [1826] (from Sir Walter Scott's *Ivanhoe*, translated by Karl Ludwig Müller)

ˈgroːsɐ ˈtʰaːt‘ən tʰaːt deːɐ̯ ˈrɪt‘ɐ fɛrn ɪm ˈhaelgən ˈlandə fiːl;
Grosser Taten tat der Ritter fern im heil'gen Lande viel;
Of great deeds did the knight far in the holy land much;
(The knight performed many great deeds far away in the holy land;)

ʊnt das kʰrɔøts ɪaof ˈzaenɐ ˈʃʊlt‘ɐ blaeçt‘ ɪm ˈraoən ˈʃlaxt‘gəvyːl.
und das Kreuz auf seiner Schulter bleicht' im rauhen Schlachtgewühl.
and the cross on his shoulder faded in the rough battle- tumult.
(and the cross on his shoulder faded in the rough tumult of battle.)

ˈmançə narp‘ ɪaof ˈzaenəm ˈʃɪldə tʰruːk‘ ɪeːɐ̯/ɪeːr ɪaos dem ˈkʰampfgəfɪldə;
Manche Narb' auf seinem Schilde trug er aus dem Kampfgefilde;
Many a scar on his shield carried he from the battlefield;
(He carried away from the battlefield many a dent in his shield;)

an deːɐ̯ ˈdaːmə ˈfɛnst‘ɐ dɪçt‘ zaŋ ɪeːɐ̯ zoː ɪm ˈmoːndənlɪçtʰ:
an der Dame Fenster dicht sang er so im Mondenlicht:
at the lady's window close sang he thus in the moonlight:
(close to his lady's window he sang thus in the moonlight:)

hael deːɐ̯ ˈʃøːnən! ɪaos deːɐ̯ ˈfɛrnə ɪɪst deːɐ̯ ˈrɪt‘ɐ ˈhaemgəkʰeːɐ̯tʰ,
Heil der Schönen! aus der Ferne ist der Ritter heimgekehrt,
Hail to the beautiful one! from the distance has the knight returned home,
("Hail to the fair lady! Her knight has returned home from far away,)

dɔx nɪçts dʊrft‘ ɪeːɐ̯ mɪt‘ zɪç ˈneːmən, ɪals zaen ˈtʰrɔøəs rɔs ɪʊnt‘ ʃveːɐ̯tʰ.
doch nichts durft' er mit sich nehmen, als sein treues Ross und Schwert.
but nothing could he with himself take, than his loyal steed and sword.
(but he could bring nothing back with him except his loyal steed and his sword.)

ˈzaenə ˈlantsə, ˈzaenə ˈʃp‘oːrən zɪnt‘ ɪaˈlaen ɪiːm ɪʊnfɛɐ̯ˈloːrən,
Seine Lanze, seine Sporen sind allein ihm unverloren,
His lance, his spurs are alone to him unlost,
(His lance and his spurs alone have not been lost to him,)

diːs ɪɪst‘ ɪal zaen ˈɪrdɪʃ glʏk‘, diːs ɪʊnt ˈtʰeːk‘las ˈliːbəsblɪkʰ.
dies ist all sein irdisch Glück, dies und Theklas Liebesblick.
that is all his earthly fortune, that and Tekla's love- look.
(those are all his earthly treasures, those—and Tekla's look of love.)

hael deːɐ̯ ˈʃøːnən! vas deːɐ̯ ˈrɪt‘ɐ tʰaːt‘, fɛɐ̯ˈdaŋk‘t‘ ɪeːɐ̯/ɪeːr ˈiːrɐ gʊnstʰ,
Heil der Schönen! was der Ritter tat, verdankt er ihrer Gunst,
Hail to the beautiful one! what the knight did, owes he to her favor,
(Hail to the fair lady! Whatever her knight accomplished he owes to her favor,)

'daːrʊm zɔl liːɐ̯ loːp' fɛɐ̯'kʰʏndən ʃt'eːt͡s dɛs 'zɛŋɐs 'zyːsə kʰʊnstʰ.
darum soll ihr Lob verkünden stets des Sängers süsse Kunst.
therefore shall her praise announce always the singer's sweet art.
(therefore shall the sweet art of the singer always proclaim her praise.)
[*Müller:* **des Minstrels** ('mɪnst'rəls, minstrel's)]

zeːt, daː lɪst' ziː, vɪrt' lɛs 'ha͡esən, vɛn ziː 'liːrə 'ʃøːnə 'pʰra͡ezən,
"Seht, da ist sie," wird es heissen, wenn sie ihre Schöne preisen,
"See, there is she," will it be to say, when they her beauty praise,
("See, there she is," they will say when they praise her beauty,) [*Müller:* **das** (das, that) **ist sie**]

'deːrən 'la͡ogən 'hɪməlsglant͡s gaːp' ba͡e 'lask'alɔn den kʰrant͡s.
"deren Augen Himmelsglanz gab bei Askalon den Kranz."
"whose eyes' heavenly radiance gave at Ascalon the wreath."
("Whose radiant, heavenly eyes gave us the wreath of victory at the Battle of Ascalon.")
[*note: Ascalon, on the coast of Palestine, was the scene of a battle in 1099*]

ʃa͡ot' liːɐ̯ 'lɛçəln, 'leːrnə 'mɛnɐ ʃt'rɛk't' lɛs 'leːp'loːs lɪn den ʃt'a͡op',
Schaut ihr Lächeln, eh'rne Männer streckt es leblos in den Staub,
See her smile, brazen men stretched it lifeless into the dust,
(See that smile of hers! It stretched out iron-hard men lifeless in the dust,)
[*Müller:* **Fünfzig** ('fʏnft͡sɪç, fifty) **Männer**]

ʊnt' li'kʰoːni̯ʊm, lɔp' za͡en 'zʊlt'aːn 'muːt'ɪç ʃt'rɪt', vart' liːm t͡sʊm ra͡op'.
und Ikonium, ob sein Sultan mutig stritt, ward ihm zum Raub.
and Iconium, though its sultan bravely fought, became for it to the booty.
(and Iconium, though its sultan fought bravely, became the booty of that smile.)

'diːzə 'lɔk'ən, viː ziː 'gɔldən 'ʃvɪmən lʊm di brʊst deːɐ̯ 'hɔldən,
Diese Locken, wie sie golden schwimmen um die Brust der Holden,
These curls, as they golden swim about the breast of the lovely one,
(Those golden curls, floating about the breast of the lovely one,)

'leːk't'ən 'mançəm 'muːzəlman 'fɛsəln lʊnt͡sɛɐ̯'ra͡esbaːɐ̯/-baːr lan.
legten manchem Muselmann Fesseln unzerreissbar an.
laid for many a mussulman chains unbreakable on.
(put unbreakable chains on many a mussulman.)

ha͡el deːɐ̯ 'ʃøːnən, diːɐ̯ gə'høːrət', 'hɔldə, vas da͡en 'rɪt'ɐ tʰaːtʰ,
Heil der Schönen, dir gehöret, Holde, was dein Ritter tat,
Hail to the beautiful one, to you belongs, lovely one, what your knight did,
(Hail to the fair lady! To you, lovely one, belongs whatever your knight accomplished,)

'daːrʊm 'lœfnə liːm di 'p͡fɔrt'ə, 'naxt'vɪnt' ʃt'ra͡eft, di 'ʃt'ʊndə naːtʰ;
darum öffne ihm die Pforte, Nachtwind streift, die Stunde naht;
therefore open to him the gate, night wind roves, the hour nears;
(therefore open the gate to him: the cold night wind is blowing, the hour approaches;)
['naxt'lʊft'] [ʃt'ʊnt' lɪst' ʃp'ɛːtʰ]
[*Müller & Schubert's repeat:* **Öffne darum;** *Müller:* **Nachtluft streift, die Stund' ist spät**]
[night air] [hour is late]

dɔrtʻ ǀɪn 'zyːrɪ̯əns ' 'ha͜esən 't͜soːnən, mʊstʻ ǀeːɐ̯ la͜eçt dɛs nɔrt͜s ǀɛntʻ'voːnən,
dort in Syriens heissen Zonen, musst' er leicht des Nords entwohnen,
there in Syria's hot zones, had to he easily of the North disaccustom,
(out there in Syria's heat he quickly had to disaccustom himself from the coldness of the North,)
[*entwohnen* = *entwöhnen* = disaccustom]

liːpʻ ǀɛɐ̯'ʃtʻɪkʻə nuːn di ʃaːm, va͜el fɔn iːm deːɐ̯ ruːm diːɐ̯ kʰaːm.
Lieb' ersticke nun die Scham, weil von ihm der Ruhm dir kam.
love stifle now the bashfulness, since from him the fame to you came.
(may love now stifle bashfulness, since fame came to you from him.)
[jɛt͜st] [liːɐ̯]
[*Müller:* **Lieb' ersticke jetzt die Scham, weil von ihr der Ruhm dir kam!**]
[now] [it (love)]

[In chapter XVII of Sir Walter Scott's novel *Ivanhoe* Richard the Lionhearted, king of England, having returned from the crusade, sings this song in a forest hermitage for Friar Tuck's entertainment, accompanying himself on the harp. Schubert's highly energetic accompaniment, however, suggests a pair of martial trumpets instead. Here is the poem, entitled "The Crusader's Return," in Scott's original words:

High deeds achieved of knightly fame, / From Palestine the champion came;
The cross upon his shoulders borne / Battle and blast had dimmed and torn.
Each dint upon his batter'd shield / Was token of a foughten field:
And thus beneath his lady's bower / He sung, as fell the twilight hour.
"Joy to the fair! — thy knight behold, / Return'd from yonder land of gold;
No wealth he brings, nor wealth can need, / Save his good arms and battle-steed;
His spurs, to dash against the foe, / His lance and sword to lay him low;
Such all the trophies of his toil, / Such — and the hope of Tekla's smile!
Joy to the fair! whose constant knight / Her favour fired to feats of might;
Unnoted shall she not remain, / Where meet the bright and noble train:
Minstrel shall sing and herald tell — / 'Mark yonder maid of beauty well;
'Tis she for whose bright eyes was won / The listed field of Askalon!'
Note well her smile! — it edged the blade / Which fifty wives to widows made.
Even vain his strength and Mahount's spell, / Iconium's turban'd Soldan fell.
Seest thou her locks, whose sunny glow / Half shows, half shades, her neck of snow?
Twines not of them one golden thread, / But for its sake a Paynim bled.
Joy to the fair! — my name unknown, / Each deed, and all its praise thine own;
Then oh, unbar this churlish gate, / The night dew falls, the hour is late.
Inured to Syria's glowing breath, / I feel the north breeze chill as death;
Let grateful love quell maiden shame, / And grant him bliss who brings thee fame."]

Rückblick see *Winterreise*

'rʏkʻveːkʻ
Rückweg
The Way Back

Posthumously published [composed 1816] (poem by Johann Mayrhofer)

t͜sʊm 'doːna͜oʃtʻroːm, t͜sʊr 'kʰa͜ezɐʃtʻatʻ geː ɪç ǀɪn 'baŋɪçkʰa͜etʰ:
Zum Donaustrom, zur Kaiserstadt geh' ich in Bangigkeit:
To the Danube-stream, to the emperor-city go I in anxiety:
(To the Danube, to the imperial city I go with a feeling of anxiety:)

dɛn vas das ˈleːbən ˈʃøːnəs hatʻ, lɛntʻˈva̯eçətʻ va̯etʻ lʊntʻ va̯etʰ. [lɛntʻˈʃvɪndətʻ]
denn was das Leben Schönes hat, entweichet weit und weit. [*poem:* **entschwindet]**
for what the life of beauty has, disappears far and far. [disappears]
(because whatever life holds of beauty is disappearing, far, far behind me.)

di ˈbɛrgə ˈʃvɪndən ˈlalgəmax, mɪtʻ ˈliːrən valtʻ lʊntʻ flʊs,
Die Berge schwinden allgemach, mit ihren Wald und Fluss,
The mountains vanish gradually, with them woods and river,
[*poem:* **weichen** (ˈva̯eçən, retreat) **allgemach... Tal** (tʰaːl, valley) **und Fluss]**

deːɐ̯ ˈkʰyːə ˈglɔkʻən ˈlɔ̯øtʻən naːx, lʊntʻ ˈhʏtʻən ˈnɪkʻən gruːs.
der Kühe Glocken läuten nach, und Hütten nicken Gruss.
the cows' bells sound after, and huts nod greeting.
(the cowbells tinkle after me, and huts nod a farewell greeting as I pass.)

vas ʃtʻart da̯en ˈla̯ogə ˈtʰrɛːnənfɔ̯øçtʻ hɪˈna̯os lɪn ˈbla̯oə fɛrn?
Was starrt dein Auge tränenfeucht hinaus in blaue Fern'?
What stares your eye tear- moist out into blue distance?
(Why do your eyes stare into the blue distance, moist with tears?)

ax, ˈdɔrtʻən va̯eltʻ ɪç, lʊnlɛɐ̯ˈra̯eçtʻ, fra̯e lʊntʻɐ ˈfra̯eən gɛrn.
Ach, dorten weilt' ich, unerreicht, frei unter Freien gern.
Ah, there stayed I, unreached, free among free people gladly.
(Ah, there I stayed happily, out of reach to the world of the city, free among free people.)

voː ˈliːbə nɔx lʊnt ˈtʰrɔ̯øə gɪltʰ, daː ˈlœfnətʻ zɪç das hɛrt͡s,
Wo Liebe noch und Treue gilt, da öffnet sich das Herz,
Where love still and loyalty is valid, there opens itself the heart,
(Where love and loyalty still mean something, there one's heart can open up;)

di frʊxtʻ lan ˈliːrən ˈʃtʻraːlən ʃvɪltʰ, lʊntʻ ˈʃtʻreːbətʻ ˈhɪməlvɛrt͡s.
die Frucht an ihren Strahlen schwillt, und strebet himmelwärts.
the fruit at its/their rays swells, and strives heavenward.
(spiritual fruit ripens and reaches toward heaven under the rays of love and loyalty.)

[The music is quite appealing; but, on first hearing and uninterpreted, the German words do not yield their full substance, unless one is familiar with the circumstances of the poet, Schubert's talented but melancholy friend, who was embittered by the increasing political repression in Vienna as he returned to the frustrations of the city after a free, happy interlude in the country.]

ˈzɛŋɐs ˈmɔrgənliːtʻ
Sängers Morgenlied
A Singer's Morning Song

Two versions, both posthumously published [composed 1815] (poem by Theodor Körner)

ˈzyːsəs lɪçtʻ! la̯os ˈgɔldnən ˈp͡fɔrtʻən brɪçst duː ˈziːgənt dʊrç di naxtʰ.
Süsses Licht! Aus gold'nen Pforten brichst du siegend durch die Nacht.
Sweet light! From golden gates break you conquering through the night.
(Sweet light! From golden gates you break through the night like a conqueror.)
[*Schubert's first version:* **goldenen** (ˈgɔldənən, golden)]

'ʃøːnɐ tʰaːk'! duː bɪst' lɛɐ̯'vaxtʰ. mɪt' gə'ha͜emnɪsfɔlən 'vɔrt'ən,
Schöner Tag! du bist erwacht. Mit geheimnisvollen Worten,
Beautiful day, you have awakened! With mysterious words,

ˈɪn me'loːdɪʃən la'kʰɔrdən, gryːs ɪç 'da͜enə 'roːzənpʰraxtʰ!
in melodischen Akkorden, grüss' ich deine Rosenpracht!
in melodious chords, greet I your rose- splendor!
(in melodious music, I greet your rosy splendor!)

ax! deːɐ̯ 'liːbə 'zanft'əs 'veːən ʃvɛlt' miːɐ̯ das bə'veːk't'ə hɛrt͜s,
Ach! der Liebe sanftes Wehen schwellt mir das bewegte Herz,
Ah! the love's gentle blowing swells for me the agitated heart,
(Ah, love's gentle breath swells my agitated heart,)

zanft', viː la͜en gə'liːp't'ɐ ʃmɛrt͜s. dʏrft' ɪç nuːɐ̯/nuːr la͜of 'gɔldnən 'høːən
sanft, wie ein geliebter Schmerz. Dürft' ich nur auf gold'nen Höhen
gently, like a beloved pain. Might I only on golden heights
(gently, like a beloved pain. Oh, if only, on golden heights, I could)

mɪç ɪm 'mɔrgənduft' lɛɐ̯'geːən! 'zeːnzuxt t͜siːt' mɪç 'hɪməlvɛrt͜s.
mich im Morgenduft ergehen! Sehnsucht zieht mich himmelwärts.
myself in the morning-fragrance stroll! Longing draws me heavenward.
(stroll in the fragrance of morning! Longing draws me heavenward.)

ʊnt deːɐ̯ 'zeːlə 'kʰyːnəs 'ʃt'reːbən tʰrɛːk't' ɪm 'ʃt'ɔlt͜sən 'riːzənla͜of
Und der Seele kühnes Streben trägt im stolzen Riesenlauf
And the soul's bold striving bears in the proud giant- run
(And in a proud, gigantic leap my soul's bold striving bears)

dʊrç di 'vɔlk'ən mɪç hɪ'na͜of. dɔx mɪt' 'zanft'əm 'ga͜est'ɐbeːbən
durch die Wolken mich hinauf. Doch mit sanftem Geisterbeben
through the clouds me up. Yet with gentle spirits- trembling
(me up through the clouds. Yet with a gentle trembling of spirits)

drɪŋk't das liːt' ɪns 'ɪnrə 'leːbən, løːst den ʃt'ʊrm me'loːdɪʃ la͜of.
dringt das Lied ins inn're Leben, löst den Sturm melodisch auf.
penetrates the song into the inner life, breaks the storm melodically up.
(the song penetrates into my inner life, dissolves the storm there into melody.)

foːɐ̯ den 'la͜ogən vɪrt' lɛs 'hɛlə; 'frɔ͜ønt'lɪç la͜of deːɐ̯ 't͜saːɐ̯t'ən ʃp'uːɐ̯
Vor den Augen wird es helle; freundlich auf der zarten Spur
Before the eyes becomes it bright; sympathetically on the delicate spoor
(Before my eyes all is growing bright; sympathetically following the delicate spoor of the song,)

veːt deːɐ̯/deːr 'la͜enkʰlaŋ deːɐ̯ na'tʰuːɐ̯, lʊnt' bə'ga͜est'ɐt' ra͜oʃt di 'kʰvɛlə,
weht der Einklang der Natur, und begeistert rauscht die Quelle,
wafts the concord of the nature, and enraptured murmurs the source,
(the harmony of Nature wafts along, and the bubbling spring murmurs in rapture,)

'mʊnt'ɐ tʰant͜st di 'flʏçt'gə 'vɛlə dʊrç dɛs 'mɔrgəns 'ʃt'ɪlə fluːɐ̯.
munter tanzt die flücht'ge Welle durch des Morgens stille Flur.
cheerfully dances the fleeting wave through the morning's quiet meadow.
(the fleeting wave dances cheerfully through the quiet meadow of the morning.)

ʊnt‘ fɔn 'zy:sɐ lʊst dʊrç'drʊŋən ve:p‘t‘ zɪç 't͡sa:ɐ̯t‘ə harmo'ni:
Und von süsser Lust durchdrungen webt sich zarte Harmonie
And by sweet pleasure penetrated weaves itself delicate harmony
(And, penetrated by sweet pleasure, delicate harmony weaves itself)

dʊrç dɛs 'le:bəns pʰoe'zi:. vas di 'ze:lə tʰi:f dʊrç'kʰlʊŋən,
durch des Lebens Poesie. Was die Seele tief durchklungen,
through the life's poetry. What the soul deeply (has) through-sounded,
(through the poetry of life. That which has sounded deeply through the soul,)

vas bə'rɑ͜oʃt de:ɐ̯ mʊnt‘ gə'zʊŋən, gly:t‘ ɪn 'ho:ɐ melo'di:.
was berauscht der Mund gesungen, glüht in hoher Melodie.
what intoxicated the mouth (has) sung, glows in sublime melody.
(that which, intoxicated, the mouth has sung, now glows in sublime melody.)

dɛs gə'zaŋəs 'mʊnt‘ɐn 'zø:nən va͜eçt‘ ɪm 'le:bən 'je:dɐ ʃmɛrt͡s,
Des Gesanges muntern Söhnen weicht im Leben jeder Schmerz,
(To) the song's cheerful sons yields in the life every pain,
(Every pain in life yields to the cheerful sons of song,)

ʊnt‘ nu:ɐ̯ 'li:bə ʃvɛlt‘ i:ɐ̯ hɛrt͡s. ɪn dɛs 'li:dəs 'ha͜elgən 'tʰø:nən
und nur Liebe schwellt ihr Herz. In des Liedes heil'gen Tönen
and only love swells their heart. In the song's holy tones
(and only love swells their hearts. In the holy tones of a song)

ʊnt‘ ɪm 'mɔrgənglant͡s dɛs 'ʃø:nən fli:k‘t di 'ze:lə 'hɪməlvɛrt͡s.
und im Morgenglanz des Schönen fliegt die Seele himmelwärts.
and in the morning-radiance of the beautiful flies the soul heavenward.
(and in the morning-radiance of the beautiful the soul flies toward heaven.)

[Schubert made two totally different settings of this poem within three days, the first fast and bubbling with charm and pearly runs, the second slow and calmly reflective.]

'ʃɛ:fɐs 'kʰla:gəli:t‘
Schäfers Klagelied
Shepherd's Lament

Op. 3, No. 1 [1814] (Johann Wolfgang von Goethe)

da: 'dro:bən ɑ͜of 'je:nəm 'bɛrgə, da: ʃt‘e: ɪç 'tʰɑ͜ozənt‘ma:l,
Da droben auf jenem Berge, da steh' ich tausendmal,
There up there on that mountain, there stand I (a) thousand times,
(Up there on that mountain I have stood a thousand times,)

an 'ma͜enəm 'ʃt‘a:bə 'hɪngəbo:gən, ʊnt‘ 'ʃɑ͜oə hɪ'nap‘ ɪn das tʰa:l. [gə'bo:gən]
an meinem Stabe hingebogen, und schaue hinab in das Tal. [*poem:* **gebogen**]
on my staff thither-bent, and look down into the valley. [bent]
(leaning on my crook, and looked down into the valley.)

dan fɔlg ɪç de:ɐ̯ 'va͜edəndən 'he:ɐ̯də, ma͜en 'hʏnt‘çən bə'va:rət‘ mi:ɐ̯ zi:;
Dann folg' ich der weidenden Herde, mein Hündchen bewahret mir sie;
Then follow I the grazing flock, my little dog guards for me it;
(Then I follow the grazing flock, which my little dog guards for me;)

ɪç bɪn heˈrʊntʻɐ gəˈkʰɔmən lʊntʻ va͜es dɔx ˈzɛlbɐ nɪçtʻ viː.
ich bin herunter gekommen und weiss doch selber nicht wie.
I am down come and know though myself not how.
(I have come down here, and I don't even know how myself.)

daː ˈʃtʻeːət fɔn ˈʃøːnən ˈbluːmən, daː ʃtʻeːt di ˈgant͜sə ˈviːzə zoː fɔl.
Da stehet von schönen Blumen, da steht die ganze Wiese so voll.
There stands of beautiful flowers, there stands the whole meadow so full.
(Here the whole meadow is so full of beautiful flowers.) [*1st version:* **steht** (*both times*)]
[*poem:* **Da stehet von schönen Blumen die ganze Wiese so voll.**]

ɪç ˈbrɛçə ziː, ˈloːnə t͜suː ˈvɪsən, veːm lɪç ziː ˈgeːbən zɔl.
Ich breche sie, ohne zu wissen, wem ich sie geben soll.
I pick them, without to know, to whom I them give shall.
(I pick them without knowing whom I can give them to.)

ʊntʻ ˈreːgən, ʃtʻʊrm lʊntʻ gəˈvɪtʻɐ fɛɐ̯ˈpʰas ɪç ˈlʊntʻɐ dem ba͜om.
Und Regen, Sturm und Gewitter verpass' ich unter dem Baum.
And rain, storm, and thunder pass I under the tree.
(And I sit out a rainy thunderstorm under the tree.)

di ˈtʰyːrə dɔrtʻ ˈbla͜ebətʻ fɛɐ̯ˈʃlɔsən; dɔx ˈlaləs lɪstʻ ˈla͜edɐ(r) la͜en tʰra͜om.
Die Türe dort bleibet verschlossen; doch alles ist leider ein Traum.
The door there remains locked; but all is unfortunately a dream.
(The door there remains locked; but, alas, it is all just a dream that brought me here.)
[*1st version:* **und** (ʊntʻ, and) **alles ist leider ein Traum**]

ɛs ˈʃtʻeːətʻ la͜en ˈreːgənboːgən voːl ˈlyːbɐ ˈjeːnəm ha͜os!
Es stehet ein Regenbogen wohl über jenem Haus!
There stands a rainbow to be sure above that house!
(To be sure, there is a rainbow over that house;)

ziː ˈlaːbɐ(r) lɪstʻ ˈfɔrtʻgət͜soːgən, lʊntʻ va͜etʻ lɪn das lantʻ hɪˈna͜os. [ˈvɛkgəˈt͜soːgən]
sie aber ist fortgezogen, und weit in das Land hinaus. [*poem:* **weggezogen**]
she however has left, and far into the country out. [moved away]
(but she has moved away, far out into the country.) [*1st version:* **gar** (gaːɐ̯, very) **weit**]

hɪˈna͜os lɪn das lantʻ lʊntʻ ˈva͜etʻɐ, fiˈla͜eçtʻ gaːɐ̯/gaːr ˈlyːbɐ di zeː.
Hinaus in das Land und weiter, vielleicht gar über die See.
Out into the country and farther, perhaps even over the sea.

foˈryːbɐ(r), liːɐ̯ ˈʃaːfə, nuːɐ̯ foˈryːbɐ! dem ˈʃɛːfɐ(r) lɪstʻ gaːɐ̯ zoː veː.
Vorüber, ihr Schafe, nur vorüber! Dem Schäfer ist gar so weh. [*poem without* **nur**]
Past, you sheep, just past! To the shepherd is entirely so aching.
(Let's pass this place, you sheep, just keep moving! Your shepherd is aching so badly.)

[Goethe wrote the poem to fit the melody of a folksong with the same opening words that happened to strike his fancy. Schubert's artful setting is one of those that was sent to the great poet, who failed to ackowledge them. The *Gesamtausgabe* prints a "first" version (so identified above) in E minor with a four-bar introduction and a "second" version in C minor. Apparently Schubert composed the song in C minor, then transposed it upwards and added the prelude for a public performance, the very first of any Schubert song. The date was February 28, 1819.]

ˈʃatsgrɛːbɐs bəˈgeːɐ̯
Schatzgräbers Begehr
The Treasure-Seeker's Desire

Op. 23, No. 4 [1822] (Franz von Schober)

ɪn ˈtʰiːfstɐ(r) ˈleːɐ̯də ruːtʻ la͡en ǀaltʻ gəˈzɛts, deːm tʰra͡epʻtʻ mɪçs ˈrastʻloːs ˈnaːxtsuʃpʻyːrən;
In tiefster Erde ruht ein alt Gesetz, dem treibt mich's rastlos nachzuspüren;
In deepest earth rests an old law, that drives me it restlessly to track down:
(Deep down in the earth an old law is buried; something drives me to track it down without rest;)

ʊntʻ ˈgraːbəntʻ kʰan ǀɪç ˈlandrəs nɪçtʻ fɔlˈfyːrən.
und grabend kann ich Andres nicht vollführen.
and digging can I anything else not carry out.
(and when I am digging for it I can accomplish nothing else.)

voːl ʃpʻantʻ ǀa͡ox miːɐ̯ di vɛltʻ ǀiːɐ̯ ˈgɔldnəs nɛts,
Wohl spannt auch mir die Welt ihr goldnes Netz,
To be sure, spreads also for me the world its golden net,
(To be sure, for me too the world spreads out its golden net;)

voːl tʰøːntʻ ǀa͡ox miːɐ̯ deːɐ̯ ˈkʰluːkʻha͡etʻ za͡eçtʻ gəˈʃvɛts:
wohl tönt auch mir der Klugheit seicht Geschwätz:
to be sure, sounds also to me the prudence's shallow chatter:
(to be sure, the shallow chatter of common sense rings in *my* ears too:)

duː vɪrst di myː ǀʊnt tsa͡etʻ ǀʊmˈzɔnstʻ fɛɐ̯ˈliːrən!
"Du wirst die Müh' und Zeit umsonst verlieren!"
"You will the effort and time in vain lose!"
("You will waste the effort and the time for nothing!")

das zɔl mɪç nɪçtʻ ǀɪn ˈma͡enɐ(r) ˈǀarba͡etʻ ˈǀɪrən; ǀɪç ˈgraːbə ˈglyːəntʻ fɔrtʰ,
Das soll mich nicht in meiner Arbeit irren; ich grabe glühend fort,
That shall me not in my work mislead; I dig fervently forth,
(But that shall not mislead me in my work; I shall keep digging, fervently,)

[das ˈhɛmə nɪçtʻ ma͡en ˈǀɛmzɪgəs hanˈtʰiːrən]
[*poem:* **Das hemme nicht mein emsiges Hantiren, ich grabe...**]
[That let hinder not my diligent operating]
[(Let that not hinder my diligent task, I shall keep digging fervently,)]

zoː nuːn, viː ʃtʻeːts. ǀʊntʻ zɔl mɪç niː dɛs ˈfɪndəns ˈvɔnə ˈlaːbən,
so nun, wie stets. Und soll mich nie des Findens Wonne laben,
so now, as always. And shall me never the finding's joy refresh,
(now as always. And if the joy of discovery never will reward me,)

zɔltʻ ɪç ma͡en graːpʻ mɪt ˈdiːzɐ ˈhɔfnʊŋ ˈgraːbən,
sollt' ich mein Grab mit dieser Hoffnung graben,
should I my grave with this hope dig,
(if I should be digging my *grave* with this hope,)

ɪç ˈʃtʻa͜egə gɛrn hɪˈnapʻ, gəˈʃtʻɪltʻ ɪst dan ma͜en ˈzeːnən.
ich steige gern hinab, gestillt ist dann mein Sehnen.
I climb gladly down, stilled is then my longing.
(then I shall gladly climb down into it; my longing will at least be stilled.)
[ɛs lœʃt di ˈflamən dɔx, diː ˈmartʻɐntʻ ˈbrɛnən.]
[*poem:* **es löscht die Flammen doch, die marternd brennen.]**
[it extinguishes the flames, after all, which tormentingly burn.]

drʊm ˈlasətʻ ˈruːə miːɐ̯/miːr ɪn ˈma͜enəm ˈʃtʻreːbən!
Drum lasset Ruhe mir in meinem Streben!
Therefore leave peace to me in my striving!
(Therefore leave me to my endeavor in peace!)

a͜en graːpʻ maːkʻ man voːl ˈjeːdəm ˈgɛrnə ˈgeːbən, [dɔx]
Ein Grab mag man wohl jedem gerne geben, [*poem:* **mag man doch]**
A grave may one no doubt to everyone gladly give, [surely]
(No doubt one may willingly give a grave to anyone;)

vɔltʻ iːɐ̯ ɛs dɛn nɪçtʻ miːɐ̯/miːr, iːɐ̯ ˈliːbən, ˈgœnən?
wollt ihr es denn nicht mir, ihr Lieben, gönnen? [*poem:* **es mir denn nicht]**
would you it then not to me, you dear people, not begrudge?
(would you then begrudge *me* one, dear people?)

[Schubert's powerful and fascinating music lifts his friend's enigmatic and sometimes awkward poem to a higher level, as he portrays a man who vigorously pursues his vision in a task that may never accomplish its goal, ignoring the temptations, incomprehension, and ridicule of the world.]

ˈʃɪfɐs ˈʃa͜edəliːtʻ

Schiffers Scheidelied

A Sailor's Song of Farewell

Posthumously published [composed 1827] (poem by Franz von Schober)

di ˈvoːgən am gəˈʃtʻaːdə ˈʃvɛlən, ɛs kʰlatʃt deːɐ̯ vɪntʻ ɪm ˈzeːgəltʰuːx,
Die Wogen am Gestade schwellen, es klatscht der Wind im Segeltuch,
The waves at the shore swell, there chats the wind in the sailcloth,
(The waves are swelling, down at the shore; the wind chatters in the canvas sails)

ʊntʻ ˈmʊrməltʻ ɪn den ˈva͜esən ˈvɛlən; ɪç ˈhøːrə ˈza͜enən ˈvɪldən ʃpʻrʊx.
und murmelt in den weissen Wellen; ich höre seinen wilden Spruch.
and murmurs in the white waves; I hear its wild verdict.

ɛs ruːftʻ mɪç fɔrtʻ, ɛs vɪŋkʻt deːɐ̯ kʰaːn, foːɐ̯/foːr ˈʊngədʊltʻ ˈʃa͜okʻəlntʻ,
Es ruft mich fort, es winkt der Kahn, vor Ungeduld schaukelnd,
Something calls me forth, there beckons the boat, in impatience rocking,
(Something is calling me away; the boat is beckoning, rocking in its impatience,)
[*poem:* **Er** (eːɐ̯, it–*masc., for "Spruch"*) **ruft...es winkt mir** (miːrɐ̯, to me) **der Kahn]**

a͜of ˈva͜etʻə baːn. dɔrtʻ ʃtʻrɛkʻtʻ zi zɪç ɪn ˈløːdɐ ˈfɛrnə, duː kʰanstʻ nɪçtʻ
auf weite Bahn. Dort streckt sie sich in öder Ferne, du kannst nicht
onto broad way. There stretches it itself into empty distance, you can not (come)
(onto the vast pathway of the sea. There it stretches out into the empty distance, you can't come)

mɪt‘, ziːst duː, ma͜en kʰɪnt‘. viː la͜eçt‘ fɛɐ̯ˈzɪŋk‘ən ˈma͜enə ˈʃt‘ɛrnə, viː la͜eçt‘
mit, siehst du, mein Kind. Wie leicht versinken meine Sterne, wie leicht
with (me), see you, my child. How easily set my stars, how easily
(with me, you see, my child. How easily my stars may set, how easily)

|ɛɐ̯ˈvɛkst t͜sʊm ʃt‘ʊrm deːɐ̯ vɪnt‘. dan droːt‘ |ɪn ˈtʰa͜ozənt‘ gəˈʃt‘alt‘ən deːɐ̯ tʰoːt‘;
erwächst zum Sturm der Wind. Dann droht in tausend Gestalten der Tod;
grows to the storm the wind. Then threatens in thousand forms the death;
(the wind can grow to a storm! Then death threatens in a thousand forms;)

viː tʰrɔt͜st‘ |ɪç |iːm, vʏst‘ |ɪç dɪç |ɪn noːtʰ? |oː ˈ|øːzə ˈda͜enɐ(r) ˈ|armə ˈʃlɪŋə
wie trotzt’ ich ihm, wüsst’ ich dich in Not? O löse deiner Arme Schlinge
how defied I it, knew I you in danger? O loosen your arms’ noose
(how would I be able to defy it, if I knew you were in danger? Oh, loosen the noose of your arms)

|ʊnt‘ ˈ|øːzə |a͜ox fɔn miːɐ̯ da͜en hɛrt͜s; va͜es |ɪç |ɛs dɛn, |ɔp‘ |ɪçs fɔlˈbrɪŋə
und löse auch von mir dein Herz; weiss ich es denn, ob ich’s vollbringe
and untie also from me your heart; know I it then, whether I it accomplish
(and untie your heart too from me; do I know whether I can accomplish what I attempt)
[*Peters:* **weiss ich denn**]

ʊnt‘ ˈziːk‘ra͜eç ˈkʰeːrə ˈha͜emaːt‘vɛrt͜s? di ˈvɛlə, diː jɛt͜st‘ zoː ˈlɔk‘ənt‘ zɪŋt‘,
und siegreich kehre heimatwärts? Die Welle, die jetzt so lockend singt,
and victoriously turn homeward? The wave, which now so enticingly sings,
(and turn homeward victoriously? The wave that is singing now so enticingly)

fiˈla͜eçt‘ |ɪst͜s diˈzɛlbə, diː mɪç fɛɐ̯ˈʃlɪŋtʰ. nɔx |ɪst͜s |ɪn ˈda͜enə hant‘ gəˈgeːbən,
vielleicht ist’s dieselbe, die mich verschlingt. Noch ist’s in deine Hand gegeben,
perhaps is it the same, which me swallows. Still is it into your hand given,
(is perhaps the same that will swallow me up. The decision is still in your hands,)

nɔx gɪŋst duː nɪçt͜s |ʊnˈløːsbaːɐ̯/-baːr |a͜en, |oː ˈtʰrɛnə ʃnɛl da͜en ˈjʊŋəs ˈleːbən
noch gingst du nichts unlösbar ein, o trenne schnell dein junges Leben
yet went you nothing inextricably into, O separate quickly your young life
(you have not entered into anything inextricably yet; Oh, quickly separate your young life)

fɔn ˈma͜enəm ˈ|ʊngəvɪsən za͜en, |oː ˈvɔlə, |oː ˈvɔlə, bəˈfoːɐ̯ duː mʊst‘,
von meinem ungewissen Sein, o wolle, o wolle, bevor du musst,
from my uncertain existence, O want, O want, before you must,
(from my uncertain existence. Do so voluntarily—before you are *forced* to!)
[*poem:* **o wolle, wolle, bevor du musst**]

|ɛnt‘ˈzaːgʊŋ |ɪst‘ ˈla͜eçt‘ɐ(r) |als fɛɐ̯ˈlʊstʰ!
Entsagung ist leichter als Verlust!
resignation is easier than loss!
(resignation is easier to bear than loss!)

oː las mɪç |ɪm bəˈvʊst‘za͜en ˈʃt‘ɔ͜øɐn, das |ɪç |aˈla͜en |a͜of ˈleːɐ̯dən bɪn,
O lass mich im Bewusstsein steuern, dass ich allein auf Erden bin,
O let me in the consciousness steer, that I alone on earth am,
(Oh, let me steer my course in the consciousness that I am alone on earth,)
[*poem:* **Und** (ʊnt‘, and) **lass mich**]

dan bɔ͡øk‘t‘ zɪç foːɐ̯ dem lʊngəˈhɔ͡øɐn, foːɐ̯m ˈlʊnlɛɐ̯høːɐ̯t‘ən nɪçt‘ ma͡en zɪn.
dann beugt sich vor dem Ungeheuern, vorm Unerhörten nicht mein Sinn.
then bends itself before the monstrous, before the unheard of not my mind.
(then my mind will not falter when faced with monstrous, unknown dangers.)

ɪç ˈtʰra͡ebə mɪt dem lɛnt‘ˈzɛt͡sən ʃp‘iːl lʊnt‘ ˈʃt‘eːə ˈpʰlœt͡slɪç fiˈla͡eçt‘ lam t͡siːl.
Ich treibe mit dem Entsetzen Spiel und stehe plötzlich vielleicht am Ziel.
I carry on with the horror (a) game and stand suddenly perhaps at the goal.
(I shall play a game with horror as my opponent, and perhaps suddenly find myself at my goal.)

dɛn hoːx la͡of ˈma͡enɐ ˈmast‘ə ˈʃp‘ɪt͡sən vɪrt ʃt‘eːt͡s da͡en bɪlt‘ bəˈga͡est‘ɐnt‘ ʃt‘eːn,
Denn hoch auf meiner Maste Spitzen wird stets dein Bild begeisternd steh'n,
For high on my masts' tips will always your image inspiringly stand,
(For your image will always be like a pennant flying from my masthead, inspiring me,)
[*GA:* **auf meiner Masten** (ˈmast‘ən, masts'–*different form of plural*) **Spitzen**]

ʊnt‘, ˈlangəflamət‘ fɔn den ˈblɪt͡sən, mɪt‘ ˈza͡enəm glant͡s den muːt‘ lɛɐ̯ˈhøːn;
und, angeflammet von den Blitzen, mit seinem Glanz den Mut erhöh'n;
and, at-flamed by the lightnings, with its radiance the courage lift;
(and, illuminated by lightning flashes, it will lift my courage with its radiance;)

deːɐ̯ ˈvɪndə ˈhɔ͡ølən, la͡ox nɔx zoː baŋ, lyːbɐˈtʰɔ͡øbət‘ nɪçt ˈda͡enɐ ˈʃt‘ɪmə kʰlaŋ.
der Winde Heulen, auch noch so bang, übertäubet nicht deiner Stimme Klang.
the winds' howling, even still so fearful, drowns out not your voice's sound.
(the howling of the winds, however fearful, will not drown out the sound of your voice.)
[ʊnt‘] [di] [ziː lyːbɐˈtʰɔ͡øbən]
[*poem:* **Und heulen die Winde auch noch so bang, sie übertäuben nicht**]
[And howl (*verb*) the] [they drown out not]

ʊnt‘ kʰan lɪç dɪç nuːɐ̯ zeːn lʊnt‘ ˈhøːrən, dan hat͡s mɪt‘ miːɐ̯ nɔx ˈkʰa͡enə noːtʰ,
Und kann ich dich nur seh'n und hören, dann hat's mit mir noch keine Not,
And can I you only see and hear, then has it with me still no emergency,
(And as long as I can see you and hear you, then I am not yet in urgent trouble,)
[*poem:* **so** (zoː, then) **hat's mit mir**]

das ˈleːbən vɪl lɪç nɪçt‘ lɛnt‘ˈbeːrən, lʊnt‘ ˈkʰɛmp͡fən vɪl lɪç mɪt dem tʰoːt‘.
das Leben will ich nicht entbehren, und kämpfen will ich mit dem Tod.
the life want I not to be deprived of, and fight want I with the death.
(then I shall not want to lose my life, and I shall want to fight with death.)

viː ˈvʏrdə miːɐ̯/miːr ˈla͡enə vɛlt t͡sʊr last,
Wie würde mir eine Welt zur Last,
How would become to me a world to the burden,
(How could a world become burdensome to me)
[*poem:* **Wie würde mir je** (jeː, ever) **eine Welt**]

diː ˈlɛŋəl zoː ʃøːn viː dɪç lʊmˈfastʰ? la͡ox duː zɔlst‘ nɪçt‘ ma͡en bɪlt t͡sɛɐ̯ˈʃlaːgən,
die Engel so schön wie dich umfasst? Auch du sollst nicht mein Bild zerschlagen,
which angels as lovely as you contains? Also you shall not my image destroy,
(that contains angels as lovely as you? You too should not destroy my image either;)

mɪt‘ ˈfrɔ͜ønt‘ʃaftsthrɛːnən vae lɛs laen, lɛs zɔl lɪn ʃmɛrts lʊnt‘ ˈfrɔ͜ødətha:gən
mit Freundschaftstränen weih' es ein, es soll in Schmerz- und Freudetagen
with friendship- tears consecrate it ..., it shall in pain and joy- days
(consecrate it with tears of friendship; in days of sorrow and joy it shall)
[*poem:* **Freudentagen** (ˈfrɔ͜ødənthaːgən, days of joys); *einweihen* = consecrate]

daen thro:st‘ lʊnt daen fɛɐ̯ˈthrɑot‘ɐ zaen. ja: ˈblaebə, vɛn mɪç lɑox ˈlaləs fɛɐ̯ˈli:s,
dein Trost und dein Vertrauter sein. Ja bleibe, wenn mich auch alles verliess,
your comfort and your confidant be. By all means remain, if me even all forsakes,
(be your comfort and your confidant. Even if all else forsakes me, by all means remain)

maen frɔ͜ønt‘ lɪm ˈhaemɪʃən pharaˈdi:s.
mein Freund im heimischen Paradies.
my friend in the native paradise.
(my friend in that paradise that has been my homeland.)

ʊnt‘ ʃp‘y:lt dan lɑox di ˈfalʃə ˈvɛlə mɪç tho:t tsuˈrʏk‘ tsʊm ˈblu:mənʃt‘rant‘,
Und spült dann auch die falsche Welle mich tot zurück zum Blumenstrand,
And washes then even the treacherous wave me dead back to the flower- shore,
(And then even if a treacherous wave washes my dead body back to that flowery shore,)

zo: vaes lɪç dɔx lan ˈli:bɐ ˈʃt‘ɛlə nɔx ˈlaenə, ˈlaenə ˈthrɔ͜øə hant‘,
so weiss ich doch an lieber Stelle noch eine, eine treue Hand,
then know I at least at dear place yet one, one faithful hand
(then at least I shall know that at that dear place there will still be one, *one* faithful hand)

de:ɐ̯ ˈve:dɐ fɛɐ̯-/fɛrˈlaxt‘ʊŋ nɔx ʃmɛrts lɛs ve:ɐ̯t‘,
der weder Verachtung noch Schmerz es wehrt,
to which neither contempt nor sorrow it prevents,
(that neither contempt nor sorrow will prevent)

das zi: ˈmaenən ˈrɛst‘ən laen gra:p bəˈʃe:ɐ̯th.
dass sie meinen Resten ein Grab beschert.
that it [the hand] to my remains a grave gives.
(from giving my remains a decent burial.)

[The stormy accompaniment suggests the wind and the waves and the depth of the sea, as well as the agitation of the young sailor as he takes a serious leave of his girl, telling us much about himself as he does so. The poet was one of the composer's closest friends; Schober took Schubert in when his father turned him out of the house, and again later in his all too short life.]

ˈʃlaxt‘gəzaŋ
Schlachtgesang
Battle Song

Posthumously published [composed 1816] (poem by Friedrich Gottlieb Klopstock)

mɪt‘ ˈlʊnzɐm larm lɪst‘ nɪçts gəˈtha:n, ʃt‘e:t‘ lʊns de:ɐ̯ ˈmɛçt‘ɪgə nɪçt‘ bae,
Mit unserm Arm ist nichts getan, steht uns der Mächtige nicht bei,
With our arm is nothing done, stands us the Mighty One not by,
(Our own strength can accomplish nothing, unless the Almighty is with us,)

deːɐ̯/deːr ˈǀaləs ˈǀa͡osfyːɐ̯tʰ! ǀʊmˈzɔnst‘ ǀɛntˈflamt‘ ǀʊns ˈkʰyːnɐ muːt‘,
der Alles ausführt! Umsonst entflammt uns kühner Mut,
who all works out! In vain inflames us bold courage,
(who determines everything! In vain are we fired by bold courage,)

vɛn ǀʊns deːɐ̯ ziːk‘ fɔn deːm nɪçt‘ vɪrt, deːɐ̯/deːr ˈǀaləs ˈǀa͡osfyːɐ̯tʰ!
wenn uns der Sieg von Dem nicht wird, der Alles ausführt!
if to us the victory from Him not will (come), who all works out!
(if victory will not come to us from Him, who determines everything!)

fɛɐ̯ˈgeːbəns ˈfliːsət‘ ˈǀʊnzɐ bluːt‘ fyːɐ̯s ˈfaːt‘ɐlant‘, vɛn deːɐ̯ nɪçt‘ hɪlft‘,
Vergebens fliesset unser Blut fürs Vaterland, wenn Der nicht hilft,
In vain flows our blood for the fatherland, if He not helps,
(In vain our blood will flow for the fatherland, if He does not help,)

deːɐ̯/deːr ˈǀaləs ˈǀa͡osfyːɐ̯tʰ! fɛɐ̯ˈgeːbəns ˈʃt‘ɛrbən viːɐ̯ den tʰoːt‘ fyːɐ̯s ˈfaːt‘ɐlant‘,
der Alles ausführt! Vergebens sterben wir den Tod fürs Vaterland,
who all works out! In vain die we the death for the fatherland,
(He who determines everything! In vain we die the death for the fatherland,)

vɛn deːɐ̯ nɪçt‘ hɪlft, deːɐ̯/deːr ˈǀaləs ˈǀa͡osfyːɐ̯tʰ! ʃt‘røːm hɪn, ǀoː bluːt‘,
wenn Der nicht hilft, der Alles ausführt! Ström' hin, o Blut,
if He not helps, who all works out! Stream forth, O blood,
(if He does not help, He who determines everything! Stream forth, O blood,)

ǀʊnt tʰøːt‘, ǀoː tʰoːt‘ fyːɐ̯s ˈfaːt‘ɐlant‘! viːɐ̯ ˈtʰra͡oən deːm,
und töt', o Tod fürs Vaterland! Wir trauen Dem,
and kill, O death for the fatherland! We trust in Him,

deːɐ̯/deːr ˈǀaləs ˈǀa͡osfyːɐ̯tʰ! ǀa͡of, ǀɪn den ˈflaməndamp͡f hɪˈna͡en!
der Alles ausführt! Auf, in den Flammendampf hinein!
who all works out! Up, into the flame- steam into!
(who determines everything! Up! Into the flames and smoke!)

viːɐ̯ ˈǀɛçəlt‘ən dem ˈtʰoːdə t͡suː ǀʊnt‘ ˈǀɛçəln, fa͡ent‘, ǀɔ͡øç t͡suː!
Wir lächelten dem Tode zu und lächeln, Feind', euch zu!
We smiled to the death at and smile, enemy, you at!
(We smiled at death, and we are smiling at you, enemy!)

deːɐ̯ tʰant͡s, deːn ˈǀʊnzrə ˈtʰrɔməl ʃlɛːk‘t, deːɐ̯ ˈǀa͡ot‘ə, ˈʃøːnə ˈkʰriːgəstʰant͡s,
Der Tanz, den unsre Trommel schlägt, der laute, schöne Kriegestanz,
The dance, that our drum beats, the loud, beautiful war- dance,
(The dance that our drum is beating, that loud, beautiful dance of war,)

eːɐ̯ ˈtʰant͡sət‘ hɪn naːx ǀɔ͡øç! diː dɔrt tʰrɔmˈpʰeːt‘ən, ˈha͡oət‘ ǀa͡en,
er tanzet hin nach euch! Die dort trompeten, hauet ein,
it dances hence after you! Those who there trumpet, hew into,
(will dance along with you! Those playing the trumpet there, attack) [*einhauen* = attack, charge]

voː ˈǀʊnzɐ ˈroːt‘ɐ ʃt‘aːl das tʰoːɐ̯/tʰoːr ǀɔ͡øç va͡et‘ hat‘ ˈǀa͡ofgətʰaːn!
wo unser roter Stahl das Tor euch weit hat aufgetan!
where our red steel the gate for you wide has opened!
(where our bloodied steel has opened the gate wide for you!)

den flu:k‘, de:n di tʰrɔmˈpʰe:t‘ə blɛ:st, den ˈlɑ͜ot‘ən, ˈʃø:nən ˈkʰri:gəsflu:k,
Den Flug, den die Trompete bläst, den lauten, schönen Kriegesflug,
The flight, which the trumpet blows, the loud, beautiful war- flight,
(The call to fly that the trumpet is blowing, that loud, beautiful call to fly into battle, to charge,)

fli:k‘t‘, fli:k‘t‘ li:n ʃnɛl hɪˈna͜en! vo: ˈlʊnzrə ˈfa:nən ˈfo:ɐ̯vɛrt͜s ve:n,
fliegt, fliegt ihn schnell hinein! Wo unsre Fahnen vorwärts weh'n,
fly, fly it quickly into! Where our banners forward flutter,
(let it fly quickly through that gate! Where our banners are fluttering forward,)

da: ve: lɑ͜ox di ʃt‘anˈdart‘ hɪˈna͜en, da: ˈzi:gə rɔs lʊnt‘ man!
da weh' auch die Standart' hinein, da siege Ross und Mann!
there may wave also the standard into, there may triumph horse and man!
(may our standard of victory also wave there, may horse and man triumph there!)

ze:t‘ li:ɐ̯ den ˈho:ən ˈva͜esən hu:tʰ? ze:t‘ li:ɐ̯ das ˈlɑ͜ofgəho:bnə ʃve:ɐ̯t?
Seht ihr den hohen weissen Hut? Seht ihr das aufgehobne Schwert?
See you the high white hat? See you the raised sword?
(Do you see that high white hat? Do you see that raised sword,)

dɛs ˈfɛlt‘hɛrn hu:t‘ lʊnt‘ ʃve:ɐ̯tʰ? fɛrn ˈlɔrdnət‘ le:ɐ̯ di ˈkʰy:nə ʃlaxt‘,
des Feldherrn Hut und Schwert? Fern ordnet' er die kühne Schlacht,
the commander-in-chief's hat and sword? Far away orders he the bold battle,
(the hat and sword of our commander-in-chief? From afar he orders the bold battle;)

lʊnt‘ ˈjɛt͜so, da:s lɛnt‘ˈʃa͜edʊŋ gɪlt, tʰu:t‘ le:ɐ̯s dem ˈtʰo:də na:.
und jetzo, da's Entscheidung gilt, tut er's dem Tode nah.
and now, when it decision calls for, does he it to the death near.
(and now, at the decisive moment, he does so close to the zone of death.)

dʊrç li:n lʊnt‘ lʊns lɪst‘ nɪçt͜s gəˈtʰa:n, ʃt‘e:t‘ lʊns de:ɐ̯ ˈmɛçt‘ɪgə nɪçt‘ ba͜e,
Durch ihn und uns ist nichts getan, steht uns der Mächtige nicht bei,
Through him and us is nothing done, stands us the Mighty One not by,
(Nothing is accomplished through him or through us, unless the Almighty is with us,)

de:ɐ̯/de:r ˈlaləs ˈlɑ͜osfy:ɐ̯tʰ! dɔrt dampft‘ lɛs nɔx. hɪˈna͜en, hɪˈna͜en!
der Alles ausführt! Dort dampft es noch. Hinein, hinein!
who all works out! There steams it yet. Into, into!
(who determines everything! The battle is still smoking there: go on! Get into it!)

vi:ɐ̯ ˈlɛçəlt‘ən dem ˈtʰo:də t͜su: lʊnt‘ ˈlɛçəln, fa͜ent‘, lɔ͜øç t͜su:!
Wir lächelten dem Tode zu und lächeln, Feind', euch zu!
We smiled to the death at and smile, enemy, you at!
(We smiled at death, and we are smiling at you, enemy!)

[This martial song, marked "fiery, fast" and *fortissimo*, is clearly not a *Lied*, although it is included among the lieder in the *Gesamtausgabe*. It is notated as a partsong, and in 1827 Schubert arranged it for a performance with double chorus. The poem is entitled *Schlachtlied*. It describes in poetic terms a typical 18th-century battle: the infantry column marches with fixed bayonets into the smoke of battle to the beat of the drum; then, at the trumpet signal, the cavalry starts its attack; then, at "*Hinein! Hinein!*" the rest of the troops join the furious fighting.]

'ʃlaːfliːt' / 'ʃlʊmɐliːt'
Schlaflied / Schlummerlied
Lullaby / Slumber Song

Op. 24, No. 2 [1817] (Johann Mayrhofer)

ɛs maːnt deːɐ̯ valt', lɛs ruːft deːɐ̯ ʃt'roːm: duː 'liːbəs 'byːp'çən, tsuː lʊns kʰɔm!
Es mahnt der Wald, es ruft der Strom: "Du liebes Bübchen, zu uns komm!"
There exhorts the woods, there calls the stream: "You dear little boy, to us come!"
(The woods are summoning you, the river is calling: "Dear little boy, come to us!")
[*poem:* **Du holdes** ('hɔldəs, lovely) **Bübchen]**

deːɐ̯ 'kʰnaːbə kʰɔmt', lʊnt' 'ʃt'ɑ͜ʊnənt' va͜elt', lʊnt' lɪst' fɔn 'jeːdəm ʃmɛrts gə'ha͜eltʰ.
Der Knabe kommt, und staunend weilt, und ist von jedem Schmerz geheilt.
The boy comes, and being astonished lingers, and is from every pain healed.
(The boy comes, and lingers in astonishment; and he is cured of every pain.)
[*GA & poem:* **und staunt** (ʃt'ɑ͜ʊnt', is astonished)**, und weilt]**
[*poem:* **Der Knabe naht** (naːt', approaches)**; von allem** ('laləm, all) **Schmerz]**

ɑ͜ʊs 'bʏʃən 'fløːt'ət' 'vaxt'əlʃlaːk', mɪt' 'lɪrən 'farbən ʃp'iːlt deːɐ̯ tʰaːk',
Aus Büschen flötet Wachtelschlag, mit irren Farben spielt der Tag,
From Bushes flutes quail- song, with confused colors plays the day,
(The quail's flute-like song wafts from the bushes, the day plays with confused colors,)
[*GA & poem:* **Aus Saaten** ('zaːt'ən, standing corn)**]**
[*Peters (error):* **mit ihren** ('liːrən, their) **Farben]**
[*poem:* **mit irren Lichtern** ('lɪçt'ɐn, lights)**]**

ɑ͜ʊf 'blyːmçən roːt', lɑ͜ʊf 'blyːmçən blɑ͜ʊ lɛɐ̯'glɛntst dɛs 'hɪməls 'fɔ͜øçt'ɐ tʰɑ͜ʊ.
auf Blümchen rot, auf Blümchen blau erglänzt des Himmels feuchter Tau.
on little flowers red, on little flowers blue gleams the heaven's moist dew.
(the moist dew of heaven sparkles on little red and blue flowers.)
[ʊnt' lɑ͜ʊf den 'blyːmla͜en lɪn deːɐ̯/deːr lɑ͜ʊ]
[*poem:* **und auf den Blümlein in der Au]**
[and on the little flowers in the meadow]

ɪns 'frɪʃə graːs leːk't' leːɐ̯ zɪç hɪn: lɛst' 'lyːbɐ zɪç di 'vɔlk'ən tsiːn —
Ins frische Gras legt er sich hin: lässt über sich die Wolken zieh'n —
Into the fresh grass lays he himself down: lets over himself the clouds drift —
(He lies down in the fresh grass and lets the clouds drift over him —)
[*poem:* **Ins hohe** ('hoːə, high) **Gras]**

an 'za͜enə 'mʊt'ɐ(r) 'langəʃmiːk't' hat' liːn deːɐ̯ 'tʰrɑ͜ʊmgɔt' 'la͜engəviːk'tʰ.
an seine Mutter angeschmiegt hat ihn der Traumgott eingewiegt.
against his mother nestled has him the dream-god lulled to sleep.
(the god of dreams has lulled him to sleep, nestled against his mother.)
[*poem:* **an Mutter Erde** ('mʊt'ɐ(r) 'leːɐ̯də, Mother Earth) **angeschmiegt]**

[The version of this song first published in 1823 was actually Schubert's revision in 12/8 time of an earlier effort in 2/2, composed in 1817. The harmony is identical, the melody virtually the same except for some details of rhythm. The first version bore the title *Abendlied.* Both can be found in the *Neue Schubert Ausgabe*, Lieder, Volume 2. The Peters title is *Schlummerlied.*]

'ʃvaːnəngəzaŋ

Schwanengesang

Swan Song (Cycle)

Fourteen songs, posthumously published as Schubert's "Swan Song" [composed 1828]
(seven poems by Ludwig Rellstab, six by Heinrich Heine, and one by Johann Gabriel Seidl)

1. (Ludwig Rellstab)

'liːbəsboːt'ʃafth

Liebesbotschaft

Message of Love

'raoʃəndəs 'bɛçlaen, zoː 'zɪlbɐn lʊnt' hɛl, laelst tsʊr gə'liːp't'ən
Rauschendes Bächlein, so silbern und hell, eilst zur Geliebten
Murmuring brooklet, so silvery and bright, hurry to the beloved [female]
(Murmuring brooklet, so silvery and bright, are you hurrying to my beloved)

zoː 'mʊnt'ɐ(r) lʊnt' ʃnɛl? lax, 'thraot'əs 'bɛçlaen, maen 'boːt'ə zae duː;
so munter und schnell? Ach, trautes Bächlein, mein Bote sei du;
so cheerfully and quickly? Ah, dear brooklet, my messenger be you;
(so cheerfully and so quickly? Ah, dear brooklet, be my messenger,)
[*Peters:* **mein Bote bist** (bɪst, are) **du**]

'brɪŋə di 'gryːsə dɛs 'fɛrnən liːɐ tsuː. lal 'liːrə 'bluːmən lɪm 'gart'ən gə'pfleːk'th,
bringe die Grüsse des Fernen ihr zu. All' ihre Blumen im Garten gepflegt,
bring the greetings of the distant one to her to. All her flowers in the garden tended,
(bring her the greetings of her far away friend. All of the flowers that she tends in the garden,)

diː ziː zoː 'liːp'lɪç lam 'buːzən thrɛːk'th, lʊnt' 'liːrə 'roːzən lɪn 'phʊrp'ʊrnɐ gluːt',
die sie so lieblich am Busen trägt, und ihre Rosen in purpurner Glut,
which she so charmingly on the bosom wears, and her roses in purple fire,
(and wears so charmingly on her bosom, and her roses that glow with a purple fire,)

'bɛçlaen, lɛɐ'khvɪk'ə mɪt' 'khyːləndɐ fluːth. vɛn ziː lam 'luːfɐ(r), [van]
Bächlein, erquicke mit kühlender Flut. Wenn sie am Ufer, [*Schubert MS:* **Wann**]
brooklet, refresh with cooling flood. If she on the bank, [When]
(refresh them, brooklet, with your cooling waters. If on your banks she)

lɪn 'thrɔømə fɛɐ'zɛŋk'th, 'maenɐ gə'dɛŋk'ənt das 'khœpfçən hɛŋth,
in Träume versenkt, meiner gedenkend das Köpfchen hängt,
in dreams sunk, of me thinking the little head hangs,
(hangs her little head, sunk in dreams and thinking of me,)

'thrøːst'ə di 'zyːsə mɪt' 'frɔønt'lɪçəm blɪkh, dɛn deːɐ gə'liːp't'ə
tröste die Süsse mit freundlichem Blick, denn der Geliebte
comfort the sweet one [female] with friendly look, for the beloved one [male]
(comfort the sweet girl with a friendly look, for her beloved)

kheːɐt' balt tsu'rʏkh. naek't' zɪç di 'zɔnə mɪt' 'røːt'lɪçəm ʃaen,
kehrt bald zurück. Neigt sich die Sonne mit rötlichem Schein,
turns soon back. Bends itself the sun with reddish gleam,
(will soon return. If the sun is setting with a reddish gleam,)

ˈviːɡə das ˈliːpʻçən ɪn ˈʃlʊmɐ(r) l̲a̲e̲n. ˈr̲a̲ʊ̲ʃə ziː ˈmʊrməlntʻ
wiege das Liebchen in Schlummer ein. Rausche sie murmelnd
lull the sweetheart into slumber in. Babble her murmuringly
(lull my sweetheart to sleep. Softly babbling, murmur her) [*rauschen* = *murmeln* = murmur]

ɪn ˈzyːsə ruː, ˈflʏstʻrə liːɐ̯ ˈtʰrɔ̲ø̲mə deːɐ̯ ˈliːbə tsuː.
in süsse Ruh', flüstre ihr Träume der Liebe zu.
into sweet rest, whisper to her dreams of the love to.
(into sweet rest, whisper dreams of love to her.)

[The Rellstab songs do not tell a continuous story. *Schwanengesang* is not a true song cycle in that sense, like *Die schöne Müllerin* or *Winterreise*. "Swan Song" refers to the ancient belief that the swan sings as it dies; that title was given to Schubert's last group of songs, published six months after his death. *Liebesbotschaft* is the last, and one of the loveliest, of Schubert's songs inspired by the rippling water of a brook.]

2. (Ludwig Rellstab)
ˈkʰriːɡɐs ˈlaːnʊŋ
Kriegers Ahnung
Warrior's Premonition

ɪn ˈtʰiːfɐ ruː liːkʻtʻ lʊm mɪç heːɐ̯ deːɐ̯ ˈvafənbryːdɐ kʰra̲e̲s;
In tiefer Ruh' liegt um mich her der Waffenbrüder Kreis;
In deep rest lies around me hither the weapon-brothers circle;
(My comrades in arms lie in a circle all around me in deep repose;)

miːɐ̯/miːr lɪst das hɛrts zoː baŋ lʊntʻ ʃveːɐ̯, fɔn ˈzeːnzuxtʻ miːɐ̯ zoː ha̲e̲s.
mir ist das Herz so bang und schwer, von Sehnsucht mir so heiss.
to me is the heart so anxious and heavy, from longing to me so hot.
(my heart is so anxious and heavy, so ardent with longing.)

viː haːb ɪç lɔftʻ zoː zyːs ɡəˈruːtʻ lan ˈliːrəm ˈbuːzən varm!
Wie hab' ich oft so süss geruht an ihrem Busen warm!
How have I often so sweetly rested on her bosom warm!
(How often I have rested so sweetly on her warm bosom!)
[*Schubert & Peters:* **so süss geträumt** (ɡəˈtʰrɔ̲ø̲mtʻ, dreamed)]

viː ˈfrɔ̲ø̲ntʻlɪç ʃiːn dɛs ˈheːɐ̯dəs gluːtʻ, laːkʻ ziː lɪn ˈma̲e̲nəm larm!
wie freundlich schien des Herdes Glut, lag sie in meinem Arm!
how friendly shone/seemed the hearth's glow, lay she in my arm!
(How friendly the glow of the hearth, as she lay in my arms!)

hiːɐ̯, voː deːɐ̯ ˈflamən ˈdyːstʻrɐ ʃa̲e̲n lax! nuːɐ̯/nuːr la̲ʊ̲f ˈvafən ʃpʻiːltʰ,
Hier, wo der Flammen düst'rer Schein ach! nur auf Waffen spielt,
Here, where the flames' gloomy shine ah! only on weapons plays,
(Here, where the gloomy light of the flames plays only on weapons, alas,)
[*poem:* **der Flamme** (ˈflamə, flame's–*singular*)]

hiːɐ̯ fyːlt di brʊstʻ zɪç gants laˈla̲e̲n, deːɐ̯ ˈveːmuːt ˈtʰrɛːnə kʰvɪltʰ.
hier fühlt die Brust sich ganz allein, der Wehmut Träne quillt.
here feels the breast itself entirely alone, the melancholy's tear wells up.
(here my heart feels all alone, and tears of melancholy well up.)

hɛrt͡s, das deːɐ̯ tʰroːst dɪç nɪçt‘ fɛɐ̯ˈlɛstʰ! lɛs ruːft‘ nɔx ˈmançə ʃlaxtʰ.
Herz, dass der Trost dich nicht verlässt! es ruft noch manche Schlacht.
Heart, that the comfort you not forsakes! there calls still many a battle.
(Heart, don't let comfort forsake you! Many a battle will still be calling.)

balt‘ ruː ɪç voːl lʊnt‘ ˈʃlaːfə fɛstʰ, hɛrt͡sˈliːpst‘ə — ˈguːt‘ə naxtʰ!
Bald ruh' ich wohl und schlafe fest, Herzliebste — gute Nacht!
Soon rest I probably and sleep soundly, dearest sweetheart — good night!
(Soon enough I may be at rest and sleeping soundly. Dearest sweetheart, good night!)

[On the eve of battle, while his comrades are sleeping, this soldier cannot fall asleep. He thinks longingly of his sweetheart. A premonition of death chills his heart. If not tomorrow, then soon: more battles than one lie ahead. Schubert set each of the four stanzas in a different musical form.]

3. (Ludwig Rellstab)
ˈfryːlɪŋszeːnzʊxtʰ
Frühlingssehnsucht
Spring Longing

ˈzɔ͡øzəlndə ˈlʏft‘ə ˈveːənt‘ zoː mɪlt‘, ˈbluːmɪgɐ ˈdʏft‘ə ˈlaːt‘mənt‘ lɛɐ̯ˈfʏltʰ!
Säuselde Lüfte wehend so mild, blumiger Düfte atmend erfüllt!
Murmuring airs blowing so mildly, of flowery scents breathing impregnated!
(Murmuring breezes blowing so mildly, impregnated with flower fragrances and exhaling them!)

viː hɑ͡oxt‘ liːɐ̯ mɪç ˈvɔnɪç bəˈgryːsənt‘ lan!
Wie haucht ihr mich wonnig begrüssend an!
How breathe you me blissfully greeting upon!
(How blissful I feel when you beathe your greeting upon me!)

viː haːp‘t‘ liːɐ̯ dem ˈpʰɔxəndən ˈhɛrt͡sən gəˈtʰaːn?
wie habt ihr dem pochenden Herzen getan?
how have you to the pounding heart done?
(What have you done to my pounding heart?)

ɛs ˈmœçt‘ə lɔ͡øç ˈfɔlgən lɑ͡of ˈlʊft‘ɪgɐ baːn! voˈhɪn? ˈbɛçlɑ͡en,
es möchte euch folgen auf luftiger Bahn! Wohin? Bächlein,
it would like you to follow on airy course! Whither? Brooklets,
(It would like to follow you on your airy course! But where? Little brooks,)

zoː ˈmʊnt‘ɐ ˈrɑ͡oʃənt t͡suˈmaːl, ˈvɔlən hɪˈnʊnt‘ɐ ˈzɪlbɐn lɪns tʰaːl. di ˈʃvɛləndə
so munter rauschend zumal, wollen hinunter silbern ins Tal. Die schwellende
so cheerfully babbling especially, want down silvery into the valley. The swelling
(silver, babbling so especially cheerfully, want to go down into the valley. The swelling)
[*poem:* **wallen** (ˈvalən, wander) **hinunter**]

ˈvɛlə, dɔrt‘ lɑ͡elt‘ ziː daˈhɪn! tʰiːf ˈʃp‘iːgəln zɪç ˈfluːrən lʊnt‘ ˈhɪməl daˈrɪn.
Welle, dort eilt sie dahin! Tief spiegeln sich Fluren und Himmel darin.
wave, there hurries it thither! Deeply reflect themselves meadows and sky in it.
(wave, there it is, hurrying down! Meadows and sky are deeply reflected in it.)

vas t͡siːst duː mɪç, ˈzeːnənt‘ fɛɐ̯ˈlaŋəndɐ zɪn, hɪˈnap‘?
Was ziehst du mich, sehnend verlangender Sinn, hinab?
Why draw you me, yearningly desiring mind, down?
(Why do you draw me down, my yearning, desiring mind?)

ˈgryːsəndɐ ˈzɔnə ˈʃpʻiːləndəs gɔltʻ, ˈhɔfəndə ˈvɔnə ˈbrɪŋəst duː hɔltʻ.
Grüssender Sonne spielendes Gold, hoffende Wonne bringest du hold.
Greeting sun's opalescent gold, hoping rapture bring you charmingly.
(Opalescent gold of the welcoming sun, you bring hopeful rapture so charmingly!)

viː laːpʻtʻ mɪç da͜en ˈzeːlɪç bəˈgryːsəndəs bɪltʻ!
Wie labt mich dein selig begrüssendes Bild!
How refreshes me your blessedly greeting image!
(How your image refreshes me with its blessed greeting!)

ɛs ˈlɛçəltʻ |am ˈtʰiːfbla͜oən ˈhɪməl zoː mɪltʻ
es lächelt am tiefblauen Himmel so mild
it smiles on the deep blue sky so gently
(It smiles so gently up there in the deep blue sky)

ʊntʻ hatʻ miːɐ̯ das ˈla͜ogə mɪt ˈtʰrɛːnən gəˈfʏltʰ! vaˈrʊm?
und hat mir das Auge mit Tränen gefüllt! Warum?
and has for me the eye with tears filled! Why?
(and has filled my eyes with tears! Why?)

ˈgryːnəntʻ |ʊmˈkʰrɛnt͜sətʻ ˈvɛldɐ(r) |ʊntʻ høː! ˈʃɪmɐntʻ |ɛɐ̯ˈglɛnt͜sətʻ ˈblyːtʻənʃneː!
Grünend umkränzet Wälder und Höh'! schimmernd erglänzet Blütenschnee!
Greeningly around-garlands forests and heights! shimmeringly gleams blossom-snow!
(Forests and heights are garlanded with green! The snow-white blossoms gleam and shimmer!)

zoː ˈdrɛŋətʻ zɪç ˈlaləs t͜sʊm ˈbrɔ͜øtʻlɪçən lɪçtʰ; |ɛs ˈʃvɛlən di ˈkʰa͜emə,
So dränget sich alles zum bräutlichen Licht; es schwellen die Keime,
Thus presses itself all to the bridal light; there swell the sprouts,
(Thus all things surge toward the bridal light; the sprouts are swelling,)

di ˈkʰnɔspʻə brɪçtʰ; ziː ˈhaːbən gəˈfʊndən, vas ˈliːnən gəˈbrɪçtʰ: |ʊnt duː?
die Knospe bricht; sie haben gefunden, was ihnen gebricht: und du?
the bud breaks (open); they have found what for them is wanting: and you?
(the bud bursts open; they have found what they were needing; and you?)

ˈrastʻloːzəs ˈzeːnən! ˈvʏnʃəndəs hɛrt͜s, ˈlɪmɐ nuːɐ̯ ˈtʰrɛːnən, ˈkʰlaːgə |ʊntʻ ʃmɛrt͜s?
Rastloses Sehnen! wünschendes Herz, immer nur Tränen, Klage und Schmerz?
Restless longing! wishing heart, always only tears, complaint and pain?
(Restless longing! My wishful heart, must there always be only tears, complaints, and pain?]

a͜ox |ɪç bɪn miːɐ̯ ˈʃvɛləndɐ ˈtʰriːbə bəˈvʊstʰ! veːɐ̯ ˈʃtʻɪlətʻ miːɐ̯/miːr ˈlɛntʻlɪç
Auch ich bin mir schwellender Triebe bewusst! Wer stillet mir endlich
Also I am in me of swelling drives conscious! Who stills for me at last
(I too am conscious of swelling drives! Who will at last appease in me)

di ˈdrɛŋəndə lʊstʰ? nuːɐ̯ duː bəˈfra͜est den lɛnt͜s lɪn deːɐ̯ brʊstʰ, nuːɐ̯ duː!
die drängende Lust? Nur du befreist den Lenz in der Brust, nur du!
the urging desire? Only you free the spring in the breast, only you!
(this urgent desire? Only you can set free the spring in my heart, only you!)

[*poem:* **befreiest** (bəˈfra͜eəst, free)]

[This song is an exuberant expression of spring fever. The impetuous forward drive is halted effectively at each question. In performance, two of the musically identical verses can be left out without too great a loss.]

4. (Ludwig Rellstab)
ˈʃtʻɛntʻçən
Ständchen
Serenade

ˈla͜ezə ˈfleːən ˈma͜enə ˈliːdɐ dʊrç di naxt t͜suː diːɐ̯;
Leise flehen meine Lieder durch die Nacht zu dir;
Softly plead my songs through the night to you;
(My songs are softly pleading through the night to you;)

ɪn den ˈʃtʻɪlən ha͜en hɛɐ̯ˈniːdɐ, ˈliːpʻçən, kʰɔm t͜suː miːɐ̯!
in den stillen Hain hernieder, Liebchen, komm' zu mir!
into the quiet grove down, sweetheart, come to me!
(come down to me, sweetheart, into the quiet grove!)

ˈflʏstʻɐntʻ ˈʃlaŋkʻə ˈvɪp͜fəl ˈra͜oʃən ɪn dɛs ˈmoːndəs lɪçtʰ;
Flüsternd schlanke Wipfel rauschen in des Mondes Licht;
Whispering slender treetops rustle in the moon's light;
(Slender treetops are whispering, as they rustle in the moonlight;)

dɛs fɛɐ̯ˈrɛːtʻɐs ˈfa͜entʻlɪç ˈla͜oʃən ˈfʏrçtʻə, ˈhɔldə, nɪçtʰ.
des Verräters feindlich Lauschen fürchte, Holde, nicht.
the betrayer's hostile eavesdropping fear, lovely one, not.
(do not be afraid that some hostile eavesdropper will betray us, lovely one.)

høːɐ̯st di ˈnaxtʻɪgalən ˈʃlaːgən? |ax! ziː ˈfleːən dɪç,
Hörst die Nachtigallen schlagen? ach! sie flehen dich,
Hear the nightingales sing? ah! they entreat you,
(Do you hear the nightingales singing? Ah, they are entreating you,)

mɪt deːɐ̯ ˈtʰøːnə ˈzyːsən ˈkʰlaːgən ˈfleːən ziː fyːɐ̯ mɪç.
mit der Töne süssen Klagen flehen sie für mich.
with the tones' sweet lamenting plead they for me.
(they are pleading for me with the sweet lamenting of their tones.)

ziː fɛɐ̯ˈʃtʻeːn dɛs ˈbuːzəns ˈzeːnən, ˈkʰɛnən ˈliːbəsʃmɛrt͜s,
Sie versteh'n des Busens Sehnen, kennen Liebesschmerz,
They understand the bosom's yearning, know love- pain,
(They understand the yearning of the heart, they know love's pain,)

ˈryːrən mɪt den ˈzɪlbɐtʰøːnən ˈjeːdəs ˈva͜eçə hɛrt͜s.
rühren mit den Silbertönen jedes weiche Herz.
touch with the silver tones every soft heart.
(with their silvery tones they touch every soft heart.)

las |a͜ox diːɐ̯ di brʊstʻ bəˈveːgən, ˈliːpʻçən, ˈhøːrə mɪç!
Lass auch dir die Brust bewegen, Liebchen, höre mich!
Let also for you the breast be moved, sweetheart, hear me!
(Let your breast, too, be moved: sweetheart, hear me!)

ˈbeːbəntʻ har ɪç diːɐ̯/diːr |ɛntʻˈgeːgən! kʰɔm, bəˈglʏkʻə mɪç!
bebend harr' ich dir entgegen! komm, beglücke mich!
trembling wait I to you toward! come, make happy me!
(Trembling, I am waiting here for you! Come, make me happy!)

[The Serenade is surely one of Schubert's two or three most familiar melodies, along with *Ave Maria* and possibly the song-like theme from the first movement of the "Unfinished" Symphony, thanks to a certain operetta. This seductive serenade ought to melt almost any susceptible heart.]

5. (Ludwig Rellstab)
ˈɑ͜oflɛnt‘haltʰ
Aufenthalt
My Abode

ˈrɑ͜oʃəndɐ ʃt‘ro:m, ˈbrɑ͜ozəndɐ valt‘, ˈʃt‘arəndɐ fɛls, ma͜en ˈlɑ͜oflɛnt‘ˈhaltʰ.
Rauschender Strom, brausender Wald, starrender Fels, mein Aufenthalt.
Rushing stream, raging forest, rigid rock, my abode.

vi: zɪç di: ˈvɛlə lan ˈvɛlə ra͜ehtʰ, ˈfli:sən di ˈtʰrɛ:nən mi:ɐ̯/mi:r ˈle:vɪç lɛɐ̯ˈnɔ͜øtʰ.
Wie sich die Welle an Welle reiht, fliessen die Tränen mir ewig erneut.
As itself the wave on wave ranks, flow the tears for me eternally renewed.
(As wave follows wave, so my tears are flowing, eternally replenished.)

ho:x lɪn den ˈkʰro:nən ˈvo:gənt‘ zɪçs re:k‘t‘, zo: ˈlʊnlɑ͜ofhø:ɐ̯lɪç ma͜en ˈhɛrt͜sə ʃlɛ:k‘tʰ.
Hoch in den Kronen wogend sich's regt, so unaufhörlich mein Herze schlägt.
High in the crowns waving itself it stirs, thus ceaselessly my heart beats.
(High above, the treetops are swaying in agitated rhythms, just as my heart is ceaselessly beating.)

ʊnt‘ vi: dɛs ˈfɛlzən lu:ɐ̯-/lu:rˈlalt‘əs* le:ɐ̯t͜s, ˈle:vɪç de:ɐ̯ˈzɛlbə ˈbla͜ebət‘ ma͜en ʃmɛrt͜s.
Und wie des Felsen uraltes Erz, ewig derselbe bleibet mein Schmerz.
And like the rock's primeval ore, eternally the same remains my pain.
(And like the primeval ore of the rock, my pain remains eternally the same.)
[**normally accented on the first syllable:* ˈlu:ɐ̯lalt‘əs]

[The distraught poet feels in harmony with the violent moods of nature: a thundering mountain stream, a storm in the forest, the sheer, unyielding face of a cliff—there is his natural home. Schubert captures the grim, majestic turbulance in one of his most powerful masterpieces.]

6. (Ludwig Rellstab)
ɪn de:ɐ̯ ˈfɛrnə
In der Ferne
At a Distance

ˈve:ə dem ˈfli:əndən vɛlt‘ hɪˈnɑ͜os ˈt͜si:əndən! — ˈfrɛmdə dʊrçˈmɛsəndən,
Wehe dem Fliehenden Welt hinaus ziehenden! — Fremde durchmessenden,
Woe to the fugitive world out emigrating! — Foreign land traversing,
(Woe to the fugitive who tries to move away from the world! Those traversing foreign lands,)

ˈha͜ema:t‘ fɛɐ̯ˈgɛsəndən, ˈmʊt‘ɐhɑ͜os ˈhasəndən, ˈfrɔ͜øndə fɛɐ̯ˈlasəndən
Heimat vergessenden, Mutterhaus hassenden, Freunde verlassenden
homeland forgetting, mother-house hating, friends forsaking
(forgetting their native land, hating their family home, forsaking their friends, —)

ˈfɔlgət‘ kʰa͜en ˈze:gən, lax! lɑ͜of ˈli:rən ˈve:gən na:x! ˈhɛrt͜sə, das ˈze:nəndə,
folget kein Segen, ach! auf ihren Wegen nach! Herze, das sehnende,
follows no blessing, ah! on their ways after! Heart, the yearning,
(no blessing follows after them on their various ways, alas! The yearning heart,)

ˈlɑo̯gə, das ˈtʰrɛːnəndə, ˈzeːnzʊxtʻ, niː ˈlɛndəndə, ˈhɑe̯mvɛrt͜s zɪç ˈvɛndəndə,
Auge, das tränende, Sehnsucht, nie endende, heimwärts sich wendende,
eye, the weeping, longing, never ending, homewards itself wending,
(the weeping eyes; the never-ending longing, turning homewards;)

ˈbuːzən, deːɐ̯ ˈvaləndə, ˈkʰlaːgə, fɛɐ̯ˈhaləndə, ˈlaːbəntʻʃtʻɛrn, ˈblɪŋkʻəndɐ,
Busen, der wallende, Klage, verhallende, Abendstern, blinkender,
bosom, the seething, lament, fading away, evening star, twinkling,
(the seething bosom; the lament, fading away; the twinkling evening star,)

ˈhɔfnʊŋsloːs ˈzɪŋkʻəndɐ! ˈlʏftʻə, liːɐ̯ ˈzɔ̯ø̯zəlndən, ˈvɛlən, zanftʻ ˈkʰrɔ̯ø̯zəlndən,
hoffnungslos sinkender! Lüfte, ihr säuselnden, Wellen, sanft kräuselnden,
hopelessly sinking! Breezes, you murmuring, waves, gently curling,
(hopelessly sinking! You murmuring breezes, you gently curling waves,)

ˈzɔnənʃtʻraːl, ˈlɑe̯ləndɐ, ˈnɪrgəntʻ fɛɐ̯ˈvɑe̯ləndɐ:
Sonnenstrahl, eilender, nirgend verweilender:
sunbeam, hurrying, nowhere lingering:
(you hurrying sunbeam, nowhere lingering, — all of you:)

diː miːɐ̯ mɪtʻ ˈʃmɛrt͜sə, lax! diːs ˈtʰrɔ̯ø̯ə ˈhɛrt͜sə braːx — gryːstʻ
die mir mit Schmerze, ach! dies treue Herze brach — grüsst
her who for me with pain, ah! this true heart broke — greet
(greet the one who broke so painfully this faithful heart of mine,)

fɔn dem ˈfliːəndən vɛltʻ hɪˈnɑo̯s ˈt͜siːəndən!
von dem Fliehenden Welt hinaus ziehenden!
from the fugitive world out emigrating one!
(give her a greeting from the fugitive who is leaving the world behind!)

[On the surface, the poem seems a rather artificial exercise in rhyme and rhythm. Schubert gives it poignance, empathizing with the desperation—verging on madness—of the rejected lover.]

7. (Ludwig Rellstab)
ˈapʻʃiːtʻ
Abschied
Farewell

aˈdeː! duː ˈmʊntʻrə, duː ˈfrøːlɪçə ʃtʻatʰ, laˈdeː! ʃoːn ˈʃarətʻ mɑe̯n ˈrœslɑe̯n
Ade! du muntre, du fröhliche Stadt, Ade! Schon scharret mein Rösslein
Farewell! you cheerful, you merry town, farewell! Already paws my little horse
(Farewell, you cheerful, merry town, farewell! Already my little horse is pawing the ground)

mɪtʻ ˈlʊstʻɪgəm fuːs; jɛt͜stʻ nɪm nɔx den ˈlɛt͜stʻən, den ˈʃɑe̯dəndən gruːs!
mit lustigem Fuss; jetzt nimm noch den letzten, den scheidenden Gruss!
with merry foot; now take yet the last, the parting greeting!
(with a merry hoof; now take my last, my parting greeting!)
[*poem:* **nimm meinen** (ˈmɑe̯nən, my) **letzten**]

duː hastʻ mɪç voːl ˈniːmaːls nɔx ˈtʰrɑo̯rɪç gəˈzeːn,
Du hast mich wohl niemals noch traurig geseh'n,
You have me probably never yet sad seen,
(You have probably never yet seen me sad,)
[*poem:* **wohl nimmermehr** (ˈnɪmɐmeːɐ̯, nevermore/never) **traurig**]

zoː kʰan lɛs lɑ͜ox jɛt͜st' nɪçt' ba͜em 'lap'ʃiːt' gə'ʃeːn. la'deː!
so kann es auch jetzt nicht beim Abschied gescheh'n. Ade!
so can it also now not at the farewell happen. Farewell!
(so that cannot happen now at parting either. Farewell!)

a'deː! liːɐ̯ 'bɔ͜ømə, liːɐ̯ 'gɛrtən zoː gryːn, la'deː! nuːn ra͜et' ɪç
Ade! ihr Bäume, ihr Gärten so grün, Ade! Nun reit' ich
Farewell! you trees, you gardens so green, farewell! Now ride I
(Farewell, you trees, you gardens so green, farewell! Now I am riding)

lam 'zɪlbɐnən 'ʃt'roːmə lɛnt''laŋ, va͜et''ʃalənt' lɛɐ̯'tʰøːnət' ma͜en 'lap'ʃiːt͜sgəzaŋ;
am silbernen Strome entlang, weitschallend ertönet mein Abschiedsgesang;
by the silver river along, far- resounding sounds my farewell- song;
(alongside the silver river; my song of farewell reverberates into the distance;)

niː haːp't' liːɐ̯/liːr la͜en 'tʰrɑ͜orɪgəs liːt' gə'høːɐ̯tʰ, ['kʰlaːgəndəs]
nie habt ihr ein trauriges Lied gehört, [*poem:* ein klagendes Lied]
never have you a sad song heard, [lamenting]
(you never heard a sad song from me,)

zoː vɪrt' lɔ͜øç lɑ͜ox 'kʰa͜enəs ba͜em 'ʃa͜edən bə'ʃeːɐ̯tʰ. la'deː!
so wird euch auch keines beim Scheiden beschert. Ade!
so will to you also none at the parting be given. Farewell!
(so none will be given to you at parting either. Farewell!)

a'deː! liːɐ̯ 'frɔ͜ønt'lɪçən 'mɛːk't'la͜en dɔrtʰ, la'deː! ['mɛːk'dəla͜en]
Ade! ihr freundlichen Mägdlein dort, Ade! [*poem:* Mägdelein]
Farewell! you friendly girls there, farewell! [girls]

vas ʃɑ͜ot' liːɐ̯/liːr lɑ͜os 'bluːmənlʊmdʊft'ət'əm hɑ͜os mɪt' 'ʃɛlmɪʃən,
Was schaut ihr aus blumenumduftetem Haus mit schelmischen,
Why look you from flower-around-scented house with roguish,
(Why do you look out from your house, surrounded by fragrant flowers, with such roguish,)

'lɔk'əndən 'blɪk'ən hɛ'rɑ͜os? viː zɔnst', zoː gryːs ɪç lʊnt' 'ʃɑ͜oə mɪç lʊm,
lockenden Blicken heraus? Wie sonst, so grüss' ich und schaue mich um,
enticing glances out? As usual, so greet I and look me about,
(enticing glances? As usual I greet you and *look* around,)

dɔx 'nɪmɐ vɛnd ɪç ma͜en 'rœsla͜en lʊm. la'deː! ['nɪmɐmeːɐ̯]
doch nimmer wend' ich mein Rösslein um. Ade! [*poem:* nimmermehr]
but never turn I my little horse around. Farewell! [nevermore]
(but I shall never turn my little *horse* around.)

a'deː! 'liːbə 'zɔnə, zoː geːst duː t͜sʊr ruː, la'deː!
Ade! liebe Sonne, so gehst du zur Ruh', Ade!
Farewell! dear sun, so go you to the rest, farewell!
(Farewell, dear sun; so you are going to your rest! Farewell!)

nuːn 'ʃɪmɐt deːɐ̯ 'blɪŋk'əndən 'ʃt'ɛrnə gɔlt'.
Nun schimmert der blinkenden Sterne Gold.
Now shimmers the twinkling stars' gold.
(Now the golden light of the twinkling stars is shimmering.)

vi: bɪn lɪç lɔ͜øç ˈʃtʻɛrnla͜en lam ˈhɪməl zo: hɔltʻ; dʊrçˈt͜si:n vi:ɐ̯ di vɛltʻ
Wie bin ich euch Sternlein am Himmel so hold; durchzieh'n wir die Welt
How am I to you little stars in the sky so favored; traverse we the world
(How you little stars in the sky seem to favor me: even if my horse and I traverse the world)
[*poem:* **durchziehen** (dʊrçˈt͜si:ən, traverse) **die Welt wir**]

la͜ox va͜etʻ lʊntʻ bra͜etʻ, li:ɐ̯ ge:pʻtʻ ˈly:bɐ(r)lal lʊns das ˈtʰrɔ͜øə gəˈla͜etʰ. laˈde:!
auch weit und breit, ihr gebt überall uns das treue Geleit. Ade!
even far and wide, you give everywhere to us the faithful guidance. Farewell!
(far and wide, wherever we go you give us faithful guidance. Farewell!)

aˈde:! du: ˈʃɪmɐndəs ˈfɛnstʻɐla͜en hɛl, laˈde:! du: ˈglɛnt͜səstʻ zo: ˈtʰra͜olɪç
Ade! du schimmerndes Fensterlein hell, Ade! Du glänzest so traulich
Farewell! you shimmering little window bright, farewell! You gleam so cozily
(Farewell, you brightly shimmering little window! You gleam so cozily)

mɪt ˈdɛmɐndəm ʃa͜en, lʊntʻ ˈla:dəstʻ zo: ˈfrɔ͜øntʻlɪç lɪns ˈhʏtʻçən lʊns la͜en.
mit dämmerndem Schein, und ladest so freundlich ins Hüttchen uns ein.
with dawning/dimming light, and invite so cordially into the little cottage us in.
(with a soft light, and invite us into the little cottage so cordially.)

foˈry:bɐ(r), lax, rɪtʻ lɪç zo: ˈmançəs ma:l
Vorüber, ach, ritt ich so manches mal
Past, ah, rode I so many a time
(I've ridden past you so many a time,)

ʊntʻ vɛ:ɐ̯/vɛ:r lɛs dɛn ˈhɔ͜øtʻə t͜sʊm ˈlɛt͜stʻən ma:l? laˈde:! laˈde:! li:ɐ̯ ˈʃtʻɛrnə,
und wär' es denn heute zum letzten mal? Ade! Ade! ihr Sterne,
and were it then today for the last time? Farewell! Farewell! you stars,
(and today would it be for the last time? Farewell! Farewell, you stars,)

fɛɐ̯ˈhʏlətʻ lɔ͜øç gra͜o! laˈde:! dɛs ˈfɛnstʻɐla͜en ˈtʰry:bəs, fɛɐ̯ˈʃɪmɐndəs lɪçtʰ
verhüllet euch grau! Ade! des Fensterlein trübes, verschimmerndes Licht
veil yourselves grey! Farewell! the little window's dim, away-shimmering light
(veil yourselves in grey! Farewell! The light of that little window, growing dim in the distance,)
[*poem:* **des Fensterleins** (ˈfɛnstʻɐla͜ens, window's)]

ɛɐ̯ˈzɛt͜stʻ li:ɐ̯/li:r lʊnˈt͜sɛ:lɪgən ˈʃtʻɛrnə mi:ɐ̯ nɪçtʰ; darf lɪç hi:ɐ̯ nɪçtʻ ˈva͜elən,
ersetzt ihr unzähligen Sterne mir nicht; darf ich hier nicht weilen,
replace you innumerable stars for me not; may I here not linger,
(you innumerable stars cannot take the place of that for me; if I may not linger here,)
[*Peters:* **Sterne uns** (lʊns, for us) **nicht**

mʊs hi:ɐ̯ fo:ɐ̯ˈba͜e, vas hɪlftʻ lɛs, fɔlkʻtʻ li:ɐ̯ mi:ɐ̯ nɔx zo: tʰrɔ͜ø! laˈde:!
muss hier vorbei, was hilft es, folgt ihr mir noch so treu! Ade!
must here past, what helps it, follow you me yet so faithfully! Farewell!
(if I must ride by, what help is it if you follow me, however faithfully? farewell!)
[*poem:* **was hilft es mir** (mi:ɐ̯, me)]

[The young man leaves town on horseback, heading out into the world, with a backward glance but no turning around, no regrets, no tears. He was happy there. But life and adventure lie ahead!]

8. (Heinrich Heine)
deːɐ̯ ˈlatˈlas
Der Atlas
Atlas

ɪç ˈlʊnglʏkˈzeːlgɐ(r) ˈlatˈlas!
Ich unglücksel'ger Atlas!
I unhappy Atlas!
(I am the unhappy Atlas!)

ˈa͜enə vɛlt, di ˈgant͜sə vɛlt deːɐ̯ ˈʃmɛrt͜sən, mʊs lɪç ˈtʰraːgən,
eine Welt, die ganze Welt der Schmerzen, muss ich tragen,
a world, a whole world of the sorrows, must I bear,
(I must bear a world, a whole world of sorrows;)

ɪç ˈtʰraːgə lʊnlɛɐ̯ˈtʰrɛːkˈlɪçəs, lʊntˈ ˈbrɛçən vɪl miːɐ̯ das hɛrt͜s lɪm ˈla͜ebə.
ich trage Unerträgliches, und brechen will mir das Herz im Leibe.
I bear (the) unbearable, and to break wants for me the heart in the body.
(I bear the unbearable, and my heart threatens to break in my body.)

duː ˈʃtˈɔlt͜səs hɛrt͜s, duː hastˈ lɛs jaː gəˈvɔltʰ! duː ˈvɔltˈəstˈ ˈglʏkˈlɪç za͜en,
Du stolzes Herz, du hast es ja gewollt! Du wolltest glücklich sein,
You proud heart, you have it after all wanted! You wanted happy to be,
(You proud heart, you wanted this, after all! You wanted to be happy,)

lʊnˈlɛntˈlɪç ˈglʏkˈlɪç, ˈloːdɐ(r) lʊnˈlɛntˈlɪç ˈleːlənt, ˈʃtˈɔlt͜səs hɛrt͜s,
unendlich glücklich, oder unendlich elend, stolzes Herz,
endlessly happy, or endlessly wretched, proud heart,

lʊntˈ ˈjɛt͜so bɪst duː ˈleːləntˈ.
und jetzo bist du elend.
and now are you wretched.
(and now you are wretched.)

[Unlike the Rellstab songs, the first seven in this so-called "cycle," the Heine songs can be thought of as telling the story of one man's unhappy love. The poems, without individual titles, were originally published as part of a collection entitled *Die Heimkehr* ("The Homecoming"); there their sequence is as follows (using Schubert's titles for convenience): *Das Fischermädchen, Am Meer, Die Stadt, Der Doppelgänger, Ihr Bild, Der Atlas.* In Heine's concept, *Der Atlas* was a culmination, not a beginning. Nevertheless, Schubert's Heine songs are among his greatest achievements, each one a unique masterpiece. Atlas was a Titan (one of his brothers was Prometheus). He ruled over an immense kingdom, called Atlantis. The gods sent a deluge. In one day and one night Atlantis sank beneath the waves. Atlas, who escaped, led a revolt against the gods. When he was defeated, his punishment was to support the heavens on his powerful shoulders for the rest of eternity. Here Heine uses Atlas as the archetype of a man who wants too much, who wants to experience everything to the fullest degree, and who is doomed to bear an unbearable burden, to bear the weight of a world of suffering on his shoulders.]

9. (Heinrich Heine)
iːɐ̯ bɪlt‘
Ihr Bild
Her Picture

ɪç ʃt‘ant‘ ǀɪn 'dʊŋk‘əln 'tʰrɔ͜ømən ǀʊnt‘ ʃt‘art‘ iːɐ̯ 'bɪlt‘nɪs ǀan, ['ʃtart‘ə]
Ich stand in dunkeln Träumen und starrt' ihr Bildnis an, [*poem:* **starrte]**
I stood in dark dreams and stared her portrait at, [stared]
(I stood in dark dreams and stared at her portrait,)

ʊnt das gə'liːp‘t‘ə 'ǀant‘lɪt͡s 'ha͜emlɪç t͡suː 'leːbən bə'gan.
und das geliebte Antlitz heimlich zu leben begann.
and the beloved countenance secretly to live began.
(and that beloved face secretly began to come alive.)

ʊm 'liːrə 'lɪp‘ən t͡soːk‘ zɪç la͜en 'lɛçəln 'vʊndɐbaːɐ̯,
Um ihre Lippen zog sich ein Lächeln wunderbar,
Around her lips pulled itself a smile wondrously,
(Miraculously, a smile took shape around her lips,)

ʊnt‘ viː fɔn 'veːmuːt͡stʰrɛːnən ǀɛɐ̯'glɛnt͡st‘ə iːɐ̯/iːr 'ǀa͜ogənpʰaːɐ̯.
und wie von Wehmutstränen erglänzte ihr Augenpaar.
and as (if) from melancholy-tears glistened her eyes- pair.
(and her eyes were glistening as if with tears of melancholy.)

a͜ox 'ma͜enə 'tʰrɛːnən 'flɔsən miːɐ̯ fɔn den 'vaŋən hɛ'rap‘ —
Auch meine Tränen flossen mir von den Wangen herab —
Also my tears flowed for me from the cheeks down —
(My tears, too, were flowing down my cheeks —)

ʊnt‘ ǀax, ǀɪç kʰan ǀɛs nɪçt‘ 'gla͜obən, das ǀɪç dɪç fɛɐ̯'loːrən haːp‘!
und ach, ich kann es nicht glauben, dass ich dich verloren hab'!
and ah, I can it not believe, that I you lost have!
(and—ah!—I cannot believe that I have lost you!)

[The grey loneliness of the opening unison, the color added by harmony as her picture seems to come alive, the return of bare octaves as tears of loss begin to flow, and the moving outburst at the end with its *forte* postlude create a remarkably concise union of poetry and music.]

10. (Heinrich Heine)
das 'fɪʃɐmɛːt‘çən
Das Fischermädchen
The Fisher Girl

duː 'ʃøːnəs 'fɪʃɐmɛːt‘çən, 'tʰra͜ebə den kʰaːn ǀans lant‘;
Du schönes Fischermädchen, treibe den Kahn ans Land;
You lovely fisher girl, drive the boat to the land;
(You lovely fisher girl, row your boat to the shore;)

kʰɔm t͡suː miːɐ̯/miːr ǀʊnt‘ 'zɛt͡sə dɪç 'niːdɐ, viːɐ̯ 'kʰoːzən hant‘ ǀɪn hant‘.
komm zu mir und setze dich nieder, wir kosen Hand in Hand.
come to me and set yourself down, we talk amorously hand in hand.
(come to me, sit down beside me, and we shall talk of love, hand in hand.)

leːk‘ ɪan maen hɛrts daen 'kʰœpfçən ɪʊnt‘ 'fʏrçt‘ə dɪç nɪçt tsuː zeːɐ̯;
Leg' an mein Herz dein Köpfchen und fürchte dich nicht zu sehr;
Lay on my heart your little head and fear yourself not too much;
(Lay your little head against my heart and don't be too afraid;)

fɛɐ̯'tʰraost duː dɪç dɔx 'zɔrk‘loːs 'tʰɛːk‘lɪç dem 'vɪldən meːɐ̯.
vertraust du dich doch sorglos täglich dem wilden Meer.
entrust you yourself after all unconcernedly daily to the wild sea.
(after all, without a worry you entrust yourself daily to the wild sea.)

maen hɛrts glaeçt‘ gants dem 'meːrə, hat‘ ʃt‘ʊrm ɪʊnt‘ ɪɛp‘ ɪʊnt‘ fluːtʰ,
Mein Herz gleicht ganz dem Meere, hat Sturm und Ebb' und Flut,
My heart is like exactly to the sea, has storm and ebb and flood,
(My heart is just like the sea: it has storms and ebb tide and flood;)

ʊnt‘ 'mançə 'ʃøːnə 'pʰɛrlə ɪɪn 'zaenɐ 'tʰiːfə ruːtʰ.
und manche schöne Perle in seiner Tiefe ruht.
and many a beautiful pearl in its depths rests.
(and many a beautiful pearl rests in its depths.)

[You, who face the wind and the waves every day with such confidence, should not be afraid of the stormy heart of a poet; you may find an unexpected pearl or two inside.]

11. (Heinrich Heine)
di ʃt‘atʰ
Die Stadt
The Town

am 'fɛrnən hori'tsɔnt‘ə ɪɛɐ̯'ʃaent‘, viː ɪaen 'neːbəlbɪlt‘, di ʃt‘at‘ mɪt‘ 'iːrən 'tʰʏrmən,
Am fernen Horizonte erscheint, wie ein Nebelbild, die Stadt mit ihren Türmen,
On the far horizon appears, like a mist- image, the town with its towers,
(The town with its towers appears on the far horizon like a misty vision,)

ɪn 'aːbəntdɛmrʊŋ gə'hʏltʰ. ɪaen 'fɔøçt‘ɐ 'vɪnttsuːk 'kʰrɔøzəltʰ di 'graoə 'vasɐbaːn;
in Abenddämm'rung gehüllt. Ein feuchter Windzug kräuselt die graue Wasserbahn;
in evening twilight veiled. A moist wind-gust ruffles the grey waterway;
(veiled in evening twilight. A moist gust of wind ruffles the grey surface of the water;)

mɪt 'tʰraorɪgəm 'tʰak‘t‘ə 'ruːdɐtʰ deːɐ̯ 'ʃɪfɐ(r) ɪɪn 'maenəm kʰaːn. di 'zɔnə heːp‘t‘ zɪç
mit traurigem Takte rudert der Schiffer in meinem Kahn. Die Sonne hebt sich
with sad strokes rows the boatman in my boat. The sun raises itself
(the boatman in my boat rows with mournful strokes. The sun rises)

nɔx 'ɪaenmaːl 'ɪɔøçt‘ənt‘ fɔm 'boːdən ɪɛm'pʰoːɐ̯, ɪʊnt tsaek‘t‘ miːɐ̯ 'jeːnə 'ʃt‘ɛlə,
noch einmal leuchtend vom Boden empor, und zeigt mir jene Stelle,
still once shining from the ground upwards, and shows to me that place,
(radiantly out of the earth once more, and shows me that place)

voː ɪɪç das 'liːpst‘ə fɛɐ̯'loːɐ̯.
wo ich das Liebste verlor.
where I the dearest lost.
(where I lost what was dearest to me.)

[*das Liebste* (neuter): *Liebchen, Mädchen* (all diminutives are neuter), *Gut*?]

[Schubert created an uncanny atmosphere for *Die Stadt*: an ominous quiet at twilight; whisps of mist; brief gusts of wind; grey, ruffled water; the downward strokes of the boatman's oar; the sudden *forte* when the rays of the sun expose the place where the poet lost the love of the girl he loved; his *fortissimo* cry of pain and despair; in the postlude, the quiet indifference of the water.]

12. (Heinrich Heine)
am meːɐ̯
Am Meer
By the Sea

das meːɐ̯/meːr lɛɐ̯ˈglɛnt͜stʻə va͜etʻ hɪˈnɑ͜os lɪm ˈlɛt͜stʻən ˈlaːbəntʻʃa͜enə;
Das Meer erglänzte weit hinaus im letzten Abendscheine;
The sea gleams far out in the last evening light;
(The sea stretches far away into the distance, gleaming in the last rays of evening;)

viːɐ̯ ˈzaːsən lam ˈla͜enzaːmən ˈfɪʃɐhɑ͜os, viːɐ̯ ˈzaːsən ʃtʻʊm lʊntʻ laˈla͜enə.
wir sassen am einsamen Fischerhaus, wir sassen stumm und alleine.
we sat by the lonely fisherman's house, we sat without speaking and alone.
(we were sitting by that lonely fisherman's house, sitting there in silence and alone.)

deːɐ̯ ˈneːbəl ʃtʻiːkʻ, das ˈvasɐ ʃvɔl, di ˈmøːvə floːkʻ hɪn lʊntʻ ˈviːdɐ;
Der Nebel stieg, das Wasser schwoll, die Möve flog hin und wieder;
The mist rose, the water swelled, the seagull flew hence and again;
(The mist rose, the waters swelled, now and then a gull flew by;) [*hin und wieder* = now and then]

ɑ͜os ˈda͜enən ˈlɑ͜ogən ˈliːbəfɔl ˈfiːlən di ˈtʰrɛːnən ˈniːdɐ.
aus deinen Augen liebevoll fielen die Tränen nieder.
from your eyes love-full fell the tears down.
(tears fell from your eyes, full of love.)

ɪç zaː ziː ˈfalən lɑ͜of ˈda͜enə hantʻ lʊntʻ bɪn lɑ͜ofs kʰniː gəˈzʊŋkʻən;
Ich sah sie fallen auf deine Hand und bin aufs Knie gesunken;
I saw them fall onto your hand and am [= have] onto the knee sunk;
(I saw them falling onto your hand, and I sank down onto my knees;)

ɪç haːpʻ fɔn ˈda͜enɐ ˈva͜esən hant di ˈtʰrɛːnən ˈfɔrtʻgətʰrʊŋkʻən.
ich hab' von deiner weissen Hand die Tränen fortgetrunken.
I have from your white hand the tears away-drunk.
(I drank the tears away from your white hand.)

za͜etʻ ˈjeːnɐ ˈʃtʻʊndə fɛɐ̯ˈt͜seːɐ̯tʻ zɪç ma͜en la͜epʻ, di ˈzeːlə ʃtʻɪrpʻtʻ foːɐ̯ ˈzeːnən; —
Seit jener Stunde verzehrt sich mein Leib, die Seele stirbt vor Sehnen; —
Since that hour consumes itself my body, the soul dies of longing; —
(Since that hour my body is wasting away, my soul is dying with longing; —)

mɪç hat das ˈlʊnglʏkʻzeːlgə va͜epʻ fɛɐ̯ˈgɪftʻətʻ mɪtʻ ˈliːrən ˈtʰrɛːnən.
mich hat das unglücksel'ge Weib vergiftet mit ihren Tränen.
me has the unhappy woman poisoned with her tears.
(that unhappy woman has poisoned me with her tears.)

[The opening discords hint at danger. The hauntingly beautiful melody that starts the song suggests the surenity of the broad seascape. He is remembering, he speaks to her in imagination. A soft tremolo begins in the piano as the mist is rising; a *crescendo* paints the swelling of the sea; poignant accents accompany the woman's tears. The serene melody returns, as he recalls how he drank the tears from her hand, an enigmatic gesture (gallantry? an attempt to comfort and console her? a ritual partaking of her sorrow?). Then the tremolo recurs, to shudder with him as he tells himself that her tears have poisoned him. Again the accents, again the ominous chords.]

13. (Heinrich Heine)
deːɐ̯ ˈdɔpʻəlgɛŋɐ
Der Doppelgänger
The Wraithe / The Phantom Double

ʃtʻɪl lɪst di naxtʰ, lɛs ˈruːən di ˈgasən, lɪn ˈdiːzəm ˈha͜ozə ˈvoːntʻə ma͜en ʃa͜ts;
Still ist die Nacht, es ruhen die Gassen, in diesem Hause wohnte mein Schatz;
Still is the night, there rest the alleys, in this house lived my treasure;
(The night is still, nothing stirs in the streets; my treasure used to live in this house;)

ziː hatʻ ʃoːn lɛŋst di ʃtʻatʻ fɛɐ̯ˈlasən, dɔx ʃtʻeːtʻ nɔx das ha͜os
sie hat schon längst die Stadt verlassen, doch steht noch das Haus
she has already long since the town left, but stands still the house
(she has long since left town; but the house is still standing)

a͜of demˈzɛlbən pʰla͜ts. daː ʃtʻeːtʻ la͜ox la͜en mɛnʃ, lʊntʻ ʃtʻartʻ lɪn di ˈhøːə,
auf demselben Platz. Da steht auch ein Mensch, und starrt in die Höhe,
on the same place. There stands also a human being, and stares into the height,
(in the same place. A man is standing there too, and staring up at a window,)

ʊntʻ rɪŋt di ˈhɛndə foːɐ̯ ˈʃmɛrtsənsgəvaltʰ; miːɐ̯ gra͜ostʻ lɛs,
und ringt die Hände vor Schmerzensgewalt; mir graust es,
and wrings the hands for pain- power; to me makes shudder it,
(and wringing his hands in overpowering agony; I shudder) [*mir graust es* = I shudder]

vɛn lɪç za͜en ˈlantʻlɪts ˈzeːə — deːɐ̯ moːnt tsa͜ekʻtʻ miːɐ̯ ˈma͜enə ˈla͜egnə gəˈʃtʻaltʰ.
wenn ich sein Antlitz sehe — der Mond zeigt mir meine eig'ne Gestalt.
when I his countenance see — the moon shows to me my own form.
(when I see his face — the moon shows me my own form!)

duː ˈdɔpʻəlgɛŋɐ, duː ˈbla͜eçɐ gəˈzɛlə! vas lɛfst duː naːx ma͜en ˈliːbəsla͜etʻ,
Du Doppelgänger, du bleicher Geselle! was äffst du nach mein Liebesleid,
You double, you pale companion! why ape you after my love- suffering,
(My double, my pale companion, why do you mock the pain of my love)
[*nachäffen* = to ape, to mimic, to mock]

das mɪç gəˈkʰvɛːltʻ la͜of ˈdiːzɐ ˈʃtʻɛlə zoː ˈmançə naxtʻ, lɪn ˈaltʻɐ tsa͜etʰ?
das mich gequält auf dieser Stelle so manche Nacht, in alter Zeit?
that me tormented on this spot so many a night, in old time?
(that tormented me on this very spot so many a night, long ago?)

[A deathly stillness. Someone is standing there where I used to stand. A *crescendo* of pain. A horrified whisper, growing to a triple *forte* discord as I recognize — myself! *Accelerando,* bitter resentment of the mockery. Another triple *forte* in the pause, a stab of intense pain, then again as I remember those many nights, followed immediately by slow torture, *piano*, in the lingering *melisma*, drawing out the aching regret for a time that vanished so long ago. A shattering song!]

14. (Johann Gabriel Seidl)
di ˈtʰɑo̯bənpʰɔstʰ
Die Taubenpost
The Pigeon Post

ɪç haːpʻ ˈlae̯nə ˈbriːftʰɑo̯pʻ lɪn ˈmae̯nəm zɔltʻ, diː lɪstʻ gaːɐ̯/gaːr lɛɐ̯ˈgeːbən lʊnt tʰrɔø̯;
Ich hab' eine Brieftaub' in meinem Sold, die ist gar ergeben und treu;
I have a carrier pigeon in my pay, it is thoroughly devoted and faithful;

ziː nɪmtʻ miːɐ̯ niː das tsiːl tsuː kʰʊrts, lʊntʻ fliːkʻtʻ lɑo̯x niː foːɐ̯ˈbae̯.
sie nimmt mir nie das Ziel zu kurz, und fliegt auch nie vorbei.
it takes for me never the goal too short, and flies also never past.
(it never flies short of my goal, and never flies past it, either.)

ɪç ˈzɛndə ziː fiːlˈtʰɑo̯zəntʻmaːl lɑo̯f ˈkʰʊntʻʃaft ˈtʰɛːkʻlɪç hɪˈnɑo̯s,
Ich sende sie vieltausendmal auf Kundschaft täglich hinaus,
I send it many thousand times on reconnaissance daily out,
(I send it out on reconnaissance many thousands of times every day,)

foːɐ̯ˈbae̯ lan ˈmançəm ˈliːbən lɔrtʰ, bɪs tsuː deːɐ̯ ˈliːpstʻən hɑo̯s.
vorbei an manchem lieben Ort, bis zu der Liebsten Haus.
past by many a dear place, till to the dearest one's house.
(past many a dear spot, as far as my sweetheart's house.)

dɔrtʻ ʃɑo̯tʻ ziː tsʊm ˈfɛnstʻɐ ˈhae̯mlɪç hɪˈnae̯n, bəˈlɑo̯ʃtʻ ˈliːrən blɪkʻ lʊntʻ ʃrɪtʰ,
Dort schaut sie zum Fenster heimlich hinein, belauscht ihren Blick und Schritt,
There looks it at the window secretly in, eavesdrops (on) her glance and step,
(There it secretly looks in at the window, and eavesdrops on her every glance and step,)

giːpʻtʻ ˈmae̯nə ˈgryːsə ˈʃɛrtsəntʻ lapʻ, lʊntʻ nɪmt di ˈliːrən mɪtʰ.
gibt meine Grüsse scherzend ab, und nimmt die ihren mit.
gives my greetings jokingly over, and takes the hers with.
(playfully delivers *my* greetings, and takes *hers* away with it.) [*abgeben* = to deliver]

kʰae̯n ˈbriːfçən brɑo̯x ɪç tsuː ˈʃrae̯bən meːɐ̯, di ˈtʰrɛːnə zɛlpstʻ geːb ɪç liːɐ̯;
Kein Briefchen brauch' ich zu schreiben mehr, die Träne selbst geb' ich ihr;
No little letter need I to write (any) more, the tear even give I to it;
(I don't need to write any notes any more, I can even give it a tear to deliver;)

oː ziː fɛɐ̯ˈtʰrɛːkʻtʻ ziː ˈzɪçɐ nɪçtʰ, gaːɐ̯/gaːr ˈlae̯frɪç diːntʻ ziː miːɐ̯.
o sie verträgt sie sicher nicht, gar eifrig dient sie mir.
O it miscarries it certainly not, very zealously serves it me.
(Oh, it certainly will not carry that tear to the wrong address: it serves me very zealously.)

bae̯ tʰaːkʻ, bae̯ naxtʻ, lɪm ˈvaxən, lɪm tʰrɑo̯m, liːɐ̯ gɪlt das ˈlaləs glae̯ç,
Bei Tag, bei Nacht, im Wachen, im Traum, ihr gilt das alles gleich,
By day, by night, in the waking, in the dream, to it means that all (the) same,
(By day, by night, waking, in dreams — it's all the same to my pigeon,)
[*poem:* **im Wachen und** (lʊnt, and) **Traum**]

vɛn ziː nuːɐ̯ ˈvandɐn, ˈvandɐn kʰan, dan lɪstʻ ziː ˈlyːbɐˌrae̯ç.
wenn sie nur wandern, wandern kann, dann ist sie überreich.
if it just wander, wander can, then is it extremely rich.
(as long as it can keep flying missions, it considers itself extremely rich.)

ziː vɪrtʻ nɪçtʻ myːtʻ, ziː vɪrtʻ nɪçtʻ matʰ, deːɐ̯ veːkʻ lɪstʻ ʃtʻeːt͜s liːɐ̯ nɔ͜ø,
Sie wird nicht müd', sie wird nicht matt, der Weg ist stets ihr neu,
It grows not tired, it grows not weak, the way is always to it new,
(It does not grow tired, it does not grow weak, the way is always new to it,)

ziː bra͜oxtʻ nɪçtʻ ˈlɔkʻʊŋ, bra͜oxtʻ nɪçtʻ loːn, diː tʰa͜opʻ lɪstʻ zoː miːɐ̯ tʰrɔ͜ø!
sie braucht nicht Lockung, braucht nicht Lohn, d i e Taub' ist so mir treu!
it needs no enticement, needs no reward, *that* pigeon is so to me true!
(it needs no enticement, needs no reward, *that* pigeon is so faithful to me!)

drʊm heːg ɪç ziː la͜ox zoː tʰrɔ͜ø lan deːɐ̯ brʊstʻ, fɛɐ̯ˈzɪçɐt dɛs ˈʃøːnstʻən gəˈvɪns;
Drum heg' ich sie auch so treu an der Brust, versichert des schönsten Gewinns;
For that cherish I it also so loyally at the breast, assured of the finest prize;
(That's why I cherish it in my heart, also so faithfully, assured of the most beautiful prize;)

ziː ha͜estʰ: di ˈzeːnzʊxtʰ — kʰɛntʻ liːɐ̯ ziːʔ — di ˈboːtʻɪn ˈtʰrɔ͜øən zɪns.
sie heisst: die Sehnsucht — kennt ihr sie? — die Botin treuen Sinns.
it is called: the longing — know you it? — the messenger of faithful feeling.
(the pigeon's name is — "Longing." Do you know it? — the messenger of faithful feelings.)

[Love is a carrier pigeon that never goes astray, in this charming piece, the last "Swan Song." (The two following songs, both called "Swan Songs," are not a part of the "*Schwanengesang*" cycle put together and published under that title after Schubert's death.)]

ˈʃvaːngəzaŋ / ˈɛntʻlɪç ʃtʻeːn di ˈp͜fɔrtʻən ˈlɔfən

Schwangesang / Endlich steh'n die Pforten offen

Swan Song / At Last the Gates Stand Open

Posthumously published [composed 1815] (poem by Ludwig Kosegarten)

ˈɛntʻlɪç ʃtʻeːn di ˈp͜fɔrtʻən ˈlɔfən, ˈlɛntʻlɪç vɪŋkʻt das ˈkʰyːlə graːpʻ,
Endlich steh'n die Pforten offen, endlich winkt das kühle Grab,
At last stand the gates open, at last beckons the cool grave,
(At last the gates stand open, at last the cool grave beckons,)
[*poem:* **endlich winket mir** (ˈvɪŋkʻətʻ miːɐ̯, beckons to me) **das Grab**]

ʊntʻ naːx ˈlaŋəm ˈfʏrçtʻən, ˈhɔfən, na͜eg ɪç mɪç di naxtʻ hɪˈnapʻ.
und nach langem Fürchten, Hoffen, neig' ich mich die Nacht hinab.
and after long fearing, hoping, bend I myself the night down.
(and after a long time of fearing and hoping I bend down into the night.)
[*die Nacht hinab* = down the night (as in "down the river," etc.)]

ˈdʊrçgəvaxtʻ zɪntʻ nuːn di ˈtʰaːgə ˈma͜enəs ˈleːbəns, [ˈa͜osgəvaxtʻ]
Durchgewacht sind nun die Tage meines Lebens, [*poem:* **Ausgewacht**]
Through-watched are now the days of my life, [Out-watched, watched-out]
(I have stood my watch through the days of my life, and that duty is now over;)

ˈzyːsə ruː drʏkʻtʻ naːx ˈla͜osgəva͜entʻɐ ˈkʰlaːgə miːɐ̯ di ˈmyːdən ˈvɪmpʻɐn t͜suː.
süsse Ruh' drückt nach ausgeweinter Klage mir die müden Wimpern zu.
sweet rest presses after out-wept lament for me the weary eyelashes closed.
(after my eyes have wept away all their tears of lamentation, sweet rest closes my weary lids.)
[*poem:* **milde** (ˈmɪldə, gentle) **Ruh'... Wimper** (no longer correct)]

'ɑo̯gə, ʃlɔ͡øs dɪç! ʃt'ra:l de:ɐ̯ 'zɔnən, 'vɛk'ə nɪçt den 'ʃlɛ:fɐ me:ɐ̯!
Auge, schleuss dich! Strahl der Sonnen, wecke nicht den Schläfer mehr!
Eye, shut yourself! Ray of the suns, wake not the sleeper (any) more!
(Close, my eyes! Sunbeams, do not waken the sleeper any more!) [*schleuss* = *schliess'* = close]
[*poem:* **den Schlummrer** ('ʃlʊmrɐ, slumberer) **mehr]**

'za̯enə 'zant'lu:ɐ̯/-lu:r lɪst' fɛɐ̯'rɔnən, 'za̯enɐ 'kʰrɛft'ə 'ʃp'ru:dəl le:ɐ̯.
Seine Sanduhr ist verronnen, seiner Kräfte Sprudel leer.
His hourglass has run out, his powers' bubbling souce (is) empty.
(His hourglass has run out, the once-bubbling spring from which he drew his strength is dry.)
['ma̯enə lu:ɐ̯/lu:r lɪst' 'lɑo̯sgərɔnən. 'ma̯enəs 'le:bəns brʊn lɪst' le:ɐ̯.]
[*poem:* **Meine Uhr ist ausgeronnen. Meines Lebens Brunn ist leer.]**
[my clock has run down. My life's well is empty.]

'dʊrçgərant' zɪnt' 'za̯enə 'ʃraŋk'ən, 'dʊrçgəkʰɛmp͡fət' lɪst' za̯en kʰamp͡f.
Durchgerannt sind seine Schranken, durchgekämpfet ist sein Kampf.
Through-run are his barriers, through-fought is his battle.
(He has run through the barriers, he has finished fighting his battle.)
[*poem:* **meine** ('ma̯enə, my) **Schranken... mein** (ma̯en, my) **Kampf]**

ze:t, de:ɐ̯/de:r 'le:ɐ̯də 'p͡fa̯elɐ 'vaŋk'ən. ze:t, di vɛlt' fɛɐ̯'valt' vi: damp͡f.
Seht, der Erde Pfeiler wanken. Seht, die Welt verwallt wie Dampf.
See, the earth's pillars waver. See, the world boils away like steam.

'dʊŋk'əl vɪrt' ma̯en blɪk' lʊnt 'tʰry:bə, tʰɑo̯p' das lo:ɐ̯/lo:r, lʊnt' ʃt'ar das hɛrt͡s;
Dunkel wird mein Blick und trübe, taub das Ohr, und starr das Herz;
Dark becomes my gaze and dim, deaf the ear, and benumbed the heart;
(My eyes grow dim and dark, my ear grows deaf, and my heart grows numb;)
[*poem:* **mein** (ma̯en, my) **Ohr... mein** (ma̯en, my) **Herz]**

ɪn li:m kʰlɔp͡ft' nɪçt' me:ɐ̯ di 'li:bə, lɪn li:m be:p't' nɪçt' me:ɐ̯ de:ɐ̯ ʃmɛrt͡s.
in ihm klopft nicht mehr die Liebe, in ihm bebt nicht mehr der Schmerz.
in it beats no more the love, in it trembles no more the pain.
(love no longer beats there, pain no longer trembles in my heart.)

'ɑo̯sgəli:bət', 'lɑo̯sgəlɪt'ən ha:b ɪç, lʊnt di 'la̯edənʃaft tʰo:p't' nɪçt' me:ɐ̯,
Ausgeliebet, ausgelitten hab' ich, und die Leidenschaft tobt nicht mehr,
Out-loved, out-suffered have I, and the passion rages not (any) more,
(I have no more love to give, I have suffered all I can, and passion no longer rages inside me;)

ʊnt' 'lap'gəʃnɪt'ən dɔrt' ma̯en 're:bən, la̯est' ma̯en zaftʰ.
und abgeschnitten dorrt mein Reben, eis't mein Saft.
and off-cut withers my vine, ices my sap.
(my vine is cut off and withers away; my sap is freezing.) [*Reben* short for *Rebenstock* = vine]

'œfnə 'da̯enə 'ʃat'ənp͡fɔrt'ən, 'lœfnə, 'lɛŋəl tʰo:t', zi: nu:n!
Öffne deine Schattenpforten, öffne, Engel Tod, sie nun!
Open your shadow- portals, open, Angel Death, them now!
(Open your shadowy gates, Angel of Death, open them now!)
[*poem:* **Öffne deines Dunkels Pforten** ('da̯enəs 'dʊŋk'əls 'p͡fɔrt'ən, your darkness's gates)]

'laŋə vɪl lɪç, 'laŋə 'dɔrt'ən bae di:ɐ̯/di:r lɪn de:ɐ̯ 'kʰamɐ ru:n.
Lange will ich, lange dorten bei dir in der Kammer ruh'n.
Long want I, long there with you in the chamber to rest.
(I want to rest for a long, long time there with you in that chamber.)

zy:s, gə'rɔøʃlo:s, kʰy:l lʊnt' 'ʃt'ɪlə zɔls lɪn 'daenɐ 'kʰamɐ zaen.
Süss, geräuschlos, kühl und stille soll's in deiner Kammer sein.
Sweet, noiseless, cool and quiet shall it in your chamber be.
(It is believed to be sweet, noiseless, cool, and quiet in your chamber.)
[*poem:* **Sanft** (zanft', gentle)**, geräuschlos]**

o: zo: 'laelə, 'tʰraot'ɐ, 'hʏlə lɪn daen 'ʃla:fgəvant' mɪç laen!
O so eile, Trauter, hülle in dein Schlafgewand mich ein!
O then hurry, dear one, wrap in your sleep- garment me up!
(Oh, then hurry, dear angel of death, and wrap me in your sleeping garment!)

di: mɪç gɛrn lʊnt' 'li:bənt' 'ʃaotən, mo:nt' lʊnt' 'zɔnə, 'le:bət' vo:l!
Die mich gern und liebend schauten, Mond und Sonne, lebet wohl!
(You) who me gladly and lovingly see, moon and sun, fare well!
(You who gladly and lovingly look down at me, moon and sun, farewell!)

di: mi:ɐ̯ 'zy:sə 've:mu:t 'tʰaot'ən, fry: lʊnt' 'ʃp'ɛ:t'ro:t', 'le:bət' vo:l!
Die mir süsse Wehmut tauten, Früh- und Spätrot, lebet wohl!
(You) who me sweet melancholy dew, early- and late-red, fare well!
(You who bedew me with sweet melancholy, dawn and sunset, farewell!)

'le:bət' vo:l, li:ɐ̯ 'gry:nən 'fɛldɐ, du: maen 'tʰaozənt'ʃø:nən- tʰa:l!
Lebet wohl, ihr grünen Felder, du mein Tausendschönchen-Tal!
Fare well, you green fields, you my daisy- valley!
(Farewell, you green fields, and you, my valley of daisies!)
[*poem:* **ihr Saatenfelder** ('za:t'ənfɛldɐ, fields of standing corn)]

'dy:st'rə, 'faeɐlɪçə 'vɛldɐ, bɛç lʊnt' 'hy:gəl 'laltsuma:l!
Düstre, feierliche Wälder, Bäch' und Hügel allzumal!
Dark, solemn forests, brooks and hill/hills altogether!
(Dark, solemn forests, brooks, and hills, I bid you all farewell!)

di: li:ɐ̯ 'tsɛ:ɐ̯t'lɪç mɪç lʊm'ʃlaŋətʰ, mɪt' mi:ɐ̯ 'tʰaelət' ve: lʊnt' vo:l,
Die ihr zärtlich mich umschlanget, mit mir teiltet Weh und Wohl,
Who you tenderly me twined about, with me shared woe and weal,
(You who embraced me tenderly, who shared my good times and bad,)

mɪt' mi:ɐ̯ 'kʰɛmpft'ət', mɪt' mi:ɐ̯ 'raŋət', 'le:bət', 'frɔøndə, 'le:bət' vo:l!
mit mir kämpftet, mit mir ranget, lebet, Freunde, lebet wohl!
with me fought, with me struggled, live, friends, fare well!
(who fought with me and struggled with me, my friends, live and fare well!)

di: du: 'maenən ʃt'aop' lɛɐ̯'ʃu:fəst', lʊnt'
Die du meinen Staub erschufest, und
Who you my dust created, and
(You who created my dust, and)

li:n hɔ͜øt‘ ɪn 'da͜enən ʃo:s, 'mʊt‘ɐ(r) 'le:ɐ̯də, 'vi:dɐ 'ru:fəst‘, hʏl li:n zanft‘ lʊnt‘
ihn heut' in deinen Schoss, Mutter Erde, wieder rufest, hüll' ihn sanft und
it today into your womb, Mother Earth, again call, cover it gently and
(who call it back today into your womb, Mother Earth, cover it gently and)

'ʃt‘ø:rʊŋslo:s! 'le:vɪç vɪrt di naxt‘ nɪçt 'da͜oɐn, 'le:vɪç 'di:zɐ 'ʃlʊmɐ nɪçtʰ.
störungslos! Ewig wird die Nacht nicht dauern, ewig dieser Schlummer nicht.
undisturbed! Eternally will the night not last, eternally this slumber not.
(let it be undisturbed! The night will not last forever, nor will this slumber.)

'hɪnt‘ɐ 'je:nən 'grɛ:bɐʃa͜oɐn 'dɛmɐt‘ 'lʊnla͜oslœʃlɪç lɪçtʰ.
Hinter jenen Gräberschauern dämmert unauslöschlich Licht.
Beyond those graves- shudders dawns inextinguishable light.
(Beyond those shudders of the grave an inextinguishable light will dawn.)
['hɪnt‘ɐ 'je:nɐ 'grɛ:bɐ 'ʃa͜oɐn 'dɛmɐt‘ mi:ɐ̯/mi:r la͜en 'nɔ͜øəs lɪçtʰ]
[*poem:* **Hinter jener Gräber Schauern dämmert mir ein neues Licht]**
[Beyond those graves' shudders dawns for me a new light]

'a:bɐ bɪs das lɪçt‘ mi:ɐ̯ 'fʊŋk‘lə, bɪs la͜en 'ʃø:nrɐ tʰa:k‘ mi:ɐ̯ laxt‘,
Aber bis das Licht mir funkle, bis ein schön'rer Tag mir lacht,
But till the light for me sparkles, till a more beautiful day for me laughs,
(But till that light sparkles for me, till a more beautiful day smiles on me,)
[*poem:* **bis der junge** (de:ɐ̯ 'jʊŋə, the young [=Judgment]) **Tag erwacht** (lɛɐ̯'vaxtʰ, wakes)]

zɪŋk‘ ɪç 'ru:ɪç ɪn di 'dʊŋk‘lə, 'ʃt‘ɪlə, 'kʰy:lə 'ʃlʊmɐnaxtʰ. [ʃt‘a͜ek‘]
sink' ich ruhig in die dunkle, stille, kühle Slummernacht. [*poem:* **steig' ich ruhig]**
sink I calmly into the dark, quiet, cool slumber- night. [descend]
(I sink calmly into that dark, quiet, cool night of slumber.)

[The poem sounds like the ruminations of an old man, ready to lay down his burden; the poet was only seventeen years old! Schubert's simple strophic setting has some haunting moments.]

'ʃvanəngəzaŋ / vi: kʰla:g ɪçs la͜os
Schwanengesang / Wie klag' ich's aus
Swan Song / How Shall I Express

Op. 23, No. 3 [1822?] (Johann Chrysostomus Senn)

vi: kʰla:g ɪçs la͜os das 'ʃt‘ɛrbəgəfy:l, das la͜of'lø:zənt dʊrç di 'gli:dɐ rɪntʰ?
"Wie klag' ich's aus das Sterbegefühl, das auflösend durch die Glieder rinnt?
" How lament I it out the dying- feeling, that dissolving through the limbs runs?
("How shall I express in my lament the feeling of dying that runs through my limbs, dissolving?)

vi: zɪŋ lɪçs la͜os das 've:ɐ̯dəgəfy:l, das lɛɐ̯'lø:zənt dɪç, lo: ga͜est‘, 'lanve:tʰ?
Wie sing' ich's aus das Werdegefühl, das erlösend dich, o Geist, anweht?"
How sing I it out the becoming-feeling, that redeeming you, O spirit, at-wafts?"
(How shall I express in song the feeling of becoming, that wafts over you, O spirit, redeeming?")

e:ɐ̯ kʰla:k‘t‘, le:ɐ̯ zaŋ fɛɐ̯'nɪçt‘ʊŋsbaŋ, fɛɐ̯'kʰlɛ:rʊŋsfro:, bɪs das 'le:bən flo:.
Er klagt', er sang vernichtungsbang, verklärungsfroh, bis das Leben floh.
He lamented, he sang annihilation-fearful, transfiguration-glad, till the life fled.
(He lamented and sang, fearful of annihilation, rejoicing in transfiguration, till his life fled.)
[*poem:* **Es** (ɛs, It) **klagt', es sang]**

das bəˈdɔ͜øtʻət dɛs ˈʃvaːnən gəˈzaŋ. [lɪst]
Das bedeutet des Schwanen Gesang. [*poem:* **Das ist des Schwanen Gesang.**]
That means the swan's song. [is]
(That is what the swan's song means.)

[There is an ancient belief that the swan—without a song in life—sings on his journey into death. There is depth in this short song. The plaintive opening chords prepare the way for the mystery of death: the body's fear of dying, the soul's yearning for transfiguration and redemption.]

ˈʃva͜et͜sɐliːtʻ
Schweizerlied
Swiss Song

Posthumously published [composed 1817] (poem in Swiss dialect by J. W. von Goethe)

ˈuːfm ˈbɛːrkli bɪn ɪ ˈksæːssɛ, haː dɛ ˈfœglɛ ˈt͜suːəkʃa͜ut; [kəˈzæssɛ]
Uf'm Bergli bin i g'sässe, ha de Vögle zugeschaut; [*poem:* **gesässe**]
On the little mountain have I sat, have the birds at-looked; [sat]
(I was sitting on the little mountain, watching the birds;)

hænt kəˈsʊŋŋɛ, hænt kəˈʃprʊŋŋɛ, hænt ˈsnæʃtli kəˈba͜ut. [*unvoiced b* (*throughout*)]
hänt gesunge, hänt gesprunge, hänt 'sNästli gebaut.
(they) have sung, have hopped, have the little nest built.
(they were singing, hopping about, and building their little nest.)

in æ ˈgartə bɪn ɪ ˈkʃtantɛ, haː tɛn ˈɪːmpli ˈt͜suːəkʃa͜ot ; [kəˈʃtantɛ]
In a Garte bin i g'stande, ha de Imbli zugeschaut; [*poem:* **gestande**]
In a garden have I stood, have the little bees at-looked; [stood]
(I was standing in a garden, watching the little bees;)

hænt kəˈprʊmmət, hænt kəˈsʊmmət, hænt ˈt͜sælli kəˈba͜utʰ. [*t, k, p never aspirated*]
hänt gebrummet, hänt gesummet, hänt Zelli gebaut.
(they) have hummed, have buzzed, have little cells built.
(they were humming, they were buzzing, they were building cells.)

uːf t ˈviːəsə bɪn ɪ ˈkaŋŋə, ˈluːəkt ɪ ˈsʊmmər fœglɛn aː; [*n inserted to avoid hiatus*]
Uf d' Wiese bin i gange, lugt' i Summervögle a;
On the meadow have I walked, looked I butterflies at;
(I was walking on the meadow, looking at the butterflies;)

hænt kəˈsoːkɛ, hænt kəˈfloːkɛ, kaːr t͜sʃœːn hænt͜s kəˈtaː. [*s always unvoiced*]
hänt gesoge, hänt gefloge, gar z' schön hänt's getan.
(they) have sucked, have flown, really too beautifully have it done.
(they were sucking nectar, they were flitting about, they were doing it all so beautifully.)
[*Peters:* **gar zu schön** (t͜suː ʃøːn, too beautifully)]

unt daː kxʊmt nʊ dɛ ˈhannsl̩, unt daː t͜sæ͜ik ɪːn ɛm froː, [*n inserted to avoid hiatus*]
Unt da kummt nu der Hansel, und da zeig' i em froh,
And there comes now the Hansel, and there show I him happily,
(And now along comes Hansel, and I happily show him)

'viə 'ziəs 'mɑxxɛ, unt mər 'lɑxxɛ unt 'mɑxxəs 'ɑ͜uə so:. [*s always unvoiced*]
wie sie's mache, und mer lache und mache's au so.
how they it do, and we laugh and do it also so.
(what they are doing; and we laugh and do the same.)

[The poem is in Goethe's version of a Swiss dialect. The pronunciation is quite different from standard German. The b, g, and d are pronounced more like *unaspirated* p, k, and t, respectively. There is no glottal stop before vowels; on the contrary, an n is often inserted to avoid a hiatus. Schubert's setting is utterly delightful, gracefully capturing the lilt of Swiss mountain music.]

'ʃve:ɐ̯t'li:t'
Schwertlied
Sword Song

Posthumously published [composed 1815] (poem by Theodor Körner)

du: ʃve:ɐ̯t' lan 'ma͜enɐ 'lɪŋk'ən, vas zɔl da͜en 'ha͜et'rəs 'blɪŋk'ən?
Du Schwert an meiner Linken, was soll dein heitres Blinken?
You sword at my left (side), what means your bright shining?
(You sword at my left side, why are you gleaming so brightly?)

ʃɑ͜ost' mɪç zo: 'frɔ͜ønt'lɪç lan, ha:p' 'ma͜enə 'frɔ͜ødə dran. — 'hʊra!
Schaust mich so freundlich an, hab' meine Freude dran. — Hurrah!
(You) look me so friendly at, (I) have my joy thereat. — Hurrah!
(You look at me in such a friendly way, it gives me joy. — Hurrah!)

mɪç tʰrɛ:k't' la͜en 'vak'rɐ 'ra͜et'ɐ, drʊm blɪŋk' ɪç lɑ͜ox zo: 'ha͜et'ɐ,
"Mich trägt ein wackrer Reiter, drum blink' ich auch so heiter,
"Me carries a valiant rider, therefore shine I also so brightly,
("A valiant cavalryman is carrying me, that's why I shine so brightly,)

bɪn 'fra͜eən 'manəs ve:ɐ̯; das frɔ͜øt dem 'ʃve:ɐ̯t'ə ze:ɐ̯. — 'hʊra!
bin freien Mannes Wehr; das freut dem Schwerte sehr." — Hurrah!
(I) am free man's weapon; that gladdens the sword very much." — Hurrah!
(I am the weapon of a free man; that makes a sword very glad." — Hurrah!)

ja:, 'gu:t'əs ʃve:ɐ̯t', fra͜e bɪn lɪç, lʊnt' 'li:bə dɪç hɛrt͜s'lɪnɪç,
Ja, gutes Schwert, frei bin ich, und liebe dich herzinnig,
Yes, good sword, free am I, and love you cordially,
(Yes, good sword, I am free, and I love you sincerely,)

als vɛ:ɐ̯st du: mi:ɐ̯ gə'tʰrɑ͜ot', lals 'la͜enə 'li:bə brɑ͜otʰ. — 'hʊra!
als wärst du mir getraut, als eine liebe Braut. — Hurrah!
as (if) were you to me married, as a dear bride. — Hurrah!
(as if you were married to me, as a dear bride. — Hurrah!)

di:ɐ̯ ha:b ɪçs ja: lɛɐ̯'ge:bən, ma͜en 'lɪçt'əs 'la͜ezənle:bən.
"Dir hab' ich's ja ergeben, mein lichtes Eisenleben.
"To you have I it after all yielded, my bright iron- life.
("To you, after all, I have yielded my bright iron life.)

ax ˈvɛːrən viːɐ̯ gəˈtʰrɑ͜ot‘! van hoːlst duː ˈdɑ͜enə brɑ͜otʰ? — ˈhʊra!
Ach wären wir getraut! Wann holst du deine Braut?" — Hurrah!
Ah were we married! When fetch you your bride?" — Hurrah!
(Ah, if we were only married! When will you fetch your bride?"— Hurrah!)

t͜sʊr ˈbrɑ͜ot‘naxt͜s- ˈmɔrgənrøːt‘ə ruːft‘ ˈfɛst‘lɪç di tʰrɔmˈpʰet‘ə;
Zur Brautnachts-Morgenröte ruft festlich die Trompete;
To the bridal nights- dawn calls festively the trumpet;
(The trumpet calls to celebrate the coming of dawn in the bridal night;)

vɛn di kʰaˈnoːnən ʃrɑ͜en, hoːl ɪç das ˈliːp‘çən lɑ͜en. — ˈhʊra!
wenn die Kanonen schrei'n, hol' ich das Liebchen ein. — Hurrah!
when the cannons shout, fetch I the sweetheart .... — Hurrah!
(when the cannons roar I shall fetch my sweetheart. — Hurrah!) [*einholen* (here) = go to fetch]

oː ˈzeːlɪgəs lʊmˈfaŋən! lɪç ˈharə mɪt‘ fɛɐ̯ˈlaŋən.
"O seliges Umfangen! Ich harre mit Verlangen.
"O blissful embrace! I wait with desire.

duː ˈbrɔ͜øt‘gam, ˈhoːlə mɪç, mɑ͜en ˈkʰrɛnt͜sçən blɑ͜ep‘t‘ fyːɐ̯ dɪç. — ˈhʊra!
Du Bräut'gam, hole mich, mein Kränzchen bleibt für dich." — Hurrah!
You bridegram, fetch me, my little wreath remains for you." — Hurrah!
(My bridegroom, fetch me, my bridal wreath will be yours." — Hurrah!)

vas kʰlɪrst duː lɪn deːɐ̯ ˈʃɑ͜edə, duː ˈhɛlə ˈlɑ͜ezənfrɔ͜ødə,
Was klirrst du in der Scheide, du helle Eisenfreude,
Why clank you in the sheath, you bright iron- joy,
(Why are you clanking in your sheath, you bright iron joy,)

zoː vɪlt‘, zoː ˈʃlaxt‘ənfroː? mɑ͜en ʃveːɐ̯t‘, vas kʰlɪrst duː zoː? — ˈhʊra!
so wild, so schlachtenfroh? Mein Schwert, was klirrst du so? — Hurrah!
so wild, so battle- happy? My sword, why clank you so? — Hurrah!
(so wild, so battle-happy? My sword, why are you clanking like that? — Hurrah!)

voːl kʰlɪr ɪç lɪn deːɐ̯ ˈʃɑ͜edə; lɪç ˈzeːnə mɪç t͜sʊm ˈʃt‘rɑ͜et‘ə,
"Wohl klirr' ich in der Scheide; ich sehne mich zum Streite,
"Indeed clank I in the sheath; I long myself to the fight,
("I am indeed clanking in my sheath; I am longing for a fight,)

rɛçt‘ vɪlt‘ lʊnt‘ ˈʃlaxt‘ənfroː. drʊm, ˈrɑ͜et‘ɐ, kʰlɪr ɪç zoː. — ˈhʊra!
recht wild und schlachtenfroh. Drum, Reiter, klirr' ich so." — Hurrah!
quite wild and battle- happy. Therefore, rider, clank I so." — Hurrah!
(quite wild and battle-happy. That's why I am clanking like that, cavalryman."— Hurrah!)

blɑ͜ep‘ dɔx lɪm ˈlɛŋən ˈʃt‘yːp‘çən. vas vɪlst duː hiːɐ̯, mɑ͜en ˈliːp‘çən?
Bleib doch im engen Stübchen. Was willst du hier, mein Liebchen?
Stay though in the narrow little room. What want you here, my sweetheart?
(Just stay in that narrow little room. What would you want here, my sweetheart!)

blɑ͜ep‘ ʃt‘ɪl lɪm ˈkʰɛmɐlɑ͜en, blɑ͜ep‘, balt‘ hoːl ɪç dɪç lɑ͜en. — ˈhʊra!
Bleib still im Kämmerlein, bleib, bald hol' ich dich ein. — Hurrah!
Stay quietly in the little chamber, stay, soon fetch I you .... — Hurrah!
(Stay quietly in your little chamber, stay there; I shall soon come to fetch you. — Hurrah!)

las mɪç nɪçt‘ 'laŋə 'vart‘ən! lo: 'ʃø:nɐ 'li:bəsgart‘ən,
“Lass mich nicht lange warten! O schöner Liebesgarten,
“Let me not long wait! O beautiful love- garden,
(“Do not make me wait long! Oh beautiful garden of love,)

fɔl 'rø:sla͜en 'blu:t‘ɪçro:t‘, lʊnt‘ 'la͜ofgəbly:t‘əm tʰo:t‘. — 'hʊra!
voll Röslein blutigrot, und aufgeblühtem Tod.” — Hurrah!
full (of) little roses bloody red, and open-blossomed death.” — Hurrah!
(full of little blood-red roses where the blossoms of death open wide.” — Hurrah!)

zo: kʰɔm dɛn la͜os de:ɐ̯ 'ʃa͜edə, du: 'ra͜et‘ɐs 'la͜ogənva͜edə.
So komm denn aus der Scheide, du Reiters Augenweide.
So come then out of the sheath, you rider’s eye- pasture.
(Then come out of your sheath, you welcome sight to a cavalryman’s eyes.)

hɛ'ra͜os, ma͜en ʃve:ɐ̯t‘, hɛ'ra͜os! fy:ɐ̯ dɪç lɪns 'fa:t‘ɐha͜os. — 'hʊra!
Heraus, mein Schwert, heraus! Führ’ dich ins Vaterhaus. — Hurrah!
Out, my sword, out! Guide yourself into the paternal house. — Hurrah!
(Out, my sword, out! Enter your natural home. — Hurrah!)

ax 'hɛrlɪç lɪst͜s lɪm 'fra͜eən, lɪm 'rʏst‘gən 'hɔxt͜sa͜et͜sra͜egən.
“Ach herrlich ist’s im Freien, im rüst’gen Hochzeitsreihen.
“Ah glorious is it in the open air, in the vigorous wedding round dance.
(“Ah, it is glorious to be out of doors, in the vigorous wedding dance.)
[*GA:* **Hochzeitreihen** ('hɔxt͜sa͜et‘ra͜egən, wedding round dance)]

vi: glɛnt͜st‘ lɪm 'zɔnənʃt‘ra:l zo: 'brɔ͜øt‘lɪç hɛl de:ɐ̯ ʃt‘a:l! — 'hʊra!
Wie glänzt im Sonnenstrahl so bräutlich hell der Stahl!” — Hurrah!
How gleams in the sunbeam so bridally bright the steel!”— Hurrah!
(How bridally bright my steel gleams in the sunlight!” — Hurrah!)

vo:l'la͜of, li:ɐ̯ 'kʰɛk‘ən 'ʃt‘ra͜et‘ɐ, vo:l'la͜of, li:ɐ̯ 'dɔ͜øt͜ʃən 'ra͜et‘ɐ!
Wohlauf, ihr kecken Streiter, wohlauf, ihr deutschen Reiter!
Come on, you bold fighters, come on, you German cavalrymen!

vɪrt‘ lɔ͜øç das hɛrt͜s nɪçt‘ varm? ne:mt‘ 'sli:p‘çən lɪn den larm. — 'hʊra!
Wird euch das Herz nicht warm? Nehmt ’s Liebchen in den Arm. — Hurrah!
Becomes for you the heart not warm? Take the sweetheart into the arm. — Hurrah!
(Is your heart not growing warm? Take your sweetheart into your arms. — Hurrah!)

e:ɐ̯st tʰa:t‘ lɛs lan de:ɐ̯ 'lɪŋk‘ən nu:ɐ̯ gant͜s fɛɐ̯'ʃt‘o:lən 'blɪŋk‘ən;
Erst tat es an der Linken nur ganz verstohlen blinken;
First did she at the left (side) only quite furtively shine;
(First, at your left side, she gleamed only very furtively, peeking out of the sheath;)

dɔx lan di 'rɛçt‘ə tʰra͜ot‘ gɔt‘ 'zɪçt‘ba:ɐ̯lɪç di bra͜otʰ. — 'hʊra!
doch an die Rechte traut Gott sichtbarlich die Braut. — Hurrah!
but in your right hand trusts God [obj.] visibly the bride [subj.]. — Hurrah!
(but in your right hand the bride can be seen to have brave confidence in God. — Hurrah!)

drʊm drʏk'tʼ den ˈliːbəhaesən ˈbrɔøt'lɪçən mʊnt' fɔn ˈlaezən
Drum drückt den liebeheissen bräutlichen Mund von Eisen
Therefore press the love-ardent bridal mouth of iron
(Therefore press the passionate iron mouth of your bride)
[*The word* "bräutlichen" *does not fit the musical phrase unless the rhythm is altered.*]

an ˈlɔørə ˈlɪp'ən fɛst'. fluːx! veːɐ̯ di braot' fɛɐ̯ˈlɛstʰ! — ˈhʊra!
an eure Lippen fest. Fluch! wer die Braut verlässt! — Hurrah!
to your lips firmly. Curse! (him) who the bride forsakes! — Hurrah!
(firmly to your lips. Curse him who forsakes his bride! — Hurrah!)

nuːn last das ˈliːp'çən ˈzɪŋən, das ˈhɛlə ˈfʊŋk'ən ˈʃp'rɪŋən!
Nun lasst das Liebchen singen, dass helle Funken springen!
Now let the sweetheart sing, (so) that bright sparks leap!
(Now let your sweetheart sing, so that bright sparks will dance!)

deːɐ̯ ˈhɔxtsaetmɔrgən graot'. *ˈhʊra/hʊˈraː, duː ˈlaezənbraotʰ! — ˈhʊra!
Der Hochzeitmorgen graut. Hurrah, du Eisenbraut! — Hurrah!
The wedding morning dawns. Hurrah, you iron bride! — Hurrah!
*[*The accentuation varies, first* ˈhʊra, *then at the repeat* hʊˈraː (*both correct*)]

[The poem is a dialogue between the cavalryman and his sword, with a male chorus shouting "Hurrah!" at the end of each short verse (both poem and song add the instruction: "with clanking swords"). The poet was killed in battle shortly after writing this poem (at Gladebusch, August 23, 1813, fighting against Napoleon's army). The sword is seen as the soldier's eager bride.]

ˈʃvɛst'ɐgruːs
Schwestergruss
Sisterly Greeting

Posthumously published [composed 1822] (poem by Franz von Bruchmann)

ɪm ˈmoːndənʃaen val ɪç laof lʊnt' lap', zeː ˈtʰoːt'ənbaen lʊnt' ˈʃt'ɪləs graːp'.
Im Mondenschein wall' ich auf und ab, seh' Totenbein' und stilles Grab.
In the moonlight wander I up and down, see dead bones and quiet grave.
(In the moonlight I wander up and down, seeing dead bones and the quiet grave.)

ɪm ˈgaest'ɐhaox foˈryːbɐ ʃveːp'ts, viː flam lʊnt' raox foˈryːbɐ beːp'ts;
Im Geisterhauch vorüber schwebt's, wie Flamm' und Rauch vorüber bebt's;
In the ghosts- breath past hovers it, like flame and smoke past trembles it;
(Something hovers past in a ghostly breeze, something trembles by me, like flame and vapor;)
[*Peters:* **vorüber webt's** (veːp'ts, weaves)**... vorüber schwebt's**]

aos ˈneːbəltʰruːk' ʃt'aek't' ˈlaenə gəˈʃt'alt', loːn zʏnt' lʊnt' luːk' foˈryːbɐ valtʰ,
aus Nebeltrug steigt eine Gestalt, ohn' Sünd' und Lug vorüber wallt,
out of mist- deceit rises a form, without sin and falsehood past floats,
(out of an illusion of mist a form without sin or falsehood rises and floats by,)
[*Lug* = *Lüge* = lie, falsehood (now used only in the combination "*Trug und Lug*")]

das laok' zoː blao, deːɐ̯ blɪk' zoː groːs viː lɪn ˈhɪməlslao, viː lɪn ˈgɔt'əs ʃoːs;
das Aug' so blau, der Blick so gross wie in Himmelsau, wie in Gottes Schoss;
the eye so blue, the gaze so big as in heaven- meadow, as in God's lap;
(the eyes so blue, the gaze as wide as in the meadows of heaven, as in the lap of God;)

a͜en va͜es gəˈvantʻ bəˈdɛkʻt das bɪltʻ, lɪn ˈt͜saːɐ̯tʻɐ hantʻ ˈla͜enə ˈliːliə kʰvɪltʰ,
ein weiss Gewand bedeckt das Bild, in zarter Hand eine Lilie quillt,
a white garment covers the image, in delicate hand a lily rises up,
(a white garment covers the apparition, a lily rises from a delicate hand;)

ɪn ˈga͜estʻɐha͜ox ziː t͜suː miːɐ̯ ʃpʻrɪçtʰ: lɪç ˈvandrə ʃoːn lɪm ˈra͜enən lɪçtʻ,
in Geisterhauch sie zu mir spricht: "Ich wand're schon im reinen Licht,
in spirit- breath she to me speaks: "I wander already in the pure light,
(she speaks to me in a spirit's whisper: "I already wander in pure light,)

zeː moːntʻ lʊntʻ zɔn t͜suː ˈma͜enəm fuːs, lʊntʻ leːpʻ lɪn vɔn, lɪn ˈlɛŋəlkʰʊs;
seh' Mond und Sonn' zu meinem Fuss, und leb' in Wonn', in Engelkuss;
see moon and sun at my foot, and live in bliss, in angel-kiss;
(I see the moon and the sun beneath my feet, and live in bliss, kissed by the angels;)

ʊntʻ lal di lʊst, diː lɪç lɛmˈp͜fɪntʻ, nɪçt ˈda͜enə brʊstʻ kʰɛntʻ, ˈmɛnʃənkʰɪntʻ!
und all' die Lust, die ich empfind', nicht deine Brust kennt, Menschenkind!
and all the joy, which I feel, not your breast knows, human being!
(and your breast, human as you are, cannot know all the joy that I feel,)

vɛn duː nɪçtʻ lɛst den ˈleːɐ̯dəngɔtʻ, bəˈfoːɐ̯ dɪç fast deːɐ̯ ˈgra͜ozə tʰoːtʻ.
wenn du nicht lässt den Erdengott, bevor dich fasst der grause Tod."
if you not leave the earth- god, before you seizes the gruesome death."
(unless you abandon the god of earthly materialism, before gruesome death seizes you.")

zoː tʰøːnt di lʊftʻ, zoː za͜ost deːɐ̯ vɪnt, t͜suː den ˈʃtʻɛrnən ruːft das ˈhɪməlskʰɪntʻ, lʊntʻ
So tönt die Luft, so saust der Wind, zu den Sternen ruft das Himmelskind, und
So sounds the air, so moans the wind, to the stars calls the heaven- child, and
(So speaks the air, so moans the wind; the child of heaven calls up to the stars, and)

leː ziː fliːtʻ, di va͜es gəˈʃtʻaltʻ, lɪn ˈfrɪʃɐ blyːtʻ ziː zɪç lɛntʻˈfaltʰ: lɪn ˈra͜enɐ
eh' sie flieht, die weiss' Gestalt, in frischer Blüt' sie sich entfalt': in reiner
before she flees, the white form, in fresh bloom she herself unfurls: in pure
(before she flees, that white form, she expands in a fresh blossoming: as pure)

flam ʃveːpʻtʻ ziː lɛmˈpʰoːɐ̯, ˈloːnə ʃmɛr͜ts lʊntʻ harm, t͜suː deːɐ̯/deːr ˈlɛŋəl kʰoːɐ̯.
Flamm' schwebt sie empor, ohne Schmerz und Harm, zu der Engel Chor.
flame soars she aloft, without pain and sorrow, to the angel choir.
(flame she soars aloft, without pain and sorrow, to the angel choir.)

di naxtʻ fɛɐ̯ˈhʏlt den ˈha͜elgən lɔrtʰ, fɔn gɔtʻ lɛɐ̯ˈfʏltʻ zɪŋ lɪç das vɔrtʰ.
Die Nacht verhüllt den heil'gen Ort, von Gott erfüllt sing' ich das Wort.
The night veils the holy place, by God filled sing I the word.
(Night veils the holy place; filled with a sense of God, I sing the Word.)

[The poem was written after the death of the poet's sister. Bruchmann was one of Schubert's classmates at the *Stadtkonvikt*, later the host for a number of "Schubertiads." The poem, with its bones and graveyard, typical of the period, is transfigured by some very fine music.]

ˈzeːnzʊxtʰ / ax, la͜os ˈdiːzəs ˈtʰaːləs ˈɡrʏndən
Sehnsucht / Ach, aus dieses Tales Gründen
Longing / Ah, Out of the Depths of This Valley

Op. 39 (the later version) [1813, 1819?] (Friedrich von Schiller)

ax, la͜os ˈdiːzəs ˈtʰaːləs ˈɡrʏndən, diː deːɐ̯ ˈkʰaltʻə ˈneːbəl drʏkʻtʰ,
Ach, aus dieses Tales Gründen, die der kalte Nebel drückt,
Ah, out of this valley's depths, which the cold mist oppresses,
(Ah, if I could only find a way out of the depths of this valley, oppressed by cold mist,)

kʰœntʻ ɪç dɔx den ˈla͜osɡaŋ ˈfɪndən, lax, viː fyːltʻ ɪç mɪç bəˈɡlʏkʻtʰ!
könnt' ich doch den Ausgang finden, ach, wie fühlt' ich mich beglückt!
could I only the way out find, ah, how felt I myself blessed!
(ah, how fortunate I would feel!)

dɔrtʻ lɛɐ̯blɪkʻ ɪç ˈʃøːnə ˈhyːɡəl, ˈleːvɪç jʊŋ lʊntʻ ˈleːvɪç ɡryːn!
Dort erblick' ich schöne Hügel, ewig jung und ewig grün!
There see I beautiful hills, eternally young and eternally green!
(I can see beautiful hills up there, eternally young and eternally green!)

hɛtʻ ɪç ˈʃvɪŋən, hɛtʻ ɪç ˈflyːɡəl, naːx den ˈhyːɡəln t͜søːɡ ɪç hɪn.
Hätt' ich Schwingen, hätt' ich Flügel, nach den Hügeln zög' ich hin.
Had I pinions, had I wings, toward the hills would depart I hence.
(If I had wings I would leave this place and fly toward those hills.)

harmoˈniːən høːr ɪç ˈkʰlɪŋən, ˈtʰøːnə ˈzyːsɐ ˈhɪməlsruː,
Harmonien hör' ich klingen, Töne süsser Himmelsruh',
Harmonies hear I sounding, tones of sweet heaven- peace,
(I can hear harmonies, tones of sweet heavenly peace,)

ʊnt di ˈla͜eçtʻən ˈvɪndə ˈbrɪŋən miːɐ̯ deːɐ̯ ˈdʏftʻə ˈbalzaːm t͜suː,
und die leichten Winde bringen mir der Düfte Balsam zu,
and the light winds bring to me the scents' balm to,
(and the light breezes bring me the balm of sweet scents,)

ˈɡɔldnə ˈfrʏçtʻə zeː ɪç ˈɡlyːən, ˈvɪŋkʻənt ˈt͜svɪʃən ˈdʊŋkʻəlm la͜opʻ,
gold'ne Früchte seh' ich glühen, winkend zwischen dunkelm Laub,
golden fruits see I glow, beckoning between dark foliage,
(I see golden fruit glowing, beckoning out of dark foliage,)

ʊnt di ˈbluːmən, diː dɔrtʻ ˈblyːən, ˈveːɐ̯dən ˈkʰa͜enəs ˈvɪntʻɐs ra͜opʻ.
und die Blumen, die dort blühen, werden keines Winters Raub.
and the flowers, that there bloom, become no winter's prey.
(and the flowers that bloom there never become the prey of winter.)

ax, viː ʃøːn mʊs zɪçs lɛɐ̯ˈɡeːən dɔrtʻ lɪm ˈleːvɡən ˈzɔnənʃa͜en,
Ach, wie schön muss sich's ergehen dort im ew'gen Sonnenschein,
Ah, how beautiful must itself it stroll there in the eternal sunshine,
(Ah, how beautiful it must be to stroll there in the eternal sunshine,)

[*GA (both later versions):* **O** (oː, oh) **wie schön**]

ʊnt di lʊft‘ lɑ̯of ˈjeːnən ˈhøːən, loː viː ˈlaːbənt‘ mʊs lɛs zɑ̯en!
und die Luft auf jenen Höhen, o wie labend muss es sein!
and the air on those heights, O how refreshing must it be!
(and the air on those heights, oh, how refreshing it must be!)

dɔx miːɐ̯ veːɐ̯t dɛs ˈʃt‘roːməs ˈtʰoːbən, deːɐ̯/deːr lɛɐ̯ˈgrɪmt daˈt̮svɪʃən brɑ̯ostʰ,
Doch mir wehrt des Stromes Toben, der ergrimmt dazwischen braust,
But to me hinders the stream's raging, which infuriated there-between roars,
(But I am hindered by the raging river that is furiously roaring between me and my goal,)

ˈzɑ̯enə ˈvɛlən zɪnt‘ gəˈhoːbən, das di ˈzeːlə miːɐ̯/miːr lɛɐ̯ˈgrɑ̯ostʰ.
seine Wellen sind gehoben, dass die Seele mir ergraust.
its waves are raised, that the soul in me becomes terrified.
(its waves so high that my soul is terrified.)

ˈɑ̯enən ˈnaxən zeː ɪç ˈʃvaŋk‘ən, ˈlaːbɐ(r) lax! deːɐ̯ ˈfɛːɐ̯man feːltʰ.
Einen Nachen seh' ich schwanken, aber ach! der Fährmann fehlt.
A small boat see I rocking, but ah! the ferryman is lacking.
(I see a small boat rocking there; but, alas, there is no ferryman in sight.)

frɪʃ hɪˈnɑ̯en lʊnt‘ ˈloːnə ˈvaŋk‘ən! ˈzɑ̯enə ˈzeːgəl zɪnt‘ bəˈzeːltʰ.
Frisch hinein und ohne Wanken! seine Segel sind beseelt.
Lively into (it) and without wavering! its sails are animated.
(Quick! Into it without hesitation! Its sails are billowing.)

duː mʊst‘ ˈglɑ̯obən, duː mʊst‘ ˈvaːgən, dɛn di ˈgœt‘ɐ lɑ̯en kʰɑ̯en p̮fant‘;
Du musst glauben, du musst wagen, denn die Götter leih'n kein Pfand;
You must believe, you must risk, for the gods lend no security;

nuːɐ̯/nuːr lɑ̯en ˈvʊndɐ kʰan dɪç ˈtʰraːgən lɪn das ˈʃøːnə ˈvʊndɐlant‘.
nur ein Wunder kann dich tragen in das schöne Wunderland.
only a miracle can you carry into the beautiful miracle-land.
(only a miracle of faith can take you to that beautiful land of miracles.)

[Schiller's poem expresses his longing to reach a higher spiritual plane, to escape from the limitations of mundane life through a leap of faith. Schubert made two settings. Both the *Neue Schubert Ausgabe* and the *Gesamtausgabe* offer three choices: a first attempt from 1813, then two slightly variant versions of a fine new one from several years later (the date is unknown).]

ˈzeːnzʊxtʰ / deːɐ̯ ˈlɛrçə ˈvɔlk‘ənnaːə ˈliːdɐ
Sehnsucht / Der Lerche wolkennahe Lieder
Longing / The Lark's Songs From Near the Clouds

Op. 8, No. 2 [1817?] (Johann Mayrhofer)

deːɐ̯ ˈlɛrçə ˈvɔlk‘ənnaːə ˈliːdɐ(r) lɛɐ̯ˈʃmɛt‘ɐn t̮suː dɛs ˈvɪnt‘ɐs flʊxtʰ.
Der Lerche wolkennahe Lieder erschmettern zu des Winters Flucht.
The lark's cloud- near songs warble to the winter's flight.
(The lark's songs, from near the clouds, warble a fanfare to winter's flight.)

di ˈleːɐ̯də hʏlt‘ lɪn zamt di ˈgliːdɐ(r), lʊnt‘ ˈblyːt‘ən ˈbɪldən ˈroːt‘ə frʊxtʰ.
Die Erde hüllt in Sammt die Glieder, und Blüten bilden rote Frucht.
The earth covers in velvet the limbs, and blossoms form red fruit.
(The earth covers her limbs in velvet, and blossoms form red fruit.)

nuːɐ̯ duː, loː ˈʃtʻʊrmbəveːkʻtʻə ˈzeːlə, bɪstʻ ˈblyːtʻənloːs, ˌɪn dɪç gəˈkʰeːɐ̯tʰ,
Nur du, o sturmbewegte Seele, bist blütenlos, in dich gekehrt,
Only you, O storm-tossed soul, are blossomless, into yourself turned,
(Only you, my storm-tossed soul, are without blossoms, turned in upon yourself,)

ʊntʻ vɪrstʻ ˌɪn ˈgɔldnɐ ˈfryːlɪŋshɛlə fɔn ˈtʰiːfɐ ˈzeːnzʊxtʻ ˈlɑofgətseːɐ̯tʰ.
und wirst in gold'ner Frühlingshelle von tiefer Sehnsucht aufgezehrt.
and become in golden spring- brightness by deep longing consumed.
(and, amidst the golden brightness of spring, are consumed by a deep longing.)

niː vɪrtʻ, vas duː fɛɐ̯ˈlaŋstʻ, lɛntʻˈkʰaemən dem ˈboːdən, lideˈaːlən frɛmtʻ,
Nie wird, was du verlangst, entkeimen dem Boden, Idealen fremd,
Never will, what you desire, sprout from the ground, to ideals alien,
(What you desire will never sprout from that ground, so alien to idealism,)

deːɐ̯ ˈtʰrɔtsɪç ˈdaenən ˈʃøːnən ˈtʰrɔømən di ˈroːə kʰraftʻ lɛntʻˈgeːgənʃtʻɛmtʰ. [ˈrɑoə]
der trotzig deinen schönen Träumen die rohe Kraft entgegenstemmt. [*poem:* **die rauhe**]
that defiantly to your beautiful dreams, the raw power opposes, [rough]
(that defiantly opposes raw power to your beautiful dreams,)

duː rɪŋst dɪç matʰ mɪtʻ ˈzaenɐ ˈhɛrtʻə, fɔm ˈvʊnʃə ˈhɛftʻɪgɐ(r) lɛntʻˈbrantʰ:
Du ringst dich matt mit seiner Härte, vom Wunsche heftiger entbrannt:
You wrestle yourself weary with its hardness, by the wish more fervently inflamed:
(You exhaust yourself wrestling with its hardness, all the more fervently inflamed by this wish:)

mɪt ˈkʰraːnɪçən laen ˈʃtʻreːbəndɐ gəˈfɛːɐ̯tʻə tsuː ˈvandɐn ˌɪn laen ˈmɪldɐ lantʻ.
mit Kranichen ein strebender Gefährte zu wandern in ein milder Land.
with cranes a striving companion to wander into a gentler land.
(to migrate with the cranes, as their striving companion, to a gentler land.)
[*GA:* **ein sterbender** (ˈʃtʻɛrbəndɐ, dying—*misprint!*) **Gefährte**]

[Mayrhofer was a highly gifted poet, but also a melancholy pessimist who eventually committed suicide; this fine poem inspired his friend and sometime roommate to compose an exqisite song!]

ˈzeːnzʊxtʰ / di ˈʃaebə friːɐ̯tʰ
Sehnsucht / Die Scheibe friert
Longing / The Windowpane Freezes

Op. 105, No. 4 [1826] (Johann Gabriel Seidl)

di ˈʃaebə friːɐ̯tʰ, deːɐ̯ vɪntʻ lɪstʻ rɑo, deːɐ̯ ˈnɛçtʻgə ˈhɪməl raen lʊntʻ blɑo:
Die Scheibe friert, der Wind ist rauh, der nächt'ge Himmel rein und blau:
The windowpane freezes, the wind is rough, the nocturnal sky clear and blue:

ɪç zɪts lɪn ˈmaenəm ˈkʰɛmɐlaen lʊntʻ ʃɑo lɪns ˈraenə blɑo hɪˈnaen!
ich sitz' in meinem Kämmerlein und schau' ins reine Blau hinein!
I sit in my little room and look into the pure blue into!
(I sit in my little room and look out into the pure blue!)

miːɐ̯ feːltʻ lɛtʻˈvas*, das fyːl ɪç guːtʰ, miːɐ̯ feːltʻ maen liːpʻ, das ˈtʰrɔøə bluːtʰ:
Mir fehlt etwas, das fühl' ich gut, mir fehlt mein Lieb, das treue Blut:
To me is lacking something, that feel I well, to me is missing my love, the true blood:
(Something is missing, that I feel all too well; I miss my love, that faithful soul:)
[**normal pronunciation:* ˈlɛtʻvas]

ʊnt‘ vɪl lɪç ɪn di ˈʃt‘ɛrnə zeːn, mʊs ʃt‘eːts das laok‘ miːɐ̯/miːr ˈyːbɐgeːn!
und will ich in die Sterne seh'n, muss stets das Aug' mir übergeh'n!
and want I into the stars to look, must always the eye for me overflow!
(and if I want to look at the stars, my eyes continually have to brim over with tears!)

maen liːp‘, voː vaelst duː nuːɐ̯ zoː fɛrn, maen ˈʃøːnɐ ʃt‘ɛrn, maen ˈlaogənʃt‘ɛrn?
Mein Lieb, wo weilst du nur so fern, mein Schöner Stern, mein Augenstern?
My love, where linger you only so far, my lovely star, my eye-star?*
(My love, wherever are you lingering, so far from me, my beautiful star, my darling?)
[**Augenstern* = the pupil of the eye; also, as here, a term of endearment]

duː vaest, dɪç liːp‘ lʊnt‘ braox ɪç jaː, — di ˈtʰrɛːnə tʰrɪt‘ miːɐ̯ ˈviːdɐ naː.
Du weisst, dich lieb' und brauch' ich ja, — die Träne tritt mir wieder nah'.
You know, you love and need I really, — the tear steps to me again near.
(You know that I really love you and need you—tears are coming back again.)

daː kʰvɛːlt‘ ɪç mɪç zoː ˈmançən tʰaːk‘, vael miːɐ̯ kʰaen liːt‘ gəˈlɪŋən maːk‘,
Da quält' ich mich so manchen Tag, weil mir kein Lied gelingen mag,
Here tormented I myself so many a day, because for me no song to succeed wants,
(I have tormented myself here for so many a day because no song wants to turn out right for me,)

vaels ˈnɪmɐ zɪç lɛɐ̯ˈtsvɪŋən lɛst‘ lʊnt‘ frae hɪnˈzɔøzəlt‘, viː deːɐ̯ vɛstʰ!
weil's nimmer sich erzwingen lässt und frei hinsäuselt, wie der West!
because it never itself be forced lets and freely away-whispers, like the west (wind)!
(because inspiration can never be forced, and it goes whispering away freely like the west wind!)

viː mɪlt‘ mɪçs ˈviːdɐ graːt dʊrçˈglyːtʰ! —
Wie mild mich's wieder grad' durchglüht! —
How gently me it again just now through-glows! —
(How gently it is glowing through me again right now! —)

ziː nuːɐ̯, das lɪst‘ jaː ʃoːn laen liːt‘!
Sieh' nur, das ist ja schon ein Lied!
See just, that is indeed already a song!
(Just see! This is indeed already a song!)

vɛn mɪç maen loːs fɔm ˈliːp‘çən varf, dan fyːl ɪç, das lɪç ˈzɪŋən darf.
Wenn mich mein Los vom Liebchen warf, dann fühl' ich, dass ich singen darf.
When me my lot from the sweetheart cast, then feel I, that I to sing am allowed.
(When my lot has cast me far from my sweetheart, then I feel at least that I am allowed to sing.)

[The poem portrays the birth of a song out of loneliness and longing. Schubert's lovely setting alternates minor-mode loneliness with major-key warmth when the poet thinks lovingly of his sweetheart—and when he realizes that inspiration for a poem has come to him after all.]

Sehnsucht (Gedicht aus "Wilhelm Meister") see *Nur wer die Sehnsucht kennt*

ˈzeːnzʊxtʰ / vas t͜siːt‘ miːɐ̯ das hɛrt͜s zoː?
Sehnsucht / Was zieht mir das Herz so?
Longing / What Tugs At My Heart So?

Posthumously published [composed 1814] (poem by Johann Wolfgang von Goethe)

vas t͜siːt‘ miːɐ̯ das hɛrt͜s zoː? vas t͜siːt‘ mɪç hɪˈna͜os, ǀʊnt‘ ˈvɪndət‘
Was zieht mir das Herz so? was zieht mich hinaus, und windet
What tugs for me the heart so? what draws me outside, and winds
(What is tugging so at my heart? What draws me outside, wrenching)

ǀʊnt‘ ʃra͜op‘t‘ mɪç ǀa͜os ˈt͜sɪmɐ(r) ǀʊnt‘ ha͜os? viː dɔrt‘ zɪç di ˈvɔlk‘ən
und schraubt mich aus Zimmer und Haus? Wie dort sich die Wolken
and twists me out of room and house? As there themselves the clouds
(and twisting me out of my room and my home? Like the clouds there,)

ǀam ˈfɛlzən fɛɐ̯ˈt͜siːn, daː mœçt‘ ɪç hɪˈnyːbɐ, daː mœçt‘ ɪç voːl hɪn!
am Felsen verzieh'n, da möcht' ich hinüber, da möcht' ich wohl hin!
at the cliff disperse, there would like I over, there would like I indeed hence!
(dispersing at the cliff, I would like to go over there, I would really like to go there!)
[*poem:* **um Felsen** (ǀʊm ˈfɛlzən, around rocks—*plural*)]

nuːn viːk‘t‘ zɪç deːɐ̯ ˈraːbən gəˈzɛlɪgɐ fluːk‘; ǀɪç ˈmɪʃə mɪç ˈdrʊnt‘ɐ(r)
Nun wiegt sich der Raben geselliger Flug; ich mische mich drunter
Now rocks itself the ravens' gregarious flight; I mix myself there-among
(Now the ravens are rocking to and fro in gregarious flight; I mingle among them)

ǀʊnt‘ ˈfɔlgə dem t͜suːk‘. ǀʊnt‘ bɛrk‘ ǀʊnt‘ gəˈmɔ͜øɐ(r) ǀʊmˈfɪt‘ɪgən viːɐ̯;
und folge dem Zug. Und Berg und Gemäuer umfittigen wir;
and follow the migration. And mountain and masonry around-wing we;
(and follow their migration. And we wing about, over mountains and masonry;)
[*note: Peters omits the 2-bar repeat of* **und Berg und Gemäuer umfittigen wir**]

ziː ˈva͜elət daː ˈdrʊnt‘ən, ǀɪç ˈʃp‘ɛːə naːx ǀiːɐ̯. daː kʰɔmt‘ ziː ǀʊnt‘ ˈvandəltʰ;
sie weilet da drunten, ich spähe nach ihr. Da kommt sie und wandelt;
she lingers there below, I look out for her. There comes she and wanders;
(she is staying there, down below, I look out for her. There she comes, strolling about;)

ɪç ˈǀa͜elə zoˈbalt‘, ǀa͜en ˈzɪŋəndɐ ˈfoːgəl, ǀɪm ˈbʊʃɪçt‘ən valt‘.
ich eile sobald, ein singender Vogel, im buschigten Wald.
I hurry as soon as (I see her), a singing bird, in the bushied [obs.] woods.
(I fly faster, a singing bird in the bushy woods, as soon as I see her.)
[*poem:* **zum** (t͜sʊm, to the) **buschigten**; *Peters:* **im buschigen** (ˈbʊʃɪgən, bushy)]

ziː ˈva͜elət‘ ǀʊnt‘ ˈhɔrçət‘ ǀʊnt‘ ˈlɛçəlt‘ mɪt‘ zɪç: ǀeːɐ̯ ˈzɪŋət‘ zoː ˈliːp‘lɪç
Sie weilet und horchet und lächelt mit sich: "Er singet so lieblich
She lingers and listens and smiles to herself: "He sings so charmingly

ǀʊnt‘ zɪŋt‘ ǀɛs ǀan mɪç. di ˈʃa͜edəndə ˈzɔnə fɛɐ̯ˈgʏldət di høːn; [fɛɐ̯ˈgʊldət]
und singt es an mich." Die scheidende Sonne vergüldet die Höh'n; [*poem:* **verguldet**]
and sings it to me." The departing sun gilds the heights; [gilds]
(and he is singing for me." The departing sun gilds the heights;)
[*vergulden* (obs.) = *vergülden* (poetic) = *vergolden* = to gild]

di ˈzɪnəndə ˈʃøːnə, ziː lɛstʻ lɛs gəˈʃeːən. ziː ˈvandəltʻ lam ˈbaxə [gəˈʃeːn]
die sinnende Schöne, sie lässt es geschehen. Sie wandelt am Bache [*poem:* **gescheh'n]**
the musing beauty, she lets it happen. She wanders by the brook [happen]
(the young beauty, lost in thought, pays no heed. She wanders by the brook)

di ˈviːzən lɛntʻˈlaŋ, lʊntʻ ˈfɪnstʻɐ(r) lʊntʻ ˈfɪnstʻrɐ(r) lʊmˈʃlɪŋtʻ zɪç deːɐ̯ gaŋ.
die Wiesen entlang, und finster und finst'rer umschlingt sich der Gang.
the meadow along, and dark and darker winds itself the way.
(along the meadow, and her winding path grows darker and darker.)

a͜of ˈla͜enmaːl lɛɐ̯ˈʃa͜en ɪç, la͜en ˈblɪŋkʻəndɐ ʃtʻɛrn. [ˈblyːəndɐ]
Auf einmal erschein' ich, ein blinkender Stern. [*Peters:* **ein blühender Stern]**
At once appear I, a twinkling star. [blooming]
(All at once I appear, a twinkling star.)

vas ˈglɛnt͡səṭ daː ˈdroːbən, zoː naː lʊntʻ zoː fɛrn? lʊntʻ hast duː mɪtʻ ˈʃtʻa͜onən
"Was glänzet da droben, so nah und so fern?" Und hast du mit Staunen
"What glitters there above, so near and so far?" And have you with astonishment
("What is glittering up there, so near yet so far?" And when with astonishment you)

das ˈlɔ͜øçtʻən lɛɐ̯ˈblɪkʻtʰ: lɪç liːkʻ diːɐ̯ t͡suː ˈfyːsən, daː bɪn lɪç bəˈglʏkʻtʰ!
das Leuchten erblickt: ich lieg' dir zu Füssen, da bin ich beglückt!
the shining seen: I lie for you at feet, there am I made happy!
(have seen that light: I shall lie at your feet, and there I shall be happy!)

[In his attempt to illustrate everything he could find in this fantasy, Schubert makes eleven tempo changes in 69 bars, including four recitatives and several changes of key. The effect is a bit patchy; but no song by Schubert is without interest. The *Gesamtausgabe* prints the song in G, its original key; Peters follows the first published edition, in F (and omits a two-bar repeat).]

ˈzeːnzʊxt deːɐ̯ ˈliːbə
Sehnsucht der Liebe
Love's Longing

Posthumously published [composed 1815] (poem by Theodor Körner)

viː di naxtʻ mɪtʻ ˈha͜elgəm ˈbeːbən la͜of deːɐ̯ ˈʃtʻɪlən ˈleːɐ̯də liːkʻtʰ! viː ziː zanft
Wie die Nacht mit heil'gem Beben auf der stillen Erde liegt! wie sie sanft
How the night with holy trembling on the silent earth lies: how it gently
(How the night lies on the silent earth with a holy trembling! How gently it)

deːɐ̯ ˈzeːlə ˈʃtʻreːbən, ˈlʏpʻgə kʰraftʻ lʊntʻ ˈfɔləs ˈleːbən lɪn den ˈzyːsən ˈʃlʊmɐ viːkʻtʰ!
der Seele Streben, üpp'ge Kraft und volles Leben in den süssen Schlummer wiegt!
the soul's striving, exuberant strength and full life into the sweet slumber lulls!
(lulls the soul's striving, man's exuberant strength, and full vitality into sweet slumber!)

ˈaːbɐ mɪtʻ ˈleːvɪç ˈnɔ͜øən ˈʃmɛrt͡sən reːkʻtʻ zɪç di ˈzeːnzʊxtʻ lɪn ˈma͜enɐ brʊstʰ.
Aber mit ewig neuen Schmerzen regt sich die Sehnsucht in meiner Brust.
But with eternally new pains stirs itself the longing in my breast.
(But longing is roused in my breast with eternally renewed pain.)

'ʃlʊmɐn lɑ͜ox 'lalə gə'fy:lə lɪm 'hɛrt͜sən,
Schlummern auch alle Gefühle im Herzen,
Slumber even all feelings in the heart,
(Even if all other feelings in my heart are asleep,)

ʃva͜ek‘t‘ lɪn de:ɐ̯ 'ze:lə kʰva:l lʊnt‘ lʊstʰ: 'ze:nzʊxt de:ɐ̯ 'li:bə
schweigt in der Seele Qual und Lust: Sehnsucht der Liebe
is silent in the soul torment and pleasure: longing of the love
(even if torment and pleasure are silent in my soul: love’s longing)

'ʃlʊmɐt‘ ni:, 'ze:nzʊxt de:ɐ̯ 'li:bə vaxt‘ ʃp‘ɛ:t‘ lʊnt‘ fry:.
schlummert nie, Sehnsucht der Liebe wacht spät und früh.
slumbers never, longing of the love wakes late and early.
(never sleeps, love’s longing is awake both early and late.)

la͜es, vi: 'lɛ:ɔlsharfəntʰø:nə, ve:t‘ la͜en 'zanft‘ɐ hɑ͜ox mɪç lan.
Leis’, wie Äolsharfentöne, weht ein sanfter Hauch mich an.
Softly, like aeolian-harp-tones, wafts a gentle breath me at.
(As soft as the tones of an aeolian harp, a gentle breeze wafts toward me.)

hɔlt‘ lʊnt‘ 'frɔ͜ønt‘lɪç glɛnt͜st‘ ze'le:nə,
Hold und freundlich glänzt Selene,
Graciously and amiably gleams Selene (the Greek goddess of the moon)
(Selene gleams graciously and amiably,)

ʊnt‘ lɪn 'mɪldɐ, 'ga͜est‘gɐ 'ʃø:nə ge:t di naxt di 'ʃt‘ɪlə ba:n.
und in milder, geist’ger Schöne geht die Nacht die stille Bahn.
and in mild, spiritual beauty goes the night the quiet course.
(and the night takes its quiet course in mild, spiritual beauty.)

'a:bɐ(r) la͜en 'kʰy:nəs, 'ʃt‘ʏrmɪʃəs 'le:bən 'ʃɛŋk‘ət di 'li:bə dem 'tʰrʊŋk‘ənən zɪn.
Aber ein kühnes, stürmisches Leben schenket die Liebe dem trunkenen Sinn.
But a bold, stormy life [obj.] gives the love [subj.] to the intoxicated mind.
(But love gives the intoxicated mind a bold and stormy life.)
['ab:ɐ(r) lɑ͜of 'kʰy:nən 'ʃt‘ʏrmɪʃən 've:gən fy:ɐ̯t di 'li:bə den 'trʊŋk‘ənən zɪn.]
[*poem:* **Aber auf kühnen stürmischen Wegen führt die Liebe den trunkenen Sinn.]**
[But on bold stormy paths leads the love the intoxicated mind.]
[(But love leads the intoxicated mind along bold and stormy pathways.)]

'dɔ͜øt‘lɪçɐ ze: ɪç da͜en bɪlt‘ mi:ɐ̯/mi:r lɛnt‘'ʃve:bən,
Deutlicher seh’ ich dein Bild mir entschweben,
More clearly see I your image from me float away,
(I see your image more clearly, floating away from me,)
[vi: 'lalə 'kʰrɛft‘ə gə'valt‘ɪç zɪç 're:gən!]
[*poem:* **Wie alle Kräfte gewaltig sich regen!]**
[How all energies powerfully themselves stir!]
[(How powerfully all of one’s energies are stirred!)]

ax! lʊnt di 'ru:ə de:ɐ̯ brʊst‘ lɪst da'hɪn: 'ze:nzʊxt de:ɐ̯ 'li:bə 'ʃlʊmɐt‘ ni:...
ach! und die Ruhe der Brust ist dahin: Sehnsucht der Liebe schlummert nie...
ah! and the peace of the breast is gone: longing of the love slumbers never...
(and peace, alas, is gone from my breast: love’s longing never sleeps...)

tʰiːf, lɪm ˈzyːsən, ˈhaelgən ˈʃvaegən, ruːt di vɛltˈ lʊntˈ ˈlaːtˈmətˈ kʰaom,
Tief, im süssen, heil'gen Schweigen, ruht die Welt und atmet kaum,
Deeply, in the sweet, holy silence, rests the world and breathes scarcely,
(The world is resting deeply in sweet, holy silence, scarcely breathing,)

ʊnt di ˈʃøːnstˈən ˈbɪldɐ ˈʃtˈaegən laos dɛs ˈleːbəns ˈbʊntˈən ˈraegən,
und die schönsten Bilder steigen aus des Lebens bunten Reigen,
and the loveliest images rise from the life's colorful round dances,
(and the loveliest images arise from life's colorful dance,)

ʊntˈ leˈbɛndɪç vɪrt deːɐ̯ tʰraom. ˈlaːbɐ(r) laox lɪn dɛs ˈtʰraoməs gəˈʃtˈaltˈən
und lebendig wird der Traum. Aber auch in des Traumes Gestalten
and alive becomes the dream. But even in the dream's forms
(and our dream seems to be a living experience. But even in the form of dreams)

vɪŋkˈtˈ miːɐ̯ di ˈzeːnzʊxt, di ˈʃmɛrtslɪçə, tsuː, lʊntˈ loːn lɛɐ̯ˈbarmən,
winkt mir die Sehnsucht, die schmerzliche, zu, und ohn' Erbarmen,
beckons to me the longing, the painful, to, and without mercy,
(longing beckons me, painful longing, and, without mercy,)

mɪt ˈtʰiːfən gəˈvaltˈən, ʃtˈøːɐ̯tˈ ziː das hɛrts laos deːɐ̯ ˈvɔnɪgən ruːː
mit tiefen Gewalten, stört sie das Herz aus der wonnigen Ruh':
with deep powers, disturbs it the heart from the blissful rest:
(with deep powers, it disturbs my heart from its blissful rest:)

ˈzeːnzʊxt deːɐ ˈliːbə ˈʃlʊmɐtˈ niː...
Sehnsucht der Liebe schlummert nie...
longing of the love slumbers never...
(love's longing never sleeps...)

zoː lɛntˈˈʃveːpˈt deːɐ̯ kʰraes deːɐ̯ ˈhoːrən, bɪs deːɐ̯ tʰaːkˈ lɪm ˈlɔstˈən graot.
So entschwebt der Kreis der Horen, bis der Tag im Osten graut.
Thus floats by the circle of the Horae*, till the day in the east dawns.
(Thus the circle of the hours floats by, till day dawns in the east.)
[**the Horae were goddesses of the seasons; here they represent the passing hours*]

daː lɛɐ̯ˈheːpˈtˈ zɪç, ˈnɔøgəboːrən, laos dɛs ˈmɔrgəns ˈroːzəntʰoːrən, ˈglyːəntˈ hɛl di
Da erhebt sich, neugeboren, aus des Morgens Rosentoren, glühend hell die
Then raises itself, new born, from the morning's rose- gates, glowing brightly the
(Then from the roseate portals of the morning the newborn sun will rise, glowing brightly, the)

ˈhɪməlsbraotʰ. ˈlaːbɐ di ˈzeːnzʊxtˈ naːx diːɐ̯/diːr lɪm ˈhɛrtsən lɪstˈ mɪt dem ˈmɔrgən
Himmelsbraut. Aber die Sehnsucht nach dir im Herzen ist mit dem Morgen
heaven's bride. But the longing for you in the heart is with the morning
(bride of heaven. But with the morning the longing for you in my heart has)
[*poem:* **Aber die Sehnsucht in meinem** (lɪn ˈmaenəm, in my) **Herzen]**

nuːɐ̯ ˈʃtˈɛrkˈɐ(r) lɛɐ̯ˈvaxtʰ; ˈleːvɪç fɛɐ̯ˈjʏŋən zɪç ˈmaenə ˈʃmɛrtsən,
nur stärker erwacht; ewig verjüngen sich meine Schmerzen,
only stronger wakened; eternally rejuvenate themselves my pains,
(only wakened all the stronger; my pains are eternally renewed;)

ˈkʰvɛːlən den tʰaːk‘ lʊnt‘ ˈkʰvɛːlən di naxtʰ: ˈzeːnzʊxt deːɐ̯ ˈliːbə ˈʃlʊmɐt‘ niː...
quälen den Tag und quälen die Nacht: Sehnsucht der Liebe schlummert nie...
torment the day and torment the night: longing of the love slumbers never...
(they torment my day and torment my night: love's longing never sleeps...)

[The first verse is printed with the music in the *Gesamtausgabe*; the other verses fit the faster second part of the music only when the note values of the vocal line are adjusted to the rhythm of the words. The song is beautiful and worth the trouble.]

zae̯ miːɐ̯ gəˈgryːstʰ
Sei mir gegrüsst
I Greet You

Op. 20, No. 1 [1822] (Friedrich Rückert)

oː duː lɛnt‘ˈrɪsnə miːɐ̯/miːr lʊnt‘ ˈmae̯nəm ˈkʰʊsə! zae̯ miːɐ̯ gəˈgryːst‘, zae̯ miːɐ̯ gəˈkʰʏstʰ!
O du Entriss'ne mir und meinem Kusse! sei mir gegrüsst, sei mir geküsst!
O you torn away from me and my kiss! be by me greeted, be by me kissed!
(O you who were torn from me and my kiss, I greet you, I kiss you!)

ɛɐ̯ˈrae̯çbaːɐ̯ nuːɐ̯ ˈmae̯nəm ˈzeːnzʊxt͡sgruːsə, zae̯ miːɐ̯ gəˈgryːst‘, zae̯ miːɐ̯ gəˈkʰʏstʰ!
Erreichbar nur meinem Sehnsuchtsgrusse, sei mir gegrüsst, sei mir geküsst!
accessible only to my longing- greeting, be by me greeted, be by me kissed!
(You who are accessible to the greeting only of my longing, I greet you, I kiss you!)

duː fɔn deːɐ̯ hant deːɐ̯ ˈliːbə ˈdiːzəm ˈhɛrt͡sən gəˈgeːbnə!
Du von der Hand der Liebe diesem Herzen gegeb'ne!
You from the hand of the love to this heart given!
(You who were given to my heart by the hand of love,)

duː, fɔn ˈdiːzɐ brʊst‘ gəˈnɔmnə miːɐ̯! mɪt ˈdiːzəm ˈtʰrɛːnəngʊsə
du, von dieser Brust genomm'ne mir! mit diesem Tränengusse
you, from this breast taken from me! with this tears- gush
(you who were taken away from this breast of mine, with this gush of tears)

zae̯ miːɐ̯ gəˈgryːst‘, zae̯ miːɐ̯ gəˈkʰʏstʰ! t͡sʊm tʰrɔt͡s deːɐ̯ ˈfɛrnə,
sei mir gegrüsst, sei mir geküsst! Zum Trotz der Ferne,
be by me greeted, be by me kissed! To the defiance of the distance,
(I greet you, I kiss you! In defiance of the distance)

diː zɪç, ˈfae̯nt‘lɪç ˈtʰrɛnənt‘, hat ˈt͡svɪʃən mɪç lʊnt dɪç gəˈʃt‘ɛlt‘;
die sich, feindlich trennend, hat zwischen mich und dich gestellt;
which itself, hostilely separating, has between me and you placed;
(that is placed between you and me, hostilely separating us,)

dem nae̯t deːɐ̯ ˈʃɪk‘zaːlsmɛçt‘ə t͡sʊm fɛɐ̯ˈdrʊsə zae̯ miːɐ̯ gəˈgryːst‘, zae̯ miːɐ̯ gəˈkʰʏstʰ!
dem Neid der Schicksalsmächte zum Verdrusse sei mir gegrüsst, sei mir geküsst!
to the envy of the fate- powers to the dismay be by me greeted, be by me kissed!
(and to the frustration of the envious powers of fate, I greet you, I kiss you!)

viː duː miːɐ̯ jeː lɪm ˈʃøːnst‘ən lɛnt͡s deːɐ̯ ˈliːbə
Wie du mir je im schönsten Lenz der Liebe
As you to me ever in the loveliest spring of the love
(As ever you came toward me in the loveliest springtime of our love)

mɪt‘ gruːs |ʊnt‘ k^{h}ʊs |ɛnt‘ˈgeːgən k^{h}aːmst‘,
mit Gruss und Kuss entgegen kamst,
with greeting and kiss toward came,
(with a greeting and a kiss,)

mɪt‘ ˈma͜enɐ ˈzeːlə ˈglyːənt͜st‘əm |ɛɐ̯ˈgʊsə za͜e miːɐ̯ gəˈgryːst‘, za͜e miːɐ̯ gəˈk^{h}ʏst^h!
mit meiner Seele glühendstem Ergusse sei mir gegrüsst, sei mir geküsst!
with my soul’s most glowing outpouring be by me greeted, be by me kissed!
(with my soul’s most glowing outpouring of emotion I greet you, I kiss you!)

a͜en ha͜ox deːɐ̯ ˈliːbə ˈt^{h}ɪlgət‘ rɔ͜øm |ʊnt ˈt͜sa͜et‘ən, |ɪç bɪn ba͜e diːɐ̯, duː bɪst‘ ba͜e miːɐ̯,
Ein Hauch der Liebe tilget Räum’ und Zeiten, ich bin bei dir, du bist bei mir,
A breath of the love cancels spaces and times, I am with you, you are with me,
(A breath of love cancels space and time: I am with you, you are with me,)

ɪç ˈhalt‘ə dɪç |ɪn ˈdiːzəs |arms |ʊmˈʃlʊsə, za͜e miːɐ̯ gəˈgryːst‘, za͜e miːɐ̯ gəˈk^{h}ʏst^h!
ich halte dich in dieses Arms Umschlusse, sei mir gegrüsst, sei mir geküsst!
I hold you in this arm’s embrace, be by me greeted, be by me kissed!
(I hold you these arms of mine, I greet you, I kiss you!)

[The poem is part of a collection called *Östliche Rosen* (“Eastern Roses”), and its form—with its recurring phrase—is an attempt to imitate a type of oriental love poem called a *ghazal*. The song is lovely and well known (Schubert returned to its melody in his Fantasy in C major for violin and piano); the singer’s challenge is to avoid either monotony or a too-effusive sentimentality.]

ˈzeːlɪgə vɛlt^h
Selige Welt
Blessed World

Op. 23, No. 2 [1822?] (Johann Chrysostomus Senn)

ɪç ˈt^{h}ra͜ebə |a͜of dɛs ˈleːbəns meːɐ̯, |ɪç ˈzɪt͜sə gəˈmuːt‘ |ɪn ˈma͜enəm k^{h}aːn,
Ich treibe auf des Lebens Meer, ich sitze gemut in meinem Kahn,
I drift on the life’s sea, I sit calmly in my boat,
(I drift on life’s sea, I sit calmly im my boat,) [*gemut* (obs., still found in *wohlgemut* = cheerful)]

nɪçt t͜siːl nɔx ˈʃt‘ɔ͜øɐ, hɪn |ʊnt‘ heːɐ̯, viː di ˈʃt‘røːmʊŋ ra͜est‘,
nicht Ziel noch Steuer, hin und her, wie die Strömung reisst,
not goal nor helm, to and fro, as the current rips,
(without a goal, without a rudder, to and fro, as the current pulls me,)

viː di ˈvɪndə gaːn. ˈ|a͜enə ˈzeːlɪgə ˈ|ɪnzəl zuːxt deːɐ̯ vaːn, dɔx ˈ|a͜enə |ɪst‘ |ɛs nɪçt^h.
wie die Winde gahn. Eine selige Insel sucht der Wahn, doch eine ist es nicht.
as the winds go. A blessed island seeks the folly, but one is there not.
(as the winds blow. Folly seeks a blessed island; but there isn’t any.) [*gahn* (dial.) = *geh’n* = go]

duː ˈ|andə ˈglɔ͜øbɪç ˈ|yːbɐ(r)|al |an, voː zɪç ˈvasɐ(r) |an ˈ|eːɐ̯də brɪçt^h.
Du lande gläubig überall an, wo sich Wasser an Erde bricht.
You land full of faith everywhere at, where itself water at earth breaks.
(Just land your boat anywhere, full of faith, wherever the water breaks against a shore.)

[The poet was one of Schubert’s schoolmates at the imperial *Stadtkonvikt*; later his room in Vienna was raided by the police while Schubert happened to be present. Senn was accused of having written subversive materials. He refused to hand over his private papers. Both young men were arrested. Schubert was soon released; but Senn spent fourteen months in jail and was then banished from Vienna to Tirol, his native region. He and his friend never met again; but another schoolmate, Bruchmann, visited Senn in Innsbruck, and probably brought back to Vienna the two poems that Schubert set. The music of this song is in the bold spirit of *Mut* in *Winterreise*.]

ˈzeːlɪçkʰa͜etʰ
Seligkeit
Bliss

Posthumously published [composed 1816] (poem by Ludwig Hölty)

ˈfrɔ͜ødən ˈzɔndɐ t͡saːl blyːn lɪm ˈhɪməlszaːl ˈlɛŋəln lʊntʻ fɛɐ̯ˈkʰlɛːɐ̯tʻən,
Freuden sonder Zahl blüh'n im Himmelssaal Engeln und Verklärten,
Joys without number bloom in the heavenly hall for angels and transfigured souls,

viː di ˈfɛːtʻɐ ˈleːɐ̯tʻən. loː daː mœçtʻ ɪç za͜en, lʊntʻ mɪç ˈleːvɪç frɔ͜øn!
wie die Väter lehrten. O da möcht' ich sein, und mich ewig freu'n!
as the fathers taught. O there would like I to be, and myself eternally to make happy!
(as the fathers of the church have taught us. Oh, I would like to be there, and be eternally happy!)

ˈjeːdəm ˈlɛçəlt tʰra͜otʰ ˈla͜enə ˈhɪməlsbra͜otʰ; harf lʊntʻ ˈpsaltʻɐ ˈkʰlɪŋətʰ, lʊnt
Jedem lächelt traut eine Himmelsbraut; Harf' und Psalter klinget, und
For each smiles intimately a heavenly bride; harp and psaltery sounds, and
(For each a heavenly bride is intimately smiling; the harp and psaltery are sounding, and)

man tʰant͡stʻ lʊntʻ ˈzɪŋətʰ. loː daː mœçtʻ ɪç za͜en, lʊntʻ mɪç ˈleːvɪç frɔ͜øn!
man tanzt und singet. O da möcht' ich sein, und mich ewig freu'n!
one dances and sings. O there would like I to be, and myself eternally to make happy!
(everyone dances and sings. Oh, I would like to be there, and be eternally happy!)

ˈliːbɐ bla͜eb ɪç hiːɐ̯, ˈlɛçəltʻ ˈla͜ora miːɐ̯ ˈla͜enən blɪkʻ, deːɐ̯ ˈzaːgətʰ,
Lieber bleib' ich hier, lächelt Laura mir einen Blick, der saget,
Rather remain I here, (if) smiles Laura at me a look, that says,
(I would rather remain *here*, on earth, if Laura will smile at me with a look that says)

das lɪç ˈla͜osgəkʰlaːgətʰ. ˈzeːlɪç dan mɪtʻ liːɐ̯, bla͜eb ɪç ˈleːvɪç hiːɐ̯!
dass ich ausgeklaget. Selig dann mit ihr, bleib' ich ewig hier!
that I (have) out-lamented. Blissful then with her, remain I eternally here!
(that I have no more reason to lament. Then, blissful, I shall stay here forever with her!)

[This utterly delicious little song, bubbling with charm, is irresistible when sung with the artistry of an Elisabeth Schumann or Elisabeth Schwarzkopf. Some female singers have changed the sex of the addressee, substituting "*der Liebste*" for "Laura" (no slur on "*lächelt*") and "*dir*" for "*ihr*."]

'zɛlma lʊnt' 'zɛlmar
Selma und Selmar
Selma and Selmar

Posthumously published [composed 1815] (poem by Friedrich Gottlieb Klopstock)

'vaenə du: nɪçt', lo: di: lɪç 'lɪnɪç 'li:bə, das laen 'tʰraorɪgɐ tʰa:k'
Weine du nicht, o die ich innig liebe, dass ein trauriger Tag
Weep you not, O whom I ardently love, that a sad day
(Oh, do not weep, you whom I ardently love, that a sad day)

fɔn di:ɐ mɪç 'ʃaedətʰ! vɛn nu:n 'vi:dɐ 'hɛsp'erʊs di:ɐ dɔrt' 'lɛçəltʰ,
von dir mich scheidet! Wenn nun wieder Hesperus dir dort lächelt,
from you me separates! When now again Hesperus on you there smiles,
(separates me from you! Now when Hesperus, the evening star, smiles on you there again,)

kʰɔm ɪç 'glʏk'lɪçɐ 'vi:dɐ! 'la:bɐ(r) lɪn 'dʊŋk'lɐ naxt'
komm' ich Glücklicher wieder! Aber in dunkler Nacht
come I fortunate man again! But in dark night
(I—fortunate man—shall come back! But in the dark night)

lɛɐ'ʃt'aekst du: 'fɛlzən, ʃve:pst' lɪn 'tʰɔøʃəndɐ 'dʊŋk'lɐ naxt' laof 'vasɐn!
ersteigst du Felsen, schwebst in täuschender dunkler Nacht auf Wassern!
climb you rocks, hover in deceptive dark night on waters!
(you climb up on rocks, you hover on the water in the treacherous darkness of night!)

tʰaelt' ɪç nu:ɐ mɪt di:ɐ di gə'fa:ɐ tsu: 'ʃt'ɛrbən, vʏrd ɪç 'glʏk'lɪçə 'vaenən?
Teilt' ich nur mit dir die Gefahr zu sterben, würd' ich Glückliche weinen?
Shared I only with you the danger to die, would I fortunate one weep?
(If only I could share with you the mortal danger, would I—fortunate man—weep?)
[*GA, 2nd version:* **Teilt' ich nun** (nu:n, now) **mit dir**]

[The name Selma is borrowed from Macpherson's Ossianic prose poems (one of which is "The Song of Selma"), which had created a sensation a few years before Klopstock wrote the above (in 1766). The atmosphere of rocks and sea and wild nature at night was undoubtedly inspired by the world of Ossian. The *Gesamtausgabe* prints two versions, nearly identical except that the second has a two-bar prelude and a faster tempo marking (Peters follows the second version).]

ser'ba:te, o 'd:dɛ:i ku'stɔ:di
Serbate, o dei custodi
Preserve, O Custodian Gods

Posthumously published (in 1940) [composed 1812] (poem by Pietro Metastasio)

ser'ba:te, o 'd:dɛ:i ku'stɔ:di 'del:la ro'ma:na 'sɔrte, in 't:ti:to,‿il 'dʒu:sto,‿il 'fɔrte
Serbate, o dei custodi della romana sorte, in Tito, il giusto, il forte,
Preserve, O gods custodians of the Roman destiny, in Titus, the just, the strong,
(You gods who are custodians of the destiny of Rome, preserve in Titus, the just, the strong,)

lo'no:re di 'nɔstra e'ta:, 'vo:i ʎ:ʎimor'ta:li‿ a'l:lɔ:ri su la tʃe'za:rea 'kjɔ:ma,
l'onor di nostra età. Voi gl'immortali allori su la cesarea chioma,
the honor of our age. You the immortal laurels upon the imperial brow,
(—preserve in him the honor of our era. You, immortal laurels on the imperial brow,)

'vo:i kusto'di:te a 'r:ro:ma la 'su:a felitʃi'ta. [konser'va:te]
voi custodite a Roma la sua felicità. [*variant version:* **conservate a Roma]**
you guard for Rome the its happiness. [conserve]
(guard and preserve the happiness of Rome.)

fu 'vɔstro un si gran 'do:no, 'si:a 'luŋgo‿il 'do:no 'vɔstro,
Fu vostro un sì gran dono, sia lungo il dono vostro.
Was yours a so great gift, be long the gift yours.
(Yours was so great a gift—may it last long!)

lin'vi:di:‿ al 'mondo 'nɔstro‿il 'mondo ke v:ve'r:ra.
L'invidii al mondo nostro il mondo che verrà.
It may envy of the world ours the world that will come [= the future world].
(May the world to come be envious of our world for that gift!)

[The text comes from a chorus in Act I, Scene 5, of Metastasio's opera libretto, *La clemenza di Tito* ("The Clemency of Titus"). Both Gluck and Mozart composed operas based on that libretto, but neither included this particular number. While studying with Antonio Salieri, Schubert made at least two versions for solo voice and one for chorus. One of the solo versions was published in *Der junge Schubert* by Alfred Orel (Vienna, 1940), as an appendix; another has been arranged and privately printed by Reinhard Van Hoorickx.]

'zɔ͜øftsɐ
Seufzer
Sighs

Posthumously published [composed 1815] (poem by Ludwig Hölty)

di 'naxt'ɪgal zɪŋt' 'ly:bɐ(r)|al |a͜of 'gry:nən 'ra͜ezən di 'bɛst'ən 'va͜ezən.
Die Nachtigall singt überall auf grünen Reisen die besten Weisen,
The nightingale sings everywhere on green sprigs the best melodies,

das 'rɪŋslʊm valt' |ʊnt' 'lu:fɐ ʃaltʰ. manç 'jʊŋəs pʰa:ɐ̯ ge:t dɔrt',
dass ringsum Wald und Ufer schallt. Manch junges Paar geht dort,
that round around forest and bank resounds. Many a young pair goes there,
(so that, all around, the woods and the banks resound. Many a young couple goes walking there,)

vo: kʰla:ɐ̯ das 'bɛçla͜en 'ra͜oʃətʰ, |ʊnt' ʃt'e:t', |ʊnt' 'la͜oʃətʰ mɪt' 'fro:əm zɪn
wo klar das Bächlein rauschet, und steht, und lauschet mit frohem Sinn
where clear the brooklet murmurs, and stands, and listens with happy mind
(where the clear brooklet is murmuring, and they stand and listen in a happy mood)

de:ɐ̯ 'zɛŋərɪn. |ɪç 'hø:rə baŋ |ɪm 'dy:st'ɐn gaŋ de:ɐ̯ 'naxt'ɪgalən
der Sängerin. Ich höre bang' im düstern Gang der Nachtigallen
to the singer. I hear anxiously in the dark walk the nightingale's
(to the singer. But as I walk along the dark pathway I hear with anxiety the nightingale's)

gə'zɛŋə 'ʃalən; denn |ax! |a'la͜en |ɪr ɪç |ɪm ha͜en.
Gesänge schallen; denn ach! allein irr' ich im Hain.
songs sounding; for, ah! alone stray I in the grove.
(songs; for, alas, I stray all alone in the grove.)

[This lovely song is one of three Hölty poems that Schubert set on the same day, May 22, 1815.]

ˈʃɪlrɪk‘ lʊnt‘ ˈvɪnvela
Shilrik und Vinvela
Shilric and Vinvela

Posthumously published [composed 1815] (prose poem by James Macpherson—"Ossian")
(German translation by Edmund von Harold)

VINVELA:

ma͜en gəˈliːp‘t‘ɐ(r) lɪst‘ la͜en zoːn dɛs ˈhyːgəls. lɛɐ̯ fɛɐ̯ˈfɔlk‘t di ˈfliːəndən ˈhɪrʃə.
Mein Geliebter ist ein Sohn des Hügels. Er verfolgt die fliehenden Hirsche.
My beloved is a son of the hill. He pursues the fleeing deer.
(*Macpherson's original:* My love is a son of the hill. He pursues the fleeing deer.)

di ˈdɔgən ˈʃna͜ʊbən lʊm liːn, di zɛn ˈza͜enəs ˈboːgəns ʃvɪrt‘ lɪn dem vɪnt‘.
Die Doggen schnauben um ihn, die Senn' seines Bogens schwirrt in dem Wind.
The mastuffs pant around him, the string of his bow whirs in the wind.
(His grey dogs are panting around him; his bow-string sounds in the wind.)
[*Peters:* **die Sehne** (ˈzeːnə, strings) **seines Bogens**]
[*Senne* (obs.) = *Sehne* = sinew, string of a bow]
[*Harold:* **Seine grauen** (ˈza͜enə ˈgra͜ʊən, his grey) **Doggen... in den** (lɪn den, into the) **Wind**]

ruːst duː ba͜e deːɐ̯ ˈkʰvɛlə dɛs ˈfɛlzən, ˈloːdɐ ba͜e dem ˈra͜ʊʃən dɛs ˈbɛrk‘ʃt‘roːms?
Ruhst du bei der Quelle des Felsen, oder bei dem Rauschen des Bergstroms?
rest you by the spring of the rock, or by the roaring of the mountain-stream?
(Dost thou rest by the fount of the rock, or by the noise of the mountain-stream?)
[*Peters:* **des Felsens** (ˈfɛlzəns, rock—more correct modern German)]

deːɐ̯ ʃilf na͜ek‘t‘ zɪç lɪm ˈvɪndə, deːɐ̯ ˈneːbəl fliːk‘t‘ ˈlyːbɐ di ˈha͜edə;
Der Schilf neigt sich im Winde, der Nebel fliegt über die Heide;
The reed bends itself in the wind, the mist flies over the heath;
(The rushes are nodding to the wind, the mist flies over the hill;)
[*Peters:* **Das Schilfrohr** (das ˈʃɪlfroːɐ̯, the reed) **neigt sich**]
[*Harold:* **der Nebel fliegt über den Hügel** (den ˈhyːgəl, the hill)]

ɪç vɪl liːm ˈlʊngəzeːən naːn, lɪç vɪl liːn bəˈtʰraxt‘ən fɔm ˈfɛlzən hɛˈrap‘.
ich will ihm ungesehen nah'n, ich will ihn betrachten vom Felsen herab.
I want to him unseen to approach, I want him to observe from the rock down.
(I will approach my love unseen; I will behold him from the rock.)
[*Harold:* **ich will mich** (mɪç, myself) **ungeseh'n** (ˈlʊngəzeːn, unseen) **ihm nah'n**]

ɪç zaː dɪç t͜suˈleːɐ̯st‘ ˈliːp‘ra͜eç ba͜e deːɐ̯ fɛɐ̯-/fɛrˈlalt‘ət‘ən ˈla͜eçə fɔn ˈbrano.
Ich sah dich zuerst liebreich bei der veralteten Eiche von Branno.
I saw you first love-rich by the aged oak of Branno.
(Lovely I saw thee first by the aged oak of Branno;) ["*Branno*" *is the name of a mountain stream*]
[lɪm ha͜en] [fɛɐ̯ˈvɪt‘ɐt‘ən]
[*Peters:* **Ich sah dich zuerst im Hain bei der verwitterten Eiche von Branno**]
[in the grove] [weathered]
[*Harold:* **Sah ich dich zuerst liebreich bei der veralteten Eiche von Branno**]

ʃlaŋk ˈkʰeːɐ̯t‘əst duː fɔm ˈjaːgən t͜suˈrʏkʰ, ˈlʊnt‘ɐ(r) ˈlalən ˈda͜enən ˈfrɔ͜ʏndən deːɐ̯ ˈʃøːnst‘ə.
Schlank kehrtest du vom Jagen zurück, unter allen deinen Freunden der Schönste.
Slender turned you from the chase back, among all your friends the fairest.
(thou wert returning tall from the chase; the fairest among thy friends.)

SHILRIK:

vas ɪsts fyːɐ/fyːr ˈlaenə ˈʃtʻɪmə, diː lɪç ˈhøːrə? ziː glaeçt dem ˈhaoxə dɛs ˈzɔmɐs.
Was ist's für eine Stimme, die ich höre? Sie gleicht dem Hauche des Sommers.
What is it for a voice, that I hear? It is like to the breath of the summer.
(What voice is that I hear? that voice like the summer wind!)

ɪç zɪts nɪçtʻ baem ˈnaegəndən ˈʃilfə, lɪç høːɐ nɪçt di ˈkʰvɛlə dɛs ˈfɛlzən;
Ich sitz' nicht beim neigenden Schilfe, ich hör' nicht die Quelle des Felsen;
I sit not by the bending reed, I hear not the spring of the rock;
(I sit not by the nodding rushes; I hear not the fount of the rock.)

[nɪçtʻ bɪrkʻtʻ mɪç das ˈnaegəndə ˈʃɪlfroːɐ, nɪçtʻ høːr ɪç] [ˈfɛlzəns]
[*Peters:* **Nicht birgt mich das neigende Schilfrohr, nicht hör' ich die Quelle des Felsens]**
[not shelters me the bending reed, not hear I] [rock]
[(the bending reed does not shelter me, I do not hear the spring of the rock)]

ˈfɛrnə, ˈfɛrnə, loː ˈvɪnvela, geː ɪç tsuː dem ˈkʰriːgɐn fɔn ˈfɪŋgal; [tsiː]
ferne, ferne, o Vinvela, geh' ich zu den Kriegern von Fingal; [*Peters:* **zieh' ich]**
far, far, O Vinvela, go I to the warriors of Fingal; [go]
(Afar, Vinvela, afar, I go to the wars of Fingal.)
[*Harold: without "o"*; **zu den Kriegen** (ˈkʰriːgən, wars)]

ˈmaenə ˈdɔgən bəˈglaetʻən mɪç nɪçtʰ, lɪç ˈtʰreːtʻə nɪçtʻ meːɐ/meːr laof den ˈhyːgəl,
meine Doggen begleiten mich nicht, ich trete nicht mehr auf den Hügel,
my mastiffs accompany me not, I step not more onto the hill,
(My dogs attend me no more. No more I tread the hill.)
[*Peters:* **ich seh' dich** (zeː dɪç, see you) **nicht mehr auf dem** (dem, [on] the) **Hügel]**

ɪç zeː dɪç nɪçtʻ meːɐ fɔn deːɐ ˈhøːə, ˈtsiːɐlɪç ˈʃraetʻəntʻ lam ˈʃtʻroːmə deːɐ ˈflɛçə,
ich seh' dich nicht mehr von der Höhe, zierlich schreitend am Strome der Fläche,
I see you not more from the height, gracefully striding by the stream of the plain,
(No more from on high I see thee, fair-moving by the stream of the plain;)
[*Harold:* **beim** (baem, by the) **Strome]**

ˈʃɪmɐntʻ viː deːɐ ˈboːgən dɛs ˈhɪməls, viː deːɐ moːntʻ laof deːɐ ˈvɛstʻlɪçən ˈzaetʻə.
schimmernd wie der Bogen des Himmels, wie der Mond auf der westlichen Seite.
shimmering like the bow of the heaven, like the moon on the western side.
(bright as the bow of heaven; as the moon on the western wave.)
[*Harold:* **auf der westlichen Welle** (ˈvɛlə, wave)]
[ˈlyːbɐ ˈdʊŋkʻləm gəˈbɪrgə]
[*Peters:* **wie der Mond über dunklem Gebirge]**
[over dark mountain-range)]

VINVELA:

zoː bɪst duː gəˈgaŋən, loː ˈʃɪlrɪkʰ, lɪç bɪn laˈlaen laof dem ˈhyːgəl,
So bist du gegangen, o Shilrik, ich bin allein auf dem Hügel,
Then are you gone, O Shilric, I am alone on the hill,
(Then thou art gone, O Shilric! I am alone on the hill!)

man ziːt di ˈhɪrʃə lam ˈrandə dɛs ˈgɪpfəls, ziː ˈgraːzən ˈfʊrçtʻloːs hɪnˈvɛkʻ,
man sieht die Hirsche am Rande des Gipfels, sie grasen furchtlos hinweg,
one sees the deer on the edge of the peak, they graze fearlessly away,
(The deer are seen on the brow; void of fear they graze along.)

['zɑ͜omə] ['valdəs] [ba͜em kʰvɛl]
[*Peters:* **man sieht die Hirsche am Saume des Waldes, sie grasen furchtlos beim Quell]**
[edge] [woods] [by the spring]

ziː 'fʏrçt'ən di 'vɪndə nɪçt' meːɐ̯, nɪçt' meːɐ̯ den 'brɑ͜ozəndən bɑ͜om.
sie fürchten die Winde nicht mehr, nicht mehr den brausenden Baum.
they fear the winds not more, not more the roaring tree.
(No more they dread the wind; no more the rustling tree.)
[*Peters:* **den rauschenden** ('rɑ͜oʃəndən, rustling) **Baum]**

deːɐ̯ 'jɛːgɐ(r) lɪst' va͜et' lɪn deːɐ̯ 'fɛrnə, leːɐ̯/leːr lɪst' lɪm 'fɛldə deːɐ̯ 'grɛːbɐ.
Der Jäger ist weit in der Ferne, er ist im Felde der Gräber.
The hunter is far in the distance, he is in the field of the graves.
(The hunter is far removed, he is in the field of graves.)

iːɐ̯ 'frɛmdən, liːɐ̯ 'zøːnə deːɐ̯ 'vɛlən, loː ʃoːnt' 'ma͜enəs 'liːp'ra͜eçən 'ʃɪlrɪkʰ!
Ihr Fremden, ihr Söhne der Wellen, o schont meines liebreichen Shilrik!
You strangers, you sons of the waves, O spare my love-rich Shilric!
(Strangers! sons of the waves! spare my lovely Shilric!) [*Harold: without "o"*]
[*Peters:* **o schont meines holden Geliebten** ('hɔldən gə'liːp't'ən, lovely beloved)]

SHILRIK:

vɛn lɪç lɪm 'fɛldə mʊs 'falən, heːp' hoːx, loː 'vɪnvela, ma͜en graːp'!
Wenn ich im Felde muss fallen, heb' hoch, o Vinvela, mein Grab!
If I in the field must fall, raise high, O Vinvela, my grave!
(If fall I must in the field, raise high my grave, Vinvela.)
[lɪn deːɐ̯ ʃlaxt' lɪç] ['tʰʏrmə]
[*Peters:* **Wenn in der Schlacht ich muss fallen, türme hoch...]**
[in the battle I] [pile]

'grɑ͜oə 'ʃt'a͜enə lʊnt' la͜en 'hyːgəl fɔn 'leːɐ̯də 'zɔlən mɪç ba͜e deːɐ̯ 'naːxvɛlt' bə'ts͜a͜eçnən.
Graue Steine und ein Hügel von Erde sollen mich bei der Nachwelt bezeichnen.
grey stones and a hill of earth shall me to the posterity mark.
(Grey stones and heaped-up earth shall mark me to future times.)
[*Peters:* **bei der Nachwelt verkünden** (fɛɐ̯'kʰʏndən, make known)]

vɛn deːɐ̯ 'jɛːgɐ ba͜em 'hɑ͜ofən vɪrt' 'zɪts͜ən, vɛn leːɐ̯ ts͜uː 'mɪt'aːk' 'za͜enə 'ʃp'a͜ezə gə'nɔ͜øst',
Wenn der Jäger beim Haufen wird sitzen, wenn er zu Mittag seine Speise geneusst,
When the hunter by the mound will sit, when he at noon his food enjoys,
(When the hunter shall sit by the mound, and produce his food at noon,)
[*Harold:* **bei dem** (ba͜e dem, by the) **Haufen;** *geneusst* (obs.) = *geniesst* = enjoys]
[lam 'hyːgəl] [lʊnt' lɛnt''ʃvʊndənɐ 'ts͜a͜et'ən gə'dɛŋk'tʰ,]
[*Peters:* **Wenn der Jäger am Hügel wird sitzen und entschwundener Zeiten gedenkt,]**
[at the hill (= grave)] [and of vanished times thinks,]

vɪrt' leːɐ̯ 'zaːgən: la͜en 'kʰriːgɐ ruːt' hiːɐ̯, lʊnt' ma͜en ruːm zɔl 'leːbən lɪn 'za͜enəm loːp'.
wird er sagen: "Ein Krieger ruht hier," und mein Ruhm soll leben in seinem Lob.
will he say: "A warrior rests here," and my fame shall live in his praise.
("Some warrior rests here," he will say; and my fame shall live in his praise.)

ɛɐ̯-/ɛɾˈlɪnrə dɪç ˈmaɐ̯nɐ(r), lo: ˈvɪnvela, vɛn lɪç laʊ̯f ˈle:ɐ̯dən lɛɐ̯ˈli:k‘.
Erinn're dich meiner, o Vinvela, wenn ich auf Erden erlieg'.
Remember yourself of me, O Vinvela, when I on earth am brought low.
(Remember me, Vinvela, when low on earth I lie!)

[*Harold: without "o"*; **auf der Erde** (laʊ̯f de:ɐ̯ ˈle:ɐ̯də, on the earth)]
[mɪç de:ɐ̯ ˈra:zən laɐ̯nst dɛk‘tʰ]
[*Peters:* **wenn mich der Rasen einst deckt]**
[me the grass once covers]
[(when the grass one day covers me)]

VINVELA:

ja:, lɪç ve:ɐ̯t‘ mɪç ˈdaɐ̯nɐ(r) lɛɐ-/lɛɾˈlɪnɐn; lax, maɐ̯n ˈʃɪlrɪk‘ vɪrt‘ ˈfalən,
Ja, ich werd' mich deiner erinnern; ach, mein Shilrik wird fallen,
Yes, I shall myself of you remember; ah, my Shilric will fall,
(Yes! I will remember thee; alas! my Shilric will fall!)

maɐ̯n gəˈli:p‘t‘ɐ! vas zɔl lɪç tʰu:n, vɛn du: laʊ̯f ˈle:vɪç fɛɐ̯ˈgɪŋstʰ?
mein Geliebter! Was soll ich tun, wenn du auf ewig vergingest?
my beloved! What shall I do, when you for ever perish?
(What shall I do, my love! when thou art for ever gone?)

ɪç ˈve:ɐ̯də ˈdi:zə ˈhy:gəl lam ˈmɪt‘a:k‘ dʊrçˈʃt‘raɐ̯çən,
Ich werde diese Hügel am Mittag durchstreichen,
I shall these hills at the noon through-roam,
(Through these hills I will go at noon:) [ve:ɐ̯t‘] [lɪm] [dʊrçˈʃtraɐ̯fən]

[*Harold:* **Ich werd' diese Hügel im Mittag durchstreifen]**
[shall] [in the] [through-roam]
[vo:l ve:ɐ̯d ɪç ˈdi:zən] [dʊrçˈzu:xən]
[*Peters:* **Wohl werd' ich diesen Hügel am Mittag durchsuchen,]**
[Probably shall I this] [through-search]
[(I shall probably search through this hill at noon)]

di ˈʃvaɐ̯gəndə ˈhaɐ̯də dʊrçˈtsi:n. dɔrt‘ ve:ɐ̯d ɪç den pʰlats ˈdaɐ̯nɐ ru:,
die schweigende Heide durchzieh'n. Dort werd' ich den Platz deiner Ruh',
the silent heath traverse. There shall I the place of your rest,
(I will go through the silent heath. There I will see the place of thy rest,)

[*Harold:* **durchgehen** (dʊrçˈge:ən, go through)]

vɛn du: fɔn de:ɐ̯ ja:k‘t tsuˈrʏk,kʰe:ɐ̯t‘əst‘, bəˈʃaʊ̯n. lax, maɐ̯n ˈʃɪlrɪk‘ vɪrt‘ ˈfalən,
wenn du von der Jagd zurückkehrtest, beschau'n. Ach, mein Shilrik wird fallen,
when you from the chase return, look at. Ah, my Shilric will fall,
(returning from the chase. Alas! my Shilric will fall;)

[*Peters:* **zurücke kehrtest** (tsuˈrʏk‘ə ˈke:ɐ̯t‘əst‘, back turn = come back)]

ˈla:bɐ(r) lɪç ve:ɐ̯t‘ ˈmaɐ̯nəs ˈʃɪlrɪks gəˈdɛŋk‘ən. [ˈve:ɐ̯də]
aber ich werd' meines Shilriks gedenken. [*Harold:* **aber ich werde]**
but I shall of my Shilric think. [shall]
(but I will remember Shilric.)

[The text comes from a German translation of an excerpt from *Carric-Thura*, one of the "Poems of Ossian" that James Macpherson passed off as translations of actual ancient Celtic documents, but that were later shown to be his own work, with borrowings from Milton, Pope, and other writers. These "Ossian" poems were exceptionally popular in Germany, and much admired by Goethe himself (they play a significant role in *The Sorrows of Young Werther*). Schubert set a number of them ("Cronnan" continues the story: Shilric returns from the battle alive to find Vinvela a ghost). As indicated above, there are major differences between the standard Harold translation and the version of the text in the Peters edition; there are musical differences as well, between the Peters version and that of the *Gesamtausgabe*, in both the vocal and the piano parts.]

zi: lɪn ˈjeːdəm ˈliːdə
Sie in jedem Liede
She in Every Song

Privately published [sketch composed 1827] (poem by Karl Gottfried von Leitner)

neːm ɪç di ˈharfə, ˈfɔlgənt dem ˈdraŋə ˈzyːsɐ gəˈfyːlə dɛŋkʻ ɪç lɑo̯x dae̯n,
Nehm' ich die Harfe, folgend dem Drange süsser Gefühle denk' ich auch dein',
Take I the harp, following the urge of sweet feelings think I also of you,
(When I take up my harp, following the urging of sweet feelings I am also thinking of you,)

ˈmɛːtʻçən! lʊntʻ glɑo̯pʻ, lɛs ˈkʰœnən jaː ˈlaŋə ˈloːnə di ˈharfə ˈzɛŋɐ nɪçtʻ zae̯n.
Mädchen! und glaub', es können ja lange ohne die Harfe Sänger nicht sein.
girl! and believe, there can surely long without the harp singers not be.
(girl! And believe me, without the harp there can surely not be minstrels much longer.)

vɛːn ɪç lɪm ˈliːdə ˈziːdlɐ(r) lʊntʻ ˈkʰlɑo̯zə, bʊrkʻ lʊnt tʰʊrˈniːrə ˈviːdɐ t͡suː ʃɑo̯n:
Wähn' ich im Liede Siedler und Klause, Burg und Turniere wieder zu schau'n:
Imagine I in the song settler and hermitage, castle and tourney again to see:
(If I imagine that I see a hermit and his cell in the song, or a castle and a tournament,)
[*Siedler* (here) may stand for *Einsideler* = hermit]

pʰraŋstʻ mɪtʻ baˈrɛtʻə lʊntʻ ˈʃtʻarəndɐ ˈkʰrɑo̯zə duː lam balˈkʰoːnə ˈt͡svɪʃən den frɑo̯n.
prangst mit Barette und starrender Krause du am Balkone zwischen den Frau'n.
shine with cap and stiff ruff you on the balcony among the ladies.
(you are there, replendent in a medieval cap and a stiff ruff among the ladies on the balcony.)

pʰrae̯z ɪç deːɐ̯/deːr ˈlalpʻən ˈfriːtʻlɪçə ˈlʏftʻə, hoːx lɔpʻ dɛs ˈtʰaːləs ˈvɪldəm gəˈbrɑo̯s:
Preis' ich der Alpen friedliche Lüfte, hoch ob des Tales wildem Gebraus:
Praise I the alps' peaceful airs, high over the valley's wild roaring:
(If I intend to praise the peaceful air of the alps, high above the wild roar of the valley,)

fʏlst duː lals ˈzɛnɪn ˈtʰrɪlɐnt di ˈkʰlʏftʻə, laxstʻ lɑo̯s dem ˈkʰlae̯nən, ˈhœlt͡sɐnən hɑo̯s.
füllst du als Sennin trillernd die Klüfte, lachst aus dem kleinen, hölzernen Haus.
fill you as dairy-maid trilling the gorges, laugh from the little, wooden house.
(I hear you as alpine dairy-maid fill the gorges with trills, see you smile from your little chalet.)

zɪŋ ɪç fɔn ˈʃøːnən ˈvasɐjʊŋfrɑo̯ən ˈlae̯nzaːm lɪm ˈmoːntʻʃae̯n ˈʃvɪməntʻ lɪm
Sing' ich von schönen Wasserjungfrauen einsam im Mondschein schwimmend im
Sing I of lovely water- virgins lonely in the moonlight swimming in the
(If I sing of lovely water nymphs, swimming alone by moonlight in the)

zeː: ʃveːpst duː bae̯ ˈliːnən ˈlʊntʻən lɪm ˈblɑo̯ən, ʃtʻrɛkstʻ miːɐ̯/miːr lɛntʻˈgeːgən ˈlarmə fɔn
See: schwebst du bei ihnen unten im Blauen, streckst mir entgegen Arme von
lake: float you with them below in the blue, stretch to me toward arms of
(lake, I see you floating with them in the blue depths, stretching toward me your arms white as)

ʃneː. ˈyːbɐ(r)ˌal ˈnaːə ˈvaeləst, duː ˈliːbə, miːɐ̯/miːr ˌɪn deːɐ̯ ˈdɪçtˈʊŋ ˈroːzɪgəm lantˈ,
Schnee. Überall nahe weilest, du Liebe, mir in der Dichtung rosigem Land',
snow. Everywhere near linger, you love, to me in the poetry's roseate land,
(snow. Everywhere you, my love, are lingering near to me in the roseate land of poetry;)

ˌax! nuːɐ̯/nuːr ˌɪm ˈleːbən, ˈʃtˈrɛŋə ˌʊnt ˈtʰryːbə, tʰrɛntˈ ˌʊns dɛs ˈʃɪkˈzaːls ˈfaentˈlɪçə hantˈ!
ach! nur im Leben, strenge und trübe, trennt uns des Schicksals feindliche Hand!
ah! only in the life, severe and dreary, parts us the fate's hostile hand!
(ah, only in life, so severe and dreary, does the hostile hand of fate keep us apart!)

[No matter what the minstrel plans to sing, he always finds his beloved somewhere in every song. Schubert wrote out the voice part, the bars for piano alone, and some indications of the accompaniment. His sketch does not include the words. The poem was identified by Reinhard Van Hoorickx, who then created a performing version of the song, which he published privately. His realization has been recorded (DG 1981007). The *tessitura* of the song is high, up to a top C.]

ˈskˈoːliə / lastˈ ˌɪm ˈmɔrgənʃtˈraːl dɛs maen
Skolie / Lasst im Morgenstrahl des Mai'n
Drinking Song / In the Sunlight of a May Morning

Posthumously published [composed 1815] (poem by Johann Ludwig von Deinhardstein)

lastˈ ˌɪm ˈmɔrgənʃtˈraːl dɛs maen ˌʊns deːɐ̯ ˈbluːmə ˈleːbən frɔøn,
Lasst im Morgenstrahl des Mai'n uns der Blume Leben freu'n,
Let in the morning ray of the May us in the flower life rejoice
(In the sunlight of a May morning let us rejoice in the flower that is life)

ˌeː ˌiːɐ̯ dʊftˈ ˌɛntˈˈvaeçətʰ! haoxtˈ ˌeːɐ̯/ˌeːr ˌɪn den ˈbuːsən kʰvaːl,
eh' ihr Duft entweichet! Haucht er in den Busen Qual,
before its fragrance fades away! Breathes it into the bosom torment,
(before its fragrance fades! Even if that scent breathes torment into our hearts,)

glyːtˈ ˌaen ˈdɛːmɔn ˌɪm pʰoˈkʰaːl, deːɐ̯ ziː ˌlaeçtˈ fɛɐ̯ˈʃɔøçətʰ.
glüht ein Dämon im Pokal, der sie leicht verscheuchet.
glows a daemon in the goblet, who it easily chases away.
(there is a daemon glowing in the wine-cup who will easily chase the pain away.)

ʃnɛl viː ˌʊns di ˈfrɔødə kʰʏstˈ, vɪŋkˈt deːɐ̯ tʰoːtˈ, ˌʊntˈ ziː tsɛɐ̯ˈfliːstʰ;
Schnell wie uns die Freude küsst, winkt der Tod, und sie zerfliesst;
Quickly as us the joy kisses, beckons the death, and it melts away;
(As quickly as we are kissed by joy, we are beckoned by Death, and that joy melts away;)

ˈdʏrfən viːɐ̯/viːr ˌiːn ˈʃɔøən? fɔn den ˈmɛːtˈçənlɪpˈən vɪŋkˈtˈ ˈleːbənsˌaːtˈəm;
dürfen wir ihn scheuen? Von den Mädchenlippen winkt Lebensatem;
may we him shun? From the girl- lips beckons life- breath;
(may we shun him? The breath of life beckons from a girl's lips;)

veːɐ̯/veːr ˌiːn tʰrɪŋkˈtˈ, ˈlɛçəltˈ ˈzaenəm ˈdrɔøən.
wer ihn trinkt, lächelt seinem Dräuen.
whoever it drinks, smiles at his threatening.
(whoever drinks that can smile at Death's menace.)

[The title "*Skolie*" is a form of *Skolion* (plural *Skolien*), the term derived from an old Greek word for drinking song, often sung as a round. The toast "Skoal!" comes from the same source.]

ˈskʻoːli̯ə / ˈmɛːtʻçən lɛntʻˈziːgəltʻən, ˈbryːdɐ, di ˈflaʃən

Skolie / Mädchen entsiegelten, Brüder, die Flaschen

Drinking Song / Girls Have Unsealed the Bottles, Brothers

Posthumously published [composed 1816] (poem by Friedrich von Matthisson)

mɛːtʻçən lɛntʻˈziːgəltʻən, ˈbryːdɐ, di ˈflaʃən; lɑo̯f!
Mädchen entsiegelten, Brüder, die Flaschen; auf!
Girls unsealed, brothers, the bottles; up!
(Girls have unsealed the bottles, brothers! Come)

di gəˈflyːgəltʻən ˈfrɔ̯ødən t͡suː ˈhaʃən, ˈlɔkʻən lʊntʻ ˈbɛçɐ fɔn ˈroːzən lʊmˈglyːtʰ.
die geflügelten Freuden zu haschen, Locken und Becher von Rosen umglüht.
the winged joys to snatch, curls and glasses by roses around-glowed.
(and snatch the wingéd joys, curls and glasses encircled by glowing roses.)

ɑo̯f! leː di ˈmoːzɪgən ˈhyːgəl lʊns ˈvɪŋkʻən, ˈvɔnə fɔn ˈroːzɪgən ˈlɪpʻən t͡suː ˈtʰrɪŋkʻən;
Auf! eh' die moosigen Hügel uns winken, Wonne von rosigen Lippen zu trinken;
Up! before the mossy hills to us beckon, bliss from rosy lips to drink;
(Before the mossy grave beckons to us, come and drink bliss from rosy lips;)

ˈhʊldɪgʊŋ ˈlaləm, vas ˈjuːgəntʻlɪç blyːtʰ!
Huldigung Allem, was jugendlich blüht!
homage to all, what youthful blooms!
(pay homage to all that is youthfully blooming!) [note: *Hügel* is often a synonym for "grave"]

[This "Skolion" is a catchy drinking song of the type much loved by German students of that era.]

zoː lastʻ mɪç ˈʃa͜enən / liːt deːɐ̯ mɪnˈjõ / mɪnˈjõ t͡sva͜e

So lasst mich scheinen / Lied der Mignon / Mignon II

Such Let Me Seem / Mignon's Song / Mignon II

Op. 62, No. 3 [1826] (poem included in *Wilhelm Meister* by Johann Wolfgang von Goethe)

zoː lastʻ mɪç ˈʃa͜enən, bɪs lɪç ˈveːɐ̯də; t͡siːtʻ miːɐ̯ das ˈva͜esə kʰla͜etʻ nɪçtʻ lɑo̯s!
So lasst mich scheinen, bis ich werde; zieht mir das weisse Kleid nicht aus!
So let me appear, till I become; take from me the white dress not off!
(Such let me seem until I become such: do not make me take off this white dress!)
[*ausziehen* = undress, take off (clothes, etc.)]

ɪç ˈla͜elə fɔn deːɐ̯ ˈʃøːnən ˈleːɐ̯də hɪˈnapʻ lɪn ˈjeːnəs ˈfɛstʻə hɑo̯s.
Ich eile von der schönen Erde hinab in jenes feste Haus.
I hurry from the beautiful earth down into that firm house.
(I shall soon leave this beautiful earth and go down into that firm house below.)
[*variant (not by Goethe):* **jenes dunkle** (ˈdʊŋkʻlə, dark) **Haus**]

dɔrtʻ ruː lɪç ˈla͜enə ˈkʰla͜enə ˈʃtʻɪlə, dan ˈlœfnətʻ zɪç deːɐ̯ ˈfrɪʃə blɪkʰ,
Dort ruh' ich eine kleine Stille, dann öffnet sich der frische Blick,
There rest I a little quiet (time), then opens itself the fresh gaze,
(There I shall rest for a quiet little time; then my refreshed eyes will open,)

ɪç ˈlasə dan di ˈra͜enə ˈhʏlə, den ˈgʏrtʻəl lʊnt den kʰrant͜s t͜suˈrʏkʰ.
ich lasse dann die reine Hülle, den Gürtel und den Kranz zurück.
I leave then the pure covering, the girdle and the wreath behind.
(then I shall leave behind this pure white dress, the girdle, and the wreath.)

ʊntʻ ˈjeːnə ˈhɪmlɪʃən gəˈʃtʻaltʻən ziː ˈfraːgən nɪçtʻ naːx man lʊntʻ va͜epʻ,
Und jene himmlischen Gestalten sie fragen nicht nach Mann und Weib,
And those heavenly forms they ask not after man and woman,
(And those heavenly beings will not ask who is a man, who is a woman;)

ʊntʻ ˈkʰa͜enə ˈkʰla͜edɐ, ˈkʰa͜enə ˈfaltʻən lʊmˈgeːbən den fɛɐ̯ˈkʰlɛːɐ̯tʻən la͜epʻ.
und keine Kleider, keine Falten umgeben den verklärten Leib.
and no clothes, no folds surround the transfigured body.
(and no clothes, no draperies will enclose the transfigured body.)

t͜svaːɐ̯ leːpʻtʻ ɪç ˈloːnə zɔrkʻ lʊntʻ ˈmyːə, dɔx fyːltʻ ɪç ˈtʰiːfən ʃmɛrt͜s gəˈnʊŋ;
Zwar lebt' ich ohne Sorg' und Mühe, doch fühlt' ich tiefen Schmerz genung;
To be sure lived I without care and trouble, but felt I deep pain enough;
(True, I lived without care and trouble; but I nevertheless felt deep pain often enough.)
[*genung* (obs., poetic) = *genug* = enough]

foːɐ̯ ˈkʰʊmɐ(r) ˈlaltʻɐtʻ ɪç t͜suː ˈfryːə; maxtʻ mɪç la͜of ˈleːvɪç ˈviːdɐ jʊŋ!
vor Kummer altert' ich zu frühe; macht mich auf ewig wieder jung!
for sorrow aged I too early; make me for ever again young!
(through sorrow I became old too early; make me young again forever!)

[In *Wilhelm Meister*, Book VIII, Chapter 2, the girl Mignon, little more than a child but old for her years, is dressed in an angel costume and asked to present gifts to some children during a birthday celebration. –"Are you an angel," asked one child. –"I wish I were," answered Mignon. –"Why are you carrying a lily?" –"My heart should be that pure and open, then I would be happy." –"What are those wings like? Let us see them!" –"They represent more beautiful ones, that have not yet unfurled." After the little celebration Mignon is asked to remove her costume; she begs to be allowed to keep it on. Until recently she had always preferred to dress like a boy. But she has been very ill. Mignon has a premonition of her death; still in her angel dress, she makes up a song, accompanying herself on the zither, in which she describes intuitively what dying will be like. Hers is a beautiful and touching vision: a little time of rest and oblivion in the grave, then an awakening to a new state of existence in which no clothes are needed to cover the transfigured body, and none of the angels will ask if she is a boy or a girl. Schubert made four attempts to set this haunting poem: the first two, in 1816, are fragments (but have been completed by Reinhard Van Hoorickx); the third (1821) and fourth (1826, the best known) are both beautiful—but the third ("Mignon II" in the *Gesamtausgabe*) is particularly touching, and fits the rhythm of the poem much more naturally than the fourth version, musically lovely as it is, which gives too much weight to such words as *eine* ("an"), *und* ("and"), and *den* ("the").]

zoˈnɛtʰ la͜ens / aˈpʰɔlo, ˈleːbətʻ nɔx da͜en hɔltʻ fɛɐ̯ˈlaŋən
Sonett I / Apollo, lebet noch dein hold Verlangen
Sonnet I / Apollo, If Your Sweet Desire Still Lives

Posthumously published [composed 1818] (Italian original by Petrarch)
(German translation by August Wilhelm von Schlegel)

aˈpʰɔlo, ˈleːbətʻ nɔx da͜en hɔltʻ fɛɐ̯ˈlaŋən
Apollo, lebet noch dein hold Verlangen,
Apollo, lives still your lovely desire, / (Apollo, if your sweet desire for her still lives,)

das ǀan tʰɛ'saːlʃɐ fluːt di 'blɔndən 'haːrə ǀɪn diːɐ̯/diːr ǀɛnt''flamtʰ,
das an thessal'scher Flut die blonden Haare in dir entflammt,
which by Thessalian waters the blond hairs in you kindled,
(the desire that her blond hair kindled in you by the Thessalian river,)

ʊnt' ǀɪsts ǀɪm lɑ͡ɔf deːɐ̯ 'jaːrə nɪçt' 'ǀʊnt'ɐ(r) ǀɪn fɛɐ̯'gɛsənha͡ɛt' gə'gaŋən:
und ist's im Lauf der Jahre nicht unter in Vergessenheit gegangen:
and is it in the course of the years not under in oblivion gone:
(and if that desire has not been submerged in oblivion, in the course of the years,—)

foːɐ̯ frɔst' ǀʊnt' 'neːbəln, 'vɛlçə 'fa͡ɛnt'lɪç 'haŋən,
vor Frost und Nebeln, welche feindlich hangen,
from frost and mists, which hostilely hang,
(from frost and mist that hang hostilely in the air)

zoː laŋ zɪç ǀʊns da͡ɛn 'ǀant'lɪt͡s bɪrk't, das 'kʰlaːrə, jɛt͡st
so lang' sich uns dein Antlitz birgt, das klare, jetzt
as long (as) itself from us your countenance conceals, the bright, now
(as long as your bright face is hidden from us, now)

diːs gə'leːɐ̯t'ə 'ha͡ɛlgə lɑ͡ɔp bə'vaːrə, voː duː t͡su'leːɐ̯stʰ ǀʊnt' ǀɪç dan vart' gə'faŋən.
dies geehrte heil'ge Laub bewahre, wo du zuerst und ich dann ward gefangen.
this honored sacred foliage preserve, where you first and I then were captured.
(preserve this honored, sacred foliage, wherein first your heart and then mine were captured.)

ʊnt dʊrç di kʰraft' fɔn dem fɛɐ̯'liːp't'ən 'hɔfən,
Und durch die Kraft von dem verliebten Hoffen,
And through the power of the in-love hoping,
(And through that power of amorous hope)

das ǀɪn deːɐ̯ 'juːgənt' nɪçt dɪç liːs fɛɐ̯'geːən,
das in der Jugend nicht dich liess vergehen,
which in the youth not you let perish,
(that would not let you die of love in your youth,)

las, fɔn dem drʊk' bə'fra͡etʰ, di lʊft' ǀɛɐ̯'varmən. zoː 'veːɐ̯dən viːɐ̯,
lass, von dem Druck befreit, die Luft erwarmen. So werden wir,
let, from the pressure freed, the air become warm. Then shall we,
(let the air, freed from this oppression, become warm again. Then we shall,)

fɔm 'ʃt'ɑ͡ɔnən froː gə'tʰrɔfən, ǀɪm 'gryːnən 'ǀʊnzrə 'hɛrɪn 'zɪt͡sən zeːn,
vom Staunen froh getroffen, im Grünen uns're Herrin sitzen seh'n,
by the marveling gladly struck, in the greening our lady sit see,
(joyfully struck by wonderment, see our lady sitting in the greenery,)

[*Schlegel:* **sehen** ('zeːən, see)]

ʊnt' zɪç bə'ʃat'ən mɪt den 'la͡egnən 'ǀarmən.
und sich beschatten mit den eig'nen Armen.
and herself shade with the own arms.
(and shading herself with her own arms—with the branches of your immortal laurel!)

[The text is a translation of Petrarch's Sonnet XXXIV, which is preceded by these words: "Pray to Apollo that he, as god of medicine, as the sun, and as the lover of the tree consecrated to him and to the sun, may think of Laura." Petrarch, of course, was famously in love with a lady named Laura; and her name is derived from the Latin word for laurel. Apollo had pursued the nymph

Daphne ("laurel" in Greek); when she was transformed into a laurel tree, he decreed that ever afterward the leaves of that tree would crown those who achieved greatness in art or athletics. The German translator added the following to his version: "The general opinion is that this sonnet was written for the planting of a young laurel tree; it can, however, be understood merely allegorically as a plea to Apollo to aid Laura's convalescence by granting good weather." Schubert's setting, a mixture of expressive recitative and graceful *arioso*, has lovely moments.]

zo'nɛtʰ t͜svae / a'laen, 'na:xdɛŋk'lɪç, vi: gə'lɛ:mt' fɔm 'kʰramp͜fə
Sonett II / Allein, nachdenklich, wie gelähmt vom Krampfe
Sonnet II / Alone, Pensive, as if Disabled by a Cramp

Posthumously published [composed 1818] (original Italian poem by Petrarch)
(German translation by August Wilhelm von Schlegel)

a'laen, na:x'dɛŋk'lɪç*, vi: gə'lɛ:mt' fɔm 'kʰramp͜fə, dʊrç'mɛs ɪç 'lø:də 'fɛldɐ,
Allein, nachdenklich, wie gelähmt vom Krampfe, durchmess' ich öde Felder,
Alone, pensive, as (if) disabled by the cramp, traverse I barren fields,
(Alone, pensive, as if disabled by a cramp, I cross the barren fields,) [**normally* 'na:xdɛŋk'lɪç]

'ʃlaeçənt 'tʰrɛ:gə, ʊnt' vɛnt' ʊm'he:ɐ̯ den blɪk', t͜su: fli:n di 'ʃt'e:gə,
schleichend träge, und wend' umher den Blick, zu flieh'n die Stege,
skulking sluggishly, and turn around the gaze, to flee the footpaths,
(skulking sluggishly, and turn to look around, to avoid any paths)

vo: 'laenə 'mɛnʃənʃp'u:ɐ̯ den zant' nu:ɐ̯ 'ʃt'amp͜fə.
wo eine Menschenspur den Sand nur stampfe.
where a human- trace the sand only might stamp.
(where even one human footprint might have marked the sand.)

nɪçt' 'landrə 'ʃʊt͜sve:ɐ̯ fɪnd ɪç mi:ɐ̯/mi:r ɪm 'kʰamp͜fə fo:ɐ̯ dem ɛɐ̯'ʃp'ɛ:n
Nicht andre Schutzwehr find' ich mir im Kampfe vor dem Erspäh'n
Not other defensive weapon find I for me in the battle against the espying
(I can find no other defense in my battle against the prying and spying)

dɛs fɔlks ɪn 'alə 've:gə, vael man ɪm tʰu:n, vo: 'kʰaenə 'frɔødə 're:gə,
des Volks in alle Wege, weil man im Tun, wo keine Freude rege,
of the people into all paths, because one in the doing, where no joy stirs,
(of people into all my paths, because in my actions, when there is no joy stirring, one)

fɔn 'aosən 'li:zət', vi: ɪç 'ɪnən 'damp͜fə. zo: das ɪç 'glaobə jɛt͜st',
von aussen lieset, wie ich innen dampfe. So dass ich glaube jetzt,
from outside reads, how I inside steam. So that I believe now,
(can read from outward signs how I am steaming within. So that I now believe)

bɛrk' ʊnt' gə'fɪldə, ʊnt' flʊs ʊnt' 'valdʊŋ vaes, aos 'vɛlçən 'ʃt'ɔfən
Berg und Gefilde, und Fluss und Waldung weiss, aus welchen Stoffen
mountain and field, and river and woodland knows, from which materials
(that mountain and field and river and woodland know from what materials)

maen 'le:bən zae, das zɪç fɛɐ̯'he:lt' je:t''ve:dən dɔx fɪnd ɪç nɪçt'
mein Leben sei, das sich verhehlt jedweden. Doch find' ich nicht
my life be, which itself conceals from each and all. But find I not
(my life is made, though concealed from everyone. But I do not find)

zo: 'rɑ̯oə ve:ɐ̯k' lʊnt' 'vɪldə, das nɪçt de:ɐ̯ 'li:bəsgɔtʰ mɪç ʃt'e:ts gə'tʰrɔfən,
so rauhe Weg' und wilde, dass nicht der Liebesgott mich stets getroffen,
such rough paths and wild, that not the love- god me constantly (has) met,
(any paths so rough and wild that the god of love has not constantly encountered me on them,)

ʊnt' fy:ɐ̯t' mɪt' mi:ɐ̯, lʊnt' lɪç mɪt' li:m dan 're:dən.
und führt mit mir, und ich mit ihm dann Reden.
and conducts with me, and I with him then discourse.
(and on which he has not then carried on a conversation with me, and I with him.)

[ʊnt' fy:ɐ̯t mɪt' mi:ɐ̯ dan 're:dən.]
[*Schubert adds a final line:* **und führt mit mir dann Reden.]**
[and conducts with me then discourse.]
[(and on which he has not then carried on a conversation with me.)]

[When he is unhappy, he tries to conceal his inner feelings, tries to avoid all contact with others; but no matter how obscure or rough the path he chooses, he cannot hide from the god of love. The opening music—descriptive and darkly beautiful—realistically portrays the poet "skulking sluggishly"; there is a brief recitative; then an *arioso* marked "restless, uneasy." The song ends lyrically, as he yields to thoughts of love.The poem is a translation of Petrarch's Sonnet XXXV.]

zo'nɛtʰ drae̯ / nu:n'me:ɐ̯, da: 'hɪməl, 'le:ɐ̯də ʃvae̯k'tʰ
Sonett III / Nunmehr, da Himmel, Erde schweigt
Sonnet III / Now that Heaven and Earth are Silent

Posthumously published [composed 1818] (poem by Petrarch, Sonnet CLXIV)
(German translation by Johann Diederich Gries)

nu:n'me:ɐ̯, da: 'hɪməl, 'le:ɐ̯də ʃvae̯k't' lʊnt' 'vɪndə, gə'fi:dɐ, vɪlt,
Nunmehr, da Himmel, Erde schweigt und Winde, Gefieder, Wild,
Now, when heaven, earth is silent and winds, feathers, game,
(Now that heaven and earth are silent, and winds, birds, and animals)

dɛs 'ʃlʊmɐs 'bandə 'tʰra:gən, di naxt' lɪm 'kʰrae̯zə fy:ɐ̯t den 'ʃt'ɛrnənva:gən,
des Schlummers Bande tragen, die Nacht im Kreise führt den Sternenwagen,
the slumber's bonds bear, the night in the circle guides the star- chariot,
(bear the bonds of slumber, night guides her chariot of stars in its great circular course,)

ʊnt' ʃt'ɪl das me:ɐ̯ zɪç zɛŋk't' lɪn 'zae̯nə 'grʏndə: nu:n vax ɪç, nu:n zɪn lɪç,
und still das Meer sich senkt in seine Gründe: nun wach' ich, nun sinn' ich,
and quietly the sea itself sinks into its depths: now wake I, now think I,
(and the sea quietly settles down into its depths: now I am awake, now I am thinking,)
[*Gries:* **nun wach' ich, sinne** ('zɪnə, think),**]**

gly: lʊnt' vae̯n lʊnt' 'fɪndə nu:ɐ̯ zi:, di: mɪç fɛɐ̯'fɔlk't' mɪt' 'zy:sən 'pʰla:gən.
glüh' und wein' und finde nur sie, die mich verfolgt mit süssen Plagen.
burn and weep and find only her, who me pursues with sweet torments.
(burning, and weeping, and finding only her, pursuing me with sweet torments.)
[*Gris:* **glühe**('gly:ə, burn)**, wein', und finde]**

kʰri:k' lɪst' mae̯n 'ts̯u:ʃt'ant', ts̯ɔrn lʊnt' 'mɪsbəha:gən; nu:ɐ̯, dɛŋk' ɪç zi:,
Krieg ist mein Zustand, Zorn und Missbehagen; nur, denk' ich sie,
War is my condition, anger and discontent; only, think I (of) her,
(War is my condition, anger and discontent; but, if I think about her,)

vɪŋk'tʻ 'fri:də mi:ɐ̯ gə'lɪndə. zo: ʃtrø:mtʻ, vas mɪç lɛɐ̯'nɛ:ɐ̯tʰ, das zy:s lʊntʻ 'hɛrbə,
winkt Friede mir gelinde. So strömt, was mich ernährt, das Süss' und Herbe,
beckons peace to me gently. Thus streams, what me nourishes, the sweet and bitter,
(peace beckons gently. Thus that which nourishes me, both sweet and bitter, flows)

ɑ̯os 'la̯enəs 'la̯ent̯sgən kʰvɛls le'bɛndgəm 'ʃtʻra:lə, di'zɛlbə hantʻ gi:pʻtʻ 'ha̯elʊŋ mi:ɐ̯/mi:r
aus eines einz'gen Quells lebend'gem Strahle, dieselbe Hand gibt Heilung mir
from one single source's living beam, the same hand gives healing to me
(from the living stream of one single source; the same hand gives me healing)

lʊntʻ 'vʊndən. lʊnt das ma̯en 'la̯edən ni: la̯en t̯si:l lɛɐ̯'ra̯eçə, ʃtʻɛrpʻ lʊntʻ lɛɐ̯'ʃtʻe: ɪç
und Wunden. Und dass mein Leiden nie ein Ziel erreiche, sterb' und ersteh' ich
and wounds. And that my suffering never a goal reaches, die and arise I
(and wounds. And since my suffering never reaches a goal, I die and rise again)
[*Gries:* **nie ein Ziel erwerbe** (lɛɐ̯'vɛrbə, gain—"*erwerbe*" fits the sonnet rhyme-scheme)]

'tʰɛ:kʻlɪç 'tʰɑ̯ozəntʻma:lə, zo: va̯etʻ lɛntʻ'fɛrntʻ nɔx, zo: va̯etʻ bɪn lɪç, t̯su: gə'zʊndən.
täglich tausendmale, so weit entfernt noch, so weit bin ich, zu gesunden.
daily (a) thousand times, so far distanced still, so far am I, to get well.
(a thousand times a day, so far am I still from getting well.)
[*Gries:* **so weit entfernt noch bin ich zu gesunden.**]

[In the *Gesamtausgabe* the sonnet is mistakenly attributed to Dante (Schubert's error), and the translation to A.W. von Schlegel (who had included it in his collection of Italian, Spanish, and Portuguese verse). Of Schubert's three settings of Petrarch, this one, or at least the first page, sounds most Italian, almost like a melody from an undiscovered opera by Bellini or Donizetti.]

son fra 'londe
Son fra l'onde
I Am Among The Waves

Posthumously published [composed 1813] (poem by Pietro Metastasio)

son fra 'londe‿ in 'mɛd:dzo‿al 'ma:re, e‿ al fu'ro:re di 'dop:pjo 'vɛnto;
Son fra l'onde in mezzo al mare, e al furor di doppio vento;
I am among the waves in middle of the sea, and of the fury of double wind;
(I am among the waves in the midst of the sea, in the fury of winds at war with each other;)

or re'sisto, or mi zgo'mento fra la 'spɛme, e fra lo'r:ro:r.
or resisto, or mi sgomento fra la speme, e fra l'orror.
now I resist, now me dismays between the hope, and between the horror.
(one moment I resist, the next I am dismayed, caught between hope and horror.)

per la fe, per la 'tu:a 'vi:ta or pa'vɛnto, or 'so:no‿ ar'di:ta,
Per la fè, per la tua vita or pavento, or sono ardita,
For the faith, for the your life now I fear, now I am emboldened [*female speaker*]
(One moment I fear for your faith, for your life, the next I am emboldened;)

e ri'trɔvo‿e'gwal mar'ti:re nel:lar'di:re‿ e nel ti'mo:r.
e ritrovo equal martire nell' ardire e nel timor.
and I find equal torture in the daring and in the fear.
(and I find equal torture, whether I am brave or afraid.)

[The above text is an aria of Venere (Venus) from *Gli orti Esperidi* ("The Gardens of the Hesperides"), one of the assignments given by Antonio Salieri to his sixteen-year-old pupil.]

ˈʃp‘raːxə deːɐ̯ ˈliːbə
Sprache der Liebe
The Language of Love

Op. 115, No. 3 [1816] (August Wilhelm von Schlegel)

las dɪç mɪt‘ gəˈlɪndən ˈʃlɛːgən ˈryːrən, ˈma͜enə ˈt͡saːɐ̯t‘ə ˈla͜ot‘ə!
Lass dich mit gelinden Schlägen rühren, meine zarte Laute!
Let yourself with gentle strokes be touched, my delicate lute!
(Let me touch you with gentle strokes, my tender lute!)

daː di naxt‘ hɛɐ̯ˈniːdɐ ˈtʰa͜ot‘ə, ˈmʏsən viːɐ̯ gəˈlɪsp‘əl ˈp͡fleːgən.
Da die Nacht hernieder taute, müssen wir Gelispel pflegen.
Since the night downward dews, must we whispering cultivate.
(Since the night descends with the dew, we must communicate in whispers.)

viː zɪç ˈda͜enə ˈtʰøːnə ˈreːgən, viː ziː ˈlaːt‘mən, ˈkʰlaːgən, ˈʃt‘øːnən,
Wie sich deine Töne regen, wie sie atmen, klagen, stöhnen,
As themselves your tones stir, as they breathe, lament, moan,
(As your tones are stirred, as they breathe, lament, and moan,)

valt das hɛrt͡s t͡suː ˈma͜enɐ ˈʃøːnən, brɪŋt‘ liːɐ̯/liːr la͜os deːɐ̯ ˈzeːlə ˈtʰiːfən
wallt das Herz zu meiner Schönen, bringt ihr aus der Seele Tiefen
floats the heart to my lovely one, brings her from the soul's depths
(my heart floats away to my lovely one, bringing her from the depths of my soul)

ˈalə ˈʃmɛrt͡sən, ˈvɛlçə ˈʃliːfən; ˈliːbə dɛŋk‘t‘ ɪn ˈzyːsən ˈtʰøːnən.
alle Schmerzen, welche schliefen; Liebe denkt in süssen Tönen.
all pains, which slept; love thinks in sweet tones.
(all of the pain that was sleeping there; love thinks in sweet tones.)

[Although the poem has three more verses, Schubert intended only that the first be sung. The others do not fit the music except with more or less extensive alterations (the *Gesamtausgabe* prints all four). Besides, the climax is very effective once, but would be ruined by repetition.]

ˈʃtɛnt‘çən / hɔrç, hɔrç! di lɛrç
Ständchen / Horch, horch! die Lerch'
Serenade / Hark, Hark! The Lark

Posthumously published [composed 1826] (poem by William Shakespeare)
(German translation by August Wilhelm von Schlegel)
(Two additional verses by Friedrich Reil)

hɔrç, hɔrç! di lɛrç ɪm ˈɛːt‘ɐbla͜o; ʊnt‘ ˈføːbʊs, nɔ͜ø lɛɐ̯ˈvɛk‘t‘,
Horch, horch! die Lerch' im Äterblau; und Phöbus, neu erweckt,
Hark, hark! the lark in the ether-blue; and Phoebus, newly wakened,
(Hark, hark! The lark sings in the blue ether, and Phoebus, the sun god, wakened anew,)

tʰrɛŋk'tʼ 'zaenə 'rɔsə mɪt dem tʰao, deːɐ̯ 'bluːmənkʰɛlçə dɛk'tʰ;
tränkt seine Rosse mit dem Tau, der Blumenkelche deckt;
waters his horses with the dew, that flower- chalices covers;
(waters the horses that draw his chariot with the dew that covers the chalices of the flowers;)

di 'rɪŋəlbluːmə 'kʰnɔsp'ə ʃlɔøst di 'gɔldnən 'lɔøk'laen laof;
die Ringelblume Knospe schleusst die gold'nen Äuglein auf;
the marigold bud opens the golden little eyes up:
(the marigold bud opens up its little golden eyes:) [*schleusst auf* = *schliesst auf* = unlocks]

mɪt' 'laləm, vas daː 'raetsənt' haest, duː 'zyːsə maet', ʃt'eː laof! ʃt'eː laof, ʃt'eː laof!
mit allem, was da reizend heisst, du süsse Maid, steh' auf! Steh' auf, steh' auf!
with all, what there charming is called, you sweet maid, get up! Get up, get up!
(with everything that we call charming, sweet girl, wake up!)
[*Peters:* **was da reizend ist** (lɪst, is)]

[vɛn ʃoːn di 'liːbə 'gantsə naxt deːɐ̯ 'ʃt'ɛrnə 'lɪçt'əs heːɐ̯
[Wenn schon die liebe ganze Nacht der Sterne lichtes Heer
[If already the dear whole night the stars' bright army
[(If already the whole night long the bright host of stars)

hoːx 'lyːbɐ diːɐ̯/diːr lɪm 'vɛksəl vaxt', zoː 'hɔfən ziː nɔx meːɐ̯,
hoch über dir im Wechsel wacht, so hoffen sie noch mehr,
high above you in the succession keeps watch, then hope they still more,
(has been keeping watch high above you, each star in succession, then they hope all the more)

das laox daen 'laogənʃt'ɛrn ziː gryːst'. lɛɐ̯'vax! ziː 'vart'ən draof,
dass auch dein Augenstern sie grüsst. Erwach! Sie warten drauf,
that also your eye- star [= pupil] them greets. Awake! They wait for that,
(that the stars in your eyes will greet them too. Wake up! They are waiting for you,)

vael duː dɔx gaːɐ̯ zoː 'raetsənt' bɪst, duː 'zyːsə maet', ʃt'eː laof!
weil du doch gar so reizend bist, du süsse Maid, steh' auf!
because you after all really so charming are, you sweet maid, get up!
(because after all you really are so charming! Sweet girl, wake up!)

ʊnt' vɛn dɪç 'laləs das nɪçt' vɛk't',
Und wenn dich alles das nicht weckt,
And if you all that not wakes,
(And if all that does not wake you,)

zoː 'veːɐ̯də dʊrç den tʰoːn deːɐ̯ 'mɪnə 'tsɛːɐ̯t'lɪç 'laofgənɛk't'!
so werde durch den Ton der Minne zärtlich aufgeneckt!
then be through the tone of the courtly love tenderly up-teased!
(then let me tenderly tease you awake in the tones of courtly love!)

loː dan lɛɐ̯'vaxst duː ʃoːn! viː lɔft' ziː dɪç lans 'fɛnst'ɐ tʰriːp', das vaes lɪç,
O dann erwachst du schon! Wie oft sie dich ans Fenster trieb, das weiss ich,
O then awake you all right! How often they you to the window drove, that know I,
(Oh, then you will surely wake up! I know how often they have brought you to your window,)

drʊm ʃtʻeː lɑ͡ʊf, lʊntʻ ˈhaːbə ˈda͡enən ˈzɛŋɐ liːpʻ, duː ˈzyːsə ma͡etʻ, ʃtʻeː lɑ͡ʊf!]
drum steh' auf, und habe deinen Sänger lieb, du süsse Maid, steh' auf!]
therefore get up, and have your singer dear, you sweet maid, get up!]
(therefore get up and love your singer! Sweet girl, wake up!)]

[The poem is a "song" from *Cymbeline*, Act II, Scene 3. When Schubert's popular setting was published, after his death, two more verses were commissioned, in brackets above. The original English words, which actually fit the music (if "heaven's" becomes "heav'n's"), are as follows:

Hark, hark! the lark at heaven's gate sings, / And Phoebus 'gins arise,
His steeds to water at those springs / On chaliced flowers that lies;
And winking Mary-buds begin / To ope their golden eyes;
With everything that pretty is / My lady sweet, arise:
Arise, arise!]

Ständchen (Leise flehen meine Lieder) see *Schwanengesang*

ˈʃtʻɪmə deːɐ̯ ˈliːbə / ˈaːbəntʻgəvœlkʻə ˈʃveːbən hɛl
Stimme der Liebe / Abendgewölke schweben hell
The Voice of Love / Evening Clouds Float Brightly

Posthumously published [2 versions, composed 1815, 1816] (poem by Friedrich von Matthisson)

ˈaːbəntʻgəvœlkʻə ˈʃveːbən hɛl lam bəˈpʰʊrpʻʊrtʻən ˈhɪməl;
Abendgewölke schweben hell am bepurpurten Himmel;
Evening clouds float brightly in the purpled sky;
(Bright evening clouds are floating in the purple sky:)

ˈhɛspʻerʊs ʃɑ͡ʊtʻ, mɪtʻ ˈliːbəsblɪkʻ, dʊrç den ˈblyːəndən ˈlɪndənha͡en,
Hesperus schaut, mit Liebesblick, durch den blühenden Lindenhain,
Hesperus looks, with love- gaze, through the blooming linden grove,
(Hesperus, the evening star, looks through the blossoming linden grove with the gaze of love,)

ʊntʻ za͡en pʻroˈfeːtʻɪʃəs ˈtʰrɑ͡ʊɐliːt t͡sɪrpʻtʻ lɪm ˈkʰrɑ͡ʊtʻə das ˈha͡emçən.
und sein prophetisches Trauerlied zirpt im Kraute das Heimchen.
and its prophetical mourning-song chirps in the plants the cricket.
(and the cricket is chirping its prophetical threnody among the plants.)

ˈfrɔ͡ødən deːɐ̯ ˈliːbə ˈharən da͡en! ˈflʏstʻɐn ˈla͡ezə di ˈvɪndə;
Freuden der Liebe harren dein! flüstern leise die Winde;
Joys of the love wait of you! whisper softly the winds;
("The joys of love are waiting for you!" the winds softly whisper;)

ˈfrɔ͡ødən deːɐ̯ ˈliːbə ˈharən da͡en! tʰøːnt di ˈkʰeːlə deːɐ̯ ˈnaxtʻɪgal;
Freuden der Liebe harren dein! tönt die Kehle der Nachtigall;
Joys of the love wait of you! sounds the throat of the nightingale;
("The joys of love are waiting for you!" sounds from the throat of the nightingale;)

hoːx fɔn dem ˈʃtʻɛrnəngəvœlpʻ hɛˈrapʻ haltʻ miːɐ̯ ˈʃtʻɪmə deːɐ̯ ˈliːbə!
hoch von dem Sternengewölb' herab hallt mir Stimme der Liebe!
high from the star- vault down resounds to me voice of the love!
(down from the high starry vault the voice of love resounds to me!)

ɑ͜os deːɐ̯ pʻlaˈtʰaːnən labyˈrɪntʻ ˈvandəltʻ ˈlɑ͜ora, di ˈhɔldə!
Aus der Platanen Labyrinth wandelt Laura, die Holde!
Out of the plane trees' labyrinth wanders Laura, the lovely one!
(Laura the Lovely wanders out from the labyrinth of plane trees!)

ˈbluːmən lɛntʻˈʃpʻriːsən dem ˈt͜seːfyːɐ̯tʰrɪtʰ, lʊntʻ viː ˈsfɛːrəngəzaŋəstʰoːn
Blumen entspriessen dem Zephyrtritt, und wie Sphärengesangeston
Flowers sprout from the zephyr-step, and like spheres- song- tone
(Flowers spring up from her zephyr-light footsteps, and like the music of the spheres)

beːpʻtʻ fɔn den ˈroːzən deːɐ̯ ˈlɪpʻə miːɐ̯ ˈzyːsə ˈʃtʻɪmə deːɐ̯ ˈliːbə!
bebt von den Rosen der Lippe mir süsse Stimme der Liebe!
trembles from the roses of the lip to me sweet voice of the love!
(the sweet voice of love trembles to me from the roses of her lips!)

[Schubert wrote two totally different versions, both lovely. The earlier setting has the simple charm of a German folk song, the later a richer, fuller accompaniment of repeated chords.]

ˈʃtʻɪmə deːɐ̯ ˈliːbə / ˈma͜enə zeˈlɪndə!
Stimme der Liebe / Meine Selinde!
The Voice of Love / My Selinde!

Posthumously published [composed 1816] (poem by Friedrich Leopold, Graf zu Stolberg)

ˈma͜enə zeˈlɪndə! dɛn mɪtʻ ˈlɛŋəlʃtʻɪmə zɪŋt di ˈliːbə miːɐ̯ t͜suː:
Meine Selinde! denn mit Engelstimme singt die Liebe mir zu:
My Selinde! for with angel-voice sings the love to me to:
(My Selinde! For love sings to me with its angelic voice:)

ziː vɪrt di ˈda͜enə! ziː vɪrt di ˈma͜enə! ˈhɪməl lʊntʻ ˈleːɐ̯də ˈʃvɪndən!
sie wird die Deine! Sie wird die Meine! Himmel und Erde schwinden!
she becomes the yours! she becomes the mine! Heaven and earth disappear!
("She will be yours!" She will be mine! Heaven and earth are disappearing!)
[*poem:* **sie wird die Deine! wird die Meine!**]

ˈma͜enə zeˈlɪndə! ˈtʰrɛːnən deːɐ̯ ˈzeːnzʊxt, diː lɑ͜of ˈblasən ˈvaŋən ˈbeːpʻtʻən,
Meine Selinde! Tränen der Sehnsucht, die auf blassen Wangen bebten,
My Selinde! Tears of the longing, which on pale cheeks trembled,
(My Selinde! Tears of longing that were trembling on my pale cheeks)

ˈfalən hɛˈrapʻ lals ˈfrɔ͜ødəntʰrɛːnən! dɛn miːɐ̯ tʰøːnt di ˈhɪmlɪʃə ˈʃtʻɪmə:
fallen herab als Freudentränen! Denn mir tönt die himmlische Stimme:
fall down as joy- tears! For to me sounds the heavenly voice:
(now fall as tears of joy! For a heavenly voice is sounding in my ears:)

ˈda͜enə vɪrtʻ ziː! di ˈda͜enə!
Deine wird sie! die Deine!
Yours becomes she! the yours!
("She will be yours! Yours!")

[Ecstatic passion blazes through this brief, beautiful song, with its throbbing accompaniment.]

zuˈla͜ekʻa a͜ens / vas bəˈdɔ͜øtʻət di bəˈveːɡʊŋ?
Suleika I / Was bedeutet die Bewegung?
Suleika I / What Does this Stirring Mean?

Op. 14, No. 1 [1821] (Marianne von Willemer, revised by Goethe)

vas bəˈdɔ͜øtʻət di bəˈveːɡʊŋ? brɪŋt deːɐ̯/deːr |ɔstʻ miːɐ̯ ˈfroːə ˈkʰʊndə?
Was bedeutet die Bewegung? Bringt der Ost mir frohe Kunde?
What means the movement? Brings the east (wind) to me glad tidings?
(What does this stirring mean? Does the east wind bring me glad tidings?)

ˈza͜enɐ ˈʃvɪŋən ˈfrɪʃə ˈreːɡʊŋ kʰyːlt dɛs ˈhɛrt͜səns ˈtʰiːfə ˈvʊndə.
Seiner Schwingen frische Regung kühlt des Herzens tiefe Wunde.
Its wings' fresh stirring cools the heart's deep wound.
(The fresh oscillation of its wings cools the deep wound in my heart.)

ˈkʰoːzəntʻ ʃpʻiːltʻ |eːɐ̯ mɪt dem ˈʃtʻɑ͜obə, jaːkʻtʻ |iːn |ɑ͜of |ɪn ˈla͜eçtʻən ˈvœlkʻçən,
Kosend spielt er mit dem Staube, jagt ihn auf in leichten Wölkchen,
Caressingly plays it with the dust, chases it up in light little clouds,
(it plays caressingly with the dust, chasing it up in light little clouds,)

tʰra͜epʻt t͜sʊr ˈzɪçɐn ˈreːbənlɑ͜obə deːɐ̯/deːr |ɪnˈzɛkʻtʻən ˈfroːəs ˈfœlkʻçən.
treibt zur sichern Rebenlaube der Insekten frohes Völkchen.
drives to the secure grape-arbor the insects' happy little folk.
(driving the happy little insects into the security of the grape-arbor.)

ˈlɪndɐtʻ zanft deːɐ̯ ˈzɔnə ˈɡlyːən, kʰyːltʻ |ɑ͜ox miːɐ̯ di ˈha͜esən ˈvaŋən,
Lindert sanft der Sonne Glühen, kühlt auch mir die heissen Wangen,
Tempers gently the sun's burning, cools also for me the hot cheeks,
(It gently tempers the burning heat of the sun, and cools my hot cheeks as well;)

kʰʏst di ˈreːbən nɔx |ɪm ˈfliːən, diː |ɑ͜of fɛltʻ |ʊntʻ ˈhyːɡəl ˈpʰraŋən.
küsst die Reben noch im Fliehen, die auf Feld und Hügel prangen.
kisses the vines still in the fleeing, which on field and hill are resplendent.
(even in fleeing it kisses the vines that sparkle on field and hillside.)

ʊntʻ miːɐ̯ brɪŋtʻ za͜en ˈla͜ezəs ˈflʏstʻɐn fɔn dem ˈfrɔ͜øndə ˈtʰɑ͜ozəntʻ ˈɡryːsə;
Und mir bringt sein leises Flüstern von dem Freunde tausend Grüsse;
And to me brings its soft whispering from the friend (a) thousand greetings;
(And its soft whisper brings me a thousand greetings from my friend;)

eː nɔx ˈdiːzə ˈhyːɡəl ˈdyːstɐn, ˈɡryːsən mɪç voːl ˈtʰɑ͜ozəntʻ ˈkʏsə.
eh' noch diese Hügel düstern, grüssen mich wohl tausend Küsse.
before still these hills darken, greet me probably (a) thousand kisses.
(probably a thousand kisses will still greet me before this hill grows dark.)

ʊntʻ zoː kʰanst duː ˈva͜etʻɐ ˈt͜siːən! ˈdiːnə ˈfrɔ͜øndən |ʊntʻ bəˈtʰryːpʻtʻən.
Und so kannst du weiter ziehen! diene Freunden und Betrübten.
And then can you farther move on! serve friends and troubled ones.
(And then, wind, you can move on and serve other lovers and those who are troubled.)

dɔrt‘, dɔrt‘, voː ˈhoːə ˈmɑ͜oɐn ˈglyːən, dɔrt‘ fɪnd ɪç balt den fiːlgəliːp‘t‘ən.
Dort, dort, wo hohe Mauern glühen, dort find’ ich bald den Vielgeliebten.
There, there, where high walls glow, there find I soon the much-loved one.
(There, there, where the high walls are gleaming, there I shall soon find my dearly beloved.)
[*poem:* **Dort wo hohe Mauern glühen, find’ ich bald...**]

ax, di ˈvaːrə ˈhɛrt͜sənskʰʊndə, ˈliːbəshɑ͜ox, lɛɐ̯ˈfrɪʃt‘əs ˈleːbən
Ach, die wahre Herzenskunde, Liebeshauch, erfrischtes Leben
Ah, the true heart- tidings, love- breath, refreshed life
(Ah, the true tidings of the heart, the breath of love, and refreshed life)

vɪrt‘ miːɐ̯ nuːɐ̯/nuːr lɑ͜os ˈza͜enəm ˈmʊndə, kʰan miːɐ̯ nuːɐ̯ za͜en ˈlaːt‘əm ˈgeːbən.
wird mir nur aus seinem Munde, kann mir nur sein Atem geben.
will to me only from his mouth, can to me only his breath give.
(will come to me only from his mouth, only his breath can give them to me.)

[Goethe incorporated the two “Suleika” songs into his collection of poems called *Der West-östliche Divan* (“The Western-Eastern Divan,” divan, in this sense, meaning “a book of many leaves” and pronounced dɪˈvæn in English and ˈdiːvaːn in German); but they are not originally by Goethe: they are the work of his mistress at that time, Marianne von Willemer. He revised a few words only. In his cycle, inspired by oriental poetry, the lovers are named Hatem and Suleika, hence the name given to both poem and song. The east wind brings messages from Hatem; the west wind, in “Suleika II,” will convey *her* feelings to *him*. The piano plays the part of the love-laden wind.]

ˈzuˈla͜ek‘a t͜sva͜e / ax, lʊm ˈda͜enə ˈfɔ͜øçt‘ən ˈʃvɪŋən / zuˈla͜ek‘as ˈt͜sva͜et‘ɐ gəˈzaŋ
Suleika II / Ach, um deine feuchten Schwingen / Suleikas zweiter Gesang
Suleika II / Ah, Your Moist Wings / Suleika’s Second Song

Op. 31 [1821? 1824?] (Marianne von Willemer, revised by Goethe)

ax, lʊm ˈda͜enə ˈfɔ͜øçt‘ən ˈʃvɪŋən, vɛst‘, viː zeːɐ̯/zeːr lɪç dɪç bəˈna͜edə:
Ach, um deine feuchten Schwingen, West, wie sehr ich dich beneide:
Ah, on account of your moist wings, west (wind), how much I you envy:
(Ah, how I envy you your moist wings, west wind,)

dɛn duː kʰanst‘ liːm ˈkʰʊndə ˈbrɪŋən, vas lɪç lɪn deːɐ̯ ˈtʰrɛnʊŋ ˈla͜edə!
denn du kannst ihm Kunde bringen, was ich in der Trennung leide!
for you can to him tidings bring, what I in the separation suffer!
(for you can bring him tidings of how I am suffering in this separation!)

di bəˈveːgʊŋ ˈda͜enɐ ˈflyːgəl vɛk‘t‘ lɪm ˈbuːzən ˈʃt‘ɪləs ˈzeːnən;
Die Bewegung deiner Flügel weckt im Busen stilles Sehnen;
The movement of your wings wakens in the bosom quiet longing;
(The movement of your wings wakens quiet longing in my bosom;)

ˈbluːmən, ˈlɑ͜oən, valt‘ lʊnt‘ ˈhyːgəl ʃt‘eːn ba͜e ˈda͜enəm hɑ͜ox lɪn ˈtʰrɛːnən.
Blumen, Auen, Wald und Hügel steh’n bei deinem Hauch in Tränen.
flowers, meadows, forest and hill stand at your breath in tears.
(Your breath brings tears to flowers, meadows, woods, and hills.) [*i.e.: brings rain*]
[*poem:* **Blumen, Augen** (ˈlɑ͜ogən, eyes)]

dɔx da͜en ˈmɪldəs ˈzanftʻəs ˈveːən kʰyːlt di ˈvʊndən ˈla͜oɡənliːdɐ;
Doch dein mildes sanftes Wehen kühlt die wunden Augenlider;
But your gentle soft blowing cools the sore eyelids;
(But your soft, gentle blowing cools my burning eyelids;)

ax, fyːɐ̯ la͜etʻ mʏstʻ ɪç fɛɐ̯ˈɡeːən, hɔftʻ ɪç nɪçt t͜suː zeːn liːn ˈviːdɐ.
ach, für Leid müsst' ich vergehen, hofft' ich nicht zu seh'n ihn wieder.
ah, for sorrow would have I to perish, hoped I not to see him again.
(ah, I should die of sorrow if I did not have the hope of seeing him again.*)

ˈa͜elə dɛn t͜suː ˈma͜enəm ˈliːbən, ˈʃpʻrɛçə zanft t͜suː ˈza͜enəm ˈhɛrt͜sən;
Eile denn zu meinem Lieben, spreche sanft zu seinem Herzen;
Hurry then to my love, speak softly to his heart;

dɔx fɛɐ̯ˈma͜etʻ liːn t͜suː bəˈtʰryːbən lʊntʻ fɛɐ̯ˈbɪrkʻ liːm ˈma͜enə ˈʃmɛrt͜sən.
doch vermeid' ihn zu betrüben und verbirg ihm meine Schmerzen.
but avoid him to distress and hide from him my pains.
(but avoid distressing him, and hide my pain from him.)

zaːkʻ liːm, ˈlaːbɐ zaːks bəˈʃa͜edən: ˈza͜enə ˈliːbə za͜e ma͜en ˈleːbən;
Sag' ihm, aber sag's bescheiden: seine Liebe sei mein Leben;
Tell him, but say it unassumingly: his love be my life;
(Tell him—but say it with humility—that his love is my life;)

ˈfrɔ͜ødɪɡəs ɡəˈfyːl fɔn ˈba͜edən vɪrtʻ miːɐ̯ ˈza͜enə ˈnɛːə ˈɡeːbən.
freudiges Gefühl von beiden wird mir seine Nähe geben.
joyful feeling of both will to me his nearness give.
(His nearness will give me a joyful feeling, both of love and of life.)

[See "Suleika I" for the circumstances behind the poem. *Marianne and Goethe never met again, though they corresponded during the rest of his life. The date of Schubert's song is in dispute: most sources claim 1821, when Schubert's other settings from the "Divan" were composed; but there is good reason to believe that *this* song, which is dedicated to the famous singer Anna Milder-Hauptmann and was sent to her by the composer, was a response to a request from her in December 1824; in any case, it was published in 1825, and not with the other "Suleika" song. This is a big song with a high B flat at the end, and was introduced by the diva at a concert.]

ˈst͜seːnə la͜os ˈɡøːtʻəs fa͜ostʰ

Szene aus Goethes "Faust"

A Scene from Goethe's *Faust*

Posthumously published [composed 1814] (scene from *Faust* by Johann Wolfgang von Goethe)

BÖSER GEIST (ˈbøːzɐ ɡa͜estʰ, Evil Spirit):
viː ˈlandɐs, ˈɡrɛːtʻçən, vaːɐ̯ diːɐ̯s, lals duː nɔx fɔl ˈlʊnʃʊltʻ
Wie anders, Gretchen, war dir's, als du noch voll Unschuld
How different, Gretchen, was for you it, when you still full of innocence
(How different it used to be for you, Gretchen, when you, still full of innocence,)

hiːɐ̯ t͜sʊm *ˈlaltʻaːɐ̯ tʰraːtstʰ, la͜os dem fɛɐ̯ˈɡrɪfnən ˈbyːçəlçən ɡəˈbeːtʻə ˈlaltʻəstʰ,
hier zum Altar trat'st, aus dem vergriff'nen Büchelchen Gebete lalltest,
here to the altar stepped, out of the wrongly held little book prayers babbled,
(stepped up to the altar here and babbled prayers out of an upside-down prayer book,)

[**normally pronounced* lalˈtʰaːɐ̯]

halp‘ 'kʰɪndɐʃp‘iːlə, halp‘ gɔt‘ |ɪm 'hɛrt͜sən. 'greːt‘çən! voː ʃt‘eːt da͜en kʰɔp͜f?
halb Kinderspiele, halb Gott im Herzen. Gretchen! wo steht dein Kopf?
half child- games, half God in the heart. Gretchen! where stands your head?
(half childish play, half God in your heart. Gretchen, where is your head? Can’t you remember?)

ɪn 'da͜enəm 'hɛrt͜sən 'vɛlçə 'mɪsətʰaːtʰ? beːt͜st duː fyːɐ̯ 'da͜enɐ 'mʊt‘ɐ 'zeːlə,
In deinem Herzen welche Missetat? Bet’st du für deiner Mutter Seele,
In your heart what sin? Pray you for your mother’s soul,
(What sin is in your heart? Are you praying for the soul of your mother,)

diː dʊrç dɪç t͜sʊr 'laŋən, 'laːŋən pʰa͜en hɪ'nyːbɐʃliːf?
die durch dich zur langen, langen Pein hinüberschlief?
who through you to the long, long pain slept into the other side?
(who—through *your doing*—crossed over in her sleep to a long, long torment?)
[*Gretchen had been persuaded to give her mother the sleeping potion that killed her.*]

a͜of 'da͜enɐ 'ʃvɛlə 'vɛsən bluːtʰ? |ʊnt‘ '|ʊnt‘ɐ 'da͜enəm 'hɛrt͜sən reːk‘t‘ zɪçs nɪçt‘
Auf deiner Schwelle wessen Blut? Und unter deinem Herzen regt sich’s nicht
On your threshold whose blood? And beneath your heart stirs itself it not
(Whose blood is on your threshold? And beneath your heart is not something stirring)
[*Her lover killed her brother at her doorstep; she is pregnant.*]

'kʰvɪlənt‘ ʃoːn, |ʊnt‘ '|ɛŋst‘ɪçt dɪç |ʊnt‘ zɪç mɪt‘ '|aːnʊŋsfɔlɐ 'geːgənvartʰ?
quillend schon, und ängstigt dich und sich mit ahnungsvoller Gegenwart?
swellingly already, and frightens you and itself with ominous presence?
(already, swelling, and does its ominous presence not frighten you and that unborn child itself?)
[*Goethe:* **ängstet** ('|ɛŋst‘ət, frightens—*archaic form*)]

GRETCHEN ('greːt‘çən, diminutive of Margarete):
veː! veː! vɛːr ɪç deːɐ̯ gə'daŋk‘ən loːs, diː miːɐ̯ hɛ'ryːbɐ(r) |ʊnt‘ hɪ'nyːbɐ 'geːən
Weh! Weh! Wär’ ich der Gedanken los, die mir herüber und hinüber gehen
Woe! Woe! Were I of the thoughts free, that in me this way and that way go
(Alas, alas! If only I were free of the thoughts that run about in my mind, this way and that,)
[*first version:* **geh’n** (geːn, go)]

'viːdɐ mɪç!
wider mich!
against me!
(against my will!)

CHOR (kʰoːɐ̯, choir—*in the cathedral*):
'diːɛs 'iːrɛ, 'diːɛs 'ilːla, 'sɔlvɛt 'sɛklʊm ɪn fa'vilːla.
Dies irae, dies illa, solvet saeclum in favilla.
Day of wrath, day that, dissolves (the) world [subj.] into glowing ashes.
(Day of wrath, that day, the world will dissolve into ashes.)
[*note: German pronunciation of church Latin is necessary in this scene.*]

BÖSER GEIST:
grɪm fast dɪç! di pʰo'za͜onə tʰøːntʰ! di 'grɛːbɐ 'beːbən! |ʊnt da͜en hɛrt͜s,
Grimm fasst dich! Die Posaune tönt! Die Gräber beben! Und dein Herz,
Anger seizes you! The trombone sounds! The graves quake! And your heart,
(Divine anger seizes you! The final trumpet sounds! Graves are quaking! And your heart,)

lɑ͜os 'laʃən,ruː tsuː 'flamən,kʰvaːlən 'viːdɐ(r) 'lɑ͜ofgəʃafən, beːp'tʻ lɑ͜of!
aus Aschenruh' zu Flammenqualen wieder aufgeschaffen, bebt auf!
from ashes- peace to flames- torments again up-created, trembles up!
(brought back from the peace of ashes to the torments of flame, trembles convulsively!)
[*GA first version, NSA both versions:* **wieder aufgeschreckt** ('lɑ͜ofgəʃrɛkʻtʻ, startled)]

GRETCHEN:
vɛːr ɪç hiːɐ̯ vɛkʻ! miːɐ̯/miːr lɪstʻ, lals lɔpʻ di 'lɔrgəl miːɐ̯ den 'laːtʻəm fɛɐ̯'zɛt͜stʻə,
Wär' ich hier weg! Mir ist, als ob die Orgel mir den Atem versetzte,
Were I here away! To me is, as if the organ from me the breath removed,
(If only I were away from here! I feel as if the organ has taken away my ability to breathe,)
[*first version:* **mir ist's** (lɪst͜s, is it)]

gə'zaŋ ma͜en hɛrt͜s lɪm 'tʰiːfstʻən 'løːstʻə.
Gesang mein Herz im Tiefsten löste.
song my heart in the deepest loosened.
(as if that chant has shaken the deepest recesses of my heart.)

CHOR:
'juːdeks 'ɛrgɔ kʊm sɛ'deːbɪt, 'kvɪtkvɪt 'laːtɛt apːpa'reːbɪt, [*note German Latin qu*]
Judex ergo cum sedebit, quidquid latet adparebit,
(the) judge then when will sit, whatever is hidden will appear,
(Then, when the judge will have taken his seat, whatever is hidden will be revealed,)

niːl i'nlultum rɛma'neːbɪt. [*note glottal stop in "inultum"— German Latin*]
nil inultum remanebit.
nothing unpunished will remain.
(nothing will remain unpunished.)

GRETCHEN:
miːɐ̯ vɪrtʻ zoː lɛŋ! di 'mɑ͜oɐn,pf͜a͜elɐ bə'faŋən mɪç!
Mir wird so eng! Die Mauernpfeiler befangen mich!
To me becomes so confined! The walls- columns constrain me!
(I feel so confined, so closed in! The walls, the columns imprison me!)
[*GA, NSA, both versions:* **Die Mauerpfeiler** ('mɑ͜oɐpf͜a͜elɐ, wall-columns)]
[*NSA, both versions:* **Mir wird so bang!** (baŋ, afraid)]

das gə'vœlbə drɛŋtʻ mɪç!— lʊftʰ!
Das Gewölbe drängt mich!—Luft!
The vault presses me!— Air!
(The vault presses down on me!—Air!)

BÖSER GEIST:
fɛɐ̯'bɪrkʻ dɪç! zʏntʻ lʊntʻ 'ʃandə bla͜ep'tʻ nɪçtʻ fɛɐ̯'bɔrgən. lʊftʰ? lɪçtʰ? 'veːə diːɐ̯!
Verbirg dich! Sünd' und Schande bleibt nicht verborgen. Luft? Licht? Wehe dir!
Hide yourself! Sin and shame remain not hidden. Air? Light? Woe to you!
(Go, hide yourself! Sin and shame will not remain hidden. You want air? Light? Woe unto you!)
[*Goethe:* **Weh** (veː, woe) **dir!**]

CHOR:
kvɪt sʊm 'misɛr tʊŋk dik'tuːrʊs? kvɛm pa'tronʊm rɔga'tuːrʊs?
Quid sum miser tunc dicturus? Quem patronum rogaturus?
What I am wretched then to say? What protector to call upon?
(What am I then to say, wretch that I am? What protector can I call upon,)

kʊm viːks 'justʊs sit sɛ'kuːrʊs.
Cum vix justus sit securus.
when scarcely (the) just man will be fearless.
(when even the just man is scarcely without fear.)

BÖSER GEIST:
iːɐ̯/iːr 'lant'lɪt͡s 'vɛndən fɛɐ̯'kʰlɛːɐ̯t'ə fɔn diːɐ̯/diːr lap'.
Ihr Antlitz wenden Verklärte von dir ab.
Their countenance turn transfigured beings from you away.
(The blest turn their faces away from you.)

di 'hɛndə diːɐ̯ t͡suː 'ra͜eçən, 'ʃa͜oɐt͡s den 'ra͜enən. veː!
Die Hände dir zu reichen, schauert's den Reinen. Weh!
The hands to you to extend, shudders it the pure. Woe!
(Those who are pure shudder at the thought of extending a hand to you. Woe!)
[*NSA, both versions:* **schaudert's** ('ʃa͜odɐn, shudders it)]

CHOR:
kvɪt sʊm 'misɛr tʊŋk dik'tuːrʊs? kvɛm pa'tronʊm rɔga'tuːrʊs?
Quid sum miser tunc dicturus? Quem patronum rogaturus?
What I am wretched then to say? What protector to call upon?
(What am I then to say, wretch that I am? What protector can I call upon,)
[*Goethe: without* **Quem patronum rogaturus?**]

[GRETCHEN (*fainting*):
'naxbarɪn!— 'lɔ͜øɐ 'fɛʃçən!]
Nachbarin!— Euer Fläschchen!]
Neighbor woman!—Your little flask!]
(Neighbor!—Your smelling salts!)]

[This famous, highly dramatic scene is from Part I of Goethe's masterpiece. It bears the heading "*Dom*" (cathedral), to indicate the location, followed by "service, organ, and singing; Gretchen is among the congregation; the Evil Spirit is behind Gretchen." Schubert did not set the last line, in brackets above, which is a familiar quotation to all Germans. Pregnant, abandoned by her lover, cursed by her dying brother, Gretchen turns to the church for solace; instead she hears the choir evoke the horrors of Judgment Day and the voice of the devil Mephistopheles, playing the role of her tormented conscience. Schubert made two versions, the first calling for chorus, organ, and trombones, the second as a song for voice and piano. Both versions are offered by the *Gesamtausgabe* (the text partially corrected to conform with Goethe) and the *Neue Schubert Ausgabe* (NSA, above, with the words as Schubert wrote them down); Peters prints the second.]

'tʰɛːk'lɪç t͡suː 'zɪŋən
Täglich zu singen
To Be Sung Daily

Posthumously published [composed 1817] (poem by Matthias Claudius)

ɪç 'daŋk'ə gɔt' lʊnt' 'frɔ͜øə mɪç viːs kʰɪnt t͡sʊr 'va͜enaxt͡sgaːbə,
Ich danke Gott und freue mich wie's Kind zur Weihnachtsgabe,
I thank God and gladden myself like the child at the Christmas- gift,
(I thank God and rejoice like a child at the distribution of gifts at Christmas,)

das lɪç hiːɐ̯ bɪn lʊnt das lɪç dɪç, ʃøːn ˈmɛnʃlɪç ˈlantʻlɪt͡s ˈhaːbə.
dass ich hier bin und dass ich dich, schön menschlich Antlitz habe.
that I here am and that I you, fair human countenance have.
(that I am here and that I have *you*, fair countenance of humanity;)
[*poem:* **dass ich bin, bin! Und dass ich dich, schön menschlich Antlitz! habe;**]

das lɪç di ˈzɔnə, bɛrkʻ lʊntʻ meːɐ/meːr lʊntʻ la͡ɔpʻ lʊntʻ graːs kʰan ˈzeːən,
Dass ich die Sonne, Berg und Meer und Laub und Gras kann sehen,
That I the sun, mountain and sea and foliage and grass can see,
(that I can see the sun, the mountains, the sea, the foliage, and the grass,)

ʊntʻ ˈlaːbənt͡s ˈlʊntʻɐm ˈʃtʻɛrnənheːɐ̯/-heːr lʊntʻ ˈliːbən ˈmoːndə ˈgeːən.
und Abends unterm Sternenheer und lieben Monde gehen.
and evenings under the star- host and dear moon walk.
(and can walk in the evening beneath the starry host and the dear moon.)

ɪç ˈdaŋkʻə gɔtʻ mɪtʻ ˈza͡etʻənʃpʻiːl, das lɪç kʰa͡en ˈkʰøːnɪç ˈvɔrdən;
Ich danke Gott mit Saitenspiel, dass ich kein König worden;
I thank God with string music, that I no king (have) become;
(I thank God to the sound of the lyre that I was not made a king;)

ɪç vɛːɐ̯ gəˈʃma͡eçəltʻ ˈvɔrdən fiːl, lʊntʻ vɛːɐ̯ viˈla͡eçtʻ fɛɐ̯ˈdɔrbən.
ich wär' geschmeichelt worden viel, und wär' vielleicht verdorben.
I would have flattered been much, and would be perhaps spoiled.
(I would have been very much flattered, and would perhaps be spoiled.)

gɔtʻ ˈgeːbə miːɐ̯ nuːɐ̯ ˈjeːdən tʰaːkʻ, zoː fiːl lɪç darf t͡sʊm ˈleːbən.
Gott gebe mir nur jeden Tag, so viel ich darf zum Leben.
God give me only each day, as much (as) I am allowed for the living.
(May God give me each day only as much as I need to live.)

eːɐ̯ giːpʻt͡s dem ˈʃpʻɛrlɪŋ la͡ɔf dem dax; viː zɔltʻ leːɐ̯s miːɐ̯ nɪçtʻ ˈgeːbən!
Er gibt's dem Sperling auf dem Dach; wie sollt' er's mir nicht geben!
He gives it to the sparrow on the roof; how should He it to me not give!
(He gives that to the sparrow on the roof; why would He not also give it to me?)

[A simple, cheerful sentiment with appropriately pleasant music.]

Täuschung see *Winterreise*

ˈtʰeːkʻla. ˈla͡enə ˈga͡estʻɐʃtʻɪmə

Thekla. Eine Geisterstimme

Thekla: A Voice from the Other World

Op. 88, No. 2 [1817—earlier version 1813] (Friedrich von Schiller)

voː lɪç za͡e, lʊntʻ voː mɪç ˈhɪngəvɛndətʻ, lals ma͡en ˈflʏçtʻgɐ ˈʃatʻə
Wo ich sei, und wo mich hingewendet, als mein flücht'ger Schatte
Where I be, and where myself hence-turned, when my fleeting shadow
(Where am I, you ask, and where did I go when my fleeting shadow)
[*Peters:* **Schatten** (ˈʃatʻən, shadow—*current form of the word*)]

diːɐ̯/diːr lɛntʼʃveːpʼtʰ? haːb ɪç nɪçtʼ bəˈʃlɔsən lʊntʼ gəˈlɛndətʼ, haːb ɪç nɪçtʼ gəˈliːbətʼ
dir entschwebt? Hab' ich nicht beschlossen und geendet, hab' ich nicht geliebet
from you soared away? Have I not concluded and ended, have I not loved
(floated away from you? Was my mortal existence not concluded, had I not loved)

lʊntʼ gəˈleːpʼtʰ? vɪlst duː naːx den ˈnaxtʼɪgalən ˈfraːgən, diː mɪtʼ ˈzeːlənfɔlɐ meloˈdiː
und gelebt? Willst du nach den Nachtigallen fragen, die mit seelenvoller Melodie
and lived? Want you after the nightingales to ask, that with soulful melody
(and lived? Would you ask that of the nightingales that with their soulful melody)

dɪç lɛntˈt͜sʏkʼtʼən lɪn dɛs ˈlɛnt͜səs ˈtʰaːgən? nuːɐ̯ zoː laŋ ziː ˈliːpʼtʼən, ˈvaːrən ziː.
dich entzückten in des Lenzes Tagen? Nur so lang' sie liebten, waren sie.
you delighted in the spring's days? Only as long (as) they loved, were they.
(charmed you in the days of spring? They were alive only as long as they loved.)

ɔpʼ lɪç den fɛɐ̯ˈloːrənən gəˈfʊndən? ˈgla͜obə miːɐ̯/miːr, lɪç bɪn mɪtʼ liːm fɛɐ̯-/fɛrˈla͜entʰ,
Ob ich den Verlorenen gefunden? Glaube mir, ich bin mit ihm vereint,
Whether I the lost one (have) found? Believe me, I am with him united,
(You ask whether I have found the one I lost? Believe me, I am united with him,)

voː zɪç nɪçtʼ meːɐ̯ tʰrɛntʼ, vas zɪç fɛɐ̯ˈbʊndən, dɔrtʼ, voː ˈkʰa͜enə ˈtʰrɛːnə vɪrtʼ
wo sich nicht mehr trennt, was sich verbunden, dort, wo keine Träne wird
where itself not more parts, what itself bound, there, where no tear becomes
(where that which is joined will not be parted any more, there where no tear is)

gəˈva͜entʰ. ˈdɔrtʼən vɪrstʼ la͜ox duː lʊns ˈviːdɐ ˈfɪndən, vɛn da͜en ˈliːbən ˈlʊnzɐm ˈliːbən gla͜eçtʰ;
geweint. Dorten wirst auch du uns wieder finden, wenn dein Lieben unserm Lieben gleicht;
wept. There will also you us again find, if your loving our loving equals;
(shed. There you too will find us again, if your love is like ours;)

dɔrtʼ lɪstʼ la͜ox deːɐ̯ ˈfaːtʼɐ, fra͜e fɔn ˈzʏndən, deːn deːɐ̯ ˈbluːtʼgə mɔrtʼ nɪçtʼ meːɐ̯/meːr
dort ist auch der Vater, frei von Sünden, den der blut'ge Mord nicht mehr
there is also the father, free from sins, whom the bloody murder not more
(my father is there too, free from any sins, whom the bloody murder no more)

lɛɐ̯ˈra͜eçtʰ. lʊntʼ leːɐ̯ fyːlt, das liːn kʰa͜en vaːn bəˈtʰroːgən, lals leːɐ̯/leːr ˈla͜ofvɛrt͜s t͜suː den
erreicht. Und er fühlt, dass ihn kein Wahn betrogen, als er aufwärts zu den
reaches. And he feels, that him no delusion betrayed, when he upwards to the
(harm. And he feels that it was no delusion that betrayed him when he looked up at the)

ˈʃtʼɛrnən zaː; dɛn viː ˈjeːdɐ vɛːkʼtʼ, vɪrtʼ liːm gəˈvoːgən, veːɐ̯/veːr lɛs gla͜opʼtʼ, deːm
Sternen sah; denn wie jeder wägt, wird ihm gewogen, wer es glaubt, dem
stars looked; for as each weighs, is for him weighed, who it believes, for him
(stars; for as each of us judges, so shall he be judged: whoever truly believes that)

lɪst das ˈha͜elgə naː. vɔrtʼ gəˈhaltʼən vɪrtʼ lɪn ˈjeːnən ˈrɔ͜ømən ˈjeːdəm ˈʃøːnən ˈglɔ͜øbɪgən
ist das Heil'ge nah. Wort gehalten wird in jenen Räumen jedem schönen gläubigen
is the holy near. Word kept is in those spaces for each beautiful devout
(is near to holiness. In those realms where we now exist promises are kept to each noble, devout)

gəˈfyːl; ˈvaːgə duː, t͜suː ˈlɪrən lʊnt t͜suː ˈtʰrɔ͜ømən: ˈhoːɐ zɪn liːkʼtʼ lɔftʼ lɪn ˈkʰɪntʼʃəm ʃpʼiːl.
Gefühl; wage du, zu irren und zu träumen: hoher Sinn liegt oft in kind'schem Spiel.
feeling; dare you, to stray and to dream: high sense lies often in childish play.
(feeling; dare to make mistakes and to dream: often a higher purpose hides in children's play.)

[*Peters:* **hoher Sinn liegt oft im kind'schen** (|ım ˈkʰınt‘ʃən, in the childish) **Spiel]**

[Schubert made three versions; all can be found in the *Gesamtausgabe* and *Neue Schubert Ausgabe*. Peters gives the final, definitive version. The poem was written in response to those who wondered about the fate of Thekla, Wallenstein's gentle daughter in Schiller's well-known trilogy (*Wallensteins Lager, Die Piccolomini, Wallensteins Tod*). Wallenstein led the forces of the Austrian emperor during the Thirty Years' War. He believed in astrology, in the power of the planets to influence human destiny, hence Thekla's remark about the stars. When he attempted to negotiate with the enemy, he was betrayed, accused of treason, and eventually murdered. Schubert's song, sensitively interpreted, can be deeply moving. It is touched with the sublime.]

ˈtʰiːfəs la͜et‘
Tiefes Leid
Deep Sorrow

Posthumously published [composed 1825 or 1826] (poem by Ernst Schulze)

ıç bın fɔn ˈ|alɐ ruː gəˈʃiːdən |ʊnt tʰra͜ep‘ |ʊmˈheːɐ̯/-heːr |a͜of ˈvıldɐ fluːtʰ;
Ich bin von aller Ruh' geschieden und treib' umher auf wilder Flut;
I am from all peace severed and drift about on wild waters;
(I have been severed from all peace and drift about on wild waters;)
[*Peters:* **...von aller Ruh' geschieden, ich** (ıç, I) **treib' umher...]**

an ˈ|a͜enəm |ɔrt‘ nuːɐ̯ fınd ıç ˈfriːdən, das |ıst deːɐ̯/deːr |ɔrt‘, voː ˈ|aləs ruːtʰ.
an einem Ort nur find' ich Frieden, das ist der Ort, wo alles ruht.
in one place only find I peace, that is the place, where everything rests.
(I shall find peace in one place only, that is the place where all things are at rest.)

ʊnt‘ vɛn di vınt‘ |a͜ox ˈʃa͜orıç ˈza͜ozən, |ʊnt‘ kʰalt deːɐ̯ ˈreːgən ˈniːdɐfɛltʰ,
Und wenn die Wind' auch schaurig sausen, und kalt der Regen niederfällt,
And if the winds even horribly roar, and cold the rain down- falls,
(And even if the winds are howling horribly, and a cold rain is falling,)

dɔx vıl |ıç dɔrt‘ fiːl ˈliːbɐ ˈha͜ozən, |als |ın deːɐ̯/deːr ˈ|ʊnbəʃt‘ɛndgən vɛltʰ.
doch will ich dort viel lieber hausen, als in der unbeständ'gen Welt.
yet want I there much rather house, than in the inconstant world.
(I nevertheless would rather lodge there than in this inconstant world.)
[*poem* **doch mag** (maːk‘, like to/may) **ich dort]**

dɛn viː di ˈtʰrɔ͜ømə ˈʃp‘uːɐ̯loːs ˈʃveːbən, |ʊnt‘ ˈ|a͜enɐ ʃnɛl dɛn ˈ|andɐn tʰra͜ep‘tʰ,
Denn wie die Träume spurlos schweben, und einer schnell den andern treibt,
For as the dreams traceless float, and one quickly the other drives (away),
(For just as dreams float on and leave no trace, and as one dream quickly drives the other away,)

ʃp‘iːlt‘ mıt‘ zıç zɛlpst das ˈ|ırə ˈleːbən, |ʊnt‘ ˈjeːdəs naːt‘ |ʊnt‘ ˈkʰa͜enəs bla͜ep‘tʰ.
spielt mit sich selbst das irre Leben, und jedes naht und keines bleibt.
plays with it- -self the confused life, and everything approaches and nothing remains.
(life plays confused games with itself, and everything draws near, but nothing remains.)
[*GA:* **und jeder** (ˈjeːdɐ, everyone—*a misprint?*) **naht und keines bleibt]**

niː vıl di ˈfalʃə ˈhɔfnʊŋ ˈva͜eçən, niː mıt deːɐ̯ ˈhɔfnʊŋ fʊrçt‘ |ʊnt‘ myː;
Nie will die falsche Hoffnung weichen, nie mit der Hoffnung Furcht und Müh;
Never wants the false hope to withdraw, never with the hope fear and trouble;
(False hope will never fade away, nor will fear and trouble, along with that hope;)

di ˈleːvɪçʃt'ʊmən, ˈleːvɪçblae̯çən fɛɐ̯ˈhae̯sən lʊnt' fɛɐ̯ˈzaːgən niː.
die Ewigstummen, Ewigbleichen verheissen und versagen nie.
the eternally mute, eternally pale promise and refuse never.
(the eternally silent, eternally pale, never promise and never refuse.)

nɪçt' vɛk' ɪç ziː mɪt' ˈmae̯nən ˈʃrɪt'ən lɪn ˈliːrɐ ˈdʊŋk'lən ˈlae̯nzaːmkʰae̯tʰ;
Nicht weck' ich sie mit meinen Schritten in ihrer dunklen Einsamkeit;
Not wake I them with my steps in their dark solitude;
(I shall not wake them in their dark solitude with the sound of my steps;)

ziː ˈvɪsən nɪçt', vas lɪç gəˈlɪt'ən, lʊnt' ˈkʰae̯nən ʃt'øːɐ̯t' mae̯n ˈtʰiːfəs lae̯t'.
sie wissen nicht, was ich gelitten, und keinen stört mein tiefes Leid.
they know not, what I (have) suffered, and none [obj.] disturbs my deep sorrow.
(they do not know what I have suffered, and my deep sorrow will disturb none of them.)

dɔrt' kʰan di ˈzeːlə ˈfrae̯ɐ ˈkʰlaːgən bae̯ ˈjeːnɐ, diː lɪç tʰrɔ̯ø gəˈliːp'tʰ;
Dort kann die Seele freier klagen bei Jener, die ich treu geliebt;
There can the soul more freely lament to that woman, whom I faithfully (have) loved;
(There my soul can more freely lament to her whom I have faithfully loved;)

nɪçt' vɪrt deːɐ̯ ˈkʰalt'ə ʃt'ae̯n miːɐ̯ ˈzaːgən, lax, das lɑo̯x ziː mae̯n ʃmɛrts bəˈtʰryːp'tʰ!
nicht wird der kalte Stein mir sagen, ach, dass auch sie mein Schmerz betrübt!
not will the cold stone to me say, ah, that also her my pain grieves!
(the cold stone will not tell me, alas, that my pain also grieves *her*!)

[The poet has been deeply hurt and would rather die than live; the woman he loved made a promise and broke it, she came so near yet would not stay; the dead are no longer tormented by false hope; the dead make no promises; in death he will never be told that his pain may have touched her, for he knows in his bitter heart that that will not be so. The poem is from a diary in verse, and is headed simply "*Am 17ten Januar 1817*" ("On the 17th of January, 1817"); Schubert gave his manuscript the title "*Im Jänner* [Austrian dialect] *1817*." The present title was added by another hand, before publication. The song clearly foreshadows the atmosphere of *Winterreise*.]

tʰiːf lɪm gəˈtʰʏməl deːɐ̯ ʃlaxtʰ
Tief im Getümmel der Schlacht
Deep in the Tumult of the Battle

Posthumously published [composed 1822] (text by Franz von Schober)
(from the opera *Alfonso and Estrella*)

tʰiːf lɪm gəˈtʰʏməl deːɐ̯ ʃlaxt', lʊmˈrʊŋən fɔn ˈgrɔ̯øəl lʊnt' bluːtʰ,
Tief im Getümmel der Schlacht, umrungen von Gräuel und Blut,
Deep in the tumult of the battle, surrounded by horror and blood,
[*in context of the opera:* **Doch** (dɔx, but) **im Getümmel...]**

gaːp' miːɐ̯ nɪçt' ˈleːrə lʊnt' maxt tsuː ˈziːgən den ˈblɪtsəndən muːtʰ.
gab mir nicht Ehre und Macht zu siegen den blitzenden Mut.
gave to me not honor and power to conquer the flashing courage [obj.].
(it was not honor or the power to conquer that gave me that flaming courage:)

nuːɐ̯ ˈdae̯nə ˈzyːsə gəˈʃt'altʰ, diː miːɐ̯/miːr lɪm ˈkʰampfə lɛɐ̯ˈʃiːn,
Nur deine süsse Gestalt, die mir im Kampfe erschien,
Only your sweet form, which to me in the battle appeared,
(only your sweet image, which appeared to me in the midst of the battle,)

t͡soːkʻ mɪç mɪtʻ ˈhɪməlsgəvalt dʊrç di ˈdroːəndən ˈfa͜endə daˈhɪn.
zog mich mit Himmelsgewalt durch die drohenden Feinde dahin.
drew me with heaven- force through the threatening enemies thither.
(drew me onward with heavenly force through the threatening ranks of the enemy.)

nuːɐ̯ da͜en ˈlɛçəlndɐ blɪkʰ gaːpʻ miːɐ̯ di ˈʃtʻɛrkʻə, den ziːkʻ,
Nur dein lächelnder Blick gab mir die Stärke, den Sieg,
Only your smiling gaze gave me the strength, the victory,

nuːɐ̯ da͜en ˈliːbəndɐ blɪkʰ giːpʻtʻ miːɐ̯ bəˈloːnʊŋ |ʊntʻ glʏkʰ.
nur dein liebender Blick gibt mir Belohnung und Glück.
only your loving look gives me reward and happiness.

[Schubert and his friend Schober collaborated on an opera. Schober wrote the libretto; Schubert completed the music, thirty-four musical numbers, within five months; but *Alfonso und Estrella* was rejected in Vienna, later in Dresden as well. Because Schober was persistent, it was eventually presented by Liszt in Weimar in 1854, long after the composer had died.]

ˈtʰɪʃlɐliːtʻ
Tischlerlied
Cabinetmaker's Song

Posthumously published [composed 1815] (author unknown)

ma͜en ˈhantʻvɛrk geːt dʊrç ˈ|alə vɛltʻ |ʊntʻ brɪŋtʻ miːɐ̯ ˈmançən ˈtʰaːlɐ gɛltʻ,
Mein Handwerk geht durch alle Welt und bringt mir manchen Taler Geld,
My handiwork goes through all (the) world and brings me many a thaler money,
(My handiwork travels all over the world and brings me many a silver coin,)

dɛs bɪn |ɪç hoːx fɛɐ̯ˈgnyːkʻtʰ. den ˈtʰɪʃlɐ bra͜oxtʻ |a͜en ˈjeːdɐ ʃtʻantʻ.
dess bin ich hoch vergnügt. Den Tischler braucht ein jeder Stand.
of that am I highly pleased. The cabinetmaker [obj.] needs an every rank [subj.].
(which makes me very gratified. The cabinetmaker is needed by people of every rank.)

ʃoːn vɪrt das kʰɪnt dʊrç ˈma͜enə hantʻ |ɪn ˈzanftʻən ʃlaːf gəˈviːkʻtʰ.
Schon wird das Kind durch meine Hand in sanften Schlaf gewiegt.
Already is the child through my hand in gentle sleep rocked.
(Already at the start of life, a baby is gently rocked to sleep in the work of my hand.)

das ˈbɛtʻə t͡suː deːɐ̯ ˈhɔxt͡sa͜etʻnaxtʻ vɪrtʻ |a͜ox dʊrç ˈma͜enən fla͜es gəˈmaxtʻ
Das Bette zu der Hochzeitnacht wird auch durch meinen Fleiss gemacht
The bed for the wedding night is also through my diligence made
(My diligence also makes the bed for the wedding night,)

|ʊntʻ ˈkʰʏnstʻlɪç ˈangəmaːltʰ. |a͜en ˈga͜et͡shals za͜e |a͜ox nɔx zoː kʰarkʻ,
und künstlich angemalt. Ein Geizhals sei auch noch so karg,
and artfully painted. A skinflint be even ever so stingy,
(and paints it artfully. However stingy a skinflint may be,)
[*auch noch so* = ever so; *künstlich:* today = artificial; earlier = artful, ingenious]

|eːɐ̯ bra͜oxtʻ |am ˈ|ɛndə ˈ|a͜enən zarkʻ, |ʊnt deːɐ̯ vɪrtʻ guːtʻ bəˈt͡saːltʰ.
er braucht am Ende einen Sarg, und der wird gut bezahlt.
he needs at the end a coffin, and that will be well paid.
(he still will need a coffin in the end, and that will cost him plenty.)

drʊm ha:b ɪç ˈɪmɐ ˈfro:ən mu:tʻ lʊntʻ ˈmaxə ˈma͜enə ˈlarba͜etʻ gu:tʻ,
Drum hab' ich immer frohen Mut und mache meine Arbeit gut,
Therefore have I always cheerful spirit and do my work well,
(Therefore I am always in a good humor and do my work well,)

lɛs za͜e tʰɪʃ ˈlo:dɐ ʃraŋkʰ. lʊntʻ ve:ɐ̯ ba͜e mi:ɐ̯ bra:f fi:l bəˈʃtʻɛltʻ
es sei Tisch oder Schrank. Und wer bei mir brav viel bestellt
it be table or cabinet. And whoever by me uprightly much orders
(whether it be a table or a cabinet. And whoever orders a lot from me in good faith,)

lʊnt t͜sa:ltʻ mi:ɐ̯/mi:r ˈɪmɐ ˈba:rəs gɛlt, de:m za:g ɪç ˈgro:sən daŋkʰ.
und zahlt mir immer bares Geld, dem sag' ich grossen Dank.
and pays me always ready money, to him say I big thanks.
(and always pays me in cash, to that person I say "Many thanks!")

[The Peters version of this amusing song, based on the first publication, has a brief prelude, different voice and piano parts for the last phrase and its repeat, and a totally different postlude, two bars shorter than the one in the *Gesamtausgabe*, which is based on Schubert's first draft.]

ˈtʰɪʃli:tʻ
Tischlied
Drinking Song

Op. 118, No. 3 [1815] (Johann Wolfgang von Goethe)

mɪç lɛɐ̯ˈgra͜eftʻ, lɪç va͜es nɪçtʻ vi:, ˈhɪmlɪʃəs bəˈha:gən.
Mich ergreift, ich weiss nicht wie, himmlisches Behagen.
Me seizes, I know not how, heavenly well-being.
(I am overcome—I don't know why!—by a heavenly sense of well-being.)

vɪl mɪçs ˈlɛtʻva ga:ɐ̯ hɪˈna͜of t͜su: den ˈʃtʻɛrnən ˈtʰra:gən?
Will mich's etwa gar hinauf zu den Sternen tragen?
Wants me it perhaps even up to the stars to carry?
(Is this feeling going to carry me up to the stars?)

dɔx lɪç ˈbla͜ebə ˈli:bɐ hi:ɐ̯, kʰan lɪç ˈre:tʻlɪç ˈza:gən,
Doch ich bleibe lieber hier, kann ich redlich sagen,
Yet I stay rather here, can I honestly say,
(Yet I can honestly say that I would rather stay here,)

ba͜em gəˈzaŋ lʊntʻ ˈgla:zə va͜en la͜of den tʰɪʃ t͜su: ˈʃla:gən.
beim Gesang und Glase Wein auf den Tisch zu schlagen.
with the song and glass wine on the table to pound.
(to pound on the table while singing and enjoying a glass of wine.)

ˈvʊndɐtʻ lɔ͜øç, li:ɐ̯ ˈfrɔ͜øndə, nɪçtʻ, vi: lɪç mɪç gəˈbɛ:ɐ̯də;
Wundert euch, ihr Freunde, nicht, wie ich mich gebärde;
Surprise yourselves, you friends, not, how I myself conduct;
(Do not be surprised, my friends, by my behavior;)

ˈvɪrkʻlɪç lɪstʻ lɛs ˈlalɐˌli:pstʻ la͜of de:ɐ̯ ˈli:bən ˈle:ɐ̯də:
wirklich ist es allerliebst auf der lieben Erde: [*GA:* **wirklich es ist**]
really is it all- lovely on the dear earth:
(it is really very lovely on this dear old earth of ours:)

'da:rʊm ʃvø:r ɪç 'fa͜eɐlɪç lʊnt' lo:n 'lalə 'fɛ:ɐ̯də,
darum schwör' ich feierlich und ohn' alle Fährde,
therefore swear I solemnly and without all danger,
(therefore I solemnly swear, without any danger of perjury,)

das lɪç mɪç nɪçt' 'fre:fənt'lɪç 'vɛk'bəge:bən 've:ɐ̯də.
dass ich mich nicht freventlich wegbegeben werde.
that I myself not criminally withdraw shall.
(that I shall never leave it: that would be a crime!)

da: vi:ɐ̯/vi:r 'la:bɐ(r) 'lal͡tsu,ma:l zo: ba͜e'zamən 'va͜elən,
Da wir aber allzumal so beisammen weilen,
Since we however all at once thus together linger,
(However, since we are all lingering here together at the same time,)

dɛçt' ɪç, 'kʰlɛŋə de:ɐ̯ pʰo'kʰa:l t͡su: dɛs 'dɪçt'ɐs 't͡sa͜elən.
dächt' ich, klänge der Pokal zu des Dichters Zeilen.
would think I, would sound the cup to the poet's lines.
(I should have thought that the drinking cup would be sounding in time with the poet's verses.)

'gu:t'ə 'frɔ͜ødə 't͡si:ən fɔrtʰ, vo:l la͜en 'hʊndɐt' 'ma͜elən,
Gute Freunde ziehen fort, wohl ein hundert Meilen,
Good friends move away, maybe a hundred miles,
(Good friends are going away, maybe a hundred miles or so,)
[*note: the poem was written as a farewell toast to a friend leaving town to join the army*]

'da:rʊm zɔl man hi:ɐ̯/hi:r lam lɔrtʰ 'lant͡suʃt'o:sən 'la͜elən.
darum soll man hier am Ort anzustossen eilen.
therefore shall one here at the place to clink glasses hurry.
(therefore at this time and place we should hurry to clink glasses together.)

['le:bə ho:x, ve:ɐ̯ 'le:bən ʃaft'! das lɪst' 'ma͜enə 'le:rə.
[Lebe hoch, wer Leben schafft! Das ist meine Lehre.
[Live high, who life creates! That is my teaching.
[(Long may he live who creates life! That is my teaching.) [*lebe hoch* = long live / here's to ...]

'lʊnzɐ 'kʰø:nɪç dɛn fo'ran, li:m gə'by:ɐ̯t di 'le:rə.
Unser König denn voran, ihm gebührt die Ehre.
Our king then foremost, to him is due the honor.
(The first toast, then, to our king: that honor is due to *him*.)

'ge:gən lɪn lʊnt' 'lɔ͜øsɐn fa͜ent' zɛt͡st' le:ɐ̯ zɪç t͡sʊr 've:rə;
Gegen inn- und äussern Feind setzt er sich zur Wehre;
Against inner and outer enemy sets he himself to the defense;
(He defends the state against domestic and foreign enemies;)

ans lɛɐ̯'halt'ən dɛŋk't' le:ɐ̯ t͡sva:ɐ̯, me:ɐ̯ nɔx vi: le:ɐ̯ 'me:rə.
ans Erhalten denkt er zwar, mehr noch wie er mehre.
about the preservation thinks he of course, more yet as he propagates.
(he thinks about preservation, of course, all the more, the more he propagates.)
[*note: the king was evidently a rather prolific father.*]

nu:n bəˈgry:s ɪç zi: zoˈgla͜eç, zi: di ˈla͜entsɪç ˈla͜enə.
Nun begrüss' ich sie sogleich, sie die einzig Eine.
Now greet I her at once, her the unique and only one.
(Next I toast *her*, right away, the one and only one.)

ˈje:dɐ ˈdɛŋkʻə ˈrɪtʻɐlɪç zɪç daˈba͜e di ˈza͜enə.
Jeder denke ritterlich sich dabei die Seine.
Every man think (her) chivalrously for himself thereby the his [fem.].
(And, when I toast her, let every man chivalrously imagine for himself that she is his.)

ˈmɛrkʻətʻ la͜ox la͜en ˈʃø:nəs kʰɪntʻ, ve:n lɪç ˈle:bən ˈma͜enə,
Merket auch ein schönes Kind, wen ich eben meine,
Notices also a beautiful child, whom I just now mean,
(If a beautiful girl happens to note whom I have in mind right now,)

nu:n zo: ˈnɪkʻə zi: mi:ɐ̯ tsu:: le:pʻ la͜ox zo: de:ɐ̯ ˈma͜enə!
nun so nicke sie mir zu: leb' auch so der Meine!
well then nod she to me to: live also thus the mine [masc.]!
(well, then let her nod to me: "Long live my man too!")

ˈfrɔ͜øndən gɪlt das ˈdrɪtʻə gla:s, ˈtsva͜eən ˈlo:dɐ ˈdra͜eən,
Freunden gilt das dritte Glas, zweien oder dreien,
For friends is intended the third glass, for two or three,
(The third round is intended for friends, for two or three special friends,)

di: mɪtʻ lʊns, lam ˈgu:tʻən tʰa:kʻ, zɪç lɪm ˈʃtʻɪlən ˈfrɔ͜øən
die mit uns, am guten Tag, sich im Stillen freuen
who with us, on the good day, themselves in the quiet rejoice
(who quietly rejoice with us when the day is good) [*sich freuen* = rejoice, be glad]

ʊnt de:ɐ̯ ˈne:bəl ˈtʰry:bə naxtʰ, la͜es lʊntʻ la͜eçt, tsɛɐ̯ˈʃtʻrɔ͜øən;
und der Nebel trübe Nacht, leis und leicht, zerstreuen;
and the mists' dark night, softly and lightly, disperse;
(and, softly and lightly, disperse the mist of melancholy when the night is dark;)

ˈdi:zən za͜e la͜en ho:x gəˈbraxtʰ, ˈlaltʻən ˈlo:dɐ ˈnɔ͜øən.
diesen sei ein Hoch gebracht, alten oder neuen.
to these be a toast brought, to old or new (friends).
(let a toast be raised to them, whether they be old friends or new.) [*ein Hoch* = a toast / a cheer]

ˈbra͜etʻɐ ˈvalətʻ nu:n de:ɐ̯ ʃtʻro:m, mɪtʻ fɛɐ̯ˈme:ɐ̯tʻən ˈvɛlən.
Breiter wallet nun der Strom, mit vermehrten Wellen.
Broader flows now the stream, with increased waves.
(The river is flowing more broadly now, with more and bigger waves.)

ˈle:bən jɛtstʻ, lɪm ˈho:ən tʰo:n, ˈre:tʻlɪçə gəˈzɛlən!
Leben jetzt, im hohen Ton, redliche Gesellen!
(Long) live now, in the high tone, honest companions!
(Now a toast to honest companions: may they live well, highly regarded, and long!)

di: zɪç, mɪtʻ gəˈdrɛŋtʻɐ kʰraftʰ, bra:f tsuˈzamən ˈʃtʻɛlən
die sich, mit gedrängter Kraft, brav zusammen stellen
who themselves, with dense power, uprightly together place
(To those who, with combined strength, assemble together freely)

ɪn dɛs 'glʏk'əs 'zɔnənʃa͜en lʊnt' lɪn 'ʃlɪmən 'fɛlən.
in des Glückes Sonnenschein und in schlimmen Fällen.
in the good fortune's sunshine and in bad cases.
(in the sunshine of good fortune and when times are bad as well!)

viː viːɐ̯ nuːn t͜su'zamən zɪnt', zɪnt t͜su'zamən 'fiːlə.
Wie wir nun zusammen sind, sind zusammen viele.
As we now together are, are together many.
(Many have gathered together elsewhere, just as we have now.)

voːl gə'lɪŋən dɛn, viː lʊns, 'landɐn 'liːrə 'ʃp'iːlə! [dan]
Wohl gelingen denn, wie uns, andern ihre Spiele! [*GA:* **dann**]
Well prosper then, as for us, for others their games! [then—*more specific as to time*]
(May the games of others, then, prosper well, like ours!)

fɔn deːɐ̯ 'kʰvɛlə bɪs lans meːɐ̯ 'maːlət' 'mançə 'myːlə,
Von der Quelle bis ans Meer mahlet manche Mühle,
From the source till to the sea grinds many a mill,
(From the source of the stream to the sea many a mill is grinding the grain,)

ʊnt das voːl deːɐ̯ 'gant͜sən vɛltʰ lɪst͜s, vo'ra͜ʊf lɪç 't͜siːlə.]]
und das Wohl der ganzen Welt ist's, worauf ich ziele.]
and the welfare of the whole world is it, whereat I aim.]
(and the goal of my thoughts is the welfare of the entire world.)]

[There are differences between the *Gesamtausgabe* and the Peters version: four bars in the voice part are not the same in the two editions. Further, the *Gesamtausgabe* prints all eight verses, whereas Peters only the first three (the rest are in brackets, above). Goethe's "parody" was written to fit a pre-existing tune. Schubert's setting is one of the twenty-seven of his Goethe-songs that his friends sent to the sage of Weimar (without, however, receiving any answer).]

'tʰoːdəsmuˌziːkʰ
Todesmusik
The Music of Death

Op. 108, No. 2 [1822] (Franz von Schober)

ɪn dɛs 'tʰoːdəs 'fa͜eɐʃt'ʊndə, vɛn lɪç la͜enst' fɔn 'hɪnən 'ʃa͜edə,
In des Todes Feierstunde[, wenn ich einst von hinnen scheide,
In the death's solemn hour, when I one day from hence depart,
(In the solemn hour of death, when one day I depart from this life,)
[*note: lines in brackets not in the published poem.*]

lʊnt den kʰamp͜f, den 'lɛt͜st'ən 'la͜edə, 'zɛŋk'ə, 'ha͜elɪgə kʰa'møːnə,
und den Kampf, den letzten leide,] senke, heilige Kamöne,
and the battle, the last suffer, sink, holy Camena,
(and suffer that last battle, send down, holy Camena,)
[*note: the Camenae were originally Roman nature deities, later the Roman equivalent of the Greek Muses. Schober uses a Gothic version of the name; here the muse is invoked to ease the struggle of the dying.*]

nɔx ˈlaenmaːl di ˈʃtʻɪlən ˈliːdɐ, nɔx ˈlaenmaːl di ˈzyːsən ˈtʰøːnə ['raenən]
noch einmal die stillen Lieder, noch einmal die süssen Töne [*poem:* **die reinen Töne**]
yet once the quiet songs, yet once the sweet tones [pure]
(once more your quiet songs, once more your sweet tones)

aof di ˈtʰiːfə ˈlapʻʃiːtsvʊndə ˈmaenəs ˈbuːzəns ˈhaeləntʻ ˈniːdɐ.
auf die tiefe Abschiedswunde meines Busens heilend nieder.
onto the deep parting- wound of my bosom healingly down.
(to heal the deep wound of parting in my heart.)

ˈheːbə lɑos dem ˈlɪrdʃən ˈrɪŋən di bəˈdrɛŋtʻə ˈraenə ˈzeːlə,
Hebe aus dem ird'schen Ringen die bedrängte reine Seele,
Lift from the earthly struggle the afflicted pure soul,
(Lift my pure, afflicted soul above this earthly stuggle,)

ˈtʰraːgə ziː lɑof ˈdaenən ˈʃvɪŋən, das ziː zɪç dem lɪçtʻ fɛɐ̯ˈmɛːlə.
trage sie auf deinen Schwingen, dass sie sich dem Licht vermähle.
bear it on your wings, that it itself to the light be wedded.
(bear it on your wings to be united with the light.)

oː daː ˈveːɐ̯dən mɪç di ˈkʰlɛŋə zyːs lʊntʻ ˈvɔnəfɔl lʊmˈveːən
O da werden mich die Klänge süss und wonnevoll umwehen
O there will me the sounds sweetly and blissfully about-waft
(Oh, there those sounds will waft about me sweetly and blissfully)

[*poem:* **traut** (tʰrɑotʻ, intimately) **und wonnevoll**]

ʊnt di ˈkʰɛtʻən, diː lɪç ˈʃpʻrɛŋə, ˈveːɐ̯dən ʃtʻɪl lʊntʻ laeçtʻ fɛɐ̯ˈgeːən.
und die Ketten, die ich sprenge, werden still und leicht vergehen.
and the chains, which I burst, will quietly and lightly vanish.

ˈaləs groːsə veːɐ̯d ɪç ˈzeːən, das lɪm ˈleːbən mɪç bəˈglʏkʻtʻə,
Alles Grosse werd' ich sehen, das im Leben mich beglückte,
Everything great shall I see, that in the life me made happy,
(I shall see everything great and noble that made me happy in life,)

ˈaləs ˈʃøːnə, vas miːɐ̯ ˈblyːtʻə, vɪrtʻ fɛɐ̯ˈhɛrlɪçtʻ foːɐ̯ miːɐ̯ ˈʃtʻeːən.
alles Schöne, was mir blühte, wird verherrlicht vor mir stehen.
everything beautiful, that for me bloomed, will glorified before me stand.
(all the beauty that ever blossomed for me will appear before me, glorified.)

ˈjeːdən ʃtʻɛrn, deːɐ̯ miːɐ̯/miːr lɛɐ̯ˈglyːtʻə, deːɐ̯ mɪtʻ ˈfrɔøntʻlɪçəm gəˈfʊŋkʻəl
Jeden Stern, der mir erglühte, der mit freundlichem Gefunkel
Every star, that for me glowed, that with friendly glittering
(Every star that ever glowed for me, that with its friendly glitter ever)

dʊrç das ˈgrɑoənfɔlə ˈdʊŋkʻəl ˈmaenəs ˈkʰʊrtsən ˈveːgəs ˈblɪkʻtʻə,
durch das grauenvolle Dunkel meines kurzen Weges blickte,
through the dreadful darkness of my short pathway gazed,
(gazed through the dreadful darkness of my short journey through life,)

[*poem:* **durch das hoffnungslose** (ˈhɔfnʊŋsloːzə, hopeless) **Dunkel**]

'je:də 'blu:mə, di: li:n 'ʃmʏk'tʻə, 'je:dən ʃtʻɛrn, de:ɐ̯ mi:ɐ̯/mi:r lɛɐ̯'gly:tʻə,
jede Blume, die ihn schmückte, [jeden Stern, der mir erglühte,]
every flower, that it adorned, every star, that for me glowed,
(every flower that brightened my path, every star that glowed for me,)
[*line in brackets (a repeat) added by Schubert*]

've:ɐ̯dən mi:ɐ̯ di 'tʰø:nə 'brɪŋən. lʊnt di 'ʃrɛkʻlɪçən mi'nu:tʻən,
werden mir die Töne bringen. Und die schrecklichen Minuten,
will to me the tones bring. And the frightful minutes,
(your tones will bring back to me. And the frightful minutes)

vo: lɪç 'ʃmɛrt͜slɪç 'kʰœntʻə 'blu:tʻən, 've:ɐ̯dən mɪç mɪtʻ lʊstʻ lʊm'kʰlɪŋən,
wo ich schmerzlich könnte bluten, werden mich mit Lust umklingen,
when I painfully could bleed, will me with pleasure around-sound,
(when I could be painfully bleeding will envelop me in pleasing sound,)

ʊntʻ fɛɐ̯'kʰlɛ:rʊŋ ve:ɐ̯d ɪç 'ze:ən 'lɑ͜osgəgɔsən 'ly:bɐ(r) 'lalən 'dɪŋən.
und Verklärung werd' ich sehen ausgegossen über allen Dingen.
and transfiguration shall I see out-poured over all things.
(and I shall see all things bathed in transfiguring light.)

zo: lɪn 'vɔnə ve:ɐ̯d ɪç 'lʊntʻɐge:ən, zy:s fɛɐ̯'ʃlʊŋən fɔn de:ɐ̯ 'frɔ͜ødə 'flu:tʻən.
So in Wonne werd' ich untergehen, süss verschlungen von der Freude Fluten.
Thus in bliss shall I go under, sweetly engulfed by the joy's floods.
(Thus shall I sink into bliss, sweetly engulfed in floods of joy.)

[This is a big song that should be better known (though several prominent commentators show little enthusiasm). The title may be misleading, may suggest something depressing, like a funeral march. On the contrary, the song offers a beatific vision of the transition from death to a new state of being, a transition expressed in many modulations, like waves of new impressions, lifted veils, stages of the transformation. The poet was one of Schubert's close friends. The opening melody has a noticeable resemblance to that of Florestan's famous aria in Beethoven's *Fidelio.*]

'tʰo:tʻəngrɛ:bɐli:tʻ
Totengräberlied
Gravedigger's Song

Posthumously published [composed 1813] (poem by Ludwig Hölty)

'gra:bə, 'ʃpʻa:tʻən, 'gra:bə! 'laləs, vas lɪç 'ha:bə, daŋkʻ ɪç, 'ʃpʻa:tʻən, di:ɐ̯!
Grabe, Spaten, grabe! Alles, was ich habe, dank' ich, Spaten, dir!
Dig, spade, dig! All, what I have, thank I, spade, to you!
(Dig, spade, dig! I have you to thank, spade, for all that I have!)

ra͜eç lʊntʻ 'larmə 'lɔ͜øtʻə 've:ɐ̯dən 'ma͜enə 'bɔ͜øtʻə, 'kʰɔmən la͜enst t͜su: mi:ɐ̯.
Reich' und arme Leute werden meine Beute, kommen einst zu mir.
Rich and poor people become my booty, come one day to me.
(Both rich and poor become my booty; one day they all come to me.)

'va͜elantʻ gro:s lʊntʻ 'le:dəl, 'nɪkʻtʻə 'di:zɐ 'ʃɛ:dəl 'kʰa͜enəm 'gru:sə daŋkʰ.
Weiland gross und edel, nickte dieser Schädel keinem Grusse Dank.
Formerly great and noble, nodded this skull to no greeting thanks.
(This skull belonged to a nobleman too grand to acknowledge a greeting with a nod of thanks.)

'di:zəs 'baengərɪp'ə 'lo:nə vaŋ lʊnt' 'lɪp'ə 'hat'ə gɔlt' lʊnt' raŋ.
Dieses Beingerippe ohne Wang' und Lippe hatte Gold und Rang.
This bone-skeleton without cheek and lip had gold and rank.
(This skeleton without cheeks or lips once had gold and rank.)

'je:nɐ kʰɔpf mɪt' 'ha:rən va:ɐ fo:ɐ 've:nɪç 'ja:rən ʃø:n, vi: 'lɛŋəl zɪnt'.
Jener Kopf mit Haaren war vor wenig Jahren schön, wie Engel sind.
That head with hairs was before few years beautiful, as angels are.
(That head that still has hair was beautiful a few years ago, as beautiful as the head of an angel.)

'tʰaozənt' 'jʊŋə 'fɛnt'çən 'lɛk't'ən li:m das 'hɛnt'çən, 'gaft'ən zɪç halp blɪnt'.
Tausend junge Fäntchen leckten ihm das Händchen, gafften sich halb blind.
(A) thousand young little fops licked for it the little hand, gaped themselves half blind.
(A thousand young little fops used to lick its owner's little hand, gaping themselves half blind.)

[Schubert presents us with a very jolly gravedigger in this effective song for a bass voice.]

'tʰo:t'əngrɛ:bɐs 'haemve:
Totengräbers Heimweh
Gravedigger's Homesickness

Posthumously published [composed 1825] (poem by Jacob Nicolaus Craigher)

o: 'mɛnʃhaetʰ, lo: 'le:bən, vas zɔls? lo: vas zɔls? 'gra:bə laos, 'ʃarə tsu:,
O Menschheit, o Leben, was soll's? o was soll's? Grabe aus, scharre zu,
O mankind, O life, what shall it? O what means it? Dig out, fill up,
(O mankind, O life, what does it all mean, oh, what does it all mean? Dig a hole, fill it up,)

tʰa:k' lʊnt' naxt' 'kʰaenə ru:! das 'drɛŋən, das 'tʰraebən, vo'hɪn? lo: vo'hɪn?
Tag und Nacht keine Ruh'! Das Drängen, das Treiben, wohin? o wohin?
day and night no rest! The hurrying, the driving, whither? O whither?
(no rest day or night! This hurrying, this pushing, where, oh where does it lead?)
[*GA:* **Das Treiben, das Drängen** (reversed order from that of the poem)]

ɪns gra:p', lɪns gra:p' tʰi:f hɪ'nap'! lo: 'ʃɪk'za:l, lo: 'tʰraorɪgə pflɪçt',
"Ins Grab, ins Grab tief hinab!" O Schicksal, o traurige Pflicht,
"Into the grave, into the grave, deep down!" O fate, O mournful duty,

lɪç tʰra:ks 'lɛŋɐ nɪçtʰ! van vɪrst du: mi:ɐ 'ʃla:gən, lo: 'ʃt'ʊndə de:ɐ ru:?
ich trag's länger nicht! Wann wirst du mir schlagen, o Stunde der Ruh'?
I bear it longer not! When will you for me strike, O hour of the rest?
(I can bear it no longer! When will you strike for me, O hour of rest?)

o: tʰo:t'! kʰɔm lʊnt 'drʏk'ə di 'laogən mi:ɐ tsu:! lɪm 'le:bən, da: lɪsts, lax! zo:
o Tod! komm' und drücke die Augen mir zu! Im Leben, da ist's, ach! so
O death! come and press the eyes for me closed! In the life, there is it, ah! so
(O death, come and close my eyes! In life, alas, all is so)
[*poem:* **Im Leben da ist es** (lɪst' lɛs, is it) **so schwül!**]

ʃvy:l! lɪm 'gra:bə zo: 'fri:t'lɪç, zo: kʰy:l! dɔx lax! ve:ɐ le:k't' mɪç hɪ'naen?
schwül! im Grabe so friedlich, so kühl! Doch ach! wer legt mich hinein?
sultry! in the grave so peaceful, so cool! But ah! who lays me into it?
(oppressively sweaty, in the grave so peaceful, so cool! But, alas, who will lay me into it?)

ıç ˈʃtʻeːə laˈla͜en, zoː gants laˈla͜en! fɔn ˈlalən fɛɐ̯ˈlasən, dem tʰoːtʻ nuːɐ̯ fɛɐ̯ˈvantʻ,
ich stehe allein, so ganz allein! Von allen verlassen, dem Tod nur verwandt,
I stand alone, so utterly alone! By all forsaken, to the death only related,
(I am alone, so utterly alone! Forsaken by all, kin only to death,)

fɛɐ̯ˈva͜el ıç lam ˈrandə, das kʰrɔ͜ø͡ts lın deːɐ̯ hantʻ, lʊntʻ ˈʃtʻarə mıtʻ ˈzeːnəndən
verweil' ich am Rande, das Kreuz in der Hand, und starre mit sehnenden
linger I at the edge, the cross in the hand, and stare with longing
(I linger at the edge, the cross in my hand, and stare—with a longing)

blıkʻ hıˈnapʻ lıns ˈtʰiːfə graːpʻ! loː ˈha͜emaːt dɛs ˈfriːdəns, deːɐ̯ ˈzeːlıgən lantʻ,
Blick hinab ins tiefe Grab! O Heimat des Friedens, der Seligen Land,
gaze down into the deep grave! O homeland of the peace, the blessed's land,
(gaze—down into the deep grave! O homeland of peace, land of the blessed dead,)

lan dıç kʰnʏp͡ft di ˈzeːlə la͜en ˈmaːgıʃəs bantʻ! duː vıŋkstʻ miːɐ̯ fɔn ˈfɛrnə,
an dich knüpft die Seele ein magisches Band! du winkst mir von ferne,
to you ties the soul a magical bond! you beckon to me from afar,
(a magical bond binds my soul to you! You beckon me from afar,)

duː ˈleːvıgəs lıçtʰ! lɛs ˈʃvındən di ˈʃtʻɛrnə, das ˈla͜ogə ʃoːn brıçtʰ!
du ewiges Licht! Es schwinden die Sterne, das Auge schon bricht!
you eternal light! There disappear the stars, the eye already breaks!
(eternal light! The stars are disappearing, my eyes already grow dim!)

ıç ˈzıŋkʻə, lıç ˈzıŋkʻə! liːɐ̯ ˈliːbən, lıç ˈkʰɔmə, liːɐ̯ ˈliːbən, lıç kʰɔm!
Ich sinke, ich sinke! ihr Lieben, ich komme, ihr Lieben, ich komm'!
I sink, I sink! you dear ones, I come, you dear ones, I come!
(I am sinking, I am sinking! Oh my dear ones, I am coming to you...)

[The poor man is dying before our eyes in this pathetic, musically rich and remarkable song.]

ˈtʰoːtʻəngrɛːbɐva͜ezə
Totengräberweise
Gravedigger's Song

Posthumously published [composed 1826] (poem by Franz Xaver von Schlechta)

nıçtʻ zoː ˈdyːstʻɐ(r) lʊntʻ zoː bla͜eç, ˈʃleːfɐ(r) lın deːɐ̯ ˈtʰruːə,
Nicht so düster und so bleich, Schläfer in der Truhe,
Not so gloomy and so pale, sleeper in the chest,
(Be not so gloomy and so pale, sleeper in the chest;)

ˈʊntʻɐ ˈʃɔlən la͜eçtʻ lʊntʻ va͜eç leːg ıç dıç t͡sʊr ˈruːə.
unter Schollen leicht und weich leg' ich dich zur Ruhe.
under clods of earth light and soft lay I you to the rest.
(I lay you to your rest beneath light, soft clods of earth.)

[ˈvoːnəstʻ nuːn lım ˈʃtʻılən ra͜eç ˈgɔtʻgəva͜etʻɐ ˈruːə!]
[*poem:* **wohnest nun im stillen Reich Gottgeweihter Ruhe!**]
[(you) dwell now in the quiet realm of God-consecrated rest!]

vɪrt deːɐ̯ lae̯p‘ dɛs 'vʊrməs rɑo̯p‘ lʊnt‘ lae̯n ʃp‘iːl deɐ̯ 'vɪndən,
Wird der Leib des Wurmes Raub und ein Spiel der Winden,
Becomes the body the worm's prey and a sport of the winds,
(Though your body will become the prey of the worms, and your dust the sport of the winds,)

mʊs das hɛrt͡s zɛlpst‘ nɔx lals ʃt‘ɑo̯p‘ 'leːbən lʊnt‘ lɛm'p͡fɪndən.
muss das Herz selbst noch als Staub leben und empfinden.
must the heart even still as dust live and feel.
(your heart, even as dust, is still required to continue to live and feel.)

dɛn deːɐ̯ hɛr zɪt͡st t͡suː gə'rɪçt‘; 'glae̯çənt 'dae̯nəm 'leːbən, [jɛt͡st‘ bə'gɪnət dae̯n]
Denn der Herr sitzt zu Gericht; gleichend deinem Leben, [*p.* **Jetzt beginnet dein Gericht]**
For the Lord sits in judgment; resembling your life, [Now begins your]
(For the Lord sits in judgment; according to how you lived your life,)

'veːɐ̯dən, 'dʊŋk‘əl 'loːdɐ lɪçt, 'tʰrɔ̯ø̯mə dɪç lʊm'ʃveːbən.
werden, dunkel oder licht, Träume dich umschweben.
will, dark or light, dreams you about-hover.
(dreams, dark or bright, will hover about you.)

'jeːdɐ lɑo̯t, deːɐ̯ dɪç fɛɐ̯'kʰlaːk‘tʰ lals den kʰvɛl deːɐ̯ 'ʃmɛrt͡sən,
Jeder Laut, der dich verklagt als den Quell der Schmerzen,
Every sound, that you accuses as the source of the pains,
(Every sound that accuses you of being a source of pain)

vɪrt‘ lae̯n 'ʃarfɐ dɔlç lʊnt‘ naːk‘t‘ zɪç t͡suː 'dae̯nəm 'hɛrt͡sən.
wird ein scharfer Dolch und nagt sich zu deinem Herzen.
becomes a sharp dagger and gnaws itself to your heart.
(will become a sharp dagger that incrementally twists its way into your heart.)

dɔx deːɐ̯ 'liːbə 'tʰrɛːnəntʰɑo̯, deːɐ̯ dae̯n graːp bə'ʃp‘ryːətʰ,
Doch der Liebe Tränentau, der dein Grab besprühet,
But the love's tear- dew, which your grave [obj.] besprinkles,
(But the dewy tears of love that are sprinkled on your grave)

fɛrp‘t‘ zɪç lan dɛs 'hɪməls blɑo̯, 'kʰnɔsp‘ət‘ lɑo̯f lʊnt‘ 'blyːətʰ.
färbt sich an des Himmels Blau, knospet auf und blühet.
colors itself to the heaven's blue, buds up and blooms.
(will reflect the blue of heaven, will bring forth buds and blossoms.)

ɪm gə'zaŋə leːp‘t deːɐ̯ hɛlt‘, lʊnt t͡suː 'zae̯nəm 'ruːmə
Im Gesange lebt der Held, und zu seinem Ruhme
In the song lives the hero, and to his fame
(The hero lives on in song, and to his fame)

'ʃɪmɐt‘ hoːx lɪm 'ʃt‘ɛrnənfelt‘ 'lae̯nə 'fɔ̯ø̯ɐbluːmə. ['brɛnət‘]
schimmert hoch im Sternenfeld eine Feuerblume. [*poem:* **brennet hoch]**
shimmers high in the star- field a fire- flower. [burns]
(a flower of fire shimmers on high in the field of stars.)

'ʃlaːfə bɪs deːɐ̯/deːr 'lɛŋəl ruːftʰ, bɪs pʰo'zɑo̯nən 'kʰlɪŋən,
Schlafe bis der Engel ruft, bis Posaunen klingen,
Sleep till the angel calls, till trombones sound,
(Sleep till the angel calls, till the trumpets sound,)

ʊnt di ˈla͜ebɐ zɪç deːɐ̯ grʊftʻ ˈjuːgəntʻlɪç lɛntʻˈʃvɪŋən.
und die Leiber sich der Gruft jugendlich entschwingen.
and the bodies themselves from the grave youthfully away-soar.
(and the bodies rise up in renewed youth from their graves.) [*sich entschwingen* = soar away]

[There is strength and firmeness of faith in the music as in the sturdy philospher who sings it. Schubert shifts from minor to major and back according to the darker or lighter aspects of death.]

ˈtʰoːtʻənkʰrant͜s fyːɐ̯ la͜en kʰɪntʻ
Totenkranz für ein Kind
Funeral Wreath for a Child

Posthumously published [composed 1815] (poem by Friedrich von Matthisson)

zanftʻ veːn, lɪm ha͜ox deːɐ̯/deːr ˈlaːbəntʻlʊft, di ˈfryːlɪŋshalm la͜of ˈda͜enɐ grʊftʻ,
Sanft weh'n, im Hauch der Abendluft, die Frühlingshalm' auf deiner Gruft,
Gently wave, in the breath of the evening air, the spring blades on your grave,
(In the evening breeze the spring grasses are waving gently on your grave,)

voː ˈzeːnzʊxt͜stʰrɛːnən ˈfalən. niː zɔl, bɪs lʊns deːɐ̯ tʰoːtʻ bəˈfra͜et, di ˈvɔlkʻə deːɐ̯
wo Sehnsuchtstränen fallen. Nie soll, bis uns der Tod befreit, die Wolke der
where yearning- tears fall. Never shall, till us the death frees, the cloud of the
(where tears of yearning fall. Never, till death frees us, shall the cloud of)

fɛɐ̯ˈgɛsənha͜et da͜en ˈhɔldəs bɪltʻ lʊmˈvalən. voːl diːɐ̯/diːr, lɔpʻgla͜eç lɛntʻˈkʰnɔspʻətʻ kʰa͜om,
Vergessenheit dein holdes Bild umwallen. Wohl dir, obgleich entknospet kaum,
oblivion your lovely image about-float. Good for you, although out-budded barely,
(oblivion float over your lovely image. You are well-off, though your bud has barely blossomed,)

fɔn ˈleːɐ̯dənlʊstʻ lʊntʻ ˈzɪnəntʰra͜om, fɔn ʃmɛrt͜s lʊntʻ vaːn gəˈʃiːdən! duː ʃlɛːfstʻ
von Erdenlust und Sinnentraum, von Schmerz und Wahn geschieden! Du schläfst
from earth-pleasure and senses-dream, from pain and delusion separated! You sleep
(you are separated from earthly pleasure, the dream of the senses, pain, and delusion! You sleep)

lɪn ruː; viːɐ̯ ˈvaŋkʻən lɪr lʊntʻ ˈlʊnʃtʻɛːtʻbaŋ lɪm ˈvɛltʻgəvɪr, lʊntʻ ˈhaːbən ˈzɛltʻən ˈfriːdən.
in Ruh'; wir wanken irr und unstätbang im Weltgewirr, und haben selten Frieden.
in peace; we waver lost and uncertain in the world-maze, and have seldom peace.
(in peace; we stumble, lost and uncertain in the confusion of the world, and seldom find peace.)
[*unstätbang* (dialect) = *unstetbang* = fearful of instability]

[A sometimes chromatic bass line and subtle harmonies give a special poignance to this song.]

ˈtʰoːtʻənlɔp͜fɐ / lɛɐ̯ˈlɪnərʊŋ
Totenopfer / Erinnerung
An Offering to the Dead / Memory

Posthumously published [composed 1814] (poem by Friedrich von Matthisson)

kʰa͜en ˈroːzənʃɪmɐ ˈlɔ͜øçtʻət dem tʰaːkʻ t͜sʊr ruː! deːɐ̯/deːr ˈlaːbəntʻneːbəl
Kein Rosenschimmer leuchtet dem Tag zur Ruh'! der Abendnebel
No roseate shimmer lights the day to the rest! the evening mist
(No roseate shimmer lights the day to rest! The evening mist) **[*poem:* den** (den, the) **Tag]**

ʃvɪlt‘ lam gəˈʃt‘aːt‘ lɛmˈpʰoːɐ̯, voː dʊrç fɛɐ̯ˈdɔrt‘ə ˈfɛlzəngrɛːzɐ
schwillt am Gestad' empor, wo durch verdorrte Felsengräser
swells by the shore aloft, where through withered field grasses
(rises up by the shore, where through withered field grasses)

ˈʃt‘ɛrbəndɐ ˈlʏft‘ə gəˈzɔ͜øzəl ˈvandəltʰ. nɪçt‘ ˈʃveːɐ̯muːt͡sfɔlɐ
sterbender Lüfte Gesäusel wandelt. Nicht schwermutsvoller
dying breezes' murmur wanders. Not more melancholy
(the murmur of dying breezes wanders. Not more melancholy than this)

ˈbeːp‘t‘ə dɛs ˈhɛrpst‘əs veːn dʊrçs ˈtʰoːtə graːs lam ˈzɪŋk‘əndən ˈraːzənmaːl,
bebte des Herbstes Weh'n durch's tote Gras am sinkenden Rasenmal,
quivered the autumn's blowing through the dead grass on the sinking turf- memorial,
(was the autumn wind that quivered through the dead grass on the sinking memorial mound,)
[*NSA:* **tönte** (ˈtʰøːnt‘ə, sounded) **des Herbstes Weh'n**]

voː ˈma͜enəs ˈjuːgənt‘liːp‘lɪŋs ˈlaʃə ˈlʊnt‘ɐ den ˈtʰra͜oɐndən ˈva͜edən ˈʃlʊmɐtʰ.
wo meines Jugendlieblings Asche unter den trauernden Weiden schlummert.
where my youth- darling's ash(es) under the mourning willows slumbers.
(where the ashes of the darling of my youth are slumbering under the weeping willows.)
[*poem:* **unter der** (deːɐ̯, the–*singular*) **trauernden Weide** (ˈva͜edə, willow)]

iːm ˈtʰrɛːnən ˈlɔp͡fɐn veːɐ̯d ɪç ba͜em ˈblɛt‘ɐfal, liːm, vɛn das ˈma͜ela͜op‘
Ihm Tränen opfern werd' ich beim Blätterfall, ihm, wenn das Mailaub
To him tears sacrifice shall I at the leaf- fall, to him, when the May foliage
(I shall offer him tears when the leaves are falling and when the May foliage)

ˈviːdɐ den ha͜en lʊmˈra͜oʃtʰ, bɪs miːɐ̯, fɔm ˈʃøːnɐn ʃt‘ɛrn, di ˈleːɐ̯də
wieder den Hain umrauscht, bis mir, vom schönern Stern, die Erde
again the grove about-rustles, till to me, from the more beautiful star, the earth
(is rustling again around the grove, until I have gone to a more beautiful star and the earth)

ˈfrɔ͜ønt‘lɪç lɪm ˈra͜egən deːɐ̯ ˈvɛlt‘ən ˈʃɪmɐtʰ.
freundlich im Reigen der Welten schimmert.
amiably in the round-dance of the worlds shimmers.
(will be shimmering in the round-dance of the stars, to me, then, only one world among many.)

[The sentiment is sad, but the music is grateful, well-made, appealingly unpretentious, and far from depressing. The original (and more appropriate) title of the poem was "*Erinnerung*" ("Memory"), changed in a later publication. The *Gesamtausgabe* chose "*Totenopfer*," the *Neue Schubert Ausgabe* uses the earlier title.]

Tränenregen see *Die schöne Müllerin*

ˈtʰra͜oɐ deːɐ̯ ˈliːbə
Trauer der Liebe
Love's Grief

Posthumously published [composed 1816] (poem by Johann Georg Jacobi)

voː di tʰa͜op‘ lɪn ˈʃt‘ɪlən ˈbuːxən ˈliːrən ˈtʰa͜obɐ zɪç lɛɐ̯ˈvɛːltʰ, voː
Wo die Taub' in stillen Buchen ihren Tauber sich erwählt, wo
Where the female dove in quiet beech trees her male dove for herself chooses, where
(There where the female dove chooses herself a mate among the silent beech trees, where)

zɪç 'naxt'ɪgalən 'zu:xən, |ʊnt di 're:bə zɪç fɛɐ̯'mɛ:ltʰ; vo: di 'bɛçə
sich Nachtigallen suchen, und die Rebe sich vermählt; wo die Bäche
each other nightingales search for, and the grapevine itself marries; where the brooks
(nightingales search for one another, and the grapevines are joined in an embrace; where brooks)

zɪç fɛɐ̯'-/fɛr'|a͜enən, gɪŋ |ɪç |ɔft' mɪt' 'la͜eçt'əm ʃɛrt͜s, [ʃmɛrt͜s]
sich vereinen, ging ich oft mit leichtem Scherz,* [*variant:* **Schmerz]**
themselves unite, went I often with light jest, [pain]
(flow together, I often went in a light, jesting mood,)

[**note:* *"Scherz" in both GA and Peters; in reproducing the poem, Schochow prints "Schmerz," yet also claims "no divergence" between song and poem! "Schmerz" makes better sense: "I often went in mild pain, often with anxious weeping"; is it Schubert's mistake, or their misprint?*]

gɪŋ |ɪç |ɔft' mɪt' 'baŋəm 'va͜enən, 'zu:xt'ə mi:ɐ̯/mi:r |a͜en 'li:bənt' hɛrt͜s.
ging ich oft mit bangem Weinen, suchte mir ein liebend Herz.
went I often with anxious weeping, sought for me a loving heart.
(often with anxious weeping, and sought for myself a loving heart.)

o:, da: ga:p' di 'fɪnst'rə 'la͜obə 'la͜ezən tʰro:st' |ɪm 'a:bənt'ʃa͜en;
O, da gab die finstre Laube leisen Trost im Abendschein;
O, there gave the dark arbor soft consolation in the sunset glow;
(Oh, there the dark arbor in the glow of sunset gave me soft consolation;)

o:, da: kʰa:m |a͜en 'zy:sɐ 'gla͜obə mɪt dem 'mɔrgənglant͜s |ɪm ha͜en;
o, da kam ein süsser Glaube mit dem Morgenglanz im Hain;
O, there came a sweet faith with the morning-radiance in the grove;
(Oh, there a sweet faith came to me with the radiance of morning in the grove;)

da: fɛɐ̯'na:m |ɪçs |ɪn den 'vɪndən, |i:ɐ̯ gə'flʏst'ɐ 'le:ɐ̯t'ə mɪç:
da vernahm ich's in den Winden, ihr Geflüster lehrte mich:
there heard I it in the winds, their whispering taught me:
(there I heard it in the winds, their whispering taught me:)

das |ɪç 'zu:xən zɔlt' |ʊnt' 'fɪndən, 'fɪndən, 'hɔldə 'li:bə, dɪç!
dass ich suchen sollt' und finden, finden, holde Liebe, dich!
that I search should and find, find, lovely love, you!
(that I should seek and find—find *you*, lovely love!)

'a:bɐ(r), |ax! vo: bli:p' |a͜of 'le:ɐ̯dən, 'hɔldə 'li:bə, 'da͜enə ʃp'u:ɐ̯?
Aber, ach! wo blieb auf Erden, holde Liebe, deine Spur?
But, ah! where remained on earth, lovely love, your trace?
(Ah, but where on earth, lovely love, did any trace of you remain?)

'li:bən, |ʊm gə'li:p't t͜su: 've:ɐ̯dən, |ɪst das lo:s de:ɐ̯/de:r '|ɛŋəl nu:ɐ̯.
Lieben, um geliebt zu werden, ist das Los der Engel nur.
To love, so as loved to be, is the lot of the angel only.
(To love with the expectation of being loved in return, that is the lot of an angel only.)

ʃt'at de:ɐ̯ 'vɔnə fant' |ɪç 'ʃmɛrt͜sən, hɪŋ |an de:m, vas mɪç fɛɐ̯'li:s;
Statt der Wonne fand ich Schmerzen, hing an dem, was mich verliess;
Instead of the bliss found I pains, clung to that, which me deserted;
(Instead of bliss I found pain; I clung to that which deserted me;)

ˈfri:dən gi:p‘t dem ˈtʰrɔ͜øən ˈhɛrt͜sən nu:ɐ̯/nu:r la͜en ˈkʰʏnft‘ɪç pʰaraˈdi:s.
Frieden gibt dem treuen Herzen nur ein künftig Paradies.
peace [obj.] gives to the faithful heart only a future paradise.
(only a future paradise will give peace to a faithful heart.)

[Schubert speaks for this disappointed seeker after love in his most charming, Mozartean vein.]

ˈtʰrɪŋk‘li:t‘/ ˈbaxʊs, ˈfa͜est‘ɐ fʏrst dɛs va͜ens
Trinklied / Bachus, feister Fürst des Weins
Drinking Song / Bacchus, Plump Prince of Wine

Posthumously published [composed 1826] (poem by William Shakespeare)
(German translation by Ferdinand Mayerhofer von Grünbühel and Eduard von Barernfeld)
(German second verse probably by Friedrich Reil)

ˈbaxʊs, ˈfa͜est‘ɐ fʏrst dɛs va͜ens, kʰɔm mɪt‘ ˈla͜ogən ˈhɛlən ʃa͜ens,
Bachus, feister Fürst des Weins, komm mit Augen hellen Scheins,
Bacchus, plump prince of the wine, come with eyes of bright shine,
(Bacchus, plump prince of wine, come with your brightly shining eyes,)

ˈʊnzrə zɔrk‘ lɛɐ̯ˈzɔ͜øf da͜en fas, lʊnt da͜en la͜op‘ lʊns ˈkʰrø:nən las.
unsre Sorg' ersäuf dein Fass, und dein Laub uns krönen lass.
our care [obj.] may drown your vat [subj.], and your foliage us crown let.
(may your vat drown our cares, and let your vine-leaves crown us.)

fʏl lʊns, bɪs di vɛlt‘ zɪç dre:tʰ, fʏl lʊns, bɪs di vɛlt‘ zɪç dre:tʰ,
Füll' uns, bis die Welt sich dreht, füll' uns, bis die Welt sich dreht!
Fill us, till the world itself turns, fill us, till the world itself turns!
(Fill us, till the world goes round, fill us, till the world goes round!)

[ˈʊnzɐ zaŋ lɛɐ̯ˈʃalə ho:x! va͜en mɪt‘ zaŋ ʃmɛk‘t‘ ˈbɛsɐ nɔx.
[Unser Sang erschalle hoch! Wein mit Sang schmeckt besser noch.
[Our song resound high! Wine with song tastes better yet.
[(Let our song resound to the sky! Wine with song tastes better yet.)

zo: lɛntˈˈfli:ət‘ fro: di t͜sa͜et‘, ve:ms nɪçt‘ ˈmʊndət‘, ˈfli:ə va͜etʰ.
So entfliehet froh die Zeit, wem's nicht mundet, fliehe weit.
Thus flees away happily the time, (he) to whom it not tastes good, may flee far.
(Thus time will pass happily; let him who does not like it hurry far away.)

ho:x de:ɐ̯/de:r ˈle:dlə ˈgœt‘ɐtʰraŋkʰ! ho:x de:ɐ̯/de:r ˈle:dlə ˈgœt‘ɐtʰraŋkʰ!
Hoch der edle Göttertrank! Hoch der edle Göttertrank!]
High the noble gods- drink! High the noble gods- drink!] [*Hoch* = toast or cheer]
(A toast to the noble nectar of the gods! A toast to the noble nectar of the gods!)]

[The words are from *Antony and Cleopatra*, Act II, Scene 7. Schubert wrote a repeat mark at the end, though the poem has only one verse; so the first publisher added a second (in brackets, above), not from Shakespeare. Peters includes that second verse, the *Gesamtausgabe* does not. Schubert's melody happens to fit the original English in a perfectly natural way:

Come, thou monarch of the vine, / Plumpy Bacchus with pink eyne!
In thy vats our cares be drown'd / With thy grapes our hairs be crown'd;
Cup us, till the world go round, / Cup us, till the world go round!]

'tʰrɪŋk'liːt'/ 'bryːdɐ! 'ʊnzɐ 'leːɐ̯dənvalən

Trinklied / Brüder! unser Erdenwallen

Drinking Song / Brothers! Our Pilgrimage on Earth

Op. 131, No. 2 [1815] (Ignaz Franz Castelli)

'bryːdɐ(r)! 'ʊnzɐ(r) 'leːɐ̯dənvalən ɪst' la̯en 'leːvgəs 'ʃt'a̯egən, 'falən,
Brüder! unser Erdenwallen ist ein ew'ges Steigen, Fallen,
Brothers! our earth- pilgrimage is an eternal climbing, falling,
(Brothers, our pilgrimage on earth is an eternal climbing and falling,)

balt' hɪ'na̯of ʊnt' balt' hɪ'nap': ɪn dem 'drɛŋəndən gə'vyːlə
bald hinauf und bald hinab: in dem drängenden Gewühle
soon up and soon down: in the pressing tumult
(one minute you're up, the next you're down; in the crowded turmoil)

giːp'ts deːɐ̯ 'gruːbən gaːɐ̯ zoː 'fiːlə, ʊnt di 'lɛtst'ə ɪst das graːp'.
gibt's der Gruben gar so viele, und die letzte ist das Grab.
are there of the pits absolutely so many, and the last is the grave.
(there are so darn many pits to fall into, and the last one is the grave.)

CHOR (kʰoːɐ̯, chorus):
'daːrʊm 'bryːdɐ! 'ʃɛŋk'ət' la̯en, mʊs ɛs ʃoːn gə'zʊŋk'ən za̯en,
Darum Brüder! schenket ein, muss es schon gesunken sein,
Therefore brothers! pour (it) in, must it already sunk be, [*einschenken* = pour a drink]
(Therefore, brothers, fill your glasses! If everything has to end up in the ground,)

'zɪŋk'ən viːɐ̯ bə'ra̯oʃt' fɔm va̯en.
sinken wir berauscht vom Wein.
sink we intoxicated from the wine.
(then at least let's sink down drunk from wine!)

[The "chorus" is marked "two tenors and bass." A good drinking song needs a catchier tune.]

'tʰrɪŋk'liːt'/ iːɐ̯ 'frɔ̯ø̯ndə ʊnt duː 'gɔldnɐ va̯en

Trinklied / Ihr Freunde und du gold'ner Wein

Drinking Song / You Friends and You Golden Wine

Posthumously published [composed 1815] (poem by Alois Zettler)

SOLO:
iːɐ̯ 'frɔ̯ø̯ndə ʊnt duː 'gɔldnɐ va̯en, fɛɐ̯'zyːsət' miːɐ̯ das 'leːbən;
Ihr Freunde und du gold'ner Wein, versüsset mir das Leben;
You friends and you golden wine, sweeten for me the life;
(You, friends, and you, golden wine, sweeten my life;)

oːn ɔ̯ø̯ç, bə'glʏk'ɐ, 'vɛːrə fa̯en ɪç ʃt'eːts ɪn aŋst' ʊnt' 'beːbən.
ohn' euch, Beglücker, wäre fein ich stets in Angst und Beben.
without you, happy makers, were acutely I constanly in fear and trembling.
(without you, happy makers, I would constantly be in an acute state of fear and trembling.)
[fɔn ɔ̯ø̯ç gə'tʰrɛnt' ʊnt' kʰraŋk' tsuː za̯en!—diːs 'dɛŋk'ən maxt' mɪç 'beːbən.]
[*poem:* **Von euch getrennt und krank zu sein!— dies denken macht mich beben.]**
[from you parted and sick to be!— that to think makes me tremble.]

CHOR (kʰoːɐ̯, chorus):
ˈoːnə ˈfrɔ͡øndə, ˈloːnə va͡en, mœçtʻ ɪç nɪçtʻ lɪm ˈleːbən za͡en. [maːkʻ]
Ohne Freunde, ohne Wein, möcht' ich nicht im Leben sein. [*poem:* **mag ich nicht**]
Without friends, without wine, would like I not in the life to be. [like]
(Without friends, without wine, I wouldn't like to be alive.)

SOLO:
veːɐ̯ ˈtʰa͡ozəndə lɪn ˈkʰɪstʻən ʃliːstʻ, naːx ˈmeːrərəm nuːɐ̯ ˈtʰraxtʻətʰ,
Wer Tausende in Kisten schliesst, nach Mehrerem nur trachtet,
He who thousands in coffers locks, to more only aspires,
(He who locks up thousands in his coffers, who only aspires to acquire more,)

deːɐ̯ ˈfrɔ͡øndə noːtʻ lʊntʻ zɪç fɛɐ̯ˈgɪstʻ, za͡e ra͡eç! fɔn lʊns fɛɐ̯-/fɛrˈlaxtʻətʰ.
der Freunde Not und sich vergisst, sei reich! von uns verachtet.
the friends' need and himself forgets, be rich! by us despised.
(who forgets the need of his friends and forgets his own, let him be rich!—we despise him.)
[*poem:* **vergiesst** (fɛɐ̯ˈgiːstʻ, forgets—*dialect, for the rhyme; vergiessen* = spills, pours out)]

CHOR:
ˈoːnə ˈfrɔ͡øndə, ˈloːnə va͡en, maːkʻ la͡en ˈlandrɐ ˈra͡eçɐ za͡en.
Ohne Freunde, ohne Wein, mag ein Andrer Reicher sein.
Without friends, without wine, may an other rich man be.
(Without friends, without wine, let someone else—not me!—be a rich man.)

SOLO:
oːn ˈlalən frɔ͡øntʻ, vas lɪst deːɐ̯ hɛltʻ? vas zɪnt dɛs ra͡eçs maˈgnaːtʻən?
Ohn' allen Freund, was ist der Held? Was sind des Reichs Magnaten?
Without all friend, what is the hero? What are the state's magnates?
(Without a friend, what is a hero, what are the magnates of the state?)

vas lɪstʻ la͡en hɛr deːɐ̯ ˈgant͡sən vɛltʻ? zɪntʻ ˈlalə ʃlɛçtʻ bəˈraːtʻən!
Was ist ein Herr der ganzen Welt? Sind alle schlecht beraten!
What is a lord of the whole world? Are all ill advised!
(What is a lord of the whole world? They are all in need of good advice!)

CHOR:
ˈoːnə ˈfrɔ͡øndə, ˈloːnə va͡en, maːk lɪç zɛlpstʻ nɪçtʻ ˈkʰa͡ezɐ za͡en!
Ohne Freunde, ohne Wein, mag ich selbst nicht Kaiser sein!
Without friends, without wine, would like I even not emperor to be!
(Without friends, without wine, I wouldn't even want to be an emperor!)

SOLO:
ʊntʻ mʊs la͡enstʻ lan deːɐ̯ ˈt͡suːkʰʊnftʻ pʰɔrt dem la͡epʻ di zeːl lɛntʻˈʃveːbən:
Und muss einst an der Zukunft Port dem Leib die Seel' entschweben:
And must one day at the future's harbor from the body the soul soar away:
(And when one day at the harbor of the future the soul must soar away from the body:)

zoː vɪŋkʻ miːɐ̯/miːr la͡os deːɐ̯ ˈzeːlgən hɔrtʻ la͡en frɔ͡øntʻ lʊntʻ zaft deːɐ̯ ˈreːbən.
so wink' mir aus der Sel'gen Hort ein Freund und Saft der Reben.
then may beckon to me from the blest's retreat a friend and juice of the vines.
(then may a friend and the juice of the vine beckon to me from the retreat of the blest.)

CHOR:

zɔnst‘ maːk‘ ˈloːnə frɔ͜ønt‘ lʊnt‘ va͜en lɪç la͜ox nɪçt‘ lɪm ˈhɪməl za͜en.
Sonst mag ohne Freund und Wein ich auch nicht im Himmel sein.
Otherwise like without friend and wine I even not in the heaven to be.
(Otherwise, without a friend, without wine, I wouldn’t even like to be in heaven.)

[This drinking song has a catchy tune, and Schubert’s friends must have enjoyed singing it.]

ˈtʰrɪŋk‘liːt‘ foːɐ̯ deːɐ̯ ʃlaxtʰ
Trinklied vor der Schlacht
Drinking Song Before the Battle

Posthumously published [composed 1815] (poem by Theodor Körner)

ʃlaxt, duː brɪçst‘ lan! gryːst‘ ziː lɪn ˈfrɔ͜ødɪgəm ˈkʰra͜ezə, la͜ot‘ naːx
Schlacht, du brichst an! Grüss’t sie in freudigem Kreise, laut nach
Battle, you start ... ! Greet it in joyful circle, loudly according to
(Battle, you are about to start! Brothers, greet it in a joyful circle, loudly, in the time-honored)
[*anbrechen* = to start; to dawn]

gɛrˈmaːnɪʃɐ ˈva͜ezə. ˈbryːdɐ, hɛˈran! nɔx pʰɛrlt deːɐ̯ va͜en; leː di
germanischer Weise. Brüder, heran! Noch perlt der Wein; eh’ die
Germanic way. Brothers, come on! Still pearls the wine; before the
(Germanic way. Brothers, come on! The wine is still sparkling; before the)

pʰoˈza͜onən lɛɐ̯ˈdrøːnən, last‘ lʊns das ˈleːbən fɛɐ̯ˈzøːnən. ˈbryːdɐ, ʃenk‘t‘ la͜e!
Posaunen erdröhnen, lasst uns das Leben versöhnen. Brüder, schenkt ein!
trombones resound, let us the life reconcile. Brothers, pour (wine) in (your glass)!
(last trump sounds, let us make peace with life. Brothers, fill your glasses!)

gɔt‘ ˈfaːt‘ɐ høːɐ̯tʰ, vas lan dɛs ˈgraːbəs ˈtʰoːrən ˈfaːt‘ɐlants ˈzøːnə gəˈʃvoːrən.
Gott Vater hört, was an des Grabes Toren Vaterlands Söhne geschworen.
God Father hears, what at the grave’s gates fatherland’s sons (have) sworn.
(God the Father hears what the sons of the fatherland have sworn at the gates of death.)

ˈbryːdɐ, liːɐ̯ ʃvøːɐ̯tʰ! ˈfaːt‘ɐlants hɔrtʰ, vɔln viːɐ̯s la͜os ˈglyːəndən ˈkʰɛt‘ən
Brüder, ihr schwört! Vaterlands Hort, woll’n wir’s aus glühenden Ketten
Brothers, you swear! Fatherland’s shield, want we it from burning chains
(Brothers, swear! As our fatherland’s shield, we want to rescue its people from burning chains,)

tʰoːt‘ ˈloːdɐ ˈziːgənt‘ lɛɐ̯ˈrɛt‘ən. ˈhantʃlaːk‘ lʊnt‘ vɔrtʰ! høːɐ̯t‘ liːɐ̯ ziː naːn?
tot oder siegend erretten. Handschlag und Wort! Hört ihr sie nah’n?
dead or victorious rescue. Handclasp and word! Hear you them approaching?
(dead or victorious. Swear and shake hands on that! Do you hear them coming,)

ˈliːbə lʊnt‘ ˈfrɔ͜ødən lʊnt‘ ˈla͜edən! tʰoːt! duː kʰanst‘ lʊns nɪçt‘ ˈʃa͜edən!
Liebe und Freuden und Leiden! Tod! du kannst uns nicht scheiden!
love and joys and suffering! Death! you can us not separate!
(love, joys and sorrows? Death, you can not separate us!)

'bry:dɐ, ʃt'o:st' lan! ʃlaxt' ru:ft'! hɪ'nɑ͜os! hɔrç, di tʰrɔm'pʰe:t'ən 'vɛrbən.
Brüder, stosst an! Schlacht ruft! Hinaus! Horch, die Trompeten werben.
Brothers, clink ... ! Battle calls! Out! Hark, the trumpets recruit.
(Brothers, clink glasses! Battle is calling us! Let's go! Listen, the trumpets are summoning us.)
[*anstossen* = to clink glasses]

fo:ɐ̯vɛrts, lɑ͜of 'le:bən lʊnt' 'ʃt'ɛrbən! 'bry:dɐ, tʰrɪŋk't' lɑ͜os!
Vorwärts, auf Leben und Sterben! Brüder, trinkt aus!
Forward, to live and die! Brothers, drink out!
(Forward! Some to live and some to die! Brothers, drink up!)

[Shortly after writing these verses, the young poet fell in battle. Schubert's darkly vigorous song, though included with the *Lieder* in the *Gesamtausgabe*, is actually intended for a double chorus.]

Trock'ne Blumen see *Die schöne Müllerin*

tʰro:stʰ / 'hœrnɐkʰlɛŋə 'ru:fən

Trost / Hörnerklänge rufen

Consolation / Horn Calls Are Sounding

Posthumously published [composed 1819] (poem by Johann Mayrhofer)

'hœrnɐkʰlɛŋə 'ru:fən 'kʰla:gənt' lɑ͜os dɛs 'fɔrst'əs 'gry:nɐ naxtʰ,
Hörnerklänge rufen klagend aus des Forstes grüner Nacht,
Horn- sounds call lamentingly from the forest's green night,
(Horn calls are sounding, plaintively, from the green night of the forest;)

in das lant de:ɐ̯ 'li:bə 'tʰra:gənt', 'valt'ət' 'li:rə 'ts͜ɑ͜obɐmaxtʰ.
in das Land der Liebe tragend, waltet ihre Zaubermacht.
into the land of the love carrying, rules their magic power.
(their magic power holds sway, reaching into the land of love.)

'ze:lɪç, ve:ɐ̯/ve:r lɑ͜en hɛrts gə'fʊndən, das zɪç 'li:bənt' li:m lɛɐ̯'ga:p'!
Selig, wer ein Herz gefunden, das sich liebend ihm ergab!
Blest, whoever a heart (has) found, that itself lovingly to him yielded!
(Blest is he who found a heart that lovingly yielded itself to him!)

mi:ɐ̯/mi:r lɪst' 'je:dəs glʏk' lɛnt''ʃvʊndən, dɛn di 'tʰɔ͜ørə dɛk't das gra:p.
Mir ist jedes Glück entschwunden, denn die Teure deckt das Grab.
For me is every happiness vanished, for the dear one [obj.] covers the grave [subj.]
(For me all happiness has vanished, for the grave covers my dear one.)

'tʰø:nən lɑ͜os dɛs 'valdəs 'grʏndən 'hœrnɐkʰlɛŋə lan mɑ͜en lo:ɐ̯,
Tönen aus des Waldes Gründen Hörnerklänge an mein Ohr,
Sound from the woods' depths horn- sounds to my ear,
(When the sound of the horns reaches my ear from the depths of the woods,)

glɑ͜ob ɪç 'vi:dɐ zi: ts͜u: 'fɪndən, ts͜i:t' lɛs mɪç ts͜u: li:ɐ̯/li:r lɛm'pʰo:ɐ̯.
glaub' ich wieder sie zu finden, zieht es mich zu ihr empor.
believe I again her to find, draws it me to her upwards.
(I imagine that I am finding her again, it lifts me up toward her.)

'je:nzaets/'jenzaets vɪrt' zi: mi:ɐ/mi:r lɛɐ'ʃaenən, di: zɪç 'li:bənt' mi:ɐ/mi:r lɛɐ'ga:p',
Jenseits wird sie mir erscheinen, die sich liebend mir ergab,
On the other side will she to me appear, who herself lovingly to me yielded,
(She who lovingly yielded herself to me will appear to me again in the next world:)

o: vɛlç 'ze:lɪgəs fɛɐ-/fɛr'laenən, 'kʰaenə 'ʃrɛk'ən hat das gra:p'.
o welch' seliges Vereinen, keine Schrecken hat das Grab.
O what blissful uniting, no terrors has the grave.
(oh, what a blissful reunion that will be! For me the grave holds no terrors.)

[The first published version indicates the tempo as *"lebhaft"* ("lively"); but the manuscript is marked *"mässig,"* which seems more appropriate to the elegiac, nostalgic mood of the song. In the prelude we hear the horn calls, softened by distance, coming from the depths of the woods.]

tʰro:stʰ / 'nɪmɐ 'laŋə vael ɪç hi:ɐ
Trost / Nimmer lange weil' ich hier
Consolation / Not Much Longer Shall I Linger Here

Posthumously published [composed 1817] (author unknown)

'nɪmɐ 'laŋə vael ɪç hi:ɐ, 'kʰɔmə balt' hɪ'naof tsu: di:ɐ;
Nimmer lange weil' ich hier, komme bald hinauf zu dir;
No more long linger I here, (I) come soon up to you;
(Not much longer shall I linger here: I shall soon come up to you;)

tʰi:f lʊnt' ʃt'ɪl fy:l ɪçs lɪn mi:ɐ: 'nɪmɐ 'laŋə vael ɪç hi:ɐ.
tief und still fühl' ich's in mir: nimmer lange weil' ich hier.
deeply and quietly feel I it in me: no more long linger I here.
(I feel it deeply and quietly in my heart: not much longer shall I linger here.)

'kʰɔmə balt' hɪ'naof tsu: di:ɐ, 'ʃmɛrtsən, 'kʰva:lən, fy:ɐ/fy:r lʊnt' fy:ɐ
Komme bald hinauf zu dir, Schmerzen, Qualen, für und für
(I) come soon up to you, pains, torments for and for
(I shall soon come up to you; pain and torment forever and ever)

'vy:t'ən lɪn dem 'bu:zən mi:ɐ; 'kʰɔmə balt' hɪ'naof tsu: di:ɐ. [den]
wüten in dem Busen mir; komme bald hinauf zu dir. [*GA:* **in den Busen]**
rage in the bosom of me; (I) come soon up to you. [into the]
(are raging in my bosom; I shall soon come up to you.)

tʰi:f lʊnt' ʃt'ɪl fy:l ɪçs lɪn mi:ɐ: 'laenəs 'haesən 'draŋəs gi:ɐ
Tief und still fühl' ich's in mir: eines heissen Dranges Gier
Deeply and quietly feel I it in me: a hot craving's eagerness
(I feel it deeply and quietly in my heart: an eager, passionate craving)

tse:ɐt di flam lɪm 'lɪnɐn hi:ɐ, tʰi:f lʊnt' ʃt'ɪl fy:l ɪçs lɪn mi:ɐ.
zehrt die Flamm' im Innern hier, tief und still fühl' ich's in mir.
consumes the flame in the inside here, deeply and quietly feel I it in me.
(feeds on the flame inside me here; deeply and quietly I feel that within me.)

[In this strophic song, Schubert's heartfelt harmonies ennoble the simple, touching little poem.]

tʰroːstʻ lan leˈliːza
Trost an Elisa
Consolation for Elisa

Posthumously published [composed 1814] (poem by Friedrich von Matthisson)

leːnst duː ˈdaenə ˈblaeçgəhɛrmtʻə ˈvaŋə ˈɪmɐ nɔx lan ˈdiːzən ˈlaʃənkʰruːkʻ?
Lehnst du deine bleichgehärmte Wange immer noch an diesen Aschenkrug?
Lean you your pale- afflicted cheek ever still against this ashes- urn?
(Are you still leaning your pale, pining cheek against that funeral urn,)

ˈvaenəntʻ lʊm den ˈtʰoːtʻən, deːn ʃoːn ˈlaŋə
Weinend um den Toten, den schon lange
Weeping for the dead man, whom already long since
(weeping for your beloved dead, whom already long since)

tsuː deːɐ̯ ˈzeːrafiːm tʰriˈʊmfgəzaŋə deːɐ̯ fɔlˈlɛndʊŋ ˈflyːgəl tʰruːkʻ? ziːst duː
zu der Seraphim Triumphgesange der Vollendung Flügel trug? Siehst du
to the seraphim's triumph- song the perfection's wings bore? See you
(the wings of perfection have borne aloft to join the triumphant song of the seraphim? Do you see)

ˈgɔtʻəs ˈʃtʻɛrnənʃrɪft dɔrtʻ ˈflɪmɐn, diː deːɐ̯ ˈbaŋən ˈʃveːɐ̯muːt tʰroːstʻ fɛɐ̯ˈhaestʰ?
Gottes Sternenschrift dort flimmern, die der bangen Schwermut Trost verheisst?
God's star- writing there glitter, which to the anxious melancholy comfort promises?
(God's handwriting, glittering there in the stars, which promises consolation to anxious sadness?)

ˈhɛlɐ vɪrt deːɐ̯ ˈglaobə diːɐ̯ nuːn ˈʃɪmɐn, das
Heller wird der Glaube dir nun schimmern, dass [*poem:* **nun dir schimmern**]
More brightly will the faith for you now shimmer, that
(Faith will shimmer for you more brightly now, faith that)

hoːx ˈlyːbɐ ˈzaenɐ ˈhʏlə ˈtʰrʏmɐn ˈvalə dɛs gəˈliːpʻtʻən gaestʰ! voːl,
hoch über seiner Hülle Trümmern walle des Geliebten Geist! Wohl,
high above his cloak's remains be floating the beloved's spirit! Well-being,
(your beloved's spirit is floating high above the remains of his mortal frame! Happy,)

loː voːl dem ˈliːbəndən gəˈfɛːɐ̯tʻən ˈdaenɐ ˈzeːnzʊxtʰ, leːɐ̯/leːr lɪstʻ ˈleːvɪç daen!
o wohl dem liebenden Gefährten deiner Sehnsucht, er ist ewig dein!
O well-being for the loving companion of your longing, he is eternally yours!
(oh, happy the loving companion of your longing: he is eternally yours!)

ˈviːdɐzeːn lɪm ˈlandə deːɐ̯ fɛɐ̯ˈkʰlɛːɐ̯tʻən, vɪrst duː, ˈdʊldərɪn, den laŋ lɛntʻˈbeːɐ̯tʻən,
Wiederseh'n im Lande der Verklärten, wirst du, Dulderin, den lang Entbehrten,
See again in the land of the transfigured, will you, endurer, the long missed one,
(Suffering woman, you will see again in the land of the blest the one you have missed so long,)

ʊntʻ viː leːɐ̯/leːr lʊnˈʃtʻɛrpʻlɪç zaen!
und wie er unsterblich sein!
and as he immortal be!
(and you will be immortal, as he is!)

[Schubert's setting is mostly a very beautiful, expressive recitative, with subtle harmonies. The singer is urged to add the appoggiaturas that would have been expected in Schubert's day.]

tʰroːst‘ |ɪm ˈliːdə
Trost im Liede
Consolation in Song

Op. 101, No. 3 [1817] (Franz von Schober)

bra͜ost dɛs ˈ|ʊnglʏks ʃt‘ʊrm |ɛmˈpʰoːɐ̯: halt‘ |ɪç ˈma͜enə ˈharfə foːɐ̯.
Braust des Unglücks Sturm empor: halt ich meine Harfe vor.
Roars the misfortune's storm up: hold I my harp before.
(When a storm of misfortune starts to roar I hold up my harp before me.)

ˈʃʏt͜sən ˈkʰœnən ˈza͜et‘ən nɪçt, diː |eːɐ̯ la͜eçt‘ |ʊnt‘ ʃnɛl dʊrçˈbrɪçtʰ;
Schützen können Saiten nicht, die er leicht und schnell durchbricht;
Protect can strings not, which it easily and quickly through-breaks;
(The harpstrings, which the storm would easily and quickly breach, cannot protect me;)
[*poem:* **schnell und leicht**]

ˈ|aːbɐ dʊrç dɛs ˈzaŋəs tʰoːɐ̯ ʃlɛːk‘t‘ |eːɐ̯ ˈmɪldɐ(r) |an ma͜en |oːɐ̯.
aber durch des Sanges Tor schlägt er milder an mein Ohr.
but through the song's gate strikes it more mildly at my ear.
(but through the gate of song the roar of the storm strikes my ear more mildly.)

ˈzanft‘ə ˈla͜ot‘ə hø̈ːr ɪç ˈkʰlɪŋən, diː miːɐ̯/miːr |ɪn di ˈzeːlə ˈdrɪŋən,
Sanfte Laute hör' ich klingen, die mir in die Seele dringen,
Soft sounds hear I sounding, which for me into the soul penetrate,
(I then hear soft tones sounding, which penetrate into my soul,)

diː miːɐ̯/miːr |a͜of dɛs ˈvoːlla͜ots ˈʃvɪŋən ˈvʊndɐbaːrə ˈtʰrøːst‘ʊŋ ˈbrɪŋən;
die mir auf des Wohllauts Schwingen wunderbare Tröstung bringen;
which to me on the harmony's wings wondrous consolation bring;
(which bring me wondrous consolation on the wings of harmony;)

ʊnt‘ |ɔp‘ ˈkʰlaːgən miːɐ̯/miːr |ɛnt‘ˈʃveːbən, |ɔp‘ |ɪç ʃt‘ɪl |ʊnt‘ ˈʃmɛrt͜slɪç ˈva͜enə,
und ob Klagen mir entschweben, ob ich still und schmerzlich weine,
and though laments from me hover away, though I quietly and painfully weep,
(and though laments may escape from my lips, though I may be quietly and grievously weeping,)

fyːl ɪç mɪç dɔx zoː |ɛɐ̯ˈgeːbən, das |ɪç fɛst‘ |ʊnt‘ ˈglɔ͜øbɪç ˈma͜enə:
fühl' ich mich doch so ergeben, dass ich fest und gläubig meine:
feel I myself nevertheless so resigned, that I firmly and devoutly believe:
(I nevertheless feel so reconciled that I firmly and devoutly believe:)

ɛs gəˈhøːɐ̯t t͜suː ˈma͜enəm ˈleːbən, das zɪç ʃmɛrt͜s | |ʊnt‘ ˈfrɔ͜ødə ˈ|a͜enə.
es gehört zu meinem Leben, dass sich Schmerz und Freude eine.
it belongs to my life, that themselves pain and joy should unite.
(it is a necessary aspect of my life that pain and joy are united.)

[The poem celebrates the power of music to console the heart during difficult times. In the same month, March of 1817, Schubert set two such poems by his friend and benefactor. The other, *An die Musik*, is far more famous; but this song is also lovely, and carries a spiritual message.]

tʰroːstʼ ˈɪn ˈtʰrɛːnən
Trost in Tränen
Consolation in Tears

Posthumously published [composed 1814] (poem by Johann Wolfgang von Goethe)

viː kʰɔmts͜, das duː zoː ˈtʰrɑ͜ʊrɪç bɪst, daː ˈlaləs froː lɛɐ̯ˈʃa͜ent ʰ?
Wie kommt's, dass du so traurig bist, da alles froh erscheint?
How comes it, that you so sad are, when all happy appears?
(How does it happen that you are so sad, when everything appears to be happy?)

man ziːt diːɐ̯s lan den ˈlɑ͜ʊgən lan, gəˈvɪs duː hastʼ gəˈva͜entʰ.
Man sieht dir's an den Augen an, gewiss du hast geweint.
One sees in you it at the eyes at, surely you have wept.
(One can see from your eyes: surely you have been weeping.)

ʊntʼ haːb ɪç ˈla͜enzaːm lɑ͜ʊx gəˈva͜entʼ, zoː lɪsts͜ ma͜en ˈla͜egnɐ ʃmɛrts͜,
"Und hab' ich einsam auch geweint, so ist's mein eig'ner Schmerz,
"And have I alone even wept, so is it my own sorrow,
("And if I have been weeping, it is my *own* sorrow, it concerns only *me*,)

ʊnt ˈtʰrɛːnən ˈfliːsən gaːɐ̯ zoː zyːs, lɛɐ̯ˈla͜eçtʼɐn miːɐ̯ das hɛrts͜.
und Tränen fliessen gar so süss, erleichtern mir das Herz."
and tears flow very so sweetly, ease to me the heart."
(and, besides, tears flow so very sweetly, they ease my heart.")

di ˈfroːən ˈfrɔ͜øndə ˈlaːdən dɪç, loː kʰɔm lan ˈlʊnzrə brʊstʰ!
Die frohen Freunde laden dich, o komm an uns're Brust!
The happy friends invite you, O come to our breast!
(Your happy friends invite you, come to our breast for an embrace!)

ʊntʼ vas duː lɑ͜ʊx fɛɐ̯ˈloːrən hastʼ, fɛɐ̯ˈtʰrɑ͜ʊə den fɛɐ̯ˈlʊstʰ.
Und was du auch verloren hast, vertraue den Verlust.
And what you ever lost have, confide the loss.
(And whatever it is that you have lost, confide the loss to us.)

[*Peters:* **vertraure** (fɛɐ̯ˈtʰrɑ͜ʊrə, mourn away) **den Verlust**]

iːɐ̯ lɛrmtʼ lʊntʼ rɑ͜ʊʃtʼ lʊntʼ ˈlaːnətʼ nɪçtʼ, vas mɪç, den ˈlarmən, kʰvɛːltʰ.
"Ihr lärmt und rauscht und ahnet nicht, was mich, den Armen, quält.
"You make noise and roar and imagine not, what me, the poor man, torments.
("You make a fuss and lots of noise and have no idea what is tormenting me, poor fellow.)

ax na͜en, fɛɐ̯ˈloːrən haːb ɪçs nɪçtʼ, zoː zeːɐ̯/zeːr lɛs miːɐ̯/miːr lɑ͜ʊx feːltʰ.
Ach nein, verloren hab' ich's nicht, so sehr es mir auch fehlt."
Ah no, lost have I it not, as much (as) it to me also is missing."
(Ah no, I have not *lost* the thing that makes me sad, however much I may miss it.")

zoː ˈrafə dɛn dɪç ˈla͜elɪç lɑ͜ʊf, duː bɪstʼ la͜en ˈjʊŋəs bluːtʰ.
So raffe denn dich eilig auf, du bist ein junges Blut.
So snatch then yourself hurriedly up, you are a young blood.
(Then pull yourself together right away: you are a young man.)

ɪn 'da͜enən 'ja:rən hat' man kʰraft' lʊnt t͜sʊm lɛɐ̯'vɛrbən mu:tʰ.
In deinen Jahren hat man Kraft und zum Erwerben Mut.
In your years has one strength and to the acquiring courage.
(At your age one has the strength and the courage to get what one wants.)

ax na͜en, lɛɐ̯'vɛrbən kʰan lɪçs nɪçt', lɛs ʃt'e:t' mi:ɐ̯ ga:ɐ̯ t͜su: fɛrn.
"Ach nein, erwerben kann ich's nicht, es steht mir gar zu fern.
"Ah no, acquire can I it not, it stands from me absolutely too far.
("Ah no, I cannot acquire it, it is absolutely too far away from me.)

ɛs va͜elt' zo: ho:x, lɛs blɪŋk't' zo: ʃø:n, vi: 'dro:bən 'je:nɐ ʃt'ɛrn.
Es weilt so hoch, es blinkt so schön, wie droben jener Stern."
It stays so high, it sparkles so beautifully, as up there that star."
(It stays as high above me, it sparkles as beautifully as that star up there.")

di 'ʃt'ɛrnə, di: bə'ge:ɐ̯t' man nɪçt', man frɔ͜øt' zɪç 'li:rɐ pʰraxtʰ,
Die Sterne, die begehrt man nicht, man freut sich ihrer Pracht,
The stars, them desires one not, one gladdens oneself in their splendor,
(One does not *desire* the stars: one rejoices in their splendor;)

ʊnt' mɪt' lɛnt't͜sʏk'ən blɪk't' man la͜of lɪn 'je:dɐ 'ha͜et'ɐn naxtʰ.
und mit Entzücken blickt man auf in jeder heitern Nacht.
and with delight looks one up in every serene night.
(and one looks up at them with delight on every cloudless night.)

ʊnt' mɪt' lɛnt't͜sʏk'ən blɪk' ɪç la͜of zo: 'mançən 'li:bən tʰa:k';
"Und mit Entzücken blick' ich auf so manchen lieben Tag;
"And with delight look I up so many an agreeable day;
("And I do look up with delight on many an agreeable day;)

fɛɐ̯'va͜enən last di 'nɛçt'ə mɪç, zo: laŋ lɪç 'va͜enən ma:k'.
verweinen lasst die Nächte mich, so lang' ich weinen mag."
weep away let the nights me, as long (as) I to weep like."
(so let me weep the nights away, as long as I still want to weep.")

[The well-meaning friends pose their questions and offer their solutions in the major key; the young man who likes to weep gives his evasive answers mostly in the minor. The Peters edition, based on the first publication, is transposed down from F to D, and adds a brief introduction.]

'y:bɐ 'lalən 't͜sa͜obɐ 'li:bə
Über allen Zauber Liebe
Love Is Above All Magic

Posthumously published, incomplete [composed 1819, 1820?] (poem by Johann Mayrhofer)

zi: 'hʏp͜ft'ə mɪt' mi:ɐ̯/mi:r la͜of 'gry:nəm pʰla:n, lʊnt' za: di 'falbəndən 'lɪndən lan
Sie hüpfte mit mir auf grünem Plan, und sah die falbenden Linden an
She skipped with me on green plain, and looked the yellowing lindens at
(She skipped with me on the green plain, and looked at the yellowing linden trees)
[*poem:* **Sie hüpfte vor** (fo:ɐ̯, before) **mir... die fahlenden** ('fa:ləndən, fading) **Linden**]

mɪt 'tʰrɑ͜oɐndən 'kʰɪndəslɑ͜ogən: di 'ʃt'ɪlən 'lɑ͜obən zɪnt' lɛnt''lɑ͜op'tʰ,
mit trauernden Kindesaugen: "Die stillen Lauben sind entlaubt,
with grieving child- eyes: "The quiet arbors are defoliated,
(with the eyes of a grieving child: "The silent arbors are leafless;)

di 'blu:mən hat de:ɐ̯ hɛrpst' gə'rɑ͜op'tʰ, de:ɐ̯ hɛrpst' vɪl ga:ɐ̯ nɪçt͡s 'tʰɑ͜ogən.
die Blumen hat der Herbst geraupt, der Herbst will gar nichts taugen.
the flowers has the autumn stolen, the autumn wants at all nothing to be good for.
(autumn has stolen the flowers, autumn is good for nothing at all.)

ax, du: bɪst' la͜en 'ʃø:nəs dɪŋ, 'fry:lɪŋ! ['ly:bɐ(r) 'lalən 't͡sɑ͜obɐ 'fry:lɪŋ!
Ach, du bist ein schönes Ding, Frühling! [über allen Zauber Frühling!"
Ah, you are a beautiful thing, spring! [above all magic spring!"
(Ah, spring, you are a beautiful thing, [better than any magic!")

das 't͡si:ɐ̯lɪçə kʰɪnt', vi:s fo:ɐ̯ mi:ɐ̯ ʃve:p't'! lɑ͜os 'li:l̯iən lʊnt' 'ro:zən t͡sa:ɐ̯t' gə've:p't',
Das zierliche Kind, wie's vor mir schwebt! aus Lilien und Rosen zart gewebt,
The dainty child, how it before me hovers! from lilies and roses delicately woven,
(That dainty child, how her image, delicately woven of lilies and roses, hovers before me,)

mɪt' 'lɑ͜ogən gla͜eç den 'ʃt'ɛrnən: — bly:t' mi:ɐ̯ da͜en 'hɔldəs 'langəzɪçtʰ,
mit Augen gleich den Sternen: — "Blüht mir dein holdes Angesicht,
with eyes like to the stars: — "Blooms for me your lovely countenance,
(her eyes like stars, as she said: — "When your dear face is blooming like a flower for me,)

dan ma:k', fy:ɐ̯'va:ɐ̯/-va:r lɪç 't͡sa:gə nɪçtʰ, de:ɐ̯ 'ma͜eən zɪç lɛnt''fɛrnən.
dann mag, fürwahr ich zage nicht, der Maien sich entfernen.
then may, truly I hesitate not, the May itself remove.
(then—I don't mind saying it!—May can stay away.) [*sich entfernen* = remove itself, go away]

'fɛrbət' nu:ɐ̯ dɛs 'le:bəns 'tʰry:bə 'li:bə: 'ly:bɐ(r) 'lalən 't͡sɑ͜obɐ 'li:bə.]
Färbet nur des Lebens Trübe Liebe: über allen Zauber Liebe."]
Colors only the life's gloom love: above all magic love."]
(Only love can bring color into life's gloomy moments: love is above all magic!")]

[This beautiful song, with a most exquisite accompaniment, would be very popular if Schubert had bothered to finish it; as it is, his manuscript breaks off after thirty bars, just before the last line of the first verse. Presumably, the second verse would have been a repeat (with slight modifications). Reinhard Van Hoorickx has completed the song and published it privately. There is a recording of his version.]

'y:bɐ 'vɪldəman
Über Wildemann
Above Wildemann

Op. 108, No. 1 [1826] (Ernst Shulze)

di 'vɪndə 'zɑ͜ozən 'lam 'tʰanənhaŋ, di 'kʰvɛlən 'brɑ͜ozən das tʰa:l lɛnt''laŋ; lɪç
Die Winde sausen am Tannenhang, die Quellen brausen das Tal entlang; ich
The winds roar at the fir-tree slope, the springs rage the valley along; I
(The winds roar through the fir-trees on the slope, the streams rage through the valley; I)

ˈvandrə |ɪn ˈlaelə dʊrç valt‘ |ʊnt‘ ʃne:, vo:l ˈmançə ˈmaelə fɔn hø: tsu: hø:.
wand're in Eile durch Wald und Schnee, wohl manche Meile von Höh' zu Höh'.
wander in haste through forest and snow, probably many a mile from height to height.
[*poem:* **wandr' in** (ˈvandrɪn, wander in) **Eile**]

ʊnt‘ vɪl das ˈle:bən |ɪm ˈfraeən tʰa:l zɪç |aox ʃo:n ˈhe:bən tsʊm ˈzɔnənʃt‘ra:l;
Und will das Leben im freien Tal sich auch schon heben zum Sonnenstrahl;
And wants the life in the free valley itself even already to raise to the sunbeam;
(And even if life down in the open valley is already rising at the sun's early rays;)

ɪç mʊs foˈry:bɐ mɪt‘ ˈvɪldəm zɪn |ʊnt‘ ˈblɪk‘ə ˈli:bɐ tsʊm ˈvɪnt‘ɐ hɪn. |aof ˈgry:nən
ich muss vorüber mit wildem Sinn und blicke lieber zum Winter hin. Auf grünen
I must (go) past with wild mind and look rather to the winter hence. On green
(I must go on with wild emotions in my mind and look rather toward the winter. On green)

ˈhaedən, |aof ˈbʊnt‘ən |aon, mʏst‘ ɪç maen ˈlaedən nu:ɐ̯/nu:r ˈ|ɪmɐ ʃaon,
Heiden, auf bunten Au'n, müsst' ich mein Leiden nur immer schau'n,
moors, on many-colored pastures, would have I my suffering only always to see,
(moors, on many-colored meadows, I would always have to see only what makes me suffer:)

das zɛlpst‘ |am ˈʃt‘aenə das ˈle:bən ʃp‘ri:st‘, |ʊnt‘ |ax, nu:ɐ̯/nu:r ˈ|aenə |i:ɐ̯ hɛrts fɛɐ̯ˈʃli:stʰ.
dass selbst am Steine das Leben spriesst, und ach, nur Eine ihr Herz verschliesst.
that even on the stone the life sprouts, and ah, only one her heart locks up.
(that life is sprouting even out of stone, and—alas!—that only *one* creature locks up her heart.)

o: ˈli:bə, ˈli:bə, |o: ˈmaeənhaox! du: drɛŋst di ˈtʰri:bə |aos baom |ʊnt‘ ʃt‘raox!
O Liebe, Liebe, o Maienhauch! du drängst die Triebe aus Baum und Strauch!
O love, love, O May- breath! you press the shoots out of tree and bush!
(O love, love! O breath of May! You bring forth the young shoots from tree and bush!)

di ˈfø:gəl ˈzɪŋən |aof ˈgry:nən hø:n, di ˈkʰvɛlən ˈʃp‘rɪŋən bae ˈdaenəm ve:n!
Die Vögel singen auf grünen Höh'n, die Quellen springen bei deinem Weh'n!
The birds sing on green heights, the springs leap up at your blowing!
(The birds sing on green heights, the springs leap up at your caress!)

mɪç lɛst du: ˈʃvaefən |ɪm ˈdʊŋk‘lən va:n dʊrç ˈvɪndəspfaefən |aof ˈraoɐ ba:n.
Mich lässt du schweifen im dunklen Wahn durch Windespfeifen auf rauher Bahn.
Me let you roam about in the dark madness through wind-whistling on rough path.
(You let me roam about in dark madness through the whistling wind on a rough pathway.)

o: ˈfry:lɪŋsʃɪmɐ(r), |o: ˈbly:t‘ənʃaen, zɔl |ɪç dɛn ˈnɪmɐ mɪç daen |ɛɐ̯ˈfrɔøn?
O Frühlingsschimmer, o Blütenschein, soll ich denn nimmer mich dein erfreu'n?
O spring- shimmer, O blossom-gleam, shall I then never myself of you rejoice?
(O shimmer of spring, O gleam of blossoms, shall I then never be able to rejoice in you again?)

[In his bitter distress, the poet seeks winter in the snow on mountain peaks, because the spring that has come to the valley below only reminds him, in its teeming life, that the one he loves has rejected him and closed her heart to the power that makes the meadows blossom. The full heading of the poem (part of a diary in verse) is "Above Wildemann, a village in the Harz Mountains, April 28, 1816." Schubert's powerful music rages like the storm in the poet's heart.]

ʊm ˈmɪtʻɐnaxtʰ
Um Mitternacht
At Midnight

Op. 88, No. 3 [1825] (Ernst Schulze)

ˈkʰa͜enə ˈʃtʻɪmə hø:r ɪç ˈʃalən, ˈkʰa͜enə ʃrɪtʻ la͜of ˈdʊŋkʻlɐ ba:n,
Keine Stimme hör' ich schallen, keinen Schritt auf dunkler Bahn,
No voice hear I sound, no step on dark pathway,
(I hear no voice sounding, no step on the dark pathway,)

zɛlpst de:ɐ̯ ˈhɪməl hat di ˈʃø:nən ˈhɛlən ˈlɔ͜økʻla͜en ˈt͜su:gətʰa:n.
selbst der Himmel hat die schönen hellen Äuglein zugetan.
even the sky has the beautiful bright little eyes closed.
(even the sky has closed it beautiful, bright little eyes.)

ɪç nu:ɐ̯ ˈvaxə, ˈzy:səs ˈle:bən, ˈʃa͜oə ˈze:nəntʻ lɪn di naxtʻ,
Ich nur wache, süsses Leben, schaue sehnend in die Nacht,
I only wake, sweet life, look longingly into the night,
(Only I am awake, sweet love, and I look longingly into the night,)

bɪs da͜en ʃtʻɛrn lɪn ˈlø:dɐ ˈfɛrnə ˈli:pʻlɪç ˈlɔ͜øçtʻəntʻ mi:ɐ̯/mi:r lɛɐ̯ˈvaxtʰ.
bis dein Stern in öder Ferne lieblich leuchtend mir erwacht.
until your star in deserted distance sweetly shining for me awakens.
(until your star will awaken for me, shining sweetly in the distance, now deserted.)

ax, nu:ɐ̯/nu:r ˈla͜enma:l, nu:ɐ̯ fɛɐ̯ˈʃtʻo:lən da͜en gəˈli:pʻtʻəs bɪlt t͜su: ze:n,
Ach, nur einmal, nur verstohlen dein geliebtes Bild zu seh'n,
Ah, just once, just furtively your beloved image to see,
(Ah, just once more, even if only furtively to see your beloved image,)

vɔltʻ ɪç gɛrn lɪm ʃtʻʊrm lʊntʻ ˈvɛtʻɐ bɪs t͜sʊm ˈʃpʻɛ:tʻən ˈmɔrgən ʃtʻe:n!
wollt' ich gern im Sturm und Wetter bis zum späten Morgen steh'n!
would I gladly in the storm and bad weather till to the late morning stand!
(I would gladly stand here in the bad, stormy weather all night long till as late as the dawn!)
[*GA:* **in** (lɪn, in—*not "in the"*) **Sturm und Wetter**]

ze: ɪçs nɪçtʻ fɔn ˈfɛrnə ˈlɔ͜øçtʻən? na:tʻ lɛs nɪçtʻ ʃo:n na:x lʊntʻ na:x?
Seh' ich's nicht von ferne leuchten? naht es nicht schon nach und nach?
See I it not from afar shining? approaches it not already little by little?
(Do I not see your image shining from afar? Is it not already approaching, little by little?)
[*poem:* **Seh' ich's nicht schon** (ʃo:n, already) **ferne leuchten?**]

ax, lʊntʻ ˈfrɔ͜øntʻlɪç hø:r ɪçs ˈflʏstʻɐn: zi:, de:ɐ̯ frɔ͜øntʻ lɪstʻ la͜ox nɔx vax.
Ach, und freundlich hör' ich's flüstern: sieh', der Freund ist auch noch wach.
Ah, and friendly hear I it whisper: see, the friend is also still awake.
(Ah, and I hear its friendly whisper: "Look, my friend is also still awake.")
[*note: he is "der Freund"; she would be "die Freundin" ("her" star could also be the friend).*]

ˈzy:səs vɔrtʻ, gəˈli:pʻtʻə ˈʃtʻɪmə, de:ɐ̯ ma͜en hɛrt͜s lɛntʻˈge:gənʃlɛ:kʻtʻ!
Süsses Wort, geliebte Stimme, der mein Herz entgegenschlägt!
Sweet word, beloved voice, to which [*i.e.: the voice*] my heart toward- beats!
(Sweet words, beloved voice, at which my anticipating heart is beating faster!)

ˈtʰa͜ozənt‘ ˈzeːlgə ˈliːbəsbɪldɐ hat da͜en ha͜ox miːɐ̯/miːr ˈla͜ofgəreːk‘tʰ.
tausend sel’ge Liebesbilder hat dein Hauch mir aufgeregt.
thousand blissful love- images has your breath for me up-stirred.
(Your breath has stirred in me a thousand blissful images of love.)

ˈalə ˈʃt‘ɛrnə zeː ɪç ˈglɛnt͜sən la͜of deːɐ̯ ˈdʊŋk‘lən, ˈbla͜oən baːn, [ˈdʊŋk‘əln]
Alle Sterne seh’ ich glänzen auf der dunklen, blauen Bahn, [*GA:* **dunkeln]**
All stars see I glitter on the dark, blue course, [dark]
(I now see *all* the stars glittering in their dark, blue courses,)
[*poem:* **auf der dunkelblauen** (ˈdʊŋk‘əlbla͜oən, dark blue) **Bahn]**

ʊnt‘ ɪm ˈhɛrt͜sən hat‘ ʊnt ˈdroːbən zɪç deːɐ̯ ˈhɪməl ˈla͜ofgətʰaːn.
und im Herzen hat und droben sich der Himmel aufgetan.
and in the heart has and up there itself the heaven opened.
(and heaven has opened, both in my heart and up above.)

ˈhɔldɐ ˈnaːxhal, ˈviːgə ˈfrɔ͜ønt‘lɪç jɛt͜st‘ ma͜en ha͜op‘t‘ ɪn ˈmɪldə ruː,
Holder Nachhall, wiege freundlich jetzt mein Haupt in milde Ruh’,
Lovely echo, lull kindly now my head into gentle rest,
(Lovely echo, lull my head now into gentle, kindly rest,)

ʊnt‘ nɔx ɔft‘, iːɐ̯ ˈtʰrɔ͜ømə, ˈlɪsp‘əlt‘ iːɐ̯ gəˈliːp‘t‘əs vɔrt‘ miːɐ̯ t͜suː!
und noch oft, ihr Träume, lispelt ihr geliebtes Wort mir zu!
and again often, you dreams, whisper her beloved word to me to!
(and you, dreams, whisper her beloved words to me often, over and over again!)

[This poem, like the previous one and several others that Schubert set, comes from Schulze’s diary in verse, where it is headed “On March 5th, 1815, at 12 o’clock in the night.” An unusual feature of the vocal line in the song is the leap of a ninth in four of the poem’s seven verses.]

Ungeduld see *Die schöne Müllerin*

uˈraːni̯əns flʊxtʰ
Uraniens Flucht
Urania’s Flight

Posthumously published [composed 1817] (poem by Johannes Mayrhofer)

last‘ ʊns, iːɐ̯ ˈhɪmlɪʃən, la͜en fɛst‘ bəˈgeːən! gəˈbiːt‘ət t͜sɔ͜øs. ʊnt‘ fɔn deːɐ̯/deːr
“Lasst uns, ihr Himmlischen, ein Fest begehen!” gebietet Zeus. Und von der
“Let us, you heavenly ones, a feast celebrate!” orders Zeus. And from the
(“Immortals, let us have a feast!” Zeus orders. And from)
[za͜en ˈraʃɐ ˈboːt‘ə la͜elt‘]
[*poem:* **gebietet Zeus — sein rascher Bote eilt — und]**
[his swift messenger hurries]

ˈʊnt‘ɐvɛlt, den høːn ʊnt‘ ˈzeːən, ʃt‘a͜ek‘t‘ ˈaləs t͜sʊm oˈlʏmp‘ʊs ʊnfɛɐ̯va͜eltʰ. deːɐ̯
Unterwelt, den Höh’n und Seen, steigt Alles zum Olympus unverweilt. Der
underworld, the heights and seas, climbs everyone to the Olympus without delay. The
(the underworld, the heights, and the seas, every divinity ascends Olympus without delay. The)

ˈreːbəngɔtʻ fɛɐ̯ˈlɛst, deːn lеːɐ̯ bəˈt͡svʊŋən, dɛs ˈɪndʊs ˈbluːmənraeçən ˈfaːbəlʃtʻrantʻ;
Rebengott verlässt, den er bezwungen, des Indus blumenreichen Fabelstrand;
vine- god leaves, which he conquered, the Indus's flower- rich fable-shore;
(god of wine leaves the flowered, fabled shore of the Indus, which he has conquered;)

dɛs ˈheːlikʰɔns lɛɐ̯ˈhaːbnə ˈdɛmərʊŋən laˈpʰɔl, lʊnt t͡syːpʻria liːɐ̯/liːr ˈɪnzəllantʻ, di
des Helikons erhabne Dämmerungen Apoll, und Cypria ihr Inselland, die
the Helicon's exalted twilights Apollo, and Cypria her island country, the
(Apollo leaves the exalted twilight of Mount Helicon, and Cypria her island home, the)

ˈʃtʻrøːmərɪnən ˈmoːsbəzɔ͜ømtʻɐ ˈkʰvɛlən, dryˈaːdəngrʊpʻən lɑ͜os dem ˈʃtʻɪlən haen, lʊnt deːɐ̯
Strömerinnen moosbesäumter Quellen, Dryadengruppen aus dem stillen Hain, und der
naiads of moss-rimmed springs, dryad- groups from the quiet grove, and who
(naiads of moss-rimmed springs, groups of dryads from the quiet grove, and he who)

[*poem:* **wie** (viː, as well as) **der**]

bəˈhɛrʃt dɛs lot͡seˈaːnəs ˈvɛlən, ziː ˈfɪndən ˈvɪlɪç zɪç t͡sʊm ˈfɛstʻə laen. lʊntʻ viː
beherrscht des Ozeanes Wellen, sie finden willig sich zum Feste ein. Und wie
rules the ocean's waves, they find willingly themselves to the feast in. And as
(rules the ocean's waves, they all willingly put in an appearance at the feast. And as)

ziː nuːn lɪn ˈglɛnt͡səndən gəˈvandən den ˈleːvgən kʰraes, lan deːm kʰaen ˈvɛksəl t͡seːɐ̯tʰ,
sie nun in glänzenden Gewanden den ew'gen Kreis, an dem kein Wechsel zehrt,
they now in glittering garments the eternal circle, at which no change gnaws,
(they now in their glittering garments form an eternal, changeless circle,)

den ˈblyːəndən, lʊm ˈlʊnzɐn ˈdɔnrɐ ˈvandən, daː ʃtʻraːltʻ zaen ˈlɑ͜ogə ˈjuːgəntʻlɪç
den blühenden, um unsern Donn'rer wanden, da strahlt sein Auge jugendlich
the blossoming, around our thunderer wind, then beams his eye youthfully
(ever blossoming, around our thunderer, his eyes are radiant, youthfully)

[*poem:* **unsren** (ˈlʊnzrən, our)]

fɛɐ̯ˈkʰlɛːɐ̯tʰ. leːɐ̯ vɪŋkʻtʻ: lʊntʻ ˈheːbə fʏlt di ˈgɔldnən ˈʃaːlən; leːɐ̯ vɪŋkʻtʻ: lʊnt ˈt͡seːrɛs
verklärt. Er winkt: und Hebe füllt die goldnen Schalen; er winkt: und Ceres
transfigured. He beckons: and Hebe fills the golden bowls; he beckons: and Ceres

[ˈfʏlətʻ kʰryːkʻ lʊntʻ] [deːɐ̯ ˈtʰroːjɐ]

[*poem:* **und Hebe füllet Krüg' und Schalen; er winkt: der Trojer**]

[fills pitchers and] [the Trojan (Ganymede)]

raeçtʻ lamˈbroːzia; leːɐ̯ vɪŋkʻtʻ: lʊntʻ ˈzyːsə ˈfrɔ͜ødənhʏmnən ˈʃalən, lʊntʻ vas leːɐ̯/leːr ˈlɪmɐ(r)
reicht Ambrosia; er winkt: und süsse Freudenhymnen schallen, und was er immer
passes ambrosia; he waves: and sweet joy- hymns sound, and what he ever
(serves ambrosia; he waves his hand: and sweet hymns of joy resound; and whatever he)

ˈlɔrdnətʰ, das gəˈʃaː. ʃoːn ˈrøːtʻətʻ lʊst deːɐ̯ ˈgɛstʻə ʃtʻɪrn lʊntʻ ˈvaŋə, deːɐ̯ ˈʃlɑ͜oə
ordnet', das geschah. Schon rötet Lust der Gäste Stirn und Wange, der schlaue
ordered, that happened. Already reddens pleasure the guests' brow and cheeks, the sly
(ordered, happened. Already pleasure reddens the brows and cheeks of the guests, the sly)

[*poem:* **ordnete** (ˈlɔrdnətʻə, ordered)**, geschah**]

ˈleːrɔs ˈlɛçəltʻ ʃtʻɪl fyːɐ̯ zɪç: di ˈflyːgəl ˈlœfnən zɪç, lɪm ˈzactʻən ˈgaŋə
Eros lächelt still für sich: die Flügel öffnen sich, im sachten Gange
Eros smiles silently to himself: the double doors open themselves, in the soft walk
(Eros smiles silently to himself. The double doors open: walking softly,)

ǀa͜en ˈleːdləs va͜ep‘ ǀɪn di fɛɐ̯ˈzamlʊŋ ʃlɪç. ǀʊnˈʃt‘ra͜et‘ɪç ǀɪst‘ ziː deːɐ̯/deːr ǀuraˈniːdən
ein edles Weib in die Versammlung schlich. Unstreitig ist sie der Uraniden
a noble woman into the assembly crept. Incontestably is she of the Uranides’
(a noble woman crept into the assembly. She is incontestably a daughter of Uranus, the sky:)

gəˈʃlɛçt‘, ǀiːɐ̯ ha͜op‘t‘ ǀʊmˈhɛlt‘ ǀa͜en ˈʃt‘ɛrnənkʰrant͜s; ǀɛs ˈlɔ͜ødçt‘ət‘ ˈhɛrlɪç ǀa͜of dem
Geschlecht, ihr Haupt umhellt ein Sternenkranz; es leuchtet herrlich auf dem
family, her head about-brightens a star- wreath; it shines gloriously on the
(a wreath of stars radiates light around her head; it shines gloriously on her)

ˈleːbənsmyːdən ǀʊnt‘ bla͜eç gəˈfɛrp‘t‘ən ˈǀant‘lɪt͜s ˈhɪməlsglant͜s. dɔx ˈǀiːrə ˈgɛlbən
lebensmüden und bleich gefärbten Antlitz Himmelsglanz. Doch ihre gelben
life- weary and pale colored countenance heaven- splendor. But her yellow
(pale, life-weary face, with heavenly splendor. But her blond)

ˈhaːrə zɪnt‘ fɛɐ̯ˈʃnɪt‘ən, ǀa͜en ˈdʏrft‘ɪç kʰla͜et dɛk‘t‘ ˈǀiːrən ˈra͜enən la͜ep‘; di ˈvʊndən ˈhɛndən
Haare sind verschnitten, ein dürftig Kleid deckt ihren reinen Leib; die wunden Händen
hairs are cropped, a shabby dress covers her pure body; the sore hands
(hair is roughly cropped, a shabby dress covers her pure body; her scarred hands)

ˈdɔ͜øt‘ən, das gəˈlɪt‘ən deːɐ̯ ˈkʰnɛçt‘ʃaft‘ ˈʃveːrə ʃmaːx das ˈgœt‘ɐva͜ep‘.
deuten, dass gelitten der Knechtschaft schwere Schmach das Götterweib.
show, that (has) suffered the servitude’s heavy shame the gods- woman.
(show that the goddess has suffered the heavy shame of servitude.)

ɛs ˈʃp‘ɛːət‘ ˈjuːpit‘ɐ(r) ǀɪn ˈǀiːrən ˈt͜syːgən: duː bɪst‘, duː bɪst‘ ǀɛs nɪçt‘, ǀuˈraːnia!
Es spähet Jupiter in ihren Zügen: “du bist, du bist es nicht, Urania!”
There scouts Jupiter in her features: “You are, you are it not, Urania!”
(Jupiter scrutinizes her features: “It is not, it *cannot* be you, Urania!”)

ɪç bɪns! di ˈgœt‘ɐ ˈtʰa͜oməln fɔn den ˈkʰryːgən ǀɛɐ̯ˈʃt‘a͜ontʰ, ǀʊnt‘ ˈruːfən: viː? ǀuˈraːnia?
“Ich bin’s!” Die Götter taumeln von den Krügen erstaunt, und rufen: Wie? Urania?
“I am it!” The gods reel from the jugs astounded, and call: How? Urania?
(–“It is I!” The gods turn from their cups, astounded and reeling, and cry out: “What? Urania?!”)

ɪç ˈkenə dɪç nɪçt‘ meːɐ̯! ǀɪn ˈhɔldɐ ˈʃøːnə, ʃp‘rɪçt t͜sɔ͜øs, t͜soːkst duː fɔn miːɐ̯ deːɐ̯
“Ich kenne dich nicht mehr! In holder Schöne,” spricht Zeus, “zogst du von mir der
“I know you not more! In gracious beauty,” speaks Zeus, “went you from me to the
(–“I do not recognize you any more!” says Zeus; you were sent by me to the)

[*poem: without* **von mir**]

ˈleːɐ̯də t͜suː; den ˈgœt‘lɪçən bəˈfrɔ͜øndən ˈǀiːrə ˈzøːnə, ǀɪn ˈma͜enə ˈvoːnʊŋ ˈla͜et‘ən ˈzɔlt‘əst duː.
Erde zu; den Göttlichen befreunden ihre Söhne, in meine Wohnung leiten solltest du.
earth to; for the divine ones befriend her sons, into my dwelling lead should you.
(earth; you were to acquaint her sons with the gods and lead them to my abode.)

[**dem Göttlichen** (dem ˈgœt‘lɪçən, with the divine—*singular*)]

voˈmɪt‘ pʰanˈdoːra ˈǀa͜enst‘əns zɪç gəˈbrʏst‘ətʰ, ǀɪst‘ ˈǀʊnbədɔ͜øt‘ənt‘ ˈvaːɐ̯lɪç ǀʊnt‘ gəˈrɪŋ,
Womit Pandora einstens sich gebrüstet, ist unbedeutend wahrlich und gering,
With which Pandora once herself gave airs, is insignificant truly and trifling,
(The adornment in which Pandora once gave herself such airs is truly insignificant and trifling,)

[*sich brüsten* = to give oneself airs, to brag, to boast]

ɛɐ̯'vɛːɡə lɪç, vo'mɪt' lɪç dɪç ɡə'rʏst'ət, den ʃmʊkʰ, deːn 'maenə 'liːbə lʊm dɪç hɪŋ.
erwäge ich, womit ich dich gerüstet, den Schmuck, den meine Liebe um dich hing."
consider I, with which I you equipped, the jewelry, which my love about you hung."
(when I consider the jewelry with which I equipped you and which my love hung about you.")

vas duː, loː hɛr, miːɐ̯ 'daːmaːls 'laofɡətʰraːɡən, vo'tsuː dɛs 'hɛrtsəns 'laeɡnɐ draŋ
"Was du, o Herr, mir damals aufgetragen, wozu des Herzens eig'ner Drang
"What you, O lord, to me then gave as a task, to which the heart's own impulse
(–"That which you, my lord, gave me as a task, and to which the impulse of my own heart)

mɪç tʰriːp', fɔl'tsoːk' lɪç 'vɪlɪç, jaː lɪç darf lɛs 'zaːɡən; dɔx das maen 'vɪrk'ən 'loːnə
mich trieb, vollzog ich willig, ja ich darf es sagen; doch das mein Wirken ohne
me drove, carried out I willingly, yes I may it say; but that my work without
(drove me, I carried out willingly, yes, I may say that; but that my work remained without)

'frʏçt'ə bliːp', maːkst duː, loː 'hɛrʃɐ, mɪt dem 'ʃɪk'zaːl 'rɛçt'ən, deːm 'laləs,
Früchte blieb, magst du, o Herrscher, mit dem Schicksal rechten, dem alles,
fruits remained, may you, O ruler, with the fate remonstrate, to which all,
(good results, my sovereign, you may remonstrate with fate, to which all)

vas lɛnt'ʃt'ant', lɪst' 'lʊnt'ɐtʰaːn: deːɐ̯ mɛnʃ fɛɐ̯'vɪrt das 'ɡuːt'ə mɪt dem 'ʃlɛçt'ən,
was entstand, ist untertan: der Mensch verwirrt das Gute mit dem Schlechten,
that existed, is subject: the human being confuses the good with the bad,
(that ever existed is subject: the human being confuses the good with the bad,)

iːn hɛlt' ɡə'faŋən 'zɪnlɪçkʰaet' lʊnt' vaːn. dem 'laenən must' ɪç 'zaenə 'lɛk'ɐ 'pflyːɡən,
ihn hält gefangen Sinnlichkeit und Wahn. Dem Einen musst' ich seine Äcker pflügen,
him holds captive sensuality and delusion. For the one had to I his fields plow,
(sensuality and delusion hold him captive. For one man I had to plow his fields,)

dem 'landɐn 'ʃafnərɪn lɪm 'haozə zaen, deːm 'zaenə 'kʰɪnt'laen lɪn di 'ruːə 'viːɡən,
dem Andern Schaffnerin im Hause sein, dem seine Kindlein in die Ruhe wiegen,
for the other housekeeper in the house be, for this his babies into the rest rock,
(for another to be housekeeper in his home, for this one to rock his babies to sleep,)

dem 'landɐn zɔlt' ɪç 'loːp'ɡədɪçt'ə ʃt'rɔøn. deːɐ̯/deːr 'laenə 'ʃp'ɛrt'ə mɪç lɪn 'tʰiːfə
dem Andern sollt' ich Lobgedichte streu'n. Der Eine sperrte mich in tiefe
for the other should I praise-poems scatter. The one locked me into deep
(for that one I was told to scatter poems of praise. One man locked me into deep)

'ʃaxt'ən, liːm 'laostsubɔøt'ən 'kʰlɪŋəndəs me'tʰal; deːɐ̯/deːr 'landrə 'jaːk't'ə mɪç dʊrç
Schachten, ihm auszubeuten klingendes Metall; der Andre jagte mich durch
shafts, for him to exploit clanging metal; the other chased me through
(mine shafts, to dig out clanging metal; another drove me through)

'bluːt'ɡə 'ʃlaxt'ən lʊm ruːm, zoː 'vɛksəlt'ə deːɐ̯/deːr 'larmən kʰvaːl. jaː, 'diːzəs
blut'ge Schlachten um Ruhm, so wechselte der Armen Qual. Ja, dieses
bloody battles for fame, thus changed the poor woman's torment. Yes, this
(bloody battles for the sake of fame; thus the form of my torment changed. Yes, this)

dia'deːm, di 'ɡɔldnən 'ʃt'ɛrnə, das duː deːɐ̯ 'ʃaedəndən hast 'tsuːɡəvantʰ, ziː
Diadem, die gold'nen Sterne, das du der Scheidenden hast zugewandt, sie
diadem, the golden stars, that you upon the departing one have bestowed, they
(diadem, these golden stars, that you bestowed upon me at my departure, they)

ˈhɛtʻən ɛs t͡sʊr ˈfɔ͜øərʊŋ gant͡s ˈgɛrnə ba͜e ˈvɪntʻɐlɪçəm ˈfrɔstʻə ˈvɛkgəbrantʰ.
hätten es zur Feuerung ganz gerne bei winterlichem Froste weggebrannt."
would have it as the fuel quite gladly during wintery frosts away-burned."
(would have gladly burned it up as fuel during winter frosts.")

fɛɐ̯ˈvʏnʃtʻə bruːtʻ! hɛrʃt t͡sɔ͜øs mɪtʻ ˈvɪldɐ ˈʃtʻɪmə, dem ˈʃnɛlstʻən ˈʊntʻɐgaŋ za͜e
"Verwünschte Brut!" herrscht Zeus mit wilder Stimme, "dem schnellsten Untergang sei
"Accursed brood!" rules Zeus with wild voice, "to the quickest downfall be
("Accursed rabble!" Zeus commands in a furious voice: "To the quickest downfall be)
[*poem:* **ruft** (ruːft, calls) **Zeus**]

ziː gəˈva͜etʰ! di ˈvɔlkʻənbʊrkʻ ɛɐ̯ˈbeːpʻtʻ fɔn ˈza͜enəm ˈgrɪmə, ʊntʻ lʊftʻ ʊntʻ meːɐ̯/meːr
sie geweiht!" Die Wolkenburg erbebt von seinem Grimme, und Luft und Meer
it consecrated!" The cloud- castle trembles from his anger, and air and sea
(they doomed!" The cloud-castle quakes at his anger, and air and sea)
[*poem:* **du** (duː, you) **geweiht**]

ʊntʻ lantʻ ɛɐ̯ˈt͡sɪtʻɐn va͜etʰ. leːɐ̯ ra͜est den blɪt͡s gəˈvaltʻzaːm a͜os den ˈfɛŋən dɛs ˈaːdlɐs,
und Land erzittern weit. Er reisst den Blitz gewaltsam aus den Fängen des Adlers,
and land tremble far. He tears the lightning forcefully from the talons of the eagle,
(and land tremble far and wide. He tears a lightning bolt forcefully from the talons of his eagle,)

ˈyːbɐm ˈhoːən ˈha͜opʻtʻə ʃvɛŋkʻt di ˈloːə leːɐ̯, di ˈeːɐ̯də t͡suː fɛɐ̯ˈzɛŋən, diː
überm hohen Haupte schwenkt die Lohe er, die Erde zu versengen, die
above the high head brandishes the flame he, the earth to scorch, which
(brandishes the flame above his lofty head, intending to scorch the earth, which)

ˈza͜enən ˈliːpʻlɪŋ ˈʊnlɛɐ̯høːɐ̯tʻ gəˈkʰrɛŋkʻtʰ. leːɐ̯ ˈʃra͜etʻətʻ ˈfoːɐ̯vɛrt͡s ʊm ziː t͡suː fɛɐ̯ˈdɛrbən,
seinen Liebling unerhört gekränkt. Er schreitet vorwärts um sie zu verderben,
his darling scandalously insulted. He strides forward in order it to ruin,
(has so scandalously insulted his darling. He strides forward to destroy it,)

ɛs drɔ͜øt deːɐ̯ ˈroːtʻə blɪt͡s, nɔx meːɐ̯ za͜en blɪkʰ; di ˈbaŋə vɛltʻ bəˈra͜etʻətʻ zɪç
es dräut der rote Blitz, noch mehr sein Blick; die bange Welt bereitet sich
there threatens the red lightning, still more his gaze; the anxious world prepares itself
(the red lightning is threatening, still more his gaze; the anxious world prepares itself)

t͡suː ˈʃtʻɛrbən — ɛs zɪŋkʻt deːɐ̯ ˈrɛçɐ(r)arm, leːɐ̯ tʰrɪt t͡suˈrʏkʰ, ʊntʻ ha͜estʻ uˈraːniən
zu sterben — es sinkt der Rächerarm, er tritt zurück, und heisst Uranien
to die — there sinks the avenger-arm, he steps back, and bids Urania
(to die. Suddenly the arm of the avenger sinks down, he steps back, and bids Urania)
[*poem:* **des Rächers Arm** (dɛs ˈrɛçɐs arm, the avenger's arm)]

hɪˈnʊntʻɐ ˈʃa͜oən. ziː ziːtʻ ɪn ˈva͜etʻɐ fɛrn a͜en ˈliːbəntʻ pʰaːɐ̯, a͜of ˈa͜enɐ ˈgryːnən,
hinunter schauen. Sie sieht in weiter Fern' ein liebend Paar, auf einer grünen,
down to look. She sees in far distance a loving couple, on a green,
(look down. In the far distance she sees a loving couple on a green)

ˈʃtʻroːmʊmflɔsənən ˈa͜oə, iːɐ̯ ˈbɪltʻnɪs t͡siːɐ̯t den ˈlɛntʻlɪçən alˈtʰaːɐ̯, foːɐ̯ deːm di
stromumflossnen Aue, ihr Bildnis ziert den ländlichen Altar, vor dem di
stream-about-flowed meadow, her image adorns the rustic altar, before which the
(meadow, surrounded by streams; she sees her image adorning a rustic altar, before which the)
[*poem:* **Auen** (ˈa͜oən, meadow)]

ˈba͜edən ˈlɔp͜fənt‘ ˈni:dɐkʰni:ən, di ˈhɪmlɪʃə lɛɐ̯ˈze:nənt, di: lɛnt‘ˈflo:n. lʊnt‘
beiden opfernd niederknieen, die Himmlische ersehnend, die entflohn. Und
both sacrificing down-kneel, the heavenly one longing for, who (has) fled. And
(two are kneeling and offering sacrifices, longing for the heavenly one who has fled. And)

vi: la͜en ˈmɛçt‘ɪç me:ɐ̯ fɔn harmoˈni:ən lʊmˈvo:k‘t di ˈgœt‘ɪn ˈli:rəs ˈfle:əns tʰo:n;
wie ein mächtig Meer von Harmonien umwogt die Göttin ihres Flehens Ton;
like a mighty sea of harmonies about-waves the goddess their pleading's tone;
(the sound of their plea surges about the goddess like a mighty sea of harmonies;)
[*poem:* **Und wie ein Ozean** (ˈlo:t͜sea:n, ocean) **von Harmonien**]

i:ɐ̯ ˈdʊŋk‘ləs ˈla͜ogə ˈfʏlət‘ ˈla͜enə ˈtʰrɛ:nə; de:ɐ̯ ʃmɛrt͜s de:ɐ̯ ˈli:bəndən hat‘ zi: lɛɐ̯ˈra͜eçtʰ,
ihr dunkles Auge füllet eine Träne; der Schmerz der Liebenden hat sie erreicht,
her dark eye fills a tear; the pain of the loving ones has her reached,
(a tear fills her dark eye; the pain of that loving couple has reached her,)

i:ɐ̯/i:r ˈlʊnmu:t‘ vɪrt‘, vi: ˈla͜enəs ˈbo:gəns ˈze:nə fɔm ˈfɔ͜øçt‘ən ˈmɔrgəntʰa͜oə, nu:n lɛɐ̯ˈva͜eçtʰ.
ihr Unmut wird, wie eines Bogens Sehne vom feuchten Morgentaue, nun erweicht.
her anger becomes, as a bow's string by the moist morning dew, now softened.
(her displeasure is now softened, like a bowstring in the moist morning dew.)
[*poem:* **vom Morgentaue** (*without* **feuchten**)]

fɛɐ̯ˈt͜sa͜eə, ha͜eʃt di ˈgœt‘lɪçə fɛɐ̯ˈzø:nt‘ə, lɪç va:ɐ̯ t͜su: raʃ lɪm t͜sɔrn, ma͜en
"Verzeihe," heischt die göttliche Versöhnte, "ich war zu rasch im Zorn, mein
"Forgive," requests the divine reconciled one, "I was too quick in the anger, my
("Forgive!" the reconciled goddess requests, "I was too hasty in my anger; my)

di:nst‘, le:ɐ̯ gɪlt‘ nɔx la͜of de:ɐ̯/de:r ˈle:ɐ̯də; vi: man mɪç la͜ox ˈhø:nt‘ə, manç ˈfrɔməs
Dienst, er gilt noch auf der Erde; wie man mich auch höhnte, manch frommes
service, it matters still on the earth; how one me ever mocks, many a devout
(service is still of value on the earth; however much some may mock me, many a devout)

hɛrt͜s lɪst‘ nɔx fɔn mi:ɐ̯/mi:r lɛɐ̯ˈfʏltʰ. lo: las mɪç t͜su: den ˈlarmən ˈmɛnʃən ˈʃt‘a͜egən, zi:
Herz ist noch von mir erfüllt. O lass mich zu den armen Menschen steigen, sie
heart is still with me filled. O let me to the poor humans descend, them
(heart is still filled with me. Oh let me go down to those poor human beings, to teach them)

ˈle:rən, vas da͜en ˈho:ɐ ˈvɪlə lɪstʰ, lʊnt‘ ˈli:nən ˈmʏt‘ɐlɪç lɪn ˈtʰrɔ͜ømən ˈt͜sa͜egən das lant‘,
lehren, was dein hoher Wille ist, und ihnen mütterlich in Träumen zeigen das Land,
teach, what your high will is, and to them motherly in dreams show the land,
(your sublime will, and like a mother to show them in dreams the land)

vo: de:ɐ̯ fɔlˈlɛndʊŋ ˈblu:mə ʃp‘ri:stʰ. lɛs za͜e! ru:ft t͜sɔ͜øs, ra͜eç vɪl lɪç dɪç bəˈʃt‘at‘ən;
wo der Vollendung Blume spriesst." "Es sei!" ruft Zeus, "reich will ich dich bestatten;
where the perfection's flower sprouts." "It be!" calls Zeus, "richly want I you to equip;
(where the flower of perfection blooms." –"So be it!" cries Zeus, "I want to deck you out richly;)

t͜sɔ͜øç, ˈtʰɔxt‘ɐ, hɪn, mɪt‘ ˈfrɪʃəm, ˈʃt‘ark‘əm zɪn, lʊnt‘ ˈkʰɔmə, fy:lst du: ˈda͜enə kʰraft‘
zeuch, Tochter, hin, mit frischem, starkem Sinn, und komme, fühlst du deine Kraft
go, daughter, thither, with fresh, strong mind, and come, feel you your strength
(go there, my daughter, with a fresh, strong mind; and, if you feel your strength weaken, come)
[*poem:* **und komm** (kʰɔm, come)**, gewahrst** (gəˈva:ɐ̯st, see) **du;** *zeuch* (poetic) = *ziehe*]

|ɛɐ̯ˈmat‘ən, t͜su: |ʊns hɛˈrɑ͜ɔf, dɛs ˈhɪməls ˈbʏrgərɪn. |ɔft‘ ˈze:ən vi:ɐ̯ dɪç ˈkʰɔmən, ˈvi:dɐ
ermatten, zu uns herauf, des Himmels Bürgerin. Oft sehen wir dich kommen, wieder
weaken, to us up, the heaven's citizeness. Often see we you come, again
(back to us, a citizen of heaven. Often we shall see you come, and again)

ˈʃa͜edən, |ɪn ˈ|ɪmɐ ˈlɛŋɐn ˈrɔ͜ømən bla͜epst du: |ɑ͜os, |ʊnt‘ ˈ|ɛnt‘lɪç ga:ɐ̯, |ɛs ˈ|ɛndən ˈda͜enə
scheiden, in immer längern Räumen bleibst du aus, und endlich gar, es enden deine
depart, in ever longer spaces remain you out, and finally even, there end your
(depart, for ever longer intervals you will remain away, and finally, even, your sorrows will end;)

ˈla͜edən, di ˈva͜et‘ə ˈ|e:ɐ̯də nɛnst du: |a͜enst da͜en hɑ͜os. da:, ˈdʊldərɪn, vɪrst du: gəˈ|axt‘ət‘
Leiden, die weite Erde nennst du einst dein Haus. Da, Dulderin, wirst du geachtet
sorrows, the vast earth name you one day your house. There, endurer, will you respected
(you will one day call the whole vast earth your home. There, patient one, you will live respected,)
[*poem:* **Du** (du:, you)**, Dulderin! wirst dort** (dɔrt‘, there) **geachtet wohnen]**

ˈvo:nən, nɔx me:ɐ̯/me:r |als vi:ɐ̯; fɛɐ̯ˈgɛŋlɪç |ɪst di maxtʰ, di: |ʊns |ɛɐ̯ˈfrɔ͜øtʰ; de:ɐ̯ ʃt‘ʊrm
wohnen, noch mehr als wir; vergänglich ist die Macht, die uns erfreut; der Sturm
dwell, still more than we; transient is the power, that us gladdens; the storm
(still more than we are; for the power in which we now rejoice is transient; a storm)

fɛlt‘ ˈ|ʊnzrə ˈtʰro:nən, dɔx ˈda͜enə ˈʃt‘ɛrnə ˈlɔ͜øçt‘ən dʊrç di naxtʰ.
fällt unsre Thronen, doch deine Sterne leuchten durch die Nacht."
fells our thrones, but your stars shine through the night."
(may bring down our thrones; but your stars will continue to shine through the night.")
[*poem:* **der Sturm droht unsren** (dro:t‘ ˈ|ʊnzrən, threatens our) **Thronen]**

[The "Urania" of this poem is Aphrodite Urania, the personification of pure, noble love (not the other Urania, the muse of astronomy). This "celestial" Aphrodite was worshipped at different sites from those of the goddess of sexual love and feminine beauty, best known as Venus (her Roman name) and referred to above as "Cypria," after Cyprus, her favorite island. The Urania of the poem is called a uranid, because, in one version of her origin, her father was Uranus, the ancient god of the sky (actually, all the gods were descended from him). He was brutally castrated by his own son Cronus, and his severed genitals were cast into the sea; Aphrodite was born of the foam that rose then to the surface. Zeus, the "thunderer," son of Cronus, inherited the sky and made his home on the highest peak of Mount Olympus, abode of the gods. Jupiter is his Roman name. Helicon was a mountain sacred to Apollo, god of poetry and music, and the muses, who personified the arts. Nymphs of the streams were called naiads; the dryads were the nymphs that inhabited trees. Hebe, goddess of youth and a daughter of Zeus and Hera, his queen, was cup-bearer to the gods. Ceres was the goddess of the fruits of the earth. Eros is the Greek name of Cupid. Pandora, the first mortal woman, was created to be as beautiful as a goddess, adorned with gifts from all the gods, and sent to earth to marry Epimetheus, brother of Prometheus (who had created man out of clay and water in one version of his story). Pandora was warned not to open a certain jar; but curiosity got the better of her: when she removed the lid a plague of evils swarmed out to infest the earth. Her legend corresponds to that of Eve in the Judeo-Christian tradition. Mayrhofer used these myths to illustrate his own idealistic vision of the direction in which man should develop spiritually. Schubert's setting is a solo cantata seventeen pages long, with many interesting moments that are waiting for an adventurous singer to bring them to life.]

ˈfaːtʻɐlantsliːtʻ
Vaterlandslied
Song of the Fatherland

Posthumously published [composed 1815] (poem by Friedrich Gottlieb Klopstock)

ɪç bɪn laen ˈdɔøtʃəs ˈmɛːtʻçən! maen laok‘ lɪst‘ blao lʊnt‘ zanft‘ maen blɪkʰ,
Ich bin ein deutsches Mädchen! Mein Aug' ist blau und sanft mein Blick,
I am a German girl! My eye is blue and gentle my glance,
(I am a German girl! My eyes are blue, my glance is gentle,)

ɪç haːp‘ laen hɛrts das ˈleːdəl lɪst‘, lʊnt‘ ʃtʻɔlts lʊnt‘ guːtʰ.
ich hab' ein Herz das Edel ist, und stolz und gut.
I have a heart that noble is, and proud and good.
(I have a heart that is noble, proud, and good.)

ɪç bɪn laen ˈdɔøtʃəs ˈmɛːtʻçən! tsɔrn blɪkʻtʻ maen ˈblaoəs laok‘ laof deːn,
Ich bin ein deutsches Mädchen! Zorn blickt mein blaues Aug' auf den,
I am a German girl! Anger looks my blue eye on him,
(I am a German girl! My blue eyes dart anger at him,)

ɛs hast‘ maen hɛrts deːn, deːɐ̯ zaen ˈfaːtʻɐlant‘ fɛɐ̯ˈkʰɛntʰ!
es hasst mein Herz den, der sein Vaterland verkennt!
it hates my heart him, who his fatherland fails to appreciate!
(my heart hates him, who fails to appreciate his fatherland!)

ɪç bɪn laen ˈdɔøtʃəs ˈmɛːtʻçən! lɛɐ̯ˈkʰøːrə miːɐ̯ kʰaen ˈandɐ lant‘
Ich bin ein deutsches Mädchen! Erköre mir kein ander Land
I am a German girl! Would choose for myself no other land
(I am a German girl! I would choose for myself no other land)

tsʊm ˈfaːtʻɐlant‘, vɛːɐ̯ miːɐ̯/miːr laox frae di ˈgroːsə vaːl!
zum Vaterland, wär' mir auch frei die grosse Wahl!
as the fatherland, were to me even free the great choice!
(as my fatherland, even if that big choice were free to me!)

ɪç bɪn laen ˈdɔøtʃəs ˈmɛːtʻçən! maen ˈhoːəs ˈlaogə blɪkʻtʻ laox ʃpʻɔtʰ,
Ich bin ein deutsches Mädchen! Mein hohes Auge blickt auch Spott,
I am a German girl! My high eye looks also scorn,
(I am a German girl! My proud eyes also look with scorn,)

blɪkʻtʻ ʃpʻɔtʻ laof deːn, deːɐ̯ ˈzɔøməns maxt‘ bae ˈdiːzɐ vaːl.
blickt Spott auf den, der Säumens macht bei dieser Wahl.
looks scorn on him, who delay makes in this choice.
(looks with scorn at him who hesitates at such a choice.) [*Säumens* (obs.) = *Säumnis* = delay]

duː bɪst‘ kʰaen ˈdɔøtʃɐ ˈjʏŋlɪŋ! bɪst ˈdiːzəs ˈlaoən ˈzɔøməns veːɐ̯tʰ,
Du bist kein deutscher Jüngling! Bist dieses lauen Säumens wert,
You are no German youth! Are of this lukewarm delaying worthy,
(You are not a true German youth! You are worthy of that lukewarm shilly-shallying,)

dɛs 'faːt'ɐlant͡s nɪçt' veːɐ̯t', vɛn duːs nɪçt' liːpst', viː lɪç!
des Vaterlands nicht wert, wenn du's nicht liebst, wie ich!
of the fatherland not worthy, if you it not love, as I!
(not worthy of the fatherland, if you do not love it as I do!)

duː bɪst' kʰa͡en 'dɔ͡ʏtʃɐ 'jʏŋlɪŋ! ma͡en 'gant͡səs hɛrt͡s fɛɐ̯-/fɛr'laxt'ət dɪç,
Du bist kein deutscher Jüngling! Mein ganzes Herz verachtet dich,
You are no German youth! My whole heart despises you,

deːɐ̯s 'faːt'ɐlant' fɛɐ̯'kʰɛnt, dɪç 'frɛmt'lɪŋ lʊnt dɪç tʰoːɐ̯!
der's Vaterland verkennt, dich Fremdling und dich Tor!
who the fatherland fails to appreciate, you stranger and you fool!
(who fail to appreciate the fatherland, you stranger and you fool!)

ɪç bɪn la͡en 'dɔ͡ʏtʃəs 'mɛːt'çən! ma͡en 'guːt'əs, 'leːdləs, 'ʃt'ɔlt͡səs hɛrt͡s
Ich bin ein deutsches Mädchen! Mein gutes, edles, stolzes Herz
I am a German girl! My good, noble, proud heart

ʃlɛːk't' la͡ot' lɛm'pʰoːɐ̯ ba͡em 'zyːsən 'naːmən: 'faːt'ɐlant'!
schlägt laut empor beim süssen Namen: Vaterland!
beats loudly up at the sweet name: fatherland!
(leaps up and beats loudly at the sweet name: fatherland!)

zoː ʃlɛːk't' miːɐ̯s la͡enst' ba͡em 'naːmən dɛs 'jʏŋlɪŋs nuːɐ̯,
So schlägt mir's einst beim Namen des Jünglings nur,
Thus beats for me it one day at the name of the youth merely,
(Thus it will one day beat for me at the mere name of the young man)

deːɐ̯ ʃt'ɔlt͡s viː lɪç la͡ofs 'faːt'ɐlant', guːt', 'leːdəl lɪst', la͡en 'dɔ͡ʏtʃɐ(r) lɪstʰ!
der stolz wie ich aufs Vaterland, gut, edel ist, ein Deutscher ist!
who proud as I of the fatherland, good, noble is, a German is!
(who is as proud of the fatherland as I am, who is good and noble, who is a German!)

[Schubert made two settings, not very different, of this ultra-nationalistic, oddly negative poem.]

Vedi quanto adoro see *Arie*

fɛɐ̯'geːp'lɪçə 'liːbə
Vergebliche Liebe
Love in Vain

Op. 173, No. 3 [1815] (Carl Joseph Bernard)

jaː, lɪç va͡es lɛs, 'diːzə 'tʰrɔ͡ʏə 'liːbə heːk't' lʊm'zɔnst' ma͡en 'vʊndəs hɛrt͡s! vɛn
Ja, ich weiss es, diese treue Liebe hegt umsonst mein wundes Herz! Wenn
Yes, I know it, this true love conceals in vain my wounded heart! If
(Yes, I know it, my wounded heart conceals this loyal love in vain! If)

miːɐ̯ nuːɐ̯ di 'kʰla͡enst'ə 'hɔfnʊŋ 'bliːbə, ra͡eç bə'loːnət' vɛːɐ̯ ma͡en ʃmɛrt͡s!
mir nur die kleinste Hoffnung bliebe, reich belohnet wär' mein Schmerz!
for me only the smallest hope might remain, richly rewarded were my pain!
(even the smallest hope were left for me, my pain would be richly rewarded!)

'a:bɐ(r) |ao͜x di 'hɔfnʊŋ |ɪst' fɛɐ̯'ge:bəns, kʰɛn ɪç dɔx |i:ɐ̯ 'grao͜za:m ʃp'i:l!
Aber auch die Hoffnung ist vergebens, kenn' ich doch ihr grausam Spiel!
But also the hope is in vain, know I after all its cruel game!
(But hope is also in vain; I know its cruel game, after all!)

tʰrɔts de:ɐ̯ 'tʰrɔ͜ø̯ə 'maenəs 'ʃt'reːbəns 'fli:ət' 'le:vɪç mɪç das tsi:l! 'dɛnɔx
Trotz der Treue meines Strebens fliehet ewig mich das Ziel! Dennoch
Despite the constancy of my striving flees eternally me the goal! Nevertheless
(Despite the constancy of my striving, the goal seems ever farther from me! And yet)

li:b ɪç, 'dɛnɔx hɔf ɪç 'ɪmɐ(r), 'lo:nə 'li:bə, 'lo:nə 'hɔfnʊŋ tʰrɔ͜ø;
lieb' ich, dennoch hoff' ich immer, ohne Liebe, ohne Hoffnung treu;
love I, nevertheless hope I always, without love, without hope faithful;
(I love, and yet I always hope, faithful without love, without hope;)

'lasən kʰan |ɪç 'di:zə 'li:bə 'nɪmɐ, mɪt' |i:ɐ̯ brɪçt das hɛrts |ɛnt'tsvae!
lassen kann ich diese Liebe nimmer, mit ihr bricht das Herz entzwei!
leave can I this love never, with it breaks the heart in two!
(I can never leave this love, with it my heart is breaking in two! It will be with me till I die!)

[Schubert composed his highly expressive setting in C minor, as in the *Gesamtausgabe*; it was published in A minor, the version reproduced in the Peters edition.]

fɛɐ̯'gɪsmaennɪçtʰ
Vergissmeinnicht
Forget-me-not

Posthumously published [composed 1823] (poem by Franz von Schober)

als de:ɐ̯ 'fry:lɪŋ zɪç fɔm 'hɛrtsən de:ɐ̯/de:r |ɛɐ̯'bly:t'ən 'le:ɐ̯də rɪs,
Als der Frühling sich vom Herzen der erblühten Erde riss,
When the spring itself from the heart the blossomed earth tore,
(When Spring tore himself away from the heart of the blossoming earth,)

tso:k' |e:ɐ̯ nɔx |aen'ma:l mɪt' 'ʃmɛrtsən dʊrç di vɛlt, di: |e:ɐ̯ fɛɐ̯'li:s.
zog er noch einmal mit Schmerzen durch die Welt, die er verliess.
went he yet once with sorrows through the world, which he forsook.
(he wandered with sorrow one more time through the world that he was forsaking.)
[*poem:* **durch die Flur** (flu:ɐ̯, meadow)]

'vi:zənʃmɛlts |ʊnt' 'za:t'əngry:nə 'gry:sən |i:n mɪt' 'hɛləm bly:n,
Wiesenschmelz und Saatengrüne grüssen ihn mit hellem Blüh'n,
Meadow-enamel and crops- green greet him with bright blooming,
(The many-colored meadows and the green crops greet him with their bright blooming,)

ʊnt di 'ʃat'ənbalda͵xi:nə 'dʊŋk'lən valts |ʊm'zɔ͜øzəln |i:n.
und die Schattenbaldachine dunklen Walds umsäuseln ihn.
and the shadow- canopy of dark woods about-rustles him.
(and the canopy of shadows in the dark woods rustles all around him.)

da: ɪm 'vaeçən zamt dɛs 'mo:zəs zi:t' |e:ɐ̯, halp' fɔm gry:n fɛɐ̯'dɛk't',
Da im weichen Sammt des Mooses sieht er, halb vom Grün verdeckt,
There in the soft velvet of the moss sees he, half by the green concealed,
(There, in the soft velvet of the moss, he sees, half concealed by greenery,)

'ʃlʊmɐzyːs, laen 'kʰʊmɐloːzəs 'hɔldəs 'veːzən 'hɪngəʃt'rɛk'tʰ.
schlummersüss, ein kummerloses holdes Wesen hingestreckt.
slumber- sweet, an untroubled lovely being stretched out.
(a lovely creature, seemingly without a care in the world, stretched out and sleeping sweetly.)

ɔps laen kʰɪnt' nɔx, lɔps laen 'mɛːt'çən, vaːk't' leːɐ̯ nɪçt zɪç tsuː gə'ʃt'eːn.
Ob's ein Kind noch, ob's ein Mädchen, wagt er nicht sich zu gesteh'n.
Whether it a child still, whether it a girl, dared he not to himself to admit.
(He wouldn't venture to say whether it was still a child or whether it was a very young woman.)

'kʰʊrtsə 'blɔndə 'zaedənfɛːt'çən lʊm das 'rʊndə 'kʰœpfçən veːn.
Kurze blonde Seidenfädchen um das runde Köpfchen weh'n.
Short blond silk- little-threads about the round little head waft.
(Short blond hair like delicate threads of silk waft about her round little head.)

tsaːɐ̯t' nɔx zɪnt di 'ʃlaŋk'ən 'gliːdɐ(r), lʊnlɛnt''falt'ət di gə'ʃt'alt',
Zart noch sind die schlanken Glieder, unentfaltet die Gestalt,
Delicate still are the slender limbs, un-unfolded the form,
(Her slender limbs are still quite delicate, her form has not yet ripened to maturity,)
[*poem:* **unentwickelt** (lʊnlɛnt''vɪk'əlt, undeveloped)]

ʊnt dɔx ʃaent deːɐ̯ 'buːzən 'viːdɐ ʃoːn fɔn 'reːgʊŋən dʊrç'valtʰ.
und doch scheint der Busen wieder schon von Regungen durchwallt.
and yet seems the bosom again already from stirrings through-undulated.
(and yet again her bosom seems already to swell with some inner stirring.)

'roːzɪç ʃt'raːlt deːɐ̯ 'vaŋən 'fɔøɐ, 'lɛçəlnt' lɪst deːɐ̯ mʊnt' lʊnt' ʃlao,
Rosig strahlt der Wangen Feuer, lächelnd ist der Mund und schlau,
Rosy radiates the cheeks' fire, smiling is the mouth and sly,
(The fire of her cheeks radiates a rosy glow, her mouth is smiling and sly,)

dʊrç deːɐ̯ 'vɪmp'ɐn 'dʊft'gən 'ʃlaeɐ(r) 'lɔøgəlt' 'ʃalk'haft' 'hɛləs blao.
durch der Wimpern duft'gen Schleier Äugelt schalkhaft helles Blau.
through the lashes' fragrant veil ogles roguishly bright blue.
(A bright blue is peeking roguishly through the fragrant veil of her lashes.)

ʊnt deːɐ̯ 'fryːlɪŋ, 'vɔnətʰrʊŋk'ən ʃt'eːt' leːɐ̯, lʊnt dɔx tʰiːf gə'ryːɐ̯t';
Und der Frühling, wonnetrunken steht er, und doch tief gerührt;
And the spring, bliss- drunk stands he, and yet deeply touched;
(And Spring stands there, drunk with bliss, and yet deeply touched;)

ɪn das 'hɔldə bɪlt' fɛɐ̯'zʊŋk'ən, fyːlt' leːɐ̯ gants, vas leːɐ̯ fɛɐ̯'liːɐ̯tʰ!
in das holde Bild versunken, fühlt er ganz, was er verliert!
into the lovely picture sunk, feels he completely, what he loses!
(sunk in contemplation of the lovely picture, he feels keenly what he is losing!)

'aːbɐ 'drɪŋənt' maːnt di 'ʃt'ʊndə, das leːɐ̯ ʃnɛl fɔn 'hɪnən mʊs.
Aber dringend mahnt die Stunde, dass er schnell von hinnen muss.
But urgently reminds the hour, that he quickly from hence must.
(But the hour urgently reminds him that he must quickly leave here.)

ax, daː brɛnt‘ lɑ͡ʊf 'liːrəm 'mʊndə 'glyːənt‘ ha͡ɛs deːɐ̯ 'ʃa͡ɛdəkʰʊs.
Ach, da brennt auf ihrem Munde glühend heiss der Scheidekuss.
Ah, then burns on her mouth glowingly hot the parting-kiss.
(Ah, then his parting kiss burns on her mouth with glowing ardor.)
[*poem:* **sein** (za͡ɛn, his) **Scheidekuss]**

ʊnt‘ lɪn dʊft‘ lɪst‘ leːɐ̯/leːr lɛnt‘'ʃvʊndən. dɔx das kʰɪnt‘ lɛnt‘'fɛːɐ̯t dem ʃlaːf,
Und in Duft ist er entschwunden. Doch das Kind entfährt dem Schlaf,
And in fragrance is he vanished. But the child slips out from the sleep,
(And he has vanished in a fragrant mist. But the child slips out of sleep,)
[viː leːɐ̯/leːr] [fɛɐ̯'ʃvɪndət‘, fɛːɐ̯t] [lɑ͡ʊs 'tʰiːfəm]
[*poem:* **Und wie er in Duft verschwindet, fährt das Kind aus tiefem Schlaf,]**
[as he] [disappears, goes] [out of deep]
[(And as he disappears in fragrance, the child comes out of her deep sleep)]

tʰiːf hat‘ ziː deːɐ̯ kʰʊs lɛnt'ts͡ʊndən, viː la͡ɛn 'blɪts͡ʃt‘raːl, deːɐ̯ ziː tʰraːf.
tief hat sie der Kuss entzunden, wie ein Blitzstrahl, der sie traf.
deeply has her the kiss ignited, like a lightning ray, which her struck.
(that kiss has set her afire in the depths of her being, as if she had been struck by lightning.)
[dɛn lɛs hat] [gə'ts͡ʏndət‘]
[*poem:* **denn es hat der Kuss gezündet, wie...]**
[for it (*the child–obj.*) has] [ignited]
[(for that kiss has set the child on fire)]

'alə 'kʰa͡ɛmə zɪnt‘ lɛnt‘'falt‘ət, diː liːɐ̯ 'kʰla͡ɛnɐ 'buːzən bark‘,
Alle Keime sind entfaltet, die ihr kleiner Busen barg,
All buds are unfurled, which her little bosom concealed,
(All the buds that had been concealed in her little bosom have unfurled,)

ʃnɛl ts͡ʊr 'jʊŋfra͡ʊ lʊmgə'ʃt‘alt‘ət‘, ʃt‘a͡ɛk‘t‘ ziː la͡ʊs deːɐ̯ 'kʰɪnt‘ha͡ɛt‘ zark‘.
schnell zur Jungfrau umgestaltet, steigt sie aus der Kindheit Sarg.
quickly to the virgin transformed, rises she from the childhood's coffin.
(suddenly transformed into a young woman, she rises from the coffin of her childhood.)

'iːrə 'bla͡ʊən 'la͡ʊgən 'ʃlaːgən lɛrnst‘ lʊnt‘ 'liːbəlɪçt‘ lɛm'pʰoːɐ̯,
Ihre blauen Augen schlagen ernst und liebelicht empor,
Her blue eyes open earnestly and love-light up,
(Her blue eyes open wide with earnestness and bright with love,)

naːx dem glʏk‘ ʃa͡ɛnt‘ ziː ts͡uː 'fraːgən, vas ziː 'lʊngəkʰant‘ fɛɐ̯'loːɐ̯. [das ziː]
nach dem Glück scheint sie zu fragen, was sie ungekannt verlor. [*poem:* **das sie]**
after the happiness seems she to ask, what she unknown lost. [that she]
(she seems to be asking about the unknown happiness that she has lost.)

'aːbɐ 'niːmant‘ giːp‘t‘ liːɐ̯ 'kʰʊndə, 'lalə zeːn ziː 'ʃt‘a͡ʊnənt‘ lan,
Aber niemand gibt ihr Kunde, alle seh'n sie staunend an,
But no one gives her information, all look her astonished at,
(But no one gives her any information; they all look at her in astonishment,)

ʊnt di 'ʃvɛst‘ɐ(r) lɪn deːɐ̯ 'rʊndə 'vɪsən nɪçt‘, viː liːɐ̯ gə'tʰaːn.
und die Schwester in der Runde wissen nicht, wie ihr getan.
and the sisters in the round know not, what to her done.
(and her sisters, all around her, do not know what has happened to her.)

ax! ziː vae̯s ǀɛs zɛlpstʻ nɪçtʰ! ˈtʰrɛːnən ˈʃpʻrɛçən ˈliːrən ʃmɛrt͡s nuːɐ̯/nuːr ǀao̯s,
Ach! sie weiss es selbst nicht! Tränen sprechen ihren Schmerz nur aus,
Ah! she knows it herself not! Tears speak her pain only out,
(Ah, she does not know what it is herself! Tears only express her pain,)

ʊntʻ ǀae̯n ˈǀʊnlɛɐ̯grʏntʻlɪç ˈzeːnən tʰrae̯pʻtʻ ziː ǀao̯s zɪç zɛlpstʻ hɛˈrao̯s;
und ein unergründlich Sehnen treibt sie aus sich selbst heraus;
and an unfathomable longing drives her out of her- self out;
(and an unfathomable longing drives her beyond the self she has known,)

tʰrae̯pʻtʻ ziː fɔrt, das bɪlt t͡suː ˈfɪndən, das ǀɪn ˈǀiːrəm ˈǀɪnɐn leːpʻtʻ, [ˈǀɪnrən]
treibt sie fort, das Bild zu finden, das in ihrem Innern lebt, **[*GA:* Inn'ren]**
drives her forth, the image to find, that in her inside lives, [inside]
(drives her away to find the image that now lives inside of her,)

das liːɐ̯/liːr ˈǀaːnʊŋən fɛɐ̯ˈkʰʏndən, das ǀɪn ˈtʰrɔ͜ømən ziː ǀʊmˈʃveːpʻtʰ.
das ihr Ahnungen verkünden, das in Träumen sie umschwebt.
that to her inklings announce, that in dreams her about-hovers.
(that offers her inklings of something yet unknown, that hovers about her in dreams.)

ˈfɛlzən hatʻ ziː ǀyːbɐˈkʰlɔmən, ˈbɛrgə ʃtʻae̯kʻtʻ ziː ǀapʻ ǀʊntʻ ǀao̯f,
Felsen hat sie überklommen, Berge steigt sie ab und auf,
Rocks has she over-climbed, mountains climbs she down and up,
(She has climbed over rocks, she climbs up and down mountains,)

bɪs ziː ǀan den flʊs gəˈkʰɔmən, deːɐ̯/deːr liːɐ̯ hɛmt den ˈʃtʻreːbəǀao̯f.
bis sie an den Fluss gekommen, der ihr hemmt den Strebelauf.
till she to the river (has) come, which for her obstructs the strive- course.
(until she has come to a river that obstructs the course of her striving.)

dɔx ǀɪm ˈǀuːfɐgraːs, dem ˈfɔ͜øçtʻən, vɪrtʻ liːɐ̯ ˈhae̯sɐ fuːs gəˈkʰyːltʻ,
Doch im Ufergras, dem feuchten, wird ihr heisser Fuss gekühlt,
But in the bank-grass, the moist, becomes her hot foot cooled,
(But her hot feet are cooled in the moist grass by the riverside,)

[*poem:* **Hier** (hiːɐ̯, here)**, im Ufergras**]

ʊntʻ ǀɪm ˈvɛlənʃpʻiːgəl ˈǀɔ͜øçtʻən ˈziːətʻ ziː liːɐ̯/liːr ˈǀae̯gnəs bɪltʻ.
und im Wellenspiegel leuchten siehet sie ihr eig'nes Bild.
and in the waves-mirror shining sees she her own image.
(and she sees her own reflection shining in the mirror of the waves.)

[*GA:* **und in seinem Spiegel** (ǀɪn ˈzae̯nəm ˈʃpʻiːgəl, in its mirror)]

ziːt dɛs ˈhɪməls ˈblao̯ə ˈfɛrnə, ziːt deːɐ̯ ˈvɔlkʻən ˈpʰʊrpʻʊrʃae̯n,
Sieht des Himmels blaue Ferne, sieht der Wolken Purpurschein,
Sees the sky's blue distance, sees the clouds' purple- gleam,
(she sees the blue distance of the sky, the purple gleam of the clouds,)

ziːt den moːntʻ ǀʊntʻ ˈǀalə ˈʃtʻɛrnə; — ˈmɪldɐ fyːltʻ ziː ˈǀiːrə pʰae̯n.
sieht den Mond und alle Sterne; — milder fühlt sie ihre Pein.
sees the moon and all stars; — milder feels she her pain.
(sees the moon and all the stars; — her pain feels milder.)

dɛn lɛs lɪst' liːɐ̯/liːr 'lɑ͜ofgəgaŋən, das ziː 'la͜enə 'zeːlə fant',
Denn es ist ihr aufgegangen, dass sie eine Seele fand,
For it has on her dawned, that she a soul found,
(For it has dawned on her that she has found a soul)

diː liːɐ̯/liːr 'ɪnɐst'əs fɛɐ̯'laŋən, 'liːrən 'tʰiːfst'ən ʃmɛrt͜s fɛɐ̯'ʃt'ant'.
die ihr innerstes Verlangen, ihren tiefsten Schmerz verstand.
that her most inner desire, her deepest pain understood.
(that understood her most inner desire, her deepest pain.)
[*GA:* **innigstes** ('ɪnɪçst'əs, most intimate) **Verlangen**]

gɛrn maːk' ziː lan 'diːzɐ 'ʃt'ɛlə zɪç di 'ʃt'ɪlə 'voːnʊŋ bɑ͜on,
Gern mag sie an dieser Stelle sich die stille Wohnung bau'n,
Gladly may she on this spot for herself the quiet dwelling build,
(Gladly she will build herself a quiet dwelling on this spot,)

deːɐ̯ fɛɐ̯'kʰlɛːɐ̯t'ən 'zanft'ən 'vɛlə kʰan ziː 'rʏk'halt͜sloːs fɛɐ̯'tʰrɑ͜on.
der verklärten sanften Welle kann sie rückhaltslos vertrau'n.
in the transfigured soft wave can she unreservedly confide.
(she can freely confide in the radiant, gentle waves.)

ʊnt' ziː fyːlt' zɪç gant͜s gə'neːzən, vɛn ziː t͜suː dem 'vasɐ ʃp'rɪçt',
Und sie fühlt sich ganz genesen, wenn sie zu dem Wasser spricht,
And she feels herself completely healed, when she to the water speaks,
(And she feels completely healed of her pain when she says to the water,)

viː t͜suː dem gə'laːnt'ən 'veːzən: loː fɛɐ̯'gɪs, fɛɐ̯'gɪs ma͜en nɪçtʰ!
wie zu dem geahnten Wesen: O vergiss, vergiss mein nicht!
as to the imagined being: Oh forget, forget me not!
(as if to the lover of her dreams: "Oh, do not forget me! Forget me not!")

[The song, eleven pages long in the *Gesamtausgabe* (ten in Peters), has many lovely moments, especially in its final section; but its length is a handicap, considering the slightness of the subject matter. It is one of the two rather verbose "flower ballads" by his friend Schober upon which Schubert lavished his inexhaustible facility (the other is "*Viola*").]

fɛɐ̯'kʰlɛːrʊŋ
Verklärung
Transfiguration

Posthumously published [composed 1813] (poem by Alexander Pope)
(German translation by Johann Gottfried Herder)

'leːbənsfʊŋk'ə, fɔm 'hɪməl lɛnt''glyːtʰ, deːɐ̯ zɪç 'loːst͜suvɪndən myːtʰ,
Lebensfunke, vom Himmel entglüht, der sich loszuwinden müht,
Life- spark, from the heaven away-glowed, which itself free to twist troubles,
(Spark of life, which had its origin in heaven's glow, which now struggles to wrest itself free,)
[*Herder:* **erglüht** (lɛɐ̯'glyːtʰ, kindled)]

't͜sɪt'ɐnt', kʰyːn, foːɐ̯ 'zeːnzʊxt' 'la͜edənt', gɛrn lʊnt dɔx mɪt' 'ʃmɛrt͜sən 'ʃa͜edənt':
zitternd, kühn, vor Sehnen leidend, gern und doch mit Schmerzen scheidend:
trembling, bold, from the longing suffering, gladly and yet with pains departing:
(trembling, yet brave, suffering with longing, gladly departing, yet in pain:)
[*Herder:* **zitternd-kühn** (trembling-bold)]

ɛnt', lo: lɛnt den kʰampf, na'tʰu:ɐ̯! zanft' lɪns 'le:bən 'laofvɛrts 'ʃve:bən,
end', o end' den Kampf, Natur! Sanft ins Leben aufwärts schweben,
end, O end the battle, nature! Gently into the life upwards soar,
(end, oh end this battle, Nature! Let me gently soar upwards into life,)

zanft' hɪn'ʃvɪndən las mɪç nu:ɐ̯! hɔrç, mi:ɐ̯ 'lɪsp'əln 'gaest'ɐ tsu::
sanft hinschwinden lass mich nur! Horch, mir lispeln Geister zu:
gently thither-disappear let me only! Hark, to me whisper spirits to:
(just let me softly disappear! Listen, spirits are whispering to me:)

'ʃvɛst'ɐ- 'ze:lə, kʰɔm tsʊr ru:. 'tsi:ət' vas mɪç zanft' fɔn 'hɪnən,
"Schwester-Seele, komm zur Ruh." Ziehet was mich sanft von hinnen,
"Sister- soul, come to the rest." Draws something me gently from hence,
("Sister soul, come to your rest." Something draws me gently away,)

vas lɪsts, vas mi:ɐ̯ 'maenə 'zɪnən, mi:ɐ̯ den haox tsu: 'raobən dro:tʰ?
was ist's, was mir meine Sinnen, mir den Hauch zu rauben droht?
what is it, that from me my senses, from me the breath to rob threatens?
(what is this that threatens to steal away my senses and my breath?)
[*GA:* **Sinne** ('zɪnə, senses—*correct plural in ordinary German, but no rhyme*)]

'ze:lə! ʃp'rɪç, lɪst das de:ɐ̯ tʰo:t'? di vɛlt' lɛnt''vaeçtʰ, zi: lɪst' nɪçt' me:ɐ̯, —
Seele! sprich, ist das der Tod? Die Welt entweicht, sie ist nicht mehr. —
Soul! speak, is that the death? The world disappears, it is no more. —
(My soul, speak: is this death? The world is disappearing, it exists no more. —)

'ɛŋəl- 'laenkʰlaŋ lʊm mɪç he:ɐ̯! lɪç ʃve:p' lɪm 'mɔrgənro:tʰ!
Engel-Einklang um mich her! ich schweb' im Morgenrot!
Angel- harmony around me hither! I hover in the dawn!
(Angelic harmony is all around me! I float in the light of dawn!)
[harmo'ni:ən] [ʃvɪm]
[*Herder:* **Harmonien um mich her! Ich schwimm' im Morgenrot**]
[Harmonies] [swim]

laet', lo: laet' mi:ɐ̯/mi:r 'lɔørə 'ʃvɪŋən, li:ɐ̯ 'bry:dɐ, 'gaest'ɐ, hɛlft' mi:ɐ̯,
Leiht, o leiht mir eure Schwingen, ihr Brüder, Geister, helft mir,
Lend, O lend me your wings, you brothers, spirits, help me,
(Lend, oh lend me your wings, brothers, spirits, help me,)
[*Herder:* **ihr Brüder-Geister** (brother-spirits)]

hɛlft' mi:ɐ̯ 'zɪŋən: lo: gra:p', vo: lɪst daen zi:k'? vo: lɪst daen pfael, lo: tʰo:t'?
helft mir singen: "O Grab, wo ist dein Sieg? wo ist dein Pfeil, o Tod?"
help me to sing: "O grave, where is your victory? Where is your arrow, O death?"

[Pope's title is "*The Dying Christian to his Soul.*" His magnificent poem is a precious jewel of English literature. In Schubert's setting, made when he was sixteen years old, twenty-one of the forty-two bars, exactly half, are recitative, including the famous final lines. Here is the original:

Vital spark of heav'nly flame! / Quit, oh quit this mortal frame;
Trembling, hoping, ling'ring, flying, / Oh the pain, the bliss of dying!
Cease, fond Nature, cease thy strife, / And let me languish into life.
Hark! They whisper: Angels say, / Sister spirit, come away.
What is this absorbs me quite, / Steals my senses, shuts my sight,
Drowns my spirits, draws my breath? / Tell me, my Soul, can this be Death?
The world recedes, it disappears! / Heav'n opens on my eyes, my ears

With sounds seraphic ring: / Lend, lend your wings! I mount, I fly!
O Grave, where is thy victory? / O Death, where is thy sting?]

fɛɐ̯ˈzʊŋkʻən
Versunken
Sunk in a Sea of Hair

Posthumously published [composed 1821] (poem by Johann Wolfgang von Goethe)

fɔl ˈlɔkʻənkʰrɑ͜os la͜en hɑ͜opʻtʻ zoː rʊntʻ! — ʊnt darf lɪç dan
Voll Lockenkraus ein Haupt so rund! — Und darf ich dann
Full of locks- curly a head so round! — And may I then
(A head so round and full of curly locks! — And when I may)

lɪn ˈzɔlçən ˈra͜eçən ˈhaːrən mɪtʻ ˈfɔlən ˈhɛndən hɪn lʊntʻ ˈviːdɐ ˈfaːrən,
in solchen reichen Haaren mit vollen Händen hin und wieder fahren,
in such rich hairs with full hands hence and again go,
(run my full hands through such rich hair now and then,) [*hin und wieder* = now and then]
[*Peters:* **hin- und widerfahren** (hɪn- lʊntʻ ˈviːdɐfaːrən, go to and fro)]

daː fyːl ɪç mɪç fɔn ˈhɛrtsənsgrʊntʻ gəˈzʊntʻ. lʊntʻ kʏs ɪç ˈʃtʻɪrnə,
da fühl' ich mich von Herzensgrund gesund. Und küss' ich Stirne,
then feel I myself from heart's-depths healthy. And kiss I brow,
(then a feeling of well-being fills me from the bottom of my heart. And when I kiss that brow,)

ˈboːgən, ˈlɑ͜ogə, mʊntʻ, dan bɪn lɪç frɪʃ lʊntʻ ˈlɪmɐ ˈviːdɐ vʊntʻ.
Bogen, Auge, Mund, dann bin ich frisch und immer wieder wund.
curve, eye, mouth, then am I freshly and ever again wounded.
(that curve, those eyes, that mouth, then I am freshly wounded again and again.)

deːɐ̯ ˈfʏnfgətsakʻtʻə kʰam, voː zɔltʻ leːɐ̯ ˈʃtʻɔkʻən? leːɐ̯ kʰeːɐ̯tʻ ʃoːn ˈviːdɐ
Der fünfgezackte Kamm, wo sollt' er stocken? Er kehrt schon wieder
The five-toothed comb, where should it stop? It returns already again
(This five-toothed comb, my hand, where should it stop? It already returns)

tsuː den ˈlɔkʻən. das loːɐ̯ fɛɐ̯ˈzaːkʻtʻ zɪç nɪçt dem ʃpʻiːl,
zu den Locken. Das Ohr versagt sich nicht dem Spiel,
to the locks. The ear denies itself not to the game,
(to that curly hair. That ear too does not refuse to be kissed in this game,)

[hiːɐ̯ lɪstʻ nɪçtʻ fla͜eʃ, hiːɐ̯ lɪstʻ nɪçtʻ hɑ͜otʰ,]
[*not in the song:* **hier ist nicht Fleisch, hier ist nicht Haut,]**
[here is not flesh, here is not skin,]
[(this is not flesh, this is not skin,)]

zoː tsaːɐ̯t tsʊm ʃɛrts, zoː ˈliːbəfiːl! dɔx viː man lɑ͜of dem ˈkʰœɐ̯pfçən kʰrɑ͜otʻ,
so zart zum Scherz, so liebeviel! Doch wie man auf dem Köpfchen kraut,
so delicate in the fun, so love-much! But as one on the little head gently rubs,
(so tender in fun, so much to love! But as one gently strokes that little head,)

man vɪrtʻ lɪn ˈzɔlçən ˈra͜eçən ˈhaːrən fyːɐ̯/fyːr ˈleːvɪç lɑ͜of lʊntʻ ˈniːdɐ ˈfaːrən.
man wird in solchen reichen Haaren für ewig auf und nieder fahren.
one will in such rich hairs for ever up and down travel.
(one will travel up and down in such rich hair forever.)

[zo: hast du:, 'ha:fɪs, laox gə'tʰa:n, vi:ɐ̯ 'faŋən lɛs fɔn 'fɔrnən lan.]
[*omitted:* **So hast du, Hafis, auch getan, wir fangen es von vornen an.]**
[Thus have you, Hafiz, also done, we start it from (the) beginning ... .]
[(Thus have you also done, Hafiz, centuries ago; we shall now start again from the beginning.)]
[*anfangen* = to start]

[Schubert devised an exquisite accompanient in perpetual motion that suggests the rippling hair as well as the lover's excited enthusiasm. The vocal melody, too, is full of charm. The poem is from *Der West-östliche Divan* (see the note after *Suleika I*), a collection of poetry inspired by the 14th-century Persian poet Hafiz (mentioned above in one of the lines that Schubert left out).]

fi:ɐ̯ kʰan'tso:nən
Vier Canzonen
Four Songs

Posthumously published [composed 1820] (poems by Jacopo Vitorelli and Pietro Metastasio)

I
non tak:ko'sta:r a'l:lurna
Non t'accostar all'urna
Do Not Apporach the Urn

non tak:ko'sta:r a'l:lurna, ke 'lɔs:sa 'mi:e rin'sɛr:ra. 'kwesta pje'to:sa 'tɛr:ra
Non t'accostar all'urna, che l'ossa mie rinserra. Questa pietosa terra
Not yourself approach to the urn, that the bones mine encloses. This compassionate earth
(Do not approach the urn that encloses my bones. This compassionate plot of earth)
[*GA:* **che l'osse** ('lɔs:se—*error*, bones) **mie]**
[tak:ko'sta:re‿ a'l:lurna, ke‿il 'tʃener 'mi:o]
[*poem:* **Non t'accostare all'urna, che il cener mio rinserra]**
[yourself approach to the urn, that the ash(es) mine]
[(Do not approach the urn that encloses my ashes)]

ɛ 'sakra‿ al 'mi:o do'lo:r. ri'ku:zo‿i 'twɔ:i dʒa'tʃinti, non 'vɔʎ:ʎo‿i 'pjanti 'twɔ:i,
è sacra al mio dolor. Ricuso i tuoi giacinti, non voglio i pianti tuoi,
is sacred to the my grief. I refuse the your hyacinths, not want the tears yours,
(is sacred to my grief. I refuse your hyacinths, I do not want your tears,) [*GA:* **i tuoi pianti]**
['ɔdjo ʎ:ʎi‿a'f:fan:ni 'twɔ:i]
[*poem:* **Odio gli affanni tuoi, ricuso i tuoi giacinti.]**
[I hate the anxieties yours]
[(I hate your anxiety)]

ke 'dʒ:ʒo:van 'aʎ:ʎi‿e'sti:nti 'du:e 'la:grime, 'du:e fjo:r? 'empja! do'vevi‿ a'l:lo:r
che giovan agli estinti due lagrime, due fior? Empia! dovevi allor
what use are to the dead two tears, two flowers? Cruel one! you should have then
(what use to the dead are two tears, two flowers? Cruel woman! You should have then)
[*poem:* **due lagrime, o** (o, or) **due fior?.. dovevi allora** (a'l:lo:ra, then)]

'pɔrdʒermi un fi:l da'i:ta, 'kwando tra'e:a la 'vi:ta in 'grɛmbo de:i so'spi:r.
porgermi un fil d'aita, quando traéa la vita in grembo dei sospir.
give me a thread of help, when drew the life in womb of the sighs.
(given me a thread of help, when life drew me into the womb of sighs.)
[*poem:* **la vita nell'ansia e nei** (ne'l:lansja‿ e 'ne:i, into anxiety and into) **sospir.]**

aː ke diˈnuːtil ˈpjanto aˈsːsordi la foˈrɛsta? [foˈrɛsto]
Ah che d'inutil pianto assordi la foresta? [*Peters (in error):* **foresto]**
Ah why with useless weeping do you deafen the forest? [forest (*misspelled*)]
(Ah, why do you deafen the forest with useless weeping?)

riˈspɛtːa‿un ˈombra ˈmɛsta e ˈlaʃːʃala dorˈmiːr.
Rispetta un ombra mesta e lasciala dormir.
Respect a shade melancholy and let it sleep.
(Respect a melancholy shade and let it sleep.)

[Schubert mistakenly believed that the author of the above verses was Metastasio; recently the author of this song and the next has been identified as Jacopo Vittorelli (1749-1835)]

II
ˈgwarda ke ˈbːbjaŋka ˈluːna
Guarda che bianca luna
Look How White the Moon

ˈgwarda ke ˈbːbjaŋka ˈluːna, ˈgwarda ke ˈnːnɔtːte‿aˈdʒːʒurːra!
Guarda che bianca luna, guarda che notte azzurra!
Look what white moon, look what night blue!
(Look how white the moon, how blue the night!)

uˈnɑːura non suˈsurːra, nɔ, non ˈtrɛːmola ˈuːno stɛːl.
Un'aura non susurra, no, non tremola uno stel. [*poem: without* **no]**
A light breeze not whispers, no, not trembles a stem.
(Not a breeze is whispering, no, not a single stem is trembling.)

luziɲːɲoˈletːto ˈsolo va ˈdalːla ˈsjɛːpe aˈlːlorno, e sospiˈrando‿inˈtoːrno
L'usignoletto solo va dalla siepe all'orno, e sospirando intorno
The nightingale alone goes from the hedge to the mountain-ash, and sighing all around
(The nightingale, all alone, goes from the hedge to the mountain-ash, and sighing all around)
[*poem:* **L'usignuoletto** (luziɲːɲwɔˈletːto, the little nightingale)]

ˈkjaːma la ˈsuːa feˈdeːl. ˈelːla, ke‿ il ˈsɛntə‿aˈpːpeːna, vjɛːn di ˈfrona‿ in ˈfronda
chiama la sua fedel. Ella, che il sente appena, vien di fronda in fronda
calls the his faithful. She, who him hears scarcely, comes from leafy branch to branch
(calls to his faithful mate. She, as soon as she hears him, comes from branch to branch)
[*GA (in error):* **ch' el sente oppena;** *poem:* **già** (dʒa, already) **vien]**

e ˈpaːre ke ʎːʎi ˈdiːka, nɔ, non ˈpjandʒere, son kwi.
e pare che gli dica, no, non piangere, son qui.
and it seems that to him she may say, no, not weep, I am here.
(and seems to be saying to him: "No, don't weep! I am here.")
[*poem:* **e par** (par, seems) **che gli risponda** (riˈsponda, may answer), **non piangere]**

ke ˈdʒːʒɛːmiti son ˈkwesti, ke ˈdːdoltʃi ˈpjanti‿ iˈrɛne, ke ˈdːdoltʃi ˈpjanti son ˈkwesti?
Che gemiti son questi, che dolci pianti, Irene, che dolci pianti son questi?
What moans are these, what sweet tears, Irene, what sweet tears are these?
[*poem:* **Che dolci affetti, o** (aˈfːfɛtːti‿o‿ , emotions, O) **Irene, che gemiti son questi!]**

tu 'maːi non me sa'pesti ri'spondere ko'si.
Tu mai non me sapesti rispondere così.
You never not me could answer thus.
(You never answered me like that before.)
[*poem:* **Ah** (aː, ah) **mai tu non sapesti respondermi** (ri'spondermi, answer me) **così!]**

[This poem, like the previous one, is by Jacopo Vittorelli, and not by Metastasio, as Schubert had erroneously believed when he wrote these four delightful songs in Italian *bel canto* style.]

III

da kwel sem'bjante a'pːpreːsi

Da quel sembiante appresi

From That Face I Learned to Sigh

da kwel sem'bjante a'pːpreːsi a sospi'raːr da'moːre; [sospi'raːre‿a'mante]
Da quel sembiante appresi a sospirar d'amore; [*poem:* **a sospirare amante;]**
From that countenance I learned to sigh for love; [sigh lovingly/as a lover]
(From that face I learned to sigh for love;)
[*GA (in error):* **a sospirand' amore;** *Peters (in error):* **a sospiran d'amore]**

'sɛmpre per kwel sem'bjante sospire'rɔ da'moːrə. [da'moːr]
sempre per quel sembiante sospirerò d'amore. [*poem:* **d'amor]**
always for that countenance I shall sigh for love. [for love]
(I shall always sigh with love for that face.)

la 'faːtʃe‿a 'kuːi ma'tːtʃeːsi 'soːla ma'lːlɛtːta‿e 'pjaːtʃe;
La face a cui m'accesi sola m'alletta e piace;
The torch at which myself I lighted only me allures and pleases;
(Only that torch that ignited my passion allures and pleases me;)
[*GA & Peters (in error):* **solo** ('soːlo, alone–*masculine; but refers to "la face"–feminine*)]

ɛ 'fredːda‿ɔ'ɲːɲaltra 'faːtʃe per riscal'darmi‿il 'kwɔːre. ['ɔɲːɲi‿'altra... il kɔːr]
è fredda ogn' altra face per riscaldarmi il cuore. [*poem:* **ogni altra... il cor]**
is cold every other torch for warming me the heart. [every other... the heart]
(every other torch is too cold to warm my heart.)

[The text is from Metastasio's libretto, *L'eroe cinese* ("The Chinese Hero"), Act I, Scene 3. The Chinese princess Lisinga is speaking to her sister about her lover, Siveno. Schubert made two errors in transcribing the Italian (at the same time destroying the rhyme): "*a sospirand' amore*" (*Gesamtausgabe*) and "*a sospiran d'amore*" (Peters) are both impossible. "*A sospirar d'amore*" is perfectly acceptable Italian, but does not rhyme with "*sembiante*." Also, it should be "*sola*" and not "*solo*." The singer should follow Metastasio's original words: "*a sospirare amante*."]

IV

miːo bɛːn, ri'kordati

Mio ben ricordati

My Love, Remember

miːo bɛːn, ri'kordati, se‿a'vːvjɛːn 'kiːo 'mɔːraː 'kwanto kwe'staːnima fe'deːl
Mio ben, ricordati, se avvien ch'io mora: quanto quest' anima fedel
My love, remember yourself, if it happens that I should die: how much this soul faithful
(My love, remember, if it happens that I should die, how much this faithful soul of mine)

ta'mɔ. e se pu'ra:mano le 'fred:de 'tʃe:neri: ne'l:lurna‿an'ko:ra tadore'rɔ.
t'amò. E se pur amano le fredde ceneri: nell'urna ancora t'adorerò.
you loved. And if too love the cold ashes: in the urn still you I shall adore.
(loved you. And if cold ashes can also love, then in my funeral urn I shall still adore you.)

[The words are from Metastasio's libretto, *Alessandro nell'Indie* ("Alexander in the Indies"), Act III, Scene 7, during Alexander the Great's campaign in India; Gandarte, a general in the army of an Indian king, bids farewell to Erissena, the king's sister, on his way to a dangerous mission.]

Vier Refrainlieder see *Bei dir allein, Die Männer sind méchant,*
Die Unterscheidung, and *Irdisches Glück*

vi̯o:la
Viola
Violet

Op. 123 [1823] (Franz von Schober)

'ʃne:glœk'la̯en, lo: 'ʃne:glœk'la̯en! lɪn den 'la̯oən 'lɔ̯ øt'əst du:,
Schneeglöcklein, o Schneeglöcklein! In den Auen läutest du,
Little snow bell, O little snow bell! In the meadows ring you,
(Little snow bell, little snow bell, you are ringing in the meadows,)
[note: *Schneeglöcklein*, "little snow bell," is the German name of the snowdrop flower]

'lɔ̯øt'əst' lɪn dem 'ʃt'ɪlən ha̯en, 'lɔ̯øt'ə 'lɪmɐ, 'lɔ̯øt'ə t̮su:.
läutest in dem stillen Hain, läute immer, läute zu.
(you) ring in the quiet grove, ring always, ring on.
(you are ringing in the quiet grove! Ring always, keep ringing!)

dɛn du: 'kʰʏndəst' 'fro:ə t̮sa̯etʰ, 'fry:lɪŋ na:t, de:ɐ̯ 'brɔ̯øt'ɪga:m,
Denn du kündest frohe Zeit, Frühling naht, der Bräutigam,
For you announce happy time, spring approaches, the bridegroom,
(For you are announcing a happy time: Spring, the bridegroom, is approaching,)

kʰɔmt' mɪt' zi:k' fɔm 'vɪnt'ɐʃt'ra̯etʰ, de:m le:ɐ̯ 'za̯enə 'la̯esve:ɐ̯ na:m.
kommt mit Sieg vom Winterstreit, dem er seine Eiswehr nahm.
comes with victory from the winter-fight, from whom he his ice-weapon took.
(coming in triumph from his battle with Winter, whom he has stripped of his weapon of ice.)

'da:rʊm ʃvɪŋt de:ɐ̯ 'gɔldnə ʃt'ɪft, das da̯en 'zɪlbɐhɛlm lɛɐ̯'ʃaltʰ,
Darum schwingt der gold'ne Stift, dass dein Silberhelm erschallt,
Therefore swing the golden rod, that your silver helmet resounds,
(Therefore swing your golden clapper, so that your silver bell will resound,)

ʊnt da̯en 'li:p'lɪçəs gə'dʏftʰ la̯es, vi: 'ʃma̯eçəlru:f lɛnt''valt:
und dein liebliches Gedüft leis', wie Schmeichelruf entwallt:
and your lovely fragrance softly, like flattering- call away floats:
(and your lovely fragrance will softly float out of you, like an enticing call:)

das di 'blu:mən lɪn de:ɐ̯/de:r le:ɐ̯t' 'ʃt'a̯egən la̯os dem 'dy:st'ɐn nɛstʰ,
dass die Blumen in der Erd' steigen aus dem düstern Nest
that the flowers in the earth rise out of the dark nest
(a call to the flowers in the earth to rise out of their dark nest)

ʊnt dɛs ˈbrɔ͜øtʻɪgaːms zɪç veːɐ̯tʻ ˈʃmʏkʻən t͜suː dem ˈhɔxt͜sa͜et͜sfɛstʰ.
und des Bräutigams sich wert schmücken zu dem Hochzeitsfest.
and of the bridegroom themselves worthy adorn for the wedding celebration.
(and adorn themselves for the wedding celebration in a manner worthy of their bridegroom.)

ˈʃneːglœkʻla͜en, ǀoː ˈʃneːglœkʻla͜en! ǀɪn den ˈǀa͜ʊən ˈlɔ͜øtʻəst duː,
Schneeglöcklein, o Schneeglöcklein! In den Auen läutest du,
Little snow bell, O little snow bell! In the meadows ring you,
(Little snow bell, little snow bell, you are ringing in the meadows,)

ˈlɔ͜øtʻəstʻ ǀɪn dem ˈʃtʻɪlən ha͜en, lɔ͜øt di ˈbluːmən ǀa͜ʊs deːɐ̯ ruː! [lɔ͜øtʰ]
läutest in dem stillen Hain, läut' die Blumen aus der Ruh! [*Schubert: an extra* läut]
(you) ring in the quiet grove, ring the flowers out of the rest! [ring]
(you are ringing in the quiet grove! Ring the flowers out of their sleep!)

duː viˈoːla, t͜saːɐ̯tʻəs kʰɪntʻ, høːɐ̯st t͜suˈleːɐ̯st den ˈvɔnəla͜ʊtʰ,
Du Viola, zartes Kind, hörst zuerst den Wonnelaut.
You Violet, delicate child, hear as the first the bliss- sound.
(You, Violet, delicate child, are the first to hear that blessed sound.)

ʊntʻ ziː ˈʃtʻeːətʻ ǀa͜ʊf gəˈʃvɪntʻ, ˈʃmʏkʻətʻ ˈzɔrkʻlɪç zɪç ǀals bra͜ʊtʰ,
Und sie stehet auf geschwind, schmücket sorglich sich als Braut.
And she stands up quickly, adorns carefully herself as bride.
(And she rises quickly, carefully adorns herself as a bride.)

ˈhʏlətʻ zɪç ǀɪns ˈgryːnə kʰla͜etʻ, nɪmt den ˈmantʻəl ˈzamətʻbla͜ʊ,
Hüllet sich ins grüne Kleid, nimmt den Mantel sammetblau,
wraps herself in the green dress, takes the cloak velvet- blue,
(She wraps herself in her green dress, takes out her blue velvet cloak,)

nɪmt das ˈgʏldənə gəˈʃma͜etʻ, ǀʊnt den brɪliˈantʻəntʰa͜ʊ. [brɪlˈjantʻəntʰa͜ʊ]
nimmt das güldene Geschmeid, und den Brilliantentau [*sic*]. [*normally:* Brillantentau]
takes the gold jewelry, and the diamond- dew. [diamond-dew]
(puts on her gold jewelry and diamond dew.)

[*poem:* **Diamantentau** (diaˈmantʻəntʰa͜ʊ, diamond dew)]

a͜elt dan fɔrtʻ mɪtʻ ˈmɛçtʻgəm ʃrɪtʻ, nuːɐ̯ den frɔ͜øntʻ ǀɪm ˈtʰrɔ͜øən zɪn,
Eilt dann fort mit mächt'gem Schritt, nur den Freund im treuen Sinn,
Hurries then forth with powerful step, only the friend in the faithful mind,
(Then she hurries away with energetic steps, with only thoughts of her friend in her loyal mind,)

[*poem:* **mit ems'gem** (ˈǀɛmzgəm, active/eager) **Schritt]**

gant͜s fɔn ˈliːbəsgluːt dʊrçˈglyːtʻ, ziːtʻ nɪçtʻ heːɐ̯/heːr ǀʊntʻ ziːtʻ nɪçtʻ hɪn.
ganz von Liebesglut durchglüht, sieht nicht her und sieht nicht hin.
totally from the love- fire through-glowed, looks not hither and looks not hence.
(glowing throughout with the fire of love, looking neither to the right nor to the left.)

[*poem:* **Liebesglück** (ˈliːbəsglʏkʻ, love's happiness)]

dɔx ǀa͜en ˈǀɛŋstʻlɪçəs gəˈfyːl ˈiːrə ˈkʰla͜enə brʊst dʊrçˈvaltʻ,
Doch ein ängstliches Gefühl ihre kleine Brust durchwallt,
But an anxious feeling her little breast through-seethes,
(But a feeling of anxiety begins to seethe through her little breast,)

dɛn lɛs lɪst‘ nɔx rɪŋs zoː ʃt‘ɪl, lʊnt di 'lʏft‘ə veːn zoː kʰaltʰ. [nɔx]
denn es ist noch rings so still, und die Lüfte weh'n so kalt. [*poem:* **noch kalt]**
for it is still all around so quiet, and the breezes blow so cold. [still]
(for it is still quiet all around her, and the breezes are so cold.)

ʊnt‘ ziː hɛmt den 'ʃnɛlən lɑ͜ɔf, ʃoːn bə'ʃt‘raːlt‘ fɔn 'zɔnənʃa͜en,
Und sie hemmt den schnellen Lauf, schon bestrahlt von Sonnenschein,
And she stops the quick course, already radiated by sunshine,
(And she stops in her quick course, already radiated by sunshine,)

dɔx mɪt‘ 'ʃrɛk‘ən blɪk‘t‘ ziː lɑ͜ɔf, — dɛn ziː 'ʃt‘eːət‘ gant͡s la'la͜en.
doch mit Schrecken blickt sie auf, — denn sie stehet ganz allein.
but with fright looks she up, — for she stands all alone.
(and looks up in fright, for she is standing there all by herself.)

'ʃvɛst‘ɐn nɪçtʰ, — nɪçt‘ 'brɔ͜øt‘ɪgaːm, — 't͡suːgədrʊŋən lʊnt‘ fɛɐ̯'ʃmɛːtʰ! —
Schwestern nicht, — nicht Bräutigam, — zugedrungen und verschmäht! —
Sisters not, — not bridegroom, — importuned and rejected! —
(No sisters to be seen, no bridegroom! Urged on and then rejected!)

daː dʊrç'ʃɑ͜oɐt‘ ziː di ʃaːm, 'fliːət‘ viː fɔm ʃt‘ʊrm gə'veːtʰ,
Da durchschauert sie die Scham, fliehet wie vom Sturm geweht,
Then through-shudders her the shame, flees as from the storm blown,
(Then shame shudders through her, and she flees as if blown by a windstorm,)

'fliːət‘ lan den 'fɛrnst‘ən lɔrtʰ, voː ziː graːs lʊnt‘ 'ʃat‘ən dɛk‘tʰ,
fliehet an den fernsten Ort, wo sie Gras und Schatten deckt,
flees to the farthest place, where her grass and shadow covers,
(flees to the farthest place she can find, where grass and shadows will cover her,)

ʃp‘ɛːt‘ lʊnt‘ 'lɑ͜oʃət‘ 'lɪmɐfɔrtʰ, lɔp‘ vas 'rɑ͜oʃət‘ lʊnt‘ zɪç reːk‘tʰ.
späht und lauschet immerfort: ob was rauschet und sich regt.
scouts and listens constantly: whether something rustles and itself stirs.
(constantly on the look-out and listening to hear whether anything is rustling or stirring.)

ʊnt‘ gə'kʰrɛŋk‘ət‘ lʊnt‘ gə'tʰɔ͜øʃtʰ 'zɪt͡sət‘ ziː lʊnt‘ ʃlʊxt͡st‘ l lʊnt‘ va͜entʰ;
Und gekränket und getäuscht sitzet sie und schluchzt und weint;
And offended and disappointed sits she and sobs and weeps;
(And she sits there, offended and disappointed, sobbing and weeping,)

fɔn deːɐ̯ 'tʰiːfst‘ən laŋst t͡sɛɐ̯'fla͜eʃtʰ, lɔp‘ kʰa͜en 'naːəndɐ(r) lɛɐ̯'ʃa͜entʰ.
von der tiefsten Angst zerfleischt, ob kein Nahender erscheint.
by the deepest fear lacerated, whether no approacher appears.
(torn apart by the most intense fear, wondering whether someone might not be approaching.)
[*Schubert MS:* **ob kein Nahender sich zeigt** (zɪç t͡sa͜ek‘tʰ, himself shows–*no rhyme*)

'ʃneːglœk‘la͜en, loː 'ʃneːglœk‘la͜en! lɪn den 'lɑ͜oən 'lɔ͜øt‘əst duː,
Schneeglöcklein, o Schneeglöcklein! In den Auen läutest du,
Little snow bell, O little snow bell! In the meadows ring you,
(Little snow bell, little snow bell, you are ringing in the meadows,)

ˈlɔ͡øtˈəstˈ lɪn dem ˈʃtˈɪlən ha͡en, lɔ͡øt di ˈʃvɛstˈɐn liːɐ̯ hɛɐ̯ˈt͡suː!
läutest in dem stillen Hain, läut' die Schwestern ihr herzu!
(you) ring in the quiet grove, ring the sisters to her hither!
(you are ringing in the quiet grove! Call her sisters to come to her!)

ˈroːzə ˈnaːətˈ(ʰ), ˈliːli̯ə ʃvaŋtˈ(ʰ), tʰʊlpˈ lʊntˈ hyaˈt͡sɪntˈə ʃvɛltˈ,
Rose nahet, Lilie schwankt, Tulp' und Hyazinthe schwellt,
Rose approaches, Lily totters, Tulip and Hyacinth swell,
(Rose approaches, Lily totters, Tulip and Hyacinth rise up,)

ˈvɪntˈlɪŋ kʰɔmt daˈheːɐ̯ gəˈraŋkˈtˈ, lʊntˈ narˈt͡sɪs hatˈ zɪç gəˈzɛltʰ.
Windling kommt daher gerankt, und Narziss' hat sich gesellt.
Bindweed comes along crept, and Narcissus has itself joined.
(Bindweed comes creeping along, and Narcissus has joined the group.)

daː deːɐ̯ ˈfryːlɪŋ nuːn lɛɐ̯ˈʃa͡entʰ, lʊnt das ˈfroːə fɛstˈ bəˈgɪntʰ,
Da der Frühling nun erscheint, und das frohe Fest beginnt,
Since the spring now appears, and the happy celebration begins,
(Since Spring has arrived now, and the happy celebration is beginning,)
[*poem:* **Als** (als, when) **der Frühling]**

ziːtˈ leːɐ̯/leːr ˈlalə, diː fɛɐ̯-/fɛrˈla͡entˈ, lʊntˈ fɛɐ̯ˈmɪstˈ za͡en ˈliːpstˈəs kʰɪntˈ.
sieht er alle, die vereint, und vermisst sein liebstes Kind.
sees he all, that (are) united, and misses his dearest child.
(he sees all of the flowers that are united there and misses his dearest child.)

ˈalə ʃikˈtˈ leːɐ̯ ˈzuːxəntˈ fɔrtˈ, lʊm di ˈla͡enə, diː liːm veːɐ̯tʰ.
Alle schickt er suchend fort, um die Eine, die ihm wert.
All sends he searching forth, for the one, which to him dear.
(He sends them all to search for that *one*, who is dear to him.)

ʊntˈ ziː ˈkʰɔmən lan den lɔrtˈ, voː ziː ˈla͡enzaːm zɪç fɛɐ̯ˈt͡seːɐ̯tʰ.
Und sie kommen an den Ort, wo sie einsam sich verzehrt.
And they come to the place, where she in solitude herself consumes.
(And they come to the place where she is wasting away in solitude.)

dɔx lɛs zɪt͡st das ˈliːbə hɛrt͡s ʃtˈʊm lʊntˈ bla͡eç, das ha͡ʊptˈ gəˈbʏkˈtʰ —
Doch es sitzt das liebe Herz stumm und bleich, das Haupt gebückt —
But there sits the dear heart mute and pale, the head bowed —
(But the dear heart is sitting there pale and mute, her head bowed down—)
[*Peters:* **das liebe Kind** (kʰɪntˈ, child)]

ax! deːɐ̯ liːpˈ lʊntˈ ˈzeːnzʊxtˈ ʃmɛrt͡s hat di ˈt͡sɛːɐ̯tˈlɪçə lɛɐ̯ˈdrʏkˈtʰ.
ach! der Lieb' und Sehnsucht Schmerz hat die zärtliche erdrückt.
ah! the love's and longing's pain has the delicate one crushed.
(ah, the pain of love and longing has crushed the delicate creature.)

ˈʃneːglœkˈla͡en, loː ˈʃneːglœkˈla͡en! lɪn den ˈla͡ʊən ˈlɔ͡øtˈəst duː,
Schneeglöcklein, o Schneeglöcklein! In den Auen läutest du,
Little snow bell, O little snow bell! In the meadows ring you,
(Little snow bell, little snow bell, you are ringing in the meadows,)

ˈlɔ͜ø̯tʻəstʻ ɪn dem ˈʃtʻɪlən ha͜en, lɔ͜ø̯tʻ viˈoːla ˈzanftʻə ruː!
läutest in dem stillen Hain, läut' Viola sanfte Ruh!
(you) ring in the quiet grove, ring Violet gentle rest!
(you are ringing in the quiet grove. Ring Violet to a gentle, final rest!)
[*note: there should be no commas before and after "Viola." (an error in Peters)*]

[This poem, like *Vergissmeinnicht*, is subtitled *Blumenballade* ("Flower ballad"). The soft ringing of the "snowbells" is heard in Schubert's introduction, and their theme is a recurring refrain. The through-composed setting is full of delightful touches. It deserves an occasional performance, despite its daunting length (sixteen pages in Peters, fifteen in the *Gesamtausgabe*.]

fɔlˈɛndʊŋ
Vollendung
Fulfillment

Posthumously published in 1970 [composed 1817] (poem by Friedrich von Matthisson)

vɛn ɪç la͜enst das t͜siːl ɛɐ̯ˈrʊŋən ˈhaːbə, ɪn den ˈlɪçtʻgəfɪldən ˈjeːnɐ vɛltʻ,
Wenn ich einst das Ziel errungen habe, in den Lichtgefilden jener Welt,
When I one day the goal reached have, in the light-fields of that world,
(When one day I have reached my goal in the radiant fields of that other world,)

ha͜el, deːɐ̯ ˈtʰrɛːnə dan an ˈma͜enəm ˈgraːbə, diː a͜of ˈhɪngəʃtʻrɔ͜ø̯tʻə ˈroːzən fɛltʰ!
heil, der Träne dann an meinem Grabe, die auf hingestreute Rosen fällt!
hail, to the tear then on my grave, that on scattered roses falls!
(then hail to the tear that falls onto scattered roses on my grave!)

ˈzeːnzʊxt͜sfɔl, mɪtʻ ˈbaŋɐ(r) ˈaːnʊŋsvɔnə, [ˈhoːɐ ˈaːndʊŋsvɔnə]
Sehnsuchtsvoll, mit banger Ahnungswonne, [*poem:* **mit hoher Ahndungswonne**]
Longing-full, with anxious surmisal-bliss, [lofty surmisal (obs.)-bliss]
(Full of longing, with mingled fear and bliss in the anticipation,)

ˈruːɪç, viː deːɐ̯ ˈmoːntʻbəglɛnt͜stʻə ha͜en, ˈlɛçəlntʻ, viː ba͜em ˈniːdɐgaŋ deːɐ̯ ˈzɔnə,
ruhig, wie der mondbeglänzte Hain, lächelnd, wie beim Niedergang der Sonne,
calm, as the moon-beglittered grove, smiling, as at the descent of the sun,
(calm as the grove that glitters in the moonlight, smiling, as if at a sunset,)

har ɪç, ˈgœtʻlɪçə fɔlˈɛndʊŋ, da͜en! a͜el, oː ˈa͜elə mɪç ɛmˈpʰoːɐ̯ t͜suː ˈflyːgəln, voː
harr' ich, göttliche Vollendung, dein! Eil', o eile mich empor zu flügeln, wo
wait I, divine fulfillment, for you! Hasten, O hasten me aloft to wing, where
(I am waiting for you, divine fulfillment! Hasten, oh hasten to wing me aloft where)

zɪç ˈʊntʻɐ miːɐ̯ di ˈvɛltʻən dreːn, voː ɪm ˈleːbənskʰvɛl zɪç ˈpʰalmən
sich unter mir die Welten dreh'n, wo im Lebensquell sich Palmen
themselves below me the worlds turn, where in the life-spring themselves palms
(worlds are spinning below me, where in the fountainhead of life palms)

ˈʃpʻiːgəln, voː diː ˈliːbəndən zɪç ˈviːdɐ zeːn.
spiegeln, wo die Liebenden sich wieder seh'n.
reflect, where the loving ones one another again see.
(are reflected, where loving souls will see one another again.)

['sk'la:fənkʰɛt'ən zɪnt de:ɐ̯/de:r 'le:ɐ̯də 'la͜edən, ǀɔft', ǀax! 'ǀœft'ɐs brɪçt' zi: nu:ɐ̯ de:ɐ̯ tʰo:t'!
[Sklavenketten sind der Erde Leiden, oft, ach! öfters bricht sie nur der Tod!
[slave- chains are the earth's sorrows, oft, ah! often breaks them only the death!
[(Earth's sorrows are the chains of a slave; often, oh, so often only death will break them!)

'blu:mənkʰrɛnt͜sən 'gla͜eçən 'li:rə 'frɔ͜ødən, di: ǀa͜en 'vɛst'hɑ͜ox t͜su: ǀɛnt''blɛt'ɐn dro:tʰ!]
Blumenkränzen gleichen ihre Freuden, die ein Westhauch zu entblättern droht!]
Flower- garlands resemble her joys, which a west-breath to defoliate threatens!]
(Earth's joys are like garlands that the breath of the west wind threatens to strip of petals!)]

[This song, long believed lost, is not in Peters or the *Gesamtausgabe*. It was discovered by Christa Landon in 1968 and published by Bärenreiter in 1970. Schubert set only three of the four verses (the omitted stanza is in brackets, above). The title of the poem is *Die Vollendung*.]

fɔm 'mɪt'la͜edən ma'ri:ɛ
Vom Mitleiden Mariä*
Of Mary's Suffering at the Cross

Posthumously published [composed 1818] (poem by Friedrich von Schlegel)

als ba͜e dem kʰrɔ͜øt͜s ma'ri:a ʃt'ant', ve: 'ly:bɐ ve: ǀi:ɐ̯ hɛrt͜s ǀɛm'p͜fant'
Als bei dem Kreuz Maria stand, Weh über Weh ihr Herz empfand
When by the cross Mary stood, woe upon woe her heart felt
(When Mary stood at the foot of the cross her heart felt sorrow upon sorrow,)

ʊnt' 'ʃmɛrt͜sən 'ly:bɐ 'ʃmɛrt͜sən; das 'gant͜sə 'la͜edən 'kʰrɪsti ʃt'ant' gə'drʊk't'
und Schmerzen über Schmerzen; das ganze Leiden Christi* stand gedruckt
and pains upon pains; the whole suffering of Christ stood printed
(and agony upon agony; the whole suffering of Christ was imprinted)
[**note: in German the genitive of* Christus *is* Christi*, and of* Maria *is* Mariä]

ǀɪn 'li:rəm 'hɛrt͜sən. zi: 'li:rən zo:n mʊs bla͜eç ǀʊnt tʰo:tʰ, ǀʊnt' 'ly:bɐ(r)ǀal
in ihrem Herzen. Sie ihren Sohn muss bleich und tot, und überall
in her heart. She her son must pale and dead, and everywhere
(upon her heart. She has to see her son, deathly pale, and all over)

fɔn 'vʊndən ro:tʰ ǀam 'kʰrɔ͜øt͜sə 'la͜edən 'ze:ən. gə'dɛŋk', vi: 'di:zɐ 'bɪt'rə tʰo:t'
von Wunden rot am Kreuze leiden sehen. Gedenk, wie dieser bitt're Tod
from wounds red on the cross suffer see. Think, how this bitter death
(red with wounds, suffering on the cross. Think how this bitter death)

t͜su: 'hɛrt͜sən ǀi:ɐ̯ mʊst' 'ge:ən. ǀɪn 'kʰrɪsti hɑ͜op't dʊrç ba͜en ǀʊnt' hɪrn,
zu Herzen ihr musst' gehen. In Christi Haupt durch Bein und Hirn,
to heart to her had to go. In Christ's head through bone and brain,
(must have gone to her heart! Into Christ's head, through bone and brain,)

dʊrç 'ǀɑ͜ogən, 'ǀo:rən, dʊrç di ʃt'ɪrn, fi:l 'ʃarfə 'dɔrnən 'ʃta:xən;
durch Augen, Ohren, durch die Stirn', viel scharfe Dornen stachen;
through eyes, ears, through the forehead, many sharp thorns stabbed;
(through eyes, ears, through his forehead, many sharp thorns pierced;)

dem zo:n di 'dɔrnən hɑ͜op't' lʊnt' hɪrn, das hɛrt͜s de:ɐ̯ 'mʊt'ɐ 'bra:xən.
dem Sohn die Dornen Haupt und Hirn, das Herz der Mutter brachen.
for the son the thorns (broke) head and brain, the heart of the mother (they) broke.
(those thorns stabbed the head and brain of her son, and broke the mother's heart.)

[The song, in its noble simplicity and deep compassion, is in the tradition of the finest sacred music, moving, free of sentimentality, and fully worthy of the poignant subject. Peters follows the first published version in F minor; the original key is G minor, as in the *Gesamtausgabe*.]

fɔn 'i:da
Von Ida
About Ida

Posthumously published [composed 1815] (poem by Ludwig Kosegarten)

de:ɐ̯ 'mɔrgən bly:t; de:ɐ̯/de:r 'lɔst'ən gly:t';
Der Morgen blüht; der Osten glüht;
The morning blooms; the east glows;
(The day is dawning, the east begins to glow;)

lɛs 'lɛçəlt' lɑ͜os dem 'dʏnən flo:ɐ̯ di 'zɔnə mat' lʊnt' kʰraŋk' hɛɐ̯'fo:ɐ̯.
es lächelt aus dem dünnen Flor die Sonne matt und krank hervor.
there smiles from the thin gauze the sun dim and sickly out.
(a dim and sickly sun smiles wanly through the thin gauze of the clouds.)

dɛn, lax, ma͜en 'li:p'lɪŋ fli:t(ʰ)! lɑ͜of 'vɛlçɐ flu:ɐ̯/flu:r, lɑ͜of 'vɛsən ʃp'u:ɐ̯,
Denn, ach, mein Liebling flieht! Auf welcher Flur, auf wessen Spur,
For, ah, my darling flees! On which meadow, on of what track,
(For, alas, my darling has left me alone! On what meadow, in trace of what,)

zo: fɛrn fɔn 'li:dən valst du: lɪt͜st', lo: du:, de:ɐ̯ gant͜s ma͜en hɛrt͜s bə'zɪt͜st,
so fern von Iden wallst du itzt, o du, der ganz mein Herz besitzt,
so far from Ida wander you now, O you, who entirely my heart possess,
(are you wandering now, so far from your Ida, O you, who possess my heart entirely,)
[*revised poem:* **so fern von Agnes** ('lagnɛs) **weilst** (va͜elst, linger) **du jetzt** (jɛt͜st', now)]

du: 'li:p'lɪŋ de:ɐ̯ na't͜ʰu:ɐ̯? fɛɐ̯'nɪmst du: lɑ͜ox lɪm 'mɔrgənhɑ͜ox das lax,
du Liebling der Natur? Vernimmst du auch im Morgenhauch das Ach,
you darling of the nature? Perceive you also in the morning breath the sigh
(you darling of Nature? In the sound of the morning breeze do you also hear the sigh)

das 'li:dəns brʊst' lɛnt''lɛçt͜st, das 'ze:nən, drɪn li:ɐ̯ hɛrt͜s t͜sɛɐ̯'lɛçt͜st',
das Idens Brust entächzt, das Sehnen, drin ihr Herz zerlechzt,
that Ida's breast out-moans, the longing, therein her heart languishes away,
(that comes moaning out of Ida's breast, the longing in which her heart is pining away,)
[*note: in the revised poem the name is* **Agnes** *throughout*]

ɪm 'kʰy:lən 'mɔrgənhɑ͜ox? vas 'la:ndəst du:, ['la:nəst]
im kühlen Morgenhauch? Was ahndest du, [*revised poem:* **ahnest** (*ahndest obs.*)]
in the cool morning breath? What surmise you, [surmise]
(can you feel it in the cool morning breeze? Have you any inkling of what I am feeling,)

de:ɐ̯/de:r ˈ|i:dəns ru: |ʊnt‘ ˈ|i:dəns ˈfrɔ͜ødən mɪt‘ zɪç na:m?
der Idens Ruh' und Idens Freuden mit sich nahm?
who Ida's peace and Ida's joys with himself took?
(you who took away with you Ida's peace and all of Ida's joys?)

|ax, ˈ|a:ndəst du: vo:l ˈ|i:dəns gra:m, |ʊnt‘ fle:st‘ fy:ɐ̯/fy:r ˈ|i:dəns ru:?
Ach, ahndest du wohl Idens Gram, und flehst für Idens Ruh'?
Ah, surmise you perhaps Ida's grief, and pray for Ida's peace?
(Ah, do you perhaps surmise Ida's grief, and are you praying for Ida's inner peace?)
[*revised poem:* **Und** (|ʊnt‘, and) **ahnest** (ˈ|a:nəst, surmise) **du**]

o: ˈkʰe:rə |ʊm! kʰe:r |ʊm, kʰe:r |ʊm! t͜su ˈda͜enɐ(r) ˈ|a͜enza:mtʰra͜orəndən!
O kehre um! Kehr' um, kehr' um! zu deiner Einsamtraurenden!
O turn around! Turn back, come back! to your lonely- grieving one!
(Oh, come back! Come back, come back to your lonely, grieving Ida,)
[*revised poem:* **Einsamtrauernden** (ˈ|a͜enza:mtʰra͜oɐndən, lonely-grieving one)]

t͜su: ˈda͜enɐ(r) ˈ|a:ndʊŋʃa͜orəndən! ma͜en ˈ|a͜ent͜sɪgɐ, kʰe:r |ʊm!
zu deiner Ahndungschaurenden! Mein Einziger, kehr' um!
to your foreboding-shivering one! My only one, come back!
(to your Ida who is shivering with foreboding! My only love, come back!)
[ˈ|a:ndʊŋʃa͜oɐndən! t͜su: ˈda͜enɐ(r) ˈ|a:gnɛs |ʊm!]
[*revised poem:* **zu deiner Ahnungschauernden! zu deiner Agnes um!]**
[foreboding-shivering one! to your Agnes back!]
[(come back to your Agnes, who is shivering with foreboding!)]

[The published poem, as available today, is called *Von Agnes*; apparently Schubert's source was an older version, in which the lady's name was Ida, and in which various forms of the word *Ahnung* appear in the obsolete variant *Ahndung* (which now means something quite different). In performing the song that *d* should be omitted, to make the meaning clear. Schubert wrote the following instruction on his manuscript: "If this song is sung by a tenor, then the accompaniment should be transposed down an octave throughout"; but the words are clearly for a female singer.]

fo:ɐ̯ ˈma͜enɐ ˈvi:gə
Vor meiner Wiege
Before My Cradle

Op. 106, No. 3 [1827] (Karl Gottfried von Leitner)

das ˈ|alzo, das |ɪst de:ɐ̯/de:r ˈ|ɛŋə ʃra͜en, da: la:k‘ |ɪç ˈ|a͜est‘əns |als kʰɪnt daˈra͜en,
Das also, das ist der enge Schrein, da lag ich einstens als Kind darein,
That then, that is the narrow chest, there lay I once as child therein,
(That, then, is the narrow chest in which I once lay as a baby,)
[*poem:* **da lag ich in Windeln** (|ɪn ˈvɪndəln, in swaddling bands) **als Kind darein]**

da: la:k‘ |ɪç gəˈbrɛçlɪç, ˈhɪlflo:s |ʊnt‘ ʃt‘ʊm,
da lag ich gebrechlich, hilflos und stumm,
there lay I frail, helpless and mute,
(lay there frail, helpless, and mute,)

ʊnt t͜so:k‘ nu:ɐ̯ t͜sʊm ˈva͜enən di ˈlɪp‘ən kʰrʊm. |ɪç ˈkʰɔnt‘ə nɪçt͜s ˈfasən
und zog nur zum Weinen die Lippen krumm. Ich konnte nichts fassen
and pulled only to the crying the lips crooked. I could nothing grasp
(and twisted my lips only to cry. I could not grasp anything)

mɪt' 'hɛnt'çən tsa:ɐt', lʊnt' va:ɐ dɔx gə'bʊndən na:x 'ʃelmənlartʰ;
mit Händchen zart, und war doch gebunden nach Schelmenart;
with little hands delicate, and was yet bound according to rogue- fashion;
(with my delicate little hands, and yet I was bound like a rogue;)

ɪç 'hat'ə 'fy:sçən, lʊnt' la:k' dɔx vi: la:m, bɪs 'mʊt'ɐ
ich hatte Füsschen, und lag doch wie lahm, bis Mutter
I had little feet, and lay yet as (if) lame, till Mother
(I had little feet, and yet I lay there as if I were lame, till Mother)

lan 'li:rə brʊst' mɪç na:m. dan 'laxt'ə lɪç 'zaogənt tsu: li:ɐ/li:r lɛm'pʰo:ɐ,
an ihre Brust mich nahm. Dann lachte ich saugend zu ihr empor,
to her breast me took. Then laughed I sucking to her up,
(took me to her breast. Then I smiled up at her as I suckled,)

zi: zaŋ mi:ɐ fɔn 'ro:zən lʊnt' 'lɛŋəln fo:ɐ. zi: zaŋ lʊnt' zi: 'vi:k't'ə mɪç
sie sang mir von Rosen und Engeln vor. Sie sang und sie wiegte mich
she sang to me of roses and angels before. She sang and she rocked me
(she sang to me of roses and angels. She sang and rocked me) [*vorsingen* = to sing for someone]
[*poem:* **Engelein** ('lɛŋəlaen, little angels)]

'zɪŋənt' lɪn ru:, lʊnt' 'kʰʏst'ə mi:ɐ 'li:bənt di 'laogən tsu:. zi: 'ʃp'ant'ə
singend in Ruh, und küsste mir liebend die Augen zu. Sie spannte
singing into rest, and kissed me lovingly the eyes closed. She spread
(to sleep, singing; and she closed my eyes lovingly with a kiss. She spread)

laos 'zaedə, ga:ɐ 'dɛmərɪç gry:n, laen 'kʰy:lɪgəs tsɛlt' ho:x 'ly:bɐ mɪç hɪn.
aus Seide, gar dämmerig grün, ein kühliges Zelt hoch über mich hin.
out of silk, very dusky green, a coolish canopy high above me out.
(out a cool canopy of dusky green silk high above me.)

vo: fɪnd ɪç nu:ɐ 'vi:dɐ zɔlç 'fri:t'lɪç gə'ma:x? fi'laeçt', vɛn
Wo find' ich nur wieder solch' friedlich Gemach? Vielleicht, wenn
Where find I only again such peaceful chamber? Perhaps, when
(Where shall I find again such a peaceful chamber? Perhaps when)
[*poem:* **Wann** (van, when) **find' ich nun** (nu:n, now) **wieder**]

das 'gry:nə gra:s maen dax! lo: 'mʊt'ɐ, li:p' 'mʊt'ɐ, blaep' 'laŋə nɔx hi:ɐ!
das grüne Gras mein Dach! O Mutter, lieb Mutter, bleib' lange noch hier!
the green grass my roof! O Mother, dear Mother, stay long still here!
(the green grass is my roof! Oh Mother, dear Mother, stay here a long time yet!)

ve:ɐ 'zɛŋə dan 'tʰrø:st'lɪç fɔn 'lɛŋəln mi:ɐ? ve:ɐ 'kʰʏst'ə
wer sänge dann tröstlich von Engeln mir? Wer küsste
who would sing then comfortingly of angels to me? Who would kiss
(Who would comfort me with songs of angels then? Who would kiss)

mi:ɐ 'li:bənt di 'laogən tsu:, tsʊr 'laŋən, tsʊr 'lɛtst'ən lʊnt 'tʰi:fəst'ən ru:?
mir liebend die Augen zu, zur langen, zur letzten und tiefesten Ruh'?
me lovingly the eyes closed, to the long, to the last and deepest rest?
(my eyes closed so lovingly, for the long, last, and deepest sleep?)

[Schubert touchingly expresses nostalgia for all-embracing mother-love. The shift from minor to major during thoughts of death brings a beautiful serenity and acceptance to the final measures.]

Waldesnacht see *Im Walde* (Schlegel)

'vandrɐs 'naxt'li:t' l̯aens / de:ɐ̯ du: fɔn dem 'hɪməl bɪstʰ
Wandrers Nachtlied I / Der du von dem Himmel bist
Wayfarer's Night Song I / You Who Are From Heaven

Op. 4, No. 3 [1815] (Johann Wolfgang von Goethe)

de:ɐ̯ du: fɔn dem 'hɪməl bɪst', 'laləs laet' lʊnt' 'ʃmɛrtsən ʃt'ɪlst', ['ʃt'ɪləst']
Der du von dem Himmel bist, alles Leid und Schmerzen stillst, [*poem:* **stillest**]
You who from the heaven are, all sorrow and pain [*infinitive*] allay, [allay]
(Sweet peace, you who come to us from heaven, who allay all sorrow and pain,)

de:n, de:ɐ̯ 'dɔp'əlt' 'le:lənt' lɪst, 'dɔp'əlt' mɪt' lɛnt'tsʏk'ʊŋ fʏlst',
den, der doppelt elend ist, doppelt mit Entzückung füllst,
him, who doubly wretched is, doubly with delight fill,
(who fill him who is doubly wretched with doubled delight,)
[*poem:* **mit Erquickung** (lɛɐ̯'kʰvɪk'ʊŋ, refreshment) **füllest** ('fʏl əst', fill)]

ax, lɪç bɪn dɛs 'tʰraebəns 'my:də! vas zɔl lal de:ɐ̯ ʃmɛrts lʊnt' lʊst'?
ach, ich bin des Treibens müde! Was soll all der Schmerz und Lust?
ah, I am of the activity weary! What means all the pain and pleasure?
(ah, I am weary of constant meaningless activity! What is the use of all the pain and pleasure?)

'zy:sɐ 'fri:də, kʰɔm, lax kʰɔm lɪn 'maenə brʊstʰ!
Süsser Friede, komm', ach komm' in meine Brust!
Sweet peace, come, oh come into my breast!

[Goethe, who led a very active life with many interests and many obligations, longs here for the inner peace that has eluded him. These are thoughts that come at night to the tired wayfarer.]

'vandrɐs 'naxt'li:t' tsvae / 'y:bɐ 'lalən 'gɪpfəln lɪst' ru:
Wandrers Nachtlied II / Über allen Gipfeln ist Ruh'
Wayfarer's Night Song II / Above All the Peaks There Is Peace

Op. 96, No. 3 [1822?] (Johann Wolfgang von Goethe)

'y:bɐ(r) 'lalən 'gɪpfəln lɪst' ru:, lɪn 'lalən 'vɪpfəln 'ʃp'y:rəst du: kʰaom 'laenən haox;
Über allen Gipfeln ist Ruh', in allen Wipfeln spürest du kaum einen Hauch;
Above all peaks is peace, in all tree-tops notice you scarcely a breath;
(Above all the mountain peaks there is peace, in all the tree-tops you can scarcely sense a breath;)

di 'fø:glaen 'ʃvaegən lɪm 'valdə. 'vart'ə nu:ɐ̯, 'vart'ə nu:ɐ̯, 'baldə 'ru:əst du: laox.
die Vöglein schweigen im Walde. Warte nur, warte nur, balde ruhest du auch.
the little birds are silent in the forest. Wait just, wait just, soon rest you too.
(the little birds are silent in the forest. Just wait, just wait! Soon you too will find rest.)
[*poem:* **Vögelein** ('fø:gəlaen, little birds); **Warte nur** *once only and with* **!**]

[Goethe wrote those lines on the wall of a mountain chalet when he was thirty-one; he returned there when he was sixty-four, read the words again and wept. In fourteen bars Schubert created a matching masterpiece. The *Gesamtausgabe* includes an optional turn between the first two notes of "*balde*" (both times) that is missing in Peters (on the grounds that it may be a later addition).]

vas bə'le:p't di 'ʃø:nə vɛltʰ?
Was belebt die schöne Welt?
What Animates the Beautiful World?

Posthumously published [composed 1819 or 1820] (poem by Georg Edler von Hofmann)

vas bə'le:p't di 'ʃø:nə vɛltʰ? 'li:bə nu:ɐ̯ fɛɐ̯'ʃaft' li:ɐ̯ 'le:bən,
Was belebt die schöne Welt? Liebe nur verschafft ihr Leben,
What animates the beautiful world? Love only provides for it life,
(What animates this beautiful world? Love alone provides it with life,)

nu:ɐ̯ de:ɐ̯ 'li:bə 'ʃt'ra:lən 'ge:bən 'hɛləs lɪçt dem 'ʃat'ənfɛlt'.
nur der Liebe Strahlen geben helles Licht dem Schattenfeld.
only the love's beams give bright light to the shadow- field.
(only the radiance of love gives bright light in this field of shadows.)

'kʰla:gənt 'tʰrɑ͜oɐt di na'tʰu:ɐ̯, fy:lt' zi: nɪçt de:ɐ̯ 'li:bə 'vɔnə,
Klagend trauert die Natur, fühlt sie nicht der Liebe Wonne,
Lamenting grieves the nature, feels it not the love's bliss,
(Nature grieves, lamenting, if she does not feel the bliss of love.)

'li:bə ɪst de:ɐ̯ 'vɛlt'ən 'zɔnə, zi: ɛɐ̯'kʰvɪk'ət' ha͜en ʊnt' flu:ɐ̯.
Liebe ist der Welten Sonne, sie erquicket Hain und Flur.
Love is the worlds' sun, it revives grove and meadow.
(Love is the sun that lights all the worlds; it revives grove and meadow.)

'angəlaxt' fɔn 'i:rəm blɪkʰ, 'ju:bəln 'le:ɐ̯də, lʊft' ʊnt' 'me:rə —
Angelacht von ihrem Blick, jubeln Erde, Luft und Meere —
At- laughed by its gaze, rejoice earth, air and seas —
(The earth, the air, and the sea rejoice when smiled upon by the eyes of love —)
[*angelacht* = laughed at; in poetry = *angelächelt* = smiled at]

'hɔldə 'li:bə, di:ɐ̯ za͜e 'le:rə, 'ʃp'ɛndəst' 'le:vɪç 'le:bənsglʏkʰ.
holde Liebe, dir sei Ehre, spendest ewig Lebensglück.
lovely love, to you be honor, (you) bestow eternally life- happiness.
(lovely love, we honor you, who eternally bestow the happiness of life.)

[This beautiful, grateful song celebrating happy love can be found in Volume VII of the Peters collection. It was written as incidental music for the "melodrama" *Die Zauberharfe* ("The Magic Harp"), a play with music that failed after eight performances at the Theater an der Wien.]

Wasserflut see *Winterreise*

've:mu:tʰ
Wehmut
Melancholy

Op. 22, No. 2 [1822?] (Matthäus von Collin)

vɛn lɪç dʊrç valt' ʊnt' 'flu:rən ge:, lɛs vɪrt' mi:ɐ̯ dan zo: vo:l ʊnt' ve:
Wenn ich durch Wald und Fluren geh', es wird mir dann so wohl und weh
When I through woods and meadows go, it becomes for me then so happy and sad
(When I walk through the woods and fields I feel both happy and sad)
[*poem:* **Wenn ich auf hohem Berge steh'** (lɑ͜of 'ho:ən 'bɛrgə ʃt'e:, on high mountains stand)]

ɪn lʊnruːfɔlɐ brʊstʰ. zoː voːl, zoː veː, vɛn lɪç ['tʰiːfɐ, 'ʃt'ɪlɐ]
in unruhvoller Brust. So wohl, so weh, wenn ich [*poem:* **in tiefer, stiller Brust]**
in unrest-full breast. So happy, so sad, when I [deep, quiet]
(in my uneasy heart. So happy, so sad, when I)

di lɑo lɪn 'liːrɐ 'ʃøːnhaet' 'fʏlə ʃɑo, lʊnt' lal di 'fryːlɪŋslʊstʰ.
die Au in ihrer Schönheit Fülle schau', und all die Frühlingslust.
the meadow in its beauty's fullness see, and all the spring- pleasure.
(see the meadow in the fullness of its beauty, and all the pleasure of spring.)
[*poem:* **all die grüne** ('gryːnə, green) **Lust]**

dɛn vas lɪm 'vɪndə 'tʰøːnənt' veːt', vas 'lɑofgətʰʏrmt' gɛn 'hɪməl ʃt'eːt',
Denn was im Winde tönend weht, was aufgetürmt gen Himmel steht,
For what in the wind sounding blows, what piled up toward heaven stands,
(For whatever is sounding in the wind, whatever is piled up toward heaven,)
[*poem:* **zum** (tsʊm, to the) **Himmel]**

lʊnt' lɑox deːɐ mɛnʃ zoː hɔlt' fɛɐ'tʰrɑot' [lɛŋ]
und auch der Mensch so hold vertraut [*poem:* **so eng vertraut]**
and also the human being so charmingly familiar [intimately, closely]
(and man himself, so pleasingly familiar)

mɪt' lal deːɐ 'ʃøːnhaet, diː leːɐ ʃɑot', lɛnt''ʃvɪndət'(ʰ), lʊnt' fɛɐ'geːtʰ.
mit all' der Schönheit, die er schaut, entschwindet, und vergeht.
with all the beauty, that he sees, disappears, and perishes.
(with all the beauty that he sees, will disappear and perish.)

[The title of the published poem is *Naturgefühl* ("Feeling for Nature"); Schubert chose to title his marvelously expressive setting *Wehmut* and added the words *Alles vergeht* ("all is transitory").]

veːɐ kʰɑoft' 'liːbəsgœt'ɐ?
Wer kauft Liebesgötter?
Whe Will Buy These Cupids?

Posthumously published [composed 1815] (poem by Johann Wolfgang von Goethe)

fɔn 'lalən 'ʃøːnən 'vaːrən, tsʊm 'mark't'ə 'heːɐgəfaːrən, vɪrt' 'kʰaenə meːɐ bə'haːgən,
Von allen schönen Waren, zum Markte hergefahren, wird keine mehr behagen,
Of all lovely wares, to the market hither brought, will none more please,
(Of all the lovely wares brought here to the market, none will give more pleasure)

lals diː viːɐ/viːr lɔøç gə'tʰraːgə lɑos 'fɛrnən 'lɛndɐn 'brɪŋən! loː 'høːrət', vas viːɐ
als die wir euch getragen aus fernen Ländern bringen! O höret, was wir
than those we to you carried from distant lands bring! O hear, what we
(than these which we bring to you, transported from distant lands! Oh hear what we)

'zɪŋən! lʊnt' zeːt di 'ʃøːnən 'føːgəl, ziː 'ʃt'eːən tsʊm fɛɐ'kʰɑof. tsu'leːɐst' bə'zeːt den
singen! und seht die schönen Vögel, sie stehen zum Verkauf. Zuerst beseht den
sing! and see the lovely birds, they stand to the sale. First look at the
(are singing, and see the lovely birds! They are for sale. First look at the)

ˈgroːsən, den ˈlʊstˈɪgən, den ˈloːzən! leːɐ̯ ˈhʏp͡fət', la͜eçt' lʊnt' ˈmʊnt'ɐ
grossen, den lustigen, den Losen! Er hüpfet, leicht und munter
big one, the merry, the loose! He hops, lightly and cheerfully
(big one, the merry one, the wanton! He hops lightly and cheerfully)

fɔn ba͜om lʊnt' bʊʃ hɛˈrʊnt'ɐ; gla͜eç lɪst' leːɐ̯ ˈviːdɐ ˈdroːbən. viːɐ̯
von Baum und Busch herunter; gleich ist er wieder droben. Wir
from tree and bush down; right away is he again up there. We
(down from a tree or a bush, then right away he is back up there again. We)

ˈvɔlən liːn nɪçt' ˈloːbən. loː zeːt den ˈmʊnt'ɐn ˈfoːgəl! leːɐ̯ ʃt'eːt' hiːɐ̯ t͡sʊm fɛɐ̯ˈkʰa͜of.
wollen ihn nicht loben. O seht den muntern Vogel! Er steht hier zum Verkauf.
want him not to praise. O see the cheerful bird! He stands here to the sale.
(don't need to sing his praises. Just look at the lively bird! He is for sale.)

bəˈtʰraxt'ət' nuːn den ˈkʰla͜enən, leːɐ̯ vɪl bəˈdɛçt'ɪç ˈʃa͜enən, lʊnt dɔx lɪst' leːɐ̯ deːɐ̯ ˈloːzə,
Betrachtet nun den kleinen, er will bedächtig scheinen, und doch ist er der lose,
Consider now the little one, he wants discreet to appear, and yet is he the loose,
(Consider this little one now; he wants to appear discreet; and yet he is a rakish one,)

zoː guːt' lals viː deːɐ̯ ˈgroːsə; leːɐ̯ ˈt͡sa͜egət' ma͜est' lɪm ˈʃt'ɪlən den ˈlalɐbɛst'ən ˈvɪlən.
so gut als wie der grosse; er zeiget meist im stillen den allerbesten Willen.
as well as like the big one; he shows mostly in the quiet the very best will.
(just as much so as the big bird; he shows his very good will mostly in a quiet way.)

deːɐ̯ ˈloːzə ˈkʰla͜enə ˈfoːgəl, leːɐ̯ ʃt'eːt' hiːɐ̯ t͡sʊm fɛɐ̯ˈkʰa͜of. loː zeːt das ˈkʰla͜enə ˈtʰɔ͜øp'çən,
Der lose kleine Vogel, er steht hier zum Verkauf. O! seht das kleine Täubchen,
The loose little bird, he stands here to the sale. O see the little dove,
(This free-and-easy little bird is for sale. Oh, see the little dove,)

das ˈliːbə ˈtʰʊrt'əlva͜ep'çən! di ˈmɛːt'çən zɪnt' zoː ˈt͡siːɐ̯lɪç, fɛɐ̯ˈʃt'ɛndɪç lʊnt' maˈniːɐ̯lɪç;
das liebe Turtelweibchen! Die Mädchen sind so zierlich, verständig und manierlich;
the dear turtledove-female! The girls are so dainty, sensible and mannerly;
(the dear female turtledove! The girl-birds are so dainty, so sensible and mannerly;)

ziː maːk' zɪç ˈgɛrnə ˈpʰʊt͡sən lʊnt' ˈlɔ͜ørə ˈliːbə ˈnʊt͡sən. deːɐ̯ ˈkʰla͜enə ˈt͡saːɐ̯t'ə ˈfoːgəl,
sie mag sich gerne putzen und eure Liebe nutzen. Der kleine zarte Vogel,
she likes herself gladly to dress up and your love to use. The little delicate bird,
(she likes to dress up and to take advantage of your love. This delicate little bird)

leːɐ̯ ʃt'eːt' hiːɐ̯ t͡sʊm fɛɐ̯ˈkʰa͜of. viːɐ̯ ˈvɔlən ziː nɪçt' ˈloːbən, ziː ʃt'eːn t͡suː ˈlalən ˈpʰroːbən.
er steht hier zum Verkauf. Wir wollen sie nicht loben, sie steh'n zu allen Proben.
it stands here to the sale. We want them not to praise, they stand to all tests.
(is for sale. We don't need to sing their praises: they pass all tests. Try them out!)

ziː ˈliːbən zɪç das ˈnɔ͜øə; dɔx ˈlyːbɐ(r) ˈliːrə ˈtʰrɔ͜ø fɛɐ̯ˈlaŋt' nɪçt' briːf lʊnt'
Sie lieben sich das Neue; doch über ihre Treue verlangt nicht Brief und
They love for themselves the new; but about their constancy demand not letter and
(They love anything new; but as for their constancy, do not ask for any guarantee, signed and)

ˈziːgəl; ziː ˈhaːbən ˈlalə ˈflyːgəl. viː ˈlart'ɪç zɪnt di ˈføːgəl, viː ˈra͜et͡sənt' lɪst deːɐ̯ kʰa͜of!
Siegel; sie haben alle Flügel. Wie artig sind die Vögel, wie reizend ist der Kauf!
seal; they have all wings. How pretty are the birds, how charming is the sale!
(sealed; they all have wings, after all. How pretty the birds are, and what a charming sale!)

[The above poem is actually a duet for Papageno and Papagena in Goethe's unfinished sequel to Mozart's *Die Zauberflöte*! Papageno, of course, is a bird-catcher, and both he and his mate are traditionally dressed entirely in feathers. Peters, following the first publication as usual, gives the song in A major; the *Gesamtausgabe* offers C major, the key of Schubert's original manuscript.]

Wer nie sein Brot mit Tränen ass see *Harfenspieler III*

Wer sich er Einsamkeit ergibt see *Harfenspieler I*

ˈviːdɐʃa͜en / hartʻ ǀa͜en ˈfɪʃɐ ǀɑ͜of deːɐ̯ ˈbrʏkʻə / tʰɔm leːntʻ ˈharəntʻ ǀɑ͜of deːɐ̯ ˈbrʏkʻə
Widerschein / Harrt ein Fischer auf der Brücke / Tom lehnt harrend auf der Brücke
Reflection / A Fisherman Waits on the Bridge / Tom, Waiting, Leans against the Bridge

Posthumously published [composed 1819/1820, 1828] (poem by Franz Xaver von Schlechta)

Gesamtausgabe:
hartʻ ǀa͜en ˈfɪʃɐ ǀɑ͜of deːɐ̯ ˈbrʏkʻə,
Harrt ein Fischer auf der Brücke,
Waits a fisherman on the bridge,
(A fisherman is waiting on the bridge)

Peters:
tʰɔm leːntʻ ˈharəntʻ ǀɑ͜of deːɐ̯ ˈbrʏkʻə,
Tom lehnt harrend auf der Brücke,
Tom leans waiting on the bridge,
(Tom is leaning against the bridge, waiting)

di gəˈliːpʻtʻə zɔ͜ømtʰ, ˈʃmɔlənt tʰɑ͜oxtʻ leːɐ̯ ˈza͜enə ˈblɪkʻə ǀɪn den bax ǀʊnt tʰrɔ͜ømtʰ.
die Geliebte säumt, schmollend taucht er seine Blicke in den Bach und träumt.
the beloved delays, sulking plunges he his glances into the brook and dreams.
(for his sweetheart, who is late; sulking, he looks down into the brook and dreams.)

dɔx diː lɑ͜oʃtʻ ǀɪm ˈnaːən ˈfliːdɐ, ǀʊntʻ liːɐ̯ ˈbɪltʻçən ʃtʻraːltʻ jɛt͜stʻ ǀɑ͜os ˈkʰlaːrən
Doch die lauscht im nahen Flieder, und ihr Bildchen strahlt jetzt aus klaren
But she eavesdrops in the nearby lilac, and her little image beams now out of clear
(But she is eavesdropping in the nearby lilacs, and her little image now beams out of the clear)

ˈvɛlən ˈviːdɐ, ˈtʰrɔ͜øɐ niː gəˈmaːltʰ. ǀʊntʻ leːɐ̯ ziːt͜s! ǀʊntʻ leːɐ̯ kʰɛnt di ˈbɛndɐ,
Wellen wieder, treuer nie gemalt. Und er sieht's! Und er kennt die Bänder,
waves back, more faithfully never painted. And he sees it! And he knows the ribbons,
(waves back at him, more faithfully never painted. And he sees it! And he knows those ribbons,)

[*poem* (*without* **Und er sieht's**):
Und der Fischer (deːɐ̯ ˈfɪʃɐ, the fisherman) **kennt die Bänder**
(*also in Schubert at the repeat*)]

kʰɛnt den ˈzyːsən ʃa͜en: ǀʊntʻ leːɐ̯ hɛltʻ zɪç ǀam gəˈlɛndɐ, zɔnst t͜siːt͜s ǀiːn hɪˈna͜en.
kennt den süssen Schein: und er hält sich am Geländer, sonst zieht's ihn hinein.
knows the sweet look: and he holds himself on the railing, else draws it him in.
(knows that sweet look: and he holds onto the railing so that look won't draw him into the water.)

[Schubert paints the scene, the waiting and looking this way and that, the stealthy approach of the girl, the rippling water, the surprise that nearly makes him tumble, the power of the alluring reflection that seems to draw him downwards toward the water. The history of the song is curious: an early version of the poem "with music by Franz Schubert in Vienna" was published in 1820 in the supplement to "Becker's Pocket Book for Sociable Pleasure." The scenario was the same; but the words were different, except for the last two lines. Then, in 1828, Schubert rewrote the song to accommodate a second version of the poem, that had been published in 1824. After Schubert's death, but before his second version was published, Schlechta made further revisions (including a new opening line) which were incorporated in the printed song. When the

Gesamtausgabe appeared in 1895 the editor reverted to the opening line of the poet's second version, but retained other changes made after the composer's death.]

ˈviːdɐzeːn
Wiedersehn
Reunion

Posthoumously published [composed 1825] (poem by August Wilhelm von Schlegel)

deːɐ̯ ˈfryːlɪŋszɔnə ˈhɔldəs ˈlɛçəln ɪstʻ ˈma͜enɐ ˈhɔfnʊŋ ˈmɔrgənroːtʰ;
Der Frühlingssonne holdes Lächeln ist meiner Hoffnung Morgenrot;
The spring- sun's lovely smile is my hope's dawn;
(The lovely smile of the spring sun is the dawn of my hope;)

miːɐ̯ ˈflʏstʻɐtʻ ɪn dɛs ˈvɛstʻəs ˈfɛçəln deːɐ̯ ˈfrɔ͜ødə ˈla͜ezəs ˈla͜ofgəboːtʰ.
mir flüstert in des Westes Fächeln der Freude leises Aufgebot.
to me whispers in the west's fanning the joy's soft proclamation.
(a soft proclamation of joy is being whispered to me in the fanning of the west wind.)

ɪç kʰɔm, ʊntʻ ˈyːbɐ tʰaːl ʊntʻ ˈhyːgəl, oː ˈzyːsə ˈvɔnəgeːbərɪn,
Ich komm', und über Tal und Hügel, o süsse Wonnegeberin,
I come, and over valley and hill, O sweet bliss-giving woman,
(I am coming, and over hill and dale, you sweet giver of bliss,)

ʃveːpʻtʻ, a͜of dɛs ˈliːdəs ˈraʃəm ˈflyːgəl, deːɐ̯ gruːs deːɐ̯ ˈliːbə t͜suː diːɐ̯ hɪn.
schwebt, auf des Liedes raschem Flügel, der Gruss der Liebe zu dir hin.
soars, on the song's quick wing, the greeting of the love to you hence.
(love's greeting is soaring toward you on the quick wings of song.)

deːɐ̯ gruːs deːɐ̯ ˈliːbə fɔn dem ˈtʰrɔ͜øən, deːɐ̯/deːr ˈoːnə ˈgeːgənliːbə ʃvuːɐ̯,
Der Gruss der Liebe von dem Treuen, der ohne Gegenliebe schwur,
The greeting of the love from the faithful one, who without returned-love swore,
(Love's greeting from a faithful lover, who swore, even without the assurance of being loved,)

diːɐ̯/diːr ˈleːvɪç ˈhʊldɪgʊŋ t͜suː ˈva͜eən viː deːɐ̯/deːr ˈalˈvaltʻəndən naˈtʰuːɐ̯;
dir ewig Huldigung zu weihen wie der allwaltenden Natur;
to you eternal homage to consecrate as to the all-governing Nature;
(to consecrate an eternal homage to you and to all-governing Nature;)

deːɐ̯ ʃtʻeːt͜s, viː naːx dem ˈlaŋəlʃtʻɛrnə deːɐ̯ ˈʃɪfɐ(r), ˈla͜enzaːm blɪkʻtʻ ʊntʻ la͜oʃtʰ,
der stets, wie nach dem Angelsterne der Schiffer, einsam blickt und lauscht,
who constantly, as toward the North Star the sailor, alone looks and listens,
(who, in solitude, is constantly looking and listening, as the sailor toward the North Star,)

ɔpʻ nɪçt t͜suː iːm ɪn naxtʻ ʊntʻ ˈfɛrnə dɛs ˈʃtʻɛrnəs kʰlaŋ hɛɐ̯ˈniːdɐ ra͜oʃtʰ.
ob nicht zu ihm in Nacht und Ferne des Sternes Klang hernieder rauscht.
whether not to him in night and distance the star's sound hither-down murmurs.
(to hear whether in the night, from afar, the music of my star will come murmuring down to me.)

ha͜el miːɐ̯/miːr! ɪç ˈlaːtʻmə ˈkʰyːnəs ˈzeːnən, ʊntʻ ˈlaːtʻmɛs baltʻ an ˈda͜enɐ brʊstʰ,
Heil mir! ich atme kühnes Sehnen, und atm' es bald an deiner Brust,
Hail to me! I breathe bold longing, and breathe it soon on your breast,
(Happy me! I breath bold longing, and shall soon be breathing that on your breast,)

ʊnt‘ za͜ok‘ |ɛs |a͜en mɪt 'da͜enən 'tʰøːnən, |ɪm 'pʰʊlsʃlaːk‘ 'naːmənloːzɐ lʊstʰ.
und saug’ es ein mit deinen Tönen, im Pulsschlag namenloser Lust.
and suck it in with your tones, in the pulse-beat of nameless pleasure.
(and drink it in, along with the sound of your voice, to the pulse-beat of inexpressible pleasure.)

duː 'lɛçəlst‘, vɛn ma͜en hɛrt͜s, |ʊm'faŋən fɔn 'da͜enɐ nɛː, dan 'vɪldɐ ʃt‘reːp‘tʰ,
Du lächelst, wenn mein Herz, umfangen von deiner Näh’, dann wilder strebt,
You smile, when my heart, surrounded by your nearness, then more wildly aspires,

ɪn'dɛs das 'zeːlɪgə fɛɐ̯'laŋən deːɐ̯ gyːt‘ |ʊm 'da͜enə 'lɪp‘ə ʃveːp‘tʰ.
indes das selige Verlangen der Güt’ um deine Lippe schwebt.
while the blessed desire of the goodness about your lips hovers.
(while the blessed desire of goodness hovers about your lips.)

duː liːpst‘ mɪç, 'gœt‘lɪç 'hoːəs 'veːzən! duː liːpst‘ mɪç, 'zanft‘əs, 't͜saːɐ̯t‘əs va͜ep‘!
Du liebst mich, göttlich hohes Wesen! Du liebst mich, sanftes, zartes Weib!
You love me, divinely noble creature! You love me, gentle, tender woman!

ɛs gnyːk‘t‘. |ɪç 'fyːlə mɪç gə'neːzən, |ʊnt‘ 'leːbənsfʏl |an zeːl |ʊnt‘ la͜ep‘.
Es gnügt. Ich fühle mich genesen, und Lebensfüll’ an Seel’ und Leib.
It is enough. I feel myself get well, and life- abundance in soul and body.
(That is enough! I feel myself being healed, I feel life’s abundance in my soul and my body.)

na͜en, nɔx mɪt dem gə'ʃɪk‘ t͜suː 'haːdɐn, das ʃnɛl mɪç 'viːdɐ fɔn diːɐ̯ ra͜estʰ,
Nein, noch mit dem Geschick zu hadern, das schnell mich wieder von dir reisst,
No, still with the fate to wrangle, that quickly me again from you tears,
(No, to wrangle with the fate that once again suddenly tears me away from you)

fɛɐ̯'ʃmeːt‘ ma͜en bluːt, das dʊrç di 'laːdɐn mɪt‘ 'ʃt‘ɔlt͜sən, 'la͜eçt‘ən 'vɛlən kʰra͜estʰ.
verschmäht mein Blut, das durch die Adern mit stolzen, leichten Wellen kreist.
disdains my blood, that through the veins with proud, light waves circulates.
(my blood, which circulates through my veins in proud, light waves, disdains.)

[It is spring, and soon the poet will return to his beloved, too happy to deplore the fate that sometimes keeps them apart. Schubert’s manuscript gives the first verse and repeat marks; later, when he made a fair copy of this exquisite song, he added two more of the poem’s four verses.]

'viːgənliːt‘ / 'ʃlaːfə, 'ʃlaːfə, 'hɔldɐ, 'zyːsɐ kʰnaːbə
Wiegenlied / Schlafe, schlafe, holder, süsser Knabe
Cradle Song / Sleep, Sleep, Lovely, Sweet Boy

Op. 98, No. 2 [1816] (author unknown)

'ʃlaːfə, 'ʃlaːfə, 'hɔldɐ, 'zyːsɐ kʰnaːbə, 'la͜ezə viːk‘t dɪç 'da͜enɐ 'mʊt‘ɐ hant‘;
Schlafe, schlafe, holder, süsser Knabe, leise wiegt dich deiner Mutter Hand;
Sleep, sleep, lovely, sweet boy, softly rocks you your mother’s hand;
(Sleep, sleep, lovely, sweet boy; your mother’s hand is softly rocking you;)

'zanft‘ə 'ruːə, 'mɪldə 'laːbə brɪŋt diːɐ̯ 'ʃveːbənt 'diːzəs 'viːgənbant‘.
sanfte Ruhe, milde Labe bringt dir schwebend dieses Wiegenband.
gentle rest, mild comfort brings to you floating this cradle strap.
(this swaying cradle strap will bring you gentle rest and sweet comfort.)

ˈʃlaːfə lɪn dem ˈzyːsən ˈgraːbə, nɔx bəˈʃʏtst dɪç ˈdaenɐ ˈmʊtʻɐ(r) larm;
Schlafe in dem süssen Grabe, noch beschützt dich deiner Mutter Arm;
Sleep in the sweet grave, still protects you your mother's arm;
(Sleep in this sweet grave; your mother's arm is still protecting you;)

ˈalə ˈvʏnʃə, ˈlalə ˈhaːbə fastʻ ziː ˈliːbəntʻ, ˈlalə ˈliːbəvarm.
alle Wünsche, alle Habe fasst sie liebend, alle liebewarm.
all wishes, all possession grasps she lovingly, all love-warm.
(all her wishes, all that she possesses she holds lovingly, all with the warmth of love.)

ˈʃlaːfə lɪn deːɐ ˈflaomən ˈʃoːsə, nɔx lʊmˈtʰøːnt dɪç ˈlaotʻɐ ˈliːbəstʰoːn;
Schlafe in der Flaumen Schosse, noch umtönt dich lauter Liebeston;
Sleep in the down's womb, still around-sounds you pure love- tone;
(Sleep in your downy feather-bed; the tones of pure love are still surrounding you;)

ˈaenə ˈliːliə, ˈlaenə ˈroːzə, naːx dem ˈʃlaːfə veːɐtʻ ziː diːɐ tsʊm loːn.
eine Lilie, eine Rose, nach dem Schlafe werd' sie dir zum Lohn.
a lily, a rose, after the sleep will it (be) for you as the reward.
(a lily, a rose—after your sleep that will be your reward.)

[*grammatical note: the rose and the lily collectively get a verb in the singular.*]

[Schubert ascribed the authorship to Matthias Claudius, but the poem does not appear among his published works. The song is one of the loveliest of all lullabies. Richard Strauss confessed to stealing the opening phrase for a trio of nymphs—a musical gem—in his *Ariadne auf Naxos*.]

ˈviːgənliːtʻ / ˈʃlʊmrə zanftʰ
Wiegenlied / Schlumm're sanft
Cradle Song / Slumber Softly

Posthumously published [composed 1815] (poem by Theodor Körner)

ˈʃlʊmrə zanftʻ! nɔx lan dem ˈmʊtʻɐhɛrtsən fyːlst duː nɪçt dɛs ˈleːbəns kʰvaːl lʊntʻ
Schlumm're sanft! Noch an dem Mutterherzen fühlst du nicht des Lebens Qual und
Slumber softly! Still at the mother-heart feel you not the life's torment and
(Slumber softly! Still at your mother's heart, you do not feel life's torment and)

lʊst; ˈdaenə ˈtʰrɔømə ˈkʰɛnən ˈkʰaenə ˈʃmɛrtsən, ˈdaenə vɛltʻ lɪst ˈdaenɐ ˈmʊtʻɐ brʊstʰ.
Lust; deine Träume kennen keine Schmerzen, deine Welt ist deiner Mutter Brust.
pleasure; your dreams know no pains, your world is your mother's breast.

ax! viː zyːs tʰrɔømtʻ man di ˈfryːən ˈʃtʻʊndən, voː man fɔn deːɐ ˈmʊtʻɐliːbə leːpʻtʻ;
Ach! wie süss träumt man die frühen Stunden, wo man von der Mutterliebe lebt;
Ah! how sweetly dreams one the early hours, when one from the mother-love lives;
(Ah, how sweetly one dreams in the early hours of life, when one lives from mother-love;)

di lɛɐ-/ɛrˈlɪnərʊŋ lɪstʻ miːɐ fɛɐˈʃvʊndən, ˈlaːnʊŋ blaepʻtʻ lɛs nuːɐ, di
die Erinnerung ist mir verschwunden, Ahnung bleibt es nur, die
the memory has for me vanished, surmisal remains it only, which
(the memory of that time has vanished for me, all that remains is a surmisal that)

mɪç dʊrçˈbeːpʻtʰ. ˈdraemaːl darf deːɐ mɛnʃ zoː zyːs lɛɐˈvarmən, ˈdraemaːl lɪsts
mich durchbebt. Dreimal darf der Mensch so süss erwarmen, dreimal ist's
me through-trembles. Three times may the human so sweetly be warmed, three times is it
(trembles through me. Three times man is allowed to be so sweetly warmed, three times it is)

dem ˈglʏkˈlɪçən lɛɐ̯ˈlɑo̯pˈt, das leːɐ̯/leːr lɪn deːɐ̯ ˈliːbə ˈgœtˈɐ(r)larmən
dem Glücklichen erlaubt, dass er in der Liebe Götterarmen
to the fortunate one permitted, that he in the love's divine arms
(granted to fortunate man, so that he, in the divine arms of love,)

an dɛs ˈleːbəns ˈhøːrə ˈdɔ̯øtˈʊŋ glɑo̯pˈtʰ. ˈliːbə giːpˈtˈ liːm ˈliːrən ˈleːɐ̯stˈən ˈzeːgən,
an des Lebens höh're Deutung glaubt. Liebe gibt ihm ihren ersten Segen,
in the life's higher meaning believes. Love gives him her first blessing,
(believes in life's higher meaning. Love gives him her first blessing,)

lʊnt deːɐ̯ ˈzɔ̯økˈlɪŋ blyːtˈ lɪn frɔ̯øtˈ lʊntˈ lʊstˈ, ˈlaləs laxt dem ˈfrɪʃən blɪkˈ lɛntˈgeːgən;
und der Säugling blüht in Freud' und Lust, alles lacht dem frischen Blick entgegen;
and the infant blooms in joy and pleasure, all smiles to the fresh gaze toward;
(and the infant blossoms in joy and pleasure, everything greets his fresh gaze with a smile;)

ˈliːbə hɛltˈ liːn lan deːɐ̯ ˈmʊtˈɐbrʊstʰ. vɛn zɪç dan deːɐ̯ ˈʃøːnə ˈhɪməl ˈtʰryːpˈtˈə, lʊntˈ
liebe hält ihn an der Mutterbrust. Wenn sich dann der schöne Himmel trübte, und
love holds him at the mother-breast. When itself then the fair sky darkens, and
(love holds him at his mother's breast. Then, when the fair sky darkens, and)

lɛs vœlkˈtˈ zɪç nuːn dɛs ˈjʏŋlɪŋs lɑo̯f: daː, t͡sʊm ˈt͡svae̯tˈən maːl,
es wölkt sich nun des Jünglings Lauf: da, zum zweiten Mal,
it clouds itself now the youth's path: then, for the second time,
(the pathway of the young man becomes overcast: then for the second time)

nɪmtˈ lals gəˈliːpˈtˈə liːn di liːpˈ lɪn ˈliːrə ˈlarmə lɑo̯f. dɔx lɪm ˈʃtˈʊrmə
nimmt als Geliebte ihn die Lieb' in ihre Arme auf. Doch im Sturme
takes as beloved him the love into her arms up. But in the storm
(love lifts him up into her arms as her beloved. But in a storm)

brɪçt deːɐ̯ ˈblyːtˈənʃtˈɛŋəl, lʊntˈ lɪm ˈʃtˈʊrmə brɪçt dɛs ˈmɛnʃən hɛrt͡s: daː
bricht der Blütenstengel, und im Sturme bricht des Menschen Herz: da
breaks the blossom-stem, and in the storm breaks the human heart: then
(the stem of a blossom may break, and in a storm the human heart will one day break: then)

lɛɐ̯ˈʃae̯nt di liːpˈ lals ˈtʰoːtˈənlɛŋəl, lʊntˈ ziː tʰrɛːkˈtˈ liːn ˈjuːbəlntˈ ˈhɪməlvɛrt͡s.
erscheint die Lieb' als Todesengel, und sie trägt ihn jubelnd himmelwärts.
appears the love as death-angel, and she bears him rejoicing heavenward.
(love will appear as the angel of death, and she will bear him, rejoicing, heavenward.)

[This song is not really a lullaby at all, but rather a contemplation of love as it is experienced at three crucial stages in life: by the baby, by the young man, and by the soul at the hour of death.]

ˈviːgənliːtˈ / viː zɪç deːɐ̯ ˈlɔ̯økˈlae̯n ˈkʰɪntˈlɪçɐ ˈhɪməl
Wiegenlied / Wie sich der Äuglein kindlicher Himmel
Cradle Song / How the Little Eyes' Childlike Heaven

Op. 105, No. 2 [1826?] (Johann Gabriel Seidl)

viː zɪç deːɐ̯/deːr ˈlɔ̯økˈlae̯n ˈkʰɪntˈlɪçɐ ˈhɪməl, ˈʃlʊmɐbəlastˈətˈ ˈlɛsɪç
Wie sich der Äuglein kindlicher Himmel, Schlummerbelastet, lässig
How themselves the little eyes' childlike heaven, slumber- laden, lazily
(How the childlike heaven of those little eyes, heavy with sleep, lazily)

fɛɐ̯ˈʃliːstʰ! ˈʃliːsə ziː la͜enstʻ zoː, lɔkʻt dɪç di ˈleːɐ̯də: ˈdrɪnən lɪstʻ ˈhɪməl, ˈla͜osən
verschliesst! Schliesse sie einst so, lockt dich die Erde: drinnen ist Himmel, aussen
closes! Close them one day so, lures you the earth: inside is heaven, outside
(closes! If the earth lures you one day, then close them like that; inside is heaven, outside)

lɪstʻ lʊstʰ! viː diːɐ̯ zoː ˈʃlaːfroːtʻ ˈglyːət di ˈvaŋə! ˈroːzən la͜os ˈleːdən ˈha͜oxtʻən ziː lan:
ist Lust! Wie dir so schlafrot glühet die Wange! Rosen aus Eden hauchten sie an:
is pleasure! How for you so sleep- red glows the cheek! Roses from Eden breathed it at:
(is pleasure! How your cheeks are glowing, red with sleep! Roses from Eden breathed on them:)

ˈroːzən di ˈvaŋən, ˈhɪməl di ˈla͜ogən, ˈha͜etʻərɐ ˈmɔrgən, ˈhɪmlɪʃɐ tʰaːkʻ!
Rosen die Wangen, Himmel die Augen, heiterer Morgen, himmlischer Tag!
roses the cheeks, heaven the eyes, serene morning, heavenly day!
(your cheeks are roses, your eyes are heaven, a serene morning promises a heavenly day!)

viː dɛs gəˈlɔkʻəs ˈgɔldɪgə ˈvalʊŋ ˈkʰyːlət deːɐ̯ ˈʃlɛːfə ˈglyːəndən za͜om!
Wie des Gelockes goldige Wallung kühlet der Schläfe glühenden Saum!
How the curl's golden undulation cools the temple's glowing edge!
(How the golden undulation of your curls cools the edge of your glowing temples!)

ʃøːn lɪst das ˈgɔltʻhaːɐ̯, ˈʃøːnɐ deːɐ̯ kʰrant͜s dra͜of: tʰrɔ͜ʏm duː fɔm ˈlɔrbeːɐ̯,
Schön ist das Goldhaar, schöner der Kranz drauf: träum' du vom Lorbeer,
Beautiful is the golden hair, more beautiful the wreath on it: dream you of the laurel,
(Golden hair is beautiful; more beautiful still is a wreath of achievement on it: dream of laurel,)

bɪs leːɐ̯ diːɐ̯ blyːtʰ. ˈliːpʻlɪçəs ˈmʏntʻçən, ˈlɛŋəl lʊmˈveːn dɪç: ˈdrɪnən di ˈlʊnʃʊltʻ,
bis er dir blüht. Liebliches Mündchen, Engel umweh'n dich: drinnen die Unschuld,
till it for you blooms. Lovely little mouth, angels about-waft you: inside the innocence,
(till it blooms for you. Lovely little mouth, angels hover about you: inside is innocence,)

ˈdrɪnən di liːpʻ; ˈvaːrə ziː, ˈkʰɪntʻçən, ˈvaːrə ziː ˈtʰrɔ͜ʏlɪç: ˈlɪpʻən zɪntʻ ˈroːzən,
drinnen die Lieb'; wahre sie, Kindchen, wahre sie treulich: Lippen sind Rosen,
inside the love; keep them, little child, keep them faithfully: lips are roses,
(inside is love; keep them, little child, keep that love and that innocence faithfully: lips are roses,)

ˈlɪpʻən zɪntʻ gluːtʰ. viː diːɐ̯/diːr la͜en ˈlɛŋəl ˈfaltʻət di ˈhɛntʻçən, ˈfaltʻə ziː la͜enstʻ zoː,
Lippen sind Glut. Wie dir ein Engel faltet die Händchen, falte sie einst so,
lips are fire. As for you an angel folds the little hands, fold them one day thus,
(lips are fire. As an angel has folded your little hands for you, fold them like that one day,)

geːst duː t͜sʊr ruː; ʃøːn zɪnt di ˈtʰrɔ͜ʏmə, vɛn man gəˈbeːtʻətʰ:
gehst du zur Ruh; schön sind die Träume, wenn man gebetet:
go you to the rest; beautiful are the dreams, if one prays:
(when you go to your rest; dreams are beautiful if you have prayed;)

ʊnt das lɛɐ̯ˈvaxən loːntʻ mɪt dem tʰra͜om.
und das Erwachen lohnt mit dem Traum.
and the awakening rewards with the dream.
(and your awakening will reward you along with the dream.)

[This lullaby is considered by some to be dangerously soothing: no singer—except the mother at the cradle—wants to lull an audience to sleep; but the music is exquisite and there are subtle variations in each of the verses, for instance the hint of danger at "outside is pleasure" (worldly temptation), and at "lips are fire." The song was published on the day of Schubert's funeral.]

vi: 'ʊlfru fɪʃtʰ
Wie Ulfru fischt
How Ulfru Fishes

Op. 21, No. 3 [1817] (Johann Mayrhofer)

de:ɐ̯/de:r 'laŋəl t͡sʊk't, di 'ru:t'ə be:p't, dɔx la͜eçt' fɛ:ɐ̯t' zi: hɛ'ra͜os.
Der Angel zuckt, die Rute bebt, doch leicht fährt sie heraus.
The line jerks, the rod quivers, but easily goes it out.
(The fishing line jerks, the rod quivers, but it comes up easily, empty.)

i:ɐ̯/i:r 'la͜egənzɪŋgən 'nɪksən ge:p't dem 'fɪʃɐ 'kʰa͜enən ʃma͜os!
Ihr eigensinn'gen Nixen gebt dem Fischer keinen Schmaus!
You self-willed water-sprites give to the fisherman no feast!
(You capricious water-sprites don't give the fisherman any feast!)

vas 'frɔmət' li:m za͜en 'kʰlu:gɐ zɪn, di 'fɪʃə 'ba͜oməln 'ʃp'ɔt'ənt' hɪn —
Was frommet ihm sein kluger Sinn, die Fische baumeln spottend hin —
What is of use to him his clever mind, the fish dangle mockingly away —
(What use to him is his clever mind, the fish—so to speak—dangle tantalizingly out of reach;)
[*poem:* **die Fischlein** ('fɪʃla͜en, little fish) **baumeln**]

e:ɐ̯ ʃt'e:t' lam 'lu:fɐ 'fɛst'gəbant', kʰan nɪçt' lɪns 'vasɐ(r), li:n hɛlt das lant'.
er steht am Ufer festgebannt, kann nicht ins Wasser, ihn hält das Land.
he stands on the bank rooted to the spot, can not into the water, him holds the land.
(he stands on the bank as if rooted to the spot, can't go into the water; dry land holds him fast.)

di 'glat'ə 'flɛçə 'kʰrɔ͜øzəlt' zɪç, fɔm 'ʃʊp'ənfɔlk' bə've:k'tʰ,
Die glatte Fläche kräuselt sich, vom Schuppenvolk bewegt,
The smooth surface ruffles itself, by the scale- folk stirred,
(The smooth surface is ruffled, stirred by the scaly folk)

das 'za͜enə 'gli:dɐ 'vɔnɪk'lɪç lɪn 'zɪçɐn 'flu:t'ən re:k'tʰ.
das seine Glieder wonniglich in sichern Fluten regt.
that its limbs blissfully in safe waters moves.
(that blissfully exercise fins and tails in the safety of the water.)

fo'rɛlən 't͡sap'əln hɪn lʊnt' he:ɐ̯, dɔx bla͜ep't dɛs 'fɪʃɐs 'laŋəl le:ɐ̯.
Forellen zappeln hin und her, doch bleibt des Fischers Angel leer.
Trout wriggle that way and this, but remains the fisherman's hook empty.
(Trout are darting this way and that, but the fisherman's hook remains empty.)

zi: 'fy:lən, vas di 'fra͜eha͜et' lɪstʰ, 'frʊxt'lo:s lɪst' 'fɪʃɐs 'laltə lɪstʰ.
Sie fühlen, was die Freiheit ist, fruchtlos ist Fischers alte List.
They feel, what the freedom is, fruitless is fisherman's old cumming.
(They feel what freedom is; the ancient cunning of fishermen is fruitless.)

di 'le:ɐ̯də lɪst' gə'valt'ɪç ʃø:n, dɔx 'zɪçɐ(r) lɪst' zi: nɪçtʰ!
Die Erde ist gewaltig schön, doch sicher ist sie nicht!
The earth is powerfully beautiful, but safe is it not!
(The earth is immensely beautiful — but *safe* it is *not*!)

ɛs 'zɛndən 'ʃt'ʏrmə 'la͜ezəshøːn; deːɐ̯ 'haːgəl lʊnt deːɐ̯ frɔst t͜sɛɐ̯'brɪçt'
Es senden Stürme Eiseshöh'n; der Hagel und der Frost zerbricht
There send storms [obj.] ice-heights [subj.]; the hail and the frost smash
(Icy peaks send down storms; hail and frost destroy)

mɪt' 'la͜enəm 'ʃlaːgə, 'la͜enəm drʊk', das 'gɔldnə kʰɔrn, deːɐ̯ 'roːzən ʃmʊkʰ —
mit einem Schlage, einem Druck, das gold'ne Korn, der Rosen Schmuck —
with one blow, one squeeze, the golden grain, the roses' finery —
(at one stroke, with one blow, the golden grain, the delicate beauty of the roses —)

den 'fɪʃla͜en 'lʊnt'ɐm 'va͜eçən dax, kʰa͜en ʃt'ʊrm fɔlk't' 'liːnən fɔm 'landə naːx.
den Fischlein unterm weichen Dach, kein Sturm folgt ihnen vom Lande nach.
for the little fishes under the soft roof, no storm follows them from the land after.
(but no storm from the land pursues the little fishes that are under their soft roof of water.)
[*poem:* **unters weiche Dach** ('lʊntɐs 'va͜eçə dax, *as far as* under the soft roof)]

[Schubert dedicated this catchy, vigorous song with its many kaleidoscopic modulations to the poet, his friend and sometime roommate. It was published along with two others as "Three Fishing Songs...for Bass Voice." Peters prints the vocal part in the treble cleff. The words seem light-hearted; but there may be a political message: Mayrhofer longed to feel "what freedom is."]

vɪl'kʰɔmən lʊnt' 'lap'ʃiːt'
Willkommen und Abschied
Hail and Farewell

Op. 56, No. 1 [1822] (Johann Wolfgang von Goethe)

ɛs ʃluːk' ma͜en hɛrt͜s, gə'ʃvɪnt t͜suː pf͜eːɐ̯də! lɛs vaːɐ̯ gə'tʰaːn, fast' leː gə'daxtʰ;
Es schlug mein Herz, geschwind zu Pferde! Es war getan, fast eh' gedacht;
There beat my heart, quickly to horse! It was done, almost before thought;
(My heart was beating, quick, to horse! No sooner thought than done.)

deːɐ̯/deːr 'laːbənt' 'viːk't'ə ʃoːn di 'leːɐ̯də, lʊnt' lan den 'bɛrgən hɪŋ di naxtʰ;
der Abend wiegte schon die Erde, und an den Bergen hing die Nacht;
the evening lulled already the earth, and on the mountains hung the night;
(Evening had already lulled the earth, and night hung on the mountains;)

ʃoːn ʃt'ant' lɪm 'neːbəlkʰla͜et di 'la͜eçə, la͜en 'la͜ofgətʰʏrmt'ə 'riːzə, daː,
schon stand im Nebelkleid die Eiche, ein aufgetürmte Riese, da,
already stood in the mist-dress the oak, a towering giant, there,
(the oak stood there, already clad in mist, a looming giant,)

voː 'fɪnst'ɐnɪs la͜os dem gə'ʃt'rɔ͜øçə mɪt' 'hʊndɐt' 'ʃvart͜sən 'la͜ogən zaː.
wo Finsternis aus dem Gesträuche mit hundert schwarzen Augen sah.
where darkness out of the bushes with hundred black eyes looked.
(where darkness peered out of the bushes with a hundred pitch-black eyes.)

deːɐ̯ moːnt' fɔn 'la͜enəm 'vɔlk'ənhyːgəl zaː 'kʰlɛːk'lɪç la͜os dem dʊft' hɛɐ̯'foːɐ̯,
Der Mond von einem Wolkenhügel sah kläglich aus dem Duft hervor,
The moon from a cloud- hill looked dolefully out of the vapor out,
(From a hill of clouds the moon gazed out dolefully through the mist,)

di ˈvɪndə ˈʃvaŋən ˈla͜ezə ˈflyːgəl, ǀʊmˈza͜ost‘ən ˈʃa͜oɐlɪç ma͜en loːɐ̯;
die Winde schwangen leise Flügel, umsausten schauerlich mein Ohr;
the winds swung soft wings, about-whistled horridly my ear;
(the winds softly flapped their wings and whistled horridly about my ears;)

di naxt‘ ʃuːf ˈtʰa͜ozənt‘ ˈǀʊngəhɔ͜øɐ; dɔx frɪʃ ǀʊnt‘ ˈfrøːlɪç vaːɐ̯ ma͜en muːtʰ;
die Nacht schuf tausend Ungeheuer; doch frisch und fröhlich war mein Mut;
the night created thousand monsters; but fresh and happy was my mood:
(the night created a thousand monsters; but my mood was fresh and happy;)

ɪn ˈma͜enən ˈlaːdɐn ˈvɛlçəs ˈfɔ͜øɐ! ǀɪn ˈma͜enəm ˈhɛrt͜sən ˈvɛlçə gluːtʰ!
in meinen Adern welches Feuer! in meinem Herzen welche Glut!
in my veins what fire! in my heart what ardor!
(what a fire was in my veins, what ardor in my heart!)

dɪç zaː ǀɪç, ǀʊnt di ˈmɪldə ˈfrɔ͜ødə flɔs fɔn dem ˈzyːsən blɪk‘ ǀa͜of mɪç;
Dich sah ich, und die milde Freude floss von dem süssen Blick auf mich;
You saw I, and the gentle joy flowed from the sweet glance onto me;
(I saw you, and a gentle joy flowed to me from your sweet gaze;)

gant͜s vaːɐ̯ ma͜en hɛrt͜s ǀan ˈda͜enɐ ˈza͜et‘ə ǀʊnt‘ ˈjeːdɐ(r) ˈǀaːt‘əmt͜suːk‘ fyːɐ̯ dɪç.
ganz war mein Herz an deiner Seite und jeder Atemzug für dich.
completely was my heart at your side and every breath for you.
(my whole heart was at your side, and my every breath was for you.)

a͜en ˈroːzənfarbnəs ˈfryːlɪŋsvɛt‘ɐ ǀʊmˈgaːp‘ das ˈliːp‘lɪçə gəˈzɪçtʰ,
Ein rosenfarb'nes Frühlingswetter umgab das liebliche Gesicht,
A rose- colored spring- weather surrounded the lovely face,
(An atmosphere of rose-colored springtime framed your lovely face,)

ʊnt ˈt͜sɛːɐ̯t‘lɪçkʰa͜et‘ fyːɐ̯ mɪç — ǀiːɐ̯ ˈgœt‘ɐ! ǀɪç hɔft‘ ǀɛs, ǀɪç fɛɐ̯ˈdiːnt‘ ǀɛs nɪçtʰ!
und Zärtlichkeit für mich — ihr Götter! ich hofft' es, ich verdient' es nicht!
and tenderness for me — ye gods! I hoped it, I deserved it not!
(and tenderness for me — ye gods! I had hoped for this, but I never felt that I deserved it!)

dɔx ǀax! ʃoːn mɪt deːɐ̯ ˈmɔrgənzɔnə fɛɐ̯-/fɛrˈlɛŋt deːɐ̯/deːr ˈǀap‘ʃiːt‘ miːɐ̯ das hɛrt͜s:
Doch ach! schon mit der Morgensonne verengt der Abschied mir das Herz:
But ah! already with the morning sun constricts the farewell to me the heart:
(But alas, already with the morning sun farewell constricts my heart:)

ɪn ˈda͜enən ˈkʰʏsən ˈvɛlçə ˈvɔnə! ǀɪn ˈda͜enəm ˈǀa͜ogə ˈvɛlçɐ ʃmɛrt͜s!
in deinen Küssen welche Wonne! in deinem Auge welcher Schmerz!
in your kisses what bliss! in your eye what pain!
(in your kisses what bliss, in your eyes what pain!)

ɪç gɪŋ, duː ʃt‘ant͜st‘ ǀʊnt‘ zaːst t͜sʊr ˈleːɐ̯dən, ǀʊnt‘ zaːst‘ miːɐ̯ naːx mɪt‘ ˈnasəm blɪkʰ:
Ich ging, du stand'st und sahst zur Erden, und sahst mir nach mit nassem Blick:
I went, you stood and looked at the earth, and looked me after with moist gaze:
(I left, you were standing there, downcast, and you looked after me with tears in your eyes:)

ʊnt dɔx, vɛlç glʏk‘ gəˈliːp‘t t͜suː ˈveːɐ̯dən! ǀʊnt‘ ˈliːbən, ˈgœt‘ɐ, vɛlç ǀa͜en glʏkʰ!
und doch, welch Glück geliebt zu werden! und lieben, Götter, welch ein Glück!
and yet, what happiness loved to be! and to love, gods, what a happiness!
(and yet, what happiness to be loved! And, ye gods, what happiness to love!)

[Schubert's exciting song captures the lover's impetuosity magnificently. Goethe was a student in Strasbourg, wildly in love with a pastor's daughter thirty miles to the north, when he wrote the poem. Schubert's first version was in D major. Because of the taxing *tessitura* leading to the high notes, he transposed it to C major for publication. The *Gesamtausgabe* gives both versions.]

'vɪnt'ɐliːt'
Winterlied
Winter Song

Posthumously published [composed 1816] (poem by Ludwig Hölty)

'kʰa͜enə 'bluːmən blyːn; nuːɐ̯ das 'vɪnt'ɐgryːn blɪk't dʊrç 'zɪlbɐhʏlən;
Keine Blumen blüh'n; nur das Wintergrün blickt durch Silberhüllen;
No flowers bloom; only the wintergreen looks through silver-covers;
(No flowers are blooming; only the wintergreen peeks out through its covering of silvery ice;)

nuːɐ̯ das 'fɛnst'ɐ 'fʏlən 'bluːmən roːt' lʊnt' va͜es, 'la͜ofgəblyːt' la͜os la͜es. ['blyːmçən]
nur das Fenster füllen Blumen rot und weiss, aufgeblüht aus Eis. [*poem:* **Blümchen]**
only the window fill flowers red and white, up-bloomed out of ice. [little flowers]
(only red and white flowers, blossoming up out of ice, fill the windowpanes.)

ax! kʰa͜en 'foːgəlzaŋ tʰøːnt' mɪt' 'froːəm kʰlaŋ; nuːɐ̯ di 'vɪnt'ɐva͜ezə
Ach! kein Vogelsang tönt mit frohem Klang; nur die Winterweise
Ah! no birdsong sounds with happy tone; only the winter-melody
(Ah, no birdsong rings out with happy tones; only the wintry melody)

'jeːnɐ 'kʰla͜enən 'ma͜ezə, diː lam 'fɛnst'ɐ ʃvɪrt', lʊnt' lʊm 'fʊt'ɐ gɪrtʰ.
jener kleinen Meise, die am Fenster schwirrt, und um Futter girrt.
of that little titmouse, who at the window whirs, and for feed coos.
(of that little titmouse, who flutters about at the window and chirps for food.)

'mɪnə fliːt den ha͜en, voː di 'føgəla͜en zɔnst' lɪm 'gryːnən 'ʃat'ən
Minne flieht den Hain, wo die Vögelein sonst im grünen Schatten
Romantic love flees the grove, where the little birds formerly in the green shadows
(Romantic love flees the grove, where in the green shadows little birds formerly)

'iːrə 'nɛst'ɐ 'hat'ən; mɪnə fliːt den ha͜en, kʰeːɐ̯t' lɪns 't͜sɪmɐ(r) la͜en.
ihre Nester hatten; Minne flieht den Hain, kehrt ins Zimmer ein.
their nests built; love flees the grove, turns into the room into.
(built their nests; love flees the grove and takes up lodging in this room.)
[*einkehren* = to stop at (an inn, etc.), enter]

'kʰalt'ɐ 'januaːɐ̯, hiːɐ̯ veːɐ̯d ɪç fyːɐ̯'vaːɐ̯/-vaːr 'lʊnt'ɐ 'mɪnəʃp'iːlən
Kalter Januar, hier werd' ich fürwahr unter Minnespielen
Cold January, here shall I truly among love- play
(Cold January, here in the midst of love-play I shall truly)

'da͜enən frɔst' nɪçt' 'fyːlən! 'valt'ə 'lɪmɐdaːɐ̯, 'kʰalt'ɐ 'januaːɐ̯!
deinen Frost nicht fühlen! Walte immerdar, kalter Januar!
your frost not feel! Reign forever, cold January!
(not feel your frost! May you reign forever, cold January!)

[At first glance the music looks like a children's ditty; but the song turns out to be strangely haunting. With *Frühlingslied* and *Erntelied* this song could make a mini-cycle of the seasons.]

ˈvɪntʻɐraezə

Winterreise

Winter Journey

Song Cycle, Op. 89 [1827] (Wilhelm Müller)

1.

ˈguːtʻə naxtʰ

Gute Nacht

Good Night

fremtʻ bɪn lɪç ˈlaengətsoːgən, frɛmt tsiː lɪç ˈviːdɐ(r) laos.
Fremd bin ich eingezogen, fremd zieh' ich wieder aus.
Foreign am I moved in, foreign move I again out.
(I came as a stranger, I leave as a stranger.)

deːɐ̯ mae vaːɐ̯ miːɐ̯ gəˈvoːgən mɪtʻ ˈmançəm ˈbluːmənʃtʻraos.
Der Mai war mir gewogen mit manchem Blumenstrauss.
The May was toward me well-disposed with many a flower- bouquet.
(The month of May was friendly to me, with many a bouquet of flowers.)

das ˈmɛːtʻçən ʃpʻraːx fɔn ˈliːbə, di ˈmʊtʻɐ gaːɐ̯ fɔn leː —
Das Mädchen sprach von Liebe, die Mutter gar von Eh' —
The girl spoke of love, the mother even of marriage —

nuːn lɪst diː vɛltʻ zoː ˈtʰryːbə, deːɐ̯ veːk gəˈhʏltʻ lɪn ʃneː.
nun ist die Welt so trübe, der Weg gehüllt in Schnee.
now is the world so dreary, the way covered in snow.
(now the world is so dreary, the way covered in snow.)

ɪç kʰan tsuː ˈmaenɐ ˈraezən nɪçtʻ ˈvɛːlən mɪt deːɐ̯ tsaetʰ,
Ich kann zu meiner Reisen nicht wählen mit der Zeit,
I can to my journey not choose with the time,
(I cannot choose the time for my journey,)

mʊs zɛlpst den veːkʻ miːɐ̯ ˈvaezən lɪn ˈdiːzɐ ˈdʊŋkʻəlhaetʰ.
muss selbst den Weg mir weisen in dieser dunkelheit.
must myself the way for me indicate in this darkness.
(I must find the way for myself in this darkness.)

ɛs tsiːtʻ laen ˈmoːndənˈʃatʻən lals maen gəˈfɛːɐ̯tʻə mɪtʰ,
Es zieht ein Mondenschatten als mein Gefährte mit,
There moves a moon- shadow as my companion with,
(A moon-cast shadow moves along with me as my companion,)

ʊntʻ laof den ˈvaesən ˈmatʻən zuːx ɪç dɛs ˈvɪldəs tʰrɪtʰ.
und auf den weissen Matten such' ich des Wildes tritt.
and on the white mat seek I the deer's step.
(and on the white mat I look for the tracks of a deer.)

vas zɔl lɪç ˈlɛŋɐ ˈvaelən, das man mɪç tʰriːpʻ hɪˈnaos? [bɪs]
Was soll ich länger weilen, dass man mich trieb hinaus? [*poem:* **bis man**]
Why shall I longer stay, that one me might drive out? [till]
(Why should I stay any longer, for them to drive me away?)

las 'ɪrə 'hʊndə 'hɔ͜ølən foːɐ̯/foːr 'liːrəs 'hɛrən hɑ͜us!
Lass irre Hunde heulen vor ihres Herren Haus!
Let mad dogs howl before their master's house!

di 'liːbə liːp't das 'vandɐn — gɔt' hat' ziː zoː gə'maxtʰ —
Die Liebe liebt das wandern — Gott hat sie so gemacht —
The love loves the wandering — God has it so made —
(Love loves wandering — God has made it so —)

fɔn 'la͜enəm t͜suː dem 'andɐn. fa͜en 'liːp'çən, 'guːt'ə naxtʰ.
von einem zu dem andern; fein Liebchen, gute Nacht.
from one to the other; fine sweetheart, good night.

vɪl dɪç ɪm tʰrɑ͜om nɪçt' 'ʃt'øːrən, vɛːɐ̯ ʃaːt' ʊm 'da͜enə ruː,
Will dich im Traum nicht stören, wär Schad' um deine Ruh,
(I) want you in the dream not to disturb, would be shame for your rest,
(I do not want to disturb you while you are dreaming; it would be a shame to mar your rest.)

zɔlst' 'ma͜enən tʰrɪt' nɪçt' 'høːrən — zaxt', zaxt diː 'tʰyːrə t͜suː!
Sollst meinen Tritt nicht hören — sacht, sacht die Türe zu!
You shall my step not hear — softly, softly the door shut!
(You shall not hear my step — softly, softly I shut the door!)

ʃra͜ep' ɪm fo'ryːbɐgeːən ans tʰoːɐ̯ diːɐ̯ 'guːt'ə naxtʰ,
Schreib im Vorübergehen ans Tor dir: gute Nacht,
(I) write in the past- going onto the gate to you: "Good night,"
(As I pass by I write on your gate: "Good night,")

da'mɪt duː 'møːgəst' 'zeːən, ɪan dɪç haːb ɪç gə'daxtʰ. [ɪɪç haːp' ɪan dɪç gə'daxtʰ]
damit du mögest sehen, an dich hab' ich gedacht. [*poem:* ich hab' an dich gedacht]
so that you might see, of you have I thought. [I have of you thought]
(so that you might see that I have thought of you.)

[*Winterreise* is the Everest of song cycles, a daunting challenge: twenty-four variations on cold and ice and bleak despair. In this first song the rejected lover begins his journey away from the town where he has fallen in love, a journey without a conscious destination. He sets out at night. Snow has obliterated all the roads. His moon-cast shadow is his only companion. With bitter sarcasm, he reflects that love is destined to be inconstant, always wandering from one love-object to another. A bittersweet tenderness mixed with irony colors his words when he addresses his "fine sweetheart": "I do not want to disturb you while you are dreaming" (sung very softly). Unlike *Die schöne Müllerin*, this cycle does not tell a story in any clear sequence: it is rather a masterful series of pictures of a desolate inner landscape to match the wintry surroundings.]

2.
di 'vɛt'ɐfaːnə
Die Wetterfahne
The Weather-Vane

deːɐ̯ vɪnt' ʃp'iːlt' mɪt deːɐ̯ 'vɛt'ɐfaːnə ɪɑ͜of 'ma͜enəs 'ʃøːnən 'liːp'çəns hɑ͜os.
Der Wind spielt mit der Wetterfahne auf meines schönen Liebchens Haus.
The wind plays with the weather-vane on my beautiful sweetheart's house.

da: daxtʻ ɪç ʃo:n lɪn 'ma͜enəm 'va:nə, zi: pfɪf den 'larmən 'flʏçtʻlɪŋ la͜os.
Da dacht' ich schon in meinem Wahne, sie pfiff den armen Flüchtling aus.
There thought I already in my madness, it whistled the poor fugitive out.
(There in my madness I thought: it is hissing the poor fugitive off the stage.)
[*auspfeifen* = what a European audience does when displeased]

e:ɐ̯ hɛtʻ lɛs 'le:ɐ bə'mɛrkʻən 'zɔlən, dɛs 'ha͜ozəs 'la͜ofgəʃtʻɛkʻtʻəs ʃiltʻ,
Er hätt' es eher bemerken sollen, des Hauses aufgestecktes Schild,
He would have it sooner to notice been obliged, the house's affixed sign-board,
(He should have noticed it sooner, that sign attached to the house;)

zo: hɛtʻ e:ɐ̯ 'nɪmɐ 'zu:xən 'vɔlən lɪm ha͜os la͜en 'tʰrɔ͜ øəs 'fra͜oənbɪltʻ.
so hätt' er nimmer suchen wollen im Haus ein treues Frauenbild.
then would have he never to seek wanted in the house a faithful woman(-picture).
(then he would never have tried to find a faithful woman in that house.)

de:ɐ̯ vɪntʻ ʃpʻi:lt 'drɪnən mɪt den 'hɛrt͜sən vi: la͜of dem dax, nu:ɐ̯ nɪçtʻ zo: la͜otʰ.
Der Wind spielt drinnen mit den Herzen wie auf dem Dach, nur nicht so laut.
The wind plays inside with the hearts as on the roof, only not so loudly.
(Inside, the wind plays with hearts just as it plays on the roof, only not so loudly.)

vas 'fra:gən zi: na:x 'ma͜enən 'ʃmɛrt͜sən? li:ɐ̯ kʰɪntʻ lɪstʻ 'la͜enə 'ra͜eçə bra͜otʰ.
Was fragen sie nach meinen Schmerzen? Ihr Kind ist eine reiche Braut.
What ask they after my pains? Their child is a rich bride.
(What do they care about my pain? Their child will be a rich bride.)

[Now we know why he is so desperate: the young woman he loves is about to marry a rich man. On this windy night the wooden weather-vane on her roof is flapping this way and that, a symbol of her unstable affections; and when it creaks, it sounds as if the house is whistling him out of town. Schubert has created a vividly picturesque description of the turning, flapping weather-vane, reacting to gusts of wind from opposite directions, with rattling, shivering trills, the thud of detached chords, the creak of high, octave *acciaccature*, and the *legato* moan of the wind.]

3.
gə'fro:rnə 'tʰrɛ:nən
Gefror'ne Tränen
Frozen Tears

gə'fro:rnə 'tʰrɛ:nən 'falən fɔn 'ma͜enən 'vaŋən lapʻ: lɔpʻ lɛs mi:ɐ̯ dɛn lɛntʻ'gaŋən,
Gefror'ne Tränen fallen von meinen Wangen ab: ob es mir denn entgangen,
Frozen tears fall from my cheeks down: if it by me then went unnoticed,
(Frozen tears fall from my cheeks: is it possible that I did not even notice)

das lɪç gə'va͜enətʻ ha:pʻ? la͜e 'tʰrɛ:nə, 'ma͜enə 'tʰrɛ:nə, lʊntʻ za͜etʻ li:ɐ̯ ga:ɐ̯ zo: la͜o,
dass ich geweinet hab'? Ei Tränen, meine Tränen, und seid ihr gar so lau,
that I wept have? Ah tears, my tears, and are you really so tepid,
(that I have been weeping? Oh my tears, my tears, are you really so very tepid)

das li:ɐ/li:r lɛɐ̯'ʃtʻart t͜su: 'la͜ezə, vi: 'kʰy:lɐ 'mɔrgəntʰa͜o?
das ihr erstarrt zu Eise, wie kühler Morgentau?
that you congeal to ice, like cool morning dew?

ʊnt drɪŋt dɔx la͜os deːɐ̯ 'kʰvɛlə deːɐ̯ brʊst' zoː 'glyːənt' ha͜es, [iːɐ̯]
Und dringt doch aus der Quelle der Brust so glühend heiss, [*at the repeat:* **ihr dringt]**
And rush yet from the source of the breast so burning hot, [you]
(And yet you gush up from your source in my breast, so burning hot,)

als 'vɔlt'ət' liːɐ̯ tsɛɐ̯'ʃmɛltsən dɛs 'gantsən 'vɪnt'ɐs la͜es.
als wolltet ihr zerschmelzen des ganzen Winters Eis.
as (if) wanted you to melt the whole winter's ice.
(as if you wanted to melt all the ice of the entire winter.)

[It is an effort to move, but he is on his way. The tears congeal on his cheek. How could they cool so quickly, coming as they do from the searing fire in his heart? The soft, low notes at "*Ei Tränen,*" as he wonders at the mystery, start the build-up to a powerful, high climax of despair.]

4.
ɛɐ̯'ʃt'arʊŋ
Erstarrung
Numbness

ɪç zuːx lɪm ʃneː fɛɐ̯'geːbəns naːx 'liːrɐ 'tʰrɪt'ə ʃp'uːɐ̯, voː ziː lan 'ma͜enəm 'larmə
Ich such' im Schnee vergebens nach ihrer Tritte Spur, wo sie an meinem Arme
I search in the snow in vain after her steps' trace, where she on my arm
(I search in the snow in vain for the trace of her steps, where she, on my arm,)

dʊrç'ʃt'rɪç di 'gryːnə fluːɐ̯. lɪç vɪl den 'boːdən 'kʰʏsən, dʊrç'drɪŋən la͜es lʊnt'
durchstrich die grüne Flur. Ich will den Boden küssen, durchdringen Eis und
through-roamed the green meadow. I want the ground to kiss, to penetrate ice and
(used to roam through the green meadow. I want to kiss the ground, to penetrate the ice and)

ʃneː mɪt' 'ma͜enən 'ha͜esən 'tʰrɛːnən, bɪs lɪç di 'leːɐ̯də zeː. voː fɪnd ɪç 'la͜enə 'blyːt'ə,
Schnee mit meinen heissen Tränen, bis ich die Erde seh'. Wo find' ich eine Blüte,
snow with my hot tears, till I the earth see. Where find I a blossom,
(snow with my hot tears, till I can see the earth. Where shall I find a blossom?)

voː fɪnd ɪç 'gryːnəs graːs? di 'bluːmən zɪnt' lɛɐ̯'ʃt'ɔrbən, deːɐ̯ 'raːzən ziːt' zoː blas.
wo find' ich grünes Gras? Die Blumen sind erstorben, der Rasen sieht so blass.
where find I green grass? The flowers have died, the turf looks so pale.
(Where shall I find green grass? The flowers have died, the turf looks so pale.)

zɔl dɛn kʰa͜en 'langədɛŋk'ən lɪç 'neːmən mɪt' fɔn hiːɐ̯? vɛn 'ma͜enə 'ʃmɛrtsən
Soll denn kein Angedenken ich nehmen mit von hier? Wenn meine Schmerzen
Shall then no keepsake I take with (me) from here? If my pains
(Am I then to take no keepsake away with me? If my pain)

'ʃva͜egən, veːɐ̯ zaːk't' miːɐ̯ dan fɔn liːɐ̯? ma͜en hɛrts lɪst' viː lɛɐ̯'froːrən, kʰalt'
schweigen, wer sagt mir dann von ihr? Mein Herz ist wie erfroren,* kalt
are silent, who tells me then of her? My heart is as (if) frozen, coldly
(is silent who will speak to me of her? My heart is as if frozen, coldly)

[******poem & GA:* **erfroren** (frozen); *Peters* (*Schubert's error*): **erstorben** (lɛɐ̯'ʃt'ɔrbən, died)]

ʃt‘art‘ li:ɐ̯ bɪlt da'rɪn: ʃmɪlt͡st‘ je: das hɛrt͡s mi:ɐ̯ 'vi:dɐ, fli:st‘ l̯ɑo̯x li:ɐ̯ bɪlt da'hɪn!
starrt ihr Bild darin: schmilzt je das Herz mir wieder, fliesst auch ihr Bild dahin!
congeals her image in it: thaws ever the heart for me again, flows also her image away!
(her image congeals inside it: if my heart ever thaws again, her image will melt and flow away!)
[*poem:* **fliesst auch das** (das, the) **Bild dahin**]

[There is a sense of frantic rushing about in the music (Schubert originally called for “not too fast,” later changed to “rather fast”), as the desperate lover retraces the path they used to take during the time of their happiness. He longs for something tangible to remind him of those days, yet can find nothing but ice and snow. If his frozen heart ever thaws, will the image of her that he carries inside it also melt and flow away? The singer should correct Schubert’s error and sing “*Mein Herz is wie erfroren*” to make the meaning of the last few lines completely clear.]

5.
de:ɐ̯ 'lɪndənbɑo̯m
Der Lindenbaum
The Linden-Tree

am 'brʊnən fo:ɐ̯ dem 'tʰo:rə da: ʃt‘e:t‘ l̯a̯en 'lɪndənbɑo̯m; lɪç tʰrɔ̯ø̯mt‘
Am Brunnen vor dem Tore da steht ein Lindenbaum; ich träumt’
By the well in front of the gate there stands a linden- tree; I dreamt

lɪn 'za̯enəm 'ʃat‘ən zo: 'mançən 'zy:sən tʰrɑo̯m. lɪç ʃnɪt‘ lɪn 'za̯enə 'rɪndə
in seinem Schatten so manchen süssen Traum. Ich schnitt in seine Rinde
in its shade so many a sweet dream. I carved into its bark

zo: 'mançəs 'li:bə vɔrtʰ; lɛs t͡so:k‘ lɪn frɔ̯ø̯t‘ lʊnt‘ 'la̯edə t͡su: li:m mɪç 'lɪmɐfɔrtʰ.
so manches liebe Wort; es zog in Freud’ und Leide zu ihm mich immerfort.
so many a dear word; something drew in joy and sorrow to it me continually.
(so many a word of love; in joy and sorrow I was continually drawn to that tree.)

ɪç mʊst‘ l̯ɑo̯x 'hɔ̯ø̯t‘ə 'vandɐn fo:ɐ̯'ba̯e lɪn 'tʰi:fɐ naxtʰ, da: ha:b ɪç
Ich musst’ auch heute wandern vorbei in tiefer Nacht, da hab’ ich
I had to also today wander past in deep night, then have I
(Today I had to pass by that tree in the dead of night; as I did, I)

nɔx lɪm 'dʊŋk‘əl di 'lɑo̯gən 't͡su:gəmaxtʰ. lʊnt‘ 'za̯enə 't͡sva̯egə 'rɑo̯ʃt‘ən,
noch im Dunkel die Augen zugemacht. Und seine Zweige rauschten,
even in the dark the eyes closed. And its branches rustled,
(kept my eyes closed, even in the dark. And its branches rustled)

als 'ri:fən zi: mi:ɐ̯ t͡su:: kʰɔm he:ɐ̯ t͡su: mi:ɐ̯, gə'zɛlə, hi:ɐ̯ fɪnt͡st du: 'da̯enə ru:!
als riefen sie mir zu: komm her zu mir, Geselle, hier find’st du deine Ruh!
as (if) called they to me to: come hither to me, companion, here find you your rest!
(as if they were calling to me: “Come here to me, my friend, here you will find your rest!”)

di 'kʰalt‘ən 'vɪndə 'bli:zən mi:ɐ̯ gra:t‘ lɪns 'langəzɪçtʰ, de:ɐ̯ hu:t‘ flo:k‘ mi:ɐ̯ fɔm 'kʰɔp͡fə,
Die kalten Winde bliesen mir grad’ ins Angesicht, der Hut flog mir vom Kopfe,
The cold winds blew to me right into the face, the hat flew me from the head,
(The cold winds blew right in my face, my hat flew off my head,)

ɪç ˈvɛndət‘ə mɪç nɪçtʰ. nuːn bɪn lɪç ˈmançə ˈʃt‘ʊndə lɛnt‘ˈfɛrnt‘ fɔn ˈjeːnəm lɔrtʰ,
ich wendete mich nicht. Nun bin ich manche Stunde entfernt von jenem Ort,
I turned myself not. Now am I many an hour distant from that place,
(but I didn't turn back. Now I am many hours distant from that place,)

ʊnt‘ ˈɪmɐ høːr ɪçs ˈraoʃən: duː ˈfɛndəst‘ ˈruːə dɔrtʰ!
und immer hör' ich's rauschen: du fändest Ruhe dort!
and always hear I something rustling: you would find rest there!
(and yet I always hear the sound of that rustling, telling me: "There you would find rest!")

[This is surely the most famous of the *Winterreise* songs. The first verse, without introduction or postlude, can be found in older German collections of popular folk melodies, though Schubert's music is definitely his own creation. The rustling leaves of the linden murmur sweetly in the piano prelude; their sound shifts to the minor mode when the lover starts his journey; it becomes a desolate moan in the rising wind, then fades away in the major key of a beautiful memory at the end. The voice of the tree, as the lover hears it, is infinitely touching as it calls him back.]

6.
ˈvasɐfluːtʰ
Wasserflut
Flood

ˈmançə tʰrɛːn laos ˈmaenən ˈlaogən lɪst‘ gəˈfalən lɪn den ʃneː;
Manche Trän' aus meinen Augen ist gefallen in den Schnee;
Many a tear from my eyes has fallen into the snow;

ˈzaenə ˈkʰalt‘ən ˈflɔk‘ən ˈzaogən ˈdʊrst‘ɪç laen das ˈhaesə veː.
seine kalten Flocken saugen durstig ein das heisse Weh.
its cold flakes suck thirstily in the hot pain.
(its cold flakes thirstily drink the hot pain.)

vɛn di ˈgrɛːzɐ ˈʃp‘rɔsən ˈvɔlən, veːt daˈheːɐ̯/-heːr laen ˈlaoɐ vɪnt‘,
Wenn die Gräser sprossen wollen, weht daher ein lauer Wind,
When the grasses to sprout want, blows hither a warm wind,
(When the grass is ready to grow again, a warm wind will blow this way,)

[*poem:* **Wann** (van, when) **die Gräser**]

ʊnt das laes tsɛɐ̯ˈʃp‘rɪŋt‘ lɪn ˈʃolən, lʊnt deːɐ̯ ˈvaeçə ʃneː tsɛɐ̯ˈrɪntʰ.
und das Eis zerspringt in Schollen, und der weiche Schnee zerrinnt.
and the ice splits into chunks, and the soft snow melts away.
(the ice will split into chunks, and the soft snow will melt away.)

ʃneː, duː vaest‘ fɔn ˈmaenəm ˈzeːnən, zaːk‘, voˈhɪn dɔx geːt daen laof?
Schnee, du weisst von meinem Sehnen, sag', wohin doch geht dein Lauf?
Snow, you know about my longing, say, whither though goes your course?
(Snow, you know about my longing, tell me, where will your course take you?)

[*poem:* **sag' mir** (miːɐ̯, me)**, wohin geht dein Lauf?**]

ˈfɔlgə naːx nuːɐ̯ ˈmaenən ˈtʰrɛːnən, nɪmt dɪç balt das ˈbɛçlaen laof.
Folge nach nur meinen Tränen, nimmt dich bald das Bächlein auf.
Follow after just my tears, takes you soon the brooklet up.
(Just follow my tears, the brooklet will soon receive you.)

vɪrst‘ mɪt‘ liːm di ʃt‘at dʊrç'ts̮iːən, 'mʊnt‘rə 'ʃt‘raːsən la̯en lʊnt‘ la̯os;
Wirst mit ihm die Stadt durchziehen, muntre Strassen ein und aus;
(You) will with it the town traverse, lively streets in and out;
(With the brook you will flow through the town, in and out of lively streets;)

fyːlst duː 'ma̯enə 'tʰrɛːnən 'glyːən, daː lɪst‘ 'ma̯enɐ 'liːpst‘ən ha̯os.
fühlst du meine Tränen glühen, da ist meiner Liebsten Haus.
feel you my tears burning, there is my dearest one's house.
(if you feel my tears burning, you will know that you are passing the home of my dearest one.)

[The cold snow soaks up his hot tears; when the snow melts, the mingled water and tears will flow toward the town; when they near his sweetheart's house, the snow-water will feel the tears burning again. There has been much discussion about the rhythm of the accompaniment: many commentators believe that the dotted eighths and sixteenths should be assimilated to the triplets, since the notes are spaced that way on Schubert's manuscript. The effect is smoother, but blander.]

7.
a̯of dem 'flʊsə
Auf dem Flusse
On the River

deːɐ̯ duː zoː 'lʊst‘ɪç 'ra̯oʃt‘əst‘, duː 'hɛlɐ, 'vɪldɐ flʊs, viː ʃt‘ɪl bɪst duː gə'vɔrdən,
Der du so lustig rauschtest, du heller, wilder Fluss, wie still bist du geworden,
Who you so merrily rippled, you clear, wild river, how quiet have you become,
(You who used to ripple along so merrily, you clear, wild stream, how quiet you have become,)

giːpst‘ 'kʰa̯enən 'ʃa̯edəgruːs! mɪt‘ 'hart‘ɐ, 'ʃt‘arɐ 'rɪndə hast duː dɪç lyːbɐ'dɛk‘t‘,
gibst keinen Scheidegruss! Mit harter, starrer Rinde hast du dich überdeckt,
(you)give no parting greeting! With hard, rigid crust have you yourself covered,
(you give me no parting greeting! You are covered over with a hard, rigid crust,)

liːkst‘ kʰalt‘ lʊnt‘ 'lʊnbəveːk‘lɪç lɪm 'zandə 'la̯osgəʃt‘rɛk‘tʰ. lɪn 'da̯enə 'dɛk‘ə graːb ɪç
liegst kalt und unbeweglich im Sande ausgestreckt. In deine Decke grab' ich
(you) lie cold and motionless in the sand outstretched. Into your covering carve I
(and lie there, cold and motionless, stretched out in the sand. Into your covering I carve)

mɪt‘ 'la̯enəm 'ʃp‘ɪts̮ən ʃt‘a̯en den 'naːmən 'ma̯enɐ 'liːpst‘ən lʊnt‘ ʃt‘ʊnt‘ lʊnt tʰaːk‘ hɪ'na̯en:
mit einem spitzen Stein den Namen meiner Liebsten und Stund und Tag hinein:
with a sharp stone the name of my dearest and hour and day into:
(with a sharp stone the name of my dearest, the hour and the day:)

den tʰaːk‘ dɛs 'leːɐ̯st‘ən 'gruːsəs, den tʰaːk‘, lan deːm lɪç gɪŋ; lʊm naːm lʊnt 'ts̮aːlən
den Tag des ersten Grusses. den Tag, an dem ich ging; um Nam' und Zahlen
the day of the first greeting, the day, on which I went; around name and numbers
(the day of our first meeting, the day I went away; around her name and the dates)

'vɪndət‘ zɪç la̯en ts̮ɛɐ̯'brɔxnɐ rɪŋ. ma̯en hɛrts̮, lɪn 'diːzəm 'baxə lɛɐ̯'kʰɛnst duː
windet sich ein zerbrochner Ring. Mein Herz, in diesem Bache erkennst du
winds itself a broken ring. My heart, in this brook recognize you
(a broken ring is entwined. My heart, in this brook do you recognize)

nu:n dae̯n bɪlt‘? lɔps 'lʊnt‘ɐ 'zae̯nɐ 'rɪndə vo:l lɑo̯x zo: 'rae̯sənt‘ ʃvɪltʰ?
nun dein Bild? Ob's unter seiner Rinde wohl auch so reissend schwillt?
now your image? Whether it under its crust perhaps also so laceratingly swells?
(your image now? Under its crust is it also swelling so laceratingly?)

[The river that once rushed along its course so wildly is now covered with rigid, motionless ice. The poet compares the river to his frozen heart: perhaps the current is still raging violently underneath that inert surface too. The range of the song is from low A sharp to high A natural.]

8.

'rʏk‘blɪkʰ
Rückblick
A Look Back

ɛs brɛnt‘ mi:ɐ̯/mi:r 'lʊnt‘ɐ 'bae̯dən 'zo:lən, tʰre:t‘ ɪç lɑo̯x ʃo:n lɑo̯f lae̯s lʊnt‘ ʃne:,
Es brennt mir unter beiden Sohlen, tret' ich auch schon auf Eis und Schnee,
It burns for me under both soles, step I even already on ice and snow,
(The soles of both my feet are burning, even though I step on ice and snow,)

ɪç mœçt‘ nɪçt‘ 'vi:dɐ(r) 'la:t‘əm 'ho:lən, bɪs lɪç nɪçt‘ me:ɐ̯ di 'tʰʏrmə ze:,
ich möcht' nicht wieder Atem holen, bis ich nicht mehr die Türme seh',
I would like not again breath to fetch, till I not more the towers see,
(I don't even want to draw a breath until I can no longer see the towers of that town,)

ha:p‘ mɪç lan 'je:dən ʃt‘ae̯n gə'ʃt‘o:sən, zo: lae̯lt‘ ɪç tsu: de:ɐ̯ ʃt‘at‘ hɪ'nɑo̯s;
hab' mich an jeden Stein gestossen, so eilt' ich zu der Stadt hinaus;
(I) have myself into every stone bumped, so hurried I at the town out;
(I rushed through town in such a hurry that I stubbed my toe on every cobblestone;)
[*poem:* **an jedem Stein** (lan 'je:dəm ʃt‘ae̯n, at every stone)]
[*zu der Stadt hinaus* = through the town / out of the town]

di 'kʰrɛ:ən 'varfən bɛl lʊnt‘ 'ʃlo:sən lɑo̯f 'mae̯nən hu:t‘ fɔn 'je:dəm hɑo̯s.
die Krähen warfen Báll' und Schlossen auf meinen Hut von jedem Haus.
the crows tossed balls and hailstones onto my hat from every house.
(the crows tossed snow and hailstones onto my hat from every rooftop.)

vi: 'landɐs hast du: mɪç lɛm'pfaŋən, du: ʃt‘at de:ɐ̯/de:r 'lʊnbəʃt‘ɛndɪçkʰae̯tʰ!
Wie anders hast du mich empfangen, du Stadt der Unbeständigkeit!
How differently have you me received, you city of the inconstancy!
(How differently you once received me, city of inconstancy!)

an 'dae̯nən 'blaŋk‘ən 'fɛnst‘ɐn 'zaŋən di lɛrç lʊnt‘ 'naxt‘ɪgal lɪm ʃt‘rae̯tʰ.
An deinen blanken Fenstern sangen die Lerch' und Nachtigall im Streit.
At your bright windows sang the lark and nightingale in the contest.
(At your bright windows the lark and the nightingale would sing in competition with each other.)

di 'rʊndən 'lɪndənbɔ̯ø̯mə 'bly:t‘ən, di 'kʰla:rən 'rɪnən 'rɑo̯ʃt‘ən hɛl,
Die runden Lindenbäume blühten, die klaren Rinnen rauschten hell,
The round linden- trees blossomed, the clear gutters murmured brightly,
(The round linden-trees blossomed, clear rills babbled brightly,)

ʊnt‘ |ax, zvae̯ 'mɛ:t‘çənlɑ̯ogən 'gly:t‘ən! da: va:ɐ̯s gə'ʃe:n |ʊm dɪç, gə'zɛl!
und ach, zwei Mädchenaugen glühten! da war's gescheh'n um dich, Gesell!
and ah, two girl- eyes glowed! then was it happened for you, comrade!
(and ah, two girlish eyes were glowing! At that moment you were done for, my friend!)
[*es war um dich geschehen* (idiom) = you were done for!]

kʰœmt mi:ɐ̯ de:ɐ̯ tʰa:k‘ |ɪn di gə'daŋk‘ən, mœçt‘ ɪç nɔx 'laenma:l 'rʏk‘vɛrts ze:n,
Kömmt mir der Tag in die Gedanken, möcht' ich noch einmal rückwärts seh'n,
Comes to me the day into the thoughts, would like I yet once backwards to look,
(When that day comes into my thoughts, I would like to look back once more,)
[*kömmt* (poetical, obsolete, or dialect) = *kommt* = comes]

mœçt‘ ɪç tsu'rʏk‘ə 'vi:dɐ 'vaŋk‘ən, fo:ɐ̯/fo:r 'li:rəm 'hɑ̯ozə 'ʃt‘ɪlə ʃt‘e:n.
möcht' ich zurücke wieder wanken, vor ihrem Hause stille steh'n.
would like I back again to stagger, in front of her house still to stand.
(I would like to stagger back again and stop in front of her house.)

[He can't wait to get far away from the town, the soles of his feet are burning to flee; yet the memory of her look on the day he fell in love makes him want to go back. The unsynchronous treble and bass in the piano part at the beginning and end of the song express his desperate, stumbling haste as well as the conflict between the determination to flee and the urge to return. In the introduction we can picture him rushing headlong, pausing to catch a panting breath—or perhaps for that backward glance—then running again. The lyrical, *legato* middle section recalls a time of happiness, made more poignant by present misery. The next to the last bar in the piano part should continue the syncopations in the treble, according to Schubert's manuscript; the Peters edition, based as usual on the first publication, is in error there.]

9.

'ɪrlɪçtʰ

Irrlicht

Will-o'-the Wisp

ɪn di 'tʰi:fst‘ən 'fɛlzəngrʏndə 'lɔk‘t‘ə mɪç lae̯n 'lɪrlɪçt‘ hɪn:
In die tiefsten Felsengründe lockte mich ein Irrlicht hin:
Into the deepest rocky depths lured me a will-o'-the-wisp hence:
(A will-o'-the-wisp has lured me into the deepest chasm in the mountains:)

vi: |ɪç 'lae̯nən 'lɑ̯osgaŋ 'fɪndə, li:k‘t‘ nɪçt‘ ʃve:ɐ̯ mi:ɐ̯/mi:r |ɪn dem zɪn.
wie ich einen Ausgang finde, liegt nicht schwer mir in dem Sinn.
how I an out-way find, lies not heavily for me in the mind.
(how I find a way out is not a grave concern in my mind.)

bɪn gə'vo:nt das 'lɪrəge:ən, sfy:ɐ̯t‘ ja: 'je:dɐ ve:k‘ tsʊm tsi:l:
Bin gewohnt das Irregehen, 's führt ja jeder Weg zum Ziel:
Am used to the stray-going, it leads after all every path to the goal:
(I am used to going astray; all paths, after all, will eventually lead to my goal:)

'ʊnzrə 'frɔ̯ødən, 'lʊnzrə 've:ən, 'laləs 'lae̯nəs 'lɪrlɪçts ʃp‘i:l!
unsre Freuden, unsre Wehen,* alles eines Irrlichts Spiel!
our joys, our pains, all a will-o'-the-wisp's game!
(our joys, our pains — they are all a will-o'-the-wisp's game!)
[**Peters & Schubert's MS (in error):* **unsre Freuden, unsre Leiden** ('lae̯dən, sorrows)]

dʊrç dɛs ˈbɛrkʻʃtʻroːms ˈtʰrɔkʻnə ˈrɪnən vɪntʻ lɪç ˈruːɪç mɪç hɪˈnapʻ;
Durch des Bergstroms trockne Rinnen wind' ich ruhig mich hinab;
Through the mountain-stream's dry channels wind I calmly myself downwards:
(Through the dry channel of a mountain stream I shall calmly wend my way downwards:)

ˈjeːdɐ ʃtʻroːm vɪrt͜s meːɐ̯ gəˈvɪnən, ˈjeːdəs ˈla͜edən la͜ox za͜en graːpʻ.
jeder Strom wird's Meer gewinnen, jedes Leiden auch sein Grab.
every stream will the sea gain, every suffering also its grave.
(every stream will find the sea, every sorrow, too, will reach its grave.)

[*poem:* **auch ein** (la͜en, a) **Grab]**

[Will-o'-the-wisp, or *ignis futuus* ("foolish fire"), is a spontaneous combustion of methane gas that sometimes causes a mysterious darting flash over a marsh, often misleading travelers. The jilted lover has numbly followed the elusive, illusory little light into a rocky ravine. Will he ever find his way out? He is stoically indifferent. But he sees the dry bed of a mountain stream. That would eventually lead to the sea, just as suffering will eventually lead to a grave. The piano imitates the flickering will-o'-the-wisp (the triplets on the third beats of bars 3, 7, 19, and 42 should *all* be *staccato*, as in the *Gesamtausgabe*). The dotted rhythms should *not* be assimilated to the singer's triplets. Schubert made a mistake in transcribing the words, substituting "*Leiden*" for "*Wehen*," which rhymes with "*Irregehen*." The singer should correct the composer's error.]

10.
rastʰ
Rast
Rest

nuːn mɛrkʻ ɪç leːɐ̯stʻ, viː myːtʻ lɪç bɪn, daː lɪç t͜sʊr ruː mɪç ˈleːgə;
Nun merk' ich erst, wie müd' ich bin, da ich zur Ruh' mich lege;
Now notice I first, how tired I am, when I to the rest myself lay;
(Only now that I lie down to rest do I notice how tired I am;)

das ˈvandɐn hiːltʻ mɪç ˈmʊntʻɐ hɪn la͜of ˈlʊnvɪrtʻbaːrəm ˈveːgə.
das Wandern hielt mich munter hin auf unwirtbarem Wege.
the wandering held me lively hence on inhospitable road.
(walking kept me lively on the inhospitable road.)

di ˈfyːsə ˈfruːgən nɪçtʻ naːx rastʰ, lɛs vaːɐ̯ t͜suː kʰalt t͜sʊm ˈʃtʻeːən;
Die Füsse frugen nicht nach Rast, es war zu kalt zum Stehen;
The feet asked not for rest, it was too cold for the standing;
(My feet did not ask to rest: it was too cold to stand still;)

deːɐ̯ ˈrʏkʻən ˈfyːltʻə ˈkʰa͜enə lastʰ, deːɐ̯ ʃtʻʊrm half fɔrtʻ mɪç ˈveːən.
der Rücken fühlte keine Last, der Sturm half fort mich wehen.
the back felt no burden, the storm helped forth me to blow.
(my back felt no burden, the storm-wind helped by blowing me onward.)

ɪn ˈla͜enəs ˈkʰøːlɐs ˈlɛŋəm ha͜os haːpʻ ˈlɔpʻdax lɪç gəˈfʊndən;
In eines Köhlers engem Haus hab' Obdach ich gefunden;
In a charcoal-burner's narrow house have shelter I found;
(I have found shelter in a charcoal-burner's narrow hut;)

dɔx ˈma͜enə ˈgliːdɐ ruːn nɪçtʻ l͜ɑos, zoː ˈbrɛnən ˈliːrə ˈvʊndən.
doch meine Glieder ruh'n nicht aus, so brennen ihre Wunden.
but my limbs rest not out, so burn their wounds.
(but my limbs find no rest, their wounds are burning so.)

ɑ͜ox duː, ma͜en hɛrt͜s, lɪn kʰampf lʊntʻ ʃtʻʊrm zoː vɪltʻ lʊntʻ zoː fɛɐ̯ˈveːgən,
Auch du, mein Herz, in Kampf und Sturm so wild und so verwegen,
Also you, my heart, in battle and storm so wild and so bold,
(You too, my heart, so wild and so bold in battle and storm,)

[*poem:* **im** (lɪm, in the) **Kampf und Sturm**]

fyːlstʻ lɪn deːɐ̯ ʃtʻɪl leːɐ̯st ˈda͜enən vʊrm mɪtʻ ˈha͜esəm ʃtʻɪç zɪç ˈreːgən!
fühlst in der Still' erst deinen Wurm mit heissem Stich sich regen!
feel in the stillness first your worm with hot sting itself stir!
(only now in the stillness do you fully feel the worm stirring inside you and its burning sting!)

[He has found shelter in the humble house of a charcoal-burner. The words—"*da ich zur Ruh mich lege*"—tell us that he is lying down, *not* walking; the dragging steps in the introduction are a memory, constantly returning to his mind. He had not realized how tired he was until now that he is trying to rest. His aching body and the throbbing wound in his heart keep him awake.]

11.
ˈfryːlɪŋstʰr͜ɑom
Frühlingstraum
Dream of Spring

ɪç ˈtʰr͜ɔømtʻə fɔn ˈbʊntʻən ˈbluːmən, zoː viː ziː voːl ˈblyːən lɪm ma͜e;
Ich träumte von bunten Blumen, so wie sie wohl blühen im Mai;
I dreamt of brightly colored flowers, so as they indeed bloom in the May;
(I dreamt of brightly colored flowers, just as they bloom in May;)

ɪç ˈtʰr͜ɔømtʻə fɔn ˈgryːnən ˈviːzən, fɔn ˈlʊstʻɪgəm ˈfoːgəlgəʃra͜e.
ich träumte von grünen Wiesen, von lustigem Vogelgeschrei.
I dreamt of green meadows, of merry bird- calls.

ʊntʻ lals di ˈhɛːnə ˈkʰrɛːtʻən, daː vartʻ ma͜en ˈl͜ɑogə vax;
Und als die Hähne krähten, da ward mein Auge wach;
And when the cocks crowed, then became my eye awake;
(And when the cocks crowed my eyes awoke;)

daː vaːɐ̯/vaːr lɛs kʰaltʻ lʊntʻ ˈfɪnstʻɐ, lɛs ˈʃriːən di ˈraːbən fɔm dax.
da war es kalt und finster, es schrieen die Raben vom Dach.
here was it cold and dark, there shrieked the ravens on the roof.
(it was cold and dark here, and ravens were croaking on the roof.)

dɔx lan den ˈfɛnstʻɐʃa͜ebən, veːɐ̯ ˈmaːltʻə di ˈblɛtʻɐ daː?
Doch an den Fensterscheiben, wer malte die Blätter da?
But on the window-panes, who painted the leaves there?
(But who painted those leaves on the window-panes?)

iːɐ̯ laxtʻ voːl ˈlyːbɐ den ˈtʰr͜ɔømɐ, deːɐ̯ ˈbluːmən lɪm ˈvɪntʻɐ zaː?
Ihr lacht wohl über den Träumer, der Blumen im Winter sah?
You laugh probably at the dreamer, who flowers in the winter saw?
(Are you perhaps laughing at the dreamer who saw flowers in the winter?)

ɪç ˈtʰrɔ͜ømtʻə fɔn liːpʻ lʊm ˈliːbə, fɔn ˈla͜enɐ ˈʃøːnən ma͜etʻ,
Ich träumte von Lieb' um Liebe, von einer schönen Maid,
I dreamt of love for love, of a beautiful girl,

fɔn ˈhɛrt͜sən lʊntʻ fɔn ˈkʰʏsən, fɔn ˈvɔnə lʊntʻ ˈzeːlɪçkʰa͜etʰ.
von Herzen und von Küssen, von Wonne und Seligkeit.
of embracing and of kissing, of rapture and bliss.
[*poem:* **von Wonn'** (vɔn, rapture) **und Seligkeit]**

ʊntʻ lals di ˈhɛːnə ˈkʰrɛːtʻən, daː vartʻ ma͜en ˈhɛrt͜sə vax;
Und als die Hähne krähten, da ward mein Herze wach;
And when the cocks crowed, then became my heart awake;
(And when the cocks crowed my heart awoke;)

nuːn zɪt͜s ɪç hiːɐ̯/hiːr laˈla͜enə, lʊnt ˈdɛŋkʻə dem ˈtʰra͜omə naːx.
nun sitz' ich hier alleine, und denke dem Traume nach.
now sit I here alone, and think the dream after.
(now I am sitting alone here and thinking about that dream.)

di ˈla͜ogən ʃliːs ɪç ˈviːdɐ, nɔx ʃlɛːkʻt das hɛrt͜s zoː varm.
Die Augen schliess' ich wieder, noch schlägt das Herz so warm.
The eyes close I again, still beats the heart so warmly.
(I close my eyes again, my heart is still beating so warmly.)

van gryːntʻ liːɐ̯ ˈblɛtʻɐ(r) lam ˈfɛnstʻɐ? van haltʻ ɪç ma͜en ˈliːpʻçən lɪm larm?
Wann grünt ihr Blätter am Fenster? wann halt' ich mein Liebchen im Arm?
When turn green you leaves on the window? when hold I my darling in the arm?
(When will you leaves on the window turn green? When shall I hold my darling in my arms?)
[*poem:* **wann halt' ich dich** (dɪç, you)**, Liebchen, im Arm?]**

[Finally having fallen asleep in the charcoal-burner's hut, he dreams about spring and love, wakes to find frost on the windows. Schubert's masterpiece of a song portrays marvelously the contrasts between the innocent joy of the dream, the harsh reality on awakening, and the almost unbearable poignance of the lover's sadness.]

12.
ˈa͜enzaːmkʰa͜etʰ
Einsamkeit
Loneliness

viː ˈla͜enə ˈtʰryːbə ˈvɔlkʻə dʊrç ˈha͜etʻrə ˈlʏftʻə geːtʰ,
Wie eine trübe Wolke durch heitre Lüfte geht,
As a gloomy cloud through serene airs goes,
(Like a dark cloud moving slowly across a serene sky)

vɛn lɪn deːɐ̯ ˈtʰanə ˈvɪpf͜əl la͜en ˈmatʻəs ˈlʏftʻçən veːtʰ:
wenn in der Tanne Wipfel ein mattes Lüftchen weht:
when in the fir-tree's crown a feeble breeze blows;
(when a feeble breeze is blowing through the top of the fir-tree,)
[*poem:* **wann** (van, when) **in der Tanne Wipfel;** *GA:* **in der Tannen** (ˈtʰanən, fir-trees')]

zoː tsiː lɪç ˈmaenə ˈʃt‘raːsə daˈhɪn mɪt ˈtʰrɛːgəm fuːs,
so zieh' ich meine Strasse dahin mit trägem Fuss,
so move I my street along with sluggish foot,
(that is how I trudge down the road, dragging sluggish feet,)

dʊrç ˈhɛləs, ˈfroːəs ˈleːbən, ˈlaezaːm* lʊnt‘ ˈloːnə gruːs.
durch helles, frohes Leben, einsam und ohne Gruss.
through bright, happy life, lonely and without greeting.
(passing in lonely solitude and without any greeting through scenes of bright, happy life.)
[**note: the singer should give weight to the upbeat to match the natural stress of the word.*]

ax, das di lʊft‘ zoː ˈruːɪç! lax, das di vɛlt‘ zoː lɪçtʰ!
Ach, dass die Luft so ruhig! ach, dass die Welt so licht!
Ah, that the air so calm! ah, that the world so light!
(Alas, that the air is so calm! Alas, that the world is so full of light!)

als nɔx di ˈʃt‘ʏrmə ˈtʰoːp‘t‘ən, vaːɐ̯/vaːr lɪç zoː ˈleːlənt‘ nɪçtʰ.
Als noch die Stürme tobten, war ich so elend nicht.
When still the storms raged, was I so wretched not.
(When the storms were still raging I felt less wretched.)

[He is back on the road, trudging along. The weather is too mild. The world is too full of light. He felt less miserable when the storm matched the storm in his heart. This was originally the end of Schubert's cycle, since he had seen only the first twelve poems of Müller's *Die Winterreise* (*sic*; Schubert dropped the article); he wrote the song in D minor to round out the cycle with a return to its opening key. Later, when he discovered the complete publication of the poems, he changed the key to B minor, altering four of the notes. The *Gesamtausgabe* prints both versions.]

13.
di pʰɔstʰ
Die Post
The Post

fɔn deːɐ̯ ˈʃt‘raːsə heːɐ̯/heːr laen ˈpʰɔst‘hɔrn kʰlɪŋtʰ.
Von der Strasse her ein Posthorn klingt.
From the street hither a posthorn sounds.
(A posthorn sounds from the road.)

vas hat‘ lɛs, das lɛs zoː hoːx ˈlaofʃp‘rɪŋt‘*, maen hɛrts? di pʰɔst‘ brɪŋt‘ ˈkaenən briːf
Was hat es, dass es so hoch aufspringt, mein Herz? Die Post bringt keinen Brief
What has it, that it so high up-leaps, my heart? The post brings no letter
(What's the matter with my heart, that it should leap up so high? The post brings no letter)
[**note: do not stress the second syllable; most bars need only one stress.*]

fyːɐ̯ dɪç. vas drɛŋst duː dɛn zoː ˈvʊndɐlɪç, maen hɛrts? nuːn jaː, di pʰɔst‘
für dich. Was drängst du denn so wunderlich, mein Herz? Nun ja, die Post
for you. Why surge you then so strangely, my heart? Well, after all, the post
(for you. Why are you throbbing so strangely then, my heart? Well, after all, the post coach)

kʰɔmt‘ laos deːɐ̯ ʃt‘atʰ, voː lɪç laen ˈliːbəs ˈliːp‘çən hat‘, maen hɛrts! vɪlst‘
kommt aus der Stadt, wo ich ein liebes Liebchen hatt', mein Herz! Willst
comes from the town, where I a dear sweetheart had, my heart! Want (you)
(is coming from the town where I used to have a dear sweetheart, my heart! Do you want)

voːl ˈlaenˈmaːl hɪˈnyːbɐzeːn, ˈlʊnt‘ ˈfraːgən, viː ˈlɛs dɔrt‘ maːk geːn, maen hɛrts?
wohl einmal hinübersehʼn, und fragen, wie es dort mag gehʼn, mein Herz?
maybe once over-there-to-look, and ask, how it there may go, my heart?
(maybe to have a look over there, and ask how things are going back in that town, my heart?)

[He hears the bugle-call of the post coach. The mail has arrived in the town—or at the inn—where he is lodging at the moment. Why does his heart leap up? He knows that there can be no mail for him. And yet... Perhaps he could just ask how things are going in the town where he used to live. This song is a welcome change of mood in the middle of the cycle. The piano offers the rhythm of the horses hoofs and the melody of the posthorn. The voice expresses the sudden excitement and the impossible hope. This song has had an independent life, apart from the cycle.]

14.
deːɐ̯ ˈgraezə kʰɔpf
Der greise Kopf
The Hoary Head

deːɐ̯ raef hat‘ ˈlaenən ˈvaesən ʃaen miːɐ̯/miːr ˈlyːbɐs haːɐ̯ gəˈʃt‘rɔøətʰ.
Der Reif hat einen weissen Schein mir übers Haar gestreuet.
The hoarfrost has a white sheen for me over the hair strewn.
(The hoarfrost spread a white sheen over my hair.) [*poem:* **hattʼ** (hat‘, had–*past perfect*) **einen**]

daː glaop‘t‘ ɪç ʃoːn laen graes tsuː zaen, lʊnt‘ haːp‘ mɪç zeːɐ̯ gəˈfrɔøətʰ.
Da glaubtʼ ich schon ein Greis zu sein, und habʼ mich sehr gefreuet.
Then believed I already an old man to be, and have myself very gladdened.
(I believed I was already an old man, and I was very glad.) [*poem:* **Da meintʼ** (maent‘, thought)]

dɔx balt‘ lɪst‘ leːɐ̯ hɪnˈvɛkgətʰaotʰ, haːp‘ ˈviːdɐ ˈʃvartsə ˈhaːrə,
Doch bald ist er hinweggetaut, habʼ wieder schwarze Haare,
But soon is it away- thawed, have again black hairs,
(But soon it melted away; I have black hair again,)

das miːɐs foːɐ̯ ˈmaenɐ ˈjuːgənt‘ graotʰ — viː vaet‘ nɔx bɪs tsʊr ˈbaːrə!
dass mirʼs vor meiner Jugend graut — wie weit noch bis zur Bahre!
so that for me it at my youth shudders — how far still till to the bier!
(so that I have to shudder at my youth — how far it is still to the grave!)

fɔm ˈlaːbənt‘roːt tsʊm ˈmɔrgənlɪçt‘ vart‘ ˈmançɐ kʰɔpf tsʊm ˈgraezə.
Vom Abendrot zum Morgenlicht ward mancher Kopf zum Greise.
From the sunset to the morning-light became many a head to the hoary.
(Between sunset and dawn many a head has become hoary.)

veːɐ̯ glaop‘ts? lʊnt‘ ˈmaenɐ vart‘ lɛs nɪçt‘ laof ˈdiːzɐ ˈgantsən ˈraezə!
Wer glaubtʼs? Und meiner ward es nicht auf dieser ganzen Reise!
Who believes it? And mine became it not on this entire journey!
(Who would believe it? And mine has not turned white on this entire journey!)

[He is back on the road, has slept out in the open somewhere. He wakes up to find his hair covered with hoarfrost. Good! I'm an old man! Less time to wait! But no, the frost melts away. He has heard tales of hair turning white overnight from shock or from some great grief; how is it possible that his hair is still black after such an eternity of torment? The great arching phrase that introduces the song expresses the depth and immensity of the sort of experience that might turn a head grey overnight; when the voice takes over the theme, the singer should avoid stressing the word "*übers*" at the crest, or "*hab*" in the next phrase, since those are not the words that carry the actual meaning of the thoughts, in spite of their apparent prominence in the shape of the melody.]

15.
di ˈkʰrɛːə
Die Krähe
The Crow

ˈa͜enə ˈkʰrɛːə vaːɐ̯ mɪt‘ miːɐ̯/miːr |ɑ͜os deːɐ̯ ʃt‘at‘ gəˈt͜soːgən,
Eine Krähe war mit mir aus der Stadt gezogen,
A crow had with me out of the town moved,
(A crow left town with me;)

ɪst‘ bɪs ˈhɔ͜øt‘ə fyːɐ̯/fyːr |ʊnt‘ fyːɐ̯/fyːr |ʊm ma͜en hɑ͜op‘t‘ gəˈfloːgən.
ist bis heute für und für um mein Haupt geflogen.
has till today for ever and ever around my head flown.
(until now it has circled above my head over and over again.)

ˈkʰrɛːə, ˈvʊndɐlɪçəs tʰiːɐ̯, vɪlst‘ mɪç nɪçt‘ fɛɐ̯ˈlasən?
Krähe, wunderliches Tier, willst mich nicht verlassen?
Crow, strange beast, want me not to forsake?
(Crow, you strange beast, you don't want to leave me, do you?)

ma͜enst‘ voːl balt‘ |als ˈbɔ͜øt‘ə hiːɐ̯ ˈma͜enən la͜ep‘ t͜suː ˈfasən?
Meinst wohl bald als Beute hier meinen Leib zu fassen?
(You) think perhaps soon as prey here my body to seize?
(Are you perhaps expecting to seize my body soon as your prey?)

nuːn, |ɛs vɪrt‘ nɪçt‘ va͜et‘ meːɐ̯ geːn |an dem ˈvandɐʃt‘aːbə.
Nun, es wird nicht weit mehr geh'n an dem Wanderstabe.
Well, it will not far more go with the walking-stick.
(Well, I will not be going very much farther with this walking-stick.)

ˈkʰrɛːə, las mɪç ˈ|ɛnt‘lɪç zeːn ˈtʰrɔ͜øə bɪs t͜sʊm ˈgraːbə!
Krähe, lass mich endlich seh'n Treue bis zum Grabe!
Crow, let me at last see constancy till to the grave!
(Crow, let me at last see constancy until death!)

[Ever since he left town a crow has been circling above his head, waiting for carrion. With bitter irony he comments on such constancy. Maybe, for once, he will find an example of constancy until death. The eerie, ominous circles, even the soft flapping of the wings, can be heard in the piano part; the voice often follows the instumental melody, as the eyes of the traveler follow the circling bird. Does the *diminuendo* at the end suggest that the bird gives up and flies away?]

16.
ˈlɛt͜st‘ə ˈhɔfnʊŋ
Letzte Hoffnung
Last Hope

hiː |ʊnt daː |ɪst‘ |an den ˈbɔ͜ømən ˈmançəs ˈbʊnt‘ə blat t͜suː zeːn,
Hie und da ist an den Bäumen manches bunte Blatt zu seh'n,
Here and there is on the trees many a colored leaf to be seen,
(Here and there many a colored leaf can still be seen on the trees,)

[*poem:* **Hier** (hiːɐ̯, here) **und da ist an den Bäumen noch ein buntes** (nɔx la̯en ˈbʊntʻəs, still a colored) **Blatt zu seh'n]**

ʊntʻ lɪç ˈbla̯ebə foːɐ̯ den ˈbɔ̯ømən ˈlɔftʻmaːls lɪn gəˈdaŋkʻən ʃtʻeːn.
und ich bleibe vor den Bäumen oftmals in Gedanken steh'n.
and I remain in front of the trees oftentimes in thoughts stand(ing).
(and I often remain standing deep in thought in front of those trees.)

ˈʃɑ̯ɔə naːx dem ˈla̯enən ˈblatʻə, ˈhɛŋə ˈma̯enə ˈhɔfnʊŋ dran;
Schaue nach dem einen Blatte, hänge meine Hoffnung dran;
(I) look toward the one leaf, hang my hope on it;
(I look at one individual leaf, I hang my hope onto it;)

ʃpʻiːlt deːɐ̯ vɪntʻ mɪtʻ ˈma̯enəm ˈblatʻə, ˈt͡sɪtʻrɪç, vas lɪç ˈt͡sɪtʻɐn kʰan.
spielt der Wind mit meinem Blatte, zittr' ich, was ich zittern kann.
plays the wind with my leaf, tremble I, whatever I tremble can.
(if the wind plays with my leaf, I tremble from head to toe.)
[*was ich zittern kann* (idiomatic construction) = tremble as hard as I can]

ax, lʊntʻ fɛlt das blat t͡suː ˈboːdən, fɛltʻ mɪtʻ liːm di ˈhɔfnʊŋ lapʻ,
Ach, und fällt das Blatt zu Boden, fällt mit ihm die Hoffnung ab,
Ah, and falls the leaf to ground, falls with it the hope off,
(Ah, and if that leaf will fall to the ground, if my hope will fall with it,)

fal ɪç ˈzɛlbɐ mɪt t͡suː ˈboːdən, va̯en, va̯en lɑ̯ɔf ˈma̯enɐ ˈhɔfnʊŋ graːpʻ.
fall' ich selber mit zu Boden, wein', wein' auf meiner Hoffnung Grab.
fall I myself with to ground, weep, weep on my hope's grave.
(I shall fall to the ground with them myself and weep, weep on the grave of my hope.)
[*poem: only one* **wein']**

[He stares obsessively at a particular leaf, *his* leaf, left over from autumn, on a particular tree. That leaf will be a symbol of his tenuous hope: when it finally falls, his last hope will die. The piano introduction suggests the leaves that flutter in a light breeze, break off, and fall. We hear his trembling as his leaf quivers in the wind, feel his fearful suspense in the silence that follows.]

17.
ɪm ˈdɔrfə
Im Dorfe
In the Village

ɛs ˈbɛlən di ˈhʊndə, lɛs ˈrasəln di ˈkʰɛtʻən; lɛs ˈʃlaːfən di ˈmɛnʃən
Es bellen die Hunde, es rasseln die Ketten; es schlafen die Menschen
There bark the dogs, there rattle the chains; there sleep the human beings
(Dogs are barking, their chains are rattling; the people are sleeping)
[*poem:* **die Menschen schnarchen** (ˈʃnarçən, snore)**]**

lɪn ˈliːrən ˈbɛtʻən, ˈtʰrɔ̯ømən zɪç ˈmançəs, vas ziː nɪçtʻ ˈhaːbən,
in ihren Betten, träumen sich manches, was sie nicht haben,
in their beds, dream themselves many a thing, what they not have,
(in their beds, dreaming themselves many a thing that they don't have,)

tʰuːn zɪç ɪm ˈguːtˈən ʊntˈ ˈargən ɛɐ̯ˈlaːbən; ʊntˈ ˈmɔrgən fryː ɪstˈ ˈaləs t͡sɛɐ̯ˈflɔsən.
tun sich im Guten und Argen erlaben; und morgen früh ist alles zerflossen.
do themselves in the good and bad refresh; and tomorrow early is all dissolved.
(refreshing themselves in good and bad times; and tomorrow morning all will have melted away.)

jeː nuːn, ziː ˈhaːbən iːɐ̯ tʰa͜el gəˈnɔsən, ʊntˈ ˈhɔfən, vas ziː nɔx ˈyːbrɪç ˈliːsən,
Je nun, sie haben ihr Teil genossen, und hoffen, was sie noch übrig liessen,
Oh well, they have their share enjoyed, and hope, what they still over left,
(Oh well, at least they enjoyed their share and can hope that whatever was still left over)

dɔx ˈviːdɐ t͡suː ˈfɪndən a͜of ˈiːrən ˈkʰɪsən. bɛltˈ mɪç nuːɐ̯ fɔrtˈ, iːɐ̯ ˈvaxən ˈhʊndə,
doch wieder zu finden auf ihren Kissen. Bellt mich nur fort, ihr wachen Hunde,
after all again to find on their pillows. Bark me just away, you wide-awake dogs,
(they will find again on their pillows. Go on and bark me away, you watchdogs,)

lastˈ mɪç nɪçtˈ ruːn ɪn deːɐ̯ ˈʃlʊmɐʃtˈʊndə! ɪç bɪn t͡suː ˈɛndə mɪtˈ ˈalən ˈtʰrɔ͜ømən —
lasst mich nicht ruh'n in der Schlummerstunde! Ich bin zu Ende mit allen Träumen —
let me not rest in the slumber- hour! I am at end with all dreaming —
(don't let me rest in these hours of sleep! I am finished with all dreaming —)

vas zɔl ɪç ˈʊntˈɐ den ˈʃlɛːfɐn ˈzɔ͜ømən?
was soll ich unter den Schläfern säumen?
what shall I among the sleepers linger?
(why should I linger among the sleepers?)

[In his aimless wandering he is passing through a sleeping village at night. The watchdogs do well to bark him away: he is finished with dreams, why should he linger among the sleepers? The piano gives us the growling dogs, the rattling chains, perhaps even the snores of the people.]

18.

deːɐ̯ ˈʃtˈʏrmɪʃə ˈmɔrgən

Der stürmische Morgen

The Stormy Morning

viː hat deːɐ̯ ʃtˈʊrm t͡sɛɐ̯ˈrɪsən dɛs ˈhɪməls ˈgra͜oəs kʰla͜etˈ!
Wie hat der Sturm zerrissen des Himmels graues Kleid!
How has the storm torn to pieces the sky's grey dress!
(How the storm has ripped to pieces the sky's grey dress!)

di ˈvɔlkˈənfɛt͡sən ˈflatˈɐn ʊmˈheːɐ̯/-heːr ɪn ˈmatˈəm ʃtˈra͜etʰ.
Die Wolkenfetzen flattern umher in mattem Streit.
The cloud-tatters flutter about in feeble fight.
(The tattered bits of cloud flutter about, putting up a feeble fight against the raging winds.)

ʊntˈ ˈroːtˈə ˈfɔ͜øɐflamən t͡siːn ˈt͡svɪʃən ˈiːnən hɪn.
Und rote Feuerflammen zieh'n zwischen ihnen hin.
And red fire- flames move between them hence.
(And red flashes of lightning dart between them.)

das nɛn ɪç ˈla͜enən ˈmɔrgən zoː rɛçtˈ naːx ˈma͜enəm zɪn!
Das nenn' ich einen Morgen so recht nach meinem Sinn!
That name I a morning so right after my mind!
(I call this a morning right after my own heart!)

ma͜en hɛrt͜s zi:t' ǀan dem 'hɪməl gə'ma:lt' za͜en 'ǀa͜egnəs bɪlt' —
Mein Herz sieht an dem Himmel gemalt sein eignes Bild —
My heart sees in the sky painted its own image —
(My heart sees its own image painted in the sky —)

ɛs ǀɪst' nɪçt͜s ǀals de:ɐ̯ 'vɪnt'ɐ, de:ɐ̯ 'vɪnt'ɐ kʰalt' ǀʊnt' vɪlt'.
es ist nichts als der Winter, der Winter kalt und wild.
it is nothing but the winter, the winter cold and wild.
(an image of nothing but winter, cold, wild winter.)

[A violent storm corresponds to the storm in his heart and rages graphically in Schubert's music.]

19.
'tʰɔ͜øʃuŋ
Täuschung
Delusion

a͜en lɪçt tʰant͜st' 'frɔ͜ønt'lɪç fo:ɐ̯ mi:ɐ̯ he:ɐ̯; ǀɪç fɔlk' ǀi:m na:x di kʰrɔ͜øt͜s ǀʊnt' kʰve:ɐ̯;
Ein Licht tanzt freundlich vor mir her; ich folg' ihm nach die Kreuz und Quer;
A light dances friendly before me hither; I follow it after the cross and diagonal;
(A light dances before me invitingly; I follow after it, hither and thither, wherever it leads;)
[*die Kreuz und Quer* (idiom) = hither and thither, to and fro]

ɪç fɔlk' ǀi:m gɛrn ǀʊnt' ze:s ǀi:m ǀan, das ǀɛs fɛɐ̯'lɔk't den 'vandɐsman.
ich folg' ihm gern und seh's ihm an, dass es verlockt den Wandersmann.
I follow it gladly and see it in it ... , that it lures astray the wandering man.
(I follow it gladly, even though I can tell by looking at it, that it lures the wanderer astray.)
[*ich seh's ihm an* = I can tell by looking at him/it]

ax, ve:ɐ̯ vi: ǀɪç zo: 'ǀe:lənt' ǀɪstʰ, gi:p't' gɛrn zɪç hɪn de:ɐ̯ 'bʊnt'ən lɪstʰ,
Ach, wer wie ich so elend ist, gibt gern sich hin der bunten List,
Ah, whoever as I so wretched is, gives gladly himself up to the bright guile,
(Ah, one as wretched as I am is willing to be taken in by this gay deception)
[*sich hingeben* = to give oneself up, to surrender]

di: 'hɪnt'ɐ(r) ǀa͜es ǀʊnt' naxt' ǀʊnt' gra͜os ǀi:m va͜est' ǀa͜en 'hɛləs, 'varməs ha͜os,
die hinter Eis und Nacht und Graus ihm weist ein helles, warmes Haus,
that behind ice and night and horror to him shows a bright, warm house,
(that shows him—beyond ice and night and horror—a brighly-lighted, warm house)

ʊnt' 'ǀa͜enə 'li:bə 'ze:lə drɪn — nu:ɐ̯ 'tʰɔ͜øʃʊŋ ǀɪst' fy:ɐ̯ mɪç gə'vɪn!
und eine liebe Seele drin — nur Täuschung ist für mich Gewinn!
and a dear soul in it — only delusion is for me gain!
(and a dear soul inside — only delusion has something to offer me now!)

[Is this light that leads travelers astray another will-o'-the-wisp? Is it some sort of mirage? In any case, the music could not be more different from that of *Irrlicht*. Here is a lilting dance, alluring and cheerful, and the wanderer follows it willingly, even though he knows that he is following an illusion. He *wants* to be deceived, because reality has nothing to offer him. Schubert stole the music from himself, from his unsuccessful opera *Alfonso und Estrella*. The song provides contrast and relief, before the marvelous but heart-breaking music ahead on this winter journey.]

20.

deːɐ̯ ˈveːkʻvaezɐ

Der Wegweiser

The Signpost

vas fɛɐ̯ˈmaed ıç dɛn di ˈveːgə, voː di ˈlandɐn ˈvandrɐ geːn,
Was vermeid' ich denn die Wege, wo die andern Wandrer geh'n,
Why avoid I then the roads, where the other wanderers walk,
(Why do I avoid the roads where other wanderers are walking?) [*poem:* **andren** (ˈlandrən, other)]

ˈzuːxə miːɐ̯ fɛɐ̯ˈʃtʻɛkʻtʻə ˈʃtʻeːgə dʊrç fɛɐ̯ˈʃnaetʻə ˈfɛlzənhøːn?
suche mir versteckte Stege durch verschneite Felsenhöh'n?
seek for me hidden footpaths through snow-covered rock- heights?
(Why do I seek out hidden footpaths through rocky, snow-covered heights?)

ˈhaːbə jaː dɔx nıçts bəˈgaŋən, das lıç ˈmɛnʃən ˈzɔltʻə ʃɔøn —
Habe ja doch nichts begangen, dass ich Menschen sollte scheu'n —
(I) have really after all nothing committed, that I human beings should shun —
(I have not committed any crime, after all; why should I shun my fellow man?)

vɛlç laen ˈtʰøːrıçtʻəs fɛɐ̯ˈlaŋən tʰraepʻtʻ mıç lın di ˈvyːstʻənaeən?
welch ein törichtes Verlangen treibt mich in die Wüsteneien?
what a foolish longing drives me into the wildernesses?
(What sort of foolish longing drives me into wildernesses?)
[*poem & Schubert's repeat:* **Wüstenei'n** (ˈvyːstʻənaen, wildernesses)]

ˈvaezɐ ˈʃtʻeːən laof den ˈʃtʻraːsən, ˈvaezən laof di ˈʃtʻɛːtʻə tsuː,
Weiser stehen auf den Strassen,* weisen auf die Städte zu,
Signposts stand on the roads, point to the towns to.
(There are signposts by the roads, pointing the way to various towns.)
[**Schubert's error & Peters:* **Weiser stehen auf den Wegen** (ˈveːgən, roads/paths–*no rhyme*)

ʊntʻ lıç ˈvandrə ˈzɔndɐ ˈmaːsən, ˈloːnə ruː, lʊntʻ ˈzuːxə ruː.
und ich wandre sonder Massen, ohne Ruh', und suche Ruh'.
and I wander without measures, without rest, and seek rest.
(and I wander on with no measure of the distance, no moderation, without rest, and seeking rest.)

ˈaenən ˈvaezɐ zeː ıç ˈʃtʻeːən lʊnfɛɐ̯ˈrʏkʻtʻ foːɐ̯ ˈmaenən blıkʰ;
Einen Weiser seh' ich stehen unverrückt vor meinen Blick;
A signpost see I standing fixed in front of my gaze;
(I see one signpost that is constantly fixed in front of my gaze;)

ˈaenə ˈʃtʻraːsə mʊs lıç ˈgeːən, diː nɔx ˈkʰaenɐ gıŋ tsuˈrʏkʰ.
eine Strasse muss ich gehen, die noch keiner ging zurück.
a road must I walk, (on) which as yet no one went back.
(I must take a road on which no one as yet has ever come back.)

[This deeply moving song is one of the towering peaks of the cycle. What has he done, that he should avoid his fellow man? Why does he seek out hidden, inaccessible trails? Signposts point in all directions; but there is only one road that he is compelled to travel, and one destination. Many sequences of repeated tones run through the song, obsessively; till one becomes prominent in the voice and in the piano, one tone repeated inexorably, over and over, under a very slowly descending chromatic scale, as he sees, fixed before his eyes, the signpost that points to death. The singer should correct Schubert's error (in brackets above) and preserve the poet's rhyme.]

21.

das ˈvɪrt͜shɑ͜os

Das Wirtshaus

The Inn

ɑ͜of ˈla͜enən ˈtʰoːt‘ənlak‘ɐ hat‘ mɪç ma͜en veːk ɡəˈbraxtʰ.
Auf einen Totenacker hat mich mein Weg gebracht.
Onto a graveyard has me my way brought.
(My path has brought me to a graveyard.)

alˈhiːɐ̯ vɪl lɪç ˈla͜enkʰeːrən, haːb ɪç ba͜e miːɐ̯ ɡəˈdaxtʰ.
Allhier will ich einkehren, hab' ich bei mir gedacht.
Here want I to lodge, have I to myself thought.
(I want to lodge here, I thought to myself.)

iːɐ̯ ˈɡryːnən ˈtʰoːt‘ənkʰrɛnt͜sə kʰœnt‘ voːl di ˈt͜sa͜eçən za͜en,
Ihr grünen Totenkränze könnt wohl die Zeichen sein,
You green funeral wreaths could well the signs be,
(You green funeral wreaths could well be the signs)

diː ˈmyːdə ˈvandrɐ ˈlaːdən lɪns ˈkʰyːlə ˈvɪrt͜shɑ͜os la͜en.
die müde Wandrer laden ins kühle Wirtshaus ein.
that tired wanderers [obj.] invite into the cool inn ... .
(that invite tired travelers to come into the inn.) [*einladen* = to invite]

zɪnt dɛn ɪn ˈdiːzəm ˈhɑ͜ozə di ˈkʰamɐn lal bəˈzɛt͜stʰ?
Sind denn in diesem Hause die Kammern all' besetzt?
Are then in this house the rooms all occupied?
(Are all the rooms in this house then occupied?)

bɪn mat t͜sʊm ˈniːdɐzɪŋk‘ən, bɪn ˈtʰøːt‘lɪç ʃveːɐ̯ fɛɐ̯ˈlɛt͜stʰ. [lʊnt]
bin matt zum Niedersinken, bin tödlich schwer verletzt. [*poem:* **und tödlich**]
(I) am weary to the down- sinking, am mortally severely wounded. [and]
(I am weary to the point of collapse, I am mortally and severely wounded.)

oː ˈlʊnbarmhɛrt͜sɡə ˈʃɛŋk‘ə, dɔx ˈva͜ezəst duː mɪç lap‘?
O unbarmherz'ge Schenke, doch weisest du mich ab?
O uncompassionate inn, yet turn you me away?
(O merciless inn, do you nonetheless turn me away?)

nuːn ˈva͜et‘ɐ dɛn, nuːɐ̯ ˈva͜et‘ɐ, ma͜en ˈtʰrɔ͜øɐ ˈvandɐʃt‘aːp‘!
Nun weiter denn, nur weiter, mein treuer Wanderstab!
Now farther then, only farther, my faithful walking stick!
(Then, my trusty staff, we must continue farther, only farther, on our way!)

[The hymnlike setting has been called "conventional," but a heavenly beauty and infinite sadness make this song one of the most moving in the entire cycle. The exhausted traveler finds himself at the gate of a country cemetery. That place of peace fills him with an aching longing. Must he go on and on in his misery? Is there no room in the inn? No, he must resign himself to his fate. A striking feature of *Winterreise* is the irony in many of the individual titles; someone reading them casually could imagine the subjects to be pleasant ones, lyrical or bucolic: "Good Night," "The Linden-Tree," "On the River," "Rest," "Spring Dream," "In the Village," and "The Inn."]

22.
muːtʰ
Mut
Courage

fliːkʻt deːɐ̯ ʃneː miːɐ̯/miːr |ɪns gəˈzɪçtʰ, ʃʏtʻlɪç |iːn hɛˈrʊntʻɐ. vɛn maen hɛrts
Fliegt der Schnee mir ins Gesicht, schüttl' ich ihn herunter. Wenn mein Herz
Flies the snow to me into the face, shake I it down. If my heart
(If snow flies in my face I shake it off. If my heart)

|ɪm ˈbuːzən ʃpʻrɪçtʰ, zɪŋ ɪç hɛl |ʊntʻ ˈmʊntʻɐ. ˈhøːrə nɪçtʻ, vas |ɛs miːɐ̯ zaːkʻtʰ,
im Busen spricht, sing' ich hell und munter. Höre nicht, was es mir sagt,
in the bosom speaks, sing I brightly and cheerfully. (I) hear not, what it to me says,
(speaks in my bosom, I sing brightly and cheerfully. I do not hear what it says to me,)

ˈhaːbə ˈkʰaenə ˈloːrən, ˈfyːlə nɪçtʻ, vas |ɛs miːɐ̯ kʰlaːkʻtʰ, ˈkʰlaːgən |ɪstʻ fyːɐ̯ ˈtʰoːrən.
habe keine Ohren, fühle nicht, was es mir klagt, Klagen ist für Toren.
(I) have no ears, feel not, what it to me complains, complaining is for fools.
(I have no ears; I do not feel what it bemoans to me: moaning is for fools.)

ˈlʊstʻɪç |ɪn di vɛltʻ hɪˈnaen ˈgeːgən vɪntʻ |ʊntʻ ˈvɛtʻɐ!
Lustig in die Welt hinein gegen Wind und Wetter!
Merrily into the word hence against wind and weather!
(Merrily onward, out into the world against wind and weather!)

vɪl kʰaen gɔtʻ |aof ˈleːɐ̯dən zaen, zɪntʻ viːɐ̯ ˈzɛlbɐ ˈgœtʻɐ!
Will kein Gott auf Erden sein, sind wir selber Götter!
wants no god on earth to be, are we ourselves gods!
(If no god wants to rule on earth then we ourselves are gods!)

[The wretched wanderer summons all his courage for a defiant burst of uncharacteristic bravado before his final inner collapse. The song is forceful, sharply rhythmical, with powerful accents.]

23.
di ˈneːbənzɔnən
Die Nebensonnen
The Mock Suns

drae ˈzɔnən zaː |ɪç |am ˈhɪməl ʃtʻeːn, haːpʻ |aŋ |ʊntʻ fɛstʻ ziː ˈlangəzeːn;
Drei Sonnen sah' ich am Himmel steh'n, hab' lang und fest sie angeseh'n;
Three suns saw I in the sky standing, (I) have long and fixedly them at-looked;
(I saw three suns in the sky; I stared at them for a long time;)

ʊntʻ ziː |aox ˈʃtʻandən daː zoː ʃtʻiːɐ̯, |als ˈvɔltʻən ziː nɪçtʻ vɛkʻ fɔn miːɐ̯.
und sie auch standen da so stier, als wollten sie nicht weg von mir.
and they too stood there so fixedly, as (if) would (go) they not away from me.
(and they stared back at me, fixedly, as if they did not want to leave me.)
[*poem:* **als könnten** (ˈkʰœntʻən, could) **sie nicht**]

ax, ˈmaenə ˈzɔnən zaetʻ liːɐ̯ nɪçtʰ! ʃaotʻ ˈlandɐn dɔx |ɪns ˈlangəzɪçtʰ!
Ach, meine Sonnen seid ihr nicht! Schaut andern doch ins Angesicht!
Ah, my suns are you not! Look others for goodness' sake into the face!
(Ah, you are not *my* suns! Go and look somebody else in the face!)

ja:, ˈnɔ͜ølɪç hat‘ ɪç ˈa͜ox vo:l dra͜e; nu:n zɪnt‘ hɪˈnap‘ di ˈbɛst‘ən tsva͜e.
Ja, neulich hatt' ich auch wohl drei; nun sind hinab die besten zwei.
Yes, recently had I also indeed three; now are down the best two.
(Yes, until recently I also had three suns; now the best two have set.)

gɪŋ nu:ɐ̯ di drɪt‘ le:ɐ̯t‘ hɪnt‘ɐˈdra͜en! ˈɪm ˈdʊŋk‘əln vɪrt‘ mi:ɐ̯ ˈvo:lɐ za͜en.
Ging' nur die dritt' erst hinterdrein! Im Dunkeln wird mir wohler sein.
Went only the third just after (them)! In the darkening will for me better be.
(If only the third would just follow them! I will be better off in the dark.)

[*poem:* **Im Dunkel** (ˈdʊŋk‘əl, dark)]

[Mock suns are a phenomenon that sometimes occurs in nature when a conformation of clouds partially hides the sun in such a way as to create the illusion of two or more suns. Here the poet ruefully thinks of the two bright eyes that used to light his world and are now lost to him. If the sun in the sky would also disappear for him, he would be better off. The conductor Bruno Walter had a different interpretation: he thought of the three suns as Faith, Hope, and Love: the first two were gone, for the rejected lover; if love would also die in him, he would not feel so wretched.]

24.
de:ɐ̯ ˈla͜eɐman
Der Leiermann
The Organ-Grinder

ˈdry:bən ˈhɪnt‘ɐm ˈdɔrfə ʃt‘e:t‘ ˈa͜en ˈla͜eɐman, ˈʊnt‘ mɪt‘ ˈʃt‘arən ˈfɪŋɐn
Drüben hinterm Dorfe steht ein Leiermann, und mit starren Fingern
Yonder behind the village stands an organ-grinder, and with stiff fingers
(Over there behind the village an organ-grinder is standing, and with stiff fingers)

dre:t‘ ˈe:ɐ̯, vas ˈe:ɐ̯ kʰan. ˈba:ɐ̯fu:s ˈa͜of dem ˈa͜ezə vaŋk‘t‘ ˈe:ɐ̯ hɪn ˈʊnt‘ he:ɐ̯;
dreht er, was er kann. Barfuss auf dem Eise wankt er hin und her;
turns he, what he can. Barefoot on the ice staggers he to and fro;
(he grinds away as best he can. Barefoot on the ice, he staggers to and fro;)

[*poem:* **schwankt** (ʃvaŋk‘t‘, sways/staggers) **er**]

ʊnt‘ za͜en ˈkʰla͜enɐ ˈtʰɛlɐ bla͜ep‘t‘ ˈi:m ˈɪmɐ le:ɐ̯. ˈkʰa͜enɐ ma:k ˈi:n ˈhø:rən,
und sein kleiner Teller bleibt ihm immer leer. Keiner mag ihn hören,
and his little plate remains for him always empty. No one wants him to hear,
(and his little plate for offerings remains always empty. No one wants to hear him,)

ˈkʰa͜enɐ zi:t‘ ˈi:n ˈan; ˈʊnt‘ di ˈhʊndə ˈkʰnʊrən ˈʊm den ˈalt‘ən man.
keiner sieht ihn an; und die Hunde knurren um den alten Mann.
no one looks him at; and the dogs growl around the old man.
(no one looks at him; and dogs are growling around the old man.)

[*poem:* **und die Hunde brummen** (ˈbrʊmən, growl/grumble)]

ʊnt‘ ˈe:ɐ̯ lɛst‘ ˈɛs ˈge:ən ˈaləs, vi: ˈɛs vɪl, dre:t‘, ˈʊnt‘ ˈza͜enə ˈla͜eɐ
Und er lässt es gehen alles, wie es will, dreht, und seine Leier
And he lets it go all, as it will, turns, and his hurdy-gurdy
(And he lets everything go on as it will; he just keeps turning the handle, and his hurdy-gurdy)

ʃt‘e:t‘ ˈi:m ˈnɪmɐ ʃt‘ɪl. ˈvʊndɐlɪçɐ(r) ˈalt‘ɐ, zɔl ˈɪç mɪt di:ɐ̯ ge:n?
steht ihm nimmer still. Wunderlicher Alter, soll ich mit dir geh'n?
stands for him never still. Remarkable old man, shall I with you go?
(never stops playing for him. Remarkable old man, shall I go with you?)

vɪlst t͜su: ˈma͜enən ˈli:dɐn ˈda͜enə ˈla͜eɐ dre:n? [du: ˈma͜enə]
Willst zu meinen Liedern deine Leier dreh'n? [*GA:* **Willst du meinen Liedern**]
Want to my songs your hurdy-gurdy to turn? [you to my]
(Do you want to grind your hurdy-gurdy to my songs?)

[What ending could possibly be more striking—or more original! The piano imitates the never-ending, expressionless drone of the hurdy-gurdy. The singer sings without nuance in the tone of a man who has lost his mind. Is the barefoot old man really there, standing on the ice? Is it a madman, or a phantom in the unhinged mind of the wanderer, who longed for death but is too young to die? After so many powerful emotions, this eerie stillness, this emptiness, is devastating!]

Wohin? see *Die schöne Müllerin*

ˈvɔlk'ə lʊnt' ˈkʰvɛlə
Wolke und Quelle
The Cloud and the Stream

Sketch, privately published [composed 1827?] (poem by Karl Gottfried von Leitner)

a͜of ˈma͜enən ˈha͜emɪʃən ˈbɛrgən da: zɪnt di ˈvɔlk'ən t͜su: ha͜os;
Auf meinen heimischen Bergen da sind die Wolken zu Haus';
On my native mountains there are the clouds at home;
(Clouds are at home on my native mountains;)

bɪn mɪt'ən'lɪnə gə'ʃt'andən, lʊnt' za: lɪns tʰa:l hɪ'na͜os.
bin mitteninne gestanden, und sah ins Tal hinaus.
(I) have right in the middle stood, and looked into the valley out.
(I have stood right in the middle of them, and looked out into the valley.)

zi: ˈla:bɐ ˈflo:gən fɔn ˈdanən, vi: ˈʃvɛ:nə zo: lɪçt' lʊnt' la͜eçtʰ;
Sie aber flogen von dannen, wie Schwäne so licht und leicht;
They however flew from thence, like swans so light (in color) and light (in weight);
(They, however, flew away, as light in color and as lightly-soaring as swans;)

vɛ:ɐ̯ ˈgɛrnə mɪt' ˈli:nən gə'tso:gən, zo: va͜et de:ɐ̯ ˈhɪməl ra͜eçtʰ.
wär' gerne mit ihnen gezogen, so weit der Himmel reicht.
(I) were gladly with them gone, so far the sky reaches.
(I would gladly have gone with them as far as the sky may extend.)

ɛs ˈdrɛŋt'ə mɪç fɔrt' lɪn di ˈfrɛmdə t͜sʊr ˈfɛrnə la͜en ˈvɪldɐ tʰri:p';
Es drängte mich fort in die Fremde zur Ferne ein wilder Trieb;
There urged me forth into the foreign lands to the far-off a wild impetus;
(A wild impetus urged me forth into foreign lands, to that which is far away;)

dɔx jɛt͜st' lɛɐ̯ˈʃa͜enən mi:ɐ̯ ˈha͜ema:t' lʊnt' ˈnɛ:ə nu:ɐ̯ ˈha͜elɪç lʊnt' li:b.
doch jetzt erscheinen mir Heimat und Nähe nur heilig und lieb.
but now seem to me homeland and nearness only sacred and dear.
(but now only my homeland and that which is near seem sacred and precious to me.)

nu:n ze:n ɪç mɪç ˈnɪmɐ(r) lɪns ˈva͜et'ə, hɪ'na͜os lɪns ˈne:bəlndə bla͜o;
Nun sehn' ich mich nimmer ins Weite, hinaus ins nebelnde Blau;
Now long I myself never into the distance, out into the misting blue;
(Now I never long to go into the distance, out into the misty blue;)

nu:n ʃp‘ɛ: lɪç mɪt‘ 'ʃt‘ɪləm fɛɐ̯'laŋən hɪ'nap‘ lɪn di 'ʃma:lə lɑo̯.
nun späh' ich mit stillem Verlangen hinab in die schmale Au.
now scout I with quiet desire down into the narrow meadow.
(now, with quiet desire, I am on the lookout for something down in the narrow meadow.)

vas nɪk‘t dɔrt‘ 'lʊnt‘ən lam 'fɛnst‘ɐ? lʊnt‘ 'bly:ət‘ vi: 'mɔrgənlɪçtʰ?
Was nickt dort unten am Fenster? und blühet wie Morgenlicht?
What nods there below at the window? and blooms like morning light?
(What is nodding down there at that window, and blossoming like the dawn?)

ɪsts 'li:rə ro:s lam gə'zɪmzə? 'lo:dɐ(r) li:ɐ̯ 'hɔldəs gə'zɪçtʰ?
Ist's ihre Ros' am Gesimse? oder ihr holdes Gesicht?
Is it her rose at the window sill? or her lovely face?
(Is it her rose on the window sill? Or is it her lovely face?)

fi:l glʏk‘, li:ɐ̯ 'vɔlk‘ən, tsʊr 'raezə! lɪç 'tsi:ə 'nɪmɐ mɪt‘ lɔø̯ç;
Viel Glück, ihr Wolken, zur Reise! Ich ziehe nimmer mit euch;
Much luck, you clouds, on the journey! I go never with you;
(Good luck, you clouds, on your journey! I shall not be going with you any more;)

vas 'la:bɐ 'lɔk‘ət‘ lʊnt‘ 'lɪsp‘əlt da: 'dry:bən lɪm 'lɛntsəsgəʃt‘rɔø̯ç?
was aber locket und lispelt da drüben im Lenzesgesträuch?
what however lures and whispers there yonder in the spring-bushes?
(but what is that, that entices and murmurs over there in the springtime greenery?)

bɪst du: lɛs, 'kʰvɛlə, di: 'flʏst‘ɐtʰ? ja:, ja:! lɪç 'laelə mɪt di:ɐ̯;
Bist du es, Quelle, die flüstert? Ja, ja! ich eile mit dir;
Are you it, stream, that whispers? Yes, yes! I hurry with you;
(Is it you, stream, who are whispering? Yes, yes! I shall hurry with you;)

du: kʰɛnst‘ ja: di 'kʰʏrtsəst‘ən 've:gə hɪ'nʊnt‘ɐ, hɪ'nʊnt‘ɐ tsu: li:ɐ̯.
du kennst ja die kürzesten Wege hinunter, hinunter zu ihr.
you know after all the shortest ways down, down to her.
(you, after all, know the shortest ways down the mountain, down to *her*.)

[Schubert's sketch gives the complete vocal part, without the text, and with indications of the prelude, general accompaniment, interludes, and postlude. A performing version was created by Reinhard Van Hoorickx, who also identified the poet, and found the poem that fit the music.]

'vɔnə de:ɐ̯ 've:mu:tʰ
Wonne der Wehmut
The Joy of Melancholy

Op. 115, No. 2 [1815] (Johann Wolfgang von Goethe)

'tʰrɔk‘nət‘ nɪçt, 'tʰrɔk‘nət‘ nɪçt, 'tʰrɛ:nən de:ɐ̯/de:r 'le:vɪgən 'li:bə!
Trocknet nicht, trocknet nicht, Tränen der ewigen Liebe!
Dry not, dry not, tears of the eternal love!
(Do not dry, do not dry, tears of eternal love!)

ax, nu:ɐ̯ dem 'halp‘gətʰrɔk‘nət‘ən 'lɑo̯gə vi: 'lø:də, vi: tʰo:t di vɛlt‘ li:m lɛɐ̯'ʃaent(ʰ)!
Ach, nur dem halbgetrockneten Auge wie öde, wie tot die Welt ihm erscheint!
Ah, only to the half-dried eye how barren, how dead the world to it appears!
(Ah, how barren, how dead the world appears only to half-dried eyes!)

ˈtʰrɔkʻnətʻ nɪçt, ˈtʰrɔkʻnətʻ nɪçt, ˈtʰrɛːnən ˈʊnˈglʏkʻlɪçɐ ˈliːbə! [*normally:* ˈʊnglʏkʻlɪçɐ]
Trocknet nicht, trocknet nicht, Tränen unglücklicher Liebe!
Dry not, dry not, tears of unhappy love!
(Do not dry, do not dry, tears of unhappy love!)

[The title gives a clue to the meaning: as long as I am weeping over this unhappy love my love seems eternal, and I rejoice in the soul-filling, enduring fullness of what I feel. If these tears were to dry, my love would be dying, and the world would start to look bleak and empty to me. Beethoven, of course, made *the* famous setting of this poem. It is totally different from Schubert's, which has been strangely disparaged by most commentators, since it can be very expressive and haunting if one takes the trouble to explore its subtle beauty with some empathy.]

Zufriedenheit see *Lied / Ich bin vergnügt*

t͡sʊm ˈpʰʊnʃə
Zum Punsche
To Be Sung When Drinking Punch

Posthumously published [composed 1816] (poem by Johann Mayrhofer)

ˈvoːgətʻ ˈbra͜ozəntʻ, harmoˈniːən, ˈkʰeːrə ˈviːdɐ(r), ˈaltʻə t͡sa͜etʰ; ˈpʰʊnʃgəˈfʏltʻə ˈbɛçɐ,
Woget brausend, Harmonien, kehre wieder, alte Zeit; Punschgefüllte Becher,
Swell effervescently, harmonies, return again, old time; punch- filled beakers,
(Swell effervescently, harmonies! Come back, old times! Punch-filled glasses,)

ˈvandɐtʻ ɪn dɛs ˈkʰra͜ezəs ˈha͜etʻɐkʰa͜etʰ! mɪç lɛɐ̯ˈgra͜efən ʃoːn di ˈvɛlən, bɪn
wandert in des Kreises Heiterkeit! Mich ergreifen schon die Wellen, bin
wander in the circle's cheerfulness! Me seize already the waves, am
(pass around among the cheerful circle! The waves already engulf me, I am)

deːɐ̯/deːr ˈleːɐ̯də va͜etʻ lɛntʻˈrʏkʻtʰ; ˈʃtʻɛrnə ˈvɪŋkʻən, ˈlʏftʻə ˈzɔ͜øzəln, ʊnt di ˈzeːlə ɪstʻ bəˈglʏkʻtʰ!
der Erde weit entrückt; Sterne winken, Lüfte säuseln, und die Seele ist beglückt!
from the earth far carried away; stars beckon, airs whisper, and the soul is blessed!
(carried far away from the earth; stars are beckoning, breezes whisper, and the soul is blessed!)

vas das ˈleːbən ˈa͜ofgəbʏrdətʻ, liːkʻtʻ ˈam ˈuːfɐ ˈneːbəlʃveːɐ̯; ˈʃtʻɔ͜ørə fɔrtʻ, la͜en ˈraʃɐ
Was das Leben aufgebürdet, liegt am Ufer nebelschwer; steu're fort, ein rascher
What the life burdens, lies on the shore mist-heavy; steer forth, a fast
(That with which life burdens us lies on the mist-heavy shore; steer onwards, a fast)

ˈʃvɪmɐ(r), ɪn das ˈhoːə ˈfriːdənsmeːɐ̯. vas dɛs ˈʃvɪmɐs lʊstʻ fɛɐ̯ˈmeːrətʻ, ɪst das
Schwimmer, in das hohe Friedensmeer. Was des Schwimmers Lust vermehret, ist das
swimmer, in the high peace- sea. What the swimmer's pleasure increases, is the
(swimmer on the high seas of peace. What especially increases the swimmer's pleasure is the)
[*poem:* **des Schwimmens** (ˈʃvɪməns, swimming's)]

ˈpʰlɛt͡ʃɐn ˈhɪntʻɐdra͜en; dɛn lɛs ˈfɔlgən di gəˈnɔsən, ˈkʰa͜enɐ vɪl deːɐ̯ ˈlɛt͡stʻə za͜en.
Plätschern hinterdrein; denn es folgen die Genossen, keiner will der letzte sein.
splashing behind; for there follow the comrades, no one wants the last to be.
(splashing he hears behind him, for his friends are following him; no one wants to be last.)

[A drinking song in a minor key, the words by Schubert's melancholy friend in a lively mood.]

t͜sʊr ˈnaːmənsfa͜eɐ dɛs hɛrn ǀanˈdreːas ˈzɪlɐ
Zur Namensfeier des Herrn Andreas Siller
For the Name Day of Herr Andreas Siller

Posthumously published [composed 1813] (author unknown)

dɛs ˈføːbʊs ˈʃtʻraːlən zɪnt dem ǀɑ͜ok‘ ǀɛnt‘ˈʃvʊndən, hɪnˈvɛk‘ fɔm horiˈt͜sɔnt^{h}
Des Phöbus Strahlen sind dem Aug' entschwunden, hinweg vom Horizont
The Phoebus's rays have to the eye disappeared, away from the horizon
(Phoebus's rays have vanished to the eye from the horizon)

ʊnt‘ ǀoː! dɛs ˈfa͜eɐ(r)ǀaːbənt͜s ˈfroːə ˈʃt‘ʊndən bəˈlɔ͜øçt‘ət‘ nuːn deːɐ̯ moːnt‘.
und o! des Feierabends frohe Stunden beleuchtet nun der Mond.
and O! the leisure-evening's happy hours illumines now the moon.
(and—oh!—now the moon illumines the happy hours of our evening leisure.)

[This charming novelty for voice, violin, and harp was written to celebrate the name day of a certain Herr Andreas Siller, who seems to have left us no other trace of his existence. The music is marked "*Da capo*," but no second verse has as yet been discovered, nor the name of the poet.]

Zwei Szenen aus "Lacrimas" see *Florio* and *Delphine*

Index to Volume II, song titles and first lines: **page**

Errata, Volume I

Page x: the actual number of different song texts turned out to be 608 instead of 615. Also Reinhard Van Hoorickx writes his name with a capital V.

Page 36, **Adelwold und Emma**, *2nd line of page 36: "rigid" is misspelled (literal version).*

Page 46, **Amalia**, *3rd line: "paradisiacal" is more usual than "paradisaical" (literal version).*

Page 86, **An die Natur**: *in commentary after the text "expresses" should be "express."*

Page 107, **Aria di Abramo**: *title:* 'arja di a'braːmo; *first line:* di 'tante 'peːne (*note: the first consonant should not be doubled after "di," after personal pronouns, or after articles.*); *fourth line:* del pja'tʃeːr.

Page 108, **Arie aus Metastasio's "Didone": Vedi quanto adoro**: *in title as in first line:* 'veːdi; *4th line:* di ki mi fide'rɔ (*no doubling after "di" or "mi"*); *5th line:* di 'viːta (*same*).

Page 109, **Atys**, *4th line: "homesickness" is misspelled in the literal translation.*

Page 140, **Blumenlied**, *4th line: "lovelier" is misspelled in the literal translation.*

Page 147, **Cronnan**: *last line;* page 148, *first line;* and page 149, *in the commentary after the song: the name should be spelled "Shilric" in the English version.*

Page 197, **Der Alpenjäger,** *5th line: "He is" (not "ist") in the literal translation.*

Page 205, **Der XIII. Psalm**: *the German title is a misprint: "VIII" should of course be "XIII."*

Page 235, **Der Hirt auf dem Felsen**, *5th line: "therefore" is misspelled in the literal version.*

Page 299, **Der Unglückliche**: *in commentary after text: "noted in Vienna"* (*not "iln Vienna"*).

Page 342, **Die Erde**: *sixth line:* 'vʊndɐfɔlɐ(r) (*the ending was inadvertently omitted*).

Page 383, **Die Nacht**, *7th line of page 383: should read "through thorns" (literal version).*

Pages 501, 503, index, **Am Meer**: *the word should be* erglänzte. Das Meer erglänzte.

Pages 502, 504, index, **Auf dem Flusse**: *word should be* rauschtest. Der du so lustig rauschtest.

From **Terresa Berganza**
Plaza San Lorenzo del Escorial
Madrid Spain
February 25, 1980

La competencia profesional del señor BEAUMONT GLASS me es conocida desde hace muchos años. Su profunda experiencia musicológica, sus dotes personales, su variado dominio lingüistico y su inigualable capacidad en el trabajo diario han sido para mí en repetidas ocasiones, el mejor apoyo y el mejor estímulo para mi propio trabajo...

...su extraordinaria labor en el Festival Internacional de Opera de Aix-en-Provence 1978, cuando en mi interpretación del personaje "Ruggiero" de la ópera "ALCINA" de Haendel pude y debí recurrir a él a fin de lograr una mejor y más perfecta elaboración artística de mi personaje.

Así mismo, mi debut en el personaje de "Charlotte" de la ópera "WERTHER" de Massenet, en la ópera de Zürich, debut que estuvo acompañado de un extraordinario éxito, sólo fué posible gracias a su eficaz trabajo y asistencia. Sus insinuaciones y consejos me fueron siempre de inestimable valía.

Podría citar, por último, mis largas sesiones de refinadísimo trabajo en la preparación de la obra "Frauenliebe und Leben" de Schumann, destinada a figurar en mi repertorio de recitales. Y no puedo dejar de hacer observar que fué también el señor Beaumont Glass quien cuido de escoger entre los Liedern de Brahms, aquellos que mejor se adecuaban a mis especiales cualidades vocales...

English Translation

"The professional competence of Mr. BEAUMONT GLASS has been known to me for many years. His profound musicological experience, his personal talents, his command of various languages and his matchless capability in the daily routine have been for me on repeated occasions the greatest support and the greatest stimulation for my own work...

...his extraordinary work in the International Opera Festival of Aix-en-Provence 1978 when for my interpretation of the character, Ruggiero, in the opera, *Alcina* by Handel I was able to turn to him in order to achieve a better and more perfect artistic working-out of my role...

Similarly, my debut in the part of Charlotte in the opera *Werther* by Massenet at the Zurich Opera, which was accompanied by an extraordinary success, was only possible thanks to his efficacious work and assistance. His suggestions and advice were always of inestimable value to me...

I could cite, finally, my long sessions of most detailed work in the preparation of the cycle *Frauenliebe und Leben* by Schumann, destined to be featured in my recital repertoire. And I must mention that it was also Mr. Beaumont Glass who chose among the Lieder of Brahms those which were best suited to my particular vocal qualities..."

Teresa Berganza

Leyerle Publications is pleased to share the full review by the noted author, singer and teacher, Dr. Richard Dale Sjoerdsma,* of SCHUBERT'S COMPLETE SONG TEXTS by Beaumont Glass, which recently appeared in The Journal of Singing.

Beaumont Glass,
Schubert's Complete Song Texts, Volume I.
Leyerle Publications, Box 384,
Geneseo, New York 14454, 1996
Hardbound, xiv, 513 pp.,
$60.00 + $5.00 shipping and handling.
ISBN 1-878617-19-2

Song preparation, as detailed in the text reviewed above, is predicated upon an approach that begins with the poem. It is irrefutable that the singer and accompanist must each understand not only the message of the poem, but also the exact meaning of each word, before (s)he can use the music to lift the form to a new spiritual dimension. Since the musician cannot be expected to attain equal proficiency in all languages, definitive works of the caliber of the Glass reference are welcome, indeed essential.

In an earlier "Bookshelf" column, Candace A. Magner's *Phonetic Readings of Schubert* (Metuchen: Scarecrow Press, 1994; reviewed in *JOS* 52:3, January/February 1996, p. 75) was recommended as a pronouncing reference for the *Lieder* of that composer. *Schubert's Complete Song Texts* replicates that function, but offers considerably more. Following a brief essay on "Schubert and his Songs" and a section on interpreting *Lieder* that raises a number if issues elaborated upon in the Stein/Spillman volume [an earlier review], the author details the format of the book and offers a guide to German diction. In this first volume, about half of Schubert's more than 600 songs are presented in alphabetical order by title. After the title and its translation appear the opus number, if any, the year of composition, and the name of the poet. The German text of each poem is delineated in bold type; above each word is a transcription of the pronunciation based on the symbols of the International Phonetic Alphabet; beneath each word is its literal translation; beneath that, usually, is a fourth line expressing the meaning of the translation in idiomatic English. At the end of each song is a commentary of varying length, ranging from a single sentence to a modest paragraph, depending upon circumstances. These exceptionally valuable interpolations contain observations on the nature of the song, interpretive hints, background information, identification of descrepancies or unusual references, and the like. Sometimes a song is listed by more than one title, in which case it is cross-referenced, both in the commentary and in the index of titles and first lines that concludes the volume.

The beauty of the IPA lies in its allowing for no ambiguity of sound: [u] is the same whether one sings in English, German, Russian, or Sanskrit, as long as there is agreement on what [u] represents. When one compares a number of pronunciation guides, however, it appears that there is considerably less consistency in the application of symbol to sound than one would expect. This is especially true with the German diphthongs and the *r*. Glass takes his diphthongs from *Siebs—Deutsche Hochsprache* [ae, ɑo, ɔø] rather than from *Duden—Das Aussprachewörterbuch* [ai, au, ɔy], asserting, "that version works better for singers." Other authors evince bewildering variations, combinations, and alternative spellings: William Odom, *German for Singers (NY: Schirmer Books, 1981),* has [ɑe, ɑo, ɔø]; John Moriarty, *Diction* (Boston: E.C. Schirmer, 1975) has [ɑːi, ɑːɛ; ɑːʊ, ɑːo; ɔːy, ɔːø]; Joan Wall, et al., *Diction for Singers* (Dallas: *Pst...Inc.*, 1990), has [aɪ, ɑʊ, ɔʏ]; Magner, *op cit.*, has [ae, ao, ɔø]. As far as the *er* ending is concerned, Glass is consistent in his use of [ɐ], although he does not clearly articulate the differences among [ɐ], [ɐ̯], [ɐ(r)]: aen 'zʏːsɐ 'haelɪgɐ(r) la'k^{h}ɔrtʻ fɔn diːɐ̯. The other writers treat the *er* as follows: Odom [ɑ], Moriarty [r], Wall [ɐ], Magner [r]; Josephine Barber, *German for Musicians* (Bloomington: Indiana University Press, 1985) uses [ɐ] and follows *Duden* in her representation of diphthongs.

Glass is meticulously uniform, however, in his application of the symbols, giving particular attention to eliminating common faults among English-speaking interpreters of *Lieder*. One example has to do with the careless aspiration of certain consonants. To address this, the author indicates both strongly aspirated [t^h, k^h, p^h] and lightly aspirated [tʻ, kʻ, pʻ] consonants. Further instruction is proffered concerning the German [l], the closed [e], and the final *s* after a voiced consonant. Such attention to idiosyncratic detail, as well as the exemplary transcriptions and translations assure that this publication will quickly become the definitive reference in its field. No musician actively concerned with Schubert *Lieder* can afford to be without this highly recommended text.

Few could be considered as qualified as Professor Glass for an undertaking of this nature. A summary of his academic, performance, and publication credits and experiences would by itself constitute a lengthy review. Suffice it to say that he has worked extensively in Switzerland and France; he has accompanied numerous internationally prominent singers in recitals; he is fluent in German, Italian, and French; he has translated eighteen complete operas; and he has created over 150 singing translations of German, French, Spanish, Russian, Finnish, and Norwegian art songs. The second volume, expected to appear early in 1997, is awaited with eager anticipation.

Richard Dale Sjoerdsma, ***The Journal of Singing***,
Vol. 52, No. 2 *November/December 1996, pp. 56-57*
*This is a *corrected version* made by Dr. Sjoerdsma.

More words of praise for SCHUBERT'S COMPLETE SONG TEXTS by Beaumont Glass:

From CHOICE:

[A monthly review service published by the Association of College and Research Libraries]

Schubert, Franz. **Schubert's complete song texts, v. 1,** with international phonetic alphabet transcriptions, word for word translations and commentary by Beaumont Glass. Leyerle, 1996. 513 p. ISBN 1-878617-19-2, $60.00

In recent years, there has been a trend toward providing students of voice and vocal literature with publications that include or consist entirely of International Phonetic Alphabet (IPA) transcriptions and literal translations of the masterworks of song literature and opera. IPA has been a significant tool in providing accurate foreign-language pronunciation guidance to students in all schools, but especially for those in schools with limited voice programs and in schools where grammar courses in German, French, and Italian (at least) are not offered or, for curricular reasons, cannot be taken by music majors. Such publications are immensely valuable and schools should consider each new entry carefully. Glass (Univ. of Iowa, Iowa City) makes an especially strong contribution to this field. He has taken on the whole of Schubert's more than 600 songs. (Volume 2 will be published sometime in 1997.)[‡] His transcriptions are precise and thorough, his literal translations are very careful, and his idiomatic translations are useful. The format is clear and the text has for the most part been carefully edited. Entries contain the date of composition and poet of each song lyric and brief (sometimes very brief) supplemental information on some aspect of the song. There are other translations and transcriptions available but none as comprehensive as this one will be when volume 2 is published. ***—M.S. Roy, Pennsylvania State University, University Park Campus.***

[‡Note: We expect Volume II to be available late March, 1997]

From Nico Castel

"Thanks ever so much for sending me the Schubert book by Beaumont Glass. What a stupendous reference work! It's THE work to consult. Such detail and scholarship, such care with the matter of lines from the original poem not set to music...in short, it's a ***masterpiece*** *and* ***invaluable.*** *It will make all those other books (........) obsolete.*
And it ***looks*** *so good and solid, made to last on a book shelf for life. Congratulations! With the Gartside Ravel and Fauré books we are beginning to avail ourselves with a substantial reference library of Lieder and Mélodies for future generations. Onward with Brahms, Schumann, Wolf, Loewe and Strauß! (****Please*** *don't ask me to do it...I'm somewhat occupied with another project for the next few years...)"* *

*[Professor Castel's "project" for the next few years is his gigantic operatic libretti series, already consisting of the two-volume set, *The Complete Puccini Libretti* (minus *TURANDOT*) and the four-volume set, *The Complete Verdi Libretti*. He is currently preparing the first of two volumes of Mozart's opera libretti of his completed operas, which we expect to be ready about April or May, 1997. After the Mozart, he plans to do twenty-four or more volumes which will contain all the opera libretti of the still-performed operas of the major composers of the world. The project is expected to take him well into the 21st century. Castel is, himself, no stranger to critical acclaim. For 27 years he has sung over 200 roles at the Metropolitan Opera. For 17 of those years he has held the post of principal multi-language diction coach at the Met. He has been bombarded by kudos from his colleagues at the Met and internationally, as well as by all music critics and observers who are familiar with his prodigious work.]